Modern Times
A History of the World
from the 1920s to the 1990s

PAUL JOHNSON

PHOENIX
GIANT

A PHOENIX GIANT PAPERBACK

First published in Great Britain in 1983
by George Weidenfeld & Nicolson Limited

This paperback edition published in 1996
by Phoenix, a division of Orion Books Ltd, Orion House,
5 Upper St Martin's Lane, London WC2H 9EA

ISBN 1 85799 450 7

Printed and bound in Great Britain by
The Guernsey Press Co. Ltd, Guernsey, C.I.

British Library Cataloguing in Publication Data is
available.

Paul Johnson was born in 1928 and educated at Stonyhurst and Magdalen College, Oxford. After army service, in which he reached the rank of Captain, he worked in Paris, as Assistant Editor of the French monthly *Realités*. From 1955-70 he was on the staff of the *New Statesman*, for the last six years as Editor. He has contributed to many of the world's most famous newspapers and magazines and has visited all five continents to report events, interview presidents and prime ministers for the press and TV, and to lecture to academic and business audiences. Paul Johnson is married to the public affairs administrator Marigold Johnson and has four grown-up children. He lives in London and Somerset, and his hobbies are painting and hill-walking.

This book is dedicated
to the memory of my father,
W. A. Johnson,
artist, educator and enthusiast

CONTENTS

ACKNOWLEDGEMENTS

Among the many institutions and individuals to whom I am beholden I would especially like to thank the American Enterprise Institute for Public Policy Research in Washington, which gave me hospitality as a Resident Scholar; Dr Norman Stone, who read the manuscript and corrected many errors; my editor at Weidenfeld, Linda Osband; the copy-editor, Sally Mapstone; and my eldest son, Daniel Johnson, who also worked on the manuscript.

'Thou shalt break them with a rod of iron;
thou shalt dash them in pieces like a potter's vessel.
Be wise now therefore, O ye kings:
be instructed, ye judges of the earth'

Psalms, 2: 9–10

ONE

A Relativistic World

The modern world began on 29 May 1919 when photographs of a solar eclipse, taken on the island of Principe off West Africa and at Sobral in Brazil, confirmed the truth of a new theory of the universe. It had been apparent for half a century that the Newtonian cosmology, based upon the straight lines of Euclidean geometry and Galileo's notions of absolute time, was in need of serious modification. It had stood for more than two hundred years. It was the framework within which the European Enlightenment, the Industrial Revolution, and the vast expansion of human knowledge, freedom and prosperity which characterized the nineteenth century, had taken place. But increasingly powerful telescopes were revealing anomalies. In particular, the motions of the planet Mercury deviated by forty-three seconds of arc a century from its predictable behaviour under Newtonian laws of physics. Why?

In 1905, a twenty-six-year-old German Jew, Albert Einstein, then working in the Swiss patent office in Berne, had published a paper, 'On the electrodynamics of moving bodies', which became known as the Special Theory of Relativity.[1] Einstein's observations on the way in which, in certain circumstances, lengths appeared to contract and clocks to slow down, are analogous to the effects of perspective in painting. In fact the discovery that space and time are relative rather than absolute terms of measurement is comparable, in its effect on our perception of the world, to the first use of perspective in art, which occurred in Greece in the two decades c. 500–480 BC.[2]

The originality of Einstein, amounting to a form of genius, and the curious elegance of his lines of argument, which colleagues compared to a kind of art, aroused growing, world-wide interest. In 1907 he published a demonstration that all mass has energy, encapsulated in the equation $E = mc^2$, which a later age saw as the starting point in the race for the A-bomb.[3] Not even the onset of the European war prevented scientists from following his quest for an all-embracing

1

General Theory of Relativity which would cover gravitational fields and provide a comprehensive revision of Newtonian physics. In 1915 news reached London that he had done it. The following spring, as the British were preparing their vast and catastrophic offensive on the Somme, the key paper was smuggled through the Netherlands and reached Cambridge, where it was received by Arthur Eddington, Professor of Astronomy and Secretary of the Royal Astronomical Society.

Eddington publicized Einstein's achievement in a 1918 paper for the Physical Society called 'Gravitation and the Principle of Relativity'. But it was of the essence of Einstein's methodology that he insisted his equations must be verified by empirical observation and he himself devised three specific tests for this purpose. The key one was that a ray of light just grazing the surface of the sun must be bent by 1.745 seconds of arc – twice the amount of gravitational deflection provided for by classical Newtonian theory. The experiment involved photographing a solar eclipse. The next was due on 29 May 1919. Before the end of the war, the Astronomer Royal, Sir Frank Dyson, had secured from a harassed government the promise of £1,000 to finance an expedition to take observations from Principe and Sobral.

Early in March 1919, the evening before the expedition sailed, the astronomers talked late into the night in Dyson's study at the Royal Observatory, Greenwich, designed by Wren in 1675–6, while Newton was still working on his general theory of gravitation. E.T. Cottingham, Eddington's assistant, who was to accompany him, asked the awful question: what would happen if measurement of the eclipse photographs showed not Newton's, nor Einstein's, but *twice* Einstein's deflection? Dyson said, 'Then Eddington will go mad and you will have to come home alone.' Eddington's notebook records that on the morning of 29 May there was a tremendous thunderstorm in Principe. The clouds cleared just in time for the eclipse at 1.30 pm. Eddington had only eight minutes in which to operate. 'I did not see the eclipse, being too busy changing plates . . . We took sixteen photographs.' Thereafter, for six nights he developed the plates at the rate of two a night. On the evening of 3 June, having spent the whole day measuring the developed prints, he turned to his colleague, 'Cottingham, you won't have to go home alone.' Einstein had been right.[4]

The expedition satisfied two of Einstein's tests, which were reconfirmed by W.W. Campbell during the September 1922 eclipse. It was a measure of Einstein's scientific rigour that he refused to accept that his own theory was valid until the third test (the 'red shift') was met. 'If it were proved that this effect does not exist in nature', he wrote to Eddington on 15 December 1919, 'then the whole theory would have to be abandoned'. In fact the 'red shift' was confirmed by the Mount Wilson observatory in 1923, and thereafter empirical proof of relativity theory accumulated steadily, one of the most striking instances being the gravitational lensing system of quasars, identified in 1979–80.[5] At the time, Einstein's professional heroism did not go unappreciated. To the young philosopher Karl Popper and his friends at Vienna University, 'it was a great experience for us, and one which had a lasting influence on my intellectual development'. 'What impressed me most', Popper wrote later, 'was Einstein's own clear statement that he would regard his theory as untenable if it should fail in certain tests . . . . Here was an attitude utterly different from the dogmatism of Marx, Freud, Adler and even more so that of their followers. Einstein was looking for crucial experiments whose agreement with his predictions would by no means establish his theory; while a disagreement, as he was the first to stress, would show his theory to be untenable. This, I felt, was the true scientific attitude.'[6]

Einstein's theory, and Eddington's much publicized expedition to test it, aroused enormous interest throughout the world in 1919. No exercise in scientific verification, before or since, has ever attracted so many headlines or become a topic of universal conversation. The tension mounted steadily between June and the actual announcement at a packed meeting of the Royal Society in London in September that the theory had been confirmed. To A.N. Whitehead, who was present, it was like a Greek drama:

We were the chorus commenting on the decree of destiny as disclosed in the development of a supreme incident. There was dramatic quality in the very staging: the traditional ceremonial, and in the background the picture of Newton to remind us that the greatest of scientific generalizations was now, after more than two centuries, to receive its first modification . . . a great adventure in thought had at last come home to shore.[7]

From that point onward, Einstein was a global hero, in demand at every great university in the world, mobbed wherever he went, his wistful features familiar to hundreds of millions, the archetype of the abstracted natural philosopher. The impact of his theory was immediate, and cumulatively immeasurable. But it was to illustrate what Karl Popper was later to term 'the law of unintended consequence'. Innumerable books sought to explain clearly how the General Theory had altered the Newtonian concepts which, for ordinary men and women, formed their understanding of the world about them, and how it worked. Einstein himself summed it up thus: 'The "Principle of Relativity" in its widest sense is contained in the statement: The totality of physical phenomena is of such a character that it gives no basis for the introduction of the concept of "absolute motion"; or, shorter but less precise: There is no absolute motion.'[8] Years later, R. Buckminster Fuller was to send a famous cable to the Japanese artist Isamu Noguchi explaining Einstein's key equation in exactly 249 words, a masterpiece of compression.

But for most people, to whom Newtonian physics, with their straight lines and right angles, were perfectly comprehensible, relativity never became more than a vague source of unease. It was grasped that absolute time and absolute length had been dethroned; that motion was curvilinear. All at once, nothing seemed certain in the movements of the spheres. 'The world is out of joint', as Hamlet sadly observed. It was as though the spinning globe had been taken off its axis and cast adrift in a universe which no longer conformed to accustomed standards of measurement. At the beginning of the 1920s the belief began to circulate, for the first time at a popular level, that there were no longer any absolutes: of time and space, of good and evil, of knowledge, above all of value. Mistakenly but perhaps inevitably, relativity became confused with relativism.

No one was more distressed than Einstein by this public misapprehension. He was bewildered by the relentless publicity and error which his work seemed to promote. He wrote to his colleague Max Born on 9 September 1920: 'Like the man in the fairy-tale who turned everything he touched into gold, so with me everything turns into a fuss in the newspapers.'[9] Einstein was not a practising Jew, but he acknowledged a God. He believed passionately in absolute standards of right and wrong. His professional life was devoted to the quest not only for truth but for certitude. He insisted the world could be divided into subjective and objective spheres, and that one must be able to make precise statements about the objective portion. In the scientific (not the philosophical) sense he was a determinist. In the 1920s he found the indeterminacy principle of quantum mechanics not only unacceptable but abhorrent. For the rest of his life until his death in 1955 he sought to refute it by trying to anchor physics in a unified field theory. He wrote to Born: 'You believe in a God who plays dice, and I in complete law and order in a world which objectively exists and which I, in a wildly speculative way, am trying to capture. I firmly *believe*, but I hope that someone will discover a more realistic way or rather a more tangible basis than it has been my lot to find.'[10] But Einstein failed to produce a unified theory, either in the 1920s or thereafter. He lived to see moral relativism, to him a disease, become a social pandemic, just as he lived to see his fatal equation bring into existence nuclear warfare. There were times, he said at the end of his life, when he wished he had been a simple watchmaker.

The emergence of Einstein as a world figure in 1919 is a striking illustration of the dual impact of great scientific innovators on mankind. They change our perception of the physical world and increase our mastery of it. But they also change our ideas. The second effect is often more radical than the first. The scientific genius impinges on humanity, for good or ill, far more than any statesman or warlord. Galileo's empiricism created the ferment of natural philosophy in the seventeenth century which adumbrated the scientific and industrial revolutions. Newtonian physics formed the framework of the eighteenth-century Enlightenment, and so helped to bring modern nationalism and revolutionary politics to birth. Darwin's notion of the survival of the fittest was a key element both in the Marxist concept of class warfare and of the racial philosophies which shaped Hitlerism. Indeed the political and social consequences of Darwinian ideas have yet to work themselves out, as we shall see throughout this book. So, too, the public response to relativity was one of the principal formative influences on the course of twentieth-century history. It formed a knife, inadvertently wielded by its author, to help cut society adrift from its traditional moorings in the faith and morals of Judeo-Christian culture.

The impact of relativity was especially powerful because it virtually coincided with the public reception of Freudianism. By the time Eddington verified Einstein's General Theory, Sigmund Freud was already in his mid-fifties. Most of his really original work had been done by the turn of the century. *The Interpretation of Dreams* had been published as long ago as 1900. He was a well-known and controversial figure in specialized medical and psychiatric circles, had already founded his own school and enacted a spectacular theological dispute with his leading disciple, Carl Jung, before the Great War broke out. But it was only at the end of the war that his ideas began to circulate as common currency.

The reason for this was the attention the prolonged trench-fighting focused on cases of mental disturbance caused by stress: 'shell-shock' was the popular term. Well-born scions of military families, who had volunteered for service, fought with conspicuous gallantry and been repeatedly decorated, suddenly broke. They could not be cowards, they were not madmen. Freud had long offered, in psychoanalysis, what seemed to be a sophisticated alternative to the 'heroic' methods of curing mental illness, such as drugs, bullying, or electric-shock treatment. Such methods had been abundantly used, in ever-growing doses, as the war dragged on, and as 'cures' became progressively short-lived. When the electric current was increased, men died under treatment, or committed suicide rather than face more, like victims of the Inquisition. The post-war fury of relatives at the cruelties inflicted in military hospitals, especially the psychiatric division of the Vienna General Hospital, led the Austrian government in 1920 to set up a commission of inquiry, which called in Freud.[11] The resulting controversy, though inconclusive, gave Freud the world-wide publicity he needed. Professionally, 1920 was the year of breakthrough for him, when the first psychiatric polyclinic was opened in Berlin, and his pupil and future biographer, Ernest Jones, launched the *International Journal of Psycho-Analysis*.

But even more spectacular, and in the long run far more impor-tant, was the sudden discovery of Freud's works and ideas by intellectuals and artists. As Havelock Ellis said at the time, to the Master's indignation, Freud was not a scientist but a great artist.[12] After eighty years' experience, his methods of therapy have proved, on the whole, costly failures, more suited to cosset the unhappy than cure the sick.[13] We now know that many of the central ideas of psychoanalysis have no basis in biology. They were, indeed, formu-lated by Freud before the discovery of Mendel's Laws, the chromoso-mal theory of inheritance, the recognition of inborn metabolic errors, the existence of hormones and the mechanism of the nervous impulse, which collectively invalidate them. As Sir Peter Medawar has put it, psychoanalysis is akin to Mesmerism and phrenology: it contains isolated nuggets of truth, but the general theory is false.[14] Moreover, as the young Karl Popper correctly noted at the time, Freud's attitude to scientific proof was very different to Einstein's and more akin to Marx's. Far from formulating his theories with a high degree of specific content which invited empirical testing and refutation, Freud made them all-embracing and difficult to test at all. And, like Marx's followers, when evidence did turn up which appeared to refute them, he modified the theories to accommodate it. Thus the Freudian corpus of belief was subject to continual expan-sion and osmosis, like a religious system in its formative period. As one would expect, internal critics, like Jung, were treated as heretics; external ones, like Havelock Ellis, as infidels. Freud betrayed signs, in fact, of the twentieth-century messianic ideologue at his worst – namely, a persistent tendency to regard those who diverged from him as themselves unstable and in need of treatment. Thus Ellis's disparagement of his scientific status was dismissed as 'a highly sublimated form of resistance'.[15] 'My inclination', he wrote to Jung just before their break, 'is to treat those colleagues who offer resistance exactly as we treat patients in the same situation'.[16] Two decades later, the notion of regarding dissent as a form of mental sickness, suitable for compulsory hospitalization, was to blossom in the Soviet Union into a new form of political repression.

But if Freud's work had little true scientific content, it had literary and imaginative qualities of a high order. His style in German was magnetic and won him the nation's highest literary award, the Goethe Prize of the City of Frankfurt. He translated well. The anglicization of the existing Freudian texts became an industry in the Twenties. But the new literary output expanded too, as Freud allowed his ideas to embrace an ever-widening field of human activity and experience. Freud was a gnostic. He believed in the existence of a hidden structure of knowledge which, by using the techniques he was devising, could be discerned beneath the surface of things. The dream was his starting-point. It was not, he wrote, 'differently constructed from the neurotic symptom. Like the latter, it may seem strange and senseless, but when it is examined by means of a technique which differs slightly from the free association method used in psychoanalysis, one gets from its *manifest content* to its *hidden meaning*, or to its latent thoughts.'[17]

Gnosticism has always appealed to intellectuals. Freud offered a particularly succulent variety. He had a brilliant gift for classical allusion and imagery at a time when all educated people prided themselves on their knowledge of Greek and Latin. He was quick to seize on the importance attached to myth by the new generation of social anthropologists such as Sir James Frazer, whose *The Golden Bough* began to appear in 1890. The meaning of dreams, the function of myth — into this potent brew Freud stirred an all-pervading potion of sex, which he found at the root of almost all forms of human behaviour. The war had loosened tongues over sex; the immediate post-war period saw the habit of sexual discussion carried into print. Freud's time had come. He had, in addition to his literary gifts, some of the skills of a sensational journalist. He was an adept neologian. He could mint a striking slogan. Almost as often as his younger contemporary Rudyard Kipling, he added words and phrases to the language: 'the unconscious', 'infantile sexuality', the 'Oedipus complex', 'inferiority complex', 'guilt complex', the ego, the id and the super-ego, 'sublimation', 'depth-psychology'. Some of his salient ideas, such as the sexual interpretation of dreams or what became known as the 'Freudian slip', had the appeal of new intellectual parlour-games. Freud knew the value of topicality. In 1920, in the aftermath of the suicide of Europe, he published *Beyond the Pleasure Principle*, which introduced the idea of the 'death instinct', soon vulgarized into the 'death-wish'. For much of the Twenties, which saw a further abrupt decline in religious belief, especially among the educated, Freud was preoccupied with anatomizing religion, which he saw as a purely human construct. In *The Future of an Illusion* (1927) he dealt with man's unconscious attempts to mitigate unhappiness. 'The attempt to procure', he wrote, 'a protection against suffering through a delusional remoulding of reality is made by a considerable number of people in common. The religions of mankind must be classed among the mass-delusions of this kind. No one, needless to say, who shares a delusion ever recognizes it as such.'[18]

This seemed the voice of the new age. Not for the first time, a prophet in his fifties, long in the wilderness, had suddenly found a rapt audience of gilded youth. What was so remarkable about Freudianism was its protean quality and its ubiquity. It seemed to have a new and exciting explanation for everything. And, by virtue of Freud's skill in encapsulating emergent trends over a wide range of academic disciplines, it appeared to be presenting, with brilliant panache and masterful confidence, ideas which had already been half-formulated in the minds of the élite. 'That is what I have always thought!' noted an admiring André Gide in his diary. In the early 1920s, many intellectuals discovered that they had been Freudians for years without knowing it. The appeal was especially strong among novelists, ranging from the young Aldous Huxley, whose dazzling *Crome Yellow* was written in 1921, to the sombrely conservative Thomas Mann, to whom Freud was 'an oracle'.

The impact of Einstein and Freud upon intellectuals and creative artists was all the greater in that the coming of peace had made them aware that a fundamental revolution had been and was still taking place in the whole world of culture, of which the concepts of relativity and Freudianism seemed both portents and echoes. This revolution had deep pre-war roots. It had already begun in 1905, when it was trumpeted in a public speech, made appropriately enough by the impresario Sergei Diaghilev of the *Ballets Russes*:

We are witnesses of the greatest moment of summing-up in history, in the name of a new and unknown culture, which will be created by us, and which will also sweep us away. That is why, without fear or misgiving, I raise my glass to the ruined walls of the beautiful palaces, as well as to the new commandments of a new aesthetic. The only wish that I, an incorrigible sensualist, can express, is that the forthcoming struggle should not damage the amenities of life, and that the death should be as beautiful and as illuminating as the resurrection.[19]

As Diaghilev spoke, the first exhibition of the Fauves was to be seen in Paris. In 1913 he staged there Stravinsky's *Sacre du Printemps*; by then Schoenberg had published the atonal *Drei Klavierstücke* and Alban Berg his String Quartet (Opus 3); and Matisse had invented the term 'Cubism'. It was in 1909 that the Futurists published their manifesto and Kurt Hiller founded his Neue Club in Berlin, the nest of the artistic movement which, in 1911, was first termed Expressionism.[20] Nearly all the major creative figures of the 1920s had already been published, exhibited or performed before 1914, and in that sense the Modern

Movement was a pre-war phenomenon. But it needed the desperate convulsions of the great struggle, and the crashing of regimes it precipitated, to give modernism the radical political dimension it had hitherto lacked, and the sense of a ruined world on which it would construct a new one. The elegiac, even apprehensive, note Diaghilev struck in 1905 was thus remarkably perceptive. The cultural and political strands of change could not be separated, any more than during the turbulence of revolution and romanticism of 1790–1830. It has been noted that James Joyce, Tristan Tzara and Lenin were all resident-exiles in Zurich in 1916, waiting for their time to come.[21]

With the end of the war, modernism sprang onto what seemed an empty stage in a blaze of publicity. On the evening of 9 November 1918 an Expressionist Council of Intellectuals met in the Reichstag building in Berlin, demanding the nationalization of the theatres, the state subsidization of the artistic professions and the demolition of all academies. Surrealism, which might have been designed to give visual expression to Freudian ideas – though its origins were quite independent – had its own programme of action, as did Futurism and Dada. But this was surface froth. Deeper down, it was the disorientation in space and time induced by relativity, and the sexual gnosticism of Freud, which seemed to be characterized in the new creative models. On 23 June 1919 Marcel Proust published *A l'Ombre des jeunes filles*, the beginning of a vast experiment in disjointed time and subterranean sexual emotions which epitomized the new pre-occupations. Six months later, on 10 December, he was awarded the Prix Goncourt, and the centre of gravity of French letters had made a decisive shift away from the great survivors of the nineteenth century.[22] Of course as yet such works circulated only among the influential few. Proust had to publish his first volume at his own expense and sell it at one-third the cost of production (even as late as 1956, the complete *A la Récherche du temps perdu* was still selling less than 10,000 sets a year).[23] James Joyce, also working in Paris, could not be published at all in the British Isles. His *Ulysses*, completed in 1922, had to be issued by a private press and smuggled across frontiers. But its significance was not missed. No novel illustrated more clearly the extent to which Freud's concepts had passed into the language of literature. That same year, 1922, the poet T.S.Eliot, himself a newly identified prophet of the age, wrote that it had 'destroyed the whole of the nineteenth century'.[24] Proust and Joyce, the two great harbingers and centre-of-gravity-shifters, had no place for each other in the *Weltanschauung* they inadvertently shared. They met in Paris on 18 May 1922, after the first night of Stravinsky's *Rénard*, at a party for Diaghilev and the cast, attended by the composer and his designer, Pablo Picasso. Proust, who had already insulted Stravinsky, unwisely gave Joyce a lift home in his taxi. The drunken Irishman assured him he had not read one syllable of his works and Proust, incensed, reciprocated the compliment, before driving on to the Ritz where he had an arrangement to be fed at any hour of the night.[25] Six months later he was dead, but not before he had been acclaimed as the literary interpreter of Einstein in an essay by the celebrated mathematician Camille Vettard.[26] Joyce dismissed him, in *Finnegans Wake*, with a pun: '*Prost bitte*'.

The notion of writers like Proust and Joyce 'destroying' the nineteenth century, as surely as Einstein and Freud were doing with their ideas, is not so fanciful as it might seem. The nineteenth century saw the climax of the philosophy of personal responsibility – the notion that each of us is individually accountable for our actions – which was the joint heritage of Judeo-Christianity and the classical world. As Lionel Trilling, analysing Eliot's verdict on *Ulysses*, was to point out, during the nineteenth century it was possible for a leading aesthete like Walter Pater, in *The Renaissance*, to categorize the ability 'to burn with a hard, gem-like flame' as 'success in life'. 'In the nineteenth century', Trilling wrote, even 'a mind as exquisite and detached as Pater's could take it for granted that upon the life of an individual person a judgment of success or failure might be passed.'[27] The nineteenth-century novel had been essentially concerned with the moral or spiritual success of the individual. *A la Récherche* and *Ulysses* marked not merely the entrance of the anti-hero but the destruction of individual heroism as a central element in imaginative creation, and a contemptuous lack of concern for moral balance-striking and verdicts. The exercise of individual free will ceased to be the supremely interesting feature of human behaviour.

That was in full accordance with the new forces shaping the times. Marxism, now for the first time easing itself into the seat of power, was another form of gnosticism claiming to peer through the empirically-perceived veneer of things to the hidden truth beneath. In words which strikingly foreshadow the passage from Freud I have just quoted, Marx had pronounced: 'The *final pattern* of economic relationships as seen on the surface . . . is very different from, and indeed quite the reverse of, their *inner but concealed essential pattern*.'[28] On the surface, men appeared to be exercising their free will, taking decisions, determining events. In reality, to those familiar with the methods of dialectical materialism, such individuals, however powerful, were seen to be mere flotsam, hurled hither and thither by the irresistible surges of economic forces. The ostensible behaviour of individuals merely concealed class patterns of which they were almost wholly unaware but powerless to defy.

Equally, in the Freudian analysis, the personal conscience, which stood at the very heart of the Judeo-Christian ethic, and was the principal engine of individualistic achievement, was dismissed as a mere safety-device, collectively created, to protect civilized order from the fearful aggressiveness of human beings. Freudianism was many things, but if it had an essence it was the description of guilt. 'The tension between the harsh super-ego and the ego that is subjected to it', Freud wrote in 1920, 'is called by us the sense of guilt . . . . Civilization obtains mastery over the individual's dangerous desire for aggression by weakening and disarming it and by setting up an agency within him to watch over it, like a garrison in a conquered city.' Feelings of guilt were thus a sign not of vice, but of virtue. The super-ego or conscience was the drastic price the individual paid for preserving civilization, and its cost in misery would increase inexorably as civilization advanced: 'A threatened external unhappiness . . . has been exchanged for a permanent internal unhappiness, for the tension of the sense of guilt.' Freud said he intended to show that guilt-feelings, unjustified by any human frailty, were 'the most important problem in the development of civilization'.[29] It might be, as sociologists were already suggesting, that society could be collectively guilty, in creating conditions which made crime and vice inevitable. But personal guilt-feelings were an illusion to be dispelled. None of us was individually guilty; we were all guilty.

Marx, Freud, Einstein all conveyed the same message to the 1920s: the world was not what it seemed. The senses, whose empirical perceptions shaped our ideas of time and distance, right and wrong, law and justice, and the nature of man's behaviour in society, were not to be trusted. Moreover, Marxist and Freudian analysis combined to undermine, in their different ways, the highly developed sense of personal responsibility, and of duty towards a settled and objectively true moral code, which was at the centre of nineteenth-century European civilization. The impression people derived from Einstein, of a universe in which all measurements of value were relative, served to confirm this vision – which both dismayed and exhilarated – of moral anarchy.

And had not 'mere anarchy', as W.B. Yeats put it in 1916, been 'loosed upon the world'? To many, the war had seemed the greatest calamity since the fall of Rome. Germany, from fear and ambition, and Austria, from resignation and despair, had willed the war in a way the other belligerents had not. It marked the culmination of the wave of pessimism in German philosophy which was its salient characteristic in the pre-war period. Germanic pessimism, which contrasted sharply with the optimism based upon political change and reform to be found in the United States, Britain, France and even Russia in the decade before 1914, was not the property of the intelligentsia but was to be found at every level of German society, particularly at the top. In the weeks before the outbreak of Armageddon, Bethmann Hollweg's secretary and confident Kurt Riezler made notes of the gloomy relish with which his master steered Germany and Europe into the abyss. July 7 1914: 'The Chancellor expects that a war, whatever its outcome, will result in the uprooting of everything that exists. The existing world very antiquated, without ideas.' July 27: 'Doom greater than human power hanging over Europe and our own people.'[30] Bethmann Hollweg had been born in the same year as Freud, and it was as though he personified the 'death instinct' the latter coined as the fearful decade ended. Like most educated Germans, he had read Max Nordau's *Degeneration*, published in 1895, and was familiar with the degenerative theories of the Italian criminologist Cesare Lombroso. War or no war, man was in inevitable decline; civilization was heading for destruction. Such ideas were commonplace in central Europe, preparing the way for the gasp of approbation which greeted Oswald Spengler's *Decline of the West*, fortuitously timed for publication in 1918 when the predicted suicide had been accomplished.

Further West, in Britain, Joseph Conrad (himself an Easterner) had been the only major writer to reflect this pessimism, working it into a whole series of striking novels: *Nostromo* (1904), *The Secret Agent* (1907), *Under Western Eyes* (1911), *Victory* (1915). These despairing political sermons, in the guise of fiction, preached the message Thomas Mann was to deliver to central Europe in 1924 with *The Magic Mountain*, as Mann himself acknowledged in the preface he wrote to the German translation of *The Secret Agent* two years later. For Conrad the war merely confirmed the irremediable nature of man's predicament. From the perspective of sixty years later it must be said that Conrad is the only substantial writer of the time whose vision remains clear and true in every particular. He dismissed Marxism as malevolent nonsense, certain to generate monstrous tyranny; Freud's ideas were nothing more than 'a kind of magic show'. The war had demonstrated human frailty but otherwise would resolve nothing, generate nothing. Giant plans of reform, panaceas, all 'solutions', were illusory. Writing to Bertrand Russell on 23 October 1922 (Russell was currently offering 'solutions' to *The Problem of China*, his latest book), Conrad insisted: 'I have never been able to find in any man's book or any man's talk anything convincing enough to stand up for a moment against my deep-seated sense of fatality governing this man-inhabited world .... The only remedy for Chinamen and for the rest of us is the change of hearts. But looking at the history of the last 2,000 years there is not much reason to expect that thing, even if man has taken to flying .... Man doesn't fly like an eagle, he flies like a beetle.'[31]

At the onset of the war, Conrad's scepticism had been rare in the Anglo-Saxon world. The war itself was seen by some as a form of progress, H.G.Wells marking its declaration with a catchy volume entitled *The War That Will End War*. But by the time the armistice came, progress in the sense the Victorians had understood it, as something continuous and almost inexorable, was dead. In 1920, the great classical scholar J.B.Bury published a volume, *The Idea of Progress*, proclaiming its demise. 'A new idea will usurp its place as the directing idea of humanity .... Does not Progress itself suggest that its value as a doctrine is only relative, corresponding to a certain not very advanced stage of civilization?'[32]

What killed the idea of orderly, as opposed to anarchic, progress, was the sheer enormity of the acts perpetrated by civilized Europe over the past four years. That there had been an unimaginable, unprecedented moral degeneration, no one who looked at the facts could doubt. Sometime while he was Secretary of State for War (1919–21), Winston Churchill jotted down on a sheet of War Office paper the following passage:

All the horrors of all the ages were brought together, and not only armies but whole populations were thrust into the midst of them. The mighty educated States involved conceived – not without reason – that their very existence was at stake. Neither peoples nor rulers drew the line at any deed which they thought could help them to win. Germany, having let Hell loose, kept well in the van of terror; but she was followed step by step by the desperate and ultimately avenging nations she had assailed. Every outrage against humanity or international law was repaid by reprisals – often of a greater scale and of longer duration. No truce or parley mitigated the strife of the armies. The wounded died between the lines: the dead mouldered into the soil. Merchant ships and neutral ships and hospital ships were sunk on the seas and all on board left to their fate, or killed as they swam. Every effort was made to starve whole nations into submission without regard to age or sex. Cities and monuments were smashed by artillery. Bombs from the air were cast down indiscriminately. Poison gas in many forms stifled or seared the soldiers. Liquid fire was projected upon their bodies. Men fell from the air in flames, or were smothered often slowly in the dark recesses of the sea. The fighting strength of armies was limited only by the manhood of their countries. Europe and large parts of Asia and Africa became one

vast battlefield on which after years of struggle not armies but nations broke
and ran. When all was over, Torture and Cannibalism were the only two
expedients that the civilized, scientific, Christian States had been able to
deny themselves: and they were of doubtful utility.[33]

As Churchill correctly noted, the horrors he listed were perpetrated by the 'mighty educated States'. Indeed, they were quite
beyond the power of individuals, however evil. It is a commonplace
that men are excessively ruthless and cruel not as a rule out of
avowed malice but from outraged righteousness. How much more is
this true of legally constituted states, invested with all the seeming
moral authority of parliaments and congresses and courts of justice!
The destructive capacity of the individual, however vicious, is small;
of the state, however well-intentioned, almost limitless. Expand the
state and that destructive capacity necessarily expands too, *pari
passu*. As the American pacifist Randolph Bourne snarled, on the eve
of intervention in 1917, 'War is the health of the state.'[34] Moreover,
history painfully demonstrates that collective righteousness is far
more ungovernable than any individual pursuit of revenge. That was
a point well understood by Woodrow Wilson, who had been
re-elected on a peace platform in 1916 and who warned: 'Once lead
this people into war and they'll forget there ever was such a thing as
tolerance . . . . The spirit of ruthless brutality will enter into every
fibre of our national life.'[35]

The effect of the Great War was enormously to increase the size,
and therefore the destructive capacity and propensity to oppress, of
the state. Before 1914, all state sectors were small, though most were
growing, some of them fast. The area of actual state activity averaged
between 5 and 10 per cent of the Gross National Product.[36] In 1913,
the state's total income (including local government) as a percentage
of GNP, was as low as 9 per cent in America. In Germany, which
from the time of Bismarck had begun to construct a formidable
apparatus of welfare provisions, it was twice as much, 18 per cent;
and in Britain, which had followed in Germany's wake since 1906, it
was 13 per cent.[37] In France the state had always absorbed a
comparatively large slice of the GNP. But it was in Japan and, above
all, in Imperial Russia that the state was assuming an entirely new
role in the life of the nation by penetrating all sectors of the industrial
economy.

In both countries, for purposes of military imperialism, the state
was forcing the pace of industrialization to 'catch up' with the more
advanced economies. But in Russia the predominance of the state in
every area of economic life was becoming the central fact of society.
The state owned oilfields, gold and coal mines, two-thirds of the

railway system, thousands of factories. There were 'state peasants' in the New Territories of the east.[38] Russian industry, even when not publicly owned, had an exceptionally high dependence on tariff barriers, state subsidies, grants and loans, or was interdependent with the public sector. The links between the Ministry of Finance and the big banks were close, with civil servants appointed to their boards.[39] In addition, the State Bank, a department of the Finance Ministry, controlled savings banks and credit associations, managed the finances of the railways, financed adventures in foreign policy, acted as a regulator of the whole economy and was constantly searching for ways to increase its power and expand its activities.[40] The Ministry of Trade supervised private trading syndicates, regulated prices, profits, the use of raw materials and freight-charges, and placed its agents on the boards of all joint-stock companies.[41] Imperial Russia, in its final phase of peace, constituted a large-scale experiment in state collective capitalism, and apparently a highly successful one. It impressed and alarmed the Germans: indeed, fear of the rapid growth in Russia's economic (and therefore military) capacity was the biggest single factor in deciding Germany for war in 1914. As Bethmann Hollweg put it to Riezler, 'The future belongs to Russia.'[42]

With the onset of the war, each belligerent eagerly scanned its competitors and allies for aspects of state management and intervention in the war economy which could be imitated. The capitalist sectors, appeased by enormous profits and inspired no doubt also by patriotism, raised no objections. The result was a qualitative and quantitative expansion of the role of the state which has never been fully reversed – for though wartime arrangements were sometimes abandoned with peace, in virtually every case they were eventually adopted again, usually permanently. Germany set the pace, speedily adopting most of the Russian state procedures which had so scared her in peace, and operating them with such improved efficiency that when Lenin inherited the Russian state-capitalist machine in 1917–18, it was to German wartime economic controls that he, in turn, looked for guidance.[43] As the war prolonged itself, and the losses and desperation increased, the warring states became steadily more totalitarian, especially after the winter of 1916–17. In Germany the end of civilian rule came on 9 January 1917 when Bethmann Hollweg was forced to bow to the demand for unrestricted submarine warfare. He fell from power completely in July, leaving General Ludendorff and the admirals in possession of the monster-state. The episode marked the real end of the constitutional monarchy, since the Kaiser forewent his prerogative to appoint and dismiss the chancellor, under pressure from the military. Even while still chancellor, Bethmann Hollweg discovered that his phone was tapped, and according to Riezler, when he heard the click would shout into it 'What *Schweinhund* is listening in?'[44] But phone-tapping was legal under the 'state of siege' legislation, which empowered area military commands to censor or suppress news-papers. Ludendorff was likewise authorized to herd 400,000 Belgian workers into Germany, thus foreshadowing Soviet and Nazi slave-labour methods.[45] In the last eighteen months of hostilities the German élite fervently practised what was openly termed 'War Socialism' in a despairing attempt to mobilize every ounce of productive effort for victory.

In the West, too, the state greedily swallowed up the independence of the private sector. The corporatist spirit, always present in France, took over industry, and there was a resurgence of Jacobin patriotic intolerance. In opposition, Georges Clemenceau fought successfully for some freedom of the press, and after he came to supreme power in the agony of November 1917 he permitted some criticism of himself. But politicians like Malvy and Caillaux were arrested and long lists of subversives were compiled (the notorious '*Carnet B*'), for subsequent hounding, arrest and even execution. The liberal Anglo-Saxon democracies were by no means immune to these pressures. After Lloyd George came to power in the crisis of December 1916, the full rigours of conscription and the oppressive Defence of the Realm Act were enforced, and manufacturing, transport and supply mobilized under corporatist war boards.

Even more dramatic was the eagerness, five months later, with which the Wilson administration launched the United States into war corporatism. The pointers had, indeed, been there before. In 1909 Herbert Croly in *The Promise of American Life* had predicted it could only be fulfilled by the state deliberately intervening to promote 'a more highly socialized democracy'. Three years later Charles Van Hise's *Concentration and Control: a Solution of the Trust Problem in the United States* presented the case for corporat-ism. These ideas were behind Theodore Roosevelt's 'New National-ism', which Wilson appropriated and enlarged to win the war.[46] There was a Fuel Administration, which enforced 'gasless Sundays', a War Labor Policies Board, intervening in industrial disputes, a Food Administration under Herbert Hoover, fixing prices for com-modities, and a Shipping Board which launched 100 new vessels on 4 July 1918 (it had already taken over 9 million tons into its operating control).[47] The central organ was the War Industries Board, whose first achievement was the scrapping of the Sherman Anti-Trust Act, a sure index of corporatism, and whose members (Bernard Baruch, Hugh Johnson, Gerard Swope and others) ran a kindergarten for

1920s interventionism and the New Deal, which in turn inspired the New Frontier and the Great Society. The war corporatism of 1917 began one of the great continuities of modern American history, sometimes underground, sometimes on the surface, which culminated in the vast welfare state which Lyndon Johnson brought into being in the late 1960s. John Dewey noted at the time that the war had undermined the hitherto irresistible claims of private property: 'No matter how many among the special agencies for public control decay with the disappearance of war stress, the movement will never go backward.'[48] This proved an accurate prediction. At the same time, restrictive new laws, such as the Espionage Act (1917) and the Sedition Act (1918), were often savagely enforced: the socialist Eugene Debs got ten years for an anti-war speech, and one man who obstructed the draft received a forty-year sentence.[49] In all the belligerents, and not just in Russia, the climacteric year 1917 demonstrated that private liberty and private property tended to stand or fall together.

Thus the war demonstrated both the impressive speed with which the modern state could expand itself and the inexhaustible appetite which it thereupon developed both for the destruction of its enemies and for the exercise of despotic power over its own citizens. As the war ended, there were plenty of sensible men who understood the gravity of these developments. But could the clock be turned back to where it had stood in July 1914? Indeed, did anyone wish to turn it back? Europe had twice before experienced general settlements after long and terrible wars. In 1648 the treaties known as the Peace of Westphalia had avoided the impossible task of restoring the *status quo ante* and had in large part simply accepted the political and religious frontiers which a war of exhaustion had created. The settlement did not last, though religion ceased to be a *casus belli*. The settlement imposed in 1814–15 by the Congress of Vienna after the Napoleonic Wars had been more ambitious and on the whole more successful. Its object had been to restore, as far as possible, the system of major and minor divine-right monarchies which had existed before the French Revolution, as the only framework within which men would accept European frontiers as legitimate and durable.[50] The device worked in the sense that it was ninety-nine years before another general European war broke out, and it can be argued that the nineteenth century was the most settled and productive in the whole history of mankind. But the peacemakers of 1814–15 were an unusual group: a congress of reactionaries among whom Lord Castlereagh appeared a revolutionary firebrand and the Duke of Wellington an egregious progressive. Their working assumptions rested on the brutal denial of all the innovatory political notions of the previous quarter-century. In particular, they shared avowed beliefs, almost untinged by cynicism, in power-balances and agreed spheres of interest, dynastic marriages, private understandings between sovereigns and gentlemen subject to a common code (except *in extremis*), and in the private ownership of territory by legitimate descent. A king or emperor deprived of possessions in one part of Europe could be 'compensated', as the term went, elsewhere, irrespective of the nationality, language or culture of the inhabitants. They termed this a 'transference of souls', following the Russian expression used of the sale of an estate with its serfs, *glebae adscripti*.[51]

Such options were not available to the peacemakers of 1919. A peace of exhaustion, such as Westphalia, based on the military lines, was unthinkable: both sides were exhausted enough but one, by virtue of the armistice, had gained an overwhelming military advantage. The French had occupied all the Rhine bridgeheads by 6 December 1918. The British operated an inshore blockade, for the Germans had surrendered their fleet and their minefields by 21 November. A peace by *diktat* was thus available.

However, that did not mean that the Allies could restore the old world, even had they so wished. The old world was decomposing even before war broke out. In France, the anti-clericals had been in power for a decade, and the last election before the war showed a further swing to the Left. In Germany, the 1912 election, for the first time, made the Socialists the biggest single party. In Italy, the Giolitti government was the most radical in its history as a united country. In Britain the Conservative leader A.J. Balfour described his catastrophic defeat in 1906 as 'a faint echo of the same movement which has produced massacres in St Petersburg, riots in Vienna and Socialist processions in Berlin'. Even the Russian autocracy was trying to liberalize itself. The Habsburgs anxiously sought new constitutional planks to shore themselves up. Europe on the eve of war was run by worried would-be progressives, earnestly seeking to satisfy rising expectations, eager above all to cultivate and appease youth.

It is a myth that European youth was ruthlessly sacrificed in 1914 by selfish and cynical age. The speeches of pre-war politicians were crammed with appeals to youth. Youth movements were a European phenomenon, especially in Germany where 25,000 members of the *Wandervögel* clubs hiked, strummed guitars, protested about pollution and the growth of cities, and damned the old. Opinion-formers like Max Weber and Arthur Moeller van den Bruck demanded that youth be brought to the helm. The nation, wrote Bruck, 'needs a change of blood, an insurrection of the sons against the fathers, a substitution of the old by the young'.[52] All over Europe, sociologists were assiduously studying youth to find out what it thought and wanted.

And of course what youth wanted was war. The first pampered 'youth generation' went enthusiastically to a war which their elders, almost without exception, accepted with horror or fatalistic despair. Among articulate middle-class youth it was, at the outset at least, the most popular war in history. They dropped their guitars and seized their rifles. Charles Péguy wrote that he went 'eagerly' to the front (and death). Henri de Montherlant reported that he 'loved life at the front, the bath in the elemental, the annihilation of the intelligence and the heart'. Pierre Drieu la Rochelle called the war 'a marvellous surprise'. Young German writers like Walter Flex, Ernst Wurche and Ernst Jünger celebrated what Jünger called 'the holy moment' of August 1914. The novelist Fritz von Unger described the war as a 'purgative', the beginning of 'a new zest for life'. Rupert Brooke found it 'the only life . . . a fine thrill, like nothing else in the world'. For Robert Nichols it was 'a privilege'. 'He is dead who will not fight', wrote Julian Grenfell ('Into Battle'), 'and who dies fighting has increase.' Young Italians who got into the war later were if anything even more lyrical. 'This is the hour of the triumph of the finest values,' one Italian poet wrote, 'this is the Hour of Youth.' Another echoed: 'Only the small men and the old men of twenty' would 'want to miss it.'[53]

By the winter of 1916–17, the war-lust was spent. As the fighting prolonged itself endlessly, bloodied and disillusioned youth turned on its elders with disgust and rising anger. On all sides there was talk in the trenches of a reckoning with 'guilty politicians', the 'old gang'. In 1917 and still more in 1918, all the belligerent regimes (the United States alone excepted) felt themselves tested almost to destruction, which helps to explain the growing desperation and savagery with which they waged war. Victory became identified with political survival. The Italian and Belgian monarchies and perhaps even the British would not have outlasted defeat, any more than the Third Republic in France. Of course, as soon as victory came, they all looked safe enough. But then who had once seemed more secure than the Hohenzollerns in Berlin? The Kaiser Wilhelm II was bundled out without hesitation on 9 November 1918, immediately it was realized that a German republic might obtain better peace terms. The last Habsburg Emperor, Charles, abdicated three days later, ending a millennium of judicious marriages and inspired juggling. The Romanovs had been murdered on 16 July and buried in a nameless grave. Thus the three imperial monarchies of east and central Europe, the tripod of legitimacy on which the *ancien régime*, such as it was, had rested, all vanished within a year. By the end of 1918 there was little chance of restoring any one of them, still less all three. The Turkish Sultan, for what he was worth, was finished too (though a Turkish republic was not proclaimed until 1 November 1922).

At a stroke, the dissolution of these dynastic and proprietory empires opened up packages of heterogeneous peoples which had been lovingly assembled and carefully tied together over centuries. The last imperial census of the Habsburg empire showed that it consisted of a dozen nations: 12 million Germans, 10 million Magyars, 8.5 million Czechs, 1.3 million Slovaks, 5 million Poles, 4 million Ruthenians, 3.3 million Romanians, 5.7 million Serbs and Croats, and 800,000 Ladines and Italians.[54] According to the 1897 Russian imperial census, the Great Russians formed only 43 per cent of the total population;[55] the remaining 57 per cent were subject peoples, ranging from Swedish and German Lutherans through Orthodox Latvians, White Russians and Ukrainians, Catholic Poles, Ukrainian Uniates, Shia, Sunni and Kurdish Muslims of a dozen nationalities, and innumerable varieties of Buddhists, Taoists and animists. Apart from the British Empire, no other imperial conglomerate had so many distinct races. Even at the time of the 1926 census, when many of the western groups had been prised away, there were still approximately two hundred peoples and languages.[56] By comparison, the Hohenzollern dominions were homogeneous and monoglot, but they too contained huge minorities of Poles, Danes, Alsatians and French.

The truth is that, during the process of settlement in eastern and central Europe, from the fourth to the fifteenth centuries, and during the intensive phase of urbanization which took place from the early eighteenth century onwards, about one-quarter of the area had been occupied by mixed races (including over ten million Jews) whose allegiance had hitherto been religious and dynastic rather than national. The monarchies were the only unifying principle of these multi-racial societies, the sole guarantee (albeit often a slender one) that all would be equal before the law. Once that principle was removed, what could be substituted for it? The only one available was nationalism, and its fashionable by-product irredentism, a term derived from the Italian *Risorgimento* and signifying the union of an entire ethnic group under one state. To this was now being added a new cant phrase, 'self-determination', by which was understood the adjustment of frontiers by plebiscite according to ethnic preferences.

The two principal western Allies, Britain and France, had originally no desire or design to promote a peace based on nationality. Quite the contrary. Both ran multiracial, polyglot overseas empires. Britain in addition had an irredentist problem of her own in Ireland. In 1918 both were led by former progressives, Lloyd George and

Clemenceau, who under the agony of war had learned Realpolitik and a grudging respect for the old notions of 'balance', 'compensation' and so forth. When, during the peace talks, the young British diplomat Harold Nicolson urged that it was logical for Britain to grant self-determination to the Greeks in Cyprus, he was rebuked by Sir Eyre Crowe, head of the Foreign Office: 'Nonsense, my dear Nicolson. . . . Would you apply self-determination to India, Egypt, Malta and Gibraltar? If you are *not* prepared to go as far as this, then you have not [sic] right to claim that you are logical. If you *are* prepared to go as far as this, then you had better return at once to London.'[57] (He might have added that Cyprus had a large Turkish minority; and for that reason it has still not achieved self-determination in the 1980s.) Lloyd George would have been happy to strive to keep the Austro–Hungarian empire together as late as 1917 or even the beginning of 1918, in return for a separate peace. As for Clemenceau, his primary object was French security, and for this he wanted back not merely Alsace-Lorraine (most of whose people spoke German) but the Saar too, with the Rhineland hacked out of Germany as a French-oriented puppet state.

Moreover, during the war Britain, France and Russia had signed a series of secret treaties among themselves and to induce other powers to join them which ran directly contrary to nationalist principles. The French secured Russian approval for their idea of a French-dominated Rhineland, in return for giving Russia a free hand to oppress Poland, in a treaty signed on 11 March 1917.[58] By the Sykes–Picot Agreement of 1916, Britain and France agreed to strip Turkey of its Arab provinces and divide them between themselves. Italy sold itself to the highest bidder: by the Secret Treaty of London of 26 April 1915 she was to receive sovereignty over millions of German-speaking Tyroleans, and of Serbs and Croats in Dalmatia. A treaty with Romania signed on 17 August 1916 gave her the whole of Transylvania and most of the Banat of Temesvar and the Bukovina, most of whose inhabitants did not speak Romanian. Another secret treaty signed on 16 February 1917 awarded Japan the Chinese province of Shantung, hitherto in Germany's commercial sphere.[59]

However, with the collapse of the Tsarist regime and the refusal of the Habsburgs to make a separate peace, Britain and France began to encourage nationalism and make self-determination a 'war aim'. On 4 June 1917 Kerensky's provisional government in Russia recognized an independent Poland; France began to raise an army of Poles and on 3 June 1918 proclaimed the creation of a powerful Polish state a primary objective.[60] Meanwhile in Britain, the Slavophile lobby headed by R.W.Seton-Watson and his journal, *The*

New Europe, was successfully urging the break-up of Austria–Hungary and the creation of new ethnic states.[61] Undertakings and promises were given to many Slav and Balkan politicians-in-exile in return for resistance to 'Germanic imperialism'. In the Middle East, the Arabophile Colonel T.E.Lawrence was authorized to promise independent kingdoms to the Emirs Feisal and Hussein as rewards for fighting the Turks. In 1917 the so-called 'Balfour Declaration' promised the Jews a national home in Palestine to encourage them to desert the Central Powers. Many of these promises were mutually incompatible, besides contradicting the secret treaties still in force. In effect, during the last two desperate years of fighting, the British and French recklessly issued deeds of property which in sum amounted to more than the territory they had to dispose of, and all of which could not conceivably be honoured at the peace, even assuming it was a harsh one. Some of these post-dated cheques bounced noisily.

To complicate matters, Lenin and his Bolsheviks seized control of Russia on 25 October 1917 and at once possessed themselves of the Tsarist diplomatic archives. They turned copies of the secret treaties over to western correspondents, and on 12 December the *Manchester Guardian* began publishing them. This was accompanied by vigorous Bolshevik propaganda designed to encourage Communist revolutions throughout Europe by promising self-determination to all peoples.

Lenin's moves had in turn a profound effect on the American President. Woodrow Wilson has been held up to ridicule for more than half a century on the grounds that his ignorant pursuit of impossible ideals made a sensible peace impossible. This is no more than a half-truth. Wilson was a don, a political scientist, an ex-President of Princeton University. He knew he was ignorant of foreign affairs. Just before his inauguration in 1913 he told friends, 'It would be an irony of fate if my administration had to deal chiefly with foreign affairs.'[62] The Democrats had been out of office for fifty-three years and Wilson regarded US diplomats as Republicans. When the war broke out he insisted Americans be 'neutral in fact as well as name'. He got himself re-elected in 1916 on the slogan 'He kept us out of war'. He did not want to break up the old Europe system either: he advocated 'peace without victory'.

By early 1917 he had come to the conclusion that America would have a bigger influence on the settlement as a belligerent than as a neutral, and he did draw a narrow legal and moral distinction between Britain and Germany: the use of U-boats by Germany violated 'human rights', whereas British blockade-controls violated only 'property rights', a lesser offence.[63] Once in the war he waged it vigorously but he did not regard America as an ordinary combatant.

It had entered the war, he said in his April 1917 message to Congress, 'to vindicate the principles of peace and justice' and to set up 'a concert of peace and action as will henceforth ensure the observance of these principles'. Anxious to be well-prepared for the peacemaking in September 1917 he created, under his aide Colonel Edward House and Dr S.E.Mezes, an organization of 150 academic experts which was known as 'the Inquiry' and housed in the American Geographical Society building in New York.[64] As a result, the American delegation was throughout the peace process by far the best-informed and documented, indeed on many points often the sole source of accurate information. 'Had the Treaty of Peace been drafted solely by the American experts,' Harold Nicolson wrote, 'it would have been one of the wisest as well as the most scientific documents ever devised.'[65]

However, the Inquiry was based on the assumption that the peace would be a negotiated compromise, and that the best way to make it durable would be to ensure that it conformed to natural justice and so was acceptable to the peoples involved. The approach was empirical, not ideological. In particular, Wilson at this stage was not keen on the League of Nations, a British idea first put forward on 20 March 1917. He thought it would raise difficulties with Congress. But the Bolshevik publication of the secret treaties, which placed America's allies in the worst possible light as old-fashioned predators, threw Wilson into consternation. Lenin's call for general self-determination also helped to force Wilson's hand, for he felt that America, as the custodian of democratic freedom, could not be outbid by a revolutionary regime which had seized power illegally. Hence he hurriedly composed and on 8 January 1918 publicly delivered the famous 'Fourteen Points'. The first repudiated secret treaties. The last provided for a League. Most of the rest were specific guarantees that, while conquests must be surrendered, the vanquished would not be punished by losing populations, nationality to be the determining factor. On 11 February Wilson added his 'Four Principles', which rammed the last point home, and on 27 September he provided the coping-stone of the 'Five Particulars', the first of which promised justice to friends and enemies alike.[66] The corpus of twenty-three assertions was produced by Wilson independently of Britain and France.

We come now to the heart of the misunderstanding which destroyed any real chance of the peace settlement succeeding, and so prepared a second global conflict. By September 1918 it was evident that Germany, having won the war in the East, was in the process of losing it in the West. But the German army, nine million strong, was still intact and conducting an orderly retreat from its French and

Belgian conquests. Two days after Wilson issued his 'Five Particulars', the all-powerful General Ludendorff astounded members of his government by telling them 'the condition of the army demands an immediate armistice in order to avoid a catastrophe'. A popular government should be formed to get in touch with Wilson.[67] Ludendorff's motive was obviously to thrust upon the democratic parties the odium of surrendering Germany's territorial gains. But he also clearly considered Wilson's twenty-three pronouncements collectively as a guarantee that Germany would not be dismembered or punished but would retain its integrity and power substantially intact. In the circumstances this was as much as she could reasonably have hoped for; indeed more, for the second of the 14 Points, on freedom of the seas, implied the lifting of the British blockade. The civil authorities took the same view, and on 4 October the Chancellor, Prince Max of Baden, opened negotiations for an armistice with Wilson on the basis of his statements. The Austrians, on an even more optimistic assumption, followed three days later.[68] Wilson, who now had an army of four million and who was universally believed to be all-powerful, with Britain and France firmly in his financial and economic grip, responded favourably. Following exchanges of notes, on 5 November he offered the Germans an armistice on the basis of the 14 Points, subject only to two Allied qualifications: the freedom of the seas (where Britain reserved her rights of interpretation) and compensation for war damage. It was on this understanding that the Germans agreed to lay down their arms.

What the Germans and the Austrians did not know was that, on 29 October, Colonel House, Wilson's special envoy and US representative on the Allied Supreme War Council, had held a long secret meeting with Clemenceau and Lloyd George. The French and British leaders voiced all their doubts and reservations about the Wilsonian pronouncements, and had them accepted by House who drew them up in the form of a 'Commentary', subsequently cabled to Wilson in Washington. The 'Commentary', which was never communicated to the Germans and Austrians, effectively removed all the advantages of Wilson's points, so far as the Central Powers were concerned. Indeed it adumbrated all the features of the subsequent Versailles Treaty to which they took the strongest objection, including the dismemberment of Austria–Hungary, the loss of Germany's colonies, the break-up of Prussia by a Polish corridor, and reparations.[69] What is still more notable, it not only based itself upon the premise of German 'war guilt' (which was, arguably, implicit in Wilson's twenty-three points), but revolved around the principle of 'rewards' for the victors and 'punishments' for the vanquished, which Wilson had specifically repudiated. It is true that during the October negotiations Wilson, who had never actually had to deal with the Germans before, was becoming more hostile to them in consequence. He was, in particular, incensed by the torpedoing of the Irish civilian ferry *Leinster*, with the loss of 450 lives, including many women and children, on 12 October, more than a week after the Germans had asked him for an armistice. All the same, it is strange that he accepted the Commentary, and quite astounding that he gave no hint of it to the Germans. They, for their part, were incompetent in not asking for clarification of some of the points, for Wilson's style, as the British Foreign Secretary, A.J.Balfour, told the cabinet 'is very inaccurate. He is a first-rate rhetorician and a very bad draftsman.'[70] But the prime responsibility for this fatal failure in communication was Wilson's. And it was not an error on the side of idealism.

The second blunder, which compounded the first and turned it into a catastrophe, was one of organization. The peace conference was not given a deliberate structure. It just happened, acquiring a shape and momentum of its own, and developing an increasingly anti-German pattern in the process, both in substance and, equally important, in form. At the beginning, everyone had vaguely assumed that preliminary terms would be drawn up by the Allies among themselves, after which the Germans and their partners would appear and the actual peace-treaty be negotiated. That is what had happened at the Congress of Vienna. A conference programme on these lines was actually drawn up by the logical French, and handed to Wilson by the French ambassador in Washington as early as 29 November 1918. This document had the further merit of stipulating the immediate cancellation of all the secret treaties. But its wording irritated Wilson and nothing more was heard of it. So the conference met without an agreed programme of procedure and never acquired one.[71] The *modus operandi* was made still more ragged by Wilson's own determination to cross the Atlantic and participate in it. This meant that the supposedly 'most powerful man in the world' could no longer be held in reserve, as a *deus ex machina*, to pronounce from on high whenever the Allies were deadlocked. By coming to Paris he became just a prime minister like the rest, and in fact lost as many arguments as he won. But this was partly because, as the negotiations got under way, Wilson's interest shifted decisively from his own twenty-three points, and the actual terms of the treaty, to concentrate almost exclusively on the League and its Covenant. To him the proposed new world organization, about which he had hitherto been sceptical, became the whole object of the conference. Its operations would redeem any failings in the treaty itself. This had two dire consequences. First, the French were able to get agreed much harsher terms, including a 'big' Poland which cut Prussia in two and stripped Germany of its Silesian industrial belt, a fifteen-year Allied occupation of the Rhineland, and enormous indemnities. Second, the idea of a preliminary set of terms was dropped. Wilson was determined to insert the League Covenant into the preliminary document. His Secretary of State, Robert Lansing, advised him that even such a putative agreement legally constituted a treaty and therefore required Congressional ratification. Fearing trouble in the Senate, Wilson then decided to go straight for a final treaty.[72] Of course there were other factors. Marshal Foch, the French generalissimo, feared that the announcement of agreed preliminary terms would accelerate the demobilization of France's allies, and so strengthen Germany's hand in the final stage. And agreement even between the Allies was proving so difficult on so many points that all dreaded the introduction of new and hostile negotiating parties, whose activities would unravel anything so far achieved. So the idea of preliminary terms was dropped.[73]

Hence when the Germans were finally allowed to come to Paris, they discovered to their consternation that they were not to negotiate a peace but to have it imposed upon them, having already rendered themselves impotent by agreeing to an armistice which they now regarded as a swindle. Moreover, Clemenceau, for whom hatred and fear of the Germans was a law of nature, stage-managed the imposition of the *diktat*. He had failed to secure agreement for a federated Germany which reversed the work of Bismarck, or for a French military frontier on the Rhine. But on 7 May 1919 he was allowed to preside over the ceremony at Versailles, where France had been humiliated by Prussia in 1871, at which the German delegation at last appeared, not in the guise of a negotiating party but as convicted prisoners come to be sentenced. Addressing the sullen German plenipotentiary, Count von Brockdorff-Rantzau, he chose his words carefully:

You see before you the accredited representatives of the Allied and Associated powers, both small and great, which have waged without intermission for more than four years the pitiless war which was imposed on them. The hour has struck for the weighty settlement of our accounts. You asked us for peace. We are disposed to grant it to you.[74]

He then set a time-limit for outright acceptance or rejection. The Count's bitter reply was read sitting down, a discourtesy which infuriated many of those present, above all Wilson, who had become increasingly anti-German as the conference proceeded: 'What abominable manners . . . . The Germans are really a stupid people. They always do the wrong thing . . . . This is the most tactless speech I have

ever heard. It will set the whole world against them.' In fact it did
not. A.J.Balfour did not object to Brockdorff remaining seated. He
told Nicolson, 'I failed to notice. I make it a rule never to stare at
people when they are in obvious distress.'[76] There were stirrings of
pity for the Germans among the British, and thereafter, until 28
June when the Germans finally signed, Lloyd George made strenu-
ous efforts to mitigate the severity of the terms, especially over the
German–Polish frontier. He feared it might provoke a future war –
as indeed it did. But all he got from a hostile Wilson and
Clemenceau was a plebiscite for Upper Silesia.[77] Thus the Germans
signed, 'yielding', as they put it, 'to overwhelming force'. 'It was as
if', wrote Lansing, 'men were being called upon to sign their own
death-warrants . . . . With pallid faces and trembling hands they
wrote their names quickly and were then conducted back to their
places.'[78]

The manner in which the terms were nailed onto the Germans
was to have a calamitous effect on their new Republic, as we shall
see. Lloyd George's last-minute intervention on their behalf also
effectively ended the *entente cordiale*, and was to continue to
poison Anglo–French relations into the 1940s: an act of perfidy
which General de Gaulle was to flourish bitterly in Winston Churchill's face in the Second World War.[79] At the time, many Frenchmen believed Clemenceau had conceded too much, and he was the
only politician in the country who could have carried what the
French regarded as an over-moderate and even dangerous settlement.[80] The Americans were split. Among their distinguished
delegation, some shared Wilson's anti-Germanism.[81] John Foster
Dulles spoke of 'the enormity of the crime committed by Germany'.
The slippery Colonel House was instrumental in egging on Wilson
to scrap his 'points'. Wilson's chief adviser on Poland, Robert
H.Lord, was next to Clemenceau himself the strongest advocate of
a 'big' Poland.[82] But Lansing rightly recognized that the failure to
allow the Germans to negotiate was a cardinal error and he
considered Wilson had betrayed his principles in both form and
substance.[83] His criticisms were a prime reason for Wilson's brutal
dismissal of him early in 1920.[84]

Among the younger Americans, most were bitterly critical.
William Bullitt wrote Wilson a savage letter: 'I am sorry that you
did not fight our fight to the finish and that you had so little faith in
the millions of men, like myself, in every nation who had faith in
you . . . . Our government has consented now to deliver the suffering peoples of the world to new oppressions, subjections and
dismemberments – a new century of war.'[85] Samuel Eliot Morrison,
Christian Herter and Adolf Berle shared this view. Walter

Lippmann wrote: 'In my opinion the Treaty is not only illiberal and in bad faith, it is in the highest degree imprudent.'[86]

Many of these young men were to be influential later. But they were overshadowed by a still more vehement critic in the British delegation who was in a position to strike a devastating blow at the settlement immediately. John Maynard Keynes was a clever Cambridge don, a wartime civil servant and a Treasury representative at the conference. He was not interested in military security, frontiers and population-shifts, whose intrinsic and emotional importance he tragically underestimated. On the other hand he had a penetrating understanding of the economic aspects of European stability, which most delegates ignored. A durable peace, in his view, would depend upon the speed with which the settlement allowed trade and manufacturing to revive and employment to grow. In this respect the treaty must be dynamic, not retributive.[87] In 1916 in a Treasury memorandum, he argued that the 1871 indemnity Germany had imposed on France had damaged both countries and was largely responsible for the great economic recession of the 1870s which had affected the entire world.[88] He thought there should be no reparations at all or, if there were, the maximum penalty to be imposed on Germany should be £2,000 million: 'If Germany is to be "milked",' he argued in a preparatory paper for the conference, 'she must not first of all be ruined.'[89] As for the war debts in which all the Allies were entangled – and which they supposed would be paid off by what they got out of Germany – Keynes thought it would be sensible for Britain to let her creditors off. Such generosity would encourage the Americans to do the same for Britain, and whereas Britain would be paid by the Continentals in paper, she would have to pay the USA in real money, so a general cancellation would benefit her.[90]

In addition to limiting reparations and cancelling war-debts, Keynes wanted Wilson to use his authority and the resources of the United States to launch a vast credit programme to revitalize European industry – a scheme which, in 1947–8, was to take the form of the Marshall Plan. He called this 'a grand scheme for the rehabilitation of Europe'.[91] He sold this proposal to his boss, the Chancellor of the Exchequer, Austen Chamberlain, and in April 1919 drafted two letters which Lloyd George sent to Wilson. The first argued 'the economic mechanism of Europe is jammed' and the proposal would free it; the second, that 'the more prostrate a country is and the nearer to Bolshevism, the more presumably it requires assistance. But the less likely is private enterprise to do it.'[92] It was Keynes's view that America was enjoying a unique 'moment' in world affairs, and that Wilson should avoid trying to dictate post-war boundaries and the shape of the League and, instead, use

US food supplies and economic power to aid Europe's long-term recovery. A prosperous Europe would be more likely to forget the bitter memories of the immediate past and to place in perspective the frontier adjustments which were now so fraught with passion.

There was much wisdom and some justice in Keynes's view, and he was certainly right about America's role, as some American historians now recognize.[93] But Wilson, obsessed by the League and uninterested in economic revival, brushed aside Lloyd George's pleas, and the US Treasury was horrified by Keynes's ideas. Its representatives, complained Keynes, were 'formally interdicted' from 'discussing any such question with us even in private conversation'.[94] There could be no question of cancelling war-debts. Keynes's disgust with the Americans boiled over: 'They had a chance of taking a large, or at least humane view of the world, but unhesitatingly refused it,' he wrote to a friend. Wilson was 'the greatest fraud on earth'.[95] He was even more horrified when he read the Treaty through and grasped what he saw as the appalling cumulative effect of its provisions, particularly the reparations clauses. The 'damned Treaty', as he called it, was a formula for economic disaster and future war. On 26 May 1919 he resigned from the British delegation. 'How can you expect me', he wrote to Chamberlain, 'to assist at this tragic farce any longer, seeking to lay the foundation, as a Frenchman put it, "*d'une guerre juste et durable*"?' He told Lloyd George: 'I am slipping away from this scene of nightmare.'[96]

Keynes's departure was perfectly understandable, for the settlement his wit and eloquence had failed to avert was a *fait accompli*. But what he now proceeded to do made infinitely more serious the errors of judgement he had so correctly diagnosed. Keynes was a man of two worlds. He enjoyed the world of banking and politics in which his gifts allowed him to flourish whenever he chose to do so. But he was also an academic, an aesthete, a homosexual and a member both of the secret Cambridge society, The Apostles, and of its adjunct and offspring, the Bloomsbury Group. Most of his friends were pacifists: Lytton Strachey, the unofficial leader of the Bloomsberries, Strachey's brother James, David Garnett, Clive Bell, Adrian Stephen, Gerald Shove, Harry Norton and Duncan Grant.[97] When conscription was introduced, some of them, rather than serve, preferred to be hauled before tribunals as conscientious objectors, Lytton Strachey featuring in a widely publicized and, to him, heroic case. They did not approve of Keynes joining the Treasury, seeing it as 'war work', however non-belligerent. In February 1916, he found on his plate at breakfast an insidious note from Strachey, the pacifist equivalent of a white feather: 'Dear Maynard, Why are you still at the Treasury? Yours, Lytton.' When Duncan Grant, with whom

Keynes was having an affair, was up before a tribunal in Ipswich, Keynes put the case for him, flourishing his Treasury briefcase with the royal cipher to intimidate the tribunal members, who were country small-fry. But he was ashamed of his job when with his friends. He wrote to Grant in December 1917: 'I work for a government I despise for ends I think criminal.'[98]

Keynes continued at the Treasury out of a residual sense of patriotism but the tensions within him grew. When the war he had hated culminated in a peace he found outrageous, he returned to Cambridge in a state of nervous collapse. Recovering, he sat down at once to write a scintillating and vicious attack on the whole conference proceedings. It was a mixture of truth, half-truth, misconceptions and flashing insights, enlivened by sardonic character-sketches of the chief actors in the drama. It was published before the end of the year as *The Economic Consequences of the Peace* and caused a world-wide sensation. The work is another classic illustration of the law of unintended consequences. Keynes's public motive in writing it was to alert the world to the effects of imposing a Carthaginian Peace on Germany. His private motive was to reinstate himself with his friends by savaging a political establishment they blamed him for serving. It certainly succeeded in these objects. It also proved to be one of the most destructive books of the century, which contributed indirectly and in several ways to the future war Keynes himself was so anxious to avert. When that war in due course came, a young French historian, Etienne Mantoux, pointed an accusing finger at Keynes's philippic in a tract called *The Carthaginian Peace: or the Economic Consequences of Mr Keynes*. It was published in London in 1946, a year after Mantoux himself had been slaughtered and the same year Keynes died of cancer.

The effect of Keynes's book on Germany and Britain was cumulative, as we shall see. Its effect on America was immediate. As already noted, the League of Nations was not Wilson's idea. It emanated from Britain. Or rather, it was the brain-child of two eccentric English gentlemen, whose well-meaning but baneful impact on world affairs illustrates the proposition that religious belief is a bad counsellor in politics. Walter Phillimore, who at the age of seventy-two chaired the Foreign Office committee whose report coined the proposal (20 March 1918), was an international jurist and author of *Three Centuries of Treaties of Peace* (1917). He was also a well-known ecclesiastical lawyer, a Trollopian figure, prominent in the Church Assembly, an expert on legitimacy, ritual, vestments and church furniture, as well as Mayor of leafy Kensington. As a judge he had been much criticized for excessive severity in sexual cases, though not towards other crimes. It would be difficult to conceive of a man less suited to draw up rules for coping with global Realpolitik, were it not for the existence of his political ally, Lord Robert Cecil, Tory MP and Under-Secretary of State for Foreign Affairs. Cecil reacted against the political scepticism and cynicism of his prime minister father, Lord Salisbury, who had had to cope with Bismarck, by approaching foreign affairs with a strong dosage of religiosity. He was a nursery lawyer, whom his mother said 'always had two Grievances and a Right'. He had tried to organize opposition to bullying at Eton. As Minister responsible for the blockade he had hated trying to starve the Germans into surrender, and so fell on the League idea with enthusiasm. Indeed he wrote to his wife in August 1918: 'Without the hope that [the League] was to establish a better international system I should be a pacifist.'[99] It is important to realize that the two men most responsible for shaping the League were quasi-pacifists who saw it not as a device for resisting aggression by collective force but as a substitute for such force, operating chiefly through 'moral authority'.

The British military and diplomatic experts disliked the idea from the start. Colonel Maurice Hankey, the Cabinet Secretary and the most experienced military co-ordinator, minuted: '. . . any such scheme is dangerous to us, because it will create a sense of security which is wholly fictitious . . . . It will only result in failure and the longer that failure is postponed the more certain it is that this country will have been lulled to sleep. It will put a very strong lever into the hands of the well-meaning idealists who are to be found in almost every government who deprecate expenditure on armaments, and in the course of time it will almost certainly result in this country being caught at a disadvantage.' Eyre Crowe noted tartly that a 'solemn league and covenant' would be like any other treaty: 'What is there to ensure that it will not, like other treaties, be broken?' The only answer, of course, was force. But Phillimore had not consulted the Armed Services, and when the Admiralty got to hear of the scheme they minuted that to be effective it would require more warships, not less.[100] All these warnings, made at the very instant the League of Nations was conceived, were to be abundantly justified by its dismal history.

Unfortunately, once President Wilson, tiring of the Treaty negotiations themselves, with their necessary whiff of amoral Realpolitik, seized on the League, and made it the vessel of his own copious religious fervour, doubts were swept aside. His sponsorship of the scheme, indeed, served to strip it of such practical merits as it might have had. There is an historical myth that the European powers were desperately anxious to create the League as a means of involving the United States in a permanent commitment to help keep the peace;

that Wilson shared this view; and that it was frustrated by Republican isolationism. Not so. Clemenceau and Foch wanted a mutual security alliance, with its own planning staff, of the kind which had finally evolved at Allied HQ, after infinite pains and delays, in the last year of the war. In short, they wanted something on the lines which eventually appeared in 1948–9, in the shape of the North Atlantic Treaty Organization. They recognized that a universal system, to which all powers (including Germany) belonged, irrespective of their record, and which guaranteed all frontiers, irrespective of their merits, was nonsense. They were better informed of Congressional opinion than Wilson, and knew there was small chance of it accepting any such monstrosity. Their aims were limited, and they sought to involve America by stages, as earlier France had involved Britain. What they wanted America to accept, in the first place, was a guarantee of the Treaty, rather than membership of any League.[101]

This was approximately the position of Senator Cabot Lodge, the Republican senate leader. He shared the scepticism of both the British experts and the French. Far from being isolationist, he was pro-European and a believer in mutual security. But he thought that major powers would not in practice accept the obligation to go to war to enforce the League's decisions, since nations eschewed war except when their vital interests were at stake. How could frontiers be indefinitely guaranteed by anything or anybody? They reflected real and changing forces. Would the US go to war to protect Britain's frontiers in India, or Japan's in Shantung? Of course not. Any arrangement America made with Britain and France must be based on the mutual accommodation of vital interests. Then it would mean something. By September 1919, Lodge and his supporters, known as the 'Strong Reservationists', had made their position clear: they would ratify the Treaty except for the League; and they would even accept US membership of the League provided Congress had a right to evaluate each crisis involving the use of American forces.[102]

It was at this juncture that Wilson's defects of character and judgement, and indeed of mental health, became paramount. In November 1918 he had lost the mid-term elections, and with them control of Congress, including the Senate. That was an additional good reason for not going to Paris in person but sending a bipartisan delegation; or, if he went, taking Lodge and other Republicans with him. Instead he chose to go it alone. In taking America into the war, he had said in his address to Congress of 2 April 1917: 'The world must be made safe for democracy.' His popular *History of the American People* presented democracy as a quasi-religious force, *vox populi vox dei*. The old world, he now told Congress, was suffering from a 'wanton rejection' of democracy, of its 'purity and spiritual power'. That was where America came in: 'It is surely the manifest destiny of the United States to lead in the attempt to make this spirit prevail.'[103] In that work, the League was the instrument, and he himself the agent, an embodiment of the General Will.

It is not clear how Wilson, the ultra-democrat, came to consider himself the beneficiary of Rousseau's *volonté générale*, a concept soon to be voraciously exploited by Europe's new generation of dictators. Perhaps it was his physical condition. In April 1919 he suffered his first stroke, in Paris. The fact was concealed. Indeed, failing health seems to have strengthened Wilson's belief in the righteousness of his course and his determination not to compromise with his Republican critics. In September 1919 he took the issue of the League from Congress to the country, travelling 8,000 miles by rail in three weeks. The effort culminated in a second stroke in the train on 25 September.[104] Again, there was a cover-up. On 10 October came a third, and massive, attack, which left his entire left side paralysed. His physician, Admiral Gary Grayson, admitted some months later, 'He is permanently ill physically, is gradually weakening mentally, and can't recover.'[105] But Grayson refused to declare the President incompetent. The Vice-President, Thomas Marshall, a hopelessly insecure man known to history chiefly for his remark 'What this country needs is a good five-cent cigar', declined to press the point. The private secretary, Joseph Tumulty, conspired with Wilson himself and his wife Edith to make her the president, which she remained for seventeen months.

During this bizarre episode in American history, while rumours circulated that Wilson was stricken with tertiary syphilis, a raving prisoner in a barred room, Mrs Wilson, who had spent only two years at school, wrote orders to cabinet ministers in her huge, childish hand ('The President says . . .'), sacked and appointed them, and forged Wilson's signature on Bills. She, as much as Wilson himself, was responsible for the sacking of the Secretary of State, Lansing ('I hate Lansing', she declared) and the appointment of a totally inexperienced and bewildered lawyer, Bainbridge Colby, in his place. Wilson could concentrate for five or ten minutes at a time, and even foxily contrived to deceive his chief Congressional critic, Senator Albert Fall, who had complained, 'We have petticoat government! Mrs Wilson is president!' Summoned to the White House, Fall found Wilson with a long, white beard but seemingly alert (Fall was only with him two minutes). When Fall said, 'We, Mr President, we have all been praying for you,' Wilson snapped, 'Which way, Senator?', interpreted as evidence of his continuing sharp wit.[106]

Thus America in a crucial hour was governed, as Germany was to be in 1932–3, by an ailing and mentally impaired titan on the threshold of eternity. Had Wilson been declared incapable, there is little doubt that an amended treaty would have gone through the Senate. As it was, with sick or senile pertinacity he insisted that it should accept all he demanded, or nothing: 'Either we should enter the League fearlessly,' his last message on the subject read, 'accepting the responsibility and not fearing the role of leadership which we now enjoy . . . or we should retire as gracefully as possible from the great concert of powers by which the world was saved.'[107]

Into this delicately poised domestic struggle, in which the odds were already moving against Wilson, Keynes's book arrived with devastating timing. It confirmed all the prejudices of the irreconcilables and reinforced the doubts of the reservationists; indeed it filled some of Wilson's own supporters with foreboding. The Treaty, which came before the Senate in March, required a two-thirds majority for ratification. Wilson's own proposal went down to outright defeat, 38–53. There was still a chance that Lodge's own amended text would be carried, and thus become a solid foreign policy foundation for the three Republican administrations which followed. But with a destructive zest Wilson from his sick-bed wrote to his supporters, in letters signed with a quavering, almost illegible hand, begging them to vote against. Lodge's text was carried 49–35, seven votes short of the two-thirds needed. Of the thirty-five against, twenty-three were Democrats acting on Wilson's orders. Thus Wilson killed his own first-born, and in doing so loosened the ties between Europe and even the well-disposed Republicans. In disgust, Lodge pronounced the League 'as dead as Marley's ghost'. 'As dead as Hector', said Senator James Reed. Warren Harding, the Republican presidential candidate, with a sneer at the Democrats' past, added: 'As dead as slavery.' When the Democrats went down to overwhelming defeat in the autumn of 1920, the verdict was seen as a repudiation of Wilson's European policy in its entirety. Eugene Debs wrote from Atlanta Penitentiary, where Wilson had put him: 'No man in public life in American history ever retired so thoroughly discredited, so scathingly rebuked, so overwhelmingly impeached and repudiated as Woodrow Wilson.'[108]

Thus Britain and France were left with a League in a shape they did not want, and the man who had thus shaped it was disavowed by his own country. They got the worst of all possible worlds. American membership of a League on the lines Lodge had proposed would have transformed it into a far more realistic organization in general. But in the particular case of Germany, it would have had a critical advantage. Lodge and the Republican internationalists believed the treaty was unfair, especially to Germany, and would have to be revised sooner or later. In fact the Covenant of the League specifically provided for this contingency. Article 19, often overlooked and in the end wholly disregarded, allowed the League 'from time to time' to advise the reconsideration of 'treaties which have become inapplicable' and whose 'continuance might endanger the peace of the world'.[109] An American presence in the League would have made it far more likely that during the 1920s Germany would have secured by due process of international law those adjustments which, in the 1930s, she sought by force and was granted by cowardice.

Wilson's decision to go for an international jurist's solution to Europe's post-war problems, rather than an economic one, and then the total collapse of his policies, left the Continent with a fearful legacy of inflation, indebtedness and conflicting financial claims. The nineteenth century had been on the whole a period of great price stability, despite the enormous industrial expansion in all the advanced countries. Retail prices had actually fallen in many years, as increased productivity more than kept pace with rising demand. But by 1908 inflation was gathering pace again and the war enormously accelerated it. By the time the peace was signed, wholesale prices, on a 1913 index of 100, were 212 in the USA, 242 in Britain, 357 in France and 364 in Italy. By the next year, 1920, they were two and a half times the pre-war average in the USA, three times in Britain, five times in France and six times in Italy; in Germany the figure was 1965, nearly twenty times.[110] The civilized world had not coped with hyper-inflation since the sixteenth century or on this daunting scale since the third century AD.[111]

Everyone, except the United States, was in debt. Therein lay the problem. By 1923, including interest, the USA was owed $11.8 billion. Of this, Britain alone owed the USA $4.66 billion. But Britain, in turn, was owed $6.5 billion, chiefly by France, Italy and Russia. Russia was now out of the game, and the only chance France and Italy had of paying either Britain or the United States was by collecting from Germany. Why did the United States insist on trying to collect these inter-state debts? President Coolidge later answered with a laconic 'They hired the money, didn't they?' No more sophisticated explanation was ever provided. In an essay, 'Inter-Allied Debts', published in 1924, Bernard Baruch, the panjandrum of the War Industries Board and then Economic Adviser to the US Peace Delegation, argued, 'The US has refused to consider the cancellation of any debts, feeling that if she should – other reasons outside – the major cost of this and all future wars would fall upon her and thus put her in a position of subsidizing all wars, having subsidized one.'[112] Plainly Baruch did not believe this ludicrous defence. The truth is that insistence on war-debts made no economic sense but was part of the political price paid for the foundering of

Wilsonism, leaving nothing but a hole. At the 1923 Washington conference, Britain amid much acrimony agreed to pay the USA £24 million a year for ten years and £40 million a year thereafter. By the time the debts were effectively cancelled after the Great Slump, Britain had paid the USA slightly more than she received from the weaker financial Allies, and they in turn had received about £1,000 million from Germany.[113] But of this sum, most had in fact been raised in loans in the USA which were lost in the recession. So the whole process was circular, and no state, let alone any individual, was a penny the better off.

But in the meantime, the strident chorus of claims and counter-claims had destroyed what little remained of the wartime Allied spirit. And the attempt to make Germany balance everyone else's books simply pushed her currency to destruction. The indemnity levied by Germany on France in 1871 had been the equivalent of 4,000 million gold marks. This was the sum the Reparations Commission demanded from Germany for Belgian war damage alone, and in addition it computed Germany's debt at 132,000 million GMs, of which France was to get 52 per cent. There were also deliveries in kind, including 2 million tons of coal a month. Germany had to pay on account 20,000 million GMs by 1 May 1921. What Germany actually did pay is in dispute, since most deliveries were in property, not cash. The Germans claimed they paid 45,000 million GMs. John Foster Dulles, the US member of the Reparations Commission, put it at 20–25,000 million GMs.[114] At all events, after repeated reductions and suspensions, Germany was declared (26 December 1922) a defaulter under Paragraphs 17–18 of Annex II of the Treaty, which provided for unspecified reprisals. On 11 January 1923, against British protests, French and Belgian troops crossed the Rhine and occupied the Ruhr. The Germans then stopped work altogether. The French imposed martial law on the area and cut off its post, telegraph and phone communications. The German retail price-index (1913: 100) rose to 16,170 million. The political consequences for the Germans, and ultimately for France too, were dolorous in the extreme.

Was the Treaty of Versailles, then, a complete failure? Many intellectuals thought so at the time; most have taken that view since. But then intellectuals were at the origin of the problem – violent ethnic nationalism – which both dictated the nature of the Versailles settlement and ensured it would not work. All the European nationalist movements, of which there were dozens by 1919, had been created and led and goaded on by academics and writers who had stressed the linguistic and cultural differences between peoples at the expense of the traditional ties and continuing economic interests which urged them to live together. By 1919 virtually all European intellectuals of the younger generation, not to speak of their elders, subscribed to the proposition that the right to national self-determination was a fundamental moral principle. There were a few exceptions, Karl Popper being one.[115] These few argued that self-determination was a self-defeating principle since 'liberating' peoples and minorities simply created more minorities. But as a rule self-determination was accepted as unarguable for Europe, just as in the 1950s and 1960s it would be accepted for Africa.

Indeed by 1919 there could be no question of saving the old arrangements in Central and Eastern Europe. The nationalists had already torn them apart. From the distance of seventy years it is customary to regard the last years of Austria–Hungary as a tranquil exercise in multi-racialism. In fact it was a nightmare of growing racial animosity. Every reform created more problems than it solved. Hungary got status within the empire as a separate state in 1867. It at once began to oppress its own minorities, chiefly Slovaks and Romanians, with greater ferocity and ingenuity than it itself had been oppressed by Austria. Elections were suspect, and the railways, the banking system and the principles of internal free trade were savagely disrupted in the pursuit of racial advantage immediately any reform made such action possible. Czechs and other Slav groups followed the Hungarians' example. No ethnic group behaved consistently. What the Germans demanded and the Czechs refused in Bohemia, the Germans refused and the Italians and south Slovenes demanded in the South Tyrol and Styria. All the various Diets and Parliaments, in Budapest, Prague, Graz and Innsbruck, were arenas of merciless racial discord. In Galicia, the minority Ruthenians fought the majority Poles. In Dalmatia the minority Italians fought the majority South Slavs. As a result it was impossible to form an effective parliamentary government. All of the twelve central governments between 1900 and 1918 had to be composed almost entirely of civil servants. Each local government, from which minorities were excluded, protected its home industries where it was legally empowered to do so, and if not, organized boycotts of goods made by other racial groups. There was no normality in the old empire.

But at least there was some respect for the law. In Imperial Russia there were anti-Jewish pogroms occasionally, and other instances of violent racial conflict. But the two Germanic empires were exceptionally law-abiding up to 1914; the complaint even was that their peoples were too docile. The war changed all that with a vengeance. There is truth in the historian Fritz Stern's remark that the Great War ushered in a period of unprecedented violence, and began in effect a Thirty Years' War, with 1919 signifying the continuation of war by different means.[116] Of course in a sense the calamities of the epoch were global rather than continental. The 1918–19 influenza virus strain, a pandemic which killed forty million people in Europe, Asia and America, was not confined to the war areas, though it struck them hardest.[117] New-style outbreaks of violence were to be found almost everywhere immediately after the formal fighting ended. On 27 July–1 August, in Chicago, the USA got its first really big Northern race-riots, with thirty-six killed and 536 injured. Others followed elsewhere: at Tulsa, Oklahoma, on 30 May 1921, fifty whites and two hundred blacks were murdered.[118] In Canada, on 17 June 1919, the leaders of the Winnipeg general strike were accused, and later convicted, of a plot to destroy constitutional authority by force and set up a Soviet.[119] In Britain, there was a putative revolution in Glasgow on 31 January 1919; and civil or class war was a periodic possibility between 1919 and the end of 1921, as the hair-raising records of cabinet meetings, taken down verbatim in shorthand by Thomas Jones, survive to testify. Thus, on 4 April 1921, the cabinet discussed bringing back four battalions from Silesia, where they were holding apart frantic Poles and Germans, in order to 'hold London', and the Lord Chancellor observed stoically: 'We should decide without delay around which force loyalists can gather. We ought not to be shot without a fight anyway.'[120]

Even so it was in Central and Eastern Europe that the violence, and the racial antagonism which provoked it, were most acute, widespread and protracted. A score or more minor wars were fought there in the years 1919–22. They are poorly recorded in western histories but they left terrible scars, which in some cases were still aching in the 1960s and which contributed directly to the chronic instability in Europe between the wars. The Versailles Treaty, in seeking to embody the principles of self-determination, actually created more, not fewer, minorities, and much angrier ones (many were German or Hungarian), armed with far more genuine grievances. The new nationalist regimes thought they could afford to be far less tolerant than the old empires. And, since the changes damaged the economic infrastructure (especially in Silesia, South Poland, Austria, Hungary and North Yugoslavia), everyone tended to be poorer than before.

Every country was landed with either an anguished grievance or an insuperable internal problem. Germany, with divided Prussia and lost Silesia, cried to heaven for vengeance. Austria was left fairly homogeneous – it even got the German Burgenland from Hungary – but was stripped bare of all its former possessions and left with a third of its population in starving Vienna. Moreover, under the Treaty it was forbidden to seek union with Germany, which made the Anschluss seem more attractive than it actually was. Hungary's population was reduced from 20 to 8 million, its carefully integrated industrial economy was wrecked and 3 million Hungarians handed over to the Czechs and Romanians.[121]

Of the beneficiaries of Versailles, Poland was the greediest and the most bellicose, emerging in 1921, after three years of fighting, twice as big as had been expected at the Peace Conference. She attacked the Ukrainians, getting from them eastern Galicia and its capital Lwow. She fought the Czechs for Teschen (Cieszyn), and failed to get it, one reason why Poland had no sympathy with the Czechs in 1938 and actually helped Russia to invade them in 1968, though in both cases it was in her long-term interests to side with Czech independence. She made good her 'rights' against the Germans by force, in both the Baltic and Silesia. She invaded newly free Lithuania, occupying Vilno and incorporating it after a 'plebiscite'. She waged a full-scale war of acquisition against Russia, and persuaded the Western powers to ratify her new frontiers in 1923. In expanding by force Poland had skilfully played on Britain's fears of Bolshevism and France's desire to have a powerful ally in the east, now that its old Tsarist alliance was dead. But of course when it came to the point Britain and France were powerless to come to Poland's assistance, and in the process she had implacably offended all her neighbours, who would certainly fall on her the second they got the opportunity.

Meanwhile, Poland had acquired the largest minorities problem in Europe, outside Russia herself. Of her 27 million population, a third were minorities: West Ukrainians (Ruthenians), Belorussians, Germans, Lithuanians, all of them in concentrated areas, plus 3 million Jews. The Jews tended to side with the Germans and Ukrainians, had a block of thirty-odd deputies in the parliament, and formed a majority in some eastern towns with a virtual monopoly of trade. At Versailles Poland was obliged to sign a special treaty guaranteeing rights to her minorities. But she did not keep it even in the Twenties, still less in the Thirties when her minorities policy deteriorated under military dictatorship. With a third of her population treated as virtual aliens, she maintained an enormous police force, plus a numerous but ill-equipped standing army to defend her vast frontiers. There was foresight in the remark of the Polish nobleman to the German ambassador in 1918, 'If Poland could be free, I'd give half my worldly goods. But with the other half I'd emigrate.'[122]

Czechoslovakia was even more of an artefact, since it was in fact a collection of minorities, with the Czechs in control. The 1921 census revealed 8,760,000 Czechoslovaks, 3,123,448 Germans, 747,000

Magyars and 461,000 Ruthenians. But the Germans claimed it was deliberately inaccurate and that there were, in fact, far fewer in the ruling group. In any case, even the Slovaks felt they were persecuted by the Czechs, and it was characteristic of this 'country' that the new Slovak capital, Bratislava, was mainly inhabited not by Slovaks but by Germans and Magyars.[123] In the Twenties the Czechs, unlike the Poles, made serious efforts to operate a fair minorities policy. But the Great Depression hit the Germans much harder than the Czechs – whether by accident or design – and after that the relationship became hopelessly envenomed.

Yugoslavia resembled Czechoslovakia in that it was a miniature empire run by Serbs, and with considerably more brutality than the Czechs ran theirs. In parts of it there had been continuous fighting since 1912, and the frontiers were not settled (if that is the word) until 1926. The Orthodox Serbs ran the army and the administration, but the Catholic Croats and Slovenes, who had much higher cultural and economic standards, talked of their duty to 'Europeanize the Balkans' (i.e., the Serbs) and their fears that they themselves would be 'Balkanized'. R.W.Seton-Watson, who had been instrumental in creating the new country, was soon disillusioned by the way the Serbs ran it: 'The situation in Jugoslavia', he wrote in 1921, 'reduces me to despair . . . . I have no confidence in the new constitution, with its absurd centralism.' The Serb officials were worse than the Habsburgs, he complained, and Serb oppression more savage than German. 'My own inclination', he wrote in 1928, '. . . is to leave the Serbs and Croats to stew in their own juice! I think they are both mad and cannot see beyond the end of their noses.'[124] Indeed, MPs had just been blazing away at each other with pistols in the parliament, the Croat Peasant Party leader, Stepan Radić, being killed in the process. The country was held together, if at all, not so much by the Serb political police as by the smouldering hatred of its Italian, Hungarian, Romanian, Bulgarian and Albanian neighbours, all of whom had grievances to settle.[125]

Central and Eastern Europe was now gathering in the grisly harvest of irreconcilable nationalisms which had been sown throughout the nineteenth century. Or, to vary the metaphor, Versailles lifted the lid on the seething, noisome pot and the stench of the brew therein filled Europe until first Hitler, then Stalin, slammed it down again by force. No doubt, when that happened, elderly men and women regretted the easy-going dynastic empires they had lost. Of course by 1919 the notion of a monarch ruling over a collection of disparate European peoples by divine right and ancient custom already appeared absurd. But if imperialism within Europe was anachronistic, how much longer would it seem defensible outside it?

Self-determination was not a continental principle; it was, or soon would be, global. Eyre Crowe's rebuke to Harold Nicolson at the Paris Conference echoed a point Maurice Hankey had made to Lord Robert Cecil when the latter was working on the embryo League of Nations scheme. Hankey begged him not to insist on a general statement of self-determination. 'I pointed out to him', he noted in his diary, 'that it would logically lead to the self-determination of Gibraltar to Spain, Malta to the Maltese, Cyprus to the Greeks, Egypt to the Egyptians, Aden to the Arabs or Somalis, India to chaos, Hong Kong to the Chinese, South Africa to the Kaffirs, West Indies to the blacks, etc. And where would the British Empire be?'[126]

As a matter of fact the principle was already being conceded even at the time Hankey wrote. During the desperate days of the war, the Allies signed post-dated cheques not only to Arabs and Jews and Romanians and Italians and Japanese and Slavs but to their own subject-peoples. As the casualties mounted, colonial manpower increasingly filled the gaps. It was the French Moroccan battalions which saved Rheims Cathedral. The French called it gleefully *la force noire*, and so it was but in more senses than one. The British raised during the war 1,440,437 soldiers in India; 877,068 were combatants; and 621,224 officers and men served overseas.[127] It was felt that in some way India should be rewarded; and the cheapest way to do it was in the coinage of political reform.

The capstone on British rule in India had been placed there when Disraeli made Victoria Empress in 1876. The chain of command was autocratic: it went from the district officer to provincial commissioner to governor to governor-general to viceroy. This principle had been maintained in the pre-war Morley–Minto reforms, since Lord Morley, though a liberal progressive, did not believe democracy would work in India. But his Under-Secretary, Edwin Montagu, thought differently. Montagu was another Jew with oriental longings, though rather different ones: the longing to be loved. He suffered from that corrosive vice of the civilized during the twentieth century, which we shall meet in many forms: guilt. His grandfather had been a goldsmith, his father made millions as a foreign exchange banker, and so earned himself the luxury of philanthropy. Montagu inherited all this and the feeling that he owed something to society. He was a highly emotional man; people used the term 'girlish' about his approach to public affairs. Turning down the Ireland secretaryship in 1916, he wrote, 'I shrink with horror at being responsible for punishment.' When he died a friend wrote to *The Times*: 'He never tired of being sorry for people.'[128]

Lloyd George must have had other things on his mind when he gave Montagu India in June 1917. Montagu's aim was to launch India irretrievably on the way to independence. He at once set about drafting a statement of Britain's post-war intentions. It came before the cabinet on 14 August, at one of the darkest periods of the war. On the agenda was the rapid disintegration of the entire Russian front, as well as the first really big German air raids on Britain: and the minds of the despairing men round the table were hag-ridden by the fearful losses in the Passchendaele offensive, then ending its second bloody and futile week. Elgar was writing the final bars of his Cello Concerto, his last major work, which conveys better than any words the unappeasable sadness of those days. Montagu slipped through his statement of policy which included one irrevocable phrase: 'the gradual development of free institutions in India with a view to ultimate self-government'.[129] But Lord Curzon pricked up his ears. He was the archetypal imperialist of the silver age, a former viceroy, on record as saying: 'As long as we rule India we are the greatest power in the world. If we lose it we shall drop straight away to a third-rate power.'[130] He pointed out that, to the men around that table, the phrase 'ultimate self-government' might mean 500 years, but to excitable Indians it meant a single generation. Confident in the magic of his diplomatic penmanship, he insisted on changing the statement to 'the gradual development of self-governing institutions with a view to the progressive realization of responsible government in India as an integral part of the British Empire'. In fact changing the phrase made no difference: Montagu meant self-government and that was how it was understood in India.

Indeed, that November and December, while Lenin was taking over Russia, Montagu went out to India to consult 'Indian opinion'. In his subsequent report he wrote: 'If we speak of "Indian Opinion" we should be understood as generally referring to the majority of those who have held or are capable of holding an opinion on the matter with which we are dealing.'[131] In other words, he was only interested in the 'political nation', those like Jinnah, Gandhi and Mrs Besant whom he called 'the real giants of the Indian political world' and who shared his political mode of discourse. Just as Lenin made no effort to consult the Russian peasants in whose name he was now turning a vast nation upside down, so Montagu ignored the 400 million ordinary Indians, the 'real nation', except as the subjects of his philanthropic experiment. His action, he wrote, in 'deliberately disturbing' what he called the 'placid, pathetic contentment of the masses' would be 'working for [India's] highest good'.[132] He got his Report through cabinet on 24 May and 7 June 1918, when the attention of ministers was focused on the frantic efforts to arrest the German breakthrough in France, almost to the exclusion of anything else. So it was published (1918), enacted (1919) and implemented (1921). By creating provincial legislatures, bodies of course elected by and composed of the 'political nation', Montagu drove a runaway coach through the old autocratic chain of command. Thereafter there seemed no turning back.

However, it must not be supposed that already, in 1919, the progressive disintegration of the British Empire was inevitable, indeed foreseeable. There are no inevitabilities in history.[133] That, indeed, will be one of the central themes of this volume. In 1919 the British Empire, to most people, appeared to be not only the most extensive but the most solid on earth. Britain was a superpower by any standards. She had by far the largest navy, which included sixty-one battleships, more than the American and French navies put together, more than twice the Japanese plus the Italians (the German navy was now at the bottom of Scapa Flow); plus 120 cruisers and 466 destroyers.[134] She also had the world's largest air force and, surprisingly in view of her history, the world's third largest army.

In theory at least the British Empire had gained immeasurably by the war. Nor was this accidental. In December 1916, the destruction of the frail Asquith government and the formation of the Lloyd George coalition brought in the 'Balliol Imperialists': Lord Curzon and especially Lord Milner and the members of the 'Kindergarten' he had formed in South Africa. The Imperial War Cabinet promptly set up a group under Curzon, with Leo Amery (of the Kindergarten) as secretary, called the 'Territorial Desiderata' committee, whose function was to plan the share of the spoils going not only to Britain but to other units in the empire. At the very time when Montagu was setting about getting rid of India, this group proved very forceful indeed, and secured most of its objects. General Smuts of South Africa earmarked South-West Africa for his country, William Massey of New Zealand a huge chunk of the Pacific for the antipodean dominions. Britain received a number of important prizes, including Tanganyika, Palestine and, most important, Jordan and Iraq (including the Kirkuk-Mosul oilfields), which made her the paramount power throughout the Arab Middle East. It is true that, at Wilson's insistence, these gains were not colonies but League of Nations mandates. For the time being, however, this appeared to make little difference in practice.

Britain's spoils, which carried the Empire to its greatest extent – more than a quarter of the surface of the earth – were also thought to consolidate it economically and strategically. Smuts, the most imaginative of the silver age imperialists, played a central part in the creation of both the modern British Commonwealth and the League. He saw the latter, as he saw the Commonwealth, not as an engine of self-determination but as a means whereby the white race could continue their civilizing mission throughout the world. To him the acquisition of South-West Africa and Tanganyika was not arbitrary, but steps in a process, to be finished off by the purchase or absorption of Portuguese Mozambique, which would eventually produce what he termed the British African Dominion. This huge territorial conglomerate, stretching from Windhoek right up to Nairobi, and nicely rounded off for strategic purposes, would encompass virtually all Africa's mineral wealth outside the Congo, and about three-quarters of its best agricultural land, including all the areas suitable for white settlement. This creation of a great dominion running up the east coast of Africa was itself part of a wider geopolitical plan, of which the establishment of a British paramountcy in the Middle East was the keystone, designed to turn the entire Indian Ocean into a 'British Lake'. Its necklace of mutually supporting naval and air bases, from Suez to Perth, from Simonstown to Singapore, from Mombasa to Aden to Bahrein to Trincomalee to Rangoon, with secure access to the limitless oil supplies of the Persian Gulf, and the inexhaustible manpower of India, would at long last solve those problems of security which had exercised the minds of Chatham and his son, Castlereagh and Canning, Palmerston and Salisbury. That was the great and permanent prize which the war had brought Britain and her empire. It all looked tremendously worth while on the map.

But was there any longer the will in Britain to keep this elaborate structure functioning, with the efficiency and ruthlessness and above all the conviction it required to hold together? Who was more characteristic of the age, Smuts and Milner – or Montagu? It has been well observed, 'Once the British Empire became world-wide, the sun never set upon its problems.'[135] When troubles came, not in single spies but in battalions, would they be met with fortitude? If 1919 marked the point at which the new Thirty Years' War in Europe switched from Great Power conflict to regional violence, further east it witnessed the beginning of what some historians are now calling 'the general crisis of Asia', a period of fundamental upheaval of the kind Europe had experienced in the first half of the seventeenth century.

In February 1919, while the statesmen were getting down to the red meat of frontier-fixing in Paris, Montagu's policy of 'deliberately disturbing' the 'pathetic contentment' of the Indian masses began to produce its dubious fruits, when Mahatma Gandhi's first *satyagraha* (passive resistance) campaign led to some very active disturbances. On 10 March there was an anti-British rising in Egypt. On 9 April the first serious rioting broke out in the Punjab. On 3 May there was war between British India and Afghanistan insurgents. The next day students in Peking staged demonstrations against Japan and her western allies, who had just awarded her Chinese Shantung. Later that month, Kemal Ataturk in Anatolia, and Reza Pahlevi in Persia, showed the strength of feeling against the West across a huge tract of the Middle East. In July there was an anti-British rising in Iraq. These events were not directly connected but they all testified to spreading nationalism, all involved British interests and all tested Britain's power and will to protect them. With the country disarming as fast as it possibly could, the Chief of the Imperial General Staff, Sir Henry Wilson, complained in his diary: ' . . . in no single theatre are we strong enough, not in Ireland, nor England, nor on the Rhine, nor in Constantinople, nor Batoum, nor Egypt, nor Palestine, nor Mesopotamia, nor Persia, nor India.'[136]

India: there was the rub. In 1919 there were only 77,000 British troops in the entire subcontinent, and Lloyd George thought even that number 'appalling': he needed more men at home to hold down the coalfields.[137] In India, officers had always been taught to think fast and act quickly with the tiny forces at their disposal. Any hesitation in the face of a mob would lead to mass slaughter. They would always be backed up even if they made mistakes.[138] As was foreseeable, Montagu's reforms and Gandhi's campaign tended to incite everyone, not just the 'political nation', to demand their rights. There were a great many people in India and very few rights to go round. Muslim, Hindu and Sikh fundamentalists joined in the agitation. One result was an episode at Amritsar on 9–10 April 1919. There were, in Amritsar in the Punjab, one hundred unarmed constables and seventy-five armed reserves. That should have been enough to keep order. But the police were handled in pusillanimous fashion; some were not used at all – a sign of the times. As a result the mob got out of hand. Two banks were attacked, their managers and an assistant beaten to death, a British electrician and a railway guard murdered, and a woman missionary teacher left for dead. General Dyer, commanding the nearest army brigade, was ordered in, and three days later he opened fire on a mob in a confined space called the Jalianwala Bagh. He had earlier that day toured the whole town with beat of drum to warn that any mob would be fired upon. The same month thirty-six other orders to fire were given in the province. In Dyer's case the firing lasted ten minutes because the order to cease fire could not be heard in the noise. That was not so unusual either, then or now. On 20 September 1981, again in Amritsar, government of India police opened fire for twenty minutes on a gang of sword-wielding Sikhs.[138] The mistake made by Dyer, who was used to frontier fighting, was to let his fifty men load their rifles and issue them with spare magazines. As a result 1,650 rounds were fired and 379 people were killed. Dyer compounded his error by ordering the flogging of six men and by an instruction that all natives passing the spot where the missionary had been assaulted were to crawl on the ground.[140]

Some people praised Dyer: the Sikhs, for whom Amritsar is the national shrine and who feared it would be sacked by the mob, made him an honorary Sikh. The British Indian authorities returned him to frontier duties (the Third Afghan war broke out the next month) and privately swore never to let him near a mob again. That was the traditional way of dealing with such a case. The Indian nationalists raised an uproar and Montagu ordered an inquiry under a British judge, Lord Hunter. That was the first mistake. When Dyer was questioned by the inquiry in Lahore he was shouted down by continuous Hindustani abuse which the judge failed to control and could not understand, and Dyer said some foolish things. Hunter censured his conduct and as a result Dyer was sacked from the army. This was the second mistake. It infuriated the British community and the army, who felt that Dyer had not been given a proper trial with legal representation. It left the nationalists unappeased because the punishment was too slight for what they regarded as a massacre. The right-wing *Morning Post* collected a public subscription of £26,000 for Dyer. The nationalists responded with a subscription of their own, which bought the Bagh and turned it into a public shrine of race-hatred.

Sir Edward Carson, the leader of the Ulster die-hards, organized a motion of censure on Montagu, who defended the punishment of Dyer in a hysterical speech: 'Are you going to keep hold of India by terrorism, racial humiliation and subordination and frightfulness, or are you going to rest it upon the goodwill, and the growing goodwill, of the people of your Indian Empire?' Lloyd George's secretary reported to him that, under noisy interruptions, Montagu 'became more racial and Yiddish in screaming tone and gesture' and many Tories 'could have assaulted him physically they were so angry'. Winston Churchill saved the government from certain defeat by a brilliant speech, which he later came to regret bitterly. He said that Dyer's use of force was 'an episode which appears to me to be without precedent or parallel in the modern history of the British Empire . . . a monstrous event'. 'Frightfulness', he said, using a current code-word meaning German atrocities, 'is not a remedy known to the British pharmacopoeia. . . . We have to make it clear, some way or other, that this is not the British way of doing business.' He made skilful use of Macaulay's phrase, 'the most frightful of all spectacles, the strength of civilization without its mercy'.[141] But if all this were true, why was not Dyer on trial for his life? That was what the Indian 'political nation' thought. The episode, which might have been quickly forgotten, was thus turned, by the publicity which the British government afforded it, into a great watershed in Anglo–Indian relations.

Jawaharlal Nehru, an Old Harrovian of thirty, then working for Gandhi as an agitator among the peasants, travelled in the next sleeping compartment to Dyer while the General was on his way to give evidence to the Hunter inquiry. He overheard Dyer say to other British officers that he had felt like reducing Amritsar 'to a heap of ashes' but 'took pity on it'. In the morning Dyer 'descended at Delhi Station in pyjamas with bright pink stripes and a dressing gown'. What he could never forget, wrote Nehru, was the response of the British: 'This cold-blooded approval of that deed shocked me greatly. It seemed absolutely immoral, indecent; to use public-school language, it was the height of bad form. I realized then ... how brutal and immoral imperialism was and how it had eaten into the souls of the British upper classes.'[142] As for the inquiry and the Commons debate, the British liberals might have saved their breath. All they succeeded in doing was to help turn Dyer and Amritsar into indelible hate-symbols around which nationalists could rally.

The episode was a watershed in Indian internal security too. 'From then on', one historian of British India has put it, 'it was not the first object of the government to keep order.'[143] Security officials, both British and Indian, now hesitated to deal promptly with riotous assemblies. In 1921 when the Muslim 'Moplahs' rioted against the Hindus in the Madras area, the provincial government, with Amritsar in mind, delayed bringing in martial law. As a result, over 500 people were murdered and it took a year and huge forces of troops to restore order, by which time 80,000 people had been arrested and placed in special cages, 6,000 sentenced to transportation, 400 to life-imprisonment and 175 executed. Attacks on security forces became frequent and audacious. On 4 February 1922 in the United Provinces, a mob surrounded the police station and, those inside not daring to open fire, all twenty-two of them were torn to pieces or burned alive. From that point onwards, large-scale racial, sectarian and anti-government violence became a permanent feature of Indian life.[144] There too, in the largest and most docile colony in human history, the mould of the nineteenth century had been broken.

The disturbances in Europe and the world which followed the seismic shock of the Great War and its unsatisfactory peace were, in one sense, only to be expected. The old order had gone. Plainly it could not be fully restored, perhaps not restored at all. A new order would eventually take its place. But would this be an 'order' in the sense the pre-1914 world had understood the term? There were, as we have seen, disquieting currents of thought which suggested the image of a world adrift, having left its moorings in traditional law and morality. There was too a new hesitancy on the part of established and legitimate authority to get the global vessel back under control by the accustomed means, or any means. It constituted an invitation, unwilled and unissued but nonetheless implicit, to others to take over. Of the great trio of German imaginative scholars who offered explanations of human behaviour in the nineteenth century, and whose corpus of thought the post-1918 world inherited, only two have so far been mentioned. Marx described a world in which the central dynamic was economic interest. To Freud, the principal thrust was sexual. Both assumed that religion, the old impulse which moved men and masses, was a fantasy and always had been. Friedrich Nietzsche, the third of the trio, was also an atheist. But he saw God not as an invention but as a casualty, and his demise as in some important sense an historical event, which would have dramatic consequences. He wrote in 1886: 'The greatest event of recent times – that "God is Dead", that the belief in the Christian God is no longer tenable – is beginning to cast its first shadows over Europe.'[145] Among the advanced races, the decline and ultimately the collapse of the religious impulse would leave a huge vacuum. The history of modern times is in great part the history of how that vacuum had been filled. Nietzsche rightly perceived that the most likely candidate would be what he called the 'Will to Power', which offered a far more comprehensive and in the end more plausible explanation of human behaviour than either Marx or Freud. In place of religious belief, there would be secular ideology. Those who had once filled the ranks of the totalitarian clergy would become totalitarian politicians. And, above all, the Will to Power would produce a new kind of messiah, uninhibited by any religious sanctions whatever, and with an unappeasable appetite for controlling mankind. The end of the old order, with an unguided world adrift in a relativistic universe, was a summons to such gangster-statesmen to emerge. They were not slow to make their appearance.

TWO

The First Despotic Utopias

Lenin left Zurich to return to Russia on 8 April 1917. Some of his comrades in exile accompanied him to the station, arguing. He was to travel back through Germany at the invitation of General Ludendorff, who guaranteed him a safe passage provided he undertook not to talk to any German trade unionists on the way. War breeds revolutions. And breeding revolutions is a very old form of warfare. The Germans called it *Revolutionierungspolitik*.[1] If the Allies could incite the Poles, the Czechs, the Croats, the Arabs and the Jews to rise against the Central Powers and their partners, then the Germans, in turn, could and did incite the Irish and the Russians. If the Germans used Lenin, as Churchill later put it, 'like a typhoid bacillus', they attached no particular importance to him, lumping him in with thirty other exiles and malcontents. The arguing comrades thought Lenin would compromise himself by accepting German aid and tried to dissuade him from going. He brushed them aside without deigning to speak and climbed on the train. He was a fierce little man of forty-six, almost bald but (according to the son of his Zurich landlady) 'with a neck like a bull'. Entering his carriage he immediately spotted a comrade he regarded as suspect: 'Suddenly we saw Lenin seize him by the collar and . . . pitch him out onto the platform.'[2]

At Stockholm, comrade Karl Radek bought him a pair of shoes, but he refused other clothes, remarking sourly, 'I am not going to Russia to open a tailor's shop.' Arriving at Beloostrov on Russian soil, in the early hours of 16 April, he was met by his sister Maria and by Kamenev and Stalin, who had been in charge of the Bolshevik paper *Pravda*. He ignored his sister completely, and Stalin whom he had not met, and offered no greeting to his old comrade Kamenev whom he had not seen for five years. Instead he shouted at him, 'What's this you have been writing in *Pravda*? We saw some of your articles and roundly abused you.' Late that night he arrived at the

Finland Station in Petrograd. He was given a bunch of roses and taken to the Tsar's waiting-room. There he launched into the first of a series of speeches, one of them delivered, still clutching the roses, from the top of an armoured car. The last took two hours and 'filled his audience with turmoil and terror'. Dawn was breaking as he finished. He retired to bed, said his wife, Krupskaya, hardly speaking a word.[3]

The grim lack of humanity with which Lenin returned to Russia to do his revolutionary work was characteristic of this single-minded man. Vladimir Ilich Ulyanov was born in 1870 at Simbirsk on the Volga, the son of an inspector of primary schools. When he was sixteen, his elder brother Alexander was hanged for conspiring to blow up the Tsar with a bomb which he had made himself. His supposed reaction to his brother's death, 'We shall never get there by that road', is probably apocryphal, since he did not in fact become a Marxist (which meant disavowing terrorism) until later, after he had been forced out of Kazan University for 'revolutionary activities'. His sister Anna said he was 'hardened' by his brother's execution.[4] Certainly politics now obsessed him, then and for ever, and his approach was always cerebral rather than emotional. His contemporaries refer to his 'unsociability', his 'excessive reserve' and his 'distant manner'. Aged twenty-two, he dissuaded friends from collecting money for the victims of a famine, on the grounds that hunger 'performs a progressive function' and would 'cause the peasants to reflect on the fundamental facts of capitalist society'.[5] Within a year or two he had acquired a double-bottomed suitcase for importing seditious books, and its discovery earned him a three-year sentence in Siberia. The few days before his exile he spent in the Moscow Library, scrabbling for facts and statistics with which to hammer home his theories. In Siberia he married Krupskaya, another subversive.

Men who carry through political revolutions seem to be of two main types, the clerical and the romantic. Lenin (he adopted the pen-name in 1901) was from the first category. Both his parents were Christians. Religion was important to him, in the sense that he hated it. Unlike Marx, who despised it and treated it as marginal, Lenin saw it as a powerful and ubiquitous enemy. He made clear in many writings (his letter to Gorky of 13 January 1913 is a striking example) that he had an intense personal dislike for anything religious. 'There can be nothing more abominable', he wrote, 'than religion.' From the start, the state he created set up and maintains to this day an enormous academic propaganda machine against religion.[6] He was not just anti-clerical like Stalin, who disliked priests because they were corrupt. On the contrary, Lenin had no real feelings about corrupt priests, because they were easily beaten. The men he really feared and hated, and later persecuted, were the saints. The purer the religion, the more dangerous. A devoted cleric, he argued, is far more influential than an egotistical and immoral one. The clergy most in need of suppression were not those committed to the defence of exploitation but those who expressed their solidarity with the proletariat and the peasants. It was as though he recognized in the true man of God the same zeal and spirit which animated himself, and wished to expropriate it and enlist it in his own cause.[7] No man personifies better the replacement of the religious impulse by the will to power. In an earlier age he would surely have been a religious leader. With his extraordinary passion for force, he might have figured in Mohammed's legions. He was even closer perhaps to Jean Calvin, with his belief in organizational structure, his ability to create one and then dominate it utterly, his puritanism, his passionate self-righteousness, and above all his intolerance.

Krupskaya testifies to his asceticism, and tells us how he gave up all the things he cared for, skating, reading Latin, chess, even music, to concentrate solely on his political work.[8] A comrade remarked, 'He is the only one of us who lives revolution twenty-four hours a day.' He told Gorky he refused to listen to music often because 'it makes you want to say stupid, nice things and stroke the heads of people who could create such beauty while living in this vile hell. And now you mustn't stroke anyone's head – you might get your hand bitten off.'[9] We have to assume that what drove Lenin on to do what he did was a burning humanitarianism, akin to the love of the saints for God, for he had none of the customary blemishes of the politically ambitious: no vanity, no self-consciousness, no obvious relish for the exercise of authority. But his humanitarianism was a very abstract passion. It embraced humanity in general but he seems to have had little love for, or even interest in, humanity in particular. He saw the people with whom he dealt, his comrades, not as individuals but as receptacles for his ideas. On that basis, and on no other, they were judged. So he had no hierarchy of friendships; no friendships in fact, merely ideological alliances. He judged men not by their moral qualities but by their views, or rather the degree to which they accepted his. He bore no grudges. A man like Trotsky, whom he fought bitterly in the years before the Great War, and with whom he exchanged the vilest insults, was welcomed back with bland cordiality once he accepted Lenin's viewpoint. Equally, no colleague, however close, could bank the smallest capital in Lenin's heart.

Lenin was the first of a new species: the professional organizer of totalitarian politics. It never seems to have occurred to him, from early adolescence onwards, that any other kind of human activity was

worth doing. Like an anchorite, he turned his back on the ordinary
world. He rejected with scorn his mother's suggestion that he should
go into farming. For a few weeks he functioned as a lawyer and hated
it. After that he never had any other kind of job or occupation, for
his journalism was purely a function of his political life. And his
politics were hieratic, not demotic. Lenin surrounded himself with
official publications, and works of history and economics. He made
no effort to inform himself directly of the views and conditions of the
masses. The notion of canvassing an electorate on their doorsteps
was anathema to him: 'unscientific'. He never visited a factory or set
foot on a farm. He had no interest in the way in which wealth was
created. He was never to be seen in the working-class quarters of any
town in which he resided. His entire life was spent among the
members of his own sub-class, the bourgeois intelligentsia, which he
saw as a uniquely privileged priesthood, endowed with a special
gnosis and chosen by History for a decisive role. Socialism, he wrote
quoting Karl Kautsky, was the product of 'profound scientific
knowledge . . . . The vehicle of [this] science is not the proletariat but
the bourgeois intelligentsia: contemporary socialism was born in the
heads of individual members of this class.'[10]

Individual members – or one individual member? In practice it was
the latter. In the twenty years before his Revolution, Lenin created
his own faction within the Social Democrats, the Bolsheviks, split it
off from the Mensheviks, or minority, and then made himself
absolute master of it. This process, the will to power in action, is well
documented by his more critical comrades. Plekhanov, the real
creator of Russian Marxism, through whose *Iskra* organization
Lenin first came to prominence, accused him of 'fostering a sectarian
spirit of exclusiveness'. He was 'confusing the dictatorship of the
proletariat with dictatorship over the proletariat' and seeking to
create 'Bonapartism if not absolute monarchy in the old pre-
revolutionary style'.[11] Vera Zasulich said that, soon after Lenin
joined *Iskra*, it changed from a friendly family into a personal
dictatorship. Lenin's idea of the party, she wrote, was Louis xiv's
idea of the state – *moi*![12] The same year, 1904, Trotsky called Lenin
a Robespierre and a terrorist dictator seeking to turn the party
leadership into a committee of public safety. Lenin's methods, he
wrote in his pamphlet *Our Political Tasks*, were 'a dull caricature of
the tragic intransigence of Jacobinism . . . the party is replaced by the
organization of the party, the organization by the central committee
and finally the central committee by the dictator'.[13] Six years later, in
1910, Madame Krzhizhanovskaya wrote: 'He is one man against the
whole party. He is ruining the party.'[14] In 1914 Charles Rappaport,
while praising Lenin as 'an incomparable organizer', added: 'But he

regards only himself as a socialist . . . . War is declared on anyone who differs with him. Instead of combating his opponents in the Social Democratic Party by socialist methods, i.e. by argument, Lenin uses only surgical methods, those of "blood-letting". No party could exist under the regime of this Social Democratic Tsar, who regards himself as a super-Marxist, but who is, in reality, nothing but an adventurer of the highest order.' His verdict: 'Lenin's victory would be the greatest menace to the Russian Revolution . . . he will choke it.'[15] Two years later, on the eve of the Revolution, Viacheslav Menzhinsky described him as 'a political Jesuit . . . this illegitimate child of Russian absolutism . . . the natural successor to the Russian throne'.[16]

The impressive unanimity of this critical analysis of Lenin, coming over a period of twenty years from men and women in close agreement with his aims, testifies to an awesome consistency in Lenin's character. He brushed aside the attacks, which never seem to have caused him to pause or reconsider for one second. There was no chink in his self-armour. Authoritarian? Of course: 'Classes are led by parties and parties are led by individuals who are called leaders . . . . This is the ABC. The will of a class is sometimes fulfilled by a dictator.'[17] What mattered was that the anointed individual, the man selected by History to possess the gnosis at the appointed time, should understand and so be able to interpret the sacred texts. Lenin always insisted that Marxism was identical with objective truth. 'From the philosophy of Marxism', he wrote, 'cast as one piece of steel, it is impossible to expunge a single basic premise, a single essential part, without deviating from objective truth.'[18] He told Valentinov: 'Orthodox Marxism requires no revision of any kind either in the field of philosophy, in its theory of political economy, or its theory of historical development.'[19] Believing this, and believing himself the designated interpreter, rather as Calvin interpreted scripture in his *Institutes*, Lenin was bound to regard heresy with even greater ferocity than he showed towards the infidel. Hence the astonishing virulence of the abuse which he constantly hurled at the heads of his opponents within the party, attributing to them the basest possible motives and seeking to destroy them as moral beings even when only minor points of doctrine were at stake. The kind of language Lenin employed, with its metaphors of the jungle and the farmyard and its brutal refusal to make the smallest effort of human understanding, recalls the *odium theologicum* with poisoned Christian disputes about the Trinity in the sixth and seventh centuries, or the Eucharist in the sixteenth. And of course once verbal hatred was screwed up to this pitch, blood was bound to flow eventually. As Erasmus sadly observed of the Lutherans and papists, 'The long war of words and writings will end in blows' – as it did, for a whole century. Lenin was not in the least dismayed by such a prospect. Just as the warring theologians felt they were dealing with issues which, however trivial they might seem to the uninitiated, would in fact determine whether or not countless millions of souls burned in Hell for all eternity, so Lenin knew that the great watershed of civilization was near, in which the future fate of mankind would be decided by History, with himself as its prophet. It would be worth a bit of blood; indeed a lot of blood.

Yet the curious thing is that, for all his proclaimed orthodoxy, Lenin was very far from being an orthodox Marxist. Indeed in essentials he was not a Marxist at all. He often used Marx's methodology and he exploited the Dialectic to justify conclusions he had already reached by intuition. But he completely ignored the very core of Marx's ideology, the historical determinism of the revolution. Lenin was not at heart a determinist but a voluntarist: the decisive role was played by human will: his. Indeed, for a man who claimed a special 'scientific' knowledge of how the laws of History worked, he seems to have been invariably surprised by the actual turn of events. The outbreak of the 1905 abortive Revolution in Russia astounded him. The beginning of the 1914 war came to him like a thunderclap from a clear sky; so it did to others but then they did not claim a private line to History. He was still more shaken by the total failure of the international socialist movement to unite against the war. The fall of the Tsar amazed him. He was staggered when the Germans offered to get him back to Russia. When he arrived there he predicted he would be arrested on the spot, and instead found himself clutching those roses. He was again surprised, no less agreeably, by the success of his own Revolution. But the international uprising he confidently predicted did not materialize. To the end of his days, like the early Christians awaiting the Second Coming, he expected the Apocalypse any moment. What made Lenin a great actor on the stage of history was not his understanding of its processes but the quickness and energy with which he took the unexpected chances it offered. He was, in short, what he accused all his opponents of being: an opportunist.

He was also a revolutionary to his fingertips, and of a very old-fashioned sort. He believed that revolutions were made not by inexorable historical forces (they had to be there too, of course) but by small groups of highly disciplined men responding to the will of a decisive leader. In this respect he had much more in common with the French Jacobin revolutionary tradition of 1789–95, and even with its more recent exponents, such as Georges Sorel, than with the instinctive Marxists, most of whom were German and who saw the triumph of the proletariat almost as a Darwinian process of evolution. Lenin cut through that kind of sogginess like a knife: 'Theory, my friend, is grey, but green is the everlasting tree of life.' Again: 'Practice is a hundred time more important than theory.'[20] If the whole of Marx appears in his book, wrote Trotsky, 'the whole of Lenin on the other hand appears in revolutionary action. His scientific works are only a preparation for revolutionary activity'.[21] Lenin was an activist, indeed a hyper-activist, and it was this which made him such a violent figure. He was not a syndicalist like Sorel. But the two men shared the same appetite for violent solutions, as Sorel later acknowledged when he defined revolutionary violence as 'an intellectual doctrine, the will of powerful minds which know where they are going, the implacable resolve to attain the final goals of Marxism by means of syndicalism. Lenin has furnished us with a striking example of that psychological violence.'[22] Lenin was obsessed by force, almost to the point of lip-smacking at the scent of it. 'Revolutions are the feast-days of the oppressed classes.' 'An oppressed class which does not strive to gain a knowledge of weapons, to be drilled in the use of weapons, to possess weapons, an oppressed class of this kind deserves only to be oppressed, maltreated and regarded as slaves.' His writings abound in military metaphors: states of siege, iron rings, sheets of steel, marching, camps, barricades, forts, offensives, mobile units, guerrilla warfare, firing squads. They are dominated by violently activist verbs: flame, leap, ignite, goad, shoot, shake, seize, attack, blaze, repel, weld, compel, purge, exterminate.

The truth is, Lenin was too impatient to be an orthodox Marxist. He feared the predicament foreseen by Engels when he had written, 'The worst thing that can befall a leader of an extreme party is to be compelled to take over a government in an epoch when the moment is not yet ripe for the domination of the class which he represents . . . he is compelled to represent not his party or his class, but the class for whom conditions are ripe for domination.'[23] Russia was a semi-industrialized country, where the bourgeoisie was weak and the proletariat small, and the objective conditions for the revolution not nearly ripe. It was this dilemma which led Lenin into heresy. If 'proletarian consciousness' had not yet been created, was it not the task of Marxist intellectuals like himself to speed up the process? In 1902, in *What Is To Be Done?*, he first used the term 'vanguard fighters' to describe the new role of a small revolutionary élite.[24] He drew an entirely novel distinction between a revolution created by a mature 'organization of workers', in advanced capitalist countries like Germany and Britain, and 'an organization of revolutionaries', suitable for Russian conditions. The first was occupational, broad, public: in short a mass proletarian party. The second was quite different: 'an organization of revolutionaries must contain primarily and chiefly people whose occupation is revolutionary activity . . . . This organization must necessarily be not very broad and as secret as possible.' As such it had to forgo the 'democratic principle' which required 'full publicity' and 'election to all posts'. Working within the framework of an autocracy like Russia, that was impossible: 'The one serious organizational principle for workers in our movement must be strictest secrecy, restricted choice of members, and training of professional revolutionaries. Once these qualities are present something more than democracy is guaranteed: complete comradely confidence among revolutionaries.' But in the same passage he points out grimly that revolutionaries know 'by experience that in order to rid itself of an unworthy member an organization of genuine revolutionaries recoils from nothing'.[25] If comrades must, when needs be, murder each other – a point Dostoevsky had already made in *The Devils* – was not this 'comradely confidence' a fantasy? Was it not, indeed, belied by what happened to the organization the moment Lenin joined it, and still more when he took it over?[26]

Rosa Luxemburg, the most gifted as well as one of the more orthodox of the German Marxists, recognized Lenin's heresy for what it was: so serious as to destroy the whole purpose and idealism of Marxism. She attributed it to Lenin's faults of character, both personal and national: 'The "ego", crushed and pulverized by Russian absolutism,' she wrote, 'reappeared in the form of the "ego" of the Russian revolutionary' which 'stands on its head and proclaims itself anew the mighty consummator of history.' Lenin, she argued, was in effect demanding absolute powers for the party leadership, and this would 'intensify most dangerously the conservatism which naturally belongs to every such body'. Once granted, such powers would never be relinquished.[27] When Lenin insisted that 'consciousness' had to be brought to the proletariat from without, by 'vanguard elements', and the revolution pushed forward before it was ripe by 'vanguard fighters', he was in fact contradicting the whole 'scientific' basis of Marxist theory. She denounced the idea as élitist and non-Marxist, and said it would lead inevitably to 'military ultracentralism'.[28]

Leninism was not only a heresy; it was exactly the same heresy which created fascism. Italy was also a semi-industrialized country, where Marxists were looking for ways to speed up the coming of revolution. Italian Marxists, too, were attracted by Sorel's notions of revolutionary violence. In 1903, the year after Lenin first used the term 'vanguard fighters', Roberto Michaels, in his introduction to the Italian translation of Sorel's *Saggi di critica del Marxismo*, urged the creation of a 'revolutionary élite' to push forward the proletarian socialist millennium. Such an élite, echoed his colleague Angelo Olivetti, was essential for an under-industrialized country.[29] These ideas were taken up by a third Italian Marxist, Benito Mussolini, who was thirteen years younger than Lenin and just entering politics at this time. His father, a farrier and small property owner, was a socialist-anarchist; his mother a teacher. They filled him with a wide range of political philosophy, which included Nietzsche – he knew all about 'the will to power' – and he was much more broadly read than Lenin. But his political formation was fundamentally Marxist. Marx, he wrote, was 'the father and teacher'; he was 'the magnificent philosopher of working-class violence'.[30] But, like Lenin, he advocated the formation of 'vanguard minorities' which could 'engage the sentiment, faith and will of irresolute masses'. These vanguards had to be composed of specially trained, dedicated people, élites. Such revolutionary leadership should concern itself with the psychology of classes and the techniques of mass-mobilization, and, through the use of myth and symbolic invocation, raise the consciousness of the proletariat.[31] Like Lenin, again, he thought violence would be necessary: 'Instead of deluding the proletariat as to the possibility of eradicating all causes of bloodbaths, we wish to prepare it and accustom it to war for the day of the "greatest bloodbath of all", when the two hostile classes will clash in the supreme trial.'[32] Again, there is the endless repetition of activist verbs, the militaristic imagery.

In the years before 1914, from his impotent exile in Switzerland, Lenin watched the progress of Mussolini with approval and some envy. Mussolini turned the province of Forli into an island of socialism – the first of many in Italy – by supporting the *braccianti* day-labourers against the landowners.[33] He became one of the most effective and widely read socialist journalists in Europe. In 1912, aged twenty-nine, and still young-looking, thin, stern, with large, dark, luminous eyes, he took over the Italian Socialist Party at the Congress of Reggio Emilia, by insisting that socialism must be Marxist, thoroughgoing, internationalist, uncompromising. Lenin, reporting the congress for *Pravda* (15 July 1912), rejoiced: 'The party of the Italian socialist proletariat has taken the right path.' He agreed when Mussolini prevented the socialists from participating in the 'bourgeois reformist' Giolitti government, and so foreshadowed the emergence of the Italian Communist Party.[34] He strongly endorsed Mussolini's prophecy on the eve of war: 'With the unleashing of a mighty clash of peoples, the bourgeoisie is playing its last card and calls forth on the world scene that which Karl Marx called the sixth great power: the socialist revolution.'[35]

As Marxist heretics and violent revolutionary activists, Lenin and Mussolini had six salient features in common. Both were totally opposed to bourgeois parliaments and any type of 'reformism'. Both saw the party as a highly centralized, strictly hierarchical and ferociously disciplined agency for furthering socialist objectives. Both wanted a leadership of professional revolutionaries. Neither had any confidence in the capacity of the proletariat to organize itself. Both thought revolutionary consciousness could be brought to the masses from without by a revolutionary, self-appointed élite. Finally, both believed that, in the coming struggle between the classes, organized violence would be the final arbiter.[36]

The Great War saw the bifurcation of Leninism and Mussolini's proto-fascism. It was a question not merely of intellect and situation but of character. Mussolini had the humanity, including the vanity and the longing to be loved, which Lenin so conspicuously lacked. He was exceptionally sensitive and responsive to mass opinion. When the war came and the armies marched, he sniffed the nationalism in the air and drew down great lungfuls of it. It was intoxicating: and he moved sharply in a new direction. Lenin, on the other hand, was impervious to such aromas. His isolation from people, his indifference to them, gave him a certain massive integrity and consistency. In one way it was a weakness: he never knew what people were actually going to do – that was why he was continually surprised by events, both before and after he came to power. But it was also his strength. His absolute self-confidence and masterful will were never, for a moment, eroded by tactical calculations as to how people were likely to react. Moreover, he was seeking power in a country where traditionally people counted for nothing; were mere dirt beneath the ruler's feet.

Hence when Lenin returned to Petrograd he was totally unaffected by any wartime sentiment. He had said all along that the war was a bourgeois adventure. The defeat of the Tsar was 'the least evil'. The army should be undermined by propaganda, the men encouraged 'to turn their guns on their officers', and any disaster exploited to 'hasten the destruction ... of the capitalist class'. There should be 'ruthless struggle against the chauvinism and patriotism of the bourgeoisie of all countries without exception'.[37] Lenin was dismayed by the failure of all socialists to smash the war, and as it prolonged itself he lost hope of the millennium coming soon. In January 1917 he doubted whether 'I will live to see the decisive battles of the coming revolution'.[38] So when the Tsar was sent packing six weeks later he was surprised, as usual. To his delight, the new parliamentary regime opted to continue the war, while releasing political prisoners and thus allowing his own men to subvert it. The

Bolsheviks would overturn the new government and seize power by opposing the war. *Pravda* resumed publication on 5 March. Kamenev and Stalin hurried back from Siberia to take charge of it eight days later. Then, to Lenin's consternation, the two idiots promptly changed the paper's line and committed it to supporting the war! That was why, the second Lenin set eyes on Kamenev on 3 April, he bawled him out. The *Pravda* line promptly changed back again. Lenin sat down and wrote a set of 'theses' to explain why the war had to be resisted and ended. Stalin later squared his yard-arm by confessing to 'a completely mistaken position' which 'I shared with other party comrades and renounced it completely . . . when I adhered to Lenin's theses'.[39] Most other Bolsheviks did the same. They were overwhelmed by Lenin's certainty. The war did not matter. It had served its purpose in destroying the autocracy. Now they must exploit warweariness to oust the parliamentarians. He was indifferent to how much territory Russia lost, so long as a nucleus was preserved in which to install Bolshevism. Then they could await events with confidence. A German victory was irrelevant because their German comrades would soon be in power there – and in Britain and France too – and the day of the world socialist revolution would have dawned.[40]

In outlining this continental fantasy Lenin had, almost by chance, hit upon the one line of policy which could bring him to power. He had no real power-base in Russia. He had never sought to create one. He had concentrated exclusively on building up a small organization of intellectual and sub-intellectual desperadoes, which he could completely dominate. It had no following at all among the peasants. Only one of the Bolshevik élite even had a peasant background. It had a few adherents among the unskilled workers. But the skilled workers, and virtually all who were unionized, were attached – in so far as any had political affiliations – to the Mensheviks.[41] That was not surprising. Lenin's intransigence had driven all the ablest socialists into the Menshevik camp. That suited him: all the easier to drill the remainder to follow him without argument when the moment to strike came. As one of them put it, 'Before Lenin arrived, all the comrades were wandering in the dark.'[42] The other Bolshevik with clear ideas of his own was Trotsky. In May he arrived in Petrograd from America. He quickly realized Lenin was the only decisive man of action among them, and became his principal lieutenant. Thereafter these two men could command perhaps 20,000 followers in a nation of over 160 million.

The Russian Revolution of 1917, both in its 'February' and its 'October' phases, was made by the peasants, who had grown in number from 56 million in 1867 to 103.2 million by 1913.[43] In pre-war Russia there were less than 3.5 million factory workers and miners, and even by the widest definition the 'proletariat' numbered only 15 million. Many of the 25 million inhabitants of large towns were part of extended peasant families, working in town but based on villages. This connection helped to transmit radical ideas to the peasants. But in essence they were there already, and always had been. There was a Russian tradition of peasant collectivism, based on the commune (*obshchina*) and the craftsmen's co-operative (*artel*). It had the sanction of the Orthodox Church. Private enrichment was against the communal interest. It was often sinful. The grasping peasant, the *kulak* ('fist'), was a bad peasant: the *kulaks* were not a class (that was a later Bolshevik invention). Most peasants harboured both a respect for hierarchy and an egalitarian spirit, the latter liable to surface in moments of crisis when notions of freedom (*volya*) drove them to seize and confiscate. But the peasants never evinced the slightest desire for 'nationalization' or 'socialization': they did not even possess words for such concepts. What many wanted were independent plots, as was natural. The steps taken to create peasant proprietors since 1861 merely whetted their appetites, hence the rural agitation of 1905. From 1906, a clever Tsarist minister, P.A.Stolypin, accelerated the process, partly to appease the peasants, partly to boost food supplies to the towns, thus assisting the rapid industrialization of Russia. He also helped peasants to come out of the communes. Up to the middle of 1915 nearly 2 million got title to individual plots, plus a further 1.7 million following the voluntary break-up of communes. As a result, in the decade before the war, Russian agricultural productivity was rising rapidly, the peasants becoming better educated and, for the first time, investing in technology.[44]

The war struck a devastating blow at this development, perhaps the most hopeful in all Russian history, which promised to create a relatively contented and prosperous peasantry, as in France and central Europe, while providing enough food to make industrialization fairly painless. The war conscripted millions of peasants, while demanding from those who remained far more food to feed the swollen armies and the expanded war-factories. There were massive compulsory purchases. But food prices rose fast. Hence tension between town and countryside grew, with each blaming the other for their misery. The Bolsheviks were later able to exploit this hatred. As the war went on, the government's efforts to gouge food out of the villages became more brutal. So agrarian rioting increased, with 557 outbreaks recorded up to December 1916. But food shortages increased too, and food prices rose fast. As a result there was an unprecedented rise in the number of factory strikes in 1916, despite the fact that many industrial areas were under martial law or 'reinforced security'. The strikes came to a head at the end of February 1917, and would have been smashed, but for the fact that the peasants were angry and desperate also. Nearly all the soldiers were peasants, and when the Petrograd garrison was ordered to coerce the factory workers it mutinied. About a third, some 66,000, defied their officers. As they were armed, the regime collapsed. So the first stage of the Revolution was the work of peasants.

The destruction of the autocracy inevitably carried with it the rural hierarchy. Those peasants without plots began to seize and parcel up the big estates. That might not have mattered. The Provisional Government was bound to enact a land reform anyway, as soon as it got itself organized. But in the meantime it was committed to carrying on the war. The war was going badly. The Galician offensive failed; Lwov had fallen by July. There was a change of ministry and Kerensky was made Prime Minister. He decided to continue the war, and to do this he had to get supplies out of the peasants. It was at this point that Lenin's anti-war policy, by pure luck, proved itself inspired. He knew nothing about the peasants; had no idea what was going on in the countryside. But by opposing the war he was opposing a policy which was bound to fail anyway, and aligning his group with the popular peasant forces, both in the villages and, more important, within the army. As a result, the Bolsheviks for the first time even got a foothold in the countryside: by the end of 1917 they had about 2,400 rural workers in 203 centres. Meanwhile, the attempt to enforce the war policy wrecked the Provisional Government. A decree it had passed on 25 March obliged the peasants to hand over their entire crop, less a proportion for seed, fodder and subsistence. Before the war, 75 per cent of the grain had gone onto the market and 40 per cent had been exported. Now, with the countryside in revolt, there was no chance of Kerensky collecting what he needed to keep the war going. For the first time in modern Russian history, most of the harvest remained down on the farms. Kerensky got less than a sixth of it.[45] The attempt to grab more merely drove the peasants into open revolt and the authority of the Provisional Government in the countryside began to collapse. At the same time, the failure to get the grain to the towns meant a rapid acceleration of food prices in September, no bread at all in many places, mutiny in the army and navy, and strikes in the factories. By the beginning of October, the revolt of the peasants had already kicked the guts out of Kerensky's government.[46]

The moment had now arrived for Lenin to seize power with the 'vanguard élite' he had trained for precisely this purpose. He had, of course, no mandate to destroy parliamentary government. He had no mandate for anything, not even a notional Marxist one. He was not a peasant leader. He was not much of a proletarian leader either. In any case the Russian proletariat was tiny. And it did not want Leninism. Of more than one hundred petitions submitted by industrial workers to the central authorities in March 1917, scarcely any mentioned Socialism. Some 51 per cent demanded fewer hours, 18 per cent higher wages, 15 per cent better work conditions and 12 per cent rights for workers' committees. There was no mass support for a 'revolution of the proletariat'; virtually no support at all for anything remotely resembling what Lenin was proposing to do.[47] This was the only occasion, from that day to this, when Russian factory workers had the chance to say what they really wanted; and what they wanted was to improve their lot, not to turn the world upside down. By 'workers' committees' they meant Soviets. These had first appeared in 1905, quite spontaneously. Lenin was baffled by them: according to the Marxist texts they ought not to exist. However, they reappeared in the 'February Revolution', and when he returned to Russia in April 1917 he decided they might provide an alternative vehicle to the parliamentary system he hated. He thought, and in this respect he was proved right, that some at least of the factory Soviets could be penetrated and so manipulated by his men. Hence his 'April Theses' advocated 'Not a parliamentary republic . . . but a republic of Soviets of Workers', Poor Peasants' and Peasants' Deputies throughout the country, growing from below upwards'.[48] Ever a skilful opportunist, he began to see Soviets as a modern version of the 1870 Paris Commune: they could be managed by a determined group, such as his own, and so become the instrument for the 'dictatorship of the proletariat'. Hence when the Bolsheviks met in conference later in April he got them to voice the demand that 'proletarians of town and country' should bring about 'the rapid transfer of all state power into the hands of the Soviets'.[49] When Trotsky, who had actually worked in a 1905 Soviet, arrived in May he was put in charge of an effort to capture the most important of the town Soviets, in Petrograd.

In early June 1917, the first All-Russian Congress of Soviets met with 822 delegates. The towns were absurdly over-represented. The Social Revolutionaries, who spoke for the peasants, had 285 delegates. The Mensheviks, who represented the organized workers, had 248. There were minor groups totalling 150 and forty-five with no label. The Bolsheviks had 105.[50] The anarchists staged a trial of strength on 3 July when they ordered big street demonstrations against the war. But they were scattered by loyal troops, *Pravda* was shut down and some Bolsheviks, including Kamenev and Trotsky, put in gaol. Lenin was allowed to escape to Finland: he was not yet considered a fatal enemy.[51] The decisive change came during the summer and early autumn. The war-fronts began to collapse. In August Kerensky held an all-party 'State Conference' in Moscow, attended by 2,000 delegates. It accomplished nothing. At the end of the month, a Tsarist general, Kornilov, staged a military revolt which ended in fiasco. All these events played into Lenin's hands, especially the last which allowed him to create an atmosphere of fear in which he could persuade people it was necessary to break the law to 'preserve' the new republic. But it was, above all, the failure of Kerensky to get food out of the peasants which sapped legal order. Troops were demobilizing themselves and flocking to the cities where there was no bread for them. There, they joined or formed Soviets, and were soon electing Bolshevik spokesmen who promised an immediate end to the war and the distribution of all estates to the peasants. By early September the Bolsheviks had majorities on both the Petrograd and the Moscow Soviets, the two that really mattered, and on 14 September Lenin, still in hiding, felt strong enough to issue the slogan 'All power to the Soviets'.[52] Trotsky, just out of gaol, immediately became president of the Petrograd Soviet, the focus of the coming uprising.

Trotsky, indeed, was the active agent of the Revolution. But Lenin was the master-mind, who took all the key decisions and provided the essential 'will to power'. The Bolshevik Revolution, let alone the creation of the Communist state, would have been quite impossible without him. He slipped back into Petrograd in disguise on 9 October and at a meeting of the Central Committee the next day he won a 10–2 vote for an armed rising. A Political Bureau or 'Politburo' – the first we hear of it – was created to manage the rising. But the actual military preparations were made by a 'military-revolutionary committee', formed under Trotsky from the Petrograd Soviet. The rising was timed to make use of the second All-Russian Congress of Soviets, which met on 25 October. The previous evening, Lenin formed an embryo government, and in the morning Trotsky's men went into action and seized key points throughout the city. The members of the Provisional Government were taken prisoner or fled. There was very little bloodshed. That afternoon the Bolsheviks got the Congress of Soviets to approve the transfer of power. The following day, before dispersing, it adopted a decree making peace, another abolishing landed estates and a third approving the composition of the Council of People's Commissars, or Sovnarkom for short, the first Workers' and Peasants' Government.[53] But as Stalin was later careful to point out, it was the military revolutionary committee which seized power, and the Congress of Soviets 'only *received* the power from the hands of the Petrograd Soviet'.[54] His object in making this distinction was to preserve the notion of a Marxist proletarian revolution. Certainly there was nothing legal about the way in which Lenin came to power. But it was not a revolutionary uprising either. It was an old-style *coup*, or as the Germans were soon to call it, a *putsch*. There was nothing Marxist about it.

At the time, however, Lenin astutely made the greatest possible use of the spurious legitimacy conferred upon his regime by the Soviets. Indeed for the next two months he carefully operated at two levels, which corresponded in a curious way to the Marxist perception of the world. On the surface was the level of constitutional arrangements and formal legality. That was for show, for the satisfaction of the public, and for the outside world. At a lower level were the deep structures of real power: police, army, communications, arms. That was for real. At the show level, Lenin described his government as 'provisional' until the 'Constituent Assembly', which the Kerensky government had scheduled for election on 12 November, had had a chance to meet. So the elections proceeded, with the Bolsheviks merely one of the participating groups. It was the first and last true parliamentary election ever held in Russia. As expected it returned a majority of peasant-oriented Social Revolutionaries, 410 out of 707. The Bolsheviks had 175 seats, the Mensheviks were down to sixteen, the bourgeois Kadets had seventeen and 'national groups' made up the remaining members. Lenin fixed the Assembly's first meeting for 5 January 1918. To keep up the show he invited three members of the SR left wing to join his Sovnarkom. This had the further advantage of splitting the SRs so that he now had a majority in the Congress of Soviets, and he summoned that to meet three days after the Assembly had been dealt with. He intended it would thereafter remain the tame instrument of his legitimacy. Reassured, perhaps, by these constitutional manoeuvres, the great city of Petrograd went about its business and pleasures. Even on the day Kerensky was overthrown, all the shops remained open, the trams ran, the cinemas were crowded. The Salvation Army, which the republic had admitted for the first time, played on street-corners. Karsavina was at the Mariinsky. Chaliapin sang at concerts. There were packed public lectures. Society congregated at Contant's restaurant. There was extravagant gambling.[55]

Meanwhile, down among the structures, Lenin worked very fast. It is significant that, when he had so much else to do, he gave priority to controlling the press. In September, just before the *putsch*, he had publicly called for 'a much more democratic' and 'incomparably more complete' freedom of the press. In fact under the republic the press had become as free as in Britain or France. Two days after he seized power, Lenin ended this freedom with a decree on the press. As part of 'certain temporary, extraordinary measures', any newspapers 'calling for open resistance or insubordination to the Workers' or Peasants' Government', or 'sowing sedition through demonstrably slanderous distortions of fact', would be suppressed and their editors put on trial. By the next day the government had closed down ten Petrograd newspapers; ten more were shut the following week.[56] Management of the news was entrusted primarily to the Bolshevik party newspaper, *Pravda*, and the paper of the Soviets, *Isvestia*, now taken over by Sovnarkom.

Meanwhile, with great speed if in some confusion, the physical apparatus of power was being occupied by the Bolshevik activists. The method was corporatist. Every organization, from factories to the trams, held Soviet-style elections. This was the easiest way to ensure that delegates chosen were broadly acceptable to the regime. Later, Boris Pasternak was to give a vignette of the process:

Everywhere there were new elections: for the running of housing, trade, industry and municipal services. Commissars were being appointed to each, men in black leather jerkins, with unlimited powers and an iron will, armed with means of intimidation and revolvers, who shaved little and slept less. They knew the shrinking bourgeois breed, the average holder of cheap government stocks, and they spoke to them without the slightest pity and with Mephistophelean smiles, as to petty thieves caught in the act. These were the people who reorganized everything in accordance with the plan, and company after company, enterprise after enterprise, became Bolshevised.[57]

This physical takeover was quickly given an infrastructure of decree-law. 10 November: Peter the Great's Table of Ranks abolished. 22 November: house searches authorized; fur coats confiscated. 11 December: all schools taken from the Church and handed to the state. 14 December: state monopoly of all banking activity; all industry subjected to 'workers' control'. 16 December: all army ranks abolished. 21 December: new law code for 'revolutionary courts'. 24 December: immediate nationalization of all factories. 29 December: all payments of interest and dividends stopped; bank-withdrawals strictly limited. As the novelist Ilya Ehrenburg put it later: 'Every morning the inhabitants carefully studied the new decrees, still wet and crumpled, pasted on the walls: they wanted to know what was permitted and what was forbidden.'[58]

But even at this stage some of the key moves in the consolidation of power were not reflected in public decree-laws. In the initial stages of his take-over, Lenin depended entirely on the armed bands Trotsky had organized through the Petrograd Soviet. They were composed partly of politically motivated young thugs, the 'men in black leather jerkins', partly of deserters, often Cossacks. An eye-witness described the scene in the rooms of the Smolny Institute, from which the Bolsheviks initially operated: 'The Bureau was packed tight with Caucasian greatcoats, fur caps, felt cloaks, galloons, daggers, glossy black moustaches, astounded, prawn-like eyes, and the smell of horses. This was the élite, the cream headed by "native" officers, in all perhaps five hundred men. Cap in hand they confessed their loyalty to the Revolution.'[59] These men were effective in overawing the crumbling republic. But for the enforcement of the new order, something both more sophisticated and more ruthless was required. Lenin needed a political police.

Believing, as he did, that violence was an essential element in the Revolution, Lenin never quailed before the need to employ terror. He inherited two traditions of justification for terror. From the French Revolution he could quote Robespierre: 'The attribute of popular government in revolution is at one and the same time *virtue and terror*, virtue without which terror is fatal, terror without which virtue is impotent. The terror is nothing but justice, prompt, severe, inflexible; it is thus an emanation of virtue.'[60] Brushing aside the disastrous history of the Revolutionary Terror, Marx had given the method his own specific and unqualified endorsement. There was, he wrote, 'only one means to *curtail*, simplify and localize the bloody agony of the old society and the bloody birth-pangs of the new, only one means – the revolutionary terror'.[61] But Marx had said different things at different times. The orthodox German Marxists did not accept that terror was indispensable. A year after Lenin seized power, Rosa Luxemburg, in her German Communist Party programme of December 1918, stated: 'The proletarian revolution needs for its purposes no terror, it hates and abominates murder.'[62] Indeed, one of the reasons why she opposed Lenin's 'vanguard élite' attempt to speed up the historical process of the proletarian revolution was precisely because she thought it would tempt him to use terror – as the Marxist text hinted – as a short-cut, especially against the background of the Tsarist autocracy and general Russian barbarism and contempt for life.

In fact the real tragedy of the Leninist Revolution, or rather one of its many tragedies, is that it revived a savage national method of government which was actually dying out quite fast. In the eighty years up to 1917, the number of people executed in the Russian empire averaged only seventeen a year, and the great bulk of these occurred in the earlier part of the period.[63] Wartime Russia in the last years of the Tsars was in some ways more liberal than Britain and France under their wartime regulations. The Republic abolished the death penalty completely, though Kerensky restored it at the front in September 1917. Most of Lenin's own comrades were

opposed to it. Most of the early Bolshevik killings were the work of
sailors, who murdered two former ministers on 7 January 1918,
and carried out a three-day massacre in Sevastopol the following
month, or were indiscriminate peasant slaughters deep in the countryside.[64]

  It is difficult to avoid the conclusion that the decision to use
terror and oppressive police power was taken very early on by
Lenin, endorsed by his chief military agent Trotsky; and that it was,
as Rosa Luxemburg feared it would be, an inescapable part of his
ideological approach to the seizure and maintenance of authority,
and the type of centralized state he was determined to create. And
this in turn was part of Lenin's character, that will to power he had
in such extraordinary abundance. As early as 1901 Lenin warned:
'In principle we have never renounced terror and cannot renounce
it.'[65] Again: 'We'll ask the man, where do you stand on the
question of the revolution? Are you for it or against it? If he's
against it, we'll stand him up against a wall.' Shortly after he came
to power he asked: 'Is it impossible to find among us a Fouquier-
Tinville to tame our wild counter-revolutionaries?'[66] The number of
times Lenin, as head of the government, began to use such expressions as 'shoot them', 'firing-squad', 'against the wall', suggests a
growing temperamental appetite for extreme methods.

  There was also a revealing furtiveness, or rather deliberate duplicity, in the manner in which Lenin set up the instrument to be
used, if necessary, for counter-revolutionary terror. The original
Bolshevik armed force, as already explained, was Trotsky's military-revolutionary committee of the Petrograd Soviet. Trotsky had
no scruples about continuing to use force even after the Revolution
had succeeded: 'We shall not enter into the kingdom of socialism in
white gloves on a polished floor', was how he put it.[67] Immediately
after 25–26 October 1917, this committee became a sub-committee
of the Central Executive and was given security jobs including
fighting 'counter-revolution', defined as 'sabotage, concealment of
supplies, deliberate holding up of cargoes, etc'. Its constitution was
made public in a Sovnarkom decree of 12 November 1917.[68] As it
was charged with examining suspects, it set up a special section
under Felix Dzerzhinsky, a fanatical Pole who was in charge of
security at Smolny. However, when on 7 December 1917 the
military committee was finally dissolved by another Sovnarkom
decree, Dzerzhinsky's section remained in being, becoming the
'All-Russian Extraordinary Commission' (Cheka), charged with
combating 'counter-revolution and sabotage'. The decree which
created the Cheka was not made public until more than ten years
later (*Pravda*, 18 December 1927), so that Lenin's security force

was from the beginning and remained for the rest of his life a secret police in the true sense, in that its very existence was not officially acknowledged.[69]

There was no question that, from the very start, the Cheka was intended to be used with complete ruthlessness and on a very large scale. A week before it came into official though secret existence, Trotsky was challenged about the growing numbers of arrests and searches. He defended them to the All-Russian Congress of Peasants' Deputies, insisting that 'demands to forgo all repressions at a time of civil war are demands to abandon the civil war'.[70] The Cheka had a committee of eight under Dzerzhinsky and he quickly filled up its ranks, and the corps of senior inspectors and agents, with other fanatics. Many of them were fellow Poles or Latvians, such as the sinister Latsis, or 'Peters', brother of Peter the Painter of the Sidney Street Siege, perpetrator of a series of murders in Houndsditch, and Kedrov, a sadist who eventually went mad. The speed with which the force expanded was terrifying. It was recruiting people as fast as it could throughout December 1917 and January 1918, and one of its first acts was to see set up a nationwide intelligence service by asking all local Soviets for 'information about organizations and persons whose activity is directed against the revolution and popular authority'. This decree suggested that local Soviets should themselves set up security committees to report back to professional agents, and from the first the Cheka was assisted by a growing horde of amateur and part-time informers. Its full-time ranks grew inexorably. The Tsar's secret police, the Okhrana, had numbered 15,000, which made it by far the largest body of its kind in the old world. By contrast, the Cheka, within three years of its establishment, had a strength of 250,000 full-time agents.[71] Its activities were on a correspondingly ample scale. While the last Tsars had executed an average of seventeen a year (for all crimes), by 1918–19 the Cheka was averaging 1,000 executions a month for political offences alone.[72]

This figure is certainly an understatement – for a reason which goes to the heart of the iniquity of the system Lenin created. Almost immediately after the Cheka came into being, a decree set up a new kind of 'revolutionary tribunal', to try those 'who organize uprisings against the authority of the Workers' and Peasants' Government, who actively oppose it or do not obey it, or who call on others to oppose or disobey it', and civil servants guilty of sabotage or concealment. The tribunal was authorized to fix penalties in accordance with 'the circumstances of the case and the dictates of the revolutionary conscience'.[73] This decree effectively marked the end of the rule of law in Lenin's new state, then only weeks old. It dovetailed into the Cheka system. Under the Tsars, the Okhrana was empowered to arrest, but it then had to hand over the prisoner to the courts for public trial, just like anyone else; and any punishments were meted out by the ordinary civil authorities. Under Lenin's system, the Cheka controlled the special courts (which met in secret) and carried out their verdicts. Hence once a man fell into the Cheka's hands, his only safeguard was 'the dictates of the revolutionary conscience'. As the Cheka arrested, tried, sentenced and punished its victims, there was never any reliable record of their numbers. Within weeks of its formation, the Cheka was operating its first concentration and labour camps. These arose from a Sovnarkom decree directing 'bourgeois men and women' to be rounded up and set to digging defensive trenches in Petrograd.[74] Camps were set up to house and guard them, and once the Cheka was given supervision over the forced labour programme, its prison-camps began to proliferate on the outskirts of towns, or even deep in the countryside – the nucleus of what was to become the gigantic 'Gulag Archipelago'. By the end of 1917, when Lenin had been in power only nine or ten weeks, it would be correct to say that the Cheka was already a 'state within a state'; indeed as regards many activities it was the state.

We can dismiss the notion that its origins and growth were contrary to Lenin's will. All the evidence we possess points in quite the opposite direction.[75] It was Lenin who drafted all the key decrees and Dzerzhinsky was always his creature. Indeed it was Lenin personally who infused the Cheka with the spirit of terror and who, from January 1918 onwards, constantly urged it to ignore the doubts and humanitarian feelings of other Bolsheviks, including many members of Sovnarkom. When Lenin transferred the government from Petrograd to Moscow for security reasons, and placed Sovnarkom within the Kremlin, he encouraged Dzerzhinsky to set up his own headquarters independently of Sovnarkom. A large insurance company building was taken over in Lubyanka Square; inside it an 'inner prison' was built for political suspects; and from this point on the Cheka was an independent department of state reporting directly to Lenin. He left its officials in no doubt what he wanted. In January 1918, three months before the civil war even began, he advocated 'shooting on the spot one out of every ten found guilty of idling'. A week later he urged the Cheka publicly: 'Until we apply the terror – shooting on the spot – to speculators, we shall achieve nothing.' A few weeks later he demanded 'the arrest and *shooting* of takers of bribes, swindlers, etc'. Any breach of the decree laws must be followed by 'the harshest punishment'.[76] On 22 February, he authorized a Cheka proclamation ordering local Soviets to 'seek out, arrest and shoot immediately' a whole series of categories of 'enemies, speculators, etc'.[77] He followed this general decree with his own personal instructions. Thus, by August 1918, he was telegraphing the

Soviet at Nizhni-Novgorod: 'You must exert every effort, form a *troika* of dictators . . . *instantly* introduce *mass terror, shoot and transport* hundreds of prostitutes who get the soldiers drunk, ex-officers, etc. Not a minute to be wasted.'[78] His example inspired others. The next month the army newspaper proclaimed: 'Without mercy, without sparing, we will kill our enemies in scores of hundreds, let them be thousands, let them drown themselves in their own blood . . . let there be floods of blood of the bourgeois.'[79] Lenin's incitements brought their results. In the first six months of 1918 the Cheka executed, according to its official figures, only twenty-two prisoners. In the second half of the year it carried out 6,000 executions, and in the whole of 1919 some 10,000. W.H.Chamberlain, the first historian of the revolution, who was an eye-witness, calculated that by the end of 1920 the Cheka had carried out over 50,000 death sentences.[80]

However, the most disturbing and, from the historical point of view, important characteristic of the Lenin terror was not the quantity of the victims but the principle on which they were selected. Within a few months of seizing power, Lenin had aban-doned the notion of individual guilt, and with it the whole Judeo-Christian ethic of personal responsibility. He was ceasing to be interested in *what* a man did or had done — let alone *why* he had done it — and was first encouraging, then commanding, his repress-ive apparatus to hunt down people, and destroy them, not on the basis of crimes, real or imaginary, but on the basis of generaliza-tions, hearsay, rumours. First came condemned categories: 'pros-titutes', 'work-shirkers', 'bagmen', 'speculators', 'hoarders', all of whom might vaguely be described as criminal. Following quickly, however, came entire occupational groups. The watershed was Lenin's decree of January 1918 calling on the agencies of the state to 'purge the Russian land of all kinds of harmful insects'. This was not a judicial act: it was an invitation to mass murder. Many years later, Alexander Solzhenitsyn listed just a few of the groups who thus found themselves condemned to destruction as 'insects'. They included 'former *zemstvo* members, people in the Cooper movements, homeowners, high-school teachers, parish councils and choirs, priests, monks and nuns, Tolstoyan pacifists, officials of trade unions' — soon all to be classified as 'former people'.[81] Quite quickly the condemned group decree-laws extended to whole classes and the notion of killing people collectively rather than individually was seized upon by the Cheka professionals with enthusiasm. Probably the most important Cheka official next to Dzerzhinsky himself was the ferocious Latvian M.Y. Latsis. He came nearest to giving the Lenin terror its true definition:

The Extraordinary Commission is neither an investigating commission nor a tribunal. It is an organ of struggle, acting on the home front of a civil war. It does not judge the enemy: it strikes him . . . . We are not carrying out war against individuals. We are exterminating the bourgeoisie as a class. We are not looking for evidence or witnesses to reveal deeds or words against the Soviet power. The first question we ask is – to what class does he belong, what are his origins, upbringing, education or profession? These questions define the fate of the accused. This is the essence of the Red Terror.[82]

Once Lenin had abolished the idea of personal guilt, and had started to 'exterminate' (a word he frequently employed) whole classes, merely on account of occupation or parentage, there was no limit to which this deadly principle might be carried. Might not entire categories of people be classified as 'enemies' and condemned to imprisonment or slaughter merely on account of the colour of their skin, or their racial origins or, indeed, their nationality? There is no essential moral difference between class-warfare and race-warfare, between destroying a class and destroying a race. Thus the modern practice of genocide was born.

While the Cheka was getting itself organized, Lenin proceeded to wind up the democratic legacy of the republic. The Constituent Assembly had been elected on 12 November 1917. Lenin made clear his attitude towards it on 1 December: 'We are asked to call the Constituent Assembly as originally conceived. No thank you! It was conceived against the people and we carried out the rising to make certain that it will not be used against the people.'[83] In his 'Theses on the Constituent Assembly', published anonymously in *Pravda* of 13 December, he contrasted a parliament, which 'in a bourgeois republic . . . is the highest form of the democratic principle', with a Soviet, which 'is a higher form of the democratic principle'. Hence 'any attempt . . . to look at the . . . Constituent Assembly from the formal, juridical standpoint, within the framework of bourgeois democracy' was treason to the proletariat. Unless the Assembly made 'an unconditional declaration of acceptance of the Soviet power', it would face a crisis to be 'solved only by revolutionary means'.[84] This was not so much an argument as a blunt statement by Lenin that his regime would not accept any form of democratic control by a parliament. Four days later, to underline his point, he arrested the leader of the right-wing section of the Social Revolutionaries, Avksientiev, and his chief followers, 'for the organization of a counter-revolutionary conspiracy'.[85]

By the time the Assembly met on 5 January 1918, Lenin had already put together the essentials of a repressive regime, albeit on a small scale as yet (the Cheka had only 120 full-time agents), and was

therefore in a position to treat the parliament with the contempt he felt
it deserved. He did not put in an appearance but he had written the
script down to the last line. The building was 'guarded' by the Baltic
Fleet sailors, the most extreme of the armed groups at Lenin's
disposal. *Izvestia* had warned the deputies the day before they met
that 'all power in the Russian republic belongs to the Soviets and
Soviet institutions' and that if they sought to 'usurp this or that
function of state power' they would be treated as counter-
revolutionaries and 'crushed by all means at the disposal of the Soviet
power, including the use of armed force'.[86] As soon as the deputies
gathered, Lenin's henchman, Sverdlov, simply pushed from the
tribune its oldest member, who by a Russian tradition was about to
open proceedings, and took charge. There followed a long debate,
culminating in a vote after midnight which went against the Bolsheviks and their allies, 237–138. The Bolsheviks then withdrew,
followed an hour later by their partners, the Left SRs. At 5 am on 6
January, following instructions sent direct from Lenin, the sailor in
charge of the guard told the Assembly that its meeting must close
'because the guard is tired'. It adjourned for twelve hours but never
reassembled, for later that day, after a speech by Lenin, the Central
Executive Committee formally dissolved it and a guard was placed on
the doors to tell the deputies to go back to their homes. An unarmed
demonstration in favour of the parliament was dispersed, several in
the crowd being killed.[87] Thus briefly and brutally did Lenin destroy
parliamentary democracy in Russia. Three days later, in the same
building and with Sverdlov presiding, the Soviets met to rubber-stamp
the decisions of the regime.

By the end of January 1918, after about twelve weeks in authority,
Lenin had established his dictatorship so solidly that nothing short of
external intervention could have destroyed his power. Of course by
this time the Germans were in a position to snuff him out without
difficulty. They were advancing rapidly on all fronts, meeting little
opposition. But on 3 March Lenin signed their dictated peace-terms,
having argued down Trotsky and other colleagues, who wanted to
pursue a 'no war no peace' line until the German workers' revolution
broke out. Thereafter, for the rest of the war, the Germans had an
interest in keeping Lenin going. As their Foreign Minister, Admiral
Paul von Hintze, put it in July 1918: 'The Bolsheviks are the best
weapon for keeping Russia in a state of chaos, thus allowing Germany
to tear off as many provinces from the former Russian Empire as she
wishes and to rule the rest through economic controls.'[88]

For equal and opposite reasons the Allies were anxious to oust
Lenin and get Russia back into the war. But Lenin was clearly right to
settle with the Germans, whose threat to him was near and immediate,

rather than the Allies, who were distant and divided in their aims. As early as 14 December 1917 the British War Cabinet decided to pay money to anti-Bolsheviks 'for the purpose of maintaining alive in South East Russia the resistance to the Central Powers'. On 26 December Britain and France divided up Russia into spheres of influence for this end, the French taking the south, the British the north.[89] In March 1918 the first British troops went to Archangel and Murmansk, initially to protect British war stores there. After the German armistice the Allies continued with their intervention, for Lenin had signed a separate peace with the enemy and at one time Winston Churchill hoped to persuade the Council of Ten in Paris to declare war formally on the Bolshevik regime.[90] By the end of 1918, there were 180,000 Allied troops on Russian territory – British, French, American, Japanese, Italian and Greek, as well as Serb and Czech contingents – plus 300,000 men of various anti-Bolshevik Russian forces supported by Allied money, arms and technical advisers. It may be asked: granted the slender, almost non-existent popular support Lenin enjoyed in Russia, how did his regime manage to survive?

The short answer is that it was very nearly extinguished in the late summer and early autumn of 1919. There was absolutely nothing inevitable about its endurance. A number of quite different factors worked in its favour. In the first place, with one exception none of the Allied statesmen involved even began to grasp the enormous significance of the establishment of this new type of totalitarian dictatorship, or the long-term effect of its implantation in the heart of the greatest land power on earth. The exception was Winston Churchill. With his strong sense of history, he realized some kind of fatal watershed was being reached. What seems to have brought the truth home to him was not only the murder of the entire Russian royal family on 16 July 1918, without any kind of trial or justification, but Lenin's audacity, on 31 August, in getting his men to break into the British Embassy and murder the naval attaché, Captain Crombie. To Churchill it seemed that a new kind of barbarism had arisen, indifferent to any standards of law, custom, diplomacy or honour which had hitherto been observed by civilized states. He told the cabinet that Lenin and Trotsky should be captured and hanged, 'as the object upon whom justice will be executed, however long it takes, and to make them feel that their punishment will become an important object of British policy'.[91] He told his Dundee electors on 26 November 1918 that the Bolsheviks were reducing Russia 'to an animal form of barbarism', maintaining themselves by 'bloody and wholesale butcheries and murders carried out to a large extent by Chinese executions and armoured cars .... Civilization is being completely extinguished over gigantic areas, while Bolsheviks hop and caper like troops of ferocious baboons amid the ruins of cities and corpses of their victims.' 'Of all the tyrannies in history', he remarked on 11 April 1919, 'the Bolshevik tyranny is the worst, the most destructive, the most degrading.' Lenin's atrocities were 'incomparably more hideous, on a larger scale and more numerous than any for which the Kaiser is responsible'. His private remarks to colleagues were equally vehement. Thus, to Lloyd George: 'You might as well legalize sodomy as recognize the Bolsheviks.' To H.A.L.Fisher: 'After conquering all the Huns – the tigers of the world – I will not submit to be beaten by the baboons.' Once the regime consolidated itself it would become far more expansionist than Tsarist Russia and, he warned Field Marshal Wilson, 'highly militaristic'.[92] Churchill never wavered in his view that it ought to be a prime object of the policy of the peaceful, democratic great powers to crush this new kind of menace while they still could.

But even Churchill was confused about means. He resented suggestions his colleagues fed the press that he had some kind of master-plan to suppress Bolshevism throughout the world. He wrote to Lloyd George (21 February 1919): 'I have no Russian policy. I know of no Russian policy. I went to Paris to look for a Russian policy! I deplore the lack of a Russian policy.' He admitted it was not the job of the West to overthrow Lenin: 'Russia must be saved by Russian exertions.'[93] All the other Western leaders, in varying degrees, were lukewarm about the business. On 14 February 1919 Wilson said he was for withdrawal: 'Our troops were doing no sort of good in Russia. They did not know for whom or for what they were fighting.' The French were more interested in building up their new ally, Poland, into a big state. Lloyd George was thinking in terms of public opinion at home: 'The one thing to spread Bolshevism was to attempt to suppress it. To send our soldiers to shoot down the Bolsheviks would be to create Bolshevism here.' Sir David Shackleton, head official at the Ministry of Labour, warned the cabinet in June 1919 that British intervention was the main cause of industrial unrest. The War Office warned of 'revolutionary talk in the Brigade of Guards' and General Ironside, in charge at Archangel, cabled home news of 'very persistent and obstinate' mutinies among his own troops.[94]

None of this might have mattered if Lloyd George, in particular, had regarded Leninism as the ultimate evil. But he did not. Leninism subscribed to self-determination. It was prepared to let go, had indeed already let go, all the small nations on its fringes: Finland, the Baltic states, Poland, possibly the Ukraine, the Crimean and the Georgian republics. Marshal Foch, for the French, spoke in terms of welding these new democratic states into a *cordon sanitaire* to seal off Bolshevism from civilized Europe. Unlike Churchill, most western opinion saw the Bolsheviks as non-expansionist, prepared to settle for a weak Russia, internationally minded. To them, it was the anti-Bolshevik commanders, Admiral Kolchak and General Denikin, who stood for Tsarist imperialism, the old fear-images of 'the Bear', the 'Russian Steamroller' and so forth. This view was by no means unfounded. Kolchak persistently refused to give the Allies the assurances they wanted about confirming the independence of Finland and the Baltic states after he had overthrown Lenin. He would not even promise to permit democratic elections in Russia itself. Denikin showed himself strongly anti-Polish and hotly opposed to liberty for the Ukrainians, the Caucasus and other small nations. He appeared to want to re-establish the Tsarist empire in all its plenitude and, worse, with all its traditional ferocity. What damaged the image of the White Russians in the West more than anything else, not least with Churchill himself, was Denikin's identification of Bolshevism with Jewry and the anti-Semitic atrocities of his troops: during 1919 over 100,000 Jews appear to have been murdered in south Russia, by no means all of them in peasant pogroms.[95]

The anti-Bolshevik commanders, in fact, never accommodated themselves either to the Allies or to the oppressed nationalities. Hence, when Denikin took Kiev on 31 August 1919 and advanced towards Moscow, Allied forces were already being evacuated in the north, releasing masses of Lenin's troops to move south. Again, on 16 October 1919, General Yudenich's troops were only twenty-five miles from Petrograd and Denikin was near Tula west of Moscow: within a week his Cossacks had deserted, there were nationalist risings in the Ukraine and a general rebellion in the Caucasus. From that moment the White Russian tide began to recede and by the end of the year their cause was finished.

Lenin's biggest single asset was his willingness to hand out post-dated cheques not only to the nationalists but above all to the peasants. No one was then to know that none of the cheques would be honoured. The White leaders felt they could not match these promises. General Sir Henry Rawlinson, Britain's last commander on the spot, thought the victory was due to the character and determination of the Bolshevik leaders: 'They know what they want and are working hard to get it.'[96] There were only a few thousand Bolshevik cadres, but Lenin had filled them with his will to power and given them a clear vision to strive for. They had not yet begun to murder each other. They were absolutely ruthless — far more so than their opponents — in shooting failed commanders, deserters, faint-hearts, saboteurs and anyone who argued or caused trouble. Such ferocity, it is sad to record, has nearly always paid among the Great Russians; and of course it was the Great Russians who constituted the bulk of the people behind Lenin's lines. The real intransigent elements, the minorities and racial nationalities, were all behind the lines of the Whites, who felt unable to make them any concessions. The conjunction was fatal.

Lenin, however, was not without secret friends abroad. The links of self-interest established between his regime and the German military in November 1917 seem to have been maintained, albeit sometimes in tenuous form, even after the Armistice. German military assistance to the Bolsheviks is frequently referred to by British officers advising Denikin and other White commanders.[97] The help took the immediate form of *Freikorps* officers, munitions and in due course industrial expertise in building new war factories. The last point was vital to the Germans, who under the Versailles Treaty had to dismantle their armaments industry. By secretly coaching the Bolsheviks in arms technology and developing new weapons in Russia they were maintaining a continuity of skills which, when the time was ripe, could once more be openly exploited back at home. Thus a strange, covert alliance was formed, which occasionally broke surface, as at the Rapallo Conference in 1922 and, still more sensationally, in August 1939, but which for most of the time was carefully hidden: a working relationship of generals, arms experts, later of secret police, which was to continue in one form or another until 22 June 1941. It is one of the ironies of history that German specialists first taught Soviet Communism how to make excellent tanks, a weapon used to overwhelm Germany in 1943–5. The deeper irony is that this was a marriage of class enemies: what could be further apart than Prussian generals and Bolsheviks? Yet in the final crisis and aftermath of the war, both groups saw themselves, and certainly were seen, as outlaws. There was a spirit of gangster fraternization in their arrangements, the first of many such Europe was to experience over the next twenty years.

The earliest of Lenin's post-dated cheques to be dishonoured was the one he issued to the nationalities. Here, the methodology was Lenin's but the agent he used was the former seminarist, Josef Djugashvili, or Stalin, whom he made People's Commissar of the People's Commissariat of Nationalities (Narkomnats). Throughout his career, Lenin showed a brilliant if sinister genius for investing words and expressions with special meanings which suited his political purposes – a skill with which the twentieth century was to become depressingly familiar, in many different forms. Just as, to Lenin, a parliament, which he could not control, was 'bourgeois democracy', whereas a Soviet, which he could, was 'proletarian democracy', so self-determination took on class distinctions. Finland, the Baltic states, Poland, were lost to Russia. These countries were, accordingly, termed 'bourgeois republics', the reservation being that, at some convenient future time, when Soviet power was greater, they could be transformed into 'proletarian republics' and brought into a closer relationship with the Soviet Union. The Ukraine, whose grain supplies were essential to the regime's survival, was not permitted to opt for 'bourgeois self-determination' and in 1921–2, after fearful struggles, was obliged to accept 'proletarian self-determination', that is, membership of the Soviet Union.[98]

Stalin applied this technique to the Caucasus and Russian Asia wherever Bolshevik military power made it possible. If self-determination raised its head it was branded 'bourgeois' and stamped upon. Such breakaway movements, as he put it, were simply attempts 'to disguise in a national costume the struggle with the power of the working masses'. Self-determination was a right 'not of the bourgeoisie but of the working masses' and must be used solely as an instrument in 'the struggle for Socialism'.[99] True, that is proletarian, self-determination could not manifest itself until Soviets or other authentic proletarian bodies had been formed. Then each nationality could exercise its 'right'. Using Narkomnats, Stalin created a system to implant in each nationality officials whose party loyalties were stronger than their local affiliations, a method which his deputy Pestkovsky later described as 'supporting the old tradition of Russification'.[100] When, after the defeat of Denikin, a new Council of Nationalities was formed, it was merely the mouthpiece of Narkomnats policies, and it served to guide local Soviets and representative bodies into renouncing 'the right to separate' in favour of 'the right to unite', another example of Lenin's verbal sleight.[101]

By the end of 1920, the crucial year, all the nationalities which had not already escaped had been safely locked into the Soviet state. The Ukraine followed as soon as the Red Army had finally established its control there. The key was Lenin's concept of the 'voluntary union', the local party supplying the needful element of 'volition' on orders from Party headquarters in Moscow. Thanks, then, to the principle of 'democratic centralism' within the party, Lenin and later Stalin were able to rebuild the Tsarist empire, and Stalin to expand it. A propagandist outer structure was provided by the so-called Union of Soviet Socialist Republics, which was and still remains a mask for Great Russian imperialism. For the constitution of the USSR, the first All-Union Congress of Soviets, on 10 January 1923, appointed a commission of twenty-five, including three each from the Transcaucasian and White Russian republics, five from the Ukraine and five from the autonomous republics. But as each one of them was a party official under strict orders from above, the constitution was actually drawn up in Moscow right at the top (in fact by Stalin himself). It was a federal constitution only in superficial nomenclature; it merely gave an external legal form to a highly centralized autocracy, where all real power was in the hands of a tiny ruling group.[102]

The stages by which Lenin created this autocracy are worth describing in a little detail because they became the grim model, in essentials, for so many other regimes in the six decades which have followed. His aims were fourfold. First, to destroy all opposition outside the party; second, to place all power, including government, in party hands; third, to destroy all opposition within the party; fourth, to concentrate all power in the party in himself and those he chose to associate with him. As with the constitution-making and the creation of the USSR, all four objects were pursued simultaneously, though some were attained more quickly than others.

The elimination of all non-party opposition posed few problems once Lenin had got the Cheka organized. The 1918 constitution, drafted by Stalin on Lenin's instructions, embodied 'the dictatorship of the proletariat', which Lenin once brutally described as 'a special kind of cudgel, nothing else'.[103] It contained no constitutional safeguards and gave nobody any rights against the state. The power of the state was unlimited, indivisible – no separation of legislative and executive function, no independent judiciary – and absolute. Lenin scorned the antithesis between the individual and the state as the heresy of the class society. In a classless society, the individual *was* the state, so how could they be in conflict, unless of course the individual were a state enemy? Hence there was no such thing as equality of rights; or one man, one vote. In fact, voting for the All-Russian Congress of Soviets contained a fundamental gerrymander, in that city Soviets elected a legate for every 25,000 voters, whereas rural ones (where the Bolsheviks were weaker) had a deputy for every 125,000 inhabitants. In any case entire categories of people, as well as countless individuals, were denied the vote (and all other civil 'privileges') altogether, and the constitution listed among its 'general principles' the laconic observation: 'In the general interest of the working class, [the state] deprives individuals or separate groups of any privileges which may be used by them to the detriment of the socialist revolution.'[104]

Though the Bolsheviks controlled all 'representative' organs from the early weeks of 1918 onwards, opposition politicians lingered on for a time, though thousands were shot during the civil war. In May 1920 members of a British Labour delegation visiting Moscow were allowed, according to Bertrand Russell, 'complete freedom to see politicians of opposition parties'.[105] Six months later, the eighth All-Russian Congress of Soviets was the last to admit delegates calling themselves Mensheviks or Social Revolutionaries, and even these had long since lost all voting rights. By then Martov, the only remaining Social Democrat of consequence, had left Russia and had denounced Bolshevism at the Halle congress of independent German socialists.

The last real challenge to the regime from outside the party came from the Kronstadt mutiny of 28 February 1921, which began on the battleship *Petropavlovsk*. The sailors had always been the revolutionary hotheads. They actually believed in freedom and equality. They foolishly supposed Lenin did so as well. Had they followed the advice of the few ex-Imperial officers left in the navy, they would have established a bridgehead on the mainland (Petrograd was seventeen miles away) and spread the revolt to the capital, pressing their demands by force. That might have entailed the end of the regime, for by early 1921 Bolshevism was universally unpopular, as the sailors' grievances indicated. In fact they amounted to a total indictment of the regime. They asked for the election of Soviets by secret ballot, instead of 'show of hands' at 'mass meetings'; and free campaigning by the rival candidates. They denounced all existing Soviets as unrepresentative. They called for freedom of speech and of the press for 'workers, peasants, the anarchist and the Left socialist parties', free trade unions, freedom of assembly, the formation of peasants' unions, the freeing of 'all socialist political prisoners' and anyone imprisoned 'in connection with workers' and peasants' movements', the setting up of a commission to review the cases of all those in prison or concentration camps, the abolition of 'political departments' in the army, navy and public transport, since 'no one party can enjoy privileges for the propaganda of its ideas and receive money from the state for this purpose', and, lastly, the right of the peasants to 'do as they please with all the land'. What they were objecting to, in short, was virtually everything Lenin had done since he came to power. They were naïve, to put it mildly, to assume that any single one of their demands would be granted except over gun-barrels, or indeed over Lenin's dead body.

The failure of the sailors to spread revolt to the mainland allowed the regime to get itself organized. The fortress was stormed across the ice on 18 March, Tukhachevsky, who was in charge, using young Army cadets from the military schools, who had to be driven at pistol-point by a body of 200 desperate Bolsheviks drafted from the tenth Party Congress. The regime's line was that the mutiny had been organized from abroad by White Guards and led by Tsarist ex-officers. No public trials were held but Lenin carefully selected for publication a list of thirteen 'ringleaders', which included a former priest, five ex-officers and seven peasants. Hundreds, perhaps thousands, were murdered after the mutiny was crushed, though the details will probably never be known: the episode had been entombed by official Soviet historiography beneath a massive pyramid of lies.[106]

Once the mutiny was crushed, Lenin determined he would no longer tolerate any form of political activity outside the party. All those, he said, who were not in the party were 'nothing else but Mensheviks and Social Revolutionaries dressed up in modern, Kronstadt, non-party attire'. Such creatures, he added, 'we shall either keep safely in prison or send them to Martov in Berlin for the free enjoyment of all the amenities of free democracy'.[107] After this declaration, in May 1921, the Cheka quickly moved in to break up any remaining Social Democrat activity; that summer marked the extinction of visible political opposition in Lenin's state. He had given non-Communists the choice that still faces them today sixty years later: acquiescent silence, prison or exile.

At the same time the process began whereby party membership became essential to the holding of any important position in the state and its endlessly proliferating organs. 'As the governing party,' wrote Lenin in 1921, 'we could not help fusing the Soviet "authorities" with the party "authorities" – with us they are fused, and they will be.'[108] And Kamenev: 'We administer Russia and it is only through Communists that we can administer it.' Party members were instructed to take over 'the network of the state administration (railways, food supplies, control, army, law-courts etc.)', trade unions, and all factories and workshops, even public baths and dining rooms and other welfare organs, schools and housing committees. In every sphere they were to constitute 'organized fractions' and 'vote solidly together'.[109] Communist Party membership was now essential to getting on; the party had swollen from 23,600 in 1917 to 585,000 at the beginning of 1921. From this point date the first systematic efforts to screen party members (a 'central verification committee' was set up in October), expel those lacking in zeal, subservience or connections, and turn the party card into a valuable privilege, to be earned.[110]

Thus there came into being what is, perhaps, the most important single characteristic of the Communist totalitarian state: the hierarchy of party organs in town, district, region and republic, placed at each level in authority over the corresponding organs of the state. The 'vanguardism' of the Revolution was now transformed into the 'vanguardism' of perpetual rule, the party becoming and remaining what Lenin called the 'leading and directing force' in Soviet society. Nowhere was party control more marked than in the central government, and in Sovnarkom itself, which was in theory answerable to the Soviets. S.Lieberman, one of the 'experts' employed by Lenin, testified that, by 1921–2, the two key government departments, the Council of People's Commissars and the Council of Labour and Defence, were already mere rubber-stamps for decisions taken within the party.[111] Lydia Bach, who studied the process at the time, wrote in 1923 that Sovnarkom, 'having ceased to be a body with a will of its own, does nothing but register automatically decisions taken elsewhere and place its seal on them'.[112]

Lenin had thus displaced one ruling class by another, the party. The 'new class' which the Yugoslav dissident Communist Milovan Djilas denounced in the 1950s was already in existence by 1921–2. But if the 'vanguard élite', now half a million strong, ultimately to be fifteen million, enjoyed privileges, even administrative authority, it did not share real power. That was to be the sole right of an inner vanguard, a secret élite. One of the most depressing features of the Lenin regime, as Rosa Luxemburg had feared, was the almost conscious reproduction of the very worst features of Tsardom. The Tsars, too, had periodically experimented with 'responsible government', a cabinet system like Sovnarkom. Peter the Great had had his 'Senate', Alexander I his 'Committee of Ministers' in 1802, Alexander II his 'Council of Ministers' in 1857, and there had been another such body in 1905.[113] In each case, the combination of autocracy plus bureaucracy wrecked the system, as the Tsar dealt privately with individual ministers instead of allowing the cabinet to function. The whiff of Divine Right was too strong in the Tsar's nostrils, just as now the whiff of History, and its handmaiden the Dictatorship of the Proletariat, was too strong in Lenin's.[114] When it came to the point, he did not want 'responsible government', any more than he wanted any kind of legal, constitutional or democratic restraints on his decisions.

This meant crushing all opposition within the party, the third stage in the building of Lenin's autocracy. To do Lenin justice, he had always made it clear that he believed in a small, centralized party, with real decisions in the hands of a very few. He had set this all down in a letter to party workers dated September 1902.[115] His notions of 'democratic centralism' were clear and well known, though not officially defined until a decade after his death in 1934: '(1) Application of the elective principle to all leading organs of the party from the highest to the lowest; (2) periodic accountability of the party organs to their respective party organizations; (3) strict party discipline and subordination of the minority to the majority;

(4) the absolutely binding character of the decision of the higher organs upon the lower organs and upon all party members.'[116] Now the most obvious thing about this list is that (3) and especially (4) completely cancel out (1) and (2). That in fact had been Lenin's practice. The Party Congress, though in theory sovereign, and meeting annually between 1917 and 1924, in fact took no leading part after its ratification of the Treaty of Brest-Litovsk in March 1918. It became a mere form, like the All-Russian Congress of Soviets. The Central Committee succeeded to its authority.

Lenin took advantage of the thrill of terror the Kronstadt mutiny had sent through the party to end any lingering notion of democracy within it. At the tenth Party Congress, which took place while the mutineers were still uncrushed, he told the delegates (9 March 1921) that the time had come to make the party monolithic: 'We do not need any opposition now, comrades. Now is not the time. Either on this side or on that – with a rifle, not with the opposition! No more opposition now, comrades! The time has come to put an end to opposition, to put the lid on it. We have had enough opposition!' They must end 'the luxury of discussions and disputes'. It was 'a great deal better to "discuss with rifles" than with the theses of the opposition'.[117]

Under the influence of this speech, and with the feeling perhaps that, if the mutiny succeeded, they would all be hanged in a fortnight, the comrades concentrated their minds wonderfully and passed a series of resolutions which gave Lenin everything he wanted. They included a secret rider, known as 'Point Seven', which gave the Central Committee 'full powers . . . to apply all measures of party sanctions, including expulsion from the party' when any 'breach of discipline or revival or toleration of fractionalism' took place. Such expulsion would apply even to members of the CC, by a two-thirds vote, and the CC need not even refer the matter to the Congress, which thus abdicated. Moreover, 'fractionalism' was now created an offence on a par with 'counter-revolution', so that all the newly created forces of repression, hitherto reserved for enemies of the party, could now be used against party members, who would be tried and condemned in secret. Some of those present were fully aware of the risks. Karl Radek, who had bought Lenin that pair of shoes, told the Congress: 'In voting for this resolution, I feel that it can well be turned against us. And nevertheless I support it . . . . Let the Central Committee in a moment of danger take the severest measures against the best party comrades if it find this necessary . . . . Let the Central Committee even be mistaken! That is less dangerous than the wavering which is now observable.'[118] He knew that party democracy was signing its death-warrant. What he (and many, many others present) did not realize was that he was signing his own actual death-warrant.

That was doubtless because the extent to which the Central Committee itself had forfeited power to small groups within it, including its own bureaucracy, was not yet generally realized, in even the higher reaches of the party. The party bureaucracy was a deliberate creation of Lenin's. He had not merely a distrust but a positive loathing for the old imperial bureaucracy, not least because he felt compelled to use it. He wanted his own corps of officials, rather as the Tsars (again the sinister parallel) had developed a 'Personal Chancery' to get round the system of cabinet and responsible government.[119] On 9 April 1919, in order to counter the 'evils' of the old bureaucracy, Lenin issued a decree setting up a People's Commissariat of State Control, to keep a watchful eye over state officials, and replace them when necessary by reliable people. As the Commissar of this bureau he appointed Stalin – it was in fact Stalin's first independent job of major importance.

What Lenin liked in Stalin was undoubtedly his enormous capacity for endless drudgery behind a desk. A man like Trotsky was happy enough in violent action, or in violent polemics in speech and print. What he lacked was the willingness to engage, day after day and month after month, in the hard slog of running the party or state machinery. For this Stalin had an insatiable appetite, and since he appeared to possess no ideas of his own, or rather adopted Lenin's the moment they were explained to him, Lenin piled more and more offices and detailed bureaucratic work upon this patient and eager beast of burden. At the eighth Party Congress in the spring of 1919, three new bodies of great importance emerged. These were a six-member Secretariat of the Central Committee, an Organization Bureau (Orgburo) to run the party on a day-to-day basis, and a Political Bureau or Politburo of five, to 'take decisions on questions not permitting of delay'. To avoid the dangers of a clash between these three bodies, an interlocking membership was arranged. Stalin's name appeared on both the Politburo and the Orgburo lists.

Holding this multiplicity of posts (which included membership of several other important committees), and exercising to the full his capacity for work, Stalin in the years 1919–21, and clearly on Lenin's instructions and with his full support, began to move men around within the labyrinthine hierarchies of party and government and Soviet organs, with a view to securing a more homogeneous, disciplined and docile machine, totally responsive to Lenin's will. He thus acquired an immensely detailed knowledge of personalities, throughout Russia as well as at the centre, and gradually also gained his own following since he became known as the most consistent job-provider. All this time he was Lenin's instrument. He was the perfect bureaucrat; and he had found the perfect master, with a huge will and an absolutely clear sense of direction.

It is significant that Stalin's handiwork in the recesses of the party first began to be visible at the tenth Party Congress in 1921, when Lenin got the party to abdicate power over itself. This procedure, which in effect gave the Central Committee the right to pass death sentences on any members (including its own), meant that Lenin had to possess an absolutely dependable two-thirds majority on the CC. Stalin supplied it. The newly elected Central Committee included many already closely linked to him: Komarov, Mikhailov, Yaroslavsky, Ordzhonikidze, Voroshilov, Frunze, Molotov, Petrovsky, Tuntal, and candidate-members like Kirov, Kuibyshev, Chubar and Gusev. These were the pliable legion Stalin had recruited on Lenin's behalf. He was also extremely active in the new 'Personal Chancery' or Party Secretariat, which began to grow almost as fast as the Cheka, and for similar reasons. In May 1919 it had a staff of thirty; this had risen to 150 by the ninth Party Congress of March 1920; and the next year, when Lenin killed democracy in the party, it was swollen to 602, plus its own 140-strong staff of guards and messengers.[120] Finally, at the eleventh Party Congress, Lenin gave Stalin formal possession of this little private empire he had so lovingly assembled when he made him General-Secretary of the party, with his henchmen Molotov and Kuibyshev as assistants. This was decided secretly and announced in a little tucked-away story in *Pravda* on 4 April 1922. One of the Bolsheviks, Preobrazhensky, protested against such concentration of power in Stalin's personal grip. Was it 'thinkable', he asked, 'that one man should be able to answer for the work of two commissariats as well as the work of the Politburo, the Orgburo and a dozen party committees?'[121] The protest seems to have been ignored.

Two months later Lenin had his first stroke. But his work was already complete. He had systematically constructed, in all its essentials, the most carefully engineered apparatus of state tyranny the world had yet seen. In the old world, personal autocracies, except perhaps for brief periods, had been limited, or at least qualified, by other forces in society: a church, an aristocracy, an urban bourgeoisie, ancient charters and courts and assemblies. And there was, too, the notion of an external, restraining force, in the idea of a Deity, or Natural Law, or some absolute system of morality. Lenin's new despotic utopia had no such counterweights or inhibitions. Church, aristocracy, bourgeoisie had all been swept away. Everything that was left was owned or controlled by the state. All rights whatsoever were vested in the state. And, within that state, enormous and ever-growing as it was, every single filament of power could be traced back to the hands of a minute group of men – ultimately to one man. There was, indeed, an elaborate and pretentious structure of representation. By 1922 it meant nothing whatever. You could search its echoing corridors in vain to find a spark of democratic life. How could it be otherwise? Lenin hated the essence of democracy; and he regarded its forms merely as a means to legitimize violence and oppression. In 1917, the year he took power, he defined a democratic state as 'an organization for the systematic use of violence by one class against the other, by one part of the population against another'.[122] *Who–whom?* was his paramount criterion. Who was doing what to whom? Who was oppressing whom; exploiting or shooting whom? To a man who thought in such terms, who seems to have been incapable of thinking in any other terms, how could it have been possible to envisage a set of political arrangements except as a despotism, conducted by an autocrat and ruling by violence?

At Lenin's last Party Congress, his imagery, more than ever, was militaristic: rifles, machine-guns, firing-squads. 'It is indispensable', he said, 'to punish strictly, severely, unsparingly the slightest breach of discipline.' Or again, 'Our revolutionary courts must shoot.'[123] Not 'desirable' but *indispensable*. Not 'may' but *must*. It was he himself, at this time, who drafted the paragraph which remains to this day the basis, in Soviet criminal law, of the despotism:

Propaganda or agitation or participation in an organization or co-operation with organizations having the effect ... of helping in the slightest way that part of the international bourgeoisie which does not recognize the equal rights of the Communist system coming to take the place of capitalism, and which is endeavouring to overthrow it by force, whether by intervention or blockade or by espionage or by financing of the press or by any other means – is punishable by death or imprisonment.[124]

What else was this paragraph, as all-inclusive as words could make it, but an unrestricted licence for terror? That indeed was its purpose, as he explained in a letter to the Commissar of Justice, Kursky, written 17 May 1922, on the eve of his stroke: 'The paragraph on terror must be formulated as widely as possible, since only revolutionary consciousness of justice and revolutionary conscience can determine the conditions of its application in practice.'[125] Here, Lenin was encapsulating his lifelong contempt for any system of moral law. Just as, a few years later, Adolf Hitler was to justify his actions in accordance with what he termed 'the higher law of the party', so Lenin laid down the 'revolutionary conscience' as the only moral guide to the use of the vast machine for slaughter and cruelty he had brought into existence.

It may be that Lenin believed there was such a thing as a 'revolutionary conscience'. No doubt he thought he possessed one. Up to the end of 1918 he occasionally intervened in the terror to save the life of someone he knew personally. But everything else he said and did, in speech and writing, in public pronouncements and private letters, was to goad on his subordinates to further savagery, particularly towards the end. There is no doubt whatever that Lenin was corrupted by the absolute power he forged for himself. So were his colleagues. The very process of violent revolution, and violent self-preservation thereafter, inevitably destroyed conscience and all other elements of idealism. The point had been well made a decade before, by the wise and sad old Pole Joseph Conrad, in his novel about revolution, *Under Western Eyes* (1911):

In a real revolution, the best characters do not come to the front. A violent revolution falls into the hands of narrow-minded fanatics and of tyrannical hypocrites at first. Afterwards come the turn of all the pretentious intellectual failures of the time. Such are the chiefs and the leaders. You will notice that I have left out the mere rogues. The scrupulous and the just, the noble, humane and devoted natures, the unselfish and the intelligent may begin a movement, but it passes away from them. They are not the leaders of a revolution. They are its victims: the victims of disgust, disenchantment – often of remorse. Hopes grotesquely betrayed, ideals caricatured – that is the definition of revolutionary success.

Only Lenin's curious myopia about people, springing from his fundamental lack of interest in them as individuals, prevented him from recognizing that the civil war destroyed the last vestiges of what 'revolutionary conscience' might once have existed. By that time, of course, he himself had been consumed by the organic cancer of power. The process had been described in a novel he must surely, once, have read, Dostoevsky's *House of the Dead*:

Whoever has experienced the power, the unrestrained ability to humiliate another human being . . . automatically loses power over his own sensations. Tyranny is a habit, it has its own organic life, it develops finally into a disease. The habit can kill and coarsen the very best man to the level of a beast. Blood and power intoxicate . . . . The man and the citizen die with the tyrant forever; the return to human dignity, to repentance, to regeneration, becomes almost impossible.

Certainly, Lenin never showed the slightest regrets about his lifework, though in the last two-and-a-half years of his existence he was a sick, angry, frustrated and ultimately impotent creature. It is argued that, towards the end, he recognized Stalin as the emergent monster he undoubtedly was, and sought desperately to build up Trotsky's influence as a countervailing force. One would like to think that Lenin became a victim of his own despotism. But the facts are by no means clear. There is however one suggestive and sinister element. As part of his dehumanizing process, Lenin had insisted from the beginning of his rule that the party organs take an interest in the health of senior party men, and issue them (on medical advice) with orders about leave, hospitalization and rest. In mid-1921 Lenin began to experience severe headaches. On 4 June the Orgburo ordered him to take leave; he disobeyed it. He took a month's leave in July, and began to work less thereafter; there were further orders, from the Politburo, in August. He resumed normal work on 13 September for nearly three months, but in early December his health got worse and he spent more time at his country house at Gorky outside Moscow. In the early weeks of 1922 there were more orders to do little or no work, and he was supposed to visit Moscow only with the permission of the Party Secretariat. His impress was on the tenth Party Congress throughout but ostensibly he only chaired a few committees. He had just left Moscow for a further rest when he had his first stroke on 25 May 1922. He was then completely out of action for months, and when he returned to work on 2 October, the Secretariat, in the name of the Central Committee, enforced a strict regime and prevented him from getting access to papers. There is no doubt at all that Stalin was the most active agent of this medical restriction, and on 18 December he had himself formally appointed supervisor of Lenin's health.[126]

This led directly to the Lenin–Stalin breach. Stalin discovered that Lenin had been secretly working, contrary to party orders, and, in particular, had been dictating letters to his wife. He abused Krupskaya on the phone and threatened to have her investigated by the Central Control Commission.[127] On 24 December Lenin dictated his so-called 'testament'. This discussed six Soviet leaders by name. Stalin was said to have too much power, which he might wield with too little caution. Trotsky was described as 'over-preoccupied with the purely administrative side of things' ('administrative' was Lenin's euphemism for force and terror). On the night of 30 December Lenin dictated a further note, showing increased hostility to Stalin, and his last two articles were attacks on Stalin's Control Commission. On 4 January 1923 Lenin dictated a postscript to his 'testament': 'Stalin is too rude . . . intolerable in a Secretary-General. I therefore propose to our comrades to consider a means of removing Stalin from this post.'[128] On the night of 5 March Lenin wrote to Stalin, rebuking him for abusing his wife on the phone and telling him to apologize or face 'the rupture of relations between us'. Four days later came the second, debilitating stroke which robbed Lenin of speech, movement and mind. A final stroke killed him in January 1924 but by then he had long since ceased to count.

Lenin thus bequeathed to his successor all the elements of a personal despotism in furious working order. What, in the meantime, had happened to the Utopia? In 1919 the American journalist Lincoln Steffens accompanied an official US mission sent by Wilson to Russia to find out what was going on there. On his return, Bernard Baruch asked him what Lenin's Russia was like, and Steffens replied, 'I have been over into the future – and it works!'[129] This was one of the earliest comments by a western liberal on the new kind of totalitarianism, and it set the pattern for much that was to come. What on earth can Steffens have seen? The whole object of Lenin's 'vanguard élite' revolution was to speed up the industrialization of the country and thus the victory of the proletariat. Yet once Lenin took over the reverse happened. Before the war, Russian industrial production was increasing very fast: 62 per cent between 1900 and 1913.[130] Until the end of 1916 at any rate it continued to expand in some directions. But once the peasants refused to hand over their 1917 harvest (to Lenin's delight and profit) and food ceased to flow into the towns, the industrial workers, many of them born peasants, began to drift back to their native villages. Lenin's revolution turned the drift into a stampede. Beginning in the winter of 1917–18, the population of Petrograd fell from 2.4 to 1.5 million; by 1920 it was a ghost town, having lost 71.5 per cent of its population; Moscow lost 44.5 per cent. The year Steffens 'went over into the future', the Russian industrial labour force had fallen to 76 per cent of its 1917 total, and the wastage was greatest among skilled workers. Production of iron ore and cast iron fell to only 1.6 and 2.4 per cent of their 1913 totals, and total output of manufactured goods, by 1920, was a mere 12.9 per cent of pre-war.[131] By 1922, the year Lenin had his first stroke, the more independent-minded members of the regime were talking of the de-industrialization of Russia. Maxim Gorky told a French visitor:

Hitherto the workers were masters, but they are only a tiny minority . . . the peasants are legion . . . . The urban proletariat has been declining steadily for four years . . . . The immense peasant tide will end by engulfing everything . . . . The peasant will become master of Russia, since he represents numbers. And it will be terrible for our future.[132]

What had happened? The truth is, though Lenin understood very well how to create a despotism, he had no practical vision of the Utopia at all. Marx provided no clue. He described the capitalist economy; he said nothing about the socialist economy. It would, Marx remarked vaguely, be organized by 'society'. All he was sure about was that once 'all elements of production' were 'in the hands of the state, i.e. of the proletariat organized as the ruling class', then 'productive forces would reach their peak and the sources of wealth flow in full abundance'.[133] Lenin had no ideas on this subject either. He deduced from Marx that 'the state' ought to run the industrial economy. Just as the 'vanguard élite' had to take the place of the proletariat in forcing through the revolution in an underdeveloped industrial economy, so too it would have to represent it in running 'all elements of production'. And since Lenin believed in ultra-centralism in political matters, and had created a machine with precisely this end in view, so there must be central control in industry, with the party (i.e., himself and immediate associates) exercising it. This crude line of thought underlay the 'April Theses' and his two other wartime writings, *Will the Bolshevists Retain State Power?* and *State and Revolution*. It also prompted his decision, in December 1917, to create a body called Vesenkha (Supreme Council of National Economy) and, during the next dozen or so weeks, separate ministries to control the major industries, all of them staffed by bureaucrats.

Thus, almost haphazardly, did Soviet Russia acquire a centralized 'planned' economy of the type which she has maintained ever since and exported to a third of the world. As usual, Lenin thought entirely in terms of control; not of production. He thought that provided he got the system of control right (with the Politburo taking all the key decisions), the results would flow inevitably. He was wholly ignorant of the process whereby wealth is created. What he liked were figures: all his life he had an insatiable appetite for bluebooks. One some-times suspects that inside Lenin there was a book-keeper of genius struggling to get out and bombard the world with ledgers. In all his remarks on economic matters once he achieved power, the phrase which occurs most frequently is 'strict accounting and control'. To him, statistics were the evidence of success. So the new ministries, and the new state-owned factories, produced statistics in enormous quantities. The output of statistics became, and remains to this day, one of the most impressive characteristics of Soviet industry. But the output of goods was another matter.

The shape of the Soviet economy was also determined by another accidental factor, which gave Lenin a practical vision. This was the German war-production machine. One must remember that, during the formative period of the Leninist state, its first twelve months, Russia was first the negotiating partner, then the economic puppet, of Germany. By 1917, as we have seen, the Germans had seized upon the state capitalist model of pre-war Russia and married it to their own state, now run by the military. They called it 'war socialism'. It looked impressive; indeed in many ways it was impressive, and it certainly impressed Lenin. From then on his industrial ideas were all shaped by German practice. His first industrial supremo, the former Menshevik Larin, was also an enthusiastic exponent of German methods, which of course fitted in perfectly with Lenin's notions of central control. He began to hire German experts, another example of the special relationship developing between the anti-democratic elements in both countries. When other Bolsheviks objected, Lenin replied with his pamphlet *On 'Left' Infantilism and the Petty Bourgeois Spirit*:

Yes: learn from the Germans! History proceeds by zigzags and crooked paths. It happens that it is the Germans who now, side by side with bestial imperialism, embody the principle of discipline, of organization, of solid working together, on the basis of the most modern machinery, of strict accounting and control. And this is precisely what we lack.[134]

German 'state capitalism', he said, was a 'step forward' to socialism. History had played a 'strange trick'. It had just given birth to 'two separate halves of socialism, side by side, like two chickens in one shell': political revolution in Russia, economic organization in Germany. Both were necessary to socialism. So the new Russia must study the 'state capitalism of the Germans' and 'adopt it *with all possible strength*, not to spare *dictatorial* methods in order to hasten its adoption even more than Peter [the Great] hastened the adoption of westernism by barbarous Russia, not shrinking from barbarous weapons to fight barbarism.'[135]

So one might say that the man who really inspired Soviet economic planning was Ludendorff. His 'war socialism' certainly did not shrink from barbarism. It employed slave-labourers. In January 1918 Ludendorff broke a strike of 400,000 Berlin workers by drafting tens of thousands of them to the front in 'labour battalions'. Many of his methods were later to be revived and intensified by the Nazis. It would be difficult to think of a more evil model for a workers' state. Yet these were precisely the features of German 'war socialism' Lenin most valued. What the Germans had, what he wanted, was a docile labour force. He set about getting it. The first illusion he dispelled was that the workers' Soviets which had taken over the factories were to run them. His trade union spokesman, Lozovsky, warned: 'The workers in each enterprise should not get the impression that the enterprise belongs to them.'[136] No fear of that with Lenin in control! 'Such disturbers of discipline', he said, 'should be shot.'[137] By January 1918, the Bolshevik regime had taken over the unions and brought them into the government. They were weak anyway. The only strong one was the railwaymen's, which put up some resistance and was not finally crushed till 1920–1. The other union leaders acquired jobs, offices, salaries and became tame government officials. As Zinoviev put it, the unions had become 'organs of socialist power' and 'organs of the socialist state', and for all workers 'participation in the trade unions will be part of their duty to the state'. So the closed shop was universally imposed and in return union officials (who soon had to be party members under party discipline) worked closely with ministry bureaucrats and factory managers to 'raise socialist production'. In short they became company unions of the most debased kind, the 'company' being the state. In this corporatist system their main task became 'labour discipline' and they found themselves acting as an industrial police-force.[138]

Such policing became necessary as Lenin applied his notion of 'universal labour service' on the analogy of military conscription.[139] The seventh Party Congress demanded 'the most energetic, unsparingly decisive, draconian measures to raise the self-discipline and discipline of workers'. From April 1918 the unions were set to work issuing 'regulations' to 'fix norms of productivity'. Workers who rebelled were expelled from the union, with consequent loss of job and food-rations, on the lines of Lenin's dictum 'He who does not work, neither shall he eat'.[140] Strikes became illegal. 'No strikes can take place in Soviet Russia', said the trade union confederation head, Tomsky, in January 1919, 'let us put the dot on that "i".' Strike funds were confiscated and sent to promote strikes in 'bourgeois countries'. In June 1919 'labour books', modelled on the work-passes imposed on natives by various colonial governments, were introduced in the big towns. About the same time, the first organized labour camps came into existence: 'undisciplined workers', 'hooligans' and other disaffected or idle people could be sent there by the Cheka, revolutionary tribunals or Narkomtrud, the body responsible for general labour mobilization. From January 1920 anybody could be called up for compulsory corvée: road-making, building, carting etc. As a Narkomtrud spokesman put it: 'We supplied labour according to plan, and consequently without taking account of individual peculiarities or qualifications or the wish of the worker to engage in this or that kind of work.'[142] The provincial Chekas ran the camps, whose administration was in the hands of a special section of the People's Commissariat of Internal Affairs, the NKVD. There was a second tier of camps, with a harsher regime and 'difficult and unpleasant' work (i.e. in the Arctic), supposedly for counter-revolutionaries only, but soon full of ordinary workers.[143]

The end of the civil war did not end compulsory labour. Like all Lenin's 'emergency' institutions, it became permanent. Indeed, the Third Army in the Urals promptly found itself transformed into 'the First Revolutionary Army of Labour' by a decree of 15 January 1920, and most of its 'soldiers' never saw their homes again. Trotsky exulted in what he called 'the militarization of the working class'. Radek denounced 'the bourgeois prejudice of "freedom of labour"'. The ninth Party Congress in 1920 ordered workers leaving their jobs to be branded as 'labour deserters' and punished by 'confinement in a concentration camp'.[144] The new anti-society was christened in a flourish of Leninist Newspeak: 'We know slave-labour,' Trotsky told the third Trade Union Congress, 'we know serf-labour. We know the compulsory, regimented labour of the medieval guilds, we have known the hired wage-labour which the bourgeoisie calls "free". We are now advancing towards a type of labour socially regulated on the basis of an economic plan which is obligatory for the whole country . . . . This is the foundation of socialism.' Compulsory labour under capitalism, wrote Bukharin, was quite the reverse of compulsory labour under the dictatorship of the proletariat: the first was 'the enslavement of the working class', the second the 'self-organization of the working class'.[145] Both these men were later to be murdered by the same verbal fictions.

In fact, as we have seen, the working class was organizing itself back into the villages at an alarming rate. Lenin, like the Tsars and Kerensky before him, had somehow to gouge food out of the peasants. How to do it – by the market or by bayonets? First he tried bayonets. In 1917 he had incited the peasants to seize their land. In 1918 he tried to grab the land for the state. His 'On the Socialization of the Land' law of 19 February 1918 said the object of policy was 'to develop the collective system of agriculture' at 'the expense of individual holdings' in order to bring about 'a socialist economy'.[146] But in practice, as an official of Narkomzen, the state agriculture ministry, put it, 'the land was simply seized by the local peasants'. They got 86 per cent of the confiscated land, and only 14 per cent went to the newly established state farms and communes. So for the autumn 1918 harvest, Lenin sent armed detachments of factory workers into the countryside to confiscate what food they could, and tried to encourage 'committees of poor peasants' to tyrannize over those he termed 'kulaks and rich peasants' who had 'amassed enormous sums of money'.[147] Later, Lenin grouped these devices together, into twenty-five-strong bands of 'workers and poor peasants', who got a cut of any food they managed to steal. But, said Tsuryupa, Commissar for Agriculture, as soon as they reached the country 'they begin to break out and get drunk.' Later still, Lenin invented a new category of 'middle peasants', whom he tried to set against the 'kulaks'. As these classes existed only in his own mind, and bore no relation to actual peasants in real villages, that tactic did not work either.

By the spring of 1921, when the Kronstadt sailors rose, Lenin's whole economic policy, such at it was, lay in manifest ruins. Industry was producing practically nothing. There was no food in the towns. On Lenin's own admission 'tens and hundreds of thousands of disbanded soldiers' were becoming bandits.[148] About the only thing in plentiful supply was the paper rouble, which the printing presses poured out ceaselessly, and which had now fallen to little over 1 per cent of its November 1917 value. Some of the Bolsheviks tried to make a virtue of necessity and boasted that the inflation was deliberately created to smash the old regime of money. One described the presses of the state mint as 'that machine-gun of the Commissariat of Finance pouring fire into the arse of the bourgeois system'. Zinoviev told the German Social Democrats, 'We are moving towards the *complete abolition of money*.' In a sense this was true: paper money has never recovered its old significance in the Soviet Union. But the price has been permanent shortages in the shops.

In any case, the peasants would not look at Lenin's paper rouble, and in May 1921 he threw in his hand. Plainly, if he did not get some food to the towns, his regime would collapse. He may have been short of genuine economic ideas, but he was never short of verbal ones. He now coined the phrase 'New Economic Planning'. NEP was, in fact, surrender to the peasants and the return to a market system based on barter. The goon-squads were withdrawn, and the peasants were allowed to get what they could for their food. Small factories and workshops were allowed to start up again, outside the control of the state, to produce goods the peasants were willing to accept in exchange for grain. Unfortunately, the Bolshevik capitulation came too late to affect the 1921 sowing, and a dry summer brought famine, the first in Russian history to be substantially created by government policy. It affected, according to Kalinin, about 27 million people. As many as 3 million may have died in the winter of 1921–2. In desperation, the government turned to the American Relief Administration organized under Herbert Hoover. For the first time, Russia, hitherto one of the world's greatest food-exporting countries, had to turn to American capitalist agriculture to save it from the disastrous consequences of its experiment in collectivism. Sixty years later, the same pattern was being repeated. The peasants had destroyed the Tsar and made Leninism possible. Lenin had failed to reward them, as he had promised. They exacted a price. It is still being paid.[149]

Thus ended, in total failure, the first major experiment in what it was now fashionable to call social engineering. Lenin termed it 'a defeat and retreat, for a new attack'.[150] But soon he was dead, and the 'new attack' on the peasants was to be left to the bureaucratic monster he left behind him. Lenin believed in planning because it was 'scientific'. But he did not know how to do it. He thought there must be some magical trick, which in his case took the form of 'electrification'. Fascinated, as he always was, by Germanic 'thoroughness', he greatly admired Karl Ballod's *Der Zukunftsstaat*, published in 1919. It inspired his slogan: 'Communism is Soviet power plus electrification of the whole country.' Electricity would do it! It was the last word in modern science![151] It would transform stubborn Russian agriculture. Much better to try to electrify everything than to work out a complicated general plan, which was nothing but 'idle talk', 'boring pedantry', 'ignorant conceit'.[152] He took little interest in Gosplan (1921), the new planning machinery, until it gave top priority to electrification. Then, in his last few active weeks, he became enthusiastic about it: it would build vast power-stations! Thus began a curious cult which has persisted in the Soviet Union to this day, and which has made the heavy electrical engineer the most valued figure in Soviet society (next to the arms designer). Lenin's legacy was a solidly built police state surrounded by economic ruins. But he went to eternity dreaming of electricity.

Lenin's confident expectations of Marxist risings in the advanced industrial countries have long since been buried. How would they have succeeded? Lenin's own revolution had only been made possible by a huge, inchoate, undirected and pragmatic movement among the peasants, which he did not understand and never troubled to analyse. His fellow Marxist revolutionaries in industrial Europe had no such luck. Besides, by November 1918, when the opportunity for revolutionary change in central Europe arrived, the dismal experiences of Lenin's social enginering – economic breakdown, starvation, civil war and mass terror – already constituted an awful warning, not least to the more moderate socialists. The extremists did, indeed, try their hands, and were burnt in the flames they lit. On 4 November 1918, German sailors and soldiers took over Kiel and formed workers' councils. Three days later, the Left socialist Kurt Eisner led a rising of the garrison in Munich, and overturned the Bavarian government. But the Social Democrats who came to power in Germany when the Kaiser fled did not make Kerensky's mistakes. Their military expert, Gustav Noske, turned to the army, which provided a *Freikorps* of ex-officers and NCOs. The refusal of the Leninists to seek power by parliamentary means played into his hands. On 6 January 1919 the Berlin Leninists (who called themselves Spartacists) took over the city. Noske marched on it at the head of 2,000 men. Three days after he took it, Rosa Luxemburg and her friend Karl Liebknecht were murdered by the ex-officers charged with taking them to prison. Eisner, too, was murdered on 21 February. His followers contrived to win only three seats in the Bavarian elections. When, despite this, they set up a Communist Republic on 7 April, it lasted less than a month and was destroyed by the *Freikorps* without difficulty. It was the same story in Halle, Hamburg, Bremen, Leipzig, Thuringia, Brunswick. The Communists could neither win elections nor practise violence successfully.[152]

The wind of change was blowing in rather a different direction. By the second half of 1919 new types of 'vanguard élites' were making their appearance in Europe. They too were socialists. Marx was often in their pantheon. But they appealed to something broader than an abstract 'proletariat' which was mysteriously failing to respond – at any rate as an electoral or a fighting force – and their collective dynamic was not so much class as nation, even race. They also had a powerful and immediate grievance in common: dissatisfaction with the Treaty of Versailles. In Austria, one of the big losers, they were called *Heimwehren*. In Hungary, the biggest loser of all, the national temper had not been improved by a putative Communist republic, set up in March 1919 by Lenin's disciple Béla Kun. In August it collapsed in fire and blood, and the spirit of its successor was increasingly that of the anti-Semitic leader Julius Gömbös, who called himself a National Socialist and appealed passionately for justice, revenge and a purge of 'alien elements'.[153] In Turkey, which had lost its Arab empire and appeared to be losing its western littoral also, Mustafa Kemal Pasha, soon to be 'Ataturk', likewise offered national socialism and was already proving that a settlement determined in Paris could not be enforced on the spot. Italy, too, though a big gainer, still had a grievance against Versailles: she had not got the Dalmatian coast. On 11 September, the poet and war-hero Gabriele d'Annunzio led a raggle-taggle force of army deserters into the port of Fiume. It was an impudent bluff: but Britain and France, the custodians of the settlement, backed down – an ominous portent. D'Annunzio, too, was a national socialist.

From Milan, Mussolini sniffed this new wind and liked it, just as five years earlier he had caught the whiff of wartime excitement, and liked that too. The coming of war and his own determination to bring Italy into it had taken him right out of the official socialist party. It had made him a nationalist, not merely in the romantic-Left tradition of Mazzini but in the acquisitive tradition of the old Romans, whose *fasces*, turned into a radical emblem in the French Revolution, he found a useful symbol, just as Lenin had picked on

the hammer and sickle of the old Social Democrats. It made him hate
Lenin for taking Russia out of the war and so jeopardizing Italy's
promised gains. He urged the Japanese to march through Russia with
the command '*Avanti, il Mikado!*' By 1919 Lenin's economic failure
had turned him away from the outright expropriation of industry.
He now wanted to use and exploit capitalism rather than destroy it.
But his was to be a radical revolution nonetheless, rooted in the
pre-war 'vanguard élite' Marxism and syndicalism (workers' rule)
which was to remain to his death the most important single element
in his politics. Many other young Italian former socialists shared his
radicalism while abandoning their internationalism.[154] Internationalism had not worked either in 1914, when it had failed to stop war,
or in 1917, when it had failed to respond to Lenin's call for world
revolution. But the desire to install a new economic Utopia remained.

On 23 March 1919 Mussolini and his syndicalist friends founded
a new party. Its programme was partial seizure of finance capital,
control over the rest of the economy by corporative economic
councils, confiscation of church lands and agrarian reform, and
abolition of the monarchy and senate. In compiling this list Mussolini frequently cited Kurt Eisner as a model.[155] Eisner's Bavarian
fighting-squads, themselves an imitation of Lenin's 'men in black
leather jerkins', served to inspire Mussolini's *Fasci di Combat-
timento*.[156] Indeed, he had shed none of the attachment to violent
activism he shared with Lenin. Paraphrasing Marx, he pledged
himself 'to make history, not to endure it'. His other favourite
quotation was *Vivre, ce n'est pas calculer, c'est agir*.[157] His vocabulary was very like Lenin's, abounding in military imagery and strong,
violent verbs. Like Lenin, he was impatient to get history moving,
fast – to *velocizzare l'Italia*, as the Futurists like Marinetti put it.
Indeed he radiated impatience, furiously studying his watch, turning
with anger on the agents of delay.

Yet Mussolini was changing. The lean and hungry look had gone
with his hair. On his bald head a huge cyst had emerged and a dark
oval mole on his thrusting and now fleshy chin. His teeth were the
colour of old ivory and widely separated, considered lucky in
Italy.[158] He was handsome, vigorous, well-launched in a sexual
career that would bring him 169 mistresses.[159] He was very vain and
ambitious. He wanted power and he wanted it now. D'Annunzio's
success persuaded him that radicalism, even radical nationalism, was
not enough. For fascism to succeed, it must invoke poetry, drama,
mystery. This had always been a complaint, among the Italian
Marxists, about Marx himself: he did not understand human beings
well enough. He omitted the potency of myth, especially national
myth. Now that Freud had demonstrated – scientifically, too – the

power of dark and hidden forces to move individuals, was it not time to examine their impact on mass-man? D'Annunzio wrote of 'the terrible energies, the sense of power, the instinct for battle and domination, the abundance of productive and fructifying forces, all the virtues of Dionysian man, the victor, the destroyer, the creator'.[160] Italy was not short of poetic myths. There was the nineteenth-century nationalist myth of Garibaldi and Mazzini, still enormously powerful, the Realpolitik myth of Machiavelli (another of Mussolini's favourite authors), and the still earlier myth of Rome and its empire, waiting to be stirred from its long sleep and set to march with new legions. On top of this there was the new Futurist myth, which inspired in Mussolini a vision of a socialist Italy, not unlike Lenin's electrified Russia, in which 'life will become more intense and frenetic, ruled by the rhythm of the machine'. Mussolini stirred all these volatile elements together to produce his heavy fascist brew, flavouring all with the vivifying dash of violence: 'No life without shedding blood', as he put it.[161]

But whose blood? Mussolini was a complex and in many respects ambivalent man. Unlike Lenin, he rarely did the evil thing of his own accord; he nearly always had to be tempted into it, until long years of power and flattery atrophied his moral sense almost completely. He was not capable of embarking on a deliberate course of unprovoked violence. In 1919–20 he was desperate for a fighting cause. He spoke forlornly of fascism as 'the refuge of all heretics, the church of all heresies'.[162] Then the socialists, by resorting to violence, gave him what he wanted. Their mentor was a frail young Marxist called Antonio Gramsci, who came from exactly the same intellectual tradition as Mussolini: Marxism, Sorel, syndicalism, a repudiation of historical determinism, a stress on voluntarism, the need to force history forward by an emphasis on struggle, violence and myth; plus Machiavellian pragmatism.[163] But Gramsci, though much more original than Mussolini, lacked his aplomb and self-confidence. He came from a desperately poor Sardinian family. His father had gone to jail and Gramsci, who already suffered from Pott's Disease of the lungs, had begun working a ten-hour day at the age of eleven. He was amazed when his future wife fell in love with him (and wrote her some striking love-letters). Unable to see himself in a leadership role, he drew from Machiavelli not a personal prince, like Mussolini, but a collective one: 'The modern Prince, the myth-prince, cannot be a real person, a concrete individual: it can only be an organization.'

Thus Gramsci stuck to syndicalism when Mussolini turned to romance and drama, and he preached the take-over of factories. In 1920 the socialists began to follow his advice and soon the Red Flag flew over workshops and offices scattered all over the country. There was no determined effort to take over the state. Indeed the socialists were divided about tactics, and in January 1921 they split, with a Communist Party (PCI) forging off to the left. The take-over accomplished little except to terrify the middle class. As Errico Malatesta warned the moderates: 'If we do not go on to the end, we shall have to pay with tears of blood for the fear we are now causing the bourgeoisie.'[164] There was not much violence, but enough to give Mussolini the excuse to resort to it himself. As in Germany, the socialists made a catastrophic mistake in using it at all.[165] As Mussolini boasted, the fascist leopard could easily deal with the 'lazy cattle' of the socialist masses.[166]

The fascist 'action squads' were formed mainly from ex-servicemen, but they constantly recruited students and school-leavers. They were much better disciplined and more systematic than the socialists and co-ordinated their efforts by telephone. They often had the passive or even active support of the local authorities and *carabinieri*, who would search a socialist *casa del popolo* for arms, then give the go-ahead to the squads, who would burn it down. The socialists claimed fascism was a class party, and its terror a *Jacquerie borghese*. Not so: there were thousands of working-class fascists, especially in areas like Trieste where a racial element could be invoked (the socialists there were mainly Slovenes). It was in these fringe areas that fascism first got a mass-following, spreading gradually inland to Bologna, the Po Valley and the hinterland of Venice. Mussolini, always sensitive towards people, early grasped the point that Italy was a collection of cities, each different, each to be played by ear. As he got inland, the middle-class element became more dominant. Fascism began to exercise a powerful appeal to well-to-do youth. One of the most important and dangerous recruits was Italo Balbo, who at the age of twenty-five brought Mussolini his home town, Ferrara, and soon became head of the fascist militia and by far the most ruthless and efficient of the *condottieri*.[167] In 1921 he moved through central Italy, like one of the Borgias, leaving behind the smoking ruins of trade union headquarters and a trail of corpses. It was Balbo who first terrified *bien-pensant* Italy into believing fascism might be an irresistible force.

He even terrified Mussolini, who always disliked large-scale violence, especially violence for its own sake, and wrote and spoke against it.[168] But the expansion of fascism, which pushed him and thirty-five other deputies into parliament in May 1921, had also placed him, and other former socialists, in a minority within the movement. At the fascist Congress of Rome the same year, he was forced to compromise. In return for being made *Duce*, he agreed to violence, and 1922 was the year of fascist terror. In effect, the authorities connived while a private, party army began an internal conquest. In city after city, the town halls were stormed, socialist councils driven out of office by force, and local prefects, who wished to use the police to resist fascist illegality, were dismissed. The parliamentarians could not agree to form a strong government under Giolitti, who would have snuffed Mussolini out – the *Duce* would not have fought the state – because the Vatican effectively prevented the Church-influenced parties and the moderate socialists from coalescing. The new Communist Party (as later in Germany) actually hoped for a fascist regime, which it thought would precipitate a Marxist revolution.[169] When Balbo seized Ravenna in July 1922 the socialists responded by calling a General Strike, which was a disastrous failure.

Italy was not a happy or a well-governed country. It had appalling poverty, the highest birth-rate in Europe and, after Germany, one of the highest inflation-rates. The *risorgimento* had brought disappointment instead of the promised land. The war and its victories had divided Italy rather than united it. The parliamentary regime was grievously corrupt. The monarchy was unloved. The state itself had been at daggers with the Church since 1871, and was denounced from every pulpit on Sundays. The public services were breaking down. There was genuine fear of a Red Terror, for the Catholic newspapers were full of Lenin's atrocities and the Russian famine. Mussolini was not personally identified with violence. On the contrary: he seemed to many to be the one to stop it. He had become a wonderful public speaker. He had learnt from d'Annunzio the gift of conducting a quasi-operatic dialogue with the crowd ('*A chi l'Italia?*' '*A noi!*'). But he was not just a demagogue. His speeches specialized in the wide-ranging philosophical reflections Italians love. Liberals from Benedetto Croce downwards attended his meetings. By the early autumn of 1922 his oratory had acquired a confident and statesmanlike ring. He was now in secret contact with the palace, the Vatican, the army, the police and big business. What, they all wanted to know, did he want? At Udine he told them, in the last of a series of major speeches given all over the country: 'Our programme is simple: we wish to govern Italy.'[170] He would govern Italy as it had never been governed since Roman times: firmly, fairly, justly, honestly, above all efficiently.

On 16 October 1922 Mussolini decided to force the issue, believing that if he waited, Giolitti, the one man he feared, might steal his role. He arranged for a march on Rome for the end of the month, by four divisions totalling 40,000 blackshirted men. Many army and police commanders agreed not to fire on them, and his paper, *Il Popolo d'Italia*, carried the banner: *I grigioverdi fraterniz-*

zano con le Camicie Nere! Mussolini had a lifelong capacity for hovering uneasily between grandeur and farce. By the time his ill-equipped, badly clothed and unfed army had halted outside Rome, in pouring rain, on the evening of 28 October, it did not present a very formidable spectacle. The government, though weak, had a Rome garrison of 28,000 under a reliable commander and it agreed to proclaim a state of emergency. But Rome buzzed with rumours and misinformation. The little King Victor Emmanuel, tucked up in the Quirinale Palace, was told only 6,000 ill-disciplined troops faced a horde of 100,000 determined fascists. He panicked and refused to sign the decree, which had to be torn down from the walls where it had just been posted. At that point the government lost heart.

Mussolini, for an impatient man, played his cards skilfully. When he was telephoned in Milan by the King's ADC, General Cittadini, and offered partial power in a new ministry, he simply replaced the receiver. The next day, 29 October, he graciously consented to form his own government, provided the invitation by phone was confirmed by telegram. The wire duly came, and that evening he went to Milan Station in state, wearing his black shirt, to catch the night-sleeper to Rome. As it happened, the wife of the British ambassador, Lady Sybil Graham, was also on the train. She saw Mussolini, who was surrounded by officials, impatiently consult his watch and turn fiercely on the station-master. 'I want the train to leave exactly on time', he said. 'From now on, everything has got to function perfectly.'[171] Thus a regime, and a legend, were born.

In the last decade of his life Mussolini became an increasingly tragic, even grotesque, figure. Looking back from this later perspective it is hard to grasp that, from the end of 1922 to the mid-1930s, he appeared to everyone as a formidable piece on the European chess-board. Once installed, he did not make any of Lenin's obvious mistakes. He did not create a secret police, or abolish parliament. The press remained free, opposition leaders at liberty. There were some murders, but fewer than before the *coup*. The Fascist Grand Council was made an organ of state and the Blackshirts were legalized, giving an air of menace to the April 1924 elections, which returned a large fascist majority. But Mussolini saw himself as a national rather than a party leader. He said he ruled by consent as well as force.[172] He seems to have possessed not so much the will to power as the will to office. He wanted to remain there and become respectable; he wished to be loved.

In 1924 the murder of Giacomo Matteotti, the most vigorous of the opposition deputies, ended these illusions. Mussolini was generally believed to be responsible.[173] Deputies had been killed before, and it is curious that this particular crime aroused such fury in Italy and raised

eyebrows abroad. It did Mussolini great damage, some of it permanent, and became for him a kind of Rubicon, cutting any remaining
links with the socialists and liberals and driving him into the arms of
his extremists. In a very characteristic mixture of arrogance and
fatalistic despair, he announced the beginning of fascism in a
notorious speech delivered on 3 January 1925. Opposition newspapers were banned. Opposition leaders were placed in *confino* on an
island. As Mussolini put it, opposition to the monolithic nation was
superfluous – he could find any that was needed within himself and
in the resistance of objective forces – a bit of verbal legerdemain that
even Lenin might have envied.[174] He produced a resounding totalitarian formula, much quoted, admired and excoriated then and since:
'Everything within the state, nothing outside the state, nothing
against the state.' A whole series of 'fascist laws' were drawn up,
some constitutional, some punitive, some positive, the last being the
Leggi di riforma sociale, which purported to bring the Corporate
State into existence.

But there was always something nebulous about Italian fascism. Its
institutions, like the Labour Charter, the National Council of
Corporations and the Chamber of Fasces and Corporations, never
seemed to get much purchase on the real Italy. Mussolini boasted,
'We control the political forces, we control the moral forces, we
control the economic forces. Thus we are in the midst of the
corporative fascist state.'[175] But it was a state built of words rather
than deeds. After all, if Mussolini's totalitarian definition represented reality, how was it he was able to come to terms with the
Church, which was certainly 'outside the state', and even sign a
concordat with the Vatican, something none of his parliamentary
predecessors had been able to do? He once defined fascism as
'organized, concentrated, authoritarian democracy on a national
basis'.[176] Yes: but what was all this authority *for*? One senses that
Mussolini was a reluctant fascist because, underneath, he remained a
Marxist, albeit a heretical one; and to him 'revolution' was meaningless without large-scale expropriation, something the bulk of his
followers and colleagues did not want. So the fascist Utopia tended
to vanish round the corner, leaving only the despotism. As late as
1943, just before the débâcle, an article in *Critica fascista* by the
young militant Vito Panunzio declared that the regime could still win
provided it at last brought about the 'fascist revolution'.[177] By then
Mussolini had been in apparently dictatorial power for more than
two decades.

But if Mussolini did not practise fascism, and could not even
define it with any precision, it was equally mystifying to its opponents, especially the Marxists. Sophisticated Anglo-Saxon liberals

could dismiss it as a new kind of mountebank dictatorship, less bloodthirsty than Leninism and much less dangerous to property. But to the Marxists it was much more serious. By the mid-1920s there were fascist movements all over Europe. One thing they all had in common was anti-Communism of the most active kind. They fought revolution with revolutionary means and met the Communists on the streets with their own weapons. As early as 1923 the Bulgarian peasant regime of Aleksandr Stamboliski, which practised 'agrarian Communism', was ousted by a fascist *putsch*. The Comintern, the new international bureau created by the Soviet government to spread and co-ordinate Communist activities, called on the 'workers of the world' to protest against the 'victorious Bulgarian fascist clique', thus for the first time recognizing fascism as an international phenomenon. But what exactly was it? There was nothing specific about it in Marx. It had developed too late for Lenin to verbalize it into his march of History. It was unthinkable to recognize it for what it actually was – a Marxist heresy, indeed a modification of the Leninist heresy itself. Instead it had to be squared with Marxist-Leninist historiography and therefore shown to be not a portent of the future but a vicious flare-up of the dying bourgeois era. Hence after much lucubration an official Soviet definition was produced in 1933: fascism was 'the unconcealed terrorist dictatorship of the most reactionary, chauvinistic and imperialistic elements of finance capital'.[178] This manifest nonsense was made necessary by the failure of 'scientific' Marxism to predict what was the most striking political development of the inter-war years.

In the meantime, Mussolini's Italy was now an empirical fact, just like Lenin's Russia, inviting the world to study it, with a view to imitation, perhaps, or avoidance. The historian of modern times is made constantly aware of the increasingly rapid interaction of political events over wide distances. It was as though the development of radio, the international telephone system, mass-circulation newspapers and rapid forms of travel was producing a new conception of social and political holism corresponding to new scientific perceptions of the universe and matter. According to Mach's Principle, formulated first at the turn of the century and then reformulated as part of Einstein's cosmology, not only does the universe as a whole influence local, terrestrial events but local events have an influence, however small, on the universe as a whole. Quantum mechanics, developed in the 1920s, indicated that the same principle applied at the level of micro-quantities. There were no independent units, flourishing apart from the rest of the universe.[179] 'Splendid isolation' was no longer a practicable state policy, as even the United States had implicitly admitted in 1917. There were many who welcomed this development, and saw the League of Nations as a response to what they felt was a welcome new fact of life. But the implications of global political holism were frightening as well as uplifting. The metaphor of disease was apt. The Black Death of the mid-fourteenth century had migrated over the course of more than fifty years and there were some areas it had never reached. The influenza virus of 1918 had enveloped the world in weeks and penetrated almost everywhere. The virus of force, terror and totalitarianism might prove equally swift and ubiquitous. It had firmly implanted itself in Russia. It was now in Italy.

If Lincoln Steffens could detect a working future even in Lenin's Moscow, what might not be discerned in totalitarian Rome? Mussolini could not or would not conjure a new fascist civilization out of his cloudy verbal formulae. But what he liked doing and felt able to do, and indeed was gifted at doing, was big construction projects. He tackled malaria, then the great, debilitating scourge of central and southern Italy.[180] The draining of the Pontine Marshes was a considerable practical achievement, as well as a symbol of fascist energy. Mussolini encouraged Balbo, a keen pilot, to build a large aviation industry, which won many international awards. Another fascist boss, the Venetian financier Giuseppe Volpi, created a spectacular industrial belt at Mughera and Mestre on the mainland. He also, as Minister of Finance, revalued the lira, which became a relatively strong currency.[181] Train, postal and phone services all markedly improved. There were no strikes. Corruption continued, perhaps increased; but it was less blatant and remarked upon. In Sicily, the Mafia was not destroyed, but it was effectively driven underground. Above all, there was no more violence on the streets. Some of these accomplishments were meretricious, others harmful in the long run. But taken together they looked impressive, to foreigners, to tourists, to many Italians too. No Utopia was emerging in Italy, but the contrast with hungry, terrorized Russia was striking. To those north of the Alps, who rejected alike the Bolshevism of the East and the liberalism of the West, the Italian renaissance seemed to offer a third way.

THREE

Waiting for Hitler

On 10 November 1918 the Lutheran chaplain at the Pasewalk Military Hospital in Pomerania summoned the patients to tell them that the House of Hohenzollern had fallen: Germany was now a republic. The news came like a thunderbolt to the wounded soldiers. One of them was Adolf Hitler, a twenty-nine-year-old junior NCO. He had fought on the Western Front throughout the war, had twice distinguished himself in action, and earlier that year had received the rare accolade of the Iron Cross First Class. A month before, on 13 October south of Ypres, he had been temporarily blinded in a British mustard gas attack. He had not been able to read the newspapers and had dismissed rumours of collapse and revolution as a 'local affair', got up by 'a few Jewish youths' who had 'not been at the Front' but 'in a clap hospital'. Now the aged pastor, tears pouring down his face, told them their Kaiser had fled, the war was lost and the Reich was throwing itself unconditionally upon the mercy of its enemies. The news of the surrender was, as Hitler later wrote, 'the most terrible certainty of my life. Everything went black before my eyes. I tottered and groped my way back to the dormitory, threw myself on my bunk, and dug my burning head into my blanket and pillow. Since the day I had stood on my mother's grave, I had not wept . . . . But now I could not help it.'[1]

The shock of defeat to most Germans, especially the soldiers, was enormous. It was something no one in the West understood. The Germans knew they were retreating on the Western Front. But the withdrawal was orderly; the army was intact. And it was not in the West that Germany's main anxieties and ambitions lay. Germany had fought the war principally from fear of the growing industrial and military strength of Russia, a huge, overbearing, tyrannical and barbarous neighbour, right on Germany's doorstep and threatening to overwhelm her. By the middle of 1918 Germany, despite the desperate struggles on the Western Front, had exorcized what to her was the principal spectre. Tsarist Russia had been beaten and destroyed. Its successor had signed a dictated peace. The Treaty of Brest-Litovsk gave Germany all the security she had ever needed. It deprived Russia of 70 per cent of her iron and steel capacity, 40 per cent of her total industry. It gave Germany everything in European Russia she considered of any value: as a member of the German government gloated, 'It is in the East that we shall collect the interest on our War Bonds.'[2] Indeed it gave more, because it reopened the prospect of a vast economic empire in Eastern Europe, a colonization of the great plains which had been the aim of the expanding German civilization of the Middle Ages. The 'pull of the East' had always meant more to average Germans than their belated exercise in African colonization or even the Kaiser's bid for commercial and maritime supremacy. It was Tsarist Great Russia which had blocked Germany's 'manifest destiny' to the East. Now that monstrous despotism was at last in ruins. The programme of the Teutonic Knights could again be resumed.

On 1 March 1918 Kiev fell and Ludendorff occupied the Ukraine, set up a 'Landowners' Republic' under German supervision, and laid the foundation of a satellite-colony of the Reich. The Kaiser became Duke of Courland, embracing Livonia and Estonia, to be run by their small German minorities and tied to Germany's economy. In April German troops landed in Finland, another potential satellite. On 7 May Germany forced a dictated peace on Romania, and there too economic colonization proceeded quickly. Ludendorff put troops in the Crimea, which was earmarked for a German settlement, and in September he had penetrated as far as the Baku oilfields, preparatory to a plunge into Transcaucasia, to take up a strategic position on the rim of Central Asia. Even rumours of the downfall of the Habsburgs and the break-up of Turkey were seen by German geopoliticians as opportunities for further plunder and economic penetration, in central Europe and the Middle East. In the early autumn of 1918 it appeared to them that the war, far from being lost, had in all essentials been won – and won overwhelmingly. Indeed Germany might emerge from the settlement the equal, in military and economic potential, of the United States and the British Empire, the third superpower.

Some illusions survived even the first, overwhelming shock of defeat. Leaving aside the fact that Wilson and Colonel House had already secretly accepted the Anglo-French interpretation of the 'Fourteen Points', the optimistic construction the Germans placed on them was totally unwarranted. One south German town welcomed its demobilized soldiers with the banner 'Welcome, brave soldiers, your work has been done,/God and Wilson will carry it on'.[3] The truth was finally brought home to Germany only when the terms of the Treaty were published in May 1919. In fact Versailles, for Germany, was not really a 'Carthaginian Peace'. Keynes was quite wrong in this respect. Austria and Hungary fared much worse. Versailles allowed Germany to retain all the essentials of Bismarck's work. Had she chosen the path of peace, Germany must inevitably have become, over the next two decades, the dominant economic force in the whole of central and eastern Europe.

But Germany's losses have to be seen in the perspective of the colossal gains she thought she had secured only a short time before. The thought that Tsarist Russia would have imposed infinitely worse terms on Germany (very like, no doubt, those dictated in 1945) does not seem to have occurred to the Germans. In any case Tsarist Russia had been destroyed by German arms! Why, then, was Germany being forced in the East to hand over entire German communities to the barbarous Slavs, in the Polish Corridor, in East Prussia, and above all in Silesia, rich in coal and iron and industry? It was these losses which caused the Germans the most grief and anger because they struck at their pride: it was, to them, against nature for Germans to live under Slav rule. Even the Silesian plebiscite, an important concession secured for Germany by Lloyd George, became a further source of German anger, for the government never explained to the German public that, under the Versailles Treaty, division of the province was permitted in accordance with local results. The plebiscite on 21 March 1921 gave a 60 per cent majority to Germany. But the League awarded some 40 per cent of the territory, containing a Polish majority, to Poland, and this portion included the most valuable industrial area. The Germans thought they had been swindled again; and this time their rage turned against the League.[4]

In a sense the Germans had been swindled for many years, but chiefly by their own governments, which had never told the country the truth about their foreign policy aims and methods. The full truth, indeed, did not begin to emerge until 1961 when the great German historian Fritz Fischer published his *Griff nach der Weltmacht*, in which he traced the aggressive continuities in Germany's expansive foreign and military policy.[5] A long and bitter controversy followed among German historians, culminating in the Berlin meeting of the German Historical Association in 1964.[6] During this debate, the essentials of the case for German war guilt were established beyond doubt, and in time accepted even by most of his critics. They are worth restating briefly.

In the second half of the nineteenth century Germany became an enormous and highly successful industrial power. This involved bringing into existence a vast industrial proletariat, who could not be

managed like peasants and with whom the German ruling class of
landowners and military men was unwilling to share power. Bismarck
created a dual solution to this problem. On the one hand, in the 1880s,
he expanded the traditional social welfare services of the Prussian
monarchy into the world's first welfare state.[7] On the other, after his
expansionary wars were done, he deliberately sought to preserve
domestic unity by creating largely imaginary foreign threats of 'encirclement', thus enclosing the nation in a homogeneous state of siege
mentality. Bismarck knew how to manage this artificial nightmare. His
successors did not. Indeed they came to believe in it themselves, victims
of a growing irrationalism and dread. By 1911 at the latest, Germany's
ruling group had unleashed a new ethnic nationalism: 'The aim was to
consolidate the position of the ruling classes with a successful foreign
policy; indeed it was hoped a war would resolve the growing social
tensions. By involving the masses in the great struggle those parts of the
nation that had hitherto stood apart would be integrated into the
monarchical state.'[8] The object of the 1914 war was to create a new
European order in which Germany would be dominant. As Bethmann
Hollweg's secretary, Riezler, described the proposed European economic union, it was 'The European disguise of our will to power'.[9]
Bethmann Hollweg recognized that Britain could not possibly accept
total German dominance in Europe. Therefore Britain (as well as
France and Russia) had to be defeated; and that meant Germany
exercising the role of a world superpower. As Riezler put it, echoing
Bethmann's thoughts: 'England's tragic error might consist of compelling us to rally all our strength, to exploit all our potentialities, to drive us
into world-wide problems, to force upon us – against our will – a desire
for world domination.'[10] This last formulation was very characteristic
of the German desire to shift the moral responsibility for its aggression
onto others.

If the responsibility for starting the war was shared jointly by the
military and civilian wings of the German ruling establishment, the
magnitude of the defeat was the fault of the generals and the
admirals. Germany ceased to be in any sense a civilian empire on 9
January 1917 when Bethmann Hollweg surrendered to the demand,
which he had resisted for three years, to wage unrestricted submarine
warfare. Thereafter the admirals and Ludendorff were in charge. It
was their war. They raised the stakes at the gambling table, thus
making it certain that, when the inevitable crash came, Germany
would not merely be defeated but broken, bankrupted, shamed and
humiliated. As Riezler put it: 'We will practically have to accept the
Diktat. Slavery for a hundred years. The dream about the world
finished forever. The end of all hubris. The dispersion of Germans
around the world. The fate of the Jews.'[11]

It is a pity that Keynes could not have been privy to these desperate thoughts of a man who was at the very centre of the German decision-making machine. He could then have appreciated that the so-called 'Carthaginian Peace' was in fact very much more generous than Germany's rulers secretly expected. But of course the overwhelming mass of the Germans were even more ignorant than Keynes. They had been taught, and they believed, that the war had been caused principally by Russian expansionism and British commercial jealousy. For Germany it had been a defensive war of survival. The tragedy is that, when the collapse came in 1918, the opportunity to tell the truth to the German people was missed. Even among the German Socialists, the only ones to admit German war-guilt were Kurt Eisner, who was murdered in 1919, Karl Kautsky, who had the job of putting the pre-war diplomatic documents in order, and Eduard David, who had seen the key papers when he was Under-Secretary at the Foreign Ministry immediately after the monarchy fell.[12] But none of the really revealing documents was published or made accessible. German historians, the best in the world, betrayed their profession and deluded themselves. Equally important, the chief actors in the tragedy lied or concealed the facts. Bethmann Hollweg could have told the truth about the origins of the war and the role of the military in losing it. He did not do so, despite provocation. Both Tirpitz and Ludendorff savaged him in their memoirs. But Bethmann's own account says very little: he feared to deepen the already wide divisions in German society.[13]

Not only was the truth not told: it was deliberately concealed beneath a myth that the German war-machine had been 'stabbed in the back' by civilian defeatism and cowardice. It is, looking back on it, extraordinary that this myth should have been accepted. No force in Wilhelmine Germany was capable of defying the military, let alone stabbing it in the back. Germany was in many ways the most militarized society on earth. Even the new industry was regimented in a military fashion. The factory-towns grew up around the barrack-cities of the Hohenzollern soldier-kings. The continuous military drill affected the business classes, and even the early stages of the trade union and Social Democratic movements, with their profound stress on discipline. Uniforms were everywhere. The Kaiser referred contemptuously to ministers, politicians and diplomats as 'stupid civilians'. To raise their prestige, members of the government affected military dress. Bismarck sported the rig of a cavalry general. When Bethmann Hollweg first appeared as Chancellor in the Reichstag he was dressed as a major. The Kaiser himself sat at his desk perched on a military saddle instead of a chair.[14] The idea of civilians somehow overturning this enormous and all-pervasive military structure, above all in the middle of the greatest war in history, was preposterous.

It was, in fact, the other way round. It was Ludendorff, suddenly aware the game was up, and determined to preserve the army intact while there was still time, who insisted on an armistice. It was his successor, General Wilhelm Groener, who gave the Kaiser his marching-orders, telling him the army was going home in good order 'but not under the command of Your Majesty, for it stands no longer behind Your Majesty'.[15] And it was the army, having helped to engineer the war, having raised the stakes and ensured that the defeat was calamitous, which then slipped out of its responsibilities and handed back authority to the civilians. They were left with the task and the odium of arranging the armistice and signing the peace, while the generals prepared their stab-in-the-back exculpation.

Thus, by a curious piece of national myopia, containing elements of self-deception, the Germans exonerated those who had got the country into the fearful mess in which it found itself. The Allies dropped their notion of war-crimes tribunals. They even backed down on extraditing German officers known to have broken The Hague Convention. These men were released to appear in German courts where they received ridiculously small sentences, and were then allowed to escape, returning to their homes as heroes.

Instead, it was the Socialists and the politicians of the Centre who got the blame for Germany's troubles. The Socialists had been the biggest party in the Reichstag before the war, but they were never admitted to government; and because parliament had inadequate control over finance – the central weakness of pre-war German 'democracy' – they could do nothing effective to stop German imperialism, though they voted against it. They were the only party to oppose Germany's annexations in Russia in early 1918. When the war ended, they briefly held power at last, but merely as the legal receivers of a bankrupt empire, whose sins they were made to bear. When the Centre politicians took over, as they soon did, they too were tainted with defeat, surrender, of being 'the men of the Allies'.

To a greater or lesser degree, indeed, the stigma of Versailles was attached to all the politicians of the new Republic, and even to the notion of the Republic itself, and so to the whole idea of parliamentary democracy. For the first time the Germans had the chance to run themselves. Everyone over twenty, male and female, had the vote. Elections to all public bodies were henceforth equal, secret, direct and according to proportional representation. The censorship was abolished. Rights of assembly were guaranteed.

Trade unions were recognized by employers. The eight-hour day was made mandatory.[16] When the first elections were held in January 1919, three-quarters of those who took part in the 80 per cent poll favoured a republic.

The new Weimar constitution was drawn up under the guidance of the great sociologist Max Weber. It gave parliament full financial sovereignty for the first time. It was supposed to embody all the best features of the American constitution. But it had one serious weakness. The President, elected for a seven-year term, was not the head of government: that was the Chancellor, a party figure responsible to parliament. But the President, under Article 48, was endowed with emergency powers when parliament was not in session. From 1923 onwards this article was pervertedly invoked whenever parliament was deadlocked. And parliament was often deadlocked, because proportional representation prevented the development of a two-party system and absolute majorities. To many Germans, who had been brought up on the notion that Germany and the Germans were a metaphysical, organic unity, the spectacle of a divided, jammed parliament was unnatural. The argument that parliament was the forum in which quite genuine and unavoidable conflicts of interest were peacefully resolved was alien to them, unacceptable. Instead they saw the Reichstag as a mere theatre for the enactment of 'the game of the parties', while the real, eternal, organic and honourable Germany was embodied in the person of the President and Article 48. This constitutional cleavage was apparent even under the first president, the Socialist Friedrich Ebert. He preferred to use his power rather than force parliamentarians into the habit of settling their differences. It became far worse when Field-Marshal Hindenburg replaced him.

Although Ludendorff had run the war, Hindenburg had been the nominal war-lord and public hero. In 1916 a gigantic wooden image had been made of him, to symbolize German determination to win. If you bought a War Bond you were allowed to knock a nail into it. About 100,000 nails were thus hammered into the colossus. Immediately the war was over the statue was broken up for firewood, as though to symbolize the disappearance of the military and the reign of the civilians. It was they, Weimar, and especially parliament, which were identified with the Treaty and all the post-war difficulties and shame. When the wooden titan returned as President, he personified not only wartime heroism and German unity, as opposed to party disunity, but the anti-republican counter-principle embedded in the Weimar Constitution itself. And it was under Hindenburg that presidential prerogative was used to appoint and dismiss chancellors and dissolve the Reichstag, leading in the last years to the virtual suspension of parliamentary government. Hitler climaxed the process by exploiting the article to lay the foundations of his dictatorship even before parliament disappeared in April 1933.

The cleavage within the constitution might not have mattered so much had it not reflected a much deeper division in German society, and indeed in German minds. I call this the East–West division, and it is one of the central themes of modern times, in so far as they have been influenced by Germany's destiny. The principal characteristic of the pre-war German regime of princes, generals and landowners, the law-professors who endowed it with academic legitimacy, and the Lutheran pastors who gave it moral authority, was illiberalism. This ruling caste hated the West with passionate loathing, both for its liberal ideas and for the gross materialism and lack of spirituality which (in their view) those ideas embodied. They wanted to keep Germany 'pure' of the West, and this was one motive for their plans to resume the medieval conquest and settlement of the East, carving out a continental empire for Germany which would make her independent of the Anglo-Saxon world system. These Easterners drew a fundamental distinction between 'civilization', which they defined as rootless, cosmopolitan, immoral, un-German, Western, materialistic and racially defiled; and 'culture', which was pure, national, German, spiritual and authentic.[17] Civilization pulled Germany to the West, culture to the East. The real Germany was not part of international civilization but a national race-culture of its own. When Germany responded to the pull of the West, it met disaster; when it pursued its destiny in the East, it fulfilled itself.

In point of fact, it was the Easterners who had ruled Germany throughout, who had created the war-anxiety, got Germany into war, and then lost it. In the minds of most Germans, however, the 'stab-in-the-back' mythology refuted this factual analysis because it attributed the loss of the war to the defeatism and treachery of the Westerners, who had then signed the armistice, accepted the disastrous peace, introduced the Republic and enthroned 'the rule of the parties'. It was thus the Westerners who were responsible for all Germany's misfortunes in the post-war world, as was only logical, for they were the puppets or paid agents of the politicians of the West in Paris and London, and of the international financial community in Wall Street and the City. Their outpost in Germany was the parliament in Weimar. But authentic German culture still had its redoubt within the Republic, in the person of President Hindenburg, an Easterner *par excellence*, and in the authority of Article 48. In time, that vital bridgehead could be extended.

For the moment, however, the Westerners were triumphant. Weimar was a 'Western' republic. It stood for civilization rather than culture: civilization was in office, culture in opposition. It is no coincidence, either, that German civilization reached its gaudiest flowering during the 1920s, when Germany, for a brief period, became the world-centre of ideas and art. This triumph had been building up for a long time. Germany was by far the best-educated nation in the world – as long ago as the late eighteenth century it had passed the 50 per cent literacy mark. During the nineteenth century it had progressively established a system of higher education which for thoroughness and diversity of scholarship was without equal. There were world-famous universities at Munich, Berlin, Hamburg, Göttingen, Marburg, Freiburg, Heidelberg and Frankfurt. The German liberal intelligentsia had opted out of public and political life in the 1860s, leaving the field to Bismarck and his successors. But it had not emigrated; indeed, it had spread itself, and when it began to resurface just before the Great War, and took command in 1918, what was most striking about it was its polycentral strength.

Of course Berlin, with its 4 million population, held the primacy. But, unlike Paris, it did not drain all the country's intellectual and artistic energies into itself. While Berlin had its Alexanderplatz and Kurfürstendamm, there were plenty of other cultural magnets: the Bruehl in Dresden, the Jungfernsteg in Hamburg, the Schweidnitzter-strasse in Breslau or the Kaiserstrasse in Frankfurt. The centre of architectural experiment, the famous Bauhaus, was in Weimar, later moving to Dessau. The most important centre of art studies, the Warburg Institute, was in Hamburg. Dresden had one of the finest art galleries in the world as well as a leading European opera house, under Fritz Busch, where two of Richard Strauss's operas had their first performance. Munich had a score of theatres, as well as another great gallery; it was the home of *Simplicissimus*, the leading satirical magazine, and of Thomas Mann, the leading novelist. *Frankfurter Zeitung* was Germany's best newspaper, and Frankfurt was a leading theatrical and operatic centre (as was Munich); and other cities, such as Nuremberg, Darmstadt, Leipzig and Düsseldorf, saw the first performances of some of the most important plays of the Twenties.[18]

What particularly distinguished Berlin was its theatre, by far the world's richest in the 1920s, with a strongly political tone. Its pre-eminence had begun before the war, with Max Reinhardt's reign at the Deutsche Theater, but in 1918 republicanism took over completely. Some playwrights were committed revolutionaries, like Friedrich Wolf and Ernst Toller, who worked for Erwin Piscator's 'Proletarian Theatre', for which George Grosz designed scenery. Bertholt Brecht, whose play *Drums in the Night* was first staged in

Berlin in 1922, when he was twenty-four, wrote political allegories. He was attracted to Communism by its violence, as he was to American gangsterism, and his friend Arnolt Bronnen to fascism; Brecht designed his own 'uniform', the first of the Leftist outfits – leather cap, steel-rimmed glasses, leather coat. When *The Threepenny Opera*, which he wrote with the composer Kurt Weill, was put on in 1928 it set an all-time record for an opera by receiving over 4,000 performances throughout Europe in a single year.[19] But the bulk of the Berlin successes were written by liberal sophisticates, more notable for being 'daring', pessimistic, problematical, above all 'disturbing', than directly political: men like Georg Kaiser, Carl Sternheim, Arthur Schnitzler, Walter Hasenclever, Ferdinand Bruckner and Ferenc Molnar.[20] Sometimes the 'cultural Right' went for a particular play, as when it tried to disrupt the first night of *Der fröhliche Weinberg* by Carl Zuckmayer (who also wrote the script for *The Blue Angel*). But it was really the theatre as a whole to which conservatives objected, for there were no right-wing or nationalist plays whatever put on in Berlin. After watching a Gerhart Hauptmann play, a German prefect of police summed up the reaction of *Kultur*-Germany: 'The whole trend ought to be liquidated.'[21]

Berlin was also the world-capital in the related fields of opera and film. It was crowded with first-class directors, impresarios, conductors and producers: Reinhardt, Leopold Jessner, Max Ophuls, Victor Barnowsky, Otto Klemperer, Bruno Walter, Leo Blech, Joseph von Sternberg (*The Blue Angel*), Ernst Lubitsch, Billy Wilder (*Emil and the Detectives*), Fritz Lang (*Metropolis*). In designing and making scenery and costumes, lighting-effects, the standards of orchestral playing and choral singing, in sheer attention to detail, Berlin had no rivals anywhere. When *Wozzeck*, a new opera written by Arnold Schoenberg's gifted pupil Alban Berg, received its première at the Berlin State Opera in 1925, the conductor Erich Kleiber insisted on no less than 130 rehearsals.[22] The 1929 Berlin Music Festival featured Richard Strauss, Bruno Walter, Furtwängler, George Szell, Klemperer, Toscanini, Gigli, Casals, Cortot and Thibaud.[23] Against this background of talent, craftsmanship and expertise, Germany was able to develop the world's leading film industry, producing more films in the 1920s than the rest of Europe put together; 646 in the year 1922 alone.[24]

Even more remarkable was Germany's success in the visual arts. In 1918 Walter Gropius became director of the Weimar Arts and Crafts School and began to put into practice his theory of *Gesamtkunstwerk*, or total work of art, a term first used by Wagner but applied here, on the analogy of a medieval cathedral, to the integrated use of painting, architecture, furniture, glass and metal work, sculpture, jewellery and fabrics. The notion sprang from the Gothic revival but the atmosphere at the Bauhaus was dictated by the functional use of the latest materials and construction techniques. As one of the teachers, Lothar Schreyer, put it, 'We felt that we were literally building a new world.' It attracted many fine talents: Klee, Kandinsky, Mies van der Rohe, Oskar Schlemmer, Hannes Meyer; Bartók, Hindemith, Stravinsky were among the visiting artists.[25]

Indeed, it was the institutionalization of modernism which appeared so novel in Weimar and gave it its peculiar strength. Over the whole range of the arts, Weimar was less hostile to modernism than any other society or political system. The leading German museums began to buy modern paintings and sculpture, just as the opera houses patronized atonality. Otto Dix was made an art-professor in Berlin, Klee in Düsseldorf, Kokoschka in Dresden. Equally important in making modernism acceptable was the work of the art theorists and historians, like Carl Einstein, W.R. Worringer and Max Dvořák, who placed Abstraction and Expressionism in the context of the European art tradition. As a result, Berlin rivalled and even surpassed Paris as an exhibition centre for modern painting. The gallery run by Herwath Walden and his wife Else Lasker-Schüler, who also published the magazine *Der Sturm*, was more enterprising than any on the Left Bank, showing Leger, Chagall, Klee, Kurt Schwitters, Moholy-Nagy and Campendonck. The *Neue Sachlichkeit*, or New Realism, which displaced the dying Expressionism in 1923, attracted more interest than the Paris movements.[26]

There was, in fact, a modernistic cultural paramountcy in Weimar Germany. This in itself was highly provocative to the Easterners. They called it *Kulturbolschewismus*. Throughout the war the German ultra-patriotic press had warned that defeat would bring the triumph of Western 'decadent' art, literature and philosophy, as though Lloyd George and Clemenceau could not wait to get to Berlin to ram Cubism down German throats. Now it had actually happened! Weimar was the great battleground in which modernism and traditionalism fought for supremacy in Europe and the world, because in Weimar the new had the institutions, or some of them, on its side. The law, too: the Weimar censorship law, though still strict, was probably the least repressive in Europe. Films like *The Blue Angel* could not be shown in Paris. Stage and night-club shows in Berlin were the least inhibited of any major capital. Plays, novels and even paintings touched on such themes as homosexuality, sado-masochism, transvestism and incest; and it was in Germany that Freud's writings were most fully absorbed by the intelligentsia and penetrated the widest range of artistic expression.

The Left intelligentsia often sought deliberately to incite 'right-thinking' Germany to fury. They had been smothered so long beneath the conventional wisdom of army, church, court and academia; now it was the turn of the outsiders who had, in a curious and quite unprecedented way, become the insiders of Weimar society. In the *Weltbühne*, the smartest and most telling of the new journals, sexual freedom and pacifism were exalted, the army, the state, the university, the Church and, above all, the comfortable, industrious middle classes, were savaged and ridiculed. It featured the writings of Kurt Tucholsky, a satirist whom many compared to Heine, and whose acid pen jabbed more frequently and successfully beneath the skin of the Easterners than any other writer – the verbal equivalent of George Grosz's fearsome caricatures. He wrote: 'There is no secret of the German Army I would not hand over readily to a foreign power.'[27] Tucholsky was wonderfully gifted. He intended to give pain, to arouse hatred and fury. He succeeded.

This cultural trench warfare, waged without reference to any Geneva Convention, merciless in its spite, animosity and cruelty, was calculated to arouse the atavism of the Easterners. Their approach to the public realm was paranoid. The paranoia had to some extent been deliberately manufactured by Bismarck. But long before 1914 it had become instinctive and habitual, with the Reich the object of world-wide conspiracies, political, economic, military and cultural. The catastrophe of the war, far from exorcizing the fantasies, seemed to confirm them. And now here was Germany, noble, helpless and suffering, stricken in defeat and jeeringly tormented by cosmopolitan riff-raff who appeared to control all access to the platforms of the arts and, by secret conspiracy, were systematically replacing German *Kultur* by their own, accursed *Zivilisation*. The grievance was increasingly resented throughout the 1920s and strikingly summed up in a book called *Kurfürstendamm* written by Friedrich Hussong, and published a few weeks after the Nazis came to power:

A miracle has taken place. They are no longer here . . . . They claimed they were the German *Geist*, German culture, the German present and future. They represented Germany to the world, they spoke in its name . . . . Everything else was mistaken, inferior, regrettable kitsch, odious philistinism . . . . They always sat in the front row. They awarded knighthoods of the spirit and of Europeanism. What they did not permit did not exist . . . . They 'made' themselves and others. Whoever served them was sure to succeed. He appeared on their stages, wrote in their journals, was advertised all over the world; his commodity was recommended whether it was cheese or relativity, powder or *Zeittheater*, patent medicines or human rights, democracy or bolshevism, propaganda for abortion or against the legal system, rotten Negro music or dancing in the nude. In brief, there never was a more impudent dictatorship than that of the democratic intelligentsia and the *Zivilisations-literaten*.[28]

Of course underlying and reinforcing the paranoia was the belief that Weimar culture was inspired and controlled by Jews. Indeed, was not the entire regime a *Judenrepublik*? There was very little basis for this last doxology, resting as it did on the contradictory theories that Jews dominated both Bolshevism and the international capitalist network. The Jews, it is true, had been prominent in the first Communist movements. But in Russia they lost ground steadily once the Bolsheviks came to power, and by 1925 the regime was already anti-Semitic. In Germany also the Jews, though instrumental in creating the Communist Party (KPD), were quickly weeded out once it was organized as a mass party. By the 1932 elections, when it put up 500 candidates, not one was Jewish.[29] Nor, at the other end of the spectrum, were the Jews particularly important in German finance and industry. The belief rested on the mysterious connection between Bismarck and his financial adviser, Gerson von Bleichröder, the Jew who organized the Rothschilds and other banking houses to provide the finance for Germany's wars.[30] But in the 1920s Jews were rarely involved in government finance. Jewish businessmen kept out of politics. Big business was represented by Alfred Hugenberg and the German Nationalist People's Party, which was anti-Semitic. Jews were very active at the foundation of Weimar, but after 1920 one of the few Jews to hold high office was Walther Rathenau and he was murdered two years later.

In culture however it was a different matter. There is nothing more galling than a cultural tyranny, real or imaginary, and in Weimar culture 'they' could plausibly be identified with the Jews. The most hated of them, Tucholsky, was a Jew. So were other important critics and opinion formers, like Maximilian Harden, Theodor Wolff, Theodor Lessing, Ernst Bloch and Felix Salten. Nearly all the best film-directors were Jewish, and about half the most successful playwrights, such as Sternheim and Schnitzler. The Jews were dominant in light entertainment and still more in theatre criticism, a very sore point among the Easterners. There were many brilliant and much publicized Jewish performers: Elizabeth Bergner, Erna Sack, Peter Lorre, Richard Tauber, Conrad Veidt and Fritz Kortner, for instance. Jews owned important newspapers, such as Frankfurt's *Zeitung*, the *Berliner Tageblatt* and the *Vossische Zeitung*. They ran the most influential art galleries. They were particularly strong in publishing, which (next to big city department stores) was probably the area of commerce in which Jews came closest to predominance. The best liberal publishers, such as Malik Verlag, Kurt Wolff, the

Cassirers, Georg Bondi, Erich Reiss and S. Fischer, were owned or run by Jews. There were a number of prominent and highly successful Jewish novelists: Hermann Broch, Alfred Döblin, Franz Werfel, Arnold Zweig, Vicki Baum, Lion Feuchtwanger, Bruno Frank, Alfred Neumann and Ernst Weiss, as well as Franz Kafka, whom the intelligentsia rated alongside Proust and Joyce and who was an object of peculiar detestation among the Easterners. In every department of the arts, be it architecture, sculpture, painting or music, where change had been most sudden and repugnant to conservative tastes, Jews had been active in the transformation, though rarely in control. The one exception, perhaps, was music, where Schoenberg was accused of 'assassinating' the German tradition; but even here, his far more successful and innovatory pupil, Berg, was an Aryan Catholic. However, it is undoubtedly true to say that Weimar culture would have been quite different, and infinitely poorer, without its Jewish element, and there was certainly enough evidence to make a theory of Jewish cultural conspiracy seem plausible.[31]

This was the principal reason why anti-Semitism made such astonishing headway in Weimar Germany. Until the Republic, anti-Semitism was not a disease to which Germany was thought to be especially prone. Russia was the land of the pogrom; Paris was the city of the anti-Semitic intelligentsia. Anti-Semitism seems to have made its appearance in Germany in the 1870s and 1880s, at a time when the determinist type of social philosopher was using Darwin's principle of Natural Selection to evolve 'laws' to explain the colossal changes brought about by industrialism, the rise of megalopolis and the alienation of huge, rootless proletariats. Christianity was content with a solitary hate-figure to explain evil: Satan. But modern secular faiths needed human devils, and whole categories of them. The enemy, to be plausible, had to be an entire class or race.

Marx's invention of the 'bourgeoisie' was the most comprehensive of these hate-theories and it has continued to provide a foundation for all paranoid revolutionary movements, whether fascist-nationalist or Communist-internationalist. Modern theoretical anti-Semitism was a derivative of Marxism, involving a selection (for reasons of national, political or economic convenience) of a particular section of the bourgeoisie as the subject of attack. It was a more obviously emotional matter than analysis purely by class, which is why Lenin used the slogan that 'Anti-Semitism is the socialism of fools'. But in terms of rationality there was little to choose between the two. Lenin was saying, in effect, that it was the entire bourgeoisie, not just Jewry, which was to blame for the ills of mankind. And it is significant that all Marxist regimes, based as they are on paranoid explanations of human behaviour, degenerate sooner or later into anti-Semitism. The new anti-Semitism, in short, was part of the sinister drift away from the apportionment of individual responsibility towards the notion of collective guilt – the revival, in modern guise, of one of the most primitive and barbarous, even bestial, of instincts. It is very curious that, when the new anti-Semitism made its appearance in Germany, among those who attacked it was Nietzsche, always on the lookout for secular, pseudo-rational substitutes for the genuine religious impulse. He denounced 'these latest speculators in idealism, the anti-Semites . . . who endeavour to stir up all the bovine elements of the nation by a misuse of that cheapest of propaganda tricks, a moral attitude.'[32]

But if modern anti-Semitism was by no means a specifically German phenomenon, there were powerful forces which favoured its growth there. The modern German nation was, in one sense, the creation of Prussian militarism. In another, it was the national expression of the German romantic movement, with its stress upon the *Volk*, its mythology and its natural setting in the German landscape, especially its dark, mysterious forests. The German *Volk* movement dated from Napoleonic times and was burning 'alien' and 'foreign' books, which corrupted '*Volk* culture', as early as 1817. Indeed it was from the *Volk* movement that Marx took his concept of 'alienation' in industrial capitalism. A *Volk* had a soul, which was derived from its natural habitat. As the historical novelist Otto Gemlin put it, in an article in *Die Tat*, organ of the *Volk*-romantic movement, 'For each people and each race, the countryside becomes its own peculiar landscape'.[33] If the landscape was destroyed, or the *Volk* divorced from it, the soul dies. The Jews were not a *Volk* because they had lost their soul: they lacked 'rootedness'. This contrast was worked out with great ingenuity by a Bavarian professor of antiquities, Wilhelm Heinrich Riehl, in a series of volumes called *Land und Leute* (*Places and People*), published in the 1850s and 1860s.[34] The true basis of the *Volk* was the peasant. There could of course be workers, but they had to be 'artisans', organized in local guilds. The proletariat, on the other hand, was the creation of the Jews. Having no landscape of their own, they destroyed that of others, causing millions of people to be uprooted and herded into giant cities, the nearest they possessed to a 'landscape' of their own. 'The dominance of the big city', wrote Riehl, 'will be the equivalent to the dominance of the proletariat'; moreover, the big cities would link hands across the world, forming a 'world bourgeois' and a 'world proletariat' conspiring to destroy everything that had a soul, was 'natural', especially the German landscape and its peasantry.[35]

The *Volk* movement spawned a crop of anti-Semitic 'peasant' novels, of which the most notorious was Herman Löns's *Der Wehrwolf* (1910), set in the Thirty Years' War, and showing the peasants turning on their oppressors from the towns like wolves: 'What meaning does civilization have? A thin veneer beneath which nature courses, waiting until a crack appears and it can burst into the open.' 'Cities are the tomb of Germanism.' 'Berlin is the domain of the Jews.' Jews functioned among the peasants as money-lenders, cattle-dealers and middlemen, and the first organized political anti-Semitism surfaced in the peasant parties and the *Bund der Land-wirte*, or Farmers' Union. Hitler was an avid reader of 'peasant novels', especially the works of Dieter Eckhart, who adapted *Peer Gynt* into German, and of Wilhelm von Polenz, who also identified the Jews with the cruelty and alienation of modern industrial society.

German anti-Semitism, in fact, was to a large extent a 'back to the countryside' movement. There were special *Volk* schools, which stressed open-air life. 'Mountain theatres', shaped from natural amphitheatres, were built in the Harz Mountains and elsewhere, for dramatized '*Volk* rites' and other spectacles, an activity the Nazis later adopted on a huge scale and with great panache. The first youth movements, especially the highly successful *Wandervögel*, strumming guitars and hiking through the countryside, took on an anti-Semitic coloration, especially when they invaded the schools and universities. The 'garden city' movement in Germany was led by a violent anti-Semite, Theodor Fritsch, who published the *Antisem-itic Catechism*, which went through forty editions, 1887–1936, and who was referred to by the Nazis as *Der Altmeister*, the master-teacher. Even the sunbathing movement, under the impulse of Aryan and Nordic symbols, acquired an anti-Semitic flavour.[36] Indeed in 1920s Germany there were two distinct types of nudism: 'Jewish' nudism, symbolized by the black dancer Josephine Baker, which was heterosexual, commercial, cosmopolitan, erotic and immoral; and anti-Semitic nudism, which was German, *Völkisch*, Nordic, non-sexual (sometimes homosexual), pure and virtuous.[37]

It is, indeed, impossible to list all the varieties of ingredients which, from the 1880s and 1890s onwards, were stirred into the poisonous brew of German anti-Semitism. Unlike Marxism, which was essen-tially a quasi-religious movement, German anti-Semitism was a cultural and artistic phenomenon, a form of romanticism. It was Eugen Diederichs, the publisher of *Die Tat* from 1912, who coined the phrase 'the new romanticism', the answer to Jewish Expression-ism. He published *Der Wehrwolf*, and at his house in Jena, sur-rounded by intellectuals from the Youth Movement, he wore zebra-striped trousers and a turban and launched the saying 'Demo-cracy is a civilization, while aristocracy equals culture.' He also contrived to transform Nietzsche into an anti-Semitic hero. Other audacious acts of literary theft were perpetrated. Tacitus' *Germania* was turned into a seminal *Volkisch* text; Darwin's works were tortured into a 'scientific' justification for race 'laws', just as Marx had plundered them for class 'laws'. But there were plenty of genuine mentors too. Paul de Lagarde preached a Germanistic religion stripped of Christianity because it had been Judaized by St Paul, 'the Rabbi'. Julius Langbehn taught that assimilated Jews were 'a pest and a cholera', who poisoned the artistic creativity of the *Volk*: they should be exterminated, or reduced to slavery along with other 'lower' races.[38] Both Houston Stewart Chamberlain and Eugen Dühring stressed the necessary 'barbarism' or Gothic element in German self-defence against Jewish decadence and the importance of the 'purity' and idealism of the Nordic pantheon. Chamberlain, whom Hitler was to visit on his deathbed to kiss his hands in 1927, argued that God flourished in the German and the Devil in the Jewish race, the polarities of Good and Evil. The Teutons had inherited Greek aristocratic ideals and Roman love of justice and added their own heroism and fortitude. Thus it was their role to fight and destroy the only other race, the Jews, which had an equal purity and will to power. So the Jew was not a figure of low comedy but a mortal, implacable enemy: the Germans should wrest all the power of modern technology and industry from the Jews, in order to destroy them totally.[39] Some of the German racial theorists were Marxists, like Ludwig Woltmann, who transformed the Marxist class-struggle into a world race-struggle and advocated the arousal of the masses by oratory and propaganda to mobilize the Germans into the conquests needed to ensure their survival and proliferation as a race: 'The German race has been selected to dominate the earth.'

By the 1920s, in brief, any political leader in Germany who wished to make anti-Semitism an agent in his 'will to power' could assemble his campaign from an enormous selection of slogans, ideas and fantasies, which had accumulated over more than half a century. The Versailles Treaty itself gave the controversy new life by driving into Germany a great wave of frightened Jews from Russia, Poland and Germany's surrendered territories. Thus it became an urgent 'problem', demanding 'solutions'. They were not wanting either. There were proposals for double-taxation for Jews; isolation or apartheid; a return to the ghetto system; special laws, with hanging for Jews who broke them; an absolute prohibition of inter-marriage between Aryan Germans and Jews. A 1918 best-seller was Artur Dinter's *Die Sünde wider das Blut* (*Sins Against the Blood*), describing how rich Jews violated the racial purity of an Aryan woman. Calls for the extermination of the Jews became frequent and popular, and anti-Semitic pamphlets circulated in millions. There were many violent incidents but when, in 1919, the Bavarian police asked for advice on how to cope with anti-Semitism, Berlin replied there was no remedy since 'it has its roots in the difference of race which divides the Israelitic tribe from our *Volk*'.[40]

The Jews tried everything to combat the poison. Some brought up their children to be artisans or farmers. They enlisted in the army. They attempted ultra-assimilation. A Jewish poet, Ernst Lissauer, wrote the notorious 'Hate England' hymn. They went to the other extreme and tried Zionism. Or they formed militant Jewish organizations, student leagues, duelling clubs. But each policy raised more difficulties than it removed, for anti-Semitism was protean, hydra-headed and impervious to logic or evidence. As Jakob Wassermann put it: 'Vain to seek obscurity. They say: the coward, he is creeping into hiding, driven by his evil conscience. Vain to go among them and offer them one's hand. They say: why does he take such liberties with his Jewish pushfulness? Vain to keep faith with them as a comrade in arms or a fellow-citizen. They say: he is Proteus, he can assume any shape or form. Vain to help them strip off the chains of slavery. They say: no doubt he found it profitable. Vain to counter-act the poison.'[41] Mortitz Goldstein argued that it was useless to expose the baselessness of anti-Semitic 'evidence': 'What would be gained? The knowledge that their hatred is genuine. When all calumnies have been refuted, all distortions rectified, all false notions about us rejected, antipathy will remain as something irrefutable.'[42]

Germany's defeat in 1918 was bound to unleash a quest for scapegoats, alien treachery in the midst of the *Volk*. Even without collateral evidence, the Jews, the embodiment of Westernizing 'civilization', were automatically cast for the role. But there was evidence as well! The influx of Jews in the immediate post-war period was a fresh dilution of the *Volk*, presaging a further assault on its martyred culture. And Weimar itself, did it not provide daily proof, in parliament, on the stage, in the new cinemas, in the bookshops, in the magazines and newspapers and art galleries, everywhere an ordinary, bewildered German turned, that this cosmopolitan, corrupting and ubiquitous conspiracy was taking over the Reich? What possible doubt could there be that a crisis was at hand, demanding extreme solutions?

It was at this point that the notion of a violent resolution of the conflict between culture and civilization began to take a real grip on the minds of some Germans. Here, once again, the fatal act of Lenin, in beginning the cycle of political violence in 1917, made its morbid contribution. Anti-Semitism had always presented itself as defensive. Now, its proposals to use violence, even on a gigantic scale, could be justified as defensive. For it was generally believed, not only in Germany but throughout Central and Western Europe, that Bolshevism was Jewish-inspired and led, and that Jews were in control of Communist Parties, and directed Red revolutions and risings wherever they occurred. Trotsky, the most ferocious of the Bolsheviks, who actually commanded the Petrograd *putsch*, was undoubtedly a Jew; so were a few other Russian leaders. Jews had been prominent in the Spartacist rising in Berlin, in the Munich Soviet government, and in the abortive risings in other German cities. Imagination rushed in where facts were hard to get. Thus, Lenin's real name was Issachar Zederblum. The Hungarian Red Revolution was directed not by Béla Kun but by a Jew called Cohn. Lenin's Red Terror was a priceless gift to the anti-Semitic extremists, particularly since most of its countless victims were peasants and the most rabid and outspoken of the Cheka terrorizers was the Latvian Jew Latsis. Munich now became the anti-Semitic capital of Germany, because it had endured the Bolshevist-Jewish terror of Kurt Eisner and his gang. The *Münchener Beobachter*, from which the Nazi *Völkische Beobachter* later evolved, specialized in Red atrocity stories, such as Kun or Cohn's crucifixion of priests, his use of a 'mobile guillotine' and so on. And many of the news items reported from Russia were, of course, perfectly true. They formed a solid plinth on which a flaming monument of fantasy could be set up. Hitler was soon to make highly effective use of the Red Terror fear, insisting, time and again, that the Communists had already killed 30 million people. The fact that he had added a nought in no way removed the reality of those first, terrible digits. He presented his National Socialist militancy as a protective response and a preemptive strike. It was 'prepared to oppose all terrorism on the part of the Marxists with tenfold greater terrorism'.[43] And in that 'greater terrorism' the Jews would be hunted down not as innocent victims but as actual or potential terrorists themselves.

The syphilis of anti-Semitism, which was moving towards its tertiary stage in the Weimar epoch, was not the only weakness of the German body politic. The German state was a huge creature with a small and limited brain. The Easterners, following the example of Bismarck, grafted onto the Prussian military state a welfare state which provided workers with social insurance and health-care as of right and by law. As against the Western liberal notion of freedom of choice and private provision based on high wages, it imposed the paternalistic alternative of compulsory and universal security. The state was nursemaid as well as sergeant-major. It was a towering shadow over the lives of ordinary people and their relationship towards it was one of dependence and docility. The German industrialists strongly approved of this notion of the state as guardian, watching over with firm but benevolent solicitude the lives of its citizens.[44] The philosophy was Platonic; the result corporatist. The German Social Democrats did nothing to arrest this totalitarian drift when they came briefly to power in 1918; quite the contrary. They reinforced it. The Weimar Republic opened windows but it did not encourage the citizen to venture outside the penumbra of state custody.

Who was in charge of this large and masterful apparatus, now that the Easterners were in opposition? The answer was: nobody. The bureaucrats were trained on Prussian lines. They followed the rules and when in doubt waited for orders. The architects of the Weimar Republic made no attempt to change this pattern and encourage civil servants to develop a sense of moral autonomy. Presumably they feared that the officials of the new regime might be tempted to disobey their new parliamentary masters. At all events they were exhorted to regard obedience as the supreme virtue. In a famous lecture given in 1919, Max Weber insisted: 'The honour of the civil servant is vested in his ability to execute conscientiously the order of superior authorities.' Only the politician had the right and duty to exercise personal responsibility.[45] It would be difficult to conceive of worse advice to offer to German mandarins. Naturally, it was followed, right to the bitter end in 1945.

The moral abdication of the bureaucrats might not have mattered so much if the politicians had followed the other half of Weber's counsel. But the parliamentarians never provided the vigorous and self-confident leadership needed to make Weimar a success. When in doubt they always fell back on Article 48, which was first used in August 1921 to forbid anti-republican meetings. It was as though they were conscious all the time that the bulk of the nation had reservations about Weimar, regarded its élites as lackeys of the Allies, *Erfüllungspolitiker*, men pledged to fulfil a hated treaty. Often they gave the impression that they shared these doubts themselves. The Socialists set this pattern from the start. Called to office for the first time in 1918 they made no real attempt to change the basic structures of an overwhelmingly authoritarian country. The SPD leaders were worthy, toilsome men: Ebert a saddler, Noske a basket-maker, Wels an upholsterer, Severing a locksmith, Scheidemann a printer. They were dull, unimaginative, sneered at by the Left intelligentsia, despised by the academics. They relinquished their grip on office all too easily as soon as the Centre-Right recovered its nerve. They lacked the will to power.

They were, moreover, thrown off balance right at the start by the decision of the Far Left to follow Lenin's example and opt for violence against parliamentarianism in the winter of 1918–19. We see here, once again, the disastrous consequences which flow when men use the politics of force because they are too impatient for the politics of argument. The Left *putsch* drove the Social Democrats into a fatal error. Afraid to use the regular army units, which might have proved mutinous, Gustav Noske asked the old High Command to provide him with a *Freikorps* of demobilized officers. They were, of course, produced with dispatch. The SPD ministers thus gave legitimacy to a movement which was already spreading in the East, where German settler communities were fighting the Poles, and which was from the start violently and incorrigibly anti-Weimar. Soon there were no less than sixty-eight of these bodies, sometimes called *Bunds* or *Ordens*, with burgeoning social and political aims and a taste for street-fighting. One, the *Bund Wehrwolf*, fought the French – and the Socialists – in the Ruhr. Another, the *Jungdeutscher Orden*, had 130,000 members by 1925.[46] It was from such an *Orden*, run by Karl Harrer, that the Nazis emerged, Hitler turning it into a mass-party, with the SA or Brownshirts as a reminder of its *Freikorps* origins.[47]

Almost inevitably, the abortive Left risings, leading to the legalizing of the *Freikorps* and the Right's recovery of confidence, produced in turn an army *putsch*. It came in March 1920, under Wolfgang Kapp, an old friend of Tirpitz and co-founder with him of the Fatherland Party in 1917. About half the army supported Kapp but the Right politicians and the civil servants refused to join him, and after four days he fled to Sweden. Unfortunately, the Far Left had again opted for violence instead of backing the new republican institutions. In the Ruhr they raised a 'Red Army' of 50,000 workers, the only time in the whole history of Weimar that the Marxists were able to put a sizeable military force into the field. The emergence of this body gave the army command an uncovenanted opportunity to retrieve its reputation as the custodian of law and order. In April it marched into the Ruhr and reconquered it from the Marxists, after dreadful brutalities on both sides. As a result, control of the army passed from the hands of the one reliably republican general, Walther Reinhardt, into those of a *Junker* reactionary, General Hans von Seeckt, who was dedicated to the destruction of the Versailles Treaty. Seeckt immediately set about strengthening the 'Russian connection', evading the arms-limitation clauses of the Treaty by constructing secret arms factories in Russia, a process accelerated by the signing of the Rapallo Treaty in 1922. He also purged the army of its republican elements, cashiering the NCOs and privates who had opposed the Kapp *putsch* for 'breaking discipline'.[48] He turned the army from a politically neutral instrument into the matrix of a new, anti-republican state, which would implement the old programme of the Easterners. Thus the army slipped from Weimar's control and moved into the opposition. When President Ebert asked Seeckt in 1923 where the army stood, he replied: 'The *Reichswehr* stands behind me.'[49]

The resurgence of the Right was soon reflected in politics. In the June 1920 elections the Social Democrat vote collapsed, the old Weimar coalition lost power, and thereafter the men who had created the Republic no longer controlled it. More serious was the erosion of the rule of law. The judiciary, which had never liked the Republic, decided like the army to go into opposition. The perpetrators of the Kapp *putsch* were never brought to book in the courts. Moreover, the events of spring 1920 sharply increased a tendency already observable the previous year for judges to treat political violence, which had now become endemic in Germany, on a selective political basis. They reasoned that, since violence had originated with the Left, a violent response by the Right was in a sense designed to protect public order, and therefore justified. Thanks to Lenin's terror, this view was widely shared in Germany, so that juries tended to back the judges. It was the same argument that allowed the presentation of anti-Semitism as 'defensive'. But of course it played straight into the hands of the right-wing thugs of the *Freikorps* and *Bunds* and *Orden*, and helped the transformation of Germany from an exceptionally law-abiding into an exceptionally violent society. Statistics compiled in 1922 over a four-year period (1919–22) show that there were 354 murders committed by the Right and twenty-two by the Left. Those responsible for every one of the left-wing murders were brought to court; ten were executed and twenty-eight others received sentences averaging fifteen years. Of the right-wing murders, 326 were never solved; fifty killers confessed, but of these more than half were acquitted despite confessions; and twenty-four received sentences averaging four months.[50]

The Right, in short, could practise violence with little fear of legal retribution. Judges and juries felt they were participating in the battle between German culture and alien civilization: it was right to recognize that violence might be a legitimate response to cultural provocation. Thus when the great liberal journalist Maximilian Harden, who was also a Jew, was nearly beaten to death by two thugs in 1922, the would-be killers got only a nominal sentence. The defence argued that Harden provoked the attack by his 'unpatriotic articles', and the jury found 'mitigating circumstances'.

Why did juries, representing ordinary middle-class people in Germany, tend to side with the Easterners against the Westerners? One chief reason was what they were taught in the schools, which itself reflected the political tone of the universities. The tragedy of modern Germany is an object-lesson in the dangers of allowing academic life to become politicized and professors to proclaim their 'commitment'. Whether the bias is to the Left or Right the results are equally disastrous for in either case the wells of truth are poisoned.

The universities and especially the professoriate were overwhelmingly on the side of *Kultur*. The jurists and the teachers of German literature and language were stridently nationalist. The historians were the worst of the lot. Heinrich von Treitschke had written of Germany's appointment with destiny and warned the Jews not to get in the way of the 'young nation'. His hugely influential *History of Germany in the Nineteenth Century*, a Wilhelmine classic, went into another big popular edition in 1920. Contemporary historians like Erich Marcks, Georg von Below and Dietrich Schäfer still celebrated the achievements of Bismarck (the anniversaries of Sedan and the founding of the empire were both public universities' holidays) and the lessons they drew from the Great War centred around Germany's lack of 'relentlessness'. They provided academic backing for the 'stab-in-the-back' myth. The academic community as a whole was a forcing-house for nationalist mythology. Instead of encouraging self-criticism and scepticism, the professors called for 'spiritual revivals' and peddled panaceas.[51]

By sheer bad luck, the most widely read and influential book in 1920s Germany was *The Decline of the West* by Oswald Spengler, a foolish and pedantic schoolteacher. He conceived his book in 1911 as a warning against undue German optimism. He wrote it during the war in anticipation of a German victory. Its first volume actually appeared in 1918, when defeat gave it an astonishing relevance and topicality. Thus it became a best-seller. The essence of the book was social Darwinism. He defined eight historic cultures and argued that the 'laws of morphology' applied to them. The last, the culture of the West, was already showing symptoms of decay, such as democracy, plutocracy and technology, indicating that 'civilization' was taking over from 'culture'. It seemed to explain why Germany had been defeated. It also heralded a coming age of cruel war in which would arise new Caesars, and democrats and humanitarians would have to be replaced by new élites of steel-hardened heroes who would look not for personal gain but for service to the community.[52] He followed it up in 1920 with a sensational essay, *Prussianism and Socialism*, which called for a classless, national socialism, in which the entire nation worked together under a dictator. It was exactly the sort of argument Mussolini was beginning to put forward in Italy.

Neatly complementing Spengler's analysis was the work of two other important Easterners. Carl Schmitt, Germany's leading legal philosopher, who poured out a flood of books and articles during these years, constantly stressed the argument that order could only be restored when the demands of the state were given preference over the quest for an illusory 'freedom'. The Reich would not be secure until Weimar was remodelled as an authoritarian state around the principle embodied in Article 48.[53] The point was restated in a historical perspective by the cultural historian Arthur Moeller van den Bruck in a brilliant book published in 1923. The Germans, he argued, were the leading European creators. Their first Reich, the medieval empire, had formed Europe. Their second creation, Bismarck's, was artificial because it had admitted the corruption of liberalism: that, of course, was why it had collapsed under test. Weimar was a mere interlude of chaos. Now the Germans had another opportunity: by purging society of liberalism and capitalism, they could build the third and final state which would embody all Germany's values and endure for a thousand years. He entitled this remarkable exercise in historical prophecy *The Third Reich*.[54]

Spurred on by their professors, the German student body, which averaged about 100,000 during the Weimar period, gave an enthusiastic reception to these Easterner philosophies. The notion that the student body is in some constitutional way a depository of humanitarian idealism will not survive a study of the Weimar period. Next to the ex-servicemen, the students provided the chief manpower reservoir of the violent extremists, especially of the Right. Student politics were dominated by the right-wing *Hochschulring* movement throughout the 1920s until it was replaced by the Nazis.[55] The Right extremists proceeded by converting half a dozen students on a campus, turning them into full-time activists, paid not to study. The activists could then swing the mass of the student body behind them. The Nazis did consistently better among the students than among the population as a whole and their electoral gains were always preceded by advances on the campus, students proving their best proselytizers. Students saw Nazism as a radical movement. They liked its egalitarianism. They liked its anti-Semitism too. Indeed, the students were more anti-Semitic than either the working class or the bourgeoisie. Most German student societies had excluded Jews even before 1914. In 1919 the fraternities subscribed to the 'Eisenach Resolution', which stated that the racial objection to Jews was insuperable and could not be removed by baptism. The next year they deprived Jewish students of the 'honour' of duelling. In 1922 the authorities at Berlin University cancelled a memorial service in honour of the murdered Walther Rathenau rather than risk a violent student demonstration. This policy of appeasement towards student violence became the pattern of the 1920s, the rectors and faculties always capitulating to the most outrageous demands of student leaders rather than risk trouble. By 1929 the universities had passed almost wholly into the Easterner camp.

Against this widely based array of social forces, what had the

Westerners to rely upon? Not many people were prepared to die for Weimar or even to speak out for it. The liberals, as one of them said, had 'married the Republic without loving it'. To them it simply filled the vacuum left by the disappearance of the monarchy and pending the emergence of something better. Even Max Weber, before his death in 1920, admitted he would have preferred a plebiscitory democracy under a strong man to a parliamentary one he assumed would be weak or corrupt or both. As the liberal Munich lawyer Professor Hans Nawiasky put it, the Republic was a child born in sorrow in whose arrival no one could take pride.[56] It could never be separated in people's minds from its tragic and detestable origins.

The Left had most to lose if Weimar failed – indeed they had most to gain by making it work – but the Far Left, at least, could never be persuaded to appreciate the fact. The scars of 1919 never healed and the Leninist element hated the Social Democrats, whom they began to call 'Social Fascists' from 1923 onwards, more passionately than anyone to the right of them. They not only failed to recognize fascism as a new and highly dangerous phenomenon, but refused to draw any distinction between middle-class conservatives who were pre-pared to work within the rule of law, and political savages who were right outside it. The Marxists never grasped the significance of anti-Semitism either. Here again their minds had been numbed by Marx's narcotic system. Marx had accepted much of the mythology of anti-Semitism in that he dismissed Judaism as a reflection of the money-lending era of capitalism. When the revolution came it was doomed to disappear: there would be no such person as a 'Jew'.[57] As a result of this absurd line of reasoning, the Jewish Marxists – Trotsky, Luxemburg, Paul Axelrod, Otto Bauer, Julius Martov – felt obliged to reject national self-determination for Jews while advocat-ing it for everybody else.[58] There was a grievous perversity in this crass denial of nature. As the Jewish historian Simon Dubnow put it: 'How much a Jew must hate himself who recognizes the right of every nationality and language to self-determination but doubts it or restricts it for his own people whose "self-determination" began 3,000 years ago.'[59] Seeing the Jews as a non-problem, the Marxists dismissed anti-Semitism as a non-problem too. They thus entered the greatest ideological crisis in European history by throwing their brains out of the window. It was a case of intellectual disarmament on a unilateral basis.

Nevertheless the destruction of the Republic was not inevitable. It would almost certainly have survived had not the radical Right produced a political genius. The central tragedy of modern world history is that both the Russian and the German republics, in turn, found in Lenin and Hitler adversaries of quite exceptional calibre, who embodied the will to power to a degree unique in our times. Of course the arrival of such a figure came as no surprise to the *exaltés* of the German Right. All the disciples of Nietzsche agreed a *Führer* would be necessary and would emerge, like a messiah. He was envisaged as the Knight from Dürer's famous print, *Knight, Death and the Devil*. Wilhelm Stapel in *The Christian Statesman* presented him as ruler, warrior and priest in one, endowed with charismatic qualities.[60]

The reality was rather different. Hitler was totally irreligious and had no interest in honour or ethics. He believed in biological determinism, just as Lenin believed in historical determinism. He thought race, not class, was the true revolutionary principle of the twentieth century, just as nationalism had been in the nineteenth. He had a similar background to Lenin. His father, too, was a minor bureaucrat, an Austrian customs official on the Bavarian border. Hitler, like Lenin, was the product of an age increasingly obsessed by politics. He never seriously attempted to make his living by any other means and he was only really at home, like Lenin, in a world where the pursuit of power by conspiracy, agitation and force was the chief object and satisfaction of existence. But in that barren and cheerless world he, like Lenin, was a master. He had the same intellectual egoism, lack of self-doubt, ruthlessness in personal relations, preference for force as opposed to discussion and, most important, the ability to combine absolute fidelity to a long-term aim with skilful opportunism. The two men even shared a certain puritanism: Hitler, like Lenin (and unlike Mussolini), had little personal vanity and was not corrupted by the more meretricious aspects of power.

But in one essential respect they were quite different. Whereas Lenin was the religious type of revolutionary, Hitler was a romantic. Indeed he was an artist. Liberal intellectuals were horrified, in 1939, when Thomas Mann, in a brilliant essay called *Brother Hitler*, compared him to the archetypal romantic artist (as described in, say, Henri Murger's *Vie de Bohème*) and asked: 'Must we not, even against our will, recognize in this phenomenon an aspect of the artist's character?'[61] Yet the comparison is valid and illuminating. It explains a good deal about Hitlerism which otherwise would remain obscure. Hitler practised painting with little skill and no success. His talent did not lie there. But his reactions were usually those of an artist both in recoil and response. Taken to his father's place of work, he found himself filled with 'repugnance and hatred'; it was 'a government cage' where 'old men sat crouched on top of one another, like monkeys'.[62] He grasped that he had a public mission when he first heard a performance of Wagner's earliest success, *Rienzi*, about a commoner who becomes people's tribune in fourteenth-century Rome but is destroyed by jealous nobles in a burning capitol: 'It began at that hour', he said later.[63] He seems to have conceived the 'final solution' for the Jews in the fantastic setting of the Gothic castle at Werfenstein in Austria where an unfrocked monk, Jörg Lanz von Liebenfels, was working out a systematic programme of race-breeding and extermination 'for the extirpation of the animal-man and the propagation of the higher new-man', and waged the race-struggle 'to the hilt of the castration knife'. It is significant that Lanz claimed Lenin as well as Hitler among his disciples, seeing an analogy between the extermination of classes 'thrown into the dust-bin of history' and races eliminated by breeding programmes, two forms of social Darwinism.[64] Hitler, too, was very interested in class differences, very shrewd in exploiting them to his advantage. But class did not stand near the centre of his political dream because it was not a visual concept. Race was.

Hitler appears always to have approached politics in terms of visual images. Like Lenin and still more like Stalin, he was an outstanding practitioner of the century's most radical vice: social engineering – the notion that human beings can be shovelled around like concrete. But in Hitler's case there was always an artistic dimension to these Satanic schemes. Planning a world empire radiating from Berlin, it was the colossal state structures of the capital which sprang first to mind and were then modelled down to the smallest detail.[65] When, during the war, Hitler gave directives for the political, demographic and economic transformation of tens of millions of square miles of Europe, right up to the Urals, he spoke in elaborate terms of the Babylonian gardens which were to adorn the cities of the master-race.[66] It was highly characteristic of him that he put an architect in charge of war production. Indeed he should have been an architect himself. When he spoke of his desire for the world to be 'changed thoroughly and in all its parts', he was thinking visually and in concrete terms, by extension from his lifelong wish to rebuild his 'home' town of Linz. All he actually contrived to put up was a new bridge there: but almost to the last day in the bunker he studied plans for the city's transformation. He periodically envisaged retirement, 'after the war', when, his prime mission accomplished, he would replan towns and supervise public building schemes.

Hitler's artistic approach was absolutely central to his success. Lenin's religious-type fanaticism would never have worked in Germany. The Germans were the best-educated nation in the world. To conquer their minds was very difficult. Their hearts, their sensibilities, were easier targets. Hitler's strength was that he shared with so many other Germans the devotion to national images new and old: misty forests breeding blond titans; smiling peasant villages under the shadow of ancestral castles; garden cities emerging from ghetto-like slums; riding Valkyries, burning Valhallas, new births and dawns in which shining, millennian structures would rise from the ashes of the past and stand for centuries. Hitler had in common with average German taste precisely those revered images which nearly a century of nationalist propaganda had implanted.

It is probably true to say that Hitler's cultural assets were the source of his appeal. Popular detestation of Weimar culture was an enormous source of political energy, which he tapped with relish. Lenin's notion of giving up music to concentrate on politics would have been incomprehensible to him. In Germany, music was politics; and especially music-drama. Hitler exemplifies the truth that ar-chitectural and theatrical skills are closely related. His romantic-artistic instincts led him to rediscover a truth almost as old as the *polis* itself, which certainly goes back to the Pharaohs: that the presentation of the charismatic leader, whether Renaissance mon-arch or modern democratic politician, is at least as important as the content. One of the reasons Hitler admired Wagner was that he learnt so much from him, especially from *Parsifal*, which became the model for his political spectaculars. The lesson he derived from the Western Front was that wars could be won or lost by propaganda: a thought which inspired his famous sixth chapter of *Mein Kampf*. The object of all propaganda, he wrote, was 'an encroachment upon man's freedom of will'.[67] This could be achieved by the 'mysterious magic' of Bayreuth, the 'artificial twilight of Catholic Gothic chur-ches', and both these effects he used; but he also plundered the tricks of Reinhardt and other despised Weimar producers and the cinema of Fritz Lang. The scenes of his oratory were designed and set with enviable professional skill; the attention to detail was fanatical. Hitler was the first to appreciate the power of amplification and the devilry of the searchlight: he seems to have invented *son et lumière* and used it with devastating effect at his mass night-meetings. He imported political costumery and insignia from Mussolini's Italy but improved upon them, so that Hitlerian uniforms remain the standard of excellence in totalitarian sumptuary. Both Stalinism and Maoism imitated Hitler's staging, exceeding it in scale but not in style.

As the star of these music-dramas Hitler rehearsed himself with equal professionalism. The myth of the 'mad orator' was unfounded. Hitler was always in total control of himself. He found the notion useful in dealing with foreigners, however, since people like Neville Chamberlain were hugely relieved when they actually met Hitler and found him capable of talking in a sane and reasonable manner. But all his 'mad' effects were carefully planned. He said in August 1920 that his object was to use 'calm understanding' to 'whip up and incite

. . . the instinctive'.[68] He always studied the acoustics in the halls where he spoke. He committed his speeches to an excellent memory (though he had very full notes too). He practised in front of a mirror and got the party photographer to take him in action so he could study the shots. The mind reels at what he might have done with television and it is odd he did not push its development: Berlin-Witzleben put on a TV show as early as 8 March 1929. Hitler used oratorical gestures, then rare in Germany, which he copied from Ferdl Weiss, a Munich comedian who specialized in beer-hall audiences. He timed himself to arrive late, but not too late. In the early days he dealt brilliantly with hecklers and used a lot of mordant humour.[69] Later he aimed at the inspired prophet image, and severely reduced the specific political content in his speeches. Nietzsche's sister Elizabeth, whom he visited in Weimar, said he struck her more as a spiritual than a political leader.[70] But his style was not that of a theologian so much as a revivalist: the American journalist H.R.Knickerbocker compared him to 'Billy Sunday'.[71] One observer wrote at the time: 'Hitler never really makes a political speech, only philosophical ones.'[72] In fact he did not so much outline a programme and make promises as demand a commitment. He saw politics as the mobilizing of wills. The listener surrendered his will to his leader, who restored it to him reinforced. As he put it: 'The will, the longing and also the power of thousands are accumulated in every individual. The man who enters such a meeting doubting and wavering leaves it inwardly reinforced: he has become a link in the community.'

We touch here upon an important point. Hitler, like Lenin, had nothing but contempt for parliamentary democracy or any other aspect of liberalism. But whereas Lenin insisted that an élite or even a single individual represented the will of the proletariat by virtue of their/his *gnosis*, Hitler was not averse to the democratic voice expressing itself in a less metaphysical form. In a sense he believed in participatory democracy and even practised it for a time. Indeed Hitler had no alternative but to pursue power, to some extent, by democratic means. In a rare moment of frankness, Lenin once said that only a country like Russia could have been captured so easily as he took it. Germany was a different proposition. It could not be raped. It had to be seduced.

It took Hitler some time to discover this fact. His political education is worth studying in a little detail. In pre-1914 Vienna he acquired his socialism and his anti-Semitism. The socialism he got from the famous Christian-Social mayor, Karl Lueger, who imitated and improved on Bismarck's social policy to create a miniature welfare state: in fifteen years he gave Vienna a superb transport, educational and social security system, green belts and a million new jobs. Here the whole of Hitler's domestic policy up to 1939 was adumbrated: to use the huge, paternalistic state to persuade the masses to forgo liberty in exchange for security. Lueger was also an anti-Semite, but it was another Viennese politico, the Pan-Germanist Georg von Schönerer, who taught Hitler to place the 'solution' to 'the Jewish problem' in the very centre of politics: Schönerer demanded anti-Jewish laws and his followers wore on their watch-chains the insignia of a hanged Jew.

The third element, which turned Hitler into the archetypal Easterner, was added during the war. Ludendorff believed strongly in the political education of the troops. He indoctrinated them with the idea of a vast eastward expansion, which the Brest-Litovsk Treaty showed was possible. Hitler became an enthusiastic exponent of this vision, expanded it and adapted it to include in its realization the 'final solution' for the 'Jewish problem'. It remained the biggest single element in his entire programme of action, the axis of attack around which all else revolved. Ludendorff's scheme for a politicized army was one of the many ideas which Lenin enthusiastically adopted, appointing political commissars down to battalion level. In turn, the German army readopted it after the Red risings of early 1919 had been put down. The Political Department of the Munich district command made Hitler one of their first 'political instruction officers' after the Munich Soviet had been smashed. Ernst Roehm was one of his colleagues. These two men took full advantage of the genuine anti-Red fears in Munich to turn it into the capital of German extremism.

In September 1919 Hitler took over a small proletarian group called the German Workers' Party. By April 1920, when he left the army to begin a full-time political career, he had transformed it into the nucleus of a mass party, given it a foreign policy (abrogation of Versailles, a Greater Germany, Eastern expansion, Jews to be excluded from citizenship) and reorganized its economic aims into a radical twenty-five-point programme: confiscation of war-profits, abolition of unearned incomes, state to take over trusts and share profits of industry, land for national needs to be expropriated without compensation. He also added the words 'National Socialist' to its title. Though Hitler sometimes used the words nationalism and socialism as though they were interchangeable, the radical and socialist element in his programme always remained strong. He was never in any sense a bourgeois or conservative politician or an exponent or defender of capitalism. Nor was the Nazi Party predominantly lower middle-class. Modern historians have hotly debated the extent of its working-class appeal.[73] The truth seems to be that the active Nazis were drawn from the discontented of all classes except the peasants and farmers. Out of a total of 4,800 members in 1923, 34.5 per cent were working class, 31 per cent lower middle-class, 6.2 minor officials, 11.1 clerks, 13.6 small businessmen and shopkeepers.[74]

Hitler's policy of creating a vanguard-élite party on a mass base was, of course, modelled on Lenin's experience. Indeed in important respects he remained a Leninist to the end, particularly in his belief that a highly disciplined and centralized party, culminating in an autocratic apex, was the only instrument capable of carrying through a fundamental revolution. Once in power he put in motion a systematic party take-over of all the organs of society exactly as Lenin did. And initially he planned to take power in the same way as Lenin in 1917, by a paramilitary *putsch*. He was encouraged in this resolve by the success of Mussolini's march on Rome in the autumn of 1922. A year later he thought the time had come in Germany too.

In 1923 the German currency, long teetering on the brink of chaos, finally fell into it. In 1913 the German mark had been worth 2.38 US dollars. By 1918 it had fallen to 7 cents, and by the middle of 1922 one US cent would buy 100 marks. The German financial authorities blamed the fall on the reparation clauses of the Versailles Treaty. In fact reparations had nothing directly to do with it. German public finance had been unsound since Bismarck's day, when he had paid for his wars by borrowing, afterwards liquidating the debts with the loot. The same technique was tried in 1914–18 but this time there was no loot and Germany emerged with a mountain of public debt in government bonds and a stupendous amount of paper money in circulation. The inflation began long before reparations were heard of and it had reached hyper-inflation levels by 1921 when the first payments became due. The crisis was due entirely to the reckless manner in which the Ministry of Finance, abetted by the Reichsbank, allowed credit and the money supply to expand. No one in the financial and business establishment cared a damn for the 'Republican mark'. They speculated and hedged against it, shipped capital abroad and, in the case of the industrialists, invested in fixed capital as fast as they could by borrowing paper money. When Keynes was called in to advise in the autumn of 1922 he proposed a sharp remedy which a later generation would term 'monetarism' – the government, he said, must at all costs balance the budget and curb money supply. This excellent advice was rejected and the printing presses accelerated.[75]

The final currency collapse began in January 1923 when the French occupied the Ruhr, the population stopped working and the German government accepted the financial responsibility to continue paying their wages. By the summer of 1923 a visiting US Congressman, A.P.Andrew, recorded he got 4,000 million marks for 7 dollars; a meal for two in a restaurant cost 1,500 million, plus a 400 million tip. By 30 November the daily issue was up to 4,000 quintillions. The banks were charging 35 per cent interest a day on loans, while paying depositors only 18 per cent a year. As a result, a peasant woman who deposited the price of a cow and drew it out six months later found it was worth less than the price of a herring. Small depositors and holders of government bonds lost everything. The big gainers, apart from the government itself, were the landowners, who redeemed all their mortgages, and the industrialists, who repaid their debts in worthless paper and became the absolute owners of all their fixed capital. It was one of the biggest and crudest transfers of wealth in history. The responsibilities were clear; the beneficiaries of the fraud were easily identifiable. Yet it is a depressing indication of public obtuseness in economic matters that the German public, and above all the losers, far from 'developing a proletarian consciousness' – as Marx had predicted they would in such a case – blamed the Versailles Treaty and 'Jewish speculators'.

Naturally such an upheaval had political results. On 13 August Gustav Stresemann, the only popular Weimar politician, formed a 'Great Coalition' from the Social Democrats to the fairly respectable Right. It lasted only one hundred days. A state of emergency was declared and power placed in the hands of the Defence Minister. There was talk of a 'March on Berlin'. But it was the Communists, as nearly always happened, who began the cycle of violence by an uprising in Saxony. Hitler now decided it was time to take over Bavaria. On 8 November his men surrounded a beer-hall where the local government was meeting, took its leaders into custody, formed them into a new dictatorial government with himself as political boss and Ludendorff head of the army, and then marched on the city with 3,000 men. But the police opened fire, the march dispersed, Hitler was arrested and in due course sentenced to five years in Landsberg fortress-prison.[76]

The authorities, however, had no intention he should serve his term. Hitler benefited from the double-standard which favoured all 'Easterner' criminals. 'The prisoner of Landsberg' was a popular and cosseted inmate. Instead of gaol garb he wore *Lederhosen*, a Bavarian peasant jacket and a green hunting hat with a feather. He spent up to six hours a day receiving a constant stream of visitors, including admiring women and cringing politicians. On his thirty-fifth birthday the flowers and parcels filled several rooms of the fortress, and his cell, according to one eyewitness, always 'looked like a delicatessen store'.[77] The months he spent there were just long enough for him to write *Mein Kampf*, tapping it out, as Hess's wife Ilse later testified, 'with two fingers on an ancient typewriter'.[78]

While Hitler was in Landsberg a great change came over Germany. In the short term events moved against him. The new president of the Reichsbank, Dr Hjalmar Schacht, stabilized the currency, introduced a new Reichsmark, based on gold and negotiable abroad, stopped printing money and slashed government expenditure – did, in fact, what Keynes had advised eighteen months before. The German economy, indeed the world economy, moved into smoother waters. The next five years saw steady economic expansion and in consequence a much higher degree of political stability: they were the best years of Weimar's life. Hitler realized, in Landsberg, that he was not going to get power Lenin's way. He must become a demotic politician. *Mein Kampf* acknowledged this fact and indicated exactly how he would do it. But he also sensed that the year 1923 had been a watershed, which in the long run must favour his endeavour. For millions of its victims, the legacy of the Great Inflation would be an inextinguishable, burning hatred of Weimar and its managers, of the 'Westernizing' establishment, of the Treaty and the Allies and those in Germany who had been associated with them. The German middle class had shifted its axis. Henceforth the Western cause was doomed; 'culture' would prevail over 'civilization'. Hitler noted this seismic reorientation in the remarkable fourth chapter of *Mein Kampf* describing the 'war for living space' fought against Russia. 'We stop the endless German movement to the south and west', he wrote, 'and turn our gaze towards the land in the east. At long last we break off the colonial and commercial policies of the pre-War period and shift to the soil policy of the future.'[79]

Almost at the exact moment Hitler was writing this, a strange and intuitive Englishman was coming to exactly the same conclusion. On 19 February 1924 D.H.Lawrence wrote a 'Letter from Germany'.[80] It was, he said, 'as if the Germanic life were slowly ebbing away from contact with western Europe, ebbing to the deserts of the east'. On his last visit in 1921, Germany 'was still open to Europe. Then it still looked to western Europe for a reunion . . . reconciliation. Now that is over . . . the positivity of our civilization has broken. The influences that come, come invisibly out of Tartary . . . . Returning again to the fascination of the destructive East that produced Attila.' He continued:

. . . at night you feel strange things stirring in the darkness . . . . There is a sense of danger . . . a queer, *bristling* feeling of uncanny danger . . . . The hope in peace-and-production is broken. The old flow, the old adherence is ruptured. And a still older flow has set in. Back, back to the savage polarity of Tartary, and away from the polarity of civilized Christian Europe. This, it seems to me, has already happened. And it is a happening of far more profound import than any actual *event*. It is the father of the next phase of events.

Determined to exploit this new polarity, and in his role of populist politician, Hitler – who had an undoubted streak of creative imagination – spent his last weeks in gaol thinking out the concept of spectacular scenic roads built specially for cars, the future *autobahnen*, and of a 'people's car' or *Volkswagen* to carry the nation along them.[81] He was released on 20 December 1924 and, suffering from Wagner-starvation, made straight for the house of the pianist Ernst Hanfstaengel and commanded him: 'Play the *Liebestod*.' The next morning he bought a Mercedes for 26,000 marks and thereafter, until he became Chancellor, insisted on passing every car on the road.[82]

FOUR

Legitimacy in Decadence

While the Eastern wind was blowing again in Germany, the Anglo–French alliance was coming apart. On 22 September 1922 there was an appalling scene at the Hotel Matignon in Paris between Raymond Poincaré, the French Prime Minister, and Lord Curzon, the British Foreign Secretary. Three days before, the French had pulled out their troops from Chanak, leaving the tiny British contingent exposed to the full fury of Ataturk's nationalists, and making a humiliation inevitable. Curzon had come to remonstrate.

The two men hated each other. Poincaré was the spokesman of the French *rentiers*, a Forsytian lawyer, sharp, prudent, thrifty, who liked to quote Guizot's advice to the French, *'Enrichissez-vous!'* L'Avocat de France, they called him: he had inherited the nationalism of Thiers, whose biography he was writing. His boast was incorruptibility: he insisted on writing all his letters by hand and when he sent an official messenger on private business, paid for it himself.[1] Curzon, too, wrote his own letters, thousands and thousands of them, sitting up late into the night, unable to sleep from a childhood back-injury. He, too, had a parsimonious streak, rigorously scrutinizing Lady Curzon's household accounts, keeping the servants up to the mark, not above telling a housemaid how to dust the furniture or a footman how to pour tea. But Poincaré brought out all his aristocratic contempt for middle-class vulgarity and French emotional self-indulgence. As the two men argued, Poincaré 'lost all command of his temper and for a quarter of an hour shouted and raved at the top of his voice'. Lord Hardinge, the British Ambassador, had to help the shocked Curzon to another room, where he collapsed on a scarlet sofa, his hands trembling violently. 'Charley,' he said, 'I can't bear that horrid little man. I can't bear him. I can't bear him.' And Lord Curzon wept.[2]

The underlying cause of the Anglo–French division was precisely a different estimate of the likelihood of a German military revival. Most of the British regarded French statesmen as paranoid on the subject of

138

Germany. 'I tell you,' Edouard Herriot was heard to say by Sir Austen Chamberlain, 'I look forward with terror to her making war upon us again in ten years.'[3] This French view was shared by the British members of the Inter-Allied Commission of Control, whose job was to supervise Articles 168–9 of the Versailles Treaty governing the disarmament of Germany. Brigadier-General J.H.Morgan reported privately that Germany had retained more of its pre-war characteristics, especially its militarism, than any other state in Europe.[4] The French claimed that every time they checked a statement by the Weimar War Ministry, they found it to be untrue. But the reports of the Control Commission, recording brazen violations, were never published; were, in the view of some, deliberately suppressed, to help the general cause of disarmament and cutting defence spending. The British Ambassador to Germany, Lord D'Abernon, a high-minded militant teetotaller, was passionately pro-German, the first of the Appeasers; he believed every word in Keynes's book and reported that it was impossible for Germany to conceal evasions of the Treaty.[5] He had nothing to say in his reports about holding companies set up by German firms to make weapons in Turkey, Finland, Rotterdam, Barcelona, Bilbao and Cadiz, and arrangements made by Krupps to develop tanks and guns in Sweden.[6]

French resentment at British indifference to the risks of a German revival was further fuelled on 16 April 1922 when Germany signed the Rapallo Treaty with Russia. One of the secret objects of this agreement, as the French suspected, was to extend arrangements for the joint manufacture of arms in Russia, and even to have German pilots and tank-crews trained there. It also had a sinister message to France's eastern ally Poland, hinting at a German–Soviet deal against her which finally emerged as the Nazi–Soviet Pact of August 1939. Rapallo strengthened Poincaré's determination to get reparations from Germany by force, if necessary, and it was not long after the break with Britain over Chanak that he sent French troops into the Ruhr, on 11 January 1923. Some of these troops were from French Africa, and it was one of Poincaré's boasts that France was 'a country not of 40 million but of 100 million'. The French railway system in Africa, such as it was, had as its main purpose the rapid transportation of troops to the European theatre. The fact that the Germans had a particular hatred for the Arabs and blacks in French uniform was, to the French, an additional reason for sending them there. France's harsh line brought short-term results on 26 September 1923 when the German government, in effect, capitulated to Poincaré's demands. The fierce little lawyer, who held power (with one interruption) until 1929, was the dominant figure in Western

European politics for most of the Twenties and appeared to many (including some of the British and Americans) to personify a French aggressiveness which was a greater threat to European and world stability than anything likely to emerge from Germany.

In fact all Poincaré's policy produced was a gigantic German resentment, certain to come into the open the second French power waned, and a strengthening of the very forces in Germany determined on military revival. And of course the image of a fighting-cock France, resuming the dominant role in Europe it had occupied from the time of Louis xiv to Napoleon i, was an illusion. Versailles had not broken up Bismarck's Germany. It was inevitably the only superpower in Europe, now that Russia had virtually ceased – if only temporarily – to be a European power. Sooner or later that German superiority, in numbers, industrial strength, organization and national spirit, was bound to declare itself again. The only question was whether it would do so in generous or hostile fashion.

By comparison the French were weak. Equally important, they felt they were even weaker than they actually were. The consciousness of debility, marked in the Twenties – Poincaré's bluster was an attempt to conceal it – became obsessional in the Thirties. In the seventeenth century the French population had been nearly twice as big as any other in Europe. The next largest, significantly enough, had been that of Poland.[7] The French had a melancholy awareness of the decline of their new Eastern ally, which they hoped to make great again to balance their own decline. It was engraven on French hearts that, even as late as 1800, they were still the most numerous race in Europe, Russia alone excepted. Since then they had suffered an alarming relative decline, reflected in scores of worried demographic tracts which had been appearing since the 1840s. They were overtaken by the Austrians in 1860, the Germans in 1870, the British in 1900, and the Italians were to follow in 1933, making France a mere fifth in Europe. Between 1800, when it was 28 million, and 1940, the French population increased by only 50 per cent, while Germany's quadrupled and Britain's tripled.[8]

The Great War, which (as the French saw it) Germany had willed on France in order to destroy her utterly as a major power, had tragically increased France's demographic weakness. They had had 1,400,000 men killed – 17.6 per cent of the army, 10.5 per cent of the entire active male population. Even with Alsace and Lorraine back in the fold, the French population had fallen in consequence, from 39.6 million to 39.12 million, while Britain's, for instance, had risen 2.5 million during the war years. Some 1.1 million Frenchmen had become *mutilés de guerre*, permanently disabled. The Germans had killed 673,000 peasants, seriously wounded half a million more, occupied ten *départements* with a population of 6.5 million, turned a quarter of them into refugees, wrecked farm-buildings, slaughtered livestock and removed machinery when they withdrew, as well as turning Frenchmen into slave-labourers in the factories of Ludendorff's 'War Socialism', where death-rates were nearly as high as the 10 per cent a year they reached under the Nazis in the Second World War. The French brooded on these appalling figures, which were made to seem even more terrible by the brilliance of their own war-propaganda.[9]

Those French who suffered war-damage were well compensated afterwards but the manner in which this was financed, despite all Poincaré's efforts, produced a progressive inflation which, while less spectacular than Germany's in 1923, lasted much longer and was ultimately more corrosive of national morale. Between 1912 and 1948, wholesale prices in France multiplied 105 times and the price of gold 174 times. Against the dollar, the franc in 1939 was only one-seventieth of its 1913 value.[10] For American and British tourists and expatriates, France between the wars was a bargain-basement paradise, but it was hard on the French who treated the steady erosion of their *rentes* and savings as an additional reason for having fewer children. Between 1906 and 1931 the number of French families with three or more children fell drastically and during the Thirties one-child families were commoner than any other. By 1936 France had a larger proportion of people over sixty than any other country – 147 per thousand, compared to 129 in Britain, 119 in Germany, 91 in the US and 74 in Japan.[11]

France had hoped to strengthen herself by recovering Alsace and Lorraine, the latter with a large industrial belt. But of course the economy of the two provinces had been integrated with the Ruhr and it was badly damaged by the separation. In heavily Catholic Alsace the French alienated the clergy by attacking German, the language of religious instruction. They tended to make the same mistake as the Germans and behave like colonizers. In fact they had less to offer, for French social security was much inferior to Germany's.[12] France was a poor market for industry, albeit a protected one. Strict rent controls, imposed in 1914 and never lifted, killed France's housing market. Housing stock, 9.5 million before the war, was still only 9.75 million in 1939, with nearly a third declared unfit for human habitation. Agriculture was appallingly backward. In the 1930s there were still three million horses on the farms, the same number as in 1850. France, like Italy, was a semi-industrialized country and her pre-war rate of progress was not fully sustained in the 1920s, still less in the 1930s when industrial production never returned to the 1929 levels. Between 1890 and 1904 France was the world's biggest car manufacturer. In the 1920s she still made more cars than Italy or Germany. But she failed to produce a cheap car for mass-sale. By the mid-1930s 68 per cent of cars sold in France were second-hand and there were still 1,352,000 horse-carriages on the streets, exactly as many as in 1891.[13]

The root of the problem was low investment. Here again inflation was to blame. The state was a poor substitute for the private investor. It was the biggest employer even before 1914 and the war gave the state sector new impetus. Etienne Clementel, Minister of Commerce 1915–19, wanted a national plan and an economic union of Western Europe; among his protégés were Jean Monnet and other future 'Eurocrats'. But nothing came of these ideas at the time. The state bought into railways, shipping, electricity, oil and gas to keep things going and preserve jobs, but little money was available for investment.[14] French industrialists had plenty of ideas but were frustrated by the lack of big opportunities and spent much of their time feuding with each other – thus, Ernest Mercier, head of the electricity and petrol industries, fought a bitter war with François de Wendel, the big iron-steel boss.[15] For clever men lower down the ladder the lack of opportunities was even worse (for women they were non-existent). Between the wars real wages of engineers in France fell by a third. Higher education, especially on the technical side, was tragically inadequate, bedevilled by sectarian rows and lack of funds. Most of the money went to the famous but old-fashioned 'Grandes Ecoles' in Paris: Herriot called the Polytechnique, which produced the technocrats, 'the only theology faculty which has not been abolished'. A Centre National de la Récherche Scientifique did emerge, but on an exiguous budget. The new Paris Medical Faculty building, ordered in the 1920s, was not finished till the 1950s (France had no Health Ministry until 1922), and by 1939 it had only two doctors on its staff. One striking statistic sums it up: in 1927 France spent less on higher education than on feeding cavalry horses.[16]

Moreover, in its own way France was as divided as Germany. There was no clash between civilization and culture. Quite the contrary. The French were agreed about civilization: they owned it. They were most reluctant, at Versailles, to admit English as an alternative official language. They regarded France as the originator, home and custodian of civilization – a word they themselves had coined in 1766. They envied, disliked and despised the Anglo-Saxons. Their best young novelist, François Mauriac, wrote in 1937: 'I do not understand and I do not like the English except when they are dead.' Among the popular books of the period were Henri Beraud's Faut-il reduire l'Angleterre en esclavage? (1935) and Robert

Aron and André Dandieu's *Le Cancer Americain* (1931). The Germans, oddly enough, were more acceptable. In the 1930s, young novelists like Malraux and Camus read Nietzsche and young philosophers like Sartre were attracted to Heidegger. But the official model for France was Descartes, whose methodology dominated the school philosophy classes which were the most striking feature of the French education system.[17] They were designed to produce a highly intelligent national leadership. What they did produce was intellectuals; not quite the same thing. And the intellectuals were divided not merely in their views but on their function. The most influential of the philosophy teachers, Emile Chartier ('Alain'), preached 'commitment'. But the best-read tract for the times, Julien Benda's *La Trahison des Clercs* (1927), preached detachment.[18] There was something to be said for keeping French intellectuals above the fray: they hated each other too much. Marx had assumed, in the *Communist Manifesto*, that 'intellectuals' were a section of the bourgeoisie which identified itself with the interests of the working class. This analysis appeared to be confirmed during the early stages of the Dreyfus case (the Jewish officer falsely convicted of treason), when the newly fashionable term 'intelligentsia' was identified with the anti-clerical Left. But the long Dreyfus struggle itself brought into existence an entirely new category of right-wing French intellectuals, who declared a reluctant cease-fire in 1914 but emerged foaming with rage in 1918 and helped the political Right, the next year, to win its first general election victory in a generation. Except in 1924–5, 1930–1 and 1936–8, the French Right and Centre dominated the Chambre des Deputés (and the Senate throughout), and the Right intellectuals held the initiative in the salons and on the boulevards.

There was agreement about civilization; where the French fought was over culture. Was it secular or confessional, positivist or a matter of metaphysics? The battle was bitter and destructive, savagely dividing the education system, business, local government, society. The freemasons, the militant arm of secularity, were still increasing their numbers, from 40,000 in 1928 to 60,000 in 1936.[19] Their junior arm was composed of the despised, underpaid state primary teachers, pro-republican, pacifist, anti-clerical, who fought the *curé* in every village. They used a completely different set of textbooks, especially in history, to the Catholic 'free' schools. But the Catholics were gaining in the schools. Between the wars, state secondary schools dropped from 561 to 552; Catholic ones more than doubled, from 632 in 1920 to 1,420 in 1936. The *Anciens élèves* (Old Boys) associations of these Catholic colleges were exceptionally well organized and militant, thirsting to reverse the verdict of the Dreyfus years.[20] The bifurcation in the French schools tended to produce two distinct races of Frenchmen, who had different historical heroes (and villains), different political vocabularies, different fundamental assumptions about politics and, not least, two completely different images of France.

In fact in France there were two rival types of nationalism. The secularists and republicans, who rejected the fatherhood of God and the king, had coined the term *la patrie* in the eighteenth century to denote their higher allegiance to their country. When Dr Johnson declared, at this time, that 'Patriotism is the last refuge of a scoundrel' he was denouncing a species of subversive demagoguery. French patriotism acquired a Jacobin flavour under the Revolution and this type of progressive nationalism was perpetuated by Gambetta and Clemenceau. It could be just as chauvinistic and ruthless as any other kind – more, perhaps, since it tended to admit no higher law than the interest of the Republic, thought to incarnate virtue – but it tended to evaporate into defeatism and pacifism the moment France was thought to be in the control of men who did not serve the aims of *la patrie*. In particular, it regarded the regular army, which was overwhelmingly Catholic and partly royalist, with suspicion, even hostility.

As opposed to 'patriotic France' there was 'nationalist France'. It was the Gallic equivalent of the division between Westerners and Easterners in Germany. It is a mistake to describe the inter-war French nationalists as fascists – though some of them became fascists of the most gruesome kind – because the tradition was much older. It went back to the émigrés of the Revolutionary epoch, the cultural reaction to the Enlightenment of Voltaire, Rousseau and Diderot, and it first acquired an intellectual content in the writings of Joseph de Maistre, whose masterpiece, *Les Soirées de Saint-Petersbourg*, was published in 1821. He offered a combination of irrationalism, romanticism and a Jansenist stress on original sin. Human reason is a 'trembling light', too weak to discipline a disorderly race: 'That which our miserable century calls superstition, fanaticism, intolerance etc. was a necessary ingredient of French greatness.' 'Man is too wicked to be free.' He is 'a monstrous centaur . . . the result of some unknown offence, some abominable miscegenation'.[21] To this de Maistre added the important notion of a vast conspiracy which, with the ostensible object of 'freeing' man, would in fact unleash the devil in him.

In the two decades leading up to the Dreyfus case in the 1890s, conspiracy theory became the stock-in-trade of French anti-Semites like Edouard Drumont, whose *La France juive* (1886) grossly exaggerated the power, influence and above all the numbers of Jews living in France. In fact when Drumont wrote there were only about 35,000 Jews in France. But their numbers were increasing: there were over 100,000 by 1920. Other 'aliens' poured in. France under the Third Republic, and especially between the wars, was the most agreeable country in the world in which to live, and in many ways the most tolerant of foreigners provided they did not cause trouble.[22] Between 1889 and 1940 nearly 2,300,000 foreigners received French citizenship and there were, in addition, a further 2,613,000 foreign residents in 1931, a figure which increased rapidly as refugees from Hitler, Stalin, Mussolini and the Spanish war arrived.[23] The French were not racist in the German sense, since a certain cosmopolitanism was a corollary of their proprietory rights over civilization. But they were extraordinarily susceptible to weird racial theories, which they produced in abundance. Thus in 1915 Dr Edgar Bérillon 'discovered' that Germans had intestines nine feet longer than other humans, which made them prone to 'polychesia' and bromidrosis (excessive defecation and body-smells).[24] If Paris was the world capital of Cartesian reason, it was also the capital of astrology, fringe-medicine and pseudo-scientific religiosity. There was (indeed still is) a strong anti-rationalist culture in France.

Hence the success of *Action Française*, the newspaper of the nationalist ultras. It began in 1899 among a small group of intellectuals who met on the Boulevard Saint-Germain at the Café Flore – which was, in 1944, to be 'liberated' by the Existentialists – and flourished on the talents of Charles Maurras. He publicized the idea of a multiple conspiracy: '*Quatres états confédérés: Juifs, Protestants, franc-masons, métêques*' (aliens). This was not very different from the official Vatican line during the Dreyfus case, though it substituted 'atheists' for 'aliens'. In fact though both Maurras and *Action Française* were themselves atheistic, many of their views were strongly approved of by the Catholic Church. Pius x, the last of the great reactionary popes, told Maurras' mother, 'I bless his work', and though he signed a Holy Office decree condemning his books he refused to allow it to be enforced – they were *Damnabiles, non damnandus*.[25] Vatican condemnation did come in the end, on 20 December 1926, because Pius xi had by then experience of fascism in power. But there were plenty of related groups to which faithful Catholics could belong and the nationalist movement never lost its respectability among the middle and upper classes. *Action Française*, edited by Léon Daudet, was brilliantly written and widely read: that was why Proust, though a Jew, took it, finding it 'a cure by elevation of the mind'.[26] Many leading writers were close to the movement. They included, for instance, France's leading popular historian, Jacques Bainville, whose *Histoire de France* (1924) sold over 300,000 copies, and whose *Napoléon* (1931) and *La Troisième République* were also best-sellers.

Indeed the weakness of French nationalism was that it was too intellectual. It lacked a leader with the will to power. At the end of 1933, with fascism triumphant in most of Europe, the Stavisky scandal in France gave the ultras precisely the revelation of republican corruption which they needed to justify a *coup*. Some kind of proto-fascist state would almost certainly have come into existence on 6 February 1934 had Maurras given the signal for action. But he was then sixty-six, very deaf and by temperament a sedentary word-spinner: he spent the critical day writing an editorial instead. Precisely the gifts which made him so dangerous in stirring the passions of educated Frenchmen incapacitated him from leading them into battle. There was thus no focus around which a united fascist movement could gather. Instead there was a proliferation of groups, each with a slightly different ideology and a varying degree of tolerance towards violence. They presented the mirror-image of the despised *régime des partis* in the Chambre des Deputés. Bourbon factions like *Les Camelots du Roi* jostled the Bonapartist *Jeunesses Patriotes*, the atheist *Etudiants d'Action Française* and 'pure' fascist groups such as the *Parti Populaire Français, Le Faisceau* and the *Phalanges Universitaires*, and more traditional movements like the *Croix de Feu*. Nazi-type adventurers, many of whom were later to flourish under Vichy, shopped around these mushroom growths, looking for the best bargain. It took an external catastrophe to bring them to power.

Yet Maurras and his supporters undoubtedly made this catastrophe more likely. The Third Republic had more friends in France than Weimar had in Germany. Maurras revealed that it had a host of enemies too. His favourite quotation was from the stuffy Academician and Nobel Prizewinner Anatole France: '*La République n'est pas destructible, elle est la destruction. Elle est la dispersion, elle est la discontinuité, elle est la diversité, elle est le mal.*'[27] The Republic, he wrote, was a woman, lacking 'the male principle of initiative and action'. 'There is only one way to improve democracy: destroy it.' 'Democracy is evil, democracy is death.' 'Democracy is forgetting.' His fundamental law was 'Those people who are governed by their men of action and their military leaders defeat those peoples who are governed by their lawyers and professors.' If republicanism was death, how could it be worth dying for? The Versailles Treaty was the creation of 'a combination of Anglo-Saxon finance and Judeo-German finance'. The conspiracy theory could be reformulated – anarchism, Germans, Jews: 'The barbarians from the depths, the barbarians from the East, our *Demos* flanked by its two friends, the German and the Jew.'[28] The ultra-nationalists, though jealous of French interests as they conceived them, were thus unwilling either to preserve the Europe of Versailles or to curb fascist aggression. Bainville's diaries show that he welcomed the fascist successes in Italy and Germany.[29] Maurras applauded the invasion of Ethiopia by Mussolini as the struggle of civilization against barbarism.[30] 'What can you do for Poland?' he asked his readers, a cry echoed by Marcel Déat's devastating *'Mourir pour Dantzig?'*

In effect, then, both the strains of nationalism in France, the Jacobin and the anti-republican, had reservations about the sacrifices they would be prepared to make. It was not a case of my country right or wrong, or my country Left or Right, but a case of whose country – mine or theirs? The division within France was already apparent by the early 1920s and the infirmity of will it produced soon affected actual policy. France's post-war defence posture was based on absolute military supremacy west of the Rhine, containing Germany on one side, and a military alliance of new states, to contain her on the other. Poland, Czechoslovakia, Romania, Yugoslavia all had complicated military arrangements with France down to the supply of weapons and the training of technicians. Poincaré's occupation of the Ruhr in 1923 saw the western arm of the policy in action. But it did such damage to French interests in Britain and America that it appeared to many French politicians to be unrepeatable; and the 1924 American solution to the reparations mess, the Dawes Plan, removed much of the excuse for a further resort to force. The Germans now proposed that the Franco–German frontier should be guaranteed, and Britain backed their request. The French replied that, in that case, Britain must also agree to guarantee the frontiers of Germany in the east with France's allies, Poland and Czechoslovakia. But the British Foreign Secretary, Sir Austen Chamberlain, refused, writing to the head of the Foreign Office, Sir Eyre Crowe, (16 February 1925) that Britain could not possibly guarantee the Polish Corridor 'for which no British government ever will or ever can risk the bones of a British grenadier'.[31] No *mourir pour Dantzig* there, either!

Hence the Treaty of Locarno (1925), while effectively denying France the right to contain Germany by force, failed to underwrite her system of defensive alliances either. All it did was to demilitarize the Rhineland and give Britain and France the right to intervene by force if Germany sought to restore her full sovereignty there. This, however, was bluff. Though Chamberlain boasted to the 1926 Imperial Conference that 'the true defence of our country . . . is now no longer the Channel . . . but upon the Rhine', the British Chiefs of Staff privately pointed out that they did not possess the military means to back up the guarantee.[32] Two years later the Chief of the Imperial General Staff produced a cabinet memorandum pointing out that Germany's total strength, including reserves, was not the 100,000 army allowed by Versailles but a force of 2 million.[33] The French War Office made the same kind of estimate. By 1928 Poincaré had dropped the 'forward' notion of a strategic frontier on the Rhine and had reverted to a purely defensive policy: experts were already working on the project to be known as the Maginot Line.

What, then, of Poincaré's 'country of 100 million', the imperial vision which H.G.Wells termed 'the development of "Black France"'?[34] Could the empire be invoked to redress the balance of France's weakness in Europe? Maurice Barrès, the intellectual who helped to put together the right-wing coalition which swept to victory in the 1919 elections, wrote: 'One is almost tempted to thank the Germans for opening the eyes of the world to colonial questions.' The 1919 parliament was known as the 'Chambre bleu horizon', after the colour of the army uniforms and its imperialist aspirations. Albert Sarraut, the Minister for the Colonies, produced a grandiose plan in April 1921 to turn France d'Outre-mer into the economic underpinning of la Mère-patrie.[35] But to realize this vision there were one, or possibly two, prerequisites. The first and most important was money for investment. The French had hoped to get it, under the Sykes–Picot secret agreement, from the spoils of war: a 'Greater Syria' including the Mosul oilfields. But in the scramble after the end of the war she was denied this by Britain and her Hashemite Arab protégés. All France got was the Lebanon, where she was the traditional protector of the Christian Maronite community, and western Syria, where there was no oil and a lot of ferocious Arab nationalists. She would have been better off with just the Lebanon. In Syria the mandate was a total failure, provoking full-scale rebellion, put down at enormous military expense, and culminating in 1925 with the French High Commissioner shelling Damascus with heavy artillery.[36] The Middle East carve-up remained a festering source of discord between France and her chief ally, Britain, leading to actual fighting between them in 1940–1. France never made a franc profit out of the area.

As a result, there was no money for Sarraut's plan. France's black African colonies had been acquired after 1870 for prestige not economic reasons, to keep the army employed and to paint the map blue. A law of 1900 said that each colony must pay for its own upkeep. Federations were organized in West (1904) and Equatorial (1910) Africa, but the combined population of both these vast areas was less than that of Britain's Nigeria. To make economic sense, everyone agreed, they had to be linked to France's North African territories. In 1923 the Quai d'Orsay and the Ministries of War and Colonies agreed that the building of a Trans-Sahara railway was

absolutely 'indispensable'. But there was no money. Even a technical
survey was not made until 1928. The railway was never built. More
money in fact did go into France's overseas territories; investments
increased fourfold between 1914–40, the empire's share of total
French investment rising from 9 to 45 per cent. But nearly all of this
went to France's Arab territories, Algeria getting the lion's share. In
1937 foreign trade of the Franco–Arab lands was over 15 milliard
francs, four times that of West and Equatorial Africa.[37]

The second prerequisite was some kind of devolution of power, so
that the inhabitants of the 'country of 100 million' enjoyed equal
rights. But there was no chance of this. In 1919 at the Paris Treaty
talks, Ho Chi Minh presented, on behalf of the Annamites of
Indo-China, an eight-point programme; not, indeed, of self-
determination but of civil rights, as enjoyed by metropolitan France
and expatriates. He got nowhere. Indo-China had one of the worst
forced-labour systems in the world and its oppressive system of
native taxation included the old *gabelle* or salt-tax. As Ho Chi Minh
put it, France had brought to Indo-China not progress but medieval-
ism, which the *gabelle* symbolized: 'Taxes, forced labour, exploitation,' he said in 1924, 'that is the summing up of your civilization.'[38]
There were as many (5,000) French officials in Indo-China as in the
whole of British India, with fifteen times the population, and they
worked closely with the French *colon* planters. Neither would
tolerate devolution or reforms. When in 1927 a progressive French
governor-general, Alexandre Varenne, tried to end the *corvée*, they
ganged up to get him recalled. In 1930, in Indo-China alone, there
were nearly 700 summary executions. If Gandhi had tried his passive
resistance there, Ho Chi Minh wrote, 'he would long since have
ascended into heaven'.[39]

In North Africa it was no better, in some ways worse. Algeria was
in theory run like metropolitan France but in fact it had separate
electoral colleges for French and Arabs. This wrecked Clemenceau's
post-war reforms in 1919 and indeed all subsequent ones. The
French settlers sent deputies to the parliament in Paris and this gave
them a leverage unknown in the British Empire. In 1936 the *colon*
deputies killed a Popular Front bill which would have given full
citizenship to 20,000 Muslims. Marshal Lyautey, the great French
Governor-General of Morocco, described the *colons* as 'every bit as
bad as the *Boches*, imbued with the same belief in inferior races
whose destiny is to be exploited'.[40] In Morocco he did his best to
keep them out. But this was difficult. In Morocco a French farmer
could enjoy the same living standards as one in the American
Mid-West. All Europeans there had real incomes a third above that
of France, and eight times higher than the Muslims. Moreover,

Lyautey's benevolent despotism, which was designed to protect the Muslims from French corruption, in fact exposed them to native corruption at its worst. He ruled through caids who bought their tax-inspectorates and judgeships, getting into debt thereby and being obliged to squeeze their subjects to pay the interest. The system degenerated swiftly after Lyautey's death in 1934. The greatest of the caids, the notorious El Glawi, Pasha of Marrakesh, ran a mountain-and-desert empire of rackets and monopolies, including control of Marrakesh's 27,000 prostitutes who catered for the needs of the entire Western Sahara.[41] On the front that mattered most, education, little progress was made. There were far too many French officials: 15,000 of them, three times as many as the Indian administration, all anxious to perpetuate and if possible hereditarize their jobs. In 1940, accordingly, there were still only 3 per cent of Moroccans who went to school, and even in 1958 only 1,500 received a secondary education. In 1952 there were only twenty-five Moroccan doctors, fourteen of them from the Jewish community.

It was not that the French had colour prejudice. Paris always welcomed évolués. In 1919 the old-established 'Four Communes' of West Africa sent to the Chambre a black deputy, Blaise Diagne. Two years later René Maran's Batouala, giving the black man's view of colonialism, won the Prix Goncourt. But the book was banned in all France's African territories. Clever blacks learned to write superb French; but once they got to Paris they tended to stay there. In the 1930s, Léopold Senghor, later President of Senegal, felt so at home in right-wing Catholic circles he became a monarchist.[42] There seemed no future for him in Africa. By 1936 only 2,000 blacks had French citizenship. Apart from war veterans and government clerks, the great majority of black Africans were under the indigénat – summary justice, collective fines, above all forced labour. Houphouët-Boigny, later President of the Ivory Coast, described the work-gangs as 'skeletons covered with sores'. The Governor of French Equatorial Africa, Antonelli, admitted that the building of the Congo–Ocean railway in 1926 would 'require 10,000 deaths'; in fact more died during its construction.[43] Black Africans voted with their feet, running into nearby British colonies to escape the round-ups.

Some Frenchmen with long experience of colonial affairs saw portents. Lyautey warned in 1920: 'The time has come to make a radical change of course in native policy and Muslim participation in public affairs.'[44] Sarraut himself argued that the European 'civil war' of 1914–18 had weakened the position of the whites. 'In the minds of other races,' he wrote in 1931, 'the war has dealt a terrible blow to the standing of a civilization which Europeans claimed with pride to be superior, yet in whose name Europeans spent more than four years savagely killing each other.' With Japan in mind he added: 'It has long been a commonplace to contrast European greatness with Asian decadence. The contrast now seems to be reversed.'[45] Yet nothing effective was done to broaden the base of French rule. When Léon Blum's Popular Front government introduced its reform plan to give 25,000 Algerians citizenship, the leader of the Algerian moderates, Ferhat Abbas, exulted '*La France, c'est moi!*' Maurice Viollette, a liberal Governor-General of Algeria and later, as a Deputy, one of the sponsors of the reform, warned the Chambre: 'When the Muslims protest, you are indignant. When they approve, you are suspicious. When they keep quiet, you are fearful. Messieurs, these men have no political nation. They do not even demand their religious nation. All they ask is to be admitted into yours. If. you refuse this, beware lest they do not soon create one for themselves.'[46] But the reform was killed.

The truth is colonialism contained far too many unresolved contradictions to be a source of strength. Sometimes it was seen, as indeed it partly was, as the expression of European rule. Thus in the Thirties, Sarraut, who was terrified of increasing Communist subversion in Africa, proposed a united European front, to include the Italians and even the Germans, who would get their colonies back. But as war approached the French again saw their empire as a means to fight their European enemies, resurrecting the slogan '110 million strong, France can stand up to Germany!' In September 1939, Clemenceau's former secretary, Georges Mandel, once an anti-colonialist but now Minister for the Colonies, boasted he would raise 2 million black and Arab troops. The two lines of thought were in the long run mutually exclusive. If Europe used non-whites to fight its civil wars, it could not combine to uphold continental race-superiority.

But this was only one example of the confusions which, from first to last – and persisting to this day – surrounded the whole subject of imperialism and the colonial empires. What purpose did they serve? *Cui bono?* Who benefited, who suffered? To use Lenin's phrase, who was doing what to whom? There was never any agreement. Lord Shelburne, the eighteenth-century statesman who deliberated most deeply on the question, laid down the policy that 'England prefers trade without domination where possible, but accepts trade with domination when necessary.'[47] Classical economists like Adam Smith, Bentham and Ricardo saw colonies as a vicious excuse to exercise monopoly, and therefore as contrary to the general economic interest.[48] Edward Gibbon Wakefield, in his *View of the Art of Colonization* (1849), thought the object was to provide living-space for overcrowded European populations. This was likewise the view of the greatest colonizer of all, Cecil Rhodes – without it, the unemployed would destroy social order: 'The Empire . . . is a bread and butter question: if you want to avoid civil war, you must become imperialists.'[49] On the other hand, protectionists like Joe Chamberlain argued that colonies existed to provide safe markets for exports, a return to pre-industrialist mercantilism.

It was Robert Torrens in *The Colonization of South Australia* (1835), who first put forward the view that colonies should be seen primarily as a place to invest capital. The notion of surplus capital was taken up by John Stuart Mill: 'Colonization in the present state of the world is the best affair of business in which the capital of an old and wealthy country can engage.'[50] This was also the view of practical French colonizers, like Jules Ferry, and their theorists, like Paul Leroy-Beaulieu; though the latter's book, *De la Colonization* (1874), provided categories: *colonie de peuplement* (emigration and capital combined), *colonie d'exploitation* (capital export only) and *colonies mixtes*. The German theorist, Gustav Schmoller, argued that large-scale emigration from Europe was inevitable and that colonization, as opposed to transatlantic settlement, was far preferable as it did not involve capital flying from outside the control of the mother-country. All these writers and practitioners saw the process as deliberate and systematic, and above all rational. Most of them saw it as benevolent and benefiting all concerned, including the native peoples. Indeed Lord Lugard, the creator of British West Africa, felt Europe had not merely an interest but a moral mandate to make its financial resources available to the whole world.

In 1902 however the capital-export argument was turned into a conspiracy theory by J. A. Hobson, a Hampstead intellectual, classical schoolmaster and *Manchester Guardian* journalist. Hobson's ideas were to have an important twentieth-century reverberance. In 1889 he had developed a theory of under-consumption: industry produced too much, the rich could not consume it all, the poor could not afford it, and therefore capital had to be exported. Keynes later acknowledged that Hobson's theory had a decisive influence on his *General Theory of Employment, Interest and Money* (1936), and Hobson's solutions – steeply progressive taxation, vast welfare services and nationalization – became the conventional wisdom of West European social democrats. But Hobson was also an anti-Semite, and in the 1890s he was so angered by the 'scramble' for Africa, the forcible extraction of concessions from China and, above all, by the events leading up to the Boer War, that he produced a wild book, *Imperialism* (1902), in which the process was presented as a concerted and deliberate act of wickedness by 'finance-capital', often Jewish. Imperialism was the direct consequence of under-consumption and the need to export capital to secure higher returns. In two crucial chapters, 'The Parasites' and 'The Economic Taproot of Imperialism', he presented this conspiracy theory in highly moralistic and emotional terms, arguing that the only people to gain anything from empires were the 'finance-capitalists': the natives suffered, the colonizing nations as a whole suffered and, just as the Boer War was a plot to seize control of the Rand gold mines, so the practice of imperialism and particularly competitive imperialism would tend to produce war.[51]

The actual idea of imperialism had only entered the socio-economic vocabulary about 1900. Hobson's book, which defined it as 'the use of the machinery of government by private interests, mainly capitalists, to secure for them economic gains outside the country',[52] instantly made the evil conspiracy aspect immensely attractive to Marxists and other determinists.[53] The Austrian economists, Otto Bauer and Rudolf Hilferding, argued in 1910 that imperialism made war absolutely inevitable. In 1916 Lenin put the capstone on this shaky edifice by producing his *Imperialism: the Highest Stage of Capitalism*, which fitted the concept neatly into the basic structure of Marxist theory. Hitherto, colonial empires had been approached in an empirical spirit. Colonies were judged on their merits. Colonial powers were benevolent or exploitative or a mixture of both. The process was seen as having advantages and drawbacks for all the parties concerned and, above all, as complicated and changing. Now it was all reduced to slogans, made simple, in both economic and moral terms, and certified, everywhere and always, as intrinsically evil. The process whereby this crude and implausible theory became the conventional wisdom of most of the world, over the half-century which followed the Versailles Treaty, is one of the central developments of modern times, second only in importance to the spread of political violence.

The actual historical and economic reality did not fit any of the theories, the Hobson–Lenin one perhaps least of all. If empires were created because of over-saving and under-consumption, if they represented the final stage of capitalism, how did one explain the empires of antiquity? Joseph Schumpeter, whose *Zur Soziologie des Imperialismus (On the Sociology of Imperialism)* appeared in Germany in 1919, was closer to the truth when he argued that modern imperialism was 'atavistic'. Capitalism, he pointed out, usually flourished on peace and free-trade, rather than war and protectionism. Colonies often represented 'an objectless disposition . . . to unlimited frontier expansion'. They seemed to be acquired at a certain critical stage of national and social development, reflecting the real or imagined interests of the ruling class.[54] But that was too glib also. As a matter of fact, the rise of the Japanese Empire (as we shall see) came closest to the model of a deliberately willed development by an all-powerful ruling establishment. But the Japanese model was scarcely ever considered by the European theorists. And in any case Japanese expansion was often dictated by assertive military commanders on the spot, who exceeded or even disobeyed the orders of the ruling group. That was the French pattern too. Algeria was acquired as a result of army insubordination; Indo-China had been entered by overweening naval commanders; it was the marines who got France involved in West Africa.[55] In one sense the French Empire could be looked upon as a gigantic system of outdoor relief for army officers. It was designed to give them something to do. What they actually did bore little relation to what most of the ruling establishment wanted or decided. The French cabinet was never consulted about Fashoda, the protectorate over Morocco, or the 1911 crisis. Parliament never really controlled the empire at any stage of its existence. Jules Ferry probably came close to the real truth when he described the imperial scramble as 'an immense steeplechase towards the unknown'.[56] It was said that Bismarck encouraged France to lead the steeplechase in order to forget his annexation of Alsace and Lorraine. If so, he was much mistaken. Outside the army, few Frenchmen cared about black Africa. As Déroulede put it: 'I have lost two sisters – you offer me twenty chambermaids.'[57]

There were a great many other anomalies which did not fit into Hobson–Lenin. Why, in Latin America, did the phase of capitalist investment follow, rather than precede or accompany, Spanish colonialism? Why, in this vast area, were the capitalists in league with the political liberators? Then again, some of the 'exploited' or colonized countries were themselves residual empires. China was the creation of a whole series of imperial dynasties, without benefit of 'finance-capital'. India was a product of Mughal imperialism. Turkey had been expanded from Ottoman Anatolia. Egypt was an old imperial power which, after its breakaway from Turkey, sought to be one again in the Sudan. There were half a dozen native empires south of the Sahara run by groups and movements such as the Ashanti, Fulani, Bornu, Al-Haji Umar, Futa Toro. Ethiopia was an empire competing with the European empires in the Horn of Africa, before succumbing to one of them in 1935. Burma was a kind of empire. Persia, like China, was an imperial survivor from antiquity. Colonialism itself created empires of this anomalous type. The Congo (later Zaïre) was put together by the Berlin Conference of 1884–5, and survived decolonization without benefit of any of the factors which theory said created empires. So did Indonesia, a product of Dutch tidy-mindedness, assembled from scores of quite different territories. Conspiracy theory shed no light on any of these cases.[58]

What is decisive, however, is that the theory broke down at its very core – the need for colonies to provide high-return settlement areas for capital. Indeed, the closer the actual facts are studied, the clearer it becomes that any notion of 'finance-capital' desperately looking for colonies as places to invest its huge surpluses of capital is preposterous. There was never any such thing as 'surplus' capital. Investment capital was always hard to come by, but especially in the colonies. The tropics did not yield big returns until the very end of the colonial era. There were a few big success stories. In West Africa, Lever Brothers made huge investments in communications, social services and plantations which by the 1950s employed 40,000 Africans: the company owned 350,000 hectares and actively worked 60,000.[59] There was also heavy investment and occasional high profits (but also some large-scale failures) in Malaya, whose rubber and tin made it probably the richest colony between the wars. Capital did not follow the flag. The British were at least as likely to put their money in independent Latin-American states as in crown colonies. They often lost it too. Argentina, which attracted more British money than any other 'developing' territory, taught all investors a fearful lesson during its 1890–1 financial crisis. Taking the nineteenth century as a whole, British investors in Argentina showed a net loss.[60] The Germans and Italians were keener than anyone to possess colonies but were most reluctant to sink any money in them. The French preferred Russia – or the Dutch East Indies – to their 'twenty chambermaids'. The British, too, favoured Java and Sumatra over their innumerable African territories.[61] Conspiracy theory demands the existence of a small number of very clever people making a highly rational appreciation and co-ordinating their efforts. In fact the number of investors, in France and Britain alone, was very large and their behaviour emotional, inconsistent, ill-informed and prejudiced. The City of London was incapable of planning anything, let alone a world-wide conspiracy; it simply followed what it imagined (often wrongly) to be its short-term interests, on a day-to-day basis.[62] The most consistent single characteristic of European investors throughout the colonial period was ignorance, based on laziness.

If investors had no agreed and concerted, let alone conspiratorial aim, the colonial administrators were not much clearer. In the nineteenth century, in the spirit of Macaulay's educational reforms in India, the object of colonial rule was commonly thought to be to produce imitation Europeans. Between the wars this vision faded rapidly, leaving only confusion. The so-called 'Dual Mandate' policy put forward by Lord Lugard in the 1920s, not so different to Lyautey's aims in Morocco, sought to preserve native patterns of administration, and to give paramountcy to their interests. The British task, Lugard wrote, was 'to promote the commercial and industrial progress of Africa without too careful a scrutiny of the material gains to ourselves'.[63] This element of altruism gradually became stronger but it coexisted with other aims: military strategy, emigration, defending settler interests, national prestige, national economic policy (including tariffs), which varied according to the nature of the colony, and the colonial system, and were often inconsistent with native interests and indeed with each other. There was no typical colony. Many colonial territories were not, in legal terms, colonies at all, but protectorates, mandates, Trust territories, federations of kingdoms and principalities, or quasi-sovereignties like Egypt and the states of the Persian Gulf (including Persia itself). There were about a score of different prototypes. Some colonies, especially in West Africa, contained two or more quite different legal entities, representing successive archaeological layers of Western penetration. In these circumstances pursuing a consistent colonial policy, with clear long-term aims, was impossible. No empire did so.

Hence there can be no such thing as a balance-sheet of colonialism between the wars, or at any other stage. Broadly speaking, the policy was to provide the basic infrastructure of external defence, internal security, basic roads and public health, and leave the rest to private initiative. Government's aim was to be efficient, impartial, uncorrupt and non-interventionist. Sometimes the government found itself obliged to run the economy, as Italy did in Somalia and Libya, with conspicuous lack of success.[64] It usually had to maintain a broader public sector than at home. Thus Britain, for instance, promoted the modernization and expansion of agriculture and ran public health services in all her crown colonies, and operated state railways in every African territory south of the Sahara (except Rhodesia and Nyasaland). But all this points to a scarcity, not a surplus, of capital. Government did these things from a sense of duty, not desire; they added to the debit side of the ledger.

Colonial governments did little to promote industry but they did not deliberately restrict it either. Usually there was little incentive to invest, shortage of skilled labour and lack of good local markets being the main obstacles. Where conditions were suitable, as in the Belgian Congo, industry appeared between the wars, though the money came chiefly not from Belgium but from foreign sources and foreign-owned subsidiaries – another blow to the conspiracy theory. Dakar in French West Africa was a growth point for exactly the same reason. The notion that colonialism, as such, prevented local industry from developing, breaks down on the simple fact that the free-trading British, Belgians and Dutch, on the one hand, pursued diametrically opposed policies to the protectionist French, Spanish, Italian, Portuguese and Americans on the other.

From 1923 onwards, and especially after 1932, the British broke their own rules about free trade in order to promote Indian industry. It was the Viceroy, Lord Curzon, who persuaded J.N.Tata, the Parsee cotton magnate, to set up an Indian iron and steel industry, for which Britain provided protective tariffs. By 1945 India produced 1.15 million tons annually and Indian producers virtually monopolized the market. Again, in cotton and jute, where conditions for the industry were attractive, the Indians could and did produce the capital themselves, and Britain provided protection. By the time of independence, India had a large industrial sector, with Indian firms handling 83 per cent of banking, 60 per cent of exports-imports and supplying 60 per cent of consumer goods.[65] But it is very doubtful that creating local industries behind a tariff barrier worked to the advantage of the general population of a colony. By and large, the inhabitants of the free-trading empires enjoyed higher living standards than the others, as one would expect. India and Pakistan maintained ultra-protectionist policies after independence, with protection levels of 313 and 271 per cent respectively, and that is one reason why their living standards have risen so much more slowly than in the market economies of Eastern Asia.[66]

On the whole, colonial powers served the interests of local inhabitants best when they allowed market forces to prevail over restrictive policies, however well intentioned. It usually meant moving from subsistence agriculture to large-scale production of cash-crops for export. This so-called 'distortion' of colonial economies to serve the purposes of the mother country or world markets is the basis of the charge that these territories were simply 'exploited'. It is argued that colonies became poorer than before, that their 'natural' economies were destroyed, and that they entered into a diseased phase termed 'underdevelopment'.[67] Unfortunately the statistical evidence to prove or refute this theory simply does not exist. Mungo Park's *Travels in the Interior Districts of Africa* (1799) does not give the impression of a rural Arcadia where the pursuit of wealth was eschewed: quite the contrary. The independent chiefs were not only imperialists, in their own small way, but exceptionally acquisitive. They moved into cash-crop agriculture wherever they could contrive to find a market. Indeed there was no alternative, once population increases made subsistence farming a dead-end.

The notion that industrialization, as opposed to primary production, is the sole road to high living standards is belied by the experience of former colonies like Australia, New Zealand, much of Canada and the US Midwest, where exports of meat, wool, wheat, dairy products and minerals have produced the most prosperous countries in the world. It is significant, perhaps, that during the post-colonial period none of the newly independent states with well-established plantation economies has attempted to replace them by other forms of farming. Quite the reverse in fact: all have sought to improve their export-earning potential, usually in order to finance industrial development – which was exactly what most colonial governments were seeking to do in the later phases of the era. There were rarely big and never easy profits to be made out of large-scale tropical agriculture. An analysis of export prices of coffee, cocoa, ground-nuts, cotton, palm oil, rice, gum arabic, kernels and kapok in the French West African territories during the last phase of colonial rule (1953) shows that profits were small and determined largely by the transport system.[68] The argument that the advanced economies organized a progressive deterioration in the terms of trade to depress primary prices does not square with the statistical evidence and is simply another aspect of conspiracy theory.

The worst aspects of inter-war colonialism were forced labour and land apportionment on a racial basis. Their origin was as follows. African land could be made productive, and a take-off from sub-sistence agriculture achieved, only if adequate labour, working European-style regular hours, was made available. In pre-colonial Africa the answer had been slavery. The more progressive colonial powers, Britain and to a lesser extent France, were determined to abolish it. The British preferred to push Africans into the labour market by taxation. Or they imported labour under contract. This was the easy way out. Running a world-wide empire where labour as well as goods could travel freely, they induced Indians to work in Burma, Malaya, the Pacific, Ceylon and in South, Central and East Africa, even in Central and South America; and Chinese to work in South-East Asia, the Pacific, South Africa and Australia. They also brought about big internal movements in Africa, just as the Dutch, in Indonesia, induced Javanese to work in the other islands.[69] The effect was to create a large number of intractable race and communal problems (or, in the case of Indonesia, Javanese imperialism) which are still with us. The Dutch also adopted the so-called 'culture system' which forced the inhabitants to produce by demanding payment in kind, the state being the chief plantation owner and agent.[70] The culture system was adopted by Leopold II, the creator of the Belgian Congo, and became the basis of the economy there, and the Belgians also put pressure on the chiefs to provide 'volun-teers' who signed long indentures. The French and Portuguese went the whole hog with unpaid *corvées* (forced labour) as a substitute for taxation. The worst cases of oppression occurred in Portuguese

Africa and the Congo. They had largely been ended by 1914, following exposure by British journalists and consular officials. But forced labour in some forms continued right up to the late 1940s.[71] Its scale was small, however. Indeed, until comparatively recently the vast majority of Africans remained quite outside the wage economy. As late as the 1950s, out of 170 million Africans south of the Sahara, only 8 million worked for wages at any one time in the year.[72] Where wages were high the Africans worked willingly: the Rand goldfield never had any trouble getting labour, from its origin up to this day. Elsewhere it was mostly the same old story: low returns, low investments, low productivity, low wages. No one who actually worked in Africa, white or black, ever subscribed to fantasies about surplus capital. That existed only in Hampstead and Left Bank cafés.

The biggest mistake made by the colonial powers – and it had political and moral as well as economic consequences – was to refuse to allow the market system to operate in land. Here they followed the procedures first worked out in the British colonies in America in the seventeenth century, elaborated to develop the American Midwest and West (to the destruction of the indigenous Indians) and refined, on a purely racial basis, in South Africa. It involved human engineering, and was therefore destructive of the individualistic principle which lies at the heart of the Judaeo–Christian ethic. In South Africa, by 1931, some 1.8 million Europeans had 'reserves' of 440,000 square miles, while 6 million Africans were allotted only 34,000 square miles. In Southern Rhodesia, the Land Apportionment Act of 1930 gave Europeans, already in possession of 30 million acres, the right to buy a further 34 million acres of crown lands, while Africans, with reserves of 21 million acres, had access only to 7 million more. In Northern Rhodesia the whites already had exclusive possession of 9 million acres. In Kenya this deliberate distortion of the free land market was particularly disgraceful since in 1923 the Duke of Devonshire, as Colonial Secretary, had laid down the 'Devonshire Declaration': 'Primarily Kenya is an African territory ... the interests of the African natives must be paramount.' Despite this, in a deliberate exercise in social engineering, the White Highlands was cleared of its Kikuyu inhabitants to make way for white farmers. In the 1930s, there were in Kenya 53,000 square miles of African reserves, 16,700 reserved for Europeans and 99,000 of crown lands, which the government could apportion according to arbitrary political criteria. The system was indefensible. Indeed it was only defended on the grounds that drawing racial lines was essential to good farming. The argument was false in itself (as subsequent events in

Kenya have demonstrated) and it contradicted the general free-market principles on which the British Empire had been created.

Of course in pressing for the social engineering inherent in the race-determined apportionment of land, the settlers were making a crude response to what to them was an overwhelming fact: the unequal development of human societies. It is a problem fundamental to the species, which already existed in marked form at the time of the Iron Age. The archetype European capitalist empires, which were effectively confined to the years 1870–1945, constituted an uncoordinated and spasmodic, often contradictory, series of attempts to solve the problem presented by the existence of advanced and backward societies in a shrinking world, where contacts between them were inevitable, not least because populations were rising almost everywhere – and expectations too.

The system, if it can be called that, was slow to get itself organized: even the French did not have a Colonial Ministry until 1894, Germany till 1906, Italy 1907, Belgium 1910, Portugal 1911.[73] Its 'classical age' between the wars was already a kind of twilight. Its existence was too brief to achieve results on its own terms. Developing human and natural resources is a slow, laborious and often bloody business, as the whole of history teaches. Men like Rhodes, Ferry, Lugard, Lyautey and Sarraut shared an unjustified optimism that the process could be speeded up and made relatively painless. Exactly the same illusions were shared by their successors as independent rulers: Sukarno, Nasser, Nkrumah, Nehru and scores of others, as we shall see. But most of the poor countries remained in the same position relative to the rich in the 1980s as they were in the 1870s, when the great age of colonialism started.

This leads us to a very important point. Colonialism was a highly visual phenomenon. It abounded in flags, exotic uniforms, splendid ceremonies, Durbars, sunset-guns, trade exhibitions at Olympia and the Grand Palais, postage stamps and, above all, coloured maps. It was, in essence, a cartographic entity, to be perceived most clearly and powerfully from the pages of an atlas. Seen from maps, colonialism appeared to have changed the world. Seen on the ground, it appeared a more meretricious phenomenon, which could and did change little. It came easily; it went easily. Few died either to make it or break it. It both accelerated and retarded, though marginally in both cases, the emergence of a world economic system, which would have come into existence at approximately the same speed if the Europeans had never annexed a single hectare of Asia or Africa. 'Colonialism' covered such a varied multiplicity of human arrangements that it is doubtful whether it describes anything specific at all.

Colonialism was important not for what it was but for what it was not. It bred grandiose illusions and unjustified grievances. The first had a major impact on events up to 1945; the second thereafter. If the French Empire seemed to transform a declining and exhausted France into a vigorous Samson of a hundred million, Britain's Commonwealth appeared to make her a superpower – a notion that Hitler, for instance, carried with him to his bunker. Again, it was the visual aspect which determined such perceptions. In the 1920s, the great military roads, public buildings and European quarters which Lyautey had commanded for Morocco were taking shape: formidable, durable, austerely magnificent, as indeed they still are. Simultaneously, Sir Edwin Lutyens's government quarters in Delhi, the finest of all the twentieth century's large-scale conceptions, was being completed. Significantly, both had been conceived in Edwardian times; both were made flesh only after the first of Europe's civil wars had already undermined the empires they adorned. Architecture is both the most concrete and the most emblematic of the arts. Public buildings speak: sometimes in false tones. Lutyens's splendid domes and cupolas used two voices. To most of the British, to most foreigners, to most Indians above all, they announced durability; but to the military and economic experts they increasingly whispered doubt.

A case in point was the imperial currency system. From 1912 Britain divided her empire into regional currency areas, regulated by a British Currency Board according to the Colonial Sterling Exchange Standard; from 1920 colonies had to hold 100 per cent cover (in bullion or gilt-edge bonds) in Britain for their fiduciary issue. It produced a great many complaints among the nationalists, especially in India. In fact it was a sensible system which gave most of the Commonwealth the very real blessing of monetary stability. It also worked very fairly until after 1939, when the exigencies of British wartime finance and her rapid decline into total insolvency rendered the whole system oppressive.[74] There is a vital moral here. Britain could be just to her colonial subjects so long as she was a comparatively wealthy nation. A rich power could run a prosperous and well-conducted empire. Poor nations, like Spain and Portugal, could not afford justice or forgo exploitation. But it follows from this, as many British statesmen had insisted throughout the nineteenth century, that colonies were not a source of strength but of weakness. They were a luxury, maintained for prestige and paid for by diverting real resources. The concept of a colonial superpower was largely fraudulent. As a military and economic colossus, the British Empire was made of lath and plaster, paint and gilding.

Hence the curious sense, both of heartlessness and of extravagance, but also of fragility and impermanence, which the between-the-wars empire evoked in the beholder. Malcolm Muggeridge, at Simla in the early 1920s, noted that only the Viceroy and two other officials were allowed cars, and that the roads were so steep that all the rickshaw coolies died young of heart-failure. Watching a fat man being pulled along he heard someone say, 'Look, there's one man pulling another along. And they say there's a God!'[75] In 1930 in Kenya, Evelyn Waugh came across 'a lovely American called Kiki', whom a rich British settler at Lake Navaisha in the White Highlands had given 'two or three miles of lake-front as a Christmas present'.[76] Yet Leo Amery, the most ambitious of the inter-war Colonial Secretaries, found his plan to have a separate Dominions section thwarted because the Treasury would not spend an extra £800 a year in salaries.[77] When Lord Reading was made Viceroy in 1921, the political manoeuvrings which surrounded the appointment made it clear that, in the eyes of the British government, the need to keep Sir Gordon Hewart, a good debater, on the Front Bench as Attorney-General, was much more important than who ruled India.[78] Three years later, the great imperialist editor of the *Observer*, J.L.Garvin, 'thought it quite possible that within five years we might lose India and with it – Goodbye to the British Empire'.[79] The same elegiac thought occurred to a young British police officer in Burma who was called upon, at exactly that time, to shoot an elephant to impress 'the natives': 'It was at that moment', George Orwell wrote, 'that I first grasped the hollowness, the futility of the white man's dominion in the East. Here was I, the white man with his gun, standing in front of the unarmed native crowd – seemingly the leading actor in the piece. But in reality I was only an absurd puppet pushed to and fro by the will of those yellow faces behind.'[80]

Running an empire was in great part a simple matter of determination. Years later, in 1962, Sir Roy Welensky, premier of the Rhodesian Federation, was to say 'Britain has lost the will to government in Africa'. It was not yet lost in the 1920s and 1930s, or not wholly lost. But it was being eroded. The Great War had shaken the self-confidence of the British ruling class. Losses from the United Kingdom were not so enormous: 702,410 dead. They were comparable with Italy's, which bounded with vitality in the 1920s. But of course Italy's population was still rising fast. Moreover it was widely believed that the products of Oxford and Cambridge and the public schools had been particularly heavily hit. Some 37,452 British officers had been killed on the Western Front, 2,438 killed, wounded or missing on the first day (1 July 1916) of the Battle of the Somme alone.[81] From this arose the myth of the 'lost generation', in which slaughtered paladins like Raymond Asquith, Julian Grenfell and Rupert Brooke, many of them in sober fact misfits or failures, were presented as irreplaceable.[82] The myth was partly literary in creation. The war poets were numerous

and of high quality: Wilfred Owen, Edmund Blunden, Siegfried
Sassoon, Herbert Read, Robert Graves, Isaac Rosenberg, Maurice
Baring, Richard Aldington, Robert Nichols, Wilfred Gibson and
many others; in the final years of the war they became obsessed
with death, futility and waste.[83] Their poems haunted the early
1920s; later came the prose: R.C.Sherriff's play *Journey's End*,
Blunden's *Undertones of War*, Sassoon's *Memoirs of a Fox-
Hunting Man*, all in 1928; Aldington's *Death of a Hero* the
following year. It was a literature which, while not exactly defeatist,
was unheroic and underlined the cost of defending national greatness.

In the minds of the upper class, moreover, the loss of life, which
they exaggerated, was directly linked to the crisis of the old landed
system of traditional gentry agriculture, which had been in deep
trouble since the arrival of transatlantic grain in the 1870s and was
now on its last legs. Pre-war legislation had been designed to
protect tenant-farmers against landlords. Lloyd George, who hated
the landed aristocracy, capped the system with his Agriculture Act
(1920), which brought in secure tenancy; and a further act in 1923
destroyed restrictive tenancy agreements and legalized 'freedom of
cropping'. The result was the break-up of thousands of estates, big
and small. 'England is changing hands', wrote *The Times*, 19 May
1920. 'From 1910 onwards,' H.J.Massingham claimed, 'a vindic-
tive, demagogic and purely urban legislation has crippled [the
landlord], good, bad or indifferent, responsible or irresponsible.'[84]
In February 1922 the *Quarterly Circular* of the Central Landowners' Association estimated that 700,000 acres of agricultural land
was changing hands every year. The previous year a single firm of
auctioneers had disposed of land equal in area to the average
English county. The former Liberal cabinet minister, C.F.G.
Masterman, in a much-read book published in 1923, complained:
'In the useless slaughter of the Guards on the Somme, or of the
Rifle Brigade in Hooge Wood, half the great families of England,
heirs of large estates and wealth, perished without a cry . . . .
There is taking place the greatest change which has ever occurred in
the history of the land of England since the days of the Norman
Conquest.'[85] The price of land continued to fall, agricultural debt
increased and millions of acres went out of production. The *Daily
Express* cartoonist, Strube, featured a lanky and famished wastrel
labelled 'Idle Acres'. J.Robertson Scott, editor of *The Countryman*,
gave a striking picture of rural desolation in a series of articles in
Massingham's *Nation*, which became a lugubrious best-seller under
the ironic title *England's Green and Pleasant Land* (1925). In
Norfolk in 1932, the writer-farmer Henry Williamson noted, 'a

farm of nearly a square mile, with a goodish Elizabethan house and
ten or a dozen cottages, sold for a thousand pounds'.[86] It is hard to
exaggerate the effect of this untreated and ubiquitous decay at the
heart of England's ancient system of governance.

The evidence of industrial decay was omnipresent too. After a
brief post-war recovery, the fundamental weakness of Britain's
traditional export industries – coal, cotton and textiles, shipbuilding,
engineering – all of which had old equipment, old animosities and
old work-practices, combining to produce low productivity, was
reflected in chronically high unemployment. This was attributed in
great part to the decision of Winston Churchill as Chancellor of the
Exchequer to return Britain to the gold standard in 1925. Keynes
argued fiercely against it as a form of 'contemporary mercantilism'.
We were 'shackling ourselves to gold'. Churchill replied we were
'shackling ourselves to reality', which was true, the reality of
Britain's antiquated industrial economy.[87] The effects of the move
balanced out: higher export prices, cheaper imported food and raw
materials. As Churchill said, it was primarily a political move,
designed to restore Britain's financial prestige to its pre-war level. It
was necessarily deflationary and so had the unforeseen effect of
making it easier for the government to defeat the General Strike, the
ultimate weapon of the Sorelians, talked about since 1902, which
finally took place in May 1926. There had been dress-rehearsals in
1920 and 1922, from which the Tory Party had profited more than
the union leaders. When it became inevitable, Stanley Baldwin
craftily manoeuvred the leaders of the transport, railway and mining
unions into fighting the battle at the end instead of the beginning of
winter. It collapsed ignominiously after a week. 'It was as though a
beast long fabled for its ferocity had emerged for an hour, scented
danger and slunk back to its lair.'[88] Neither going back to gold nor
the breaking of the general strike weapon had any effect on the
unemployment figures which (given as a percentage of the labour
force) remained on a grievous plateau even before the end of the
Twenties boom. From 1921–9 they were as follows: 17.0; 14.3;
11.7; 10.3; 11.3; 12.5; 9.7; 10.8; 10.4.[89]

For the workers, then, the problem was not one of a 'missing
generation'. No gaps were observable in their ranks. There were not
too few of them; too many, rather. Yet their plight helped to increase
the erosion of will among the ruling establishment by radicalizing the
Anglican clergy. The Church of England had had a bad war. It had
blown an uncertain patriotic trumpet. It had been exposed by the
Catholic clergy as amateurish in its trench-ministry. It had done no
better in the munitions factories.[90] It had lost ground during a
supreme moment; and it was uneasily aware of the fact. During the

Twenties its more eager spirits developed a new evangelism of peace and 'compassion'. Some went very far to the Left. Conrad Noel, vicar of the spectacular fourteenth-century church of Thaxted in Essex, refused to display the Union Jack inside it on the grounds that it was 'an emblem of the British Empire with all the cruel exploitation for which it stood'. He put up the Red Flag, for which he quoted biblical authority: 'He hath made of one blood all nations.' Every Sunday posses of right-wing undergraduates would come over from Cambridge to tear it down, and would be resisted by 'Lansbury Lambs', a force of radical ex-policemen who had been sacked for striking in 1919.[91] This battle of the flags convulsed establishment England, a shocking new form of entertainment.

More significant was William Temple, Bishop of Manchester from 1920 and later Archbishop of York and Canterbury, by far the most influential Christian clergyman in interwar Britain. He was the first of the Anglo-Saxon clergy to opt for progressive politics as a substitute for an evangelism of dogma, and was thus part of that huge movement which, as Nietzsche had foreseen, was transforming religious energy into secular Utopianism. Temple was a jovial, Oliver Hardy figure, with an appetite not merely for carbohydrates but for social martyrdom. In 1918 he joined the Labour Party and announced the fact. In the Twenties he created COPEC, the Conference on Christian Politics, Economics and Citizenship, prototype of many such bodies from that day to this. At its 1924 meeting in Birmingham he announced: 'With the steadily growing sense that Machiavellian statecraft is bankrupt, there is an increasing readiness to give heed to the claims of Jesus Christ that He is the Way, the Truth and the Life.'[92] His actual interventions in social politics were ineffectual. Thus, the General Strike took him by surprise and caught him at Aix-les-Bains trying to cure his gout and reduce his obesity. Puffing home, he directed an intervention by churchmen which, by persuading the miners' leaders they had the whole of Christendom behind them, had the effect of prolonging the coal strike from July to December 1926, by which time the colliers and their families were destitute and starving.[93] Nothing daunted, Temple soldiered on in the progressive cause. To George Bernard Shaw a socialist bishop in person was, he gleefully exclaimed, 'a realized impossibility'. In fact Temple was a portent of many more to come; and it was a sign of the times that his views assisted, rather than impeded, his stately progress to the throne of St Augustine.

Temple's philosophy enshrined the belief, so characteristic of the twentieth century, that Christian morality was reflected in the pursuit of secular economic 'solutions'. The Christian notion of guilt, embodied in the unease of comfortable, well-fed Anglican dignitaries, powerfully reinforced the feeling of obligation which the possessing classes and the better-off nations were beginning to entertain towards the deprived, at home and abroad. Economics was not about wealth-creation, it was about duty and righteousness. Naturally Temple found eager allies on the agnostic side of the progressive spectrum. Keynes wrote him a remarkable letter, which hotly denied that economics was a morally neutral science: '. . . economics, more properly called political economy, is a side of ethics.'[94] That was what the prelate wished to hear and the Fellow of King's was anxious to teach.

As such Keynes spoke for the insidious anti-establishment which in the 1920s emerged from the privacy of Cambridge and Bloomsbury to effect a gradual but cumulatively decisive reversal in the way the British ruling class behaved. Hitherto, the axioms of British public policy at home, and of British imperialism abroad, had reflected the moral climate of Balliol College, Oxford, under the Mastership of Benjamin Jowett. Its tone was judicial: Britain's role in the world was to dispense civilized justice, enforced if necessary in the firmest possible manner. It was epitomized in the person of Lord Curzon, fastidious, witty, urbane and immensely cultured but adamant in the upholding of British interests, which he equated with morality as such. 'The British government', he minuted to the cabinet in 1923, 'is never untrue to its word, and is never disloyal to its colleagues or its allies, never does anything underhand or mean . . . that is the real basis of the moral authority which the British Empire has long exerted.'[95] Naturally, when need arose, that moral authority had to be stiffened by tanks and aeroplanes and warships operating from the string of bases Britain maintained throughout the world.

At Cambridge a rather different tradition had developed. While Oxford sent its stars to parliament, where they became ministers and performed on the public stage, Cambridge developed private groups and worked by influence and suggestion. In 1820 a Literary Society had been formed, of twelve members known as the Apostles, which propagated the early heterodoxies of Wordsworth and Coleridge. Its recruits, collectively chosen and secretly elected – not even the mere existence of the society was ever acknowledged – were of high calibre but teachers and critics rather than major creators: the one massive talent, Alfred Tennyson, quickly slipped away in 1830.[96] The Apostles' world-picture was diffident, retiring, unaggressive, agnostic, highly critical of pretensions and grandiose schemes, humanitarian and above all more concerned with personal than with public duties. It cultivated introspection; it revered friendship. It was homosexual in tone though not often in practice. Tennyson captured its mood in his poem 'The Lotus Eaters'.

In 1902 the Apostles elected a young Trinity undergraduate called Lytton Strachey. His father had been a general in India for thirty years – Curzon's world, in fact – but his intellectual and moral formation was that of his mother, an agnostic stalwart of the Women's Progressive Movement, and a free-thinking French republican schoolmistress called Marie Silvestre.[97] Two years before being elected to the Apostles he had formed, with Leonard Woolf and Clive Bell, a 'Midnight Society' which later devolved into the Bloomsbury Group. Both the Apostles and Bloomsbury, one secret and informal, the other informal and admitting a few women, revolved for the next thirty years round Strachey. Initially, however, he was not the philosopher of the sect. That was the role of G.E.Moore, a Trinity don and fellow-Apostle whose major work, *Principia Ethica*, was published the autumn after Strachey's election. Its last two chapters, 'Ethics in Relation to Conduct' and 'The Ideal', were, by implication, a frontal assault on the Judaeo–Christian doctrine of personal accountability to an absolute moral code and the concept of public duty, substituting for it a non-responsible form of hedonism based on personal relationships. 'By far the most valuable things which we know or can imagine', Moore wrote, 'are certain states of consciousness which may be roughly described as the pleasures of human intercourse and the enjoyment of personal objects. No one, probably, who has asked himself the question, has ever doubted that personal affection and the appreciation of what is beautiful in Art and Nature are good in themselves.'[98]

Strachey, who was a propagandist of genius rather than a creator, pounced on this discreet volume with the same enthusiasm Lenin showed for Hobson's *Imperialism*, published the year before. It was just the argument he wanted and could preach. To his fellow-Apostle Keynes he wrote urgently of 'the business of introducing the world to Moorism'. The book was the ideology not of odious Victorian duty, but of friendship; and, as he confided to Keynes, with whom he was already competing for the affections of handsome young men, of a very special kind of friendship: 'We can't be content with telling the truth – we must tell the whole truth: and the whole truth is the Devil . . . . It's madness for us to dream of making dowagers understand that feelings are good, when we say in the same breath that the best ones are sodomitical . . . our time will come about a hundred years hence.'[99] Not only did friendship have higher claims than conventional morality, it was ethically superior to any wider loyalty. The point was to be made by Strachey's fellow-Apostle, E.M.Forster: 'If I had to choose between betraying my *country* and betraying my *friend*, I hope I should have the guts to betray my country.'[100]

Moore's doctrine, outwardly so un-political, almost quietist, was in practice an excellent formula for an intellectual take-over. It provided ethical justification not merely for a society of mutual admirers, as the Apostles had been in the past, but for the formation of a more positive and programmatic freemasonry, a mafia almost. The Apostles system gave it access to some of the best brains Cambridge could provide: Bertrand Russell, Roger Fry, Ludwig Wittgenstein, for instance. A network of links by friendship and marriage produced convivial metropolitan centres – 21 Fitzroy Square, 38 Brunswick Square, 10 Great Ormond Street, 3 Gower Street, 46 Gordon Square, 52 Tavistock Square – as well as hospitable Trinity and King's, and such rural hostelries as Lady Ottoline Morrell's Garsington, publicized in *Crome Yellow*. Apostles (or their relations) held strategic positions: Strachey's uncle controlled the *Spectator*, Leonard Woolf the literary pages of the *Nation*, Desmond MacCarthy (and later Raymond Mortimer) those of the *New Statesman*.[101] There were several friendly publishing houses.

Not for nothing was Strachey the son of a general. He had a genius for narcissistic élitism and ran the coterie with an iron, though seemingly languid, hand. From the Apostles he grasped the principle of group power: the ability not merely to exclude but to be seen to exclude. He perfected the art of unapproachability and rejection: a Bloomsbury mandarin could wither with a glance or a tone of voice. Within his magic circle exclusiveness became a kind of mutual life-support system. He and Woolf called it 'the Method'.[102]

Strachey, moreover, did not have to wait 'a hundred years' before his time came. The war brought his moment, for it allowed him to publicize his counter-establishment philosophy in the form of avoiding national service. His method of doing so was subtle and characteristic. With other Bloomsberries, he belonged to the No-Conscription Fellowship and the National Council against Conscription. He did not play an active part in their campaign, which might have been legally dangerous, and which he left to more energetic souls like Russell.[103] But he made a sensational appearance before a tribunal in Hampstead Town Hall in March 1916, fortified by special vitamin-food and Swedish exercise and flanked by his three adoring sisters. 'Tell me, Mr Strachey,' he was asked by the chairman, 'what would you do if you saw a German soldier attempting to rape your sister?' 'I should try to come between them.' The joke was much relished; the high, squeaky voice universally imitated; no one had transfixed a courtroom in quite that way since the days of Oscar Wilde. In fact Strachey did not in the end stand on his pacifist principles at all but obtained exemption thanks to 'sheaves of doctors' certificates and an inventory of his medical symptoms'.[104] He spent the entire war writing his quartet of biographical essays, *Eminent Victorians*, which, by holding up Thomas Arnold, Florence Nightingale, Cardinal Manning and General Gordon to ridicule and contempt, was, in effect, a wholesale condemnation of precisely those virtues and principles the men in the trenches were dying to uphold. He finished it in December 1917, just as the calamitous battle of Passchendaele ended in a sea of blood and mud. It was published the following year to immediate acclaim and lasting influence. Few books in history have ever been better timed.

Later, Cyril Connolly was to call *Eminent Victorians* 'the first book of the Twenties . . . he struck a note of ridicule which the whole war-weary generation wanted to hear . . . . It appeared to the post-war young people like the light at the end of a tunnel.' The sharper members of the old guard instantly saw it for what it was – 'downright wicked in its heart', wrote Rudyard Kipling in a private letter.[105] Everyone else loved it, often for that very reason. Even among the soft underbelly of the establishment there was a self-indulgent welcome. H.H.Asquith, once the star of Jowett's Balliol, now rosy-plump and bibulous, ousted from the premiership by Lloyd George for lack of energy, gave the book what Strachey termed 'a most noble and high-flown puff' in the course of his Romanes Lecture. It appeared as Ludendorff's last offensive tore through the British Fifth Army; new editions poured out long after the Germans had begun their final retreat, and it proved itself far more destructive of the old British values than any legion of enemies. It was the instrument by which Strachey was able to 'introduce the world to Moorism', becoming in the process the most influential writer of the Twenties. As Keynes's biographer Roy Harrod later wrote: 'The veneration which his young admirers accorded [Strachey] almost matched that due to a saint.'[106] Strachey became the ruling mandarin of the age and the Bloomsberries his court – for, as has been well observed, 'their unworldliness was in fact a disguise for a thorough-going involvement with the world of fashion'.[107]

Yet their power was not directly exerted on public policy, as a rule. Keynes said that Strachey regarded politics as no more than 'a fairly adequate substitute for bridge'. Even Keynes never sought government office. They moved behind the scenes or in print and sought to create intellectual climates rather than shape specific policies. Keynes's *Economic Consequences of the Peace* rammed home the message of *Eminent Victorians* just as it made brilliant use of Strachey's new literary techniques. In 1924 E.M.Forster published *A Passage to India*, a wonderfully insidious assault on the principle of the Raj, neatly turning upside down the belief in British superiority and maturity which was the prime justification of the Indian Empire. Two years later Forster's Apostolic mentor, Goldsworthy Lowes Dickinson, who invented the term 'A League of Nations' and founded the League of Nations Union, published his *The International Anarchy 1904–14*, a grotesquely misleading account of the origins of the Great War, which superbly reinforced the political moral of Keynes's tract.[108] The foreign policy of Bloomsbury was that Britain and Germany were on exactly the same moral plane up to 1918 and that, since then, Britain had been at a moral disadvantage, on account of an iniquitous peace, a continuing imperialism and armaments which, in themselves, were the direct cause of war. To a great mass of educated opinion in Britain this slowly became the prevailing wisdom.

In a deeper sense, too, Bloomsbury represented an aspect of the nation now becoming predominant. Like the shattered ranks of the old gentry, like the idle acres, like the dole-queues, Bloomsbury lacked the energizing principle. It is curious how often in photographs Strachey is shown, supine and comatose, in a low-slung deckchair. Frank Swinnerton recorded that, at their first meeting, 'He drooped if he stood upright, and sagged if he sat down. He seemed entirely without vitality.'[109] He 'dragged his daddy longlegs from room to room', wrote Wyndham Lewis, 'like a drug-doped stork.' Strachey himself admitted to his brother: 'We're all far too weak physically to be any use at all.'[110] Few Bloomsberries married; and even those not addicted to what was termed 'the higher sodomy' lacked the philoprogenitive urge. The circle was outraged when Keynes, for reasons which are still mysterious, married the bouncing Russian dancer Lydia Lopokova.

What is perhaps even more striking is the low productivity of Bloomsbury, so curiously akin to Britain's exhausted industries. Strachey himself produced only seven books, two of them collected articles. MacCarthy's expected major work never materialized: there were volumes of pieces but no original book. Raymond Mortimer followed exactly the same pattern. Forster, known as the *Taupe* (the Mole), was another low-voltage writer: five novels only (apart from his homosexual fiction, *Maurice*, published posthumously). He was made a Fellow of King's in 1946 and thereafter he wrote nothing, pursuing a mole-like existence for a quarter of a century, emerging only to collect honorary degrees. Another member of the group, the philosopher J.E.McTaggart, was able to work only two or three hours a day and spent the rest of his time devouring light novels at the rate of nearly thirty a week. He 'walked with a strange, crab-like gait, keeping his backside to the wall'.[111] Lowes Dickinson, too, was an etiolated, lethargic figure in a Chinese mandarin's cap. Virginia

Woolf wrote of him, 'What a thin whistle of hot air Goldie lets out through his front teeth!'[112] Above all, Moore himself became virtually sterile after he had delivered his *Principia*. All that followed was a popular version, a collection of essays, a set of lecture notes – then silence for forty years. 'I'm afraid I have nothing to say,' he wrote to Woolf, 'which is worth saying; or, if I have, I can't express it.'[113] He terminated an Apostolic paper with this characteristic Bloomsbury maxim: 'Among all the good habits which we are to form we should certainly not neglect the habit of indecision.'[114]

Significantly, of all the Cambridge Apostles of that generation, the one wholly vital and exuberantly creative figure, Bertrand Russell, was never really part of the Bloomsbury Group. Though he shared its pacifism, atheism, anti-imperialism and general progressive notions, he despised its torpid dampness; it, in turn, rejected him. He thought Strachey had perverted Moore's *Principia* to condone homosexuality. In any case he felt it was an inferior essay. 'You don't like me, do you Moore?' he asked. Moore replied, after long and conscientious thought: 'No'.[115] It was notable that Russell, unlike Strachey, actually fought for pacifism in the Great War and went to jail for it. He read *Eminent Victorians* in Brixton prison and laughed 'so loud that the officer came to my cell, saying I must remember that prison is a place of punishment'. But his considered verdict was that the book was superficial, 'imbued with the sentimentality of a stuffy girls' school'.[116] With his four marriages, his insatiable womanizing, his fifty-six books, over one of the widest selection of topics ever covered by a single writer, his incurable zest for active experience, Russell was of sterner stuff than Bloomsbury. Nor did he share its weakness for totalitarianism. On Armistice night, Bloomsbury had joined forces with the new firmament of the Sitwells and what Wyndham Lewis termed their 'Gilded Bolshevism'. They were celebrating not so much the victory of the Allies as Lenin's wisdom in signing a separate peace to 'create and fashion a new God', as Osbert Sitwell put it. At the Adelphi, Strachey was to be seen actually dancing, 'jigging with the amiable debility of someone waking from a trance' – under the ferocious scowl of D.H.Lawrence.[117] Russell would have none of it. He went to Russia himself in 1920, saw Lenin, and pronounced his regime 'a close tyrannical bureaucracy, with a spy system more elaborate and terrible than the Tsar's and an aristocracy as insolent and unfeeling'.[118] A year later he was in China. Surveying the total administrative and political chaos there, he wrote to a friend: 'Imagine . . . Lytton sent to govern the Empire & you will have some idea how China has been governed for 2000 years.'[119]

Curiously enough, it was Russell's activities and supposedly subversive remarks which the Foreign Office found alarming. No one in authority thought to take an interest in the Apostles, which was already producing such extremists as E.M.Forster's mentor, Nathaniel Wedd, Fellow of King's, described by Lionel Trilling as 'a cynical, aggressive, Mephistophelian character who affected red ties and blasphemy'.[120] During the Thirties the Apostles were to produce at least four Soviet agents: Guy Burgess, Anthony Blunt, Leo Long and Michael Whitney Straight. At the time, however, it was Russell's public antinomianism – worthy of Oxford in its openness – which fascinated Whitehall. Even his conversations on board ship were monitored, and at one time it was considered whether to invoke the War Powers Order-in-Council (not yet repealed) to get him arrested and deported from Shanghai.[121]

These symptoms of paranoia in the Foreign Office reflected a quite genuine concern, among those who knew the facts and thought seriously about Britain's future security. There was an awful lot of empire to defend, and very little with which to defend it. That was one reason why the Foreign Office hated the League, with its further universal commitments. Successive Tory Foreign Secretaries denied Robert Cecil, Minister for League Affairs, a room in the Foreign Office, and when this was conceded by the Labour government of 1924, officials prevented him from seeing important cables.[122] Senior British policy-makers were uneasily conscious that keeping the Empire together as a formidable entity was, at bottom, bluff and demanded skilful juggling. They believed they could do it – they were not yet defeatist – but greatly resented any 'sabotage' by 'our side'. Hence their resentment at people like Russell and Cecil, who came from old governing families (the first the grandson, the second the son, of Prime Ministers) and therefore ought to know better.[123]

What particularly worried British planners was the rapid absolute, and still more relative, decline in the strength of the Royal Navy from its position of overwhelming might at the end of 1918. Britain had always skimped her army. But from the days of Queen Anne she had maintained the world's largest navy, whatever the cost, as a prerequisite to keeping her empire. For most of the nineteenth century she had insisted on a 'two-power standard', that is, a navy equal or superior to those of any two other powers combined. In the end that had proved beyond her means, but she had endeavoured to mitigate any declension from the two-power standard by diplomatic arrangements. Hence, in 1902, she had finally abandoned her 'splendid isolation' by signing a treaty of alliance with Japan, the chief object of which was to allow her to concentrate more of her naval forces in European waters. The Japanese navy had been largely created with British help and advice. For Britain, with her immense Asian possessions and interests, and limited means to protect them, Japan was a very important ally. During the war, her large navy had escorted the Australian and New Zealand forces to the war-zone: indeed, the Australian Prime Minister, W.M.Hughes, thought that if Japan had 'elected to fight on the side of Germany, we should most certainly have been defeated'.[124]

America's entry into the war, however, introduced a fearful complication. America and Japan viewed each other with increasing hostility. California operated race-laws aimed at Japanese immigrants and from 1906–8 the mass-migration from Japan had been halted. So the Japanese turned to China and sought in 1915 to turn it into a protectorate. The Americans endeavoured to halt that too: they regarded themselves as the true protectors of China. At Versailles, Wilson angered the Japanese by refusing to write a condemnation of racism into the Covenant of the League.[125] Thereafter America tended to give the Pacific priority in her naval policy. As a result, she put the sharp question to Britain: whom do you want as your friends, us or the Japanese?

For Britain the dilemma was acute. America was an uncertain ally. Indeed, strictly speaking she was not an ally at all. Of course there were ties of blood. But even by 1900 the proportion of white Americans of Anglo-Saxon stock had fallen to a third: the German–Americans, with 18,400,000 out of 67 million, were almost as numerous.[126] America's original decision to build a big ocean navy appeared to have been aimed at Britain more than any other power. As late as 1931, in fact, the United States had a war plan aimed at the British Empire, 'Navy Basic Plan Red (WPL–22), dated 15 February 1931'.[127] On the other hand, there was a whole network of institutions on both sides of the Atlantic binding the two nations together, and an identity of views and interests which constituted the fundamental fact in the foreign policies of both.

The Anglo–Japanese Treaty came up for renewal in 1922. The Americans wanted it scrapped. The British cabinet was divided. Curzon thought Japan a 'restless and aggressive power . . . like the Germans in mentality'; 'not at all an altruistic power'. Lloyd George thought the Japanese had 'no conscience'. Yet both men were clear the alliance should be renewed; so were the Foreign Office and the Chiefs of Staff. So were the Dutch and the French, thinking of their own colonies. At the 1921 Commonwealth Conference, the Australians and the New Zealanders came out strongly in favour of renewal. In short, all the powers involved in the area – except America – and all those involved in British foreign and military policy formation, were adamant that the Anglo–Japanese alliance was a stabilizing, a 'taming' factor, and ought to be maintained.[128]

But Smuts of South Africa was against, for racial reasons. So was Mackenzie King of Canada, a Liberal who depended on the anti-British vote in Quebec and who was advised by the Anglophobe O.D.Skelton, permanent head of the Canadian Ministry of External Affairs.[129] This seems to have tipped the balance. Instead of renewing the Treaty, an American proposal to call a conference in Washington to limit navies was adopted. Hughes of Australia was outraged: 'You propose to substitute for the Anglo–Japanese alliance and the overwhelming power of the British navy a Washington conference?' It was worse than that. At the Conference itself in 1922 the Americans proposed a naval 'holiday', massive scrappings, no capital ships over 35,000 tons (which meant the end of Britain's superships) and a 5:5:3 capital ship ratio for Britain, the USA and Japan. When Admiral Beatty, the First Sea Lord, first heard the details, an eyewitness said he lurched forward in his chair 'like a bulldog, sleeping on a sunny doorstep, who has been poked in the stomach by the impudent foot of an itinerant soap-canvasser'.[130] The Japanese hated the proposals too, which they regarded as an Anglo-Saxon ganging up against them. Yet the scheme went through. The pressure for disarmament at almost any cost and the related fear of driving America still further from Europe proved too strong. Japan, in turn, demanded and got concessions which made matters worse. She insisted that Britain and America agree to build no main fleet bases north of Singapore or west of Hawaii. This made it impossible, in effect, for America's fleet to come to the rapid support of the British, French or Dutch possessions if they were attacked. But even more important, the fact that Japan felt she had to demand such concessions symbolized, so far as Britain was concerned, her transition from active friend into potential enemy.

This was not grasped at the time. One of those who failed to do so was Winston Churchill: indeed, though alert to danger in India, he was always blind to perils further east. In August 1919, as War Secretary, he had been instrumental in drawing up the 'Ten Year Rule', under which defence planning was conducted on the assumption there would be no major war for at least ten years. In the Twenties this was made a 'rolling' guideline, and it was not in fact scrapped till 1932. As Chancellor of the Exchequer he put on the pressure to curb naval spending, and especially to extend the 5:5:3 ratio to cruisers, the basic naval life-support system of the empire: 'We cannot have a lot of silly little cruisers', he told the Assistant Cabinet Secretary, Tom Jones, 'which would be of no use anyway.'[131] In fact at the 1927 naval conference the Admiralty fought off this attack. But in 1930, with Labour in power again, the point was conceded – indeed, extended to destroyers and submarines too. By the early 1930s, Britain was a weaker naval power, in relative terms, than at any time since the darkest days of Charles II. Nor could she look to her empire. India was a source not of strength but of weakness, absorbing a regular 60,000 men from Britain's tiny army. The rich dominions were even more parsimonious than Britain under the stern stewardship of Churchill. Their forces were tiny and hopelessly ill-equipped. The 1925–6 Defence White Paper showed that while Britain spent annually only 51s. *per capita* on her armed forces, Australia spent only half as much, 25s, New Zealand 12s 11d and Canada a mere 5s 10d. By the early 1930s, these three 'have' powers, with so much to defend against men with lean and hungry looks, had carried out a programme of virtually total unilateral disarmament. Australia had only three cruisers and three destroyers, and an air force of seventy planes. New Zealand had two cruisers and virtually no air force. Canada had four destroyers and an army of 3,600. It had only one military aircraft – on loan from the RAF.[132] Britain was not much more provident so far as the Far East was concerned. The building of a modern naval base in Singapore had been postponed, at Churchill's urging, for five years.

History shows us the truly amazing extent to which intelligent, well-informed and resolute men, in the pursuit of economy or in an altruistic passion for disarmament, will delude themselves about realities. On 15 December 1924 Churchill wrote a remarkable letter to the Prime Minister, scouting any possibility of menace from Japan. For page after page it went on, using every device of statistics and rhetoric, to convince Baldwin – already sufficiently pacific and complacent by nature – of the utter impossibility of war with Japan: 'I do not believe there is the slightest chance of it in our lifetime. The Japanese are our allies. The Pacific is dominated by the Washington Agreement . . . . Japan is at the other end of the world. She cannot menace our vital security in any way. She has no reason whatever to come into collision with us.' Invade Australia? 'That I am certain will never happen in any period, even the most remote which we or our children need foresee . . . war with Japan is not a possibility which any reasonable government need take into account.'[133]

FIVE

An Infernal Theocracy,
a Celestial Chaos

While Winston Churchill was assuring the comatose Baldwin that Japan meant no harm, its economy was growing at a faster rate than any other nation, its population was rising by a million a year and its ruler was a god-king who was also insane. The old Emperor Meiji, under whom Japan had entered the modern world, had chosen his women carefully for their health as well as their beauty, and each evening would drop a silk handkerchief in front of the one who was to occupy his bed that night. But most of the children thus begotten were sickly nonetheless and no doctor was ever allowed to touch their divine persons. His heir Yoshihito, who reigned in theory until 1926, was clearly unbalanced. Though his regnal name, Taisho, signified 'Great Righteousness', he oscillated between storms of rage, in which he would lash at those around him with his riding-crop, and spasms of terror, dreading assassination. He sported a ferocious waxed moustache, in imitation of his idol, the Kaiser Wilhelm II, but he fell off his horse on parade, and when inspecting his soldiers sometimes struck and sometimes embraced them. On his last appearance before the Diet, he had rolled up his speech and, using it as a telescope, peered owlishly at the bobbing and bowing parliamentarians. After that he had been eased out in favour of his son Hirohito, known as Showa ('Enlightened Peace'), a timid creature interested in marine biology. He too feared assassins, as did all prominent male members of the family. The statesman Prince Ito had prudently married a sturdy tea-house girl who protected him from murderous samurai by stuffing him into the rubbish hole of his house and squatting on top (but they got him in the end).[1]

No western scholar who studies modern Japan can resist the feeling that it was a victim of the holistic principle whereby political events and moral tendencies have their consequences throughout the

176

world. Japan became infected with the relativism of the West, which induced a sinister hypertrophy of its own behavioural weaknesses and so cast itself into the very pit of twentieth-century horror. At the beginning of modern times Japan was a very remote country, in some respects closer to the society of ancient Egypt than to that of post-Renaissance Europe. The Emperor, or Tenno, was believed to be *ara-hito-gami*, 'human, a person of the living present who rules over the land and its people and, at the same time, is a god'.[2] The first Tenno had begun his reign in 660 BC, at the time of the Egyptian twenty-fifth dynasty, and the line had continued, sometimes by the use of adoption, for two and a half millennia. It was by far the oldest ruling house in the world, carrying with it, imprisoned in its dynastic amber, strange archaic continuities. In the sixteenth century Francis Xavier, the 'apostle of the Indies', had considered the Japanese he met to be ideal Christian converts by virtue of their tenacity and fortitude. But the internal disputes of the missionaries had led Japan to reject Christianity. In the second quarter of the seventeenth century it sealed itself off from the European world. It failed completely to absorb the notions of individual moral responsibility which were the gift of the Judaic and Christian tradition and retained strong vestiges of the collective accountability so characteristic of the antique world. In the 1850s, the West forced its way into this self-possessed society. A decade later, a large portion of the Japanese ruling class, fearing colonization or the fate of China, took a collective decision to carry out a revolution from above, adopt such western practices as were needful to independent survival, and turn itself into a powerful 'modern' nation. The so-called Meiji Restoration of 3 January 1868, which abolished the Shogunate or rule by palace major-domo and made the Emperor the actual sovereign, was pushed through with the deliberate object of making Japan *fukoku-kyohei*, 'rich country, strong army'.

It is important to grasp that this decision by Japan to enter the modern world contained, from the start, an element of menace and was dictated as much by xenophobia as by admiration. The Japanese had always been adept at imitative absorption, but at a purely utilitarian level which, from a cultural viewpoint, was superficial. From her great innovatory neighbour, China, Japan had taken ceremonial, music, Confucian classics, Taoist sayings, types of Buddhist speculation, Tantric mysteries, Sung painting, Chinese verse-making and calendar-making. From the West, Japan now proceeded to take technology, medicine, administrative and business procedures, plus the dress thought appropriate for these new practices. But the social structure and ethical framework of Chinese civilization were largely rejected; and, while Japan displayed pragmatic voracity in swallowing Western means, it showed little interest in Western ends: the ideals of classical antiquity or Renaissance humanism exercised little influence.[3]

Indeed it is notable that Japan was attracted by modern novelty, not by ancient truth. In a sense the Japanese had always been modern-minded people: 'modern since pre-history'.[4] They took aboard gimmickry and baubles, the technical and the meretricious, rather as a society woman adopts passing fashions. But their cultural matrix remained quite unaffected: the most characteristic cultural creations of Japan have no Chinese antecedents. Similarly, the Western importations from the mid-nineteenth century onwards left the social grammar of Japan quite untouched.[5]

Nor did Japan's long isolation imply serenity. Quite the contrary. Japan had none of China's passivity and fatalistic decay. They were very different countries; wholly different peoples. The point has often been made that the Chinese live in the realm of space, the Japanese in time. China had developed, in the great northern plain where her civilization had its roots, a majestic, ordered cosmology, and was content to await its slow evolutions. It saw life in terms of repetitive cycles, like most oriental cultures. Japan was a collection of spidery, spinal islands, rather like ancient Greece, and was almost Western in its consciousness of linear development, hurrying from point to point with all deliberate speed. Japan had a concept of time and its urgency almost unique in non-Western cultures and consistent with a social stress of dynamism.[6] There was something restless, too, in Japan's climate, as changeable and unpredictable as Britain's, but far more violent. The islands are strung out from the sub-tropics to the sub-arctic; oriental monsoons and western cyclones play upon them simultaneously. As the German scholar Kurt Singer put it, 'Relentlessly this archipelago is rocked with seismic shocks, invaded by storms, showered and pelted with rain, encircled by clouds and mists . . . . It is not space that rules this form of existence, but time, duration, spontaneous change, continuity of movement.' The rapid succession of climatic extremes helps to explain, some Japanese believe, the violent oscillations in national conduct.[7]

These national attributes, and the fact that the industrialization of Japan was imposed from above as the result of deliberate decisions by its élites, help to explain the astonishing rapidity of Japan's progress. The movement was not a spontaneous reaction to market forces but an extraordinary national consensus, carried forward without any apparent dissenting voices. It thus had more in common with the state capitalism of pre-1914 Russia than the liberal capitalism of the West, though the class conflicts which tore Tsarist Russia were absent. Under the Tenno and his court, the *gumbatsu*, or military chiefs, and the *zaibatsu*, or businessmen, worked in close harmony, in accordance with the 'rich country-strong army' programme. Within two generations huge industrial groups had emerged, Mitsui, Mitsubishi, Yasuda, Sumitomo, all closely linked to the Meiji government and the armed forces by subsidies and contracts. The 1914–18 war, which deprived Japan of traditional suppliers from Europe, and opened up new markets to her, accelerated her development towards self-sufficiency and industrial maturity. Steam tonnage rose from 1.5 to over 3 million tons. The index of manufacturing production, from an average of 160 in 1915–19, jumped to 313 in 1925–9, and in foreign trade the index (100 in 1913) moved to 126 in 1919 and 199 in 1929, with exports rising from 127 to 205 during the 1920s. By 1930 Japan had a population of 64 million, exactly twice what it had been at the beginning of the revolution-from-above in 1868, and it was already a major industrial power.[8]

Comparing Japan's revolutionary development with that of, say, Turkey – also imposed from above from 1908 onwards – it is easy to see the advantages of being an island kingdom, with natural frontiers, a homogeneous racial, religious and linguistic composition and, not least, a strong and ancient tradition of unity towards outsiders, none of which Turkey possessed.[9] Japan also had an important economic advantage which was often overlooked at the time (and since): a highly developed intermediate technology, with hundreds of thousands of skilled craftsmen and a tradition of workshop discipline going back many centuries.

Yet Japan had some fundamental weaknesses too, reflecting its archaism. Until 1945 it had no system of fixed law. It had maxims, behavioural codes, concepts of justice expressed in ideograms – exactly as in ancient Egypt. But it had no proper penal code; no system of statutory law; no judge-controlled code of common law either. The relationship between authority and those subject to it was hidden, often on important points. The constitution itself was uncertain. It did not impose a definite system of rights and duties. Prince Ito, who drew up the Meiji constitution, wrote a commentary on what it meant; but this book was a matter of dispute, and often out of official favour. The law was not sovereign. How could it be in a theocracy? But then – was Japan a theocracy? Ito thought it had been in the past, but no longer was; others took a different view. The matter was left ambiguous, as were many other legal and constitutional matters in Japan, until 1946, when the Emperor publicly announced that he was not a god. There was something vague and makeshift about the whole system of order in Japan. Honour, for instance, was more important than hierarchy. It might sometimes be right to ignore the law (such as it was) and disobey a superior. But no one could quite tell until the occasion arose. Then a consensus would develop and the collective conscience would judge. Hence activist minorities, especially in the armed forces, were often able to defy their commanders, even the Emperor, and receive the endorsement of public opinion.[10]

This absence of absolute lines between right and wrong, legality and illegality, law and disorder, made Japan peculiarly vulnerable to the relativism bred in the West after the First World War. But the weakness went back further. When in 1868 Japan turned to Europe for pragmatic guidance it looked for norms of international behaviour as well as technology. What did it find? Bismarckian Realpolitik. Thereafter came the scramble for Africa, the arms-race, the ferocity of Ludendorff's war-machine and the cult of power through violence, culminating in Lenin's triumphant *putsch*.

The Japanese observed that European behaviour, however atrocious, was always internally justified by reference to some set of beliefs. Hence, to fortify themselves in a stern, competitive world, they refurbished their own ideologies, in accordance with what they perceived to be European principles of utility. This involved, in effect, inventing a state religion and a ruling morality, known as Shinto and bushido. Hitherto, in religious matters the Japanese had been syncretistic: they took elements of imported cults and used them for particular purposes – Buddhism, Taoism, Confucianism, even Christianity – without regard for logic or consistency. It is true that Shinto was first mentioned in Japanese annals as early as the reign of Yomei Tenno (585–587 AD). It signified god in a pagan sense, going back to ancestral sun-gods and sun-goddesses, the primitive worship of ancestors and the idea of divine rulers. As such it was far less sophisticated than Buddhism and the other imperial religions of the Orient and it was only one of many elements in Japanese religious culture. But it was specifically and wholly Japanese, and therefore capable of being married to national aspirations. Hence with the Meiji Revolution a conscious decision was taken to turn it into a state religion. In 1875 it was officially separated from Buddhism and codified. In 1900 Shinto shrines were placed under the Ministry of the Interior. Regular emperor-worship was established, especially in the armed forces, and from the 1920s onwards a national code of ethics, *kokumin dotoku*, was taught in all the schools. With each Japanese military victory or imperial advance (the defeat of Russia in 1904–5 was a case in point) the state religion was consolidated and elaborated, and it is significant that the process culminated in 1941, when Japan joined the Second

World War and instituted private, popular and public religious ceremonies for the entire nation. Shinto, in brief, was transformed from a primitive, obsolescent and minority cult into an endorsement of a modern, totalitarian state, and so by a peculiarly odious irony, religion, which should have served to resist the secular horrors of the age, was used to sanctify them.

Nor was this all. Shinto, as the religion of expansionist national-ism, was deliberately underpinned by a refurbished and militarized version of the old code of knightly chivalry, bushido. In the early years of the century, bushido was defined by a Samurai professor, Dr Inazo Nitobe, as 'to be contented with one's position in life, to accept the natal irreversible status and to cultivate oneself within that allotted station, to be loyal to the master of the family, to value one's ancestors, to train oneself in the military arts by cultivation and by discipline of one's mind and body'.[11] But until the twentieth century there were few references of any kind to bushido. Some doubted its very existence. Professor Hall Chamberlain, in an essay *The Inven-tion of a New Religion*, published in 1912, wrote: 'Bushido, as an institution or a code of rules, has never existed. The accounts given of it have been fabricated out of whole cloth, chiefly for foreign consumption . . . . Bushido was unknown until a decade or so ago.'[12] It may have been a series of religious exercises, accessible to very few. At all events in the 1920s it was popularized as a code of military honour, identified with extreme nationalism and militarism, and became the justification for the most grotesque practices, first the murder of individuals, later mass-cruelty and slaughter. The 'knights of bushido' were the militant leadership of totalitarian Shintoism, the equivalent, in this oriental setting, of the 'vanguard élites' of Lenin and Mussolini, the blackshirts and brownshirts and Chekists of Europe. They embodied the 'commanding moral force of [this] country . . . the totality of the moral instincts of the Japanese race', according to Nitobe.[13] Here was a concept, superficially moralistic in tone, wholly relativistic in fact, which was dangerously akin to what Lenin termed 'the revolutionary conscience' and Hitler the 'higher morality of the party'.

This new metaphysic of militarism and violence, which certainly as an organized entity had no precedent in Japanese history, was supposed to be accompanied by the systematic development of Western political institutions. In 1876 the samurai were disbanded as a class, losing their stipends and the right to bear swords; the last feudal revolt was put down the next year. Western-style parties and newspapers were introduced in the 1870s, a new British-style peerage, with barons, viscounts and marquises, was ordained in 1884 and a cabinet-system the following year. For the first Diet in

1890 only 400,000 out of 40 million had the vote. In 1918, the 'three yen tax qualification' raised it to 3.5 million out of 60 million. In 1925 Japan got the Manhood Suffrage Act, which gave the vote to all men over twenty-five, raising the suffrage to 13 million.

But authoritarian institutions advanced *pari passu* with democracy. There was a highly restrictive press law in 1875. Police supervision of political parties was established in 1880. The constitution of 1889 was deliberately restrictive, to produce, wrote its author Prince Ito, 'a compact solidity of organization and the efficiency of its administrative activity'.[14] The Diet was balanced by a powerful House of Peers and the cabinet by the institution of the *genro*, a group of former prime ministers and statesmen who gave advice directly to the Tenno. Perhaps most important of all was a regulation, drawn up in 1894 and confirmed in 1911, that the ministers of the army and the navy must be serving officers, nominated by the respective staffs. This meant not only that army and navy were independent of political control (the chiefs of staff had direct access to the Tenno) but that each service could in effect veto a civilian cabinet by refusing to nominate its own minister. This power was frequently used and was always in the background. Hence the government was really only responsible for civil matters, the army and navy conducting their own affairs, which frequently and from the 1920s increasingly impinged on foreign policy. Since army and navy were not under civil control, and officers in the field did not necessarily feel obliged in honour to obey their nominal superiors in Tokyo, there were times when Japan came closer to military anarchy than any other kind of system.

The trouble was that Japan only slowly developed the kind of civic consciousness which in Europe was the product of town life and bourgeois notions of rights. The town itself was an import. Even Tokyo was, and until very recently remained, an enormous collection of villages. Its citizens had rural not urban reflexes and attachments. Though feudalism was killed by the Meiji Revolution, it survived in a bastard version. Everyone, from the highest downwards, felt safe only as part of a clan or *batsu*. It was and is habitual for the Japanese to extend patterns of family behaviour to wider situations. The term *habatsu*, 'permanent faction', was applied to each new activity as it came into existence: schools of painting, or wrestling, or flower-arranging; then, after 1868, to industrial firms; and after 1890 to politics. The Japanese term *oyabun-kobun*, meaning parent–child or boss–follower relationship, became the cement of this bastard feudalism in politics, a man rendering service or loyalty in return for a share of any spoils going. Indeed the Japanese did not clearly distinguish between family and non-family groupings, since the perpetuation of the family line by adoption was regarded as much more important than the perpetuation of the blood line.[15] Ozaki Yukio, the most durable of Japanese politicians, who took part in the first general election of 1890 and lived to sit in the first post-1945 Diet, wrote in 1918 that in Japan 'political parties, which should be based and dissolved solely on principles and political views, are really affairs of personal connections and sentiments, the relations between the leader and the members of a party being similar to those which subsisted between a feudal lord and his liegemen'.[16] Mass-parties of the Left, based on universal economic interests, might have changed this pattern. But the Peace Preservation law of 1925, the same year that Japan got male suffrage, gave the police such formidable power to combat Marxist subversion as effectively to inhibit their development. No left-wing party ever scored more than 500,000 votes until after 1945.

As a result, Japanese political parties were legal mafias which inspired little respect and offered no moral alternative to the traditional institutions refurbished in totalitarian form. Bribery was ubiquitous since elections were costly (25,000 dollars per seat in the inter-war period) and the pay small. Corruption ranged from the sale of peerages to land speculation in Osaka's new brothel quarter. Of the two main parties, Seiyukai was financed by Manchurian railway interests, Kenseikai by Mitsubishi, in both cases illegally. Three of the most prominent political leaders, Hara (the first commoner to become Prime Minister), Yamamoto and Tanaka, were guilty of blatant corruption.[17] Politicians did not cut attractive figures compared with the bushido militarists. They fought frequently, but only in unseemly scrimmages in the Diet, sometimes with the assistance of hired ruffians. As one British eye-witness put it in 1928: 'Flushed gentlemen, clad without in frockcoats but warmed within by too-copious draughts of *sake*, roared and bellowed, and arguments frequently culminated in a rush for the rostrum, whence the speaker of the moment would be dragged in the midst of a free fight.'[18]

Moreover, if bastard feudalism persisted in the Diet, it flourished also outside it, in the form of secret societies which constituted an alternative form of political activity: non-democratic, unconstitutional, using direct action and employing weapons instead of arguments. Once the samurai lost their stipends they had either to find work or band together and offer themselves to the highest bidder. In 1881 a group of them formed the Genyosha, the first of the secret societies, which soon entered politics indirectly by providing thugs to rig Diet elections or murder rival candidates. In 1901 a Genyosha man, Mitsuru Toyama, founded the notorious Kokuryukai or Black Dragon, the prototype of many violent, ultra-nationalist sects. The real expansion of gang-politics, however, occurred after the end of the 1914–18 war, which seems to have ushered in an era of political violence almost everywhere.

Whether the Japanese took their cue from Weimar Germany and Mussolini's Italy is not clear. Certainly, like the European fascists, they used Leninist violence as an excuse for counter-violence. What was disturbing was the overlap between these societies and constitutional politics and, most sinister, the military. Thus, the Dai Nihon Kokusuikai, the Japan National Essence Society – using concepts from the totalitarianized forms of Shinto and bushido – which was founded in 1919, included among its members three future Prime Ministers and several generals. This was comparatively respectable. Others were mere gangs of ruffians. Some were radical in exactly the same way as the revolutionary syndicalists in Italy or the early Nazis in Germany. Thus, the Yuzonsha, founded by Kita Ikki in 1919, proposed a National Socialist plan of nationalization of industry and break-up of the great estates to prepare Japan for 'the leadership of Asia', her expansion being at the expense of Britain ('the millionaire') and Russia ('the great landowner'), Japan placing itself at the head of 'the proletariat of nations'. Other radical societies included the agrarian nationalists, who wished to destroy industry completely, and the Ketsumedian, led by Inoue Nissho, dedicated to the assassination of industrialists and financiers.[19]

Virtually all these societies practised assassination, or showed an extraordinary tolerance of it. One might say that though the notion of the feudal revolt died in the 1870s, assassination was its continuance by other means. The samurai might no longer impose their will as a class; but groups of them reserved the right to register their political objections not through the ballot, beneath them, but through the sword and dagger and, after it became popular in the 1920s, the Thomson sub-machine-gun. The samurai had in fact always used hired coolie-gangsters to terrorize their peasants. Now their modernized *kais*, or gangs, were hired out to the *gumbatsu* or *zaibatsu* to enforce their will on ministers. Even more disturbing was the fact that, by 1894, the *kais* were working in conjunction with the Kempei-Tai, the Special Police to Guard Security of the state. These men reported directly to Imperial Headquarters, not the government, could hold prisoners for 121 days without formal charge or warrant and were authorized to employ torture to extract confessions. Men were frequently arrested by the Kempei-Tai after secret denunciations by the *kais*.[20]

The *kais* indeed played a protean role in Japanese society, sometimes upholding state security, sometimes enforcing protection rackets in, for instance, the new film industry, where their sanguinary gangland battles, fought with two-handed swords, formed an oriental descant to such episodes as the St Valentine's Day massacre in contemporary Chicago.[21] Mitsuru Toyama, the most notorious gang-leader, founder of the Black Dragon, occupied a curiously ambivalent role in Japanese society. Born in 1855, he had the manners and affectations of a gentleman and a knight of bushido. According to the *New York Times* correspondent, Hugh Byas, he looked 'like one of the Cheeryble Brothers, exuding benignity, and made great play of the fact that his creed would not allow him to kill a mosquito'. Killing politicians was another matter. He not merely organized assassination but protected other known murderers in his house, which the police dared not enter. They included Rash Behari Bose, wanted by the British for the attempted assassination of Lord Hardinge, the Viceroy, in 1912. When he finally died in his nineties, full of years and wickedness, the *Tokyo Times* published a special supplement in his honour.[22] That was characteristic of Japanese tolerance towards even the most flagrant and vicious law-breaking which claimed credentials of honour. The very victims themselves helped to perpetuate the system. Thus the great liberal statesman Ozaki Yukio, though constantly threatened with death himself, wrote a poem which contained the defeatist lines: 'Praise be to men who may attempt my life/If their motive is to die for their country'.[23]

Hence political assassination was not necessarily severely punished in Japan; sometimes not punished at all. And, even more important, it was not morally reprobated by society. As a result it became increasingly common. Of the original Meiji Restoration government, one was murdered, another driven to *hara-kiri*; and Prince Ito, architect of the constitution, was murdered, despite the efforts of his tea-garden wife. Of Taisho Tenno's Prime Ministers during the years 1912–26, Count Okuma, Viscount Takahashi and Mr Hara were assassinated; and under Hirohito, 1926–45, three more Prime Ministers died, Mr Hamaguchi, Mr Inukai and Admiral Saito, plus a dozen cabinet ministers.[24] Some politicians accepted the risks of their profession more stoically than others. But fear of being murdered undoubtedly deterred ministers from pushing through reforming legislation. When the writer David James asked Prime Minister Hara in 1920 why he did not repeal the police regulation which provided six months' imprisonment for incitement to strike, Hara replied, 'I have no intention of committing *hara-kiri* just now.' When Hara was stabbed to death the next year at Toyko's Shimbashi station, his 'offence' was that, as a mere civilian, he had taken over the Naval Office while the Minister, Admiral Kato, was at the Washington Naval Conference.[25] The Tenno himself was not immune from charges of lack of patriotism. There was an attempt on Hirohito's life in 1923, and this naturally timid man was undoubtedly dissuaded from giving civilian Prime Ministers the support they had a right to expect under the constitution, by fear of his own officers.

The position deteriorated after 1924–5, when army reforms introduced a new type of officer, drawn from the ranks of minor officials, shopkeepers and small landowners. These men had little respect for traditional authority – or their own high commanders – and they were imbued with Leninist and fascist notions of political violence, and above all by the new totalitarian version of bushido. While quite capable of threatening Hirohito with death, they spoke of his 'restoration' to power: what they wanted was military dictatorship under nominal imperial rule. Their key word was *kokutai* or 'national policy', and any politician guilty of the slightest disloyalty to *kokutai* was as good as dead.[26] Most of them came from rural areas, where living standards were falling during the Twenties and young girls had to go out to work just for their food as no wages could be paid. Their army brothers burned with zeal and hatred and their violence enjoyed wide public support.[27]

Under these circumstances, civilian party government gradually collapsed, and elections became meaningless. In 1927 and again in 1928 Prime Ministers were forced out of office by the army. In 1930, the Prime Minister, Hamaguchi Yuko, having got a mandate to cut the armed forces, was gunned down immediately he tried to do so. His successor was forced out over the same issue. The next Prime Minister, Inukai Ki, who again tried to stand up to the Services, was murdered in May 1932 by a group of army and naval officers. They planned, in fact, to kill him together with Charlie Chaplin, who was on a visit to Tokyo and due to take tea with the Prime Minister. The naval ringleader of the plot told the judge: 'Chaplin is a popular figure in the United States and the darling of the capitalist class. We believed that killing him would cause a war with America.' When the murderers came up for trial, their counsel argued that, as their honour and future were at stake, assassination was a form of self-defence. He presented the judge with 110,000 letters, many written in blood, begging for clemency. In Niigata, nine young men chopped off their little fingers, as evidence of sincerity, and sent them to the War Minister pickled in a jar of alcohol.[28] The lenient sentences passed at this trial, and at many others, recalled the farcical court cases involving right-wing murderers in early Weimar Germany.[29]

The breakdown of constitutional government in Japan could not be regarded as an internal affair since it was inextricably bound up with foreign policy aims. Most Japanese regarded territorial expansion as an essential element of entry into the modern world. Did not every other industrial power have an empire? It was as necessary as steel-mills or iron-clads. In Japan's case there were additional and compelling reasons: the poverty of the country, its almost total lack of natural resources and the rapid, irresistible increase in population. In 1894–5, Japan struck at China, taking Korea, Formosa (Taiwan) and Port Arthur. She was forced to surrender the last by the tripartite intervention of Russia, Germany and France. Her response was to double the size of her army and make herself self-sufficient in armaments, which she had achieved by 1904. Immediately she issued an ultimatum to Russia, took Port Arthur and won the devastating naval battle of Tsushima in May 1905, assuring herself commercial supremacy in Manchuria, and taking the Sakhalin (Karafuto) islands as part of the settlement. In 1914 she entered the war solely to possess herself of Germany's ports and property in China, and the following year she presented a series of demands to the Chinese government (the 'Twenty-one Demands') which in effect made her the preponderant colonial and commercial power in the region. The paramountcy was confirmed by the Versailles Treaty, which gave her Shantung and a whole string of Pacific islands as mandates.

Japan now faced a dilemma. She was determined to expand, but under what colours? Her Meiji Revolution was at heart an anti-colonial move, to preserve herself. Her original intention, in seizing Korea, was to deny it to the European powers and set herself up as commercial, political and military head of an 'East Asian League', a defensive alliance which would modernize East Asia and prevent further Western penetration. Japan would thus have become the first anti-colonialist great power, a role occupied by Russia after 1945, and in the process win herself (as Russia has) a family of dependent allies and satellites. The difficulty was that China, whose co-operation was essential, never showed the slightest desire to provide it, regarding Japan as a junior sovereignty and a ferocious predator, in some ways to be feared more, because nearer, than any European power. Japan never wholly abandoned this line, however. It was reflected in her demand for a racial equality clause in the League covenant, in her pious insistence that all her activities on the Chinese mainland were in the interests of the Chinese themselves, and during the 1941–5 war in her creation of puppet governments in the territories she occupied, bound together in the Greater East Asia Co-prosperity Sphere. These were not wholly fictions; but they could not become wholly, or even mainly, facts either, so long as Japan was obliged to fight and conquer China in order to make her a 'partner'.[30]

That avenue closed, was Japan to be a colonial power like the rest? That was the view of the Japanese Foreign Office, the Hirohito court, the liberal political establishment. But that meant having an ally, above all Britain, biggest and most respectable of the established empires. Britain was anxious for stability, and means could doubtless be found to provide Japan with sufficient interests and possessions to bind her, too, to a stable system. And so long as Britain was Japan's ally, the latter had a prime interest in preserving her own internal respectability, constitutional propriety and the rule of law, all of which Britain had taught her.

That was why the destruction of the Anglo–Japanese alliance by the USA and Canada in 1921–2 was so fatal to peace in the Far East. The notion that it could be replaced by the Washington Naval Treaty, and the further Nine Power treaty of February 1922 (also signed by Belgium, Italy, the Netherlands and Portugal), which guaranteed China's integrity, was a fantasy. For the second agreement provided no enforcement provision, even in theory, and the first made enforcement in practice out of the question. The net result was to put Japan in the role of potential predator and cast her out of the charmed circle of respectable 'have' powers. Britain's influence with Japan disappeared, and America, emerging as China's protector, assumed the shape of Japan's irreconcilable enemy.[31] Internally, the consequence was to shift power in Japan away from the Foreign Office, whose foreign friends had let them down, and in favour of the military, especially the younger officers imbued with fanatic zeal to go it alone, something which was in any event implicit in totalitarian Shinto.

There were, however, more prosaic reasons pushing in favour of national desperation. Japan could not feed herself. In 1868, with a population of 32 million, consuming each year an average of just under 4 bushels of rice a head, Japan got by with 6 million acres under cultivation, each yielding 20 bushels. By 1940, with prodigious effort and skill, she had pushed up the yield per acre to 40 bushels, and by taking in every inch of marginal land had increased the area under rice to 8 million acres. But in the meantime average consumption had risen to $5\frac{3}{4}$ bushels a year – not a great deal – and the population to 73 million, so Japan was short of 65 million bushels of rice a year. Agricultural productivity had already levelled off in the early 1920s and there then was no way of raising it further. So between the pre-war period 1910–14, and the end of the 1920s, rice imports tripled.[32] These had to be paid for by Japan's predominantly textile exports, already meeting cut-throat competition and tariffs.

Emigration was not really an option for the Japanese. They had been restricted by treaty from entering the United States as long ago as 1894, the first national group to be so controlled. By 1920 there were 100,000 Japanese in the USA (mainly in California) and a further 100,000 in Hawaii: four years later American terror at the 'yellow peril' led to legislation precluding Japanese from receiving American citizenship, which under the new immigration law automatically excluded them even from entering the country. Australian immigration law was equally restrictive and pointedly aimed at Japan. The attitude of the American and Australian governments (which of course reflected overwhelming public feeling) caused particular bitterness among the Japanese trading community, who had European status in Asia. By the mid-1920s even some of the 'respectable' politicians were beginning to feel there was no peaceful way out of the dilemma. In his book *Addresses to Young Men*, Hashimoto Kingoro wrote:

. . . there are only three ways left to Japan to escape from the pressure of surplus population . . . emigration, advance into world markets, and expansion of territory. The first door, emigration, has been barred to us by the anti-Japanese immigration policies of other countries. The second door . . . is being pushed shut by tariff barriers and the abrogation of commercial treaties. What should Japan do when two of the three doors have been closed against her?[33]

The same point was made far more forcefully in the propaganda disseminated by the *kais* and the army and navy slush-funds. It became the theme of Sadao Araki, who by 1926 was the leader of the young officer groups and evangelist of *Kodo*, 'the imperial way', the new militant form of expansionist Shinto. Why, he asked, must Japan, with well over 60 million mouths to feed, be content with 142,270 square miles (much of it barren)? Australia and Canada, with 6.5 million people each, had 3 million and 3.5 million square miles respectively; America had 3 million square miles, France a colonial empire of 3.8 million, Britain (even without the Dominions and India) had 2.2 million, Belgium 900,000 square miles, Portugal 800,000. America, he pointed out, in addition to her huge home territories, had 700,000 square miles of colonies. Wherein lay the natural justice of these huge discrepancies? It was not as though the Japanese were greedy. They lived off fish and rice, and not much of either. They were ingeniously economic in their use of all materials. By the mid-1920s they were close to the limits of their resources and a decade later they were right up against them. Behind the romantic atavism of the military gangs, their posturings and murderous rodomontades, lay a huge and perfectly genuine sense of national grievance shared by virtually every Japanese, many millions of whom – unlike the Germans – were actually hungry.

Yet the irony is that Japan, at any rate in the first instance, did not seek to redress the balance of right by falling on the rich Western powers, whose race policies added insult to inequity, but by imposing yet another layer of oppression on what Lord Curzon called 'the great helpless, hopeless and inert mass of China'. Of course here again the European powers had set the example. They proffered all kinds of reasons for the imposition of dictated treaties on China and their occupation of her river-ports, but their only real justification was superior force. Sometimes they made the point explicitly. In 1900 the Kaiser's message instructing German troops to relieve the Peking legations had read: 'Give no quarter. Take no prisoners. Fight in such a manner that for 1,000 years no Chinaman shall dare look askance upon a German.'[35] The other powers behaved similarly, usually without the rhetoric. If the rule of force was the law of nations in China, why should Japan alone be refused the right to follow it? Japan could not accept that the Great War had ended the era of colonialism. For her, it was just beginning. China was Japan's manifest destiny. Her leading banker Hirozo Mori wrote: 'Expansion towards the continent is the destiny of the Japanese people, decreed by Heaven, which neither the world nor we the Japanese ourselves can check or alter.'[36]

But there was another reason for attacking China, which went to the roots of the Japanese dynamic impulse. 'They are peculiarly sensitive', wrote Kurt Singer, 'to the smell of decay, however well screened; and they will strike at any enemy whose core appears to betray a lack of firmness . . . . Their readiness, in the face of apparent odds, to attack wherever they can smell decomposition makes them appear as true successors of the Huns, Avars, Mongols and other "scourges of God".'[37] This shark-like instinct to savage the stricken had been proved sound in their assault upon Tsarist Russia. It was to be the source of their extraordinary gamble for Asian and Pacific paramountcy in 1941. Now, in the 1920s, it was to lead them irresistibly to China, where the stench of social and national gangrene was unmistakable.

China's plight was the result of the optimistic belief, common to intellectuals of the Left, that revolutions solve more problems than they raise. In the nineteenth century the great powers had sought to enter and modernize China; or, as the Chinese thought, plunder it. They had imposed 'unequal treaties' which the Manchu dynasty had little alternative but to accept. The imperial system of government, which had lasted for three millennia, could be seen in two ways. It represented the principle of unity, not easily replaced in a vast country with little natural focus of unity, for its people spoke many different languages (though, thanks to the imperial civil service, educated men shared a common script of ideograms). It could also be seen as the principle of weakness which made foreign penetration possible. Incapable of reforming or modernizing itself, it had allowed to happen what the Japanese ruling class had successfully prevented.

If China, too, could not have a revolution from above, then let it have a revolution from below.

That was the view of the radical intellectuals, whose leader was the Western-educated Sun Yat-sen. Like Lenin he had spent much of his life in exile. In 1896 he had been kidnapped by the staff of the Imperial Chinese Legation in London. They planned to ship him back as a lunatic in a specially chartered steamer, and once in Peking he would have been tortured to death, the punishment reserved for plotting against the Dragon Throne. But from his top-floor cell in the Legation at the corner of Portland Place and Weymouth Street, Sun had thrown out messages wrapped around half-crowns. One had been picked up by a black porter, who took it to the police; and soon after the Prime Minister, Lord Salisbury, got Sun freed.[38] He eventually returned to China. At exactly the same time as Lenin was promoting his 'vanguard élite' theory to justify middle-class intellectuals pushing a largely non-existent proletariat into revolution and Mussolini's mentors were experimenting with 'revolutionary syndicalism', Sun founded a secret society, the Hsing Chung Hui. It was based partly on European, partly on Japanese models, and its object, like Lenin's, was to overthrow the imperial autocracy by force. It exploited famines and rice-harvest failures, assassinated provincial officials, occasionally captured cities, or engaged in more general revolts in 1904 and 1906. Its opportunity came when the death of the Dowager-Empress Tzu Hsi in 1908 left the throne to a two-year-old, Pu Yi. A national assembly was convoked. There was a possibility of creating a constitutional monarchy which would have introduced the democratic principle while conserving the unifying principle of monarchy, shorn of its abuses. But Dr Sun would have none of it. On 29 December 1911 he set up a Republic in Nanking, with himself as president, and six weeks later the Manchus, the last of China's dynasties, abdicated.

Thus the principle of legitimacy was destroyed, leaving a vacuum, which could only be filled by force. The point was noted by a young peasant, Mao Tse-tung, who had been seventeen in 1910 when he heard in his Hunan village the news of the Empress's death, two years after it occurred. When the revolution came he cut off his pigtail and joined the army, discovering in the process that, in China, it was necessary to have an army to achieve anything; an *aperçu* he never forgot.[39] The owlish Dr Sun came to the same conclusion rather later, and when he did so handed over the presidency to the last commander of the imperial troops, General Yuan Shih-kai. General Yuan would almost certainly have made himself emperor, and founded a new dynasty – as had many Chinese strong-men in the past. But in 1916 he died, the cause of monarchy was lost, and China embarked on what Charles de Gaulle was later to call *les délices de l'anarchie.*

The object of overthrowing the monarchy was to restore China's possessions according to the 1840 frontiers, unify the country and curb the foreigner. It did the opposite in each case. In Outer Mongolia the Hutuktu of Urga declared himself independent and made a secret treaty with Russia (1912), a realignment never since reversed. By 1916 five other provinces had opted for home rule. Japan moved into Manchuria and the North, and many coastal areas. The other great powers settled their 'spheres of influence' at meetings from which China was excluded. The only dependable source of revenue possessed by the Chinese Republican government (when it had one) was what remained of the old Imperial Maritime Customs, created by the Irishman Sir Robert Hart and manned by Europeans, mainly from the United Kingdom, which controlled the coasts and navigable rivers, maintained buoys, lighthouses and charts and collected duties. The rest of the government's taxation system dissolved into a morass of corruption. As there was no money, there could be no central army.

Moreover, the destruction of the monarchy struck a fatal blow at the old Chinese landed gentry. They lost their privileges in law, and immediately sought to erect a system of bastard feudalism (as in Japan) to restore them in fact. Hitherto, their factions and clans had operated within the rules of the court. Without the court there was nothing. Traditional cosmology had gone with the throne. So had religion, for Confucianism revolved round monarchy. Taoism, a private cult, was no substitute as a creed of public morals. Some took refuge in Buddhism, others in Christianity. But most of the gentry aligned themselves with whatever local source of military authority they could find, becoming, with their dependents, its clients. Confronted with the state of dissolution so graphically described by Hobbes, they chose Leviathan, in the shape of the war-lord. Alas, there was not one monster but many: by 1920 four major war-lords held sway, and scores of minor ones. China entered a hateful period reminiscent of the Thirty Years' War in Europe.[40]

Dr Sun, the sorcerer's apprentice, had himself re-elected President, then in 1921 made Generalissimo. But he had no army, and no money to pay one. He wrote books, *San-min chu-i* (*The Three Principles of the People*) and *Chien-kuo fang-lueh* (*Plans for the Building of the Realm*). It was all so easy on paper. First would come the phase of struggle against the old system; then the phase of educative rule; then the phase of true democratic government. He changed his revolutionary organization into the Kuomintang (KMT), or People's Party. It was based on Three Principles: National

Freedom, Democratic Government, Socialist Economy. A master of the classroom, Sun used to draw on a blackboard a big circle with smaller circles within, Conservatism, Liberalism, Socialism and Communism – the KMT took the best out of each and combined them. The reality was rather different. Dr Sun admitted: 'Well-organized nations count votes out of ballot boxes. Badly organized nations count bodies, dead ones, on the battlefields.' To his head bodyguard, a celebrated Canadian Jew called 'Two-Gun' Cohen, he confessed his real political aim was modest: 'I want a China where there is no need to shut one's outer gate at night.'[41]

In the circumstances, the aim was too ambitious. Outer gates remained essential; so did bodyguards. Holed up in Canton, Dr Sun required six hundred men to guard him. Sometimes he could not pay them. Then they would mutiny and raid the Treasury, to see what they could find. When Sun and other military and civil leaders moved about, they did so in big American Packards, with gun-toting heavies mounted on the running-boards. Sometimes Sun was forced to go into hiding, in weird disguises. Once he fled to Hong Kong, in a British gunboat. Indeed, he would dearly have liked British help as a Protecting Power – so much for China's independence – but Lord Curzon vetoed it. He then turned to America, and urged Jacob Gould Schurman, the US Minister in Canton, for a five-year American intervention, with power to occupy all railway junctions and provincial capitals, authority over the army, police, sanitation, flood-control, and the right to appoint key administrative experts. But this too was turned down, in 1923 and again in 1925.[42]

Baffled, Sun turned to the Soviet government in 1923. A Chinese Communist Party had been formed in 1920–1, but joint membership with the KMT was permitted by both. Indeed the Soviet regime insisted on this alliance, forcing the CCP, at its third Congress, to declare: 'The KMT must be the central force in the national revolution and assume its leadership.'[43] So Moscow (that is, Stalin) welcomed Sun's request, and in October 1923 sent him one Michael Borodin, also known as Berg and Grisenberg, to reorganize the KMT on Leninist lines of democratic centralism, and a military expert, 'Galen', also known as 'General Blucher', to create an army. They brought with them many 'advisers', the first instance of a new Soviet form of political imperialism. Galen sold Sun Soviet rifles, at US $65 each, then gave the cash to Borodin who put it into the CCP's organization. Galen also set up a military academy at Whampoa, and put in charge of it was Sun's ambitious brother-in-law, a former invoice-clerk called Chiang Kai-shek (they had married sisters of the left-wing banker, T.V. Soong).

The arrangement worked, after a fashion. The academy turned out

five hundred trained officers, whom Chiang made the élite of the
KMT's first proper army. Then he decided to turn war-lord on his
own account. The trouble with Chinese armies was discipline.
Generals, indeed whole armies, often just ran away. In 1925 Chiang,
promoted chief-of-staff to Generalissimo Sun, issued his first orders:
'If a company of my troops goes into action and then retreats
without orders, the company commander will be shot. This rule will
also apply to battalions, regiments, divisions and army corps. In the
event of a general retreat, if the commander of the army corps
personally stands his ground and is killed, all the divisional commanders will be shot.' And so on down the line. This was followed up by
drumhead courts-martial and mass-shootings.[44]

In 1924 Sun had held the first KMT Congress, and it emerged as a
mass party organized on CP lines, with over 600,000 members. But
he died in March 1925, lamenting the way that CP militants were
taking over, and deploring the failure of Britain or America to help
him save China from Communism. In the circumstances, the KMT's
own war-lord, Chiang, was bound to take over, and did so. There
now followed one of those decisive historical turning-points which,
though clear enough in retrospect, were complicated and confused at
the time. How should the revolution be carried through, now that
Dr Sun was dead? The KMT controlled only the Canton area. The
Communists were divided. Some believed revolution should be
carried through on the slender basis of the small Chinese proletariat,
concentrated in and around Shanghai. Others, led by Li Ta-chao,
librarian of Peking University (whose assistant Mao Tse-tung became), thought revolution should be based on the peasants, who
formed the overwhelming mass of the Chinese population. Orthodox
Communist doctrine scouted this notion. As Ch'en Tu-hsiu, co-
founder of the Chinese party, put it, 'over half the peasants are
petit-bourgeois landed proprietors who adhere firmly to private
property consciousness. How can they accept Communism?'[45] Stalin
agreed with this. The Russian peasants had defeated Lenin; he
himself had not yet settled their hash. He took the view that, in the
circumstances, the Chinese CP had no alternative but to back the
KMT and work through Chinese nationalism.

In the vast chaos of China, everyone was an opportunist, Chiang
above all. At the Whampoa Academy, whose object was to produce
dedicated officers, he worked closely with a young Communist,
Chou en-Lai, head of its political department. There was virtually no
difference between KMT and CP political indoctrination. Indeed, the
KMT at this stage could easily have become the form of national
Communism which Mao Tse-tung was eventually to evolve. It was
Chiang, not the Communists, who first grasped that hatred of

foreigners and imperialism could be combined with hatred of the oppressive war-lords to mobilize the strength of the peasant masses. Mao Tse-tung, who was a member of the KMT Shanghai bureau, found this idea attractive, and he was made head of the Peasant Movement Training Institute, with an overwhelming stress on military discipline (128 hours out of the total course of 380 hours). His views and Chiang's were very close at this time. In some ways he was much more at home in the KMT, with its stress on nationalism, than in the CCP, with its city-oriented dogmatism. He collaborated with the KMT longer than any other prominent Communist, which meant that after he came to power in the late 1940s he had to 'lose' a year out of his life (1925–6) in his official biographies.[46] An article Mao wrote in February 1926, which forms the first item in the official Maoist Canon, is remarkably similar to a declaration by Chiang in Changsha the same year: 'Only after the overthrow of imperialism', said Chiang, 'can China obtain freedom . . . . If we want our revolution to succeed, we must unite with Russia to overthrow imperialism . . . . The Chinese revolution is part of the world revolution.'[47]

The possibility of a merger of the KMT and the CCP into a national communist party under the leadership of Chiang and Mao was frustrated by the facts of life in China. In 1925–6 Chiang controlled only part of south China. The centre and north were in the hands of the war-lords. Marshal Sun Chuan-fang controlled Shanghai and ran five provinces from Nanking. North of the Yangtze, Marshal Wu Pei-fu ran Hankow. General Yen Hsi-shan controlled Shansi Province. Marshal Chang Tso-lin occupied Mukden and dominated the three Manchurian provinces. Marshal Chang Tsung-chang was the war-lord in Shantung, and Chu Yu-pu in the Peking-Tientsin area.

In the early spring of 1926 this pattern was broken when Marshal Feng Yu-hsiang, the ablest of the KMT commanders, marched his 300,000-strong force (known as the Kuominchun or People's Army) some 7,000 miles, circling southern Mongolia, then east through Shensu and Hunan, to attack Peking from the south. This stupendous physical and military feat (which became the model for Mao's own 'long march' in the next decade) made possible Chiang's conquest of the North in 1926–7.[48] As a result, four of the principal war-lords recognized Chiang's supremacy, and the possibility appeared of uniting China under a republic by peaceful means. The Northern campaign had been fearfully costly in life, particularly of the peasants. Was it not preferable to seek a settlement by ideological compromise now, rather than trust to the slow carnage of revolutionary attrition? If so, then instead of expelling the 'foreign capitalists', Chiang must seek their help; and being the brother-in-law of a leading banker was an advantage. But such a course must mean a break with the Communist elements within the KMT and a public demonstration that a workers' state was not just round the corner. Hence in April 1927, when he took Shanghai, Chiang turned on the organized factory workers, who had risen in his support, and ordered his troops to gun them down. The Shanghai business community applauded, and the banks raised money to pay the KMT army.

Stalin now decided to reverse his policy. He had recently ousted Trotsky and, following his usual custom, adopted the policies of his vanquished opponents. The Chinese Communist Party was ordered to break with the KMT and take power by force. It was the only time Stalin ever followed Trotsky's revolutionary line, and it was a disaster.[49] The Communist cadres rose in Canton, but the citizens would not follow them; in the fighting that followed many townsfolk were massacred and a tenth of the city burnt down. The KMT attacked in force on 14 December 1927, the Communists broke, and they were hunted down through the streets by the Cantonese themselves. Most of the staff of the Soviet consulate were murdered. Borodin returned to Moscow in disgust and told Stalin: 'Next time the Chinese shout "Hail to the World Revolution!" send in the OGPU.' Stalin said nothing; in due course he had Borodin put to death.[50]

So Chiang and Mao came to the parting of the ways. Chiang became the supreme war-lord; the KMT was reorganized as a war-lord's party, its members including (in 1929) 172,796 officers and men in the various armies, 201,321 civilians and 47,906 'overseas Chinese', who supplied much of the money and some of its worst gangsters. As it won ground among the business community and the foreign interests, it lost ground among the peasants. Dr Sun's widow left the KMT, went into exile in Europe and charged that her husband's successors had 'organized the KMT as a tool for the rich to get still richer and suck the blood of the starving millions of China . . . . Militarists and officials whom a few years ago I knew to be poor are suddenly parading about in fine limousines and buying up mansions in the Foreign Concessions for their newly acquired concubines.' Chiang was a case in point. In July 1929 the *New York Times* correspondent noted that he paid a Peking hotel bill of US $17,000, for his wife, bodyguard and secretaries, for a fifteen-day stay, forking out a further $1,500 in tips and $1,000 bribes to the local police.[51]

The moral Mao drew from Chiang's change of policy was not an ideological but a practical one. To make any political impression in China, a man had to have an army. He would become a war-lord on his own account. He was extremely well-suited for this pursuit. Mao was thirty-four in 1927: tall, powerfully built, the son of a cruel and masterful peasant who had fought and worked his way to affluence as a well-to-do farmer and grain merchant – a genuine *kulak*, in short. A contemporary at Tungshan Higher Primary School described Mao as 'arrogant, brutal and stubborn'.[52] He was not a millennarian, religious-type revolutionary like Lenin, but a fierce and passionate romantic, with a taste for crude and violent drama; an artist of sorts, cast from the same mould as Hitler, and equally impatient. Like Hitler, he was first and foremost a nationalist, who trusted in the national culture. From the philosopher Yen Fu he derived the idea that 'culturalism', the pursuit of 'the Chinese Way', was the means to mobilize her people into an irresistible force.[53] He read and used Marxist–Leninism, but his fundamental belief was closer to the axiom of his ethics teacher at Peking, Yang Chang-chi, whose daughter became his first wife: 'Each country has its own national spirit just as each person has its own personality .... A country is an organic whole, just as the human body is an organic whole. It is not like a machine which can be taken apart and put together again. If you take it apart it dies.'[54]

In Mao's thinking, a form of radical patriotism was the mainspring. He never had to make the switch from internationalism to nationalism which Mussolini carried out in 1914: he was a nationalist *ab initio*, like Ataturk. And his cultural nationalism sprang not from a sense of oppression so much as from an outraged consciousness of superiority affronted. How could China, the father of culture, be treated by European upstarts as a wayward infant – a metaphor often used by the Western press in the 1920s. Thus the *Far Eastern Review*, commenting in 1923 on attempts to tax the British–American Tobacco monopoly: 'The solution of the problem, of course, is concerted action of the powers in making it clear to these young politicians that trickery never got anything for a nation, that sooner or later the Powers grow weary of tricks and childish pranks and will set the house in order and spank the child.'[55] In 1924 Mao took a Chinese friend, newly arrived from Europe, to see the notorious sign in the Shanghai park, 'Chinese and Dogs Not Allowed'. He interrupted a soccer game (against a Yale team) with a characteristic slogan, 'Beat the slaves of the foreigners!' and used an equally characteristic metaphor, 'If one of our foreign masters farts, it's a lovely perfume!' 'Do the Chinese people know only how to hate the Japanese,' he asked, 'and don't they know how to hate England?'[56]

Mao was not cast down by the difficulty of turning China, that helpless, prostrate beast of burden, into a formidable dragon again. This big, confident man, with his flat-topped ears and broad, pale face – 'a typical big Chinese', according to a Burmese; 'like a sea-elephant', as a Thai put it – was an incurable optimist, who scrutinized the mystery of China for favourable signs. Dr Sun had thought China in a worse position than an ordinary colony: ' We are being crushed by the economic strength of the powers to a greater degree than if we were a full colony. China is not the colony of one nation but of all, and we are not the slaves of one country but of all. I think we should be called a hypo-colony.' That was Stalin's view also.[57] But Mao thought the multiplicity of China's exploiters an advantage, because one power could be set against another; he did not believe in the Leninist theory of colonialism. He argued 'disunity among the imperialist powers made for disunity among the ruling groups in China', hence there could be no 'unified state power'.[58]

But all this analysis was mere words without an army. Mao accepted Chiang's original view that the key to revolutionary success was to rouse the peasants. But peasants were as helpless as China herself until they were armed and trained, and forged into a weapon, as Genghis Khan had done. Was not Genghis a legitimate hero of a resurrected Chinese culture? It was part of Mao's romantic national-ism, so similar to Hitler's, that he scoured the past for exemplars, especially those who shared his own stress on force and physical strength.[59] His very first article declared: 'Our nation is wanting in strength. The military spirit has not been encouraged . . . . If our bodies are not strong we shall be afraid as soon as we see enemy soldiers, and then how can we attain our goals and make ourselves respected?' 'The principle aim of physical education', he added, 'is military heroism.' The martial virtues were absolutely fundamental to his national socialism.[60]

In September 1927, following the break with the KMT, Mao was ordered by the Communist leadership to organize an armed rising among the Hunan peasants. This was his opportunity to become a war-lord, and thereafter he quickly turned himself into an indepen-dent force in Chinese politics. The revolt itself failed but he preserved the nucleus of a force and led it into the mountains of Chinghanshan, on the borders of Hunan and Kiangsi. It was small, but enough; thereafter he was never without his own troops. His appeal was crude but effective, systematizing the spontaneous land-grabbing which (though he was probably unaware of the fact) had destroyed Kerensky and made Lenin's *putsch* possible. His Regulations for the Repression of Local Bullies and Bad Gentry and his Draft Resolution on the Land Question condemned the traditional enemies of poor peasants – 'local bullies and bad gentry, corrupt officials, militarists and all counter-revolutionary elements in the villages'. He classified as 'uniformly counter-revolutionary' all the groups likely to oppose his peasant-army: 'All Right-Peasants, Small, Middle and Big Land-lords', categorized as 'those possessing over 30 *mou*' (4½ acres). In fact he was setting himself up against all the stable elements in rural society, forming a war-band which was the social reverse of those commanded by gentry war-lords and their 'local bullies'.

Mao showed himself better at appealing to peasant patriotism than Chiang, as Japanese war-archives were later to show.[61] But to begin with he could not recruit more than 1,000 poor peasants. He supplemented his force with 600 bandits, recruiting deliberately from the very scum of a society in the midst of civil war, what he called his 'five *déclassé* elements': deserters, bandits, robbers, beggars and prostitutes.[62] As with other war-lords, his army fluctuated, from less than 3,000 to over 20,000. And he was as ruthless as any war-lord in killing enemies. In December 1930 he had between 2,000 and 3,000 officers and men in his army shot for belonging to the 'AB' (Anti-Bolshevik League), a KMT undercover organization within the Communist forces. Five months earlier his wife and younger sister had been executed by the KMT and there were other deaths to avenge – Chiang had killed tens of thousands of Communists in 1927–8. But Mao never hesitated to take the initiative in using force. He had by the end of 1930 already created his own secret police (as his purge revealed) and when he felt it necessary he acted with complete ruthlessness and atrocious cruelty. The comparison between his ragged and savage band and Genghis's 'horde' was not inapt, and to most of those whose fields he crossed he must have seemed like any other war-lord.[63]

Thus in the last years of the 1920s China was given over to the rival armies, motivated by a variety of ideologies or by simple greed – to their victims, what did it matter? After Chiang's Northern campaign and the meeting of war-lords in Peking in 1928, one of the KMT commanders, Marshal Li Tsung-jen, declared: 'Something new had come to changeless China . . . the birth of patriotism and public spirit.' Within months these words had been shown to be total illusion, as the war-lords fell out with each other and the Nanking government. All parties found it convenient to fly the government and the KMT flag; none paid much regard to the wishes of either. Government revenue fell; that of the war-lords rose. As the destruction of towns and villages increased, more of the dispossessed became bandits or served war-lords, great and small, for their food. In addition to the half-dozen major war-lords, many lesser generals controlled a single province or a dozen counties, with armies ranging from 20,000 to 100,000; Mao's was among the smallest of these. At the National Economic Conference on 30 June 1928, Chiang's brother-in-law, T.V.Soong, now Minister of Finance, said that whereas in 1911 under the monarchy China had an army of 400,000, more or less under single control, in 1928 it had eighty-four armies, eighteen independent divisions and twenty-one independent brigades, totalling over 2 million. The nation's total revenue, $450 million, was worth only $300 million after debt-payments. The army cost each year $360 million, and if the troops were regularly paid, $642 million – hence banditry was inevitable. Yet a disarmament conference held the following January, designed to reduce the troops to 715,000, was a complete failure. Soong told it that, in the last year, twice as much money had been spent on the army as on all other government expenditure put together.[64]

In practice, the anguished people of China could rarely tell the difference between bandits and government troops. The number of those killed or who died of exposure or starvation was incalculable. Hupeh province showed a net population loss of 4 million in the years 1925–30, though there had been no natural famine and little emigration. The worst-hit province in 1929–30 was Honan, with 400,000 bandits (mostly unpaid soldiers) out of a total population of 25 million. In five months during the winter of 1929–30, the once-wealthy city of Iyang in West Honan changed hands among various bandit armies seventy-two times. An official government report on the province said that in Miench'ih district alone 1,000 towns and villages had been looted and 10,000 held to ransom: 'When they capture a person for ransom they first pierce his legs with iron wire and bind them together as fish are hung on a string. When they return to their bandit dens the captives are interrogated and cut with sickles to make them disclose hidden property. Any who hesitate are immediately cut in two at the waist, as a warning to the others.' The report said that families were selling children and men their wives. Or men 'rented out' their wives for two or three years, any children born being the property of the men who paid the rent. 'In many cases only eight or ten houses are left standing in towns which a year ago had 400 or 450.'[65]

In desperation, the peasants built stone turrets with loopholes and crenellations, as look-outs and refuges for humans and cattle – rather like the peel towers of the fifteenth-century border in Britain. But even strongly walled towns were besieged and stormed. Choctow, only thirty miles from Peking, was besieged for eighty days and its 100,000 inhabitants starved; mothers strangled their new-born babies and girls were sold for as little as five Chinese dollars, and carried off into prostitution all over Asia. Liyang, in the heart of the Nanking government-controlled area, was stormed by a bandit force of 3,000, who looted $3 million and destroyed a further $10 million by fire. Six major towns in the Shanghai area were stormed and looted. At Nigkang the chief magistrate was bound hand and foot and murdered by pouring boiling water over him. Strange practices from the past were resumed: bamboo 'cages of disgrace' were hoisted twenty feet into the air and hung from city walls, offenders having to stand on tiptoe with their heads sticking through a hole in the top. At Fushun in Shantung, a defeated war-lord retired into the city with his 4,500 troops, taking 10,000 hostages with him. During a thirteen-day siege by KMT units, over 400 women and children were tied to posts on the city walls, the defenders firing from behind them.

Mao and other Communist war-lords, who held down about 30 million people in five provinces during 1929–30, did not rape or loot on the whole, and they suppressed gambling, prostitution and opium poppy-growing. On the other hand they ill-treated and murdered members of the middle classes, destroyed official documents, land-deeds and titles, and burned churches, temples and other places of worship, slaughtering priests and missionaries. A town might fall into the successive hands of a CCP band, a bandit-chief, an independent war-lord and a government force in turn, each exacting its due. A petition from Szechuan Province pleaded that the government's general was merely 'the leader of the wolves and tigers' and that he had 'desolated' the 'whole district' so that 'East and West for some tens of *li*, the bark of a dog or the crow of a cock is no longer heard. The people sigh that the sun and the moon might perish so that they could perish with them.' From Chengtu, capital of the province, the merchants lamented, 'We have nothing left but the grease between our bones.'[66]

In two decades, then, the pursuit of radical reform by force had led to the deaths of millions of innocents and reduced large parts of China to the misery and lawlessness that Germany had known in the Wars of Religion or France in the Hundred Years' War. Dr Sun's well-intentioned effort to create a modern Utopia had turned into a medieval nightmare. The trouble was, everyone believed in radical reform. Chiang was for radical reform. Mao was for radical reform. Many of the independent war-lords were for radical reform. Marshal Feng was known as 'the Christian General'. General Yen Hsi-shan was 'the model governor'. All these honourable gentlemen protested that they were working, and killing, for the good of China and her people. The tragedy of inter-war China illustrates the principle that when legitimacy yields to force, and moral absolutes to relativism, a great darkness descends and angels become indistinguishable from devils.

Nor were the Chinese alone in urging radical reform. As already noted, China's gangrene attracted the predatory instincts of the Japanese. And they, too, favoured radical reform. As foreign journal-

ists conceded, more progress had been achieved in Korea under thirty
years of Japanese rule than in 3,000 years of Chinese.[67] Port Arthur,
the Shantung ports and other areas occupied by Japan were havens
of order and prosperity. The young officers of this force, known as
the Kwantung army, watched with distaste and horror China's
interminable ordeal. In early 1928 two of them, Lt Colonel Kanji
Ishihara and Colonel Seishiro Itagaki, decided to force their reluctant
government into intervention. They reasoned that, while Japanese
capitalists and Chinese war-lords might benefit from the present
anarchy, it offered nothing to the Chinese people, who needed order,
and the Japanese people, who needed space. 'From the standpoint of
the proletariat,' Itagaki wrote, 'which finds it necessary to demand
equalization of national wealth, no fundamental solution can be
found within the boundaries of naturally poor Japan that will ensure
a livelihood for the people at large.' The reasoning was fundamentally similar to the Soviet exploitation of its Asian empire on behalf
of the proletariat of Great Russia. Manchuria would be freed of its
feudal war-lords and bourgeois capitalists and turned into a proletarian colony of Japan. But the instrument of change would not be a
revolutionary *putsch* but the Kwantung army.[68] On 4 June 1928 the
two colonels took the first step towards a Japanese occupation by
murdering Marshal Chang Tso-lin, the chief war-lord in Manchuria,
dynamiting his private train and blowing him to eternity while he
slept. It was the opening act in what was to become a great
international war in the East. Curiously enough, in the United States,
which had appointed itself the protector of China and the admonitor
of Japan, the episode aroused little interest. The *Philadelphia Record*
commented: 'The American people don't give a hoot in a rainbarrel
who controls North China.'[69] America was busy manufacturing its
own melodrama.

SIX

The Last Arcadia

America's proclaimed indifference to events in North China was a bluff, an elaborate self-deceit. A nation which numbered 106 'ethnic groups', which was already a substantial microcosm of world society, could not be genuinely blind to major events anywhere.[1] America's anti-Japanese policy sprang in great part from its anxiety and ambivalence about its own Japanese minority, which was only one aspect of a vast debate the nation was conducting about the nature and purpose of American society. Who was an American? What was America for? Many, perhaps most, Americans thought of their country, almost wistfully, as the last Arcadia, an innocent and quasi-Utopian refuge from the cumulative follies and wickedness of the corrupt world beyond her ocean-girded shores. But how to preserve Arcadia? That, in itself, demanded a global foreign policy. And how to create the true Arcadian? That demanded a race policy. And the two were inextricably mingled.

The notion of a fusion of races in America was as old as Hector Crevecoeur and Thomas Jefferson. It was dramatized with sensational effect in Israel Zangwill's play *The Melting-pot*, which was the New York hit of 1908. The new motion-picture industry, which was from its inception the epitome of multi-racialism, was obsessed by the idea, as many of its early epics testify. But with what proportions of ingredients should the pot be filled? By the time of the Great War, unrestricted immigration already appeared a lost cause. In 1915 an itinerant Georgian minister, William Simmons, founded the Ku Klux Klan as an organization to control minority groups which it identified with moral and political nonconformity. Its aims were powerfully assisted by the publication, the following year, of Madison Grant's presentation, in an American context, of European 'master-race' theory, *The Passing of the Great Race*. This quasi-scientific best-seller argued that America, by unrestricted immigration, had already nearly 'succeeded in destroying the privilege of birth; that is, the intellectual and moral advantages a man of good stock brings into the world with him'. The result of the 'melting-pot', he argued, could be seen in Mexico, where 'the absorption of the blood of the original Spanish conquerors by the native Indian population' had produced a degenerate mixture 'now engaged in demonstrating its incapacity for self-government'. The virtues of the 'higher races' were 'highly unstable' and easily disappeared 'when mixed with generalized or primitive characters'. Thus 'the cross between a white man and a Negro is a Negro' and 'the cross between any of the three European races and a Jew is a Jew'.[2]

This fear of 'degeneration' was used by Hiram Wesley Evans, a Dallas dentist and most effective of the Klan leaders, to build it up into a movement of Anglo-Saxon supremacist culture which at one time had a reputed 4 million members in the East and Midwest. Evans, who called himself 'the most average man in America', asserted that the Klan spoke 'for the great mass of Americans of the old pioneer stock . . . of the so-called Nordic race which, with all its faults, has given the world almost the whole of modern civilization'.[3] A racial pecking-order was almost universally accepted in political campaigning, though with significant variations to account for local voting-blocks. Thus, Senator Henry Cabot Lodge, in private an unqualified Anglo-Saxon supremacist, always used the prudent code-term 'the English-speaking people' when campaigning. Will Hays, campaign manager for Warren Harding, comprehensively summed up the candidate's lineage as 'the finest pioneer blood, Anglo-Saxon, German, Scotch–Irish and Dutch'.[4]

America's entry into the Great War gave an enormous impetus to a patriotic xenophobia which became a justification for varieties of racism and a drive against nonconformity. Wilson had feared and predicted this emotional spasm – far more violent and destructive than McCarthyism after the Second World War – but he nevertheless signed the Espionage Act of 1917 and the Sedition Act of 1918. The latter punished expressions of opinion which, irrespective of their likely consequences, were 'disloyal, profane, scurrilous or abusive' of the American form of government, flag or uniform; and under it Americans were prosecuted for criticizing the Red Cross, the YMCA and even the budget.[5] Two Supreme Court judges, Justice Louis Brandeis and Oliver Wendell Holmes, sought to resist this wave of intolerance. In *Schenk* v. *United States* (1919), Holmes laid down that restraint of free speech was legal only when the words were of a nature to create 'a clear and present danger'; and, dissenting from *Abrams* v. *United States* which upheld a sedition conviction, he argued 'the best test of truth is the power of the thought to get itself accepted in the competition of the market', a rephrasing of Milton's point in *Areopagitica*.[6] But theirs were lonely voices at the time. Patriotic organizations like the National Security League and the National Civil Federation continued their activities into the peace. The watchword in 1919 was 'Americanization'.

From the autumn of 1919, with Wilson stricken, there was virtually no government in the USA, either to prevent the brief post-war boom from collapsing into the 1920 recession, or to control the xenophobic fury which was one of its consequences. The man in charge was the Attorney-General, Mitchell Palmer. He had made himself thoroughly unpopular during the war as Alien Property Controller and in spring 1919 he was nearly killed when an anarchist's bomb blew up in front of his house. Thereafter he led a nationwide drive against 'foreign-born subversives and agitators'. On 4 November 1919 he presented Congress with a report he entitled 'How the Department of Justice discovered upwards of 60,000 of these organized agitators of the Trotzky doctrine in the US ... confidential information upon which the government is now sweeping the nation clean of such alien filth.' He described 'Trotzky' as 'a disreputable alien ... this lowest of all types known to New York City [who] can sleep in the Tsar's bed while hundreds of thousands in Russia are without food or shelter'. The 'sharp tongues of the Revolution's head', he wrote, 'were licking the altars of the churches, leaping into the belfry of the school bell, crawling into the sacred corners of American homes' and 'seeking to replace marriage vows with libertine laws'.[7] On New Year's Day 1920, in a series of concerted raids, his Justice Department agents rounded up more than 6,000 aliens, most of whom were expelled. In the 'Red scare' that followed, five members of the New York State Assembly were disbarred for alleged socialism and a congressman was twice thrown out of the House of Representatives; and two Italians, Nicola Sacco and Bartolomeo Vanzetti, anarchists who had evaded military service, were convicted of murdering a Massachusetts paymaster in a highly prejudicial case which dragged on until 1927.

A more permanent consequence was the 1921 Quota law which limited immigration in any year to 3 per cent of the number of each nationality in the USA according to the census of 1910. This device, whose object was to freeze the racial balance as far as possible, was greatly tightened by the Johnson–Reed Act of 1924, which limited the quota to 2 per cent of any nationality residing in the USA in 1890. It debarred Japanese altogether (though Canadians and Mexicans were exempt) and not only cut the earlier quota but deliberately favoured Northern and Western Europe at the expense of Eastern and Southern Europe. With a further twist of the screw in 1929, based on racial analysis of the USA population in the 1920s, the legislation of the 1920s brought mass immigration to America to an end. Arcadia was full, its drawbridge up, its composition now determined and to be perpetuated.

There were plenty who criticized the new xenophobia. On 23 July 1920 Walter Lippmann wrote to his old wartime boss, the Secretary of War Newton Baker: '. . . it is forever incredible that an administration announcing the most spacious ideals in our history should have done more to endanger fundamental American liberties than any group of men for a hundred years . . . . They have instituted a reign of terror in which honest thought is impossible, in which moderation is discountenanced and in which panic supplants reason.'[8] H.L Mencken, the Baltimore publicist (himself of German origin) who was perhaps the most influential US journalist of the 1920s, called Palmer, in the *Baltimore Evening Sun*, 13 September 1920, 'perhaps the most eminent living exponent of cruelty, dishonesty and injustice'. A fortnight later he accused the Justice Department of maintaining 'a system of espionage altogether without precedent in American history, and not often matched in the history of Russia, Austria and Italy. It has, as a matter of daily routine, hounded men and women in cynical violation of their constitutional rights, invaded the sanctuary of domicile, manufactured evidence against the innocent, flooded the land with *agents provocateurs*, raised neighbor against neighbor, filled the public press with inflammatory lies and fostered all the worst poltrooneries of sneaking and malicious wretches.'[9] The sociologist Horace Kellen, of the New School for Social Research, argued that 'Americanization' was merely a recrudescence of the anti-Catholic 'Know-Nothingism' of the 1850s, a form of Protestant fundamentalism of which the 1924 Act, 'the witch-hunting of the Quaker Attorney-General Palmer, the Tsaristically-inspired Jew-baiting of the Baptist automobile-maker Ford, the malevolent mass-mummery of the Ku-Klux Klan, the racial mumblings of Mr Madesan Grant' were manifestations, along with such innocent expressions of homely patriotism as the novels of Mrs Gertrude Atherton and the *Saturday Evening Post*.[10]

There was an important point here: America, if it was anything, was a Protestant-type religious civilization, and the xenophobia of a Palmer was merely the extreme and distorted expression of all that was most valuable in the American ethic. From this time onwards, American 'highbrows' – the term, so much more appropriate than the French *intellectuel* or *intelligentsia*, had been devised by the critic Van Wyck Brooks in 1915 – had to face the dilemma that, in attacking the distortion, they were in danger of damaging the reality of 'Americanism', which sprang from Jeffersonian democracy; and if that were lost, American culture was nothing except an expatriation of Europe. While Palmer was hunting aliens, East Coast highbrows were reading *The Education of Henry Adams*, the posthumous autobiography of the archetypal Boston mandarin, which the Massachusetts Historical Society published in October 1918. From then until spring 1920 it was the most popular non-fiction book in America, perfectly expressing the mood of educated disillusionment. It was the American equivalent of Strachey's *Eminent Victorians*, rejecting the notion of a national culture – especially one imposed by brutal repression – in favour of what Adams termed 'multiversity' but pessimistically stressing that, in the emerging America, the best-educated were the most helpless.

In fact the East Coast highbrows were by no means helpless. Over the next sixty years they were to exercise an influence on American (and world) policy out of all proportion to their numbers and intrinsic worth. But they were ambivalent about America. In the spring of 1917, Van Wyck Brooks wrote in *Seven Arts*, the journal he helped to found, 'Towards a National Culture', in which he argued that hitherto America had taken the 'best' of other cultures: now it must create its own through the elementary experience of living which alone produced true culture. America, by experiencing its own dramas, through what he termed 'the Culture of Industrialism', would 'cease to be a blind, selfish, disorderly people; we shall become a luminous people, dwelling in the light and sharing our light'.[11] He endorsed his friend Randolph Bourne's view that the whole 'melting-pot' theory was unsound since it turned immigrants into imitation Anglo-Saxons, and argued that America ought to have not narrow European nationalism but 'the more adventurous ideal' of cosmopolitanism, to become 'the first international nation'.[12] But what did this mean? D.H. Lawrence rightly observed that America was not, or not yet, 'a blood-homeland'. Jung, putting it another way, said Americans were 'not yet at home in their unconscious'. Brooks, deliberately settling into Westport, Connecticut, to find his American cosmopolitanism, together with other Twenties intellectuals whom he neatly defined as 'those who care more for the state of their minds than the state of their fortunes', nevertheless felt the strong pull of the old culture; he confessed, in his autobiography, to 'a frequently acute homesickness for the European scene'. Only 'a long immersion in American life', he wrote, 'was to cure me completely of any lingering fear of expatriation; but this ambivalence characterized my outlook in the Twenties.'[13] In May 1919, hearing that a friend, Waldo Frank, planned to settle in the Middle West, he wrote to him: 'All our will-to-live as writers comes to us, or rather stays with us, through our intercourse with Europe. Never believe people who talk to you about the west, Waldo; never forget that it is we New Yorkers and New Englanders who have the monopoly of whatever oxygen there is in the American continent.'[14]

That was an arrogant claim; to echo, though not often so frankly avowed, down the decades of the twentieth century. But without the Midwest, what was America? A mere coastal fringe, like so many of the hispanic littoral-states of South America. The hate-figure of the East Coast highbrows in the Twenties was William Jennings Bryan, the Illinois Democrat who had denounced the power of money ('You shall not crucify mankind upon a cross of gold'), opposed imperialism, resigned as Secretary of State in 1915 in protest against the drift to war and, in his old age, fought a desperate rearguard action against Darwinian evolution in the 1925 Scopes trial. Fundamentally, Bryan's aims were democratic and progressive: he fought for women's suffrage and a federal income-tax and reserve-bank, for popular election to the Senate, for the publication of campaign contributions, for freeing the Philippines, and for the representation of labour in the cabinet. Yet his values were popular ones or, to use the new term of derogation, 'populist'; he spoke the language of anti-intellectualism. His wife's diaries testify to the bitterness the couple felt at the way his work was misrepresented or completely ignored in the 'Eastern press'.[15] At the Scopes trial he was not seeking to ban the teaching of evolution but to prevent state schools from undermining religious belief: evolution should, he argued, be taught as theory not fact, parents and taxpayers should have a say in what went on in the schools, and teachers should abide by the law of the land. He saw himself as resisting the aggressive dictatorship of a self-appointed scholastic élite who were claiming a monopoly of authentic knowledge.[16]

The philosopher John Dewey, while opposing the Bryan anti-evolution crusade, warned the East Coast intelligentsia that the forces it embodied 'would not be so dangerous were they not bound up with so much that is necessary and good'. He feared the idea of a fissure, which he could see opening, between the East Coast leadership of educated opinion and what a later generation would call 'middle America' or 'the silent majority'. Evolution was a mere instance of antagonistic habits of thought. In a remarkable article, 'The American Intellectual Frontier', which he published in 1922, he warned readers of the New Republic that Bryan could not be dismissed as a mere obscurantist because he 'is a typical democratic figure – there is no gainsaying that proposition'. Of course he was mediocre but 'democracy by nature puts a premium on mediocrity'. Moreover, he spoke for some of the best, and most essential, elements in American society:

... the church-going classes, those who have come under the influence of evangelical Christianity. These people form the backbone of philanthropic social interest, of social reform through political action, of pacifism, of popular education. They embody and express the spirit of kindly goodwill towards classes which are at an economic disadvantage and towards other nations, especially when the latter show any disposition towards a republican form of government. The Middle West, the prairie country, has been the centre of active social philanthropy and political progressivism because it is the chief home of this folk ... believing in education and better opportunities for its own children ... it has been the element responsive to appeals for the square deal and more nearly equal opportunities for all .... It followed Lincoln in the abolition of slavery and it followed Roosevelt in his denunciation of 'bad' corporations and aggregations of wealth .... It has been the middle in every sense of the word and of every movement.[17]

In so far as there was an indigenous American culture, this was it. Cosmopolitanism on the East Coast was thus in danger of becoming a counter-culture and involving America in the kind of internal conflict between 'culture' and 'civilization' which was tearing apart Weimar Germany and opening the gates to totalitarianism. Indeed the conflict already existed, finding its envenomed expression in the Prohibition issue. Bryan had been presented with a vast silver loving-cup in token of his prodigious efforts to secure ratification of the eighteenth 'National Prohibition' Amendment to the constitution, which made legal the Volstead Act turning America 'dry'. The Act came into effect the same month, January 1920, that Mitchell Palmer pounced on the alien anarchists, and the two events were closely related. Prohibition, with its repressive overtones, was part of the attempt to 'Americanize' America: reformers openly proclaimed that it was directed chiefly at the 'notorious drinking habits' of 'immigrant working men'.[18] Like the new quota system, it was an attempt to preserve Arcadia, to keep the Arcadians pure. America had been founded as a Utopian society, populated by what Lincoln had, half-earnestly, half-wryly, called 'an almost-chosen people'; the eighteenth Amendment was the last wholehearted effort at millennarianism.

But if wholehearted in intention, it was not so in execution. It was another testimony to the ambivalence of American society. America willed the end in ratifying the eighteenth Amendment; but it failed to will the means, for the Volstead Act was an ineffectual compromise – if it had provided ruthless means of enforcement it would never have become law. The Prohibition Bureau was attached to the Treasury; efforts to transfer it to the Justice Department were defeated. Successive presidents refused to recommend the appropriations needed to secure effective enforcement.[19] Moreover, the Utopianism inherent in Prohibition, though strongly rooted in American society, came up against the equally strongly rooted and active American principle of unrestricted freedom of enterprise. America was one of the least totalitarian societies on earth; it possessed virtually none of the apparatus to keep market forces in check once an unfulfilled need appeared.

Hence the liquor gangsters and their backers could always command more physical and financial resources than the law. Indeed they were far better organized on the whole. Prohibition illustrated the law of unintended effect. Far from driving alien minorities into Anglo-Saxon conformity, it allowed them to consolidate themselves. In New York, bootlegging was half Jewish, a quarter Italian and one-eighth each Polish and Irish.[20] In Chicago it was half Italian, half Irish. The Italians were particularly effective in distributing liquor in an orderly and inexpensive manner, drawing on the organizational experience not only of the Sicilian, Sardinian and Neapolitan secret societies but on the 'vanguard élitism' of revolutionary syndicalism. Prohibition offered matchless opportunities to subvert society, particularly in Chicago under the corrupt mayoralty of 'Big Bill' Thompson. John Torrio, who ran large-scale bootlegging in Chicago 1920–4, retiring to Italy in 1925 with a fortune of $30 million, practised the principle of total control: all officials were bribed in varying degrees and all elections rigged.[21] He could deliver high-quality beer as cheaply as $50 a barrel and his success was based on the avoidance of violence by diplomacy – in securing agreements among gangsters for the orderly assignment of territory.[22] His lieutenant and successor Al Capone was less politically minded and therefore less successful; and the Irish operators tended to think in the short term and resort to violent solutions. When this happened gang-warfare ensued, the public became indignant and the authorities were driven to intervene.

As a rule, however, bootleggers operated with public approval, at any rate in the cities. Most urban men (not women) agreed with Mencken's view that Prohibition was the work of 'ignorant bumpkins of the cow states who resented the fact they had to swill raw corn liquor while city slickers got good wine and whiskey'. It 'had little behind it, philosophically speaking, save the envy of the country lout for the city man, who has a much better time of it in this world'.[23] City enforcement was impossible, even under reforming mayors. General Smedley Butler of the US Marine Corps, put in charge of the Philadelphia police under a 'clean' new administration in 1924, was forced to give up after less than two years: the job, he said, was 'a waste of time'. Politicians of both parties gave little help to the authorities. At the 1920 Democratic Convention in San Francisco they gleefully drank the first-class whiskey provided free by the mayor, and Republicans bitterly resented the fact that, at their Cleveland Convention in 1924, prohibition agents 'clamped down on the city', according to Mencken, 'with the utmost ferocity'. Over huge areas, for most of the time, the law was generally defied. 'Even in the most remote country districts', Mencken claimed, 'there is absolutely no place in which any man who desires to drink alcohol cannot get it.'[24]

A similar pattern of non-enforcement appeared in Norway, which prohibited spirits and strong wines by a referendum of five to three in October 1919. But Norway had the sense to drop the law by a further referendum in 1926.[25] America kept Prohibition twice as long and the results were far more serious. The journalist Walter Ligget, probably the greatest expert on the subject, testified to the House Judiciary Committee in February 1930 that he had 'a truck load of detail and explicit facts' that 'there is considerably more hard liquor being drunk than there was in the days before prohibition and . . . drunk in more evil surroundings'. Washington DC had had 300 licensed saloons before Prohibition: now it had 700 speakeasies, supplied by 4,000 bootleggers. Police records showed that arrests for drunkenness had trebled over the decade. Massachusetts had jumped from 1,000 licensed saloons to 4,000 speakeasies, plus a further 4,000 in Boston: 'there are at least 15,000 people who do nothing but purvey booze illegally in the city of Boston today.' Kansas had been the first state to go dry; had been dry for half a century, yet 'there is not a town in Kansas where I cannot go as a total stranger and get a drink of liquor, and very good liquor at that, within fifteen minutes after my arrival'. All this was made possible by universal corruption at all levels. Thus, in Detroit there were 20,000 speak-easies. He continued:

There came to my attention in the city of Detroit – and this took place last November – a wild party given at a roadhouse, and a very wild party, where the liquor was donated by one of the principal gamblers of Detroit – Denny Murphy if you want his name – and there were at that drunken revel . . . the Governor of Michigan, the chief of police of Detroit, the chief of the State Police, politicians, club men, gamblers, criminals, bootleggers, all there fraternizing in the spirit of the most perfect equality under the god Bacchus, and I will say that there were four judges of the circuit of Michigan at that drunken revel, at which naked hoochy-koochy dancers appeared later . . . you find that hypocrisy today over the length and breadth of this land.[26]

As Ligget pointed out, evasion of Prohibition generated enormous funds which were reinvested in other forms of crime such as prostitution, but above all gambling, which for the first time were organized on a systematic and quasi-legitimate basis. More recent studies confirm his view that Prohibition brought about a qualitative and – as it has turned out – permanent change in the scale and sophistication of American organized crime. Running large-scale beer-convoys required powers of organization soon put to use elsewhere. In the early 1920s, for the first time, gambling syndicates used phone-banks to take bets from all over the country. Meyer Lansky and Benjamin Siegel adapted bootlegging patterns to organize huge nationwide gambling empires. Prohibition was the 'take-off point' for big crime in America; and of course it continued after the twenty-first Amendment, which ended prohibition, was ratified in December 1933. Throughout the 1930s organized crime matured, and it was from 1944 onwards, for instance, that the small desert town of Las Vegas was transformed into the world's gambling capital. Prohibition, far from 'Americanizing' minorities, tended to reinforce minority characteristics through specific patterns of crime: among Italians, Jews, Irish and, not least, among blacks, where from the early 1920s West Indians introduced the 'numbers game' and other gambling rings, forming powerful black ghetto crime-citadels in New York, Chicago, Philadelphia and Detroit.[27] Studies by the Justice Department's Law Enforcement Assistance Administration in the 1970s indicate that the beginning of Prohibition in 1920 was the starting-point for most identifiable immigrant crime-families, which continue to flourish and perpetuate themselves in our age.[28]

The truth is, Prohibition was a clumsy and half-hearted piece of social engineering, designed to produce a homogenization of a mixed community by law. It did not of course involve the enormous cruelty of Lenin's social engineering in Russia, or Mussolini's feeble imitation of it in Italy, but in its own way it inflicted the same damage to social morals and the civilized cohesion of the community. The tragedy is that it was quite unnecessary. America's entrepreneurial market system was itself an effective homogenizer, binding together and adjudicating between ethnic and racial groups without regard to colour or national origins. The way in which the enormous German and Polish immigrations, for instance, had been absorbed within an Anglo-Saxon framework, was astounding: the market had done it. Mitchell Palmer was mistaken in thinking that aliens in the mass brought radical politics. On the contrary: they were fleeing closed systems to embrace the free one. They were voting with their feet for the entrepreneurial economy.

Indeed, at the very time Palmer expected revolution to manifest itself, American radicalism, especially of a collectivist kind, was entering a period of steady decline. It had never been strong. Marx had been unable to explain why America, which, by the end of his life, had become the most powerful and inventive of the capitalist economies, showed no sign whatever of producing the conditions for the proletarian revolution which he claimed mature capitalism made inevitable. Engels sought to meet the difficulty by arguing that socialism was weak there 'just because America is so purely bourgeois, so entirely without a feudal past and therefore proud of its purely bourgeois organization'. Lenin (1908) thought that in the USA, 'the model and ideal of our bourgeois civilization', socialism had to deal with 'the most firmly established democratic systems, which confront the proletariat with purely socialist tasks'. Antonio Gramsci blamed 'Americanism', which he defined as 'pure rationalism without any of the class values derived from feudalism'. H.G. Wells in *The Future of America* (1906) attributed the absence of a powerful socialist party to the symmetrical absence of a conservative one: 'All Americans are, from the English point of view, Liberals of one sort or another.'[29]

Until the 1920s there were some grounds for thinking, however, that an American Left might eventually come to occupy a significant role in politics. In the years before 1914 the Socialist Party had about 125,000 members, who included the leaders of the mineworkers, brewery workers, carpenters and ironworkers. It elected over 1,000 public officials, including the mayors of important towns and two congressmen; in 1912 its candidate Eugene Debs got 6 per cent of the popular vote. But thereafter the decline was continuous. The Workingmen's Party had some successes in a few cities in the 1920s and early 1930s. But the mainstream socialist parties floundered. The failure of the Socialist Party itself was attributed to its inability to decide whether it was a mass political party, a pressure group, a revolutionary sect or just an educational force, attempting to be all four at the same time.[30] Even in the desperate year 1932 Norman Thomas got only 2 per cent of the presidential vote. The Communist Party equally failed to become a new expression of American radicalism and became a mere US appendage of Soviet policy.[31] Its highest score was the 1,150,000 it helped to collect for Henry Wallace, the Progressive candidate, in 1948. During the next thirty years the decline continued. In the 1976 election, for instance, the Socialists and five other radical parties fielded candidates; none polled as many as 100,000 out of a total of 80 million votes: added together they got less than a quarter of 1 per cent of votes cast. By the beginning of the 1980s the United States was the only democratic industrialized nation in which not a single independent socialist or labour party representative held elective office.

This pattern was adumbrated by the politics of the 1920s. Whereas in Britain, Austria, France, Germany, Spain and the Scandinavian countries, Social Democratic parties became the principal opposition parties or even formed or participated in governments, in the USA the decade was a Republican one. The Republican Party was, of course, the party of Lincoln, which had emancipated the slaves and won the Civil War. Blacks, who poured into Northern cities during the First World War and after, still voted Republican in overwhelming numbers. It had also been the party of Theodore Roosevelt and progressive capital. But it was, at the same time, the party of social conservatism and free market economics. In the 1920s its mastery was overwhelming. Between 1920 and 1932, Republicans controlled the White House and the Senate for the whole time and the House except for the years 1930–2.[32] Warren Harding in 1920 got 60.2 per cent, the largest popular majority yet recorded (16,152,000 to 9,147,000), carrying every state outside the South. The Republicans took the House by 303 to 131 and won ten Senate seats to give them a majority of twenty-two.[33] In 1924 Calvin Coolidge won by 15,725,000 votes to a mere 8,386,000 for his Democrat rival, John W. Davis. In 1928 Herbert Hoover won by 21,391,000 votes to 15,016,000 for Al Smith, a landslide electoral college victory of 444 to 87; he carried all but two Northern states and five in the 'Solid South'. The Socialists polled less than 300,000, the Communists under 50,000.[34]

These repeated successes indicated what Coolidge called 'a state of contentment seldom before seen', a marriage between a democratic people and its government, and the economic system the governing party upheld and epitomized, which is very rare in history and worth examining. In order to do so effectively it is necessary to probe beneath the conventional historiography of the period, especially as it revolves round its two key figures, Harding and Coolidge.

Harding won the election on his fifty-fifth birthday, which, characteristically, he celebrated by playing a round of golf. He did not believe that politics were very important or that people should get excited about them or allow them to penetrate too far into their everyday lives. In short he was the exact opposite of Lenin, Mussolini and Hitler, and the professional Social Democratic politicians of Europe. He came from Ohio, the Republican political heartland, which had produced six out of ten presidents since 1865. He had emerged from poverty to create a successful small-town paper, the *Marion Star*, and had then become director of a bank, a phone company, a lumber firm and a building society. He was decent, small-town America in person: a handsome man, always genial and friendly, but dignified. He was not above answering the White House front door in person, and he always took a horse-ride on Sunday. He told a cheering crowd in Boston in May 1920: 'America's present need is not heroics but healing, not nostrums but normalcy; not

revolution but restoration . . . not surgery but serenity.'[35] America as
Arcadia was a reality to him; somehow, he wished to preserve it. To
get elected, he stuck old President McKinley's flagpole in front of his
house and ran a 'front porch' campaign. Many famous people made
the pilgrimage to Marion to listen to his campaign talk, Al Jolson,
Ethel Barrymore, Lillian Gish, Pearl White among them, but 600,000
ordinary folk too, thousands of them black – hence the Democrat
rumour that Harding had negro blood. Everybody liked Harding. The
worst thing about him was his sharp-faced wife, Flossie, known as
'the Duchess', of whom Harding said (not in her hearing), 'Mrs
Harding wants to be the drum-major in every band that passes'.[36]

Harding believed that America's matchless society was the creation of voluntarism and that only government could spoil it. If he
could plant a Rotary Club in every city and hamlet, he said, he would
'rest assured that our ideals of freedom would be safe and civilization
would progress'. That was a general view. 'There is only one
first-class civilization in the world', wrote the *Ladies' Home Journal*.
'It is right here in the United States.' That was also the view of most
American intellectuals, to judge not by their subsequent rationaliza-
tions in the Thirties but by what they actually wrote at the time. The
same month Harding signed the 1921 Immigration Act, Scott
Fitzgerald was writing to Edmund Wilson from London:

God damn the continent of Europe. It is of merely antiquarian interest.
Rome is only a few years behind Tyre and Babylon. The negroid streak
creeps northward to defile the Nordic race. Already the Italians have the
souls of blackamoors. Raise the bar of immigration and permit only
Scandinavians, Teutons, Anglo-Saxons and Celts to enter. France made me
sick. Its silly pose as the thing the world has to save . . . . I believe at last in
the white man's burden. We are as far above the modern Frenchman as he is
above the Negro. Even in art! Italy has no one . . . . They're thru and done.
You may have spoken in jest about New York as the capital of culture but
in 25 years it will be just as London is now. Culture follows money . . . . We
will be the Romans in the next generations as the English are now.[37]

Harding believed this cultural supremacy would arise inevitably
provided government allowed the wheels of free enterprise to turn.
Far from selecting cronies from 'the buck-eye state' (as later alleged),
he formed a cabinet of strong men: Charles Evans Hughes as
Secretary of State, Andrew Mellon at the Treasury, Hoover at
Commerce. He hurried with his cabinet list straight to the Senate,
and his choice for the Department of the Interior, Albert Fall,
Senator for New Mexico, sported a handle-bar moustache and wore
a flowing black cape and broad-brimmed stetson – normalcy itself! –
was so popular he was confirmed by immediate acclamation, the

only time in American history a cabinet member has been accorded such a vote of confidence.[38] The cabinet list was a cross-section of successful America: a car manufacturer, two bankers, a hotel director, a farm-journal editor, an international lawyer, a rancher, an engineer and only two professional politicians.

Harding inherited an absentee presidency and one of the sharpest recessions in American history. By July 1921 it was all over and the economy was booming again. Harding had done nothing except cut government expenditure, the last time a major industrial power treated a recession by classic *laissez-faire* methods, allowing wages to fall to their natural level. Benjamin Anderson of Chase Manhattan was later to call it 'our last natural recovery to full employment'.[39] But the cuts were important. Indeed, Harding can be described as the only president in American history who actually brought about massive cuts in government spending, producing nearly a 40 per cent saving over Wilsonian peacetime expenditure.[40] Nor was this a wild assault. It was part of a considered plan which included the creation of the Bureau of the Budget, under the Budget and Accounting Act of 1921, to bring authorizations under systematic central scrutiny and control. Its first director, Charles Dawes, said in 1922 that, before Harding, 'everyone did as they damn pleased'; cabinet members were 'commanchees', Congress 'a nest of cowards'. Then Harding 'waved the axe and said that anybody who didn't co-operate his head would come off'; the result was 'velvet for the taxpayer'.[41]

Harding's regime was agreeably liberal. Against the advice of his cabinet and his wife he insisted on releasing the Socialist leader Eugene Debs, whom Wilson had imprisoned, on Christmas Eve 1921: 'I want him to eat his Christmas dinner with his wife.' He freed twenty-three other political prisoners the same day, commuted death-sentences on the 'Wobblies' (Industrial Workers of the World) and before the end of his presidency had virtually cleared the gaols of political offenders.[42] He took the press into his confidence, calling reporters by their Christian names. When he moved, he liked to surround himself with a vast travelling 'family', many invited on the spur of the moment, occupying ten whole cars on his presidential train. He chewed tobacco, one of his chewing companions being Thomas Edison, who remarked, 'Harding is all right. Any man who chews tobacco is all right.' He drank hard liquor too, asking people up to his bedroom for a snort, and it was known he served whiskey in the White House. Twice a week he invited his intimates over for 'food and action' ('action' meant poker). Commerce Secretary Hoover, a stuffed shirt, was the only one who declined to play: 'It irks me to see it in the White House.'[43]

Hoover's instinct was correct: a president cannot be too careful, as had been demonstrated in virtually every presidency since. There is no evidence that Harding was ever anything other than a generous and unsuspicious man. The only specific charge of dishonesty brought against him was that the sale of the *Marion Star* was a fix; this was decisively refuted in court, the two men who bought the paper receiving $100,000 in damages. But Harding made two errors of judgement: appointing the florid Senator Fall, who turned out to be a scoundrel, and believing that his Ohio campaign-manager Harry Daugherty, whom he made Attorney-General, would screen and protect him from the influence-peddlars who swarmed up from his home state. 'I know who the crooks are and I want to stand between Harding and them,' Daugherty said. This proved an empty boast.[44]

The result was a series of blows which came in quick succession from early 1923. In February Harding discovered that Charles Forbes, Director of the Veterans Bureau, had been selling off government medical supplies at rock-low prices: he summoned him to the White House, shook him 'as a dog would a rat' and shouted 'You double-crossing bastard'. Forbes fled to Europe and resigned, 15 February.[45] On 4 March Albert Fall resigned. It was subsequently established that he had received a total of $400,000 in return for granting favourable leases of government oilfields at Elk Hills in California and Salt Creek (Teapot Dome), Wyoming. Fall was eventually gaoled for a year in 1929, though his leases later turned out well for America, since they involved building vital pipelines and installations at Pearl Harbor.[46] But that was not apparent at the time and Fall's departure was a disaster for Harding, more particularly since Charles Cramer, counsel for the Veterans Bureau, committed suicide a few days later.

Finally on 29 May Harding forced himself to see a crony of Daugherty's, Jess Smith, who together with other Ohians had been selling government favours from what became known as 'the little green house [no. 1625] on K Street'. The 'Ohio Gang', as the group was soon called, had nothing to do with Harding and it was never legally established that even Daugherty shared their loot (he was acquitted when tried in 1926–7, though he refused to take the stand). But after Harding confronted Smith with his crimes on 29 May, the wretched man shot himself the following day and this second suicide had a deplorable effect on the President's morale. According to William Allen White (not a wholly reliable witness), Harding told him, 'I can take care of my enemies all right. But my damn friends, my God-damn friends, White, they're the ones that keep me walking the floors nights.' Given time, Harding would certainly have managed to stabilize the situation and refute the rumours of guilt by association – as have several presidents since – for his own hands were completely clean, so far as the latest historical research has been able to establish. But the following month he left for a trip to Alaska and the West Coast and he died, of a cerebral haemorrhage, at the Palace Hotel, San Francisco, in early August. His wife followed him in November 1924 having first destroyed (so it was then believed) all Harding's papers, and this was taken as conclusive evidence of guilty secrets.[47]

The false historiography which presented Harding and his administration as the most corrupt in American history began almost immediately with the publication in 1924 in the *New Republic* of a series of articles by its violently anti-business editor, Bruce Bliven. This created the basic mythology of the 'Ohio Gang', run by Daugherty, who had deliberately recruited Harding as a front man as long ago as 1912 as part of a long-term conspiracy to hand over the entire nation to Andrew Mellon and Big Business. Thereafter Harding was fair game for sensationalists. In 1927 Nan Britton, daughter of a Marion doctor, published *The President's Daughter*, claiming she had had a baby girl by Harding in 1919. In 1928 William Allen White repeated the conspiracy theory in *Masks in a Pageant* and again ten years later in his life of Coolidge, *A Puritan in Babylon*. In 1930 a former FBI agent, Gaston Means, produced the best-selling *The Strange Death of President Harding*, portraying wholly imaginary drunken orgies with chorus girls at the K Street house, with Harding prominent in the 'action'. Equally damaging was the 1933 memoir *Crowded Hours*, by Theodore Roosevelt's daughter, Alice Roosevelt Longworth, which presented Harding's White House study as a speakeasy: 'the air heavy with tobacco smoke, trays with bottles containing every imaginable brand of whisky stood about, cards and poker chips ready at hand – a general atmosphere of waistcoat unbuttoned, feet on the desk and the spittoon alongside . . . . Harding was not a bad man. He was just a slob.'[48] To cap it all came an apparently scholarly work by a *New York Sun* writer, Samuel Hopkins Adams, called *Incredible Era: the Life and Times of Warren Gamaliel Harding* (1939), which welded together all the inventions and myths into a solid orthodoxy. By this time the notion of Harding as the criminal king of the Golden Calf era had become the received version of events not only in popular books like Frederick Lewis Allen's *Only Yesterday* . . . (1931) but in standard academic history. When in 1964 the Harding Papers (which had not been burnt) were opened to scholars, no truth at all was found in any of the myths, though it emerged that Harding, a pathetically shy man with women, had had a sad and touching friendship with the wife of a Marion store-owner before his presidency. The Babylonian image was a fantasy, and in all essentials Harding had been an honest and exceptionally shrewd president. But by then it was too late. A *New York Times* poll of seventy-five historians in 1962 showed that he was rated 'a flat failure' with 'very little dissent'.[49]

The treatment of Harding is worth dwelling on because, taken in conjunction with a similar denigration of his vice-president and successor Calvin Coolidge, a man of totally different temperament, it amounts to the systematic misrepresentation of public policy over a whole era. Coolidge was the most internally consistent and single-minded of modern American presidents. If Harding loved America as Arcadia, Coolidge was the best-equipped to preserve it as such. He came from the austere hills of Vermont, of the original Puritan New England stock, and was born over his father's store. No public man carried into modern times more comprehensively the founding principles of Americanism: hard work, frugality, freedom of conscience, freedom from government, respect for serious culture (he went to Amherst, and was exceptionally well-read in classical and foreign literature and in history). He was sharp, hatchet-faced, 'weaned on a pickle' (Alice Longworth), a 'runty, aloof little man, who quacks through his nose when he speaks . . . he slapped no man on the back, pawed no man's shoulder, squeezed no man's hand' (William Allen White).[50] He married a beautiful, raven-haired schoolteacher called Grace, about whom no one ever said a critical word. During their courtship he translated Dante's *Inferno* into English but immediately after the wedding ceremony he presented her with a bag of fifty-two pairs of socks that needed darning. He always saved his money. As Harding's vice-president he lived in four rooms in Willard's Hotel and gladly accepted the role as the Administration's official diner-out – 'Got to eat somewhere.' He ran the White House down to the smallest detail (rather like Curzon, but much more efficiently), scrutinizing and initialling all household bills, and prowling round the deepest recesses of the kitchens. He banked his salary and by 1928 had $250,000 invested.[51] He went to bed at ten, a point celebrated by Groucho Marx in *Animal Crackers*: 'Isn't it past your bedtime, Calvin?'. But the notion propagated by Mencken – 'He slept more than any other president, whether by day or by night. Nero fiddled but Coolidge only snored' – was misleading.[52] No president was ever better briefed on anything that mattered or less often caught unprepared by events or the doings of his team.

It suited Coolidge, in fact, to mislead people into believing he was less sophisticated and active than he was (a ploy later imitated by Dwight Eisenhower). 'A natural churchwarden in a rural parish,' wrote Harold Laski, 'who has by accident strayed into great affairs.'[53] That was exactly the impression Coolidge wished to convey. In fact few men have been better prepared for the presidency, moving up every rung of the public ladder: parish councillor, assemblyman, mayor, State Representative, State Senator, President of the State Senate, Lieutenant-Governor, Governor, Vice-President. At every stage he insisted that government should do as little as was necessary ('He didn't do anything', remarked the political comic Will Rogers, 'but that's what the people wanted done').[54] But he also insisted that, when it did act, it should be absolutely decisive. He made his national reputation in 1919 by crushing the Boston police strike: 'There is no right to strike against the public safety by anybody, anywhere, anytime.' He was elected Vice-President under the slogan 'Law and Order', and President with the messages 'Keep Cool with Coolidge', 'Coolidge or Chaos' and 'The chief business of the American people is business'. He articulated a generally held belief that the function of government is primarily to create a climate in which agriculture, manufacturing and commerce can seize the opportunities which God and nature provide. At the climax of his campaign for the presidency in 1924 a deputation of America's most successful men of affairs, led by Henry Ford, Harvey Firestone and Thomas Edison, called at his house. Edison, who as the world's best-known inventor acted as spokesman, told the crowd outside, 'The United States is lucky to have Calvin Coolidge.'[55] He won this and all his other contests handsomely, most of them by landslides.

Coolidge reflected America's Arcadian separateness during the 1920s by showing that, in deliberate contrast to the strident activism taking over so much of Europe and driven by the idea that political motion had replaced religious piety as the obvious form of moral worth, it was still possible to practise successfully the archaic virtue of *stasis*. Coolidge believed that all activity – above all of government – not dictated by pressing necessity was likely to produce undesirable results and certainly unforeseen ones. His minimalism extended even, indeed especially, to speech. It was said that he and his father, Colonel Coolidge, communicated 'by little more than the ugh-ugh of the Indian'.[56] He rejoiced in his nickname 'Silent Cal'. 'The Coolidges never slop over', he boasted. His advice as president to the Massachusetts senate was: 'Be brief. Above all, be brief.' Taking over the White House, he settled the 'Ohio Gang' scandals by acting very fast, appointing special counsel and by saying as little as possible himself. Campaigning in 1924, he noted: 'I don't recall any candidate for president that ever injured himself very much by not talking.'[57] 'The things I never say never get me into trouble', he remarked. In his *Autobiography*, he said his most important rule 'consists in never doing anything that someone else can do for you'. Nine-tenths of a president's callers at the White

House, he stressed, 'want something they ought not to have. If you keep dead still they will run out in three or four minutes.'[58]

Coolidge was as successful in handling the press as Harding but for quite different reasons. Not only did he keep no press secretary and refuse to hold on-the-record press conferences; he resented it if journalists addressed any remarks to him, even 'Good morning'. But if written questions were submitted in advance to his forbidding factotum, C. Bascom Slemp, he would write the answers himself: short, very dry, but informative and truthful.[59] The press liked his dependability, flavoured by eccentric habits: he used to get his valet to rub his hair with vaseline and, in the Oval Office, he would sometimes summon his staff by bell and then hide under his desk, observing their mystification with his curious wry detachment. Journalists also sensed he was wholly uncorrupted by power. On 2 August 1927, he summoned thirty of them, told them, 'The line forms on the left', and handed each a two-by-nine-inch slip of paper on which he had typed: 'I do not choose to run for President in 1928.' His final departure from the White House was characteristic. 'Perhaps one of the most important accomplishments of my administration', he snapped at the press, 'has been minding my own business.'[60]

Yet if Coolidge was sparing of words, what he did say was always pithy and clear, showing that he had reflected deeply on history and developed a considered, if sombre, public philosophy. No one in the twentieth century, not even his eloquent contemporary F.E. Smith, Earl of Birkenhead, defined more elegantly the limitations of government and the need for individual endeavour, which necessarily involved inequalities, to advance human happiness. 'Government cannot relieve from toil', he told the Massachusetts senate in 1914. 'The normal must take care of themselves. Self-government means self-support . . . . Ultimately, property rights and personal rights are the same thing . . . . History reveals no civilized people among whom there was not a highly educated class and large aggregations of wealth. Large profits means large payrolls. Inspiration has always come from above.'[61] Political morality, he insisted, must always be judged not by intentions but by effects: 'Economy is idealism in its most practical form', was the key sentence in his 1925 Inaugural. In an address to the New York chamber of commerce on 19 November that year he gave in lucid and lapidary form perhaps the last classic statement of *laissez-faire* philosophy. Government and business should remain independent and separate. It was very desirable indeed that one should be directed from Washington, the other from New York. Wise and prudent men must always prevent the mutual usurpations which foolish or greedy men sought on either side.

Business was the pursuit of gain but it also had a moral purpose: 'the mutual organized effort of society to minister to the economic requirement of civilization . . . . It rests squarely on the law of service. It has for its main reliance truth and faith and justice. In its larger sense it is one of the greatest contributing forces to the moral and spiritual advancement of the race.' That was why government had a warrant to promote its success by providing the conditions of competition within a framework of security. Its job was to suppress privilege wherever it manifested itself and uphold lawful possession by providing legal remedies for all wrongs: 'The prime element in the value of all property is the knowledge that its peaceful enjoyment will be publicly defended.' Without this legal and public defence 'the value of your tall buildings would shrink to the price of the waterfront of old Carthage or corner-lots in ancient Babylon'. The more business regulated itself, the less need there would be for government to act to ensure competition; it could therefore concentrate on its twin task of economy and of improving the national structure within which business could increase profits and investment, raise wages and provide better goods and services at the lowest possible prices.[62]

This public philosophy appeared to possess a degree of concordance with the actual facts of life which was rare in human experience. Under Harding and still more under Coolidge, the USA enjoyed a general prosperity which was historically unique in its experience or that of any other society. When the decade was over, and the prosperity had been, for the moment, wholly eclipsed, it was seen retrospectively, especially by writers and intellectuals, as grossly materialistic, febrile, philistine, and at the same time insubstantial and ephemeral, unmerited by any solid human accomplishment. The judgemental images were biblical: of a grotesque Belshazzar's Feast before catastrophe. 'The New Generation had matured,' Scott Fitzgerald wrote in 1931, 'to find all gods dead, all wars fought, all faiths in man shaken; all they knew was that America was going on the greatest, gaudiest spree in history.'[63] Edmund Wilson saw the Twenties as an aberration in the basic seriousness of the American conscience: 'the fireworks of the Twenties were in the nature of a drunken fiesta'.[64] In *The Epic of America*, published in 1931, James Truslow Adams summed it up: 'Having surrendered idealism for the sake of prosperity, the "practical men" bankrupted us on both of them.'[65] There were indeed some intellectuals who felt the whole attempt to spread general prosperity was misconceived and certain to invoke destruction. Michael Rostovtzeff, then finishing his monumental history of the economy of antiquity, asked: 'Is it possible to extend a higher civilization to the lower classes without debasing its standard and diluting its quality to the vanishing point? Is not every civilization bound to decay as soon as it begins to penetrate the masses?'[66]

But the view that the 1920s was a drunken spree destructive of civilized values can be substantiated only by the systematic distortion or denial of the historical record. The prosperity was very widespread and very solid. It was not universal: in the farming community particularly it was patchy, and it largely excluded certain older industrial communities, such as the textile trade of New England.[67] But it was more widely distributed than had been possible in any community of this size before, and it involved the acquisition, by tens of millions, of the elements of economic security which had hitherto been denied them throughout the whole of history. The growth was spectacular. On a 1933–8 index of 100, it was 58 in 1921 and passed 110 in 1929. That involved an increase in national income from $59.4 to $87.2 billion in eight years, with real *per capita* income rising from $522 to $716: not Babylonian luxury but a modest comfort never hitherto possible.[68] The expansion expressed itself not merely in spending and credit. For the first time, many millions of working people acquired insurance (life and industrial insurance policies passed the 100 million mark in the 1920s), savings, which quadrupled during the decade, and a stake in industry. Thus, an analysis of those buying fifty shares or more in one of the biggest public utility stock issues of the 1920s shows that the largest groups were (in order): housekeepers, clerks, factory workers, merchants, chauffeurs and drivers, electricians, mechanics and foremen.[69] The Twenties was also characterized by the biggest and longest building-boom: as early as 1924 some 11 million families had acquired their own homes.

The heart of the consumer boom was in personal transport, which in a vast country, where some of the new cities were already thirty miles across, was not a luxury. At the beginning of 1914, 1,258,062 cars had been registered in the USA, which produced 569,054 during the year. Production rose to 5,621,715 in 1929, by which time cars registered in the USA totalled 26,501,443, five-sixths of the world production and one car for every five people in the country. This gives some idea of America's global industrial dominance. In 1924 the four leading European car producers turned out only 11 per cent of the vehicles manufactured in the USA. Even by the end of the decade European registrations were only 20 per cent of the US level and production a mere 13 per cent.[70] The meaning of these figures was that the working class as a whole was acquiring the individual freedom of medium- and long-distance movement hitherto limited to a section of the middle class. Meanwhile, though rail was in decline, the numbers carried falling from 1,269 million in 1920 to 786 million in 1929, the middle class was moving into air travel: air passengers rose from 49,713 in 1928 to 417,505 in 1930 (by 1940 the figure was 3,185,278, and nearly 8 million by 1945).[71] What the Twenties demonstrates was the relative speed with which industrial productivity could transform luxuries into necessities and spread them down the class pyramid.

Indeed, to a growing extent it was a dissolvent of class and other barriers. Next to cars, it was the new electrical industry which fuelled Twenties prosperity. Expenditure on radios rose from a mere $10,648,000 in 1920 to $411,637,000 in 1929, and total electrical products tripled in the decade to $2.4 billion.[72] First the mass radio audience, signalled by the new phenomenon of 'fan mail' in autumn 1923, then regular attendance, especially by young people, at the movies (from 1927 the talkies) brought about the Americanization of immigrant communities and a new classlessness in dress, speech and attitudes which government policy, under Wilson, had been power-less to effect and which Harding and Coolidge wisely forwent. Sinclair Lewis, revisiting 'Main Street' for the *Nation* in 1924, described two working-class, small-town girls wearing 'well-cut skirts, silk stockings, such shoes as can be bought nowhere in Europe, quiet blouses, bobbed hair, charming straw hats, and easily cynical expressions terrifying to an awkward man'. One of them served hash. 'Both their dads are Bohemian; old mossbacks, tough old birds with whiskers that can't sling more English than a muskrat. And yet in one generation, here's their kids – real queens.'[73]

Such young people identified with movie-stars; for them, movies were a force of liberation, children from parents, wives from husbands. A motion-picture research survey quoted one seventeen-year-old: 'Movies are a godsend, and to express my sentiments long may they live and long may they stay in the land of the free and the home of the brave.' Another: 'I began smoking after watching Dolores Costella.'[74] Smoking was then seen as progressive and liberating, specially for women; and healthy – 'Reach for a Lucky instead of a sweet'; 'slenderize in a Sensible Way'. Advertising was a window into liberation too, especially for women of immigrant families. It educated them in the possibilities of life. The Twenties in America marked the biggest advances for women of any decade, before or since. By 1930 there were 10,546,000 women 'gainfully employed' outside the home: the largest number, as before, were in domestic/personal service (3,483,000) but there were now nearly 2 million in clerical work, 1,860,000 in manufacturing and, most encouraging of all, 1,226,000 in the professions.[75] Equally signifi-cant, and culturally more important, were the liberated housewives, the 'Blondies', to whom their appliances, cars and husbands' high wages had brought leisure for the first time. Writing on 'The New Status of Women' in 1931, Mary Ross epitomized the Blondies 'raised . . . above the need for economic activity':

They raise their children – one, two, occasionally three or four of them – with a care probably unknown to any past generation. It is they who founded the great culture-club movement . . . they who spend the great American income, sustain the movie industry, buy or borrow the novels, support the fashions and the beauty-culture businesses, keep bridge and travel and medical cults at high levels of activity and help along the two-car-family standard. Out of this sudden burst of female leisure have come many good things, much of the foundation of American philanthropy for example.[76]

The coming of family affluence was one factor in the decline of radical politics and their union base. A 1929 survey quoted a union organizer: 'The Ford car has done an awful lot of harm to the unions here and everywhere else. As long as men have enough money to buy a second-hand Ford and tires and gasoline, they'll be out on the road and paying no attention to union meetings.'[77] In 1915, 1921 and 1922 the unions lost three key Supreme Court actions, and their 1919 strikes were disastrous failures. American Federation of Labor membership dropped from a high-point of 4,078,740 in 1920 to 2,532,261 in 1932. 'Welfare capitalism' provided company sports facilities, holidays with pay, insurance and pension schemes, so that by 1927 4,700,000 workers were covered by group insurance and 1,400,000 were members of company unions.[79] The American worker appeared to be on the threshold of a hitherto unimaginable bourgeois existence of personal provision and responsibility which made collective action increasingly superfluous.

This was, as might have been expected, linked to a cultural liberation which belied the accusations of philistinism hurled (later, rather than at the time) at the Coolidge era. Perhaps the most important single development of the age was the spread of education. Between 1910 and 1930 total educational spending rose fourfold, from $426.25 million to $2.3 billion; higher education spending increased fourfold too, to nearly one billion a year. Illiteracy fell during the period from 7.7 to 4.3 per cent. The Twenties was the age of the Book of the Month Club and the Literary Guild; more new books were bought than ever before but there was a persistent devotion to the classics. Throughout the Twenties, *David Copperfield* was rated America's favourite novel, and among those voted 'the ten greatest men in history' were Shakespeare, Dickens, Tennyson and Longfellow.[80] Jazz Age it may have been but by the end of the decade there were 35,000 youth orchestras in the nation. The decade was marked

both by the historical conservation movement which restored colonial Williamsburg and the collection of contemporary painting which
created the Museum of Modern Art in 1929.[81]

The truth is the Twenties was the most fortunate decade in
American history, even more fortunate than the equally prosperous
1950s decade, because in the Twenties the national cohesion brought
about by relative affluence, the sudden cultural density and the
expressive originality of 'Americanism' were new and exciting. In
1927 André Siegfried, the French academician, published *America
Comes of Age*, in which he argued that 'as a result of the revolutionary changes brought about by modern methods of production . . . the
American people are now creating on a vast scale an entirely original
social structure'. The point might have brought a wry response from
Henry James, who had died eleven years before. In 1878 he had
written a little biography of Hawthorne which contained a celebrated and (to Americans) highly offensive passage listing all the
'items of high civilization, as it exists in other countries, which are
absent from the texture of American life' and which — so he argued —
supplied the rich social texture essential to the writing of imaginative
literature. America had, he enumerated,

No sovereign, no court, no personal loyalty, no aristocracy, no church, no
clergy, no army, no diplomatic service, no country gentlemen, no palaces,
no castles, nor manors, nor old country-houses, nor parsonages, nor
thatched cottages, nor ivied ruins; no cathedrals, nor abbeys, nor Norman
churches; no great Universities, nor public schools — no Oxford, nor Eton,
nor Harrow; no literature, no novels, no museums, no pictures, no political
society, no sporting class — no Epsom nor Ascot![82]

By the end of the Twenties America had achieved the social depth
and complexity whose absence James had mourned, and achieved it
moreover through what Hawthorne himself dismissed as the 'commonplace prosperity' of American life.[83] But it was prosperity on an
unprecedented and monumental scale, such as to constitute a social
phenomenon in itself, and bring in its train for the first time a
national literary universe of its own. The decade was introduced by
F. Scott Fitzgerald's *This Side of Paradise* (1918) and it ended with *A
Farewell to Arms* (1929) by Ernest Hemingway, who was to prove
the most influential writer of fiction in English between the wars. It
included Sinclair Lewis's *Main Street* (1920), John Dos Passos's
Three Soldiers (1921), Theodore Dreiser's *An American Tragedy*
(1926), William Faulkner's *Soldier's Pay* (1926), Upton Sinclair's
Boston (1928) and Thomas Wolfe's *Look Homeward, Angel* (1929).
The emergence of this galaxy of novels, and of playwrights like Eugene
O'Neill and Thornton Wilder, was evidence, as Lionel Trilling put it,

that 'life in America has increasingly thickened since the nineteenth century', producing not so much the 'social observation' James required of a novel but an 'intense social awareness', so that 'our present definition of a serious book is one which holds before us an image of society to consider and condemn'.[84]

This growing tendency of American culture to dispense with its umbilical source of supply from Europe began in the 1920s to produce forms of expression which were *sui generis*, not merely in cinema and radio broadcasting, where specific American contributions were present at the creation, but on the stage. The most spectacular maturing of the decade was the New York musical. It was the progeny, to be sure, of the Viennese operetta, the French boulevard music-play, English Gilbert and Sullivan comic operas and the English music-hall (its origins might be traced back, perhaps, to *The Beggar's Opera* of 1728) but the ingredients of American minstrel-show, burlesque, jazz and vaudeville transformed it into a completely new form of popular art. There had been prolific composers in the proto-genre before 1914, notably Irving Berlin and Jerome Kern. But their work then seemed so marginal and fugitive that some of Kern's earliest and best songs have disappeared without leaving any copy.[85] It was in the early Twenties that the spectacular new prosperity of the Broadway theatres combined with the new talents – George Gershwin, Richard Rodgers, Howard Dietz, Cole Porter, Vincent Youmans, Oscar Hammerstein, Lorenz Hart and E. Y. Harburg – to bring the American musical into full flower. On 12 February 1924 Gershwin's *Rhapsody in Blue* was performed by the Paul Whiteman band at the Aeolian Hall. It was the archetypal creative event of the decade. And that season, just after Coolidge had got himself elected in his own right, Gershwin's *Lady, Be Good!*, the first mature American musical, opened on 1 December in the Liberty Theatre, starring Fred Astaire and his sister Adele.[86] It was the outstanding event of a Broadway season which included Youmans' *Lollypop*, Kern's *Sitting Pretty*, Rudolph Friml's and Sigmund Romberg's *The Student Prince*, Irving Berlin's *Music Box Revue* and Sissie and Blake's *Chocolate Dandies* – among about forty musicals – as well as Marc Connelly's *Green Pastures*, Aaron Copland's First Symphony and the arrival of Serge Koussevitsky at the Boston Symphony Orchestra. Indeed, with the possible exception of Weimar Germany, the America of Coolidge prosperity was the leading theatre of western culture at this time, the place where the native creator had the widest range of opportunities and where the expatriate artist was most likely to find the freedom, the means and the security to express himself.

The trouble with Twenties expansion was not that it was philistine or socially immoral. The trouble was that it was transient. Had it endured, carrying with it in its train the less robust but still (at that time) striving economies of Europe, a global political transformation must have followed which would have rolled back the new forces of totalitarian compulsion, with their ruinous belief in social engineering, and gradually replaced them with a relationship between government and enterprise closer to that which Coolidge outlined to the business paladins of New York City. In 1929 the United States had achieved a position of paramountcy in total world production never hitherto attained during a period of prosperity by any single state: 34.4 per cent of the whole, compared with Britain's 10.4, Germany's 10.3, Russia's 9.9, France's 5.0, Japan's 4.0, 2.5 for Italy, 2.2 for Canada and 1.7 for Poland. The likelihood that the European continent would lean towards America's 'original social structure', as Siegfried termed it, increased with every year the world economy remained buoyant. Granted another decade of prosperity on this scale our account of modern times would have been vastly different and immeasurably happier.

On 4 December 1928 Coolidge gave his last public message to the new Congress:

No Congress of the United States ever assembled, on surveying the state of the Union, has met with a more pleasing prospect .... The great wealth created by our enterprise and industry, and saved by our economy, has had the widest distribution among our own people, and has gone out in a steady stream to serve the charity and business of the world. The requirements of existence have passed beyond the standard of necessity into the region of luxury. Enlarging production is consumed by an increasing demand at home and an expanding commerce abroad. The country can regard the present with satisfaction and anticipate the future with optimism.[87]

This view was not the flatulent self-congratulation of a successful politician. Nor was it only the view of the business community. It was shared by intellectuals across the whole spectrum. Charles Beard's *The Rise of American Civilization*, published in 1927, saw the country 'moving from one technological triumph to another, overcoming the exhaustion of crude natural resources and energies, effecting an ever-widening distribution of the blessings of civilization – health, security, material goods, knowledge, leisure and aesthetic appreciation . . . .'[88] Writing the same year, Walter Lippmann considered: 'The more or less unconscious and unplanned activities of businessmen are for once more novel, more daring and in a sense more revolutionary, than the theories of the progressives.'[89] John Dewey, in 1929, thought the problem was not how to prolong prosperity – he took that for granted – but how to turn 'the Great Society' into 'the Great Community'.[90] Even on the Left the feeling spread that perhaps business had got it right after all. Lincoln

Steffens, writing in February 1929, felt that both the USA and the Soviet systems might be justified: 'The race is saved one way or the other and, I think, both ways.'[91] In 1929 the *Nation* began a three-month series on the permanence of prosperity, drawing attention to pockets of Americans who had not yet shared in it; the opening article appeared on 23 October, coinciding with the first big break in the market.

It may be that Coolidge himself, a constitutionally suspicious man, and not one to believe easily that permanent contentment is to be found this side of eternity, was more sceptical than anyone else, and certainly less sanguine than he felt it his duty to appear in public. It is curious that he declined to run for president again in 1928, when all the omens were in his favour, and he was only fifty-six. He told the chief justice, Harlan Stone, 'It is a pretty good idea to get out when they still want you.' There were very severe limits to his political ambitions, just as (in his view) there ought to be very severe limits to any political activity. Stone warned him of economic trouble ahead. He too thought the market would break. His wife Grace was reported: 'Poppa says there's a depression coming.' But Coolidge assumed it would be on the 1920 scale, to be cured by a similar phase of masterly inactivity. If something more was required, he was not the man. Grace Coolidge said he told a member of the cabinet: 'I know how to save money. All my training has been in that direction. The country is in a sound financial condition. Perhaps the time has come when we ought to spend money. I do not feel I am qualified to do that.' In his view, Hoover was the Big Spender; not the last of them, the first of them. He viewed Hoover's succession to the presidency without enthusiasm: 'That man has offered me unsolicited advice for six years, all of it bad.' Coolidge was the last man on earth to reciprocate with his own. Asked, during the interregnum in early 1929, for a decision on long-term policy, he snapped, 'We'll leave that to the Wonder Boy.' He left the stage without a word, pulling down the curtain on Arcadia.

SEVEN

Dégringolade

On Friday 3 October 1929, a new under-loader took part in his first pheasant shoot on the Duke of Westminster's estate near Chester. The day before a conference of senior officials had been held in the main gun-room. As dawn was breaking, the young loader put on his new uniform and reported to the head keeper, who 'looked very impressive in green velvet jacket and waistcoat with white breeches, box-cloth leggings and a hard hat with plenty of gold braid around it'. There were eighty keepers dressed in livery: 'a red, wide-brimmed hat with a leather band, and a white smock made of a very rough material in the Farmer Giles style and gathered in at the waist by a wide leather belt with a large brass buckle'. The beaters assembled and were inspected. Next to arrive were the leather cases of the 'guns', with their engraved and crested brass name-plates. Then came the guests in their chauffeur-driven Rolls-Royces and Daimlers, and finally the Duke himself, to whom the new loader was deputed to hand his shooting stick. As soon as 'His Grace' got to his place, the head keeper blew his whistle, the beaters started off and the shoot began. 'It was all organized to the fine degree that was essential to provide the sport that His Grace wanted and expected.' At lunchtime the keepers drank ale poured from horn jugs, and in the afternoon the Duke's private narrow-gauge train, 'passenger carriages all brightly painted in the Grosvenor colours', brought the ladies to join the sport. The bag was nearly 2,000.[1]

A fortnight before this quasi-medieval scene was enacted, the Duke's good friend Winston Churchill, who until earlier that year had been Britain's Chancellor of the Exchequer for five years, wrote to his wife from America:

Now my darling I must tell you that vy gt & extraordinary good fortune has attended me lately in finances. Sir Harry McGowan asked me rather earnestly before I sailed whether he might if an opportunity came buy shares on my account without previous consultation. I replied that I could always find 2 or 3,000£. I meant this as an investment limit i.e. buying the shares outright. He evidently took it as the limit to wh I was prepared to go in a speculative purchase on margin. Thus he operated on about ten times my usual scale . . . . So here we have recovered in a few weeks a small fortune . . . . It is a relief to me to feel something behind me and behind you all.[2]

It is interesting that Churchill should have been speculating on margin right up to the brink of the crash. He was one of about 600,000 trading on margin of the 1,548,707 customers who, in 1929, had accounts with firms belonging to America's twenty-nine stock exchanges. At the peak of the craze there were about a million active speculators, and out of an American population of 120 million about 29–30 million families had an active association with the market.[3] Churchill, despite his experience and world-wide contacts, was no better informed than the merest street-corner speculator. The American economy had ceased to expand in June. It took some time for the effects to work their way through but the bull market in stocks really came to an end on 3 September, a fortnight before Churchill wrote his joyful letter. The later rises were merely hiccups in a steady downward trend. The echoes of the Duke's shoot had scarcely died away when the precipitous descent began. On Monday 21 October, for the first time, the ticker-tape could not keep pace with the news of falls and never caught up; in the confusion the panic intensified (the first margin-call telegrams had gone out the Saturday before) and speculators began to realize they might lose their savings and even their homes. On Thursday 24 October shares dropped vertically with no one buying, speculators were sold out as they failed to respond to margin calls, crowds gathered in Broad Street outside the New York Stock Exchange, and by the end of the day eleven men well known on Wall Street had committed suicide. One of the visitors in the gallery that day was Churchill himself, watching his faerie gold vanish. Next week came Black Tuesday, the 29th, and the first selling of sound stocks in order to raise desperately needed liquidity.[4]

Great stock-exchange crises, with their spectacular reversals of fortune and human dramas, make the dry bones of economic history live. But they do not help to illuminate causes and consequences of events; quite the contrary. They enormously increase the mythology which is such a potent element in economic explanation. The nature of 1920s prosperity; the reason why it ended; the cause of the Great Crash and the Great Depression which followed; and, not least, the manner and means whereby the industrial societies emerged from it –

all these are still matters of intense argument. The conventional account is largely moralistic: *hubris* followed by *nemesis*, wicked greed by salutary retribution. It is easily adapted to Marxist determinism, which of course is a form of moral, not economic, analysis. It may make an edifying tale but it does not tell us what actually happened, let alone why. The interpretation provided by the followers of Keynes, which was the received opinion of the 1950s and 1960s, no longer carries conviction, for it appeared to be refuted by the catastrophic economic events of the 1970s and early 1980s, which placed the Great Depression in an entirely new perspective. Indeed, the two episodes can no longer be usefully studied separately and it is likely that future historians will analyse them in conjunction. But it is most improbable that an agreed explanation of either, or both, will ever be forthcoming. Economic history is too closely linked to current economic theory and practice to be a matter for easy consensus. What is offered here, then, is a possible account, which seeks to remove certain misconceptions.

The first fallacy to be dispelled is that America pursued an isolationist foreign policy in the 1920s. That is not true.[5] While America's rulers would not formally underwrite the Versailles peace settlement, still less Keynes's proposal for an American government-sponsored aid programme for European recovery, they privately and unostentatiously accepted a degree of responsibility for keeping the world economy on an even keel. They agreed to share with Britain the business of providing a global currency in which world trade could be conducted, a burden carried by the City of London virtually alone up to 1914. They also took it upon themselves to promote, by informal commercial and financial diplomacy, the expansion of world trade.[6] Unfortunately, the means employed were devious and ultimately dishonest. Except during the years 1857–61, America had always been a high-tariff nation: US tariffs, which had been imitated in continental Europe, were the chief refutation of its claim to conduct its affairs on true capitalist, *laissez-faire* principles. If Harding, Coolidge and Hoover had acted on the entrepreneurial principles they proudly proclaimed, they would have resumed Wilson's abortive policy of 1913 of reducing US tariffs. In fact they did the opposite. The Fordney–MacCumber Tariff Act of 1922 and, still more, the Hawley–Smoot Act of 1930, which Hoover declined to veto, were devastating blows struck at world commerce, and so in the end at America's own.[7] The fact is that America's presidents, and her congressional leadership, lacked the political courage to stand up to the National Association of Manufacturers, the American Federation of Labour and local pressures, and so pursue internationalism in the most effective way open to them and the one which conformed most closely to the economic views they claimed to hold.

Instead, they sought to keep the world prosperous by deliberate inflation of the money supply. This was something made possible by the pre-war creation of the Federal Reserve Bank system, and which could be done secretly, without legislative enactment or control, and without the public knowing or caring. It did not involve printing money: the currency in circulation in the US was $3.68 billion at the beginning of the 1920s and $3.64 billion when the boom ended in 1929. But the expansion of total money supply, in money substitutes or credit, was enormous: from $45.3 billion on 30 June 1921 to over $73 billion in July 1929, an increase of 61.8 per cent in eight years.[8] The White House, the Treasury under Andrew Mellon, the Congress, the federal banks, and of course the private banks too, connived together to inflate credit. In its 1923 *Annual Report*, the Federal Reserve described the policy with frank crudity: 'The Federal Reserve banks are . . . the source to which the member banks turn when the demands of the business community have outrun their own unaided resources. The Federal Reserve supplies the needed additions to credit in times of business expansion and takes up the slack in times of business recession.'[9] This policy of continuous credit-inflation, a form of vulgar Keynesianism before Keynes had even formulated its sophisticated version, might have been justified if interest rates had been allowed to find their own level: that is, if manufacturers and farmers who borrowed money had paid interest at the rate savers were actually prepared to lend it. But again, the White House, the Treasury, the Congress and the banks worked in consort to keep discount and interest rates artificially low. Indeed it was the stated policy of the Federal Reserve not only to 'enlarge credit resources' but to do so 'at rates of interest low enough to stimulate, protect and prosper all kinds of legitimate business'.[10]

This deliberate interference in the supply and cost of money was used in the 1920s not merely to promote its original aim, the expansion of US business, but to pursue a supposedly benevolent international policy. While the government demanded the repayment of its war-loans, it actively assisted foreign governments and businesses to raise money in New York both by its own cheap money policy and by constant, active interference in the foreign bond market. The government made it quite clear that it favoured certain loans and not others. So the foreign loan policy was an adumbration, at the level of private enterprise, of the post-1947 foreign aid programme. The aims were the same: to keep the international economy afloat, to support certain favoured regimes and, not least, to promote America's export industries. It was made, in effect, a condition of cabinet boosting of specific loans that part of them were spent in the USA. The foreign lending boom began in 1921, following a cabinet decision on 20 May 1921 and a meeting between Harding, Hoover and US investment bankers five days later, and it ended in late 1928, thus coinciding precisely with the expansion of the money supply which underlay the boom. America's rulers, in effect, rejected the rational *laissez-faire* choice of free trade and hard money and took the soft political option of protective tariffs and inflation. The domestic industries protected by the tariff, the export industries subsidized by the uneconomic loans and of course the investment bankers who floated the bonds all benefited. The losers were the population as a whole, who were denied the competitive prices produced by cheap imports, suffered from the resulting inflation, and were the universal victims of the ultimate *dégringolade*.[11]

Moreover, by getting mixed up in the foreign loan business, the government forfeited much of its moral right to condemn stock-exchange speculation. Hoover, who was Commerce Secretary throughout the 1920s until he became President, regarded Wall Street as a deplorable casino – but he was the most assiduous promoter of the foreign bond market. Even bad loans, he argued, helped American exports and so provided employment.[12] Some of the foreign bond issues, however, were at least as scandalous as the worst stock-exchange transactions. Thus, in 1927, Victor Schoepperle, Vice-President for Latin-American loans at National City Company (affiliated to National City Bank), reported on Peru: 'Bad debt record; adverse moral and political risk; bad internal debt situation; trade situation about as satisfactory as that of Chile in the past three years. National resources more varied. On economic showing Peru should go ahead rapidly in the next ten years.' Nevertheless National City floated a $15 million loan for Peru, followed shortly afterwards by a $50 million loan and a $25 million issue. Congressional investigation, in 1933–4, established that Juan Leguia, son of the president of Peru, had been paid $450,000 by National and its associates in connection with the loan. When his father was overthrown Peru defaulted.[13] This was one example among many. The basic unsoundness of much of the foreign loan market was one of the principal elements in the collapse of confidence and the spread of the recession to Europe. And the unsoundness was the consequence not, indeed, of government *laissez-faire* but of the opposite: persistent government meddling.

Interventionism by creating artificial, cheap credit was not an American invention. It was British. The British called it 'stabilization'. Although Britain was nominally a *laissez-faire* country up to 1914, more so than America in some respects since it practised free trade, British economic philosophers were not happy with the business cycle, which they believed could be smoothed out by deliberate and combined efforts to achieve price stabilization. It must not be thought that Keynes came out of a clear non-interventionist sky: he was only a marginal 'advance' on the orthodox British seers. Since before the war Sir Ralph Hawtrey, in charge of financial studies at the Treasury, had argued that the central banks, by creating international credit (that is, inflation), could achieve a stable price level and so enormously improve on the nineteenth century's passive acceptance of the cycle, which he regarded as immoral. After 1918, Hawtrey's views became the conventional wisdom in Britain and spread to America via Versailles. In the 1920 recession the Stable Money League (later the National Monetary Association) was founded, attracting the American financial establishment and, abroad, men like Emile Moreau, Governor of the Bank of France, Edouard Benes, Lord Melchett, creator of ICI, Louis Rothschild, head of the Austrian branch, A.J.Balfour and such British economists as A.C.Pigou, Otto Kahn, Sir Arthur Salter and Keynes himself.[14]

Keynes put the case for a 'managed currency' and a stabilized price-level in his *Tract on Monetary Reform* (1923). By then, stabilization was not merely accepted but practised. Hawtrey had inspired the stabilization resolutions of the Genoa Conference in 1922; the Financial Committee of the League of Nations was stabilizationist; most of all, the Bank of England was stabilizationist. Montagu Norman, its governor, and his chief international adviser Sir Charles Addis, were both ardent apostles of the creed. Their principal disciple was Benjamin Strong, governor of the New York Federal Reserve Bank, who until his death in 1928 was all-powerful in the formation of American financial policy. Hoover called Strong, justly, 'a mental annex to Europe', and he was the effective agent in America's covert foreign policy of economic management. Indeed it is not too much to say that, for most of the 1920s, the international economic system was jointly supervised by Norman and Strong.[15] It was Strong who made it possible for Britain to return to the gold standard in 1925, by extending lines of credit from the New York Federal Reserve Bank and getting J.P.Morgan to do likewise: the London *Banker* wrote: 'no better friend of England exists'. Similar lines of credit were opened later to Belgium, Poland, Italy and other countries which met the Strong–Norman standards of financial rectitude.[16]

Of course the 'gold standard' was not a true one. That had gone for good in 1914. A customer could not go into the Bank of England and demand a gold sovereign in return for his pound note. It was the same in other European gold-standard countries. The correct term was 'gold bullion standard': the central banks held gold in large bars but ordinary people were not considered sufficiently responsible to handle gold themselves (although in theory Americans could demand gold dollars until 1933). Indeed, when a plan was produced in 1926 to give India a real gold standard, Strong and Norman united to kill it, on the grounds that there would then be a disastrous world-wide gold-drain into Indian mattresses. In short, the 1920s gold-standard movement was not genuine *laissez-faire* at all but a 'not in-front-of-the-servants' *laissez-faire*.[17] It was a benevolent despotism run by a tiny élite of the Great and the Good, in secret. Strong regarded his credit-expansion and cheap money policy as an alternative to America backing the League, and he was pretty sure US public opinion would repudiate it if the facts were made public: that was why he insisted the periodic meetings of bankers should be strictly private. A financial policy which will not stand the scrutiny of the public is suspect in itself. It is doubly suspect if, while making gold the measure of value, it does not trust ordinary people – the ultimate judges of value – to apply that measurement themselves. Why did the bankers fear that ordinary men and women, if given the chance, would rush into gold – which brought no return at all – when they could invest in a healthy economy at a profit? There was something wrong here. The German banker Hjalmar Schacht repeatedly called for a true gold standard, as the only means to ensure that expansion was financed by genuine voluntary savings, instead of by bank credit determined by a tiny oligarchy of financial Jupiters.[18]

But the stabilizers carried all before them. Domestically and internationally they constantly pumped more credit into the system, and whenever the economy showed signs of flagging they increased the dose. The most notorious occasion was in July 1927, when Strong and Norman held a secret meeting of bankers at the Long Island estates of Ogden Mills, the US Treasury Under-Secretary, and Mrs Ruth Pratt, the Standard Oil heiress. Strong kept Washington in the dark and refused to let even his most senior colleagues attend. He and Norman decided on another burst of inflation and the protests of Schacht and of Charles Rist, Deputy-Governor of the Bank of France, were brushed aside. The New York Fed reduced its rate by a further half per cent to 3½; as Strong put it to Rist, 'I will give a little *coup de whiskey* to the stock-market' – and as a result set in motion the last culminating wave of speculation. Adolph Miller, a member of the Federal Reserve Board, subsequently described this decision in Senate testimony as 'the greatest and boldest operation ever undertaken by the Federal Reserve System [which] resulted in one of the most costly errors committed by it or any other banking system in the last seventy-five years.'[19]

The German objection, influenced by the monetarists of the Viennese school, L. von Mises and F. A. Hayek, was that the whole inflationary policy was corrupt. The French objection was that it reflected British foreign economic policy aims, with the Americans as willing abettors. As Moreau put it in his secret diary:

England, having been the first European country to re-establish a stable and secure money, has used that advantage to establish a basis for putting Europe under a veritable financial domination . . . . The currencies will be divided into two classes. Those of the first class, the dollar and sterling, based on gold, and those of the second class based on the pound and the dollar – with part of their gold reserves being held by the Bank of England and the Federal Reserve of New York, the local currencies will have lost their independence.[20]

Moreau was making a general point that economic policies shaped for political purposes, as Anglo–American currency management un-doubtedly was, are unlikely to achieve economic objectives in the long run. That is unquestionably true, and it applies both in the domestic and the international field. At home, both in America and Britain, the object of stabilization was to keep prices steady and so prevent wages from dropping, which would mean social unrest; abroad, cheap money and easy loans kept trade flowing despite US protectionism and Britain's artificially strong pound. The aim was to avoid trouble and escape the need to resolve painful political dilemmas.

The policy appeared to be succeeding. In the second half of the decade, the cheap credit Strong–Norman policy pumped into the world economy perked up trade, which had failed to reach its pre-war level. Whereas in 1921–5 the world-trade growth rate, compared with 1911–14, was actually minus 1.42, during the four years 1926–9 it achieved a growth of 6.74, a performance not to be exceeded until the late 1950s.[21] Prices nevertheless remained stable: the Bureau of Labor Statistics Index of Wholesale Prices, taking 1926 as 100, shows that the fluctuation in the US was merely from 93.4 in June 1921 to a peak of 104.5 in November 1925 and then down to 95.2 in June 1929. So the notion of deliberate controlled growth within a framework of price stability had been turned into reality. This was genuine economic management at last! Keynes described 'the successful management of the dollar by the Federal Reserve Board from 1923–8' as a 'triumph'. Hawtrey's verdict was: 'The American experiment in stabilization from 1922 to 1928 showed that early treatment could check a tendency either to inflation or to depression . . .. The American experiment was a great advance upon the practice of the nineteenth century.'[22]

Yet in fact the inflation was there, and growing, all the time. What no one seems to have appreciated is the significance of the phenomenal growth of productivity in the US between 1919 and 1929: output per worker in manufacturing industry rising by 43 per cent. This was made possible by a staggering increase in capital investment which rose by an average annual rate of 6.4 per cent a year.[23] The productivity increase should have been reflected in lower prices. The extent to which it was not reflected the degree of inflation produced by economic management with the object of stabilization. It is true that if prices had not been managed, wages would have fallen too. But the drop in prices must have been steeper; and therefore real wages – purchasing power – would have increased steadily, *pari passu* with productivity. The workers would have been able to enjoy more of the goods their improved performance was turning out of the factories. As it was, working-class families found it a struggle to keep up with the new prosperity. They could afford cars – just. But it was an effort to renew them. The Twenties boom was based essentially on the car. America was producing almost as many cars in the late 1920s as in the 1950s (5,358,000 in 1929; 5,700,000 in 1953). The really big and absolutely genuine growth-stock of the 1920s was General Motors: anyone who in 1921 had bought $25,000 of GM common stock was a millionaire by 1929, when GM was earning profits of $200 million a year.[24] The difficulty about an expansion in which cars are the leading sector is that, when money is short, a car's life can be arbitrarily prolonged five or ten years. In December 1927 Coolidge and Hoover proudly claimed that average industrial wages had reached $4 a day, that is $1,200 a year. But their own government agencies estimated that it cost $2,000 a year to bring up a family of five in 'health and decency'. There is some evidence that the increasing number of women in employment reflected a decline in real incomes, especially among the middle class.[25] As the boom continued, and prices failed to fall, it became harder for the consumer to keep the boom going. The bankers, in turn, had to work harder to inflate the economy: Strong's 'little *coup de whiskey*' was the last big push; next year he was dead, leaving no one with either the same degree of monetary adventurism or the same authority.

Strong's last push, in fact, did little to help the 'real' economy. It fed speculation. Very little of the new credit went through to the mass-consumer. As it was, the spending-side of the US economy was unbalanced. The 5 per cent of the population with the top incomes had one-third of all personal income: they did not buy Fords or Chevrolets. Indeed the proportion of income received in interest, dividends and rents, as opposed to wages, was about twice as high as post-1945 levels.[26] Strong's *coup de whiskey* benefited almost solely the non-wage earners: the last phase of the boom was largely speculative. Until 1928 stock-exchange prices had merely kept pace with actual industrial performance. From the beginning of 1928 the element of unreality, of fantasy indeed, began to grow. As Bagehot put it, 'All people are most credulous when they are most happy.'[27] The number of shares changing hands, a record of 567,990,875 in 1927, went to 920,550,032.

Two new and sinister elements emerged: a vast increase in margin-trading and a rash of hastily cobbled-together investment trusts. Traditionally, stocks were valued at about ten times earnings. With high margin-trading, earnings on shares, only 1 or 2 per cent, were far less than the 8–12 per cent interest on loans used to buy them. This meant that any profits were in capital gains alone. Thus, Radio Corporation of America, which had never paid a dividend at all, went from 85 to 420 points in 1928. By 1929 some stocks were selling at fifty times earnings. As one expert put it, the market was 'discounting not merely the future but the hereafter'.[28] A market-boom based on capital gains is merely a form of pyramid-selling. The new investment trusts, which by the end of 1928 were emerging at the rate of one a day, were archetypal inverted pyramids. They had what was called 'high leverage' through their own supposedly shrewd investments, and secured phenomenal growth on the basis of a very small plinth of real growth. Thus, the United Founders Corporation was built up into a company with nominal resources of $686,165,000 from an original investment (by a bankrupt) of a mere $500. The 1929 market value of another investment trust was over a billion dollars, but its chief asset was an electric company worth only $6 million in 1921.[29] They were supposed to enable the 'little man' to 'get a piece of the action'. In fact they merely provided an additional superstructure of almost pure speculation, and the 'high leverage' worked in reverse once the market broke.

It is astonishing that, once margin-trading and investment-trusting took over, the Federal bankers failed to raise interest rates and persisted in cheap money. But many of the bankers had lost their sense of reality by the beginning of 1929. Indeed, they were speculating themselves, often in their own stock. One of the worst offenders was Charles Mitchell (finally indicted for grand larceny in 1938), the Chairman of National City Bank, who, on 1 January 1929, became a director of the Federal Reserve Bank of New York. Mitchell filled the role of Strong, at a cruder level, and kept the boom going through most of 1929. Of course many practices which contributed to the crash, and were made illegal by Congress and the new Securities and Exchange Commission in the 1930s, were regarded as acceptable in 1929. The ferocious witch-hunt begun in 1932 by the Senate Committee on Banking and the Currency, which served as a prototype for the witch-hunts of the 1940s and early

1950s, actually disclosed little law-breaking. Mitchell was the only major victim and even his case revealed more of the social *mores* of high finance than actual wickedness.[30] Henry James would have had no complaints; but the Marxist zealots were disappointed. 'Every great crisis', Bagehot remarked, 'reveals the excessive speculations of many houses which no one before suspected.'[31] The 1929 crash exposed in addition the naivety and ignorance of bankers, business-men, Wall Street experts and academic economists high and low; it showed they did not understand the system they had been so confidently manipulating. They had tried to substitute their own well-meaning policies for what Adam Smith called 'the invisible hand' of the market and they had wrought disaster. Far from demonstrating, as Keynes and his school later argued – at the time Keynes failed to predict either the crash or the extent and duration of the Depression – the dangers of a self-regulating economy, the *dégringolade* indicated the opposite: the risks of ill-informed meddling.

The credit inflation petered out at the end of 1928. The economy went into decline, in consequence, six months later. The market collapse followed after a three-month delay. All this was to be expected; it was healthy; it ought to have been welcomed. It was the pattern of the nineteenth century and of the twentieth up to 1920–1: capitalist 'normalcy'. A business recession and a stock-exchange drop were not only customary but necessary parts of the cycle of growth: they sorted out the sheep from the goats, liquidated the unhealthy elements in the economy and turned out the parasites; as J.K. Galbraith was to put it: 'One of the uses of depression is to expose what the auditors fail to find.'[32] Business downturns serve essential purposes. They have to be sharp. But they need not be long because they are self-adjusting. All they require on the part of governments, the business community and the public is patience. The 1920 recession had adjusted itself within a year. There was no reason why the 1929 recession should have taken longer, for the American economy was fundamentally sound, as Coolidge had said. As we have seen, the Stock Exchange fall began in September and became panic in October. On 13 November, at the end of the panic, the index was at 224, down from 452. There was nothing wrong in that. It had been only 245 in December 1928 after a year of steep rises. The panic merely knocked out the speculative element, leaving sound stocks at about their right value in relation to earnings. If the recession had been allowed to adjust itself, as it would have done by the end of 1930 on any earlier analogy, confidence would have returned and the world slump need never have occurred. Instead, the market went on down, slowly but inexorably, ceasing to reflect

economic realities – its true function – and instead becoming an
engine of doom, carrying to destruction the entire nation and, in its
wake, the world. By 8 July 1932 *New York Times* industrials had
fallen from 224 at the end of the panic to 58. US Steel, selling at 262
before the market broke in 1929, was now only 22. GM, already one
of the best-run and most successful manufacturing groups in the
world, had fallen from 73 to 8.[33] By this time the entire outlook for
the world had changed – infinitely for the worse. How did this
happen? Why did the normal recovery not take place?

To find the answer we must probe beneath the conventional view
of Herbert Hoover and his successor as president, Franklin
Roosevelt. The received view is that Hoover, because of his ideological attachment to *laissez-faire*, refused to use government money to
reflate the economy and so prolonged and deepened the Depression
until the election of Roosevelt, who then promptly reversed official
policy, introducing the New Deal, a form of Keynesianism, and
pulled America out of the trough. Hoover is presented as the symbol
of the dead, discredited past, Roosevelt as the harbinger of the
future, and 1932–3 the watershed between old-style free market
economics and the benevolent new managed economics and social
welfare of Keynes. Such a version of events began as the quasi-
journalistic propaganda of Roosevelt's colleagues and admirers and
was then constructed into a solid historical matrix by two entire
generations of liberal-democrat historians.[34]

This most durable of historical myths has very little truth in it. The
reality is much more complex and interesting. Hoover is one of the
tragic figures of modern times. No one illustrated better Tacitus's
verdict on Galba, *omnium consensu capax imperii nisi imperasset*
(by general consent fit to rule, had he not ruled). As we have seen, the
First World War introduced the age of social engineering. Some
pundits wished to go further and install the engineer himself as king.
Thorstein Veblen, the most influential progressive writer in America
in the first quarter of the twentieth century, had argued, both in *The
Theory of the Leisure Class* (1899) and *The Engineers and the Price
System* (1921) that the engineer, whom he regarded as a disinterested
and benevolent figure, should replace the businessman, eliminating
both the values of the leisure class and the motives of profit, and run
the economy in the interests of consumers.[35] In the Soviet Union,
which has embraced social engineering more comprehensively and
over a longer period than any other society, this is more or less what
has happened, engineers becoming the paramount element in the
ruling class (though not as yet with much advantage to the consumer).

Hoover, born in 1874, not only believed in a kind of social

engineering; he actually was an engineer. An orphan from a desperately poor Iowa farming background, his was a classical American success-story. He worked his way through Stanford University with an engineering degree and then, from 1900 to 1915, made $4 million in mining all over the world.[36] Recruited to Wilson's war-team, he became its outstanding member, absorbed its philosophy of forceful government direction and planning, and then as head of America's post-war Commission of Relief (an adumbration of the later Marshall Aid and Point Four programmes) achieved a world-wide reputation for benevolent interventionism. Maxim Gorky wrote to him: 'You have saved from death 3,500,000 children and 5,500,000 adults.'[37] In fact he used food diplomacy selectively, to defeat both Béla Kun's Communist regime in Hungary and a Habsburg come-back in Austria, while propping up the regimes the Anglo-Saxon powers favoured.[38] Keynes wrote of him as 'the only man who emerged from the ordeal of Paris with an enhanced reputation . . . [who] imported in the councils of Paris, when he took part in them, precisely that atmosphere of reality, knowledge, magnanimity and disinterestedness which, if they had been found in other quarters also, would have given us the Good Peace.'[39] Franklin Roosevelt, who as Navy Under-Secretary had also been in the wartime administration and shared Hoover's general outlook, wrote to a friend: 'He is certainly a wonder and I wish we could make him President of the United States. There could not be a better one.'[40]

As Secretary of Commerce for eight years, Hoover showed himself a corporatist, an activist and an interventionist, running counter to the general thrust, or rather non-thrust, of the Harding–Coolidge administrations. His predecessor, Oscar Straus, told him he only needed to work two hours a day, 'putting the fish to bed at night and turning on the lights around the coast'. In fact his was the only department which increased its staff, from 13,005 to 15,850, and its cost, from $24.5 million to $37.6 million.[41] He came into office at the tail-end of the Depression and immediately set about forming committees and trade councils, sponsoring research programmes, pushing expenditure, persuading employers to keep up wages and 'divided time' to increase jobs and, above all, forcing 'co-operation between the Federal, state and municipal governments to increase public works'.[42] Everywhere he formed committees and study-groups, sponsoring reports and working-parties, generating an atmosphere of buzz and business. There was no aspect of public policy in which Hoover was not intensely active, usually personally: child-health, Indian policy, oil, conservation, public education, housing, social waste, agriculture – as President, he was his own

Agriculture Secretary, and the 1929 Agricultural Marketing Act was entirely his work.[43] Harding did not like this hyperactivity, but was overwhelmed by Hoover's brains and prestige – 'The smartest gink I know'.[44] Coolidge hated it; but by then Hoover was too much part of the furniture of Republican government to be removed.

Besides, Hoover's corporatism – the notion that the state, business, the unions and other Big Brothers should work together in gentle, but persistent and continuous manipulation to make life better – was the received wisdom of the day, among enlightened capitalists, left-wing Republicans and non-socialist intellectuals. Yankee-style corporatism was the American response to the new forms in Europe, especially Mussolini's fascism; it was as important to right-thinking people in the Twenties as Stalinism was in the Thirties.[45] Hoover was its outstanding impresario and ideologue. (One of his admirers was Jean Monnet, who later re-named the approach 'indicative planning' and made it the basis both for France's post-war planning system and for the European Economic Community.) Yet Hoover was not a statist. He said he was against any attempt 'to smuggle fascism into America through a back door'.[46] On many issues he was liberal. He wanted aid to flow to underdeveloped countries. He deplored the exclusion of Japanese from the 1924 immigration quotas. His wife entertained the ladies of black congressmen. He did not make anti-Semitic jokes, like Woodrow Wilson and his wife or Franklin Roosevelt.[47] To a very wide spectrum of educated American opinion, he was the leading American public man long before he got to the White House.

Hence the general belief that Hoover, as President, would be a miracle-worker. The *Philadelphia Record* called him 'easily the most commanding figure in the modern science of "engineering statesmanship"'. The *Boston Globe* said the nation knew they had at the White House one who believed in 'the dynamics of mastery'.[48] He was 'the Great Engineer'. Hoover said he was worried by 'the exaggerated idea people have conceived of me. They have a conviction that I am a sort of superman, that no problem is beyond my capacity.'[49] But he was not really disturbed. He knew exactly what to do. He ran the administration like a dictator. He ignored or bullied Congress. He laid down the law, like a character from Dickens. He was fond of telling subordinates, 'When you know me better, you will find that when I say a thing is a fact, it *is* a fact.'[50]

When Hoover became President in March 1929 the mechanism which was to create the Depression was already in motion. The only useful action he might have taken was to allow the artificially low interest rates to rise to their natural level – a high one in the circumstances – which would have killed off the Stock Exchange boom much earlier and avoided the damaging drama of the 1929 autumn. But he did not do so: government-induced cheap credit was the very bedrock of his policy. When the magnitude of the crisis became apparent, Andrew Mellon, the Treasury Secretary, at last repudiated his interventionist philosophy and returned to strict *laissez-faire*. He told Hoover that administration policy should be to 'liquidate labor, liquidate stocks, liquidate the farmers, liquidate real estate' and so 'purge the rottenness from the economy'.[51] It was the only sensible advice Hoover received throughout his presidency. By allowing the Depression to rip, unsound businesses would quickly have been bankrupted and the sound would have survived. Wages would have fallen to their natural level, and that for Hoover was the rub. He believed that high wages were an essential element in prosperity and that maintaining wages was the most important element in policy to contain and overcome depressions.[52]

From the very start, therefore, Hoover agreed to take on the business cycle and stamp on it with all the resources of government. 'No president before has ever believed there was a government responsibility in such cases,' he wrote; ' . . . there we had to pioneer a new field.'[53] He resumed credit inflation, the Federal Reserve adding almost $300 million to credit in the last week of October 1929 alone. In November he held a series of conferences with industrial leaders in which he exacted from them solemn promises not to cut wages; even to increase them if possible – promises kept until 1932. The American Federation of Labor's journal lauded this policy: never before had US employers been marshalled to act together, and the decision marked an 'epoch in the march of civilization – high wages'.[54] Keynes, in a memo to Britain's Labour Prime Minister, Ramsay MacDonald, praised Hoover's record in maintaining wage-levels and thought the Federal credit-expansion move 'thoroughly satisfactory'.[55]

Indeed in all essentials, Hoover's actions embodied what would later be called a 'Keynesian' policy. He cut taxes heavily. Those of a family man with an income of $4,000 went down by two-thirds.[56] He pushed up government spending, deliberately running up a huge government deficit of $2.2 billion in 1931, so that the government share of the Gross National Product went up from 16.4 per cent in 1930 to 21.5 per cent in 1931. This increase in government spending, by far the largest in US history in peacetime, reaching $1.3 billion in 1931, was largely accounted for ($1 billion) by a rise in transfer payments.[57] It is true that Hoover ruled out direct relief and wherever possible he channelled government money through the banks rather than direct to businesses and individuals. But that he sought to use government cash to reflate the economy is beyond question. Coolidge's advice to angry farmers' delegations had been a bleak: 'Take up religion.' Hoover's new Agricultural Marketing Act gave them $500 million of Federal money, increased by a further $100 million early in 1930. In 1931 he extended this to the economy as a whole with his Reconstruction Finance Corporation (RFC), as part of a nine-point programme of government intervention which he produced in December. More major public works were started in Hoover's four years than in the previous thirty, including the San Francisco Bay Bridge, the Los Angeles Aqueduct and the Hoover Dam; the project for a St Lawrence Seaway was a casualty of Congressional, not White House, action. In July 1932 the RFC's capital was almost doubled to $3.8 billion and the new Emergency Relief and Construction Act extended its positive role: in 1932 alone it gave credits of $2.3 billion and $1.6 billion in cash. Alas, as there was then unanimous agreement that the budget had to be brought back into balance after two years of deficit, the 1932 Revenue Act saw the greatest taxation increase in US history in peacetime, with the rate on high incomes jumping from a quarter to 63 per cent. This made nonsense of Hoover's earlier tax cuts but by now Hoover had lost control of Congress and was not in a position to pursue a coherent fiscal policy.

Hoover's interventionism was accompanied by an incessant activist rhetoric. He was perhaps the first of what was to become a great army of democratic statesmen to use military metaphors in a context of positive economic policy: 'The battle to set our economic machine in motion in this emergency takes new forms and requires new tactics from time to time. We used such emergency powers to win the war; we can use them to fight the Depression . . .' (May 1932). 'If there shall be no retreat, if the attack shall continue as it is now organized, then this battle is won . . .' (August 1932). 'We might have done nothing. That would have been utter ruin. Instead we met the situation with proposals to private business and to Congress of the most gigantic programme of economic defence and counter-attack ever evolved in the history of the Republic . . . . For the first time in the history of depression, dividends, profits and the cost of living have been reduced before wages have suffered . . . . They were maintained until . . . the profits had practically vanished. They are now the highest real wages in the world . . . . Some of the reactionary economists urged that we should allow the liquidation to take its course until we had found bottom . . . . We determined that we would not follow the advice of the bitter-end liquidationists and see the whole body of debtors of the US brought to bankruptcy and the savings of our people brought to destruction . . .' (October 1932).[58]

Hoover, the active engineer, thought in terms of tools and weapons. Tools and weapons are meant to be used. He used them. His incessant attacks on the stock exchanges, which he hated as parasitical, and his demands that they be investigated pushed stocks down still further and discouraged private investors. His policy of public investment prevented necessary liquidations. The businesses he hoped thus to save either went bankrupt in the end, after fearful agonies, or were burdened throughout the 1930s by a crushing load of debt. Hoover undermined property rights by weakening the bankruptcy laws and encouraging states to halt action-sales for debt, ban foreclosures or impose debt moratoria. This, in itself, impeded the ability of the banks to save themselves and maintain confidence. Hoover deliberately pushed federal credits into the banks and bullied them into inflating, thus increasing the precariousness of their position.

The final crisis came when America's protectionist policy boomeranged. The atrocious Smoot–Hawley tariff of 1930, which sharply increased import-duties, more than any other positive act of policy, spread the Depression to Europe. In the summer of 1931 the collapse of Austria's leading bank, the Credit Anstalt, pushed over a whole row of European dominoes (Britain had already abandoned the gold standard on 21 September 1930) and a series of debt-repudiations ensued. What remained of America's exports to Europe vanished, and her policy of foreign loans as a substitute for free trade collapsed. Foreigners lost confidence in the dollar and since the USA was still on the gold standard began to pull out their gold, a habit that spread to American customers. In a 'normal' year about 700 US banks failed. In 1931–2 there were 5,096 failures, with deposits totalling well over $3 billion, and the process culminated early in 1933 when the US banking system came to a virtual standstill in the last weeks of the Hoover presidency, adding what appeared to be the coping-stone to the President's monument of failure.[59]

By that time Hoover's interventionism had prolonged the Depression into its fourth year. The cumulative banking crisis had, in all probability, the deflationary effect which Hoover had struggled so hard and so foolishly to prevent, so that by the end of 1932 the very worst of the Depression was over. But the cataclysmic depth to which the economy had sunk in the meantime meant that recovery would be slow and feeble. The damage was enormous, though it was patchy and often contradictory. Industrial production, which had been 114 in August 1929, was 54 by March 1933. Business construction, which had totalled $8.7 billion in 1929, fell to a mere $1.4 billion in 1933. There was a 77 per cent decline in durable manufactures over the same period. Thanks to Hoover, average real wages actually increased during the Depression; the victims, of course, were those who had no wages at all.[60] Unemployment, which had been only 3.2 per cent of the labour force in 1929, rose to 24.9 per cent in 1933 and 26.7 per cent in 1934.[61] At one point it was estimated that (excluding farm families) some 34 million men, women and children were without any income at all – 28 per cent of the population.[62] Landlords could not collect rents and so could not pay taxes; city revenues collapsed, bringing down the relief system (such as it was) and services. Chicago owed its teachers $20 million. In some areas schools closed down most of the year. In New York in 1932, more than 300,000 children could not be taught because there were no funds, and among those still attending the Health Department reported 20 per cent malnutrition.[63] By 1933 the US Office of Education estimated that 1,500 higher education colleges had gone bankrupt or shut and university enrolments fell by a quarter-million.[64] Few bought books. None of the public libraries in Chicago could buy a single new book for twelve months. Total book sales fell 50 per cent and Little, Brown of Boston reported 1932–3 as the worst year since they began publishing in 1837.[65] John Steinbeck complained: 'When people are broke, the first things they give up are books.'[66]

Intellectuals bitterly resented their own plight and the misery all around which it reflected. But they reacted in different ways. Some just reported what they saw. In one of the best of the Depression articles, 'New York in the Third Winter', James Thurber noted the contrasts and the ironies. Of the eighty-six legitimate theatres in the city, only twenty-eight had shows running: but O'Neill's *Mourning Becomes Electra* had sold out even its $6 seats. About 1,600 of the 20,000 taxis had 'dropped out'; but the rest were much smarter and cleaner as a result of intensified competition. Both the Ritz and the Pierre had cut their lowest room rates to a humiliating $6; but the new Waldorf, charging the same as before, was packed. The new Empire State, the last product of the great Twenties building boom, had only rented a third of its rooms: 'Many floors were not finished at all, merely big plastery spaces'; but 550,000 people had already paid a dollar to go up to the top. The big transatlantic liners were cutting their suite prices by a third; but 'whoopee cruises' beyond the twelve-mile-limit-ban on gambling were a roaring success. So was bridge, with Ely Culbertson selling 400,000 books a year and the industry racking up a turnover of $100 million, and the new striptease shows, with dancers earning $475 a week. Above all, he reported bargains in the big stores, which slashed their prices and kept up business accordingly. Indeed, it is a significant fact that the retail trade, reacting directly to market conditions, was the least depressed sector of the economy; industry, trapped by Hoover's iron law of high wages, was sandbagged.[67] Thurber's reporting stressed that for anyone who could actually make or earn money, Depressions were the best of times.

Most intellectuals moved sharply to the Left, or rather into politics for the first time, presenting their newly discovered country in crude, ideological colours. Thomas Wolfe, the baroque writing phenomenon of the Thirties, described the public lavatories outside New York's City Hall, where an astonishing proportion of America's two million derelicts congregated:

... drawn into a common stew of rest and warmth and a little surcease from their desperation . . . . The sight was revolting, disgusting, enough to render a man forever speechless with very pity. [Nearby were] the giant hackles of Manhattan shining coldly in the cruel brightness of the winter night. The Woolworth building was not fifty yards away, and a little further down were the silvery spires and needles of Wall Street, great fortresses of stone and steel that housed enormous banks . . . in the cold moonlight, only a few blocks away from this abyss of human wretchedness and misery, blazed the pinnacles of power where a large section of the world's entire wealth was locked in mighty vaults.[68]

Edmund Wilson, whose Depression articles were collected as *The American Jitters* (1932), eschewed the rhetoric but powerfully reflected the growing anti-enterprise sentiment which was overwhelming the country. Books might not be bought but more people were reading serious ones than ever before. He recognized shrewdly that a good time – or rather an influential time – for intellectuals had come: especially for the younger ones 'who had grown up in the Big Business era and had always resented its barbarism, its crowding-out of everything they cared about'. For them, 'these years were not depressing but stimulating. One couldn't help being exhilarated at the sudden, unexpected collapse of the stupid gigantic fraud. It gave us a new sense of freedom; and it gave us a new sense of power.'[69]

For it is a curious fact that writers, the least organized in their own lives, instinctively support planning in the public realm. And at the beginning of the Thirties planning became the new *Weltanschauung*. In 1932 it dominated the booklists: Stuart Chase, so embarrassingly wrong about the 'continuing boom' in October 1929, now published *A New Deal*, its title as timely as Bruck's *The Third Reich*. George Soule demanded Hooveresque works-programmes in *A Planned Society*. Corporatist planning reached its apotheosis in Adolf Berle's and Gardiner Means's *Modern Corporation and Private Property*, which went through twenty impressions as the Depression climaxed and predicted that the 'law of corporations' would be the 'potential constitutional law' for the new economic state.

Everyone wanted planning. America's most widely read historian, Charles Beard, advocated 'A Five Year Plan for America'.[70] Businessmen like Gerard Swope, head of General Electric, produced their own. Henry Harriman, Chairman of the New England Power Company, declared, 'We have left the period of extreme individualism . . . . Business prosperity and employment will be best maintained by an intelligent planned business structure.' Capitalists who disagreed would be 'treated like any maverick . . . roped and branded and made to run with the herd'. Charles Abbott of the American Institute of Steel Construction declared the country could no longer afford 'irresponsible, ill-informed, stubborn and non-co-operative individualism'. *Business Week*, under the sneering title 'Do You Still Believe in Lazy-Fairies?', asked: 'To plan or not to plan is no longer the question. The real question is: who is to do it?'[71]

Who, in logic and justice, but the Great Engineer, the Wonder Boy? Had not, in logic and justice, his time come at last? But there is no logic or justice in history. It is all a matter of chronology. Hoover's time had come and gone. He had been in power four years, frantically acting and planning, and what was the result? By 1932 his advisers were telling him to 'keep off the front page' as his public acts were discrediting the notion that the government could intervene effectively.[72] He had warned himself in 1929 that 'If some unprecedented calamity should come upon this nation I would be sacrificed to the unreasoning disappointment of a people who had expected too much.' That fear – confidently dismissed at the time – proved abundantly justified. In 1907 Theodore Roosevelt had remarked that 'when the average man loses his money, he is simply like a wounded snake and strikes right and left at anything, innocent or the reverse, that represents itself as conspicuous in his mind'.[73] That maxim, too, was now resoundingly confirmed, with Hoover as its helpless victim, a transfixed rabbit in a boiled shirt. He had always been a dour man; now, imperceptibly, he became the Great Depressive. The ablest of his cabinet colleagues, Henry Stimson, said he avoided the White House to escape 'the ever-present feeling of gloom that pervades everything connected with this Administration'. He added: 'I don't remember there has ever been a joke cracked in a single meeting of the last year and a half.' As his party and cabinet colleagues distanced themselves from this voodoo-figure, Hoover began to keep an 'enemies list' of the disloyal.[74] Calling on the beleaguered man, H.G.Wells found him 'sickly, overworked and overwhelmed'.[75]

And as usually happens on these occasions, sheer luck deserts the ruined cause and becomes the source of further myth. In 1924 a Bonus bill had provided army veterans with service certificates and the right to borrow $22\frac{1}{2}$ per cent of their matured value. In 1931, over Hoover's veto, Congress raised that to 50 per cent. Some of the veterans were not content and the Left, reviving for the first time since 1919, organized a 'Bonus expeditionary force' of 20,000 veterans which set up a shanty-town 'camp' in the middle of Washington in 1932. But Congress refused to budge further and on 28 July Hoover, whose policy on the issue was identical to Roosevelt's when the issue was revived in 1936, ordered the camp to be dispersed. The police proving inadequate, some troops were used under Major (later General) Patton of the US Cavalry. Both General MacArthur, then Army Chief of Staff, and his aide Major Eisenhower played minor roles in the messy operation that followed.

No episode in American history has been the basis for more falsehood, much of it deliberate. The Communists did not play a leading role in setting up the camp but they organized the subsequent propaganda with great skill. There were tales of cavalry charges; of the use of tanks and poison gas; of a little boy bayonetted while trying to save his rabbit; and of tents and shelters being set on fire with people trapped inside. These were published in such works as W. W. Walters: *BEF: the Whole Story of the Bonus Army* (1933) and Jack Douglas: *Veteran on the March* (1934), both almost entirely fiction. A book of *Ballads of the BEF* appeared, including such choice items as 'The Hoover Diet Is Gas' and 'I have seen the sabres gleaming as they lopped off veterans' ears'. A characteristic Communist tract of 1940 by Bruce Minton and John Stuart, *The Fat Years and the Lean*, concluded: 'The veterans began to leave the capital. But President Hoover would not let them disband peacefully . . . . Without warning he ordered the army forcibly to eject the BEF from Washington. The soldiers charged with fixed bayonets, firing into the crowd of unarmed men, women and children.' While the camp was burning, it was said, Hoover and his wife, who kept the best table in White House history, dined alone in full evening dress off a seven-course meal. Some of the fictions were still being repeated in respectable works of history even in the 1970s.[76]

What mattered more at the time was the Administration's inept handling of the subsequent investigation, leading to a violent and public disagreement between the Attorney-General and the Superintendant of the Washington police, which took place in the closing stages of the election campaign. Hoover, loyally supporting his cabinet colleague, was made to look a liar and a monster: 'There was no question that the President was hopelessly defeated,' wrote one of his staff.[77] Not only was his credibility impugned, but the episode lost him the support of many of the churches, who had hitherto opposed the 'Wet' Roosevelt, Prohibition being the other big issue – perhaps, for most voters, the biggest issue – of the campaign.

Thus a combination of myth and alcohol, plus his own sense and image of failure, swept the Wonder Boy into oblivion in a watershed election. Reversing the huge Republican margins of the 1920s,

Roosevelt scored 22,833,000 votes to Hoover's 15,762,000, with an electoral college majority of 472 to 59, carrying all but six states. The new voting pattern of 1932 saw the emergence of the Democratic 'coalition of minorities', based on the industrial north-east, which was to last for nearly half a century and turn Congress almost into a one-party legislature. The pattern had been foreshadowed by the strong showing of Al Smith, the Democratic candidate, in the 1928 presidential and, still more, in the 1930 mid-term congressional elections. But it was only in 1932 that the Republicans finally lost the progressive image they had enjoyed since Lincoln's day and saw it triumphantly seized by their enemies, with all that such a transfer involves in the support of the media, the approval of academia, the patronage of the intelligentsia and, not least, the manufacture of historical orthodoxy.

Paradoxically, on what is now seen as the central issue of how to extricate America from Depression, there was virtually no real difference – as yet – between the parties. Both Hoover and Roosevelt were interventionists. Both were planners of a sort. Both were inflationists. It is true that Roosevelt was inclined to favour some direct relief, which Hoover still distrusted; on the other hand he was (at this stage) even more insistent than Hoover on the contradictory need for a strictly balanced budget. The actual Democratic campaign platform was strictly orthodox. Roosevelt himself was seen as an unstable lightweight in economic matters. Indeed he appeared a lightweight generally compared to his fifth cousin, Theodore. He was an aristocrat, the only child of a Hudson River squire, descended from seventeenth-century Dutch and the 'best' Anglo-Saxon stock; the proud owner of the magnificient Hyde Park estate half-way between New York and the state capital, Albany. He had been educated by governesses to the age of fourteen; then at Groton, the American Eton, where he acquired a slight English accent and learned Latin, Greek and European history. He had four years at Harvard, 'on the Gold Coast' (high-priced dormitories and clubs), developing an outlook which was, says his best biographer, 'a mixture of political conservatism, economic orthodoxy and anti-imperialism, steeped in a fuzzy altruism and wide ignorance' – a brew from which he was never wholly weaned.[78]

By 1932 Roosevelt was an experienced administrator, with over seven years in the Navy Department behind him and a moderately successful governorship of New York. But no one regarded him as a Wonder Boy. At the beginning of 1932 Lippmann described him as 'a highly impressionable person without a firm grasp of public affairs and without very strong convictions . . . not the dangerous enemy of anything. He is too eager to please . . . no crusader . . . no tribune of the people . . . no enemy of entrenched privilege. He is a pleasant man who, without any important qualifications for the office, would very much like to be President.'[79] *Time* called him 'a vigorous, well-intentioned gentleman of good birth and breeding'.

In no sense was Roosevelt the cynosure of the left-wing intelligentsia. *Common Sense*, one of their favourite journals, thought the election a non-choice between 'the laughing boy from Hyde Park' and 'the great glum engineer from Palo Alto'. Theodore Dreiser, Sherwood Anderson, Erskine Caldwell, Edmund Wilson, John Dos Passos, Lincoln Steffens, Malcolm Cowley, Sidney Hook, Clifton Fadiman and Upton Sinclair backed the Communist candidate William Z. Foster. They signed a joint letter insisting that 'It is capitalism which is destructive of all culture and Communism which desires to save civilization and its cultural heritage from the abyss to which the world crisis is driving it.' Other intellectuals such as Reinhold Neibuhr, Stuart Chase, Van Wyck Brooks, Alexander Woolcott, Edna St Vincent Millay and Paul Douglas voted for the Socialist, Norman Thomas.[80] Even after Roosevelt was well established in the White House, some of them continued to note a lack of specific gravity which he never wholly lost. 'Washington seems much more intelligent and cheerful than under any recent administration,' Edmund Wilson wrote, 'but as one lady said to me, it is "pure Chekhov". Where the Ohio Gang played poker, the brain trustees get together and talk. Nothing really makes much sense, because Roosevelt has no real policy.'[81]

There was an element of truth in the remark. Indeed, it was essentially Hoover's campaign rhetoric which opened an ideological gap between the men. Hoover had never reciprocated Roosevelt's admiration, and thought him a frivolous fellow who might easily become a dangerous one. During the campaign, feeling he was losing, he worked himself up into a fine froth about minor differences on direct relief (which Roosevelt had practised in New York) and proposed meddling in public utilities. 'My countrymen,' he roared, 'the proposals of our opponents represent a profound change in American life . . . a radical departure from the foundations of 150 years which have made this the greatest nation in the world. This election is not a mere shift from the ins to the outs. It means deciding the direction our nation will take over a century to come.' 'This campaign', he warned, 'is more than a contest between the two men. It is more than a contest between the two parties. It is a contest between two philosophies of government.'[82] Roosevelt, delighted to see some spice attributed to a programme which the *New York Times* found contained 'not one wild nostrum or disturbing proposal in the whole list' and which the *New Republic* dismissed as 'a puny answer to the challenge of the times', took the same bellicose line: 'Never before in modern history have the essential differences between the two major American parties stood out in such striking contrast as they do today.'[83] It was all baloney. It illustrates the degree to which oratory engenders myths and myths, in turn, breed realities.

And not only oratory: personalities, too. Hoover, who had made his money by honest toil, and grown dour in the process, first despised, then hated the grinning and meretricious Whig who had simply inherited his wealth and then used it as a platform to attack the industrious. He had been incensed by a Roosevelt remark in 1928, which he never forgot, that he was 'surrounded by material-istic and self-seeking advisers'.[84] Roosevelt acquired a grievance in turn. He had been crippled by poliomyelitis since the early 1920s, and, at a White House reception for governors in spring 1932, had been kept waiting by Hoover for half an hour. He had refused to ask for a chair, seeing the incident as a trial of strength and believing – it is astonishing how paranoid politicians can become in election year – that Hoover had planned it deliberately. As it happened, Roosevelt's successful struggle over his disability was the one aspect of his character Hoover admired; it is inconceivable that he could have sought to take advantage of it.[85] But Roosevelt and his wife remembered the half-hour with hatred.

The mutual antipathy proved of great historical importance. Roosevelt seems to have been quite unaware that Hoover genuinely regarded him as a public menace; not taking politics too seriously himself, he dismissed Hoover's Cassandra-cries as partisan verbiage, the sort he might employ himself. There was then a huge hiatus between the election and the transfer of power, from early November to March. Both men agreed action was urgent; except on details, they agreed what it should be – more of the same. Roosevelt conceived the fantastic notion that Hoover ought to appoint him Secretary of State immediately, so that he and his vice-president could both resign and Roosevelt could constitutionally move into the White House immediately. Hoover, equally optimistically, thought Roosevelt should be persuaded to disavow some of his campaign remarks and promises, which he thought had made a bad situation still worse, and humbly endorse, in public, measures which the President proposed to take, thus restoring confidence and ensuring continuity of (Hoover's) policy. Granted these ludicrous misap-prehensions, it is not surprising that their contacts over the long interregnum were confined to icy epistles and a mere courtesy call by Roosevelt on 3 March 1933, the eve of the transfer. It terminated in an arctic exchange which would have warmed Henry James's heart.

When Roosevelt, who was staying at the Mayflower, said Hoover was obviously too busy to return his call, the stricken Jupiter unleashed his last thunderbolt: 'Mr Roosevelt, when you have been in Washington as long as I have, you will learn that the President of the United States calls on nobody.'[86] Roosevelt took his revenge by refusing to give the departing President, whose life was under constant threat, a Secret Service bodyguard to accompany him back to Palo Alto.[87]

The public lack of co-operation between the two men during the long interregnum worked decisively in Roosevelt's political favour by drawing a profound, if wholly false, distinction between the two regimes. Roosevelt was a new face at exactly the right time and it was a smiling face. Hence he got all the credit when the recovery, under way during Hoover's last semester, became visible in the spring in the form of what was promptly dubbed 'the Roosevelt Market'. The historian hates to admit it, but luck is very important. Hoover had asked Rudy Vallee in 1932 for an anti-Depression song; the wretched fellow produced 'Brother, Can You Spare a Dime?' Roosevelt's campaign song, actually written for MGM's *Chasing Rainbows* on the eve of the great stock market crash, struck just the right button: 'Happy Days Are Here Again'. He had a lot of the intuitive skills of Lloyd George, a politician he greatly resembled. He could coin a phrase, or get others to coin one for him, as his Inaugural showed ('Let me assert my firm belief that the only thing we have to fear is fear itself').[88] At the end of his first week in office he showed his mastery of the new radio medium by inaugurating his 'fireside chats'. In terms of political show-business he had few equals and he had an enviable knack of turning problems into solutions. Thus, faced with shut banks, he declared them shut by law (using an old 1917 Act) and termed it 'A bankers' holiday'. But he also had the solid advantage of an overwhelmingly Democrat and unusually subservient Congress. His first bill, the Emergency Banking Act, went through in less than a day, after a mere forty-minute debate interrupted by cries of 'Vote, vote!' From midnight on 6 April, after a mere month in office, he had America drinking legal liquor again, an immense boost to morale. His programme was rushed through Congress in record time but it was political showbiz which christened it 'the Hundred Days'.

Beyond generating the impression of furious movement, what his Treasury Secretary, William Woodin, called 'swift and staccato action', there was no actual economic policy behind the programme.[89] Raymond Moley, the intellectual who helped Roosevelt pick his cabinet, said future historians might find some principle behind the selection, but he could not.[90] This lack of real design was reflected in the measures. At Roosevelt's exciting press conferences, he boasted he played things by ear and compared himself to a quarter-back who 'called a new play when he saw how the last one had turned out'.[91] While increasing federal spending in some directions he slashed it in others, cutting the pensions of totally disabled war-veterans, for instance, from $40 to $20 a month, and putting pressure on states to slash teachers' salaries, which he said were 'too high'. He remained devoted to the idea of a balanced budget; his first message to Congress called for major cuts in expenditure and one of his first bills was a balanced-budget measure entitled 'To Maintain the Credit of the United States Government'. So far from being a proto-Keynesian, nothing made him more angry than journalistic suggestions that his finance was unsound.[92] The notion that Roosevelt was the first deliberately to practise deficit finance to reflate an economy is false. Keynes indeed urged this course on him in a famous letter to the *New York Times* at the end of 1933: 'I lay overwhelming emphasis on the increase of national purchasing power resulting from government expenditure financed by loans.'[93] But that was not actually Roosevelt's policy except by accident. When the two men met the following summer they did not hit it off, and there is no evidence, from start to finish, that Roosevelt ever read Keynes's writings – 'During all the time I was associated with him', Moley wrote, 'I never knew him read a serious book' – or was in the slightest influenced by Keynes's ideas.[94] The Federal Reserve Bank was certainly inflationary under Roosevelt; but then it had been throughout the previous decade.

Roosevelt's legislation, for the most part, extended or tinkered with Hoover policies. The Emergency Banking Act and the Loans to Industry Act of June 1934 extended Hoover's RFC. The Home Owners' Loan Act (1932) extended a similar act of the year before. The Sale of Securities Act (1933), the Banking Acts (1933, 1935) and the Securities and Exchange Act (1934) merely continued Hoover's attempts to reform business methods. The National Labour Relations Act of 1935 (the 'Wagner Act'), which made it easier to organize unions and won the Democrats organized labour for a generation, simply broadened and strengthened the Norris–La Guardia Act passed under Hoover. The First Agricultural Adjustment Act (1933) actually undermined the reflationary aspects of government policy, curtailed the production of foodstuffs and paid farmers to take land out of production. It was, moreover, in flat contradiction to other government measures to counter the drought and dust-storms of 1934–5, such as the Soil Erosion Service, the Soil Erosion Act (1935) and the Soil Conservation and Domestic Allotment Act (1936).[95] Roosevelt's agricultural policy, in so far as he had one, was statist, designed to win votes by raising farming incomes. But it also raised food-prices for the consumer and so delayed general recovery. The National Industrial Recovery Act (1933), which created a corporatist agency under General Hugh Johnson, was in essence a Hoover-type shot at 'indicative planning'. But, drawing on Roosevelt's Great War experience – the sole source of such novel ideas as he had – it had a flavour of compulsion about it, Johnson warning that if businessmen refused to sign his 'voluntary' codes, 'They'll get a sock right on the nose.' It was this which led Hoover to denounce it as 'totalitarian'.[96] Johnson's bullying made the scheme counterproductive and there was not much real regret when the Supreme Court declared it unconstitutional.[97]

Where Roosevelt really departed from Hooverism was in reviving and extending a Wilson Great War scheme for the state to provide cheap power for the Tennessee Valley. But this was an isolated item of improvization, a 'boondoggle' to keep the South solid. Asked how he would explain its philosophy to Congress, Roosevelt replied, characteristically, 'I'll tell them it's neither fish nor fowl but, whatever it is, it will taste awfully good to the people of the Tennessee Valley.'[98] Roosevelt also spent a great deal of money on public works: $10.5 billion, plus $2.7 billion on sponsored projects, employing at one time or another 8.5 million people and constructing 122,000 public buildings, 77,000 new bridges, 285 airports, 664,000 miles of roads, 24,000 miles of storm and water-sewers, plus parks, playgrounds and reservoirs.[99] But this again was an old Hoover policy on a somewhat larger scale. In all essentials, the New Deal continued the innovatory corporatism of Hoover. It was what Walter Lippmann, writing in 1935, termed 'the Permanent New Deal'. 'The policy initiated by President Hoover in the autumn of 1929 was something utterly unprecedented in American history,' he wrote. 'The national government undertook to make the whole economic order operate prosperously . . . the Roosevelt measures are a continuous evolution of the Hoover measures.'[100]

Hoover–Roosevelt interventionism was thus a continuum. Did it work? Pro-Roosevelt historians argue that the additional elements of the New Deal brought recovery. Pro-Hoover historians counter that Roosevelt's acts delayed what Hoover's were already bringing about.[101] From the perspective of the 1980s it seems probable that both men impeded a natural recovery brought about by deflation. It was certainly slow and feeble. 1937 was the only reasonably good year, when unemployment, at 14.3 per cent, actually dipped below 8 million; but by the end of the year the economy was in free fall again – the fastest fall so far recorded – and unemployment was at 19 per cent the following year. In 1937 production briefly passed 1929 levels but quickly slipped again. The real recovery to the boom atmosphere of the 1920s came only on the Monday after the Labor Day weekend of September 1939, when the news of war in Europe plunged the New York Stock Exchange into a joyful confusion which finally wiped out the memory of October 1929. Two years later the dollar value of production finally passed 1929 levels.[102] Keynes himself, addressing Americans in 1940, conceded that the war was crucial to economic recovery: 'Your war preparations, so far from requiring a sacrifice, will be a stimulus, which neither the victory nor the defeat of the New Deal could give you, to greater individual consumption and a higher standard of life.'[103] If interventionism worked, it took nine years and a world war to demonstrate the fact.

The political success of Roosevelt was due to quite other factors than the effectiveness of his economic measures, which were largely window-dressing, transposed by time into golden myth. He demonstrated the curious ability of the aristocratic *rentier* liberal (as opposed to self-made plebeians like Harding, Coolidge and Hoover) to enlist the loyalty and even the affection of the clerisy. Newspaper-owners opposed Roosevelt, but their journalists loved him, forgiving his frequent lies, concealing the fact that he took money off them at poker (which had damned Harding), obeying his malicious injunctions to give his Administration colleagues a 'hard time'.[104] There were dark corners in the Roosevelt White House: his own infidelities, his wife's passionate attachments to another woman, the unscrupulous, sometimes vicious manner in which he used executive power.[105] None was exposed in his lifetime or for long after. Even more important was his appeal to intellectuals, once the news he employed a 'brains trust' got about.[106] In fact, of Roosevelt's entourage only Harry Hopkins, a social worker not an intellectual as such, Rexford Tugwell and Felix Frankfurter were radical as well as influential; the two last disagreed violently, Tugwell being a Stalinist-type big-scale statist, Frankfurter an anti-business trust-buster, symbolizing in turn the First New Deal (1933–6) and the Second New Deal (1937–8), which were flatly contradictory.[107] There was no intellectual coherence to the Roosevelt administration, but it seemed a place where the clerisy could feel at home. Among the able young who came to Washington were Dean Acheson, Hubert Humphrey, Lyndon Johnson, Adlai Stevenson, William Fulbright, Abe Fortas, Henry Fowler and, not least, Alger Hiss, who held meetings with four other New Deal members of a Communist cell in a Connecticut Avenue music studio.[108]

Attacks on Roosevelt served only to strengthen his appeal to the intelligentsia. A curious case in point was Mencken. In 1926 the *New York Times* had described him 'the most powerful private citizen in America'. Walter Lippmann called him 'the most powerful personal influence on this whole generation of educated people'.[109] A great part of his appeal lay in his ferocious attacks on presidents. Theodore Roosevelt was 'blatant, crude, overly confidential, devious, tyrannical, vainglorious and sometimes quite childish'. Taft's characteristic was 'native laziness and shiftlessness'. Wilson was 'the perfect model of the Christian cad' who wished to impose 'a Cossack despotism'. Harding was 'a stonehead', Coolidge 'petty, sordid and dull . . . a cheap and trashy fellow . . . almost devoid of any notion of honour . . . a dreadful little cad'. Hoover had 'a natural instinct for low, disingenuous, fraudulent manipulators'.[110] These fusillades enthralled the intelligentsia and helped permanently to wound the reputations of the men at whom they were directed. Mencken excelled himself in attacking Roosevelt, whose whiff of fraudulent collectivism filled him with genuine outrage. He was 'the Führer', 'the quack', surrounded by 'an astounding rabble of impudent nobodies', 'a gang of half-educated pedagogues, non-constitutional lawyers, starry-eyed uplifters and other such sorry wizards', and his New Deal 'a political racket', 'a series of stupendous bogus miracles', with its 'constant appeals to class envy and hatred', treating government as 'a milch-cow with 125 million teats' and marked by 'frequent repudiations of categorical pledges'.* The only consequence of these diatribes was that Mencken forfeited his influence with anyone under thirty.

Intellectuals, indeed, relished the paranoia of the rich and the conventional, and the extraordinary vehemence and fertility of invention with which Roosevelt was assailed. His next-door neighbour at Hyde Park, Howland Spencer, called him 'a frustrated darling', a 'swollen-headed nitwit with a Messiah complex and the brain of a boy scout'; to Senator Thomas Schall of Minnesota he was 'a weak-minded Louis xiv'; Owen Young, Chairman of General Electric, claimed he 'babbled to himself', Senator William Borah of Idaho that he spent his time in his study cutting out paper dolls. According to rumour (often surfacing in pamphlets), he was insane, weak-minded, a hopeless drug-addict who burst into hysterical laughter at press conferences, an impostor (the real Roosevelt was in an insane-asylum), under treatment by a psychiatrist disguised as a White House footman, and had to be kept in a straitjacket most of the time. It was said that bars had been placed in the windows to

* Mencken himself was variously described as a polecat, a Prussian, a British toady, a howling hyena, a parasite, a mangy mongrel, an affected ass, an unsavoury creature, putrid of soul, a public nuisance, a literary stink-pot, a mountebank, a rantipole, a vain hysteric, an outcast, a literary renegade, and a trained elephant who wrote the gibberish of an imbecile: Charles Fecher: *Mencken: A Study of his Thought* (New York 1978), 179 footnote.

prevent him from hurling himself out (the same rumour had arisen in Wilson's last phase; the bars, in fact, had protected the children of Theodore Roosevelt). He was said to be suffering from an Oedipus complex, a 'Silver Cord complex', heart trouble, leprosy, syphilis, incontinence, impotency, cancer, comas and that his polio was inexorably 'ascending into his head'. He was called a Svengali, a Little Lord Fauntleroy, a simpleton, a modern political Juliet 'making love to the people from the White House balcony', a pledge-breaker, a Communist, tyrant, oath-breaker, fascist, socialist, the Demoralizer, the Panderer, the Violator, the Embezzler, petulant, insolent, rash, ruthless, blundering, a sorcerer, an impostor, callow upstart, shallow autocrat, a man who encouraged swearing and 'low slang' and a 'subjugator of the human spirit'.[111] Crossing the Atlantic on the *Europa*, just before the 1936 election, Thomas Wolfe recorded that, when he said he was voting for the Monster,

. . . boiled shirts began to roll up their backs like window-shades. Maidenly necks which a moment before were as white and graceful as the swan's became instantly so distended with the energies of patriotic rage that diamond dog-collars and ropes of pearls were snapped and sent flying like so many pieces of string. I was told that if I voted for this vile Communist, this sinister fascist, this scheming and contriving socialist and his gang of conspirators, I had no longer any right to consider myself an American citizen.[112]

It was against this background that Roosevelt won the greatest of electoral victories in 1936, by 27,477,000 to 16,680,000 votes, carrying all but two states (Maine and Vermont) and piling up enormous Democratic majorities in both houses of Congress. Roosevelt's attraction for the young, the progressives and the intellectuals survived even the abandonment of New Deal innovations in 1938 and his collapse into the hands of the Big City Democratic machine bosses, who ensured his re-election in 1940 and 1944.

The truth is that Roosevelt appeared to be in tune with the Thirties spirit, which had repudiated the virtues of capitalist enterprise and embraced those of collectivism. The heroes of the 1920s had been businessmen, the sort of titans, led by Thomas Edison, who had endorsed Harding and Coolidge on their front porches. The 1929 crash and its aftermath weakened faith in this pantheon. By 1931 Felix Frankfurter was writing to Bruce Bliven, editor of the *New Republic*: 'Nothing I believe sustains the present system more than the pervasive worship of success and the touching faith we have in financial and business messiahs . . . . I believe it to be profoundly important to undermine that belief . . . . Undermine confidence in their greatness and you have gone a long way towards removing some basic obstructions to the exploration of economic and social problems.'[113] By 1932 this undermining process was largely complete, helped by revelations that J.P. Morgan, for instance, had paid no income-tax for the three previous years, and that Andrew Mellon had been coached by an expert from his own Treasury Department in the art of tax-avoidance.

Loss of faith in American business leaders coincided with a sudden and overwhelming discovery that the Soviet Union existed and that it offered an astonishing and highly relevant alternative to America's agony. Stuart Chase's *A New Deal* ended with the question: 'Why should the Russians have all the fun of remaking a world?'[114] The first Soviet Five Year Plan had been announced in 1928, but it was only four years later that its importance was grasped by American writers. Then a great spate of books appeared, praising Soviet-style planning and holding it up as a model to America. Joseph Freeman: *The Soviet Worker*, Waldo Frank: *Dawn in Russia*, William Z. Foster: *Towards Soviet America*, Kirby Page: *A New Economic Order*, Harry Laidler: *Socialist Planning*, Sherwood Eddy: *Russia Today: What Can We Learn From It?* all of them published in 1932, reinforced Lincoln Steffens' best-selling pro-Soviet autobiography, which had appeared the year before, and introduced a still more influential tract, *The Coming Struggle for Power* by the British Communist John Strachey, which appeared in 1933.[115]

America was and is a millennarian society where overweening expectations can easily oscillate into catastrophic loss of faith. In the early 1930s there was net emigration. When Amtorg, the Soviet trading agency, advertised for 6,000 skilled workers, more than 100,000 Americans applied. To the comedian Will Rogers: 'Those rascals in Russia, along with their cuckoo stuff have got some mighty good ideas . . . . Just think of everybody in a country going to work.' 'All roads in our day lead to Moscow,' Steffens proclaimed; and Strachey echoed him: 'To travel from the capitalist world into Soviet territory is to pass from death to birth.' We must now explore the gruesome and unconscious irony of these remarks.

EIGHT

The Devils

At the very moment the American intelligentsia turned to totalitarian Europe for spiritual sustenance and guidance in orderly planning, it was in fact embarking on two decades of unprecedented ferocity and desolation – moral relativism in monstrous incarnation. On 21 December 1929 Stalin had celebrated his fiftieth birthday, as absolute master of an autocracy for which, in concentrated savagery, no parallel in history could be found. A few weeks earlier, while the New York Stock Exchange was collapsing, he had given orders for the forced collectivization of the Russian peasants, an operation involving far greater material loss than anything within the scope of Wall Street, and a human slaughter on a scale no earlier tyranny had possessed the physical means, let alone the wish, to bring about. By the time John Strachey wrote of fleeing capitalist death to find Soviet birth, this gruesome feat of social engineering had been accomplished. Five million peasants were dead; twice as many in forced labour camps. By that time, too, Stalin had acquired a pupil, admirer and rival in the shape of Hitler, controlling a similar autocracy and planning human sacrifices to ideology on an even ampler scale. For Americans, then, it was a case of moving from a stricken Arcadia to an active *pandaemonium*. The devils had taken over.

When Lenin died in 1924 his autocracy was complete and Stalin, as General Secretary of the Party, had already inherited it. All that remained was the elimination of potential rivals for sole power. For this Stalin was well equipped. This ex-seminarist and revolutionary thug was half-gangster, half-bureaucrat. He had no ideals; no ideological notions of his own. According to the composer Shostakovich, Stalin wanted to be tall, with powerful hands. The court painter Nalbandian satisfied this wish by fixing the angle of vision from below and getting his master to fold his hands over his stomach; several other portrait painters were shot.[1] Stalin was only five foot four inches tall, thin, swarthy and with a pockmarked face. A Tsarist

police description of him, compiled when he was twenty-two, noted
that the second and third toes of his left foot were fused together;
and in addition an accident as a boy caused his left elbow to be stiff,
with a shortening of the arm, the left hand being noticeably thicker
than the right. As Shostakovich said, he kept hiding his right hand.
Bukharin, two years before he was murdered, said that in his view
Stalin suffered bitterly from these disabilities and from real or
imagined intellectual incapacity. 'This suffering is probably the most
human thing about him'; but it led him to take revenge on anyone
with higher capacities: 'There is something diabolical and inhuman
about his compulsion to take vengeance for this same suffering on
everybody . . . . This is a small, vicious man; no, not a man, but a
devil.'² Stalin did not have Lenin's ideological passion for violence.
But he was capable of unlimited violence to achieve his purposes, or
indeed for no particular reason; and he sometimes nursed feelings of
revenge against individuals for years before executing them. He
served his apprenticeship in large-scale violence as Chairman of the
North Caucasus Military District in 1918, when he decided to act
against his 'bourgeois military specialists' whom he suspected of lack
of enthusiasm for killing. The chief of staff of the district, Colonel
Nosovich, testified: 'Stalin's order was brief, "Shoot them!" . . . . A
large number of officers . . . were seized by the Cheka and
immediately shot without trial.'³ At the time Stalin also complained
of all three Red Army commanders in the area sent to him by Trotsky
and later held this as a grudge against him. He had them all
murdered in 1937–9.⁴

However, immediately after Lenin's incapacitation and mindful of
his criticisms, Stalin sought power by posing as a moderate and a
man of the Centre. His problem was as follows. By controlling the
rapidly expanding Secretariat Stalin was already in virtual control of
the party machinery and in the process of filling the Central
Committee with his creatures. On the Politburo, however, four
important figures stood between him and autocracy: Trotsky, the
most famous and ferocious of the Bolsheviks, who controlled the
army; Zinoviev, who ran the Leningrad party – for which Stalin,
then and later, had a peculiar hatred; Kamenev, who controlled the
Moscow party, now the most important; and Bukharin, the leading
theorist. The first three leaned towards the Left, the last to the Right,
and the way in which Stalin divided and used them to destroy each
other, and then appropriated their policies as required – he seems to
have had none of his own – is a classic exercise in power-politics.

It is important to realize that, just as Lenin was the creator of the
new autocracy and its instruments and practice of mass terror, so
also there were no innocents among his heirs. All were vicious killers.

Even Bukharin, whom Lenin called 'soft as wax' and who has been presented as the originator of 'socialism with a human face',[5] was an inveterate denouncer of others, 'a gaoler of the best Communists' as he was bitterly called.[6] Zinoviev and Kamenev were wholly unscrupulous party bosses. Trotsky, who after his fall presented himself as a believer in party democracy and who was apotheosized by his follower and hagiographer Isaac Deutscher as the epitome of all that was noblest in the Bolshevik movement, was never more than a sophisticated political gangster.[7] He carried through the original October 1917 *putsch* and thereafter slaughtered opponents of the regime with the greatest abandon. It was he who first held wives and children of Tsarist officers hostage, threatening to shoot them for non-compliance with Soviet orders, a device soon built into the system. He was equally ruthless with his own side, shooting commissars and Red Army commanders who 'showed cowardice' (i.e. retreated), later to become a universal Stalinist practice; the rank-and-file were decimated.[8] Trotsky always took the most ruthless line. He invented conscript labour and destroyed the independent trade unions. He used unspeakable brutality to put down the Kronstadt rising of ordinary sailors and was even preparing to use poison gas when it collapsed.[9] Like Lenin, he identified himself with history and argued that history was above all moral restraints.

Trotsky remained a moral relativist of the most dangerous kind right to the end. 'Problems of revolutionary morality', he wrote in his last, posthumous book, 'are fused with the problems of revolutionary strategy and tactics.'[10] There were no such things as moral criteria; only criteria of political efficacy. He said it was right to murder the Tsar's children, as he had done, because it was politically useful and those who carried it out represented the proletariat; but Stalin did not represent the proletariat – he had become a 'bureaucratic excess' – and therefore it was wrong for him to murder Trotsky's children.[11] Trotsky's followers are, of course, notorious for their attachment to this subjectively defined code of ethics and their contempt for objective morality.

The term 'Trotskyist', first used as a term of abuse by Zinoviev, was defined in its mature form by Stalin, who created the distinction between 'permanent revolution' (Trotsky) and 'revolution in one country' (Stalin). In fact they all believed in immediate world revolution to begin with, and all turned to consolidating the regime when it didn't happen. Trotsky wanted to press ahead with industrialization faster than Stalin but both were, from first to last, opportunists. They had graduated in the same slaughterhouse and their quarrel was essentially about who should be its new high priest. Had Trotsky come out on top, he would probably have been even more bloodthirsty than Stalin. But he would not have lasted: he lacked the skills of survival.

Indeed Stalin found it easy to destroy him. Soviet internal struggles have always been about ambition and fear rather than policies. Although Kamenev and Zinoviev were broadly in agreement with Trotsky's Left line, Stalin formed a triumvirate with them to prevent him using the Red Army to stage a personal *putsch*. He used the two Leftists to hunt Trotsky down and afterwards was able to present them as violently impetuous and himself as the servant of moderation. All the crucial moves took place in 1923, while Lenin was still in a coma. Stalin flexed his muscles in the summer by getting the OGPU to arrest a number of party members for 'indiscipline' and persuading his two Leftist allies to endorse the arrest of the first major Bolshevist victim, Sultan-Galiyev (Stalin did not actually murder him until six years later).[12] All the time he was building up his following in local organizations and the CC.

Trotsky made every mistake open to him. During his 1920 visit Bertrand Russell had shrewdly noted the contrast between Trotsky's histrionics and vanity, and Lenin's lack of such weakness. An eye-witness account of the 1923–4 Politburo meetings says that Trotsky never bothered to conceal his contempt for his colleagues, sometimes slamming out or ostentatiously turning his back and reading a novel.[13] He scorned the notion of political intrigue and still more its demeaning drudgery. He never attempted to use the army since he put the party first; but then he did not build up a following in the party either. He must have been dismayed when for the first time he attacked Stalin in the autumn of 1923 and discovered how well-entrenched he was. Trotsky wanted the palm without the dust, a fatal mistake for a gangster who could not appeal from the mafia to the public. He was often sick or away; never there at the right time. He even missed Lenin's state funeral, a serious error since it was Stalin's first move towards restoring the reverential element in Russian life that had been so sadly missed since the destruction of the throne and church.[14] Soon Stalin was resurrecting the old Trotsky–Lenin rows. At the thirteenth Party Congress in May 1924 he branded Trotsky with the Leninist term of 'fractionalist'. Trotsky refused to retract his criticism that Stalin was becoming too powerful. But he could not dispute Lenin's condemnation of internal opposition and, like a man accused of heresy by the Inquisition, he was disarmed by his own religious belief. 'Comrades,' he admitted, 'none of us wishes to be right or can be right against the party. The party is in the last resort always right . . . I know that one cannot be right against the party. One can only be right with the party and through the party, since history has created no other paths to the realization of what is right.'[15] Since Stalin was already in control of the party, Trotsky's words forged the ice-pick that crushed his skull sixteen years later.

By the end of 1924 Stalin, with Kamenev and Zinoviev doing the dirty work, had created the heresy of 'Trotskyism' and related it to Trotsky's earlier disputes with Lenin, who had been embalmed and put into his apotheosis-tomb five months earlier. In January 1925 Stalin was thus able to strip Trotsky of the army control with the full approval of the party. Party stalwarts were now informed that Trotsky's part in the Revolution was very much less than he claimed and his face was already being blacked out of relevant photographs – the first instance of Stalinist re-writing of history.[16] Trotsky's first replacement as army boss, Frunze, proved awkward; so it seems Stalin had him murdered in October 1925 in the course of an operation his doctors had advised against.[17] His successor, a creature later to be known as Marshal Voroshilov, proved entirely obedient and accepted the rapid penetration of the army by the OGPU, which Stalin now controlled.

With Trotsky destroyed (he was expelled from the Politburo October 1926, from the party the following month, sent into internal exile in 1928 and exiled from Russia in 1929; murdered on Stalin's orders in Mexico in 1940), Stalin turned on his Leftist allies. Early in 1925 he stole Kamenev's Moscow party from under his nose by suborning his deputy, Uglanov. In September he brought in Bukharin and the Right to help in a frontal attack on Zinoviev–Kamenev, and had them decisively defeated at the Party Congress in December. Immediately afterwards, Stalin's most trusted and ruthless henchman, Molotov, was sent to Leningrad with a powerful squad of party 'heavies', to smash up Zinoviev's party apparatus there and take it over – essentially the same methods, but on a larger scale, that Al Capone was employing to extend his territory in Chicago at that very time.[18] Frightened, Zinoviev now joined forces with Trotsky, the man he had helped to break. But it was too late: they were both immediately expelled from the party, and at the fifteenth Party Congress in December 1926, Kamenev's protest was shouted down by the massed ranks of carefully drilled Stalinists who now filled the party's ranks. Consciously echoing Lenin, Stalin came out into the open against his old allies: 'Enough comrades, an end must be put to this game . . . . Kamenev's speech is the most lying, pharasaical, scoundrelly and roguish of all the opposition speeches that have been made from this platform.'[19]

The moment the Left was beaten and disarmed, Stalin began to adopt their policy of putting pressure on the peasants to speed industrialization, thus preparing the means to destroy Bukharin and the Right. The big clash came on 10 July 1928 at a meeting of the Central Committee, when Bukharin argued that while the *kulak* himself was not a threat – 'we can shoot him down with machine-guns' – forced collectivization would unite all the peasants against the government. Stalin interrupted him with sinister piety, 'A fearful dream, but God is merciful!'[20] God might be; not the General-Secretary. The next day, a scared Bukharin speaking on behalf of his allies Rykov, the nominal head of the government, and Tomsky, the hack 'trade union' leader, had a secret meeting with Kamenev and offered to form a united front to stop Stalin. He now realized, he said, that Stalin was not primarily interested in policy but in sole power: '*He* will strangle us. He is an unprincipled intriguer who subordinates everything to his appetite for power. At any given moment he will change his theories in order to get rid of someone . . . [He is] Genghis Khan!' He seems to have thought that Yagoda, of the OGPU, would come over to them; but he was misinformed.[21] None of these nervous men had the numerical support in the key party bodies to outvote Stalin; or the means, in the shape of trained men with guns, to overrule him by force; or the skill and resolution – both of which he had shown in abundance – to destroy him by intrigue. In 1929 they were all dealt with: Rykov ousted from the premiership, Tomsky from the trade union leadership, and both, plus Bukharin, forced publicly to confess their errors (Kamenev and Zinoviev had already done so). They could now be tried and murdered at leisure.

Stalin had already begun to perfect the dramaturgy of terror. Drawing on his monkish memories, he arranged party meetings to provide a well-rehearsed antiphonal dialogue between himself and his claque, with Stalin suggesting moderation in dealing with party 'enemies' and the claque insisting on severity. Thus, reluctantly demanding the expulsion of Trotsky and Zinoviev, Stalin said he had been against this before and had been 'cursed' by 'honest Bolsheviks' for being too lenient. The claque: 'Yes – and we still do curse you for it.'[22] In May–July 1929 Stalin staged the first of his show-trials, against a group of Donbass mining engineers charged with 'sabotage'. The script was written by the OGPU official Y.G.Yevdokimov, one of Stalin's creatures, and featured the twelve-year-old son of one of the accused, who denounced his father and called for his execution.[23] The actual head of the OGPU, Menzhinsky, opposed this trial, as did some Politburo members.[24] But this was the last time Stalin met genuine opposition from within the secret police or security apparatus. Towards the end of the year he ordered the shooting of the senior OGPU official Yakov Blyumkin, the first party member to be executed for an intra-party crime.[25]

Thereafter the trials went exactly as Stalin planned them, down to the last indignant crowd-scene, like some gigantic production by the Soviet cineaste Sergei Eisenstein. While the trial of the 'Industrial Party' was taking place the next year, the body of the court shouted, at carefully arranged intervals, 'Death to the wreckers!' and in the streets outside, thousands of workers marched past shouting 'Death, death, death!'[26] By 1929 Stalin had the all-purpose term *Stakhtyites* (wreckers) for anyone he wished to destroy. As he put it, '*Stakhtyites* are now lurking in all branches of our industry. Many, though far from all, have been caught . . . . Wrecking is all the more dangerous because it is linked with international capital. Bourgeois wrecking is an indubitable sign that capitalist elements . . . are gathering strength for new attacks on the Soviet Union.'[27] He was rapidly moving to the point when he had only to mention a list of names to the Central Committee and would receive the instant instructions: 'Arrest, try, shoot!'[28]

While goading on the witch-hunting and building up the paranoia and hysteria, Stalin was contriving his own apotheosis as the heir of the deified Lenin. As early as 1924–5, Yuzovka, Yuzovo and Tsaritsyn became Stalino, Stalinsky, Stalingrad; but it was the fiftieth birthday celebrations at the end of 1929 which marked the real beginning not only of Stalin's unfettered personal rule but of the Stalin cult in all its nightmare maturity, with names like Stalinabad, Stalin-Aul, Staliniri, Stalinissi, Stalino, Stalinogorsk, Stalinsk, Mount Stalin, sprouting all over the Soviet Empire, and with the first appearance of the Stalinist litanies: Man of Steel, the Granite Bolshevik, the Brass-hard Leninist, the Iron Soldier, the Universal Genius,[29] a form of ruler-worship which went back to the Egyptian pharaohs. While Soviet government became more hieratic and liturgical in its externals, and more terroristic in essentials, Soviet 'science' moved into the irrational, with quasi-religious groups of 'leading thinkers', known variously as Geneticists, Teleologists, Mechanists and Dialecticians – there were many others – struggling to win Stalin's approval for their all-embracing theories of physical progress.[30] Some of the experts at Stalin's court were ready to argue that, with the 'Man of Steel' in charge, human will could overcome anything, and what had hitherto been regarded as the laws of nature or of economics could be suspended. As one of his economists, S.G.Shumilin, put it: 'Our task is not to study economics but to change it. We are bound by no laws.'[31]

It was against this background of irrationality, and thus emancipated from any system of economics or morality, that Stalin carried through his colossal exercise in social engineering, the destruction of the independent Russian peasantry. As we have seen, it was the peasants who had made Lenin's *putsch* possible; and who had later, by defying him, forced on him the surrender he had concealed by the euphemism New Economic Planning. It was in the name of the continuity of Leninism and the NEP that Stalin had destroyed the Left in the years 1924–8. But now the time had come to exact a dreadful revenge on the rural multitudes who had humbled Soviet power.

There was no theoretical basis in Marxism, or anything else, for what Stalin now did. But it had a certain monstrous logic. There is no point of stability in a state which is socializing itself. It must go either forward or back. If it does not go forward, the power of the market system, which expresses certain basic human instincts of barter and accumulation, is such that it will always reassert itself, and capitalism will make its reappearance. Then the embryo socialist state will collapse. If socialism is to go forward, it must push ahead with large-scale industrialization. That means surplus food for the workers; and surplus food to export to raise money for capital investment. In short the peasants must pay the price for socialist progress. And since they are unwilling to pay this price voluntarily, force must be used, in ever-growing quantities, until their will is broken and they deliver what is required of them. That is the bitter logic of socialist power which Stalin grasped in the 1920s: there was no stable point of rest between a return to capitalism and the use of unlimited force.[32]

This logic formed a sinister counterpoint to the successive stages of Stalin's destruction of his opponents to Left and Right. Trotsky, Zinoviev and Kamenev had always argued that the peasant would never surrender enough food voluntarily, and must be coerced and, if need be, crushed. Stalin removed them, using the argument that they planned to 'plunder the peasantry' which was 'the ally of the working class', not to be subjected to 'increased pressure'.[33] But the harvest of 1927 was poor and that was when the logic of socialism began to operate. The peasants hoarded what food they had; they would not take the government's paper money, which bought nothing worth having. Thus Lenin's compromise, based on the theory of backing the 76.7 million 'middle peasants' and the 22.4 million 'poor peasants' against the 5 million 'kulaks' (in fact it was impossible to make these distinctions except on paper: all peasants hated the government), broke down.[34]

In January 1928, with no food in the towns, no grain exports and increasingly short of foreign currency, Stalin unleashed his first attack on the peasants, sending 30,000 armed party workers into the countryside, a repetition of the gouging process used in 1918. There were soon reports of atrocities, disguised by such phrases as 'competition between grain-collective organizations', 'regrettable lapses from Soviet legality', 'slipping into the methods of War Communism', 'administrative mistakes' and so forth. More sinister was the growing tendency of Stalin's spokesmen to lump all peasants together. Molotov spoke of forcing 'the middle peasant to come to heel'; Mikoyan accused the 'poor peasant' of being 'under *kulak* influence'. Some 1,400 'terrorist acts' by peasants (that is, resistance to seizure of food by armed force) were reported in 1928. One *kulak*, caught with a rifle, sneered, 'This is what the class war is all about.' The Smolensk region records, captured by the Nazis and later published, give us our only glimpse, through unfiltered official documents, into this seething cauldron of peasant agony. For the first time Stalin used the word 'liquidate', referring to 'the first serious campaign of capitalist elements in the countryside . . . against the Soviet power'. Anyone, he cynically remarked, who thought the policy could be carried through without unpleasantness, 'is not a Marxist but a fool'.[35]

But stealing the peasants' food led to them sowing less, and the 1928 harvest was even worse. By the autumn of 1928, Stalin's need for foreign exchange was desperate, as we know from a quite separate development, the large-scale secret sales of Russian art treasures to the West. It was in November 1928, according to one of the Leningrad Hermitage curators, Tatiana Chernavin, that 'We were commanded in the shortest possible time to reorganize the whole of the Hermitage collection "on the principles of sociological formations" . . . and set to work and pulled to pieces a collection which it had taken more than a hundred years to create.'[36] The paintings went to millionaires all over the world. The biggest purchaser was Andrew Mellon, who in 1930–1 bought for $6,654,053 a total of twenty-one paintings, including five Rembrandts, a Van Eyck, two Franz Hals, a Rubens, four Van Dycks, two Raphaels, a Velazquez, a Botticelli, a Veronese, a Chardin, a Titian and a Perugino – probably the finest hoard ever transferred in one swoop and cheap at the price. All went into the Washington National Gallery, which Mellon virtually created. It is one of the many ironies of this period that, at a time when the intelligentsia were excoriating Mellon for tax-evasion, and contrasting the smooth-running Soviet planned economy with the breakdown in America, he was secretly exploiting the frantic necessities of the Soviet leaders to form the basis of one of America's most splendid public collections.[37] The dollar value of Mellon's purchases alone came to a third of all officially recorded Soviet exports to the USA in 1930.

By a further and more fearful irony, it was the example of successful enterprise in America which finally persuaded Stalin to drop his flagging policy of extorting grain from independent peasants and to herd them all by force into collectives. Hitherto Stalin had always denied that co-operatives and collectives were different, describing the collective farm as merely 'the most pronounced type of producer co-operative'.[38] As such it was a voluntary institution. But in 1928 Stalin heard of the great Campbell farm in Montana, covering over 30,000 hectares, the biggest single grain-producer in the world.[39] He decided to set up such 'grain factories' in Russia, on a gigantic scale. One of 150,000 hectares was cobbled together the same year in the Caucasus. This unit was equipped with 300 tractors, and the tractor (as opposed to the wooden plough, of which 5.5 million were still in use in Russia in October 1927) became for Stalin a symbol of the future, as electricity was for Lenin. He got his men to accuse *kulaks* of an anti-tractor campaign, saying they spread rumours of 'anti-Christ coming to earth on a steel horse', of petrol-fumes 'poisoning' the soil and Volga sayings: 'The tractor digs deep, the soil dries up.' In fact it was the richer peasants who were buying tractors as quickly as they could afford them. Stalin's forcing of what he called 'tractor columns' and 'tractor stations' on the collectives led to what one of the few independent observers described as 'the reckless treatment of machinery in all the socialized lands' and 'fleets of disabled tractors' which 'dot the Russian landscape'.[40] But this was characteristic of Stalin's ignorance of what actually went on in the Russian countryside – an ignorance, of course, which Lenin had shared. According to Khrushchev, 'Stalin separated himself from the people and never went anywhere . . . . The last time he visited a village was in January 1928.'[41] The whole of the gigantic operation of collectivizing the peasants, involving about 105 million people, was conducted from Stalin's study in the Kremlin.

Not that there was much deliberative and rational planning about it. Quite the contrary. The case against using force to bring peasants into state farms had always been regarded as unassailable. It was based on Engels's dictum in his *The Peasant Question in France and Germany* (1894): 'When we acquire state power we shall not think of appropriating the small peasants by force.' Lenin often quoted this passage. Even Trotsky had spoken of 'agreement', 'compromise' and 'gradual transition'. As late as 2 June 1929 *Pravda* insisted: 'Neither terror nor de-kulakization, but a socialist offensive on the paths of NEP.'[42] The decision to collectivize by force was taken suddenly, without any kind of public debate, in the last weeks of 1929. It was typical of the way in which the pursuit of Utopia leads the tiny handful of men in power abruptly to assault a society many centuries in the making, to treat men like ants and stamp on their nest. Without warning, Stalin called for an 'all-out offensive against the *kulak* . . . . We must smash the *kulaks*, eliminate them as a class . . . .

We must strike at the *kulaks* so hard as to prevent them from rising to their feet again . . . . We must break down the resistance of that class in open battle.' On 27 December 1929, the Feast of St John the Apostle, he declared war with the slogan 'Liquidate the *kulaks* as a class!'[43] It was the green light for a policy of extermination, more than three years before Hitler came to power, twelve years before the ordering of the 'Final Solution'.

Collectivization was a calamity such as no peasantry had known since the Thirty Years' War in Germany. The organizing agency was the OGPU but any instrument which came to hand was used. The poorer peasants were encouraged to loot the homes of dispossessed *kulaks* and hunt them down across the fields. But soon *kulak* meant any peasant whatever who actively opposed collectivization, and entire peasant communities resisted desperately. They were surrounded by police and military units, using methods which Hitler imitated in detail when rounding up the Jews, and gunned down or forced into trucks for deportation. Deutscher, travelling in Russia, met an OGPU colonel who wept, saying, 'I am an old Bolshevik. I worked in the underground against the Tsar and then I fought in the civil war. Did I do all that in order that I should now surround villages with machine-guns and order my men to fire indiscriminately into crowds of peasants? Oh, no, no, no!'[44] The large-scale violence began at the end of 1929 and continued to the end of February, by which time the number of collectivized households had jumped to about 30 per cent. Disturbed by the scale of the resistance, Stalin suddenly reversed his policy in a *Pravda* article of 2 March 1930: 'One cannot implant collective farms by violence – that would be stupid and reactionary.' But half the collectives then voted to denationalize themselves in a few weeks, and by early summer he had resumed his 'stupid and reactionary' policy of force, this time carrying it through to the bitter end.[45]

The result was what the great Marxist scholar Leszek Kolakowski has called 'probably the most massive warlike operation ever conducted by a state against its own citizens'.[46] The number of peasants actually shot by the regime is not yet known and may not be discoverable even when, and if, scholars ever get at the Soviet archives. Churchill said that, in Moscow in August 1942, Stalin told him coolly that 'ten millions' of peasants had been 'dealt with'.[47] According to one scholarly estimate, in addition to those peasants executed by the OGPU or killed in battle, between 10 and 11 million were transported to north European Russia, to Siberia and Central Asia; of these one-third went into concentration camps, a third into internal exile and a third were executed or died in transit.[48]

The peasants who remained were stripped of their property,

however small, and herded into the 'grain factories'. To prevent them from fleeing to the towns, a system of internal passports was introduced, and any change of domicile without official permission was punished by imprisonment. Peasants were not allowed passports at all. So they were tied to the soil, *glebae adscripti*, as in the final phases of the Roman Empire or during the age of feudal serfdom. The system was more stringent than in the blackest periods of the Tsarist autocracy, and was not relaxed until the 1970s.[49]

The result was predictable: what has been termed 'perhaps the only case in history of a purely man-made famine'.[50] Rather than surrender their grain, the peasants burnt it. They smashed their implements. They slaughtered 18 million horses, 30 million cattle (45 per cent of the total), 100 million sheep and goats (two-thirds of the total). Even according to the figures in the official Soviet history, livestock production was only 65 per cent of the 1913 level in 1933, draught animals fell by more than 50 per cent, and total draught power, including tractors, did not surpass the 1928 level until 1935.[51] Despite the famine of 1932–3, Stalin managed to keep up some grain exports to pay for imported machinery, including the tooling of his new war-factories. The cost in Russian lives was staggering. Iosif Dyadkin's demographic study, 'Evaluation of Unnatural Deaths in the Population of the USSR 1927–58', which circulated in *samizdat* (underground newsletter) form in the late 1970s, calculates that during the collectivization and 'elimination of the classes' period, 1929–36, 10 million men, women and children met unnatural deaths.[52]

The re-feudalization of the Soviet peasantry, who then formed three-quarters of the population, had a calamitous effect on the morale of the Communist rank-and-file, who carried it through. As Kolakowski puts it: 'The whole party became an organization of torturers and oppressors. No one was innocent, and all Communists were accomplices in the coercion of society. Thus the party acquired a new species of moral unity, and embarked on a course from which there was no turning back.'[53] Exactly the same thing was to happen to the German National Socialists a few years later: it was Stalin who pointed the way to Hitler. Everyone in the party knew what was going on. Bukharin grumbled privately that the 'mass annihilation of completely defenceless men, women and children' was acclimatizing party members to violence and brute obedience, transforming them 'into cogs in some terrible machine'.[54] But only one person protested to Stalin's face. His second wife, Nadezhda, had left him in 1926 with her two small children, Vasily and Svetlana. Stalin persuaded her to return, but had her watched by the OGPU and, when she complained, traced her informants and had them arrested. On

7 November 1932, in front of witnesses, she protested violently to him about his treatment of the peasants, and then went home and shot herself. This was the second family drama – his first son Yakov had attempted suicide in despair in 1928 – and Svetlana later wrote: 'I believe that my mother's death, which he had taken as a personal betrayal, deprived his soul of the last vestiges of human warmth.'[55]

Stalin's response was to get the OGPU to take over the organization of his household; it hired and trained his servants, superintended his food and controlled all access to his person.[56] He operated now not through the normal government or party organs but through his personal secretariat, an outgrowth of the old party Secretariat; and through this he created a personal secret police within the official one, called the Special Secret Political Department of State Security.[57] Thus cocooned, he felt himself invulnerable; certainly others did. Though the state of Russia was so desperate in 1932 that Stalin's regime came near to foundering, as had Lenin's early in 1921, no one came even near to killing him.

As for the planning, held up as a model to the world, it was in all essentials a paper exercise. None of its figures have ever been independently verified, from 1928 to this day. The non-governmental auditing controls, which are an essential part of every constitutional state under the rule of law, do not exist in the Soviet Union. There was something fishy about the First Five Year Plan from the start. It was approved by the Central Committee in November 1928, formally adopted in May 1929, and then declared retrospectively operative since October 1928! Since from the end of 1929 the entire country was turned upside down by the sudden decision to collectivize agriculture, the 1928 Plan (assuming it ever existed in fact) was rendered totally irrelevant. Yet in January 1933, the month Hitler came to power, Stalin suddenly announced it had been completed in four-and-a-half years, with 'maximum over-fulfilment' in many respects.[58]

The Plan, held up to sophisticated Western society as a model of civilized process, was in fact a barbarous fantasy. Russia is a rich country, with a wealth and variety of raw materials unparalleled anywhere else in the world. The Soviet regime inherited an expanding population and a rapidly growing industrial base. As Wilhelmine Germany had surmised, nothing could stop Russia becoming one of the greatest, soon *the* greatest, industrial power on earth. The policies of Lenin and, still more, Stalin – or rather the series of hasty expedients which passed for policy – had the net effect of slowing down that inevitable expansion, just as Lenin–Stalin policies enormously, and in this case permanently, damaged Russia's flourishing agriculture.

But progress was made nonetheless. Great projects were completed. There was the Dnieper Dam of 1932; the Stalingrad tractor factory; the Magnitogorsk steel plant in the Urals; the Kuznetsk Basin mines of Siberia; the Baltic–White Sea Canal; and many others. Some of them, such as the canal, were built wholly or in part by slave labour. As we have seen, the use of political slaves had been part of the Lenin regime – though initially a small part – from its first months. Under Stalin the system expanded, first slowly, then with terrifying speed. Once forced collectivization got under way, in 1930–3, the concentration camp population rose to 10 million, and after the beginning of 1933 it never fell below this figure until well after Stalin's death. Among industries which regularly employed slave-labour on a large scale were gold-mining, forestry, coal, industrial agriculture and transport – especially the building of canals, railways, airports and roads. The OGPU negotiated slave-labour deals with various government agencies in exactly the same manner that the Nazi SS were later to hire such labour to Krupps, I.G.Farben and other German firms. For the big Baltic–White Sea Canal, one of Stalin's showpieces, 300,000 slaves were used.[59] Slave-labour ceased to be marginal, as in Lenin's time, and became an important and integral part of the Stalinist economy, with the OGPU administering large areas of Siberia and Central Asia.[60]

The death-rate in totalitarian slave-labour camps appears to have been about 10 per cent a year, to judge from German figures.[61] It may have been higher in Russia because so many of the camps were located within the Arctic and sub-Arctic regions. At all events the need to keep the slave-labour force supplied was undoubtedly one of the main reasons for the countless arrests of non-party workers during the years 1929–33. Periodically there were carefully staged show-trials, such as the Menshevik trial in March 1931, or the Metro-Vickers engineers trial in April 1933. These highly publicized events, which revealed in elaborate detail the existence of a series of diabolical conspiracies, each a small part of one gigantic conspiracy against the regime and the Russian people, were needed to create the xenophobia and hysteria without which the Stalinist state could not hang together at all. But of course they were only a tiny fraction of the process, the public rationale for arrests and disappearances taking place all over the country on an unprecedented scale.

Most 'trials' were not reported, although they often involved large groups of people, classified together according to occupation. Many were never tried at all. The arbitrary nature of the arrests was essential to create the climate of fear which, next to the need for labour, was the chief motive for the non-party terror. An OGPU man admitted to the *Manchester Guardian* Moscow correspondent that innocent people were arrested: naturally – otherwise no one would be frightened. If people, he said, were arrested only for specific misdemeanours, all the others would feel safe and so become ripe for treason.[62] But this apart, there seems to have been no pattern of logic or sense in many instances. An old Bolshevik recounts the case of an energy expert who, over eighteen months, was arrested, sentenced to death, pardoned, sent to a camp, released, rehabilitated and finally given a medal, all for no apparent reason.[63] But the overwhelming majority of those arrested spent the rest of their lives in the camps.

In the outside world, the magnitude of the Stalin tyranny – or indeed its very existence – was scarcely grasped at all. Most of those who travelled to Russia were either businessmen, anxious to trade and with no desire to probe or criticize what did not concern them, or intellectuals who came to admire and, still more, to believe. If the decline of Christianity created the modern political zealot – and his crimes – so the evaporation of religious faith among the educated left a vacuum in the minds of Western intellectuals easily filled by secular superstition. There is no other explanation for the credulity with which scientists, accustomed to evaluating evidence, and writers, whose whole function was to study and criticize society, accepted the crudest Stalinist propaganda at its face value. They needed to believe; they wanted to be duped.[64] Thus, Amabel Williams-Ellis wrote an introduction to a book about the building of the White Sea Canal, later so harrowingly described by Alexander Solzhenitsyn, which contains the sentence: 'This tale of accomplishment of a ticklish engineering job, in the middle of primaeval forests, by tens of thousands of enemies of the state, helped – or should it be guarded? – by only thirty-seven OGPU officers, is one of the most exciting stories that has ever appeared in print.' Sidney and Beatrice Webb said of the same project: 'It is pleasant to think that the warmest appreciation was officially expressed of the success of the OGPU, not merely in performing a great engineering feat, but in achieving a triumph in human regeneration.' Harold Laski praised Soviet prisons for enabling convicts to lead 'a full and self-respecting life'; Anna Louise Strong recorded: 'The labour camps have won a high reputation throughout the Soviet Union as places where tens of thousands of men have been reclaimed.' 'So well-known and effective is the Soviet method of remaking human beings', she added, 'that criminals occasionally now apply to be admitted.' Whereas in Britain, wrote George Bernard Shaw, a man enters prison a human being and emerges a criminal type, in Russia he entered 'as a criminal type and would come out an ordinary man but for the difficulty of inducing him to come out at all. As far as I could make out they could stay as long as they liked.'[65]

The famine of 1932, the worst in Russian history, was virtually unreported. At the height of it, the visiting biologist Julian Huxley found 'a level of physique and general health rather above that to be seen in England'. Shaw threw his food supplies out of the train window just before crossing the Russian frontier 'convinced that there were no shortages in Russia'. 'Where do you see any food shortage?' he asked, glancing round the foreigners-only restaurant of the Moscow Metropole.[66] He wrote: 'Stalin has delivered the goods to an extent that seemed impossible ten years ago, and I take off my hat to him accordingly.' But Shaw and his travelling companion, Lady Astor, knew of the political prisoners, since the latter asked Stalin for clemency on behalf of a woman who wished to join her husband in America (Stalin promptly handed her over to the OGPU) and she asked him, 'How long are you going to go on killing people?' When he replied 'As long as necessary', she changed the subject and asked him to find her a Russian nursery maid for her children.[67]

Estimates of Stalin written in the years 1929–34 make curious reading. H. G. Wells said he had 'never met a man more candid, fair and honest. . . no one is afraid of him and everybody trusts him'. The Webbs argued that he had less power than an American president and was merely acting on the orders of the Central Committee and the Presidium. Hewlett Johnson, Dean of Canterbury, described him as leading 'his people down new and unfamiliar avenues of democracy'. The American Ambassador, Joseph E. Davies, reported him as having 'insisted on the liberalization of the constitution' and 'projecting actual secret and universal suffrage'. 'His brown eye is exceedingly wise and gentle,' he wrote. 'A child would like to sit on his lap and a dog would sidle up to him.' Emil Ludwig, the famous popular biographer, found him a man 'to whose care I would readily confide the education of my children'. The physicist J.D.Bernal paid tribute both to his 'deeply scientific approach to all problems' and to his 'capacity for feeling'. He was, said the Chilean writer Pablo Neruda, 'a good-natured man of principle'; 'a man of kindly geniality', echoed the Dean.[68]

Some of these tributes can be variously explained by corruption, vanity or sheer folly. Davies, who consistently misrepresented the nature of Stalin's Russia to his government, was being in effect bribed by the Soviet regime, who allowed him to buy icons and chalices for his collection at below-market prices.[69] Anna Louise Strong was well described by Malcolm Muggeridge as 'an enormous woman with a very red face, a lot of white hair, and an expression of stupidity so overwhelming that it amounted to a kind of strange beauty'.[70] Self-delusion was obviously the biggest single factor in the presentation of an unsuccessful despotism as a Utopia in the making. But there was also conscious deception by men and women who thought of themselves as idealists and who, at the time, honestly believed they were serving a higher human purpose by systematic misrepresentation and lying. If the Great War with its unprecedented violence brutalized the world, the Great Depression corrupted it by appearing to limit the options before humanity and presenting them in garishly contrasting terms. Political activists felt they had to make terrible choices and, having made them, stick to them with desperate resolution. The Thirties was the age of the heroic lie. Saintly mendacity became its most prized virtue. Stalin's tortured Russia was the prime beneficiary of this sanctified falsification. The competition to deceive became more fierce when Stalinism acquired a mortal rival in Hitler's Germany.

There was, indeed, an element of deception right at the heart of this rivalry between the Communist and fascist forms of totalitarianism. They were organically linked in the process of historical development. Just as the war had made Lenin's violent seizure of power possible, and German 'War Socialism' had given him an economic policy, so the very existence of the Leninist state, with its one-party control of all aspects of public life and its systematized moral relativism, offered a model to all those who hated the liberal society, parliamentary democracy and the rule of law. It inspired imitation and it generated fear; and those who feared it most were most inclined to imitate its methods in constructing defensive counter-models of their own. Totalitarianism of the Left bred totalitarianism of the Right; Communism and fascism were the hammer and the anvil on which liberalism was broken to pieces. The emergence of Stalin's autocracy changed the dynamic of corruption not in kind but in degree. For Stalin 'was but old Lenin writ large'. The change in degree nonetheless was important because of its sheer scale. The arrests, the prisons, the camps, the scope, the brutality and violence of the social engineering – nothing like it had ever been seen or even imagined before. So the counter-model became more monstrously ambitious; and the fear which energized its construction more intense. If Leninism begot the fascism of Mussolini, it was Stalinism which made possible the Nazi Leviathan.

Hitler emerged from the Landsberg prison at the end of 1924 at almost exactly the same moment that Stalin completed the political destruction of Trotsky and established himself in a commanding position at the head of the Leninist state. The two events were connected, for Hitler now realized that he could not storm the Weimar state by force but would have to infiltrate it by creating a mass party; and the lengthening shadow of Stalin was an essential ally in this task. It was the Communist state of 1919 which first gave Hitler his base in Bavaria, bringing together in a unity of fear the 'black' Catholic separatists and the 'brown' radical-nationalists of Captain Roehm's private army. The core of the party was Bavarian, as well as an important group of Baltic refugees from Leninism living in Bavaria.[71] But to take power Hitler had to break out of the Bavarian enclave and move into the industrial north. In 1925 he formed an alliance with Gregor Strasser, a radical demagogue who, with his gifted lieutenant Joseph Goebbels, preached his own brand of socialist revolution to the working class. Hitler persuaded Strasser to transform his idea of a specifically 'German revolution', with its anti-capitalist but nationalist aims, into an 'anti-Jewish revolution', which had a broader middle-class appeal.[72] It was Strasser and Goebbels who first established Nazism as a broad movement in the north. But at the Bamberg Conference in 1926 Hitler was able to assert his supremacy in the party and Goebbels transferred his allegiance.

During the years 1925–9, the best years of Weimar, when Germany was enjoying an industrial revival which came close to pre-war levels and there were no economic factors working in his favour, Hitler established himself as a brilliant and innovatory speaker, a hard-working party organizer and an authoritarian leader of terrifying will-power. As with Leninism, the organization was to become the basis of control once power was assumed. Hitler divided the country into thirty-four *Gaue*, based on electoral districts, each with a *Gauleiter* – whom he chose personally – and with seven additional *Gaue* for Danzig, the Saar, Austria and the Sudetenland, the objects of the first wave of future expansion. His party, like Lenin's, was highly centralized – in himself, in effect – but it was also 'participatory', as was his future regime: so there was a Hitler Youth, a Nazi Schoolchildren's League, a Union of Nazi Lawyers, a Students' League, a Nazi Teachers' Association, an Order of German Women, a Nazi Physicians' League and scores of other societies. Hitler's method was always to deny his followers any real share in decisions but to give them endless scope for furious activity (including violence).

The violence came in increasing measure as Stalinism established itself in the international Communist movement and the once highly intellectual party of Rosa Luxemburg left the study and took to the streets. There, gleefully, the SA Brownshirts of Roehm joined them in bloody battles from which both parties derived benefit. The Communists used the violence to erode the Social Democrats (whom they called 'Social Fascists' and treated as the real enemy), presented by them as too weak and 'reformist' to stand up to the naked power of the Right. But the Nazis were bound to be the ultimate gainers because, while using violence, they posed as the defenders of 'Aryan order', with Weimar being too weak to uphold it effectively, and as the only force in Germany capable of exorcizing the 'Red Terror' and giving innocent citizens the peace of real authority. It was the constant street warfare which prevented the Weimar Republicans from deriving any permanent benefit from the boom years. Those who rejected alike a Stalinist-type tyranny and a liberal-capitalist state which could not provide national self-respect or even elementary security were always looking for a 'third way'. That, significantly, was the original title of Bruck's book *The Third Reich*. In the late 1920s 'third way' men included such influential figures as Carl Schmitt, Germany's leading jurist, who was in no way a Nazi but who argued and pleaded in a long series of widely read books that Germany must have a more authoritative constitution and system of government.[73] Another was Oswald Spengler, whose 'third way' embodied the *Führerprinzip* of authority, the *Führer* being a representative member of the race of the *Volk*, marked out by his charismatic leadership.[74] Once Hitler established himself as a major public figure, he and his party fitted this specification more closely than any other contender, especially after the rise of Stalin. Spengler had warned about the new epoch: 'It would be an age of cruel wars in which new Caesars would rise and an élite of steely men, who did not look for personal gain and happiness but for the execution of duties towards the community, would replace the democrats and humanitarians.'[75] The age had come: did not the very name 'Stalin' mean 'steel'; where was Germany's 'steely man'?

Weimar Germany was a very insecure society; it needed and never got a statesman who inspired national confidence. Bismarck had cunningly taught the parties not to aim at national appeal but to represent interests. They remained class or sectional pressure-groups under the Republic. This was fatal, for it made the party system, and with it democratic parliamentarianism, seem a divisive rather than a unifying factor. Worse: it meant the parties never produced a leader who appealed beyond the narrow limits of his own following. The Social Democrats, that worthy but dull and obstinate body, were most to blame. They might have created an unassailable Left–Centre block by dropping their nationalization and taxation schemes; but they refused to do so, fearing to lose ground on the Left to the Communists.

Only two Weimar politicians had multi-party appeal. One was Gustav Stresemann, Foreign Minister 1923–9, whose death at the age of fifty-one was a milestone to Hitler's victory. The other was Konrad Adenauer, Mayor of Cologne. By a tragic irony, Stresemann destroyed Adenauer's chances. City administration, drawing on the solid bourgeois traditions of the medieval past, was the only successful political institution in Germany. Adenauer ran the most highly rated municipal administration in the country with the help of the Socialists. In 1926, when he was fifty, he was asked to form a governing coalition on similar lines. He was later to show himself one of the ablest and most authoritative democratic statesmen of the twentieth century, skilfully mixing low cunning and high principle. It is more than likely he could have made the Weimar system work, especially since he would have taken it over at what, from an economic viewpoint, was the best possible moment. But Adenauer was a strong 'Westerner', some said a Rhineland separatist, who wished to tie Germany firmly to the civilized democracies of Western Europe, and in particular to bring about what he secretly described as 'a lasting peace between France and Germany . . . through the establishment of a community of economic interests'. Stresemann, however, was an 'Easterner', true to the then predominant German belief in the *Primat der Aussenpolitik*. Working through Ernst Scholtz, leader of the People's Party, and much helped by Marshal Pilsudski's establishment of a fierce military dictatorship in Poland, which occurred during the crisis, Stresemann successfully torpedoed Adenauer's bid to form a coalition including the Socialists. So his opportunity, which might have radically changed the entire course of history, was missed; and Hitler, the greatest 'Easterner' of them all, was the beneficiary.[76]

Weimar prosperity, 1924–9, was not as impressive as it seemed to some. The British CIGS, to judge by his reports, was terrified of Germany's growing industrial strength.[77] The inflation had cleared German industry's load of debt, and during the second half of the 1920s Benjamin Strong's bank-inflation had provided the Ruhr with huge quantities of American investment finance. German exports doubled in the five years after 1924. Production passed the pre-war level in 1927 and by 1929 it was 12 per cent higher *per capita*; Germany was investing a net 12 per cent of income.[78] But even in the best year incomes in real terms were 6 per cent below pre-war levels. Unemployment was high too. It was 18.1 per cent in 1926, dropped to 8.8 and 8.4 for the next two years, then passed the 3 million mark again in the winter of 1928–9, reaching over 13 per cent long before the Wall Street crash brought to an end cheap American finance. After the Smoot–Hawley tariff it quickly jumped to well over 20 per cent: it was 33.7 per cent in 1931 and an appalling 43.7 per cent at one point in 1932. That winter there were over 6 million permanently unemployed.[79]

Hitler was put into power by fear. In the 1928 elections the Nazi deputies fell from fourteen to twelve and he only got 2.8 per cent of the vote. Yet this election marked the turning-point for him, for it brought a

huge surge in Left, and especially Communist, support and thus
created the climate of fear in which he could flourish. By 1929 his
party had 120,000 members; by the summer of 1930 300,000; and
by early 1932 almost 800,000. The SA grew too, numbering half a
million by the end of 1932.[80] At each stage, Hitler's support among
the student and academic population rose first, then was followed by
a general increase. By 1930 he had captured the student movement;
the recruitment of graduates was also a function of unemployment –
the universities turned out 25,000 a year, adding to a total of
400,000, of whom 60,000 were officially registered as unemployed.
In 1933 one in every three of the *Akademiker* was out of a job.[81]

By 1929 Hitler was respectable enough to be taken into partnership by Alfred Hugenberg, the industrialist and leader of the
Nationalist Right, who thought he could use the Nazis on his road to
power. The effect was to give Hitler access to business finance, and
thereafter he never lacked money. The party system was visibly
failing. After the 1928 election it took a year to form a government.
In 1930 the Centre Party leader, Heinrich Brüning, tried to invoke
Article 48 to rule by Presidential decree, and when the Reichstag
refused he dissolved it. As a result, the Nazis with 107 seats and the
Communists with 77 became the second and third largest parties in
the Reichstag. Brüning, terrified of inflation, deflated vigorously,
thus helping both Nazis and Communists, and in the second half of
1931 the international monetary system, and the era of economic
co-operation, came to a startling end. Britain, followed by seventeen
other countries, went off the gold standard. The tariff barriers went
up everywhere. It was now every country for itself. America went
completely isolationist for the first time. Britain retreated into
protection and Imperial preference. Germany chose the weird combination of savage government cuts to keep up the value of the mark,
with decree-laws which fixed wages and prices and gave the government control of banking policy and through it of industry. As a
result, Brüning forfeited the confidence of German industry. There
began serious talk of bringing Hitler into some kind of right-wing
coalition. Roehm held secret talks with General Kurt von Schleicher,
the political head of the army. Hitler met Hindenburg for the first
time, after which the President said that, while he would not make
'this Bohemian corporal' Chancellor, he might employ him as
Postmaster-General.[82]

Both Left and Right totally underestimated Hitler, right up to the
second he stepped into the Chancellery. As we have seen, the Left
was dependent on an antiquated Marxist–Leninist system of analysis
which was pre-fascist and therefore made no provision for it. The
Communists thought Hitler was a mere excrescence on capitalism,

and therefore a puppet of Hugenberg and Schleicher, themselves manipulated by Krupp and Thyssen.[83] Under the influence of Stalin, the German CP at this time made no real distinction between the Social Democrats ('Social Fascists') and Hitler. Their leader, Ernst Thälmann, told the Reichstag on 11 February 1930 that fascism was already in power in Germany, when the head of the government was a Social Democrat. Their principal intellectual organ, the *Linkskurve*, virtually ignored the Nazis, as did the only real Communist film, *Kuhle Wampe* (1932). The only notice the Communists usually took of the Nazis was to fight them in the streets, which was exactly what Hitler wanted. There was something false and ritualistic about these encounters, as Christopher Isherwood noted: 'In the middle of a crowded street a young man would be attacked, stripped, thrashed and left bleeding on the pavement; in fifteen seconds it was all over and the assailants had disappeared.'[84] In the Reichstag, Thälmann and Goering combined to turn debates into riots. Sometimes collaboration went further. During the November 1932 Berlin transport strike thugs from the Red Front and the Brownshirts worked together to form mass picket-lines, beat up those who reported for work, and tear up tramlines.[85] One of the reasons why the army recommended the Nazis be brought into the government was that they thought they could not cope with Communist and Nazi paramilitary forces at the same time, especially if the Poles attacked too. Blinded by their absurd political analysis, the Communists actually wanted a Hitler government, believing it would be a farcical affair, the prelude to their own seizure of power.

The Right shared the same illusion that Hitler was a lightweight, a ridiculous Austrian demagogue whose oratorical gifts they could exploit – 1932 was his *annus mirabilis* when he made his finest speeches – while 'managing' and 'containing' him. 'If the Nazis did not exist,' Schleicher claimed in 1932, 'it would be necessary to invent them.'[86] In fact the exploitation was all the other way round. The events immediately preceding Hitler's accession to power are curiously reminiscent of Lenin's rise – albeit the first used the law and the second demolished it – in that they both show how irresistible is clarity of aim combined with a huge, ruthless will to power. Schleicher, seeking to separate Hitler from his thugs, had had the SA banned. In May 1932 he got Brüning turned out and replaced by his own candidate, the slippery diplomat Franz von Papen. Hoping to get Hitler's co-operation, Papen lifted the ban on the SA and called fresh elections. Hitler gave him nothing in return and denounced his government as 'the cabinet of the barons'. On 17 July he provoked a riot in Altona, and Papen used this as an excuse to take over the Prussian state government, with its police force, the last remaining Social-Democratic stronghold. He thought by this act to strengthen the hand of central government, but in fact it marked the end of the Weimar Republic and directly prepared the way for a government of illegality.

At the elections, Hitler doubled his vote to 37.2 per cent, and he and the Communists now held more than half the seats in the Reichstag. When Hindenburg refused to make him Chancellor, Hitler sent his men into the streets, and on 10 August five stormtroopers beat to death a Communist Party worker in front of his family. Hitler wrote an article justifying the murder and making it perfectly clear what a Nazi government meant. At yet another election in November the Nazi vote fell to 33 per cent, but the big gainers were the Communists, who now had 100 seats (the Nazis 196) in the Reichstag, so the result, paradoxically, was to make the Right more anxious to get Hitler into the government. Schleicher replaced Papen as Chancellor, hoping to tame the Nazis by splitting the Strasser wing (by now unimportant) from Hitler himself. The effect was to goad Papen into intriguing with Hindenburg to form a Papen–Hitler coalition, with General Werner von Blomberg brought in as Defence Minister as further 'containment'. The details of this manoeuvre are exceedingly complicated – a *totentanz* or 'dance of death' – but the essence is simple: on one side shifting and divided aims, and an inability to focus on the real essentials of power; on the other, an unwavering aim and a firm grasp of realities.

After two days of Byzantine negotiations, Hitler emerged as Chancellor on 30 January 1933. There were only three Nazis in a cabinet of twelve, and Hitler was thought to be further boxed in by Blomberg on the one side of him, and his 'pupper-master', Hugenberg, on the other. But Hitler, Goering and Frick, the three Nazi ministers, had the three posts that mattered: the Chancellorship, with permission to use Article 48; the Prussian Ministry of the Interior; and the National Interior Ministry. Apart from the army, the only force in the country capable of handling the half-million Brownshirts was the Prussian police. This had already been taken out of the hands of the Social Democrats, and was now given to Goering! Blomberg could not be expected to fight both. As for Hugenberg, he had been secretly betrayed by Papen, who had agreed that Hitler should have new elections (which he could now manage), certain to cut Hugenberg down to size.[87]

30 January 1933, therefore, was a point of no return, for Germany and indeed for the world. As Goebbels remarked, 'If we have the power we'll never give it up again unless we're carried out of our offices as corpses.'[88] The moment he set foot in the Chancellery Hitler acted with the same speed as Lenin in October 1917. He immediately

moved 25,000 men into the ministerial quarter of Berlin. That night a massed torchlight parade of his men took place, marching through the Brandenburg Gate and in front of the Chancellery for nearly six hours, while Hitler's own police 'specials' kept a vast, cheerful crowd in order. At one of the illuminated windows, the excited figure of Hitler could be seen. At another was the impassive shape of Hindenburg, the Wooden Titan, pounding his cane in time to the military beat of the band.[89]

The crowd was cheerful because politics were unpopular with most Germans and Hitler had promised to end them and substitute a one-party state. The great theme of his speeches throughout the previous year was that 'politicians had ruined the Reich'. Now he would use politics to wage war on politicians, his election was an election to end elections, his party a party to end parties: 'I tell all these sorry politicians, "Germany will become one single party, the party of a great, heroic nation."' What he was proposing was a revolution for stability, a revolt against chaos, a legal *putsch* for unity. As such he was in a powerful German tradition. Wagner had presented politics as an immoral, non-German activity. Thomas Mann had denounced 'the terrorism of politics'.[90] Hitler offered what the Marxist writer Walter Benjamin called 'the aestheticization of politics', the art without the substance. In 1919 the Surrealists had called for a 'government of artists'. Now they had one. Of the Nazi bosses, Hitler was not the only 'Bohemian', as Hindenburg put it. Funk wrote music, Baldar von Schirach and Hans Frank poetry, Goebbels novels; Rosenberg was an architect, Dietrich Eckart a painter. Hitler gave the Germans the unifying side of public life: spectacle, parades, speeches and ceremony; the divisive side, the debates, voting and decision-making, was either abolished completely or conducted by a tiny élite in secret. The parade on 30 January was a foretaste of the first, which Hitler did better than anyone else and which was the first aspect of his regime Stalin began to imitate.

The second began the next morning with Goering's take-over of the Prussian state machine, marked by massive changes in personnel, especially of senior police-officers, and the issue of orders for the rapid expansion of the state *Geheime Staatspolizei* (Gestapo) under Nazi officers. Four days later Hitler issued a decree, using his powers under Article 48, 'For the Protection of the German People', which gave the government complete discretion in banning public meetings and newspapers. On 22 February Goering created an additional 'auxiliary police', 50,000 strong, composed entirely from Nazi units. The idea was to break up any non-Nazi organizations capable of resisting. As he put it: 'My measures will not be qualified by legal scruples or by bureaucracy. It is not my business to do justice. It is my business to annihilate and exterminate – that's all!' He said to his police: 'Whoever did his duty in the service of the state, whoever obeyed my orders and took severe measures against the enemy of the state, whoever ruthlessly made use of his revolver when attacked, could be certain of protection . . . . If one calls this murder, then I am a murderer.'[91]

Goering's task was made much easier by the burning of the Reichstag on 28 February, now generally seen as indeed the work of the feeble-minded Martinus van der Lubbe, but in any event mighty convenient to the new regime. The same day Hitler put through the Emergency Decree of 28 February 1933, 'For the Protection of the People and the State', supplemented by another 'Against Betrayal of the German People and Treasonable Machinations'. They formed the real basis of Nazi rule, since they enabled the police to bypass the courts completely.[92] The key passage reads:

Articles 114–18, 123–4 and 153 of the Constitution of the German Reich are for the time being nullified. Consequently, curbs on personal liberty, on the right of free expression of opinion, including freedom of the press, of associations, and of assembly, surveillance over letters, telegrams and telephone communications, searches of homes and confiscations of as well as restrictions on property, are hereby permissible beyond the limits hitherto established by law.

This decree gave Hitler everything he needed to set up a totalitarian state and was indeed the basis of his rule, remaining in force until 1945. But following the elections of 5 March, which gave the Nazis 43.9 per cent of the votes (288 seats), Hitler brought in an Enabling Act, which he got debated and passed by the Reichstag (sitting temporarily in the Kroll Opera House, surrounded by SA and SS units) on 23 March. The first article transferred the right to legislate from the Reichstag to the administration, the second gave the latter power to make constitutional changes, the third passed the right to draft laws from the president to the chancellor, the fourth extended the act to treaties and the fifth limited it to four years (it was extended in 1937, 1941 and again in 1943). It was, in effect, an act for the abolition of the constitution and legal government – and Hitler never saw the need, or took the trouble, to replace the old Weimar Constitution with one of his own. It really added nothing to the 28 February decree, except in a metaphysical sense. It was actually debated, the only political debate Hitler as ruler ever allowed, just like Lenin with the solitary meeting of the Provisional Assembly. The parallels are almost uncanny, except that Hitler, unlike Lenin, took part in the debate himself – furiously retorting to

a speech on behalf of the Social Democrats, who opposed the bill
(twenty-six of them and eighty-one Communists were already under
arrest or in flight). But the Right and Centre parties voted for the
bill, which was carried 441–94, so this act of abdication marked
the moral death of a republic which had died in law already on
28 February.

Resistance was feeble or non-existent. Some of the Communist
leaders, who only a few weeks before had believed Hitler's entry
into office would be an ephemeral prelude to their own triumph,
were simply murdered. Others fled to Russia where the same fate
soon awaited them. The great mass of the Communist rank-and-file
humbly submitted and nothing more was heard of them. The
unions surrendered without the least hint of a struggle. On 10 May
the Social Democrats, insisting that the Nazis were merely 'the last
card of reaction', allowed all their property and newspapers to be
taken from them. A week later their deputies actually voted for
Hitler's foreign policy, so that Goering was able to declare: 'The
world has seen that the German people are united where their fate
is at stake.' In June all the non-Nazi parties of Right, Left and
Centre, together with their paramilitaries, were declared dissolved.
At the end of the month, Hugenberg, the great 'container' of Hitler,
was ignominiously pitched out of his office. Finally in July the
National Socialists were declared the only legal party. It had taken
Hitler less than five months to destroy German democracy completely, about the same time as Lenin. Not a soul stirred. As Robert
Musil put it: 'The only ones who give the impression of absolutely
refusing to accept it all – although they say nothing – are the
servant-girls.'[93]

With the mature Soviet model to guide him, Hitler set up the
apparatus of terror and the machinery of the police state even more
quickly than Lenin – and soon on a scale almost as large as Stalin's.
The initial agent in this endeavour was Goering, using the Prussian
police and his newly created Gestapo of SA and SS men, operating
from its Berlin HQ on Prinz Albrechtstrasse. It was Goering who
destroyed the Communist Party in the space of a few weeks by a
policy of murder – 'A bullet fired from the barrel of a police-pistol
is my bullet' was the assurance he gave his men – or internment in
the concentration camps he began setting up in March. The breathtaking brutality of Goering's campaign, conducted without the
slightest regard for legality, goes a long way to explain the silence
or compliance of those groups who might have been expected to
oppose the new regime. They were simply afraid. It was known that
people the Nazis disliked simply disappeared without trace: murdered, tortured to death, buried in a camp. All opposition was

enveloped in the blanket of fear, and that was precisely the effect Goering wished to create. Hitler praised his work as 'brutal and ice-cold'.[94]

It was Hitler's custom, however, to duplicate or double-bank all his agencies, so that he could back one against another, if need be, and rule through division. He had never quite trusted the SA, now a million strong, which was Roehm's creation. After his release from Landsberg he had created, from within the SA, a personal bodyguard of *Schutzstaffel* (SS), or security units. In 1929, when the black-shirted SS numbered 290, Hitler entrusted it to the twenty-nine-year-old Heinrich Himmler, the well-connected son of a former tutor to the Bavarian royal family. Despite his prim appearance and habits (his diaries record when he shaved, took a bath or had a haircut, and he kept all receipts and ticket stubs), Himmler was a *Freikorps* thug and violent anti-Semite, who wore his rimless pince-nez even when duelling. He had been a surveyor of the secret arms dumps hidden in the countryside to deceive the Allied Control Commission, and his army and social connections allowed him to raise the tone of the SS above that of the SA. Some of its unit commanders were noblemen. It included many doctors. Senior civil servants and industrialists were among its honorary members. Himmler, unlike Roehm, would not recruit the unemployed.[95]

With Hitler's encouragement, Himmler expanded the SS rapidly, so that it numbered 52,000 at his accession to power. Hitler's personal SS guard, the *Leibstandarte*, was a whole division. Himmler was never one of Hitler's intimates. He was treated as a functionary who could be filled with the loyalty of awe and terror; and it is a curious fact that Himmler, the one man who could have destroyed Hitler, feared him right to the end. Hitler regarded the SS as his own instrument of power, and he gave it special tasks. From 1931 it had a Race and Settlement Office, charged with practical applications of Nazi race theory, keeping stud books of party members and the drawing up of race-laws. The SS thus became the natural instrument to carry through Hitler's gigantic eastern extermination and settlement policy when the time came. At the same time, Himmler recruited a former naval officer, Reinhard Heydrich, whom he saw as the ideal Aryan type, to take charge of a new security and intelligence service, the *Sicherheitsdienst* (SD), which Hitler instructed him to set up to watch Roehm's SA.

Hence, when Hitler took power, Himmler was able quickly to expand his organization into a complete security system, with its own military units (the *Waffen* SS), and an organization called the *Totenkopfverbände* (Death's Head Units) to run concentration camps and for other special duties. The last included many criminals, such as Adolf Eichmann and Rudolf Hess, who had already served a sentence for murder.[96] Himmler's initial job was merely as police chief in Munich, and he required the permission of the Catholic Prime Minister of Bavaria, Heinrich Held, to set up his first concentration camp at Dachau, an announcement duly appearing in the press:

On Wednesday 22 March 1933, the first concentration camp will be opened near Dachau. It will accommodate 5,000 prisoners. Planning on such a scale, we refuse to be influenced by any petty objection, since we are convinced this will reassure all those who have regard for the nation and serve their interests.

Heinrich Himmler,
Acting Police-President of the City of Munich.[97]

Himmler's earliest 'protective custody' orders read: 'Based on Article 1 of the Decree of the Reich President for the Protection of People and the State of February 28 1933, you are taken into protective custody in the interests of public security and order. Reason: suspicion of activities inimical to the state.' Unlike Goering, Himmler, at this stage, showed himself anxious to observe the formalities of the Nazi state, such as they were. But the camp regulations he compiled indicated from the very start the horrifying comprehensiveness of the powers Himmler and his men enjoyed and the unrestricted use of terror:

The term 'commitment to a concentration camp' is to be openly announced as 'until further notice' . . . . In certain cases the Reichfuhrer ss and the Chief of the German Police will order flogging in addition . . . . There is no objection to spreading the rumour of this increased punishment . . . to add to the deterrent effect. The following offenders, considered as agitators, will be hanged: anyone who . . . makes inciting speeches, and holds meetings, forms cliques, loiters around with others; who for the purpose of supplying the propaganda of the opposition with atrocity stories, collects true or false information about the concentration camps.[98]

Himmler's impeccable bureaucratic paperwork and his genuflec-tions to legality (when he sent his aged parents for drives in his official car he always noted the cost and had it deducted from his salary[99]) were fraudulent, as was the similar pseudo-legal framework under which the OGPU worked in Soviet Russia. Hans Gisevius, a Gestapo official, later testified: 'It was always a favourite ss tactic to appear in the guise of a respectable citizen and to condemn vigor-ously all excesses, lies or infringements of the law. Himmler . . . sounded like the stoutest crusader for decency, cleanliness and justice.'[100] He was anxious to distance his men from the ruffianly SA street-fighters and Goering's Gestapo. Inside the camps, however, there was no difference: all was unspeakable cruelty, often sadism, and the negation of law.

A typical case-history, one of many thousands, was that of the Jewish poet Erich Muhsam. He had taken part in Eisner's reckless Bavarian Socialist Republic, and served six years in prison for it, being amnestied in 1924. Immediately after the Reichstag fire, fearing arrest, he had bought a ticket to Prague, but had then given it to another intellectual who was even more frightened than he was. He was pulled in and taken to Sonnenburg camp. They began by smashing his glasses, knocking out his teeth and tearing out chunks of his hair. They broke both his thumbs so he could not write, and beating about the ears destroyed his hearing. He was then moved to Cranienburg camp. There, in February 1934, the guards had possession of a chimpanzee which they found in the home of an arrested Jewish scientist. Assuming it was fierce, they loosed it on Muhsam, but to their fury the creature simply flung its arms round his neck. They then tortured the animal to death in his presence. The object was to drive Muhsam to suicide. But he would not comply; so one night he was beaten to death and hanged from a beam in a latrine. Muhsam had become wise in the ways of totalitarianism, and before his arrest had given all his papers to his wife, with express instructions on no account to go to Moscow. Unfortunately, she disobeyed him and took the papers with her; and as soon as the Soviet authorities got their hands on them they arrested her. She spent the next twenty years in Soviet camps as a 'Trotskyite agent', and the papers are to this day under lock and key in the so-called 'Gorky Institute for World Literature' in Moscow.[101]

The lawlessness of Hitler's Germany, beneath a thin veneer of legal forms, was absolute. As Goering put it, 'The law and the will of the Führer are one.' Hans Frank: 'Our constitution is the will of the Führer.' Hitler worked entirely through decrees and ordinances, as opposed to law, here again resembling Lenin, who never showed the slightest interest in constitution-making.[102] In any matters which were of interest to the Nazis, the Ministry of Justice did not function. Its boss Franz Guertner, who in 1924 as Bavarian Justice Minister had granted Hitler's early release, was a nonentity who claimed he stayed on to fight Hitlerism but in fact was never allowed to talk to Hitler on any subject except novels. Shortly before his death in 1941 he told Frank: 'Hitler loves cruelty. It pleases him . . . when he can torment someone. He has a diabolical sadism. Otherwise he simply could not stand Himmler and Heydrich.'[103] Hitler himself said: 'It was only with the greatest difficulty that I was able to persuade Dr Guertner . . . of the absolute necessity of exercising the utmost severity in cases of treason.'[104] But this was just talk. In fact Hitler frequently altered what he saw as 'lenient' sentences, imposing the death-penalty instead. He changed the 1933 Civil Service Law, adding paragraph 71, which empowered him to dismiss a judge if 'the manner of his official activities, in particular through his decisions . . . shows that he finds the National Socialist *Weltanschauung* alien' (an example cited was giving the minimum sentence for 'racial defilement').[105]

But Hitler did not even like removable or subservient judges. Like Marx and Lenin, he hated lawyers – 'a lawyer must be regarded as a man deficient by nature or deformed by experience', he said – and he eventually superimposed on the ordinary juridical system the Nazi 'People's Courts', a Leninist device which achieved its sombre apogee under the ferocious Roland Freisler in 1944–5.[106] No protection against Nazi encroachments on the rule of law or civil liberties was ever offered by the Interior Minister, Wilhelm Frick, who was a Nazi himself. In 1930–2 Frick was seen by outsiders as second only to Hitler in the movement, but in fact he was a weak man and since his Ministry had lost actual control of the police, neither he nor it counted for anything. The only important contribution it made to Hitler's rule was the drafting (under Dr Hans Globke, later to serve Dr Adenauer) of the 1935 Nuremberg Laws for the Jews. It remains an argument to this day whether the code had the effect of diminishing the appalling acts of violence carried out against Jews by local Nazis, as Globke claimed, or whether it gave moral and legal authority to systematic persecution.[107]

The manner in which Hitler ran internal security, using three competing systems (SS, SA, and Goering's police and Gestapo) and two ministries which did not function on important matters, was characteristic. As the state had no constitution (other than the anaesthetized Weimar one) so it had no system of government. Or rather it had several. There was the party system of forty or so *Gauleiters*, a powerful collegiate body, whom Hitler could make or break individually but whom he did not choose to defy as a group. The Düsseldorf *Gauleiter*, Florian, claimed he had never invited Himmler into his *Gau* and had forbidden his men to co-operate with the Gestapo. The actual party leader, as Hitler's deputy, was Rudolph Hess. But Hess was an ineffectual mystic. More important was Martin Bormann, a convicted murderer and a hard-working, Stalin-like party bureaucrat, who waged constant battles against the *Gauleiters*, on the one hand, and Goering and Goebbels on the other.[108]

Hitler did not object to these internal battles; on the contrary, he promoted them. 'People must be allowed friction with one another,' he said. 'Friction produces warmth, and warmth is energy.' He called it 'institutionalized Darwinism'. If Hitler met resistance from any ministry, he created a duplicate. He called the Foreign Ministry, still stuffed with aristocrats, 'an intellectual garbage heap', and from 1933 set up a rival organization under Joachim von Ribbentrop, which often stole the ministry's mail and answered it.[109] The Ministry of Labour, under Franz Seldte, was particularly obstructive. So Hitler appointed one of his *Gauleiters*, Fritz Sauckel, General Plenipotentiary for Work Mobilization.[110] Again, frustrated on the economic and financial front, Hitler created a duplicate economics ministry, called the Four Year Plan, under Goering. By 1942, in addition to the quota of ministries he had inherited from Weimar, Hitler had created fifty-eight Supreme Reich Boards, plus many other extra-governmental bureaux. Overlapping was universal and deliberate. It suited Hitler that Ribbentrop and Goebbels, for instance, should fight each over for control of external propaganda, down to the point where their men had pitched battles over radio equipment. Then both would appeal to him to arbitrate.

Any authoritarian system which abandons constitutional procedures and the rule of law is bound to contain an element of anarchy. Stalin's regime was not dissimilar, though he was more methodical than Hitler. The term 'Bohemian', which Hindenburg used of Hitler, was apt. He hated settled hours. After Hindenburg's death he combined the offices of Chancellor and President, and used this as an excuse to destroy the formal working of both. An old-fashioned civil servant called Dr Hans Lammers kept up a semblance of order in the Chancellery office, and he and his staff of ten to twelve *Beamten* answered Hitler's mail of about 600 letters a day. Hitler never seems to have written a letter or signed any official documents. As soon as he was in power he did his best to have all documents which mentioned him (including tax records) destroyed, and thereafter he was extraordinarily reluctant to issue any written directives. About the only documentary holograph of Hitler's we possess dates from before the First World War.

When Hitler first became Chancellor he got to his desk at 10 am, but he soon tired of routine and gradually took to working at night. He moved constantly around the country, like a medieval monarch, and even when in Berlin often refused to take decisions, claiming he was not a dictator.[111] He disliked cabinet meetings precisely because they were an orderly decision-making procedure. He held them at ever-growing intervals; even when they did take place, the really important business was done elsewhere. Thus when Hitler fired Hjalmar Schacht he appointed Walter Funk Minister of Economics during an interval at the opera, and introduced him without warning at the next cabinet meeting (4 February 1938), the last he ever held.[112] There is no doubt whatever that all important decisions were taken by Hitler personally, as a rule in bilateral meetings with individual ministers or bosses, but they are never reflected in the records, except indirectly. Hitler's orders were always oral, often emerging incidentally in the course of long harangues, and sometimes given on the spot to whoever happened to be around.[113]

Hitler's state was not corporatist because corporatism implies a distribution of power between different bodies, and Hitler would share power with no one. He did not mind senior members of the gang running little private empires, subject to his ultimate power to break them. But Lammers testified at Nuremberg that he would not allow them to meet together, even informally, so they were never able to resolve their differences in collegiate fashion. Hitler's regime, therefore, was marked by constant bilateral and multilateral struggles between its component parts, what Hobbes called 'a perpetual and restless desire for power after power, that ceaseth only in death'.[114] Goering tapped his colleagues' telephones from his 'research office' and acquired such useful treasures as a set of love-letters from Alfred Rosenberg to a comely Jewess.[115] Bormann spied on all. So, of course, did Himmler and Heydrich. Virtually everyone was in a position to blackmail everyone else, and as each sought to win Hitler's goodwill by betraying what he knew of the others, the Führer was kept well informed.

No government run in this fashion could hope to pursue consistent and carefully thought out policies, and Hitler naturally failed to do so, even on matters about which he felt most passionately. He promised to help small businesses, the peasants, the agricultural sector, to cut the big cities down to size, to bring womenfolk back from the factories into the home, to take back industry from the capitalists, the land from the *Junkers*, the army from the 'vons', the administration from the '*Doktors*'. He did none of these things. On the contrary: the cities, big business and industry flourished, and peasants and women continued to flock into the workshops.[116] Army, business, the civil service remained much the same.

Even on Jewish policy, which to Hitler was the most important issue of all, there was inconsistency and hesitation. In the first flush of Nazi triumph, many Jews were murdered or put in camps, or stripped of their property by the SA and allowed to flee. Some Nazi leaders wanted a policy of enforced emigration, but no systematic and effective measures were ever taken to bring this about. Nor did Hitler smash the big Jewish department stores, something he had promised countless times to do: Schacht persuaded him that 90,000 jobs would thereby be lost.[117] The Economics Ministry opposed attacks on Jewish business chiefly because it believed they would lead to attacks on big business in general, and it set up a special bureau to stop Nazi harassment.[118] The Nuremberg Laws themselves were drawn up in a hurry. Hitler announced them as the 'final settlement of the position of the Jews'. In fact many ambiguities remained, even in his own mind. He authorized signs 'Jews Not Welcome' outside towns, which were theoretically illegal, but conceded Jews could not actually be forbidden to enter. In 1936 the Interior Ministry even discussed banning *Der Stürmer*, the anti-Semitic Nazi paper. Anti-Semitism became more violent in 1938, probably because Hitler was adopting a more isolationist economic policy. The Interior Ministry produced the 'name decree', obliging all Jews to adopt Israel or Sarah as a middle name.[119] This was followed by the terrifying violence of the *Kristallnacht* on 9 November 1938, incited by Goebbels. But it is not clear whether Goebbels acted on his own initiative or, more likely, on Hitler's orders, given quite casually.[120] Only with the coming of war did Hitler fix upon the real 'final solution': he had had it in mind all along but needed war to make it possible. On his world aims, as opposed to domestic policy, he was always clear, consistent and resolute, as we shall see.

Hitler had no economic policy. But he had a very specific national policy. He wanted to rearm as fast as possible consistent with avoiding an Allied pre-emptive strike. He simply gave German industry his orders, and let its managers get on with it. Before he came to power, Otto Strasser had asked him what he would do with Krupp, and was told: 'Of course I would leave him alone. Do you think I should be so mad as to destroy Germany's economy?'[121] Hitler thought that Lenin's greatest economic mistake had been to order party members to take over the running of industry, and kill or expel its capitalist managers. He was determined that the Brownshirts and other party elements would not get their hands on business, and warned Major Walter Buch, judge of the Party Court, in 1933: 'It is your task as the highest judge within the party to put a brake on the revolutionary element.' The unwillingness to do this had led to the destruction of other revolutions, he said.[122]

There is no evidence whatever that Hitler was, even to the smallest degree, influenced by big business philosophy. He bowed to business advice only when convinced that taking it would forward his military and external aims. He regarded himself as a socialist, and the essence of his socialism was that every individual or group in the state should unhesitatingly work for national policy. So it did not matter who owned the actual factory so long as those managing it did what they were told. German socialism, he told Hermann Rauschning, was not about nationalization: 'Our socialism reaches much deeper. It does not change the external order of things, it orders solely the relationship of man to the state . . . . Then what does property and income count for? Why should we need to socialize the banks and the factories? We are socializing the people.'[123] Presenting his Four Year Plan (which, like Stalin's, was a mere propaganda exercise), he said that it was the job of the Ministry of Economics merely to 'present the tasks of the national economy' and then 'the private economy will have to fulfil them'. If it shrank from them 'then the National Socialist state will know how to solve these tasks'.[124]

Thus Hitler kept Germany's managerial class and made them work for him. Firms flourished or not exactly in accordance with the degree to which they carried out Hitler's orders. Of course he extracted money from them: but it was a blackmail–victim relationship, not that of client and patron. A case in point was the chemical firm I.G.Farben, originally caricatured by the Nazis as 'Isidore Farben' because of its Jewish directors, executives and scientists. It won Hitler's favour only by ridding itself of Jews (for instance the Nobel prize-winner Fritz Haber) and by agreeing to give absolute priority to Hitler's synthetics programme, the heart of his war-preparedness scheme, in a secret treaty signed 14 December 1933. Thereafter Farben was safe, but only at the cost of slavery to Hitler. Far from big business corrupting his socialism, it was the other way round. The corruption of I.G.Farben by the Nazis is one of the most striking individual tragedies within the overall tragedy of the German nation.[125]

Not having an economic policy was an advantage. Hitler was lucky. He took over a month before Roosevelt, and like him benefited from a recovery which had already begun shortly before. Unlike Roosevelt, however, he did not tinker with the economy by systematic public works programmes, though they existed. At a meeting on 8 February 1933 he said he rejected any such programmes which had no bearing on rearmament. He started autobahn construction in September 1933 chiefly because he wanted fast motor-roads and thought he had discovered an organizing genius to create them in Fritz Todt (he had).[126] Brüning had pursued an excessively deflationary policy because he had a paranoid fear of inflation. Hitler scrapped it. He sacked Dr Hans Luther, the Reichbank President, and replaced him by Hjalmar Schacht, whom he also made Economics Minister. Schacht was by far the cleverest financial minister any country had between the wars. He was a market economist but an empiric who believed in no theory and played every situation by ear.

Hitler hated high interest-rates and tight credit not because he was a pro-Keynesian but because he associated them with Jews. He told Schacht to provide the money for rearmament and Schacht did so, breaking the Reichbank's rules in the process. Inflation was avoided by Brüning's strict exchange-controls (which Hitler, in his pursuit of autarchy, made still more fierce), taxation (tax revenues tripled 1933–8) and general belt-tightening: German living standards were scarcely higher in 1938 than a decade earlier. The Germans did not mind because they were back at work. Over 8 million had been unemployed when Hitler took over. The number began to fall very quickly in the second half of 1933, and by 1934 there were already shortages in certain categories of skilled labour, though 3 million were still out of work. By 1936, however, there was virtually full employment, and by 1938 firms were desperate for labour at a time when Britain and the USA were again in recession.

Germany was thus the only major industrial country to recover quickly and completely from the Great Depression. The reason undoubtedly lies in the great intrinsic strength of German industry, which has performed phenomenally well from the 1860s to this day, when not mutilated by war or bedevilled by political uncertainty. Weimar had provided a disastrous political framework for business, which puts a stable and consistent fiscal background as the precondition of efficient investment. Weimar always had difficulty in getting a budget through the Reichstag and often had to administer financial policy by emergency decree. Its inherent political instability grew worse rather than better. After the 1928 election it became increasingly difficult to form a stable government, and by March 1930 it was clear the regime would not last, with a risk that a Marxist system might replace it. Hitler's coming to power, therefore, provided German industry with precisely what it wanted to perform effectively: government stability, the end of politics and a sense of national purpose. It could do the rest for itself. Hitler was shrewd enough to realize this. While he allowed the party to invade every other sphere of government and public policy, he kept it out of industry and the army, both of which he needed to perform at maximum efficiency as quickly as possible.[127]

By the mid-1930s Hitler was running a brutal, secure, conscienceless, successful and, for most Germans, popular regime. The German workers, on the whole, preferred secure jobs to civil rights which had meant little to them.[128] What did become meaningful to them were the social organizations which Hitler created in astonishing numbers, under the policy he termed 'belonging'. He also had the policy of co-ordination, which emphasized the unity of the state (under the party, of course). The Third Reich was a 'co-ordinated' state to which ordinary Germans 'belonged'. This concept of public life appealed to more Germans than the party politics of Weimar. The mood might not have lasted indefinitely, but it was still strong when

Hitler destroyed his popularity by getting Germany into war again. It was probably strongest among the humblest and poorest (though not among some Catholic peasants, who refused to give Nazi salutes and greetings, and bitterly resented attacks on Christianity).

Hitler also appealed to the moralistic nature of many Germans, that is, those who had a keen desire for 'moral' behaviour without possessing a code of moral absolutes rooted in Christian faith. Himmler, the conscientious mass-murderer, the scrupulous torturer, was the archetype of the men who served Hitler best. He defined the virtues of the ss, the embodiment of Nazi 'morality', as loyalty, honesty, obedience, hardness, decency, poverty and bravery. The notion of obeying 'iron laws' or 'a higher law', rather than the traditional, absolute morality taught in the churches, was a Hegelian one. Marx and Lenin translated it into a class concept; Hitler into a race one. Just as the Soviet cadres were taught to justify the most revolting crimes in the name of a moralistic class warfare, so the ss acted in the name of race – which Hitler insisted was a far more powerful and central human motivation than class. Service to the race, as opposed to the Marxist proletariat, was the basis of Nazi puritanism, marked by what Rudolf Hoess, commandant at Auschwitz, termed the 'cold' and 'stony' attitude of the ideal Nazi, one who 'had ceased to have human feelings' in the pursuit of duty.[129]

By early 1933, therefore, the two largest and strongest nations of Europe were firmly in the grip of totalitarian regimes which preached and practised, and indeed embodied, moral relativism, with all its horrifying potentialities. Each system acted as a spur to the most reprehensible characteristics of the other. One of the most disturbing aspects of totalitarian socialism, whether Leninist or Hitlerian, was the way in which, both as movements seeking power or regimes enjoying it, they were animated by a Gresham's Law of political morality: frightfulness drove out humanitarian instincts and each corrupted the other into ever-deeper profundities of evil.

Hitler learnt from Lenin and Stalin how to set up a large-scale terror regime. But he had much to teach too. Like Lenin, he wished to concentrate all power in his single will. Like Lenin he was a gnostic, and just as Lenin thought that he alone was the true interpreter of history as the embodiment of proletarian determinism, so Hitler had confidence only in himself as the exponent of the race-will of the German people. The regime he set up in January 1933 had one major anomaly: the sa. Hitler did not fully control it, and Roehm had visions which did not fit into Hitler's plans. The sa, already very large before the take-over, expanded rapidly after it. By the autumn of 1933 it had a million active, paid members, and reserves of 3.5 million more. Roehm's object was to make the SA the future German army, which would overthrow the Versailles settlement and secure Germany's expansionist aims. The old army, with its professional officer class, would be a mere training organization for a radical, revolutionary army which he himself would take on a voyage of conquest. Hitler was determined to reject this Napoleonic scheme. He had a high opinion of the regular army and believed it would put through rearmament quickly and with sufficient secrecy to carry the country through the period of acute danger when the French and their allies were still in a position to invade Germany and destroy his regime. Even more important, he had not the slightest intention of sharing power with Roehm, let alone surrendering it to him.

From March 1933, when he began to assist the rise of Himmler, who had a secret phone-link to him, it is clear that Hitler had a gigantic crime in mind to resolve the dilemma which Roehm's SA presented to him. He prepared it with great thoroughness. From October 1933, Himmler was authorized by Hitler to acquire in plurality the offices of chief of political police in all the German states, in addition to the city of Munich. This process, naturally seen by Himmler's enemies as empire-building, required Hitler's active assistance at every stage both because it was illegal (Frick had to be kept in the dark) and because it involved negotiations with the *Gauleiters*, whom Hitler alone controlled, in each *Gaue*. The process was completed on 20 April 1934 when Heydrich's SD revealed a 'plot' to murder Goering, which his own Gestapo had failed to uncover. Hitler then ordered Himmler to take over Goering's police (officially as his deputy). The SS organization, big in itself, now controlled all Germany's political police and was in a position to strike at even the gigantic, armed SA.

Hitler's motives for destroying the SA's leadership and independence had meanwhile been increasing. Its brutal, open street-violence alienated Hitler's supporters at home and was the chief source of criticism of his regime abroad. When Sir John Simon and Anthony Eden visited him on 21 February 1934, he had promised to demobilize two-thirds of the SA and permit inspection of the rest: 'short of the actual dissolution of the force,' wrote Eden, '. . . he could scarcely have gone further.'[130] Equally important was the hostility of the army. By spring 1934 the aged Hindenburg was clearly nearing the end. Hitler wished to succeed him, uniting presidency and chancellorship in one. The army and navy commanders agreed that he should do this, provided he emasculated the SA and destroyed its pretensions, and it is typical of the naïvety they always showed in negotiating with Hitler that they gave him something vital in return for a 'concession' which he needed to make anyway, and in which army co-operation was essential.

Hitler went ahead with his purge, an act of pure gangsterism, as soon as Himmler had achieved monopoly of the political police. He determined to murder all his immediate political enemies at once (including settling some old scores), so that the 'evidence' of conspiracy, manufactured by Heydrich's intelligence bureau, produced unlikely conjunctions worthy of a Stalin show-trial. Himmler and Heydrich prepared the final list, Hitler simply underlining in pencil those to be shot; Heydrich signed the warrants, which read simply: 'By order of the Führer and Reich Chancellor, – is condemned to death by shooting for high treason.' At a comparatively late stage Goering was brought into the plot. The Defence Minister Blomberg, together with his political assistant, General von Reichenau, were made accomplices, army units being ordered to stand by in case SA units resisted. Early on 30 June 1934 Hitler himself shook Roehm awake at the sanatorium of the Tegernsee, and then retired to the Munich Brownhouse. The Bavarian Justice Minister was not prepared to order mass shootings on the basis of a mere typed list, and Roehm and his associates were not actually murdered until 2 July, the political police carrying it out. In Berlin, meanwhile, according to the eye-witness account of the Vice-Chancellor, von Papen, the accused were taken to Goering's private house in the Leipzigerplatz, where he and Himmler identified them, ticked them off the list and ordered them to be taken away and shot immediately; Goering's private police provided the squads. Two days later, Hitler arrived from Munich at the Templehof. Himmler and Goering met him on the tarmac, under a blood-red sky, the three men then studying the lists of those already shot or about to be shot, a Wagnerian scene described by the Gestapo officer Hans Gisevius. Frick, the Interior Minister, was told to go home: the matter did not concern him. According to Gisevius, Frick said, 'My Führer, if you do not proceed at once against Himmler and his SS, as you have against Roehm and his SA, all you will have done is to have called in Beelzebub to drive out the devil.'[131] That shows how little he understood his master.

Many of those murdered had nothing to do with the SA. They included the former Bavarian Prime Minister, Gustav von Kahr, who had declined to take part in the 1923 *putsch*; Hitler's old colleague and party rival, Gregor Strasser; the slippery old brass-hat who was going to 'contain' him, General von Schleicher, plus his wife and his close associate, General von Bredow; the Berlin Catholic leader, Ernst Klausener, and many other inconvenient or dangerous people, probably about 150 in all.[132]

This act of mass murder by the government and police was a moral catastrophe for Germany. The code of honour of the German generals, such as it was, was shattered, for they had connived at the killing of two of their friends and colleagues. Justice was ridiculed for a law was passed on 3 July, authorizing the deeds *ex post facto*. Hitler was received in state at Hindenburg's deathbed, where the confused old man, who had once dismissed him as the 'Bohemian corporal', greeted him with the words 'Your Majesty'. After the Wooden Titan died on 2 August, Hitler assumed the succession by virtue of a law he had issued the day before, making him 'leader and Reich Chancellor'. The same day all officers and men of the army took a sacred oath to him, beginning: 'I will render unconditional obedience to the Führer of the German Reich and people.' The arrangement then went to a plebiscite and in August the German people rewarded the murderer-in-chief with a verdict of 84.6 per cent.[133] Not the least significant aspect of this turning-point was the presentation, to the SS men who had carried out the murders, of daggers of honour. Here was the shameless symbolism of moral relativism. The SS was thus launched upon its monstrous career of legalized killing. The Roehm affair, with the state openly engaged in mass murder, with the connivance of its old military élite and the endorsement of the electorate, directly foreshadowed the extermination programmes to come.

It was the sheer audacity of the Roehm purge, and the way in which Hitler got away with it, with German and world opinion and with his own colleagues and followers, which encouraged Stalin to consolidate his personal dictatorship by similar means. Hitherto, the party élite had permitted him to murder only ordinary Russians. Even to expel a senior party member required elaborate preparations. In 1930, Stalin had been openly criticized by Syrtsov, a Politburo candidate, and Lominadze, a Central Committee member. He had wanted both of them shot but the most he managed was their expulsion from the CC. Two years later he had called for the shooting of Ryutin, who had circulated privately a two-hundred-page document criticizing his dictatorship. Sergei Kirov, who had succeeded Zinoviev as boss of Leningrad, had insisted that Ryutin be spared and sent to an 'isolator', or special prison for top party men.[134] By summer 1934, Kirov's influence was still growing, and he appeared to be the man most likely to succeed Stalin – or oust him. The success of the Roehm purge inspired Stalin to do away with internal party restraints once and for all, and in the most ingenious manner: by having Kirov murdered, and using the crime as an excuse to strike at all his other enemies.[135]

Kirov was shot in mysterious circumstances on 1 December 1934, in the middle of the Smolny Institute, the former girls' school from which Lenin had launched his *putsch* and which had remained party HQ in Leningrad ever since. It was a heavily guarded place and it was never explained how the assassin, Leonid Nikolaev, got through the security cordon. What is even more suspicious is that, a few days before, Kirov's bodyguard had been removed on the orders of Yagoda, the NKVD head. In 1956 and again in 1961 Khrushchev hinted strongly that Stalin was responsible, and the circumstantial evidence seems overwhelming.[136]

Stalin reacted to the news of the murder with great violence but in a manner which suggests premeditation. He took the night train to Leningrad, and as dawn was breaking he was met at the Moscow station by Medved, head of the Leningrad police. Without a word, Stalin struck him heavily in the face. He then commandeered a floor of the Smolny Institute and took personal charge of the investigations. He sat behind a table, flanked by his own flunkeys: Molotov, Voroshilov, Zhdanov and others, with the Leningrad party officials on one side, the security men on the other. When Nikolaev was brought in, and Stalin asked him why he shot Kirov, the creature fell on his knees and shouted, pointing at the security men, 'But they made me do it.' They ran to him and beat him unconscious with pistol butts; then he was dragged out and revived in alternate hot and cold baths. Stalin had Borisov, the head of Kirov's bodyguards, beaten to death with crowbars; Medved was sent to a camp and murdered three years later; Nikolaev was executed on 29 December after a secret trial. More than a hundred so-called 'Whites' were shot; 40,000 Leningraders put in camps. Soon, anyone who knew the facts of the Kirov case was either dead or lost for ever in the Gulag Archipelago.[137]

That was only the beginning. Two weeks after Kirov's murder, Stalin had Zinoviev and Kamenev arrested. He formulated the charges against them in the minutest detail and revised the testimony they were to give down to the last comma. It took months to rehearse them, Stalin threatening nothing would be spared 'until they came crawling on their bellies with confessions in their teeth'.[138] They came up for trial in 1936, following a deal in which they agreed to confess everything provided their families were left alone and they themselves spared. In fact they were both shot within a day of their trial ending. The way in which Zinoviev begged for mercy was made the subject of a gruesome imitation, with strong anti-Semitic overtones, given at Stalin's intimate parties by K.V.Pauker, a former theatre-dresser promoted to be head of Stalin's personal NKVD guard and the only man permitted to shave him. Pauker performed this act regularly until he, too, was shot as a 'German spy'.[139]

Immediately Zinoviev and Kamenev were dead, Stalin ordered Yagoda to execute more than 5,000 party members already under arrest. This was the beginning of the Great Terror. Soon after this was done, Stalin sent from Sochi, where he was on holiday, the sinister telegram of 25 September 1936: 'We deem it absolutely necessary and urgent that Comrade Yezhov be nominated to the post of People's Commissar for Internal Affairs. Yagoda has definitely proved himself to be incapable of unmasking the Trotskyite–Zinovievite block. The OGPU is four years behind in this matter.'[140] This was followed by a systematic purge of the secret police, carried out by teams of two to three hundred party zealots secretly recruited by Yezhov.[141] Next Stalin eliminated his old Georgian friend Ordzhonikidze, the last Politburo member allowed to call him by his nickname 'Koba' or to argue with him: he was given the choice of shooting himself or dying in the police cells. After February 1937 Stalin could kill anyone, in any way he wished. At the CC plenum at the end of the month, it 'instructed' Stalin to arrest Bukharin and Rykov. Bukharin pleaded tearfully for his life. Stalin: 'If you are innocent, you can prove it in a prison cell!' The CC: 'Shoot the traitor!' The two men were taken straight off to prison and death; Yagoda was later heard to mutter, 'What a pity I didn't arrest all of you before, when I had the power.'[142] (It made no difference: of the 140 people present, nearly two-thirds would shortly be murdered.)

From the end of 1936 to the second half of 1938, Stalin struck at every group in the regime. In 1937 alone he killed 3,000 senior secret police officers and 90 per cent of the public prosecutors in the provinces. He had been in secret negotiations with Hitler since 1935. The following year he persuaded the Nazi government to concoct forged evidence of secret contacts between the Soviet army commander, Marshal Tukhachevsky, and Hitler's generals; it was done by the Gestapo and transmitted by one of its agents, General Skoblin, who also worked for the NKVD.[143] Stalin's first military victim was a cavalry general, Dmitry Shmidt, who had apparently abused him in 1927; Shmidt was arrested on 5 July 1936, tortured and murdered. Tukhashevsky and seven other senior generals followed on 11 June 1937, and thereafter 30,000 officers, about half the total, including 80 per cent of the colonels and generals.[144] Most officers were shot within twenty-four hours of arrest. In every group, the aim was to kill the most senior, especially those who had fought in the Revolution or who had known the party before Stalin owned it. The purge of the party itself was the most prolonged and severe. In Leningrad, only two out of its 150 delegates to the seventeenth Party Congress were allowed to live. The losses in the Moscow party were as great. About one million party members were killed in all.[145]

The crimes committed in these years have never been atoned for, properly investigated or punished (except by accident), since the successive generations of party leaders who ruled after Stalin were all involved in their commission. Yezhov, the principal assassin, was murdered himself by Stalin after the purges were over. His successor as head of the secret police, Lavrenti Beria, was gunned down by his Politburo colleagues immediately after Stalin's own death. Georgi Malenkov, who ruled Russia 1953–6, was the chief purger in Belorussia and Armenia. Khrushchev, who succeeded him and ruled 1956–64, was in charge of the purge both in Moscow and (together with Yezhov himself and Molotov) in the Ukraine. The Leningrad purge was under Zhdanov, one of his assistants (and one of the very few survivors) being Aleksei Kosygin, Prime Minister in the 1970s until his death. Kaganovich, who held high office until the 1960s, was the destroyer of the party in the Smolensk region. Leonid Brezhnev, an abetter and survivor of the Ukraine purge, ruled Russia from 1964 until his death in 1982.

All these men, who governed Russia in the thirty years after Stalin's death, worked from a blend of self-aggrandizement and fear, under Stalin's direct and detailed instructions. An NKVD man who had been in Stalin's bodyguard testified that Yezhov came to Stalin almost daily in the years 1937–9, with a thick file of papers; Stalin would give orders for arrests, the use of torture, and sentences (the last before the trial). Stalin carried out some interrogations himself. He annotated documents 'arrest'; 'arrest everyone'; 'no need to check: arrest them'. At the 1961 twenty-second Party Congress, Z.T.Serdiuk read out a letter from Yezhov: 'Comrade Stalin: I am sending for confirmation four lists of people whose cases are before the Military Collegium: List One, general; List Two, former military personnel; List Three, former NKVD personnel; List Four, wives of former enemies of the people. I request approval for first-degree condemnation (*pervaia kategoriia*, i.e. shooting).' The list was signed 'Approved, J.Stalin, V.Molotov'. Stalin's signature is appended to over 400 lists from 1937 to 1939, bearing the names of 44,000 people, senior party leaders, officials of the government, officers and cultural figures.[146]

Foreign Communists who had sought asylum in Moscow were murdered too, in large numbers. They included Béla Kun and most of the Hungarian Communist leaders, nearly all the top Polish Communists; all the Yugoslav party brass except Tito, the famous Bulgarians Popov and Tanev, heroes of the Leipzig trial with Dimitrov (who escaped by sheer luck: Stalin had a file on him); all the Koreans; many Indians and Chinese; and Communist leaders from Latvia, Lithuania, Estonia, Bessarabia, Iran, Italy, Finland, Austria, France, Romania, Holland, Czechoslovakia, the United States and Brazil. Particularly hard hit were the Germans who had taken refuge from Hitler. We know the names of 842 of them who

were arrested, but in fact there were many more, including wives and
children of the leaders, such as Karl Liebknecht's family. Some of the
Germans who survived were later able to display the marks of
torture of both the Gestapo and the NKVD, and were thus living
symbols of the furtive contacts which the security services of Nazi
Germany and Soviet Russia maintained throughout this period. On
the whole, European Communists were safer in their own fascist
homelands than in the 'Socialist mother-country'. Roy Medvedev,
the independent Soviet Marxist historian, noted: 'It is a terrible
paradox that most European Communist leaders and activists who
lived in the USSR perished, while most of those who were in prison
in their native lands in 1937–8 survived.'[147] That Stalin exchanged
lists of 'wanted' activists with the Nazis is certain, and he may have
done so with other totalitarian regimes which his propaganda
assailed with mechanical ferocity. He took a close interest in the fate
of the foreign Communists he dealt with. But then he took a close
interest in all aspects of his terror. At one point during the trial of his
old comrade and victim Bukharin, an arc-light briefly revealed to
visitors the face of Stalin himself, peering through the black glass of a
small window set high under the ceiling of the court.[148]

Arthur Koestler's brilliant novel, *Darkness at Noon* (1940), gave
the impression that Stalin's leading victims, trapped in their own
Marxist theology, and the relative morality they shared with him,
were induced to collaborate in their own mendacious testimony –
even came to believe it. Nothing could be further from the truth.
While leading 'conspirators', whose evidence was needed to build up
the basic structure of the fantasy, were brought to confess by a
mixture of threats to kill or torture wives and children, promises of
leniency, and physical violence, for the overwhelming majority of
those who were engulfed, Stalin's methods differed little from Peter
the Great's, except of course in scale, which precluded any subtlety.

During these years something like 10 per cent of Russia's vast
population passed through Stalin's penitential machinery. Famous
Tsarist prisons, such as the Lefortovskaia, which had been turned
into museums and peopled with waxwork figures, were put into
service again, the wax replaced by flesh and blood. Churches, hotels,
even bathhouses and stables were turned into gaols; and dozens of
new ones built. Within these establishments, torture was used on a
scale which even the Nazis were later to find it difficult to match.
Men and women were mutilated, eyes gouged out, eardrums perforated; they were encased in 'nail boxes' and other fiendish devices.
Victims were often tortured in front of their families. The wife of
Nestor Lakoba, a strikingly beautiful woman, preferred to die under
torture, even when faced with her weeping fourteen-year-old son,

rather than accuse her husband. Many faced a horrible death with similar stoicism. The NKVD's plan to stage a show-trial of the Youth Movement was frustrated by the fact that S.V.Kovarev and other leaders of the Komsomol Central Committee all preferred to die under torture rather than confess to a lie. Large numbers of army officers were killed in this fashion: *in extremis* they might sign their own 'confessions' but they would not implicate others. According to Medvedev, NKVD recruits, aged eighteen, 'were taken to torture-chambers, like medical students to laboratories to watch dissections'.[149]

That Hitler's example helped to spur Stalin to his great terror is clear enough, and his agents were always quick to learn anything the Gestapo and the SS had to teach. But the instruction was mutual. The camps system was imported by the Nazis from Russia. Himmler set them up with great speed; there were nearly one hundred Nazi camps before the end of 1933. But at all stages, even at the height of the SS extermination programme in 1942–5, there were many more Soviet camps, most of them much larger than the Nazi ones, and containing many more people. Indeed, the Soviet camps, as Solzhenitsyn and others have shown, constituted a vast series of substantial territorial islands within the Soviet Union, covering many thousands of square miles. Like the Nazi camps, which ranged downwards from Dachau, the 'Eton' or 'Groton' of the system, the Soviet camps were of many varieties. There was, for instance, a special camp for the widows, orphans and other relatives of slaughtered army officers; and there were prison-orphanages for the children of 'enemies of the people', who were themselves liable to be tried and sentenced, as was Marshal Tukhachevsky's daughter Svetlana, as soon as they were old enough.[150]

Most of the camps, however, served a definite economic purpose, and it was their example which inspired Himmler, from 1941 onwards, to seek to create a substantial 'socialized sector' of the Germany economy. The Soviet Union did not engage in a deliberate and systematic policy of genocide, though Stalin came close to it when dealing with the Soviet 'nationalities' in the Second World War. But the Soviet camps were (and are) 'death camps' all the same. The sign in iron letters over the camps in the Kolyma region, among the very worst, which read 'Labour is a matter of honour, valour and heroism', was as misleading as the Nazi imitation of it, hung over the entrance to Auschwitz: *Arbeit Macht Frei* (Work Wins Freedom). Within these camps the NKVD frequently carried out mass-executions, using machine-guns: 40,000 men, women and children were thus killed in the Kolyma camps alone in 1938. The 'special punishment' and gold-mine camps were the worst killers. Lenin and later Stalin built up the world's second-largest gold industry (after South Africa's) and huge gold reserves, on the backs of men working a sixteen-hour day, with no rest days, wearing rags, sleeping often in torn tents, with temperatures down to sixty degrees below zero, and with pitifully small quantities of food. Witnesses later testified that it took twenty to thirty days to turn a healthy man into a physical wreck in these camps, and some claimed that conditions were deliberately planned to achieve a high death-rate. Savage beatings were administered by the guards, and also by the professional criminal element, who were given supervisory duties over the masses of 'politicals' – another feature of the camps imitated by the Nazis.

In these circumstances, the death-rate was almost beyond the imagining of civilized men. Medvedev puts the figure of the great terror victims summarily shot at 4–500,000. He thinks the total number of victims in the years 1936–9 was about 4.5 million. Men and women died in the camps at the rate of about a million a year during this and later periods, and the total of deaths caused by Stalin's policy was in the region of 10 million.[151] Just as the Roehm purge goaded Stalin into imitation, so in turn the scale of his mass atrocities encouraged Hitler in his wartime schemes to change the entire demography of Eastern Europe. In social engineering, mass murder on an industrial scale is always the ultimate weapon: Hitler's 'final solution' for the Jews had its origins not only in his own fevered mind but in the collectivization of the Soviet peasantry.

Granted their unprecedented nature, the atrocities committed by the Nazi and Soviet totalitarian regimes in the 1930s had remarkably little impact on the world, though the nature (if not the scale) of both, and especially the former, were reasonably well known at the time. More attention was focused on Hitler's crimes, partly because they were nearer the West, partly because they were often openly vaunted, but chiefly because they were publicized by a growing émigré population of intellectuals. As a self-proclaimed enemy of civilization, as opposed to *Kultur*, Hitler was a natural target for the writers of the free world even before he became Chancellor; once in power he proceeded to confirm his image as a mortal enemy of the intelligentsia. His public book-burning started in March 1933 and reached a climax in Berlin that May, with Goebbels presiding, quoting the words of Ulrich von Hutten: 'Oh century, oh sciences, it is a joy to be alive!' Exhibitions of 'degenerate art' were held at Nuremberg (1935) and Munich (1937). Museums were bullied into disposing of some of their paintings: thus, at a sale in Lucerne in June 1939, works by Gauguin and Van Gogh went for derisory prices, and Picasso's *Absinthe-Drinker* failed to find a buyer. Regular lists of émigrés deprived of their German citizenship were published. They included Leon Feuchtwanger, Helmut von Gerlach, Alfred Kerr, Heinrich Mann, Kurt Tucholsky, Ernst Toller (August 1933), Robert Becher, Einstein, Theodor Plievier (March 1934), Bruno Frank, Klaus Mann, Piscator (November 1934), Friedrich Wolf, Berthold Brecht, Paul Bekker, Arnold Zweig, Thomas Mann (1935–6), and scores of other famous figures.[152] These, and thousands of Jewish and anti-Nazi university professors and journalists, who were prevented from making a living in Germany and were virtually obliged to emigrate, swelled the chorus of those who sought to expose conditions within Hitler's Reich.

All the same, Hitler had his vocal admirers. They included Lloyd George, the Duke of Windsor and Lord Rothermere, owner of the *Daily Mail*. Major Yeats-Brown, author of the famous *Lives of a Bengal Lancer*, testified that it was his 'honest opinion that there is more real Christianity in Germany today than there ever was under the Weimar Republic'. Among those who expressed qualified approval of fascism in its various forms were Benedetto Croce, Jean Cocteau, Luigi Piran-dello, Giovanni Gentile, James Burnham, W.B. Yeats, T.S. Eliot and Filippo Marinetti, as well as actual pro-fascist intellectuals like Charles Maurras, Louis-Ferdinand Céline, Ezra Pound, Oswald Spengler and Martin Heidegger.[153]

The overwhelming majority of intellectuals, however, veered to the Left. They saw Nazism as a far greater danger, both to their own order and to all forms of freedom. By the mid-Thirties, many intelligent people believed that fascism was likely to become the predominant system of government in Europe and perhaps throughout the world. There were quasi-fascist regimes in Germany, Italy, Spain, Portugal, Poland, Hungary, Austria, Turkey, Greece, Romania, Japan and many other states; and flourishing fascist parties virtually everywhere else. To them the Soviet Union appeared to be the only major power wholly committed to opposing, and if necessary fighting, fascism. Hence many of them were not only prepared to defend its apparent virtues but to justify the manifest ruthlessness of the Stalin regime. Very few of them, at any rate at that stage, were aware of the true nature of the regime. Jewish writers, in particular, knew little or nothing of Stalin's violent anti-Semitism. It was not known that he sent over 600 writers to the camps, many (including Isaac Babel and Osip Mandelstam) to their deaths; that he almost certainly murdered Maxim Gorky; and that he, like Hitler, took millions of books out of circulation and burnt them, though not publicly.[154]

Yet Western intellectuals knew enough about Soviet severity to oblige them to adopt a double standard in defending it. Lincoln Steffens set the tone: 'Treason to the Tsar wasn't a sin, treason to Communism is.'[155] Shaw argued: 'We cannot afford to give ourselves moral airs when our most enterprising neighbour . . . humanely and judiciously liquidates a handful of exploiters and speculators to make the world safe for honest men.'[156] André Malraux argued that 'Just as the Inquisition did not affect the fundamental dignity of Christianity, so the Moscow trials have not diminished the fundamental dignity of Communism.' Many intellectuals, including some who knew what totalitarian justice meant, defended the trials. Brecht wrote: 'Even in the opinion of the bitterest enemies of the Soviet Union and of her government, the trials have clearly demonstrated the existence of active conspiracies against the regime', a 'quagmire of infamous crimes' committed by 'All the scum, domestic and foreign, all the vermin, the professional criminals and informers . . . this rabble . . . I am convinced this is the truth.'[158] Feuchtwanger was present at the 1937 Pyatakov trial (which led up to the Bukharin and other trials) and wrote an instant book about it, *Moscow 1937*, which declared: 'there was no justification of any sort for imagining that there was anything manufactured or artificial about the trial proceedings.' Stalin immediately had this translated and published in Moscow (November 1937) and a copy of it was pressed on the wretched Bukharin on the very eve of his own trial, to complete his despair.[159]

The NKVD, indeed, made frequent use of pro-Stalin tracts by Western intellectuals to break down the resistance of their prisoners. They were assisted, too, by pro-Stalin elements in the Western embassies and press in Moscow. Ambassador Davies told his government that the trials were absolutely genuine and repeated his views in a mendacious book, *Mission to Moscow*, published in 1941. Harold Denny, of the *New York Times*, wrote of the trials: 'in the broad sense, they are not fakes' (14 March 1938). His colleague, Walter Duranty, the paper's regular Moscow correspondent, was one of the most comprehensive of Stalin's apologists. As Malcolm Muggeridge wrote: 'There was something vigorous, vivacious, preposterous about his unscrupulousness, which made his persistent lying somehow absorbing.' His favourite expression was 'I put my money on Stalin'.[160] Of the Pyatakov trial he wrote: 'It is unthinkable that Stalin and Voroshilov and Budyonny and the court martial could have sentenced their friends to death unless the proofs of guilt were overwhelming.'[161] To suggest the evidence was faked, echoed Ambassador Davies, 'would be to suppose the creative genius of Shakespeare'.[162]

The attempt by Western intellectuals to defend Stalinism involved them in a process of self-corruption which transferred to them, and so to their countries, which their writings helped to shape, some of the moral decay inherent in totalitarianism itself, especially its denial of individual responsibility for good or ill. Lionel Trilling shrewdly observed of the Stalinists of the West that they repudiated politics, or at least the politics of 'vigilance and effort':

In an imposed monolithic government they saw the promise of rest from the particular acts of will which are needed to meet the many, often clashing, requirements of democratic society . . . they cherished the idea of revolution as the final, all-embracing act of will which would forever end the exertions of our individual wills.[163]

For America, the development was particularly serious because the Stalinists then formed the salient part of the new radical movement; and as Trilling also noted:

In any view of the American cultural situation, the importance of the radical movement of the Thirties cannot be overestimated. It may be said to have created the American intellectual class as we now know it in its great size and influence. It fixed the character of this class as being, through all mutations of opinion, predominantly of the Left.[164]

This was the class which shaped the thinking of the liberal–Democratic political establishment, which was to hold power in the most powerful nation on earth until virtually the end of the 1970s.

The ramifying influence of Thirties totalitarian terror was, therefore, immense, in space and time. But at that epoch, the ultimate consequences of Hitler and Stalin seemed unimportant. What mattered was what their regimes would do in the immediate future, not merely to their helpless subjects, but to their neighbours near and far. The advent of Stalin and Hitler to absolute power dealt a decisive blow to a world structure which was already unstable and fragile. Both had limitless territorial aims, since both subscribed to imminent eschatologies, one of class, one of race, in the course of which their rival power-systems would become globally dominant. Hence the arrival of these two men on the scene introduced what may be termed the high noon of aggression.

NINE

The High Noon of Aggression

During the 1920s, the civilized Western democracies had maintained some kind of shaky world order, through the League on the one hand, and through Anglo–American financial diplomacy on the other. At the beginning of the 1930s, the system – if it could be called a system – broke down completely, opening an era of international banditry in which the totalitarian states behaved simply in accordance with their military means. The law-abiding powers were economically ruined and unilaterally disarmed. The French economy passed its peak in 1929 and thereafter went into steady decline, not recovering its 1929 levels until the early 1950s. Its unemployment figures remained comparatively low simply because the dismissed workers went back to the peasant farms on which they had been born, and migrants were ejected. France retreated into isolation and began to build her Maginot Line, itself a symbol of defeatism. The Americans and the British were obsessed by economy. In the early 1930s, the American army, with 132,069 officers and men, was only the sixteenth largest in the world, smaller than those of Czechoslovakia, Poland, Turkey, Spain and Romania.[1] The Chief of Staff, MacArthur, had the army's only limousine. Ramsay MacDonald, Britain's Labour Prime Minister, who had no car of his own and none provided by the state, had to trot to the end of Downing Street and hail a bus or taxi when he went about the nation's business.[2] In 1930, the Americans persuaded the semi-pacifist Labour government to sign the London Naval Treaty, which reduced the Royal Navy to a state of impotence it had not known since the seventeenth century. The Foreign Secretary Arthur Henderson, a Methodist Utopian who talked of 'mobilizing a democracy of diplomacy', defended the decision to cease work on the projected Singapore base, and to cut Britain's cruisers to a mere fifty, on the grounds that Japan 'had definitely pledged herself to settle her disputes by peaceful means'.[3]

Ironically it was the 1930 London Naval Treaty, which they had reluctantly signed, that finally persuaded the Japanese to break with the West and pursue their own self-interest. The 1930 Smoot–Hawley tariff, which destroyed their American trade (15 per cent of their exports) and the other tariffs which followed in retaliation, seemed to them sufficient moral reason to return to the law of the jungle. On 10 September 1931 sailors at the British naval base at Invergordon, angered by a 10 per cent pay cut, mutinied and immobilized some of Britain's main fleet units. Eight days later, the Japanese Army High Command engineered a crisis in Manchuria, leading to invasion, against the express commands of the civilian cabinet in Tokyo.[4] The cabinet surrendered and endorsed the army *coup*, declaring a new puppet state of Manchukuo.

Britain could, and did, do nothing. Its Tokyo ambassador, Sir Francis Lindley, reported that he found himself 'in the unpleasant position of seeking assurances from a government which had not the power to make them good'.[5] Britain got a League of Nations inquiry set up, under Lord Lytton, which in due course produced a report critical of Japan. The only consequence was that Japan left the League on 27 March 1933. League enthusiasts, like Lord Robert Cecil, pressed for 'action' against Japan. But they were the same men who had insisted on disarmament. On 29 February 1932 Sir Frederick Field, the First Sea Lord, said Britain was 'powerless' in the Far East; Singapore was 'defenceless'. The ten-year-rule was now quietly scrapped, but it was too late.[6] As Stanley Baldwin put it: 'If you enforce an economic boycott you will have war declared by Japan and she will seize Singapore and Hong Kong and we cannot, as we are placed, stop her. You will get nothing out of Washington but words, big words, but only words.'[7]

In fact, even with their existing forces, Britain and America in combination could have deterred and contained Japan. Pearl Harbor could only be defended by sea-power. Reinforced with British units, the American Pacific fleet might have made the base secure. Singapore harbour could be defended by adequate air power alone. With American air reinforcements, that too might have been rendered defensible.[8] A strong line with Japan would then have been feasible. But such joint planning was ruled out by America's growing isolationism – a feature of the 1930s much more than the 1920s. America was moving towards the 1935 Neutrality Act. When Roosevelt took over from Hoover he made matters worse. Hoover had helped to plan a world economic conference, to be held in London June–July 1933. It might have persuaded the 'have-not' powers that there were alternatives to fighting for a living. On 3 July Roosevelt torpedoed it. Thereafter no real effort was made to create a stable financial framework within which disputes could be settled by diplomacy. In the 1920s the world had been run by the power of money. In the 1930s it was subject to the arbitration of the sword.

A careful study of the chronology of the period reveals the extent to which the totalitarian powers, though acting independently and sometimes in avowed hostility towards each other, took advantage of their numbers and their growing strength to challenge and outface the pitifully stretched resources of democratic order. Italy, Japan, Russia and Germany played a geopolitical game together, whose whole object was to replace international law and treaties by a new Realpolitik in which, each believed, its own millennarian vision was destined to be realized. None of these wolf-like states trusted the others; each deceived when it could; but each took advantage of the depredations of the rest to enlarge its booty and strengthen its position. There was therefore a conspiracy in crime, unstable and shifting, sometimes open, more often covert. Competition in crime, too: the process whereby one totalitarian state corrupted another internally now spread to foreign dealings, so that a Gresham's Law operated here, too, driving out diplomacy and replacing it by force.

These predator-states practised Realpolitik in different ways and at different speeds. Stalin's Russia was the most Bismarckian, content to seize opportunity merely when it offered and patient enough to move according to geological time-scales, convinced all would be hers in the end. Germany was the most dynamic, with an imminent eschatology which Hitler felt must be realized in his lifetime. Mussolini's Italy was the jackal, following in the wake of the larger beasts and snatching any morsel left unguarded. Japan was the most unstable, haunted by the vision of actual mass-starvation. The world recession had cut the prices of her principal export, raw silk, by 50 per cent and she was now short of currency to buy rice. Yet by 1934 she was spending 937 million yen out of a total budget of 2,112 million, nearly half, on her army and navy.[9] All these totalitarian regimes suffered from internal predation too, the Hobbesian 'war of every man against every man'. But at least Germany, Russia and Italy had gangster dictatorships. In Japan, nobody was in charge.

The 1931 Manchurian conspiracy showed that the military could usurp decision-making and remain unpunished. The 1932 murders of the prime minister, finance minister and leading industrialists marked the effective end of government by parliamentary means. In December 1933 the Tenno himself was nearly murdered, and thereafter he went in terror. The most influential single figure in Japan in the period 1931–4 was the War Minister, General Sadao Araki, a ferocious bushido ideologue, who ran a Hitler-style youth movement and was one of the leading exponents of the new totalitarian Shinto. In a European country he would almost certainly have become a dictator, and thus created a centralized focus of decision-making and responsibility. But in a country which, in theory, was ruled by a living god-man, individual leadership was reprobated and punished by assassination. Even the most authoritarian of the Japanese, indeed especially the most authoritarian, subscribed to clan or group rule, small oligarchies meeting and arguing in secret and taking collective decisions which shrouded individual responsibility.[10] It was a system which encouraged at one and the same time both physical recklessness and moral cowardice, and which stifled the personal conscience. It made the Japanese ruling élites peculiarly susceptible to the collectivism preached, albeit in different accents, by Stalin, Mussolini and Hitler and especially to the central proposition, about which all three were unanimous, that the rights of the individual were subsumed in the rights of the state, which were total and unqualified. Since the 1860s, the British and Americans had tried hard to inculcate a different tradition; and with some success. It was upheld by and personified in Professor Tatsukichi Minobe, an authority on constitutional law at the Imperial University since 1902, and a peer of Japan by imperial nomination. His three major works on the Japanese constitution made him the mentor of Japanese parliamentary liberalism, and were objects of peculiar hatred to the *dévots* of totalitarian Shinto. Attacks on the old professor, who argued that the law existed to protect the individual in society, and that it was greater than the state, mounted steadily as Japan's own lawlessness went unpunished and, still more, when Hitler triumphantly emerged in Germany to rule without constitutional law and to defy international agreements. On 19 December 1934 Japan denounced the London Naval Treaty and followed Hitler in unrestricted rearmament. On 16 March 1935 Hitler repudiated the Versailles Treaty. On 25 April leading members of the Japanese armed services carried Tatsukichi's books to the roof of the Tokyo Military Club and burned them publicly.

This symbolic repudiation of the rule of law was rapidly followed by the adoption of what might be termed a crude Japanese form of Hegelianism, which became government doctrine and was taught in the services and the schools. It was summarized officially by the Ministry of Justice:

To the Japanese mind there has been no conception of the individual as opposed to the state.... Underlying western types of ideas exists an individualistic view of life which regards individuals as absolute, independent entities ... the standard of all values and themselves the highest of all values. [But] human beings, while having their independent existence and life, depend in a deeper sense on the whole and live in co-ordinated relationship with each other. They are born from the state, sustained by the state and brought up in the history and traditions of the state. Individuals can only exist as links in an infinite and vast chain of life called the state; they are links through whom the inheritance of ancestors is handed down to posterity . . . . Individuals participate in the highest and greatest value when they serve the state as part of it.[11]

The statement was mendacious because the philosophy in this form was an import from Europe, and misleading because those in Japan who most emphatically subscribed to it were the first to disobey and assault the state when its policies were not wholly subject to their control. In any case, the state was not an entity but a collection of warring factions, with murder as the arbiter. Putting military men in charge of ministries did not solve any problems: they were just as liable to be assassinated as civilians. Taking decisions collectively was no protection either: the gunmen developed the technique of collective assassination. Besides, the military were as divided as the civilian parties. The navy wanted a 'Southern' policy, expanding into the Far Eastern colonies and islands of the Dutch, French and British, rich in the raw materials, especially oil, which Japan lacked. The army wanted expansion into the Asian mainland. But they, too, were divided into 'Northerners', who wanted to build up Manchuria and strike at Russia; and 'Southerners', who wanted to take the Chinese cities and push up its great river valleys. None of these men, or the civilian politicians who sided with them, thought through their plans to their ultimate consequences. They were all brilliant tacticians; none was a strategist. Everyone had striking ideas about beginning a war; but from first to last, from 1931 to the hour of the bitter defeat in 1945, no Japanese, civil or military, worked out realistically how the war was likely to end. How could that be? To be known to argue that, in certain circumstances, defeat was possible, was to risk death. When debate was inhibited by physical fear, and changes of political direction brought about by slaughter, cold-blooded calculation – the essence of Realpolitik – became impossible. The truth is, as the 1930s progressed, Japan was ruled and her policies determined not by any true system of government but by an anarchy of terror.

The watershed was 1935–6. On 12 August 1935, the faction-fighting spread to the armed forces, when General Tetsuzan Nagata, Chief of the Military Affairs Bureau, was hacked to death by a radical colonel, Saburo Aizawa. Aizawa declared at his trial: 'I failed to dispatch Nagata with one stroke of my sword, and as a fencing instructor I am bitterly ashamed.'[12] But he was ashamed of nothing else and used his protracted trial to make violent anti-establishment

war propaganda. It was still going on when the elections of 20 February 1936 saw a recovery of parliamentary liberalism – for what it
was worth. Five days later there was an evening party at the house of
the American Ambassador, Joseph Grew. Grew was deaf, and it is
characteristic of the difficulties of working with Japan that, during
his audiences with the Tenno, he could not hear a word of what the
interpreter said as it was an unforgivable offence to speak above a
whisper in the Emperor's presence.[13] But Grew's wife, a grand-
daughter of the famous Commander Perry, spoke perfect Japanese,
and their house was a caravanserai of Japanese constitutionalism.
That evening their guests included Admiral Makoto Saito, the Privy
Seal, and Admiral Kantaro Suzuki, the Chamberlain. After dinner
Grew showed them the Nelson Eddy–Jeanette MacDonald film
Naughty Marietta, which was much relished, the Japanese wives
weeping copious tears of appreciation.[14]

Early the next morning, 1,500 men of the Tokyo garrison,
including the Guards, two crack infantry regiments and artillery
units, staged a *putsch*. They took the law courts, the Diet building,
and the headquarters of the army, navy and police; and they
surrounded the Imperial Palace. Assassination squads, armed with
swords (for honour) and Thomson sub-machine-guns (for efficiency),
were sent to the residences of the leading members of the government. Saito was murdered. So was the head of Military Education,
and the Finance Minister. Suzuki, though injured, was saved by the
heroism of his wife. The Prime Minister, Admiral Okada, a prime
target since he had just announced that the elections meant a return
to constitutional rule, was also saved by his wife, who locked him in
a cupboard, and the hit-squad gunned down his brother by mistake.
The ultimate object of the plot was to murder and replace the
Emperor; but he survived too, and the navy and imperial guards
forced the mutineers to surrender four days later. Thirteen leading
rebels were tried hastily and executed in secret – only two committed
hara-kiri, though all were given the chance to do so. It was notable
that throughout this grisly episode, nobody concerned – the victims,
their colleagues, the Emperor, senior army and navy officers, police,
bodyguards, and least of all the murderers themselves – behaved
with anything other than cowardice and pusillanimity. The only
exceptions were the despised womenfolk, the wives and maid-
servants of the ministers, who showed extraordinary courage and
resourcefulness.[15]

The attempted *putsch* was widely interpreted as pro-Nazi, but it is
more probable that its authors were, in some cases wittingly in others
unwittingly, servants of Soviet policy. Their manifesto denounced
the 'many people whose chief aim and purpose have been to amass

personal material wealth disregarding the general welfare and prosperity of the Japanese people . . . . The *Genro*, the senior statesmen, military cliques, plutocrats, bureaucrats and political parties are all traitors who are destroying the national essence.'[16] The young officers involved were quite prepared to introduce a form of Communism into Japan, through a mixture of Marxism and *Kodo* (the 'Imperial Way') with a Communist puppet-Emperor. This was the view of the Soviet agent Richard Sorge, who worked from within the Nazi embassy. He guessed, and so informed his masters in Moscow, that the mutiny would favour Soviet policy since it would mark a movement away from the 'Northern' tactic of confrontation with Russia along the Manchukuo border, and towards the further penetration of China. That was doubly welcome to Stalin since an all-out war between China and Japan would not only rule out an attack on his vulnerable eastern bases but, in all probability, force Chiang and the Kuomintang to drop their differences with the Chinese Communists, form a Popular Front, and thus hasten the moment when the whole of China would join the Soviet bloc.[17]

That, indeed, is exactly what happened. The mutineers had wanted a more active Japanese military policy, favouring a 'Northern' outlet for it. The Japanese military establishment, having hanged the mutineers, promptly and cravenly adopted their activism, but – as Sorge had guessed – gave it a 'Southern' twist. There is no evidence, however, that Japan ever willed an all-out war with China. Rather the contrary. It was her policy to pose as China's fellow-oriental 'protector' and 'brother', and gain her ends by trade, diplomacy, pressure and propaganda. The only great power with an interest in a Sino–Japanese war was Soviet Russia; and the only element within China which stood to gain from one was the CCP.

The chronology of events is suggestive. By the summer of 1934, the Communist armies in China, of which Chou En-lai was political commissar, were close to destruction at the hands of Chiang's KMT forces and their German advisers, von Seeckt and von Falkenhausen. In the autumn the Communist war-lords decided to begin what later became known as 'the Long March', ostensibly to fight the Japanese in the north; in fact to get away from Chiang's encircling blockhouses and barbed-wire. The details of the March, which began in October 1934 and ended in Yenan in December 1936, are Maoist legend, and may be believed or not according to taste.[18] The salient point is that during the course of it Mao, for the first time, got control of the main Communist forces. The nominal commander, Chang Kuo Tao, split off and took his men to Sikiang, and so was branded with the heresy of 'flightism'. Henceforth, as supreme Communist war-lord (with Chou as his political Merlin), Mao could accuse any Communist competitor of 'war-lordism' and concentrate all power, military and political, in himself.[19]

By the time this process of Communist concentration was complete and the March was over, towards the end of 1936, Stalin was pushing his 'Popular Front' policy of getting the CCP and the KMT to act together in war with Japan. Mao was at first reluctant: he thought Chiang should be shot. But during a visit to the northern front late in 1936, Chiang was arrested in a mysterious episode known as the 'Sian Incident'; his papers were searched and Chou En-lai got access to his diaries revealing the fierceness of his anti-Japanese feelings.[20] As a result Mao allowed himself to be persuaded; and by 1 March 1937 he had reverted to his earlier nationalism, telling a visitor, Agnes Smedley: 'The Communists absolutely do not tie their viewpoint to the interests of a single class at a single time, but are most passionately concerned with the fate of the Chinese nation.'[21]

To be pursued successfully, a nationalist line required a full-scale 'patriotic war'. On 5 July 1937, the Chinese Communists and the KMT signed a working agreement. Two days later, on the night of 7 July, came the first 'incident' between KMT and Japanese forces at Marco Polo Bridge outside Peking, the first shots coming from the Chinese side. It was this escalating episode which led to full-scale war. It is significant that the opposing commanders, Sung Chi-yuen, KMT Commander-in-Chief in North China, and the Japanese C-in-C General Gun Hashimoto, were on friendly terms and did everything in their power to damp down the affair. But repeated and inexplicable acts of violence make it clear that somebody was deliberately seeking a full-scale conflict. General Ho Ying-chin, the KMT Minister of War in 1937, believed to his dying day that it was the work of the Japanese military radicals, the same group who had staged the Tokyo mutiny the year before. But Japanese officers present during the Bridge affair thought at the time that the violence was the work of subversive elements in the Chinese forces, and after Mao's post-war triumph they were convinced that his agents, acting on Soviet instruction, provoked the war. The Japanese Soviet expert, General Akio Doi, said in 1967: 'We were then too simple to realize that this was all a Communist plot.' What is quite clear is that the Marco Polo affair was not a repetition of the Manchurian Incident of 1931. There was no conspiracy in the Japanese army. The Chinese behaved with rather more intransigence and arrogance than the Japanese once the incident took place, and they took the initiative in spreading the war.[22]

What is equally clear is that Russia was the great beneficiary of the Sino–Japanese war. The Japanese had been the last to abandon the attempt to crush the Bolshevik regime by force. Their frontier with the

Soviets remained tense, and in the late 1930s there were several very serious military encounters: in 1937 on the Amur River; in 1938 at Changkufeng, seventy miles from Vladivostok; and in May–June of 1939 on the Mongolian–Manchukuo border – the last being a large-scale armoured engagement, foreshadowing the vast tank-battles of the Second World War. Without the China war, Japan would undoubtedly have been able to engage the Russians in full-scale conflict, and drive them from the Far East. As it was, she could not divert sufficient forces; and the 1939 battle, in which General Zhukov made his reputation, was a Soviet victory and the first defeat the Japanese forces had suffered in modern times.[23]

The other gainer was Mao. In the autumn of 1937, with the war now raging uncontrollably, he told his generals:

The Sino–Japanese conflict gives us, the Chinese Communists, an excellent opportunity for expansion. Our policy is to devote 70 per cent of our effort to this end, 20 per cent to coping with the government, and 10 per cent to fighting Japanese. This policy is to be carried out in three stages. During the first stage we are to work with the KMT to ensure our existence and growth. During the second stage we are to achieve parity in strength with the KMT. During the third we are to penetrate deep into parts of China to establish bases for counter-attack against the KMT.[24]

This policy was carried out to the letter. Chiang retired to Chung-king, deep in the interior. Mao remained in the north-west, avoiding large-scale engagements with the Japanese but fighting a low-key guerrilla war and creating a military and political empire among the peasants.

For Japan, the war was a moral, political and ultimately a military and economic disaster. The Americans had always been basically pro-Chinese. The 'China lobby' already existed. Roosevelt was violently anti-Japanese. On 5 October 1937 in a speech in Chicago, he equated Japan with the Nazis and the fascists and signalled her moral isolation: 'When an epidemic of physical disease starts to spread, the community approves and joins in a quarantine of the patients.'[25] In the conduct of Japanese policy, the military were now in the saddle, the civilian ministers being no longer consulted, or even informed, of decisions. And military control was itself shaky, as the debased doctrine of totalitarian Shinto and bushido took over the army. The Chinese capital, Nanking, fell in December 1937. The Japanese commander, General Iwane Marsui, had entered China declaring: 'I am going to the front not to fight an enemy but in the state of mind of one who sets out to pacify his brother'; he ordered his men to 'protect and patronize the Chinese officials and people as far as possible'. In fact once the army entered Nanking, the radical officers took over. For four weeks the streets of the city were given over to one of the largest-scale massacres in history. Men, women and children, said an eye-witness, 'were hunted like rabbits. Everyone seen to move was shot.' Some 20,000 male Chinese civilians of military age were marched out into the countryside and killed by bayoneting and machine-guns – foreshadowing the Soviet massacres of the Poles in 1941 at Katyn and elsewhere. The killings went on until 6 February 1938, and by then between 200,000 and 300,000 Chinese were dead. Even an official Nazi embassy report described the scenes as 'the work of bestial machinery'. The atrocities got wide coverage in world newspapers. The Emperor and civilians in the cabinet claimed later that they knew nothing of these events until after the war.[26]

By now Japan had total censorship. In March 1938 the Diet abdicated, passing a Military Law which placed all power in the hands of the generals and admirals. But there was not much police terror: it was unnecessary. The Japanese appeared united behind the war policy. At all events there was no open opposition. The British ambassador, Sir George Sansom, reported: 'The difference between the extremists and the moderates is not one of destination but of the road by which that destination is to be reached and the speed at which it is to be travelled.'[27] Already, by early 1938, Japan had a total war economy including control of labour, of prices and wages, and of all major industrial decisions. Many firms were in fact run by state boards, often under military men. As the army occupied the big Chinese towns and moved up the rivers, rapidly appropriating all industrial China, a board, mainly of army officers, was formed to run the Chinese economy. But these men did not know how to end the war or win it; or indeed what the war was for. Was it to bring Japan prosperity? It did the reverse. The *New York Times* correspondent in Tokyo, Hugh Byas, reported (31 July 1938): 'Japan has reached the point where the length of a matchstick and the skin of a rat represent important economic factors in continuing the war with China.' Rationing and shortages were now, he said, more severe than in Germany in 1918. Rat skins were being tanned to find a leather-substitute. Major commodities such as raw cotton, cloth, chemical, leather, metals, oil, wool and steel had been removed from the market. It was impossible to buy toothpaste, chocolate, chewing-gum, golf balls, frying-pans. Anything made of iron, he wrote, 'is scarcer than gold'.[28] Long before the European war broke out, Japan was a tense, underfed, increasingly desperate totalitarian country, which had alienated all its neighbours, abolished its constitutional and democratic system, abandoned the rule of law, had no long-term strategy which made any sense, and had adopted the expedient of using force to smash its way out of its difficulties, which were increasingly self-created. Here, at the end of the 1930s, was one exemplar of relative morality in practice.

Another was Italy. Here again we see the process of mutual corruption at work. Mussolini's *putsch* had been inspired by Lenin's. From his earliest days as a political activist, Hitler had cited Mussolini as a precedent. His study in the Munich Brown House contained a large bust of Mussolini, and in a pamphlet published in 1935 Goebbels acknowledged in elaborate detail the debt of the Nazis to Italian fascism.[29] Such compliments were not reciprocated – at first. Mussolini, who saw himself with some justice as an educated and civilized man, regarded Hitler as a vulgar mountebank and a dangerous gangster. Italy had a small, well-integrated and much respected Jewish community. Mussolini owed a lot to Jews, especially to one of his socialist mentors, Angelica Balabanov, to Enrico Rocca, founder of Roman fascism, and to Gino Arias, a theorist of Italian corporatism.[30] Hence Hitler's racism was at first repugnant to Mussolini, and he perceived the potential dangers of the Nazi regime earlier than even the French, let alone the British. In 1934 he described it as 'one hundred per cent racism. Against everything and everyone: yesterday against Christian civilization, today against Latin civilization, tomorrow, who knows, against the civilization of the whole world.' He thought the regime 'drunk with a stubborn bellicosity'.[31] Italy had always feared invasion from the Teutonic north. Her hereditary enemy was Austria: and Hitler's policy of *Anschluss* must involve German backing for Austrian attempts to recover Italy's gains at Versailles. Italy had as much to lose from the unravelling of the Treaty as anyone; and when Hitler repudiated Versailles on 16 March 1935, Mussolini agreed to meet with Britain and France at Stresa (April 11–14) to form a 'front' against Nazi aggression.

But by this point Mussolini was already in the process of corruption. The audacity of the Roehm purge, and the lack of response to this state crime from any quarter, had impressed him; as had Hitler's apparent success in raising the German birth-rate. He noted that Japan's Manchurian conquest remained unpunished and that her repudiation of the 1930 London Naval Treaty, which meant she was building capital-ships and aircraft-carriers as fast as she could, had brought no urgent response from Britain. What he did not know, though he might have surmised, was that on 19 March 1934 the British cabinet had decided that Germany must be treated as 'the ultimate potential enemy against whom our "long-range" Defence policy must be directed'. As a result desperate consideration was given to the possibility of making friends again with Japan; but the idea was dropped as hopeless because of implacable American hostility.[32] Mussolini did not know this. But he could look at a map; he could count. He knew it was inconceivable that Britain could maintain adequate naval and air power at home to contain Germany, in the Far East to contain Japan, and in the Mediterranean too. He felt that Britain and France ought to be willing to pay some price to reward his continuing friendship. In the spirit of totalitarian Realpolitik he wanted a free hand to deal with Abyssinia, where incidents on the Italian Somaliland and Eritrean borders had occurred on 5 December 1934. Two months before the Stresa Front was formed he had moved out troops. He had a case. Abyssinia was itself an empire, ruling subject and often migratory populations by force and terror, behind shifting or indeterminate frontiers. Most of the local issues of 1935 were to be resurrected in the post-colonial period, in the late 1970s – though by that time Abyssinia had found a more resolute, if sinister, ally, the Soviet Union, and so kept her independence and empire. In 1935 the crisis did not revolve around the local issues but the credibility of the League, of which Abyssinia was a member and to which she vociferously appealed when Italy attacked on 3 October 1935. Five days later the League declared Italy the aggressor and on 19 October it imposed 'sanctions'.

The handling of the Abyssinian crisis, in which Britain was effectively in charge, is a striking example of how to get the worst of all possible worlds. Abyssinia was a primitive African monarchy which practised slavery; not a modern state at all. It should not have been in the League. The notion that the League had to guarantee its frontiers was an excellent illustration of the absurdity of the covenant which led Senator Lodge and his friends to reject it. The League should have been scrapped after the 1931 Manchurian fiasco. However, if it was felt worth preserving, and if the integrity of Abyssinia was a make-or-break issue, then Britain and France should have been prepared to go to war; in which case Italy would have backed down. The two Western powers would have lost her friendship, aroused her enmity indeed; but the League would have shown it had teeth, and could use them; and the effects might have been felt elsewhere, in central Europe particularly. But to impose sanctions was folly. Sanctions rarely work: they damage, infuriate and embitter but they do not deter or frustrate an act of aggression. In this case they made no sense because France would not agree to oil sanctions (the only type likely to have any impact on events) and America, the world's greatest oil producer, would not impose sanctions at all. Britain would not agree to close the Suez Canal or impose a naval quarantine: the First Sea Lord, Chatfield, reported only seven capital-ships were available.[33] While the cabinet argued about whether or not to try and impose oil sanctions, Hitler remilitarized the Rhineland on 7 March, making nonsense of both Versailles and the

Locarno pact. On this date Britain had only three battleships in home waters, scarcely sufficient to neutralize Germany's 'pocket battle-ships'. Mussolini took Addis Ababa on 5 May and annexed the country four days later. On 10 June the Chancellor of the Exchequer, Neville Chamberlain, described the sanctions policy as 'the very midsummer of madness', and a week later the cabinet scrapped them.[34]

The only effect of the sanctions policy was to turn Mussolini into an enemy. From mid-1936 the Germans began to court him. There were visits to Rome by Frank, Goering, Himmler and Baldar von Shirach. On 1 November Mussolini spoke of the 'Rome–Berlin Axis'. By 22 February 1937, a review by the British Chiefs of Staff noted, 'The days are past when we could count automatically on a friendly and submissive Italy.'[35] That meant existing plans to rein-force the Far East fleet in the event of a crisis with Japan by sending ships through the Mediterranean and Suez were impractical. Britain now had three major potential naval enemies: in home waters, the Mediterranean, and the Pacific–Indian Ocean theatre. There was also the possibility that they might operate in concert. Three weeks after Mussolini spoke of the Axis, Japan and Germany signed the Anti-Comintern Pact, aimed at Russia but signalling the possibility of groups of totalitarian powers acting in predatory wolf-packs. On 27 September 1937, Mussolini was in Berlin. He found Hitler's admiration irresistible. Hitler called him 'the leading statesman in the world, to whom none may even remotely compare himself'.[36] No longer content with Abyssinia, he began to imitate Hitler in the search for targets of expansion, manufacturing claims to Nice, Corsica, Tunis and Albania. He reversed his previous opposition to race-policy and in November 1938 produced his own version of the Nazi Nuremberg Laws.[37] He had already joined the Anti-Comintern Pact (6 November 1937) and left the League (11 December). In April 1939 he began a career of European aggression, invading and annexing Albania, and the process of corruption culminated the next month (22 May) when he signed the 'Pact of Steel' with the man he had considered a potential 'enemy of civilization' only five years before.

By this time Mussolini and Hitler had collaborated together in the first of the ideological proxy-wars. Their 'opponent' in this cynical ritual was Stalin. The theatre selected for their devastating perfor-mance was Spain, which had been virtually outside the European power-system since the early nineteenth century and which now became its agonized focus. This was itself extraordinary: Spain was aloof, self-contained, xenophobic, the European country most resis-tant to the holistic principle, the least vulnerable to the foreign viruses of totalitarianism, of Left or Right, social engineering, relative morality. That is what makes the Spanish Civil War so peculiarly tragic. The infection entered through the Socialist Party (PSOE) and then spread. As Salvador de Madariaga put it, 'what made the Spanish Civil War inevitable was the civil war within the Socialist Party'.[38] In the 1920s, the Spanish Socialists had been sensible, pragmatic reformists. Their most important figure, the union leader Francino Largo Caballero, worked within the Spanish republican tradition. If he looked abroad at all, he admired the British Fabians. He thought the formation of the first Labour government in 1924 'the most important event in the entire history of international socialism'.[39] He even worked, on a give-and-take basis, with the dozy, unadventurous dictatorship of Primo de Rivera (1923–30). He argued that regimes and dictators might come and go, but the object of socialism was to improve the material and moral conditions of the workers within capitalism.[40] Socialist moderation made it possible to end the dictatorship without bloodshed and, the following year, to effect a peaceful transition from monarchy to republic.

To begin with, Caballero served the Republic well. Violence or illegality by the Left, he insisted, would provoke the army and lead to another military dictatorship. He prevented his followers from burning down the house of General Mola, cynosure of the militant Right. He helped to shape the reformist constitution, which permitted nationalization but within a strict framework of law and subject to proper compensation. His great pride was in building schools. Whereas only 505 a year had been put up, on average, in the period 1908–30, in the first year of the Republic over 7,000 had been built.[41] That was what socialist ministers were for. He insisted that political strikes incited by the anarchists and the small Communist Party, and violent rural unrest, be put down, if necessary by the use of artillery.[42] Hence a military *coup* by the Right (August 1932) was a fiasco. A modest agrarian reform bill was passed. For a brief, hopeful moment, it looked as though Spain might achieve republican stability on a firm basis of gradual, humane modernization.

Then the vision fell to pieces. Caballero was the first victim of 'entryism' – the furtive penetration of party and union cadres by the organized ultra-Left. He lost control of the chief union federation (UGT), and began to move to the Left to regain it. Foreign analogies began to play their sinister role. Hitler's triumph, the ease with which the German Social Democrats were destroyed, pointed the lesson that moderation did not pay: by July 1933 Caballero was asserting that the Socialists would seize power rather than accept fascism. Early in 1934 the Austrian Catholic Chancellor Dollfuss smashed his local Socialist Party, bombarding its stronghold, the Karl Marx Hof, with field-guns. Comparisons were drawn with Spain. Warnings by central Europe socialists such as Otto Bauer and Julius Deutsch filled the Spanish socialist press.[43] The infection of extremism struck deepest in the Socialist Youth, which began to form street-mobs and engage in systematic violence. They flattered Caballero by calling him 'the Spanish Lenin'. The old reformer, rejuvenated by their adulation, allowed the militants to lead him by the nose deeper down the path of violence, enchanted by the term given to the new trend, *Caballerismo*.[44] If Mussolini was corrupted towards the Right, Caballero was corrupted towards the Left.

The process was accelerated by the gathering crisis on the land, hit by the end of emigration (100,000 were forced to return in 1933), falling prices, and controversy over the land-reform, which the landowners thought revolutionary, the anarchists a fraud, and which could not be enforced. In the countryside, 'the poor were maddened by hunger, the rich were maddened by fear'.[45] The landowners' slogan for the hungry was *Comed Republica!* – Let the Republic feed you! The civil guards used what was termed 'preventive brutality' to put down peasant risings led by anarchists. In November 1933 the Socialists lost the election, moved out of government and embarked on direct action.

This change of tactics could not succeed and was certain to destroy the republican system. It represented a denial of everything that Caballero had once represented. In May 1934 he encouraged the agricultural workers to strike. It failed: the Interior Ministry deported thousands of peasants at gunpoint and dropped them from lorries hundreds of miles from their homes. In October Caballero pulled out all the stops. In Madrid there was a half-hearted general strike. In Barcelona an 'Independent Catalan Republic' lasted precisely ten hours. In the Asturias, a Workers' Commune, with Socialist backing, survived a fortnight, the miners resisting fiercely with dynamite. But with the workers of Barcelona and Madrid refusing to rise, its suppression was inevitable. It was carried out by Spain's ablest general, Francisco Franco, using four columns of regular and colonial troops.

Franco had hitherto opposed military risings and he continued to do so. But he now saw Spain threatened by a foreign disease: 'The fronts are socialism, communism and the other formulae which attack civilization to replace it with barbarism.'[46] In 1935 he discovered that 25 per cent of army conscripts belonged to the Left parties, and that organizing and leafleting them was the primary task of Left cadres. In August 1935, at the seventh meeting of the Comintern, Dimitrov introduced the 'Popular Front' conception with the words: 'Comrades, you will remember the ancient tale of the capture of Troy . . . . The attacking army was unable to achieve victory until, with the aid of the famous Trojan Horse, it managed to penetrate to the very heart of the enemy camp.'[47] Franco feared that once the army was divided or neutralized there would be nothing to prevent a take-over by the extreme Left, leading to all the horrors of Lenin's Russia and, not least, a Stalinist forced collectivization of the peasants. Early in February 1936, with a Popular Front formed and on the eve of the elections, he told the Spanish military attaché in Paris that the army must be prepared to act 'if the worst came to the worst'. But he thought the crisis would blow over, and no military intervention was planned.[48] Even after the Popular Front victory on 16 February, he thought that the army without respectable civil backing would lack 'the moral unity necessary to undertake the task'.[49]

That the army got this backing was entirely the work of the Socialist and other Left extremists. The Left had been the first to desert democracy for violence in 1934.[50] The result was to set up a frenzy of fear in the main democratic right-wing grouping, the CEDA (Confederación Española de Derechas Autónomas), led by Gil Robles. Robles was a genuine republican; he was hated by the monarchists and fascists as much as by the socialists.[51] His party was a mass-movement of the middle class which did not need to use force to obtain what it could obtain through the ballot – security. Yet totalitarian corruption was present in the CEDA too. Its youth movement, the Juventudes de Acción Popular (JAP), responded eagerly to the violence of the Leftist youth organizations. It greeted Robles himself with cries of '*Jefe, Jefe, Jefe!*' and the slogan 'The *Jefe* is always right'. It called the Left 'anti-Spain'. It proclaimed: 'Either Acción Popular smashes Marxism or Marxism will destroy Spain. With the *Jefe* or against the *Jefe*! There can be no dialogue with anti-Spain. Us and not Them. Let us annihilate Marxism, free-masonry and separatism so that Spain may continue her immortal road!' Some of Robles's followers fought the 1936 election on a panic-programme: victory for the Left would be 'the arming of the rabble; burning of private houses and banks; distribution of private goods and lands; wild looting and the common ownership of women'.[52]

When the Left took office after the elections, it proceeded to confirm most of these fears. Although the Popular Front parties won, they actually got less than 50 per cent of the votes cast. The Left improved its position by 1 million votes; but the Right added an extra 750,000 votes too.[53] These figures dictated caution. Instead the Left brushed aside constitutional niceties, such as waiting for the second-round run-off, and formed a government the day after the first ballot. That night the first burnings of churches and convents took place; in Orvieto the gaol was opened. In parliament the Left began an immediate campaign to deprive CEDA deputies of their seats for alleged 'irregularities', and to attack the President, Alcalá Zamora, who was a perfectly decent republican.

The most alarming development was the rapidly growing influence of the Communists. They had succeeded in electing only seventeen deputies – including Dolores Ibarruri, '*La Pasionaria*', said to have cut a priest's throat with her teeth – but on 5 April they staged a *coup*. Thanks to the efforts of a skilful Comintern agent, Vittorio Codovilla, and the treachery of the Socialist Youth leader, Santiago Carrillo (who had already been attending meetings of the Communist Party Central Committee), the Socialist and Communist Youth Movements were amalgamated, which meant that 40,000 militants were swallowed by the Communists.[54] Ten days later a full-blooded Popular Front programme was announced, making no concession to the narrowness of the electoral victory or the even division of the country. When he heard its terms, Robles warned the Cortes: 'Half the nation will not resign itself to die. If it cannot defend itself by one path, it will defend itself by another . . . . Civil war is being brought by those who seek the revolutionary conquest of power . . . the weapons have been loaded by . . . a government which had not been able to fulfil its duty towards groups which have stayed within the strictest legality.'[55]

The forcing of a revolutionary programme through the Cortes would not of itself have provoked a military rising. The determining factor was the failure of the Popular Front to control its own militants or indeed to form any kind of stable government. The Socialists were hopelessly split as to what path to pursue. The leader of the moderates, Indalecio Prieto, hated Caballero and refused even to be in the same room with him: 'Let Caballero go to hell!' When he warned that Socialist violence would provoke the military he was accused of 'menopausal outbursts'.[56] The result was the worst of both worlds: a combination of weak government and strong rhetoric, mainly supplied by Caballero. The activities of the Popular Front youth movement on the streets of the cities, and of the anarchists organizing peasant take-overs in the country and anti-government strikes in the factories, made the rhetoric seem serious to the already frightened middle and artisanal classes, and ordinary army and police officers. The militant Left, meaning the youth movement street gangs, the anarchists, the newly formed revolutionary Marxist party, the POUM (*Partido Obrero de Unificación Marxista*) and the '*Syndicos Libres*' took the lead in the violence, to which emergent fascist gangs responded with enthusiasm. Attempts later made to attribute Left violence to fascist *'agents provocateurs'* are not plausible.[57] The Popular Front youth gangs undoubtedly bred sadistic killers, who later became the worst agents of the Stalinist terror during the Civil War.

In May the anarchist and POUM strikers began to take over factories, the peasants to occupy large properties (especially in Estremadura and Andalusia) and divide up the land. The Civil Guard was confined to its barracks. Most of the army was sent on leave. The new republican riot-police, the Assault Guards, sometimes joined in the violence, or stood watching while crops were burned. In June the violence became worse. On 16 June, Robles, in a final warning, read out to the Cortes a list of outrages and atrocities: 160 churches burned, 269 (mainly) political murders, 1,287 cases of assault, 69 political offices wrecked, 113 'general strikes', 228 partial strikes, 10 newspaper offices sacked. He concluded: 'A country can live under a monarchy or a republic, with a parliamentary or a presidential system, under Communism or Fascism! But it cannot live in anarchy.'[58] It was the failure of the government to respond to this plea which gave the conservative army leaders the 'respectable civil backing' they regarded as the precondition of a take-over. The last straw came on 11 July when the body of the right-wing parliamentarian, Calvo Sotelo, was discovered, murdered by Assault Guards in reprisal for the killing of two of them by a right-wing gang.[59] Two days later Robles publicly accused the government of responsibility. Civil war broke out on the 17 July and Robles, unwilling to be a party to a *putsch*, went to France.[60]

The Civil War occurred because the indecisive February election reflected accurately a country which was almost equally divided; foreign intervention prolonged the war for two-and-a-half years. No episode in the 1930s has been more lied about than this one, and only in recent years have historians begun to dig it out from the mountain of mendacity beneath which it was buried for a generation. What emerges is not a struggle between good and evil but a general tragedy. The insurgent generals quickly established control of the south and west. But they failed to take Madrid, and the government continued to control most of the north and east until well into 1938. Behind the lines thus established, each side committed appalling atrocities against their opponents, real or imaginary.

For the Republicans, the Catholic Church was the chief object of hatred. This is curious. The clergy were anti-liberal and anti-socialist; but they were not fascists. Most of them were monarchists, if anything. The Cardinal-Primate, Archbishop Pedro Segura of Toledo, was anti-fascist; he was also pro-British. It is true there were too many clergy: 20,000 monks, 60,000 nuns, 35,000 priests, out of a population of 24.5 million. But the clergy had lost their lands in 1837, being compensated in cash; and though the Church was supposed to be rich, the ordinary parish priest certainly was not. It was very rare for peasants to kill their own priest; but they might help to kill one from a different village. They were anti-clerical in general; but not in particular. Just as the Left intelligentsia of the towns were humanitarians in general; but not in particular. The Archbishop of Valladolid said of the peasants: 'These people would be ready to die for their local Virgin but would burn that of their neighbours at the slightest provocation.'[61]

Most of the Republican atrocities were carried out by killer gangs, formed from union militants, youth, political cadres, and calling themselves the 'Lynxes of the Republic', the 'Red Lions', 'Furies', 'Spartacus', 'Strength and Liberty', etc. They claimed that insurgents had fired from church towers; but this was untrue, with the exception of the Carmelite Church in Barcelona's Calle Lauria.[62] In fact the Church did not take part in the rising, and the help some clergy subsequently gave to the nationalists was the result, not the cause, of the atrocities. Eleven bishops, a fifth of the total number, were murdered, 12 per cent of the monks, 13 per cent of the priests.[63] The slaughtered were revered in Paul Claudel's famous poem, 'Aux Martyrs Espagnols':

Sœur Espagne, sainte Espagne – tu as choisi!
Onze évêques, seize-mille prêtres massacrés – et pas une apostasie!

Some 283 nuns were killed, a few being raped before execution, though assaults on women were rare in Republican Spain. In the province of Ciudad Real, the mother of two Jesuits was murdered by having a crucifix thrust down her throat. The parish priest of Torrijos was scourged, crowned with thorns, forced to drink vinegar and had a beam of wood strapped to his back – then shot, not crucified. The Bishop of Jaén was murdered with his sister in front of 2,000 people, the executioner being a ferocious militiawoman known as *La Pecosa* (the Freckled). Some priests were burned, others buried, alive; some had their ears cut off.[64]

The Republicans also murdered nationalist laity, chiefly the Falange. In Ronda 512 people were flung into the gorge which dramatically bisects the town, an episode used in Ernest Hemingway's *For Whom the Bell Tolls*. Lenin was the mentor; the Left murder-gangs were known as *checas*. But they used Hollywood argot: *dar un paseo* was 'taking for a ride'. There were dozens of these gangs in Madrid alone. The worst was led by the Communist youth boss, García Attadell, who ran the much-feared 'dawn patrol' and murdered scores of people. He lived in a palace, amassed quantities of loot, tried to make off to Latin America with it, but was captured and garotted in Seville prison, after being received back into Mother Church.[65] Many of these killers graduated into the Soviet-imposed secret police organization in Barcelona. In all, the Left appears to have murdered about 55,000 civilians (the National Sanctuary at Valladolid lists 54,594), including about 4,000 women and several hundred children.[66]

The Nationalist killings behind the lines were on a similar scale, but army units carried them out for the most part. The method was Leninist: to destroy the Left as an organized political force by killing all its activists, and to impose abject fear on its supporters. As General Mola put it, in Pamplona (19 July 1936): 'It is necessary to spread an atmosphere of terror. We have to create this impression of mastery . . . . Anyone who is overtly or secretly a supporter of the PR must be shot.'[67] Arrests took place at night and shootings in the dark, sometimes after torture. The Church insisted all must be confessed first (10 per cent refused) and this made secret murders difficult. But there were some blasphemous atrocities: one man was stretched out in the form of a cross and had his arms and legs chopped off while his wife was forced to watch – she went insane. Priests who attempted to intervene were shot.[68] The killings in Majorca were described by Georges Bernanos in his novel Les Grands cimitières sous la lune. But Arthur Koestler, in The Invisible Writing, also described how fascist atrocities were manufactured in the lie-factory run by Otto Katz from the Comintern office in Paris.[69]

The most famous Nationalist victim was the poet García Lorca, whose brother-in-law was the Socialist mayor of Granada. He was shot about 18 August 1936, but his grave has never been found. Some 571 were killed in the city the same month. An authoritative modern estimate of Nationalist killings lists about 8,000 in the province of Granada, 7–8,000 in Navarre, 9,000 in Seville, 9,000 in Valladolid, 2,000 in Saragossa, 3,000 in the Balearics. In the first six months of the war the Nationalists killed six generals and an admiral, virtually all the Popular Front deputies they captured, governors, doctors and schoolmasters – about 50,000 in all.[70] So the killings on both side were roughly equal, and both were of a totalitarian nature – that is, punishment was meted out on the basis of class, status and occupation, not individual guilt.

Foreign intervention was important from the start. Without it the military putsch would probably have failed. The rising was a fiasco in five out of the six biggest cities. The government had a large numerical superiority on land, soon increased by political militias. The navy murdered its officers: its two cruisers and two destroyers prevented the Army of Africa from crossing the straits by sea. The Nationalists had air superiority at first, but too few planes to transport more than 200 men a day into Spain. General Mola, who commanded the rising from Burgos, had too little ammunition and seriously thought of giving up and escaping.[71] Franco's first act, when he arrived at Tetuán from the Canaries on Sunday 19 July 1936, was to send to Rome for a dozen bombers; three days later he asked the Germans for air-transports. The German aircraft arrived in Tetuán on 28 July, the Italian two days later. Early in August Franco flew 600,000 rounds of ammunition to Mola, and got 3,000 men across the Straits in a single day. That turned the tide. The armies of the north and south linked up on 11 August and the following month Franco, who had achieved a stunning propaganda success by relieving the officer cadet academy in the Toledo Alcázar, was appointed Chief of State and Generalissimo, 'with all powers in the new state'.[72] He hoped that Republican morale would now collapse and he could take Madrid. But the arrival of French and Russian aircraft gave the government air-control over most of the front – the great lesson of the war was the importance of tactical air-support – and the appearance of Russian tanks in Madrid ruled out its capitulation. Thus foreign aid prevented a quick decision by either side.

The outcome of the war, however, was not determined by great power intervention, which cancelled itself out, nor by the non-intervention policy of Britain and France, since arms could always be obtained for gold or hard currency. The Germans provided a maximum of 10,000 men at any one time, including 5,000 in the Condor Legion, an experimental tank-and-aircraft unit, and suffered 300 killed. They also provided instructors, who performed a valuable service in the rapid training of army officers and pilots, 200 tanks, 600 aircraft and superb 88-millimetre anti-aircraft guns, which neutralized Republican air-superiority early in 1937. The Italian contribution was much bigger: 40–50,000 men at any one time (of whom 4,000 were killed), 150 tanks, 660 aircraft, 800 pieces of artillery, some of them of very high quality, and masses of machine-guns, rifles and other supplies. They claimed they shot down 903 aircraft and sunk 72,800 tons of Republican shipping. The Nationalists also had the help of several thousand Portuguese, 600 Irishmen under General O'Duffy, and a few French, White Russians, British, Americans and Latin-Americans, plus of course 75,000 Moroccan troops classed as 'volunteers'.[73]

The Russians supplied the Republic with 1,000 aircraft, 900 tanks, 300 armoured cars, 1,550 pieces of artillery and vast quantities of military equipment of all kinds. The French supplied about 300 aircraft. In quantity, the Republic received as much *matériel* from abroad as the Nationalists. But it was more variable in quality, was much less effectively used and far too much of it was left on the battlefield when Republican units retreated. The Russian tanks were heavier, better armed, faster and in every way superior to the German and Italian models – as the Japanese were to find in 1939 and Hitler in 1941–2 – but these too were under-exploited and easily abandoned: by the end of the war the Nationalists had an entire regiment equipped with Russian armour.[74]

The Russians also sent 1,000 pilots and about 2,000 other specialists, but no large units. They regarded Spain mainly as an international propaganda exercise, and their effort went into organizing the international brigades. Altogether 40,000 foreigners fought for the Republic, 35,000 in the brigades, though never more than 18,000 at any one time. In addition there were 10,000 doctors, nurses and civilian specialists. The largest contingent, about 10,000, came from France, followed by 5,000 Germans and Austrians, 5,000 Poles, 3,350 Italians, about 2,500 each from Britain and the United States, 1,500 each from Yugoslavia and Czechoslovakia, 1,000 each from Scandinavia, Canada and Hungary, and smaller contingents from over forty other countries. Casualties were very high, though all the figures are matters of dispute. One calculation, for instance, puts the British contribution as 2,762, of whom 1,762 were wounded, 543 killed. About 900 Americans died.[75]

Foreign aid and intervention did not tip the military balance either way. The Nationalists won primarily because of the capacity and judgement of Franco. Though Franco was an unlovable man and is unlikely ever to win the esteem of historians, he must be accounted one of the most successful public men of the century. His cold heart went with a cool head, great intelligence and formidable reserves of courage and will. His father was a drunken naval officer, his younger brother a record-breaking pilot and hell-raiser; Franco embodied all the self-discipline of the family. He was not interested in women, drinking or cards. His passion was maps. At twenty-two he was the youngest captain in the army; at thirty-three the youngest general in Europe. He saw a great deal of desperate fighting in Morocco, especially during the Rif War in the 1920s, when in 1925 he led the assault-wave of one of the biggest amphibious landings to date. His military views were very advanced for the time; he believed, like De Gaulle, in the 'war of movement'; in 1928 he reorganized the Spanish military academy and turned it into what the French War Minister, André Maginot, called 'the most modern centre of its kind in the world ... the last word in military technique and instruction'.[76]

Franco's philosophy is worth examining briefly because it was so remote from all the prevailing currents of the age, both liberal and totalitarian. The soldier-statesman he most resembled was Wellington, a figure much admired in Spain. Franco thought war a hateful business, from which gross cruelty was inseparable; it might sometimes be necessary to advance civilization. He was in the tradition of the Romans, the crusaders, the conquistadors, the *tercios* of Parma. In Africa his Foreign Legionaries mutilated the bodies of their enemies, cutting off their heads. But they were under strict discipline: Franco was a harsh, but just and therefore popular, commander. He saw Spanish Christian culture as unarguably superior; he found 'inexplicable' the Moroccan 'resistance to civilization'. Later, putting down the Asturian miners, he was puzzled that, while 'clearly not monsters or savages', they should lack 'that respect for patriotism or hierarchy which was necessary for decent men'.[77] His own motivation he invariably described as 'duty, love of country'.

For Franco, the army was the only truly national institution, ancient, classless, non-regional, apolitical, incorrupt, disinterested. If it was oppressed, it mutinied, as it had done since the sixteenth century and as recently as 1917; otherwise it served. Everything else in Spain was suspect. The Church was soft. Franco was *croyant* – he made the sceptical Mola pray for ammunition supplies – and he deliberately courted the approval of the hierarchy by setting up an 'ecclesiastical household', but he was in no sense a clericalist and never took the slightest notice of ecclesiastical advice on non-spiritual matters.[78] He hated politics in any shape. The Conservatives were reactionary and selfish landowners. The Liberals were corrupt and selfish businessmen. The Socialists were deluded, or worse. He exploited the two insurrectionary movements, the Falange and the Carlists, amalgamating them under his leadership, but their role was subservient, indeed servile. Franco was never a fascist or had the smallest belief in any kind of Utopia or system. At his headquarters only one politician had influence: his brother-in-law, Ramón Serrano Suñer, and he was a functionary. Franco said: 'Spaniards are tired of politics and of politicians.' Again: 'Only those who live off politics should fear our movement.' He spent his entire political career seeking to exterminate politics.[79]

Franco made better uses of his human and material resources because he fought a military war, and the Republicans fought a political war. He was a master of the nuts and bolts of war: topography, training, infrastructures, logistics, signals, air control. No genius but very thorough and calm; he never reinforced failure and he learnt from mistakes. Having stamped out politics he had no one nudging his elbow and he possessed, virtually throughout, unity of command. Perhaps his greatest psychological asset was that he quickly established, and was seen to do so, complete independence of his foreign allies. There is a point here often overlooked. Although idealism was an element in the war at the level of the ordinary men and women who fought it, at a nation-to-nation level it was severely hard-headed. Hitler, Mussolini and Stalin, and all other governments who supplied arms and services, expected to be paid. In one sense finance was the key to the war, and Franco and his advisers handled it shrewdly. Their greatest achievement was to maintain a respectable paper currency without the benefit of the nation's gold reserves and central banking system. The Nationalist peseta remained stable between 70 and 80 to the pound-sterling. By contrast, the Republican peseta fell from 36 in June 1936 to 226 in December 1937, and thereafter collapsed.[79] From an early stage, Franco put the bite on the monarchy, British and other foreign businesses in Spain, tycoons like Juan March and Juan Ventosa. He made prodigious and increasingly successful efforts to maintain exports. As a result, he was able to stabilize the currency, raise loans within Spain and, most important of all, obtain virtually all his foreign arms on credit. Hence both Germany, which was owed $225 million, and Italy, whose final bill was agreed at $273 million in 1940, had a strong practical interest in ensuring that Franco won the war and so survived to pay them off – as he did.

By contrast, the Republicans handled their finances with consummate folly. They started with one of the largest gold reserves in the world: 700 tons, worth £162 million (or $788 million). Instead of using this to raise loans, or for direct payments in the 'hard' arms markets of the capitalist countries of the West, while getting arms from the Russians on credit, they handed over more than two-thirds of their gold to Stalin. In return for arms of varying quality, which otherwise he might well have supplied on credit or for paper, Stalin swallowed up $500 million in gold, plus another $100 million earned in exports; and at the end of it all claimed he was still owed $50 million. In late 1938 he blandly told the Republic's negotiator that its credit was 'exhausted'. At no stage was Stalin owed large sums and therefore he never had a vested interest in ensuring that the Republic survived to pay him.[80]

Still more disastrous, from the Republic's point of view, was Stalin's insistence, while being paid in gold on the nail, on a political price for supplying arms at all. The moment the fighting started, and the need for arms became desperate, the influence of the Spanish CP rose dramatically. This might not have mattered so much if it had led an independent existence. In fact it was controlled through the Russian embassy, by NKVD and OGPU units under Alexander Orlov – who himself went in mortal terror of Yezhov – and by such

Comintern figures as the French witch-hunter André Marty, whose face, wrote Hemingway, 'had a look of decay, as if modelled from the waste material you find under the claws of a very old lion'.[81] It is not clear to this day how anxious Stalin was to win the war; but in any event he was determined to control the Republican side.

Caballero, who became Prime Minister in September 1936, though foolish and easily deceived, gave some resistance to the Stalinist take-over. He refused to allow the Communists to absorb the Socialist Party, as had happened in the youth movement, and in January 1937, having received a menacing letter from Stalin, and a demand to sack his best general, he threw the Soviet ambassador, Marcel Rosenberg, out of his office with the words 'Out you go! Out!' and in a voice so loud it could be heard outside. Spain might be poor, he said, but it would not tolerate that 'a foreign ambassador should try and impose his will on the head of the Spanish government'.[82] That was the end of Caballero (it was the end of Rosenberg too, who was immediately recalled and murdered by Stalin), though it took some time for the Soviet authorities to arrange a *coup*. It was decided at a meeting of the CP executive attended by the Soviet chargé d'affaires, Marty, Orlov and other secret police officials. It is notable that the CP Secretary-General, José Diaz, opposed ousting Caballero on Stalin's instruction, and at one point shouted at Marty, 'You are a guest at meetings of the Spanish Communist Party. If our proceedings do not please you, there is the door!' But in the shouting and the vote that followed, only Diaz and Jesús Hernández, the Minister of Education and our source for this meeting, voted against the *coup*; the other Spanish Communists were terrified of Orlov's men.[83]

Caballero's successor, Juan Negrín, had been picked by Stalin's agent, Arthur Stashevsky, the previous November, as the ideal puppet: a non-political, upper middle-class professor, with no union or working-class following, no Communist affiliations, and therefore 'respectable' in the eyes of the foreign press, with gross personal habits, and therefore easily blackmailed. Instead of making arms purchases, he would drive across France in a fast sports-car chasing girls. His greed was spectacular: sometimes he would dine three times in a single evening. To his protest that he was not popular enough to be premier, Hernández cynically replied, 'Popularity can be created' – propaganda was the one activity in which the Communists were without rival.[84] Behind Negrín's complaisant ignorance, the Communists – that is, Stalin's secret police – took over Republican Spain. The result was one of the major political tragedies of the century.

It is clear that, if the army had not staged a *putsch* in July 1936, sooner or later Spain would have had to endure a civil war fought among the Left. It broke out in Barcelona in the spring of 1937, with

the Communists fighting the POUM and the anarchists. The immediate pretext, as in the wider civil war, was a political murder, of a
leading Communist, Roldán Cortada, shot on 25 April, possibly by
an anarchist 'control patrol', possibly by the Comintern agent
Ernö Gerö. Both sides had private armies, secret police forces,
gangs of murderous thugs. The POUM slogan was 'Before renouncing the revolution, we will die on the barricades'. The Communist
chanted 'Before we capture Saragossa, we have to take Barcelona'.
There were riots and large-scale fighting in May, followed by the
intervention of the navy and 4,000 assault guards.[85] Caballero's
refusal to disband the POUM militias was the immediate pretext for
his ousting. The moment Negrín was installed as nominal premier,
the Communists took over the Interior Ministry and all the key
police and paramilitary posts, and moved forward to a *règlement
des comptes*.

The purge coincided with Stalin's massacre of his own party in
Russia, and it bore all the marks of his methods. The CP-controlled
Madrid police forced two captured Falangists to prepare a fake
plan for a Madrid rising by Franco's much-vaunted 'Fifth Column',
and they forged a letter to Franco, on the back of this plan, from
Andrés Nin, the POUM leader. A great mass of forged documents
implicating the POUM in a fascist betrayal was put in a suitcase left
in Gerona, then 'discovered' by police. On 14 June, Orlov, as head
of the Spanish NKVD, probably acting on direct instructions from
Stalin, ordered the arrest of all POUM leaders. This was despite the
protests of the Communist members of the cabinet (the non-
Communist members, least of all Negrín, were not even informed).[86]
The Commander of the 29th POUM division was recalled from the
front for 'consultations' and arrested too. The detained men were
taken straight to carefully prepared interrogation-centres and torture-chambers, most of them underground but including the former
Barcelona convent of St Ursula, known as 'the Dachau of Republican Spain'. Efforts by the cabinet to secure Nin's release were quite
unavailing. But Stalin's plans to make him the centre of a Spanish
show-trial were frustrated, since Nin, the model for Orwell's hero
Goldstein in *Nineteen Eighty-Four*, preferred to die under torture
rather than confess. (He was eventually murdered by Orlov in the
park of El Pardo, later Franco's palace.) During the rest of 1937
and well into 1938, many thousands of POUM members, and
indeed other Leftists of all descriptions, were executed or tortured
to death in Communist prisons. They included a large number of
foreigners, such as Trotsky's former secretary, Erwin Wolff, the
Austrian socialist Kurt Landau, the British journalist 'Bob' Smilie
and a former lecturer at Johns Hopkins University, José Robles.

Among those who just managed to escape were Orwell and Willy Brandt, the future German Chancellor.[87]

It was one of Spain's many misfortunes at this time that her Civil War coincided with the climax of Stalin's great terror. Many of the Barcelona murders had little to do with Spain's internal politics but were, rather, the backlash of events in Moscow and Leningrad. Thus Robles was executed because, as interpreter of General Jan Antonovich Berzin, head of the Russian military mission to Spain, he knew too much about Berzin's recall and liquidation as part of Stalin's purge of the army. Stalin was having his leading agents killed all over the world in 1937–8. And, as in Russia, virtually all the creatures who helped him to take over the Left in Spain, and then to terrorize it, were murdered in turn. The head of the NKVD's foreign department was cornered in his own office in Paris in February 1938 and forced to take cyanide. Of those who organized arms supplies to Spain, Evhen Konovalek was killed in Rotterdam in May 1938, Rudolf Clement was found, a headless corpse, in the Seine, and Walter Krivitsky, boss of Soviet military intelligence in Western Europe, was chased for three years by Stalin's hit-men until they got him in Washington on 10 February 1941.[88] In addition to General Berzin, Stalin murdered Michael Koltzov, the famous *Pravda* Spanish correspondent, Arthur Stashevky, head of the economic mission to Spain, and Antonov Ovseenko, Consul-General in Barcelona, who was told he was being recalled to Moscow to be made Minister of Justice, a joke characteristic of Stalin's gallows-humour.[89] The only man who escaped Stalin was the arch-killer Orlov himself, who defected, wrote an account of all he knew, informed Stalin that he had arranged to have it published immediately if he died violently, and so was left in peace, publishing his tale after Stalin's death.[90]

It may be asked: how was it that the atrocities against the Left in Barcelona did not cause a wave of revulsion against Stalinism throughout the world? One factor was luck. On 26 April 1937, the day after Cortada's murder in Barcelona detonated the internal crisis, forty-three aircraft of the Condor Legion bombed the historic Basque town of Guernica, whose famous oak tree had shaded the first Basque parliament. About 1,000 people were killed and 70 per cent of the buildings destroyed. It was not the first bombing of a town by either side, and Guernica was a legitimate target, though the object of the raid was terror. It was decided upon by Colonel Wolfgang von Richthofen, the Legion's Commander, in consultation with Colonel Juan Vigón, Mola's Chief of Staff. There is no evidence Mola knew about it beforehand; Franco certainly did not; and the Germans did not know of the town's historical significance.[91] For the Comintern propagandists – the best in the world – it was a stroke of uncovenanted fortune, and they turned it into the most celebrated episode of the entire war. Picasso, who had already been asked to do a large painting for the Spanish pavilion at the Paris World Fair, leapt at the subject, and the result was later taken to the New York Metropolitan. Guernica helped to push a whole segment of Western opinion, including the magazines *Time* and *Newsweek*, over to the Republican side.[92] In the subsequent hullabaloo, the echoes of which could still be heard in the 1980s, when the painting was solemnly hung in the Prado, the sounds of mass-slaughter in Barcelona went unheard.

The way in which Guernica was used to screen the destruction of the POUM was typical of the brilliancy of Comintern propaganda, handled by two inspired professional liars, Willi Muenzenberg and Otto Katz, both later murdered on Stalin's orders.[93] Throughout the Spanish war, Stalinism was assisted not only by superb public relations but by the naïvety, gullibility and, it must also be said, the mendacity and corruption of Western intellectuals, especially their willingness to overlook what W.H.Auden called 'the necessary murder'. When Orwell escaped and sought to publish an account of the POUM scandal, 'Spilling the Spanish Beans', in the *New Statesman*, its editor, Kingsley Martin, turned it down on the grounds that it would damage Western support for the Republican cause; he later argued that Negrín would have broken with the Communists over the POUM affair if the West had been willing to supply him with arms. But when Orwell's exposure appeared in the *New English Weekly*, it attracted little notice.[94] The intellectuals of the Left did not want to know the objective truth; they were unwilling for their illusions to be shattered. They were overwhelmed by the glamour and excitement of the cause and few had the gritty determination of Orwell to uphold absolute standards of morality, or the experience of the horrors that occurred when relative ones took their place. Many of them treated 'the Party' with abject subservience. Thus the poet Cecil Day-Lewis, who joined it in 1936, apologized for not having done so before, priggishly confessing to a 'refinement of bourgeois subjectivism by which I was unwilling to join the party till I was making enough money to be able to assure myself that I was joining from disinterested motives, not as one of the lean and hungry who would personally profit by revolution.' He felt he had to ask the Party's permission even before he accepted an invitation to join the selection committee of the Book Society.[95]

Besides, the Communists controlled access to Republican Spain. To get there a British writer, for instance, needed a letter from the head of the CP, Harry Pollitt, who worked closely with Victor Gollancz, the leading left-wing publisher, whose Left Book Club dominated the market. The poet W.H. Auden was saved by his 'Pollitt letter' from a prison sentence when he was arrested for indecency in a Barcelona Park.[96] A visit to 'our' Spain was essential to the self-respect of a progressive intellectual. Just as the Germans, Russians and Italians used Spain to test their new military equipment – exploitation by hardware – so writers went there to acquire material for their next novel or poem, what might be termed exploitation by software. André Malraux, whose novel about the Chinese revolution, *La Condition humaine* (1932), had made him world famous, went to Spain hoping for a sequel, which duly appeared as *L'Espoir* (1938). He brought with him a squadron of slow Potex bombers, which created a noisy splash in the papers but did little damage to the nationalists, and anyway had to be crewed by Spaniards. The commander of the Republican fighters, García Lacalle, wrote that Malraux's people were 'writers, artists, photographers, women, children and I don't know what – everything but aviators'.[97] Hemingway was in Spain too, 'researching' *For Whom the Bell Tolls*. Fancying himself hard-boiled and experienced in the cynicism of war, 'Papa' was easily duped. When his friend Dos Passos became worried about the disappearance of Robles, whom he knew well (he had in fact already been murdered), Hemingway was tipped off by his '*amigo*' in counter-espionage, the sinister Pepe Quintanilla, that Robles was a spy, and at once assumed he was guilty. He attributed Dos Passos' 'continued belief in Robles's loyalty to the good-hearted naïvety of a "typical American liberal attitude"' – but of course it was Hemingway who proved naïve.[98]

To keep the intellectuals well-disposed, the Comintern circus-masters staged all-expenses-paid international gatherings. There was the 1937 International Peace Campaign in Brussels, run by the French CP leader Marcel Cachin, which invented a Peace Day, a Peace Fair, a Peace Penny and a Peace Oath. Kingsley Martin described it – though not at the time but thirty years later – as 'the murder of honesty, enthusiasm and faith' which induced in him 'desperation'.[99] Still worse, the same year, was the Madrid Writers' Congress. Stephen Spender recorded that he and other guests were 'treated like princes or ministers . . . riding in Rolls-Royces, banqueted, feted, sung and danced to', though the climax of the proceedings was a vicious attack on André Gide, who had just published a critical book on Russia, *Retour de l'URSS*, and was now publicly excoriated as a 'fascist monster'. A burst of artillery fire restored a sense of reality:

The next morning André Chamson (head of the French delegation) announced that he and Julien Benda, author of *La Trahison des clercs*, must leave Madrid at once. For if by any chance either of them were killed, France could not choose but declare war on Franco, and this action would lead to world war. Chamson refused to accept the responsibility for such a catastrophe.[100]

Spender himself was already a veteran of the front where, at a machine-gun emplacement,

... the gunner in charge of it insisted that I should fire a few shots into the Moorish lines. I did this, positively praying that I might not by any chance hit an Arab. Suddenly the front seemed to me like a love relationship between the two sides, locked here in their opposite trenches ... and for a visitor to intervene in their deathly orgasm seemed a terrible frivolity.[101]

Meanwhile the terrible frivolity behind the Republican lines continued. As Orwell pointed out, each of the Left factions was obsessed by the need to be in a strong military position after Franco was beaten, and allowed this to affect their tactics and conduct of the war. To keep up numbers they avoided casualties, and the Communists often deliberately held up artillery or air support in order that POUM or other units which they wanted weakened should be broken.[102] After the destruction of the POUM, Republican morale declined steadily. In these circumstances, Franco opted for a war of attrition throughout the appalling winter of 1937–8, and in April he cut Republican Spain in two. Thereafter it was really a matter of time only, with Franco taking no chances and insisting on overwhelming superiority. By the autumn Stalin had tired of the war, had extracted the last ounce of propaganda value out of it, had completed his purges and was already thinking of a new deal, either with the Western democracies or, more likely, with Hitler. He had also got all the Republic's gold. So he cut off aid, and Franco was able to open his last Catalonian offensive, just before Christmas, confident that the end was near. Barcelona fell on 28 January 1939, and Madrid on 28 March. Franco had fought the war without passion, and when he heard it was over he did not even look up from his desk.[103]

The day Madrid surrendered, Hitler denounced Germany's 1934 treaty with Poland, having occupied the whole of Czechoslovakia a week before. It was obvious that a European war was inevitable and imminent. Franco's reaction was a brutal attempt to seal off Spain not only from the coming catastrophe but, as far as possible, from the whole of the twentieth century. Spain had a long tradition of crude social engineering and internal crusades. In the fifteenth and sixteenth centuries it had expelled in turn vast numbers of Moors, Jews and Protestants. By such macro-persecution it had avoided the Reformation and the horrors of the Wars of Religion. The failure to

adopt similar methods of drastic extrusion had permitted the French
Revolution to enter and thus crucified the country for fifteen years of
civil war, as Goya's drawings bore eloquent testimony. Now the
invasion by post-Christian totalitarian culture had brought another
three years of martyrdom. On the Nationalist side, 90,000 had been
killed in action; 110,000 Republican soldiers were dead; there were a
million cripples; 10,000 had died in air-raids, 25,000 from malnutrition, 130,000 murdered or shot behind the lines; now 500,000 were in
exile, half never to return.[104] The destruction of treasure had been
immense, ranging from the famous library of Cuenca Cathedral to
Goya's earliest paintings in his birthplace, Fuentodos.

Franco determined to end the destructive process of corruption by
amputating the agonized limb of Spanish collectivism. His feelings
towards the Left anticipated those of the wartime Allies towards
Nazism: he got unconditional surrender first, then de-Communized,
but in a manner closer to the drumhead purges of liberated France than
the systematic trials in Germany. It was not a Lenin-style totalitarian
massacre by classes: the Law of Political Responsibilities of 9 February
1939 dealt with responsibility for crimes on an individual basis (the
only exception was Freemasons of the eighteenth degree or higher).
Strictly speaking, there was no death penalty for political offences as
such.[105] But there was a great rage in the conquerors – the Interior
Minister, Suñer, wanted revenge for his brothers who had been shot in
Republican prisons, and he was typical of thousands – and it was not
difficult to pin capital crimes on Republican officials of all degrees.
Mussolini's son-in-law Ciano reported from Spain in July: 'Trials
going on every day at a speed which I would call summary . . . . There
are still a great number of shootings. In Madrid alone between 200 and
250 a day, in Barcelona 150, in Seville 80.'[106] Some tens of thousands
thus died, but the figure of 193,000 sometimes given for the total is
wrong, since many death-sentences passed by courts were commuted.
Franco made it clear on 31 December 1939 that many long prison
sentences (fifteen years was usual) would have to be served: 'It is
necessary to liquidate the hatred and passions left us by our past war.
But this liquidation must not be accomplished in the liberal manner,
with enormous and disastrous amnesties, which are a deception rather
than a gesture of forgiveness. It must be Christian, achieved by means of
redemption through work accompanied by repentance and
penitance.'[107] In 1941 the gaol population was still 233,375; scores of
thousands of those who had run the Republic died in prison or in exile.
Others were banned from a huge range of public or private occupations
by a decree of 25 August 1939, which put the objectives of the purge
before government efficiency or the interests of the economy.[108] Thus
ancient and traditional Spain, led by a man who regretted every second

that had passed since the old world ended in 1914, sought to immunize herself from the present. The attempt did not succeed in the long run; but it gave Spain some protection from the pandemic which now overwhelmed Europe.

TEN

The End of Old Europe

The age of aggression was bound to end in a world war. Nevertheless, it is vital to understand precisely how and why this climax
came about, for what happened in the 1930s determined the
contours of our age in the 1980s. On 5 April 1940, four days
before the Nazi invasion of Norway began the European phase of
the war in earnest, Goebbels gave a secret briefing to selected
German journalists, one of whom made a transcript. The key
passage is as follows:

Up to now we have succeeded in leaving the enemy in the dark
concerning Germany's real goals, just as before 1932 our domestic foes
never saw where we were going or that our oath of legality was just a
trick. We wanted to come to power legally, but we did not want to use
power legally .... They could have suppressed us. They could have
arrested a couple of us in 1925 and that would have been that, the end.
No, they let us through the danger zone. That's exactly how it was in
foreign policy too .... In 1933 a French premier ought to have said (and if I
had been the French premier I would have said it): 'The new Reich
Chancellor is the man who wrote *Mein Kampf*, which says this and that.
This man cannot be tolerated in our vicinity. Either he disappears or we
march!' But they didn't do it. They left us alone and let us slip through the
risky zone, and we were able to sail around all dangerous reefs. *And when
we were done, and well armed, better than they, then they started the
war!*[1]

This remarkable statement is, on the whole, an accurate summary
of what happened in the 1930s. It was adumbrated by Hitler's
secret briefing of his Service chiefs on 3 February 1933, his first
meeting with them after his assumption of supreme power. He told
them he was going to overthrow the Versailles settlement and make
Germany the greatest power in Europe, and he emphasized: 'The
most dangerous period is that of rearmament. Then we shall see

whether France has statesmen. If she does, she will not grant us time but will jump on us.'[2]

Everyone knew Hitler's aims were ambitious. The German masses believed they could and would be attained without war, by assertive diplomacy, backed by armed strength. The generals were told that war would almost certainly be necessary, but that it would be limited and short. In fact Hitler's real programme was far more extensive than the generals, let alone the masses, realized and necessarily involved not merely war but a series of wars. Hitler meant what he said when he wrote in *Mein Kampf*: 'Germany must either be a world power or there will be no Germany.' When he used the term 'world power' he meant something greater than Wilhelmine Germany, merely the dominant power in central Europe: he meant 'world' in the full sense. The lesson he had learnt from the First World War and from Ludendorff's analysis of it was that it was essential for Germany to effect a break-out from its Central European base, which could always be encircled.[3] In Hitler's view, Ludendorff had just begun to attain this, at Brest-Litovsk, when the 'stab in the back' by the Home Front wrecked everything. Hence his real plans began where Brest-Litovsk ended: the clock was to be put back to spring 1918, but with Germany solid, united, fresh and, above all, 'cleansed'.

Hitler's aims can be reconstructed not merely from *Mein Kampf* itself, with its stress on the 'East Policy', but from his early speeches and the so-called 'Second' or *Secret Book* of 1928.[4] This material makes it clear that the 'cleansing' process – the elimination of the Jews – was essential to the whole long-term strategy. Being a race-socialist as opposed to a class-socialist, Hitler believed the dynamic of history was race. The dynamic was interrupted when race-poisoning took place. The poison came, above all, from the Jews. He admired Jews as 'negative supermen'. In his *Table-Talk* he said that if 5,000 Jews emigrated to Sweden, in no time at all they would occupy all the key positions: this was because 'blood purity', as he put it in *Mein Kampf*, 'is a thing the Jew preserves better than any other people on earth'. The Germans, on the other hand, had been 'poisoned'. That was why they lost the First World War. Even he was poisoned: that was why he occasionally made mistakes – 'all of us suffer from the sickness of mixed, corrupt blood'.[5] Race-poisoning was a comparatively common obsession in the time of Hitler's youth, rather as ecological poisoning became an obsession of many in the 1970s and 1980s. The notion of ubiquitous poisoning appealed strongly to the same type of person who accepted conspiracy theories as the machinery of public events. As with the later ecologists, they thought the race-poison was spreading fast, that total disaster was imminent, and that it would take a long time to reverse even if the right policies were adopted promptly. Hitler calculated it would need a hundred years for his regime to eliminate racial poisoning in Germany: on the other hand, if Germany became the first nation-race to do so successfully, it would inevitably become 'lord of the Earth' (*Mein Kampf*).

What distinguished Hitlerian race-theory was, first, this rooted belief that 'cleansing' could make Germany the first true superpower, and ultimately the first paramount power in the world; and, secondly, his absolute conviction that 'Jewish race-poison' and Bolshevism were one and the same phenomenon. In 1928, when he wrote his Second Book, he did not appreciate that old-style 'Jewish' Bolshevism had ceased to exist and that Stalin's Russia was in essentials as anti-Semitic as Tsardom had been. On the contrary, he believed that the Soviet Union was a Jewish cultural phenomenon. Hence the object of his policy was to combat 'an inundation of diseased bacilli which at the moment have their breeding-ground in Russia'.[6] Thus the 'cleansing' fitted in perfectly with the resumption of traditional German East policy, but on a far more ambitious scale.

Hitler's full programme, therefore, was as follows. First, gain control of Germany itself, and begin the cleansing process at home. Second, destroy the Versailles settlement and establish Germany as the dominant power in Central Europe. All this could be achieved without war. Third, on this power basis, destroy the Soviet Union (by war) to rid the 'breeding-ground' of the 'bacillus' and, by colonization, create a solid economic and strategic power-base from which to establish a continental empire, in which France and Italy would be mere satellites. In the fourth stage Germany would acquire a large colonial empire in Africa, plus a big ocean navy, to make her one of the four superpowers, in addition to Britain, Japan and the United States. Finally, in the generation after his death, Hitler envisaged a decisive struggle between Germany and the United States for world domination.[7]

No one since Napoleon had thought in such audacious terms. In its gigantic scope the concept was Alexandrine. Yet until he was engulfed by the war he made, Hitler was always pragmatic. Like Lenin he was a superb opportunist, always ready to seize openings and modify his theory accordingly. This has led some historians to conclude he had no master-programme. In fact, while always adjusting the tactics to suit the moment, he pursued his long-term strategy with a brutal determination which has seldom been equalled in the history of human ambition. Unlike most tyrants, he was never tempted to relax by a surfeit of autocratic power. Quite the contrary. He was always raising the stakes on the table and seeking to hasten

the pace of history. He feared his revolution would lose its dynamism. He thought himself indispensable, and at least four of his phases
must be accomplished while he was still not only alive but at the
height of his powers. It was his impatience which made him so
dangerous in the short term and so ineffectual in the long term (the
very reverse of the Soviet strategists). In a secret speech to German
newspaper editors in November 1938, after his great Munich
triumph, he deplored the fact that his need to talk about peace had
led the German nation to relax too much. He argued that for
Germany to accept peace, and thus stability, as a permanent fact of
international life was to accept the very spirit of defeatism. Violence
was a necessity, and the public must be prepared for it.[8]

With such a monster at large, and in unfettered control of the
world's second strongest economy – the first and indeed the only one
to emerge fully from the Great Depression – what possibility was
there of maintaining the old European system? The greatest of the
legitimate powers, the United States, virtually cut itself off from
Europe. It chose Protection in 1930 and the choice was reinforced
after Roosevelt took power and made it clear, in breaking up the
proposed world economic conference in July 1933, that his New
Deal was incompatible with a negotiated world trading system: he
stood for 'Capitalism in One Country' just as Stalin stood for
'Socialism in One Country'. This isolation was formalized in 1935
when a Democratic Congress passed the Neutrality Act. The same
year, the young writer Herbert Agar epitomized the mood of many
American intellectuals, repelled by what was happening in Europe,
by bidding his countrymen to forget their European roots and be true
to their own emergent culture. During six years living in Europe, he
wrote, 'I learned that the best traits in American life are not the traits
we have copied faithfully from Europe but the traits we have freely
adapted or else originated – the traits which are our own.'[9]

Roosevelt saw himself, in some moods, as a citizen of the world,
but his internationalism was essentially verbal – indeed rhetorical –
rather than practical. He was not to blame for the state of unilateral
disarmament in which he found America in 1933; but he did nothing
to remedy matters in his first term and very little in the earlier part of
his second. As George Kennan, one of the ablest of the younger
diplomats, noted, Roosevelt's statements were made for their internal
political effect rather than their impact on world events.[10] Surrounded by his young New Dealers, whose intentions towards
Europe were benevolent but who were ignorant and hopelessly
amateurish in foreign affairs and in any case obsessed by America's
internal problems, Roosevelt was keen to appear high-minded and
'progressive'. But his high-mindedness expressed itself chiefly in

demanding that Britain stand firm for international order, and his progressiveness rated Soviet Russia, one of the totalitarian predators, as a bigger factor for world peace than Britain.

Right up to his death in 1945, there was an incorrigible element of frivolity in Roosevelt's handling of foreign policy. It was characteristic that one of his principal sources of information about Britain, and on European events generally, in the later 1930s was *The Week*, the ultra-Left conspiracy-theory bulletin put out by the *Daily Worker* journalist Claud Cockburn.[11] Some of Roosevelt's ambassadorial appointments were exceptionally ill-judged. He sent the violently anti-British Joseph Kennedy to London, and the corrupt and gullible Joseph Davies to Moscow. The latter move was particularly destructive because the US Moscow embassy was well-staffed and superbly informed, backed by a highly professional division of Eastern European affairs in the State Department. The Soviet Foreign Minister, Litvinov, admitted that this division had better records on Soviet foreign policy than the Soviet government itself.[12] Five months after Davies became ambassador in 1936, with instructions to win Stalin's friendship at all costs, the division was abolished, its library dispersed and its files destroyed. Kennan, in the Moscow embassy, thought this indicated 'the smell of Soviet influence . . . somewhere in the higher reaches of the government'. It certainly reflected a bitter power-struggle between the Secretary of State, Cordell Hull, and the Assistant-Secretary, the saturnine homosexual Sumner Welles.[13] Both men were anti-British, Hull believing that Britain's new system of imperial preference, itself a response to the avalanche of trade restrictions precipitated by the Smoot–Hawley tariff, was a bigger threat to world peace than any of the dictators.

As the diplomatic papers abundantly testify, the Roosevelt administration was never prepared to discuss specific military and diplomatic backing for Britain and France against Germany. Roosevelt's condemnatory speeches, such as his 'quarantine' oration of October 1937 or his absurd demand in April 1939 that Hitler give ten-year non-aggression guarantees to thirty-one named countries, were worse than useless. The second convinced Hitler that in no circumstances would Roosevelt actually intervene militarily, and he replied to it on 28 April, in what turned out to be his last public speech in the Reichstag, with unconcealed contempt and derision.[14]

Britain and France, even without America, might conceivably have contained Hitler in 1933–4, had both been resolute and willing to act in concert. For a short time France actually possessed the physical means to do so. But after the departure of Poincaré in 1929 there was never much chance of France carrying through a pre-emptive strike. Roosevelt's policy was bitterly anti-French, not merely in seeking to force her to disarm unilaterally but, after Roosevelt took America off the gold standard, in bringing pressure economically to break up France's pathetic attempt to create a 'gold block', which occupied her energies in 1933. Meanwhile, Hitler was consolidating himself and speeding up the secret rearmament which had been a feature of the last years of Weimar. The British were also anxious to emasculate the French army. Nothing was more likely to provoke a future war, the Foreign Secretary, Sir John Simon, told the Commons on 13 May 1932, than a 'well-armed France' facing a disarmed Germany. Even after Hitler took over, it remained British policy to bring pressure on France to cut her army. The same afternoon Hitler's Enabling Bill went through the Reichstag, Anthony Eden, for the government, announced that it was British policy to get the French army cut from 694,000 to 400,000, and rebuked Churchill for protesting against measures to 'secure for Europe that period of appeasement which is needed'. 'The House was enraged and in an ugly mood – towards Mr Churchill', noted the *Daily Dispatch*.[15] While terrified German socialists were being hunted through the streets by Goering's Gestapo squads, their British comrades sought to howl down Churchill's warning that Hitler had specifically stated in *Mein Kampf* that he would destroy France by securing British neutrality – but even the *Führer* had not counted on Britain seeking to prevent the French from defending themselves. In France, Léon Blum's socialists were equally abject, campaigning desperately to prevent conscription from being extended from one to two years. On the French Right, anti-Semitism was reviving under the Nazi stimulus, and the new slogan was 'Rather Hitler than Blum'. So far as France was concerned, Hitler was probably through his 'danger zone' by the end of 1933; that was the view of the Poles, who the next month wrote off France as an effective ally and signed – for what it was worth – a bilateral non-aggression treaty with Hitler.

Britain was not as demoralized as France in the 1930s. But there were ominous signs of decadence. Britain's weight in world affairs depended essentially on her Empire, and the Empire revolved round India. By 1931 the process set in motion by the Montagu reforms and the Amritsar débâcle had gathered pace. The British Raj was palpably breaking up. Lord Birkenhead, the Secretary of State, had warned in 1925 that concessions to the Hindus would merely provoke the Muslims to demand separation (he saw the Muslims as the Ulstermen, the Hindus as the Irish Nationalists) and predicted: 'All the conferences in the world cannot bridge over the unbridgeable, and between those two countries lies a chasm which cannot be crossed by the resources of modern political engineering.'[16] On 26 January 1931 Churchill told the Commons there were now '60,000

Indians in prison for political agitation'. Two months later, over 1,000 Muslims were massacred by Hindus in Cawnpore, followed by communal riots all over the sub-continent. It was the pattern of the 1930s. With no certain future, good British candidates no longer presented themselves for the Indian civil service, and Indians took the top places in the entrance examinations.[17] British investment was declining, and India's economic value to Britain fell steadily.[18] Churchill, who loved India and probably felt more passionately about this issue than any other in his life, feared that weak British policy would lead India into a repetition of China's tragedy: disintegration and dismemberment, with the deaths of countless millions, the scores of millions of 'untouchables' being the first victims. 'Greedy appetites', he noted on 18 March 1931, had already been 'excited', and 'many itching fingers were stretching and scratching at the vast pillage of a derelict empire'. Britain, too, would be the loser. He thought the world was 'entering a period when the struggle for self-preservation is going to present itself with great intentness to thickly populated industrial countries'. Britain would soon be 'fighting for its life' and it would be essential to retain India (May 1933).[19]

Churchill conducted the most concentrated and intense political campaign of his life against the 1935 India bill, 'a monstrous monument of shame built by pygmies', which gave India Federal Home Rule, of a type which benefited chiefly the professional Brahmin politicians, and which in practice proved unworkable. But despite his titanic efforts, he could arouse no mass public support in Britain. All his oratory was in vain. Indeed, he could not even arouse the British community in India: they had already written off the Empire. The Conservative backbenchers were apathetic and resigned to a gradual British withdrawal. Churchill was never able to persuade more than eighty-nine of them to vote against the bill, which passed by the huge majority of 264. The truth is, though the British Empire still occupied a quarter of the earth's surface, by 1935 imperialism was dead in Britain, merely awaiting the obsequies. Churchill turned from India in despair to concentrate on rearming Britain for self-survival.

That, too, looked a lost cause at times. The influence of Bloomsbury had reached upwards and downwards by the 1930s to embrace almost the entire political nation. Among the Left intelligentsia, the patriotism which Strachey had sought so successfully to destroy had been replaced by a primary loyalty to Stalin. In the 1930s the Apostles ceased to be a centre of political scepticism and became an active recruiting-ground for Soviet espionage.[20] While some Apostles like Anthony Blunt, Guy Burgess and Leo Long were encouraged to penetrate British agencies to transmit information to Moscow, the Left as a whole, led by the Communists, sought to keep Britain disarmed, a policy Stalin maintained until Hitler actually attacked him in June 1941. In the 1920s, the British Communist Party had been working class, innovatory and independent-minded. Early in the 1930s, the middle-class intellectuals moved in, and the CP rapidly became cringingly servile to Soviet foreign policy interests.[21] British Marxists, who included political thinkers like G.D.H.Cole and Harold Laski, and scientists like Joseph Needham, J.B.S.Haldane and J.D.Bernal, accepted uncritically the crude and wholly mistaken reasoning that 'capitalist Britain' and 'fascist Germany' were ruled by the same international interests and that rearmament was merely designed to perpetuate imperialism and destroy socialism. The Labour Party took the same line in diluted form. In June 1933, at the East Fulham by-election, the Labour candidate received a message from the Labour Party leader, George Lansbury: 'I would close every recruiting station, disband the Army and disarm the Air Force. I would abolish the whole dreadful equipment of war and say to the world "do your worst".'[22] Clement Attlee, who was to succeed him as leader, told the Commons, 21 December 1933: 'We are unalterably opposed to anything in the nature of rearmament.' Labour consistently voted, spoke and campaigned against rearmament right up to the outbreak of war.

Equally opposed to any policy of preparedness or firmness was the whole spectrum of British benevolence, what Shaw (who belonged to it) called 'the stage-army of the Good'. 'On every side', Trotsky wrote of it with venom, 'the slug humanitarianism leaves its slimy trail, obscuring the function of intelligence and atrophying emotion.' 'They want an outward system of nullity,' echoed D.H.Lawrence before his death, 'which they call peace and good will, so that in their own souls they can be independent little gods ... little Moral Absolutes, secure from questions .... It stinks. It is the will of a louse.'[23] The actual arguments used to justify a policy of quasi-pacifist inactivity were intellectually flimsy at the time and seem in retrospect pitiful. Hitler's savage persecution of the Jews was largely ignored. This was not so much because Britain was anti-Semitic. Unlike France, Jew-baiters like William Joyce, Henry Hamilton Beamish and Arnold Spencer Leese – who advocated mass extermination and used the term 'final solution' – were in a tiny minority.[24] It was, rather, that Hitler's anti-Semitism was rationalized into the overall 'Versailles is to blame' explanation. As Lord Lothian, a key anti-rearmer of the 'soft' Right, put it, the murder of Jews was 'largely the reflex of the external persecution to which Germans have been subjected since the war'.[25]

There was a general tendency (as with Stalin's atrocities) to ignore the actual evidence of Hitler's wickedness, which was plentiful enough, and to dismiss Hitler's ferocious statements as mere 'rhetoric', which was 'intended for home consumption' (*The Times*, 10 July 1934). Against all the evidence, the stage army persisted in believing that Hitler not only wanted peace but was a factor for it. Temple, the portly primate of York, thought he had made 'a great contribution to the secure establishment of peace'.[26] Clifford Allen wrote, 'I am convinced he genuinely desires peace.'[27] Keynes's 'Carthaginian peace' argument had so captured the minds of both Left and Right that it was felt that for Hitler to smash the Treaty by force was itself a step to peace. Versailles was 'monstrously unjust' (Leonard Woolf), 'that wicked treaty' (Clifford Allen). In remilitarizing the Rhineland, said Lothian, the Germans had 'done no more than walk into their own backyard'. Shaw agreed: 'It was if the British had reoccupied Portsmouth.'[28]

Behind all this facile rationalization, however, was simple, old-fashioned fear; a dash of cowardice, indeed. As Harold Nicolson noted during the Rhineland crisis, 'the feeling in the House is terribly pro-German, which means afraid of war'.[29] Until the coming of radar in the late 1930s, even experts accepted the views of Giulio Douhet in *The Command of the Air* (1921), that fighter aircraft could do little to prevent mass bombing. Churchill warned parliament on 28 November 1934 that up to 40,000 Londoners would be killed or injured in the first week of war. Baldwin thought the 'man in the street' ought to 'realize that there is no power on earth that can protect him from being bombed. Whatever people may tell him, the bomber will always get through.'[30] In fact people told him nothing of the sort: quite the contrary. The brilliant H.G. Wells film, *Things to Come* (1936), presented a terrifying scene of total devastation. The same year, Bertrand Russell (currently a pacifist) argued in *Which Way to Peace?* that fifty gas-bombers, using lewisite, could poison all London. General Fuller, another leading expert, predicted that London would become 'one vast, raving Bedlam', with the government 'swept away in an avalanche of terror'.

In this highly emotional atmosphere, with an ostensible concern for humanity forming a thin crust over a morass of funk – so suggestive of the nuclear scares of the late 1950s and early 1980s – the real issue of how to organize collective security in Europe was never properly debated. The mood was set by a ridiculous debate in the Oxford Union, immediately after Hitler came to power, which voted 275–153 'That this House refuses in any circumstances to fight for King and Country' – 'that abject, squalid, shameless avowal . . . a very disquieting and disgusting symptom', as Churchill called it. It was chiefly, and quite illogically, a protest against Britain's supine behaviour over Manchuria, as Michael Foot, then a Union officer (and a Liberal), explained.[31] The League of Nations Union, supposedly the hard-headed, well-informed collective security lobby group, never put the issues clearly before the public because it was unable itself to take a clear stand on when and how force could be legitimately employed in international affairs.[32] Its president and driving force, Lord Robert Cecil, knew that British abandonment of China was inevitable, but he was too devious to tell his supporters.[33] The clergy, seizing on the peace issue as a remedy for declining congregations and their own flagging faith (another precursor of the 1980s), saturated the discussion in a soggy pool of lacrymose spirituality. Three divines, the Revs Herbert Grey, Maude Royden and 'Dick' Sheppard, proposed to go to Manchuria and 'place themselves unarmed between the combatants', a ludicrous echo of Strachey's feeble witticism, but intended quite seriously.[34] The Rev. Donald Soper (Methodist) argued: 'Pacifism contains a spiritual force strong enough to repel an invader.'[35] Cosmo Gordon Lang, Archbishop of Canterbury, did not quite believe that, but he was confused enough both to oppose rearmament and to write to *The Times* wagging an admonitory finger at Mussolini.

The pacifist wing of the clergy, led by Sheppard, founded a Peace Pledge Union to collect signatures to frighten off Hitler: among those who sponsored it were Aldous Huxley, Rose Macaulay, Storm Jameson, Vera Brittain, Siegfried Sassoon, Middleton Murry and other literary luminaries. Feeling the chill wind of competition from the Left, Cecil organized, in 1934–5, a nationwide 'Peace Ballot', which produced 87 per cent approval (over 10 million votes) of the League position, and appeared to refute both the pacifists and the pro-rearmament Tories like Churchill, but which in fact never asked the question whether Britain should rearm if the dictatorships did so first, and so confused the debate still further.[36] In fact public opinion was highly volatile. In 1933–4, East Fulham was one of six by-elections fought in part on the peace issue which registered huge swings against the government (as high as 50 per cent in October 1934) and were interpreted as a public rejection of rearmament. But all these seats returned solidly to the Tory fold at the general election in 1935, just as virtually all those who voted against King and Country at Oxford fought for it when the time came. But Hitler could be excused for believing, at any rate until the end of 1938, that Britain would not oppose him by force. He therefore acted on that assumption.

Hitler's conduct of foreign and military policy between his accession to power and the end of 1938 was brilliantly forceful and — granted the complete absence of respect for any system of law and

morals – faultless. He did not make a single error of judgement. At
this stage his compulsive eschatology was an advantage: the need he
felt for speed gave his moves a pace which continually wrong-footed
his opponents and left them bewildered. 1933 and 1934 were
devoted essentially to internal consolidation and rearmament. The
action began on 13 January 1935 when Hitler won the Saar
plebiscite; eleven days after the Saar reverted to Germany on
7 March, Hitler repudiated the Versailles disarmament clauses, and
on 18 June – despite the Stresa Front – the British cravenly accepted
the *fait accompli* of a rearmed Germany by signing the Anglo–
German Naval Treaty. This inexplicable surrender not only gave
Germany the right to 35 per cent strength of Britain's surface fleet
but granted her parity in submarines. It was the beginning of positive
appeasement, as opposed to mere supine inactivity.[37] This concession infuriated the French and contributed to the breakdown in
Anglo–French policy marked by the Abyssinia crisis. Indeed, Abyssinia was an uncovenanted boon for Hitler: his one stroke of pure
luck.

It is of the essence of geopolitics to be able to distinguish between
different degrees of evil. This was a gift Anthony Eden, now Foreign
Secretary, did not possess. He could not differentiate between
Mussolini, who was corruptible but open to civilized influences too,
and Hitler, a man who had already murdered hundreds and placed
scores of thousands in concentration camps, and who openly claimed
his intention to transform Europe. 'My programme from the first
was to abolish the Treaty of Versailles . . . . I have written it
thousands of times. No human being has ever declared or recorded
what he wanted more often than me': so Hitler said, and it was
true.[38] Nor did Eden register that any threat from Italy, with her
weak and already flagging economy, was not to be compared with
the potential destructive power of Germany, with the world's second
largest industrial economy, already booming again, and a military
tradition of unparalleled ferocity. This extraordinary lack of perspective was shared by British public opinion, or at any rate that section
of it which made its voice heard. The uproar it raised over Italy's
invasion was far noisier than the hostile reaction to any of Hitler's
far more purposeful moves, then or later. The French were shaken by
such frivolity, and made it clear they could not be a party to it.

Thus Abyssinia not only destroyed the Stresa Front but created
bitter Anglo–French antagonism and ruled out any possibility of
securing joint agreement to a firm counter-move against Hitler.
France would not back Britain over Abyssinia; therefore Britain
would not back France over the Rhineland. It was the Abyssinia
crisis which enabled Hitler to bring forward his plan to remilitarize

the Rhine from 1937 to 1936, beautifully timed on 7 March at the height of Anglo–French confusion. Even so it was a risk. Hitler later admitted: 'If the French had marched into the Rhineland we would have had to withdraw with our tails between our legs.'[39] The French had the physical power to act alone, as they had done in 1923. But the will to use it was lacking.

Thereafter Hitler was in a position to resist invasion from the West. In 1936–7 he benefited greatly from the turmoils in the world. First the Spanish Civil War, then the Sino–Japanese conflict burdened the guardians of legitimacy with a multitude of fast-changing problems they could not solve. Meanwhile Hitler rearmed steadily and strengthened his alliances. The Rome–Berlin Axis of 1 November 1936, followed later that month by the Anti-Comintern Pact with Japan, altered the naval-air equations just as radically as the aircraft emerging from Hitler's new factories. By 1937 Germany had 800 bombers to Britain's forty-eight. By May that year it was calculated the German and Italian air forces could drop 600 tons of bombs a day. It was the obsession with air-raid terror, intensified by Soviet propaganda over Guernica after July 1937, which paralysed Allied diplomacy.[40]

On 5 November 1937 Hitler told his top military and foreign policy advisers that a period of active expansion could now begin, with Austria and Czechoslovakia the first targets. Von Blomberg, the War Minister, and the Army Commander, von Fritsch, protested: the French would still be too strong.[41] That was the end of them. Until this point Hitler had left the army alone, other than tell it to get on with rearmament as fast as possible. Now he decided the time had come to take it over, to clear the way for the dynamic phase of his programme. On 26 January 1938 Blomberg was dismissed: police files showed his new wife had been a prostitute and porn-model. Nine days later Fritsch went, charged with homosexuality on the evidence of a Himmler file. They were, in a sense, lucky: Stalin would have murdered them for less – he killed 200 generals in 1937–8 – or indeed for nothing at all. Some sixteen other German generals were retired, forty-four more transferred. Hitler himself took over as War Minister and head of the armed forces; the weak von Brauchitsch was made head of the army; a pliable Nazi general, Wilhelm Keitel, was told to create a new operational high command. Thus the last bastion of the old order fell to Hitler, without a murmur from anyone. He threw out Schacht from the Economics Ministry and von Neurath from the Foreign Ministry at the same time. From now on the Nazis were in total control and all was on a war footing.

A week after Fritsch was sacked, Hitler summoned the Austrian Chancellor, Kurt von Schuschnigg, to his mountain villa at Berchtesgaden. No saloon-keeper dragged to a gangster's lair could have been treated more brutally. Following the tirade, the terrified man signed a series of concessions, including the appointment of a Nazi as his Interior Minister. Afterwards, driving back to Salzburg with von Papen, the latter remarked: 'Yes – that's the way the Führer can be. Now you've seen it for yourself. But next time you'll find a meeting with him a good deal easier. The Führer can be distinctly charming.'[42] In fact the 'next time' for Schuschnigg was a summons to Dachau. Hitler's troops entered Austria thirty days after the meeting.

Hitler's treatment of his Austrian opponents was brutal and bestial in the extreme. University professors were made to scrub the streets with their bare hands (a form of 're-education' imitated by Mao Tse-tung in the 1960s).[43] The invading Nazis stole anything they could lay their hands on. When they broke into Freud's flat in Vienna, his wife put her housekeeping money on the table: 'Won't the gentlemen help themselves?' It required intervention by Roosevelt and Mussolini – and a ransom of 250,000 Austrian schillings – to get the old man permission to leave. He had to sign a statement testifying he had been well-treated, to which he appended the words 'I can heartily recommend the Gestapo to anyone.' The Germans were delighted. The bitter joke was beyond them. So was pity. Freud's four aged sisters chose not to move: all died in the gas-ovens later.[44]

On 21 April, five weeks after he swallowed Austria, Hitler instructed Keitel to prepare an invasion plan for Czechoslovakia, and told the leader of the German minority there to set the crisis in motion. The previous month, on 21 March, the British Chiefs of Staff had presented the cabinet with a paper, 'The Military Implications of German Aggression Against Czechoslovakia'. Britain was now rearming, but the paper told a fearful tale of delays and weaknesses, especially in the emotional area of air defence.[45] Two critical questions now arise. First, would the German army have overthrown Hitler if the Allies had made it clear that war was the price of his Czech policy? This is one of the great 'ifs' of history, for if the answer is 'Yes', the Second World War – and its terrible consequences – would have been averted.

It is true that some German generals believed that war over Czechoslovakia would be a disaster for Germany. A meeting convened by Brauchitsch in July 1938 agreed that the German people were against war and that the army was still too weak to defeat 'the powers'.[46] The Chief of Staff, Ludwig Beck, told the politician Ewald von Kleist-Schwenzin, who was going to Britain, 'Bring me back certain proof that England will fight if Czechoslovakia is attacked and I will put an end to this regime.'[47] Hitler assured his generals on 15 August that, so long as Chamberlain and Daladier were in power, there would be no Allied declaration of war – according to

Rauschning he referred to the Appeasers scornfully as 'My Hugen-burgs'. This did not convince Beck, who declined responsibility and resigned on 27 August. There is some evidence other generals were prepared to overthrow Hitler when and if he gave the order to attack.[48] But one must remain sceptical. The German generals had acquiesced in 1934 when Hitler murdered two of their number. They had done nothing in January when he had broken and retired their leaders. Where in the intervening months would they have found the courage they had so signally failed to possess before – and exercised it in circumstances which Hitler would have presented as desertion and treachery in the face of the enemy?

In any case, whatever the generals intended, they failed to convey the message to the British cabinet. At its decisive meeting on 30 August, only one cabinet minister, Oliver Stanley, mentioned the belief of the German generals that their country was not ready for war. What Beck and his colleagues wanted was an ultimatum – a war-threat. What the cabinet decided was exactly the opposite. As Chamberlain summed up: 'The cabinet was unanimous in the view that we should not utter a threat to Herr Hitler, that if he went into Czechoslovakia we should declare war on him. It was of the utmost importance that the decision be kept secret.' Since publicity was of the essence of a firm line being effective, the cabinet decision is incomprehensible, except on the assumption that Chamberlain and others did not want Hitler overthrown.

This raises an important point: the Hitler phenomenon cannot be seen except in conjunction with the phenomenon of Soviet Russia. Just as the fear of Communism put him in power, so it tended to keep him there. Chamberlain was not clear, at this stage, whether Hitler was a total menace or not; he was quite clear Stalin was. The British tended to underestimate the power of the Soviet army. But they rightly feared the political potential of Communist expansion. In an oblique manner Hitler had always underlined the consanguinity of the rival totalitarianisms. The moment the Nazi Party disappeared, he reiterated, 'there will be another 10 million Communist votes in Germany'. The alternative to him was not liberal democracy, he insisted, but Soviet collectivism. Chamberlain for one accepted this argument. When on 26 September, in the immediate prelude to Munich, General Gamelin gave him a more optimistic picture of Allied strength and they discussed the possibility of Hitler's over-throw, Chamberlain wanted to know: 'Who will guarantee that Germany will not become Bolshevistic afterwards?' Of course no one could give such a pledge. Daladier took a similar line: 'The Cossacks will rule Europe.'[49] So the two men chose the lesser of two evils (as they saw it): concessions to Germany.

The second question is: would the Allies have been better advised to fight in autumn 1938 over Czechoslovakia, than in autumn 1939 over Poland? This too is in dispute; but the answer is surely 'Yes'. It is true that the pace of Allied rearmament, especially of British air-power, was overtaking Germany's. But in this sense alone was the strategic equation better in 1939 than in 1938. It is important to grasp that the Munich Conference, which took place in the Brown House on 29–30 September, was not only a diplomatic surrender by Britain and France but a military disaster too. Mussolini, who appeared the star of the show – he was the only one who spoke all four languages – failed to note this point: he thought the only issue was German irridentism and that 'Hitler had no intention' of absorbing Czechoslovakia itself.[50] But the actual redrawing of the Czech frontiers at Munich was determined, at Hitler's insistence, as much on military as on racial grounds. No plebiscite was held. Some 800,000 Czechs were absorbed into Germany, and 250,000 Germans left behind as a fifth column.[51] The Czechs' elaborate frontier defences, built with French assistance, were taken over by the Germans. There was now no possibility whatever of the Czechs offering armed resistance to an outright invasion. That involved a massive shift in the strategic balance. As Churchill, who perceived the military significance of the capitulation better than anyone, pointed out in the Munich debate (5 October 1938), the annexation of Austria had given Hitler an extra twelve divisions. Now the dismantling of Czech military power released a further thirty German divisions for action elsewhere.[52]

In fact the shift was worse than this. The Czechs' forty divisions were among the best-equipped in Europe: when Hitler finally marched in he got the means to furnish equivalent units of his own, plus the huge Czech armaments industry. This 'turnaround' of roughly eighty divisions was equivalent to the entire French army.[53] The surrender, as Churchill noted, also meant the end of France's system of alliances in the east and brought about a moral collapse in the Danube basin. Seeing the Czechs abandoned by the democracies, the small states scuttled for cover or joined, like jackals, in the feast. Poland was allowed to tear off Teschen, which she had coveted since 1919. Hungary, too, got a slice of the Czech carcass. Throughout East–Central Europe and the Balkans, the friendship and favour of the Nazis was now eagerly courted by governments, and fascist parties swelled in influence and pride. German trade was everywhere triumphant. The German economy boomed. In the closing weeks of 1938 Hitler, without firing a shot, appeared to have restored all the splendour of Wilhelmine Germany. Was he not the most successful German statesman since Bismarck? So it appeared.

Yet the end of 1938 marked the watershed in Hitler's career, not least with the German people. He overestimated their will to power. They supported overwhelmingly his policy of German irridentism. They applauded the *Anschluss*: plebiscites showed 99 per cent approval in Germany and 99.75 per cent in Austria.[54] They wanted the Sudetenland back. But there is no evidence that they ever wanted to absorb large populations of non-Germans. There is ample evidence that most Germans did not want war. When on 27 September 1938 Hitler deliberately ordered the 2nd Motorized Division to pass through Berlin on its way to the Czech border, less than two hundred people came out to watch him review it from the Reichskanzlerplatz. He marched back into the building disgusted.[55] Thereafter, his brutal moves on the European chessboard, however successful or even triumphant, evoked no spontaneous applause from the German public. There was a total lack of elation when German troops marched into Prague.

Hitler sensed this vacuum in German hearts. But he no longer sought to fill it. He would go forward with or without their enthusiasm. All he insisted on was their obedience. From 1939 he ceased to play the politician, the orator, the demagogue. He became a militarist, working from army headquarters, and by means of secret gangster-pacts. His methods of government began to approximate to Stalin's, losing their public dimension of approbation and leadership. He ceased to woo: he now sought only to force and terrorize. His speech to the Reichstag on 1 September 1939, justifying his war on Poland, was short and flat; the streets were deserted as he drove to make it. Nor did the crowds turn out when the troops returned victorious. As George Kennan noted from the American embassy, the Berliners refused to cheer or even give the Nazi salute: 'Not even the most frantic efforts of professional Nazi agitators could provoke them to demonstrations of elation or approval.' It was the same even when the German troops took Paris.[56]

As German opinion ceased to keep pace with Hitler's accelerating eschatology, so British opinion swung against appeasement. It was beginning to do so even at the time of Munich itself, to judge by such newspapers as the *Manchester Guardian, News Chronicle, Daily Telegraph* and *Daily Herald. The Times*, whose editor Geoffrey Dawson was Chamberlain's closest press confidant, supported Munich; so did the left-wing *New Statesman*, whose chairman was Keynes himself.[57] But their enthusiasm soon waned. The bestial wave of anti-Semitism which Goebbels unleashed in Germany during November completed the rout of the appeasers. During the winter of 1938–9, the mood in Britain changed to accept war as inevitable. The German occupation of Prague on 15 March 1939, followed swiftly by the seizure of Memel from Lithuania six days later, convinced most British people that war was imminent. Fear gave place to a resigned despair, and the sort of craven, if misjudged, calculation which led to Munich yielded to a reckless and irrational determination to resist Hitler at the next opportunity, irrespective of its merits.

This of course was precisely the kind of hysterical response which Hitler's acceleration of history was bound to produce sooner or later. The result was to make nonsense of all his plans, and to lead him into irreparable error and the world into war. Less than a fortnight after the occupation of Prague, on 28 March, Hitler denounced his 1934 pact with Poland, and preparations went ahead for its dismemberment. Poland was to him an unfortunate geographical anomaly. It contained large subject German populations and territories he believed ought to belong to him. But more important was that it barred his invasion route into Russia and so inhibited his plans to deal with the home of 'bacillus'. It had to submit to him or be destroyed. He saw no reason why the British and the French should resist his plans. If they were not prepared to fight over Czechoslovakia, which made some kind of military sense for them, why should they fight over Poland, which made no sense at all? In any case, why should not these capitalist countries welcome his decision to move Eastwards, ultimately against the heartland of Bolshevism?

Instead, only three days later, the British gave Poland a guarantee that if 'action was taken which clearly threatened the independence of Poland so that Poland felt bound to resist with her national forces, His Majesty's Government would at once lend them all the support in their power.'[58] Chamberlain made this move without consulting the French government, although they were more or less bound to endorse it. *The Times*, briefed by Chamberlain, hastened to insist that the loosely worded pledge, one of the most ill-considered in British history, only guaranteed Poland's 'independence' not its 'integrity' – thus leaving room for the alteration of the Versailles frontiers in Germany's favour.[59] That was Hitler's interpretation. What he assumed was that the guarantee would lead Britain to put pressure on the Poles, as once on the Czechs, to satisfy his demands, including invasion routes into Russia. He had no intention of provoking war with Britain. In January 1939 he had taken the decision to build a vast high seas fleet, of ten battleships, three battlecruisers, four aircraft-carriers and no less than 249 submarines, and he told Admiral Erich Raeder that war with Britain had to be avoided until the fleet was ready in the mid-1940s.[60] He thought in fact that Britain, realizing Imperial preference was not working, was likely to be driven by economic factors to turn in conciliatory mood to Europe, now dominated by German trade; and this impression was confirmed in July by talks which Helmuth Wohlthat, Director of Goering's Four Year Plan staff, had in London – thus foreshadowing the move into Europe which did not in fact take place until the 1970s.[61]

Yet the Polish guarantee did raise problems for Hitler, because the power to invoke it was placed in the hands of the Polish government, not a repository of good sense. Therein lay the foolishness of the pledge: Britain had no means of bringing effective aid to Poland yet it obliged itself to declare war on Germany if Poland so requested. The pledge, however, might become more meaningful if Britain allied herself with Russia. This had long been the aim of the European Left, which saw it as the solution to all their dilemmas – including their desire to resist Hitler while opposing rearmament. By mid-1939 the British and French chiefs of staff favoured a Russian alliance in the sense that they favoured anything which might reduce the military odds they now faced. But following Stalin's military purges of 1938 they rated the Soviet army below Poland's, and if it came to a choice would opt for the latter. Since the Russians would not co-operate unless the Poles allowed passage of their troops, and since the Poles were no more willing to permit Soviet troops to pass through Poland to attack Germany than they were to allow German troops through to attack Russia, there was never much possibility of an Anglo–French–Russian military agreement. Nevertheless, an Anglo–French mission set off for Russia on 1 August, by sea (appropriate air transport was not available, an interesting reflection on the present state of British air-power).[62]

This was enough to determine Hitler on a momentous, if temporary, *renversement des alliances*. Hitler had all along been convinced that war was unavoidable at certain stages of his programme. But at all costs he wanted to avoid the general, unlimited war of attrition and exhaustion which Germany had experienced in 1914–18. He wanted to revert to the short, limited but politically decisive wars which Bismarck had waged in the 1860s and 1870s. The *Blitzkrieg*, for which his army was being equipped and trained, was an integral part of his whole expansionist philosophy. In his view neither the German economy nor the German people could stand more than short, fierce campaigns, of overwhelming power and intensity but very limited duration.[63] The last of these lightning wars was to be the decisive one against Russia: thereafter, with a vast Eurasian empire to exploit, Germany could build up the strength to sustain long and global conflict. But until that happened she must be careful to take on enemies singly and above all avoid protracted campaigns on two or more major fronts.

The result was what he privately termed 'a pact with Satan to drive out the devil'.[64] On 28 April, in his last big public oration, he savaged Roosevelt's windy proposal for non-aggression guarantees, and signalled in effect that all previous pacts, treaties or assumptions were now invalid. Henceforth his only guideline would be the interests of the German people, as he conceived them. Stalin's response to this speech was eager. He feared a German invasion more than any other development, internal or external. It was the absence of a German enemy in 1918–20 which alone had permitted the Bolshevik state to survive. At the Central Committee plenary session of 19 January 1925 he had laid down Soviet policy on war between capitalist states: 'Should [such a] war begin . . . we will have to take part, but we will be the last to take part so that we may throw the decisive weight into the scales, a weight which should prove the determining factor.' Since May 1935, while publicly pursuing a Popular Front policy against 'international fascism', he had privately put out periodic feelers to persuade the Nazis to relinquish their anti-Soviet crusade and settle for a totalitarian brotherhood of mutual respect and divided spoils. Germany's evident decision, in March, to carve slices out of Poland provided a promising occasion to begin such a new relationship and the prospect of the democracies fighting for Poland was an added reason for coming to terms with Hitler and keeping out of the war – for the present. On 3 May Stalin sacked the Jew Litvinov and replaced him as Foreign Minister by Molotov: a clearance of the decks for talks with Hitler. Eight days later, the outbreak of large-scale fighting with Japanese forces in the Far East gave Stalin an added incentive to make an agreement, for he, no more than Hitler, wanted a two-front struggle.[65]

The first of the gangster pacts came on 22 May: the 'Pact of Steel' between Hitler and Mussolini. The latter had already swallowed his consternation at Germany's occupation of Prague, used it as a pretext for his own invasion of Albania on 7 April, and now jointly acknowledged with Hitler that international order had finally broken down and the reign of force had begun. At this stage Hitler was still anxious to stick to his original programme of dismembering Poland first, then using it as a corridor shortly afterwards for a Blitzkrieg against Russia, with Britain observing benevolent neutrality. As late as July he hoped such an outcome was possible. But the news of the arrival of the Anglo–French military mission in Moscow forced his hand, for even the possibility of an Allied deal with Moscow would upset his Polish timetable. He decided to preempt them, and on 20 August sent a telegram to 'Herr J.V.Stalin, Moscow', asking him to receive Ribbentrop three days later. The reply came back within twenty-four hours, revealing Stalin's evident longings. The next day, 22 August, Hitler addressed the High Command at Obersalzberg. According to jottings made by some of those present, he said that the Polish operation could go ahead. They need fear nothing from the West: 'Our opponents are little worms. I saw them in Munich.' He concluded: 'I shall provide the propagandistic pretext for launching the war, no matter whether it is credible. The victor is not asked afterwards whether or not he has told the truth. What matters in beginning and waging the war is not righteousness but victory. Close your hearts to pity. Proceed brutally. Eighty million people must obtain what they have a right to. Their existence must be guaranteed. The stronger is in the right. *Supreme hardness.*'[66]

The deal with Stalin was struck the following night. It was the culmination of a series of contacts between the Soviet and German governments which went right back to the weeks following Lenin's *putsch*. They had been conducted, according to need, by army experts, secret policemen, diplomats or intermediaries on the fringe of the criminal world. They had been closer at some periods than others but they had never been wholly broken and they had been characterized throughout by total disregard for the ideological principles which either party ostensibly professed – by a contempt, indeed, for any consideration other than the most brutal mutual interest – the need of each regime to arm, to arrest and kill its opponents, and to oppress its neighbours. For two decades this evil stream of exchanges had flowed underground. Now at last it broke the surface. That night of 23–4 August there was a gruesome junket in the Kremlin. Ribbentrop reported: 'It felt like being among old party comrades.' He was as much at ease in the Kremlin, he added, 'as among my old Nazi friends'. Stalin toasted Hitler and said he 'knew how much the German people loved the Führer'. There were brutal jokes about the Anti-Comintern Pact, now dead, which both sides agreed had been meant simply to impress the City of London and 'English shopkeepers'.[67] There was the sudden discovery of a community of aims, methods, manners and, above all, of morals. As the tipsy killers lurched about the room, fumblingly hugging each other, they resembled nothing so much as a congregation of rival gangsters, who had fought each other before, and might do so again, but were essentially in the same racket.

Their agreement was termed a non-aggression pact. In fact it was a simple aggression pact against Poland. A secret protocol, which emerged in 1945 but which the Russian judges kept out of the Nuremberg trials record, divided up Eastern Europe into spheres of influence and left it open 'whether the interests of both parties make the maintenance of an independent Polish state appear desirable and how the frontiers of this state should be delimited'.[68] Thus a fourth partition of Poland was arranged, and consummated on 17 September when Soviet troops moved in, the division being solemnized by another gangster-pact, the Soviet–German Frontier and Friendship Treaty of 28 September 1939. The ground covered extended well beyond Poland, Stalin being given a free hand in Finland, most of the Baltic states and part of Romania. Hence in the autumn of 1939 he was able to impose upon Latvia, Estonia and Lithuania so-called 'security treaties', which involved the introduction of Soviet troops. He told the Latvian Foreign Minister: 'So far as Germany is concerned, we can occupy you.'[69] When the Finns resisted, Stalin unleashed war on them (30 November 1939) with Germany's acquiescence.

Stalin was delighted with the pact. He said it left Russia in a stronger position than at any time since the regime came to power. He did everything in his power to make the agreement work, to fulfil his pledge to Ribbentrop 'on his word of honour that the Soviet Union would not betray her partner'.[70] All over the world, Communist Parties reversed their anti-Nazi policy, preaching peace with Germany at any price, and actively sabotaging the war-effort when it came: at the height of the Nazi invasion of France, Maurice Thorez, head of the French CP, broadcast from Moscow begging the French troops not to resist. Stalin placed at Hitler's disposal all the immense raw material resources of the Soviet Union. This was vital to Hitler. In September 1939 Germany needed to import 80 per cent of its rubber, 65 per cent of its tin, 70 per cent of its copper, half its lead, a quarter of its zinc. Sweden, at the price of freedom from invasion (and German coal at one-third the price paid by Switzerland), provided Hitler with his iron-ore and all kinds of transit and overflight facilities.[71] But Stalin filled equally important gaps in Hitler's war-supplies: a million tons of grain, 900,000 tons of oil (including 100,000 tons of aircraft fuel), additional iron-ore, manganese and cotton. In return Russia got aero-engines, naval blueprints, torpedoes and mines.[72]

The pact brought a personal rapprochement too. Stalin presented Hitler as a man of genius, who had risen from nothing like himself. According to Ribbentrop, Hitler greatly admired Stalin, especially the way in which he held out against his own 'extremists' (a view widely shared in the West). Hitler said that Stalin had produced 'a sort of Slavonic-Muscovite nationalism', ridding Bolshevism of its Jewish internationalism. Mussolini took the view that Bolshevism was now dead: Stalin had substituted for it 'a kind of Slavonic fascism'.[73]

Yet the pact did not solve any of the problems Hitler had set himself. Indeed it involved a reversal of the original priorities on his timetable. He told Carl Burckhardt, League High Commissioner in Danzig: 'Everything that I undertake is directed against Russia. If the

West is too stupid and too blind to understand this, then I will be forced to reach an understanding with the Russians, smash the West, and then turn all my concentrated strength against the Soviet Union.'[74] Even after Hitler got the Soviet pact, he still hoped to avoid war with the West, trusting that it would stun Britain into impotent passivity. But it had no effect on British policy other than to make all concerned now assume that war was certain. It was positively welcomed by some on the British Right as visible proof that the godless totalitarian regimes were in shameless and undisguised concert, 'out in the open, huge and hideous', as Evelyn Waugh put it in his fictional trilogy, *Sword of Honour*. When Hitler invaded Poland on 1 September and the Poles invoked the guarantee, there was never any doubt that Britain would stand by it or that France, however reluctantly, would follow suit.

Thus Hitler's programme had to be drastically revised, and he found himself with a general war of the type he had hoped to avoid before disposing of Russia. From this point he ceased to nurture his image as a reasonable man, either at home or abroad, and made it clear to all that he would obtain his objectives by the ruthless application of force and terror. The same day he invaded Poland he ordered the murder of the incurably ill in German hospitals.[75] He made no attempt to reach a settlement with the Poles. He simply treated the country as occupied territory to be exploited. The victory over Poland was not an end; just a beginning. This was the exact reverse of the general German mood. After the Polish collapse General Ritter von Leeb noted in his diary, 3 October 1939: 'Poor mood of the population, no enthusiasm at all, no flags flying from the houses. Everyone waiting for peace. The people sense the needlessness of the war.' But Hitler was determined to burn Germany's bridges, to lock the nation onto an irreversible course. He told his generals, 23 November 1939: 'All hope for compromise is childish. Victory or defeat. I have led the German people to a great height even though the world now hates us. I am risking this war. I have to choose between victory or annihilation. It is not a single problem that is at stake, but whether the nation is to be or not to be.' On 17 October he ordered General Keitel to treat occupied Polish territory as 'an advanced glacis' for the future invasion of Russia.[76] So much for the security Stalin thought he had bought! But in the meantime the West had to be eliminated: France by *Blitzkrieg*, Britain by despair.

Hitler was now Generalissimo. The Polish campaign was the last prepared by the old General Staff. From now on, as with security and the civil ministries, Hitler double-banked the direction of the army, with the OKW (High Command of the Armed Forces), under his personal orders, duplicating the work of the OKH (Army High Command). The French made things easy for him. They had not wanted the war. After Munich they recognized that their Eastern policy was finished. With Poland they simply went through the motions. They thought the British pledge madness and endorsed it simply because they had no alternative.[77] They knew that to enter an all-out war with Hitlerite Germany might mean a repetition of 1870, and it took them fifty-six hours of agonized hesitation to respond to the German assault on Poland, which had been their sworn ally since 1921.[78] The military protocol which General Gamelin had signed in May 1939 with the Polish War Minister, Kasprzycki, pledged that the French air force would take immediate offensive action against Germany as soon as Poland was invaded, and that a French army invasion of Germany would follow within sixteen days. Neither promise was fulfilled. All that happened was a tentative army probe on 8 September, soon discontinued. On 22 September, on the receipt of decisively bad news from the Polish front, the French scrapped all their aggressive plans. During this time the Germans had only eleven active-service divisions in the west, but by 1 October they were transferring troops from the eastern front. Thereafter, as the minutes of the Anglo–French staff discussions show, it was the British who pressed for action on the main German front, and the French who wished to do nothing there, while planning diversionary schemes in Scandinavia, the Caucasus, Salonica, Finland and elsewhere.[79]

The French preference for passivity on the Franco–German border combined with largely meaningless activity elsewhere played straight into Hitler's hands. Hitler originally ordered the attack on France for 12 November, selecting from the alternatives offered the daring concept of an armoured thrust through the Ardennes. The restlessness of French policy forced him to command and recommand the operation twenty-nine times throughout the winter and early spring. But in the meantime he himself had conceived the brilliant Norway operation, which his military advisers pronounced impossible. Anglo–French activities gave him the pretext and he pulled off the invasion, demoralizing the Allies and discountenancing his generals, who raised no objections when he strengthened the concept of the Ardennes thrust and launched it while France was still reeling from the Norway defeat and Allied logistics were in desperate confusion.

The rapid destruction of French military power in May–June 1940 convinced Hitler that the errors of the previous autumn were not irreversible and that he could still proceed towards his ultimate targets by a series of swift Bismarckian *coups*. The campaign bore the hallmarks of both his overweening self-confidence in attack and his ingenuity in detailed invention: according to Albert Speer, it was

Hitler who thought of fitting the Stuka dive-bombers with sirens, one of the masterly psychological strokes of the *Blitzkrieg*. There were many other examples of his military inventiveness at this stage, including lengthening the gun-barrels of the tanks.[80] Just as earlier he had wrong-footed the democracies by the rapidity by which he created and exploited diplomatic opportunities, so now he gave the French commanders no chance to recover from their initial surprise. 'The ruling idea of the Germans in the conduct of this war was speed,' wrote the historian Marc Bloch, who served as staff-captain on the First Army Group. His account of those fatal weeks, *L'étrange défaite*, stressed that the collapse was a verdict on the French system as much as on its army. He praised both the populism and the intellectual calibre of Nazism:

> Compared to the old Imperial army, the troops of the Nazi regime have the appearance of being far more democratic. The gulf between officers and men seems now to be less unbridgeable . . . . The German triumph was essentially a triumph of intellect – and that is what makes it so peculiarly serious . . . . It was as though the two opposed forces belonged, each of them, to an entirely different period of history. We interpreted war in terms of assegai versus rifle made familiar to us by long years of colonial expansion. But this time it was we who were cast in the role of the savage![81]

Bloch noted that, whatever the deep-seated causes, the immediate one was 'the utter incompetence of the high command'. It is now known that General Gamelin was suffering from syphilis, which may explain the inability to make up his mind, lack of concentration, failing memory and delusions of grandeur which he exhibited during the campaign.[82] But the paralysis of senior officers was general. Bloch describes his own Army Group commander, General Blanchard, sitting 'in tragic immobility, saying nothing, doing nothing, but just gazing at the map spread on the table between us, as though hoping to find on it the decision he was incapable of taking.'[83]

As a military gamble the attack on France was a complete success. It began on 10 May and six weeks later, on 22 June, France signed an armistice which gave Hitler everything he wanted. The ratio of casualties – 27,000 German dead to 135,000 for the Allies – gives some indication of the magnitude of the German victory. On 10 June Italy had entered the war on Germany's side, and the terms of France's armistice with Mussolini, signed on 24 June, included the withdrawal of the French colonies from the war. Three days later Stalin invaded Romania and seized the provinces of Bessarabia and Bukovina; he had already appropriated the Karelian isthmus from Finland in a capitulation signed on 12 March. He was in every military sense Hitler's ally, though not his co-belligerent.

France rapidly inclined towards the Nazi camp. Disarmed by the socialists, betrayed by the fascists and, still more, by the Communists, and now deserted by the Right and the Centre, the Third Republic collapsed, friendless and unmourned. At Riom, a series of trials, against a background of approval or indifference, condemned those judged *les résponsables* for the defeat: Daladier, Reynaud, Blum, Gamelin, Mandel, Guy la Chambre and others – in effect a verdict against the kind of parliamentary politics practised in France.[84] The armistice had been signed by Maréchal Henri Philippe Pétain, and he was now invested with *pleins pouvoirs* by the rump parliament in the new capital set up in Vichy. His dictatorship had been long in coming. He had been a 1914–18 war hero and had dominated French military policy 1920–36, so in fact was as responsible as any for the *dégringolade*. But he was the most popular French general because his men felt they were less likely to be killed under his command than anyone else's. He was stupid. His books were ghosted for him by clever young officers. But he had the simple dignity of the French peasant (his father had been one). When *Le Petit Journal* held a survey in 1935 to find whom the French would most like as their dictator, Pétain came top. Second was Pierre Laval, a former socialist of the Mussolini type, whom Pétain now made Prime Minister.[85]

Pétain quickly became the most popular French ruler since Napoleon. He incarnated anti-romanticism, the anxiety to relinquish historical and global duties, the longing for a quiet and safe life which now swept over France. He was a compulsive womanizer: 'Sex and food are the only things that matter,' he said. But the Church worshipped him. Cardinal Gerlier, the French primate, announced: '*La France, c'est Pétain, et Pétain c'est la France.*'[86] In a sense it was true. He was treated like royalty. Peasants lined the rails along which his train passed. Women held out their babies for him to touch. An official report notes that at Toulouse in November 1940 a women hurled herself in front of his car to stop it so she might have the chance of touching his hand. The Prefect turned to Pétain to apologize, but found the Marshal gently asleep (he was eighty-five), 'without', said the report, 'losing his dignity or his sovereign bearing'.[87] In 1934 he had quarrelled with one of his colonels, Charles de Gaulle, who refused to write a book for him unacknowledged. Now, as Under-Secretary for War, de Gaulle refused to accept the armistice and on 5 August Britain signed an agreement with his Free French movement; but only 35,000 joined him. In its early days, the Vichy regime, composed of soldiers and civil servants, with the politicians left out, generated genuine euphoria in France, as had Hitler's in Germany in 1933.

Hitler had no difficulty in turning Vichy into an ally. On 3 July 1940, lacking adequate reassurances, the Royal Navy was instructed to sink the French fleet in Oran and other North African ports. Two days later Pétain broke off relations with Britain, and thereafter Vichy drifted inexorably into the Nazi camp, where she was ruthlessly treated as a milch-cow. Some 40 per cent of France's industrial production, 1,500,000 workers and half France's public sector revenue went to the German war-economy.[88]

Hitler was less lucky with Spain. Franco was determined to keep out of war, which he saw as the supreme evil, and especially a war waged by Hitler in association with Stalin, which he felt incarnated all the evils of the century. He declared strict neutrality in September 1939. He advised Mussolini to keep out too. He felt he had to shift to 'non-belligerency' on 13 June 1940, which he described as 'a form of national sympathy with the Axis'.[89] But as the price for entering the war he pitched his demands impossibly high: Oran, the whole of Morocco, huge territories in West Africa, massive quantities of war supplies and equipment to attack Gibraltar and defend the Canaries. When he met Hitler at Hendaye on 23 October 1940 he not only increased these demands but greeted his German benefactor with icy coldness verging on contempt. As he was himself a professional soldier, and Hitler an amateur – not even a gentleman, a corporal! – he treated Hitler's customary military *tour d'horizon* with unconcealed contempt. They talked, wrote Hitler's interpreter Paul Schmidt, 'to or rather at one another' until two in the morning and failed to agree on anything whatever. Hitler later told Mussolini he would rather have two or three teeth out than go through that again.[90]

One of Franco's collateral reasons for refusing to join Hitler was his belief that Britain had no intention of making peace. Perhaps Hitler's biggest single misjudgement was his failure to appreciate the depth of the hostility he had aroused in Britain. The main object of his *Blitzkrieg* in France was not to destroy the French army, which he felt he could do any time he wished, but to shock Britain into making terms. On 21 May, the same day he took Arras, he said he wanted 'to sound out England on dividing the world'.[91] His decision to halt his armour outside Dunkirk at the end of the month, which allowed the bulk of the British Expeditionary Force to be evacuated from the beaches, was taken for military reasons but may have been prompted by the desire to open up a line of discussion with London. On 2 June, as the last BEF units were preparing to embark, he told the staff of Army Group A in Charleville that he wanted a 'reasonable peace agreement' with Britain immediately so that he would be 'finally free' for his 'great and real task: the confrontation with Bolshevism'.[92] With the French campaign over, he spoke on 30 June of the need to give Britain one more 'demonstration of our military power before she gives up and leaves us free in the rear for the East'.[93] He continued to cling to the illusion that Britain might compromise into the late autumn. 'The Führer is obviously depressed,' noted an observer on 4 November. 'Impression that at the moment he does not know how the war ought to continue.'[94] He was waiting for a signal from London that never came.

In fact Britain became decisively more bellicose in the course of 1940. Where France chose Pétain and quietism, Britain chose Churchill and heroism. There were perfectly sound economic and military reasons for this bifurcation. Unlike France, Britain did not elect a popular front government in the mid-1930s, and the deflationary policies of the Baldwin–Chamberlain governments, though painful, eventually permitted her to make a substantial economic recovery. Although Britain's unemployment in the early 1930s was much higher than France's, there is evidence to show that much of it was voluntary as a result of the relatively high level of benefit, more than 50 per cent of average wages.[95] The economy was much healthier than it appeared in left-wing propaganda. Almost throughout the 1930s the building industry was expanding, producing over 3 million new houses, adding 29 per cent to the total stock, including a record 400,000 in one twelve-month period (1936–7).[96] The decline in union power following the failure of the General Strike in 1926, and subsequent anti-union legislation, made it possible, when the worst of the slump was over, for Britain to adopt new technologies with a speed impossible in the 1920s. Indeed for Britain the inter-war period culminated in a phase of innovatory expansion.[97] Numbers employed in the new electrical-electronics industry rose from 192,000 in 1930 to 248,000 in 1936 and Britain was the first country to create a National Grid. The chemical and petro-chemical industry expanded rapidly, with exports rising 18 per cent 1930–8. Employment in the aircraft industry had risen from 21,000 in 1930 to 35,000 in 1935, even before rearmament got under way. The number of cars produced more than doubled from 237,000 in 1930 to 508,000 in 1937.[98] These advances were all directly relevant to war-production capacity.

It is true that, in rearming, Britain experienced many set-backs and had to import machine-tools, for instance, from America, Hungary and even Germany itself.[99] But in certain key areas, especially aero-engines and above all radar, which was to prove of decisive importance both in air- and sea-power, Britain had important technological leads over Germany.[100] Rearmament accelerated in 1939 and by mid-1940 Britain was producing more aircraft, and training more air-crews, than

Germany. There were thus solid physical reasons for the transformation of Britain's mood in 1940. The emergence of Churchill, who
became Prime Minister and Minister of Defence (an important
conjunction Lloyd George had never been able to achieve in the First
World War) on 7 May, was thus natural. His resolution, energy and
oratory – he used this last gift to astonishing effect just at the point
when Hitler, his greatest rival in this respect, voluntarily relinquished
it – were a bonus. By the summer of 1940 he was at least as popular
in Britain as Pétain in France, and more popular than Hitler now was
in Germany.[101]

Churchill, though romantic and pugnacious, was not unrealistic.
He knew Britain, even with the Commonwealth, could not beat
Germany. He assumed that sooner or later the United States would
be obliged to intervene: therein lay his hope. Whatever he might say
in public he did not altogether rule out a tactical deal with Hitler. On
26 May 1940 Chamberlain's diary notes that Churchill told the War
Cabinet 'it was incredible that Hitler would consent to any terms
that we could accept though if we could get out of this jam by giving
up Malta and Gibraltar and some African colonies he would jump at
it'. The Cabinet Minutes record him saying 'if Herr Hitler was
prepared to make peace on the terms of the restoration of German
colonies and the overlordship of Central Europe', it would be
considered but 'it was quite unlikely he would make any such
offer'.[102] But this is the only evidence of his willingness to parley.
Hitler's peace offers did not get through. According to the diary of
'Chips' Channon MP, then in the government, the Foreign Office did
not even transcribe Hitler's speeches.[103]

Paradoxically, after the fall of France any possibility of a negotiated peace ended, and Churchill's political position improved
steadily. He got his first big cheer from the Conservative benches on
4 July when he announced the action against the French fleet at
Oran: hitherto, he noted, 'it was from the Labour benches that I
received the warmest welcome'. The death from cancer of Chamberlain removed his only really dangerous opponent, and on 9 October
Churchill was elected to succeed him as Conservative leader. But he
was neither able nor anxious to purge the regime of the elements who
had destroyed the Raj in India, neglected defence and appeased
Hitler. He told Cecil King, director of the *Daily Mirror*:

It was all very well to plead for a government excluding the elements that
had led us astray of recent years, but where was one to stop? They were
everywhere – not only in the political world, but among the fighting service
chiefs and the civil service chiefs. To clear all these out would be a task
impossible in the disastrous state in which we found ourselves. In any case if

one were dependent on the people who had been right in the last few years, what a tiny handful one would have to depend on! No: he was not going to run a government of revenge.[104]

Churchill's decision had important and baleful implications for the post-war composition and attitudes of the Conservative Party. But at the time it was prudent. Britain's foreign, defence and Common-wealth policies in the inter-war period had been conducted with reckless misjudgement, but Churchill himself had been a principal agent of them in the 1920s and though his record from 1930 onwards was virtually flawless, he rightly judged that an enquiry would absolve no one (least of all his new Labour allies) and would destroy the new and fragile unity over which he now presided. His magnanimity was justified. Despite the many disasters to come, Churchill's authority was never seriously challenged and of all the wartime governments his was, in combining authority with popular-ity, by far the strongest and most secure. It was this, more than any other factor, which allowed Britain to maintain the illusion of global presence and superpower status which was preserved until the Potsdam settlement in 1945.

Yet it was an illusion. The summer of 1940 brought the end of old Europe, sweeping off the stage of history the notion of a world managed by a concert of civilized European powers, within a frame of agreed international conventions and some system of moral absolutes. Britain survived but in a defensive posture, a prisoner of its relative impotence. In July, August and September 1940, Britain's fighter-squadrons and radar chains decisively defeated an attempt by Goering's *Luftwaffe* to destroy the RAF's airfields in south-east England, a necessary preliminary to any attempt to invade Britain. Thus Hitler forfeited his option of a conclusive campaign in the West. But Churchill, for his part, could carry out effective offensive operations only against Hitler's weak and embarrassing ally, Musso-lini. On 11 November the Italian fleet was crippled at Taranto by a naval air-strike, and thereafter the British never lost their general sea-control of the Mediterranean. Early in 1941 Britain began offensive operations against the Italians in Libya and proceeded to dismantle the whole of Mussolini's precarious empire in North-East Africa. But Britain's main engagement with the Nazis, the naval-air struggle to keep open the sea-lanes, was defensive. The one way of striking at Germany itself was through the air. Since fighter escorts for daylight bombing could not be provided, and since night-bombers could not guarantee to deliver their loads within a ten-mile radius of their targets, Churchill's only aggressive option was the virtually indiscriminate bombing of cities. On 8 July he wrote a sombre letter to his Minister of Aircraft Production, the newspaper proprietor Lord Beaverbrook:

When I look round to see how we can win the war I see that there is only one sure path. We have no Continental army which can defeat the German military power. The blockade is broken and Hitler has Asia and probably Africa to draw from. Should he be repulsed here or not try invasion, he will recoil eastward, and we have nothing to stop him. But there is one thing that will bring him back and bring him down, and that is an absolutely devastating, exterminating attack by very heavy bombers from this country upon the Nazi homeland.[105]

This letter is of great historical significance (it should be compared to Churchill's remarks on the corrupting effect of war on p. 13), marking the point at which the moral relativism of the totalitarian societies invaded the decision-making process of a major legitimate power. It is a matter of argument whether the British or the Germans first began the systematic bombing of civilian targets.[106] Hitler (like Lenin and Stalin) had from the very first practised and defended the use of terror to obtain any or all of his objectives. What is clear is that, long before the end of 1940, albeit under the verbal pretext of attacking 'strategic objectives', British bombers were being used on a great and increasing scale to kill and frighten the German civilian population in their homes. As the cabinet minuted on 30 October, 'the civilian population around the target areas must be made to feel the weight of the war'. The policy, initiated by Churchill, approved in cabinet, endorsed by parliament and, so far as can be judged, enthusiastically backed by the bulk of the British people – thus fulfilling all the conditions of the process of consent in a democracy under law – marked a critical stage in the moral declension of humanity in our times.

The adoption of terror-bombing was also a measure of Britain's desperation. The Treasury had warned the cabinet on 5 July 1939 that, without decisive American support, 'the prospects for a long war are becoming exceedingly grim'. Britain could not pursue Germany's economic policy of autarchy. As exports declined with the switch to war-production (taking 1938 as 100, British exports had fallen to 29 per cent by 1943, imports only to 77 per cent), gold and dollar reserves disappeared. The Roosevelt administration was verbally sympathetic to the Allies but in practice unhelpful. Pitiful French calls for help in early June 1940 were coldly dismissed by Cordell Hull as 'a series of extraordinary, almost hysterical appeals'. For some time Britain fared no better. Ambassador Joseph Kennedy, another Roosevelt campaign contributor, did not even provide verbal support: 'From the start I told them they could expect zero help. We had none to offer and I know we could not give it and, in the way of any material, we could not spare it.'[107] By the end of 1940 Britain had run out of convertible currency: she had only $12 million in her reserves, the lowest ever, and was obliged to suspend dollar purchases.[108]

On 11 March 1941 Congress enacted the Lend-Lease Act which permitted the President to 'sell, transfer title to, exchange, lease, lend or otherwise dispose of' material to any country whose defence was deemed by him vital to the defence of America. In theory this enabled Roosevelt to send Britain unlimited war-supplies without charge. But in practice Britain continued to pay for most of her arms, and in return for the agreement she virtually surrendered the remains of her export trade to the United States and (under the subsequent Master agreement of 23 February 1942) undertook to abandon Imperial Preference after the war, which for Cordell Hull had been throughout a more important foreign policy aim than the containment of totalitarian power.[109] Roosevelt's arms-supply arrangements with the Soviet Union were far more benevolent. Lend-Lease was important to Churchill simply because he believed it might tempt Hitler into conflict with the United States. Indeed, by the beginning of 1941, he recognized that the old European system of legitimacy had disappeared and that the only hope of restoring some system of law lay in Hitler's own miscalculations. Churchill was not to be disappointed.

ELEVEN

The Watershed Year

Just before dawn on 22 June 1941, German military radio inter-cepted an exchange between a Soviet forward unit and its army HQ. 'We are being fired on. What shall we do?' 'You must be insane. Why is your message not in code?'[1] Half an hour later, at 3.40 am, the Soviet Chief of Staff, G.K. Zhukov, who had received reports of German air attacks, telephoned Stalin at his villa at Kuntsevo, seven miles out of Moscow, where the dictator lived, worked and ate in a single room, sleeping on a sofa. When Zhukov announced that Russia was being invaded, there was nothing at the end of the line but a long silence and heavy breathing. Stalin finally told the general to go to the Kremlin and get his secretary to summon the Politburo. They met at 4.30, Stalin sitting pale and silent, an unlit pipe in his hands. At the Foreign Ministry, Molotov received the declaration of war from the Nazi ambassador and asked piteously, 'Have we really deserved this?' By noon, 1,200 Soviet aircraft had been destroyed on the ground. According to Nikita Khrushchev's account, Stalin gave way to hysteria and despair. Not until 3 July, eleven days later, could he bring himself to address the nation. Then he used a tone that was new to him: 'Brothers and sisters . . . my friends'.[2]

Everyone had warned Stalin of an impending Nazi attack. Churchill had sent him specific information, which had later been confirmed by the American embassy. On 15 May the Soviet spy in Tokyo, Richard Sorge, had produced details of the German invasion-plan and its correct date. Stalin also got circumstantial warnings from his own people, such as General Kirponos, commander in the Kiev district. Stalin refused to listen. He became furious if such advice was pressed. Admiral Kuznetsov later said it was dangerous to take the view invasion was likely even in private conversation with subordinates. Anyone who said so to Stalin himself, Khrushchev recalled, did so 'in fear and trepidation'.[3]

Stalin, who trusted nobody else, appears to have been the last human being on earth to trust Hitler's word. It was a case of wishful thinking. The Nazi–Soviet pact was of enormous benefit to Stalin. Though he later defended it solely as a temporary, tactical arrangement ('We secured our country peace for a year and a half and the opportunity of preparing our forces') he clearly hoped at the time that it would last indefinitely, or alternatively until the Germans and the West had mutually exhausted themselves in a prolonged war when, in accordance with his 1925 declaration, Russia could move in for the pickings. In the meantime the pact was of immense benefit to him. By mid-1940 he had recovered much of the territory Russia had lost in 1918–19. He had destroyed the structure of eastern Poland. In spring 1940, he had 15,000 Polish officers murdered, a third at Katyn near Smolensk, the rest in or near the Soviet concentration camps of Starobelsk and Ostachkov. It is possible that these mass killings were carried out at the suggestion of the Gestapo.[4] Nazi–Soviet security forces worked together very closely up to 22 June 1941. The NKVD handed over several hundred German nationals, chiefly Communists and Jews, to the Gestapo at this time.[5] The Nazis, in turn, helped Stalin to hunt down his own enemies. On 20 August 1940, after several attempts, he finally had Trotsky ice-axed to death in Mexico: as the latter had justly remarked, 'Stalin seeks to strike, not the ideas of his opponent, but at his skull.'[6] It was an approach he shared with Hitler.

Stalin rejoiced at the *Wehrmacht*'s triumph over France and promptly reorganized his own 13,000 tanks on the German pattern.[7] He took the view that the downfall of the democracies strengthened his claim for additional compensation in Eastern and Northern Europe, in return for giving Hitler a completely free hand in the West and Africa, and possibly in parts of the Middle East too. Hence when Molotov went to Berlin, 12–13 November 1940, to bring the Nazi–Soviet pact up to date, Stalin instructed him to demand, as primary requirements, Finland, Romania and Bulgaria, plus the Black Sea straits, to be allocated to the Soviet sphere of influence with, as ultimate demands, Hungary, Yugoslavia, western Poland, Sweden and a share in the Baltic Sea outlets.[8] Added up, they are not so very different to what Stalin demanded, and in most cases got, as his share of victory at the end of the Second World War. The Molotov 'package' testifies to the continuity of Soviet aims.

This list of Soviet interests was put forward on the assumption that Hitler was pursuing his acquisitive appetites chiefly in Western Europe, Africa and Asia, with the Middle East as his next strategic objective. That was a reasonable assumption at the time. Churchill's most ardent wish was that the Germans should hurl themselves upon the Soviet Union. His greatest fear was that Hitler would make the

Middle East his target. In the early months of 1941 that seemed the most likely outcome. Germany had been drawn into the Mediterranean war by Mussolini's greed and incompetence. He had invaded Greece on 28 October 1940 but the Greeks, with assistance from Britain, had humiliated and repulsed the invaders. On 9 December the British had opened an offensive in Libya, taking Benghazi on 6 February 1941.

Three days later, with furious reluctance, Hitler went to the assistance of his stricken ally, sending the Afrika Korps to Libya under General Rommel. Once committed to the theatre, the Germans moved with terrifying speed. On 28 February the Nazis, who already had Hungary and Romania as their puppets, moved into Bulgaria. Three weeks later they forced Yugoslavia to come to terms, and when a *coup d'état* in Belgrade removed the pro-Nazi government, issued ultimatums to both Yugoslavia and Greece. Rommel's first victory in North Africa took only eleven days, sending the British reeling back into Egypt. Yugoslavia collapsed after a week's fight on 17 April, Greece surrendering six days later. In eight days' desperate fighting in May, the British, already driven out of Greece, were shamed in Crete by German paratroopers. By the end of May, Cairo and the Suez Canal, the oilfields of northern Iraq, Persia and the Gulf, the world's largest refinery at Abadan and, not least, the sea and land routes to India, were all beginning to look vulnerable.

Hitler's southern venture had committed only a tiny fraction of his forces. His startling successes had been achieved at insignificant cost. Admiral Raeder and the naval high command begged him to launch a major thrust at the Middle East, which at that time was well within German capabilities. British naval, air and military power was thinly stretched over a vast area and vulnerable everywhere. Hitler's ally Japan was already contemplating an assault in the Far East. From what we now know, it seems almost certain that the Germans could have driven through the Suez barrier and on into the Indian Ocean, ready to link hands with the Japanese when they surged down into South-East Asia and up into the Bay of Bengal. Raeder's view was that such a *coup* would strike the British Empire 'a deadlier blow than the taking of London'. Hitler had 150 divisions, plus most of the *Luftwaffe*, arrayed in eastern Europe. Barely a quarter of these forces would have been enough to drive through to India.[9]

The notion opens up a disturbing line of speculation. A linkage of German and Japanese power in India would have given to the Japanese war-plan an element of long-term strategic logic which it never possessed. Anglo-Saxon power and influence would then have been eliminated from Asia, certainly for years, perhaps for good. Even Australia would have been in peril, and perhaps forced to make terms. South Africa, with its great mineral resources, would not then have been outside Hitler's range. Britain and America, instead of being able to draw resources from five-sixths of the world and its oceans, would have been largely confined to an Atlantic sphere of operations. Victory, in these circumstances, would have seemed a wearily distant if not unattainable object, and the case for coming to terms with Hitler must then have seemed, even to Churchill, almost irresistible. Here we have one of the great 'ifs' of history.

But Hitler, without hesitation, rejected the glittering Alexandrine opportunity. He clung to his view that the 'real' war, the war he had always intended to wage, was against Russia. That was what fate and the ineluctable logic of race-destiny had placed him in charge of Germany to accomplish. The destruction of Russia was not, indeed, to be the end of the story. But without it the story had no meaning, and until it had been brought about Germany could not perform its preordained world-role. He was impatient to get on. On 31 July 1940 he told General Halder that Britain's hope of survival lay in America and Russia. To destroy Russia was to eliminate both, since it would give Japan freedom of action to engage America. He seems to have thought that Roosevelt would be ready to intervene in 1942, and he wanted Russia removed from the equation before this happened. That, as he saw it, was the proper sequence of events. He told his generals on 9 January 1941 that once Russia was beaten Germany could absorb its resources and so become 'invulnerable'. She would then have the power to wage wars against whole continents. With Japan tying down America in the Pacific, he would launch a three-pronged pincer, through the Caucasus, North Africa and the Levant, which would take Germany into Afghanistan and then into the British Empire at its heart, in India. Such a strategic conception was too risky with Russia on the flank.[10]

Hence within a few days of Pétain's armistice, Hitler put his staff to work planning the Russian campaign.[11] His original idea was to launch it that autumn, and he was only with great difficulty persuaded to drop so risky a scheme – the army, the generals pleaded, must have the whole of the dry season, from early May onwards, to engulf and annihilate Russian military power before the snows came. He took the final decision to strike in December 1940, after the re-election of Roosevelt, to him an event of peculiar ill-omen, and after Molotov had presented Stalin's list of 'interests' which Hitler said made the Nazi–Soviet pact untenable 'even as a marriage of convenience'. Thereafter he did not waver from his resolve to exterminate Bolshevism at the earliest opportunity. The descent into the Mediterranean was a regrettable sideshow, made necessary by Mussolini's folly. He blamed it for what he later called

'a catastrophic delay in the beginning of the war against Russia . . . .
We should have been able to attack Russia starting 15 May 1941 and
. . . end the campaign before the winter.'[12] The assault was launched
at the earliest possible moment after the southern campaign was
over.

Surveying this watershed year of 1941, from which mankind has
descended into its present predicament, the historian cannot but be
astounded by the decisive role of individual will. Hitler and Stalin
played chess with humanity. In all essentials, it was Stalin's personal
insecurity, his obsessive fear of Germany, which led him to sign the
fatal pact, and it was his greed and illusion – no one else's – which
kept it operative, a screen of false security behind which Hitler
prepared his murderous spring. It was Hitler, no one else, who
determined on a war of annihilation against Russia, cancelled then
postponed it, and reinstated it as the centrepiece of his strategy, as,
how and when he chose. Neither man represented irresistible or even
potent historical forces. Neither at any stage conducted any process
of consultation with their peoples, or even spoke for self-appointed
collegiate bodies. Both were solitary and unadvised in the manner in
which they took these fateful steps, being guided by personal
prejudices of the crudest kind and by their own arbitrary visions.
Their lieutenants obeyed blindly or in apathetic terror, and the vast
nations over which they ruled seem to have had no choice but to
stumble in their wake towards mutual destruction. We have here the
very opposite of historical determinism – the apotheosis of the single
autocrat. Thus it is, when the moral restraints of religion and
tradition, hierarchy and precedent, are removed, the power to
suspend or unleash catastrophic events does not devolve on the
impersonal benevolence of the masses but falls into the hands of men
who are isolated by the very totality of their evil natures.

Hitler's decision to invade Russia was the most fateful of his
career. It destroyed his regime, and him with it. It was also one of the
most important in modern history, for it brought Soviet totalitarianism right into the heart of Europe. But it was a gamble that might
have succeeded. It is vital to grasp why it did not do so. Hitler
claimed early in 1945 that the five or six weeks' delay in launching
the invasion accounted for his failure to take Moscow and destroy
Stalin's regime before the winter came. But at the time he did not feel
constrained by so tight a timetable. The truth is, he grievously
underestimated Russian military capacity. There is an old and wise
diplomatic saying: 'Russia is never as strong as she looks. Russia is
never as weak as she looks.' Hitler ignored it. He was not alone in his
contempt for the Red Army. As noted, the British and French general
staffs rated its performance below Poland's. This view appeared to

be confirmed by the Finnish campaign. It was generally believed that the purge of 1937–8 had destroyed its morale. Admiral Canaris, head of the German intelligence service, the *Abwehr*, believed Heydrich's claim that his organization had deliberately framed Tukhachevsky and all the other able Soviet officers.[13] It was partly on the basis of Canaris's misleading estimates that Hitler thought the Russian campaign would be an easier proposition than the conquest of France. The Red Army, he told the Bulgarian Ambassador, Dragonoff, was 'no more than a joke'. It would be 'cut to pieces' and 'throttled in sections'. In December 1940 he estimated that 'in three weeks we shall be in St Petersburg'.[14] Though the Japanese were his allies, he made no attempt to possess himself of their far more sober estimates of Russian fighting capacity, especially in tank-warfare, based on their bitter experience in May–June 1939. German staff-work, which had been very thorough as well as brilliant in preparation for the French campaign, took the Soviet campaign lightly – there was a feeling of euphoria that Germany had at last broken out of the iron 'strategic triangle' formed by France–Poland–Czechoslovakia, and that it could now roam freely. General Marcks, the chief planner, thought it would require nine weeks at best, seventeen at worst, to destroy Soviet military resistance. The argument that Russia would withdraw into her vastness, as in 1812, was rejected on the grounds that Stalin would have to defend the industrial regions west of the Dnieper. It would prove beyond her organizational capacity to bring into play her 9–12 million reserves: Marcks thought that the Russians would at no point possess even numerical superiority.[15]

This was exactly the advice Hitler wanted, since it reinforced his belief he could wage war on the cheap. The *Blitzkrieg* was as much an economic as a military concept, based on Hitler's view that Germany could not sustain prolonged war until she possessed herself of Russia's riches. 'Operation Barbarossa', as it was called, was to be the last *Blitzkrieg*. It was cut to the bone. Even in 1941 Hitler was not prepared to put the German economy on a full war-footing. Since the occupation of Prague he had become suspicious of the will of the German people to wage total war, and he was reluctant therefore to drive women into the war-factories or to cut civilian production and consumption more than was absolutely necessary to attain his military objectives. As a result, Barbarossa was seriously underpowered in terms of the magnitude of its objectives: there were elements of 153 divisions involved, but only 3,580 tanks, 7,184 guns and 2,740 aircraft. For purposes of comparison, the Soviet offensive in January 1945 on the Berlin front alone employed 6,250 tanks, 7,560 aircraft and no less than 41,600 guns.[16] Much of the German transport was horse-powered and lack of mobility proved an increasing handicap as the campaign proceeded. The Germans found themselves fighting a Forties war with late-Thirties weaponry, and not enough even of that.

The defects were most pronounced in the air, where Goering's *Luftwaffe*, which had already revealed grave weaknesses during the Battle of Britain campaign, failed either to provide effective ground support over the whole front or to bomb Stalin's war-factories. Goering proved an increasingly idle and incompetent leader; both his chief technical officer and his staff chief were eventually driven to suicide by the exposure of their bunglings.[17] But the responsibility was also Hitler's, for failing to provide aircraft in sufficient quantity. Equally to blame was Nazi procurement policy, which was statist and bureaucratic and totally unable to produce a satisfactory heavy bomber. It is a significant fact that all the best Second World War aircraft, such as the British Mosquito and the American Mustang (P. 51), were the products of private initiative rather than government and air staff.[18] Hitler allowed the *Luftwaffe* to become the most party-dominated and totalitarian of his armed services, and dearly did he pay for it.

He also contributed his own quota of mistakes, which grew progressively as the campaign proceeded. Barbarossa was over-optimistically conceived, and its crushing early successes led Hitler to compound his error by assuming the campaign was nearly over. Russia had overwhelming weapons superiority at the start of the war: seven to one in tanks, four or five to one in aircraft.[19] But Stalin's refusal to heed warnings of the attack, his insistence that Soviet units be placed in strength right up against the frontier, and hold their ground at any cost, led to staggering losses. Before the end of the year the Germans had taken 3.5 million prisoners and killed or wounded another million.[20] Most of these big German successes came in the first month of the campaign. By 14 July Hitler was convinced that the war was won, and gave orders for war production to be switched from army to naval and air force orders.[21] Tank production actually slowed to one-third of the 600 tanks a month originally scheduled. He hoped to start pulling back some infantry divisions at the end of August, with armour following in September, leaving only fifty to sixty divisions to hold a line Astrakhan–Archangel, and to conduct punitive raids to and over the Urals. Then he would begin his descent on the Middle East and on into India.

This appreciation proved absurdly sanguine. In the second half of July Hitler decided, for economic reasons, to plunge into the Ukraine. The drive to Moscow was put off for two months. It did not actually begin until 2 October. The same day General Guderian, Hitler's best tank commander, noticed the first snowflakes. The heavy rains began four days later. The big frosts followed early, in the second week of November. The offensive slowed down. German tanks got to within twenty miles of the centre of Moscow in the north, and within thirty miles on the west. But the temperature dropped progressively, first to 20, then 60 below zero. The report Quartermaster-General Wagner produced on 27 November was summed up by General Halder in one sentence: 'We have reached the end of our human and material forces.'[22] Then, on 6 December without warning and in considerable strength, the Russians counter-attacked.

At this stage it was clear Barbarossa was a failure. A completely new strategy was needed. Hitler's response was to sack Brauchitsch and take over operational command himself. He immediately issued orders forbidding tactical withdrawals. This quickly became a settled policy, inhibiting any kind of flexibility in manœuvre. The defensive battles in which the *Wehrmacht* then engaged, through the worst of the winter, cost it over a million casualties, 31.4 per cent of the strength of the eastern army. It never recovered its *élan*. The era of the *Blitzkrieg* was over, two years after it began. The offensive was resumed in the spring. On 21 August the Germans reached the summits of the Caucasus, though they never got to the oilfields to the south. Two days later they penetrated Stalingrad on the Volga. But by then Germany's offensive capacity, in the widest sense, was exhausted. The future consisted entirely of bitter defensive warfare.

The switch from attack to defence was marked by Hitler's increasing interference in the details of the campaign. He now regularly gave direct orders to army groups, to the staffs of particular sectors, even to divisional and regimental commanders. There were furious rows with senior officers, many of whom were dismissed; one was shot. In the winter of 1941, wrote Goebbels, Hitler 'very much aged'. 'His underestimation of the enemy potentialities,' noted General Halder, 'always his shortcoming, is now gradually assuming grotesque forms.'[23] He sacked the commander of one army group, taking over detailed control himself. He refused to speak to Jodl. Eventually he quarrelled with all his commanders-in-chief, all his chiefs-of-staff, eleven out of eighteen of his field-marshals, twenty-one out of forty full generals, and nearly all the commanders of all three sectors of the Russian front.[24]

But Hitler's personal mismanagement of the campaign was not the only, or indeed the chief, reason for his failure in Russia. The cause went deeper, to the very conception of the war, to the roots indeed of Hitler's whole political purpose. In attacking Russia, he was trying to do two quite different things simultaneously, to achieve a military victory and to set in motion an enormous enterprise of social engineering. The two aims were mutually incompatible. It is not of course unusual for a military campaign to have an accompanying political purpose, to be a 'war of liberation'. That indeed would have made sense in 1941. Stalin ruled by terror alone. His regime was universally unpopular at home, and hated and feared throughout Europe. There were many in Germany, and still more outside Germany, who wished to view a war against Bolshevism as a crusade, waged on behalf of dozens of oppressed European peoples, from the Arctic to the Black Sea, who had been plundered and oppressed by half-Asiatic Russians. Taking part in Barbarossa were more than twelve divisions from Romania, two from Finland, three from Hungary, three from Slovakia; to which were later added three Italian and one Spanish division.[25] Many of these soldiers were volunteers. In addition, there were many Russians themselves, at home and abroad, who saw the occasion of Hitler's assault as an opportunity to seize their own freedom, and destroy the regime which had brought more than twenty years of misery and cost over 15 million lives.

Hitler might have put himself at the head of such a crusade. But to have done so would have been false to himself. Hitler was not in the business of liberation. Like Stalin, he was in the business of slavery. The accident of race made them opponents, and pitted their regimes against each other. But in essential respects they were fellow-ideologues, pursuing Utopias based on a fundamental division of mankind into élites and helots. Hitler's aims in Russia were in no sense idealistic. They were narrowly and ruthlessly acquisitive. He tried to explain them, on 30 March 1941, to a meeting of 250 senior German officers of all three services.[26] The war against France, he said, had been a 'conventional' war. So was the whole of the war against the West. It was military in character. The rules of war applied. But in the East things were to be quite different. Against Russia Germany would wage total war. 'We have a war of annihilation on our hands.' The purpose of the campaign was to be extermination, expansion and settlement on a colonial basis. The generals do not seem to have grasped the enormity of what Hitler proposed.[27] That did not surprise him. He was prepared for it. That was why he had embarked on a vast expansion of the ss, which was now to fulfil the real purpose for which he had created it. He formed bodies of 'specialists', 3,000 in each, which were termed *Einsatzgruppen*, and which moved in the wake of the regular army units, to begin the most audacious exercise in social engineering ever conceived.

Thus poor, tortured, misruled Eastern Europe, which had already for an entire generation borne the brunt of Lenin's ideological adventurism, and Stalin's brutally magnified version of its worst aspects, was to be the theatre of yet another totalitarian experiment.

The military object of Barbarossa was incidental. The real aim was to exterminate Bolshevism and its 'Jewish catchment area', to acquire territory for colonial settlement, to enslave the Slav masses in four 'Reich Commissariats' (termed Baltic, Ukraine, 'Muscovy' and Caucasus), and to create an autarchic economic system which would be proof against any blockade the Anglo-Saxon powers might impose.[28]

Hitler's ultimate aim was to create a German *Volk* of 250 million. He said that he proposed settling 100 million Germans on the great plains to the west of the Urals. In 1941 he envisaged that over the next decade the first 20 million would move east. Though he saw the colonization process clearly, he was vague about where the settlers were to come from. Those eligible and willing to settle, the *Volksdeutsche* from south-east Europe, numbered only 5 million, perhaps 8 million at most. His colleague Alfred Rosenberg considered the idea of 'drafting' Scandinavian, Dutch and English settlers, being racially approximate to Germans, when the war was won. Some aspects of this great population transfer, to be the most formidable and decisive in history, were determined in meticulous detail. There was to be polygamy and a free choice of women for servicemen with decorations. The Crimea, after being 'cleansed' of Slavs and Jews, was to be turned into a gigantic German spa under its old Greek name of Tauria, populated by a mass transfer of peasants from the South Tyrol.[29] Over vast areas of the Ukraine and south European Russia, a new *Volk* civilization was planned. As Hitler described it:

The area must lose the character of the Asiatic steppe. It must be Europeanized! . . . The 'Reich peasant' is to live in outstandingly beautiful settlements. The German agencies and authorities are to have wonderful buildings, the governors palaces. Around each city, a ring of lovely villages will be placed to within 30 or 40 kilometers . . . . That is why we are now building the large traffic arteries on the southern tip of the Crimea, out to the Caucasus mountains. Around these traffic strands, the German cities will be placed, like pearls on a string, and around the cities the German settlements will lie. For we will not open up *Lebensraum* for ourselves by entering the old, godforsaken Russian holes! The German settlements must be on an altogether higher level![30]

As Hitler's vision expanded, in the heady days of 1941, it came to embrace all Europe. Belgium, the Netherlands, Luxembourg, the whole of France north of the Somme were to be incorporated in a Greater Germany, the names of the cities being changed – Nancy would become Nanzig, Besançon Bisanz. Trondheim would become a major German city and naval base of 250,000 inhabitants. The Alps would be the boundary between 'the German Empire of the

North', with a new 'Germania' as its capital, and 'the Roman Empire of the South'. The Pope would be hanged in full pontificals in St Peter's Square. Strasbourg Cathedral would be turned into a giant 'Monument to the Unknown Soldier'. New crops, such as perennial rye, would be invented. He would forbid smoking, make vegetarianism compulsory, 'revive the Cimbrian art of knitting', appoint a 'Special Commissioner for the Care of Dogs' and an 'Assistant Secretary for Defence Against Gnats and Insects'.[31]

Most of these 'constructive' proposals had to wait. But from 22 June 1941 onwards, the preliminary work of destruction could begin. The 'Final Solution' for the Jews was organically linked to the Russian settlement programme. We shall examine that in the next chapter. In military terms, what was important in 1941 was the decision, embodied in orders issued by Heydrich in May and confirmed by a 'Führer's decree' exempting from punishment members of the forces who carried them out, to categorize Communist officials along with Jews, gypsies and 'Asiatic inferiors' as targets for immediate extermination. The 'Commissar Order' of 6 June 1941 insisted that Soviet functionaries 'are in principle to be disposed of by gunshot immediately'. 'Guidelines' issued just prior to Barbarossa called for 'ruthless and energetic measures against Bolshevistic agitators, guerrillas, saboteurs, Jews and total elimination of all active and passive resistance'.[32] In practice, the *Einsatzgruppen* rounded up all educated men and social leaders in areas occupied by the Germans, and began to shoot them in large numbers. About 500,000 European Russian Jews were shot in 1941, and perhaps as many Russians. Otto Ohlendorf, one of the *gruppen* commanders, admitted at Nuremberg that his unit alone murdered 90,000 men, women and children in 1941. By July, the Russian nation as a whole began to grasp the horrifying fact that they faced what appeared to be a war of extermination.

The result was the salvation of Stalin and his regime. By the time Stalin finally brought himself to speak to the Russian people on 3 July, it was clear that he could turn the struggle into the Great Patriotic War. He compared Hitler with Napoleon. He called for guerrilla warfare and a vast 'scorched earth' policy. This appeal met with some response. For the first time since 1918, the practice of religion was generally permitted. This was perhaps the biggest single factor in the recovery of a national identity. Some prisoners from the concentration camps were allowed out to form front-line 'punishment battalions'. In *Doctor Zhivago*, Boris Pasternak later gave a moving description of how the inmates welcomed the war.[33] Stalin even indulged in a little participatory 'democracy', leaving his vaulted Kremlin study, where he sat with Lenin's death-mask at his elbow, and addressing the Soviet in the safety of the Moscow underground on 6 November. Characteristically he told them a lie, that Russia had 'several times fewer tanks than the Germans': in fact the Red Army had started with 13,000.[34] The next day he spoke in Red Square, invoking the saints and warriors of imperial Russia: 'Let the manly images of our great ancestors — Alexander Nevsky, Dimitry Donskoy, Kuzma Minin, Dimitry Pozharsky, Alexander Suvorov and Mikhail Kutozov — inspire you in this war!'[35]

All the same, the regime came close to destruction in November 1941. Most government departments were evacuated to Kuibyshev on the Volga. There was a general burning of archives which could not be carried away. Once the news spread there were riots. Mobs broke into the food shops. Party officials tore up their cards and prepared to go into hiding. Only the knowledge that Stalin himself was staying in Moscow prevented dissolution.[36]

Stalin stayed for exactly the same reason Hitler concentrated all power in his hands: he did not trust the generals, and he wished to maintain personal control of the terror. It was the only way he knew how to rule. Though he played the patriotic card for all it was worth, he never relaxed the dead weight of fear he imposed on everyone. The army was held together by bonds of dread as well as loyalty. His right-hand man was his former secretary, Colonel-General L. Z. Mekhlis, now head of the Army Political Directorate, who had carried out thousands of executions during the purges. Stalin had sent him to Finland during the débâcle there in the winter of 1939–40, where he had dismissed, arrested and shot failed commanders. Under Leninist military law it was a crime to be taken prisoner. Mekhlis had arranged a grisly scene in March 1940, when thousands of returning POWs were greeted in Leningrad with a banner, 'The Fatherland Greets its Heroes', and marched straight through to railway sidings where they were hustled into cattle-trucks for the camps.[37] Under Stalin's personal orders, Mekhlis and his assistant Army Commissar E. A. Shchadenko continued to arrest, imprison and shoot selected officers throughout 1940 and 1941. The Army Group Commander in the West, D. G. Pavlov, was murdered for 'treachery'. There was another big batch of shootings in October 1941 and again in July 1942, the latter to forestall a *coup*.[38] Lesser fry were dealt with by a new and terrifying Field Security Force, Smersh, which co-operated with police blocking-battalions behind the front to prevent any retreat. Relatives of those known to have become POWs were made liable to long terms of imprisonment.[39] With the prospect of death on all sides of him, the ordinary Russian soldier had no real alternative but to fight to the last.

Anyone whose loyalty was suspect in the slightest, even in theory, was treated like an animal. Political prisoners in areas open to the German advance were massacred.[40] Stalin engaged in defensive social engineering on a scale only marginally less ambitious than Hitler's wild plans. The Germans of the Volga German Autonomous Republic, numbering 1,650,000, were hustled into Siberia. They were followed by other entire nations: the Chechens, the Ingushes, the Karachays, the Balkars of the Northern Caucasus, the Kalmyks from the north-west Caspian, the Crimean Tatars, the Meskhetians of the Soviet–Turkish border. Some of these genocidal-type crimes were enacted long after the danger from the Germans was past. The Chechens were moved as late as 23 February 1944, being carried off in American trucks supplied under Lend-Lease.[41]

Stalin's ruthlessness, combined with Hitler's folly, ensured Soviet survival. Yet as generalissimos, the two men were strangely alike, in their total indifference to casualties, however calamitous, in their refusal to visit the fronts (in both cases for security reasons) and in their personal direction of the campaigns. Stalin, like Hitler, sometimes deployed regiments himself. On 30 November 1941 Stalin received a report that the town of Dedovo-Dedovsk, twenty miles west of Moscow, had fallen. He ordered Zhukov, plus two army commanders, Rokossovsky and Govorov, to assemble a rifle company and two tanks, and retake it personally.[42] But Stalin added an extra dimension of secrecy of which even the suspicious Hitler was incapable. From the point when he recovered his nerve, early in July 1941, Stalin began quietly to accumulate secret military reserves of his own, the *Stavka*, which he commanded personally and whose very existence was concealed from the army commanders, no matter how senior.[43] The Leninist system of political control of the army, with its duplicated chains of command, made this possible. At any point in the war, therefore, Stalin had his own private army, which he directed personally, either to launch unexpected offensives, and thus retain control of the battle, or to overawe his generals, as Hitler did with the SS. He remembered Lenin's dictum: 'The unstable rear of Denikin, Kolchak, Wrangel and the imperialist agents predetermined their defeat.' Stalin 'stabilized' his rear with his *Stavka*, party and NKVD troops, and with an organization termed *Tsentral'nyi Shtab* controlling the guerrillas, which he himself commanded.[44]

In this personal struggle for survival, Stalin was greatly helped at every stage by the Western democracies. It can be said that, if Hitler's policy saved the regime, Churchill and Roosevelt saved Stalin himself. When Hitler attacked, there were some cool heads who argued that Western aid to Russia should be on a basis of simple material self-interest, highly selective and without any moral or political commitment. It should, George Kennan minuted to the State Department, 'preclude anything which might identify us politically or ideologically with the Russian war effort'. Russia should be treated as a 'fellow-traveller' rather than 'a political associate'.[45] This was sensible. On a moral plane Stalin was no better than Hitler; worse in some ways. It was practical advice too, because it formed a framework within which bargains could be struck, and it raised no assumptions that Russia would be consulted about the disposition of the post-war world.

Britain had no obligations whatever to Russia. Up to the very moment of the German invasion, the Soviet regime had done its best to assist Hitler's war-effort, fulfilling its raw-materials delivery contracts scrupulously. As late as early June 1941 the RAF was still contemplating bombing the Baku oilfields, which were supplying the *Wehrmacht*.[46] But at this point Churchill was close to despair about the long-term prospects for the war, and the likelihood of a successful German thrust right into the Middle East. When Hitler turned on Russia instead, his relief was so intense that he reacted in an irrational manner. Here was the opportunity to combine Anglo-Saxon industrial power with Russian manpower, to bleed the German army to death! It was exactly the same impulse which had prompted his Gallipoli scheme in the Great War, whose success, he still believed, would have altered the whole course of world history. The evening of the German invasion Churchill, without consulting his War cabinet, committed Britain to a full working partnership with Russia. Eden was even more enthusiastic, under the influence of his secretary, Oliver Harvey, a pro-Soviet Cambridge intellectual, who regarded the Gulag Archipelago as the necessary price for Russian modernization.[47] To launch the new alliance Churchill chose as his emissary his friend Lord Beaverbrook. He brushed aside pleas from the specialists of the British embassy, who shared Kennan's view, and who wanted hard bargaining, 'trading supplies against detailed information about Russian production and resources'. Beaverbrook laid down the policy as 'to make clear beyond a doubt the British and American intention to satisfy Russian needs to the utmost in their power, whether the Russians gave anything or not. It was to be a Christmas Tree party.'[48]

The aid was given unconditionally, being passed directly to Stalin's personal autocracy. No questions were ever asked about what he did with it. The Soviet people were never officially informed of its existence. Thus Britain and America supplied the means by which Stalin bolstered his personal power, and he repaid them in the ready coin of his soldiers' lives. Churchill and Roosevelt were content with this arrangement. Among Stalin's gifts was an enduring capacity to pose as a moderate. It served him well throughout the period 1921 to 1929, when step by step he fought his way to solitary eminence. He was always the moderate then, dealing with 'extremists' of both wings in turn. He posed as the moderate now. Churchill and Eden, Roosevelt and his envoy Averell Harriman, all accepted the view that Stalin was a statesman of the centre who, with considerable difficulty, kept his violent and fanatical followers under restraint. Stalin fed this fantasy with occasional dark hints. (Curiously enough Hitler, who had used the same tactics in the past, was taken in also; so was Mussolini.)[49] Thus Stalin and his autocracy were the sole beneficiaries of democratic aid.

How critical Western assistance was to Soviet survival cannot be determined until scholars get access to the Soviet archives, and must await the demise of the system. Under carefully controlled conditions, Stalin was fed in spectacular detail knowledge of German dispositions and plans on the Eastern Front acquired through the Enigma/Ultra intelligence system.[50] This had a major direct bearing on the campaign from 1942 onwards and helped to make possible Stalin's spectacular victories in 1943–4, for which he has been given credit. Of more decisive importance in the first instance, however, were the military supplies rushed to Archangel and Murmansk in the first autumn of the invasion, which made possible Stalin's 6 December offensive and tipped the balance during that first desperate winter. They included 200 modern fighter aircraft, intended originally for Britain's highly vulnerable base in Singapore, which had virtually no modern fighters at all. The diversion of these aircraft (plus tanks) to Russia sealed the fate of Singapore.[51] Thus, by one of the great ironies of history, Churchill, the last major British imperialist, may have sacrificed a liberal empire in order to preserve a totalitarian one.

The opening of the Soviet counter-offensive on 6 December 1941 marked the point at which Hitler lost control of the war. He had dominated world politics since he marched into the Rhineland in 1936, always keeping the initiative in his solitary hands. Now, suddenly, he was the servant of events rather than their master. Perhaps in unconscious recognition of this sombre fact – or rather to conceal it – he took five days later a decision of such insensate folly as to stagger belief.

One of the chief mysteries of Hitler's entire career is his failure to co-ordinate his war plans with the Japanese. They had been allies since the Anti-Comintern Pact of 25 November 1936. As 'have not' powers with expansionary aims they had a great deal in common, including a short-term military capacity of tremendous vehemence and almost insuperable long-term logistical weaknesses (neither had oil or access to it). For either to succeed they had to act together. Yet neither did so. Hitler gave Japan only two days' warning of his pact with Stalin in August 1939, though it made complete nonsense of the Anti-Comintern pledges.[52] When he decided to reverse the policy in 1941, he made the Japanese look even bigger fools. He knew that the Japanese ruling élite was divided between a 'Northern' strategy of attacking Russia, and a 'Southern' strategy against the old empires. Japan signed the Axis Pact on 27 September 1940. If Hitler drove first through the Middle East against Britain in 1941, then a Japanese 'Southern' strategy was to his advantage. If, as he eventually decided, he went first against Russia, then his interest was to persuade Japan to opt for a Northern attack. Early in April 1941 the Japanese Foreign Minister, Matsuoka Yosuke, who was strongly pro-Axis, was in Berlin. Hitler told him nothing about his plan to attack Russia. Matsuoka went from Berlin to Moscow and on 13 April signed a neutrality pact with Stalin, so clearing the way for a 'Southern' strategy. When Hitler invaded Russia eight weeks later, Matsuoka naïvely confessed to his colleagues: 'I concluded a neutrality pact because I thought that Germany and Russia would not go to war. If I had known they would go to war ... I would not have concluded the Neutrality Pact.'[53] Thereafter Japan moved towards a 'Southern' strategy, and by October Stalin's spy Sorge told him it was safe to move some of his twenty Eastern divisions to the Western front, where they arrived in time for the December counter-offensive.

Despite this, Hitler cleared the way for Japan's attack on America by allowing Ribbentrop, on 21 November, to give Japan an assurance that Germany would join her in war on the USA even though not required to do so under the Axis Pact.[54] From Hitler's viewpoint the Japanese surprise attack on Britain and America, at 2 am on 8 December, could not have been more ill-timed, for it came just two days after the sinister news of Stalin's offensive. Nevertheless, on 11 December, Hitler declared war on America. Ribbentrop summoned the US Chargé, Leland Morris, kept him standing, harangued him furiously and finally screamed: '*Ihr Präsident hat diesen Krieg gewollt; jetzt hat er ihn!*' (Your President wanted this war. Now he has it), and then stamped off.[55]

In fact it is most unlikely Roosevelt could have persuaded Congress to make war on Germany had not Hitler taken the initiative, still less to give the defeat of the Nazis priority. On 22 June 1941 Hitler took a tremendous gamble which did not come off, and thereafter the best outcome of the war he could hope for was a stalemate. But on 11 December 1941 he took a decision which made his defeat certain. The only short-term advantage he gained was the chance to launch a U-boat offensive in the Atlantic before America was organized to meet it. He said to Ribbentrop: 'The chief reason [for war] is that the US is already shooting at our ships.'[56] But Hitler's failure to create the 100-strong fleet of ocean-going submarines his admirals had demanded in 1939 blunted this preemptive blow; only sixty were available in December 1941, the rest were not ready until the end of 1942, by which time Allied countermeasures had made a German Atlantic victory impossible. In every other respect, short- and still more long-term, the war with America was to Germany's overwhelming disadvantage. Hitler's gesture was no more than a piece of bravado. He told the Reichstag: 'We will always strike first. We will always deal the first blow.' It was an attempt to persuade the Germans, the world, perhaps even himself, that he, Europe's leading statesman, was still in a position to dictate global events. It did the opposite, signalling the end of European hegemony and introducing the age of the extra-European superpowers.

Japan's entry into the conflict was equally short-sighted. But the background to it was more complicated. It contained elements of what might be termed rational hysteria. As the American Ambassador Joseph Grew put it, 'a national psychology of desperation develops into a determination to risk all'.[57] The Japanese were uneasily aware of their short staying-power in war, illustrated by the Russo–Japanese war of 1904–5, which began with brilliant Japanese victories but developed into a war of attrition from which Japan was, in effect, rescued by the intervention of the Great Powers. The war with China, begun in 1937, had proved a similar illusion. By 1940 Japan had occupied all China's great cities, seized the modern sector of her economy, and controlled all her main rail, road and river communications: yet the war had stalemated, China was unconquerable, all Japan's economic dilemmas remained – had, indeed, been aggravated by the effort of the China struggle. It was not a case of Japan swallowing China, as the army hotheads had predicted, but of China, in its gigantic, wallowing helplessness, swallowing Japan. The almost undefended French, British and Dutch empires of South-East Asia and the Indies, the American Philippines, the vastness of the Pacific, offered similar temptations and dangers. The point did not escape even the limited intelligence of the Tenno Hirohito. When on 5 September 1941, the two Chiefs of Staff, General Sugiyama and Admiral Nagano, told him the 'Southern strategy' could be accomplished in a ninety-day war of lightning conquest, he replied that Sugiyama had said the same thing about the China war, now three years old and unfinished. Sugiyama: 'China is a continent. The "south" consists mostly of islands.' The Tenno: 'If the interior of China is huge, is not the Pacific

Ocean even bigger? How can you be sure that war will end in three months?'[58]

There was no answer to this question. As Admiral Nagano put it: 'If I am told to fight regardless of consequences, I shall run wild considerably for six months or a year. But I have utterly no confidence in the second and third years.'[59] The ablest of the naval commanders, Admiral Yamamoto, said that Japan could not hope to win a war against Britain and America, however spectacular her initial victories. Colonel Iwakuro, a logistics expert, told one of the regular 'liaison conferences', where the top military and government bosses met, that the differentials in American and Japanese production were as follows: steel twenty to one, oil one hundred to one, coal ten to one, aircraft five to one, shipping two to one, labour-force five to one, overall ten to one. Yet to put forward such views, even in the privileged secrecy of the liaison conference, was to risk assassination or removal. It was contrary to the relativistic code of 'honour', now the dominant impulse in Japanese public life. After Yamamoto expressed his opinion, he had to be given a sea-command to get him out of range of the killers. The Colonel was promptly sent to Cambodia. Ambassador Grew reported (22 October 1940) that the Emperor was told plainly he would be murdered if he opposed the war policy.[60]

The result was to precipitate into power the reckless, indeed the emotionally unstable, such as Matsuoka. This man had been head of the Manchurian railways, prominent in the army–business network which provoked and profited from the China war. He actually embodied what was later to become the largely mythic concept of the 'military-industrial complex'. It was he who gave the 'Southern strategy' some kind of political and economic rationale, inventing the phrase 'the Great East-Asian Co-Prosperity Sphere'.[61] He epitomized the schizophrenia of Japan, the jostling incompatibility of new and old and east and west, combining Catholicism and Shinto, sophisticated business techniques and utter barbarism. He greatly resented it when, after signing the Russian agreement, Stalin (characteristically) waltzed him round the room saying, 'We are all Asiatics here – all Asiatics!' Hitler told Mussolini suspiciously that Matsuoka, though Christian, 'sacrificed to pagan gods' and combined 'the hypocrisy of an American Bible missionary with the craftiness of a Japanese Asiatic'. Roosevelt, who, thanks to 'Operation Magic' which cracked the Japanese codes, read some of Matsuoka's messages, thought them 'the product of a mind which is deeply disturbed'. This view was shared by Matsuoka's colleagues. After one liaison conference the Navy Minister asked, 'The Foreign Minister is insane, isn't he?'[62]

In Japan's governing atmosphere of heroic anarchy, however, madness went almost unnoticed. Once embarked on the China campaign, Japan had become morally isolated from the rest of the world. Hitler's destruction of France tipped the balance in favour of temptation. As the British Ambassador, Sir Robert Craigie, put it, 'How ... could Japan expect Hitler to divide the spoils with them unless she had been actively associated in the spoliation?'[63] This was the background to the Tripartite Pact with Germany and Italy which Matsuoka signed in September 1940. The way in which Japanese policy was determined inhibited sensible discussion. Democracy had been killed in 1938. The parties were abolished in 1940, being replaced by the Imperial Rule Assistance Association.[64] The cabinet ceased to function on important issues. Decisions were supposed to be taken at the liaison conferences, attended by the Tenno, the premier and Foreign Secretary, the two Service ministers (sometimes chiefs of staff also) and two court ministers. But the services would not confide in the politicians – each ran its own diplomatic network through service attachés – or in each other.

Tojo, the War Minister from 1940, concealed his plans from the navy, which he regarded as unreliable and cowardly. He sought to get his way and keep himself informed by doubling-up offices. Thus he became Home Minister, Foreign Minister in July 1941 (when Matsuoka was ousted over the Nazi invasion of Russia) and finally Prime Minister on 18 October. Even so, he knew nothing of the navy's Pearl Harbor plan until eight days before it was put into execution. It was, in fact, impossible for any one man to assert effective central control without adopting a posture of arrogance which invited instant assassination. It is significant that Tojo, the 'Southern strategy' fire-eater – he was known as 'Razor' – became much less aggressive once he took over as prime minister, and denounced the Pearl Harbor plan (when he learned of it) as 'entirely impermissible, being in contravention of accepted procedure ... hurtful to the national honour and prestige'.[65] Yet the war, and the plan, went ahead just the same.

The liaison conferences inhibited honesty. The Emperor-God sat between two incense burners, on a dais in front of a gold screen, with the mere mortals at two brocade-covered tables at right angles to him.[66] A special archaic court language had to be used. The Tenno could signify approval by banging his gold seal. Normally he did not speak; or if he did speak it was against protocol to take down his words, so the record is missing. Once (6 September 1941) he issued a warning by reading out an allusive poem written by his grandfather. He was not allowed to ask questions or express opinions: that was done for him by the President of the Council, on the basis of what he thought the Tenno intended to say.[67] Often the real decisions, if any, were taken in whispered bilateral deals, or everyone simply went ahead and acted as they thought best.

The conference of 19 September 1940, when the alliance with the Nazis was approved, showed the system at its worst. Afterwards, Hirohito called it 'the moment of truth' and said his failure to break protocol and voice his objections was 'a moral crime'. The unstable Matsuoka took this view even before Pearl Harbor, went to the Tenno to 'confess my worst mistake', warned of 'calamity' and burst into tears.[68] All found the system intolerable, and it provoked the impulse to escape into furious activity – always appealing to the impatient Japanese. Tojo, in his frustration, took to riding round the Tokyo markets on horseback, and in reply to the complaints of the fishermen that they had no petrol for their boats would shout, 'Work harder, work harder!' He told a colleague, 'There are times when we must have the courage to do extraordinary things, like jumping with eyes closed off the veranda of the Kiyomizu Temple!'[69]

Jumping blindfold off a temple is, in fact, an accurate image of the Japanese decision to go to war. The records of the policy conferences reveal four things: that all Japanese leaders believed she must obtain access to South-East Asia and its raw materials to survive; that Japan was being pushed into a corner by America and Britain; that there was a general willingness to take risks, so that mere deterrence did not work; and that there was a corresponding unwillingness to discuss the consequences of failure. When Germany knocked France out, the Japanese demanded and got airfields in Indo-China: that provoked the first American economic sanctions. At this stage only the army definitely wanted war. In 1941 Indo-China was occupied, and on 28 July America applied total sanctions, including oil. That, in effect, brought the matter to a head. Thereafter, Japan was reducing her oil reserves by 28,000 tons a day and her only prospect of replenishing them was by seizing the Dutch East Indies. The navy insisted there must be either a negotiated settlement or war. As Nagano put it: 'The Navy is consuming four hundred tons of oil an hour . . .. We want it decided one way or another quickly.'[70]

Could America have successfully 'appeased' Japan? Did it wish to? The service chiefs, General Marshall and Admiral Stark, undoubtedly did, since they thought the destruction of German power must have priority, and they wanted time to strengthen the defences of the Philippines and Malaya. Unlike the Japanese side, where the military were pushing the civilians to war, they tried to exercise restraint on the Roosevelt administration.[71] Roosevelt himself was passionately pro-Chinese. He could be termed a founder-member of the 'China Lobby', which was already in vociferous existence by 1940 and included his cronies Harry Hopkins and Henry Morgenthau. He had long believed in the existence of a secret (in fact mythical) one-hundred-year 'plan of conquest' which the Japanese had drafted in 1889.[72] In contrast to his unwillingness to take action in the European theatre, Roosevelt had always been aggressive-minded in Asia, proposing to Britain a total blockade of Japan as early as December 1937. Hostility to Japan, as he knew, was always popular in America. He regarded war with Japan as inevitable and, unlike the brass hats, saw advantages in precipitating it. Always pro-Soviet, his bellicosity increased sharply once Russia entered the war. His close colleague, the Interior Secretary Harold Ickes, wrote to him the day after Russia was invaded:

> To embargo oil to Japan would be as popular a move in all parts of the country as you could make. There might develop from the embargoing of oil to Japan such a situation as would make it, not only possible but easy, to get into this war in an effective way. And if we should thus be indirectly brought in, we would avoid the criticism that we had gone in as an ally of communistic Russia.[73]

The 'Magic' intercepts fortified Roosevelt in his war policy because they showed clearly that, in the long negotiations which followed the oil embargo and lasted until the Japanese attack itself, Japan was systematically practising deception while planning aggression. But the intercepts did not tell the whole story. If Roosevelt and Cordell Hull had possessed transcripts of the liaison conferences they would have grasped the confusion and the agonized doubts which lay behind Japanese policy. At the 1 November liaison conference, which took the final decision to go to war (while continuing to negotiate), the level of strategic debate was not high:

> *Finance Minister Kaya:* If we go along as at present without war, and three years hence the American fleet comes to attack us, will the navy have a chance of winning or won't it? (*Question asked several times.*)
> *Navy Chief of Staff Nagano:* Nobody knows.
> *Kaya:* Will the American fleet come to attack us, or won't it?
> *Nagano:* I don't know.
> *Kaya:* I don't think they will come.
> *Nagano:* We might avoid war now, but go to war three years later. Or we might go to war now and plan for what the situation will be three years hence. I think it would be easier to engage in a war now.[74]

The navy and army were quite clear what they intended to do in the initial stages of the war, to last from three to six months. Thereafter plans, and means to carry them out, became increasingly vague. The navy and army's independently calculated steel-supply requirements, for instance, each made sense only if the other's was scaled down to the point where carrying on the war became impossible.[75] After the initial operations were completed, there was a theoretical intention to move against India and Australia. But there was no plan at all to invade America, knock her out of the war or destroy her capacity to wage it. In short, there was no strategic war-winning plan at all. Instead, there was an optimistic assumption that, at some stage, America (and Britain) would negotiate a compromise peace.

Even on a tactical level, there was a huge hole in the Japanese war-plan. The navy had almost completely neglected submarine warfare, both defensive and offensive. The army's 'Southern strategy' was based on spreading its resources in occupying thousands of islands over millions of square miles of ocean, all of which would have to be supplied by sea. The contempt for the submarine meant the navy had no means of ensuring these supplies; or, conversely, of inhibiting the Allies from moving their own supplies. The last omission meant that, in the long run, Japan could not prevent America from developing a war-winning strategy. Granted America's enormous industrial preponderance there was thus no real incentive for her to seek a compromise peace, however spectacular Japan's initial success. Regarded logically, therefore, Japan's decision to go to war made no sense. It was *hara-kiri*.

Moreover, the circumstances of the Japanese attack might have been designed to create American intransigence. Throughout their calculations from 1937 onwards, Roosevelt and his advisers had always assumed that the fury of the Japanese attack would fall on the British and Dutch possessions. True, the Philippines might also be at risk. But the notion of an attack on Pearl Harbor seems never to have been considered. Ambassador Grew had reported (27 January 1941): 'There is a lot of talk around town to the effect that the Japs, in case of a break with the US, are planning to go all out in a surprise attack on Pearl Harbor.' No one took any notice.[76] Yet the idea had been knocking around since 1921, when the *Daily Telegraph* Naval correspondent, Hector Bywater, wrote *Sea Power in the Pacific*, later expanded into a novel, *The Great Pacific War* (1925). The Japanese navy had both translated and put the novel on the curriculum of its War College.[77] The idea slumbered until Yamamoto became so impressed by improvements in carrier-borne aircraft training that he decided it was feasible. In the meantime, the concept of a series of army landings in the tropics had been developed by a fanatical staff officer, Colonel Masanobu Tsuji, so full of Shinto that he had tried to blow up a prime minister with dynamite and actually burned down a brothel full of officers out of sheer moral indignation. His ideas for the invasion of Malaya, the Philippines, the Dutch East Indies and other targets required the elimination of the American Pacific Fleet during the landings period. That, in turn, gave a kind of strategic virtue to the Pearl Harbor project: the American fleet would be destroyed at anchor, and while it was being rebuilt Japan would lay hands on all of South-East Asia. The Pearl Harbor plan itself, which meant getting a huge carrier force unobserved over thousands of miles of ocean, was the most audacious and complex scheme of its kind in history, involving creating a special intelligence network, devising new means to refuel at sea, designing new torpedoes and armour-piercing shells, and training programmes of an intensity and elaboration never before undertaken. The final naval planning conference at the Naval College near Tokyo on 2 September 1941 was something of a prodigy in naval annals, since it embraced attacks and landings over several millions of square miles, involving the entire offensive phase of the war Japan intended to launch.

Yet all this ingenuity went for nothing. The Far East war began at 1.15 am on 7 December with a sea-bombardment of the Malayan landing area, the attack on Pearl Harbor following two hours later. The Pearl Harbor assault achieved complete tactical surprise. All but twenty-nine planes returned to their carriers and the fleet got away safely. But the results, though they seemed spectacular at the time, were meagre. Some eighteen warships were sunk or badly damaged, but mostly in shallow water. They were raised and repaired and nearly all returned to active service in time to take part in major operations; losses in trained men were comparatively small. As luck would have it the American carriers were out at sea at the time of the attack, and the Japanese force commander, Admiral Nagumo, had too little fuel to search and sink them, so they escaped completely. His bombers failed to destroy either the naval oil storage tanks or the submarine-pens, so both submarines and carriers – now the key arms in the naval war – were able to refuel and operate immediately.

All this was a meagre military return for the political risk of treacherously attacking a huge, intensely moralistic nation like the United States before a formal declaration of war. This may not have been the Japanese intention (it is still being argued about) for their arrangements were a characteristic mixture of breathtaking efficiency and inexplicable muddle. But it was the effect. Secretary of State Hull knew all about the Pearl Harbor attack and the ultimatum by the time the two Japanese envoys handed him their message at 2.20 pm, and had rehearsed his little verdict of history (he was a Tennessee judge): 'In all my fifty years of public service I have never seen a document that was more crowded with infamous falsehood and distortions on a scale so huge that I never imagined until today

that any government on this planet was capable of uttering them.'
Then, to the departing diplomats: 'Scoundrels and piss-pants!'[78]
Thus America, hitherto rendered ineffectual by its remoteness, its
racial diversity and its pusillanimous leadership, found itself instantly united, angry and committed to wage total war with all its
outraged strength. Hitler's reckless declaration the following week
drew a full measure of this enormous fury down upon his own
nation.

At the liaison conference of 5 November 1941, the army Chief of
Staff General Sugiyama had said, of the vast series of offensive
operations Japan planned to undertake: 'It will take fifty days to
complete the operations in the Philippines, one hundred days in
Malaya and fifty days in the Netherlands East Indies . . . the entire
operations will be completed within five months after the opening of
the war . . . we would be able to carry on a protracted war if we
could bring under our control such important military bases as
Hong Kong, Manila and Singapore, and important areas in the
Netherlands East Indies.'[79] It says a good deal about the fundamental unsoundness of the whole Japanese war-plan that these remarkably ambitious targets were all achieved – yet the net result had little
bearing on Japan's capacity to win the war or even to force a
stalemate. It was significant that, at the conference, maps of India
and Australia, the ultimate targets, were not even displayed; and
nothing was done to train technicians to exploit the Sumatran
oilfields effectively.

Singapore surrendered on 15 February 1942; the Dutch East
Indies on 8 March; the Philippines on 9 April; Corregidor on 6 May;
and a week before the Japanese had taken Mandalay in Upper
Burma. The net hardware cost of those astounding victories was 100
aircraft, a few destroyers and a mere 25,000 tons of Japan's precious
shipping. But success had been attended by a great deal of luck. The
destruction of the *Prince of Wales* and *Repulse* by air-strikes on 10
December 1941, which sank in deep water with nearly all their
experienced crews, was a greater naval victory than Pearl Harbor,
not least because it demoralized the Singapore–Malaya garrison. The
great fortress, whose inadequacies were a monument to inter-war
defence economies, delays and wishful thinking, would have survived if General Percival, the British commander, and General
Gordon Bennett, who commanded the Australians, had shown more
fighting spirit. General Tomoyuki Yamashita, who commanded the
Japanese assault force, admitted after the war that his strategy was 'a
bluff, a bluff that worked'. He was as short of water, petrol and
ammunition as Percival, who gave them as grounds for capitulation.
None of the Japanese guns had more than one hundred rounds left. It

was the Japanese belief that, had the garrison held out another week, their campaign must have failed. Churchill had plainly instructed Field-Marshal Wavell, the area commander, that 'the whole island must be fought until every single unit and every single strongpoint has been separately destroyed. Finally the city of Singapore must be converted into a citadel and defended to the death.' But Wavell, himself a melancholic defeatist, did not press these resolutions on the apathetic Percival.[80] The main-force surrender in the Philippines was also a pusillanimous act, carried out against the instructions of the commander-in-chief. The narrowness of the Japanese victories indicated that, even at this early stage, they were pressing up against the limits of their physical resources.

The notion of a Nazi–Japanese global strategy disappeared in the early summer. On 18 January 1942 the Germans and the Japanese had signed a military agreement, with longitude 70 degrees defining their respective spheres of operations. There was vague talk of linking up in India.[81] But Hitler's forces did not reach Asian territory until the end of July. By that time the Japanese, blocked at the gates of India, had moved off into the opposite direction, operating in the Aleutian Islands on the road to Alaska in early June – the furthest limit of their conquests. They had already suffered two calamitous defeats. On 7–8 May a Japanese invasion force heading for Port Moresby in New Guinea was engaged at long-range by American carrier planes in the Coral Sea, and so badly damaged that it had to return home – the first major reverse after five months of uninterrupted triumphs. On 3 June another invasion force heading for Midway Island was outwitted and defeated, losing four of its carriers and the flower of the Japanese naval air-force. The fact that it was forced to return to Japanese waters indicated that Japan had effectively lost naval–air control of the Pacific.[82] Six months into the war, Yamamoto felt obliged to reassure his staff: 'There are still eight carriers in the combined fleet. We should not lose heart. In battle as in chess it is the fool who lets himself into a reckless move out of desperation.'[83] Yet the entire war, and Hitler's insistence on joining it, were both desperate moves. The year before, Hitler had seemed to control the European chess-board, as Japan controlled that of East Asia. Yet once united in common global predation, they rapidly shrank to the status of two medium-sized powers, flailing desperately against the creeping force of economic and demographic magnitude. The imbalance was really apparent by the end of 1941. On 3 January 1942 Hitler admitted to the Japanese ambassador, General Hiroshi Oshima, that he did not yet know 'how America could be defeated'.[84] That made two of them: the Japanese did not know either. In 1945

General Jodl claimed that, 'from the start of 1942 on', Hitler knew 'victory was no longer attainable'.[85] What he did not then grasp, but what 1942 made painfully clear, was that the huge coalition he had ranged against himself and his two allies had a decisive superiority not merely in men and material but in technology. The real significance of the Battle of Midway, for example, was that it was won primarily by the Allied success in code-breaking. In launching war, the Germans and the Japanese had pushed the world over the watershed into a new age, outside their or anyone's control, full of marvels and unspeakable horrors.

TWELVE
Superpower and Genocide

Early in April 1943 the Americans determined to kill Admiral Yamamoto, master-spirit of the Japanese navy. They felt that the overwhelming moral superiority of their cause gave them the right to do so. Yamamoto, as it happened, had never believed Japan could win without the miraculous intervention of God. He told his chief of staff just before Pearl Harbor: 'The only question that remains is the blessing of heaven. If we have heaven's blessing there will be no doubt of success.' But all war-leaders had become assassination targets. That was why Hitler and Stalin never left their working headquarters. Churchill took the most risks. After the Washington Arcadia Conference in December 1941 he returned by an unescorted Boeing flying-boat, which was nearly shot down, first by the German defences in Brest, then by intercepting British Hurricanes. 'I had done a rash thing,' he admitted. The same month the Americans plotted to murder Yamamoto, the Germans destroyed a British flight from Lisbon believing Churchill was aboard: in fact they killed the film-actor Leslie Howard.[1] The difference was that, on the Allied side, morality was reinforced by technical superiority. The Germans did not know of Churchill's flights, whereas Yamamoto's movements were studied in advance by America's code-breakers.

The Americans had broken Japan's diplomatic code in 1940. But Kazuki Kamejama, head of Japan's Cable Section, proclaimed such a feat to be 'humanly impossible', and Japan continued to underrate Allied technical capacity in code-breaking.[2] When Yamamoto began his tour of Solomon Island defences on 13 April 1943 his flying schedule was radioed, the communications office claiming 'The code only went into effect on 1 April and cannot be broken.' In fact the Americans had done so by dawn the next morning. The shooting down of Yamamoto's plane was personally approved by Roosevelt. After it was accomplished, a signal was sent to the theatre comman-der, Admiral Halsey: 'Pop goes the weasel'. He was chagrined:

'What's so good about it? I'd hoped to lead that scoundrel up Pennsylvania Avenue in chains.'[3]

The skill with which Britain and America used advanced technology to illuminate global war was one of the principal reasons why the Germans and the Japanese, with all their courage and energy, were fighting an unsynchronized struggle from 1942 on. Like Bronze Age warriors facing an Iron Age power, they appeared increasingly to be survivors from a slightly earlier epoch. The British had been the leading code-breakers for half a century. It was 'Room 40' in the Old Admiralty Building in Whitehall which, early in 1917, had decoded a telegram from Arthur Zimmerman, German Foreign Minister, to the Mexican President, proposing a German-assisted Mexican re-conquest of Texas. Brilliantly publicized, this *coup* had helped to bring America into the war.[4] British intelligence, which had a continuous history since the sixteenth century, was one aspect of defence not neglected between the wars. The Germans, too, were active in this field, within limits. They intercepted and unscrambled the transatlantic telephone circuit between Britain and America, and sometimes heard Roosevelt and Churchill converse, though the talk was too guarded to yield much. They broke some Russian codes and the US military attachés' code in Cairo, Rommel making excellent use of the results. But the code was changed in 1942 and thereafter could not be broken.[5] Nor could the Germans repeat an early wartime success with British naval codes. From mid-1942 onwards, British–American communications were reasonably secure.

It was a different matter for the Germans. In 1926 their army had adopted the electrical Enigma coding machine, followed by the navy two years later. Both services remained convinced of the indestructible virtues of this encoding system. In fact Polish intelligence had reconstructed the Enigma machine, and in July 1939 they gave one each to Britain and France.[6] This became the basis for the most successful intelligence operation of the war, run from Bletchley in Buckinghamshire. 'Ultra', as it was called, remained a secret until 1974, and some aspects were concealed even in the 1980s because of their bearing on operations against Soviet codes.[7] Many of the Ultra intercepts have not yet been published and it may never be possible to assess its full impact on the course of the war.[8] But Ultra played a part as early as 1940 by helping to win the Battle of Britain. More important, the breaking of the German 'Triton' code by Bletchley in March 1943 clinched the Battle of the Atlantic, for German U-boats continued to signal frequently, confident in their communications security, and breaking the code allowed the Allies to destroy their supply-ships too. As a result, victory in the Atlantic came quite quickly in 1943, and this was important, for the U-boat was perhaps Hitler's most dangerous weapon.[9] The Ultra system was also well-adapted to the provision of false intelligence to the Axis, which became a leading feature of the Allied war-effort and was highly successful, for instance, in persuading the Germans that the D-Day Normandy landings in 1944 were a feint.[10]

Knowing how to break codes was only the core of a vast and increasingly complex operation working on the frontiers of electronic technology. It was the success of the British Post Office Research Establishment in building Colossus, the first electronic computer, which produced the acceleration in the analysis process essential to the effective use of code-breaking. From early 1942, the marriage of British and American technology and intelligence led to the early break-through in the Pacific war. Midway in June 1942 was an intelligence victory. Thereafter, the Allies knew the positions of all Japanese capital ships nearly all the time. Perhaps even more important, they were able to conduct a spectacularly successful submarine offensive against Japanese supply-ships. This turned the island empire the Japanese had acquired in their first five months of war (10 per cent of the earth's surface at its greatest extent) into an untenable liability, the graveyard of the Japanese navy and merchant marine and of their best army units: code-breaking alone raised shipping-losses by one-third.[11]

But intelligence, however complete, cannot win wars. Enigma gave the British the German order-of-battle as early as the Norway campaign in 1940; but that battle was lost because the resources were not available and in place. Where one side is outclassed in military strength, intelligence can rarely tip the balance back.[12] But where overwhelming intelligence superiority is married to quantitative advantages, the combination is devastating. Both the Nazis and the Japanese ran shortage economies. The Japanese had no alternative. Despite prodigious ingenuity, they were able to increase their total production only 2 per cent beyond its 1940 level by the beginning of 1943 (US production rose 36 per cent in the same period).[13] The Germans had a much stronger and more comprehensive economy, but Hitler was obsessed by the cost and risk of over-production, and by the need for import-substitutes. As a result, German research was devoted to ersatz materials rather than accelerating mass-production, and the economy was held back. At the end of 1941 Fritz Todt, Hitler's production chief, protested bitterly at the premature switch of production from the Russian to the Western theatres and the failure to cut back the civil economy. His death in a mysterious air crash on 2 February 1942 may not have been accidental.[14] For Germany, Jodl claimed, 'actual rearmament had to be carried out after the war began'. On 1 September 1939 Germany had only 3,906 military and naval aircraft of all types.

Only 10,392 were turned out in 1940, 12,392 in 1941 and 15,497 in 1942. Not until 1943–4, when it was too late, did the war-economy expand to its maximum (despite Allied bombing), producing 24,795 aircraft in 1943 and 40,953 in 1944.[15] Stalin argued in 1949 that Germany lost the war because 'Hitler's generals, raised on the dogma of Clausewitz and Moltke, could not understand that war is won in the factories'. Out of a population of 80 million, he continued, they put 13 million in the armed forces, and 'history tells us that no single state could maintain such an effort': the Soviet armed forces were only 11.5 million out of a population of 194 million.[16] This was a Marxist view of war which greatly exaggerates the power of the generals over Nazi war-production policy. It ignores the real reason why the German economy failed to rise into top gear until the end of 1942, which was Hitler's obstinate attachment to the military-economic doctrine of the *Blitzkrieg*. In fact many industrial workers, especially women, did not move into the war-factories until Allied bombing destroyed their civilian livelihood.

The notion that 'socialized' industry won the war is baseless. The socialized sector of German industry (e.g. the Herman Goering Steel Works) was a complete failure. The Soviet economy performed reasonably well in producing mass quantities of certain basic military items: in August 1942, at the furthest point of the Nazi advance, Soviet factories were already making 1,200 tanks a month.[17] But the troop-carrying vehicles and jeeps which gave the Red Army its growing and decisive mobility in 1943–4 came from American industry, and the Western powers jointly supplied the high technology which slowly gave Russia command of the air in the East: even in 1946 Britain was still sending Russia aero-engines, which became the basis for the highly successful post-war Mig-15. In Britain, the adoption of Ludendorff-style 'war socialism' and Keynesian macro-economics enabled the British capitalist economy to perform much more effectively than Germany's: in 1942 her war production was 50 per cent higher. But the real engine of Allied victory was the American economy. Within a single year the number of tanks built had been raised to 24,000 and planes to 48,000. By the end of the first year of the war America had raised its army production to the total of all three Axis powers together, and by 1944 had doubled it again – while at the same time creating an army which passed the 7 million mark in 1943.[18]

This astonishing acceleration was made possible by the essential dynamism and flexibility of the American system, wedded to a national purpose which served the same galvanizing role as the optimism of the Twenties. The war acted as a boom market, encouraging American entrepreneurial skills to fling her seemingly

limitless resources of materials and manpower into a bottomless
pool of consumption. One reason the Americans won Midway was
by reducing a three-month repair-job on the carrier *Yorktown* to
forty-eight hours, using 1,200 technicians round the clock.[19] The
construction programme for the defence co-ordinating centre, the
Pentagon, with its sixteen miles of corridors and 600,000 square
feet of office space, was cut from seven years to fourteen
months.[20] The war put back on his pedestal the American capitalist
folk-hero. Henry Kaiser, Henry Morrison and John McCone, the
San Francisco engineers who created the Boulder Dam (and who
had been systematically harassed during the New Deal by
Roosevelt's Interior Secretary, Harold Ickes, for breaches of federal
regulations), led the field in the wartime hustle. They built the
world's biggest cement plant and the first integrated steel mill. Told
to build ships at any cost, they cut the construction time of a
'Liberty' ship from 196 to twenty-seven days and by 1943 were
turning one out every 10.3 hours.[21] General Electric in 1942 alone
was able to raise its production of marine turbines from $1 million
to $300 million.[22] America won the war essentially by harnessing
capitalist methods to the unlimited production of firepower and
mechanical manpower. After the loss of the decisive battle of
Guadalcanal, the Tenno Hirohito asked the navy's chief of staff,
'Why was it that it took the Americans only a few days to build an
airbase and the Japanese more than a month?' All Nagano could
say was, 'I am very sorry indeed.' The truth was, the Americans had
a vast array of bulldozers and other earth-moving equipment, the
Japanese only muscle-power.[23]

The devastating combination of high technology and unrivalled
productive capacity took its most palpable and significant form in
offensive air-power. There were two reasons for this. First, the
British[24] persuaded the Americans it was the best way to make the
maximum use of their vast economic resources, while suffering the
minimum manpower losses. Second, the bombing offensive appealed
strongly to the moralistic impulse of both nations: what the British
atomic scientist P.S.M.Blackett called 'the Jupiter complex' – the
notion of the Allies as righteous gods, raining retributive thunder-
bolts on their wicked enemies.

We see here the corruptive process of moral relativism at work.
Churchill was well aware of the moral decay war brings; was
appalled by it. He had initiated the mass-bombing strategy on 2
July 1940 because he was overwhelmed by the prospect of Nazi
occupation – the ultimate moral catastrophe – and saw bombing as
the only offensive weapon then available to the British. This was
the old utilitarian theory of morals, as opposed to natural law

theory which ruled that the direct destruction of war-waging capacity was the only legitimate manner of conducting combat.[25] But all forms of moral relativism have an innate tendency to generate moral collapse since they eliminate any fixed anchorage and launch the ship of state on an ocean where there are no bearings at all. By the end of 1941, with both Russia and America in the war, the defeat of Hitler, as Churchill himself realized, was inevitable in the long run. The utilitarian rationale for attacks on cities had disappeared; the moral case had always been inadmissible. But by this time the bomber force was in being, and the economy geared to producing large numbers of long-range Lancasters. It was on 14 February 1942 that the directive was issued to Bomber Command that a primary objective was the destruction of the morale of German civilians.[26] The first major raid carried out in accordance with the new order was on Lübeck on 28 March 1942; the city 'burned like kindling', said the official report. The first 1,000-bomber raid followed on 30 May and in the summer the American Air Force joined the campaign.

Bombing used up 7 per cent of Britain's total military manpower, and perhaps as much as 25 per cent of Britain's war production.[27] The entire strategy may have been, even in military terms, mistaken. Bombing, which killed 600,000 Germans altogether, reduced but could not prevent the expansion in German war-production up to the second half of 1944, achieved by the switch from civilian consumer goods which, against an index of one hundred in 1939, fell to ninety-one in 1943 and eighty-five in 1944 – Britain's being as low as fifty-four in both years.[28] True, from the end of 1944 bombing effectively destroyed the German war-economy. Even before that, the need to defend German cities by night and day had prevented the *Luftwaffe* from keeping its air superiority on the Russian front. But the effectiveness of bombing as a war-winning weapon depended entirely on the ability to maintain indefinitely very heavy raids on the same targets night after night. The Allies came near to a strategic 'victory' in the raids on Hamburg, by far the best-protected German city, from 24 July–3 August 1943, using the 'Window' foil device which confused German radar. On the night of 27–28 July, the RAF created temperatures of 800 to 1,000 centigrade over the city, producing fire-storm winds of colossal force. Transport systems of all types were destroyed, 214,350 homes out of 414,500, 4,301 out of 9,592 factories; eight square miles were burnt out completely, and in one night alone fatal casualties in the four fire-storm districts were 40,000 or up to 37.65 of the total population.[29] Albert Speer, who had succeeded Todt as the production supremo, told Hitler that if another six cities were similarly devastated, he could not keep war-production going. But the British simply did not have the resources to enable Bomber Command to repeat raids on this scale in quick succession.

The worst aspect of terror-bombing was the appeal of the 'Jupiter complex' to the war-leaders striking their geopolitical bargains. This was the explanation for the greatest Anglo–American moral disaster of the war against Germany, the destruction of Dresden on the night of 13–14 February 1945. The origin of the raid was the desire of Roosevelt and Churchill at the Yalta Conference to prove to Stalin that the Allies were doing their best to assist the Russian effort on the Eastern front. In particular they wanted to deliver a crippling blow to German morale to help on the Russian offensive which began on 12 January. Dresden was not an industrial but a communications centre. Its population of 630,000 had been doubled by German refugees, 80 per cent of them peasants from Silesia. Stalin wanted them destroyed to facilitate his plan to 'move' Poland westwards and he also believed the city was being used as a concentration-point for troops. According to Sir Robert Saundby, deputy head of Bomber Command, the Russians specifically asked for Dresden as the target of 'Operation Thunderclap'. Not long before, the Command's chaplain, Canon L. John Collins (later to create the nuclear disarmament campaign), had invited the pious Christian socialist, Sir Stafford Cripps, who was Minister of Aircraft Production, to talk to senior officers. He took as his text 'God is my co-pilot' and told them it was essential they should be sure they were attacking military targets: 'Even when you are engaged in acts of wickedness, God is always looking over your shoulder.' This led to an angry scene, since Bomber Command believed Cripps's Ministry was deliberately starving them of aircraft for pseudo-moralistic reasons. Thereafter they were anxious to make it clear they were under politicians' orders. Hence they queried the Dresden order. It was confirmed direct from the Yalta Conference (by either Churchill or Air Chief Marshal Portal).[30]

The attack was carried out in two waves (with a third, by the USAF, to follow) in accordance with Bomber Command's tactic of the 'double blow', the second falling when relief forces had concentrated on the city. Over 650,000 incendiaries were dropped, the firestorm engulfing eight square miles, totally destroying 4,200 acres and killing 135,000 men, women and children. As it was the night of Shrove Tuesday, many of the children were still in carnival costumes. For the first time in the war a target had been hit so hard that not enough able-bodied survivors were left to bury the dead. Troops moved in and collected huge piles of corpses. The centre round the Altmarkt was cordoned off. Steel grills, twenty-five feet across, were set up, fuelled with wood and straw, and batches of five hundred corpses were piled up on each and burned. The funeral pyres were still flaming a fortnight after the raid. Goebbels claimed, 'It is the work of lunatics.' According to Speer, the attack sent a wave of terror over the whole nation. But by this stage there was no means whereby public opinion could bring pressure on an inaccessible, isolated and paranoid Hitler to negotiate surrender. And there were neither the resources nor the will to repeat the raid, which affronted the pilots themselves. One commented, 'For the first time in many operations I felt sorry for the population below.' Another said it was 'the only time I ever felt sorry for the Germans'.[31]

Germany yielded less to the Jupiter syndrome only because Hitler distrusted Goering's ability to make effective use of the vast resources a strategic bombing campaign would require. But the idea of dealing mass destruction impersonally, by remote control, appealed strongly to him. The Versailles Treaty forbade Germany to make bombers but it said nothing about ballistic missiles. Hence when Hitler came to power he found a military missile team already in existence: in 1936 its head, Walter Dornberger, was authorized to issue a directive calling for a rocket to carry one hundred times the explosive force of the Big Bertha gun of 1918 over twice the range (2,200 lbs over 156 miles).[32] In a sense Hitler was right that the coming strategic weapon would be a high-payload ballistic missile. One of the few to grasp this on the Allied side was the Tory MP Duncan Sandys, who warned on 23 November 1944: 'In future the possession of superiority in long-distance rocket artillery may well count for as much as superiority in naval or air power.' Allied orthodoxy revolved around the flexibility of the big bomber, essentially a First World War concept. The reply of Churchill's chief scientist, Lord Cherwell, 5 December 1944, was that the long-range rocket would be highly inaccurate, without a compensatory high payload. This was an unanswerable criticism so long as the explosive remained conventional.

Hitler's difficulty was that he had to choose between two possibilities. The pilotless guided aircraft (V1) appealed strongly to his highly developed sense of military economy. It was one of the most cost-effective weapons ever produced. For the price of one Lancaster bomber, crew-training, bombs and fuel, Hitler could fire well over three hundred V1s, each with a ton of high-explosive, a range of 200 miles and a better chance of reaching its target. In the period 12 June–1 September 1944, for an expenditure of £12,600,190, the V1 offensive cost the Allies £47,645,190 in loss of production, extra anti-aircraft and fighter defences, and aircraft and crews in the bombing offensive against the sites. The Air Ministry reported (4 November 1944): 'The results were greatly in the enemy's favour, the estimated ratio of our costs to his being nearly four to one.' Only 185 Germans lost their lives, against 7,810 Allies (including 1,950 trained airmen). The V1s were damaging 20,000 houses a day in July 1944 and the effect on London morale was very serious.

But Hitler did not invest early or extensively enough in this telling weapon. In the chaos of the Nazi procurement programme, it was necessary to appeal to the Führer's romanticism to get priority. That was what Dornberger's big rockets did. The V2 programme seemed the only way to gratify Hitler's intense desire to revenge himself on Roosevelt by destroying New York. The allocation of resources to it made no sense in terms of likely performance. In Germany alone it employed 200,000 workers, including a large proportion of the highest-skilled technicians. The programme deprived the Germans of advanced jets and underground oil refineries and its absorption of scarce electrical equipment interfered with production of aircraft, submarines and radar. The actual rockets used in the V2 campaign, the A4, of which only 3,000 were fired, cost £12,000 each (against £125 for the V1), carried a payload of only 12,000 lb and were hopelessly inaccurate. The projected intercontinental rocket, the A9/A10, weighing 100 tons and with a second stage ascending to 230 miles into the stratosphere, planned to be used against New York and Washington, never got beyond the drawing-board stage.[33] Even if built and fired, its conventional payload would have rendered it nugatory.

Hitler's only prospect of achieving stalemate by a decisive technical advance lay in marrying the A10 rocket to a nuclear payload. There was never much prospect of him achieving this within the time-scale of the war. Yet there was a continuing fear on the Allied side that Hitler would come into possession of atomic bombs. Many scientists believed the Second World War would become nuclear. There was a certain symmetry in the development of atomic knowledge in the inter-war period. The notion of a man-made explosion of colossal power was implicit in Einstein's Special Theory of Relativity. If the vast energy binding particles into the closely packed entity of the nucleus could be released – the heaviest elements containing the greatest energy – then uranium-235, at the top of the weight-table, was the raw material of the quest. High-energy physics was the great expanding science of the 1920s. In 1932, as Germany turned towards Hitler, the results began to come in, all over Europe and North America. That year, at the Cavendish laboratory in Cambridge, J.D.Cockcroft and E.T.S.Walton, using a £500 piece of equipment – which Lord Rutherford, head of the Cavendish, thought an outrageous sum – split the atom. Their colleague Sir James Chadwick discovered the neutron, consisting of proton and electron, with a binding energy of 1–2 million electron volts. In 1934 the Joliot-Curies, in France, made radioactive isotopes artificially and Enrico Fermi, in Italy, successfully slowed down (that is, controlled) neutrons, and went on to produce transuranic elements with even heavier masses than on the atomic table. The process of developing the theoretical notion of atomic fission, involving scientists in Germany and America as well, culminated in the first nine months of the fatal year 1939, so that by the time Hitler invaded Poland it was already clear that a man-made atomic explosion was possible. The dramatic advances of 1939, and the outbreak of war, constitute one of the most striking and sinister coincidences in history: a review article in January 1940 was able to summarize over one hundred significant publications over the previous year. The most important of them, by the Dane Nils Bohr and his American pupil J.A.Wheeler, explaining the fission process, appeared only two days before the war began.[34]

From the very beginning applied atomic physics had its ideological and moral dimensions. The concept of the bomb was born among the mainly Jewish refugee scientific community, who were terrified that Hitler might get it first. It was one of them, Leo Szilard, who proposed a self-imposed censorship of scientific publication. The bomb was created by (among others) men who put ideological considerations before national self-interest, just as it was betrayed by such men. Many of those who worked on the British project, the greatest of wartime secrets, were excluded for security reasons from other war work.[35] Fear was the primary motive. Robert Oppenheimer, a Jew, built the first A-bomb because he feared Hitler would do it first; Edward Teller, a Hungarian, built the first H-bomb because he was terrified of a Soviet monopoly.[36]

Hence the real father of the atomic bomb was Hitler and the spectres his horrifying will conjured up. In March 1940 Otto Frisch and Rudolf Peierls of Birmingham University produced an astonishing memorandum, of three typed pages, showing how to make a bomb of enriched uranium. The high-powered 'Maud' Committee (whimsically called after Maud Ray, a Kentish governess) was created to crash-develop the idea. In June it was joined by the French nuclear team, who brought with them the world's entire stock of heavy water, which they had snatched from Norway: 185 kilograms in twenty-six cans, which was first temporarily housed in Wormwood Scrubs prison, then put in the library at Windsor Castle.[37] At Einstein's request (he also feared an 'anti-Semitic bomb'), Roosevelt had set up an 'Uranium Committee' in October 1939. It was jolted into activity in the autumn of 1940 when the two leaders of the British scientific war-effort, Sir Henry Tizard and Sir John Cockcroft, went to Washington taking with them a 'black box' containing, among other things, all the secrets of the British atomic programme.

At that time Britain was several months ahead of any other nation, and moving faster. Plans for a separation plant were completed in December 1940 and by the following March the atomic bomb had ceased to be a matter of scientific speculation and was moving into the arena of industrial technology and engineering. By July 1941 the Maud Committee report, 'Use of Uranium for a Bomb', argued that such a weapon, which it thought could be ready by 1943, would be much cheaper, in cost per pound, than conventional explosives, highly economical in air-power, more concentrated in its impact and with a profound effect on enemy morale. Even if the war ended before the bomb became available, the effort was essential because no nation 'would care to risk being caught without a weapon of such decisive capabilities'.[38] Already, then, the bomb was seen in post-Hitler terms as a permanency of international life. But its supposed imminence made it a natural ingredient in the bombing policy. There can be no doubt that an all-British bomb, if available, would have been used against German cities, with the approbation of the British public, which throughout supported the area bombing policy.

In fact the optimism of the British planners was not justified. The industrial and engineering problems involved in producing pure U-235 or plutonium (the alternative fissionable material) in sufficient quantities proved daunting; as did the design of the bomb itself. The success of the project was made possible only by marrying European theory to American industrial technology and, above all, American resources and entrepreneurial adventurism. The Maud Report became the basis for America's 'Manhattan' project, with a budget of $2 billion, which spent $1 billion in 1944 alone. In order to race Hitler to the bomb (as they thought), three completely different methods of producing bomb-material, two types of uranium enrichment plants (gaseous diffusion and electro-magnetic) and a set of plutonium reactors, were pursued simultaneously. Each involved building some of the largest factories ever conceived.

The project was under the direction of an army engineer general, Leslie Groves, who shared to the full the giganticist philosophy of the new Forties phase of American capitalism.[39] Given a clear and attainable objective, he was impervious to qualitative or quantitative difficulties. He took a fierce delight in prodigality. 'We have so many PhDs now that we can't keep track of them', he boasted. He asked the American Treasury for thousands of tons of silver for electric wiring and was told: 'In the Treasury we do not speak of tons of silver. Our unit is the troy ounce.'[40] But he got the silver. The effort to invent nuclear power involved creating a series of new technologies: the first fully automated factory, the first plant operated by remote control, the first wholly sterile industrial process – 6 million square feet of leak-proof machinery – and a variety of revolutionary gadgets.[41] The waste was enormous, and much of it in retrospect seemed inexcusable. But then war is about waste; war *is* waste. The Americans were compressing perhaps three decades of scientific engineering progress into four years. There was no other way of being sure to get the bomb. There was no other country or system which could have produced this certainty. It was Hitler's bomb; it was also and above all a capitalist bomb.

It is ironic that totalitarianism, having generated the fear which made the bomb possible, made only feeble efforts of its own to justify the righteous terror of the legitimate powers. The Leningrad physicist Igor Kurchatov had asked for funds to build a reactor in the late 1930s, in response to the prodigal outpouring of Western published data. When one of his pupils noticed that this flow had halted, Kurchatov alerted his political superiors (May 1942) and eventually got a Uranium Institute established in Moscow. The Soviet programme began only a few months after the Manhattan Project, but with a low resource-priority which reflected doubt about the feasibility of a bomb.[42] According to Nikita Khrushchev it was not until the day after the Hiroshima explosion that Stalin put his secret police head, Beria, in charge of a crash project with absolute priority over all else in the state.[43] The Japanese, too, had an A-bomb project under their leading physicist, Yoshio Nishina, and built five cyclotrons. But that, too, lacked resources and in 1943 the Japanese concluded that not even the US economy could produce a bomb in the foreseeable future.[44] Germany, despite the scientific exodus, retained enough nuclear scientists to conceive a bomb. But to Hitler, the nuclear field was identified with Einstein and 'Jewish physics'. Perhaps deliberately, they failed to ignite Hitler's enthusiasm, though a nuclear explosive was exactly what he needed to make his rocket programme effective. In its colossal destructive power, it was an archetypal Hitler weapon: the destroyer-state incarnate. Even before the war he had grimly outlined to Hermann Rauschning the price of Nazi failure: 'Even as we go down to destruction we will carry half the world into destruction with us'.[45] The atomic bomb could have brought this reckless boast closer to reality. But the bomb never possessed Hitler's mind as the rocket did. The failure in the imagination of this romantic nihilist rendered groundless the fears of the scientific exiles who caused the bomb to be made.

By a further, though predictable, irony, the race to get the weapon intensified as the moral and military necessity for it diminished. As enemy power receded in 1943 and 1944, and it became clear that total victory was only a matter of time, the need to forestall Hitler was replaced by the gruesome urge to make the bomb while the war still provided the chance to use it. By the end of December 1941 it was manifest that Hitler and his Japanese allies could not win the war. By the late summer of 1942, after the Japanese disaster at Midway and the petering out of Hitler's Volga–Caucasus offensive, it was also obvious that the Axis could not achieve a stalemate either. The hinge-month was November 1942. On 2 November the British began the decisive battle of Alamein, to clear North Africa and the Mediterranean, followed by Anglo–American landings in Morocco and Algeria six days later. The next day the Japanese failed in their last major effort to win the battle of Guadalcanal Island in the Solomons, which their army commander described as the 'battle in which the rise and fall of the Japanese Empire will be decided'. Nine days after this catastrophe the Russians launched their counter-offensive at Stalingrad. Roosevelt told the *Herald Tribune:* 'It would seem that the turning point in this war has at last been reached.'

Italy was the first to accept the logic of Allied power. As early as December 1940 Mussolini had told his son-in-law Ciano that the Italians of 1914 had been superior to those of the fascist state. It reflected, he said, badly on his regime.[46] By the time the Allies invaded Sicily on 10 July 1943 he was in a mood of invincible pessimism. He did nothing to prevent his critics summoning the fascist Grand Council fifteen days later, having listened to the ten-hour debate; and waiting apathetically for his arrest, he auto-graphed a photograph for a woman '*Mussolini defunto*'.[47] While Italy hastened to make terms with the Allies, Hitler turned the country into an occupied zone, rescued the fallen dictator and allowed him to run a puppet regime. In his twilight, Mussolini reverted to his Lenin-type totalitarian socialism, always the bedrock of his political philosophy, and preached the destruction of 'pluto-cracy' and the supremacy of syndicalism. By the end of March 1945 he had carried through, albeit largely on paper, a socialist revolution which had nationalized all firms employing more than one hundred workers. And just before he was captured and hanged, upside down alongside his mistress, he had resumed his violent Germanophobia of 1914–15: '*Il tedeschi sono responsabili di tutto*' was one of his last *dicta*.[48]

It was essentially Hitler's decision to fight the war to its now inevitable finish. For a time at least Stalin was always prepared to revert to the Nazi–Soviet Pact. He offered to negotiate with Hitler in December 1942 and again in summer 1943. In the autumn, fearing that Anglo–American long-term strategy predicated a Nazi–Soviet war of exhaustion, he sent his Deputy Foreign Minister and former

Berlin ambassador, Vladimir Dekanozov, to Stockholm, with an offer of a return to the 1914 frontiers and an economic deal.[49] No doubt Stalin hoped to resurrect his 1925 strategy, pull out of the war and re-enter it later. But in November 1942, on the anniversary of his *putsch*, Hitler had said, 'There will no longer be any peace offers coming from us', and he stuck to that resolve, fulfilling the menacing prediction he had made on numerous occasions in the 1920s and 1930s that Germany had the choice only between world leadership and national destruction.

This saved the legitimate powers a damaging internal debate. It became apparent early in 1942 that official opinion in both Britain and the USA was divided into 'hard' and 'soft' armistice formulae. To resolve the dilemma, the State Department in May 1942 and the Defence Department in December 1942 recommended 'unconditional surrender' as a working principle. Roosevelt, to avoid Wilson's difficulties in 1918–19, pushed the idea on a reluctant Churchill at the Casablanca Conference on 24 January 1943, then unilaterally made it public. But there is no evidence to justify Churchill's fear that Hitler would exploit Allied intransigence to bolster German resistance.[50] No power in Germany could compel or persuade Hitler to make peace on any terms whatever. The German professional officer class, or what was left of it, made no move until it was clear that the Allied invasion of Europe, begun on 6 June 1944, had been successful. Then on 15 July Marshal Rommel sent a teletype to Hitler: 'The unequal struggle is nearing its end. I must ask you immediately to draw the necessary conclusions from this situation.'[51] When Hitler made no response, a *Junker* bomb-plot took place on 20 July. If Hitler had been killed, a military dictatorship would have followed, but it is not at all clear that Roosevelt would have been prepared to bargain with it, following the Italian example (Italy was excluded from the Casablanca 'unconditional surrender' formula).

Hitler, surviving, drew the conclusions: 'Nothing is fated to happen to me, all the more so since this isn't the first time I've miraculously escaped death . . . I am more than ever convinced that I am destined to carry on our great common cause to a happy conclusion.'[52] The plotters were mostly aristocrats, enjoying their traditional monopoly of staff jobs; as a result they had no troops. They could give orders; no one followed. Nor did they have popular support, or even contacts. Noting their narrow social base, Hitler moved emotionally, or rather returned, to the Left. In this last phase he admired Stalin more than ever. If Stalin lived ten to fifteen years he would make Russia 'the greatest power in the world'. He was a 'beast', but a beast 'on a grand scale'. Hitler added: 'I have often bitterly regretted I did not purge my officer corps in the way Stalin did.' He now gave his Lenin-type 'People's Court' and its radical hanging-judge, Roland Freisler, its moment of apotheosis: 'Freisler will take care of things all right. He is our Vishinsky.'[53] Hitler adopted the Leninist principle of 'responsibility of next of kin', while denying it was Bolshevistic – it was 'a very old custom practised among our forefathers'. The executions of suspects ('I want them to be hanged, strung up like butchered cattle'), while on a small scale compared with Stalin's killings in 1936–8, continued right up to the end of the regime.[54]

Meanwhile Goebbels, the most socialist-minded of the leading Nazis, became Hitler's closest adviser, and was allowed to radicalize the war effort, ordering total mobilization, the conscription of women, the shutting of theatres and other long-resisted measures. The *Wehrmacht* still numbered over 9 million. While some leading Nazis now sought to do a deal with the Anglo-Saxons in the name of *antibolschevismus*, Hitler clung to the image of Frederick the Great, surviving hopeless encirclement. He and Goebbels read together Carlyle's weird, multi-volume biography of the King, thus dealing a stunning blow to the already shaky reputation of the old Scotch sage.[55] Far from seeking a common front against Russia, Hitler transferred divisions to the West to launch his last offensive in the Ardennes, in December 1944, making possible the great Russian push of January 1945, which carried Soviet power into the heart of Europe.

Hitler remained to the end a socialist, though an eccentric one. Like Stalin he lived in hideous discomfort. Ciano was horrified by his Rastenburg headquarters, calling its inhabitants troglodytes: 'Smells of kitchens, uniforms, heavy boots'.[56] It was a concentration camp-monastery – the Escorial without its palatial splendour. Indeed, Hitler came to resemble Philip II in his isolation and remoteness, his resolution, above all in his cartomania, spending hours studying maps already rendered out of date by the march of war, and issuing orders for the taking of a tiny bridge or pillbox, often by imaginary soldiers. His closest companions were his Alsatian, Blondi, and her pup Wolf. Professor Morell, a smart Berlin doctor, gave him sulfanilamide and glandular injections; he took glucose, hormones, anti-depressant pills. One of his doctors, Karl Brandt, said that he aged 'four or five years every year'. His hair went grey. But his capacity for work remained impressive to the end.

Hitler moved down into his bunker under the Berlin Chancellery in January 1945, taking Goebbels with him, both breathing socialist fire. 'Under the ruins of our devastated cities,' Goebbels exulted, 'the last so-called achievements of our bourgeois nineteenth century have finally been buried.'[57] In between incessant munching of cream cakes – Hitler became 'a cake-gobbling human wreck', one of his circle said

– he voiced his radical regrets: that he had not exterminated the German nobility, that he had come to power 'too easily', not unleashing a classical revolution 'to destroy élites and classes', that he had supported Franco in Spain instead of the Communists, that he had failed to put himself at the head of a movement for the liberation of the colonial peoples, 'especially the Arabs', that he had not freed the working class from 'the bourgeoisie of fossils'. Above all he regretted his leniency, his lack of the admirable ruthlessness Stalin had so consistently showed and which invited one's 'unreserved respect' for him. One of his last recorded remarks, on 27 April 1945, three days before he killed himself (whether by bullet or poison is disputed) was: 'Afterwards, you rue the fact that you've been so kind.'[58]

Before Hitler died, deploring his benevolence, he had largely completed the greatest single crime in history, the extermination of the European Jews. The 'Jewish problem' was central to his whole view of history, political philosophy and programme of action. Next to the provision of space and raw materials for the German master-race, the destruction of the Jewish 'bacillus' and its home in Bolshevist Russia was the primary purpose of the war. For Hitler the years of peace, 1933–9, were in Jewish policy as in everything else merely years of preparation. It cannot be too strongly emphasized that Hitler's aims could not be achieved except through war and under cover of war. Like Lenin and Stalin, Hitler believed in ultimate social engineering. The notion of destroying huge categories of people whose existence imperilled his historic mission was to him, as to them, entirely acceptable. The only thing he feared was the publicity and opposition which might prevent him from carrying through his necessary task.

The war, therefore, had the great convenience of plunging Germany into silence and darkness. On 1 September 1939 he sent a note to Philip Bouhler, head of his Chancellery, ordering the extermination of the chronically insane and incurable. The work was done by ss doctors, who thus acquired experience of selecting and gassing large numbers. This programme, in which about 70,000 Germans were murdered, could not be kept completely secret. Two prominent German ecclesiastics, Bishop Wurm of Württemburg and Bishop-Count Galen of Munster, protested – the only time the German hierarchy successfully raised angry voices against Nazi crimes – and at the end of August 1941 a telephone call from Hitler ended the programme.[59] But the 'euthanasia centres' were not closed down. They continued to be used to kill insane cases from the concentration camps. In retrospect, this programme appears to have been a pilot for the larger genocide to follow.

For Hitler the war really began on 22 June 1941. That was when he could begin not only his eastern clearance programme for German expansion but large-scale genocide. There is confusion both about the sequence of events and the object of policy, reflecting the ever-changing chaos of Hitler's mind and the anarchy of Nazi administration. As early as 7 October 1939, by a secret decree, Hitler appointed Himmler to a new post as Reich Commissioner for Consolidation of German Nationhood, with instructions to undertake a 'racial clean-up' in the east, and to prepare the way for the resettlement programme. Many murders of Polish Jews were already taking place. It is not known precisely when Hitler ordered the 'final solution' to begin or exactly how he defined its scope: all his orders were verbal. In March 1941 Himmler called the first genocide conference, announcing that one of the aims of the coming Russian campaign was 'to decimate the Slav population by thirty million'.[60] At the end of the same month Hitler himself told his senior officers about the *Einsatzgruppen* extermination units which would follow in the wake of the German armies. Two days later, on 2 April, Alfred Rosenberg, after a two-hour talk with Hitler, wrote in his diary: 'Which I do not want to write down, but will never forget.'[61] The ss extermination units began their work immediately the invasion started and by the end of 1941 had murdered about 500,000 Russian Jews (as well as other Russians), chiefly by shooting. However, the key document in the genocide programmes appears to be an order issued (on the Führer's authority) by Goering on 31 July 1941 to Himmler's deputy and sd Chief, Reinhard Heydrich, whom Hitler called 'the man with an iron heart'. This spoke of a total solution, *Gesamtlösung*, and a final solution, *Endlösung*, 'to solve the Jewish problem'. Goering defined 'final' to Heydrich verbally, repeating Hitler's own verbal orders: according to the evidence given at his trial in 1961 by Adolf Eichmann, whom Heydrich appointed his deputy, it meant 'the planned biological destruction of the Jewish race in the Eastern territories'. The operative date for the programme was April 1942, to give time for preparation.[62] The executive conference, which settled the details, was organized by Eichmann and chaired by Heydrich at Wannsee on 20 January 1942. By now much evidence had been accumulated about killing methods. Since June 1941, on Himmler's instructions, Rudolf Hoess, commandant of Camp 'A' at Auschwitz-Birkenau, had been experimenting. Shooting was too slow and messy. Carbon monoxide gas was found too slow also. Then in August 1941, using 500 Soviet pows as guinea-pigs, Hoess conducted a mass-killing with Zyklon-B. This was made by a pest-control firm, Degesch, the vermin combatting corporation, a satellite of I.G.Farben. Discovering Zyklon-B, said Hoess, 'set my mind at rest'.[63] A huge ss order went out for the gas, with instructions to omit the 'indicator' component, which warned human beings of the danger. I.G.Farben's dividends from Degesch doubled, 1942–4, and at least one director knew of the use being made of the gas: the only protest from Degesch was that omitting the 'indicator' might endanger their patent.[64]

The final solution became fact from the spring of 1942. The first mass-gassings began at Belzec on 17 March 1942. This camp had the capacity to kill 15,000 a day. The next month came Sobibor (20,000 a day), Treblinka and Maidanek (25,000) and Auschwitz, which Hoess called 'the greatest institution for human annihilation of all time'. The documentation on the genocide is enormous.[65] The figures almost defy belief. By December 1941 Hitler had about 8,700,000 Jews under his rule. Of these he had by early 1945 murdered at least 5,800,000: 2,600,00 from Poland, 750,000 from Russia, 750,000 from Romania, 402,000 from Hungary, 277,000 from Czechoslovakia, 180,000 from Germany, 104,000 from Lithuania, 106,000 from the Netherlands, 83,000 from France, 70,000 from Latvia, 65,000 each from Greece and Austria, 60,000 from Yugoslavia, 40,000 from Bulgaria, 28,000 from Belgium and 9,000 from Italy. At Auschwitz, where 2 million were murdered, the process was run like a large-scale industrial operation. German firms submitted competitive tenders for the 'processing unit', which had to possess 'capacity to dispose of 2,000 bodies every twelve hours'. The five furnaces were supplied by the German firm of Topt & Co of Erfurt. The gas chambers, described as 'corpse cellars', were designed by German Armaments Incorporated, to a specification requiring 'gas-proof doors with rubber surround and observation post of double 8-millimetre glass, type 100/192'.[66] The ground over the gassing-cellars was a well-kept lawn, broken by concrete mushrooms, covering shafts through which the 'sanitary orderlies' pushed the amethyst-blue crystals of Zyklon-B. The victims marched into the cellars, which they were told were baths, and did not at first notice the gas coming from perforations in metal columns:

Then they would feel the gas and crowd together away from the menacing columns and finally stampede towards the huge metal door with its little window, where they piled up in one blue clammy blood-spattered pyramid, clawing and mauling at each other even in death. Twenty-five minutes later the 'exhauster' electric pumps removed the gas-laden air, the great metal door slid open, and the men of the Jewish *Sonderkommando* entered, wearing gas-masks and gumboots and carrying hoses, for their first task was to remove the blood and defecations before dragging the clawing dead apart with nooses and hooks, the prelude to the ghastly search for gold and the removal of the teeth and hair which were regarded by the Germans as strategic materials. Then the journey by lift or rail-waggon to the furnaces, the mill that ground the clinker to fine ash, and the lorry that scattered the ashes in the stream of the Sola.[67]

In fact, to save money inadequate quantities of the expensive gas were often used, so the healthy victims were merely stunned and were then burned alive.[68]

The 'final solution', like most Nazi schemes, degenerated into administrative muddle and cross-purposes. As in the Soviet camps, internal discipline fell into the hands of professional criminals, the dreaded *Kapos*. Eichmann and Hoess gradually lost effective control. There was a fundamental conflict of aims in concentration camp policy. Hitler wanted all the Jews (and many other groups) murdered at any cost. He rejected savagely military complaints that supplies for the desperate battles on the eastern front were being held up by the need to transport millions of victims all across Europe (often in packed trains of up to one hundred trucks or carriages, holding tens of thousands). Himmler, on the other hand, wanted to expand his ss 'state within a state' into a huge industrial and construction empire, which during the war would provide an increasing proportion of Germany's military supplies, and after it would build the infrastructure of Hitler's planned eastern settlements, with their population of 150 million. The latter task would take twenty years and require 14,450,000 slave labourers, allowing for an annual death-rate of 10 per cent.[69]

The figure is not so fantastic as it appears: in August 1944, there were 7,652,000 foreigners working in German industry alone, consisting of 1,930,000 prisoners of war, and over 5 million forced deportees or slaves.[70] Himmler wanted to use the war to create the nucleus of his slave empire and was not therefore anxious to kill Jews if he could get work out of them, particularly since he could get hard cash for his ss coffers from Krupps, Siemens, I.G.Farben, Rheinmetall, Messerschmidt, Heinkel and other big firms in return for concentration camp labour. By the end of 1944 over 500,000 camp inmates were being 'leased out' to private industry, and in addition Himmler was running his own factories, often with the use of 'hoarded' Jews whose very existence he concealed from Hitler.[71]

Himmler resolved the dilemma by a compromise, brought German industry into the death-camp system, and then worked the slaves until they were fit only to be exterminated in the ovens. Auschwitz occupies a peculiar place of dishonour in this horror story not only because of its unique size but because it was deliberately designed to embody this compromise. It was created jointly by the ss and I.G.Farben as a synthetic rubber (*Buna*) and fuel centre. The vast complex consisted of A1, the original concentration camp; A2, the extermination plant at Birkenau; A3, the *Buna* and synthetic fuel plant; and A4, I.G.Farben's own concentration camp at Monowitz. Farben had its special 'Auschwitz division', with its own firemen and camp police, armed with whips, though management complained of the noise and number of floggings carried out by the *Kapos*, demanding that these take place within the concentration camp proper and not on the work-sites.

When trains of victims arrived, they were divided into the healthy, who went to Monowitz, and the weak, sick, women and children, who went straight into the death-camp. The *Buna*–Monowitz workers started each day at 3 am, moving at the 'ss trot', even when carrying heavy materials, and confined at work in ten-metre-square zones. There were no rest-periods and anyone leaving his zone was shot, 'attempting to escape'. There were floggings every day and 'several hangings a week'. Potato-turnip soup was served at midday, a piece of bread in the evening. Fritz Saukel, head of the slave-labour system, had laid down: 'All the inmates must be fed, sheltered and treated in such a way as to exploit them to the fullest possible extent, at the lowest conceivable degree of expenditure.'[72] They were in fact worse than slaves: 25,000 were literally worked to death at Auschwitz alone. Each morning the labour allocation officer picked out the sickly for gassing. Farben kept the records, including the terminal instruction, *Nach Birkenau*. The average weight-loss was six and a half to nine pounds a week, so the hitherto normally nourished could make up the deficiency from his own body for up to three months (longer than in most Russian camps of this type). The slaves burned up their own body-weight and finally died of exhaustion. As one historian has put it:

I.G.Farben reduced slave-labour to a consumable raw material, a human one from which the mineral of life was systematically extracted. When no usable energy remained, the living dross was shipped to the gassing chambers and cremation furnaces of the extermination centre at Birkenau, where the ss recycled it into the German war economy – gold teeth for the Reichbank, hair for mattresses and fat for soap.[73]

The meagre possessions the dead brought to Auschwitz were officially 'confiscated' and sent to Germany. Over one six-week period, 1 December 1944–15 January 1945, these included 222,269 sets of men's suits and underclothes, 192,652 sets of women's clothing, and 99,922 sets of children's clothes.[74] Yet despite all this gruesome meanness, so characteristic of the totalitarian state, Auschwitz was a complete economic failure: very little synthetic fuel and no *Buna* at all were produced.

Within the general framework of genocide, which engulfed millions of Poles and Russians as well as Jews, many bizarre forms of cruelty were practised. Himmler's *Lebensborn* decree of 28 October 1939 set up stud-farms for the breeding of 'ideal Aryans', and women SS officers scoured the concentration camps to kidnap Aryan-type children to stock them, 'so that during our lifetime we shall become a people of 120 million Germanic souls'. Himmler, who admired Lord Halifax's slim figure, ordered women-breeders to be fed porridge:

Englishmen, and particularly English lords and ladies, are virtually brought up on this type of food . . . . To consume it is considered most correct. It is precisely these people, both men and women, who are conspicuous for their slender figures. For this reason the mothers in our homes should get used to porridge and be taught to feed their children on it. *Heil Hitler!*[75]

At the other end of the spectrum, 350 SS doctors (one in 300 of those practising in Germany) took part in experiments on camp inmates. Dr Sigmund Rascher, for instance, conducted low-temperature tests at Dachau, killing scores, and asked to be transferred to Auschwitz: 'The camp itself is so extensive that less attention will be attracted to the work. For the subjects howl so when they freeze!' Polish girls, termed 'rabbits', were infected with gas-gangrenous wounds for sulphonamides tests. There was mass sterilization of Russian slave-labourers, using X-rays. Other projects included injection of hepatitis virus at Sachsenhausen, of inflammatory liquids into the uterus to sterilize at Ravensbruck, the all-women camp, phlegmon-induction experiments on Catholic priests at Dachau, injections of typhus-vaccine at Buchenwald, and experimental bone-transplants and the forced drinking of seawater by gypsies. At Oranienburg selected Jews were gassed to provide specimens for Himmler's skeleton collection of 'Jewish-Bolshevik commissars who personify a repulsive yet characteristic sub-humanity'.[76]

There is a sense in which 'the crime without a name', as Churchill termed it, was a national act of wrongdoing. True, the genocide programme from first to last, despite its immense scale, was furtive. Hitler never once referred to it, even in the endless harangues to intimates which form the subjects of his *Table-talk* and other documents. Though he exulted in the slaughter of the July 1944 plotters and had film of their horrific executions played to him again and again, he never visited any of the camps, let alone the death-camps. His huge, hate-filled will set the whole process in motion and kept it going until the purpose was virtually accomplished. But the hate was abstract. It was as though he felt that even his will would dissolve if he saw the doomed millions as individual human faces:

then his capacity to carry through what he saw as his supreme service to German 'culture' would collapse. He relished his murders of the well-born generals he knew and loathed; but the massacre of entire categories of mankind was nothing more than a distasteful duty. Lenin seems to have cultivated exactly the same attitude. Even Stalin, who peered through his peep-hole at the trial-agonies of his old comrades, never visited the Lubyanka cellars or set foot in his death-camps.

From Hitler's silence downwards, the entire operation of genocide was permeated by unspoken, unspeakable guilt. Even Himmler, the archetype of the sacerdotal revolutionary, who superintended all the details of the crime, only visited Auschwitz twice. As in all totalitarian systems, a false vernacular had to be created to conceal the concrete horrors of moral relativism. ss terms for murder included 'special treatment', 'resettlement', 'the general line', 'sovereign acts beyond the reach of the judiciary', above all 'sending East'.[77] As with the murders of 1934, the major crime which was progenitor of the colossal crime, a conspiracy of silence must envelop the nation. Himmler told his ss major-generals, 4 October 1943: 'Among ourselves it should be mentioned quite frankly – but we will never speak of it publicly.' Just as in 1934 it had been their duty 'to stand comrades who had lapsed up against a wall and shoot them', so now it was their duty 'to exterminate the Jewish race'. They had never referred publicly to the 1934 killings, and now too they must keep silent. Again, he told *Gauleiters* on 29 May 1944 that before the end of the year all the Jews would be dead:

You know all about it now, and you had better keep it all to yourselves. Perhaps at some later, some very much later period we might consider whether to tell the German people a little more about this. But I think we had better not! It is we here who have shouldered the responsibility, for action as well as for an idea, and I think we had better take this secret with us into our graves.[78]

Hence security around the death-camps was elaborate. The wife of a German officer, who at a confused railway junction got onto a death-train by mistake, was ordered to the ovens nonetheless so that she could not relate what she had seen. No victim emerged alive from Auschwitz until two Slovak Jews escaped in August 1944. All the same, millions of Germans knew that something horrible was being done to the Jews. There were 900,000 people in the ss alone. Countless Germans heard and saw the endless trains rattling through the night, and knew their significance, as one recorded remark suggests: 'Those damned Jews – they won't even let one sleep at night.'[79] There was a huge overlap between the slave system and German industry. It might be recalled that the Germans had used slave-labour and working-to-exhaustion in 1916–18; it was a national response to war, a salient part of the 'war socialism' Lenin so much admired. Race paranoia was deeply rooted in German culture and had been fostered by generations of intellectuals. It antedated Hitler; dwarfed him. Forty years later it is difficult to conceive of the power and ubiquity of inter-white racism, especially anti-Semitism (and not in Germany alone). In a sense, then, it was the German people who willed the end; Hitler who willed the means.[80]

In another sense the crime had accessories throughout the civilized world. There were 150,000 non-German members of the ss. The worst massacres of Poles, for instance, were carried out by an ss division of 6,500 White Russian POWs.[81] Hitler often found willing collaborators in hunting down non-German Jews. Ironically, the safest places in Europe for Jews were fascist Spain and Portugal, and Italy until Hitler set up his puppet regime. The most dangerous was France, where the Vichy regime, anti-Semitic from the outset, became steadily more so with time. There were two types of French Jews, the assimilated Sephardis and Alsacians, and the new arrivals and refugees. In November 1941 Vichy set up the Union Générale des Israelites de France, largely staffed from the first group, which constituted a bureaucratic machine to ship the second group into the concentration camps – a miniature Jewish Vichy.[82] Vichy, in effect, took an eager part in hustling its foreign-born Jews into the death-camps; and its claim that it protected its own Jews was false, since of 76,000 Jews handed over by France to the Nazis (of whom less than 2,000 survived), a third were French by birth. Those murdered included 2,000 under six and 6,000 under thirteen.[83]

The penumbra of guilt spread wider still. In the years 1933–9, when Hitler was ambivalent about emigration and the Jews could still escape, nobody wanted them. Virtually all European governments had an anti-Semitic problem and were terrified of aggravating it. Britain firmly closed the open door to Palestine, for fear of the Arabs: the 1939 White Paper limited Jewish immigration to 75,000 over five years. Roosevelt, as usual, devoted a good deal of rhetorical sympathy to the Jews but did nothing practical to help them get into America. The first reports of genocide reached the World Jewish Congress in Lausanne in August 1942. Even Jewish officials, inured to horror, were sceptical at first. In April 1943 an Anglo–American meeting of officials in Bermuda decided, in effect, that neither nation would do anything to help the Jews and would not criticize each other for doing nothing – a mutual anti-conscience pact. By August 1943 it was known, and published, that 1,702,500 Jews had already been exterminated. On 1 November Roosevelt, Stalin and Churchill jointly warned the German leaders that they would be tried for such crimes. On 24 March 1944 Roosevelt issued a further public warning. But that was all. Though America had the space and food, he would not give asylum. Churchill alone supported action at any cost. He was overruled by his united colleagues led by Anthony Eden, whose secretary noted: 'Unfortunately A.E. is immovable on the subject of Palestine. He loves Arabs and hates Jews.' On 6 July 1944 Chaim Weizmann, president of the World Jewish Agency, begged Eden to use Allied bombers to stop the movement of Hungarian Jews, then being incinerated at the rate of 12,000 a day. Churchill minuted: 'Get anything out of the Air Force you can, and invoke me if necessary.' But nothing was done; and it is unclear whether anything effective could have been done by bombing.[84]

By this time most of the Jews were dead. What the survivors wanted was evidence that the civilized world had not forgotten them: 'We didn't pray for our life,' said a survivor, 'we had no hopes for that, but for revenge, for human dignity, for punishment to the murderers.'[85] The Jews asked for recognition of the unique enormity of the crime. It cannot be said that they got it, either from the Germans themselves, who might have absolved their shared guilt by acknowledging it, or from the Allies. The history of the punishment of German war crimes is almost as complicated and confused as the crimes themselves. Because Stalin believed, as Lenin had once done, that a Soviet Germany would emerge from the war, he underplayed German war-guilt in his public statements and encouraged his Western supporters to do the same. His private feelings were quite different. At the Teheran Conference he rebuked Churchill for distinguishing between the German leaders and the mass of the people. Equally, for home consumption he instructed Ehrenburg and other writers to publish violently racist attacks on the Germans in *Pravda*, *Red Star* and other papers.[86] Publicly, however, the Communist line in the West was to treat war-crime as a political not a moral issue. In 1942 Victor Gollancz, Britain's leading left-wing publicist, coined a famous phrase with his tract *Shall our Children Live or Die?*, which argued that guilt for the war must be placed mainly on imperialism: therefore 'everyone of us is "guilty"', though capitalists were guiltier than the mass of ordinary people.[87]

In 1945 the Allies were agreed about convicting and hanging the leading Nazis. Lower down the scale the difficulties began. The Russians were the first to reach the main death-camps. Some of the officials there disappeared, possibly to work for their captors. The links between the Nazi and Soviet security forces had always been strong, and were cordially resumed after the war. Himmler had always admired Soviet police methods (he believed Stalin had distinguished Mongol blood from Genghis Khan's horde) and his head of the Gestapo, ss General Mueller, probably went to work for the NKVD.[88] Many of the Prussian police officials, who had served Goering, went on to high office in the police of the East German People's Republic, which Stalin in due course set up.

Among the British and Americans, the ardour to punish lasted longer but was eventually damped by the march of history. By the time the I.G. Farben executives were sentenced at Nuremberg (29 July 1948), the Berlin blockade had started, Germany was now a potential ally and the resuscitation of German industry was an Anglo–American objective. So Karl Krauch, the man who Nazified the firm and personally selected Auschwitz for the *Buna* plant, got only six years. Eleven other executives got prison terms from eight years to eighteen months – 'light enough to please a chicken-thief', as the prosecutor, Josiah DuBois, angrily put it.[89] By January 1951 all the German industrialist war-criminals had been released by act of clemency by the Allies. Alfred Krupp, sentenced to forfeit all his property, got it back, since John J. McCloy, the US High Commissioner, felt that 'property forfeiture was somehow repugnant to American justice'. When the work of retribution was handed over by the Allies to the Germans themselves, the results did not indicate any intensity of collective remorse. An indemnity was paid by the new Federal Government to the new Zionist State of Israel. But individual slave-labourers who pressed their claims found the German courts unsympathetic. Out of half a million surviving slaves, 14,878, after years of litigation, eventually received sums rarely amounting to $1,250 each. Rheinmetall, after a long legal rearguard action, paid out $425 to each former slave. Krupp paid a total of $2,380,000 in 1959, after pressure from the American government. Friedrich Flick paid not a penny, and left over $1,000 million when he died, aged ninety, in 1972.[90] But who is foolish enough to believe there is justice in this world?

There were many reasons why retribution was confused and inadequate. When the Hitler regime collapsed in fragments, America and Britain were still waging an increasingly one-sided war of total destruction against Japan. The Pacific war saw the greatest naval battles in history, determined by the overwhelming advantages of resources and technology, which increased inexorably. The Japanese began with the brilliant Zero fighter. One fell intact into American hands in the Aleutians on 4 June 1942. An aircraft to counter it, the Hell-cat, was promptly designed and manufactured in prodigious numbers.[91] Japanese aircraft production reached its peak in June 1944, when 2,857 were produced; thereafter, it was steadily reduced by Allied bombing. In the whole of the war Japan made only 62,795 aircraft, of which 52,109 were lost.[92] The United States was producing more than 100,000 a year by 1943. It was the same story with warships. During the war, Japan could only get twenty carriers into commission, of which sixteen were destroyed. By the summer of 1944 the United States alone had nearly 100 carriers operating in the Pacific.[93] The imbalance was reinforced by Japan's irrational strategy. Japanese submariners were trained only to attack enemy warships. On the General Staff, only two officers were allocated to anti-submarine, mining and anti-aircraft warfare, contemptuously categorized as 'rear-line defence'. Even a limited convoy system was not adopted until 1943 and full convoying began only in March 1944; by that time the US navy had hundreds of submarines and a full-scale 'wolf-pack' system.[94] As a result, out of the 6 million tons of shipping with which Japan began the war, she lost over 5 million: 50 per cent to submarines, 40 per cent to aircraft, the rest to mines. The mistakes of the navy compounded that of the army which, in its territorial greed during the first five months of war, scattered its forces over 3,285,000 square miles, with 350 million 'subjects', garrisoned by 3,175,000 men, most of whom had to be supplied by sea. The result was that the Japanese navy destroyed itself, as well as the mercantile marine, in the increasingly futile effort to keep the army alive and armed. Many in fact starved to death or, lacking ammunition, were reduced to fighting with bamboo spears.[95]

The Japanese army strategy was to cling to its gains, arguing that US conscripts would be no match for Japanese soldiers in close-quarter fighting, and that high casualties would lead American public opinion to force its government to compromise. But once the Allies had established sea and air superiority, they adopted the 'Central Pacific strategy' of hopping or leap-frogging the Central Pacific islands, on the route to Japan itself, using amphibious landings and making maximum advantage of overwhelming fire-power.[96] The Japanese fought desperately throughout, but technology and productivity allowed the Americans to establish and maintain a colonial-era casualty-ratio. The pattern was set in the 'hinge' battle of Guadalcanal, November 1942, when the Japanese lost 25,000 against only 1,592 American fatalities. When the Central Pacific offensive began, at Tarawa Atoll in November 1943, the Americans had to kill all but seventeen of the 5,000 garrison, and lost 1,000 men themselves. As a result, they increased the fire-power and lengthened the leap-frogging. At the next island, Kwajalein, the air-sea bombardment was so cataclysmic that, an eye-witness said, 'the entire island looked as if it had been picked up to 20,000 feet and then dropped'. Virtually all the 8,500 defenders had to be killed, but firepower kept American dead down to 373.[97] These ratios were maintained. On Leyte, the Japanese lost all but 5,000 of their 70,000 men; the Americans only 3,500. At Iwojima, the Americans sustained their worst casualty ratio: 4,917 dead to over 18,000 Japanese; and in taking Okinawa they had their highest casualty-bill: 12,520 dead or missing, against Japanese losses of 185,000 killed. But in general American losses were small. Most Japanese were killed by sea or air bombardment, or cut off and starved. They never set eyes on an American foot-soldier or got within bayonet-range of him. Even in Burma, where the fighting was very severe throughout and sea-air superiority could not be used, the Indo-British 14th Army killed 128,000 Japanese, against their own total casualties of less than 20,000.[98]

The object of the Central Pacific strategy was to bring Japan itself within range of land-based heavy bombers, maintaining a round-the-clock bombardment on an ever-growing scale. In short, this was the war the air expert Douet had predicted in the 1920s, the British Appeasers had feared in the 1930s, and which Churchill had tried to wage against Germany. It started in November 1944, when the captured Guam base came into full use, and B29 Flying Fortresses, each carrying eight tons of bombs, could attack in 1,000-strong masses with fighter-escorts. In 1939 Roosevelt had sent messages to the belligerents begging them to refrain from the 'inhuman barbarism' of bombing civilians. That attitude did not survive Pearl Harbor. From March to July 1945, against virtually no resistance, the B29s dropped 100,000 tons of incendiaries on sixty-six Japanese cities and towns, wiping out 170,000 square miles of closely populated streets. On the night of 9–10 March, 300 B29s, helped by a strong north wind, turned the old swamp-plane of Musashi, on which Tokyo is built, into an inferno, destroying fifteen square miles of the city, killing 83,000 and injuring 102,000. A British eye-witness in a nearby POW camp compared it to the horror of the 1923 earthquake which he had also experienced.[99] Even before the dropping of the A-bombs, Japanese figures show that raids on sixty-nine areas had destroyed 2,250,000 buildings, made 9 million homeless, killed 260,000 and injured 412,000. These raids increased steadily in number and power; and in July the Allied fleets closed in, using their heavy guns to bombard the coastal cities from close range.

On 16 July Oppenheimer's plutonium bomb was exploded on the Almogordo bombing-range in New Mexico. It generated a fireball with a temperature four times that at the centre of the sun. Oppenheimer quoted the phrase from the *Bhagavadgita*, 'the radiance of a thousand suns . . . I am become as death, the destroyer of worlds.' Fermi, more prosaically, calculated that the shock-wave indicated a blast of 10,000 tons of TNT. The news was flashed to the new American President, Harry S. Truman, on his way back from

Potsdam. A protocol, signed by Churchill and Roosevelt at the latter's Hyde Park estate on 9 September 1944, had stated that 'when the bomb is finally available it might perhaps after mature consideration be used against the Japanese'. Truman promptly signed an order to use the bomb as soon as possible and there does not seem to have been any prolonged discussion about the wisdom or morality of using it, at any rate at the top political and military level. As General Groves put it: 'The Upper Crust want it as soon as possible.'[100] America and Britain were already hurling at Japan every ounce of conventional explosive they could deliver, daily augmented by new technology and resources; to decline to use the super-bomb would have been illogical, indeed irresponsible, since its novelty might have an impact on Japan's so far inflexible resolve to continue resistance.

The Emperor had been told that the war could not be won as early as February 1942. In 1943 the navy had reached the conclusion that defeat was inevitable. In 1944 Tojo had been thrown out by a navy *putsch*. None of this made any difference. The fear of assassination was too great. In May 1945 Russia was asked to mediate. But Stalin sat on the offer, since in January at Yalta he had been promised substantial territorial rewards to enter the Japanese war in August. On 6 June the Japanese Supreme Council approved a document, 'Fundamental Policy to be Followed henceforth in the Conduct of the War', which asserted 'we shall . . . prosecute the war to the bitter end'. The final plan for the defence of Japan itself, 'Operation Decision', provided for 10,000 suicide planes (mostly converted trainers), fifty-three infantry divisions and twenty-five brigades: 2,350,000 trained troops would fight on the beaches, backed by 4 million army and navy civil employees and a civilian militia of 28 million. They were to have weapons which included muzzle-loaders, bamboo spears and bows and arrows. Special legislation was passed by the Diet to form this army.[101] The Allied commanders assumed that their own forces must expect up to a million casualties if an invasion of Japan became necessary. How many Japanese lives would be lost? Assuming comparable ratios to those already experienced, it would be in the range of 10–20 million.

The Allied aim was to break Japanese resistance before an invasion became unavoidable. On 1 August 820 B29s unloaded 6,600 tons of explosive on five towns in North Kyushu. Five days later America's one, untested uranium bomb was dropped on Hiroshima, Japan's eighth largest city, headquarters of the 2nd General Army and an important embarkation port. Some 720,000 leaflets warning that the city would be 'obliterated' had been dropped two days before. No notice was taken, partly because it was rumoured Truman's mother had once lived nearby, and it was thought that the city, being pretty, would be used by the Americans as an occupation centre. Of the 245,000 people in the city, about 100,000 died that day, about 100,000 subsequently.[102] Some died without visible injury or cause. Others were covered with bright, multi-coloured spots. Many vomited blood. One man put his burned hand in water and 'something strange and bluish came out of it, like smoke'. Another, almost blind, regained perfect sight; but all his hair fell out.

Publicly, the Japanese government reaction was to send a protest to the world through the Swiss embassy. Having ignored international law for twenty years they now denounced 'the disregard of international law by the American government, particularly the brutality of the new land-mine used against Hiroshima'. Privately, they summoned Nishina, head of their atomic programme, to Tokyo to demand whether the Hiroshima bomb was a genuine nuclear weapon and, if so, whether he could duplicate it within six months.[103] This does not suggest that a single atomic weapon would have been decisive.

The second, plutonium-type, bomb was dropped on 9 August, not on its primary target (which the pilot could not find) but on its alternative one which, by a cruel irony, was the Christian city of Nagasaki, the centre of resistance to Shinto; 74,800 were killed by it that day. This may have persuaded the Japanese that the Americans had a large stock of such bombs (in fact only two were ready, and scheduled for dropping on 13 and 16 August). On the following day Russia, which now had 1,600,000 men on the Manchurian border, declared war, following the bargain made at Yalta. A few hours before, the Japanese had cabled accepting in principle the Allied terms of unconditional surrender. Nuclear warfare was then suspended, though conventional raids continued, 1,500 B29s bombing Tokyo from dawn to dusk on 13 August.

The final decision to surrender was taken on 14 August. The War Minister and the two chiefs of staff opposed it, and the Prime Minister, Admiral Suzuki, had to ask the Tenno to resolve the dispute. As Hirohito later put it:

At the time of the surrender, there was no prospect of agreement no matter how many discussions they had . . . . When Suzuki asked me at the Imperial conference which of the two views should be taken, I was given the opportunity to express my own free will for the first time without violating anybody else's authority or responsibilities.[104]

Hirohito then recorded a surrender message to the Japanese people which admitted that 'the war situation has developed not necessarily to Japan's advantage' and that in order to avoid 'the total extinction of human civilization' Japan would have to 'endure the unendurable and suffer what is unsufferable'.[105] Army officers broke into the palace to destroy this recording before it was broadcast, killed the head of the Imperial Guard and set fire to the homes of the Prime Minister and the chief court minister. But they failed to stop the broadcast; and immediately after it the War Minister and others committed suicide in the Palace square.[106]

The evidence does not suggest that the surrender could have been obtained without the A-bombs being used. Without them, there would have been heavy fighting in Manchuria, and a further intensification of the conventional bombardment (already nearing the nuclear threshold of about 10,000 tons of TNT a day), even if an invasion had not been required. The use of nuclear weapons thus saved Japanese, as well as Allied, lives. Those who died in Hiroshima and Nagasaki were the victims not so much of Anglo–American technology as of a paralysed system of government made possible by an evil ideology which had expelled not only absolute moral values but reason itself.

The true nature of Japan's form of totalitarianism only became apparent when the POW camps were opened up and the International Military Tribunal began its work. Its president, Sir William Webb, noted:

... the crimes of the Japanese accused were far less heinous, varied and extensive than those of the Germans accused at Nuremberg [but] torture, murder, rape and other cruelties of the most barbarous character were practised on such a vast scale and on such a common pattern that the only conclusion possible was that those atrocities were either secretly ordered or wilfully permitted by the Japanese government or its members, or by the leaders of the Armed Forces.[107]

David James, the British interpreter who visited the main camps after the surrender, noted the collapse of absolute moral values among officers of the post-1920s intakes, who had been 'thoroughly drilled in *Kodo* and state Shinto' and who were responsible for the routine cruelties: 'they had the same killing instincts in and out of action . . . . For that reason there was that common pattern of atrocity which appeared to surprise the Tribunal sitting in Tokyo.' The regime did not possess concentration camps as such: at the most it had only four hundred political prisoners of its own. But its POW camps were run on the same economic principles as Nazi and Soviet slave-camps. After visiting them James reported in September 1945:

The basic principles of Japanese POW administration were: extract the maximum amount of work at the minimum cost in food and military supplies. In the end this plunged them into an abyss of crime which engulfed the entire administration and turned Japanese into murderers pure and simple . . . . All camps were run on the same lines: they did not break any of their own regulations . . . if we try them we must bring evidence against individuals but it is the system which produced the criminals.[108]

Hence, of the 50,00 prisoners who worked on the Siam railway, 16,000 died of torture, disease and starvation. Captured Japanese field orders repeatedly emphasized that prisoners thought to be of no use were to be killed. Evidence before the courts showed that Japanese medical officers removed hearts and livers from healthy prisoners while they were still alive. Cannibalism of Allied prisoners was authorized when other food was not available. The Japanese killed more British troops in prison camps than on the field of battle. The Japanese POW record, in fact, was much worse than the Nazis': of 235,000 Anglo–American POWs held by Germany and Italy only 4 per cent died, whereas of the 132,000 in Japanese custody 27 per cent died.[109]

The Allied Tribunal in Tokyo sentenced twenty-five major war criminals, especially those responsible for planning the war and the four major horrors – the Nanking massacre, the Bataan 'death march', the Thai–Burma railway and the sack of Manila. Seven, including Tojo, were hanged. Local military commissions condemned a further 920 war-criminals to death and over 3,000 to prison. Of the non-white judges of the Tribunal, the Indian, Radhabino Pal, dissented, saying the Japanese had acted throughout only in self-defence and that the trial was 'victors' justice'. The Filipino judge, Delfin Jarahilla, said the sentences were too lenient. In fact Japanese atrocities against Indian and Filippino soldiers and against Chinese, Malay and other non-white civilians were infinitely more savage and numerous than any inflicted on the Anglo–Americans.[110] The chief victims of the system were the Japanese people, of whom more than 4 million died: for the same dogma which taught men to treat prisoners as capital criminals was responsible both for the decision to embark on suicidal war and the delay in making peace. Prime Minister Konoye, one of the guilty men, left by his deathbed a copy of Oscar Wilde's De Profundis, having carefully underlined the words: 'Terrible as was what the world did to me, what I did to myself was far more terrible still' – an epitaph for totalitarian Japan.[111] And, as we have noted time and again in this book, the holistic principle of moral corruption operates a satanic Gresham's Law, in which evil drives out good. The American aircraft which destroyed the convoy reinforcing the Lae garrison in New Guinea, 3 March 1943, machine-gunned the survivors swimming in the water, reporting: 'It was a grisly task, but a military necessity since Japanese soldiers do not surrender and, within swimming distance of shore, they could not be allowed to land and join the Lae garrison.'[112] It became commonplace for the Allies to shoot Japanese attempting to surrender. One of the defending counsel at the Tribunal, Captain Adolf Feel Jr, exclaimed bitterly: 'We have defeated our enemies on the battlefield but we have let their spirit triumph in our hearts.'[113] That was an exaggeration; but it contained an element of truth. The small-scale Japanese bombing of Chinese cities in 1937–8 had been condemned by the entire liberal establishment in America. When the time came to determine the first target for the atom bomb, it was the President of Harvard, James Conant, representing the interests of civilization on the National Defense Research Committee, who made the decisive suggestion 'that the most desirable target would be a vital war plant employing a large number of workers and closely surrounded by workers' houses'.[114]

In any case, the confusion of moral issues by the end of the war was fundamentally compounded by the presence, in the ranks of the righteous, of the Soviet totalitarian power. There was scarcely a crime the Nazis or the knights of bushido had committed, or even imagined, which the Soviet regime had not also perpetrated, usually on an even larger scale. It ran precisely the type of system which had produced the war and its horrors. More specifically, the Nazi–Soviet Pact of September 1939 and the Japanese–Soviet Pact of April 1941 had made the Axis aggressions possible.

Nevertheless, Soviet Russia not only judged the guilty of the war it had helped to create but emerged as its sole beneficiary, by virtue of precisely one of those secret wartime treaties – or bribes – which the Treaty of Versailles had so roundly condemned. And not only Versailles. The Atlantic Charter of 14 August 1941 (reiterated in the United Nations Declaration of 1 January 1942) stated that the signatories 'seek no aggrandizement, territorial or other ... they desire to see no territorial changes that do not accord with the freely-expressed wishes of the peoples concerned'. The Anglo–Russian Treaty of Alliance, 26 May 1942, stated (Article 5): ' ... they will act in accordance with the two principles of not seeking territorial aggrandizement for themselves and of non-interference in the internal affairs of other states'. Yet at the Yalta Conference of January 1945, in return for agreeing to enter the war against Japan 'two or three months after Germany has surrendered', Stalin demanded recognition of Russia's possession of Outer Mongolia; southern Sakhalin and adjacent islands; internationalization of Darien with the safeguarding of the 'pre-eminent interests of the Soviet Union'; the lease of Port Arthur as a base; the right to operate, jointly with the Chinese, the Chinese Eastern railway and the South

Manchurian railroad, with safeguards for 'the pre-eminent interests of the Soviet Union'; and, by outright annexation, the Kuril Islands. Roosevelt agreed to all these acquisitive conditions virtually without argument; and Churchill, desperate for his support on issues nearer home, acquiesced, since the Far East was largely 'an American affair . . . . To us the problem was remote and secondary.'[115]

China, the principal victim of this gross act of territorial larceny, which made the destruction of her regime possible, was not present at Yalta and, though an ally, was not even informed of these terms in principle until six months later, or in detail until 14 August, by which time Russia had declared war and the agreement was irreversible. The official Russian declaration of war was not issued until four hours after the Japanese had agreed in principle to yield.[116] Stalin got his blood-bargain for nothing, and the legitimate powers could not justify the surrender of their salient wartime principle even on grounds of iron military necessity.

What gave an additional dimension of mockery to the trials of German and Japanese war-criminals was that, at the very time when the evidence for them was being collected, Britain and America were themselves assisting Stalin to perpetrate a crime on a comparable scale, to the point of using force to deliver the victims into his hands. The Allies knew, and said nothing, about the Soviet deportation of eight entire nations in the years 1941 and 1943–4, though this was a war-crime under the definition of genocide later drawn up by the United Nations (9 December 1948). But they could not ignore the Soviet demand, made on 31 May 1944, that any Russian nationals who fell into Allied hands during the liberation of Europe must be returned to Russia, whether or not they were willing. In practice it was found that 10 per cent of 'German' prisoners were in fact Russians. Some wanted to return; some did not. They were units in a vast human convulsion few of them understood. A British intelligence report (17 June 1944) noted: 'They were never asked if they would like to join the German army but simply given German uniforms and issued with rifles . . . . These Russians never considered themselves anything but prisoners.'[117] The Americans resolved the dilemma by treating any prisoner in German uniform as German unless he insisted he was not. The British Foreign Office insisted on a pedantic rectitude. Its legal adviser, Sir Patrick Dean, minuted (24 June):

This is purely a question for the Soviet authorities and does not concern His Majesty's Government. In due course all those with whom the Soviet authorities desire to deal must be handed over to them, and we are not concerned with the fact that they may be shot or otherwise more harshly dealt with than they might be under English law.

On this basis, and despite Churchill's misgivings, the Foreign Secretary, Anthony Eden, forced through the War cabinet a decision (4 September 1944) which wholly conceded Stalin's case, and which was later written into the Yalta agreement.[118]

As a result, many hundreds of thousands of human beings were dispatched to Stalin's care. Of the first batch of 10,000, all but twelve went voluntarily. An American diplomat watched their arrival: 'They were marched off under heavy guard to an unknown destination.' With time the reluctance increased. The men aboard the *Empire Pride*, which docked at Odessa on 10 June 1945, had to be held under armed guard and included many sick and injured from desperate suicide attempts. A British observer recorded:

The Soviet authorities refused to accept any of the stretcher cases as such and even the patients who were dying were made to walk off the ship carrying their own baggage . . . [One] prisoner who had attempted suicide was very roughly handled and his wound opened up and allowed to bleed. He was taken off the ship and marched behind a packing case on the docks. A shot was heard but nothing more was seen.

He added that thirty-one prisoners were taken behind a warehouse, and fifteen minutes later machine-gun fire was heard. The senior POW on the ship, a major, informed on about 300 of those on board, all of whom were probably shot. Then the major was shot too – a typical Stalin touch.[119]

In an excess of zeal, the British Foreign Office also handed over 50,000 Cossacks who had surrendered in South Austria. These men had been refugees for over a generation and were not liable to repatriation even under the Yalta deal; but they were given to Stalin as a kind of human bonus, together with their wives and children. Some 25,000 Croats were likewise 'returned' to the Communist regime in Yugoslavia, where they became showpieces of a 'death march' through the cities: '. . . starved, thirsty, emaciated, disfigured, suffering and agonizing, they were forced to run long distances alongside their "liberators", who were riding on horses or in carts'.[120] In order to force these men, women and children across the frontiers, British troops had to use their bayonets, in some cases shooting to kill to break resistance, and occasionally employing even flame-throwers. There were large numbers of suicides, sometimes of whole families.[121] Of those presented to Stalin many were promptly shot. The rest lingered on in the camps, their existence unknown or forgotten, until in due course Solzhenitsyn drew attention to the vast scale of this particular infamy. But of course forcible repatriation was only one aspect of the problem raised for the Anglo-Saxon powers by their now triumphant totalitarian ally.

THIRTEEN

Peace by Terror

On 10 January 1946 the Tory MP and diarist 'Chips' Channon attended a society wedding in London and remarked to another guest, Lady ('Emerald') Cunard, 'how quickly normal life had been resumed. "After all", I said, pointing to the crowded room, "this is what we have been fighting for." "What," said Emerald, "are they all Poles?"'[1]

It was, indeed, all too easy to forget Poland. Yet Poland was the cause of the war in the sense that, if Poland had not existed, the war would have taken a radically different course. And Poland terminated the war too in the sense that it provoked the collapse of the wartime Alliance and the beginning of democratic–Communist confrontation. The tale was resumed where it had left off when Stalin and Hitler signed the pact of August 1939, and Soviet Russia now represented the acquisitive totalitarian principle on the world stage. Poland was the awkward piece on the global chessboard, a reminder that the war had not been so much a conflict between right and wrong as a struggle for survival.

Of course the notion that the 'Grand Alliance' was in any way altruistic had been an illusion from the start. It was largely the creation of Roosevelt, partly for his own political purposes, partly because he believed it. Those of his countrymen who had long professional experience of dealing with Stalin and his government were hotly, despairingly, opposed to Roosevelt's line. Ambassador Laurence Steinhardt, who succeeded Davies in Moscow, shared the hard-line State Department view, known as the 'Riga school':

Approaches by Britain or the United States must be interpreted here as signs of weakness . . . the moment these people here get into their heads that we are appeasing them, making up to them or need them, they immediately stop being co-operative . . . . My experience has been that they respond only to force and if force cannot be applied, to straight oriental bartering.[2]

Roosevelt would have none of this. The moment Hitler's declaration of war made Russia America's ally, he devised procedures for bypassing the State Department and the Embassy and dealing with Stalin directly.[3] His intermediary was Harry Hopkins, a political fixer who reported back that Stalin, naturally, was delighted with the idea: '[he] has no confidence in our ambassador or in any of our officials'.[4] Roosevelt also wanted to bypass Churchill, whom he thought an incorrigible old imperialist, incapable of understanding ideological idealism. He wrote to him, 18 March 1942: 'I know you will not mind my being brutally frank when I tell you that I think that I can personally handle Stalin better than either your Foreign Office or my State Department. Stalin hates the guts of all your top people. He thinks he likes me better, and I hope he will continue to do so.'[5] This vanity, so reminiscent of Chamberlain's belief that he alone could 'handle' Hitler, was compounded by an astonishing naïvety. He did not believe Stalin wanted territory. He rebuked Churchill: 'You have four-hundred years of acquisitive instinct in your blood and you just don't understand how a country might not want to acquire land somewhere if they can get it.'[6] 'I think', he said of Stalin, 'that if I give him everything I possibly can and ask nothing from him in return, *noblesse oblige*, he won't try to annex anything and will work with me for a world of democracy and peace.'[7]

The menace Roosevelt's blindness constituted to the post-war stability of Europe first became apparent at the Teheran Conference which Churchill, Roosevelt and Stalin attended in November 1943. The chairman of the British chiefs of staff, Sir Alan Brooke, summed it up: 'Stalin has got the President in his pocket.'[8] Churchill complained to one of his Ministers of State, Harold Macmillan: 'Germany is finished, though it may take some time to clean up the mess. The real problem now is Russia. I can't get the Americans to see it.'[9] Throughout 1944, though the invasion of Europe was successfully launched, Churchill's anxieties increased. After the Allied breakout of July–August 1944, the pace of the advance slowed down. General Eisenhower, the Supreme Commander, refused to accept the salient point that the degree to which his troops penetrated into Central Europe would in fact determine the post-war map: 'I would be loath to hazard American lives for purely political purposes,' he insisted.[10] As the Soviets advanced, they made their hostile intentions plain enough. Seizing the German experimental submarine station in Gdynia, they refused Allied naval experts access to its secrets, though the battle of the Atlantic was still raging and the convoys carrying arms to Russia were still under fierce U-boat attacks.[11] The American generals wanted to preserve the maximum co-operation with the Soviet armed forces so that, at the earliest possible moment, they could transfer troops to the East to finish Japan (with, they hoped, massive Soviet support), and then all go home. As Churchill saw it, that would leave the British, with twelve divisions (about 820,000 men), facing 13,000 Soviet tanks, 16,000 front-line aircraft and 525 divisions totalling over 5 million.[12] His task, as a Foreign Office memo put it, was to discover how 'to make use of American power', to steer 'this great unwieldy barge' into 'the right harbour'; otherwise it would 'wallow in the ocean, an isolated menace to navigation'.[13]

Churchill decided to pursue a two-fold policy: to bargain realistically with Stalin when he could, and to seek to screw Roosevelt up to the sticking-point at the same time. In October 1944 he went to Moscow and thrust at Stalin what he called a 'naughty document', which set out, since 'Marshal Stalin was a realist', the 'proportion of interests' of the Great Powers in five Balkan countries: Yugoslavia and Hungary were to be split 50–50 between Russia and the rest; Russia was to have 90 per cent in Romania and 75 per cent in Bulgaria; while Britain, in accord with the USA, was to have 90 per cent in Greece. According to the minutes taken by the British Ambassador, Sir Archibald Clark-Kerr, Stalin haggled over Bulgaria, where he evidently wanted 90 per cent; then he signed the paper with a tick of a blue pencil. He also agreed to hold back the Italian Communists.[14]

The 'naughty document' was in effect an attempt to exclude Russia from the Mediterranean at the price of giving her Romania and Bulgaria as satellites. Churchill calculated that Greece was the only brand to be saved from the burning, for British troops were already in place there: what he secured in Moscow was Stalin's agreement to give Britain a free hand – and it was promptly used. On 4 December, when civil war broke out in Athens, Churchill determining to use force to crush the Communists: he worked late into the night sending out cables, 'sitting gyrating in his armchair and dictating on the machine to Miss Layton, who did not bat an eyelid at the many blasphemies with which the old man interspersed his official phrases'. His key cable to General Scobie, the British commander, insisted: 'We have to hold and dominate Athens. It would be a great thing for you to succeed in this without bloodshed if possible, but also with bloodshed if necessary.'[15] Bloodshed was necessary; but Greece was saved for democracy. Indeed, though stability in the Mediterranean theatre was not assured until the Communists lost the Italian elections in April 1948, Churchill effectively, and almost singlehandedly, kept totalitarianism out of the Mediterranean for a generation by his vigorous policy in late 1944 – his last great contribution to human freedom.

But Churchill was powerless to save Eastern Europe. As he put it in a cabinet minute:

It is beyond the power of this country to prevent all sorts of things crashing at the present time. The responsibility lies with the United States and my desire is to give them all the support in our power. If they do not feel able to do anything, then we must let matters take their course.[16]

But at the critical meeting at Yalta in January 1945, Roosevelt deliberately blocked Churchill's attempts to co-ordinate Anglo–American policy in advance: he did not wish, said Averell Harriman, to 'feed Soviet suspicions that the British and Americans would be operating in concert'.[17] When Poland came up, Roosevelt settled for a Russian agreement to elections in which 'all democratic and anti-Nazi parties shall have the right to take part', but he did not back the British demand for international supervision of the poll. Instead he produced a typical piece of Rooseveltian rhetoric, a 'Declaration on Liberated Europe', with vague commitments to 'the right of all peoples to choose the form of government under which they will live'. The Russians were happy to sign it, especially after they heard Roosevelt's staggering announcement that all American forces would be out of Europe within two years: that was just what Stalin wanted to know.[18]

The Cold War may be said to date from the immediate aftermath of the Yalta Conference, to be precise from March 1945. Of course in a sense Soviet Russia had waged Cold War since October 1917: it was inherent in the historical determinism of Leninism. The pragmatic alliance from June 1941 onwards was a mere interruption. It was inevitable that Stalin would resume his hostile predation sooner or later. His mistake was to do so too quickly. It was not that he was impatient, like Hitler. He did not believe in an imminent eschatology. But he was greedy. He was too cautious to follow Hitler's example of systematically creating opportunities for plunder, but he could not resist taking such opportunities when they presented themselves. His sensible tactic was to hold his hand until the Americans had vanished to the other side of the Atlantic. Instead, seeing the Polish fruit was ripe, he could not resist taking it. Roosevelt's aide Admiral Leahy, the most hard-headed member of the American delegation, had complained even at Yalta that the Polish agreement was 'so elastic that the Russians can stretch it all the way from Yalta to Washington without ever technically breaking it'.[19] But once the commission set up by Yalta to fulfil the free election pledge met on 23 February, it became clear Stalin intended to ignore his pledges. The critical moment came on 23 March, when Molotov announced the elections would be held Soviet-style. When Roosevelt got Harriman's account of this meeting two days later, he banged his fist on his wheelchair: 'Averell is right. We can't do business with Stalin. He has broken every one of the promises he made at Yalta.'[20] Roosevelt's political education was assisted by a series of thirteen forceful messages Churchill sent him, 8 March–12 April 1945; and disillusioned at last, he went to Warm Springs to die, telling a journalist that either Stalin was not in control or was 'not a man of his word'.[21]

Nevertheless, in his last weeks Roosevelt did nothing to encourage Eisenhower to push on rapidly towards Berlin, Vienna and Prague, as the British wanted. 'The Americans could not understand', General Montgomery wrote sadly, 'that it was of little avail to win the war strategically if we lost it politically.'[22] The new President, Harry Truman, was not a member of the wealthy, guilt-ridden East Coast establishment and had none of Roosevelt's fashionable progressive fancies. He was ignorant, but he learnt fast; his instincts were democratic and straightforward. At 5.30 on 23 April he summoned Molotov to Blair House (he had not yet moved into the White House) and told him Russia must carry out what it had agreed at Yalta on Poland: 'I gave it to him straight. I let him have it. It was the straight one-two to the jaw.' Molotov: 'I have never been talked to like that in my life.' Truman: 'Carry out your agreements and you won't get talked to like that.'[23] But Truman could not transform American military policy in the last days of the war. General Bradley calculated it would cost 100,000 US casualties to take Berlin; General Marshall said that capturing Prague was not possible; General Eisenhower was opposed to anything which ended military co-operation with the Red Army; all wanted Soviet assistance against Japan.[24] So Eastern Europe and most of the Balkans were lost to totalitarianism.

It was unclear for some time whether Western Europe could be saved too. Even at the political and diplomatic level, it took precious weeks and months to reverse the Roosevelt policy. In the first half of 1945 the State Department was still trying to prevent the publication of any material critical of Soviet Russia, even straight factual journalism, such as William White's *Report on the Russians*.[25] At Potsdam, in July, Truman had at his elbow ex-Ambassador Davies, now the proud holder of the Order of Lenin, who urged, 'I think Stalin's feelings are hurt. Please be nice to him.'[26] Churchill, defeated at the elections on 25 July, had a dream in which he saw himself lying under a white sheet, his feet stretched out: dead.[27] His Labour successors, obsessed with home problems and Britain's appalling financial plight, talked vaguely of rebuilding a European alliance with France, but they were more afraid of a resurgent Germany than a Soviet steamroller.[28] There were many who thought the game was up. Harriman, back from Moscow, told the Navy Secretary, James

Forrestal, that 'half and maybe all of Europe might be Communist by the end of next winter'.[29]

Again, it was Stalin's greed which led him to overplay his hand and so reverse the process of American withdrawal. And it was a greed not only for land and power but for blood. He arrested sixteen leading non-Communist Polish politicians, accused them of 'terrorism' and set in motion the machinery for the last of his show-trials.[30] American envoys and commanders on the spot sent messages confirming the same pattern everywhere: Robert Patterson from Belgrade reported that anyone seen with a British or American was immediately arrested; Maynard Barnes cabled details about a bloodbath of 20,000 in Bulgaria; Arthur Schoenfeld described the imposition of a Communist dictatorship in Hungary; Ellery Stone in Rome advised that a Communist *putsch* was likely in Italy. William Donovan, head of the Office of Strategic Services, then America's nearest approach to an intelligence agency, advised measures to co-ordinate Western defence on the basis of the cumulatively terrifying reports flowing into his office from American agents all over Europe.[31] But it was Stalin's policies which supplied the raw material for these reports. And it was Stalin's brand of intransigent diplomacy, conducted through Molotov, which brought matters to a head at the Foreign Ministers Conference in Moscow in December 1945. There, Ernest Bevin, Britain's new Foreign Secretary, bluntly called Molotov's arguments 'Hitlerite philosophy'; and James Byrnes, Secretary of State, said Russia was 'trying to do in a slick-dip way what Hitler tried to do in domineering smaller countries by force'.[32] When Byrnes reported back on 5 January 1946, Truman made his mind up: 'I do not think we should play compromise any longer . . . . I am tired of babying the Soviets.'[33] The next month a well-timed 8,000-word cable arrived from George Kennan in Moscow, which crystallized what most people in the Administration were beginning to feel about the Soviet threat: the 'Long Telegram', as it came to be known. 'It reads exactly', its author wrote, 'like one of those primers put out by alarmed congressional committees or by the Daughters of the American Revolution, designed to arouse the citizenry to the dangers of the Communist conspiracy.'[34]

A fortnight later, on 5 March, Churchill made the Cold War a public fact when he delivered a speech, under Truman's sponsorship, at the university of Fulton:

From Stettin in the Baltic to Trieste in the Adriatic, an iron curtain has descended across the continent. Beyond that line lie all the capitals of the ancient states of Central and Eastern Europe . . . what I must call the Soviet sphere, and all are subject in one form or another, not only to Soviet influence but to a very high and in many cases increasing measure of control from Moscow.

Since, he added, the Russians respected military strength, America and Britain must continue their joint defence arrangements, so that there would be 'no quivering, precarious balance of power to offer its temptation to ambition and adventure' but an 'overwhelming assurance of security'. Afterwards, at a dinner given by the owner of *Time*, Henry Luce, the triumphant orator gobbled caviare: 'You know, Uncle Joe used to send me a lot of this. But I don't suppose I shall get any more now.' By speaking at precisely the right time – by May US polls showed that 83 per cent of the nation favoured his idea of a permanent military alliance – Churchill had averted any possibility of a repetition of the tragic American withdrawal from Europe in 1919. He claimed he lost $75 playing poker with Truman, 'But it was worth it.'[35]

Stalin continued to draw the Americans deeper into Cold War. In March 1946 he missed the deadline for the withdrawal of his troops from Iran, and finally did so only after an angry confrontation at the new United Nations Security Council. In August the Yugoslavs shot down two American transport planes and the same month Stalin began putting pressure on Turkey. The Americans responded accordingly. The prototype of the CIA was set up, and at a White House party to celebrate, Truman handed out black hats, cloaks and wooden daggers, and stuck a fake black moustache on Admiral Leahy's face.[36] America and Canada formed a joint air and anti-submarine defence system. The British and US air forces began exchanging war plans; their intelligence agencies resumed contact. By midsummer the Anglo–American alliance was in unofficial existence again. Truman undertook a purge of his Administration to eliminate the pro-Soviet elements. The last of the New Dealers in the cabinet was Henry Wallace, Agriculture Secretary, a profound admirer of Stalin, Anglophobic, anti-Churchill: 'nothing but a cat-bastard', as Truman put it. In July he sent the President a 5,000-word private letter, advocating unilateral disarmament and a massive air-and-trade programme with Russia, then leaked it. Truman confided to his diary: 'Wallace is a pacifist 100 per cent. He wants us to disband our armed forces, give Russia our atomic secrets and trust a bunch of adventurers in the Kremlin Politburo.... The Reds, phonies and the parlour pinks seem to be banded together and are becoming a national danger. I am afraid they are a sabotage front for Uncle Joe Stalin.'[37] The next day he sacked Wallace; not a mouse stirred. By October Churchill was able to claim: 'What I said at Fulton has been overpassed by the movement of events.'

In 1947–9 America undertook a series of formal commitments to Europe which became the basis of Western global policy for the next generation. The process began with a desperate signal from Britain that she could no longer support the posture of a world power. The war had cost her $30 billion, a quarter of her net wealth. She had sold $5 billion of foreign assets and accumulated $12 billion of foreign debts. America had given her a post-war loan, but this did not cover the gap in her trade – exports in 1945 were less than a third of the 1938 figure – nor her outgoings as a slender pillar of stability in Europe, the Mediterranean and the Middle East. In 1946 Britain spent 19 per cent of her Gross National Product on defence (against 10 per cent in the USA). By the beginning of 1947 she had spent $3 billion on international relief programmes, $320 million feeding Germany in 1946 alone, $330 million keeping the peace in Palestine, and cumulative totals of $540 million on Greece and $375 million on Turkey. On 6 January, a snowstorm heralded the worst winter in more than a century, which continued until the end of March. The coal froze in the pit-head stocks and could not be moved. Electricity cuts shut factories and put 2 million out of work. The Fuel Minister, Manny Shinwell, spoke of 'a condition of complete disaster'. The loan was virtually gone; $100 million were pouring from the reserves each week.

On 21 February the British informed Truman they would have to cut the Greek–Turkey commitment. Three days later Truman decided he would have to take it on. There was a tense meeting in the Oval Office on 26 February to outline the idea to leading Congressmen. General Marshall, the new Secretary of State, fumbled the job, and his deputy, Dean Acheson, decided to chip in. He said that 'Soviet pressure' on the Near East had brought it to the point where a breakthrough 'might open three continents to Soviet penetration'. Like 'apples in a barrel infected by one rotten one', the 'corruption' of Greece would 'infect Iran and all the East'. It would 'carry infection to Africa through Asia Minor and Egypt' and 'to Europe through Italy and France'. Soviet Russia 'was playing one of the greatest gambles in history at minimal cost'. It did not need to win them all: 'even one or two offered immense gains'. America 'alone' was 'in a position to break up the play'. These were the stakes that British withdrawal offered 'to an eager and ruthless opponent'. This was followed by a long silence. Then Arthur Vandenberg, a former isolationist, spoke for the Congressmen: 'Mr President, if you will say that to the Congress and the country, I will support you, and I believe most of its members will do the same.'[38]

Truman announced the 'Truman Doctrine' on 12 March. 'I believe that it must be the policy of the United States to support free peoples who are resisting attempted subjugation by armed minorities or outside pressure . . . we must assist free peoples to work out their own destinies in their own way.' The help must be 'primarily' economic. He asked for money for Greece and Turkey, plus civil and military experts, for a start: and got it with two-to-one majorities in both houses. Thus isolationism died, by act of Joseph Stalin. Two months later, on 5 June, the Secretary of State unveiled the Marshall Plan at the Harvard Commencement. It was vague; as Acheson paraphrased it: 'If the Europeans, all or some of them, could get together on a plan of what was needed to get them out of the dreadful situation . . . we would take a look at their plan and see what aid we might practically give.'[39] Eventually twenty-two European nations responded. The Czechs and Poles wished to do the same; Stalin vetoed it.

The programme began in July 1948, continued for three years, and eventually cost the American government $10.2 billion. It made excellent sense because the American export surplus, by the second quarter of 1947, was running at an annual rate of $12.5 billion. As Hugh Dalton, Britain's Chancellor of the Exchequer, put it: 'The dollar shortage is developing everywhere. The Americans have half the total income of the world, but won't either spend it in buying other people's goods or lending it or giving it away. . . . How soon will the dollar shortage bring a general crisis?' The US average consumption of 3,300 calories a day contrasted with 1,000 to 1,500 for 125 million Europeans. Marshall Aid recycled part of the surplus, narrowed the calorie difference and laid the foundation for a self-reliant Western and Southern Europe. By 1950 it was manifestly an overwhelming success.[40] It began the process of eliminating the gap between North American and European living standards and in the process opened an equally cataclysmic one between Western and Eastern Europe: the Iron Curtain became the frontier between plenty and shortage.

But as yet America had no definite military commitment to defend Europe. With successive blows, Stalin made it unavoidable. He had only about 500 soldiers in Czechoslovakia; but his men in its government controlled the police. Czechoslovakia had a mixed government. Marshall considered it part of the Soviet bloc. But for Stalin it was not enough. Greed dictated more. On 19 February 1948 he sent his Deputy Foreign Minister, V.A. Zorin, to Prague. The next day twelve non-Communist ministers submitted their resignations. After five days of crisis, a new government emerged and the country was a satellite. The US Ambassador, Laurence Steinhardt, thought the Czechs might have resisted, like the Finns and Iranians. He blamed the cowardice of President Benes and Foreign Minister Masaryk, who committed suicide after capitulating.[41] But the lack of forceful American policy was likewise a factor, and tempted Stalin further. On 24 June Stalin blocked access to the Western zones of Berlin, and cut off their electricity.

Unable to agree on a peace formula for one Germany, the rival blocs had begun creating two Germanies in 1946. On 18 June 1948 the three Western Allies announced a new German currency for their zone. That was the pretext for the Soviet move. It is significant that General Lucius Clay, head of the US zone, had been the most reluctant of the Cold Warriors. Now he changed decisively. He admitted that Allied access to Berlin was only 'oral agreement . . . implied in almost three years of application'. Now he proposed a judicious use of force to examine the 'technical difficulties' which the Russians said were blocking the route. He asked permission 'to use the equivalent of a constabulary regiment reinforced with a recoilless rifle troop and an engineer battalion . . . . Troops would be ordered to escort the convoy to Berlin. It would be directed . . . to clear all obstacles even if such an action brought on an attack.'[42]

This response was discussed at length in Washington and rejected. Forrestal, the new Secretary for Defence, told Marshall: 'the Joint Chiefs of Staff do not recommend supply to Berlin by armed convoy in view of the risk of war involved and the inadequacy of United States preparations for global conflict.'[43] What were the risks? Nikita Khrushchev later admitted that Stalin was merely 'prodding the capitalist world with the tip of a bayonet'. His real gamble was in Yugoslavia, where he had broken with Marshall Tito and expelled him from the Cominform, the co-ordinating body for national Communist parties he had set up in 1947; this took place four days after Russia blocked the Berlin routes. Khrushchev added: 'I'm absolutely sure that if the Soviet Union had a common border with Yugoslavia, Stalin would have intervened militarily.'[44] It is hard to see Stalin, involved in a showdown within his empire, allowing a Berlin probing operation – which he could cancel or resume anytime he wished – to get out of hand.

But if the risks were arguable, the inadequacy of US military power was clear enough. The Joint Chiefs of Staff calculated that the Red Army had now stabilized at 2,500,000 plus 400,000 security forces. To balance this the Americans had a nuclear monopoly. But it was a theoretical rather than an actual one. On 3 April 1947 Truman had been told, to his horror, that though materials for twelve A-bombs existed, none at all was available in assembled state. An arsenal of 400 was then ordered, to be ready by 1953, but not enough had yet been delivered by mid-1948 to carry through even the Air Force's 'Operation Pincher', which called for the complete destruction of the Soviet oil industry.[45] Some sixty B29s, known as 'Atomic Bombers', were flown to Britain in a blaze of publicity; but by no means all had atomic bombs. Instead the decision was taken to mount a technical demonstration of US air-power and to supply

Berlin by plane. It worked: the airlift was flying in 4,500 tons a day by December, and by spring 8,000 tons a day, as much as had been carried by road and rail when the cut-off came.[46] On 12 May 1949 the Russians climbed down. It was a victory of a sort. But the Americans had missed the opportunity to meet the 1940s equivalent of the 1936 Rhineland crisis and force a major surrender by the Russians.

The Berlin blockade was nevertheless a decisive event because it obliged the Western Allies to sort out their ideas and take long-term decisions. It led them to rationalize the *fait accompli* of a divided Germany and set about the creation of a West German state. Its constitution was written by February 1949, adopted in May and came into effect in the autumn. Such a Germany would have to be rearmed, and that meant embedding it in a formal Western defence structure. Hence on 4 April 1949 the North Atlantic Treaty was signed in Washington by eleven democratic powers. The assumption behind American policy was that there were only five regions on earth where the sources of modern military strength were found: the USA itself, the UK, the Rhine–Ruhr industrial area, Japan and the Soviet Union. The object of American policy must be to ensure that the Soviet leaders were limited to the one they held already. The geopolitical philosophy of 'containment' had been outlined in an article, 'The Sources of Soviet Conduct', published in *Foreign Affairs,* July 1947. Though signed 'X' it was in fact by George Kennan. It postulated that Russia, while anxious to avoid outright war, was determined to expand by all means short of it; and that America and her Allies should respond by 'a long-term, patient but firm and vigilant containment of Russian expansive tendencies', involving 'the adroit and vigilant application of counterforce at a series of constantly shifting geographical and political points'.[47] The Berlin crisis provided the impetus to give this containment philosophy practical shape.

In February–March 1949 a group of State Department and Defence officials drafted a document called 'National Security Council 68', which laid down the main lines of American foreign and defence policy for the next thirty years.[48] It enshrined the proposition that America, as the greatest free power, had moral, political and ideological obligations to preserve free institutions throughout the world, and must equip herself with the military means to discharge them. She must provide sufficient conventional as well as nuclear forces – a resolve confirmed on 3 September 1949, when a B29, on patrol at 18,000 feet in the North Pacific, produced positive evidence that the Russians had exploded their first nuclear device at the end of August.[49] The atomic monopoly was over and America must now settle down to the long haul of covering large areas of the world with her multi-purpose military protection. 'NSC-68' noted that Soviet

Russia devoted 13.8 per cent of its GNP to arms, as against America's
6–7 per cent. If necessary America could go up to a figure of 20 per
cent. The document was finally approved in April 1950. It represented a historic reversal of traditional American policy towards the
world. Gradually it produced military commitments to forty-seven
nations and led American forces to build or occupy 675 overseas
bases and station a million troops overseas.[50]

It would be a mistake, however, to give American policy a logic
and global coherence it did not actually possess. There was never a
master-plan; more a series of makeshift expedients, with huge holes
and gaps and many contradictions. It was rather like the British
Empire in fact. Moreover, like that empire, it was not all set up at the
same time. While the Americans, with some success, were laying
down the foundations of West European military and economic
stability in 1948–9, their roseate vision of the Far East, conjured up
in the light of their stupendous victory in 1945, was dissolving. Here
again they were made to pay dearly for Roosevelt's illusions and
frivolity. Roosevelt's emotional attachment to China was unlike
anything he felt for any other foreign nation. To him, China was not
a problem; it was a solution. He considered it one of the four great
powers, which ought to and could become the chief stabilizing force
in East Asia. Once America was in the war he worked hard to
convert this vision, or illusion, into reality. Stalin laughed. Churchill
fumed: 'That China is one of the world's four great powers', he
wrote to Eden, 'is an absolute farce.' He was prepared to be
'reasonably polite' about 'this American obsession' but no more.[51]
Roosevelt brought China into the Big Four system; though, characteristically, he left it out when convenient, above all in the vital Yalta
secret treaty over Japan, which let the Russians into Manchuria.
Afterwards, perhaps feeling guilty, he saw Chiang Kai-shek: 'The
first thing I asked Chiang was, "Do you want Indo-China?" He said:
"It's no help to us. We don't want it. They are not Chinese."'[52]

The notion of Chiang as the architect of East Asian post-war
stability was absurd. He never at any stage of his career effectively
controlled more than half of China itself. He was a poor administrator; an indifferent general. As a politician he lacked the sense to
grasp that what China needed was leadership which combined
radicalism with patriotic fervour. Moreover, he knew little, and
cared less, about the peasants. His ideal partner therefore was Mao
himself, with his peasant following and his radical nationalism. Mao
had worked with Chiang before and was willing to do so again;
though after the Long March had established his paramountcy in the
Communist movement his terms were higher. In February 1942 he
began his first big ideological campaign: 'rectification' he called it, to

cure the CCP of barren abstract Marxism and make it aware of Chinese history. In 1944 he praised American democracy and said 'the work we Communists are carrying on today' was essentially the same as that of 'Washington, Jefferson and Lincoln'.[53] But while Mao moved to the centre, Chiang veered off to the Right. In January 1941 his KMT forces murdered 9,000 of Mao's troops south of the Yellow River. Thereafter the two Chinese groups fought separate wars against the Japanese, neither of them very effective. Often they fought each other. In late 1943 Chiang published *China's Destiny*, in which he denounced Communism and liberalism as equally bad for China and held up the conservatism of Confucius as the ideal. The text was so hostile to the West that it had to be censored when it appeared in an English version. In 1944 the Americans worked hard to bring Chiang's and Mao's troops together, with a coalition KMT–CCP government and a joint army command, supplied and financed by America. Chiang turned it down. Mao was enthusiastic, and in October was in the curious position of openly defending the Anglo-Saxons against Chiang's attacks, a passage he later cut from his collected works.[54]

When the war ended, efforts were again made by the Americans to bring about a coalition. But Chiang insisted Mao disband his army. Stalin thought the demand reasonable. His advice to Mao was 'join the government and dissolve [the] army' since 'the development of the uprising in China has no prospect'.[55] Mao refused. He would take the number two role but he would not abase himself (and risk execution too). He had already started his own 'personality cult' with his April 1945 Party Constitution, which insisted 'the Thought of Mao Tse-tung' was essential to 'guide the entire work' of the party and praised him as 'not only the greatest revolutionary and statesman in Chinese history but also the greatest theoretician and scientist'. Most of this was written by Mao himself.[56] Mao was an ambitious romantic who had had a good war and wanted to better himself in the peace. Chiang was the man in possession who could not bear the idea of an eventual successor, especially one with intellectual pretensions. Hence there was no historical inevitability about the Chinese Civil War. It was a personal conflict.

Nor was the outcome of the war due to deep-rooted economic and class forces. The great majority of China's vast population played no part in it, from start to finish. It is true that Mao had some success in mobilizing peasant energy and discontent for his purposes. But this was due in part to the KMT's highly successful literacy programme, which by 1940 had reached most of the villages. It is true, too, that some peasants feared a victory by Chiang because they associated him with landlordism. But Mao did not lead a crusade to 'give' the

people their land. In the areas where he was strongest they already
had it. The estate system was not as widespread as outsiders
believed. Land was worked by its owners in four-fifths of the north,
three-fifths of central China, and half the south.[57] In most places
the main issue was not ownership of land, but who could provide
security and peace.

In short, the Civil War of 1945–9 was the culmination of the
war-lord period of instability introduced by the destruction of the
monarchy. Success was determined throughout by the same factors:
control of the cities and communications, and the ability to hold
together armies by keeping them paid, supplied and happy. In the
circumstances of the post-war period, Mao proved a more successful war-lord than Chiang, chiefly by keeping his armies out of the
urban economy. If any one factor destroyed the KMT it was inflation. Inflation had become uncontrollable in the last phase of the
Japanese Empire, of which urban China was a salient part. In 1945
in Japan itself, paper currency became worthless and a virtual
barter-economy developed. The disease spread to the Chinese cities
and up the great rivers. Chiang's regime, when it took over in the
last months of 1945, inherited an underlying hyper-inflation and
failed to take adequate steps to kill it. The Americans were generous in money and supplies. Chiang had been eligible for Lend-Lease
and got it in considerable quantities. He received a $500 million
economic stabilization loan and a total of $2 billion in 1945–9. But
once the Civil War began in earnest and brought the hyper-inflation
to the surface again, American assistance proved irrelevant.
Chiang's government was not only incompetent; it was also corrupt. Inflation created military weakness and military failure produced yet more inflation.

Chiang compounded the problem by denying it existed. His
strength declined slowly in 1947, rapidly in the first half of 1948. In
Peking, prices multiplied five times from mid-September to mid-
October. The *Peiping Chronicle* recorded Chiang's comment: 'Press
reports of recent price increases and panic buying were greatly
exaggerated . . . during his personal inspection of Peiping, Tientsin
and Mukden he saw nothing to support these allegations.'[58] Yet in
Manchuria and North China inflation had brought industry to a
virtual standstill. Many workers were on hunger-strike, provoked
by a chronic rice-famine. The American consul-general in Mukden
reported:

Puerile efforts have been made towards price control and to combat
hoarding . . . the results . . . have been largely to enforce requisitioning of
grain at bayonet-point for controlled prices and enable the resale of

requisitioned grain at black market prices for the benefit of the pockets of rapacious military and civil officials.[59]

In Shanghai commodity prices rose twenty times between 19 August and 8 November 1948, and on the latter date alone, rice jumped from 300 Chinese dollars per *picul* (133 pounds) in the morning to 1,000 at noon and 1800 by nightfall.[60] Hundreds died in the street every day, their bodies collected by municipal refuse trucks. Chiang put his son, General Chiang Ching-kuo, in charge as economic dictator. His 'gold-dollar' currency reform – there was nothing gold about it – changed hyper-inflation into uncontrolled panic, and he alienated one of Chiang's most faithful sources of support, Shanghai's gangster community, by squeezing $5 million (US) out of them for his own 'war chest'.[61]

Granted the principles of war-lordism, the economic collapse was reflected in army strengths. In summer 1948, in secret session, the KMT parliament was told that in August 1945 their army had been 3.7 million strong with 6,000 big guns. The CCP forces had then numbered 320,000, of which no more than 166,000 were armed. But Red units were accustomed to live off the land and scour the towns. KMT troops were paid in paper which, increasingly, did not buy enough food to feed them. So they sold their personal weapons and any other army equipment they could obtain. The officers were worse than the men and the generals worst of all. By June 1948 the KMT army was down to 2.1 million; the CCP army had risen to 1.5 million, equipped with a million rifles and 22,800 pieces of artillery, more than the KMT (21,000); virtually all these weapons had been bought from government troops. The Americans, who had supplied Chiang with $1 billion worth of Pacific War surplus, thus equipped both sides in the conflict.[62]

There was a series of clear Communist victories in the closing months of 1948, culminating in the decisive battle of Hsuchow at the end of the year. By December virtually all Manchuria and North China was in Mao's hands. Tientsin fell in January 1949 and Peking surrendered. Hsuchow cost the KMT 400,000 casualties. But of these, 200,000 prisoners, unpaid and hungry, were immediately integrated in the CCP army, with 140,000 US rifles. On 1 February 1949, the US Army Department reported that the KMT had possessed 2,723,000 troops at the beginning of 1948 and less than 1,500,000 at the end, of which half a million were non-combatants. In the same period the CCP forces had swollen to 1,622,000, virtually all combat-effective. At this point, though Chiang was already preparing to evacuate to Taiwan (Formosa), Stalin was still advising Mao to settle for a division of China, with a CCP North and a KMT South.

Chiang did not give Mao the chance for he rejected proposals for a compromise. In April 1949 Mao crossed south of the Yangtze and took Nanking the same month. By October he controlled all of mainland China and had restored, after a fashion, the precarious unity of imperial days.[63]

Thus, after forty years of ferocious civil conflict, in which millions had died, none of Sun Yat-sen's original aims, which included parliamentary democracy, freedom of the press and *habeas corpus*, had been secured, and China was back where it had started, with a despotism – albeit a much more confident and oppressive one. Mao's first act was to extend his 'land reform', already begun in the North, to the entire country. It was aimed at local bullies and evil gentry' and he urged peasants to kill 'not one or two but a goodly number' of each.[64] At least 2 million people perished, half of them the tyrannical owners of less than thirty acres. Mao, the revolutionary romantic, launched the largest nation on earth into a frenzy of violent activism which was to rival the social engineering of Hitler and Stalin.

The American policy-makers watched in bewilderment the disintegration of Roosevelt's great pillar of stability. It left behind it a gigantic vacuum. How to fill it? Though they rated Japan as one of the four key areas they had to hold, they had never hitherto conceived it as the focus of their position in the Far East, as Britain was in Europe. By miraculous dispensation of providence, the Russians had entered the war against Japan too late to make any claim to share in the occupation. So the Americans had a free hand there, under the Potsdam declaration. General MacArthur ruled the country as a surrogate constitutional Tenno. As late as the summer of 1947 it was proposed to cast Japan adrift, by signing a peace treaty and evacuating it, though the country was disarmed, had no central police system to combat Communist subversion and, since Soviet Russia controlled the Kurile Islands, south Sakhalin and North Korea, faced a semi-circle of active hostility.[65] Before this plan could be put into operation, the disaster of 1948–9 in China induced America to have second thoughts. As Soviet Russia had no official presence, America could act unilaterally and did so. Beginning in 1949, US policy was reversed: the occupation was lifted from the backs of the Japanese government and economy; the emphasis shifted from punishment to expansion, and from neutralism and de-militarization to the integration of Japan in the Western system through a generous peace treaty.

'Containment' implied precise lines, which the Russians would cross at their peril. In Europe they were now clear enough. In Asia, by 1949, Japan was firmly under the American umbrella. But where did the lines run elsewhere? On 12 January 1950 Dean Acheson made a very foolish speech to the National Press Club in Washington. In it he appeared to exclude from the American defence perimeter not only Taiwan and Indo-China but Korea, from which both Soviet and US troops had withdrawn, and which was divided into North and South zones, with only five-hundred US military training personnel in the South. Acheson's main point was that the Communization of China was not an unmitigated loss, since China and Russia would soon be at each other's throats. He thought that the Soviet 'absorption' of the whole or part of 'the four northern provinces of China' (Outer and Inner Mongolia, Sinkiang and Manchuria) was 'the most important fact in the relations of any foreign power with Asia'. America must not antagonize China and so 'deflect from the Russians to ourselves the righteous anger and the wrath and the hatred of the Chinese people which must develop'. In fact Acheson was misinformed. He relied on a briefing by General W.E.Todd, head of the Joint Chief of Staff intelligence section, that in any ranking of Soviet targets for aggression, 'Korea would be at the bottom of that list'. Nor did he know that at the time he spoke negotiations were taking place leading to the Russians handing over the Manchurian railway and Port Arthur to China.[66]

Behind Stalin's uncharacteristic generosity was his anxiety not to repeat with Mao the mistake he had made with Tito – that is, to treat him as a puppet, instead of as a fellow-dictator who had established his regime by his own efforts. Stalin seems to have decided to put his Eastern European empire in order in the summer of 1947, after the Marshall Plan was announced. He held the first meeting of the Cominform in Belgrade, to show that Yugoslavia was an integral part of the system. But its object was in fact to replace local Communist leaders with some national standing by ones who owed everything to Stalin and Russian backing. The Czech *coup* of February 1948 was part of this process. Stalin also planned to destroy Tito, whom he had never forgiven for a rude wartime message: 'If you cannot help us at least don't hinder us by useless advice.'[67] The same month as he was swallowing the Czech leadership, Stalin had gathered in Moscow Dmitrov, the Bulgarian Communist leader, whom he humiliated, and Edward Kardelj and Milovan Djilas from Yugoslavia, one of whom, if pliable enough, he intended to make Tito's replacement. He ordered them to knock Yugoslavia and Bulgaria into an economic federation on the lines of Benelux, which he thought consisted of Belgium and Luxembourg. Told that it also included the Netherlands, he denied it and shouted angrily, 'When I say no it means no!' Then, switching to bribery, he offered the Yugoslavs the bait of Mussolini's little victim: 'We agree to Yugoslavia swallowing Albania', he said and made a gesture of sucking the forefinger of his right hand.[68]

When Tito got a report of the meeting he smelt a *putsch* against himself. Like Stalin, he was an experienced political gangster familiar with the rules of survival. His first act was to cut off information from Yugoslavia's inner party organs, police and army, to their counterparts in Moscow. On 1 March he brought the crisis to the boil by having his Central Committee throw out Stalin's proposed treaty. In the subsequent theological dispute, which began on 27 March, Tito was accused of anti-Sovietism, of being undemocratic, unself-critical, lacking in class-consciousness, of having secret links with the West and engaging in anti-Soviet espionage; and eventually the entire party was branded as Menshevist, Bukharinist and Trotskyist, the accusation culminating in a crude threat to Tito's life: 'We think that the career of Trotsky is quite instructive.'[69] On 28 June the new Cominform dutifully warned that Tito's plan was to 'curry favour with the imperialists' as a prelude to setting up 'an ordinary bourgeois republic' which would in time become 'a colony of the imperialists'. It called on 'healthy elements' within the Yugoslav party to 'replace the present leaders'.

The rage and violent language of Stalin's communications reflected his growing realization that Tito was a step ahead of him at each stage of the dispute, which merely served to identify those in his party whose primary loyalty was to Moscow. Tito broke two of his principal colleagues, shot his wartime chief of staff, gaoled the deputy political head of his army and, in all, put 8,400 party, police and army suspects behind bars, the arrests continuing into 1950.[70] Stalin imposed economic sanctions, held manoeuvres on Yugoslavia's borders and, from 1949, mounted show-trials in the satellites with Tito as the arch-villain. But Tito's ability to hold his party together around a nationalist line ('no matter how much each of us loves the land of socialism, the USSR, he can in no case love his own country less') persuaded Stalin that he could not topple the regime without an open invasion by the Red Army and large-scale fighting, possibly involving the West. Tito never formally moved under the Western umbrella, but the safeguard was implicit. When he visited London in 1953, Churchill (again Prime Minister) told him: 'should our [wartime] ally, Yugoslavia, be attacked, we would fight and die with you.' Tito: 'This is a sacred vow and it is enough for us. We need no written treaties.'[71]

Khrushchev later said that the Tito row could all have been settled by discussion.[72] Stalin came to agree, though he never admitted it. The failure of his Yugoslav policy was apparent by the summer of 1948 and Zhdanov, who had presided over Tito's excommunication, died suddenly on 31 August 1948, probably murdered on Stalin's orders.[73] With Mao, recognizing that he was master in his own house, Stalin pursued quite different tactics. He seems to have decided to bind the new Chinese regime to the Soviet bloc not by threats and interlocking economic machinery but by raising the military temperature in the Far East. The Acheson speech of January 1950, with its wishful thought that, left alone by the West, China must break with Russia, suggested the danger; its pointed omission of Korea pointed to the remedy. A limited proxy war in Korea would be the means to teach China where its true military interests lay. If this was Stalin's reasoning it proved correct. The Korean War postponed the Soviet–Chinese break for a decade. Not that Stalin exactly planned the war. He seems to have agreed in the spring of 1950 that Kim Il-sung, the North Korean Communist dictator, could make a limited push across the 38th parallel in November.[74] But Kim was not a biddable man. He described himself in his own newspaper as 'the respected and beloved leader', as 'a great thinker and theoretician' responsible for 'the guiding idea of the revolution of our era', a 'great revolutionary practitioner who has worked countless legendary miracles', a 'matchless iron-willed brilliant commander who is ever-victorious', as well as 'the tender-hearted father of the people . . . embracing them in his broad bosom'. He turned Stalin's cunning probe into an attack by his entire army and launched it on 25 June, with sufficient success to panic the Americans.

The Korean War was a characteristic 20th-century tragedy. It was launched for ideological reasons, without a scintilla of moral justification or any evidence of popular support. It killed 34,000 Americans, a million Koreans, a quarter of a million Chinese. It achieved no purpose. All its consequences were unintended. Its course was a succession of blunders. Kim and Stalin underestimated America's response. Truman judged the invasion to be a prelude to an attack on Japan and a direct challenge to America's willingness to uphold international law through the United Nations. Hitherto that body had been designed to reflect great power agreement and its Security Council, with its veto system, underpinned the principle. Truman had no need to invoke the UN at all. The Potsdam agreement gave America ample powers to act alone.[75] But Truman wanted the UN's 'moral authority'. So he bypassed the Security Council and got authorization by the UN's General Assembly, which America then dominated, on a mere counting-heads basis. Thus the first long-term consequence of Korea was to undermine the concept of the UN as a useful, but limited body, and set it on a course which transformed it into an instrument of ideological propaganda. Of course the reason Truman wanted UN backing was that he took America into the war without getting Congressional approval first. This was the second unintended consequence: the elevation of the Presidency into a supra-constitutional war-making executive, especially in a Far Eastern context. A third consequence was, indeed, to place a sword between an American–Chinese rapprochement, as Stalin had wished, but in a manner he could not possibly have foreseen.

Stalin assumed the proxy war would increase China's military dependence on Soviet Russia. The reverse happened. General MacArthur quickly dealt with the North Koreans; in three months he had recaptured the capital of the South, Seoul. But he was no more biddable than Kim. He told Washington: 'Unless and until the enemy capitulates, I regard all of Korea open to our military operations' and pushed up to the Chinese frontier on the Yalu. Under cover of the crisis the Chinese first swallowed quasi-independent Tibet (21 October 1950), another unintended consequence; then attacked MacArthur with a huge 'volunteer' army (28 December). He was beaten and in April 1951 sacked, something Truman should have done the previous autumn. With difficulty the UN forces re-established the front near the 38th parallel (October 1951) and armistice talks began. But they were marked by intense bitterness and frustration on America's part. According to entries in Truman's journal, he thought of using nuclear weapons on 27 January and again on 18 May 1952. When General Eisenhower succeeded him as President, the threat of nuclear war was conveyed to China through the Indian government.[76]

As a result of the Chinese–American confrontation, Mao turned China for the first time into a military power of the front rank, something Stalin certainly never intended. Indeed Mao induced Stalin's successors to help China become a nuclear power. He refused to allow Soviet forces to establish nuclear bases on Chinese soil. Instead he pushed ahead with an independent nuclear programme, which the Russians felt obliged to assist. Khrushchev later complained Russia gave the Chinese 'almost everything they asked for. We kept no secrets from them. Our nuclear experts co-operated with their engineers and designers who were busy building a bomb.' According to his account the Russians were about to hand over a prototype bomb when they suddenly had second thoughts. The Chinese say it was 20 June 1959 when 'the Soviet government unilaterally tore up the agreement . . . and refused to provide China with a sample of an atomic bomb.'[77] But the impetus Soviet help gave to the Chinese programme could not be halted. By the time the Sino–Soviet break came, in 1963, China was on the eve of her first A-bomb test; and at only her sixth test she exploded a multi-megaton thermonuclear device. Stalin's ploy delayed the quarrel for a decade but made it far more serious when it eventually came. From that point Russia had to deal with another major military power on her south-eastern borders.

Such a change in the balance was all the more serious in that another unintended consequence of the Korean probe was a fundamental acceleration in rearmament. Although the Czech and Berlin crises pushed America into a collective security system, it was Korea which provoked the permanent arms-race. Truman had taken the decision to build the H-bomb in January 1950 but until the North Koreans started a hot war he was finding great difficulty in getting through Congress the funding for the NSC-68 programme. Defence spending in the fiscal year 1950 was only $17.7 billion. Korea revolutionized the Congressional and national attitude to defence: defence allocations jumped to $44 billion in fiscal 1952 and passed the $50 billion watershed the following year. The increases made possible the development of tactical nuclear weapons, four extra divisions for Germany, the rapid construction of overseas air-bases, a world-wide deployment of the Strategic Air Command, a nuclear carrier fleet and mobile conventional capability.[78] By February 1951 American aircraft production was back to its peak 1944 level. America's allies also rearmed and the remilitarization of Germany became a reality. If the Cold War began over Poland it reached maturity over Korea and embraced the whole world. In effect, Stalin had polarized the earth.

If Stalin had not intended to conjure up legions against himself, he cannot have regretted that his empire and its satellites were now divided from the rest of the world by an abyss of fear and suspicion. It was he who built the Iron Curtain; and it was notable that the empire had an inner iron curtain, which ran along the Soviet frontier and protected it against the bacillus of Western ideas even from the satellites themselves. Stalin hated 'Westerners' in the same way Hitler hated Jews, using the same term: 'cosmopolitanism'. This explains the extraordinary thoroughness and venom with which, in 1945–6, he destroyed or isolated in camps all those who had been in contact with non-Soviet ideas: not only prisoners of war but serving officers, technicians, journalists and party members whose wartime duties had taken them abroad. The number of foreigners permitted to visit, let alone live in, Russia was reduced to an inescapable minimum, and their contacts limited to those employed by the government and secret police. All other Russians learnt from experience that even the most innocent and casual contact with a foreigner risked engulfment in the Gulag.

Any hopes raised by victory that the vast industries created to secure it would now be used to produce some modest improvement in the life of a nation which had suffered 20 million dead and unparalleled privations, were dashed on 9 February 1946 when Stalin announced that three and possibly four more five-year plans, centred on heavy industry, would be required to increase Soviet strength and prepare it for what he grimly termed 'all contingencies'. It was clear he intended to put the entire nation under the harrow yet again and his servile Politburo colleague Andrei Zhdanov was detailed to conduct a campaign, reaching into every aspect of Russian life, to fight apoliticization and instil active commitment by fear.[79] Intellectuals of all kinds were put under pressure. The witch-hunt was launched on 14 August 1946, characteristically in Leningrad, which Stalin hated all his life as passionately as Hitler hated Vienna. Objects of the first attack were the journals *Zvezda* and *Leningrad*, the poetess Anna Akhmatova, the humourist Mikhail Zoshchenko. But it soon spread to all the arts. Aleksandr Fadaev, who got the Stalin Prize for his 1946 war novel, *The Young Guard*, was forced to rewrite it on strict party lines in 1947. Muradelli was denounced for his opera *The Great Friendship*. The hunt focused on Shostakovich's Ninth Symphony; terrified, he promptly wrote an ode lauding Stalin's forestry plan. It switched to Khachaturian's Piano Concerto; he changed his style completely. Then it turned on Eisenstein, whose film *Ivan the Terrible* was criticized for belittling its subject. In June 1947 it was the turn of the philosophers, where the failings of G.F.Aleksandrov's *History of West European Philosophy* served as pretext for a purge. In economics, Jeno Varga's book describing capitalist economies in the war served the same purpose. From 1948 on, theoretical physics, cosmology, chemistry, genetics, medicine, psychology and cybernetics were all systematically raked over. Relativity theory was condemned, not (as in Nazi Germany) because Einstein was a Jew but for equally irrelevant reasons: Marx had said the universe was infinite, and Einstein had got some ideas from Mach, who had been proscribed by Lenin. Behind this lay Stalin's suspicion of any ideas remotely associated with Western or bourgeois values. He was running what the Chinese Communists were later to term a Cultural Revolution, an attempt to change fundamental human attitudes over the whole range of knowledge by the use of naked police power.[80]

Thousands of intellectuals lost their jobs. Thousands more went into the camps. Their places were taken by creatures still more pliable, cranks and frauds. Soviet biology fell into the hands of the fanatical eccentric T.D.Lysenko, who preached a theory of inherited acquired characteristics and what he termed 'vernalization', the transformation of wheat into rye, pines into firs and so on: essentially medieval stuff. Stalin was fascinated. He edited in advance Lysenko's presidential address of 31 July 1948 to the Academy of Agricultural Science, which launched the witch-hunt in biology (Lysenko used to show to visitors a copy with corrections in Stalin's hand).[81] Scientific genetics was savaged as a 'bourgeois pseudo-science', 'anti-Marxist', leading to 'sabotage' of the Soviet economy: those who practised it had their laboratories closed down. Glorying in the reign of terror was another agricultural quack, V.R.Williams. In medicine, a woman called O.B. Lepeshinskaya preached that old age could be postponed by bicarbonate of soda enemas – an idea that briefly appealed to Stalin. In linguistics, N.Y.Marr argued that all human speech could be reduced to four basic elements: *sal, ber, yon* and *rosh*.[82] Stalin wallowed luxuriously in the oily cultural waters he had stirred, sometimes extracting its weird denizens for a brief moment of fame before wringing their necks. On 20 June 1950 he published in *Pravda* a 10,000-word article called 'Marxism and Linguistic Problems', a real collector's piece. Usually, however, he left it to others to wield the pen on his behalf. *Pravda* wrote:

If you meet with difficulties in your work, or suddenly doubt your abilities, think of him – of Stalin – and you will find the confidence you need. If you feel tired in an hour when you should not, think of him – of Stalin – and your work will go well. If you are seeking a correct decision, think of him – of Stalin – and you will find that decision.[83]

Stalin stage-managed his own apotheosis, as the embodiment of human wisdom, in the *Great Soviet Encyclopedia*, which was published from 1949 onwards. It was full of gems. The historical section on 'motor cars' began: 'In 1751–2, Leonty Shamshugenkov, a peasant in the Nizhny–Novgorod province, constructed a self-propelled vehicle operated by two men.' Stalin enjoyed editing the passages dealing with his own merits and achievements. How the ex-seminarist must have chuckled when he put up Leonid Leonov, a leading novelist who was supposed to be Christian, to propose in *Pravda* that a new calendar should be based, not on Christ's birth-date, but Stalin's! Black humour always jostled with monomania for possession of the cavity in Stalin's spirit. He rewrote the official *Short Biography of Stalin,* putting in the sentence: 'Stalin never allowed his work to be marred by the slightest hint of vanity, conceit or self-adulation.'[84]

In 1948–9 Stalin's anti-Westernism took more specific form in anti-Semitism. He had always hated Jews; he often told anti-Semitic jokes. Khrushchev said he encouraged factory workers to beat up their Jewish colleagues.[85] Stalin's last spasm of anti-Semitic fury was provoked when the arrival of Golda Meir to open Israel's first Moscow embassy was greeted with a modest display of Jewish enthusiasm. Yiddish publications were immediately banned. Wall Street bankers in Soviet cartoons suddenly sported 'Jewish' features. The Jewish actor Mikhoels was murdered in a fake car accident. Other prominent Jews vanished into the camps. Those with Russified names had their 'real' Jewish names printed in the press, an old Nazi technique. The campaign was run by tame Jews, a characteristic touch. It was mixed up in Stalin's mind with his unremitting search for enemies, real or imaginary, within the party. Zhdanov, having served his purpose, disappeared through a trap-door after the Tito fiasco. His followers were hounded down in 1949, during the so-called 'Leningrad affair', another witch-hunt against the detested city. Beria and Malenkov supplied the evidence for the purge which was carried out in secret, over 1,000 being shot.[86] The dead included the Politburo's top planner, N.A.Voznesensky, and A.A.Kuznetsov, Secretary of the Central Committee. To be Jewish was to expect arrest and death at any moment; but no one's life was safe. Marshal Zhukov had been sacked and sent to the provinces in 1946, for being too popular, and once there he kept his head down. In 1949 Stalin arrested Molotov's wife, Polina, and packed her off to Kazakhstan. She was Jewish and was accused of 'Zionist conspiracies'; but the real reason may have been her former friendship with Stalin's wife Nadya. He also sent to prison the wife of Kalinin, the Soviet Head of State. There were other cases of wife-persecution, one of the old man's last pleasures.[87] He hated the fact that so many of his relatives wished to marry Jews, and refused to meet five out of his eight grandchildren.

By the second half of 1952, by which time he was manufacturing nuclear weapons at top speed, Stalin was seeing Jewish-tinged conspiracies everywhere. The top organs of the state had virtually ceased to function. The real work was done at lugubrious supper-parties in his Kuntsevo villa, where Stalin gave verbal orders, often on the spur of the moment, to whoever happened to be there, exactly as Hitler had done. He was now an elderly man, with a pockmarked face, yellowing eyes, discoloured teeth, 'an old battle-scarred tiger', as one American visitor called him, sniffing danger everywhere. He and Beria wove about everyone in Moscow a new web of electronic surveillance. That summer a bug was found in the US Great Seal in the Ambassador's house, what Kennan described as 'for that day a fantastically advanced bit of applied electronics'.[88] But the signs are that the web was closing round Beria too; and this would be natural for Stalin always destroyed his secret police killers in the end – and he now thought Beria was a Jew.[89] Certain unmistakable signs surrounding the nineteenth Party Congress, in October 1952, indicated a new terror was about to burst upon the heads of Stalin's senior colleagues. Khrushchev later claimed that Molotov, Mikoyan and Voroshilov were among the destined victims.[90]

The storm broke on 4 November, when Jewish doctors attached to the Kremlin were arrested. Among other crimes they were accused of murdering Zhdanov. Their 'confessions' were to serve as the basis for

fresh arrests and trials, as from 1934 on. Ordering their interrogation, Stalin shouted: 'Beat, beat and beat again!' He told the security
chief, Ignatov, that if he could not get full admissions, 'We will
shorten you by a head.' Circulating copies of the preliminary
confessions to enemies, Stalin said: 'What will happen without me?
The country will perish because you do not know how to recognize
enemies.'[91] He was now completely self-isolated. He even had his
last crony, his butler Vlasik, a security police general, arrested as a
spy. His food was analysed in a laboratory before he would touch it.
He thought the air in his house might be poisoned by a deadly
vapour mentioned in the Yagoda trial in 1938. All this is curiously
reminiscent of Hitler's last years.

Stalin had completely lost touch with the normal world. His
daughter said he talked in terms of 1917 prices, and his salary
envelopes piled up unopened in his desk (from which they mysteriously vanished at his death). When she visited him on 21 December
1952, she found him sick, refusing to let any doctor near him, and
dosing himself with iodine. His personal physician for the last twenty
years, he thought, had been a British spy all the time, and was now
literally in chains.[92] Stalin had always doodled drawings of wolves
during meetings. Now the brutes obsessed him. On 17 February
1953, he told the last non-Communist visitor, K.P.S.Menon, how he
dealt with his enemies: 'A Russian peasant who sees a wolf doesn't
need to be told what the wolf intends to do – he knows! – so he
doesn't try to tame the wolf, or argue or waste time – he kills it!'[93]
The stroke came a fortnight later on 2 March, leaving Stalin
speechless. His daughter said that his death on 5 March was 'difficult
and terrible', his last gesture being to lift his left hand as if to curse,
or to ward off something.[94] As Lenin went to eternity raving of
electricity, so Stalin departed to the howling of imaginary wolves. In
the bewildered crowd-movements that followed, according to the
poet Yevtushenko, Beria's men killed hundreds of people by impro-
vising as crush-barriers their MVD lorries, whose sides dripped with
blood.[95]

The agonies of Stalin's Russia, where about 500,000 people were
judicially murdered (or just murdered) by the state in the post-war
period up to March 1953, formed a gruesome contrast to the
America against which it was pitted. While, in the immediate
post-war, Stalin was piling fresh burdens on his frightened subjects,
the Americans, contrary to predictions of government economists,
who had prophesied heavy unemployment in the conversion period,
were engaging in the longest and most intense consumer spending
spree in the nation's history. It began in autumn 1946 and accelerated the following year: 'The great American boom is on', wrote

Fortune. 'There is no measuring it. The old yardsticks will not do. . . . There is a powerful consuming demand for everything that one can eat, wear, enjoy, read, repair, paint, drink, see, ride, taste and rest in.'[96] It was the start of the longest cycle of capitalist expansion in history, spreading to Europe (as the Marshall Plan took effect) in the 1950s and to Japan and the Pacific in the 1960s; lasting, with the occasional dips, to the mid-1970s. For Americans, the taste of uninhibited prosperity was especially poignant, bringing back memories of the 1920s lost Arcadia.

There were other echoes of the Twenties. The xenophobic witch-hunting of the Woodrow Wilson administration was not repeated. Yet there was an air of patriotic tension, as Americans braced themselves to the magnitude of the global responsibility they were undertaking. Here again the contrast with Russia is marked and instructive. America was an astonishingly open society and in some ways a vulnerable one. It had possessed few defences against the systematic penetration of its organs which Stalinism practised on a huge scale in the 1930s. Agents of foreign governments had to register under the McCormack Act of 1938. Members of organizations advocating the overthrow of the US government by force or violence were open to prosecution, under both the Hatch Act of 1939 and the Smith Act of 1940. Such legislation was useless to prevent active Communists and fellow-travellers (including Soviet agents) from joining the government, which they did in large numbers during the New Deal and still more during the war. As Kennan put it,

The penetration of the American governmental services by members or agents (conscious or otherwise) of the American Communist Party in the late 1930s was not a figment of the imagination . . . it really existed; and it assumed proportions which, while never overwhelming, were also not trivial.

He says that those who served in Moscow or in the Russian division of the State Department were 'very much aware' of the danger. The Roosevelt administration was slow in reacting: 'warnings which should have been heeded fell too often on deaf or incredulous ears.'[97]

Truman was more active. In November 1946 he appointed a Temporary Commission on Employee Loyalty, and in the following March he acted on its recommendations with Executive Order 9835, which authorized inquiries into political beliefs and associations of all federal employees.[98] Once this procedure got going, in 1947, it was reasonably effective. But it was only after this date that Congress and the public became aware of the real magnitude of the wartime errors which (it was supposed) led to the 'loss' of Eastern Europe and, in 1949, of China. Roosevelt's infatuation with Stalin and his fundamental frivolity were more to blame for the weakness of American wartime policy than any Stalinist moles. But Roosevelt was dead. And the moles were being dug out as the Cold War grew more intense and the follies of the past were scrutinized.

No evidence so far uncovered suggests that Soviet agents brought about any major decision in US policy, except in the Treasury, or delivered any vital classified information, except in the nuclear weapons fields. But these were major exceptions. The Soviet agent Harry Dexter White was the most influential official in the Treasury, the man who created the post-war international monetary system, with the help of Keynes. In April 1944 he was responsible for the American government's decision to hand over to the Soviet government US Treasury plates to print occupation currency, a decision which ultimately cost the American taxpayer $225 million.[99] In 1945 Elizabeth Bentley, a former Communist spy, told the FBI of two Soviet networks in the US, one headed by the Treasury economist Nathan Gregory Silvermaster, another by Victor Perlo of the War Production Board: classified information was also transmitted from the Justice Department, the Foreign Economic Administration and the Board of Economic Warfare. FBI and Office of Strategic Services (OSS) raids also disclosed leakages from the Army and Navy departments, the Office of War Intelligence and the OSS itself. Then, from the State Department, there was Alger Hiss, who had sat at Roosevelt's elbow at Yalta and, more important, had been aide to Edward Stettinius, whom the British regarded as Stalin's biggest (if unconscious) asset in the Allied camp. In the atomic field Soviet agents included Julius and Ethel Rosenberg, Morton Sobell, David Greenglass, Harry Gold, J. Peters (alias Alexander Stevens), to whom Whittaker Chambers acted as courier, and Jacob Golos, as well as Klaus Fuchs, who had been cleared by British security.

The extent of the damage these spies caused to Western interests cannot be known until the Soviet archives are finally opened. But the fact that Soviet Russia took only four years to make an A-bomb (1945–9), no longer than the Manhattan Project itself, was a stunning shock to the Truman Administration and its Defence chiefs (though not to some of the scientific community). It was badly received by the American public. It coincided with the KMT collapse in China. It came at a period when the problem of Soviet penetration of government had in fact been overcome but when the offenders were still being brought to trial. Not until 25 January 1950 was Alger Hiss found guilty of perjury in concealing his membership of the Communist Party. His was the case which attracted most attention.

A fornight later Senator Joe McCarthy made his notorious speech in Wheeling, West Virginia, claiming that 205 known Communists were working in the State Department. That began the full-scale witch-hunt: in short, the phenomenon occurred after the realities which provoked it had been dealt with. McCarthy was a radical Republican; not a right-winger. He had become interested in espionage in the previous autumn when he had seen a confidential FBI report (already two years out of date). Shortly before the Wheeling speech he dined with Father Edmund Walsh, regent of the school of Foreign Service at Georgetown University. This was a Conservative Jesuit college (the Jesuits were not radicalized until the 1960s) which supplied large numbers of graduates to the State Department; it was concerned about the number of ultra-liberals who had entered during the period 1933–45. The Senator smelt an issue and brandished it. He was not a serious politician but an adventurer, who treated politics as a game. As his most perceptive biographer put it: 'He was no kind of fanatic . . . as incapable of true rancour, spite and animosity as a eunuch is of marriage . . . . He faked it all and could not understand anyone who didn't.'[100] Robert Kennedy, the future Attorney-General, who worked for him, denied he was evil: 'His whole method of operation was complicated because he would get a guilty feeling and get hurt after he had blasted somebody. He wanted so desperately to be liked. He didn't anticipate the results of what he was doing.'[101]

McCarthy would have been of little account had not the Korean War broken out that summer. His period of ascendancy coincided exactly with that bitter and frustrating conflict – one might say that McCarthyism was Stalin's last gift to the American people. He was rapidly destroyed once it ended. McCarthy took advantage of the Congressional committee-system which empowers investigations. For the legislature to conduct quasi-judicial inquiries is legitimate. It was an old English parliamentary procedure, which proved invaluable in establishing constitutional liberties in the seventeenth and eighteenth centuries. It was grievously abused, particularly in the conduct of political and religious witch-hunts. Two aspects were particularly objectionable: the use of inquisitorial procedure, so alien to the Common Law, and the power to punish for contempt anyone who obstructs this procedure. Congress inherited both the virtues and vices of the system, which were inseparable. In the 1930s, the Congressional liberals had hounded the Wall Street community; now it was the turn of the liberals. In the 1960s and later it would be the turn of business; and in the mid-1970s the Nixon Administration. On the whole the advantages outweigh the defects, and therefore the system is kept. Besides, it contains its own self-correcting mechanism, which worked in this case, albeit slowly: McCarthy was repudiated, censured and, in effect, extinguished by his own colleagues, the Senate. The damage inflicted by McCarthy on individual lives was due to two special factors. The first was the inadequacy of American libel laws, which permitted the press to publish his unsupported allegations with impunity, even when they were unprivileged. It was the press, especially the wire-services, which turned an abuse into a scandal, just as in the 1970s it was to magnify the Watergate case into a witch-hunt.[102] Second was the moral cowardice shown by some institutions, notably in Hollywood and Washington, in bowing to the prevailing unreason. Again, this is a recurrent phenomenon, to be repeated in the decade 1965–75, when many universities surrendered to student violence.

Without these two factors 'McCarthyism' was nothing. The contrast with Zhdanovism in Russia is instructive. McCarthy had no police. He had no executive authority at all. On the contrary: both the Truman and Eisenhower administrations did all in their power to impede him. Above all, McCarthy was not part of the legal process. He had no court. Indeed, the courts were totally unaffected by McCarthyism. As Kennan pointed out: 'Whoever could get his case before a court was generally assured of meeting there with a level of justice no smaller than at any other time in recent American history.'[103] The courts resisted McCarthyism, unlike their behaviour twenty years later when they became strongly tinged with Watergate hysteria. In the last resort, McCarthy's weapon was publicity; and in a free society publicity is a two-edged weapon. McCarthy was destroyed by publicity; and the man who orchestrated this destruction from behind the scenes was the new President, Dwight Eisenhower.

Eisenhower rightly perceived that the Korean War and the uncertainty surrounding cease-fire negotiations were the source of the frustration and fear upon which McCarthyism played. In November 1952 he had been elected to end the war. Peace has always been a vote-winning issue in the United States. Yet there is an instructive contrast in Democrat and Republican records. Wilson won in 1916 on a promise to keep America out of the war; next year America was a belligerent. Roosevelt won in 1940 on the same promise and with the same result. Lyndon Johnson won in 1964 on a peace platform (against Republican 'warmongering') and promptly turned Vietnam into a major war. Eisenhower in 1952 and Richard Nixon in 1972 are the only two Presidents in this century who have carried out their peace promises.

Yet in Eisenhower's case his achievement has been underestimated. He regarded Korea as an unnecessary and repeatedly misjudged conflict. He was appalled by the number of occasions on which the previous administration had contemplated using nuclear weapons against Manchuria and China proper, and even Russia; and by its readiness, in addition, to consider conventional bombing against China on a vast scale.[104] He set about breaking the armistice-deadlock and, instead of planning to use nuclear force in secret, he employed nuclear threats in private diplomacy. This tactic worked and within nine months he had a settlement of sorts. He was bitterly criticized at the time, and since, for doing nothing to stem anti-Communist hysteria.[105] The truth is he grasped the essential point: that it was the war which made McCarthyism possible, and that once it had been got out of the way, the Senator could soon be reduced to size. He gave the peace-effort priority and only afterwards did he organize McCarthy's downfall. With considerable cunning and in great secrecy he directed his friends in the Senate to censure McCarthy, while using his press chief, Jim Haggerty, to orchestrate the publicity. The process culminated in December 1954 and is perhaps the best example of the 'hidden hand' style of leadership which Eisenhower delighted to employ and which research brought to light many years after his death.[106]

Eisenhower was the most successful of America's twentieth-century presidents, and the decade when he ruled (1953–61) the most prosperous in American, and indeed world, history. His presidency was surrounded by mythology, much of which he deliberately contrived himself. He sought to give the impression that he was a mere constitutional monarch, who delegated decisons to his colleagues and indeed to Congress, and who was anxious to spend the maximum amount of time playing golf. His stratagem worked. His right-wing rival for Republican leadership, Senator Robert Taft, sneered, 'I really think he should have been a golf pro.'[107] His first biographer claimed that the 'unanimous consensus' of 'journalists and academics, pundits and prophets, the national community of intellectuals and critics' had been that Eisenhower's conduct of the presidency had been 'unskilful and his definition of it inaccurate . . . . [he] elected to leave his nation to fly on automatic pilot.'[108] He was seen as well-meaning, intellectually limited, ignorant, inarticulate, often weak and always lazy.

The reality was quite different. 'Complex and devious', was the summing-up of his Vice-President, Richard Nixon (no mean judge of such things); 'he always applied two, three or four lines of reasoning to a single problem and he usually preferred the indirect approach'.[109] In the late 1970s, the opening up of the secret files kept by his personal secretary, Ann Whitman, phone logs, diaries and other personal documents, revealed that Eisenhower worked very much harder than anyone, including close colleagues, supposed. A typical day started at 7.30, by which time he had read the *New York Times, Herald Tribune* and *Christian Science Monitor*, and finished close to midnight (he often worked afterwards). Many of his appointments (especially those dealing with party or defence and foreign policy) were deliberately left out of lists given to the press by Haggerty. Long and vital meetings with the State and Defence secretaries, the head of the CIA and other figures, took place unrecorded and in secret, before the formal sessions of the National Security Council. The running of defence and foreign policy, far from being bureaucratic and inflexible, as his critics supposed, in fact took place in accordance with highly efficient staff principles, contrasting strongly with the romantic anarchy of the Kennedy regime which followed. Eisenhower himself was in charge throughout.[110]

Eisenhower practised pseudo-delegation. All thought Sherman Adams, his chief of staff, took the domestic decisions. To some extent Adams shared this illusion. He said that Eisenhower was the last major world figure who actively disliked and avoided using the phone.[111] In fact the logs show he made multitudes of calls about which Adams knew nothing. Far from delegating foreign policy to John Foster Dulles, his Secretary of State, Eisenhower took advice from a number of sources of which Dulles knew nothing, and kept him on a secret, tight rein: Dulles reported back daily by phone, even when abroad. Eisenhower read a huge volume of official documents and maintained a copious correspondence with high-level friends at home and abroad in the diplomatic, business and military communities. He used Dulles as a servant; and Dulles complained that though he often worked late into the night with the President at the White House he had 'never been asked to a family dinner'.[112] The notion that Dulles and Adams were prima donnas was deliberately promoted by Eisenhower, since they could be blamed when mistakes were made, thus protecting the presidency – a technique often used in the past by crowned autocrats, such as Elizabeth I. But conversely, Eisenhower sometimes exploited his reputation for political naïvety to take the blame for mistakes made by subordinates, as, for instance, when Dulles made a series of blunders in the appointment of Winthrop Aldrich to the London embassy in 1953.[113] Kennan grasped half the truth when he wrote that on foreign affairs Eisenhower was 'a man of keen political intelligence and penetration. . . . When he spoke of such matters seriously and in a protected official circle, insights of a high order flashed out time after time through the curious military gobbledygook in which he was accustomed to expressing and concealing his thoughts.'[114] In fact Eisenhower used gobbledygook, especially at press conferences, to avoid giving answers which plain English could not conceal; he often

pretended ignorance for the same reason. Indeed he was Machiavellian enough to pretend to misunderstand his own translator when
dealing with difficult foreigners.[115] Transcripts of his secret conferences show the power and lucidity of his thoughts. His editing of
drafts by speechwriters and of speeches by Dulles betray the command
of English he could exercise when he chose. Churchill was one of the
few men who appreciated him at his correct worth. It could be said
that they were the two greatest statesmen of the mid-century.

Eisenhower concealed his gifts and activities because he thought it
essential that the autocratic leadership, which he recognized both
America and the world needed, should be exercised by stealth. He had
three quite clear principles. The first was to avoid war. Of course if
Soviet Russia was bent on destroying the West, resistance must be
made, and America must be strong enough to make it. But the
occasions of unnecessary war (as he judged Korea) must be avoided by
clarity, firmness, caution and wisdom. In this limited aim he was
successful.[116] He ended the Korean conflict. He avoided war with
China. He stamped out the Suez war in 1956, and skilfully averted
another Middle-Eastern war in 1958. Of Vietnam he said: 'I cannot
conceive of a greater tragedy for America than to get heavily involved
now in an all-out war in any of those regions.' Again: 'There is going
to be no involvement . . . unless it is as a result of the constitutional
process that is placed upon Congress to declare it.'[117] Congressional
authorization; Allied support – those were the two conditions he laid
down for American military involvement anywhere, and they were
reflected in the Middle Eastern and South-East Asian systems of
alliance he added to Nato.

Eisenhower's second and related principle was the necessity for
constitutional control over military endeavour. He used the CIA a
great deal and was the only American president to control it
effectively. He skilfully presided over the CIA operations in Iran and
Guatemala without any damage to his reputation.[118] The 1958 CIA
coup in Indonesia failed because for once the work was delegated to
Dulles. It is hard to believe Eisenhower would have allowed the 1961
Bay of Pigs operation to proceed in the form it took. He had in 1954
created a civilian Board of Consultants on Foreign Intelligence
Activities, under a wily old diplomat, David Bruce, and this was one of
a number of means he employed to keep the military establishment
under his authority.[119] He disliked generals in politics. The 1952
Chicago Republican convention, which selected him to run for the
presidency, was so thick with generals, supporters of Senator Taft and
MacArthur, that Eisenhower kept his chief aide, Colonel Bob Schultz,
and his doctor, General Howard Snyder, out of town.[120] Eisenhower
was always aware of his need to steer a difficult path between

isolationism and over-activism in world affairs. He used Dulles to satisfy the activists of the Senate. For Dulles, who was Wilson's Secretary of State Robert Lansing's nephew and had been at Versailles, the Senate's rejection of the 1919 Treaty was the never-to-be-forgotten lesson. He was always, wrote Kennan, 'intensely aware of the dependence of a Secretary of State on senatorial support for the success of his policies'.[121] Under the guidance of Eisenhower, who carefully vetted his statements in advance, Dulles used what sometimes appeared to be inflated language ('rollback', 'go to the brink', 'agonizing reappraisal') to marry legislative support to military and political realism. Only the two men knew which of America's overseas commitments were real or rhetorical.

Eisenhower's chief fear, in the tense atmosphere engendered by the Cold War, was that the government would fall into the grip of a combination of bellicose senators, over-eager brass-hats and greedy arms-suppliers – what he termed the 'military-industrial complex'. For his third principle, reflected in his diaries and other personal documents, was that the security of freedom throughout the world rested ultimately in the health of the American economy. Given time, the strength of that economy could duplicate itself in West Europe and Japan. But the US economy could itself be destroyed by intemperate spending. He said of the brass-hats: 'They don't know much about fighting inflation. This country could choke itself to death piling up military expenditures just as surely as it can defeat itself by not spending enough for protection.' Or again: 'There is no defence for any country that busts its own economy.'[122] But Eisenhower was equally fearful of reckless spending in the domestic field. He was not opposed to Keynesian measures to fight incipient recession. In 1958, to overcome such a dip, he ran up a $9.4 billion deficit, the largest ever acquired by a US government in peacetime.[123] But that was an emergency. What Eisenhower strove mightily to avoid was a huge, permanent increase in federal commitments. He put holding down inflation before social security because he thought it was ultimately the only reliable form of social security. He loathed the idea of America becoming a welfare state. He was in fact deeply conservative. He admitted in 1956: 'Taft was really more liberal than me in domestic matters.'[124] His real nightmare was a combination of excessive defence spending combined with a runaway welfare machine – a destructive conjunction that became reality in the late 1960s. While he was in charge, federal spending as a percentage of GNP, and with it inflation, was held to a manageable figure, despite all the pressures. It was a notable achievement and explains why the Eisenhower decade was the most prosperous of modern times. And that prosperity was radiating through an ever-increasing portion of the world.

The world was more secure too. In 1950–2, the risk of a major war was very considerable. By the end of the decade, a sort of stability had been reached, lines drawn, rules worked out, alliances and commitments settled across the globe. The 'containment' policy had been applied. Militant Leninism, which had expanded rapidly in the 1940s in both Europe and Asia, found its impetuous march slowed to a crawl or even halted entirely. But no sooner was the system of containment complete than it ceased to be the whole answer. For the collapse of the old liberal empires of Europe brought into existence a new category of states which raised fresh and intractable dangers.

FOURTEEN

The Bandung Generation

The same historical process which created the superpowers placed traditional powers in a dilemma. What was their role? The defeated nations, France, Germany and Japan, were driven by necessity to a fundamental reappraisal. But Britain had not been defeated. She had stood alone and emerged victorious. Could she not carry on as before? Churchill had fought desperately for British interests. He rejected utterly Roosevelt's notion of America and Russia as the two 'idealist' powers and Britain as the greedy old imperialist. He knew of the bottomless cynicism reflected in Ambassador Maisky's remark that he always added up Allied and Nazi losses in the same column.[1] He pointed out to the British Ambassador in Moscow that Russia had 'never been actuated by anything but cold-blooded self-interest and total disdain for our lives and fortunes'.[2] He was sombrely aware that Russia was anxious to tear the British Empire to pieces and feast on its members, and that America too, aided by the Dominions and especially Australia and New Zealand, favoured 'decolonization'. H.V.Evatt, Australia's cantankerous Foreign Minister, got such notions written into the UN charter.[3] Churchill snarled at Yalta: 'While there is life in my body no transfer of British sovereignty will be permitted.'[4]

Six months later Churchill had been thrown out by the electorate. His Labour successors planned to disarm, decolonize, make friends with Russia and build a welfare state. In practice they found themselves at the mercy of events. In August 1945 Lord Keynes presented them with a paper showing the country was bankrupt. Without American help, 'the economic basis for the hopes of the country is non-existent'.[5] Ernest Bevin, the trades union leader turned Foreign Secretary, began with the slogan 'Left can talk to Left' and hoped to share atomic secrets with Russia. But he was soon telling his colleague Hugh Dalton: 'Molotov was just like a Communist in a local Labour Party. If you treat him badly, he makes the most of the grievances, and if you treat him well he only puts his price up and abuses you the next day.'[6] Gradually Bevin came to embody Britain's determination to organize collective security. He told Molotov in 1949, 'Do you want to get Austria behind your Iron Curtain? You can't do that. Do you want Turkey and the Straits? You can't have them. Do you want Korea? You can't have that. You are putting your neck out and one day you will have it chopped off.'[7]

Bevin's foreign policy meant Britain had to stay in the strategic arms race. Exactly a year after Keynes delivered his bankruptcy report, the Chief of Air Staff indented with the government for nuclear bombs. Specifications for the first British atom bomber were laid down 1 January 1947.[8] Britain's leading nuclear scientist, P.S.M.Blackett, opposed a British bomb, but then he thought that Britain could and should adopt a posture of neutrality vis-à-vis America and Soviet Russia.[9] The chief scientific adviser, Sir Henry Tizard, was also against an independent nuclear force: 'We are *not* a great power and never will be again. We are a great nation but if we continue to behave like a Great Power we shall soon cease to behave like a great nation.'[10] But Tizard was staggered by the Soviet success in exploding an A-bomb as early as August 1949: he attributed it to theft of the material. At all events the decision to make the bomb was taken in January 1947, at the height of the desperate fuel crisis and just before Britain handed over the burden of Greece and Turkey to Truman. Only Attlee, Bevin and four other ministers were present.[11] The expenditure was 'lost' in the estimates and concealed from parliament. When Churchill returned to office in 1951 he was astounded to find that £100 million had been thus secretly laid out and the project well advanced.[12]

The decision to make the bomb, and the brilliant success with which it was developed and deployed, undoubtedly kept Britain in the top club for another thirty years. It was the first British A-bomb test off Monte Bello Island in October 1952 which led the Americans to resume the atomic partnership. The first British H-bomb test at Christmas Island in May 1957 formalized this partnership by persuading Congress to amend the 1946 McMahon Act: the bilateral agreements of 1955 and 1958 could not have been obtained without a British nuclear capability. Once in the club, Britain was able to play a leading part in the test-ban negotiations of 1958–63 and the process which produced the Non-Proliferation Treaty of 1970. In 1960, in a famous phrase, Aneurin Bevan defended the British bomb to his Labour Party colleagues on the grounds that, without it, a British Foreign Secretary would 'go naked into the council chambers of the world'. But this was a misformulation. Without it, Britain would not have been a party to these and other negotiations in the first place: for, like other gentlemen's clubs, the nuclear one does not admit nudes into its council chamber. In 1962 the Anglo–US Nassau agreement gave Britain title to sixty-four modern nuclear launching-platforms as opposed to 1,038 for the USA and about 265 for Soviet Russia. By 1977 the relative figures were America 11,330, Russia 3,826 and Britain 192: it was this fall in the British ratio which excluded her from the Strategic Arms Limitation Talks (SALT), even though at that time the British 'deterrent' could destroy all the major industrial and population centres in Soviet Russia and inflict 20 million casualties.[13]

In 1945–6, then, it became an axiom of British policy to engage, in conjunction with the Americans, in collective security arrangements to contain Soviet expansion, and to contribute towards them a British nuclear force. Through all the changes of mood and government, that consistent thread ran through British policy right into the 1980s. But it was the only stable element. All else was confusion and irresolution. There was a failure of vision; a collapse of will. In the late summer of 1945 the British Empire and Commonwealth seemed to have returned to the meridian of 1919. British power was stretched over nearly a third of the globe. In addition to legitimate possessions, Britain administered the Italian empire in North and East Africa, many former French colonies and many liberated territories in Europe and Asia, including the glittering empires of Indo-China and the Dutch East Indies. No nation had ever carried such wide-ranged responsibilities. Twenty-five years later, everything had gone. History had never before witnessed a transformation of such extent and rapidity.

It was often to be said, as the disintegration took place, that the collapse of the Empire was foreshadowed by the fall of Singapore early in 1941. But that is not true. There was no ignominy in 1941. Though there was a failure of leadership in the defence of the city, there was no shame in the campaign as a whole. The British in Malaya were not guilty of *hubris* in despising the Japanese. On the contrary they predicted accurately what would happen unless the garrison was reinforced and, above all, re-armed. Instead the decision was taken to save Russia. As it was, 200,000 well-equipped and very experienced Japanese troops, with an overwhelming superiority in sea- and air-power, were held at bay for seventy days by elements of only three and a half divisions of Commonwealth fighting troops. In any event, the image of Asiatic victory was wholly erased by the magnitude of Japanese defeat. Britain surrendered at Singapore with 91,000 men. When General Itagaki handed his sword to Admiral Mountbatten in 1945 he had 656,000 men in the Singapore command. Elsewhere the British received the capitulation of more than a million. More than 3,175,000 Japanese men at arms came in from the cold, the greatest defeat any Asian or non-white nation has ever undergone. In every department, Western (i.e., white) technology and organization had proved not marginally but overwhelmingly superior. It was not only a characteristic but the very archetypal colonial-style victory of fire-power over muscle-power.[14]

Nor was there any physical evidence of a collapse of loyalty towards the British empire among the subject peoples. Quite the contrary. The intense efforts made by the Japanese to establish an 'Indian National Army' and an independent regime were a total failure. A 'government' was established in October 1942 under Chandra Bose, which declared war on Britain and set up its capital in Rangoon. The INA disintegrated immediately it went into action against the Indian Army. The Japanese were never able to persuade or force more than 30,000 Indians, civil and military, to serve against Britain. Many thousands of Indian POWs preferred torture and death to changing allegiance: for instance, of the 200 officers and men of the 2/15 Punjabs captured at Kuching, virtually all were murdered by April 1945, some being beaten to death, others beheaded or bayoneted. Opposition to the war by part of India's 'political nation' had no effect on the 'military nation'. Whereas 1,457,000 Indians served in the army in 1914–18, during the Second World War the number passed the 2,500,000 mark: Indians awarded Victoria Crosses rose from eleven to thirty-one.[15]

Who spoke for India? The 'political nation'? The 'military nation'? Could anyone speak for India? In 1945 India was over 400 million people: 250 million Hindus, 90 million Muslims, 6 million Sikhs, millions of sectarians, Buddhists, Christians; 500 independent princes and maharajahs; 23 main languages, 200 dialects; 3,000 castes, with 60 million 'untouchables' at the bottom of the heap; 80 per cent of the nation lived in 500,000 villages, most of them inaccessible even by surfaced road. Yet for all practical purposes the decision had been taken in 1917, under the Montagu reforms, to begin the process of handing power over this vast and disparate nation not to its traditional or its religious or racial or economic or military leaders – or all combined – but to a tiny élite who had acquired the ideology and the techniques and, above all, the vernacular of Western politics. The decision had been confirmed by the reaction to Amritsar. That indicated the British Raj was no longer determined to enforce the rule of law at all costs. The 1935 Act set the process of abdication in motion. The British establishment, whatever public noises it might make, knew exactly what was happening. As Baldwin's *eminence grise*, J.C.C.Davidson, reported to him:

The fact is that the British government, the Viceroy and to a certain extent the states have been bounced by Gandhi into believing that a few half-baked, semi-educated urban agitators represent the views of 365 million hard-working and comparatively contented cultivators. It seems to me that the elephant has been stampeded by the flea.[16]

India illustrates the process whereby the full-time professional politician inherited the earth in the twentieth century. Reforms created an alien system of representation. A class of men, mainly lawyers, organized themselves to manipulate it. In due course the governing power was handed over to them. The dialogue was entirely between the old and the new élites. The ordinary people did not come into the play, except as a gigantic walk-on crowd in the background. The process was to be repeated all over Asia and Africa. The forms of the Westminster, Paris or Washington model were preserved. The substance was only tenuously present; or absent entirely. Lenin's Bolsheviks of 1917, Mao's CCP cadres of 1949 and the Congressmen of India came to power by different routes. But they had this in common. All three new ruling groups were men who had never engaged in any other occupation except politics and had devoted their lives to the exploitation of a flexible concept called 'democracy'.

Lenin had asserted his mandate to rule by the methods of a caudillo; Mao by those of a war-lord. Gandhi and Nehru stepped into a vacuum created by the collapse of the will to rule. The 1935 Act had made the Raj unworkable, except by permanent repression. In 1942, partly under pressure from Roosevelt, Churchill agreed to a declaration giving India self-government after the war. On 28 July he lunched with George VI, whose diary records: 'He amazed me by saying that his colleagues & both, or all 3, parties in Parlt. were quite prepared to give up India to the Indians after the war.'[17] This proved to be completely accurate. The arguments in 1945–7 were entirely about the manner and timing, not the fact, of Britain's departure. The actual Indian Independence bill, which became law 18 July 1947, was passed by both Houses of Parliament without a division and against a background of almost complete public indifference.

Indeed, had Britain not abdicated, quickly and wearily, it is difficult to see quite how Indian independence could have been secured. Gandhi was not a liberator but a political exotic, who could have flourished only in the protected environment provided by British liberalism. He was a year older than Lenin, with whom he shared a quasi-religious approach to politics, though in sheer crankiness he had much more in common with Hitler, his junior by twenty years. In his local language, Gujarati, Gandhi means 'grocer', and both he and his mother, from whom he inherited chronic constipation, were obsessed by the bodily functions and the ingress and egress of food. This preoccupation was intensified when he went to London and moved in vegetarian circles. We know more about the intimacies of his life than that of any other human being in history. He lived in public in his *ashram* or religious camp, attended by a numerous entourage of devoted women, most of them willing to describe his ways in the most minute detail. By the mid-1970s more than four hundred biographies of him were in existence, and the English edition of his utterances, compiled by fifty researchers and thirty clerks of the Indian Information Ministry, which set up a special department for this purpose, will fill eighty volumes averaging 550 pages each.[18]

Gandhi's first question, on rising, to the women who waited on him every morning was 'Did you have a good bowel movement this morning, sisters?' One of his favourite books was *Constipation and Our Civilization*, which he constantly reread. He was convinced that evil sprang from dirt and unsuitable food. So although he ate heartily – 'He was one of the hungriest men I have ever known', a disciple said – his food was carefully chosen and prepared. A mixture of bicarbonate of soda, honey and lemon-juice was his drink, and all his vegetarian dishes were assisted by munching quantities of crushed garlic, a bowl of which stood by his plate (he had no sense of smell, a useful attribute in India).[19] In middle age, Gandhi turned against his wife and children, indeed against sex itself. He thought women were better than men because he assumed they did not enjoy sex. He carried out his so-called *Brahmacharya* experiments of sleeping with naked girls solely for warmth. His only seminal emission in his middle and later years was in his sleep in 1936, when he was aged 66: it disturbed him a great deal.[20]

Gandhi's eccentricities appealed to a nation which venerates sacral oddity. But his teachings had no relevance to India's problems or aspirations. Hand-weaving made no sense in a country whose chief industry was the mass-production of textiles. His food policy would have led to mass starvation. In fact Gandhi's own *ashram*, with his own very expensive 'simple' tastes and innumerable 'secretaries' and handmaidens, had to be heavily subsidized by three merchant princes. As one of his circle observed: 'It costs a great deal of money to keep Gandhiji living in poverty.'[21] About the Gandhi phenomenon there was always a strong aroma of twentieth-century humbug. His methods could only work in an ultra-liberal empire. 'It was not so much that the British treated him forbearingly', George Orwell wrote,

as that he was always able to command publicity . . . . It is difficult to see how Gandhi's methods could be applied in a country where opponents of the regime disappear in the middle of the night and are never heard of again. Without a free press and the right of assembly, it is impossible not merely to appeal to outside opinion but to bring a mass-movement into being . . . . Is there a Gandhi in Russia at this moment?[22]

All Gandhi's career demonstrated was the unrepressive nature of British rule and its willingness to abdicate. And Gandhi was expensive in human life as well as money. The events of 1920–1 indicated that though he could bring a mass-movement into existence, he could not control it. Yet he continued to play the sorcerer's apprentice, while the casualty bill mounted into hundreds, then thousands, then tens of thousands, and the risks of a gigantic sectarian and racial explosion accumulated. This blindness to the law of probability in a bitterly divided sub-continent made nonsense of Gandhi's professions that he would not take life in any circumstances.

There was a similar element of egregious frivolity in Jawaharlal Nehru. He was a brahmin, from a priestly caste which had in modern times (characteristically) turned to law and politics. He was an only son, a mother's boy, brought up by governesses and theosophists, then as an expatriate at Harrow, where he was known as Joe, and Cambridge. As a young man he led a fashionable life in London and the spas, on £800 a year. He was easily bored. He allowed his father, a hard-working Allahabad lawyer, to pick a wife for him, another Kashmiri brahmin. But he never (like Lenin) showed the smallest desire to take a job to support his family. As his father complained:

Have you had any time to attend to the poor cows . . . reduced to the position of cows by nothing short of culpable negligence on your part and mine – I mean your mother, your wife, your child and your sisters? . . . I do not think that a man who is capable of starving his own children can be much good to the nation.[23]

Nehru drifted into politics in the wake of Gandhi's campaign, and in 1929 the Mahatma made him Congress president. He dabbled in peasant life: 'I have had the privilege of working for them, of mixing with them, of living in their mud-huts and partaking in all reverence of their lowly fare', as he put it. He was in gaol for agitation at the same time as Hitler's spell in Landsberg: 'It will be a new experience, and in this blasé world it is something to have a new experience.' India, he thought, might be saved by 'a course of study of Bertrand Russell's books'. In many ways he was a Bloomsbury figure, a politicized Lytton Strachey, transplanted to an exotic clime. 'An intellectual of the intellectuals', wrote Leonard Woolf. 'The last word in aristocratic refinement and culture dedicated to the salvation of the underdog', enthused Mrs Webb.[24] He swallowed the European Left pharmacopoeia whole, enthusing for Republican Spain, accepting Stalin's show-trials at their face-value, an Appeaser and a unilateral disarmer. He spent most of the war in gaol, following a putative revolt in 1942 which received very little support, and thus acquired an extensive knowledge of Indian penology. But of the process of wealth-creation and administration, by which 400 million people were fed and governed, he knew nothing, Until the end of the 1940s he seems to have thought that India was underpopulated.[25] Almost until the last minute he refused to believe – because he knew so little about the real India – that if the British Raj handed over power to Congress the Muslims would demand a separate state. Even more astounding was his view that violent sectarianism, which had been endemic before the nineteenth century and had begun again only after the Gandhi movement and Amritsar, had been essentially created by British rule. He told Jacques Marcuse in 1946: 'When the British go, there will be no more communal trouble in India.'[26]

In fact the post-war Indian elections, in which the Muslim League captured virtually all the seats reserved for Muslims with its programme of partition, indicated that division was inevitable and large-scale violence probable. The transfer of power has been presented as a skilful exercise in Anglo–Indian statesmanship. The reality is that the British government simply lost control. Lord Mountbatten was appointed Viceroy on 20 February 1947, with the British economy on the verge of collapse, and told to do what he liked ('*carte blanche*' as he told the King) provided he stuck to the June 1948 deadline for independence.[27] The massacres had begun even before he reached India. Churchill took the view that 'a fourteen-month time interval is fatal to an orderly transfer of power' since it gave extremists on both sides time to organize. Lord Wavell, the previous Viceroy, felt Britain should hand over a united country, leaving it to the Indians themselves to divide it if they wished. General Sir Francis Tuker, who had prepared a contingency plan for division, judged that partition was inevitable if the transfer was rushed. Mountbatten rushed the transfer. He made a decision in favour of partition within a fortnight of his arrival. Sir Cyril Radcliffe, who headed the boundary commission, had to make the awards alone as the Hindu and Muslim members were too terrified to make independent decisions.

The result was like the break-up of the Habsburg Empire in 1918–19: the unifying principle was removed and the result created more problems than it solved. The princes were abandoned. The minority sects and clans were simply forgotten. The untouchables were ignored. All the real difficulties – the Punjab, Bengal, Kashmir, the North-West Frontier, Sind, British Baluchistan – were left to resolve themselves. Mountbatten had a genius for public relations and kept up a brave front. But the transfer and partition were catastrophic shambles, an ignominious end to two centuries of highly successful rule based on bluff. Some 5 to 6 million people ran for their lives in each direction. A procession of terrified Hindus and Sikhs, for instance, stretched for fifty-seven miles from the West Punjab. The boundary force of 23,000 was too weak and some of its troops may have joined the killing themselves.[28] The carnage reached even into Lutyens's incomparable palace, for many of Lady Mountbatten's Muslim staff were murdered; she helped to move their corpses into the mortuary. Gandhi, who had made it all possible, confessed to her: 'Such a happening is unparalleled in the history of the world and it makes me hang my head in shame.'[29] Nehru, who had seen liberated Indians as so many Bloomsberries, now admitted to Lady Ismay: 'People have lost their reason completely and are behaving worse than brutes.'[30]

Gandhi was among the victims, murdered in January 1948 by one of the fanatics whose hour had come. How many went with him will never be known. Estimates of the dead at the time ranged from 1 to 2 million. More modern calculations are in the 200,000 to 600,000 range.[31] But there has been a general desire to minimize and forget the event for fear of repeating it. In the anarchy, other great injustices took place. In Kashmir, Nehru's home state, he used troops to enforce Indian rule, despite the fact that most Kashmiris were Muslims, on the grounds that the ruler was a Hindu: the Muslims there were 'barbarians'. In Hyderabad, where the majority were Hindus and the ruler a Muslim, he reversed the principle and again used troops on the grounds that 'madmen are in charge of Hyderabad's destinies'.[32] Thus Kashmir, the most beautiful province of India, was itself partitioned and remains so more than thirty years later; and the ground was prepared for two wars between India and Pakistan.

Nehru ruled India for seventeen years and founded a parliamentary dynasty. He was a popular ruler, though not an effective one. He did his best to make India's parliament, the Lok Sabha, work and spent much time there. But he was too autocratic to allow cabinet government to flourish: his rule was a one-man show – 'I think my leaving might well be in the nature of a disaster', he admitted complacently.[33] The view was generally shared abroad: 'The greatest figure in Asia', wrote Walter Lippmann. 'If he did not exist,' said Dean Acheson, 'he would have to be invented.' 'A world titan', pronounced the *Christian Science Monitor*. 'Mr Nehru, without boasting, may say that Delhi is the School of Asia', echoed the *Guardian*. Adlai Stevenson thought him one of the few men entitled 'to wear a halo in their own lifetimes'.[34] Privately Nehru came to doubt it all. 'It is terrible to think that we may be losing all our values and sinking into the sordidness of opportunist politics', he wrote in 1948. He put through a land reform but it benefited only a few richer peasants and did nothing for agricultural productivity. As for planning, he thought it would 'change the picture of the country so completely that the world will be amazed'. But nothing much happened. In 1953 he confessed that on economics 'I am completely out of touch'. At one time he liked to open a dam or two; later his interest waned. In general: 'We function more and more as the old British government did,' he wrote to Governor-General Rajagopalachari, 'only with less efficiency.'[35] Nehru did not seem to know how to rule. He spent four to five hours every day just dictating to as many as eight typists answers to the 2,000 letters which Indians with grievances wrote daily to his office.[36]

What Nehru really enjoyed was holding forth about international morality on the world stage. In the 1950s he became the leading exponent of the higher humbug. At home he practised acquisitiveness. In 1952 he subdued the Naga tribesmen by using the army (though he vetoed machine-gunning them from the air). When the Portuguese Goans obstinately refused to rise and unite themselves with India, he sent in 'volunteers' and liberated them by force. Abroad, however, he denounced 'imperialism', at any rate when practised by the West. He thought that their behaviour in Korea showed the Americans to be 'more hysterical as a people than almost any others, except perhaps the Bengalis' (who continued to massacre each other into the 1950s). The Anglo–French operations against Egypt in 1956 were 'a reversal of history which none of us can tolerate'. 'I cannot imagine a worse case of aggression.'[37]

But for the Communist world he adopted a quite different standard. To the end, his bible on Russia remained the Webbs' mendacious volumes: 'the great work', as he termed it. Visiting the country in 1955 he found the people 'happy and cheerful . . . well fed'. He thought civil liberty was not missed. There was a 'general impression' of 'contentment', with everyone 'occupied and busy'; and 'if there are complaints they are about relatively minor matters'.[38] He never showed the slightest interest in Soviet colonialism or even recognized that it existed. When Sir John Kotelawala, Prime Minister of Ceylon, criticized the Soviet system of puppet-states in Eastern Europe, Nehru turned on him furiously. He refused to condemn the Soviet invasion of Hungary in 1956, pleading 'lack of information', and contented his conscience with a tiny private complaint.[39] Of course there was nothing Nehru could do about Hungary. But he might have saved Tibet from invasion and absorption by China, whose claims were purely imperialistic. Many Indians wanted him to take action but he did nothing. He thought the aggression had to be understood in terms of 'Chinese psychology' with its 'background of prolonged suffering'.[40] He did not explain why the suffering Chinese needed to take it out on the helpless Tibetans, whose ancient society was smashed like a matchbox and whose people were hustled off into central China, being replaced by Chinese 'settlers'. The arguments Nehru used to defend China were identical with those used on Hitler's behalf in the mid-1930s: Nehru was not only the last of the Viceroys, he was also the last of the Appeasers.

At the time Nehru was anxious to act as impresario and introduce the new China to the international community. He basked in Chou En-lai's oily flattery ('Your Excellency has more knowledge of the world and Asia than I have'). He hero-worshipped the virile and militaristic Mao, and was quite taken by his fierce and sinister neighbour, Ho Chi Minh ('Fine, frank face, gentle and benign'). In China, he was 'amazed' by the 'tremendous emotional response from the Chinese people' to his visit.[41] It does not seem to have occurred to him that China and India had fundamental conflicts of interest and that in building up Chinese prestige he was knotting an almighty scourge. The first punishment came in 1959 when the Chinese, having got everything they needed out of the Pandit, started to rectify their Himalayan frontier and build military roads. Nehru was hoist with his own petard of respecting China's 'rights' in Tibet. The big crisis came in 1962 when the harassed Nehru, misled by the overconfidence of his own generals, blundered into war and was badly beaten. He was then driven to the humiliation of asking for immediate American aid, for in his panic he feared a Chinese paratroop drop on Calcutta. So the 'neo-colonialist' C130s were provided by Washington, and the 'imperialist' Seventh Fleet moved to his succour up the Bay of Bengal. Then, mysteriously, the Chinese steamroller halted and Nehru, mopping his anxious brow, was glad to take US advice and accept a ceasefire.[42] But by then he was an old man who had ceased to count much.

Up to the mid-1950s, however, he was the cynosure of a new entity which progressive French journalists were already terming *le tiers monde*. The concept was based upon verbal prestidigitation, the supposition that by inventing new words and phrases one could change (and improve) unwelcome and intractable facts. There was the first world of the West, with its rapacious capitalism; the second world of totalitarian socialism, with its slave-camps; both with their hideous arsenals of mass-destruction. Why should there not come into existence a third world, arising like a phoenix from the ashes of empire, free, pacific, non-aligned, industrious, purged of capitalist and Stalinist vice, radiant with public virtue, today saving itself by its exertions, tomorrow the world by its example? Just as, in the nineteenth century, idealists had seen the oppressed proletariat as the repository of moral excellence – and a prospective proletarian state as Utopia – so now the very fact of a colonial past, and a non-white skin, were seen as title-deeds to international esteem. An ex-colonial state was righteous by definition. A gathering of such states would be a senate of wisdom.

The concept was made flesh at the Afro–Asian Conference held 18–24 April 1955 in Bandung, at the instigation of Indonesia's President Sukarno. Some twenty-three independent states from Asia and four from Africa were present, plus the Gold Coast and the Sudan, both soon to be free. The occasion was the apogee of Nehru's world celebrity and he chose it as a brilliant opportunity to introduce Chou En-lai to the world. But the many other stars included U Nu of Burma, Norodom Sihanouk of Cambodia, Mohammed Ali of Pakistan, Kwame Nkrumah, Africa's first black president-to-be, Archbishop Makarios of Cyprus, the black Congressman Adam Clayton Powell, and the Grand Mufti of Jerusalem.[43] It was calculated that 1,700 secret police were in attendance. Some of those present were subsequently to plot to murder each other; others to end their lives in gaol, disgrace or exile. But at the time the Third World had not yet publicly besmirched itself by invasions, annexations, massacres and dictatorial cruelty. It was still in the age of innocence when it was confidently believed that the abstract power of numbers, and still more of words, would transform the world. 'This is the first inter-continental conference of coloured peoples in the history of mankind', said Sukarno in his opening oration. 'Sisters and brothers! How terrifically dynamic is our time! . . . Nations and states have awoken from a sleep of centuries!' The old age of the white man, which had ravaged the planet with its wars, was dying; a better one was dawning, which would dissolve the Cold War and introduce a new multi-racial, multi-religious brotherhood, for 'All great religions are one in their message of tolerance.' The coloured races would introduce the new morality: 'We, the people of Asia and Africa . . . far more than half the human population of the world, we can mobilize what I have called the *Moral Violence of Nations* in favour of peace.'[44] After this striking phrase, a Lucullan feast of oratory followed. Among those overwhelmed by it all was the black American writer Richard Wright: 'This is the human race speaking', he wrote.[45]

Sukarno was eminently suited to preside over this gathering. No one illustrated better than he the illusions, the political religiosity and the inner heartlessness of the post-colonial leadership. The Dutch East

Indies had been cobbled together into an administrative unit from thousands of islands. It was an empire in itself. Until 1870 it had been run on principles of pure cupidity. Thereafter, under the inspiration of the great Islamic scholar C. Snouck Hurgronje, a combination of Westernization, 'association' and the creation of native élites was introduced under the name of 'ethical policy'.[46] It was well-intended but it was really a reflection of Dutch nationalism; it had no answer when a rival, Javanese, nationalism appeared in the 1930s. This seems to have been worked out from 1927 onwards, by Sukarno and others, in the internment camp for native agitators at Upper Digul in New Guinea.[47] It was an unimpressive mixture of Islamic, Marxist and European liberal clichés, but garnished by resounding phraseology. Whatever else he was, Sukarno was the great phrase-maker of his time. When the Dutch were ousted in 1941 their will to rule collapsed. In 1945 the Javanese nationalists began to take over. The Dutch left, taking 83 per cent of the mixed races with them. The Chinese became an unrepresented and increasingly persecuted minority. The non-Javanese majority, many of them in primitive tribal confederations, found themselves colonial subjects of a Javanese empire named 'Indonesia'.

Sukarno had no more moral mandate to rule 100 millions than Nehru had in India; rather less in fact. He too was devoid of administrative skills. But he had the gift of words. Faced with a problem, he solved it with a phrase. Then he turned the phrase into an acronym, to be chanted by crowds of well-drilled illiterates. He ruled by *Konsepsi*, concepts. His party cadres painted buildings with the slogan 'Implement President Sukarno's Concepts'. His first concept in 1945 was *Pantja Sila*, or the Five Fundamental Principles: Nationalism, Internationalism (Humanitarianism), Democracy, Social Prosperity, Belief in God. These were 'the Essence of the Indonesian Spirit'.[48] The cabinet was NASAKOM, uniting the three main streams of the 'revolution': *Nasionalisme*, *Agama* (religion) and *Komunisme*. The constitution was USDEK. His political manifesto was MANIPOL. A cabinet coalition was *gotong-rojong*, 'mutual help'. Then there were *musjawarah* and *mufakat*, 'Deliberation leading to Consensus' and 'functional representation' (his term for corporatism). Dissatisfied with party government, he made a 'Bury the Parties' speech, followed by the introduction of what he termed 'guided democracy' or *Demokrasi Terpimpin*. This introduced a 'Guided Economy' or *Ekonomi Terpimpin* which expressed 'Indonesian identity', *Kepribadian Indonesia*. He felt himself called to do the guiding or, as he put it, 'President Sukarno has called on Citizen Sukarno to form a government.'[49]

As Sukarno's internal difficulties mounted in the 1950s, he spent more time and words on foreign matters. He spoke of 'Free and active neutralism'; then of the dichotomy of 'old established' and 'new emerging forces'; then of the 'Djakarta–Phnom-Penh–Peking–Pyongyang Axis'. He harassed his Chinese subjects. He attacked the international Boy Scout movement. One of his axioms was 'A Nation Always Needs an Enemy'. So he introduced another *Konsepsi*, 'Greater Indonesia', which meant expansion into Dutch New Guinea, which he re-christened West Irian, Malaysia, Portuguese Timor and the Australian territories. For this purpose he invented the term 'confrontation', coined the phrase *Ganjang Malaysia*, 'Crush Malaysia!' and developed a technique of staging 'controlled demonstrations' outside foreign embassies, occasionally letting them become 'over-enthusiastic' (as in 1963 when the British Embassy was burned down). The crowd was given a slogan for every occasion. For foreign abuse there was NEKOLIM ('Neo-Colonialism, Colonialism and Imperialism'). When foreign aid was cut off or he was criticized by the UN there was BERDIKARI ('standing on one's own feet'). 1962, when he got hold of West Irian, was 'the year of triumph'; 1963, when he failed with Malaysia, was 'the year of living dangerously'. This last, *Tahun Vivere Pericoloso*, and his stock RESOPIM ('Revolution, Indonesian socialism, natural leadership') reflect the curious amalgam of Dutch, Indonesian, French, Italian and English words (and ideas) with which Sukarno kept his tottering empire going.[50]

If anyone believed in living dangerously it was the talkative, hyperactive, pleasure-loving Sukarno. Practising multiracialism, he acquired a notably varied collection of wives and mistresses, and extended his research still further on his numerous foreign jaunts. The Chinese secret police filmed him in action and so preserved his sexual *Konsepsi* for posterity. Khrushchev, already briefed in this respect by private Tass reports, was still deeply shocked, on his visit in 1960, to see the President chatting gaily with a naked woman.[51] But as the 1960s progressed, the Indonesian economy moved closer to collapse. The virtual extinction of the Chinese minority destroyed the internal distribution system. Food rotted in the countryside. The towns starved. Foreign investment vanished. Apart from oil, which still flowed, industry was nationalized and slowly subsided under a rapacious bureaucracy. By autumn 1965 foreign debt amounted to over $2,400 million, and credit was exhausted. Sukarno had run out even of slogans. Not knowing what to do, Sukarno appears to have given the go-ahead to a *coup* by the Indonesian Communist Party (PKI).

The *putsch* took place in the early hours of 1 October. The plan was to destroy the leadership of the armed forces. General Abdul Yani, the Army Chief of Staff, and two other generals were shot on the spot. The

Defence Minister, General Nasution, escaped by climbing over the wall of his house, though his daughter was murdered. Three other generals were captured and then tortured to death, in ritual fashion, by the women and children of the PKI: their eyes were gouged out and their genitals sliced off, then their bodies thrown into the Lubang Buaja, the Crocodile Hole.[52] The events were later investigated by a special military tribunal, whose voluminous transcripts leave no doubt about Communist guilt.[53] But the movement, termed *Gestapu*, was a failure. General Suharto, the Strategic Reserve Commander, took over. A fearful retribution followed. The revenge killings began on 8 October when the PKI Djakarta headquarters was burned. The massacres were organized in the local collective fashion, so that all were equally involved in responsibility, and entire families expiated the guilt. It was one of the great systematic slaughters of the twentieth century, the age of slaughter. The toll may have been as high as 1 million, though the consensus of authorities puts it in the region of 200,000 to 250,000.[54] Sukarno, under house arrest in his palace, repeatedly but impotently called for an end to the killing, for the dead were essentially his supporters. But he was ignored, and his offices gradually stripped from him by a process of slow political torture. At each progressive stage in his degradation, one of his wives left him, and only one remained when he died, of kidney disease, on 21 June 1970, forgotten and speechless.

But this, too, was in the future. At Bandung in 1955 the all-conquering word still held sway. Among those present was the Egyptian president, Gamal Abdul Nasser, a handsome newcomer to the new humbug but already an accomplished rhetorician in his own right. Israel, undoubtedly an Afro–Asian state, was not represented at the Conference. Therein lay a long and complex tale, produced by the bisection of two of the strongest and most paranoid twentieth-century forces: the insatiable demand for oil and the evil of anti-Semitism.

Britain had moved into the Middle Eastern oilfields in 1908 and had been followed by America in 1924. By 1936 Britain controlled 524 million tons of proven reserves, against 93 million by America; in 1944 the figures had jumped to 2,181 million and 1,768 million; and by 1949 American output, coming chiefly from the richest fields of all in Saudi Arabia, had passed British.[55] By the early 1940s it was already recognized that the Middle East held most of the world's oil reserves: 'The centre of gravity of world oil production', said Everett DeGolyer, head of the US Petroleum Commission in 1944, 'is shifting until it is firmly established in that area.' At the same time there were the first hints that America might run out of domestic oil – by 1944 the calculation was that only fourteen years' supply remained.[56] Four years later Defence Secretary Forrestal was telling the oil industry: 'Unless we had access to Middle East oil, the American automobile companies would have to devise a four-cylinder motor car.'[57] European dependence increased much faster. By the time of Bandung its oil consumption was growing by 13 per cent annually, and the Middle East proportion had jumped from 25 per cent in 1938 to 50 per cent in 1949 and now stood at over 80 per cent.[58]

The growing dependence of US and European industry on a single source of oil was itself worrying. What turned it into an intractable problem was its conflation with the irreconcilable claims of Arabs and Jews to Palestine. The Balfour Declaration and the idea of a Jewish National Home was one of the post-dated cheques Britain signed to win the Great War. It might conceivably have been honoured without detriment to the Arabs – for it did not imply a Zionist state as such – but for one critical British mistake. In 1921 they authorized a Supreme Muslim Council to direct religious affairs; and it appointed Mohammed Amin al-Husseini, head of the biggest landowning clan in Palestine, to be senior judge or Mufti of Jerusalem for life. It was one of the most fatal appointments in modern history. The year before he had been given ten years' hard labour for provoking bloody anti-Jewish riots. He had innocent blue eyes and a quiet, almost cringing manner, but he was a dedicated killer who devoted his entire adult life to race-murder. There is a photograph of him taken with Himmler: the two men smile sweetly at one another; beneath, a charming inscription by the ss chief to 'His Eminence the Grossmufti': the date was 1943 when the 'Final Solution' was moving into top gear.

The Mufti outrivalled Hitler in his hatred for Jews. But he did something even more destructive than killing Jewish settlers. He organized the systematic destruction of Arab moderates. There were many of them in 1920s Palestine. Some of them even welcomed Jewish settlers with modern agricultural ideas, and sold land to them. Arabs and Jews might have lived together as two prosperous communities. But the Mufti found in Emile Ghori a terrorist leader of exceptional ability, whose assassination squads systematically murdered the leading Arab moderates – the great majority of the Mufti's victims were Arabs – and silenced the rest. By the end of the 1930s Arab moderate opinion had ceased to exist, at least in public, the Arab states had been mobilized behind Arab extremism, the British Foreign Office had been persuaded that continued access to oil was incompatible with continued Jewish immigration, and the 1939 White Paper virtually brought it to an end and, in effect, repudiated the Balfour Declaration: 'a gross breach of faith', as Churchill put it.[59]

Then in 1942 came the first authenticated reports of the 'Final Solution'. They aroused not pity but fear. America tightened its visa regulations. Seven Latin-American countries followed suit; so did Turkey.[60] At this stage Chaim Weizmann still believed agreement could be reached with Britain to resume the flow of immigrants. In October 1943, Churchill (with Attlee present to represent the Labour Party) told him that partition was acceptable, and on 4 November 1944 he promised Weizmann that 1 to 1.5 million Jews could go to Palestine over ten years.[61] But Churchill was virtually the only Zionist at the top of British politics. More worthwhile, because concrete and immediate, was his creation, within the British army, of an independent Jewish brigade, whose members ultimately formed the professional nucleus of the Haganah, the defence force of the Jewish Agency, when it turned itself into an army.

At this stage Churchill still thought Britain could control the destiny of Palestine. In fact it was already slipping from her grasp. There were two main factors. The first was Jewish terrorism. This was created by Abraham Stern, a Polish Jew who had become a fascist and an Anglophobe at Florence University, and later tried to get Nazi finance for his organization through Vichy Syria. Stern was killed by police in 1942 but his gang continued, as did a much bigger terrorist group, the Irgun, commanded from 1944 by Menachem Begin. This was a fateful development, because for the first time modern propaganda was combined with Leninist cell-structure and advanced technology to advance political aims through murder. During the next forty years the example was to be followed all over the world: a cancer of modern times, eating at the heart of humanity. Churchill, with his unfailing gift for driving to the root of events, warned of the tragedy 'if our dreams of Zionism are to end in the smoke of an assassin's pistol and the labours for its future produce a new set of gangsters worthy of Nazi Germany'. Weizmann promised that the Jewish people 'will go to the utmost limits of its power to cut off this evil from its midst'.[62] Haganah, in fact, attempted to destroy both Irgun and the Stern gang. But as the war ended and the efforts of Jews to reach Palestine became more frantic, it devoted its energies to the legitimate object of assisting illegal immigration. The 'Final Solution' did not end anti-Semitism. Thus, on 5 July 1946 in the Polish town of Kielce, a rumour that Jews were engaged in the ritual killing of Gentile children stirred up a mob which, with the connivance of the Communist police and army, beat to death forty Jews.[63] This was one of many incidents which accelerated the stampede.

With Haganah preoccupied, the gangs flourished, egged on by the rabid elements in the American press. Typical was what Ruth Gruber wrote in the *New York Post* of the Palestine police:

These men who loathed the idea of fighting their friends, the Nazis, embraced with passion the idea of fighting Jews. They walked around the streets of Jerusalem and Tel Aviv, the city built by Jews, singing the *Horst Wessel Song*. They marched into crowded markets giving the *Heil Hitler* salute.[64]

On 22 July 1946 Irgun blew up Jerusalem's principal hotel, the King David, killing forty-one Arabs, twenty-eight British, seventeen Jews and five others. Part of the hotel was a British government office and Begin claimed that the object of the bomb was to destroy secret records. But in that case, as Haganah pointed out, the bomb should have been exploded outside office hours. Begin claimed a warning was given: in fact it reached the phone-operator two minutes before, and as he was telling the hotel manager the bomb went off.[65] This crime became the prototype terrorist outrage for the decades to come. The first to imitate the new techniques were, naturally, the Arab terrorists: the future Palestine Liberation Organization was an illegitimate child of Irgun.

Jewish terrorism was counterproductive in other respects. On 30 July 1947 two captured British sergeants were murdered in cold blood, and their bodies booby-trapped. The Jewish Agency called it 'the dastardly murder of two innocent men by a set of criminals'.[66] There were anti-Semitic riots in Manchester, Liverpool, Glasgow and London; in Derby a synagogue was burnt down. But the effect of this particular episode, coming on top of others, was to turn the British Army anti-Jewish. As in India, Britain had used too little severity. The figures show that, from August 1945 to 18 September 1947 (leaving out the King David deaths), 141 British died, forty-four Arabs, twenty-five Jewish non-terrorists; in addition thirty-seven Jewish terrorists were killed in gun-fights but only seven executed (two committed suicide in prison).[67] The British troops knew they were being unjustly judged. As a result, when the evacuation took place, officers and men conspired to hand over weapons, posts and supplies to the Arabs. The military consequences were very serious. In effect, Jewish terrorism cost the Jewish state the Old City of Jerusalem and the West Bank of the Jordan, which were not taken until 1967, and then without legal title.

Terrorism led Britain to wash her hands, like Pilate, of the Palestine problem. Ernest Bevin, in charge from July 1945, was an old-fashioned working-class anti-Semite, though not a vicious one. He told the Labour Party congress in 1946 that the American idea for another 100,000 immigrants in Palestine was proposed from 'the purest motives – they did not want too many Jews in New York'.[68] Terrorism made him bitter. He thought that if Britain pulled out the Jews would all be massacred, and that British troops were being murdered by those whose lives they were protecting. But by the beginning of 1947 he had had enough. The fuel crisis tipped the balance in favour of scuttle. On 14 February – the same month Attlee decided to get out of India straight away and hand over responsibility for Greece and Turkey to America – Bevin had the Jewish leaders into his office and told them he was transferring the problem to the UN. There was no electricity; only candles. Bevin joked, 'There's no need for candles as the Israel*ites* are here.'[69]

The second factor was the impingement of America. David Ben-Gurion visited the US in 1941 and felt 'the pulse of her great Jewry with its five millions'.[70] For the first time he sensed that, with the help of America's Jews, Zionism could be achieved in the immediate future, and thereafter he hustled Weizmann along towards this object. Whether it was right to turn the concept of a Jewish national home into a state is still a matter of argument. Weizmann had the magnanimity to recognize that the cost to the Arabs must be heavy. He told the Anglo–American Committee of Inquiry set up after the war that it was not a choice between right and wrong but between greater and lesser injustice. Ben-Gurion took a deterministic view: 'History had decreed that we should return to our country and re-establish here the Jewish state.'[71] But this was to speak with the voice of Lenin or Hitler. There is no such person as History. It is human beings who decree.

The truth is, during the war years the American Jewish community first developed its collective self-confidence and began to exert the political muscle its numbers, wealth and ability had created. In the immediate post-war it became the best-organized and most influential lobby in America. It was able to show that it held the voting key to swing states like New York, Illinois and Pennsylvania. Roosevelt had a strong enough political base to ignore this pressure. With characteristic frivolity, he seems to have turned anti-Zionist when, on returning from Yalta, he had a brief meeting with the King of Saudi Arabia. 'I learned more about the whole problem', he told Congress, ' . . . by talking with Ibn Saud for five minutes than I could have learned in an exchange of two or three dozen letters.'[72] David Niles, the passionately pro-Zionist presidential assistant, testified: 'There are serious doubts in my mind that Israel would have come into being if Roosevelt had lived.'[73] Truman was politically much weaker. He felt he had to have the Jewish vote to win the 1948 election. He was genuinely pro-Zionist too, and distrusted the Arabism of 'the "striped-pants boys" in the State Department'.[74] In the event it was his will which pushed the partition scheme through the UN (29 November 1947) and recognized the new Israeli state which Ben-Gurion declared the following May. There were vast forces against it. Max Thornburg of Cal-Tex, speaking for the oil interests, wrote that Truman had 'prevailed upon the Assembly to declare racial and religious criteria the basis of political statehood' and thereby 'extinguished' the 'moral prestige of America' and 'Arab faith in her ideals'.[75] The State Department prophesied ruin. Defence Secretary Forrestal was appalled: 'no group in this country', he wrote bitterly of the Jewish lobby, 'should be permitted to influence our policy to the point where it could endanger our national security.'[76]

It is likely, indeed, that if the crisis had come a year later, after the Cold War had really got into its stride, the anti-Zionist pressures on Truman would have been too strong. American backing for Israel in 1947–8 was the last idealistic luxury the Americans permitted themselves before the Realpolitik of global confrontation descended. The same time-scale influenced Russia. It backed Zionism in order to break up Britain's position in the Middle East. It not only recognized Israel but, in order to intensify the fighting and the resultant chaos, it instructed the Czechs to sell it arms.[77] These considerations would not have prevailed a year later, when the rush for Cold War allies was on. Israel slipped into existence through a crack in the time continuum.

Hence the notion that Israel was created by imperialism is not only wrong but the reverse of the truth. Everywhere in the West, the foreign offices, defence ministries and big business were against the Zionists. Even the French only sent them arms to annoy the British, who had 'lost' them Syria. The Haganah had 21,000 men but, to begin with, virtually no guns, armour or aircraft. It was the Communist Czechs, on Soviet instructions, who made Israel's survival possible, by turning over an entire military airfield to shuttle arms to Tel Aviv.[78] Virtually everyone expected the Jews to lose. There were 10,000 Egyptian troops, 4,500 in Jordan's Arab Legion, 7,000 Syrians, 3,000 Iraqis, 3,000 Lebanese, plus the 'Arab Liberation Army' of Palestinians. That was why the Arabs rejected the UN partition scheme, which gave the Jews only 5,500 square miles, chiefly in the Negev Desert. By accepting it, despite its disadvantages (it would have created a state with 538,000 Jews and 397,000 Arabs), the Zionists showed they were willing to abide by the arbitration of international law. The Arabs chose force.

It was a small-scale, heroic struggle. Like the Trojan War, it involved many famous personalities: General Neguib, Colonel Nasser, Hakim Amir, Yigal Allon, Moshe Dayan. At the heart of the Arab failure was the hatred between their field commander, Fawzi al-Qawukji, and the Mufti and his gruesome family. The Mufti accused Qawukji of 'spying for Britain . . . drinking wine and running after women'.[79] The Iraqis and the Syrians had no maps of Palestine. Some of the Arab armies had good equipment, but all were badly trained except for the Jordanians, and King Abdullah of Jordan only wanted Old Jerusalem, which he got. He had no desire to see an Arab Palestinian state with the Mufti in charge. As he told Golda Meir at a secret meeting: 'We both have a common enemy – the Mufti.'[80] In retrospect it is clear that the only chance the Arabs had was an overwhelming success in the first days of the war. Ben-Gurion took this from them by a pre-emptive strike in April 1948, the most important decision of his life, which he was able to carry through with Czech Communist weapons.[81] Thereafter, despite anxious moments, Israeli power increased steadily: by December it had a properly equipped army of 100,000 and had established a military ascendency it retained into the 1980s.

The creation of Israel finally ended European anti-Semitism, except behind the Iron Curtain. It created the Arab refugee problem. This was the work of extremists, on both sides. The Arab population of Palestine was 93 per cent in 1918, when the Balfour Declaration first began to take effect, and 65 per cent in 1947, when the crisis broke. The Arabs could then have had their independent state, plus a major share in the running of Israel. But by then the Mufti and his assassination squads had done their work. On 14 October 1947, when Azzam Pasha, Secretary-General of the Arab League, met the Jewish negotiator Abba Eban in London, he told him bluntly that the time for reason was past: if he accepted the partition he would, he said, be 'a dead man within hours of returning to Cairo'.[82]

Here we see a classic case of the evil which political murder brings. For by the beginning of the actual fighting, Azzam himself was speaking the language of horror on the radio: 'This will be a war of extermination and a momentous massacre', he announced.[83] Even before the fighting began, 30,000 mainly well-to-do Arabs had left Palestine temporarily, expecting to return in triumph. They included the muhktars, judges and caids. With no administration to protect them, many poor Arabs fled. When the Jews captured Haifa, 20,000 Arabs had gone and most of the remaining 50,000 left afterwards despite Jewish pleas to remain. Elsewhere the Arab League ordered the Arabs to remain in their homes; there is no evidence to justify Jewish claims that Arab governments were responsible for the flight of the refugees.[84] The Arab exodus was undoubtedly assisted by the fearful massacre carried out by the Irgun at the village of Deir Yassin on 9 April 1948, right at the start of the fighting. About 250 men, women and children were murdered. An Irgun spokesman said on the evening of this atrocity: 'We intend to attack, conquer and keep until we have the whole of Palestine and Transjordan in a greater Jewish state . . . . We hope to improve our methods in future and make it possible to spare women and children.'[85] The Irgun units were thrown out of the Israeli Army during the June truce in the middle of the fighting; and it was the honourable soldiers of the Haganah who, for all practical purposes, created and saved Israel.

By then the damage had been done. When the smoke cleared there were over half a million Arab refugees (the UN figure was about 650,000; the Israeli figure 538,000).[86] To balance this, 567,000 Jews in ten Arab countries were forced to flee in the years 1948–57.[87] Nearly all went to Israel and all who did had been resettled by 1960. The Arab refugees might likewise have been resettled, as were comparable numbers of refugees, on both sides, after the Greek–Turkish conflicts of 1918–23. Instead the Arab states preferred to keep the refugees in the camps, where they and their descendants remained, as human title-deeds to a Palestinian reconquest, and the justification for further wars in 1956, 1967 and 1973.

Granted Abdullah's willingness to compromise, the Arab–Israeli conflict might have been quickly resolved. He had the best historical title to leadership of the Arab cause. But his country had only 300,000 indigenous inhabitants and an income of less than £1,200,000. It was the British who, to assist their war effort, had encouraged the Arabs to create a League; and since they directed the war from Cairo, and since Egypt was the largest country in the area, the League had become an essentially Egyptian and Cairene institution. Hence Egypt led the pack against Israel. This was both an anomaly and a tragedy. For geographical reasons, Egypt and Israel were natural allies; and in antiquity they had been so. The 'pure' Arabs of the Hejaz, like Abdullah, did not regard Egyptians as Arabs at all: he said they were poor, miserable and backward Africans. Egypt's playboy king, Farouk, aroused his particular contempt: when he mentioned his name to visitors, Abdullah would spit into the corner of his carpeted tent.[88] The Egyptians, by contrast, saw themselves as the inheritors of the oldest civilization in the world and the natural leaders of the Arab cause: Farouk had a vision of Egypt as an authoritarian Muslim state embracing gradually all Arabs, even all Muslims. Hence he identified the continuing campaign against Israel with Egypt's own self-respect and aspirations for leadership in the region. From this essentially frivolous set of notions sprang the tragedy which turned Egypt into Israel's bitter enemy for a quarter-century.

The element of instability was increased by Britain's growing disinclination to act as paramount power in the area. As early as October 1946 Britain decided to pull most of its troops out of the Middle East to East Africa, with Simonstown near Capetown replacing the big naval base at Alexandria. Attlee disliked the Arab leaders: 'I must say I had a very poor view of the governing classes.'[89] The Palestine mess, even more than the débâcle in India, disgusted

British public opinion with the whole idea of imperial responsibilities. It shook even Churchill: 'Simply such a hell-disaster', he told Weizmann in 1948, 'that I cannot take it up again . . . and must, as far as I can, put it out of my mind.'[90] But that was only the start. Farouk's grotesquely luxurious lifestyle and the corruption of his regime (the 1948 defeat was blamed on an arms scandal) had led to growing criticism, which came to a head when he married a new queen, Princess Narriman, and took her on a much-publicized honeymoon during Ramadhan in 1951. To distract the public, he unilaterally abrogated the Anglo–Egyptian Treaty on 8 October. Early the next year he began guerrilla warfare against the Canal Zone, where Britain had a vast base: thirty-eight camps and ten airfields, capable of accommodating forty-one divisions and thirty-eight squadrons. Old-style monarchs are ill-advised to invite the mob on stage. On 26 January it took over Cairo, murdering Europeans, Jews and the rich of all nations. The young officers, who had bitterly resented the higher direction of the war against Israel, saw an opening. Six months later their Free Officers Committee sent Farouk packing on his yacht, loaded with his lifetime collection of trinkets and pornography.

The leading spirit was Colonel Gamal Abdul Nasser, who soon elbowed aside the popular general, Mohammed Neguib, initially set up as figurehead. The son of a postal-clerk and a coal-merchant's daughter, he began with some radical ideals. In the disaster of 1948 he told an Israeli staff officer that he envied the socialist *kibbutz* system of farming, which he contrasted with Egypt's absentee landlordism. As this stage he blamed the British, not the Jews: 'They manoeuvred us into this war. What is Palestine to us? It was all a British trick to divert us from their occupation of Egypt.'[91] His *Philosophy of the Revolution* was a frothy mixture of Marxist tags, western liberalism and Islam: good, flatulent stuff. He was an archetypal member of the 'Bandung generation': adept at words, but not much else. Like Sukarno, he was brilliant at devising slogans and titles: he often changed the name of the party he created and of the gimcrack Arab federations he negotiated. His particular speciality was crowd-manipulation. His windy rhetoric went down well, especially with the students, and he seems to have been able to goad the Cairo mob into chanting any slogans he wished, often changing them from day to day.[92]

Once in power, Nasser was soon corrupted by it. Like Sukarno, he dissolved the parties. He set up People's Courts and accumulated 3,000 political prisoners. He always maintained a modest degree of terror. It was 'necessary'. Egypt was a poor country with a rapidly growing population (40 million by the 1970s) and a cultivable area smaller than Belgium. Nasser's philosophy did not embrace workable ideas for the creation of wealth. Such ideas as he had promoted its consumption. So terror was not enough. Like Sukarno, he needed a foreign enemy; preferably several. His rule was a deafening series of overseas crises to cover the sad silence of misery at home. First he intensified the campaign against the Suez base. But the British agreed to evacuate it, leaving behind only care and maintenance units. The agreement signed 27 July 1954 gave Nasser almost everything he asked for. When Churchill's colleagues defended it in the Commons, the old man sat with head bowed. So Nasser turned on the Sudan, a potential satellite. But it slipped from his grasp and moved towards independence.

Then Nasser went to Bandung. It completed his corruption, as it did for other young nationalist politicians. Why sweat at the thankless task of keeping a poor country fed and clothed when the world stage beckoned? Bandung opened Nasser's eyes to the opportunities the age offered to an expert publicist and sloganizer, especially one prepared to play the anti-colonialist card. And he had been holding one in his hand all the time: the Jews! Israel was easily rationalized into a general imperialist conspiracy theory. Azzam Pasha had produced the exculpatory mythology as long ago as 16 July 1948. The Arabs had lost because of the West: 'England and America followed every Arab effort to obtain arms and opposed it with all their force, while at the same time they worked resolutely and vigorously to assure the flow of war materials and troops to the Jews.'[93] After Bandung, then, Nasser reversed his earlier analysis. He worked to build up a coalition of 'anti-imperialist' Arab states, to overthrow the decision of 1948 and then to create an Arab superstate with himself at the helm.

The Cold War played into his hands. As part of the containment of the Soviets, Britain and America had been constructing a Middle Eastern alliance, embracing Turkey, Iran and Pakistan. It was known as the 'northern tier'. Much against America's will, Britain was anxious to tie this grouping to its own system of Arab clients, notably Iraq and Jordan. Anthony Eden, who had at last succeeded Churchill as Prime Minister, wanted to bolster Britain's sagging leadership in the area with American assistance. The new regime in Russia of Nikita Khrushchev, eager to retrieve Stalin's mistakes in 1948, saw Nasser's emergence as a chance to leap over the northern tier and create client states of their own. The Russians offered to back Nasser's anti-Israeli coalition with a huge supply of Iron Curtain arms on credit. Nasser was delighted. So at one bound, the Russians were over the tier, and he was in business as a Third World soldier-statesman.

Nasser did not forget the other lesson of Bandung: non-alignment. The idea was to play off East and West against each other. That meant dealing with both and being the property of neither. The Bandung philosophy was for the new nations to create their own industrial bases as fast as possible, making themselves independent of 'imperialism'. Provided the money is there, it is actually easier and quicker – and of course much more spectacular – to build a steel plant than raise agricultural productivity. Nasser returned from Bandung determined to hasten a project to build a giant high dam on the Nile at Aswan. It would provide power for industrialization and extra water for irrigation, raising the cultivable area by 25 per cent.[94] But the dam required a World Bank loan of $200 million, mainly from America. There were a great many economic and environmental objections to the scheme, objections which in the end proved fully justified – the net effect of the dam, completed by the Russians in 1970, was actually to increase unemployment and lower agricultural productivity. At all events, after much havering, the Americans turned down the project on 19 July 1956. This was the kind of blow a high-risk regime like Nasser's could not suffer in silence. He retaliated by nationalizing the Anglo–French Suez Canal.

The Suez crisis of 1956–7 was one of those serio-comic international events, like Abyssinia in 1935, which illustrate historical trends rather than determine them. Britain's decline as a world power was perhaps inevitable. The rate of decline, however, was determined by its own national will. Post-war events had suggested the will was virtually non-existent. Relative industrial decline had also been resumed, with a vengeance, as the economic crisis of autumn 1955 suggested. Sir Anthony Eden, who had waited so long in Churchill's shadow, was not the man to retrieve a lost game. He was nervous, excitable, intermittently sick, and with a fatal propensity to confuse the relative importance of events. In the 1930s he had, at one time, considered Mussolini more formidable than Hitler. Now, obsessed with the need for Britain to play a Middle Eastern role independently of America, he saw Nasser as another Duce. 'I have never thought Nasser a Hitler,' he wrote to Eisenhower, 'but the parallel with Mussolini is close.'[95] This was the wrong way to play it. Nasser needed and wanted dramas. Indifference was the easiest way to shrivel him. That was Eisenhower's tactic, mainly because it was election year and 'peace' has always proved the highroad to American voters' hearts. The difficulty was that Eden needed a drama himself. His first year in power out of Churchill's shadow had been a let-down. He was criticized, especially in his own party, for lacking 'the smack of firm government'. As the *Daily Telegraph* put it: 'There is a favourite gesture with the Prime Minister. To emphasize a point, he will clench one fist to smack the open palm of the other hand. But the smack is seldom heard.' It was a measure of Eden's unfitness that he allowed himself to be mortally rattled by this jibe, which evoked from him 'a pained and pungent oath'.[96] He would give them a smack all right!

The evening Eden got the news of Nasser's nationalization decree, he called the service chiefs to Downing Street. He asked them to prepare an invasion of Egypt. They reported back that it was impossible in under six weeks. That should have settled the matter. A country which cannot invade a small Arab state in less than six weeks is not a great power and had better devise other ways of pursuing its interests. Besides, it was not clear that Nasser had done anything illegal. He had not broken the 1888 convention which governed the Canal. To nationalize foreign assets with due compensation (as he proposed) was the right of every sovereign state. When the Iranian regime of Mohammed Mussadeq had nationalized the British oil refinery at Abadan in 1951, Britain – after, it must be said, much huffing – had sensibly left it to the CIA to knock Mussadeq off his perch. In any case the Canal agreement was due to run out in twelve years. By the time the first flush of anger had worn off, all this had become clear. Eden should have tied Nasser up in negotiations, waited until Eisenhower was re-elected and then concerted with him means to pick the Colonel off. But the Prime Minister wanted his smack. The French were of like mind. The Fourth Republic was on its last legs. It had lost Indo-China; it had lost Tunisia and was in the process of losing Morocco; it was embroiled in an Algerian revolt which Nasser was noisily abetting. The French wanted to pull him down and they preferred to do it by frontal assault rather than intrigue. They, too, wanted a drama.

An Anglo–French seizure of Alexandria, termed 'Operation Musketeer', was ready for 8 September.[97] This scheme, though crude, would probably have worked if pursued with resolution. But Eden kept postponing and eventually scrapped it, in favour of a much slower and more difficult occupation plan for the Canal itself, which seemed to him more legal. The truth is, Eden could not make up his mind either to go right outside legality, or stick firmly within it. A perfectly viable alternative was to allow the Israelis to dislodge Nasser. She and the Arab states were still technically at war. The Egyptians were blockading Israel's access to the Indian Ocean, in itself an act of war, and they refused her ships passage through the Canal, in flagrant breach of the 1888 convention. Much more serious, however, was that Nasser was clearly building up the military strength, with Soviet help, and the systematic military and diplomatic alliances, to launch a concerted assault on Israel, which would end in genocide. The process was actually concluded on 25 October 1956, when he formed a unified Egypt–Syrian–Jordan command. This process provided moral justification for an Israeli pre-emptive strike at Egypt. The French approved such a course and were in fact supplying Israel with arms to pursue it, including modern fighters. But she lacked the bombers to knock out Egypt's air force and so guarantee her cities from air attack. Only Britain could supply those. But Eden turned this option down too. It went against his deepest instincts, which were pro-Arab.

The scheme he finally settled for, after much dithering, might have been calculated to get him the worst of all possible worlds. On 22–24 October, at secret meetings in Sèvres, near Paris, British, French and Israeli representatives cooked up an immensely complicated plot, under which Israel would attack Egypt on 29 October. This would provide Britain with a righteous pretext to reoccupy the Canal to protect lives and shipping there. Britain would issue an ultimatum which Israel would accept. Egypt's refusal would allow Britain to bomb the airfields. Then the Anglo–French would land by force at Port Said. Much ink has been spilt over this 'collusion', which both Eden and his Foreign Secretary, Selwyn Lloyd, denied to their dying day.[98] But the French and Israeli participants later insisted there was a concerted scheme. General Moshe Dayan, the Israeli army commander, reported Lloyd as urging 'that our military action not be a small-scale encounter but a "real act of war", otherwise there would be no justification for the British ultimatum and Britain would appear in the eyes of the world as an aggressor'.[99]

Even this absurd scheme might have worked if Eden had possessed the will to go through with it to the bitter end. But he was an honourable man. He made a half-hearted Machiavelli. As a proxy-aggressor he was wholly incompetent. The transparency of the plot was obvious to all. The Labour opposition repudiated it and set up an uproar. The cabinet, kept imperfectly informed, was uneasy from the start and terrified at the violence of the American reaction once the invasion got under way. In letters of 2 and 8 September Eisenhower had warned Eden in the most emphatic terms not to use force, which he was sure would be counter-productive: 'Nasser thrives on drama.'[100] He was infuriated by Eden's springing this ill-conceived mine beneath him in the last stages of his election campaign. He literally ground his teeth, a habit of his when angry, and instructed the US Treasury to sell sterling, something a great many other people were already doing. This had an immediate effect on Eden's cabinet, where he was already sandwiched between two would-be successors: the old Appeaser, R.A.Butler, who wished to pull the party in the direction of the Left, and Harold Macmillan, who wished to pull it in the direction of himself. Both behaved in character. Butler said nothing but opposed the scheme behind the scenes. Macmillan urged boldness; then, when failure loomed, switched sides and, as Chancellor of the Exchequer, urged that there was no alternative but to comply with Eisenhower's wishes for a cease-fire. Eden collapsed on 6 November, only a week after the adventure was launched and twenty-four hours after the first Anglo–French landings took place. His capitulation followed a particularly fierce message from Eisenhower, which may have included the threat of oil sanctions.[101] Thereafter he retreated into sickness and resignation.

The episode was a striking victory for the Bandung generation. Nehru, administering moral rebukes all round, was in his element. Nasser emerged with enhanced prestige because in all the excitement it was scarcely noticed that the Israelis had inflicted a shattering defeat, in less than a week, on his large, Soviet-armed forces. Any Egyptian discomfort was attributed to the Anglo–French forces. Thus what might have been a fatal blow to Nasser's prestige actually enhanced it, for 'collusion' gave solid substance to the Arab mythology that Israel was merely an imperialist proxy. Suez confirmed the Bandung view of the world, mythology made flesh.

Suez is often said to have dealt the final blow to Britain's status as a great world power. That is not true. The status had been lost in 1947. Suez simply made it plain for all the world to see. The underlying cause was a failure of will, not of strength, and the Suez fiasco merely reflected that failure, of which Eden was a pathetic sacrificial victim. Macmillan, who succeeded him, drew the moral that in a world of superpowers, a medium-sized power survives by virtue of good public relations rather than battleships. The real loser in the long term was the United States. Eisenhower appeared to act decisively, and he got his way fast enough. Britain came to heel. He preserved his reputation as a man of peace. But in the process he helped to prepare a mighty scourge for America's own back, in the shape of the tendentious concept of 'world opinion' first articulated at Bandung and now, by Eisenhower's own act, transferred to the UN.

Until the early 1950s, the Americans had controlled the UN. Their first mistake was to involve it in Korea, especially through the forum of the General Assembly, a pseudo-representative body which spoke only for governments, a growing proportion of which were undemocratic. Korea broke Trygve Lie, the Norwegian Secretary-General, who was loyal to the principles of the old Western alliance. He resigned when the Russians boycotted him and got the Left to stir up his own Secretariat against him. At this point the Western democracies should have dropped the UN and concentrated instead on expanding NATO into a world-wide security system of free nations.

Instead, after much bad temper, the powers appointed a senior Swedish diplomat called Dag Hammarskjöld. A worse choice could not be imagined. He came from a highly successful family of public servants in a nation uneasily aware that it had grown immensely prosperous by staying out of two world wars. He was guilt personified and he was determined that the West should expiate it. Severe, well-read, humourless, unmarried (though not homosexual: 'In Hammarskjöld's life', wrote his official biographer, 'sex played little or no part'[102]), he exuded a secular religiosity. It was characteristic of him and of the advanced Fifties good taste he faithfully reflected, that he transformed the old UN Meditation Room, a plain and unpretentious chamber, into a dark and dramatic cavern, with striking perspective and lighting and, in its centre, a vast rectangular block of iron-ore illuminated by a single shaft of light. What did it symbolize? Relative morality perhaps. It was Hammarskjöld's manifest intention to cut the umbilical cord which linked the UN to the old wartime Western alliance, and to align the organization with what he regarded as the new emergent force of righteousness in the world: the 'uncommitted' nations. In short he too was a member of the Bandung generation, despite – or rather because of – his pallid face. When Eisenhower turned on Eden at Suez, broke him, and handed the whole problem to the UN, he gave Hammarskjöld exactly the opportunity he had been waiting for.

The Secretary-General set to work to oust the Anglo–French force and the Israelis and replace them with a multi-nation UN 'peace-keeping' contingent. He saw a role for himself as a world statesman, driven by the engine of non-alignment. Hence, though affecting impartiality, he threw his weight entirely behind the Afro–Asian camp. That meant treating Israel not as a small and vulnerable nation but as an outpost of imperialism. There was on record a 1951 UN resolution, passed before his time, calling on Egypt to allow Israeli vessels through the Canal. At no point did Hammarskjöld make any attempt to get the resolution implemented. Nor would he allow that Arab denial of freedom of navigation to Israeli shipping in the Gulf of Aqaba was a threat to peace – though in fact it was this denial, tightened by the three-power Arab military pact of 25 October 1956, which was the immediate cause of the Israeli attack. He repeatedly declined to condemn Nasser's seizure of the canal, and other arbitrary acts. So far as he was concerned, the Israeli attack and the Anglo–French intervention were wholly unprovoked acts of aggression. He said he was 'shocked and outraged' by such behaviour. On 31 October he took the unprecedented step of publicly rebuking the British and French governments. The Soviet invasion of Hungary, which took place under cover of the Suez crisis, he treated as a tiresome distraction. His friendliness to the Egyptians throughout, and his cold hostility to Britain, France and Israel, made it plain where his emotional sympathies lay. He set his heart on the public humiliation of the three powers and he got it. In deploying the UN emergency force, to move into the vacuum created by the three-power withdrawal, he insisted that its presence was by grace and favour of Egypt: as he put it, 'the very basis and starting point has been the recognition by the General Assembly of the full and unlimited sovereign rights of Egypt'.[103] It had therefore to be withdrawn at Egypt's simple request, a right exercised by Egypt in 1967 as soon as it believed itself strong enough to destroy Israel. Hammarskjöld thus bequeathed another Middle Eastern war to his successors. More important still, however, was his demonstration of the way in which the UN could be used to marshal and express hatred of the West. In 1956 it was the turn of Britain and France. Soon it would be America's own.

America was also the loser by the impact of Suez on France. If Suez simply pushed Britain slightly faster down its chosen slope, in France it helped to bring to a head the national crisis created by the agony of French Algeria. Algeria was the greatest and in many ways the archetype of all the anti-colonial wars. In the nineteenth century the Europeans won colonial wars because the indigenous peoples had lost the will to resist. In the twentieth century the roles were reversed, and it was Europe which lost the will to hang onto its gains. But behind this relativity of wills there are demographic facts. A colony is lost once the level of settlement is exceeded by the growth-rate of the indigenous peoples. Nineteenth-century colonialism reflected the huge upsurge in European numbers. Twentieth-century decolonization reflected European demographic stability and the violent expansion of native populations.

Algeria was a classic case of this reversal. It was not so much a French colony as a Mediterranean settlement. In the 1830s there were only 1.5 million Arabs there, and their numbers were dwindling. The Mediterranean people moved from the northern shores to the southern ones, into what appeared to be a vacuum: to them the great inland sea was a unity, and they had as much right to its shores as anyone provided they justified their existence by wealth-creation. And they did: they expanded 2,000 square miles of cultivated land in 1830 to 27,000 by 1954.[104] These *pieds noirs* were only 20 per cent French in origin (including Corsicans and Alsacians). They were predominantly Spanish in the west, Italian (and Maltese) in the east. But rising prosperity attracted others: Kabyles, Chaouias, Mzabite, Mauritanians, Turks and pure Arabs, from the mountains, the west, the south, the east. And French medical services virtually eliminated malaria, typhus and typhoid and effected a prodigious change in the non-European infant mortality rates. By 1906 the Muslim population had jumped to 4.5 million; by 1954 to 9 million. By the mid-1970s it had more than doubled again. If the French population had risen at the same rate, it would have been over 300 million by 1950. The French policy of 'assimilation', therefore, was nonsense, since by the year 2000 Algerian Muslims would have constituted more than half the French population, and Algeria would have 'assimilated' France rather than the reverse.[105]

By the 1950s there were not enough *pieds noirs* for long-term survival as a dominant class or even an enclave. Only a third of Algiers' 900,000 inhabitants were Europeans. Only in Oran were they in a majority. Even in and most heavily settled part, the Mitidja, the farms were worked by Muslim labour. In 1914 200,000 Europeans had lived off the land; by 1954 only 93,000. By the 1950s most *pieds noirs* had ordinary, poorly paid city jobs Arabs could do just as well. The social structure was an archaeological layer-cake of race prejudice: 'the Frenchman despises the Spaniard, who despises the Italian, who despises the Maltese, who despises the Jew; all in turn despise the Arab.'[106] There was no pretence at equality of opportunity: in 1945 1,400 primary schools catered for 200,000 European children, 699 for 1,250,000 Muslims. Textbooks began: 'Our ancestors, the Gauls . . . .'

More serious, however, was the fraudulence of the electoral system. Either the reforms passed by the French parliament were not applied at all, or the votes were cooked by the local authorities themselves. It was this which cut the ground beneath the many well-educated Muslim moderates who genuinely wanted a fusion of French and Muslim culture. As one of the noblest of them, Ahmed Boumendjel, put it: 'The French Republic has cheated. She has made fools of us.' He told the Assembly: 'Why should we feel ourselves bound by the principles of French moral values . . . when France herself refuses to be subject to them?'[107] The elections of 1948 were faked; so were those of 1951. In such circumstances, the moderates had no effective role to play. The men of violence moved forward.

There was a foretaste in May 1945, when the Arabs massacred 103 Europeans. The French reprisals were on a savage scale. Dive-bombers blew forty villages to pieces; a cruiser bombarded others. The Algerian Communist Party journal *Liberté* called for the rebels to be 'swiftly and pitilessly punished, the instigators put in front of the firing-squad'. According to the French official report, 1,020 to 1,300 Arabs were killed; the Arabs claimed 45,000. Many demobilized Arab soldiers returned to find their families dead, their homes demolished. It was these former NCOs who formed the leadership of the future Front de Libération Nationale (FLN). As the most conspicuous of them, Ahmed Ben Bella, put it: 'The horrors of the Constantine area in May 1945 persuaded me of the only path:

Algeria for the Algerians.' The French commander, General Duval, told the *pieds noirs*: 'I have given you peace for ten years.'

That proved to be entirely accurate. On 1 November 1954, the embittered NCOs were ready: Ben Bella, by now an experienced urban terrorist, linked forces with Belkacem Krim, to launch a national rising. It is important to grasp that the object, from start to finish, was not to defeat the French Army. That would have been impossible. The aim was to destroy the concept of assimilation and mutli-racialism by eliminating the moderates on both sides. The first Frenchman to be murdered was a liberal, Arabophile schoolteacher, Guy Monnerot. The first Arab casualty was a pro-French local governor, Hadj Sakok. Most FLN operations were directed against the loyal Muslim element: employees of the state were murdered, their tongues cut off, their eyes gouged out, then a note, 'FLN', pinned to the mutilated bodies.[108] This was the strategy pioneered by the Mufti in Palestine. Indeed many of the rebel leaders had served him. The ablest, Mohamedi Said, commander of 'Wilaya 3' in the Kabyle mountains, had joined the Mufti's 'Muslim SS legion', had parachuted into Tunisia as an *Abwehr* agent, and declared: 'I believed that Hitler would destroy French tyranny and free the world.' He still wore his old SS helmet from time to time. His disciples included some of the worst killers of the twentieth century, such as Ait Hamouda, known as Amirouche, and Ramdane Abane, who had sliced off breasts and testicles in the 1945 massacres, read Marx and *Mein Kampf* in jail, and whose dictum was: 'One corpse in a suit is always worth more than twenty in uniform.' These men, who had absorbed everything most evil the twentieth century had to offer, imposed their will on the villages by sheer terror; they never used any other method. Krim told a Yugoslav paper that the initiation method for a recruit was to force him to murder a designated 'traitor', *mouchard* (police spy or informer), French gendarme or colonialist: 'An assassination marks the end of the apprenticeship of each candidate.' A pro-FLN American reporter was told: 'When we've shot [the Muslim victim] his head will be cut off and we'll clip a tag on his ear to show he was a traitor. Then we'll leave the head on the main road.' Ben Bella's written orders included: 'Liquidate all personalities who want to play the role of *interlocuteur valable*.' 'Kill any person attempting to deflect the militants and inculcate in them a *bourguibien* spirit.' Another: 'Kill the *caids* . . . . Take their children and kill them. Kill all those who pay taxes and those who collect them. Burn the houses of Muslim NCOs away on active service.' The FLN had their own internal *reglements des comptes*, too: the man who issued the last order, Bachir Chihani, was accused (like Roehm) of pederasty and sadistic sex-murders, and chopped to pieces along with eight of his lovers. But it was the Muslim men of peace the FLN killers really hated. In the first two-and-a-half years of war, they murdered only 1,035 Europeans but 6,352 Arabs (authenticated cases; the real figure was nearer 20,000).[109] By this point the moderates could only survive by becoming killers themselves or going into exile.

The FLN strategy was, in fact, to place the mass of the Muslims in a sandwich of terror. On one side, the FLN killers replaced the moderates. On the other, FLN atrocities were designed to provoke the French into savage reprisals, and so drive the Muslim population into the extremist camp. FLN doctrine was spelt out with cold-blooded precision by the Brazilian terrorist Carlos Marighela:

It is necessary to turn political crisis into armed conflict by performing violent actions that will force those in power to transform the political situation of the country into a military situation. That will alienate the masses, who, from then on, will revolt against the army and the police . . . . The government can only intensify its repression, thus making the lives of its citizens harder than ever . . . police terror will become the order of the day . . . . The population will refuse to collaborate with the authorities, so that the latter will find the only solution to their problems lies in the physical liquidation of their opponents. The political situation of the country will [then have] become a military situation.[110]

Of course this odious variety of Leninism, if pursued ruthlessly enough, has a certain irresistible force. The French government in 1954 was composed, on the whole, of liberal and civilized men, under the Radical-Socialist Pierre Mendès-France. They shared the illusion – or the vision – that Algeria could become a genuine multi-racial society, on the principles of liberty, equality and fraternity. Mendès-France, who had happily freed Indo-China and Tunisia, told the Assembly: 'The Algerian *départements* are part of the French Republic . . . they are irrevocably French . . . there can be no conceivable secession.' On Algeria, said his Interior Minister, François Mitterrand, 'the only possible negotiation is war'.[111] Both men believed that, if France's own principles were now at last fully and generously turned into an Algerian reality, the problem would be solved. They sent out as Governor-General Jacques Soustelle, a brilliant ethnologist and former resistance-fighter, to create this reality. What they did not realize was that the FLN's object was precisely to transform French generosity into savagery.

Soustelle saw the FLN as fascists. He thought he could defeat them by giving the Arabs genuine democracy and social justice. He created 400 detachments of *Képis bleus* (SAS) in remote areas to protect loyalists. He brought in dedicated liberals like Germaine Tillion and Vincent Monteil to set up networks of *centres sociaux* and maintain contacts with Muslim leaders of opinion.[112] He sought desperately to bring Muslims into every level of government. His instructions to the police and army forbade terror and brutality in any form and especially collective reprisals.[113] It is unlikely that Soustelle's policy of genuine integration could have succeeded anyway, once the French themselves realized what it involved: France did not want to become a half-Arab, half-Muslim nation, any more than most Arabs wanted to become a French one. But in any case the FLN systematically murdered the instruments of Soustelle's liberal policy, French and Arab. They strove hardest to kill those French administrations who loved the Arabs; and usually succeeded. One such victim was Maurice Dupuy, described by Soustelle as a 'secular saint'. At his funeral Soustelle was in tears as he pinned the *Légion d'honneur* on the eldest of Dupuy's eight orphaned children, and it was then he first used the word 'revenge'.[114]

In the summer of 1955 the FLN went a stage further and adopted a policy of genocide: to kill all French without distinction of age or sex. On 20 August the first massacres began. As always, they embraced many Arabs, such as Allouah Abbas, nephew of the moderate nationalist leader Ferhat Abbas, who had criticized FLN atrocities. But the main object was to provoke French army reprisals. At Ain-Abid near Constantine, for instance, thirty-seven Europeans, including ten under fifteen, were literally chopped to pieces. Men had their arms and legs cut off; children their brains dashed out; women were disemboweled – one *pied-noir* mother had her womb opened, her five-day-old baby slashed to death, and then replaced in her womb. This 'Philippeville massacre' succeeded in its object: French paratroopers in the area were given orders to shoot all Arabs and (by Soustelle's account) killed 1,273 'insurgents', which FLN propaganda magnified to 12,000. It was the 1945 massacre over again. As Soustelle put it, 'there had been well and truly dug an abyss through which flowed a river of blood'. French and Muslim liberals like Albert Camus and Ferhat Abbas, appearing on platforms together to appeal for reason, were howled down by all sides.[115]

From this point the Soustelle experiment collapsed. The war became a competition in terror. The focus switched to the Algiers Casbah, where every square kilometre housed 100,000 Algerians. It began with the execution of a crippled murderer, Ferradj, who had killed a seven-year-old girl and seven other civilians. The FLN commander, Ramdane Abane, ordered one hundred French civilians to be murdered for every execution of an FLN member. On 21–24 June 1956, his chief killer, Saadi Yacef, who controlled a network of bomb-factories and 1,400 'operators', carried out forty-nine murders. The violence grew steadily through the second half of 1956 –

parallel with the build up to the Suez adventure. The French Mayor of Algiers was murdered, and a bomb carefully exploded in the middle of the funeral ceremony: Yacef secretly ordered all his operators out of the area in advance, to make certain that in the subsequent wild reprisals only innocent Muslims were killed.[116]

The Suez débâcle was important because it finally convinced the army that civilian governments could not win the war. Robert Lacoste, Soustelle's socialist successor, conceded the point. On 7 January 1957 he gave General Jacques Massu and his 4,600 men absolute freedom of action to clean the FLN out of Algiers. For the first time all restraints on the army, including the banning of torture, were lifted. Torture had been abolished in France on 8 October 1789. Article 303 of the Penal Code imposed the death penalty for anyone practising it. In March 1955 a secret report written by a senior civil servant recommended the use of supervised torture as the only alternative to prevent much more brutal unauthorized torture. Soustelle had flatly rejected it. Now Massu authorized it, as he later admitted: 'In answer to the question: "was there really torture?" I can only reply in the affirmative, although it was never either institutionalized or codified.'[117] The argument was that successful interrogation saved lives, chiefly of Arabs; that Arabs who gave information would be tortured to death, without restraint, by the FLN, and it was vital for the French to make themselves feared more. It was the Arab belief that Massu operated without restraints, as much as the torture itself, which caused prisoners to talk. But non-Muslims were tortured too. One, a Communist Jew called Henri Alleg, wrote a best-selling book which caused an outburst of moral fury throughout France in 1958.[118] Massu claimed that interrogations by his men left no permanent damage. On seeing Alleg, looking whole and well, on the steps of the Palais de Justice in 1970, he exclaimed:

Do the torments which he suffered count for much alongside the cutting off of the nose or of the lips, when it was not the penis, which had become the ritual present of the *fellaghas* to their recalcitrant 'brothers'? Everyone knows that these bodily appendages do not grow again![119]

But the notion that it was possible to supervise limited torture effectively during a war for survival is absurd. In fact, the liberal Secretary-General of the Algiers Prefecture, Paul Teitgen, testified that about 3,000 prisoners 'disappeared' during the Algiers battle. At all events Massu won it. It was the only time the French fought the FLN with its own weapons. Algiers was cleansed of terrorism. Moderate Arabs dared to raise their voices again. But the victory was thrown away by a new policy of *regroupement* of over a million poor *fellahs*, a piece of crude social engineering calculated to play into FLN hands. Besides, the Massu experiment set up intolerable strains within the French system. On the one hand, by freeing army units from political control and stressing the personalities of commanders, it encouraged private armies: colonels increasingly regarded themselves as proprietors of their regiments, as under the monarchy, and began to manipulate their generals into disobedience. In the moral confusion, officers began to see their primary obligation as towards their own men rather than the state.[120]

At the same time, news leaking out of what the army had done in Algiers began to turn French liberal and centre opinion against the war. From 1957 onwards, many Frenchmen came to regard Algerian independence, however distasteful, as preferable to the total corruption of the French public conscience. Thus the demand for the restoration of political control of the war – including negotiations with the FLN – intensified just as the French army was, as it believed, winning by asserting its independence. This irreconcilable conflict produced the explosion of May 1958 which returned General de Gaulle to power and created the Fifth Republic.

De Gaulle was not a colonialist. He thought the age of colonies was over. His body seemed in the past but his mind was in the future. He claimed that at Brazzaville in 1944, when marshalling black Africa behind the Resistance, he had sought 'to transform the old dependent relationships into preferential links of political, economic and cultural co-operation'.[121] He saw the half-hearted continuation of French colonialism as the direct result of the weakness of the Fourth Republic's constitution, which he despised, and the 'regime of the parties', incapable of 'the unequivocal decisions decolonization called for'. 'How could it', he asked, 'have surmounted and if necessary broken all the opposition, based on sentiment, habit or self-interest, which such an enterprise was bound to provoke?' The result was vacillation and inconsistency, first in Indo-China, then in Tunisia and Morocco, finally and above all in Algeria. Naturally, he said, the army 'felt a growing resentment against a political system which was the embodiment of irresolution'.[122]

The *coup* was detonated, probably deliberately, by the FLN decision on 9 May 1958 to 'execute' three French soldiers for 'torture, rape and murder'. Four days later, white students stormed the government headquarters in Algiers. Massu asked Lacoste, who had fled to France, whether he had permission to fire on the white mob. He was not given it. That night, at a Brecht play attacking generals, a left-wing audience applauded deliriously.[123] But not one was actually prepared to fight for the Fourth Republic. In Algiers, the generals took over, and called for de Gaulle's return. Some 30,000

Muslims went to the government forum to demonstrate their appro-val. They sang the '*Marseillaise*' and the army song, '*Chant des Africains*': a spontaneous demonstration in favour of French civiliza-tion and against the barbarism of the FLN. Massu said: 'Let them know that France will never abandon them.'[124] When the generals called for de Gaulle they were lying, for they saw him merely as a battering-ram, to smash the Republic and take power themselves. De Gaulle thought Algeria was untenable and would destroy the French army. Indeed, he feared even worse might happen. On 24 May a detachment from Algeria landed in Corsica. The local authorities fraternized. Police sent from Marseilles allowed themselves to be disarmed. De Gaulle took over to avert an invasion of France itself, which would probably have succeeded or, alternatively, produced civil war. He saw ominous parallels with the beginning of the Spanish catastrophe in 1936. It would, he thought, finally destroy France as a great civilizing power. If Paris was worth a mass, France herself was worth a few lies.

So, having taken power, he went to Algiers to deceive. On 4 June he told the howling *colon* mob in Algiers: '*Je vous ai compris.*' 'I tossed them the words,' he wrote, 'seemingly spontaneous but in reality carefully calculated, which I hoped would fire their enthusi-asm without committing me further than I was willing to go.'[125] He had said the previous year, privately: 'Of course independence will come but they are too stupid there to know it.' 'Long live French Algeria!' he chanted publicly in June 1958; privately: '*L'Afrique est foutue et l'Algérie avec!*' He called French Algeria 'a ruinous Utopia'. Publicly he continued to reassure the *colons* and the army. 'Independence? In twenty-five years' (October 1958). 'The French army will never quit this country and I will never deal with those people from Cairo and Tunis' (March 1959). 'There will be no Dien Bien Phu in Algeria. The insurrection will not throw us out of this country.' 'How can you listen to the liars and conspirators who tell you that in granting free choice to the Algerians, France and de Gaulle want to abandon you, to pull out of Algeria and hand it over to the rebellion?' (January 1960). 'Independence . . . a folly, a monstrosity' (March 1960).[126]

Meanwhile, he got an ever-tighter grip on the state. On 28 September 1958 the French adopted the constitution of the Fifth Republic, concentrating power in the president. On 21 December he was elected President. The same referendum which created the new constitution gave all French overseas territories the right of associa-tion or departure. The notion of consent thus became universal. One by one, de Gaulle broke or removed the men who had hoisted him to office. In February 1960 he demanded and received 'special powers'.

Four months later he opened secret talks with the FLN leaders. In January 1961 he held a referendum offering Algeria freedom in association with France, and got an overwhelming 'Yes' vote. It was the end of *Algérie française* and it brought its extremist supporters out into the open, bombs in hand.

If the army leadership had insisted on taking power in May 1958, it could have done so, with or without de Gaulle. By April 1961, when it finally grasped de Gaulle's deception and sought to overthrow him, the chance had been missed. French opinion had moved on. The conscripts had transistor radios; they could hear the news from Paris; they refused to follow their officers. The revolt collapsed; its leaders surrendered or were hunted down and gaoled. That left the way open for a complete scuttle. Captured FLN leaders were released from prisons to join the talks just as the rebel French generals were beginning their sentences.

White terrorism, the OAS (*Organization de l'Armée Secrète*), took longer to deal with. It operated at full blast for over a year, using bombs, machine-guns and bazookas, killing over 12,000 civilians (mainly Muslims) and about 500 police and security men. It illustrates the fearful power of political violence to corrupt. Indeed, in many ways it was the mirror-image of the FLN. On 23 February 1962, its leader General Salan, who had had a distinguished career as an honourable soldier, issued orders for

a generalized offensive . . . . The systematic opening of fire against CRS and gendarmerie units. "Molotov cocktails" will be thrown against their armoured vehicles . . . night and day . . . . [The objective is] to destroy the best Muslim elements in the liberal professions so as to oblige the Muslim population to have recourse to ourselves . . . to paralyse the powers that be and make it impossible for them to exercise authority. Brutal actions will be generalized over the whole territory . . . at works of art and all that represents the exercise of authority in a manner to lead towards the maximum of general insecurity and the total paralysis of the country.[127]

Nor did the corruption stop at the OAS. For in order to beat them and to protect de Gaulle himself (twice nearly murdered), the state built up its own official terror units, which murdered and tortured prisoners with impunity, and on a wide scale.[128] In this case, neither liberal France nor the international community raised a whisper of protest. OAS terrorism finally killed the idea of a white settlement. At the end of 1961 de Gaulle's closest adviser, Bernard Tricot, reported back from Algiers: 'The Europeans . . . are so hardened in opposition to everything that is being prepared, and their relations with the majority of the Muslims are so bad, that . . . the essential thing now is to organize their return.'[129]

The end came in March 1962, in an orgy of slaughter and intolerance. The Muslim mob, scenting victory, had already sacked the Great Synagogue in the heart of the Casbah, gutting it, ripping the Torah scrolls, killing the Jewish officials and chalking on the walls 'Death to the Jews' and other Nazi slogans. On 15 March the OAS raided Germaine Tillion's social centre, where handicapped children were trained, took out six men and shot them to death, beginning with the legs. One of them was Mouloud Feraoun, friend of Camus, who had termed him 'last of the moderates'. He had written: 'There is French in me, there is Kabyle in me. But I have a horror of those who kill . . . . Vive la France, such as I have always loved! Vive l'Algérie, such as I hope for! Shame on the criminals!'[130] The cease-fire with the FLN, 19 March 1962, brought a further burst of OAS killing: eighteen gendarmes and seven soldiers were murdered. The French commander, General Ailleret, retaliated by destroying the last redoubt of Algérie française, the pied noir working-class quarter of Bab-el-Oued, with its 60,000 inhabitants. He attacked it with rocket-firing dive-bombers, tanks firing at point-blank range and 20,000 infantry. It was the suppression of the 1870 Commune all over again; but this episode does not figure in the Marxist textbooks.[131] That was effectively the end of Algeria as a multiracial community. The exodus to France began. Many hospitals, schools, laboratories, oil terminals and other evidence of French culture and enterprise – including the library of the University of Algiers – were deliberately destroyed. About 1,380,000 people (including some Muslims) left in all. By 1963, of a large and historic Mediterranean community, only about 30,000 remained.[132]

The Evian Agreements, under which France agreed to get out, contained many clauses designed to save France's face. They were meaningless. It was a straight surrender. Not even paper protection, however, was given to 250,000 Muslim officials, many of a very humble kind, who had continued to serve France faithfully to the end. De Gaulle was too busy saving France by extricating it from the horror, to give them a thought. When a Muslim deputy, ten of whose family had already been murdered by the FLN, told de Gaulle that, with self-determination, 'we shall suffer', he replied coldly: 'Eh, bien – vous souffrirez.' They did. Only 15,000 had the money and means to get out. The rest were shot without trial, used as human mine-detectors to clear the minefields along the Tunisian border, tortured, made to dig their own tombs and swallow their military decorations before being killed; some were burned alive, castrated, dragged behind trucks, fed to the dogs; there were cases where entire families including tiny children were murdered together. The French army units that remained, their former comrades-in-arms, stood by, horrified and powerless, for under the Agreements they had no right to interfere. French soldiers were actually employed to disarm the Muslim *harkis*, telling them they would be issued with more modern weapons, although in fact they were about to be slaughtered. It was a crime of betrayal comparable to the British handing over Russian POWs to Stalin's wrath; worse, indeed. Estimates of the number put to death vary from 30,000 to 150,000.[133]

Who knows? A great darkness descended over many aspects of the new Algeria, a darkness which has never been lifted since. The lies continued to the end. 'France and Algeria', said de Gaulle on 18 March 1962, would 'march together like brothers on the road to civilization'.[134] The truth is, the new nation owed its existence to the exercise of cruelty without restraint and on the largest possible scale. Its regime, composed mainly of successful gangsters, quickly ousted those of its members who had been brought up in the Western tradition; all were dead or in exile by the mid-1960s.

Exactly twenty years after the independence agreement was reached, one of the chief signatories and Algeria's first President, Ben Bella himself, summed up the country's first two decades of independent existence. The net result, he said, had been 'totally negative'. The country was 'a ruin'. Its agriculture had been 'assassinated'. 'We have nothing. No industry – only scrap iron.' Everything in Algeria was 'corrupt from top to bottom'.[135] No doubt Ben Bella's bitterness was increased by the fact that he had spent most of the intervening years imprisoned by his revolutionary comrades. But the substance of his judgement was true enough. And unfortunately the new Algeria had not kept its crimes to itself. It became and for many years remained the chief resort of international terrorists of all kinds. A great moral corruption had been planted in Africa. It set a pattern of public crime and disorder which was to be imitated throughout the vast and tragic continent which was now made master of its own affairs.

FIFTEEN

Caliban's Kingdoms

In March 1959 Evelyn Waugh, visiting East Africa, wrote to his wife:
'I spent one day with the Masai . . . . They had a lovely time during
the Mau Mau rising. They were enlisted and told to bring in all the
Kikuyus' arms. Back they proudly came with baskets of severed
limbs.'[1] Waugh had provided a gruesomely imaginative foretaste of
independent Africa in his pre-war novels *Black Mischief* and *Scoop*.
Now the anarchist in him joyfully scented fiction come true: the
confusion of aims and tongues, the disintegration of ephemeral
order, the return to chaos.

We have seen in Chapter Four that it is impossible to make any
truthful generalization about colonialism. The same is true of the
decolonizing process. The most that can accurately be said is: it
occurred. All the rest is propaganda; *ex post facto* rationalization.
Colonialism has been presented as a conspiracy of capitalist states;
decolonization as a further conspiracy when it became economically
more prudent to switch to 'neo-colonialism'. But if there was a
conspiracy, why did the conspirators never meet or exchange plans
and ideas? The truth is colonialism was born in intense rivalry and
died in it. The colonial powers did not conspire against the natives.
They conspired against each other. Each colonial power hated all the
rest, despised their methods, rejoiced in their misfortunes and
happily aggravated them when convenient. They would not co-
operate even when imperative self-interest demanded. In August
1941, on the eve of the Japanese onslaught, it was found that, though
Britain and the Netherlands had been wartime allies for fourteen
months, nothing whatever had been done to co-ordinate the defence
plans of their South-East Asian empires.[2] During the entire process
of decolonization, 1945–75, the colonial powers never once met
together to decide how they were going to do it, nor do there seem to
have been even informal efforts at co-ordination. The historian who
looks for evidence of such contacts finds nothing but a hole.

One reason there was no alignment of policy for decolonization was that neither of the two biggest colonial powers, Britain and France, actually possessed one. Both made logical noises. In reality all was expediency. When de Gaulle set up his Free French standard in 1940, France's Arab and Indo-Chinese territories stuck to Vichy; only black Africa rallied to him. As a result, at the January 1944 Brazzaville Conference, he opened for them the road to freedom. But the colonial officials who attended it made a different interpretation: 'The formation of independent governments in the colonies, however far off, cannot be contemplated,' they reported. 'We visualize empire in the Roman, not the Anglo-Saxon sense of the term.'[3] De Gaulle's post-war government abolished forced labour and the hated penal code for natives; but a rising in Madagascar in 1947 was put down with astonishing ferocity, 80,000 natives dying.[4] As late as 1957, François Mitterrand declared: 'Without Africa, France will have no history in the twenty-first century.' Until the débâcle in Algeria, French policy was a maze of contradictions: old-style paternalism in the jungle and the bush, with *colon* firebrands and highly educated black nationalists sitting cheek by jowl in the Paris Assembly. Sometimes an 'African' deputy moved from a 'white' to a 'black' constituency, as did the Colonial Under-Secretary, Dr Aujoulat, in 1951, changing his politics in the process and campaigning under the slogan 'His face may be white but his heart is as black as a black man's.'[5]

When de Gaulle returned to power in May 1958 and surveyed the shattered Fourth Republic and the mess in Algeria, he abruptly decided to turn French black Africans loose. In the 28 September referendum, they were given the choice of voting 'Yes' (interdependence) or 'No' (separation). All but Guinea and Madagascar voted 'Yes'; but it was independence by another name. De Gaulle wanted to keep some kind of union together. On 12 December 1959, at a meeting of French African heads of state at St Louis, he told them: 'As the Pilgrims of Emmaus said to the traveller: "Abide with us: for it is towards evening, and the day is far spent."'[6] But they chose 'association', meaning aid and military backing, rather than 'community'. Some of these African leaders, such as Houphouët-Boigny (Ivory Coast), Philibert Tsiranana (Malagasy), Léopold Senghor (Senegal), Hamani Diori (Niger), Ahmadou Ahidjo (Cameroon), Leon M'Ba (Gabon), François Tombalbaye (Chad), and Mokhtar Ould Daddah (Mauritania), formed a personal relationship with the mesmeric general: they 'became my intimates' as he put it.[7] But this was transitory; all went their separate ways. All these territories, the Ivory Coast excepted, were very poor. Some were more 'fit' for independence than others; some not at all. But it is impossible to discern any principles behind the process by which they secured it, other than France's decision to have done with them.

In theory the British Empire, latterly Commonwealth, had always worked on a quite different supposition: that all territories were to be prepared for independence, and given it when ready. The British White Paper of June 1948 stated: 'The central purpose of British colonial policy . . . is to guide the colonial territories to responsible self-government within the Commonwealth in conditions that ensure to the people concerned both a fair standard of living and freedom from oppression in any quarter.'[8] But both qualifications were invariably abandoned when expediency beckoned. Up to the mid-1950s the pace was too slow; from 1960 it was too fast. In neither case did it reflect the real readiness and needs of the territories concerned, but rather the pressures on the British government and its will, or lack of it, to resist them. The forces set up by the Bandung movement were the decisive factor. While France decided to cut and run in 1958, Britain followed a year later, when Harold Macmillan felt free to follow de Gaulle's example. As Sir Michael Blundell, the shrewdest of the Kenya settlers' leaders, put it, '. . . a dramatic change was to take place in the policy of the British government after the general election in October 1959 . . . the decision was taken to withdraw from Africa as quickly as decency would permit.'[9] But even this switch, though rationalized in Macmillan's 'Winds of Change' speech in Cape Town on 3 February 1960, was more a series of violent wobbles than a smooth U-turn. Macmillan's agent, the Colonial Secretary Iain Macleod, later admitted there was no 'resounding decision' but more 'a score of different deliberate decisions'.[10]

When Macleod used the term 'deliberate', he meant that the formalities of negotiations were preserved, ending in a grandiose orgy of constitution-making, usually at Lancaster House in London. One thing decolonization did not lack was paper constitutions. It is ironic that Britain, which had never had one, produced (by my calculation) more than 500 for its colonial territories in the years 1920–75, most of which lasted only a few years, some a few months, some never being applied at all; none surviving into the 1980s. The European empires began in paternalism and a denial of the spirit of politics. They ended at the opposite extreme, in over-democratization and political elephantiasis. The silver age of empire was completely dominated by endless conferences and constitution-making. Thus, the two Rhodesias and Nyasaland dithered for thirty years over whether or not to have a federation. There was the Hilton–Young Commission of 1927–9, the Bledisloe Commission of 1948–9, the Settlers' Constitution of 1936 (never implemented), two separate conferences in 1951 (boycotted by Africans), a third in 1953. This produced the 'final' constitution, which was too complex for most voters to understand and was out of date by the time it was put into practice.

With voting rolls depending on a weird mixture of property, income, residence and literacy qualifications, and electoral districts and candidatures 'balanced' to the point of incomprehensibility, men and women did not always know whether they had a vote or where or how to cast it. There were often several tiers of government and a multiplicity of parties at each. Thus a country's destiny could be settled by a handful of people or by sheer muddle. In the 1962 election which led to the long Rhodesia crisis, and scores of thousands of dead, only 12,000 Africans out of a possible 65,500 actually voted; a mere 500 more African votes would have put in the moderates, and the whole of the country's history for the next twenty years would have been different.[11] Most of the Africans, and a good many whites, did not know what they were doing.

Constitutional complexities proliferated even when there were no fundamental problems of race. Thus Tanzania's 1955 'reform' produced one of the most complicated constitutions ever devised for a colonial territory, mainly to exclude the more belligerent nationalists. Further changes in 1957–8 added yet more subtleties, including a tripartite voting provision that each voter on the roll had to cast his vote for one person of each race (African, European, Asian), on pain of invalidation. A new kind of bureaucracy, expert at 'balanced' multiracial constitutions, emerged, invaded the UN Secretariat, and so internationalized itself. From 1956, under UN pressure, the Belgians in Ruanda-Urundi constructed one of the most rococo constitutions ever devised by man, with multi-roll elections to the Councils of Sub-Chiefs, Councils of Chiefs, Territorial Councils, African Council and, on top, a General Council to advise the Vice-Governor-General: a five-tier system. Here was one of the world's most primitive countries with a political structure more elaborate than that of the United States.[12]

Colonies had once been under-governed. Now they were over-governed. One reason was that 'independence' meant full sovereignty, with all that such a status implied. The Gambia, with a population of 300,000, which was really one town, Bathurst, and its hinterland, surrounded on three sides by Senegal, became a fully-fledged state burdened with the entire apparatus of government, which finally flattened it into bankruptcy in 1981. The alternative was to hammer these small, separate chunks of colonialism into federations. But they seldom worked for long or at all. They involved, too, extra tiers of government, often with two legislative chambers each, and elaborate safeguards to calm the mutual hatreds and fears of territories at different stages of development and with different racial mixes. Thus the British West Indies were over-administered, for historical reasons, even while still crown colonies. Independence added another tier, federation a third, so that while it lasted – generally not long – these islands, most of them poor and backward, probably had more legislators per head than any other community in history.

The former colonies thus became superlative prey for the great human scourge of the twentieth century: the professional politician. Indeed, if decolonization did possess an ethical principle, it was that political forms were the ultimate standard of value, the only true criteria of statehood. The principle had been adumbrated in India. The Montagu Report of 1918, which introduced it, condescendingly observed: 'If we speak of "Indian opinion", we should be understood as generally referring to the majority of those who have held or are capable of holding an opinion on the matter with which we are dealing.'[13] But every adult, even if he or she is an illiterate living in a remote village, is capable of holding an opinion about the future of the society to which they belong. What the Report was really saying, and this remained the conventional wisdom down to the tragic and savage end of the decolonization process, was that, in negotiating independence, the only valid mode of discourse was that of those who made their living by full-time politics: that unless an opinion could be expressed within the vocabulary and terms of reference and assumptions of that mode of discourse, it was not really an opinion at all, and could therefore be ignored or, if necessary, trampled on.

Hence the assumptions on which decolonization rested, and still more the constitutional clutter which accompanied it, tended to widen the gap between the 'real' and the 'political' nation, and to define the latter in the narrowest, most sectarian sense. The beneficiaries of decolonization were therefore the vote-manipulators. Therein lay the seeds of a great deception. The professional politicians see the *res publica* in terms of votes, ordinary people in terms of justice. For the 'real' nation, democracy matters less than the rule of law: the first is the form, the second the substance. When the ex-colonial peoples received independence, they thought they were being given justice: all they got was the right to elect politicians. Colonialism, of course, could not produce political equality; what it could, and at its best did, provide was equality before the law. But the process of transfer, by making the vote the yardstick of progress, left the law to take care of itself, so that in the long run the vast majority of Africans ended with nothing.

This helps to explain why those territories where the process of transfer was longest and most elaborate fared no better, as a rule, than those where it was rushed. The outstanding and perhaps the most pathetic example was the Gold Coast. In the post-1945 period it was the richest black state in Africa. It was generally regarded as the most promising. It had no race problem. It was the first to get independence. The road to freedom was a long one. It had had a legislative council since 1850, a black (nominated) member as long ago as 1888; there were six by 1916. Full elections in local government came in 1925. In 1946 the Legislative Council got an African majority. 1948: constitutional inquiry commission. 1949: African-majority committee to devise new constitution. 1951: elections under new constitution. 1952: Kwame Nkrumah Prime Minister. 1954: final 'independence constitution'. 1956: new elections. 1957: full independence. This was the slow, sure, copy-book progress to self-rule; and Nkrumah was regarded as the model African statesman, his new country, Ghana, the prototype for African self-rule. Young, handsome, ultra-articulate, he cut a notable figure at Bandung.

Yet there were portents even before independence. Ghana's drive for independence had been the work of the barrister J.B.Danquah, who had hired Nkrumah as a full-time party organizer. Nkrumah was thus from the start a professional politician, nothing else. He hijacked the party organization, turned it into a mass-movement revolving round his own personality, and persuaded the British that he was the best, or simplest, man to back in the independence stakes. They made it easy for him. The Local Government Ordinances of 1951 and 1953, by creating political councils, which immediately fell into the hands of Nkrumah's Convention People's Party, broke the power of the chiefs, the traditional authorities. Thus Ghana was an embryo one-party state even before the hand-over. Once in power, Nkrumah used British devices, such as 'judicial enquiries', and employed left-wing British legal and political advisers, to destroy all other centres of influence, and the constitutional restraints on his personal rule, and to drive the opposition into illegality. Having concentrated power in his party and himself, he then destroyed the rule of law. The decisive point came in December 1963. On the 9th, three opposition leaders (former colleagues of Nkrumah) were acquitted of treason by three judges in a special court. A careful five-hour judgement, a model of English judicial reasoning, was read by the Chief Justice, Sir Arku Korsah. He had been a Middle Temple barrister for forty-four years, a judge since 1945, Chief Justice since 1956. He was a symbol of the most vital governing principle of all: that in a civilized community, everyone and every institution, including, indeed above all, the state, is equal before and subject to the law. He was, in a real sense, the end-result of a millennium of British constitutional development. On 11 December Nkrumah sacked him. The three men were tried again and convicted. Two years later, old Danquah died in gaol, where he was being held without trial.[14]

This destruction of the rule of law was paralleled by the moral destruction of Nkrumah and by the economic destruction of the country. The three were closely connected. In the heady atmosphere of Bandung in 1955, Nkrumah absorbed two fatal fallacies. The first was that all economic problems can be solved by political means. Colonies and ex-colonies were poor and backward not for intrinsic physical and human reasons but because of the political fact of colonization. The theory was emerging, and Bandung gave it enormous impetus, that colonialism did not merely hold back economic advance but actually subjected the colony to a deliberate process of 'underdevelopment'.[15] What politics had done, politics could undo. 'Underdevelopment' could be reversed by large-scale, politically motivated investment programmes. Continental prosperity could be promoted by the political process. Nkrumah preached this doctrine at the Pan-African Congresses he inaugurated at Accra in 1958. He summed it up at Addis Ababa in May 1963: 'African unity is above all a political kingdom, which can only be gained by political means. The social and economic development of Africa will come only within the political kingdom, not the other way round.' He therefore called for a Union Government of African States, a Common Market, a Pan-African Currency, an African Monetary Zone, a Central Bank, a continental communications system and a common foreign policy: 'We shall thus begin the triumphant march of the Kingdom of African personality.'[16] Nkrumah not only preached these fantasies: he tried to practise them in Ghana. The territory had been one of colonialism's success-stories. By diligent housekeeping, its modest level of prosperity might have been consolidated and even raised. By politicizing the economy, Nkrumah rapidly eliminated Ghana's balance of payments surplus; by the mid-1960s it had accumulated a mountain of foreign debt and a low international credit-rating.

The second fallacy or disease which Nkrumah (and others) contracted at Bandung, which operated as a mutual-admiration society, was the notion that the emergence of the new nations from the malign process of 'underdevelopment' required leadership by charismatic personalities. This idea was implicit in Leninism, which endowed vanguard élites (and their guiding spirit) with quasi-sacral insights into the historical process. It was also implicit in Gandhiism, which gave a determining political role to the self-elect 'holy man' and was a primary influence on the Bandung generation. Nehru,

Sukarno, U Nu, and then Nasser and Nkrumah – and many others – were not just political leaders: they were spiritual leaders too, in the sense that the nation incarnated the spiritual yearnings of a people, and the 'liberators' incarnated the nation.

It was not long after he returned from Bandung that Nkrumah began to allow his followers to refer to him as *Osagyefo*, 'the Redeemer'. The corruption set in rapidly; a form of bastardized Stalinism made its appearance. In 1960 an authorized biography recorded: 'He is our father, teacher, our brother, our friend, indeed our life, for without him we would no doubt have existed but we would not have lived . . . . What we owe him is greater even than the air we breathe, for he made us as surely as he made Ghana.'[17] The Redeemer began to believe this nonsense himself. 'All Africans know', he said in 1961, 'that I represent Africa and that I speak in her name. Therefore no African can have an opinion that differs from mine.'[18] It was against this background that Nkrumah crushed opposition and wrecked the rule of law. The charisma held for a time, especially at international conferences. But even there, as the 1960s progressed, newer, more up-to-date and fashionable figures arose and became the cynosure. Nkrumah lost his lustre. At home, the very fact of arrogating to himself quasi-divine powers made him vulnerable when the gradual, then rapid, fall in living-standards proved the magic did not work. But by the mid-1960s there was no constitutional means of removing the Redeemer. He fell to a military *coup* in February 1966, and died in exile in 1972.

The collapse of black Africa's first and model state into military rule was a distressing blow, more particularly since its huge near-neighbour, Nigeria, had itself lapsed from constitutionalism into militarism the month before. Nigeria's population made it by far the most important of the black African states and, during the 1960s, the development of oil made it economically the most secure. It, too, had emerged from a long process of preparation for self-rule, beginning with the first elected Africans in 1922–3. It was the masterpiece of Lord Lugard's 'dual mandate' system, the most conscientious and high-minded exercise in colonial administration ever devised. Internal tension between the dominant tribes, the Hausa and Fulani of the north, the Ibo of the east and the Yoruba of the west, long antedated British sovereignty. Despite the most elaborate efforts to devise a fool-proof federal system, they survived it. Nigeria's history, indeed, illustrates the essentially superficial and ephemeral impact of colonialism. A far bigger impact, indeed, was made by the arrival of nationalism, in its Afro–Asian form, with its emphasis on the 'rights' of each ethnic community. If all these had been conceded, Nigeria would have had to be a federation of some 200 states.[19] The assertion of 'rights' to the point of fracture made Nigeria unworkable by the normal processes of democratic debate and compromise. Breakdown nearly came in 1964, only four years after independence, and finally in 1966; and military rule in turn led to the secession of the east, which termed itself 'Biafra', on 30 May 1967, followed by two years' civil war and immense loss of life.

This tragic conflict divided Africa. Only Tanzania, Zambia, Gabon and the Ivory Coast backed Biafra. The other African states supported the Nigerian military regime, most of them because they feared similar secessions which they calculated would work to the advantages of the 'imperialists'. But if Balkanization was an imperial aim, why had the colonial powers striven so hard to create unitary states or, that failing, viable federations; and why did all the great powers (as it happened) support Nigeria against the secessionists, the chief reason why Biafra was crushed? There were no answers to these questions. The political philosophy of African nationalism was based upon a theory of colonialism which was not merely false but fundamentally and systematically misleading. It was bound to lead to disillusion, frustration and war.

Unfortunately, in the watershed years 1959–60, when the colonial powers began to pull out of Africa at a rapidly accelerating rate, this false theory became the prevailing wisdom of the UN, under the impact of the Bandung generation and, above all, Dag Hammarskjöld. The critical moment came when Belgium was persuaded against its better judgement to pull out of the Congo on 30 June 1960. Belgium had run this vast and valuable though primitive region with excessive political paternalism but, from 1920 onwards, with increasing economic success. The returns of heavy industrial investment began to come in during the 1950s. The index of industrial production rose, 1948–58, from 118 to 350, with productivity increasing two and a half times during these years. Directly contradicting all the Leninist-type theories of imperialism, industrial production was growing at an annual rate of 14.3 per cent in the 1950s, tailing off only at the prospect of independence.[20] As a result, at the time of independence, the Congo had, for instance, a higher ratio of hospital beds, 560 per 100,000 inhabitants, than any other African country (higher than Belgium's own in fact) and the highest literacy rate, 42 per cent (rates in British colonies ranged from 30 per cent in Uganda to 15 per cent in Tanganyika and Nigeria; French rates averaged 10 per cent).[21] But Belgium's educational effort was concentrated overwhelmingly in the primary sector: there was no Congolese doctor, engineer or senior administrator, and above all there was not a single African officer in the 25,000-strong *Force Publique*.

What the system had rapidly produced, in its last frantic years of impending abdication, was a crop of professional politicians, all concealing deep tribal affiliations beneath a veneer of European-style ideology. The three most important, Joseph Kasavubu the President, Patrice Lumumba the Prime Minister, and Moise Tshombe, premier of Katanga, the richest of the provinces, were bitter tribal and populist rivals.[22] All three were volatile personalities but Lumumba was by far the most unstable. He was a former postal-clerk and brewery worker turned full-time political agitator, and now Minister of Defence as well as head of the government. The Belgian legacy was fragile enough but it might conceivably have lasted a few years. Lumumba, however, chose the independence ceremonies to make a rabble-rousing attack on white rule; five days later on 5 July the garrison in Leopoldville, the capital, mutinied and threw out its white officers, prior to surging forth to loot, rape and kill Europeans and Africans alike. The Belgians waited for five days, while the terror spread and increased, and while Hammarskjöld, at UN headquarters in New York, did nothing, though his own UN staff in the Congo were thrown out of their hotel rooms at gunpoint by the exultant mutineers. Only on 10 July did the Belgians send in their own troops to restore order. Immediately Hammarskjöld saw his chance, turned angrily and decisively on the Belgians, and on 13 July, in front of the Security Council, denounced their troops as a threat to peace and order.[23] The Secretary-General had been looking for an opportunity to expand the UN's role, and to ride to world government on a swelling tide of Third World emotion. As the great Belgian statesman, Paul-Henri Spaak, said of him: '*Il a vécu l'anticolonialisme exacérbé et triomphant. Il y participait par devoir, mais aussi, j'en suis sûre, par conviction.*'[24] He believed that the UN was to be the catalyst of the new Africa. France's relations with Africa, he told André Malraux, were like a good martini: 'France might be the gin, but the UN was definitely the angostura' (suggesting that he was as confused about martinis as he was about Africa). In the affairs of Afro–Asia, he said, 'Only the UN, of which they are themselves members, breaks the colonial spell and puts the matter outside the orbit of the Cold War.'[25] If Hammarskjöld had done nothing and allowed Belgium to restore order, the crisis might have been quickly resolved, with the minimum of bloodshed. Tshombe, to extract the Katanga mining industry from the chaos, had declared the province independent on 11 July. This problem, too, might have been resolved by negotiation. Instead the Secretary-General immediately set about creating and deploying a UN army, taken not from the Security Council powers (as the UN Charter clearly intended) but from the 'non-aligned' states from whom Hammarskjöld drew his following. Moreover, he sought to use this expeditionary force not merely to restore order, which the Belgians were far more capable of doing, but to reunite Katanga to the Congo by violence. He saw himself as king-maker, and Lumumba as the king. Nor is it difficult to see why he backed Lumumba, who seems to have had little following, and that purely tribal, among the Congolese themselves, but whose rhetoric appealed strongly to Pan-African intellectuals and to the Afro—Asian leaders to whom the Secretary-General looked for backing.

In this forlorn endeavour, Hammarskjöld paid scant regard to the lives, black or white, he was risking. Cold, detached, consumed by an overwhelming ambition masquerading as an ideal, he thought in terms of a political abstraction, not human beings. He formulated what became a characteristic UN double-standard: that whereas the killing of Africans by whites (as at Sharpeville in South Africa on 21 March 1960) was of international concern and a threat to peace, the killing of Africans by Africans (or of whites by Africans, or of Asians by Africans or all three races by Africans) was a purely internal matter outside the purview of the UN. Thus the UN became identified with a form of inverted racism, which was to cost an incalculable number of African lives over the next two decades. Even in Hammarskjöld's time the toll was heavy. His UN army became a source of further instability rather than the reverse. His protégé, Lumumba, tried to set up his own secessionist state, fell into the hands of the Congolese army, now controlled by a former NCO, 'General' Mobutu, was tossed to the Katangese and murdered, 17–18 January 1961. The eclipse of this worthless scoundrel, responsible for the deaths of thousands, was described by Hammarskjöld as 'a revolting crime against the principles for which this Organization stands'.[26] In fact it was no more than a meaningless incident in a long power-struggle. The Secretary-General lost his emotional detachment and became obsessed with the need to revenge the death of the king he had failed to make by using his UN troops to expel the whites from Katanga and change its regime, the first instance of what might be termed imperialism by international bureaucracy. But in the process he made the error of leaving the abstract make-believe world of his UN offices and descending into the real world of the Congo basin. It cost him his life when his aircraft hit a tree near Ndola in September 1961.

Hammarskjöld, like many other outsiders, assumed one could discern, and respond to, Western-type political principles and situations in what was, in fact, nothing more than a seething cauldron of tribal and personal politics. All the Congolese politicians shifted their positions as expediency and self-preservation dictated. It was absurd that UN policy should be tied to any one of them. The Algerians, and other Afro—Asian busy-bodies, made the same mistake. Ben Bella (soon to vanish into an oubliette himself) dismissed Tshombe as 'a travelling museum of imperialism'.[28] In fact he proved a popular prime minister when Kasavubu, reversing all his previous views, appointed him. But not for long. The Congolese street-mob was as volatile as Shakespeare's Roman mob (or a Cairo mob rehearsed by Nasser). One moment the cry was, 'Long live Tshombe, Arabs go home!' The next it was: 'Down with Tshombe, Arabs send him home!' (He had since been condemned to death for treason.)[29] The watershed was in December 1965 when, as was probably inevitable, Mobutu ended the political era with a military *coup*. He then went on, at the next Independence Day celebrations, to salute the man for whose murder he was responsible: 'Glory and honour to an illustrious citizen of the Congo, to a great African, and to the first martyr of our independence – Patrice Emery Lumumba, who was the victim of the colonialist plot!' Thereafter, Mobutu, now president, ruled with the support of Western interests, to the enrichment of many hundreds of friends, supporters and relatives and not least of himself: by the early 1980s he was reckoned to be a billionaire, perhaps the world's wealthiest man, richer than King Leopold of Belgium, who once owned the country.[30]

The watershed years 1959–60, culminating in the long Congolese crisis, to which the UN made so disastrous a contribution, probably destroyed any chance, however remote, that constitutionalism would become the norm in the new African states. Too many hopes had been invested in the new class of professional politicians. They could not deliver. They broke, or were broken, under the strain. The military men took over. The same thing had happened in the first 'liberated' continent, Latin America, in the early decades of the nineteenth century: the generation of Bolivar, the *Liberador*, was succeeded by the first generation of *Caudillos*. The phenomenon was repeated in the Arab world, where the military, led by Colonel Nasser and his colleagues, began to take over from 1952. In black Africa, the first successful military *coup* took place in Togo in January 1963, when Sylvanus Olympio was murdered. Six months later Fulbert Youlou was ousted in Brazzaville. Two months after that Hubert Maga was overthrown in Cotonou. There were mutinies in Kenya, Uganda and Tanzania in January 1964, followed the next month by the ousting of Leon Mba in Gabon (reversed by de Gaulle's paratroopers). Mobutu's Zaïre *coup* followed in November 1965, accompanied by two in Dahomey in quick succession, *coups* in the Central African Republic and in Upper Volta the following January and in Ghana in February. The first Togo *coup* attracted immense and world-wide publicity; by the time it was repeated, exactly five years later, no one outside the country took any notice. By this date (January 1968) black Africa had undergone sixty-four military *coups*, attempted *coups* and mutinies.[31] By the end of the 1960s, the decade of independence, Dahomey had already experienced six *coups*, Nigeria and Sierra Leone three each, and with two each for Ghana, Congo-Brazzaville, Togo, Upper Volta and Zaïre; many others had had one. During the 1970s, indeed, the military *putsch* became the chief means of changing political direction or the personnel of élites throughout black Africa; and already by 1975 twenty of the forty-one states were ruled by military or military-civil juntas.[32]

Even when military power did not become the normal arbiter of politics, parliamentary democracy in the Western sense, including the essential right to remove a government by electoral process, disappeared within a few years of independence, being replaced by Leninist one-party systems. In a very few cases, Kenya being the outstanding example, virtual one-party rule was accompanied by the survival of free market economics and the rule of law, at any rate up to a point. There, the ruling party became simply a non-idealistic organization for promoting the careers of élites from the dominant tribe.[33] Even in these quasi-constitutional states, corruption has been institutionalized, with the *signes extérieures de la richesse* interpreted as evidence of capacity to lead. President Jomo Kenyatta of Kenya, one of the few terrorist leaders to make successfully the transition to responsible rule, actually upbraided one of his opponents, the Leftist Bildad Kaggia, at a public meeting, for failing to enrich himself:

We were together with Paul Ngei in gaol. If you go to Ngei's home [you will find] he has planted a lot of coffee and other crops. What have you done for yourself? If you go to Kubai's home, he has a big house and has a nice *shamba*. Kaggia, what have *you* done for yourself? We were together with Kungu Karumba in gaol. Now he is running his own buses. What have *you* done for yourself?[34]

In fact a modest degree of corruption, provided it operated within well-understood African conventions, breach of which was answerable in the courts, was the least of the post-independence evils. Where the market system was allowed to operate, and the role of the state was restricted accordingly, corruption could be conventionalized (as, for instance, in eighteenth-century England) and so contained. It became an organic cancer only where the state took upon itself Utopian roles, as became increasingly the mode in Africa during the 1960s and still more in the 1970s. For this the assumptions of Leninism were partly responsible; still more the Bandung interpretation of Leninism, exalting the omni-competence of the political process to produce beneficial results, as preached by its eager acolytes such as Nkrumah.

But it was not collectivist philosophies alone which encouraged the fragile African state to expand and so corrupt itself. Some aspects of colonialism were also to blame. It is true that most colonies, in most respects, were conducted on harmless *laissez-faire* principles. That was certainly the theory throughout the British colonial empire, for instance. Government protected the colony from external aggression, policed it and ran its currency. The market did the rest. Unfortunately there were innumerable exceptions to these principles, which in some cases amounted to an alternative system.

The great temptation of colonialism, the worm in its free-market apple, was the itch to indulge in social engineering. It was so fatally easy for the colonial administrator to persuade himself that he could improve on the laws of supply and demand by treating his territory as an ant-hill and its inhabitants as worker-ants who would benefit from benevolent organizing. The Belgian Congo, where white settlers were given no political powers at all for fear they would oppress the natives, was a monument to well-meaning bossiness. The law instructed firms to behave like 'a good head of family'. As in Soviet Russia, there were restrictions on native movement, especially in the big cities, and in Elizabethville natives had to observe a curfew. The notion was that the African could be shoved around for his own good. Practice, of course, was much less benevolent than theory. Until 1945, the French used social engineering on a huge scale in the form of forced labour and native penal codes. It was infinitely less savage and extensive than the Gulag Archipelago but it rested on some of the same assumptions.

The most dedicated of the social engineers were the Portuguese, who ran the first and the last of the empires. In Angola and Mozambique they adopted slavery from the Africans, institutionalized it and integrated it with their administrative system. The slave-trade, especially to Brazil, was the economic mainstay of these two territories for three hundred years. The treaties the Portuguese signed with the African chiefs were for labour, not products (though in Mozambique the Arabs acted as middlemen). The Portuguese were the only primary producers of slaves among the European powers. They defended the trade desperately and resisted its suppression, abolishing it only when compelled by the British, and replacing it by a commercialized system of forced labour. This they maintained to the end in the 1970s, still with the co-operation of the African chiefs, who in the slave-days ran the labour-gangs or *shabalos*.

Cecil Rhodes wanted to absorb Angola and Mozambique in the free British system, regarding Portuguese colonialism as an anachronism: in his innocence he did not realize it was a portent of twentieth-century totalitarianism. In the post-1945 period the Portuguese provided every year 300,000 contracted labourers from Mozambique and 100,000 from Angola, mainly for South Africa. Every African who had not been assimilated and granted citizenship (the

Portuguese had no colour-bar as such) had to possess a *caderneta* or pass-book with his work record. Bad workers were sent to the local *jefe de posto* for corporal punishment on the hand with a *palmatoria* or perforated ping-pong bat. The ultimate deterrent was hard labour on 'the islands' (Sao Tome or Principe). Like the Belgians, the Portuguese had a curfew, and Africans could not normally leave the house after nine.[35]

The Portuguese authorities hotly defended their methods on moral grounds. They argued that in return for exporting labour, the two colonies were getting ports and railways and other investment unobtainable by any other means. They claimed they took their civilizing mission seriously: Africans were not children but adults who must be made to accept social responsibilities. This meant taking the men out of idleness into work, and the women out of the bondage of the fields into their proper role in the home.[36] But like most forms of moralizing interference it had unforeseen side-effects. In 1954 the Bishop of Beira complained that exporting labour was totally destructive of family life since 80 per cent of the men in his diocese were habitually away from home, either in Rhodesia and South Africa or on work-projects within the territory.[37]

Even the British-influenced territories used large-scale social engineering in the form of land-apportionment to underpin racial divisions. In Kenya the expulsion of the Kikuyu from the 'White Highlands' between the wars (which we have noted in Chapter Four) raised some of the same moral objections as Stalin's collectivization of the farms. It was the direct cause of the ferocious Mau Mau outbreak in the 1950s. Land apportionment legislation in Southern Rhodesia, a similar policy, was one of the underlying causes of the guerrilla war there which dominated Rhodesian history in the 1970s and was ended only with the change to black rule in 1979. But the outstanding example was South Africa, where social engineering was raised into the central principle (indeed philosophy) of government in the form of apartheid.

In South Africa pass-laws (and books) as forms of social control went back to the eighteenth century, being supposedly abolished in 1828 but creeping back in again, until in the 1970s arrests under movement-restriction laws averaged more than 600,000 a year.[38] Their origins lay in Elizabethan regulations to control 'sturdy beggars', themselves provoked by rapid population increase. But it is ironic that South Africa's first positive measures of social engineering were the work of Jan Christian Smuts, who was one of the principal architects both of the League of Nations and of the UN, and who personally at San Francisco in 1945 drafted the UN Declaration on Human Rights.[39]

Smuts was one of the Boer moderates who, in the liberal peace settlement after the Boer War, were associated with the British in the re-creation of the country. These men laid the legislative foundations of a semi-totalitarian state based upon the principle of racial-ordering. In 1911 strikes by contract workers (i.e. blacks) were made illegal, while the Mines and Works Act reserved certain job-categories for whites. In 1913 the Natives Land Act introduced the principle of territorial segregation by skin-colour. This Act was the key to all that followed, not least because it determined the nature of the African response which was to create their own proliferating varieties of Zionist religious sects.[40] In 1920 the Native Affairs Act introduced segregated political institutions for Africans, setting up the Native Conference of African leaders, nominated by government, and guided by the all-white Native Affairs Commission of 'experts'. In 1922 an Act restricted skilled apprenticeships to those with minimum educational qualifications (i.e. non-Africans). In 1923 the Native (Urban Areas) Act created segregated African residential areas in and near towns. In 1925 the Industrial Conciliation Act denied collective bargaining rights to Africans. The 1925 Wages Act and the 1926 Colour Bar Act were specifically designed to draw a gulf between poor whites and the African masses.[41]

It was Smuts, again, who moved South Africa in a directly opposite direction to that followed by the government of India after Amritsar. In 1921 he massacred an African 'Israelite' sect which engaged in a mass-squat on forbidden land at Bulhoek, and the following year he put down a black labour rebellion in the Rand with 700 casualties. This ruthless policy was reinforced with further legislation. The 1927 Native Administration Act made the Governor-General (i.e. the government) Supreme Chief over all Africans, with authoritarian powers to appoint headmen, define tribal boundaries, move tribes and individuals, and control African courts and land-ownership. Its Section 29 punished 'any person who utters any words or does any other act or thing whatever with intent to promote any feeling of hostility between Natives and Europeans'. Government police powers were further increased by the Mines and Works Act and Riotous Assemblies Act of 1930.[42] This granitic massing of totalitarian power took place at exactly the same time Stalin was erecting his tyranny on the Leninist plinth, gave government comparable powers and was designed to produce the same results.

During the Second World War, Smuts, who had earlier destroyed the hopes of the coloured and mixed races of securing political equality with white voters, extended social engineering to them. In 1943 he set up a Coloured Affairs Department to 'administer' the Cape coloureds, and the same year he introduced the Pegging Act to stop Indians moving into white areas. Far from making common cause between the whites, Asians and coloureds, against the overwhelming majority of blacks, it was Smuts's United Party which drove both into the arms of the black nationalists (who hated them more than whites), and the Indian element was vital in swinging Asian and UN opinion against South Africa.[43] Hence all the structural essentials of white supremacy and physical segregation existed before the United Party lost power to the Boer Nationalists in May 1948.

What the Nationalists did was to transform segregation into a quasi-religious philosophical doctrine, apartheid. In many ways they were a similar development to African nationalism itself. Their earliest slogan, *Afrika voor de Afrikaaners*, was identical with the black 'Africa for the Africans' of the 1960s and 1970s. Their religious sectarianism flourished at the same time as African Zionism and for the same purpose: to bring together in collective defence the oppressed, the unwanted and the discriminated against. It was remarkably similar to Jewish Zionism too, in both its origins and consequences. The Boers created their own Zion, which then served as the focus of hatred and unifying force for the Africans, as Israel did for the Arabs. The first Boer nationalist institutions, 1915–18, were created to provide help for poor whites through job agencies, credit banks and trade unions. They were fiercely anti-Semitic as well as anti-black and anti-British. The movement began with the defence of the underdog, then broadened to promote the political, economic and cultural interests of the Afrikaaners as a whole, then in 1948 suddenly made itself overdog, with a vengeance.[44]

Apartheid first appeared as a political programme in 1948, treating the Reserves as the proper homeland for Africans where their rights and citizenship were rooted, but its origins went back to the foundation in 1935 of the *Suid-Afrikaanse Bond vir Rassestudie*. It was therefore directly influenced by Hitler's racial ideas and his plans for segregated settlement in Eastern Europe, though it added a Biblical underpinning lacking in Hitler's atheist panorama. Beneath the surface, apartheid was a muddle, since it combined incompatible elements. As pseudo-scientific racism, it derived, like Hitlerism and Leninism, from social Darwinism; as a religious racism, it derived from fundamentalist beliefs which denied Darwinism in any form. On the surface, however, it had a certain clarity and simplicity; and the political system Smuts had created, reinforced by the Separate Representation of Voters Act (1951), which knocked the coloureds off the Common Roll, gave the

Nationalists a secure tenure of power which is now well into its fourth decade. They have thus had the means to embark on a course of social engineering which, for consistency and duration, is rivalled only by Soviet Russia's own.

The object of apartheid was to reverse the tide of integration and create wholly separate communities. The Prohibition of Mixed Marriages Act (1949) extended the ban from white-African to all unions across the colour lines. The Immorality Act made extra-marital sex illegal in any circumstances but more severely punished if it involved miscegenation. The Population Registration Act (1950) allocated everyone to a racial group, like the Nuremberg Laws. The Group Areas Act, the same year, empowered the government to designate residential and business areas for particular racial groups. It began the process of shoving human beings around like loads of earth and concrete, and flattening their homes and shops with bulldozers. The first phase of apartheid was consolidated by the security provisions of the Suppression of Communism Act (1950), which defined Communism not only as Marxism-Leninism but 'any related form of that doctrine' and any activity whatever which sought to bring about 'any political, industrial, social or economic change within the Union by the promotion of disturbance or disorder'. This turned the authoritarian elements of the state, for the first time, against a significant portion of the white population.

The second phase followed the appointment of the ideologist H.F.Verwoerd as Minister of Native Affairs in 1950. He was an intellectual, Professor of Social Psychology at Stellenbosch, who significantly was not an inward-looking old-style Boer but had been born in Holland and educated in Germany. He gave the system a new unity, especially after he became premier in 1958.[45] His Bantu Education Act of 1954 imposed government control over all African schools, brought the missions to heel, introduced differential sylla-buses and an educational system specifically designed to prepare Bantu-speakers for their place in society. At the same time, the systematic creation of separate living areas, the 'Bantustans', was begun. Segregation began to penetrate every aspect of life, including sport, culture and, not least, church services; and by 1959 the government had effectively segregated higher education.

During the years 1959–60, which in effect created the black African continent, many observers believed apartheid was doomed to collapse in the near future. That was Harold Macmillan's view when he gave his 'Winds of Change' speech in Pretoria on 3 February 1960, followed almost immediately by the Sharpeville shooting, in which sixty-nine Africans were killed.[46] It was thought that an Amritsar syndrome would now at last set in, that the tide of African advance was irresistible, that the Boers would lose their will and their nerve. There was a flight of capital. South Africa left the Commonwealth. There was likewise a belief that apartheid, even on its own terms, was unworkable. It conflicted with many of the demands of the market economy, on which South Africa depended for survival. It conflicted, too, with the ineluctable logic of demography. The central blueprint for progressive apartheid was the so-called Tomlinson Report of 1956, probably the most elaborate description of and justification for large-scale social engineering ever put together. It stated that 'the dominant fact of the South African situation' was that there was 'not the slightest ground for believing that the European population, either now or in the future, would be willing to sacrifice its character as a national entity and a European racial group'. And it proceeded from there to knock the country into an appropriate shape.[47] The Report was criticized at the time for its absurd over-optimism, both about the ease with which industry could be sited near Bantu areas and about the growth of the black population. The accumulating evidence of the 1960s appeared to confirm these *caveats*. In 1911, when race policy started, Europeans were nearly a third of the black population (1,276,242 whites against 4 million blacks, 500,000 coloureds and 150,000 Asians). In 1951, when apartheid had got going, there were 2,641,689 whites, 8,560,083 blacks, 1,103,016 coloureds and 366,664 Asians. By 1970 the whites had risen only to 3,752,528, the blacks had jumped to 15,057,952, the coloureds to 2,018,453 and the Asians to 620,436. It was calculated that, by the year 2000, Africans and coloureds would outnumber whites by ten to one.[48] This made the relative areas assigned to whites and blacks seem unrealistic, particularly since the creation of industrial jobs near Bantu areas was proceeding at only 8,000 a year against the Tomlinson projection of 50,000. The moral inequities of the system were gruesomely apparent. By 1973 only 1,513 white families had been forced to move out of the 'wrong' race areas, while 44,885 coloured and 27,694 Indian families had been engineered out of their homes, some of them occupied since the days of the Dutch East India Company.[49] There was a constant process of African squatting in forbidden areas, accompanied by equally constant bulldozing, under heavily armed police and army guard, horribly reminiscent of Russia, 1929–32. Presiding over this exercise in perverted Utopianism were Boer intellectuals, trained in the social sciences. Granted its internal contradictions and implausibilities, and the fact that African, and increasingly, world opinion were mobilized against it, the experiment seemed destined to collapse.

Yet the lesson of Soviet collectivization has been that such schemes, however morally and economically indefensible, can endure, if pursued with sufficient ruthlessness and brute physical power. Moreover, there were certain factors working in favour of the regime. Like Russia, South Africa is immensely rich in minerals: gold, coal, diamonds, manganese and copper (in order of importance), plus antimony, asbestos, chromium, fluor-spar, iron ore, manganese, mica, platinum, phosphates, tin, titanium, uranium, vanadium, zinc and many others.[50] Far from declining, as had been predicted in 1960, the South African economy flourished mightily from 1962 onwards, throughout the boom of the 1960s and early 1970s. When the boom ended in 1973–4, world inflation produced a price-revolution in gold from which South Africa, the world's largest producer (gold forms more than half the total of her mineral wealth), was the principal beneficiary. While incomes over virtually all the rest of Africa, including those of her most dedicated and active enemies, fell, South Africa's rose. Between 1972 and 1980, for instance, a standard sixty-pound gold ingot rose in retail value from $250,000 to $2.5 million, a tenfold increase.[51] The price-revolution benefited government revenues by over $1 billion a year and also provided funds for a huge rise in capital investments.

This steady growth in South Africa's income in the two decades after the 'Winds of Change' struck the continent enabled the regime to construct shelters against it in the form of a self-contained arms industry, which made South Africa virtually independent of reluctant foreign suppliers, and a military nuclear-weapons programme. By the early 1980s South Africa was spending $2.5 billion annually on defence, but this was no more than 6 per cent of GNP, a tolerable burden (by this point many black and Arab African countries were spending 25–50 per cent of GNP on their armed forces).[52] South African forces were periodically involved in maintaining security in South-West Africa, a former German colony Smuts had failed to secure outright at Versailles in 1919, South Africa being given it in trusteeship, a formula which (by another irony) he had invented himself. But in general South Africa survived with remarkably little damage, either to the military power or to the morale of the white ruling class, the decolonization by force of Angola, Mozambique and Southern Rhodesia (Zimbabwe) during the 1970s.

The Boer nationalists, as opposed to Smuts, had always criticized his unrealized scheme to create a 'great white dominion' including Rhodesia and Mozambique, and running from the Cape up to Kenya. They argued in the 1920s that this would merely 'engulf' the whites in a future black Africa. In the 1970s their caution was proved justified, when the ratio of white to black even within South Africa fell to 1:5. The South African regime refused to commit its own fortunes to the preservation of the crumbling bastions of colonialism to the north. When, in due course, they fell, the white *laager* contracted. This brought triumphant, militant and armed black nationalism to South Africa's own frontiers, backed by overwhelming majorities in the UN, the Organization of African Unity and a growing measure of Soviet-bloc physical support, chiefly in the form of Cuban troops and advisers.

Yet the 'confrontation' between South African apartheid and black nationalism was verbal and political rather than military, still less economic. The nearer the African states were to South Africa, the more they felt the pull of her immense and prosperous economy and the less inclination did they display in carrying their resolve to destroy apartheid further than words. Ordinary Africans voted with their feet, not indeed in favour of apartheid but for the jobs the South African economy provided. At the time of the boycott organized by the AUO in 1972, the South African Chamber of Miners employed 381,000 blacks, one-third of whom came from north of latitude 22 degrees S, and one-third from Mozambique. The number of blacks coming to South Africa increased steadily in the 1970s, not least because real wages for blacks in the Rand rose rapidly at a time when they were falling in most of black Africa. The neighbouring regimes called themselves 'front line states' and kept up the anti-apartheid rhetoric, but in practice the governments of Zambia, Malawi, Zimbabwe and, above all, Mozambique made themselves systematic collaborators with the apartheid system by deliberately increasing their exports of labour to the Rand. Malawi, Botswana and Zambia pulled out of the AUO boycott; other states simply broke it, as they had earlier broken the boycott of Southern Rhodesia. South Africa built Malawi's new capital at Lilongwe and the Cabora Bassa dam in Mozambique; and when one front-line president, Seretse Khama of Botswana, fell ill, he was immediately flown to a 'whites only' hospital in Johannesburg.[53]

It is significant that by the early 1980s the most active of South Africa's enemies was remote Nigeria, the only major black oil producer. Its royalties, which exceeded $23 billion in 1980, preserved it (as gold did South Africa) from the 1970s recession and gave it the luxury of preserving an independent foreign-economic policy. But states south of the Congo and the Great Lakes could not resist the pull of the Rand magnet and, in practice, adjusted their ideological policies accordingly.

In any case, differences between Pretoria's policy and those of most black African states were more theoretical than real. All African states practised racist policies. In the 1950s and 1960s, Egypt, Libya, Algeria, Morocco and Tunisia expelled more than a quarter of a million Jews and ghettoed the few thousand who remained. In the 1960s the United Republic of Tanzania expelled its

Arabs or deprived them of equal rights. In the 1970s Asians were expelled from most states in the Horn and East-Central Africa and they were discriminated against everywhere; even in Kenya they were threatened with expulsion in 1982. In most cases race-discrimination was a deliberate act of government policy rather than a response to popular demand. When the Uganda government expelled the Asians in 1972 the motive was to provide its members and supporters with free houses and shops, not to please ordinary black Ugandans, whose relations with the Asians had been friendly.[54] Anti-Asian racism was usually propagated by official or semi-official newspapers controlled by governments. In the 1970s they regularly published racist material: that Asian women had feelings of superiority, hence their refusal to sleep with black men; that Asians smuggled currency out of the country in suitcases; that Asian businessmen were monopolists and exploiters; a typical headline read 'Asian Doctors Kill their Patients'.[55]

From independence onwards, most black African states practised anti-white discrimination as a matter of government policy. In the second half of the 1970s Kenya and the Ivory Coast were virtually the only exceptions. Houphouët-Boigny, President of the latter, drew attention to anti-white racism at the OAU, telling the other heads of state:

It is true, dear colleagues, that there are 40,000 Frenchmen in my country and that this is more than there were before Independence. But in ten years I hope the position will be different. I hope that then there will be 100,000 Frenchmen here. And I would like at that time for us to meet again and compare the economic strength of your countries with mine. But I fear, dear colleagues, that few of you will be in a position to attend.[56]

But the commonest, indeed the universal, form of racism in black Africa was inter-tribal, and it was this form of racism, for which one euphemism is social control, which led a growing number of African states, in the 1960s and still more in the 1970s, to exercise forms of social engineering not unlike apartheid. One of the merits of colonial rule in Africa (except where white supremacy policies dictated otherwise) was that it geared itself to tribal nomadic movements, both cyclical and permanent. It permitted a high degree of freedom of movement. As populations rose, and pressures on food resources increased, this *laissez-faire* policy became more difficult to maintain. But it was a tragedy that, when independence came in the early 1960s, the successor-states chose to imitate not colonial-style liberalism but white-supremacist control. The Bandung–Leninist doctrine of the big, omnicompetent state joined in unholy matrimony with segregationism. But of course the Soviet state had always controlled all internal movement and settlement, not least its own Asian tribes. Leninist and South African practice fitted in comfortably together. Throughout black Africa, the documentation of social control – work permits, internal and external passports, visa requirements, residence permits, expulsion orders – proliferated rapidly with independence. And, as South African experience testified, once documents appear, the bulldozer is never far behind. In the early 1970s it emerged in many places in West Africa, to shift squatters from coastal towns back into the interior.[57]

The great drought which struck a dozen Central African countries near the desert-bush border in the 1970s increased nomadic movement and so the practice of violent social control. There had long been racial enmity along the desert line, since nomadic tribes (especially Touregs) had seized southerners for slavery. One of the first acts of independent Mali, which straddled the line, was to massacre its northern Touregs. When drought-relief funds became available, Mali (and other states) used them to finance control systems. As the Secretary of the International Drought Relief Committee in Mali put it: 'We have to discipline these people and to control their grazing and their movements. Their liberty is too expensive for us. This disaster is our opportunity.'[58] Control of movement, in Mali and elsewhere, was accompanied by other forms of social engineering. In such states development plans were deliberately drawn up in the late 1960s and 1970s to force everyone, nomads included, into the money economy by taxation. They did not differ in essentials from the old forced-labour system devised by the French, Spanish, Portuguese and Belgian colonizers.[59]

The most suggestive case of a new African state moving towards totalitarianism was provided by Tanzania. Its leader, Julius Nyerere, was a professional politician of the Nkrumah generation. In the 1960s, when the politicians were bowled over by the soldiers, he contrived to survive by militarizing his rhetoric and his regime. In 1960, in reaction to the Congo crisis, he said: 'There is not the slightest chance that the forces of law and order in Tanganyika will mutiny.'[60] In January 1964 they did so, and Nyerere barely survived with the help of white British troops who disarmed his black army. He then disbanded it and recreated it from scratch as a party army: 'I call on all members of the Tanu Youth League, wherever they are, to go to the local Tanu office and enrol themselves: from this group we shall try to build the nucleus of a new army.'[61] Four days later he announced the appointment of a Political Commissar for the Tanzania People's Defence Forces.

This conscious imitation of Leninism was accompanied by the erection of a one-party state. In 1961 Nyerere had said he would welcome an opposition party to Tanu: 'I would be the first to defend its rights.'[62] But in January 1964, with the party youth being reorganized as an army, he appointed a commission to design what he termed 'a democratic one-party state', observing that its job was not 'to consider whether Tanzania should be a one-party state. That decision has already been taken. Their task is to say what kind of a one-party state we should have.'[63] At the subsequent election, there was a choice of candidates, but under the same party label (meaning they needed Nyerere's approval to stand) and they were not free to raise issues.[64]

The way in which Nyerere, the former pacifist, used militaristic terminology to further his authoritarian state was ingenious and helped to explain his remarkable appeal to the Western intelligentsia, which led one black sociologist to coin the term 'Tanzaphilia'.[65] Defending his suppression of human rights, such as the freedom of speech, of the press and of assembly, Nyerere observed: 'Until our war against poverty, ignorance and disease has been won, we should not let our unity be destroyed by somebody else's book of rules.' But of course such a 'war', by definition, could never be 'won'. Moreover, such a 'war' was easily extended from internal to external opponents: Nyerere followed Sukarno's advice to find an enemy. From the post-mutiny period onwards he was in the forefront of the African leaders who demanded a concerted politico-military campaign against Rhodesia, the Portuguese territories and South Africa. The philosophy of his new authoritarian state was summed up in the 'Arusha Declaration' of February 1967, which stated bluntly: 'We are at war' and was full of militaristic imagery and sloganizing.[66]

Of course Tanzania was not at war with anybody. But the fiction was used to justify wartime restrictions and suspension of rights. The Arusha Declaration was an updated and Africanized version of Bandung, and similarly redolent of the higher humbug. Anything 'inconsistent with the existence of a classless society' was banned. 'No one must be allowed to live off the work done by others': that permitted widespread arrests of 'capitalists', especially Asians. The government 'must be chosen and led by peasants and workers': that allowed Nyerere to exclude anyone he wished from political activity. 'Laziness, drunkenness and idleness' were condemned: a pretext for forced labour. 'It is necessary for us to be on guard against internal stooges who could be used by external enemies who aim to destroy us': a pretext for a permanent political witch-hunt. 'Loitering' was specifically condemned: a pretext for the sweep-and-search operations beloved of all black African governments, slavishly copied from the South African police-manuals. The machinery for control was contained in the party structure: 'the ten-house cell' being the basic unit, moving up through the ward, the district, the region to the nation. The philosophy behind Arusha was termed by Nyerere *ujamaa*, 'familyhood', based upon a mythic past: 'In our traditional African society, we were individuals within a community. We took care of the community and the community took care of us. We neither needed nor wished to exploit our fellow men.'[67] *Ujamaa* was designed to recapture that spirit. Yet in practice it was as anti-family as any other totalitarian doctrine. Offenders were brought before 'ten-house cell' courts. 'Political education officers' handed out tracts which, for example, stated:

The cell leader has to keep a close watch so as to detect any new faces in his ten houses. When he sees a stranger, he must make enquiries and find out who he is, where he came from, where he is going, how long he will remain in the area and so on. Usually the host reports to the cell leader about his guests and gives all the necessary information. If the leader doubts the stories of these strangers, he must report the matter to the branch officials or to the police.[68]

Cell-leaders were given the right to detain anyone classified as 'runaway' (usually from forced labour) and to order 'round-ups' of 'miscreants'. A favourite phrase was *e serikali yeze kuyesula*, 'the government know how to unearth'. Indeed, after the 1964 mutinies Nyerere seems not only to have flung off his British democratic trappings but to have descended into the colony's Prussian past. His party militia learned the goose-step. He introduced sumptuary legislation and sartorial uniformity. In 1968 he decided that the Masai could not be allowed into Arusha wearing 'limited skin clothing or a loose blanket' or indeed any kind of clothing termed 'awkward' or 'soiled pigtailed hair'.[69] But having banned the traditional African garb, he switched the attack eight months later to 'remnants of foreign culture', authorizing the Tanu Youth League to manhandle and strip African girls wearing mini-skirts, wigs and tight trousers.[70] So girls were forbidden to wear trousers while men had to put them on: more or less the old white missionary standard. When the Masai complained, they were told God had forced Adam and Eve to dress before he drove them out of Eden.[71] But the missionaries had not set political spies in everyone's house.

Nyerere's *ujamaa* was merely the most elaborate and sanctimonious of the new authoritarian philosophies developed by the charismatic petty tyrants of black Africa. At the village level it was merely a euphemism for forced collectivization. In Zambia, the same process was termed 'village regrouping'. Its one-party dictator, Kenneth Kaunda, termed the national philosophy 'humanism'. This was derived, he said, from the truth that all people are 'human under the skin'. But some turned out to be more human than others. 'Zambian humanism', he declared, 'aims at eradicating all evil tendencies in Man . . . the attainment of human perfection', by ridding society of 'negative human inclinations such as selfishness, greed, hypocrisy, individualism, laziness, racism, tribalism, provincialism, nationalism, colonialism, neo-colonialism, fascism, poverty, diseases, ignorance and exploitation of man by man'.[72] The list gave the state endless scope for authoritarian action. Elsewhere, other 'isms' appeared. Ghana produced 'Consciencism', Senegal 'Negritude'. In the Congo, President Mobutu was at a loss until he hit upon the ideal ideology: 'Mobutuism'.

Once the tyrannies began to appear in the early 1960s, they swiftly graduated from the comparatively sophisticated (and bloodless) despotisms of Nyerere's Tanzania to resurrected horrors from Africa's darkest past. The gruesome comedy Evelyn Waugh had fabricated in *Black Mischief* became fact. On 'Kenyatta Day', October 1965, the President of Kenya, once termed by the British governor 'the leader of darkness and death', now called by relieved white settlers 'the old man', held a 'Last Supper', to commemorate the meal before his arrest as a Mau Mau terrorist.[73] In Malawi, Dr Hastings Banda, known as 'Conqueror' and 'Saviour', used witchcraft to sacralize his rule. In Zaïre, Joseph Mobutu banned Christian names and re-named himself Monutu Sese Seko Kuku Ngbendu Wa Za Banga, freely translated as 'the cock that leaves no hens alone'.[74] President Bongo of Gabon banned the word pygmy (he was under five feet tall) but kept a bodyguard of giant German ex-Foreign Legionaries, whose delight was to sing the *Horst Wessel Lied* at the main hotel.[75] As the 1960s progressed, violence struck the new African élites with increasing frequency. Two Prime Ministers of Burundi were murdered in quick succession. The 1966 Nigerian *coup* cost the lives of the Federal Prime Minister and two of the three regional premiers. Would-be *Caudillos* died too: in the Congo People's Republic an executed brass-hat was displayed dead on TV, his mouth crammed with dollars. Rulers showed an inclination to carry out retribution personally. The President of Benin (formerly Dahomey) murdered his Foreign Minister when he found him in bed with the Presidential wife. Another Foreign Minister, this time in Equatorial Guinea, was clubbed to death by his own head of state.

This last incident was one of the innumerable crimes committed by President Francisco Macias Nguema. In the poorer African states, of which there are nearly thirty, rulers set up one-party states and in theory disposed of absolute authority. But in practice they tended to have little power to influence intractable events or even to arbitrate tribal quarrels. All they could do was to tyrannize, usually by personal violence. Macias was a case in point. He was born in the Spanish colony in 1924, served in the administration, became President on independence in 1968 and made himself President for life in 1972. During the next seven years he turned the country into a virtual prison-camp; many of its inhabitants simply fled for their lives. A Spanish-mounted *coup* overthrew him on 3 August 1979, and he was tried for 'genocide, treason, embezzlement and systematic violation of human rights'. His execution was carried out by a Moroccan firing-squad flown in when local troops complained his spirit was too strong for mere bullets and would return 'as a tiger'.[76]

The case of President (later Emperor) Bokassa of the Central African Republic was similar. When the French gave the colony independence they put in a hand-picked professional politician, David Dako, as president. Ineffectually he tried to balance the head of the police, Izamo, against Bokassa, who led the army, and Bokassa proved the most agile of the trio.[77] From 1965 Bokassa was life President and from 1977 Emperor, holding an elaborate coronation ceremony in December attended by 3,500 foreign guests and featuring an eagle-shaped throne, a crown with 2,000 diamonds and regalia modelled on Napoleon's coronation. It cost $30 million, a fifth of the country's meagre revenues. His friendship with the expansive President Giscard d'Estaing of France, to whom he gave diamonds, was not the least of the factors which buttressed his regime. He celebrated his first anniversary by sacking and exiling his eldest son, Prince Georges, for anti-paternal remarks. Two months later, in January 1979, he slaughtered forty schoolchildren who rioted when forced to buy uniforms made in Bokassa's factory. In April, between thirty and forty more children were murdered in the Ngaragba prison, apparently in Bokassa's presence and partly by him, a fact established by a commission of Francophone lawyers under Youssoupha Ndiaya of Senegal. When Giscard, alarmed by the publicity, sent out his adviser on African affairs, René Journiac, to ask the Emperor to abdicate, he was whacked on the head by the imperial sceptre. In retaliation Giscard landed troops at Bangui on 21 September 1979, with Dako in their luggage as replacement-president. Bokassa was given asylum in the Ivory Coast at Giscard's request, and was later condemned to death *in absentia* for murder, cannibalism, 'intelligence with Libya' and fraud in gold and diamonds.

The Sékou Touré regime in the Republic of Guinea was little better; Colonel Gadafy's in Libya considerably worse; both committed the additional crime of exporting their horrors to their neighbours. The most instructive case, however, was that of 'General'

Amin in Uganda, because it illustrated so many weaknesses of the
world system in the 1970s. It was also the most tragic, for it virtually
destroyed Uganda, once the most delightful country in Africa.
Churchill, who visited it as Colonial Under-Secretary in 1908, called
it 'that paradise on earth', 'that tropical garden'. 'Uganda is a
fairy-tale,' he wrote. 'You climb up a railway instead of a beanstalk
and at the top there is a wonderful new world.'[78] Uganda's independence was rushed through in October 1963 in accordance with
Macmillan's 'Winds of Change' policy. The Baganda ruling tribe
were well-educated and always impressed Europeans by their charm.
But the country was in many ways primitive, riven by complex tribal
rivalries, racial enmity between Muslim north and Christian south
and long-standing sectarianism within the Christian communities.
Violent magic was ubiquitous. The Kakwa and Nubi of the Muslim
north drank their victims' blood and ate their livers and believed in
the Mahdist 'Yakan of Allah water', which when drunk makes
soldiers invulnerable. But the sophisticated Baganda kings also
mutilated bodies for purposes of politico-religious terror.[79] To make
matters worse, Milton Obote, the professional politician installed as
Prime Minister on independence, was a narrow-minded anti-Baganda
sectarian of exceptional administrative incompetence. In 1966 he
destroyed the constitution by using Amin to storm the Kabaka's
palace and eject him by force. When Obote, in turn, was toppled by
Amin in January 1971, many people greeted military rule with
approval as the lesser of two evils.

It is important to grasp that even at this stage Idi Amin was known
to be an exceptionally cunning and wicked man. The giant son of a
Lugbara witchwoman, he had become a Muslim at sixteen and drew
his power from the northern Kakwas and Nubis. He enlisted in the
King's African Rifles as a boy and his promotion to officer, though
he was virtually uneducated, reflected the desperate need to avoid a
Congo-type mutiny as independence neared. He quickly acquired an
evil reputation in Kenya, fighting against cattle-rustlers. It was
discovered he had murdered Pokot tribesmen and left them to be
eaten by hyenas, got information from Karamajog tribesmen by
threatening to cut off their penises with a *panga*, and had actually
sliced off the genitals of eight of them to obtain confessions. He was
also known to have murdered twelve Turkana villagers. The British
authorities were themselves reluctant to prosecute one of the few
black officers on the eve of independence, and referred the case to
Obote, already Prime Minister-designate. Obote settled for a 'severe
reprimand', a curious punishment for mass-murder.[80] Indeed, he
promoted Amin colonel, used him to put down the Baganda and
permitted him to build up a military tribal base in the north, to

engage in large-scale smuggling of gold and ivory, to recruit Muslims without reference to the government, to murder the only other senior black officer, Brigadier Okoya (and his wife) in January 1970, and thereafter to treat the army as his own. When Obote was told by the auditor-general that £2.5 million was missing from army funds, the Prime Minister left for a conference in Singapore, telling Amin he wanted a 'full explanation' by his return. That was to invite a *coup*, which Amin had already been pressed to undertake by Colonel Gadafy and the Palestinian leader Yasser Arafat, who wished to oust Obote's Israeli advisers.

Amin's was a racist regime, operated in the Muslim–Arab interest from the start, since he began massacres of the Langi and Acholi tribes within weeks of taking over. In July 1971 he asked the Israelis to help him invade Tanzania by seizing the port of Tanga; they responded by pulling out. The British repented their support at the same time, and thereafter Amin was Gadafy's client. Muslims form only 5 per cent of the population and only Libyan support made the long tyranny possible, though Palestinian terrorists provided Amin with his personal bodyguard and the most adapt of his executioner-torturers. Gadafy persuaded Amin to throw out the Asians, and it was at that point, in August 1972, that the real looting of the country began. But it ought to be on record that Britain was shipping armoured cars to Amin as late as December 1972.[81] Indeed, freighting of scarce luxuries to Uganda from Stansted airport, an important traffic which enabled Amin to keep up the morale of his soldiers, continued with British government approval almost to the end of the terror.

Surviving cabinet minutes give a unique glimpse of the emergence of a primitive tribal tyranny in the outward forms of British bureaucratic constitutionalism. Thus cabinet minute 131, dated 14 March 1972, read: 'Should any minister feel that his life was in danger from unruly crowd or dissatisfied persons, he was at liberty to shoot to kill.'[82] In fact it was not dissatisfied persons but the President whom ministers feared. His Minister of Education, Edward Rugumayo, who escaped in 1973, sent a memorandum to all African heads of state which claimed Amin had 'no principles, moral standards or scruples' and would 'kill or cause to be killed anyone without hesitation'.[83] His Attorney-General, Godfrey Lule, wrote: 'He kills rationally and coolly.' Henry Kyemba, Minister of Health, said that it was the murder of Michael Kagwar, President of the Industrial Court, in September 1971, which 'revealed to the country as a whole that the massacres were not to be limited to the army or the Acholi and Langi'.[84] The dead soon included any public figure who in any way criticized or obstructed Amin: the governor of the

Bank of Uganda, the vice-chancellor of Makerere University, the Foreign Minister, the Chief Justice, dragged out of his court in broad daylight, Archbishop Janan Luwum – the last beaten to death, along with two cabinet ministers, by Amin himself. Amin often participated in atrocities, sometimes of a private nature. Kyemba's wife Teresa, matron-in-charge of Mulago hospital, was present when the fragmented body of Amin's wife Kay was brought in: Amin appears not only to have murdered but dismembered her, for he kept collections of plates from anatomical manuals. He is also said to have killed his son and eaten his heart, as advised by a witchdoctor he flew in from Stanleyville.[85] There can be little doubt he was a ritual cannibal, keeping selected organs in his refrigerator.

The image of refrigerated cannibalism encapsulated the regime, which was a grotesque caricature of a Soviet-type terror. The traditional police simply faded away, as their senior officers were murdered for investigating Amin's crimes. Like Stalin, Amin had competing security services. They included his personal creation, the Public Safety Unit, the military police and his equivalent of the KGB, an organization called the State Research Centre which had evolved out of the old Cabinet Research Section and still retained its bound volumes of the *Economist*. The SRC was run on the advice of Palestinians and Libyans who had themselves, in some cases, had Russian training. It usually killed with sledgehammers but it was by no means primitive in all respects. It was linked by tunnel to Amin's villa so that intended victims who came to see him (he liked to ask them to cocktails) could be taken away without being seen again. SRC beatings were regular affairs, carried out at specific times every day. In contrast to Amin's impulsive nature, there was an element of totalitarian routine and bureaucratic order about the terror. As in the Soviet bloc, at least two SRC agents were attached to Ugandan overseas missions. Like the KGB, the SRC financed itself by commercial activities (including drug rackets) and often killed for hard currency.[86] Amin was not just a case of a reversion to African primitivism. In some respects his regime was a characteristic reflection of the 1970s. His terror was a Muslim–Arab phenomenon; his regime was in many ways a foreign one, run by Nubians, Palestinians and Libyans.

It could be argued that the UN power-politics of the 1970s, the ugly consequences of the relativistic morality impressed on the organization by Hammarskjöld and his school, were responsible for prolonging the Amin regime by six terrible years. According to one authority, the failure to take international action in 1972, when the nature of the regime was already glaringly apparent, cost the lives of 200,000 Ugandans. Britain bore a heavy responsibility. The SRC records revealed how important the 'Stansted whisky run' was to the regime. British appeasement reached its nadir in June 1975 when Amin threatened to execute a British lecturer, Denis Hills, for calling him 'a village tyrant'. James Callaghan, a weak Prime Minister even by the standards of the 1970s, sent out General Sir Chandos Blair with a letter from the Queen begging for clemency, and later he flew to Kampala himself. But he allowed the Stansted run to continue until 4 March 1979, the very eve of Amin's overthrow. The only government to emerge with credit was Israel's, which acted vigorously to save lives when Amin and the Palestinians hijacked an airliner at Entebbe in June 1976.

Most African states actually supported Amin, in accordance with the old Latin-American principle of '*Caudillos* stick together'. Despite the revelations of his genocidal atrocities by his ex-ministers, the OAU elected him its president and all except three of its members attended the OAU summit he held in Kampala. Nyerere objected, not so much on moral grounds as because he was an Obote ally and rightly feared an Amin invasion. 'By meeting in Kampala,' he protested, 'the heads of state of the OAU are giving respectability to one of the most murderous administrations in Africa.' Furious, the OAU even considered a motion condemning Tanzania. The heads of state showered Amin with congratulations during the summit when, having consumed parts of his earlier wife, he married a new one, a go-go dancer from his Suicide Mechanized Unit. They applauded when Amin was carried on a litter by four white businessmen, a Swede holding a parasol over his head, and when the Ugandan Air Force made a demonstration bombing on Lake Victoria against a target labelled 'Cape Town' (the bombs all missed and the Air Force commander was murdered as soon as the delegates had left). OAU heads of state again gave Amin a warm reception in 1977, and there was no criticism of Amin whatever by the OAU until 1978; even then it was muted.[87]

Most members of the UN, where the Afro–Asian–Arab and Soviet blocs formed a majority, behaved equally cynically. As chairman of the OAU, he addressed the General Assembly on 1 October 1975 in a rabid speech which denounced the 'Zionist–US conspiracy' and called not only for the expulsion of Israel but for its 'extinction' (i.e. genocide). The Assembly gave him a standing ovation when he arrived, applauded him throughout, and again rose to its feet when he left. The following day the UN Secretary-General and the President of the General Assembly gave a public dinner in Amin's honour.[88] Attempts to raise Uganda's violation of human rights at the UN in 1976 and 1977 were blocked by African votes, which rendered Amin the same service at the Commonwealth Conference in 1977. Even when he invaded Tanzania on 30 October 1978, an act which led to his downfall five months later, the OAU refused to condemn him and told Nyerere to accept mediation. For once the Tanzanian socialist dictator dropped his verbal guard:

Since Amin usurped power he has murdered more people than Smith in Rhodesia, more than Vorster in South Africa. But there is this tendency in Africa that it does not matter if an African kills other Africans . . . . Being black is now becoming a certificate to kill fellow Africans.[89]

That, indeed, was the consequence of the morally relativistic principle introduced by Hammarskjöld that killing among Africans was not the UN's business; and Amin could be forgiven for thinking the UN had given him a licence for mass-murder, indeed genocide. The Amin regime was made possible by the philosophy of the Bandung generation as well as by the re-emergent barbarism of Africa. But within a year of his fall history was being rewritten. It was claimed the applause which greeted him at the UN was 'ironic'. The terror was being linked to 'imperialism'.[90] Nor did Uganda's sorrows end when Tanzania's 'army of liberation' arrived, with Obote in its baggage. The first thing the Tanzanians did when they got to Kampala was to loot it. Though Amin himself was given sanctuary in the Muslim world (Libya, then Saudi Arabia), his tribal forces continued to occupy and terrorize part of the country. With Nyerere's armed backing Obote 'won' the 1980s elections. Obote's UPC party and the Nyerere-controlled 'military commission' gerrymandered constituency boundaries; illegally declared 17 seats uncontested UPC victories; killed one opposition (Democratic Party) candidate and beat up others; illegally removed fourteen returning officers who were not UPC stooges; sacked the Chief Justice and other officials to intimidate the judiciary; and finally, after it became clear on election night that the DP was nevertheless winning, announced on the official radio that all results would be 'vetted' by the military – whereupon the secretary to the election commission fled for his life. The army subsequently destroyed evidence of DP victories and Obote was declared the winner.[91] The result was regional and tribal civil war; and mass-terrorism by three undisciplined and mostly unpaid 'armies' prolonged indefinitely the agony of Churchill's 'fairy-tale land'.[92]

The case of Uganda illustrated the tendency of post-colonial Africa, from the mid-1960s onwards, to engage in internal and external wars, and for both the OAU and the UN, far from arbitrating such disputes, to exacerbate the drift to violence. This was not fortuitous. The militarization of the OAU began at Addis Ababa in 1963, when passive resistance was renounced, force was adopted as the means to end the remaining colonial regimes and a 'liberation committee' was formed with Tanzania in the chair. The next year, at Cairo, it was the ex-pacifist Nyerere who called for the expulsion of Portugal by force, and in 1965 it was his second-in-command, Rashidi Kawawa, who told the UN Committee on Colonialism in Dar es Salaam that its function was identical with that of the OAU committee, 'two liberation committees of historical importance in the struggle against colonialism'. M.Coulibaly of Mali, the UN chairman, at first protested: the UN could not be identified with a regional military body, he said. Then he capitulated, and his committee ruled that it was legitimate for any state to use force to expel the Portuguese. This was the first time the UN had committed itself to the military as opposed to the peaceful solution of political problems. Four months later, in November 1965, Nyerere persuaded the OAU to extend the principle to Rhodesia.[93]

With both the UN and the OAU not merely endorsing but inciting, indeed commanding, violence, individual African states employed it increasingly to resolve their inter-tribal civil wars and frontier disputes, which colonialism had frozen. Africa appears to have the greatest linguistic and ethnic variety of any continent. Of the forty-one independent states, only Egypt, Tunisia, Morocco, Lesotho and Somalia were basically homogeneous, and even these had debatable borders.[94] Most African civil wars, since they involve transfrontier tribal conflicts, tend to become foreign wars also. One of the earliest of them, the 1958 Hutu race-revolt in Rwanda against their Tutsi overlords, involved Burindi, and this pattern was repeated three times over the next fifteen years. The revolt of the Polisarios against Morocco and Mauritania, the struggle between northern Muslims and southern Christians in Chad, the civil wars in Angola, the Sudan and Nigeria, five of the longer and more serious conflicts, all involved foreign intervention. The UN and the OAU, not surprisingly, proved wholly unable to arbitrate these conflicts. A typical example was the partition in December 1975 of the old Spanish Sahara between Morocco and Mauritania, which recalled the partitions of Poland in the eighteenth century (or in 1939). Algeria was left out, and thereupon backed the Polisario insurgents. The UN passed two mutually exclusive resolutions, one supporting Morocco, the other Algeria. The OAU has never seriously attempted to enforce its primary maxim that states should not interfere in each other's internal affairs, except (interestingly enough) in the case of Amin's Uganda. It failed to censure Gadafy of Libya for his attempts to overthrow Sadat in Egypt, Niheimi in the Sudan, Bourguiba in Tunisia, Francis Tombalbaye and Felix Malloum in Chad and his blatant intervention in half a dozen other states. Nor was the OAU able to prevent incursions by non-African powers, since nobody wanted to repeat the Congo's disastrous involvement with the UN, and it was the individual states themselves which invited the help of foreign troops, as did Kenya, Uganda and Tanzania with Britain and the Ivory Coast, Gabon and Senegal with France.[94]

The trans-border complexities increased markedly after 1973–4 when Soviet Russia, with its satellite Cuba, first committed large numbers of troops to the African theatre. A case in point was Ethiopia, where the old Emperor Haile Selasse had run a semi-feudal, semi-liberal regime by a careful balance of foreign help. The Indians trained his army, the British and Norwegians the navy, the Swedes the air force, the French ran the railway, the Australians the hotels, the Yugoslavs the port, the Russians the oil refinery, the Bulgars his fishing fleet, the Italians the breweries, the Czechs the shoe factories and the Japanese the textile mills.[95] The Russians seized their chance to overthrow the old man in 1974 – he was smothered to death with a pillow – and gain a monopoly of influence, dropping their Somalian protégé in the process. The worst that could be said about the Emperor's censorship was that he had cut the death of the King from *Macbeth*; after his fall Shakespeare was no longer performed at all. The regime became totalitarian, massacred its opponents by the tens of thousands, and engaged in large-scale frontier wars which continued into the 1980s. After Russia extended the Cold War to Africa, it became the classic theatre of Realpolitik, of abrupt formations and reversals of alliances, and of the principle 'my enemy's enemy is my friend'. A characteristic instance was the Katangan invasion of Zaïre across the Angolan frontier in 1977–8, with the Communists, replacing the 'imperialist secessionists' of 1960, helping the Katangans with Cuban and Russian troops, and Morocco and France backing Zaïre.

The thirty-odd civil and foreign wars the new African states fought in their first two decades produced a swelling total of refugees. By 1970 there were a million of whose existence the UN was statistically aware. The figure leapt to 4.5 million in 1978, plus 2 million described as 'unsettled' after returning to their home country. In 1980 there were 2,740,300 UN-recorded refugees in seventeen African countries, plus 2 million 'displaced persons', the vast majority of them the result of the military activities of Soviet Russia, Cuba and Libya.[96] The possibility of a significant proportion of these people being resettled was remote. By the early 1980s, all the newly independent states, with the exception of the Ivory Coast, Kenya and the three oil-bearing territories, Algeria, Libya and Nigeria, were poorer than under the colonial system. Some had moved out of the market economy altogether.

In these circumstances, the quite rapid material progress which had been a feature of the final phase of colonialism, 1945–60, was reversed. Though independence was fertile in regional pacts, such as the six-power Casablanca Group, the fifteen-power Monrovia Group and the Brazzaville Twelve, these were largely verbal agreements for political purposes, and they proved ephemeral. Meanwhile the specific and practical inter-state arrangements for currencies, transport and communications were disrupted or lapsed. Wars, 'emergencies' and the shutting of frontiers disrupted road and rail links. Rolling-stock was not renewed. Roads deteriorated. Travel patterns tended to revert to those of the 1890s, with links chiefly between the coastal cities (though by air rather than by sea) but with little long-distance movement inland. Mobility became patchy and unreliable. In the late 1970s, the greatest traffic jams so far contrived by man took place not in the advanced West but in Lagos: it was said that the head of state, General Mohammed, died because he could not solve the jam even for himself and his car got stuck at the same time, 8 am, each morning, making it easy to plan his murder. In 1976, after the Nigerian government had ordered 18 million tons of cement, the approaches to Lagos harbour were jammed by nearly five hundred ships, and by the time most of them landed their cargo it was unusable.[97]

But in many inland areas, even in Nigeria, land traffic declined. As one account put it, 'More and more of the observable life of Africa takes place within twenty miles of its three dozen international airports.'[98] With the decline in air traffic control standards and the frequent closings of internal air-space, it often became easier and cheaper to travel between African capitals via Europe than direct. The same was true of phone-links: for instance, it was impossible to phone Abidjan from Monrovia, four hundred miles away, except through Europe or North America. The suggestion was made that this decline actually benefited authoritarian governments by immobilizing critics, for most African governments maintained for their exclusive use military transport and communications networks on the Iron Curtain model. But the state suffered too. In 1982 the Chad ambassador in Brussels complained he had not heard from his government for more than a year.[99]

Equally marked was the deterioration in medical standards. The progress made in eliminating malaria, which had been spectacular in the late 1940s and 1950s, was reversed. WHO's twenty-year programme launched in 1958 was a failure. By the end of the 1970s there were 200 million cases in the world and 1 billion people living in malaria-risk areas. The reversal was by no means confined to Africa; results in Central America and Asia were in some ways even more disappointing.[100] But the late 1970s saw a disquieting increase in malarial cases returning from African capitals where the disease had been stamped out in the 1950s.[101] The return of traditional scourges reflected the growth of malnutrition and famine, the breakdown of public health and hospital services and the shortage of qualified doctors. In 1976 WHO reversed its policy and announced that henceforth 'village healers' would be employed in rural health services, though a distinction was still made between African-type midwives, bonesetters and herbalists, on the one hand, and 'witch-doctors' using 'spells and superstitions' on the other. In 1977, however, this distinction was dropped and 'witch-doctors', patronized by 90 per cent of the rural population, were given the same status as scientifically trained practitioners.[102] In Lagos, within the penumbra of the world's largest traffic-jam, a joint teaching-hospital was opened for doctors practising medicine and 'healing'.

The varied but on balance sombre pattern of the African continent a generation after independence was reflected in the following summary of events in the last year of the 1970s decade and the first of the 1980s. For 1979: *Sudan:* attempted *coup. Morocco:* War in Western Sahara against Polisario guerrillas cost £750,000 a day. *Ethiopia:* 20,000 Cubans plus Ethiopian troops were fighting wars on three fronts against Eritrea and Somalia, where refugees passed the 1 million mark. *Djibouti:* uprising in Adar region. *Kenya:* successful multi-party elections. *Tanzania:* 40,000 troops invaded *Uganda,* when Amin, supported by 2,500 troops from *Libya,* was ousted. *Ghana: coup* by Flight-Lieutenant Jerry Rawlings. Three former heads of state and many other politicians executed by firing-squad; public floggings and canings of corrupt citizens; police strike; country declared officially bankrupt. *Nigeria:* return to civilian rule. *Liberia:* food riots; seventy killed. *Senegal:* a fourth legal party created. *Mauritania: coup.* Ould Salack, who had ousted Ould Daddah in 1978, ousted in turn by Ould Hardallah. Peace signed with Polisario guerrillas. *Mali:* single-party elections. *Guinea:* release of political prisoners, including Archbishop of Conakry. *Benin:* single-party elections. *Togo:* single-party elections; political show-trials of so-called 'Brazilian élitists'. *Cameroon:* attempted *coup* followed by small massacre. *Chad:* civil war. *People's Republic of Congo: coup. Equatorial Guinea:* overthrow of dictator Macias. *Central African Republic:* overthrow of Bokassa. *Zaïre:* most major roads reported unusable; two-thirds of road vehicles unusable for lack of spare parts; Benguela railway closed; 38 per cent of foreign exchange earmarked for debt-servicing; 42 per cent of under-fives suffering from malnutrition. *Burundi:* fifty-two missionaries expelled for 'subversion'. *Guinea-Bissau:* revenue covered only 65 per cent of expenditure. *Cape Verde:* over 90 per cent of food consumed imported. *Mozambique:* death-penalty extended to sabotage, terrorism and mercenary activities; many political executions; President Machel attacked men with long hair and women with tight clothes. Catholic and Anglican churches closed. *Angola:* civil war. *Zambia:* many political arrests. *Malawi:* import controls. *Zimbabwe:* end of white rule after decade of civil war; 20,000 dead. *Namibia:* guerrilla warfare. *Lesotho:* guerrilla warfare. *Swaziland:* economy under pressure from refugees. *Botswana:* ditto. *South Africa:* guerrilla warfare.

In 1980: *Sudan:* one-party elections. *Tunisia:* attempted *coup.* *Morocco:* war against Polisario. *Algeria:* Soviet-style concentration on heavy industry abandoned as failure. *Ethiopia:* Soviet helicopter gunships used against Somalis, Oromo, Gallas and other non-Amharic races. *Somalia:* refugees pass 1.5 million mark. *Tanzania:* Nyerere, sole candidate, elected president; famine. *Zanzibar:* attempted *coup.* *Uganda:* cost of maintaining 20,000 Tanzania army of occupation, plus 6,000 Uganda army, rose to 37 per cent of revenue; fifty political murders a week in Kampala; famine. *Ghana:* 114 per cent inflation; universities closed. *Nigeria:* attempted *coup;* 1,000 killed. *Gambia:* opposition parties banned; many arrests. *Liberia: coup;* many executions by firing-squad. *Senegal:* voluntary retirement of Senghor after twenty-year rule. *Mauritania: coup:* Ould Hardallah ousted by Ould Louly. *Mali:* schools on strike; economy described as 'catastrophic'. *Guinea*-financed coup in *Bissau,* following dispute over oil-rights. *Ivory Coast:* one-party elections. *Upper Volta: coup.* *Niger:* invasion by Libyan-financed nomads. *Benin:* President Kerekou 'converted' to Islam during visit to Gadafi. *Cameroon:* economy under pressure by refugees from Chad. *Chad:* civil war and invasion by Libya. *Zaïre:* Mobutu declared 4 February: 'As long as I live I will never tolerate the creation of another party.' *Guinea-Bissau: coup.* *Sao Tomé:* threatened invasion by exiles; 1,000 Angolans and 100 Cubans moved in. *Angola:* civil war. *Zambia:* attempted *coup.* *Zimbabwe:* British-supervised free elections. *Namibia:* guerrilla war. *Lesotho:* invasion by 'Lesotho Liberation Army'. *South Africa:* guerrilla warfare.[103]

The summary conceals many nuances. But it confirms a downtrend in the recurrent cycle of interest in Africa. The first cycle, what might be called the Rhodes period, ran from the 1880s up to the First World War, when many believed Africa's resources would be the mainstay of future European prosperity. This was briefly sustained in the early 1920s, then evaporated. A further cycle of interest began in the late 1940s and reached its peak in the early 1960s, during the transfer from colonial rule to independence. It began to collapse with militarization in the late 1960s. By the early 1980s it was dead: that is, the interest of the outside world in Africa was confined largely to certain major primary producers, especially Nigeria and South Africa. By then it was apparent that the great bulk of the continent had become and would remain politically unstable and incapable of self-sustained economic growth, or even of a place within the international economy. Africa had become simply a place for proxy wars, like Spain in the 1930s. In Africa, the professional political caste and the omnicompetent state had proved costly and sanguinary failures. We must now examine to what extent the same pattern had been repeated in Asia, especially in the two stricken giants which housed nearly half the world's population, China and India.

SIXTEEN

Experimenting with Half Mankind

In the summer of 1966, the official Peking press reported that on 16 July Mao Tse-tung, the Chairman of the Chinese Communist Party, then in his seventieth year, had organized and led a mass swim in the Yangtze. Somewhat fuzzy photographs were published of what appeared to be his large round head bobbing in the water. Reports said he had swum nearly ten miles in just over sixty minutes and he was described as 'radiant with vigour and in buoyant spirits'.[1] This was merely one of the prodigies which appeared to have taken place in China in the quarter-century between Mao's accession to power and his death in 1976. It was widely believed China was steadily overcoming the economic problems facing large, backward and heavily populated countries, and was doing so within the framework of an enthusiastic national consensus.

Visitors returned fervent admirers of Mao's brand of Communism. China, one of them wrote, was 'a kind of benign monarchy ruled by an emperor-priest who had won the complete devotion of his subjects'. Its people, another predicted, would be 'the incarnation of the new civilization of the world'. Simone de Beauvoir testified: 'life in China today is exceptionally pleasant'. The country had become, said another witness, 'almost as painstakingly careful about human lives as New Zealand'. David Rockefeller praised 'the sense of national harmony' and argued that Mao's revolution had succeeded 'not only in producing more efficient and dedicated administration, but also in fostering high morale and community of purpose'. Another American visitor found the changes 'miraculous . . . . The Maoist revolution is on the whole the best thing that happened to the Chinese people in centuries.' What attracted most admiration was the improvement in moral tone. 'Of the many communes I visited,' Felix Greene reported, 'all except one denied any knowledge of any children born out of wedlock.' 'Law and order', another American visitor found, '. . . are maintained more by the prevailing high moral code than by any threat of police action.' Yet another insisted that government tax collectors had become 'incorruptible' and that intellectuals were anxious to prove their lack of 'contempt for peasants' by 'lugging buckets of manure in their free time'.[2]

These testimonies recalled the uncritical praise lavished by visitors on Stalin and his regime during the horrors of collectivization and the great purges. When taxed on this point, admiring visitors replied that the lessons of Soviet mistakes had been learnt, largely through the extraordinary genius of Mao. He was, Jan Myrdal wrote, 'third in line with Marx and Lenin' and had solved the problem of how 'the revolution can be prevented from degenerating'. He 'combined', wrote an American political scientist, 'qualities which rarely coexist in one being in such intensity'. Han Suyin argued that, unlike Stalin, Mao 'is extremely patient, and believes in debate and re-education', and had 'an ever-present concern with the practical application of democracy'. When a problem arose, an American sinologist reported, Mao 'invariably' responded 'in a uniquely creative and profoundly ethical way'. Felix Greene believed that the hunger for power had been eliminated and that there was 'no evidence of that jockeying for power or of the personal rivalry that we have so often seen in the Kremlin'. Mao was not merely a soldier, a leader, a poet, philosopher, teacher, thinker and charismatic: he was also a kind of saint. What struck Hewlett Johnson most about him was 'something no picture has ever caught, an inexpressible look of kindness and sympathy, an obvious preoccupation with the needs of others . . . these formed the deep content of his thoughts.'[3]

Needless to say, these travellers' tales, as in Stalin's Russia, bore little or no relation to the truth, which was more interesting and infinitely more depressing. And Mao's public image, too, was as remote from the reality as Stalin's. Mao was not a saint. There was nothing of the scholar or the mandarin about him. He was a big, coarse, brutal, earthy and ruthless peasant, a *kulak* indeed; an educated version of his father. Khrushchev, not unjustly, compared him to 'a bear, swaying from side to side as he moved, calmly and slowly'.[4] Talking to the Politburo in 1956, Mao warned: 'We must not blindly follow the Soviet Union . . . . Every fart has some kind of smell, and we cannot say that all Soviet farts smell sweet.'[5] Three years later, admitting the failure of the 'Great Leap', he told the same group: 'Comrades, you must all analyse your own responsibility. If you have to shit, shit! If you have to fart, fart! You will feel much better for it.'[6] Again, in 1974, reviewing the shortcomings of the Cultural Revolution he philosophized: 'The need to shit after eating does not mean that eating is a waste of time.'[7] A Belgian Communist described him, during the great Red Guards rally in Heavenly Peace

Square on 18 August 1966, retiring from time to time to take off his vest and wipe his chest and armpits, remarking, 'It's unhealthy to let sweat dry on your body.'[8]

Beneath this coarse exterior, however, there beat a strong – indeed a wild – romantic heart. It is probably true, as Stalin insisted in 1949, that Mao was not really a Marxist at all: 'He doesn't understand the most elementary Marxist truths.'[9] While he used the Marxist formulations, and indeed considered himself a great Marxist thinker, much superior to Stalin's contemptible successors, he never in practice attempted to apply objective Marxist analysis. He did not believe in 'objective situations' at all. It was all in the mind: he might be described as a geopolitical Emile Coué who believed in 'mind over matter'. On the basis of 'the tremendous energy of the masses', he argued, 'it is possible to accomplish any task whatever'.[10] 'There is only unproductive thought,' he said, 'no unproductive regions. There are only poor methods of cultivating the land, no such thing as poor land.'[11] This contempt for objective reality explains his willingness to accept the prospect of nuclear war, and his conviction that China would win it. 'The East wind prevails over the West wind,' he said in 1957. 'If imperialism insists on fighting a war, we will have no alternative but to make up our minds and fight to the finish before going ahead with our construction.'[12] The same year, in Moscow, he shocked his Communist colleagues by the same argument: 'We may lose more than 300 million people. So what? War is war. The years will pass and we'll get to work producing more babies than ever before' (according to Khrushchev, he 'used an indecent expression').[13] He later took a similar view of war with Russia: 'Even if it goes on for ever, the sky won't fall, trees will grow, women will give birth and fishes will swim.'[14] He seems to have believed all his life that the true dynamic of history was not so much the maturation of classes (that might be the outward expression) as heroic determination. He saw himself as the Nietzschean superman made flesh.

In his artistic longings, in his romanticism and in his belief that will is the key not only to power but to accomplishment, Mao was an oriental Hitler. Though the cult of Mao bore a superficial resemblance to Stalinism, it actually had a far more creative and central role in the Maoist state. Like Hitler, Mao loved politics as theatre. The *décor* of his regime was far more striking and original than Stalin's lacklustre imitations of Nazi pomp. He drew on and transformed the majesty of the imperial era. The crowds were trained to greet him with the ritual chant 'Boundless life to Chairman Mao'. Like the emperors, he ploughed a symbolic annual furrow, used the Imperial City for his residence and gave calligraphic instructions for monuments.[15] But to this he added a sun-culture of his own, reflected in his hymn 'The East is Red', which he imposed on China as a second national anthem:

> From the Red East rises the sun:
> There appears in China a Mao Tse-tung.

His round, sun-like face appeared on huge posters; and, like the sun, he appeared at dawn to inspect a million Red Guards in the summer of 1966.

These occasions, of which there were eight within a few weeks, allowing the sun to shine on over 11 million people, strongly resembled the Nuremberg rallies. The Red Guards rhythmically chanted Maoist slogans, while Lin Piao (rather like Goebbels) called out the litanies: 'Beat down the capitalist roaders in power! Beat down the reactionary bourgeois authorities! Sweep away all wicked devils and evil spirits! Do away with the Four Old Things: old thought, old culture, old customs, old habits. The Thought of Mao Tse-tung must rule and transform the spirit, until the power of the spirit transforms matter!' (18 August 1966).[16] Mao's thought was 'the sun of our heart, the root of our life, the source of our strength', 'his thought is a compass and spiritual food', it was 'like a massive cudgel swung by a golden monkey', a 'brilliant beam of light' exposing 'monsters and goblins', a series of 'magic mirrors to detect demons', and he himself was 'the source of all wisdom'. The Revolution and its achievements were (in a manner of speaking) a gigantic thought-form of Mao's, since 'all our victories are victories of the Thought of Mao Tse-tung'.[17]

The *Little Red Book* played a similar role to *Mein Kampf* and, like Hitler, Mao used military drill, massed bands and *son et lumière* to produce illusion and hysteria. For his 1966 rallies, 1,000-piece bands played 'The East is Red', and a film of the ninth National Congress of the CCP in 1969 showed delegates, holding the *Little Red Book* aloft, jigging up and down in frenzy, tears rolling down their cheeks, yelping and baying like animals, in the Great Hall of the People.[18] The virulently abusive language Mao and his henchmen used to evoke violent and intolerant activism was very reminiscent of Hitler's anti-Semitism.

The most important respect in which Mao recalled Hitler was in his imminent eschatology. Mao was, above all, a violently impatient man. He lacked the unhurried stoicism with which Stalin remorselessly pursued his objectives and his hatreds. Mao, like Hitler, wanted to speed up history. He thought his successors would prove poltroons and faint-hearts and that unless things were done in his own lifetime, they would not be done at all. He always heard time's winged chariot at his back, and his impetuosity found expression in his complementary and insatiable love of drama. In a sense, Mao never made the transition from revolution to administration. He lacked Stalin's bureaucratic appetite. For him, history was a cosmic play, a succession of spectacular episodes, in which he was actor, impresario and spectator. No sooner had the curtain come crashing down on one scene – 'the Long March', say, or 'the Fall of the KMT' – than he clamoured for it to rise again and the action to recommence, faster and more furious than before.

Hence Mao's reign was a lurid melodrama, sometimes degenerating into farce but always, in the deepest sense, a tragedy: for what he caused to be enacted was not theatre but a gigantic series of experiments on hundreds of millions of real, living, suffering people. The first drama after the defeat of the KMT seems to have occurred towards the end of 1950. Initially, the land reform introduced in the south under the law of 1949 was not radical. A speech of Lin Piao's as late as 14 June 1950 applied the brakes. The benevolent term 'prosperous middle peasant' replaced 'rich peasant' and new categories of 'enlightened gentry' and 'small landlords' were coined to keep efficient farmers in business.[19] Then the coming of the Korean War gave Mao the pretext for his first post-war cataclysm. In 1951 and still more in 1952–3, the land reform was continually accelerated and conducted with great savagery. There was 'the Three-Antis campaign', quickly followed by 'the Five-Antis campaign'. On 21 February 1951 new 'Regulations regarding the punishment of counter-revolutionaries' provided death and life-sentences for a wide range of 'crimes'. All major towns held mass rallies at which social 'enemies' were publicly denounced and sentenced. Over a few months, nearly 30,000 such meetings were held in Peking alone, attended by 3 million people. The papers published long lists of names every day of executed 'counter-revolutionaries'. In October 1951 it was stated that 800,000 cases had been dealt with in the first six months of the year (Chou En-lai later said that 16.8 per cent had received death-sentences, which would mean 135,000 executions, or 22,500 a month, a high rate even by Stalin's worst standards). The total number of killed during this first post-war drama of Mao's may have been as high as 15 million, though a figure of 1 to 3 million is more likely.[20]

This gigantic piece of social engineering was also accompanied by Mao's first shot at mental engineering, or brainwashing, which he termed 'thought reform'. It was designed to replace traditional family piety with filial piety to the state as the central moral value of the nation and to elevate Mao into a substitute father-figure.[21] Mao defined 'thought reform' (23 October 1951) as a vital precondition for 'the thoroughgoing democratic transformation and the progressive industrialization of our country'. He set up a nationwide 'Movement for the study of Mao Tse-tung's Thoughts'; those who rejected them were branded as 'Westerners' and 'reformed' in prison, often shackled for varying periods with heavy, painful irons.[22] The drama, however, embraced not only the victims of the 'land reform' and those who criticized the way it was done. Many of the total of eight 'Antis' were directed at merchants, industrial managers and bureaucrats: the campaign in fact embraced virtually the whole nation.

Like all Mao's successive dramas, it fizzled out as he lost interest or confidence in its results, or as the disastrous consequences became apparent in lower agricultural productivity and famine. But by 1955 Mao's impatience was rising again. In a speech of 31 July 1955 he suddenly announced a speed-up in the rate of collectivization of farms and the abrupt nationalization of all commerce and industry still in private hands. He called 1955 'the year of decision in the struggle between socialism and capitalism'.[23] This campaign, too, was to change mentalities: the 'poor peasants' would acquire 'control' and then 'strengthen unity' with the 'middle peasants', even the 'upper-middle peasants', against the 'infiltration' of 'counter-revolutionaries', 'rascals' and 'devils'. Disappointed by the response, Mao produced with equal suddenness his 'Let a hundred flowers bloom' policy in 1956, to persuade a variety of voices to speak out. As he put it, 'Correct ideas, if pampered in hot-houses without exposure to the elements or immunization against disease, will not win against wrong ones.' Khrushchev took the view that the whole 'hundred flowers' episode was a mere 'provocation'. Mao merely 'pretended to be opening wide the floodgates of democracy' to 'goad people into expressing their innermost thoughts', so he could 'destroy those whose thinking he considered harmful'.[24] At all events the campaign was brutally reversed without warning. 'Rightist elements' were sent to work-camps; professors who had briefly 'bloomed' found themselves cleaning lavatories; and in 1957 the tentative protections of 'socialist legality' were withdrawn.[25]

These confused events, or abortive mini-dramas, should be seen against the background of Mao's increasing dissatisfaction with the policies of Stalin's successors in Moscow. He had disliked and disagreed with Stalin: his reaction to Stalin's death was to instigate the suicide or murder of Kao Kang, the Stalinist agent and head of the State Planning Committee, in February 1954. But he objected strongly to 'deStalinization' as an attempt to blame collective mistakes on the character of a single man. He thought Khrushchev's 'secret session speech' repudiating Stalinism of 1956 a hypocrisy.

The others, Khrushchev included, had been up to their necks in Stalin's crimes. How did Khrushchev, he demanded, see his role 'when he beats his breast, pounds the table and shouts abuse at the top of his voice'? Was he a 'murderer' and a 'bandit' himself? Or merely a 'fool' and an 'idiot'?[26] Mao was clearly afraid that the Moscow campaign against 'the cult of personality' might be used against himself. More fundamentally, however, he felt that the sheer intellectual poverty of the new Moscow leadership strengthened his claim, now Stalin was dead, to the pontifical primacy of the bloc. He determined to astound the comrades, east and west, by the sheer audacity of his next move, and in September–October 1957 announced the new drama of the Great Leap Forward, which was launched with tremendous publicity the following spring.

The Great Leap was perhaps the purest expression of Mao's chronic impatience, his belief in mind over matter, his confidence that, granted the will, the age of miracles was not over. He wanted to move to Communism in one bound, even to the stage when the state would 'wither away'. He projected his itch to telescope history onto the peasants: they were 'poor and blank', and this was 'a good thing – poor people want change, want to do things, want revolution. A clean sheet of paper has no blotches and so the newest and most beautiful words can be written on it.'[27] As a piece of social engineering, the Leap was reckless and impulsive even by Mao's standards. He justified it by arguing that Stalin had walked 'only on one leg' – that is, he created industrial and agricultural areas, each separate and monoped. China would begin 'walking on two legs', moving directly to self-reliant communes (modelled historically on the Paris Commune of 1870), each with its own industrial, agricultural and service sectors and its own defence militia: 'unity of work and arms'.[28]

The scale and speed of this experimental theatre was almost beyond belief. In January–February 1958, then after a brief pause to sort out the confusion, between August and December, about 700 million people (90 per cent of the population) had their economic, political and administrative life completely transformed. In Henan Province, for instance, 5,376 agricultural collectives were knocked into 208 large 'people's communes' with an average of 8,000 households in each. These units were expected to be virtually self-supporting and, in particular, to produce their own steel. It was a case, as Khrushchev put it, of Mao 'acting like a lunatic on a throne and turning his country upside down'. He said that Chou En-lai came to Moscow and admitted that the Chinese steel industry was in a mess as a result. A.F.Zasyadki, deputy-chairman of the State Planning Commission, was sent out to investigate. He reported to

Khrushchev that the Soviet-trained steel engineers were now being forced to work in agriculture and the steel industry was 'a shambles'. The steel mill he visited was 'in the charge of an old man'. All Russia's equipment, money and effort was being wasted.[29] Khrushchev seems to have concluded that Mao was another Stalin and worse; a madman who would wreck his country and blow up the world if he had the means. The Great Leap therefore led directly to the end of Russia's technical assistance programme (including nuclear weapons) in 1959 and to the open admission of the Sino–Soviet breach the following year at the Romanian Party Congress, when Khrushchev denounced the Chinese leadership as 'madmen', 'pure nationalists' who wanted to unleash a nuclear war.

In China itself the Great Leap movement came to a juddering halt on 23 July 1959, Mao ringing down the curtain with an abrupt 'The chaos caused was on a grand scale, and I take responsibility'.[30] But the consequences of the drama had their own irresistible momentum. Nineteen-fifty-nine was a year of natural disasters, and combining with the unnatural disaster of the Great Leap produced a man-made famine on the scale of Stalin's catastrophe in the early 1930s, which lasted till 1962.[31] To this day outsiders do not know exactly what happened to Chinese agriculture during these terrible years. The steel industry was wrecked and had to be rebuilt virtually from its foundations. Agriculture was yet again reorganized by a return to co-operatives and a fall in the size of commune units to 2,000 households. But the crops and livestock lost were lost for good. People just starved. How many millions died from the Leap is a matter of conjecture: figures are not available.

The Great Leap disaster seems to have exhausted a large portion of the political capital Mao had banked with his colleagues during the successful revolutionary war. He never held the supreme and solitary power of a Hitler and a Stalin, both because of the intractable nature of China's problems, her lack of centralization and modern communications, and because he never possessed a terror apparatus on the same scale as the KGB or the Gestapo-ss. The party was more regionalized than in Russia; in particular, there was a profound polarity between the conservatism of Peking and the radicalism of Shanghai. After the curtain came down on the drama of 1959, Mao eschewed histrionics for a while; he seems to have been 'resting'. From this point dated the beginning of 'the two-line struggle', with 'revisionists' temporarily on top. They never again allowed Mao to touch the productive process directly, either in agriculture or in heavy industry. Instead he brooded on culture and education. He had always disliked mandarinism and the cultural establishment. In a sense, he hated 'civilization' as much as Hitler did. In China it represented not the international Jewish conspiracy but the dead hand, the insufferable, insupportable weight of a 4,000-year past. In this respect his revolution appeared to have changed nothing – and it was because of this cultural failure, he reasoned, that the Great Leap had proved impractical.

By 13 February 1964 Mao was making ominous noises: 'The present method of education ruins talent and ruins youth. I do not approve of reading so many books. The method of examination is a method of dealing with the enemy. It is most harmful and should be stopped.'[32] Nine months later he betrayed unmistakable signs of impatience and a hankering for a new drama: 'We cannot follow the old paths of technical development of every country in the world, and crawl step by step behind the others. We must smash conventions . . . when we talk of a Great Leap Forward, we mean just this.'[33] Thus the Leap was transmuted from a physical to a mental one: by the beginning of 1965 Mao's interest in brainwashing had revived and was to be the dominant feature of his next and greatest drama.

By this point China was effectively run by a triumvirate: Mao himself, the head of state Liu Shao-chi, in charge of the Party and in particular of the Peking apparatus, and the army head, Lin Piao. Mao chose to open the new play indirectly, by pushing onto centre-stage his film-actress wife, Chiang Ching. She was well cast for the star role in what was soon termed the 'Cultural Revolution'. It was characteristic of Mao's romanticism that he always had a soft spot for actresses. He had had an affair, for instance, with the famous Lily Wu. His then wife, Ho Tzu-chen, found out, brought an action and got a divorce at a special Central Committee court, which then banished both women.[34] In 1939 Mao married Chiang Ching, who had acted in Shanghai in the 1930s under the stage name of Lan Ping. According to her account, she went into the profession at the age of thirteen, became a party member at nineteen, and was twenty-three when Mao sought her out in Yenan, by offering her a free ticket to a lecture he was giving at the Marxist–Leninist institute.[35] But other versions make her older and say she was married three if not four times in 1930s Shanghai, had numerous affairs in the film world and acquired many hatreds and enmities.

Chiang Ching kept, or was kept, very much in the background for the first twenty years of her marriage. There is a deep-rooted suspicion of the scheming political wife in China, what might be called the 'Dowager Empress syndrome'. In the early 1960s it was considered remarkable that Wang Kwang-mei, the wife of the head of state, Liu, should dress fashionably, wear pearls and even dance (she had been born in the USA) while accompanying her husband abroad, and this may have excited Chiang's jealousy. She herself became the centre of a group of disgruntled pseudo-intellectuals, failed writers and minor actors and film-directors, mainly from Shanghai, who wanted to take over the arts and radicalize them. There was a certain party mandate for their 'line'. In 1950, following the Zhdanov cultural purges in Soviet Russia, an 'opera reform bureau' was set up in China, drawing its inspiration from a theatre group founded at the Red Army Academy in 1931 and the so-called 'Chinese Blue Blouse Regiment' which used impromptu theatre to project ideology from mobile stages. In 1952 the Peking People's Art Theatre was set up to produce 'modern' didactic drama.[36] But little came of this. Well into the 1960s, Chinese classics remained dominant and many independent theatres flourished, performing Ibsen, O'Neill, Shaw, Chekhov and using the Stanislavsky method.[37] Chiang's own group, the League of Left-Wing Dramatists, found it difficult to get their works performed and was even suspected of Trotskyism.[38] She seems to have brought to the Chinese scene, already envenomed by the bitter sectarian factionalism inherent in Marxist–Leninist politics, the spirit of the theatrical vendetta.

She got her breakthrough in June–July 1964 when the frustrated Mao allowed her to put on the Festival of Peking Opera on Contemporary Themes in the Great Hall of the People. This consisted of thirty-seven new operas (thirty-three on the Revolution, four on earlier revolts), performed by twenty-eight proletarian companies from nineteen provinces. Even more surprisingly, Mao allowed her to deliver a speech, the first by a woman since he took power. She said there were 3,000 professional theatrical companies in China, including ninety supposed to be dealing with 'modern' drama. Nevertheless, the Chinese stage was dominated by old themes, heroes and heroines, 'by emperors, princes, generals, ministers, scholars and beauties, and on top of these, ghosts and monsters'. There were 'well over 600 million workers, peasants and soldiers in our country' as opposed to 'only a handful of landlords, rich peasants, counter-revolutionaries, bad elements, Rightists and bourgeois'. Why should the theatre serve these few and not the 600 million? She recommended for universal performance certain 'model operas', such as *Raid on the White Tiger Regiment* and *Taking Tiger Mountain by Strategy*.[39] None of this went down well in Peking, the repository and guardian of Chinese culture. Its mayor and party boss, the ultra-mandarin Peng Chen, called her operas 'still at the stage of wearing trousers with a slit-seat and thumb-sucking'. Everyone disliked her burgeoning habit of phoning her opponents and critics in order to 'struggle with them'. When she asked Peng to give her an opera troupe 'to reform on my own' and showed him a new revolutionary opera with which she proposed to reform it, he flatly refused, snatched the score from her hands and challenged her 'to take up a strong position if she pleased'.[40]

Her strong position was to persuade Mao to leave Peking and spend most of 1965 in Shanghai. There a number of themes came together in his head: hatred of Soviet Russia and its leadership, and of the new class of bourgeois bureaucrats who had frustrated his Great Leap, the longing of an elderly hero to appeal to the young again, his contempt for formal education, his loathing for the people who flourished by virtue of mandarinism, his jealousy of Liu. Liu's book, *How to be a Good Communist*, sold fifteen million copies 1962–6, as many as Mao's books at that time. Official editorials urged the comrades to study Liu on a par with Mao. The two men had quarrelled violently over the reasons for the failure of the Leap.[41] Thus to the suppressed ambitions of a failed actress were added the grievances of an injured author. Mao gave up reading the Peking *People's Daily*, turning instead to the forces paper, *Liberation Army Daily*. He was gearing up for another dramatic explosion. He observed grimly to André Malraux: 'I am alone with the masses – waiting.' To the sycophantic French ambassador, who told him youth was with him, Mao retorted: 'The things you saw represented only one side of the situation – you didn't see the other side.' He told a group of Albanians that the new privileged élite in Russia had sprung first from literary and artistic circles and the same was happening in China: 'Why are there so many literary and artistic associations in Peking? They have nothing to do . . . army performances are the best, local troupes rank second and those from Peking are the worst.' Official culture groups, he said to a group of planners, were 'just transplants from the Soviet Union . . . all ruled by foreigners and dead men'. Peking's Academy of Sciences was 'fairyland', stuffed with 'antiquarians' who 'read unreadable journals'.[42] He would rely on the earthy, peasant army. He broke its chief of staff, Luo Rui-qing, for alleged pro-Soviet activities. He built up its head, Lin Piao, against Liu and his Peking 'clique'. The shape of things to come was his permission to Chiang Ching to convene in Shanghai a 'Forum on Work in Literature and Art in the Armed Forces'. Before it took place, a nervous Lin held a briefing of senior officers:

> She is very sharp politically on questions of literature and art . . . . She has many opinions which are valuable. You should pay good attention to them and see that they are applied ideologically and organizationally. From now on, all the army's documents concerning literature and art should be sent to her.[43]

Having lined up the army behind himself, Mao went over to the attack. The actual detonator to what soon became known as the

'Cultural Revolution' was personal pique – Mao's reaction to a play, *Hai Jui Dismissed from Office*, actually written in 1961 by Wu Han, Deputy-Mayor of Peking, and another official mandarin.[44] It was about an upright Ming-dynasty official who disagreed with the Emperor's land policy and was unjustly punished for being frank. When Mao finally saw it he could not but regard it as a clear attack on himself, plainly inspired by Liu and all the more galling in that the agricultural disasters for which he was thus publicly blamed had undeniably occurred. His attack was launched with a review of the play in the Shanghai daily, *Literary Currents*, 10 November 1965. Back in Peking near the end of the year, he saw the Soviet premier, Alexei Kosygin, and sneeringly asked him if Soviet Russia would come to China's help if America attacked her over the Vietnam War: Kosygin had no answer. But Mao admitted to him frankly that he was at loggerheads with his colleagues. Indeed he made little attempt to conceal the coming explosion. Back in Shanghai early in the new year, he snarled at Teng Hsiao-ping and other senior colleagues (who had travelled down from Peking) in front of an amazed delegation of Japanese Communists, addressing them as 'You weak-kneed people in Peking' for being 'soft on Russia'. The Japanese 'cringed in amazement'.[45]

From that point on, the Cultural Revolution gathered momentum. Mao (as he later put it) 'gave the nod'. In February 1966 Lin, now Chiang Ching's firm if apprehensive ally, appointed her 'Cultural Adviser' to the entire army forces. The obnoxious mandarin Mayor of Peking was dismissed and moved, along with Liu, into the shadows, though the two men, Teng and others were not arrested until the next year. On 20 March Mao, the old wizard, decided to conjure the brutal force of unlettered youth out of the earth. 'We need determined people who are young, have little education, a firm attitude and the political experience to take over the work', he said. 'When we started to make revolution, we were mere twenty-three-year-old boys, while the rulers of that time ... were old and experienced. They had more learning – but we had more truth.'[46] On 16 May, Chiang Ching, now the leading spirit in a group of activists, mainly from Shanghai, whom Mao had officially designated as in charge of the Cultural Revolution, issued her first circular. It attacked 'scholar-tyrants' who had 'abstruse' language to silence the class struggle and keep politics out of academia, using the fallacy 'everyone is equal before the truth'. Its sixth point was an open invitation to vandalism: 'Chairman Mao often says that there is no construction without destruction. Destruction means criticism and repudiation – it means revolution.' The *People's Daily* and other Peking papers refused to print it. Two days later Lin Piao made a remarkable speech about power to the Politburo, analysing the history of *coups d'état*. Echoing Goebbels, he argued that force and propaganda were irresistible in conjunction: 'Seizure of political power depends upon gun-barrels and inkwells.' And what was power for? 'Political power is an instrument by which one class oppresses another. It is exactly the same with revolution and with counter-revolution. As I see it, *political power is the power to oppress others.*'[47] That was frank enough; and, coming from the man who was supposed to be in charge of the nation's stability, it might well make the men round the table tremble. Even worse news was that the man in charge of the secret police, Kang Sheng, had thrown in his lot with the cultural revolutionaries. That meant there would be no restraint on the new 'gun-barrels and inkwells', which in the second half of May rapidly made their appearance, in the shape of Red Guards and wall-posters.

Scholastic violence and political change had long been linked in China. The student revolt in Peking had detonated the 4th May Movement in 1919 and the 9th December Movement in 1935. There had been a similar upsurge during the 'hundred flowers', eventually put down (by Teng and Liu, among others, eagerly reacting to Mao's 'nod') with the sacking of 100,000 teachers in 1957–8.[48] But this was something on an altogether different scale. With a population of 800 million, China now had 90 million children in primary schools, 10 million in middle schools and 600,000 in university.[49] The first Red Guards appeared on 29 May. They were from the middle school, aged about twelve to fourteen, wearing red cotton armbands with the characters 'Hung Wei Ping' (Red Guards) on them in yellow. Their first act was to attack Tsinghua University.[50] Soon they were joined by children from younger and older age-groups, by students and, most important, by members of the CCP Youth Leagues who, with Mao's encouragement, revolted against their official leadership and took to the streets in gangs. During the early summer, the entire educational system in China came to a standstill, as dons and teachers fled in terror (when they were lucky enough to escape capture and 're-education') and juvenile lynch-law took over.

There was later some misunderstanding of the Cultural Revolution in the West. It was represented as a revolt of intellectuals. In fact it was quite the reverse. It was a revolution of illiterates and semi-literates against intellectuals, the 'spectacle-wearers' as they were called. It was xenophobic, aimed at those who 'think the moon is rounder abroad'. The Red Guards had a great deal in common with Roehm's Brownshirts, and the entire movement with Hitler's campaign against 'cosmopolitan civilization'. It was the greatest witch-hunt in history, which made the Zhdanov purges in post-war

Russia seem almost trivial. Nevertheless, it is significant that this great upsurge of vandalism attracted a certain type of radical academic, who was to become depressingly familiar in Europe and North America over the next few years. At Peking, the first 'big-character poster', addressed to and attacking the university authorities, was put up by a woman philosophy don, Nieh Yuan-tzu, who was to become the Madame Defarge of the campus horrors. It read: 'Why are you so afraid of big-character posters? This is a life and death struggle to counter the Black Gang!' Within a week, 10,000 students had put up 100,000 posters, 'as big as doors', often with characters four feet high.[51] The phrases were reiterated: 'You absolutely won't get away with this . . . our patience is exhausted.' The first violence began at the same time. The rampaging street-gangs seized girls with long braided hair and cut it short; boys with foreign-style stove-pipe pants had them ripped off. Hairdressers were told not to give 'duck-tail' cuts, restaurants to simplify menus, shops to stop selling cosmetics, dresses with slit skirts, sunglasses, fur-coats and other finery. Neon signs were smashed. There were huge street bonfires of forbidden goods, which included (as an exhibition of 'confiscations' showed) bolts of silk and brocade, gold and silver bars, chess-sets, ancient trunks and chests, playing-cards, mah-jong sets, gowns, frock-coats, top-hats, jazz records and a vast range of works of art. The Red Guards shut down teashops, coffee-houses, independent private theatres and all private restaurants, they put itinerant musicians, acrobats and strolling actors out of business, and they forbade weddings and funerals, holding hands and kite-flying. In Peking the ancient walls were pulled down, Bei Hai Park and the National Gallery of Fine Arts closed. Libraries were ransacked and shut, books burnt. Even when libraries remained open, few dared to visit them. Ten years later, Teng said that of the eight hundred technicians of the Research Institute for Non-ferrous Metals, for example, only four had the courage to use the library during the Cultural Revolution; he said that any of the 150,000 technical cadres of the Academy of Sciences who visited their laboratories during this dark time were denounced as 'white specialists'.[52]

There was no authority to prevent these activities. When shop-keepers and other injured parties sought police protection, they were reminded of 'The Decision of the Central Committee of the Chinese Communist Party Concerning the Great Proletarian Cultural Revolution' (1 August 1966), which read: 'The only method is for the masses to liberate themselves . . . trust the masses, rely on them and respect their initiative . . . . Don't be afraid of disturbances . . . . Let the masses educate themselves . . . no measures should be taken against students at universities, colleges, middle and primary schools . . . .'[53] In fact party leaders who sought to curb the Red Guards were paraded through the streets wearing dunces' caps and placards. Every single school superintendent seems to have been dismissed.

As the movement got under way, violence became common, then universal. Red Guard leaders seem to have come from the lowest social strata.[54] Some of them were mere street-thieves and hooligans, sporting thick leather belts with brass buckles. Their posters urged 'Boil him in oil', 'Smash his dog's head' and so on. Men and women classified as 'ghosts and monsters', 'bad elements' and 'counter-revolutionaries' had their heads shaved. Snippets of 'political debates' were later reported: 'Of course he is a capitalist. He has a sofa and two matching armchairs.'[55] Hundreds of thousands of private homes were broken into and ransacked for such reasons. But Red Guards raided government offices too, and forced officials to give them their archives on pain of being denounced as 'tools of the revisionists'. The Foreign Ministry was taken over by a gang led by Yao Teng-shan, a former petty official. He recalled every ambassador except one, stripped them of rank and assigned them to minor tasks. His notes to foreign powers, written in the style of Red Guard posters, were politely returned with the request that future communications be signed by Premier Chou. But Chou himself, normally the still centre of Chinese life through all Mao's dramas, seems to have been in danger at one stage. While it is true that, at the very top level, the Red Guards were not allowed to kill anyone, many died in gaol. Liu himself was left to die (1973) in his own excrement, naked on the freezing floor of his concrete cell.[56] But at a lower level the loss of life was catastrophic. The Agence France Presse, in the most widely respected figure, estimated (3 February 1979) that the Red Guards had murdered about 400,000 people.

Meanwhile Chiang Ching had been ruling the world of culture and addressing mass meetings at which she denounced capitalism (which she said destroyed art), jazz, rock and roll, striptease, Impressionism, Symbolism, abstract art, Fauvism, Modernism – 'in a word, decadence and obscenity, to poison and corrupt the minds of the people'. Her platform oratory was modelled on that of the secret police boss, Kang Sheng, with whom she often appeared. 'Do you want to study the Communiqué and the Sixteen-Point Directive?' 'Yes.' 'Do you want to study them again and again?' 'Yes.' 'Do you want to learn them thoroughly?' 'Yes.' 'Do you want to understand them?' 'Yes.' 'Do you want to apply them?' 'Yes.' 'Do you want to use them to carry out the Cultural Revolution in your school?' 'Yes, Yes, Yes!'[57] During the second half of 1966, virtually every main cultural organization in China was brought under her army organization. All her old scores against the theatre and film world, some dating from the 1930s, were worked off. Leading directors, playwrights, poets, actors and composers were accused of 'fawning on foreigners', praising 'secondary foreign devils', 'ridiculing the Boxers' (now seen as cultural heroes), and portraying ordinary Chinese as 'prostitutes, opium smokers, jugglers and women with bound feet', thus breeding a 'national inferiority complex'. The Red Guards were ordered by her to 'dig up the roots of the Black Line', 'rip off the masks', destroy films, songs and plays of the 'national defence line' and 'drag out' members of the 'Black Gang'.

On 12 December 1966 many 'public enemies', the ex-mayor of Peking and leading cultural mandarins – including, it seems, every film and theatre director who had ever crossed Chiang Ching – were marched to the Workers' Stadium in front of 10,000 people, with heavy wooden placards round their necks.[58] One of the worst aspects of the Cultural Revolution was the treatment of wives, who were often more brutally humiliated than their husbands. On 10 April 1967, for instance, Liu's wife was dragged in front of 300,000 people on the campus of Tsinghua University, dressed in a tight evening gown, with stiletto-heel shoes, an English straw hat and a necklace of ping-pong balls decorated with skulls, while the mob bayed, 'Down with ox-devils and snake-gods!'[59]

Chiang Ching's squads took over radio and TV stations, newspapers and magazines; they seized cameras and films, ransacked studios for evidence, confiscated all existing films and issued them re-edited, and impounded scripts, prompt-copies and musical scores. Painters no longer dared to sign work with their own name but instead used the slogan 'Ten Thousand Years to Chairman Mao'.[60] 'With hammer in hand', said Chiang Ching, 'I set out to attack all the old conventions.' She attended rehearsals of the Central Philharmonic Orchestra and interrupted them, goading the conductor Li Te-lun into a furious shriek 'You're attacking me with a big hammer!' She made composers write works which were then tried out on 'the masses' and altered to take account of their reaction. She claimed she had to 'hit them with a hammer' to make them obey and eliminate 'foreign influences'.[61] Some of her followers took her imagery literally, and one Western-trained concert pianist had his hands smashed. Hammers, fists, thumping and smashing were the emblems of revolutionary art. Taking over the ballet, Chiang Ching banned 'orchid fingers' and upturned palms, favouring instead clenched fists and violent movements to show 'hatred of landlord class' and 'determination to seek revenge'.[62]

Having banned virtually all forms of artistic expression in 1966, Chiang Ching strove desperately to fill the void. But not much was produced: two orchestral works, the Yellow River piano concerto and the Shachiaping symphony, four operas and two ballets, all eight classified as *yang-pan hsi* or 'model repertory', on the analogy of model farms. There was a sculpture series called The Rent-Collectors' Courtyard and a few paintings, of which the best known was a portrait of Mao wearing a blue gown, investigating mining conditions in the early 1920s, which was 'composed' by a collective of Peking students and actually painted by the son of a 'poor peasant'. Few films were made because (she later claimed), there was 'sabotage'; her actors, actresses and directors were given 'bad dormitories', no hot meals and power was cut off from her stages and film-sets.[63]

After the heady days of 1966, when Mao did his swim and the cult of his personality reached its apogee, China began to lurch into civil war. On 5 February 1967, Mao's protégés in Shanghai set up a 'commune', an indication he was still hankering after the Great Leap policy. It was based upon the dockers, especially the militant 2,500 of the Fifth Loading and Unloading District, who in a single day (in June 1966) had written and put up 10,000 big-character posters. Of this district, 532 workers resisted. They had posters written against them and were made to wear tall dunces' hats and carry opprobrious posters with mysterious slogans such as 'Four-Family Village' and 'Anti-Party Clique'; they also had their houses ransacked and were sentenced to 'symbolic' death sentences, which might easily become real ones.[64] The Shanghai commune was supposed to detonate others across the country. But the workers did not rise. Indeed they often resisted Red Guard invasions of their factories. Even in Shanghai the city authorities fought back with their own Scarlet Guards. Each side had enormous banks of loud-speakers, whose slogans battled it out deafeningly from dawn to dusk: 'The February seizure of power is illegal', 'The February seizure of power is admirable'. There were kidnappings, torture and gang-warfare, using bicycle chains and knuckle-dusters, 'troops' being rushed from one part of the city to another.

At the universities, private armies were formed. The 'Chingkanshang regiment' of Tsinghua University, an 'élite group' of the Far Left, fought pitched battles against 'ghosts and monsters' using bamboo spears and home-made armoured cars and cannon. Other units included the Five-One-Six, the New Peita commune, the Geological Institute's 'East is Red' commune, and the 'Sky' faction of the Aeronautical Institute. These were imitated in the factories and the non-university towns, and a kind of feudal anarchy began to develop, as China lurched back into organized gang-warfare and war-lordism. In July 1967 there was a 'mutiny', as it was called, in Wuhan, actually a large-scale battle between a Red Guard workers' force and a conservative group known as the Million Heroes. The local army commander backed the Heroes. Chou En-lai was sent down to restore peace. He was lucky to escape with his life and two of his companions were arrested and tortured. As a result, Chiang Ching produced the slogan 'Offend by reason and defend by force', and quantities of arms were issued to Red Guard groups.[65]

The violence seems to have reached a climax in the late summer of 1967. As that point Mao, as usual, became both alarmed at what he had done and bored with the incessant wrangling. He seems to have told Chiang Ching to call it all off. In September she announced that violence must be verbal only; machine-guns were to be used only when 'absolutely necessary'. Those who disobeyed were accused of 'mountain-strongholdism'. Attacks on the British Embassy and its staff were the work of 'ultra-Leftists instigated by the May Sixteenth clique'.[66] Mao also took a hand. 'The situation developed so rapidly as to surprise me,' he told the Central Committee. 'I cannot blame you if you have complaints against me.' He was annoyed that the Foreign Minister, Chen Yi, had lost twenty-seven pounds during a Red Guard grilling, adding, 'I cannot show him to foreign visitors in this condition.' He told the 'young firebrands' and 'little devils' to go back to school. He broke the Shanghai commune. 'China is now like a country divided into eight hundred princely states,' he complained.[67]

In the autumn of 1967 Mao withdrew official support for the Cultural Revolution, at any rate in its active Red Guard form, and used the People's Liberation Army (PLA) to restore order and take over from groups he now denounced as 'incompetent' and 'politically immature'. He justified this use of force by remarking, 'Soldiers are just workers and peasants wearing uniforms.' Fighting continued in some places in 1968, but in diminishing volume. In the summer, at his home in South-and-Central Lakes, he had a curious 'dawn dialogue' with Red Guard leaders: 'I have never made any tape recordings before, but I am doing it today. Otherwise you will interpret what I say today in the way you wish after you go home . . . . Too many people were arrested, because I nodded my head.' Police Minister: 'I am the one to blame for excessive arrests.' Mao: 'Don't try to free me from my mistakes or cover up for me.' Chen Boda (left-wing theorist): 'Follow the Chairman's teaching closely.' Mao (snappish): 'Don't talk to me about teachings.' Later he threatened that if Red Guards fought the army, killed people, 'destroyed means of transportation' or 'lit fires', they would be 'annihilated'. But he was unwilling to drop his anarchism entirely: 'Let the students fight for another ten years. The earth will revolve as usual. Heaven is not going to fall.' All the same, the five chief Red Guard leaders were soon at work on pig-farms deep in the countryside.[68] The drama was over.

The years which followed the collapse of the Cultural Revolution, when the bill for it was being paid by the economy and ordinary Chinese, were grim. Someone had to take the blame. On 12 September 1971, a Trident aircraft crashed 250 miles beyond the Chinese border in the Mongolian People's Republic. It contained the bodies of the PLA commander, Lin Piao, and his second wife, Yeh Chun. Everyone on board was dead and some of the corpses were riddled with bullets. According to Peking, Lin had been fleeing after the discovery of a plot of his to murder Mao. 'Captured documents', in which Mao was referred to by the code-name 'B-52', were produced, proving that Lin had sought to kill Mao in a traffic-accident, poison his food, use the air force to bomb his house, and blow up his train. He had written: 'B-52 is a paranoid and a sadist ... the greatest dictator and tyrant in China's history .... Those who are his greatest friends today will be his prisoners tomorrow .... Even his own son has been driven mad by him.' The plot was allegedly betrayed to Chou En-lai by Lin's daughter by an earlier marriage, 'Little Bean', who hated her stepmother.[69] A more plausible version had it that Lin had been killed some time before by his colleagues, at a meeting in the Great Hall of the People – a real-life revolutionary drama this time. The next year a major plot was 'exposed' within the army, and a score of senior officers tried to escape to Hong Kong. A great many books and documents in which Lin had had a hand were recalled, together with his 'epitaphs' and portraits. Eleven famous photos of Mao, with Lin on them, were withdrawn. The episode, about which the truth remains obscure, closed with a note in the Chinese press, 20 February 1974, revealing that 'Little Bean' had been shot to death near Canton, a strip of red cloth pinned to the body reading 'Treason and heinous crime'.[70]

By this time the Mao era was drawing to its close. Chou was already suffering from cancer, Mao himself from Parkinson's Disease. His last phase was marked by acrimony, consciousness of failure and confusion. He quarrelled with Chiang Ching and by 1973 they had ceased to live together. She had to submit in writing requests to see him, stating her reasons. A note from him to her dated 21 March 1974 read: 'It is better not to see each other. You have not carried out what I have been telling you for many years. What is the good of seeing each other any more? You have books by Marx and Lenin and you have my books. You stubbornly refuse to study them.' He told her her 'demands' had injured his health. 'I am already eighty years old. Even so you bother me by saying various things. Why don't you have sympathy? I envy Chou En-lai and his wife.' What must have frightened her as much was the reappearance of her enemy Teng, back from the dead and thereafter known as 'Lazarus'; he told journalists he had been at 'reform school' in Jiangsi Province. In 1975 Mao produced his final slogan, 'Three Mores and One Less': 'Chou should rest more, Teng should work more, Wang should study more and Chiang Ching should talk less.' He appended a maxim: 'The ears are made so as to remain open but the mouth may shut.'[71]

Sometimes, in his last period, Mao was perky: 'People say that China loves peace. That's boasting. In fact the Chinese love struggle. I do for one.' He kept his hatred of formal education: 'The more books one reads, the stupider one becomes.' On the other hand, just before his death he received a report on the education system from the head of Qinghua University, who had been purged by Chiang Ching, then rehabilitated. Mao told him to speak only for three minutes. He was told, grimly: 'Thirty seconds will be enough. College students study the textbooks of secondary schools, and *their* academic level is that of primary schools.' Mao (sadly): 'If this situation goes on, not only will the Party fail, but the nation itself will perish.'[72] His mind wandered between religious and secular belief. 'My body is riddled with diseases. I have an appointment with God.' On another occasion he asked colleagues: 'Are there not some of you who thought I would go to see Marx sooner?' 'None.' 'I don't believe it.'[73] His last saying was enigmatic: 'The people do not support the reversals of verdicts.'

The watershed year of 1976 opened an era of opaque confusion. Chou died early in April. This discreet mandarin, much respected abroad, who kept himself curiously detached from the failures and murderous squalor of the regime, seems to have been the only member of it to have aroused genuine popular feelings in China. When, on 5 April, the authorities removed wreaths placed in his memory in Peking's main square, 100,000 people rioted. Teng was immediately blamed for this disturbance and disgraced for the second time. Mao died on 9 September. During the last months of his life there was intense faction-fighting around his bedside. As soon as he was dead, Chiang Ching claimed a reconciliation had taken place. She produced a bit of paper which she claimed was a poem Mao had written to her *in extremis*: 'You have been wronged,' it said. 'I have tried to reach the peak of revolution but I was not successful. But you could reach the top.'[74]

However, another bit of paper was waved by Hua Kuo-Feng, who had succeeded Chou as premier. Hua was then fifty-five, a relative newcomer, having been on the Central Committee only since 1969 and Minister of Public Security since the previous year. He was almost a 'helicopter', a term more usually applied to Chiang Ching's fast-rising protégé Wang Hung-wen, now the party boss of Shanghai.

Mao liked Hua partly because he was a peasant from his favourite province, Hunan, chiefly because he was cunningly sycophantic. On 30 April the old tyrant had scratched out for Hua six characters: 'With you in charge I have no worries.' Hua's bit of paper was undoubtedly authentic. In any case he had more impressive credentials: control of the top security unit in Peking, Number 8341, which protected Mao himself and which Hua had inherited from the old security boss Kang Sheng, who had died in December 1975.

The showdown came on 6 October, a month after Mao's death, at a Politburo meeting held in the home of his old comrade Yeh Chien-ying, the Defence Minister and effective second man of the regime. Chiang Ching was present with Wang and two other leading Shanghai cronies. She brandished her paper and demanded the chairmanship for herself, with her 'brains', the Shanghai journalist Chang Chun-chiao, as premier, and Wang as head of the National People's Congress. But the 'Gang of Four', as henceforth they were known, lost the 'argument', and were taken straight from the meeting to prison. In Shanghai, their stronghold, their followers planned to arm 30,000 leftist militia-members, but the local party leadership and the garrison commander were removed before anything decisive could be done. Hua had the security services and Chiang Ching had made herself much hated in the army.[75] She may have had a following in Shanghai but in Peking the mob loathed her and called her 'the Empress', a term of abuse since Boxer days; the 5 April riot had been directed against her and her friends. It was unfortunate for her, too, that 1976 was a year of appalling natural disasters, which the Chinese associate with a change in the dynasty. In April the largest meteor ever recorded fell on Kirin Province. In July and August three earthquakes hit north China, destroying parts of Peking and the whole of the nearby industrial centre of Tangshan, killing about 665,000 people (775,000 more were injured) – the second-worst earthquake disaster in China's history.

It was a simple matter to blame such things, and genuine man-made catastrophes – economic failure, the collapse of the education system, the destruction of art treasures and China's cultural life – upon the malign influence of 'the Empress' and her gang. Soon posters were up: 'Cut Chiang Ching into Ten Thousand Pieces', 'Deep-fry the Gang of Four in Oil'. For her trial in 1980–1, the eventual indictment ran to forty-eight pages. All four were accused of an astonishing variety of crimes, and each separately of specific acts of wickedness, vanity and extravagance – the last to emphasize that their puritanical reign of terror had been hypocritical. Chang had even been 'a spy in the pay of Chiang Kai-shek'. Wang was accused of philandering, importing expensive stereophonic equipment and, only four days before his arrest, having no less than 114 photographs taken of himself. Yao Wen-yuan, the fourth member of the gang, had spent $500 on a sumptuous banquet to celebrate Chou's death. Chiang Ching herself had drunk saffron water, dined off golden carp, kept an entire truckload of pornographic films, including the notorious *Sound of Music*, which she watched every night, ridden a horse then changed into a limousine, taken out library books on empresses, said that 'Even under Communism there can still be an Empress', closed a Canton shipyard because the noise disturbed her, prohibited planes landing so she could get to sleep, called the Empress-Dowager 'a legalist', had diverted traffic, ordered the leaves in Canton to be dusted before she arrived, said 'it is better to have socialist trains which run late than revisionist trains which run on time', hastened Mao's death by shifting him from one bed to another, played poker while he lay dying and said, 'The man must abdicate and let the woman take over.' She and the others were 'bad eggs' who 'worshipped things foreign, fawned on foreigners and maintained illicit foreign relations' and had 'engaged in flagrant capitulationism and national betrayal'. They were 'the evil lords of literature and the theatre'.[76] Chiang Ching remained defiant throughout her seven-week trial, which ended early in 1981, even extracting further drama from the proceedings at one point by suddenly stripping naked.[77] She was found guilty on all charges and condemned to death, sentence being provisionally suspended for two years.

By this time Hua himself was in the shadows, elbowed aside by Teng, old Lazarus himself, who had re-emerged into public life in 1977 and from the end of 1978 was clearly in charge. He was a rough, hard man from Szechuan, with something of Mao's own coarse brutality but without a suspicion of romanticism or any interest in politics as an art-form. Teng had been the most consistent opponent of Mao's political dramas, though he had sometimes been obliged to play bit-parts in them. He had spoken out grittily and often against the excesses of the Cultural Revolution. Now that it was disavowed and punished, his emergence at the top was logical and perhaps inevitable. He despised people for whom politics was the only thing in life that mattered, especially the hard Left: 'They sit on the lavatory and can't even manage to shit.' 'One should not talk of class struggle every day. In real life, not everything is class struggle.' He had nothing but contempt for proletarian art. 'You just see a bunch of people running to and fro on the stage. Not a trace of art . . . . Foreigners clap them only out of courtesy.' Having heard the Vienna Philharmonic Orchestra, he said, '*This* is what I call food for the spirit.' Chinese operas 'nowadays', he added, were nothing more than 'gong-and-drum shows'. 'You go to a theatre and you find yourself on a battlefield.' Teng had no particular animosities: 'Let bygones by bygones. Those dismissed from office should be reinstated.' He said he wanted an end to the 'shouting and yelling'. The country must get back to work again. 'Most college students now carry nothing but one brush for all posters. They can't do anything else.' 'Scientists today are not given time for research. How can they create or invent things?' Not least, the army was demoralized, as in Chiang Kai-shek's day, and liable to revert to war-lordism. It had become 'thick-skinned, disunited, arrogant, lazy and soft'.[78]

Teng, in short, was an old-fashioned, reactionary disciplinarian, now in his late seventies, who believed in law and order and hard work. He promptly sent the army into Vietnam, partly to punish the Vietnamese pro-Soviet leadership for persecuting its Chinese minority, but mainly to teach the PLA that life was a serious business: undisciplined units were put in the van and suffered appalling casualties. That done, he set about clearing up some of the mess Mao's long reign had left behind in the economy. It was now admitted publicly that the Mao era had been characterized, not by the puritanical austerity of which it had boasted, but by appalling corruption in high places.[79] The Peking People's Daily apologized to readers for 'all the lies and distortions' it had carried and, more remarkably, warned them against 'the false, boastful and untrue reports' which it 'still often prints'.[80]

In 1978–9 decisions were taken to move away from a Stalinist–Maoist stress on heavy industry and towards an economic structure more suited to a semi-developed country. The percentage of GNP invested was to fall from the unsustainable 38 per cent of 1978 to about 25 per cent by the mid-1980s. Profit-motives and bonuses were to be introduced; the law was to be reformed with emphasis on civil rights; democratic means were to be devised to check bureaucratic abuse; above all, market forces were to be allowed to exert their beneficent force.[81] The party was to cease to be the all-powerful force in national life. Its membership, 39 million in 1982, had apparently doubled in size during the Cultural Revolution, and Teng warned that many of these people had not been properly 'educated' and were 'below standard'. In a report issued in spring 1981, he claimed that many party members 'loved flattery', were 'complacent and fuzzy-minded', had stopped 'caring about the hardships of the masses', were 'covered in the dust of bureaucracy' and were 'arrogant, conservative, lazy, interested only in pleasure and imbued with an ideology of privilege'.[82] The 'new realism' coincided with more natural disasters, including a drought which dominated agriculture in 1980 and 1981 and forced a proud regime to beg the West for help. As the 1980s opened, therefore, China ceased to be the miraculous new superpower and finally rang down the curtain on the make-believe world of Maoist romanticism, which had ended in horrific melodrama. Instead it entered the real world of slow, painful and pragmatic progress.

Mao's regime in China was a tragedy. But it did not always seem so at the time, at least to the outside world. During the 1950s and 1960s it was fashionable to contrast his authoritarian centralism, which had given China unity, stability and (it was asserted) steadily rising living-standards, with the ineffectiveness of Indian parliamentary democracy. As we have seen, the Nehru era in world affairs, when he appeared the leading international statesman, the one most attuned to the needs of the times, was based on a series of illusions, the most important of which was his belief that India and China, the two most populous nations, could act together, what he termed *Hindi-Chini-Bhai-Bhai* (India and China brothers). The policy was undermined by the first India–China conflict in 1959 and collapsed in ruins during the far more serious Chinese invasion of 1962. For Nehru, now seventy-three, it was an unrelieved personal disaster and he never recovered from it. When he died in his sleep in May 1964, he was a sad and bewildered man.

With large, overpopulated, poor and industrially backward countries like India and China, the chief problem of state is an elementary one: how to preserve the integrity of the state? How to maintain any system of government the bulk of the population will respect and acknowledge? Equally, the chief temptation of government is to bolster its popularity by taking advantage of its neighbour's misfortunes. Mao succumbed to this urge in 1959 and 1962, taking advantage of India's weakness and division. It intensified India's difficulties, though in the long run it did nothing to lessen his own.

From the moment of partition in 1947–8, both India and Pakistan were cast as mutual enemies. For a quarter of a century, economists have continued to debate whether British rule hastened or impeded India's economic progress.[83] Nehru had believed unquestioningly that 'Most of our problems today are due to . . . arrested growth and the prevention by British authority of normal adjustments.'[84] But this was to ignore the main British contribution of imposing unity on the sub-continent and preventing the 'normal adjustments' of disintegration. British rule had been a progressive process of economic integration. Partition marked the first stage in its reversal. The internal conflicts within Pakistan, especially between its east and west wings, and comparable strains between Indian central government and the provinces, suggested that a fate like China's in the 1920s was only just round the corner. Pakistan showed an inherent tendency towards war-lordism in the shape of ephemeral military dictatorships. India evinced a contrary preference for weak parliamentary rule.

When Nehru died, a group of Congress Party and provincial bosses, known as 'the Syndicate', ganged up to prevent the succession of his most formidable follower, Morarji Desai. The man they picked instead, Lal Badahur Shastri, seemed to symbolize impotence. He was known as 'the Little Sparrow' and was so small that he only came up to the bottom of General de Gaulle's paunch. In the autumn of 1965 India and Pakistan drifted into war over Kashmir. Militarily it was inconclusive; economically, immensely destructive to both sides. It was settled by a meeting between the Pakistan dictator, Marshal Ayub Khan, and Shastri at Tashkent in January 1966, and the effort so exhausted the Little Sparrow that he died the following night.

Bewildered, the Congress bosses turned to Nehru's daughter, Mrs Gandhi, who had served as Shastri's Minister of Information. Many Hindus believed she was her father reincarnated, and shouted *Jawaharlal ki jai* ('Long live Nehru!').[85] She kept five Irish wolfhounds, each bigger than her predecessor, and there was nothing small or weak about her. With China hostile, she saw India's future as linked to a Soviet alliance, and took the country towards the Left. In 1969 she quarrelled with Desai, her Finance Minister, sacked him, nationalized the banks, smashed up the old Congress Party and created a new one around her personal faction. She broke the financial power of the princely class, and when the Supreme Court ruled her actions unconstitutional, she dissolved parliament in March 1971 and won an overwhelming victory, taking 350 out of 525 seats.

Yet Mrs Gandhi, calculating and unscrupulous behind her hooded kestrel eyes, had no more grasp of economic realities than her father, and like him turned to foreign affairs for relief. She found the answer in the growing distress of Pakistan. The two wings had never had anything in common except the Muslim religion, and fear of Hindu India. The country was ruled from the west, and this was reflected in an increasing disparity of *per capita* income: in the west it rose 1959–67 from 366 to 463 rupees, in the east only from 278 to 313. Although the bulk of the population lived in the east (70 out of 125 million in the late 1960s), and produced most of the country's exports, the west got the imports. It had five to six times the power production of the east, and 26,000 hospital beds to 6,900 in the east.[86] It was one of the many grievances of the east wing that the Pakistani government had taken no effective flood-control measures in the Bay of Bengal. On the night of 12 November 1970 a cyclone struck the area, producing one of the greatest natural disasters of the century. A fifty-mile-wide wave swept inland, drowning hundreds of villages, turned itself into an ocean of mud, then swept out again, carrying with it hundreds more: over 300,000 people lost their lives.

The effect was to inspire the East Pakistan leader, Sheikh Mujib Rahman, to demand a federal system, and he won elections on this programme. The Pakistan government sent out General Tikka Khan, known as 'the butcher of Baluchistan' from his activities in the west wing, as martial law administrator, with instructions from the current dictator, Yahya Khan, 'to sort those fellows out'. On 25 March 1971 he unleashed his troops on Dacca University, and the next day Mujib proclaimed an independent Bangladesh Republic. India could probably not have kept out of the civil war in any case, for by mid-1971 there were 10 million refugees in her territory. But Pakistan resolved Mrs Gandhi's dilemma by launching a pre-emptive strike on Indian air bases. On 4 December she declared war, India recognized Bangladesh, and invaded the east wing. For the Indian Army it was an easy campaign, ending in Pakistani surrender. The Indian Commander-in-Chief and the Pakistani commander in the east wing had been at the Sandhurst military academy together. The former sent the latter his ADC with a message: 'My dear Abdullah, I am here. The game is up. I suggest you give yourself up to me and I'll look after you.'

The victory over Pakistan was the high tide of Mrs Gandhi's career. Thereafter events moved against her. The friendship with Bangladesh did not last long. As an independent power it soon became a natural ally of Pakistan. Her own regional problems multiplied, exacerbated by the natural disasters which broke up Pakistan. In 1972 the monsoon failed, bringing drought and then famine. In 1973 the security forces in Uttar Pradesh mutinied. She had to turn to the army and take over the state. The following year she had to put down a revolt in Gujarat, and take that over too. The same year, in Bihar, she used the Border Security Force and the Central Reserve Police against dissenters led by her father's old colleague Jayaprakash Narayan, who employed the Gandhi-like tactics of a *gherao*, or peaceful blockade, of the state parliament, and a *bundh*, or enforced closure, of shops and offices. All the disruptive and regional opposition forces in the nation began to congregate together in a new Janata Front, and in 1975 Narayan led demonstrations throughout India, threatening to set up *Janata Sarkars* (people's governments) all over the north. At the same time Mrs Gandhi ran into trouble over electoral offences with the high court, which declared her 1971 election void. This was precisely the combination which destroyed British India: concerted agitation to make normal administration impossible, and the difficulty of controlling it within the framework of the rule of law.

As an exponent of ruthlessness, Mrs Gandhi was more than a match for any viceroy. In Bihar alone she sent in 60,000 police and paramilitaries to break up Narayan's *gherao*. She met a rail strike with mass arrests without warrants. Since the Pakistan war she had benefited from a State of External Emergency, but this did not enable her to ignore or reverse court verdicts. On 25 June 1975 she stopped the newspapers and arrested Narayan, Desai and most of her other opponents. The next day she declared a State of Internal Emergency, in effect a *putsch* by the government against the opposition. She invited her frightened party leaders to her house to put some courage into them. She said: 'Do you know the famous proverb, "When the great eagle flies under the stars, the small birds hide"?' Then, turning to one MP, she asked fiercely: 'What was that proverb? Repeat it!' Petrified, he replied: 'Madam, when the great evil fries under the stars, the small birds hide.'[87]

Since independence India had clung tenaciously to democracy and had drawn condescending comparisons with militaristic Pakistan. One reason why Mrs Gandhi dabbled in authoritarianism was that she felt she had to compete with the populist demagoguery of Zulfikar Ali Bhutto. Bhutto was a professional politician, thrust into power as an alternative to military incompetence after the Bangladesh débâcle. He ruled Pakistan with considerable *éclat*, mainly by bending all the regulations in his favour, firing judges, suppressing newspapers and fiddling with top army appointments.[88] But, precisely because Bhutto was a civilian, Mrs Gandhi felt she could not desert parliamentarianism completely. The result was that the emergency period was a succession of *ad hoc* arrangements, without any real chain of command or clear legal responsibilities, answerable to the courts: the perfect formula for cruelty and corruption. Many thousands of political activists were held in prison, often in horrible conditions. They included prominent people, such as the dowager queens of Gwalior and Jaipur, and Snehalata Reddy, the socialist daughter of a famous film-producer, who died from her experiences. George Fernandez, who had organized the rail strike, went underground, but his brother was arrested and tortured.

Even before the emergency Mrs Gandhi had been faced with many charges of corruption, especially against her son Sanjay, and in the lawless confusion the decay of Indian public life spread rapidly. She now made Sanjay head of the Youth Congress and put him in charge of the more radical aspects of her birth-control schemes, which since 1970 she had considered the most important of all India's domestic programmes. Sanjay and his friends took the opportunity to engage in social engineering on the Maoist model. He brutally moved slum-dwellers from Delhi's open spaces to the outer suburbs and, more important, set up huge sterilization camps in which hundreds of thousands of Indian males were, by a combination of bribes and bullying, subjected to vasectomy operations carried out under the most primitive conditions. With the press and radio curbed, Indians had to turn to the BBC to discover what was happening in their own country. Since, by her own admission, Mrs Gandhi did not listen to the BBC ('the BBC had always been hostile to me'), she was often ill-briefed herself.[89] When Bhutto announced elections for March 1977, she felt she had to compete and hold one herself, believing (from the reports of sycophantic regional officials) that she could win and so legitimize her emergency. The results, in fact, were disastrous for both of them. Bhutto won handsomely, but the uproar over the way in which this was achieved led in turn to martial law and another military *coup*. He was charged with conspiracy to murder and, after two long and controversial trials, was hanged in April 1979.[90] Mrs Gandhi lost the elections and her seat, dragged down by Sanjay's social engineering and a multitude of other liabilities.

The victorious Janata Party, however, was not so much an alternative to Gandhiism as a coalition of the discontented. Its most considerable figure, Desai, had many of Gandhi's vices and none of his virtues. He did not drink or smoke and loudly asserted that the British had introduced liquor and tobacco to corrupt the natives. He made great play with his spinning-wheel. He declined the use of modern medicine. To keep himself fit he drank a glass of his own urine every morning. The Health Minister, Raj Narain, also believed in the urine treatment and commended it officially. Asked about birth-control, he said that women should eat herbs to prevent pregnancy. Such eccentricities were unaccompanied by solid administrative gifts or probity. Indeed Janata rule was even more corrupt than Mrs Gandhi's Congress Party. Attempts to conduct a Commission of Inquiry into her misdeeds or to bring her to trial (she spent a week in gaol) merely stirred up an immense sea of mud which flung itself in all directions. Returned to parliament at a by-election, then expelled, she was able to reverse the roles and present herself as the victim of persecution, making inspired use of the 1939 hit by the Lancashire singer Gracie Fields, 'Wish me luck as you wave me goodbye' – a weird instance of the survival of colonial 'values'.[91] At the election of 3 January 1980 the Indians were faced by a choice between familiar evils, and their instinct led them to vote for the nearest thing they knew to a royal dynasty. Mrs Gandhi won by a landslide, her party taking 351 seats out of 524. The 1977 result was a verdict against tyranny even at the risk of chaos; that of 1980 a vote against chaos even at the risk of tyranny again.

The history of post-independence India tended to stress the intractable nature of the problem Britain had faced: how to keep the peace among a vast and enormously diverse collection of peoples while preserving constitutional and legal safeguards? Nehru's assumption that the problem would ease after independence proved wholly unfounded. In fact it grew steadily more difficult, not least because population doubled during the next generation. According to government calculations, it was 683,810,051 in January 1981.[92] Under the pressure of these heaving masses, the structure of civil liberties created under British rule began to subside, though it never collapsed completely. Mrs Gandhi's emergency was, however, an important stage in this decline. Effective civil control over the police and the security forces was not re-established. Order of a sort was maintained, but more by terror than by justice. In November 1980, the press revealed that in the state of Bihar the police systematically used acid and bicycle spokes to blind suspects. Some thirty authenticated cases were brought to light. The following January, cases were reported from the holy city of Benares of police breaking the legs of men in custody.[93] The police were also accused of murder in their efforts to put down dacoitry, and their use of torture became a matter of frequent censure by the judiciary. As a judge of the Allahabad High Court put it: 'There is no better organized force for crime in India than the Indian police.'[94]

What made such savagery particularly detestable was that it appeared to reflect the bias of caste. The boast of British rule was that, while unable to eliminate caste, its worst consequences were mitigated by the British principle of equality before the law. It had been Churchill's great fear, his principal reason for resisting rapid independence, that the lower castes would be its principal victims, just as the higher castes (especially Brahmins like the Nehrus) were its undoubted beneficiaries. The most reprehensible aspect of police atrocities was that the police themselves, and still more the politicians who protected them, came from higher castes while, in almost every case, their victims were low-caste. Independence did nothing for the 'untouchables', who numbered over 100 million by the beginning of the 1980s. Their token representation in parliament and government was itself an aspect of their exploitation. Their way of life, their capacity to survive at all, remained a mystery, the least explored corner of Indian society.[95] There were many indications that police terror, to which authority seemed increasingly indifferent, was a form of social control rooted in the infinite gradations of privilege.

More than half the human race lives in the great mainland nations of Asia. By the 1980s the Chinese population alone had passed the 1,000 million mark. All, since securing independence or escaping foreign tutelage, engaged in 'social' experiments. China opted for Communism, including collectivized agriculture and the total nationalization of industry. Burma chose one-party socialism, consolidated from 1962 by a further layer of military control under General (later President) Ne Win. Pakistan under Bhutto carried through a sweeping programme of nationalization. Both Pakistan and India kept out market forces by high tariff barriers. India's predominantly socialist economy was planned with a conventional, Stalinist stress on heavy industry, and even its substantial and vigorous private sector was subjected to intense regulation, made bearable only by ubiquitous corruption. After a generation, the results in each case were depressingly similar and meagre. These powers viewed each other with varying degrees of hostility, though China and Pakistan were in an uneasy alliance dictated by their common hatred for India. China made her first nuclear weapons in 1964, India in 1974, Pakistan in 1978. All these nations (including Bangladesh, the poorest) spent a much higher proportion of their GNP on defence than during the colonial period. In Burma, for instance, chiefly on account of Chinese backing for Communist rebel groups, military spending by 1980 absorbed one-third of the budget and almost all foreign exchange earnings.[96] In every case, the high hopes raised by the Bandung generation, of a sudden and spectacular attainment of Western-style living standards, against a background of peace and non-alignment, had been abandoned by the end of the 1970s.

In the late 1940s, the Asian half of the human race had been told that there was a direct, immediate and essentially political solution to their plight. Experience exposed this belief as a fallacy. There were strong grounds for concluding, indeed, that politics, and especially ideological politics, was a primary contributor to human misery. No better illustration could be provided than the grim entity covered by the words the Calcutta Metropolitan District, in and around which were grouped 150 million of the poorest people on earth. Even in colonial times it inspired administrative horror. Kipling, with his customary prescience, called it the 'City of Dreadful Night'. 'It had', he wrote, a peculiar attribute, 'the BCS or Big Calcutta Stink'.[97] In the early 1940s it was becoming difficult for the municipal authorities, leaving politics aside, to keep even most of the city properly sewered. Partition dealt the city a blow from which it never recovered. It wrecked the economy of large parts of Bengal, pushing 4 million virtually unemployable refugees into the western half, one million into Calcutta itself. Between the 1921 and 1961 censuses, the population had trebled and the effort to run standard modern services had been abandoned.

By the end of the 1960s, an observer wrote that most of the District 'is without municipally organized sewerage systems, without piped water, drains or sewers, and even without privately owned means of sewage disposal, like septic tanks'. There were about 200,000 primitive communal lavatories, 'low, cramped open brick sheds with platforms above earthenware bowls or dirt floors'.[98] As we have noted, the Bangladesh crisis tipped another 10 million homeless people into Indian Bengal, a great proportion of whom ended up on the streets of Calcutta, so that by the late 1970s a million souls were sleeping in the open in the city centre alone. The fiercely partisan and doctrinaire politics of West Bengal, run by Marxists in the 1960s and 1970s, when not under constitutional suspension and direct 'presidential rule', generated limitless improvidence and corruption.

Calcutta's plight attracted many voluntary workers, who joined the efforts of Mother Teresa and her Missionaries of Charity, who had set up their stations in Calcutta in 1948. But often the Marxist government seemed more anxious to drive out volunteer medical bodies, who drew attention to its failures, than to tackle the problem at its root.[99] Calcutta became the realized anti-Utopia of modern times, the city of shattered illusions, the dark not the light of Asia. It constituted an impressive warning that attempts to experiment on half the human race were more likely to produce Frankenstein monsters than social miracles.

SEVENTEEN

The European Lazarus

If post-war history took the new nations of Africa and Asia down a series of blind alleys, often terminating in horror and savagery, Europe's experience offered more comfort. This was unexpected. The prevailing mood in 1945 was despair and impotence. The European era in history was over. In a sense Hitler had been the last truly European leader, able to initiate world events from a Euro-centric vision. He lost that power at the end of 1941. The vacuum opened by his colossal fall could not be filled by European rivals. At the end of the war, the two non-European superpowers stood, as it were, on the rim of a spent volcano, peering contemptuously into its still smouldering depths, uninvolved in its collapse but glad it no longer had the daemonic energy to terrify humanity.

On 26 October 1945, at the opening of the new ballet at the Théâtre des Champs-Elysées, the drop-curtain by Picasso was hissed by the packed high-society audience.[1] That was the old Paris. Three days later, at the Club Maintenant, Jean-Paul Sartre delivered a lecture, 'Existentialism is a Humanism'. Here was the new Paris. This occasion, too, was packed. Men and women fainted, fought for chairs, smashing thirty of them, shouted and barracked. It coincided with the launching of Sartre's new review, Les Temps modernes, in which he argued that literary culture, plus the haute couture of the fashion shops, were the only things France now had left – a symbol of Europe, really – and he produced Existentialism to give people a bit of dignity and to preserve their individuality in the midst of degradation and absurdity. The response was overwhelming. As his consort, Simone de Beauvoir, put it, 'We were astounded by the furore we caused.'[2] Existentialism was remarkably un-Gallic; hence, perhaps, its attractiveness. Sartre was half-Alsacian (Albert Schweit-zer was his cousin) and he was brought up in the house of his grandfather, Karl Schweitzer. His culture was as much German as French. He was essentially a product of the Berlin philosophy school and especially of Heidegger, from whom most of his ideas derived. Sartre had had a good war. Despite the surface enmities, there was a certain coming together of the French and German spirit. Paris was not an uncongenial place for an intellectual to be, provided he could ignore such unpleasantnesses as the round-up of Jews, as most contrived to do without difficulty.[3] As the Jewish intellectual Bernard-Henri Levy was later to point out, radical, proto-fascist forms of racialism were rarely repugnant to the French, not least to French intellectuals: he even called it 'the French ideology'.[4]

The Paris theatre flourished under the Nazis. André Malraux later snarled: 'I was facing the Gestapo while Sartre, in Paris, let his plays be produced with the authorization of the German censors.'[5] Albert Büssche, theatre critic of the Nazi forces' newspaper, *Pariser Zeitung*, called Sartre's play *Huis Clos* 'a theatrical event of the first order'. He was not the only beneficiary of German approval. When a new play by the *pied-noir* writer Albert Camus, *Le Malentendu*, was presented at the Théâtre des Mathurins on 24 June 1944, it was hooted by the French intellectual élite (then largely fascist) because Camus was known to be in the Resistance. Büssche found it 'filled with profound thoughts ... a pioneering work'.[6] Camus did not share Sartre's aloofness to the war; he was in fact one of only 4,345 Frenchmen and women who received the special Rosette of the Resistance medal. But his thinking reflected the growing contiguity of French and German philosophy which the Occupation promoted and which was an important strand in the post-war pattern. The most important influence in his life was Nietzsche, whom in effect, through his novels *L'Étranger* and *La Peste*, he gallicized for an entire generation of French youth.

Sartre and Camus came together in 1943–4, protagonists – and eventually antagonists – in a cult centred on St Germain-des-Prés which sought to relate philosophy and literature to public action. Their caravanserai was the Café Flore, itself a symbol of the ambiguities of French intellectual life. St Germain had been a haunt of Diderot, Voltaire and Rousseau, who had congregated in the old Café Procope. The Flore dated from the Second Empire, when it had been patronized by Gautier, Musset, Sand, Balzac, Zola and Huysmans; later by Apollinaire and later still by the circle of *Action Française*, led by Maurras himself: Sartre occupied his still-warm seat.[7] Existentialism in its post-war presentation was derived from Kant's 'Act as if the maxim of your action were to become through your will a general natural law'. Our positive acts, Sartre taught, created 'not only the man that we would like to be ourselves' but also 'an image of man such as we think he ought to be'. Man could shape his own essence by positive political acts. He thus offered a rationalized human gesture of defiance to despair – what Karl Popper called 'a new theology without God'. It contained an element of German pessimism, characteristic of both Heidegger and Nietzsche, in that it placed exaggerated emphasis upon the fundamental loneliness of man in a godless world, and upon the resulting tension between the self and the world.[8] But for young people it was magic. It was a form of Utopian romanticism with much the same attractions as the Romantic movement 150 years before. Indeed it was more attractive because it offered political activism too. As Popper complained, it was a respectable form of fascism which, needless to add, could easily be allied to forms of Marxism. Camus insisted he was never an Existentialist, and in 1951 he and Sartre quarrelled mortally over the latter's defence of various forms of totalitarian violence. But it was Camus's re-creation, in modern terms, of the solitary Byronic hero, who resists fate and an alien world by defiant acts, which brought the cult so vividly to life and gave it actual meaning to youth on both sides of the Rhine.

Thus Existentialism was a French cultural import, which Paris then re-exported to Germany, its country of origin, in a sophisticated and vastly more attractive guise. The point is worth stressing, for it was the first time since the age of Goethe, Byron and De Stael that young people in France and Germany felt a spontaneous cultural affinity, a shared *Weltanschauung*. It served, then, as a preparation for a more solid economic and political harmonization, for which circumstances were also propitious. Yet this might not have come about but for two further circumstances. The first was the final (and possibly terminal) maturing of Christian activism in politics, which for a vital generation became the dominant mode in Europe. The second was the emergence of a group of European titans – not Byronic, not young, not romantic, not indeed heroic in any obvious still less Existentialist sense – who were to revivify the corpse of a Europe which had slain itself. Both the agency, Christianity, and the agents, Adenauer, de Gasperi, de Gaulle, were by nature abhorrent to the founders of Existentialist activism. But then history habitually proceeds by such ironies.

Adenauer, de Gasperi, de Gaulle were great survivors; men whose turn failed to come, might never have come, then did come by gift of catastrophe and in rich plenitude. At the end of the war in 1945, Alcide de Gasperi was sixty-five, Adenauer sixty-nine. Both were men from the borders, devout Catholics, anti-nationalists, men who revered the family as the social unit, hated the state (except as a minimal, regrettable necessity), and believed the most important characteristic of organized society to be the rule of law, which must reflect Natural Law, that is the ascendancy of absolute values. In short they set their faces against many of the salient features of the twentieth century. And theirs were obstinate faces; strange faces. A terrible accident in 1917 had given Adenauer's the mahogany impassiveness of a cigar-store Indian.[9] De Gasperi, like Adenauer, tall and excessively thin in youth, faced life with the scowl of a guard-dog. Both were confederalists. Adenauer represented the poly-centrist Germany of the Holy Roman Empire, de Gasperi the northern Italy of the Habsburgs.

De Gasperi, indeed, was born under Austrian rule. As his father commanded the local gendarmes, he felt a secular loyalty to a royal house rather than to a nation state. But his primary allegiance was spiritual. Throughout his life he went to Mass every day if possible. In the remarkable letter proposing marriage to his future wife, Francesca Romani, in 1921, he wrote: 'The personality of the living Christ pulls me, enslaves me and comforts me as though I were a child. Come, I want you with me, to be drawn to that same attraction, as though to an abyss of light.'[10] He went to Vienna University and admired the city's famous mayor, Karl Lueger, though for quite different reasons to Hitler. He believed Lueger had indicated ways in which the 'social encyclicals' of the more progressive popes could be realized. His formation was thus German Catholic populism and his earliest writing was in the Austrian Catholic paper, the *Reichspost*. De Gasperi, indeed, was almost immune to the two great diseases of modern times: ethnic national-ism and the belief that states based upon it can be transformed into Utopias. In his first speech, made in Trento in 1902, he urged his listeners: 'Be Catholic first, then Italian!' He said he 'deplored' the 'idolization' of the nation and the *religione della patria*. His motto was 'Catholic, Italian, then democratic!' – in that order.[11]

Hence de Gasperi was the natural antipode to Mussolini. The two men debated 'Socialism in History' in a Merano beer-hall in 1909, Mussolini urging the need for violence, de Gasperi the necessity for basing political action on absolute principle. He had to leave early to catch a train, followed to the door by Mussolini's fluent jeers. 'He called de Gasperi: 'A man of slovenly, ungrammatical prose, a superficial man who invokes an Austrian timetable to avoid an embarrassing debate.'[12] De Gasperi, for his part, never recognized in Mussolini anything except a destructive radical: 'Bolshevism in black', as he put it. His own *Partito Popolare Trentino* was welcomed by Don Luigi Sturzo into the Catholic Popular Party, which might have ruled inter-war Italy but for Mussolini's *putsch*. De Gasperi disliked Italian parliamentary politics ('an equestrian circus'), with their theatricals and oratorial tricks, which he always spurned. But he hated the big totalitarian state still more. As he said at the last *Partito Popolare* National Congress, 28 June 1925: 'The theoretical and practical principles of fascism are the antithesis of the Christian concept of the State, which lays down that the natural rights of personality, family and society exist before the State.' Fascism was just 'the old Police State reappearing in disguise, holding over Christian institutions the sword of Damocles'. Hauled before a fascist tribunal in November 1926, he insisted: 'It is the very concept of the fascist state I cannot accept. For there are natural rights which the state cannot trample upon.'[13] De Gasperi was lucky. Mussolini threw him into the Regina Coeli prison in 1927. He might not have survived the regime any more than Gramsci. But the signature of the Lateran Treaty in 1929 enabled Pius XI to get de Gasperi out of custody and into the Vatican library, where he was sheltered for the next fourteen years.

Hence when fascism collapsed, de Gasperi was the only unsullied major figure to offer the Italian people an alternative to it which was not another form of statism. He formed the first post-war coalition government in December 1945, and in the elections to the Constituent Assembly took his new Christian Democratic Party to the front with 35.2 per cent (against 20.7 for the Socialists and 18.9 for the Communists). His real breakthrough came in January 1947, when the Social Democrats, under Giuseppe Saragat, split from the Marxist socialists under Pietro Nenni. This enabled de Gasperi to form a homogeneous Christian Democratic government, which won the first, crucial elections under the new constitution, in April 1948, with 48.5 per cent of the votes and an absolute majority of the seats (304 out of 574). This was one of the most important of the post-war European elections, for it set a pattern of relative stability in Italy for a generation. During the 'de Gasperi era', 1945–53, Italy achieved political respectability as a centrist member of European society, accepted the Marshall Plan, entered NATO, joined the Council of Europe and the European Coal and Steel Community and launched its own economic *miracolo*, symbolized by the Vespa, Emilio Pucci colours, Pininfarina car-bodies, Necchi sewing-machines and Olivetti typewriters, and by the morning greeting in the power-house of industrial recovery, Milan – '*Buon' lavoro!*'

De Gasperi's success undoubtedly helped to pave the way for Konrad Adenauer in Germany. Both men constituted possible alternatives to the inter-war totalitarian regimes of their countries. As we have seen, Adenauer might have become Chancellor in 1926. But he did not think he could have made a success of it. Weimar and the chancellorship were held in low esteem and in his view its problems were insoluble. He was out of sympathy with the prevailing wisdom in Germany. He was not a Rhineland separatist – he was a federalist rather – but he had absolutely no confidence in any 'German genius'. 'Germans are Belgians with megalomania,' he insisted. The Prussians were the worst: 'A Prussian is a Slav who has forgotten who his grandfather was.' He used to say: 'Once the night-train from Cologne to Berlin crossed the Elbe, I got no more sleep.'[14] Under Weimar, the Mayor of Cologne was the unofficial head of the German Catholic community and that was enough for Adenauer. He had no trace of German racial feeling, no particle of respect for the Bismarckian state. What had it given German Catholics? The miseries of the *Kulturkampf*. Hitler dismissed him on 13 March 1933, and he was lucky not to be killed along with Schleicher under cover of the Roehm purge. He thought Hitler was insane to go to war and bound to lose it. According to his youngest daughter, Libeth Werhahn, the family prayed for defeat.[15] He did not believe in a German resistance and had no complaints about the Allied unconditional surrender policy, which he thought necessary.

Adenauer's post-war career illustrates the importance of luck in politics. When the Americans took Cologne it had practically ceased to exist. Population had fallen from 750,000 to 32,000; André Gide, visiting the ruins, was so horrified he immediately asked to be driven away. It was Allied policy to restore those (if available) who had held office until the Nazis sacked them. So the Americans put Adenauer back in charge of the city. A few months after it became part of the British zone, he was sacked and expelled (October 1945), for reasons which were never satisfactorily explained.[16] No doubt Britain, now under a Labour government, favoured Social Democrats where possible. British administrators saw Germany as united and disarmed, mildly socialist, with industry taken out of the hands of such men as Krupps and nationalized. The education and political branches of the British military government were staffed with socialist-leaning officers, who ensured that Social Democrats ran the radio, the news-agency and quasi-official papers like *Die Welt*.

Backing the Social Democrats was the first of many serious errors in British foreign policy towards Europe. It meant putting their money on the SPD leader, Kurt Schumacher. A tragic victim of the past, he had only one arm and was soon to have a leg amputated; his incessant pain made him bitter, excitable, impatient and often unreasonable. He was in many ways the opposite to Adenauer: a Prussian, a Protestant, a believer in a big state, a 'big' Germany.[17] He refused to grasp that his vision for Germany depended essentially on Soviet agreement to reunification: it would not work for the truncated Western zones. Equally important, he refused to see (and the British with him) that the real alternative to Hitlerian Germany, something which would get the poison out of the system, was not a reconstruction of Bismarckian Germany on Social Democratic lines, with an all-powerful paternalist state, a Leninist centralized direction of nationalized industry, a huge, Prussian-style bureaucracy and a stress on equality, uniformity and collectivity. That was the formula the Russians chose for East Germany, and all it produced was a radicalized version of the Nazi state, the sort of version Goebbels (and Hitler in his final stage) would have favoured. The real antithesis to National Socialism was individualism, a society where private arrangements took priority over public, where the family was the favoured social unit and where the voluntary principle was paramount.

These were precisely the ideals in which Adenauer believed with life-long conviction. As a member, then the patriarch, of a vast, close and ramifying family, he had come to regard it (as many millions behind the Iron Curtain were also discovering) as the one reliable refuge from totalitarian invasion. Of course it could be destroyed utterly – Hitler had indeed wiped out entire Jewish families – but it could not be corrupted and perverted. Even if it lost many of its members, it closed ranks and re-formed itself with remarkable fortitude, as the Jewish experience proved. A society in which the family, as opposed to the political party and the ideological programme, was the starting-point for reconstruction, was the answer to the totalitarian evil. Schumacher's assertion that Adenauer's ideas would lead to a 'restoration' of all that was worst in Germany was one of the great misjudgements of history. It would be difficult to conceive of a man more out of sympathy with the German conventional wisdom from the 1860s onward.

If the British had allowed Adenauer to remain in charge of Cologne, he might never have entered the new national politics. They drove him there. The Soviet authorities helped by excluding his most dangerous rival, Andreas Hermes. During the summer and autumn of 1945 Christian Democrat groupings emerged in various parts of Germany. Adenauer's sacking in Cologne might have been deliberately timed to enable him to get control of the New Christian Democratic Union by constructing it as a West German federal party with its power-base in the Cologne area. He thus created a party organism precisely suited to the salient features of the new German state which was emerging.[18] In March 1946, in his first public speech, he outlined his aims. The new state must no longer dominate the individual. Everyone must be allowed to take the initiative in every facet of existence. The Christian ethic must be the basis of the German community. The state must be federal, and conceived with the view to an eventual creation of a United States of Europe.[19]

This speech, one of the most important in the post-war world, which marked the real beginning of post-war German and indeed West European politics, was made at Cologne University. Adenauer had delivered another remarkable speech there, twenty-seven years before, in June 1918: 'Whatever the ultimate shape of the peace treaty,' he had then warned, 'here on the Rhine, at the ancient international crossroads, German civilization and the civilization of the Western democracies will meet during the decades to come. Unless a genuine reconciliation is possible between them ... European leadership will be lost for ever.'[20] That opportunity had been missed; European leadership had gone, probably for ever. But European stability and prosperity were still realizable aims. In 1919 Adenauer had conceived the idea of a Rhine–Ruhr state within a German federation. In July 1946, the British created the *Land* of North Rhine–Westphalia, uniting industrial Rhineland and agricultural Westphalia, along almost identical boundaries with his 1919 conception and so handing him the perfect instrument for his design: his luck again.

For the next three years Adenauer played the cards Britain had unwittingly handed him with consummate finesse. He was a tough old bird; he had learnt patience. He kept his dignity and his temper. He was flexible, quiet, never banged the table or fawned, but charmed and sometimes discreetly flattered. He had taken to heart Churchill's saying, 'The Germans are always either at one's throat or one's feet'; he was neither. As one British minister put it, he had 'a power to stand outside the Germans'; he knew 'the weaknesses that had betrayed them'.[21] Events played into his hands. The tighter the Russians screwed down the Iron Curtain, the more committed the Allies became to the creation of the West German state he wanted. He ruled out Berlin as a capital: 'Whoever makes Berlin the new capital will be creating a new spiritual Prussia.' The capital must be 'where Germany's windows are wide open to the west'.[22] The first Berlin crisis reinforced this view. Adenauer blocked Social Democrat plans for the general nationalization of German industry, which initially had British support. By rejecting Marshall Aid for East Germany, the Russians did Adenauer a double favour: they undermined Jakob Kaiser, the Christian Democrat union leader and his chief party rival, and they made possible the separate economic development of West Germany which Adenauer required for his long-term aims. For he recognized, even at this early stage, that France would never consent to a United States of Europe which included a paramount Germany with its undivided industrial base and all its 80 million people. The Russians were the real creators of Adenauer's Germany by their policy of keeping Germany divided; and their successive moves to intensify the Cold War in 1947–8 accelerated the formation of the West German state. Adenauer paid lip-service to reunification, then and later, as every German was conventionally supposed to do. But in reality he wanted to keep it divided, and the Russians did his work for him.

Adenauer's crowning mercy was that, as President of the Parliamentary Council, he was able to write his own constitution. He took a lot of time and trouble over it and eventually produced one of the best constitutions ever drawn up for a modern state, which skilfully balances sufficient authority for the Chancellor against the entrenched powers of its federal constituents. By comparison with the Weimar constitution it was a masterpiece. For the first elections, set for 14 August 1949, he formed an alliance with Professor Ludwig Erhard, head of the Bizonal Economic Council, whose free market economic philosophy, based on low tariffs, free trade, cheap imports and high exports, was exactly suited to his own political philosophy and was, indeed, already producing results by the summer of 1949. The British, wrong to the end, assumed the Social Democrats would win easily. In fact the CDU vote was 7,360,000, against fewer than 7 million for the Socialists, and Adenauer, in rejecting the idea of a non-party coalition government, was able to argue that a total of 13 million Germans had voted for free enterprise – that is, for Erhard's ideas – and only 8 million for nationalization. What emerged, after the election, was that Adenauer was in total control of his party (and of Erhard). In getting himself made Chancellor and forming his government he behaved in an authoritative, not to say high-handed, manner. He said that, on doctor's advice, he could only remain in office for two years.[23] He remained for fourteen. The August election was thus one of the critical events of the post-war world. An SPD government, with the economic philosophy and programme it then possessed, could never conceivably have achieved the German *Wirtschaftswunder*. The Adenauer–Erhard combination was essential to it. By the time the SPD finally achieved power, in 1969, they had already renounced Marxist collective ownership and had, in effect, embraced the Erhardian market philosophy.

Adenauer enjoyed a further critical advantage, again thanks to the British. Hitler had destroyed the German trade union movement completely. The British believed it essential to the refounding of German democracy, and encouraged unions to come into existence in 1945 long before they would permit parties. The man they backed to do it was a Rhineland metal-workers' leader, Hans Boeckler. He thought in terms of one big union, a weird syndicalist notion going back to pre-1914 days. The British sent over Will Lawther, president of the mineworkers, and Jack Tanner of the engineering workers, to persuade Boeckler to go for industrial unions. What in effect Germany was given, by a *diktat* which any normal process of historical development would have made impossible, was a perfected version of the British trade union model, shorn of all its weaknesses, anomalies, contradictions and inefficiencies. By an act of suicidal generosity unique in history, a union structure exactly designed for the needs of modern industry, which Britain had tried and failed to achieve over half a century by democratic consultation, was handed by her *gratis* to her chief commercial competitor.

Some sixteen industrial unions were created, within a single federation, the DGB (*Deutscher Gewerkschaftsbund*). At British urging, the DGB was given not only constitutional powers of expulsion but the financial leverage of a fixed percentage of all union subscriptions, enabling it to hold vast financial reserves, on which unions could, and in case of strikes were obliged to, draw. To strike at all, a 75 per cent secret ballot was necessary, and the DGB in effect had a further veto.[24] Strikes for political purposes were ruled out as was any organic connection between unions and political movements. Thus West Germany acquired the most effective union structure of any leading industrial nation, with no rival federations (as in the USA), no religious-Marxist divisions (as in Italy and France), no political unions (as in Britain) and, above all, no craft unions, that disastrous relic of an earlier industrial phase which constituted the chief institutional barrier to raising productivity.

Adenauer capitalized skilfully on this gift from Britain. Boeckler, elected first Chairman of the DGB in October 1949, and thereafter its virtual dictator, had served with Adenauer on the Cologne city council. The new Chancellor made him, along with Erhard, the co-architect of his social and economic policy. He persuaded Boeckler to renounce public ownership in favour of *Mitbestimmung* (co-partnership of labour and capital) and a high-wage policy based on productivity agreements.[25] Adenauer got the co-partnership law through the Bundestag in 1951 with the help of SPD votes and at the risk to his coalition, but it paid handsome economic and political dividends. By the next year Germany was already rich enough for Adenauer to reorganize German social security in a way which secured most of the objects of SPD policy.[26] By the mid-1950s, German labour had settled for what was essentially a non-political policy based on high profits, high wages and bonuses, high productivity, excellent social security and seats on policy-forming boards. In the process the class-war in West Germany died, and one consequence of its demise was the rejection by the Social Democrats in 1959 of their original Marxist philosophy.

Adenauer was one of the most gifted statesmen of modern times; certainly the most wholly successful in recent German history. During his chancellorship, real incomes in Germany tripled. In 1953 he won a majority of seats in the Bundestag and in 1957, by which time Germany's currency was the strongest in Europe, an absolute majority of votes cast. He placed German democracy on an almost unassailable base and not only brought it back into the concert of civilized powers but made it a pillar of the legitimate establishment. He could not have achieved these things without both a strong streak of genuine idealism and ample reserves of cynical cunning. Erhard thought he had *Menschenverachtung*, a contempt for mankind. It was, rather, a vivid awareness of human weakness, and especially of German vices. In the new Bundestag, whose *décor* he supervised and made spectacular ('like a Max Reinhardt set for a production of *Julius Caesar*'), the ink-wells and desk-tops were screwed down to prevent hooliganism. Even so the scenes were awful, enhancing by contrast Adenauer's own imperturbability, dignity and maturity; though he shared with Calvin Coolidge a curious taste for practical jokes, which included hiding the block of wood on which the stocky Dr Eugen Gerstenmaier, President of the Bundestag, addressed the assembly. Adenauer did not think the Germans were a people to be trusted, either collectively or as individuals. He shadowed his ministers, tracking one down to a Paris brothel and accordingly ruling him out for the Foreign Ministry.[27] He had little affection beyond his own family circle and his closest associate was Hans Globke, co-author of the Nuremberg Laws, who ran the Chancellery and Adenauer's private intelligence service. 'And who knows', Adenauer would smirk, 'what Herr Globke may have in his safe?'[28] He thought democratic statesmen ought to be smarter and better informed than their totalitarian rivals. Collectively, he felt the Germans could only be trusted within the iron framework of the absolute rule of law, overawing even the state; his establishment of this framework will in the long run prove, perhaps, his chief contribution to German political culture.

It was because the Soviet leaders, like Hitler, hated and ridiculed law that Adenauer set his face implacably against any deal with them which could not be guaranteed and supervised down to the smallest print. He used to say that the Soviet regime had appropriated during and since the war 500,000 square miles of territory, all of it in Europe; it was the only expansionist power left. Over forty years it had broken or revoked forty-five out of the fifty-eight treaties it had signed.[29] By insisting on testing Soviet intentions, he exposed their 'reunification' proposals of 1952, 1955 and 1959 as fraudulent. He could not forget that 1,150,000 German prisoners of war had vanished into Soviet Russia, of whom only 9,628, classified as 'war criminals', had ever been accounted for.[30] Hence he used every means to persuade Germans to seek refuge in the West, where he could give them law and freedom and work. After the East German

workers' rising of June 1953, put down with great ferocity by the
Red Army, the Soviet leaders turned Walter Ulbricht's Communist
regime into a complete satellite. It did not prosper, and Adenauer's
policy of encouraging refugees was bleeding it to death at the rate of
1,000 a day by July 1961. On 13 August Ulbricht, with Soviet
permission, began building the Berlin Wall. It was illegal, and
Truman and Eisenhower would certainly have knocked it down. But
under a weak president, Jack Kennedy, the *fait accompli* was
accepted. There was nothing Adenauer could do about it, for he had
no jurisdiction in Berlin, which remained a four-power responsibility. He watched in sadness, in the last years of his life, while the
flow of refugees was cut off, and the wall saved the East German
economy, turning it from a crushing liability into a growing Soviet
asset, the one reliable industrial workshop of the bloc.

By then, however, Adenauer's work was complete, for he had tied
the West Germans, economically, militarily and politically, to Western culture and legitimacy as tightly and as permanently as human
ingenuity could devise. Therein lay the real idealism which balanced
his Realpolitik. He was the first German statesman to put European
before German interests. It may be true, as one of his critics put it,
that he was 'a good European but a bad German'.[31] In that sense he
wanted to be a 'bad' German; he hated Professor Kallmann's portrait
of him because it made him, he said, 'look just like a Hun'. He
thought that German reunification was not available at a price
Germany or the West could afford to pay. That he was right was
amply demonstrated by the failure of his successors, over twenty
years, to obtain any other result. By contrast, integration with the
West was a realizable object, and he realized it. But here again he was
fortunate. Adenauer grasped, intellectually rather than emotionally,
that Germany's future lay with France. He had no feelings for
France; no French tastes; knew very little about the country, and up
to the age of seventy had only once visited it, for a two-day
conference. Yet, as always, he saw political facts realistically: 'There
is no European policy without France or against France, just as there
can be no European policy without or against Germany.'[32]

The partner Adenauer hoped to work with in France, Robert
Schuman, had much in common with de Gasperi and himself. He
came from Luxembourg, and had been a German citizen, though
he refused to serve in the German army during the First World
War. Until 1919, when he was already middle-aged, he was not
even a French citizen. Adenauer saw him as a citizen of the
Kingdom of Lothar, Charlemagne's grandson, the so-called
'Middle Kingdom', to which both Lorraine and Cologne had
belonged. On 9 May 1950 he sold Schuman the idea of a

European coal-steel pool, which became the germ of the European Economic Community, and it was largely thanks to Schuman that the marginal but emotionally vital problem of the Saar was finally resolved in October 1955. But Schuman was too unrepresentative a Frenchman to 'deliver' France for the more grandiose project Adenauer had in mind. In any case the Fourth Republic itself could not deliver France; it was too weak to deliver anything permanently. For France to embrace Germany it required the self-confidence born of renewed strength; and a man and a regime which embodied that confidence. It was Adenauer's great fortune that he survived long enough to capitalize on de Gaulle's triumphant return to power and the birth of the Fifth Republic.

The recovery of France in the 1960s and 1970s is one of the most striking phenomena of modern times. In the 1930s, as we have seen, it would have appeared inconceivable. And the road which led to it is complex and paradoxical. The Third Republic in its last phase had been the embodiment of the notion 'small is beautiful': declining population, low production, productivity, investment, wages and consumption; the cult – the exaltation almost – of the 'little man', the small factory, the small farm, the small town. It was dead even before the Germans defeated it, and collapsed into a heap of dust in the summer of 1940. It is important to grasp that Vichy was the beginning of the recovery, because it was created not only by French fascists and collaborators but by all those who deplored the rottenness and inadequacy of its predecessor. Pétain himself may have leaned to archaism, as he indicated when he said: 'France will never be great again until the wolves are howling round the doors of her villages.'[33] But many of those who held key posts in the regime were radical modernizers. Under the guidance of Jean Coutrot, founder in 1930 of the Polytechnique's Centre for Economic Studies, a new generation of technocrats came to the fore under Vichy. They included the Minister of Industrial Production, Bichelonne, Henri Culman, Vichy's chief economic theorist, Jacques Rueff, Laval's adviser in 1934 and later de Gaulle's, Roland Boris, who also was to be influential with de Gaulle (and Pierre Mendès-France) and Pierre Massé, later Commissioner for Planning in the Fifth Republic.[34]

Indeed, amidst its extraordinary confusions, contradictions and treachery, Vichy, by the mere fact of overthrowing the existing order, was a time of experiment and risk. One of its beneficiaries was the go-ahead younger French peasant, prototype of the new farmers who were later to do so well out of the EEC. For the first time peasants became interested in modernization, machinery and productivity.[35] A system of quasi-voluntary planning ('indicative planning'), the embryo of the

Commissariat général du Plan, came into existence. It was Vichy which first put into effect the idea of tax-funded Family Allowances, conceived in 1932 by the demographer Adolphe Landry to raise the birth-rate; and under Vichy, for the first time in more than a century, the French birth-rate actually began to increase again. The psychological effect was profound. Vichy was devoted to youth, a craze it caught from the Germans. It spent far more on education than the Third Republic. It was Vichy which effectively created popular sport in France, especially football: there were only thirty professional footballers in France in 1939, ten times as many by 1943.[36] One of the most striking features of Vichy were the 'Youth Workshops' or *Chantiers de la Jeunesse* (literally 'shipyards'), with a stress on technical education which had hitherto been lacking. The aim was a rejuvenation of France. As Pétain's Minister of Information, Paul Marion, put it, 'Thanks to us, the France of camping, of sports, of dances, of travel and group hikes will sweep away the France of aperitifs, of tobacco dens, of party congresses and long digestions.'[37] To a great extent this prophecy was fulfilled.

Much of the achievement of Vichy was thrown away in its own débâcle and in the division of the nation which followed. About 170,000 French worked in the Resistance; more – 190,000 – were accused of collaboration, and about 100,000 sent to gaol. Nobody to this day knows how many were murdered in 1944: about 4,500 cases were authenticated.[38] The Communists, who had actually opposed the war in 1939–40, were the great beneficiaries of 1944, when they were able to murder most of their enemies. They claimed the title of the *parti des fusillés*, claiming 75,000 'Communist patriots' had been shot by the Nazis and Vichy. But at the Nuremberg trials the official French figure of the total killed under the Occupation was only 29,660, and the Communists never produced the actual names of more than 176 CP 'heroes'.[39] In fact leading Communists offered to give evidence against Socialist leaders at the Riom trial, and the party newspaper *l'Humanité* protested when Vichy released anti-Nazis from jail.[40] Unlike other parties, it never purged collaborators, who would have included its leader, Maurice Thorez; the only people it got rid of in 1944–5 were those who disobeyed the Stalin line in 1939–40 and fought the Nazis. Yet the CP emerged from the war, because of its belated Resistance enthusiasm, by far the richest and best-organized, and in many respects the biggest, of the French parties. It pushed its vote from 1.5 million in 1936 to over 5 million in 1945 and 5.5 million in 1946; the total went on rising until 1949, and in the late-1940s the CP had around 900,000 paid-up members. The French CP was wholly Stalinist, and remained so after Stalin's death; it was systematically corrupted, intellectually and morally, by Thorez, an archetype of the twentieth-century professional politician, who became a full-time party functionary at the age of twenty-three and never did anything else – was, in effect, a Moscow civil servant all his life.[41] He ghettoized the party vote, erecting little iron curtains round its enclaves, so that the CP became a society within France, with its own newspapers, plays, novels, poems, women's magazines, children's comics, cookery books and farmers' almanacs.[42]

The existence of this huge, intransigent party, which owed its primary allegiance to a foreign power, posed almost insuperable problems of governing France. De Gaulle, who had (as he put it) 'picked the Republic out of the gutter', found that he could not in practice entrust the 'big three' ministries to Communist members of his coalition. He could not, he said on the radio, 'concede to them any of the three posts which determine foreign policy: diplomacy, which expresses it; the army, which supports it; and the police, which covers it'.[43] The inability to secure a national, as opposed to a party-ideological, approach to defence led to his resignation in January 1946. As a result he played no direct part in shaping the new constitution, which was primarily the work of Communists and Socialists. The consequences were tragic. Ever since the end of its divine-right monarchy, France had found it impossible to devise a constitution which reconciled the demands of central authority and the rights of representation; it veered between dictatorship and chaos, according as the constitution pushed the balance one way or the other. The first twelve constitutions were failures. That of the Third Republic, in 1875, was passed by one vote in an Assembly which in fact had a majority of monarchists but could not agree on a particular king. It lasted, shakily, for sixty-five years, but it ended in complete failure and half the nation had never accepted it in spirit – one reason why Vichy was greeted with such rapture. Pétain had been entrusted with devising a new constitution but (like Hitler) had never done so. De Gaulle had his own ideas, based upon a strong presidency, which he outlined in a speech at Bayeux ('the Bayeux constitution') in June 1946. But this was never put to the vote.

The first proposed constitution for the new Fourth Republic, drawn up by the Communists and Socialists, was rejected in a referendum. A modified version, which got the grudging support of the Catholic Centre Party (MRP), was finally approved by the French, but only 9 million voted for it – fewer than for the earlier version. Over 8 million voted against, and 8.5 million abstained in disgust.[44] Drawn up in a hurry, against the clock, amid acrimonious haggling, it was one of the worst constitutions ever foisted on a great and intelligent nation. Even its grammar was atrocious. Many provisions were mutually contradictory; others were so complicated as to be incomprehensible. Some details were simply left out. Whole chapters (on the French Union and 'local collectives') were never implemented. A number of the procedures, for instance for forming a government, votes of no confidence and parliamentary dissolutions, proved unworkable. It had so many muddled compromises that even those who recommended it did not like it.[45] It retained most of the chaotic vices of the Third Republic and added new ones.

Constitution-making is a thankless task. Constitutional analysis is a tedious aspect of history. But constitutions matter. Weimar failed because its constitution was clumsy. The Federal Republic succeeded because Adenauer gave it a skilfully balanced foundation. The constitution turned the Fourth Republic into a mere arena for what de Gaulle contemptuously called 'the ballet of the parties'. Thanks to its proportional representation system, no party could form a homogeneous government. The President was a cipher, the Prime Minister, as a rule, largely impotent and often a nonentity. The shifting coalition system ruled out continuity and stability of government and, more important, made it exceedingly difficult to push through big decisions, especially unpopular measures resisted by powerful inter-party lobbies, above all colonial ones. It was no accident that the regime drifted into an unwinnable war in Indo-China, ending in the surrender at Dien Bien Phu (1954), or that it finally came to grief over *Algérie française* four years later.

Yet the twelve years of the Fourth Republic were not entirely wasted. The technocratic revolution, begun under Vichy, continued. Indeed it accelerated, thanks largely to the efforts of one industrious enthusiast, Jean Monnet. His family had run a small Cognac business of the most old-fashioned, thoroughly French kind, but exporting to the world and thus possessing international horizons. He was in business abroad from the age of sixteen, usually in merchant banking and state loans, but he spent much of the Great War in the office of Etienne Clementel, the Minister of Commerce, the first Frenchman to believe that government should help capitalist enterprise to plan, and that the 'democratic peoples' (by which he meant West Europe and America) should form an 'economic union'.[46] In the Second World War Monnet performed outstanding services in co-ordinating Allied arms production, and was a natural choice for de Gaulle to put in charge of rebuilding France's shattered economy. Monnet set up the *Commissariat général du Plan*, and from this base went on to construct the first organs of the future European Economic Community. He was that great rarity: a man of ideas and passionate conviction who did not believe in ideology. He thought that the only kind of industrial planning which worked was by persuasion and consent. To him, planning machinery was a mere framework. Regulations should be designed to produce perfect competition, not Utopias. The function of planning staff was not to issue orders but to bring minds together. Planning was essentially economic diplomacy. The virtue of Monnet's approach was that it made possible a reconciliation between planning and the market system. It reduced to a minimum the planning bureaucracy and the tyranny it breeds: at his Commissariat he had only thirty senior officials in all.[47] Monnet was small, mousy, quiet, colourless, rhetoric-hating: in appearance and manner the exact opposite of de Gaulle. What the two men shared was huge persistence and will; and, equally important, the ability to inspire and lead the young. De Gaulle bred Gaullists; Monnet, the Eurocrats.

Monnet's system of 'indicative planning' was the one major achievement of the Fourth Republic. But to produce its full results it required a framework of political stability capable of producing a strong currency and certain harsh and basic decisions affecting whole categories of people. That the Fourth Republic could not provide. Equally, Monnet set in motion the European Economic Community, though he did not invent it. As a customs-union (its essential characteristic), it had a long history. The Prussian common external tariff of 1818, expanded into the *Zollverein* (customs union) of 1834, had been the basis of German unity finally achieved in 1871. Experience seemed to show that common tariffs were the surest road to political unity. Luxembourg, originally a member of the *Zollverein*, had signed a convention with Belgium in 1921, involving common customs and balance of payments. After the Second World War it was extended to the Netherlands, with a common external tariff adopted by the three states on 1 January 1948 and a 'harmonization process' of internal tariffs beginning 15 October 1949. It was Monnet's idea to expand the Benelux concept to include the three major powers of West Europe (he wanted Britain too), beginning with coal and steel. His German friends sold it to Adenauer, who did not claim to understand the economic details but recognized the political importance of the principle. The Treaty of Paris, signed in April 1951 by Benelux, France, Germany and Italy, brought into existence a common market in coal and steel products. Six years later, on 25 March 1957, the Six agreed to the Treaty of Rome, creating a general common market, with proposals for external and internal tariffs, the end of all restrictions on movements of persons, service and capital, 'harmonization' procedures to produce perfect competition and, most difficult of all, a common agricultural price-support system.

The Fourth Republic was capable of bringing France into the EEC but lacked the resolution to make the system work. For the working of the system depended essentially on mutual sacrifices, above all from France and Germany. To survive within a common market, France had not merely to industrialize fast; it had to cut its traditional, inefficient peasant-type agricultural sector by three-quarters. In the early 1950s, France still had only one industrial worker per agricultural worker (in Britain it was nine to one). Out of a total working population of 20.5 million, 9.1 million lived in tiny rural communes and of these 6.5 million actually worked in agriculture; a further 1.25 million lived in semi-rural communes.[48] Most of these people had to be persuaded to move into the factories, involving a social upheaval quite beyond the capacity of the Fourth Republic to carry through. To make the voluntary revolution in agriculture possible, palatable and in the end profitable, enormous sums of money had to be made available for agricultural investment. The French calculation was that this should be provided by West Germany, in the form of transfer payments or internal market taxes, under a system known as the Common Agricultural Policy. In return, Germany's highly efficient manufacturing industry would get access to French consumer markets. The Treaty of Rome was thus a bargain of mutual sacrifice but a finely balanced one. The French agricultural revolution had to be carried through fast enough to justify the CAP. Equally, French industry had to modernize and expand with sufficient conviction to prevent Germany getting the best of the deal and turning France into an economic colony. Both processes required strong, self-confident government of the kind the Fourth Republic could not provide.

Even more was required: a reassertion of French nationhood. In the France of the 1950s, the 'Europeans' were essentially an élitist minority. The tone of French politics was often xenophobic, indeed racist, with the Communists leading the pack. They talked of 'Schuman le boche'. A CP trade union leader shouted at Léon Blum: 'Blum – in Yiddish that means a flower!' A CP provincial newspaper wrote: 'Blum, Schuman, Moch, Mayer do not smell of good French soil.' L'Humanité published a cartoon of 'men of the American party' – Schuman, Moch and Mayer – with crooked noses, remarking in embarrassment while Communists sang the 'Marseillaise': 'Do we know that tune?' 'No, it must be one of those French songs.'[49] Even in the centre and the Right, the coal–steel plan was attacked as 'A Europe under German hegemony', and on the Left as the 'Europe of the Vatican'. A centre Radical like old Daladier insisted: 'When they say Europe they mean Germany, and when they say Germany they mean Greater Germany.' On the right, Pierre-Etienne Flandin, the old Municher, argued that 'European federation' meant 'the suicide of France'. The splendidly named Léon Gingembre of the Association of Small and Medium Businesses (Petites et moyennes enterprises) – perhaps the most characteristic institution of the old

France – epitomized the proposed EEC as 'the Europe of trusts, international business and high finance'. It was, argued one historian, a reactionary attempt to resurrect 'the idea of the Holy Roman Empire'. 'The past is not dead,' he argued, 'but survives in the German cultural world of Adenauer, Schuman and de Gasperi.'[50]

This combination of enemies would have made the EEC unworkable, especially since it had powerful xenophobic opponents within West Germany also: Schumacher called the Treaty of Paris 'petty European, I mean a Pan-French conception . . . he who signs this treaty ceases to be a German', since it was the work of Adenauer, 'the Chancellor of the Allies'.[51] Had the Fourth Republic survived, the resolution needed to prove that a Franco–German bargain could be just to both parties would have been missing.

Hence the return of de Gaulle to power in May 1958 was a watershed not only in French but in post-war European history. At first glance he did not seem the man to push forward European economic unity, any more than he was the man to dissolve *l'Algérie française*. But then de Gaulle was never exactly what he seemed. He was one of the master-intelligences of modern times, infinite in subtlety, rich in paradox, fathomless in his sardonic ironies. He was a pre-war figure with a post-war mind, indeed a futurist mind. He was a monarchist who believed Dreyfus was innocent. He was born to love the French Empire and provincial France, *la France des villages* – in fact he ended both.

The most important point to be grasped was that the essential de Gaulle was not a soldier or even a statesman but an intellectual. He was an intellectual of a special kind, whose entire life was a meditation on the theme of mind, power and action. He had, moreover, the historian's capacity to see current events *sub specie aeternitatis*. He had been taught by his father: 'Remember what Napoleon said: "If Pierre Corneille were alive today, I would make him a prince."'[52] He was always anxious to woo intellectuals, not merely because in France so many were officially classified as such: over 1,100,000 in the 1954 census.[53] In 1943 in Algiers, he won over a deputation of intellectuals, led by Gide, by telling him: 'Art has its honour, in the same way France has hers': they realized he was an intellectual like themselves.[54] On his return to power in 1958 he gave pre-eminent place to André Malraux, who sat at his right hand in cabinet and who carried more weight with de Gaulle's inner feelings than any of his prime ministers. As for Malraux, as Gaston Palewski said, he 'entered into the epic of de Gaulle, as we all did, like a man entering a religious order'.[55]

It was characteristic of de Gaulle's intellectualism that his approach to military matters, when he was a theorist, was through philosophical and political ideas. 'The true school of command', he wrote in

L'Armée de métier, lies 'in the general culture', adding: 'Behind the victories of Alexander, one always finds Aristotle.' The same approach determined his statesmanship. His favourite quotation (with which he opened his *War Memoirs*) was the famous 'hymn to power' from Goethe's *Faust*, in which Faust rejects 'In the beginning was the Word' for 'In the beginning was the Deed'.[56] He used this to make the point that the French had clarity of thought but lacked the will to action. Hence France's need, in the first instance, for a strong state: 'Nothing effective and solid can be done without the renewal of the state ... for that is where it is necessary to begin.'[57] The state's 'role and *raison d'être* is to serve the general interest'. Only it could personify the whole community, a Leviathan with more than the strength of its composing atoms. It was the centripetal force, balancing the centrifugal forces which, especially in France, threatened general break-up. To de Gaulle, the state was not totalitarian. On the contrary, it symbolized moral and cultural values: especially, in France, idealism, 'the principal trait in her character and the essential element of her influence'. He identified it with liberty and the classical civilization, seeing French civilization as the democratic civilization *par excellence*, combining a long history of cultural advance with liberty. Democracy at its best brought people together in a consciousness of moral community, what he termed *rassemblement*. Democratic rituals were a concrete symbol of unity. Consensus preceded democratic forms. 'There is a pact twenty centuries old between the greatness of France and the liberty of the world.' Hence 'democracy is inextricably intertwined with the best understood interests of France'.[58]

De Gaulle's view of the state, then, was essentially pre-totalitarian. He identified the state with legitimacy, best embodied in the person of a sacral ruler. The monarch was the only individual whose personal interests were bound up inextricably, indeed organically, with the interests of the whole community, not just one or more sections of it (like a party leader). Hence the advice he gave to Queen Elizabeth II of England when she asked him about her role in a modern society: 'In that station to which God has called you, be who you are, Madam! That is to say, the person in relation to whom, by virtue of the principle of legitimacy, everything in your kingdom is ordered, in whom your people perceives its own nationhood, and by whose presence and dignity the national unity is upheld.'[59] In extremity, and for want of a better, he himself had had to take on this role in 1940: 'de Gaulle, alone and almost unknown, had had to assume the burden of France', as he put it. Again, in 1958, when the hideous Algeria crisis threatened France with a Spanish-type civil war, he took the role again: 'de Gaulle, now well-known but with no other weapon save his legitimacy, must take destiny in his hands.'[60] He had 'disappeared' in 1946 with precisely this purpose, to keep 'a pure image', for (as he put it) 'if Joan of Arc had married, she would no longer be Joan of Arc'.[61] He developed, indeed, the capacity to dissociate himself as a person from his public persona ('de Gaulle interests me only as a historical personality'), so that he could say: 'There were many things I would have liked to do but could not for they would not have been fitting for General de Gaulle.'[62]

The logical consequence of this theory of the state was for de Gaulle to set up his own monarchy, as he undoubtedly would have done a century before. In 1958, however, he rejected monarchy in favour of a plebiscitory democracy, using referenda and (from 1962) direct universal election of a president endowed with strong actual powers as well as a transcendental symbolic role. His 1958 constitution, adopted by 17.5 million to 4.5 (with 15 per cent abstentions), and based on the Bayeux proposals, was by far the clearest, most consistent and skilfully balanced France had ever received.[63] It induced, as intended, a polarization of the party system into two huge blocs of Left and Right (albeit with a four-party structure), forcing voters, on the second ballot, to make unambiguous choices. It reinvigorated the executive, enabling it to take decisions authoritatively and to pursue policies consistently. Above all, the 1962 presidential election system, approved by 13.15 million to 7.97 million, gave the head of state, bypassing the parties, a direct mandate from the entire electorate. As a result, France enjoyed the longest period of political stability in her entire modern history. It was twenty-three years from 1958 before there was, effectively, a change in governmental philosophy. Even after the victory of the Socialists in the presidential election of May 1981, the constitution continued to work smoothly, indicating that it was one for all seasons. France, like Germany, had got a first-class public framework at last.

This new stability made possible what had merely been hinted at under Vichy and the Fourth Republic: the 'renewal' of France. The long decadence of more than a century was not only reversed, but spectacularly seen to be reversed. In economic matters, de Gaulle proceeded with his paradoxical blend of traditionalism and modernity. The technocrat he made Chairman of the Economic Commission, and the real architect of his economic success, was Jacques Rueff, a man who placed his confidence in gold as the best available measure of value and who first put into practice the neo-conservative policies which, in the 1970s, were to become internationally fashionable under the misleading name of 'monetarism'. Rueff's plan of 8 December 1958 embraced deflation, severe cuts in government expenditure, devaluation, convertibility and a 'new franc' at 100 times its previous value; and the plan was linked to the wholesale reduction or removal, from 1 January 1959, of external tariffs and quotas. France, in short, was delivered over to free enterprise and the market. 'It was the coherence and fervour of the plan,' de Gaulle remarked later, 'as well as its daring and ambition, which won me over.' Its object, he told the nation on television, was to 'establish the nation on a basis of truth and severity'.[64]

France is fundamentally a rich country; its people highly intelligent and industrious. All that is needed to make France work effectively is a stable framework and energetic leadership. Results came fast. GNP rose by 3 per cent in the second half of 1959, by 7.9 per cent in 1960, 4.6 in 1961, 6.8 in 1962; living standards began to improve at the rate of 4 per cent a year. For the first time since the Industrial Revolution, France became an economic pace-setter. What in effect Gaullism did was to accelerate the modest economic progress under the Fourth Republic, and then stabilize it on a high plateau, within a framework of currency stability and (by French standards) very low inflation. Exports doubled, 1956–62, and during the twenty-year period beginning 1952, industrial production tripled. The franc became a hard currency and early in 1968 French reserves reached the extraordinary total of 35,000 million (new) francs.[65] These results accompanied and reinforced other long-term trends. Population, which had been 41 million in 1946, rose to 52 million by 1974. These new millions were better educated and housed than ever before. The number of housing units, stagnant between 1914 and 1939, increased at ten times the inter-war rate during the 1960s, so that by 1968 it numbered 18.25 million, double the 1939 number. From the 1960s, too, dated the general use of modern drugs in France and the emergence of an effective health service.[66] The number of state secondary school teachers rose from 17,400 in 1945 to 67,000 in 1965, and the private sector (thanks to the famous *Loi Debré*, named after de Gaulle's first prime minister) also expanded fast. High-quality mass education in France dates from the late 1950s. The number of college and university students, only 78,691 in 1939, had risen to 563,000 by 1968.[67]

Under de Gaulle, in short, France became for the first time a modern, industrialized country, in the forefront of technical progress and the assimilation of new ideas. It was the very antithesis of France in the 1930s. Such a reversal of deep historical trends is very rare in history, particularly for an old nation. It gives de Gaulle a claim to be considered the outstanding statesman of modern times. The transformation, of course, was not accomplished without pain, ugliness and shock; and protest. But the very consciousness of French people that their country was again a dynamic force, as under the young Louis XIV or Napoleon I, reconciled them to the destruction of traditional rural France and, equally important, steeled them to the acceptance of co-partnership with Adenauer's Germany in a European community.

De Gaulle did not share Monnet's passion for integration and supranationality. Publicly, he always spoke of Europe as *'l'Europe des patries'*. Yet, as always, de Gaulle's ostensible behaviour often masked quite different and subtler aims. He remained pragmatic. He was not against larger entities for specific purposes if, within them, French interests could be more surely upheld. In spring 1950 he had pondered on the battle of the Catalonian Plains, 'in which Franks, Gallo-Romans and Teutons jointly routed the hordes of Attila . . . . It is time for the Rhine to become a meeting-place and not a barrier . . . . If one did not force oneself to look coolly at things, one would be almost dazzled at the prospect of what German qualities and French values, extended to Africa, might jointly yield. That is a field of common development which might transform Europe even beyond the Iron Curtain.'[68]

In a sense, de Gaulle was more than a French nationalist; he was a Carolingian. He shared the view of the French historians of the new *Annales* school, like Fernand Braudel, that history is essentially determined by geography. Indeed, it was not new: it went back at least to Albert Sorel, who had argued in his great book, *L'Europe et la Révolution française* (1885), that 'The policy of the French state was determined by geography. It was based on a fact – the empire of Charlemagne. The starting-point for the great lawsuit which fills the history of France is the insoluble dispute over the inheritance of the emperor.'[69] From the time of Philippe le Bel, under the Valois, Henri IV and Sully, Richelieu and Mazarin, Louis XIV and into the age of Danton and Napoleon, France had sought to recreate that empire by force and under a solitary French aegis. Was it not now possible, with a truncated Germany, deprived of its non-Carolingian accretions, to recreate it peacefully, fraternally and in a non-proprietory sense? That was just the kind of pragmatic idea to appeal to de Gaulle. Unlike most modern French intellectuals, he detested Nietzsche; his approach to Germany was through Madame de Staël's *De l'Allemagne* (1810), which began in France the cult of the 'good' Germans, the Westerners. He shared her passionate admiration for Goethe. He perceived in Adenauer a man who fitted into this aspect of Germany, another *homme providentiel* like himself, whose fortunate tenure of power provided an opportunity for France which might never recur. Adenauer, he wrote, was a Rhinelander,

. . . imbued with a sense of the complementary nature of the Gauls and the Teutons which once fertilized the presence of the Roman Empire on the Rhine, brought success to the Franks and glory to Charlemagne, provided the rationale for Austria, justified the relations between the King of France and the Electors, set Germany afire with the flame of the Revolution, inspired Goethe, Heine, Madame de Staël and Victor Hugo, and in spite of the fierce struggles in which the two peoples were locked, continued to seek a path gropingly through the darkness.

That was the spirit in which de Gaulle summoned Adenauer to his château at Colombey-les-deux-églises on 14 September 1958 for what he termed 'the historic encounter between this old Frenchman and this very old German'.[70]

The meeting was an unqualified success. De Gaulle warmed to *der Alte* when he was told he would regain his youth in office, 'as has been the case with myself'.[71] Adenauer approved of the Frenchman: 'so clearly upright, correct, moral'. This was the first of forty meetings between the two men which took place in growing amity until Adenauer retired in 1962. They laid the foundation of the Franco–German axis which endured until the early 1980s. It was based upon downgrading the supranational aspects of the EEC while at the same time making its economic aspects work superlatively by the mutual interlocking of the French and German economies. Thus the balanced bargain, on which the success of the EEC depended, was turned into working reality by these two old-fashioned conservative Catholics, whose politics pre-dated the era of Christian Democracy, whose view of the world had been formed before 1914, but who had remained astonishingly alert to the changes and opportunities which the tragic events of their lifetimes had brought about. It was a genuine friendship, and an example of the way in which personalities and, still more, personal relationships, radically affect the course of international affairs.

Like many friendships, it was sealed by a common antipathy: Britain. De Gaulle did not regard Britain as a true Continental power. It was Atlanticist, 'Anglo-Saxon' as he put it, the junior member of that English-speaking partnership which had excluded him and France from their rightful place in the decision-making bodies of the wartime alliance. It was de Gaulle's aim to use the Carolingian concept of the EEC to create in Europe an alternative centre of power to the USA and Soviet Russia. He did not wish a British intrusion which would inevitably challenge France's claim to sit on Charlemagne's throne. In the first decade after the war, British foreign policy had been confused and unrealistic, and made sense only on the assumption that France would remain weak and West

Germany wholly dependent on the USA. The leadership of a European federation was hers for the asking. But with a traditional cheap-food policy based on Commonwealth imports, and in the confidence of a 'special relationship' with America, Britain did not want such a role. At Zurich in 1946 it was Churchill himself who called for 'something which will astonish you . . . a kind of United States of Europe' based on 'a partnership between France and Germany'. France and Germany, he said, 'must take the lead together. Great Britain . . . America and I trust Soviet Russia . . . must be the friends and sponsors of the new Europe.'[72]

This condescending view was based on the assumption that Britain could still be an independent great power, occupying the unique geopolitical position a world empire had once given her: as Churchill put it (in 1950), Britain was the intersection of three overlapping circles, the English-speaking world, the Commonwealth and Europe. The assessment was barely plausible in 1950. It made no sense after Suez, which had demonstrated that neither the Commonwealth nor the 'special relationship' had any value in helping Britain to protect what she regarded as a vital interest. The way then pointed clearly to a European policy. Harold Macmillan, having succeeded Eden as Prime Minister in January 1957, had an opportunity to embark on an entirely fresh course and seek to join the negotiations for the still-uncompleted Rome Treaty. He missed it. He himself still had delusions of grandeur. In February 1959 he went to Moscow, as the self-appointed spokesman for the alliance, *The Times* (no doubt suitably briefed) commenting that, with President Eisenhower 'a declining force, the German chancellor an old, unhappy man, and the French president fully preoccupied with other problems, the responsibility falling on the British prime minister to lead the alliance sensibly and yet strongly . . . is paramount'.[73]

The Moscow visit itself achieved nothing (nor did the Big Power summit in Paris in 1960), but it proved a costly error, for it persuaded Adenauer that Britain in general, and Macmillan in particular, were unreliable partners, capable of doing a deal with Russia behind Germany's back and at her expense.[74] It brought out his Anglophobia. He saw Britain as an international con-man, pretending to a status unjustified by her resources or her efforts. 'England', he wrote, 'is like a rich man who has lost all his property but does not realize it.'[75] He said his three chief dislikes were 'the Russians, the Prussians and the British'. Macmillan was trying to exploit 'us poor, dumb Continentals'. British policy was just *ein einziges Feilschen*, one long fiddle.[76] De Gaulle, during their long and frequent talks together, played skilfully on Adenauer's antipathy and suspicions. Macmillan finally applied for Britain to join the EEC in

July 1961, by which time it was a working community, becoming set in its ways. Britain's adherence meant structural changes which threatened the delicate balance of Franco–German advantage. When this became apparent, de Gaulle vetoed British entry, at a spectacular press conference on 14 January 1963. If Britain entered, he said, it would be as a Trojan horse and 'in the end there would appear a colossal Atlantic Community under American dependence and leadership which would soon completely swallow up the EEC'. This would jeopardize 'the friendship of Germany and France, the union of Europe as they both wish it and their common action in the world', which rested 'on incomparable popular support'.[77] To Britain's chagrin, Adenauer signified his silent approbation of the French *non*.

Nevertheless, the way in which these two old men saw the world was not the only reason for rejecting British membership. With every year that passed Britain was growing poorer relative to the members of the EEC. This posed a different set of problems. For if the structure of the Community (especially the CAP) was based on a bargain between France and Germany, the bargain would apply even more forcibly to Britain, which would have to pay for expensive EEC food in return for access to markets for its manufactured goods. Would these prove competitive enough to make the bargain work? In November 1967 de Gaulle again vetoed British entry, and this time he pointed to chronic weaknesses in the British economy, and the difficulty of correcting them, as his justification.[78]

Structural weakness in the British economy, *vis-à-vis* her main industrial competitors, had become apparent in the period 1870–1914 and again in the 1920s. But there had been a recovery in the second half of the 1930s, especially in high-technology areas; the economy had performed well during the Second World War, and it continued to do so up to 1950, when exports were 144 on a 1938 index of 100.[79] In 1950 the British GNP was $47 billion against only $75 billion for all six future EEC powers. British exports, at $6.3 billion, were more than two-thirds those of the Six ($9.4 billion) and GNP *per capita* was nearly twice as high ($940 to $477). Twenty years later, in 1970, British GNP *per capita* had rather more than doubled, to $2,170. That of the Six had multiplied more than five times, to $2,557. While British exports had tripled, those of the Six had multiplied nearly ten times. Their reserves, smaller than Britain's in 1950 ($2.9 billion against $3.4 billion), had also increased by ten times, while Britain's had shrunk.[80] By any conceivable continental standard of measurement, the British economy had performed badly. The gap widened throughout the 1970s, despite the fact that Britain actually joined the EEC on 1 January 1973.

Why this chronic weakness? Britain had been the first to industrialize, a process starting on a large scale in the 1760s. In the two hundred years since, it was the only major industrial power which had not suffered the convulsion of revolution, foreign conquest or civil war: those fundamental breaks with the past which, as the post-war history of France and Germany indicated, promote social and economic dynamism. Britain had no constitutional bill of rights, no written guarantees designed to protect the assumptions of a liberal society. It had instead the Common Law tradition, arbitrated by the judges, which effectively upheld rights of liberty and property and was, indeed, the legal framework within which the British created the first modern industrial society. This continued to function throughout the nineteenth century as an effective legal setting for industrial enterprise. In 1900, however, the trade unions, which already reflected the anachronisms and anomalies of early industrialization, especially in the multiplicity of ancient craft unions, created the Labour Party, to promote 'legislation in the direct interest of labour' and oppose 'measures having an opposite tendency'.[81] The salient characteristic of the British Labour Party, as opposed to other socialist movements in the West, was that it was not primarily Marxist or even socialist but a form of parliamentary syndicalism. The unions owned it. They directly sponsored a hard core of Labour MPs (128 in 1975, for instance) and, more important, paid about three-quarters of the party's national funds and 95 per cent of its election expenses.[82] The party constitution, by a system of union membership affiliations expressed in block votes, made the unions the overwhelmingly dominant element in the formation of party policy.

Parliamentary power was quickly reflected in statutory measures to destroy the Common Law balance within Britain's unwritten constitution, and tilt it decisively towards organized labour. In 1906, the first year Labour was strongly represented in parliament, it passed the Trade Disputes Act, which gave unions complete immunity from civil actions for damages (torts) 'alleged to have been committed by or on behalf of the trade unions'. Such immunity existed nowhere else in the West, for in effect it made unions impervious to actions for breach of contract, though the other parties to the contract, the employers, might be sued by the unions. Even the Webbs regarded it as 'an extraordinary and unlimited immunity'. The constitutional lawyer A.V.Dicey protested: 'It makes a trade union a privileged body exempted from the ordinary law of the land. No such privileged body has ever before been deliberately created by an English parliament.'[83] This critical act, giving unions a special status in law, became the plinth on which was subsequently erected a weighty and complex superstructure of union statutory privilege. The Trade Union Act of 1913 legalized the spending of trade union funds on political objectives, that is the Labour Party, and laid down that union members with other party affiliations had to 'contract out' of their political dues (a difficult and unpopular procedure) if they did not want to contribute to Labour funds. This procedure was reversed to 'contracting in' by the Conservative Trade Disputes Act of 1927, which also made political strikes illegal. But as soon as Labour got an absolute majority in parliament in 1945, it repealed the 1927 act and went on to give the unions special status within the nationalized industries it created and, indeed, within all its social and economic policy acts. The judges continued, from time to time, to uphold Common Law protection for individuals against unions. But whenever they found a hole in union privilege law, the unions were able to lean directly on a Labour-dominated parliament to plug it. Thus, the House of Lords in *Rookes v. Barnard* (1964) held that an unofficial strike in breach of contract was actionable. The next year, a new Labour government legalized it in the 1965 Trade Disputes Act.

In the 1960s and 1970s, growing union power was exerted in a variety of ways. In 1969, the unions vetoed the so-called 'In Place of Strife' legislation the Labour Prime Minister, Harold Wilson, proposed to enact to reduce the number of strikes. In 1972 the unions introduced new forms of direct action, including 'mass picketing', 'flying pickets' and 'secondary picketing', which the police were unwilling or unable to curb. In 1974 they used these devices to destroy a Conservative government responsible for the 1971 Industrial Relations Act which attempted, albeit ineffectually, to introduce a statutory code of union conduct. The Labour government which followed not only repealed the 1971 Act but pushed through parliament a mass of legislation extending union privileges, of which the Trade Union and Labour Relations Acts of 1974 and 1976 and the Employment Protection Acts of 1975 and 1979 were merely the most important. These extended immunity to tort actions to cases where unions induced other parties to break contracts, obliged employers to recognize unions and uphold 'closed shops' (to the point where an employee could be dismissed without legal remedy for declining to join one) and to provide facilities for union organization. The effect of this mass of legislation was to increase the number of 'closed-shop' industries and to push unionization above the 50 per cent barrier of the workforce for the first time, compared with 25 per cent or less in the United States, France and West Germany. Even more important, however, was that it removed virtually all inhibitions on union bargaining power. As the Master of the Rolls, Lord Denning, remarked: 'All legal restraints have been lifted so that they can now do as they will.'[84] In the early months of 1979, under chaotic leadership, the uninhibited unions effectively destroyed their beneficiary, the Labour government. Its Conservative successor thereupon introduced minor abridgements of union privileges in the Employment Acts of 1980 and 1982.

Excessive union legal privilege and political power contributed to Britain's slow growth in three main ways. First, it promoted restrictive practices, inhibited the growth of productivity and so discouraged investment. In the quarter-century 1950–75, Britain's investment and productivity record was the worst of any major industrial power. Second, it greatly increased the pressure of wage inflation, especially from the late 1960s onwards.[85] Thirdly, trade union social and legislative demands on government had a cumulative tendency to increase the size of the public sector and government share of GNP. Britain had traditionally been a minimum-government state: that was part of the benevolent framework which made the industrial revolution possible. The census of 1851 registered less than 75,000 civil public employees, mostly customs, excise and postal workers, with only 1,628 manning the central departments of civil government, at a time when the corresponding figure for France (1846) was 932,000. In the century that followed the proportion of the working population employed in the public sector rose from 2.4 per cent to 24.3 per cent in 1950. To put it another way, during the 120 years 1790–1910, proportion of GNP accounted for by public expenditure never rose over 23 per cent and averaged 13 per cent. After 1946 it never fell below 36 per cent.[86]

The really damaging increase, however, occurred after 1964, during a period when Labour was in office in eleven years out of fifteen. In the 1950s and early 1960s it had been just over 40 per cent. In 1965 it passed 45 per cent and in 1967 50 per cent. The 55-per-cent mark was exceeded immediately after Labour returned to office in 1974 and the following year it rose to 59.06 per cent. In 1975–6 public sector borrowing alone had reached 11.5 per cent of total output, and the total of new public borrowing over the past five years alone exceeded £31 billion.[87] By this stage the combination of public overspending and wage-inflation was in danger of pushing the British inflation rate into the 40 per cent band. In the autumn of 1976 Britain was obliged to call in the broker's men of the International Monetary Fund and submit to their *diktat*. Thereafter there was some retrenchment and, after the Conservative electoral victory of 1979, a systematic attempt to reduce public borrowing, restrain the public sector and expose the economy to the deflationary discipline of market forces. This, combined with the impact of the

North Sea offshore oilfields, which made Britain self-sufficient in oil by 1980 and a substantial net exporter by 1981, stabilized the economy and raised productivity to competitive levels, though on the lowest level of economic activity since the late 1960s. By 1983 Britain was recovering, but very slowly, and unlikely to be able to exert any form of leadership, inside or outside the EEC, for some time to come.

Britain's relative failure, however, was an exception. Over the whole of Europe west of the Iron Curtain, the four post-war decades saw a spectacular social and economic improvement. It was accomplished, moreover, against a background of constitutional legality and political peace. The contrast with the inter-war period was stunning, even in the most favoured areas. The Scandinavian countries had one of the worst records for unemployment throughout the 1920s and 1930s. In the winter of 1932–3 the percentage of the labour force out of work rose to 31.5 in Sweden, 42.4 in Norway and 42.8 in Denmark.[88] It was a period of intense class-warfare. Paramilitary forces had to be created to maintain order, and it was from the bitterness of social strife that Vidkun Quisling built his Nazi-type movement with its uniformed *birdmenn* modelled on the SA.[89]

The change came in the second half of the 1930s. In Norway (1935), Sweden and Denmark (1936) and Finland (1937), Social Democratic governments emerged which introduced comprehensive social security programmes. They were financed by rapid economic recovery. In Norway by 1938 GNP was 75 per cent above its 1914 figure and in Sweden it increased 50 per cent in the years 1932–9, though Social Democracy was no more able than any other pre-war system (Hitlerism alone excepted) to solve mass unemployment.[90] Already, in the later 1930s, British and American observers, such as Marquis Childs and Lord Simon of Wythenshawe, were drawing attention to what Simon called 'the most encouraging thing in the world today'.[91] The Social Democrats continued to dominate Scandinavian politics until the late 1970s, achieving prodigious democratic continuity. In Sweden Tage Erlander held the premiership for a record twenty-three years. Einar Gerhardsen had a comparable record in Norway until his retirement in 1965. The Social Democrats retained power from 1936–76 in Sweden and in Norway from 1935 to 1981 (except 1965–71); and they were dominant throughout this period in Denmark and Finland. This social and political stability enabled Scandinavia to make a striking contribution, in relation to its numbers, to the world economy. In the mid-1970s, 22 million Scandinavians produced nearly 20 million tons of grain, 5.6 million tons of fish (twice America's and five times Britain's production),

25.2 million tons of iron ore (more than Britain, France and Germany combined) and 49 million tons of wood and paper (a quarter of US production). Scandinavia generated more electric energy than France, and its shipbuilding exceeded that of America, Britain, France and Germany together.[92] But in the 1970s the growing cost of welfare services, the exigencies of the powerful trade union movements, as in Britain, and the impact of very high taxes combined with the energy crisis to destroy the dynamism of the Scandinavian economies, especially in Sweden, and ended the Social Democratic power monopoly. Non-socialists recovered office from 1976–82 in Sweden, in Denmark and in 1981 even in Norway, which had benefited from North Sea oil. The Scandinavian experience indicated that, even in the most favourable circumstances, there were severe practical limits to what a social welfare democracy could offer.

It was notable, indeed, that during the 1970s Switzerland overtook Sweden as the country with the highest socially balanced living standards, a result achieved by what might be termed plebiscitory conservatism. Industrialization came to Switzerland from 1800 onwards and by 1920 over 40 per cent of the employed population were in industry (plus a large service element in hotels and banks), against only 25 per cent in agriculture. Universal male suffrage was introduced as early as 1848, together with a constitutional referendum system, augmented by further referenda options in 1874 and 1891, making direct voting by the mass electorate the normal process of legislative change. This was accompanied by a device known as 'concordance democracy', which entails representation of all major parties on the government executive, the Federal Council, and public acknowledgement of pressure-groups.[93] This system had two very important political consequences. First, referenda forced conservatives to build up mass parties, which have always been populist rather than élitist. The anti-Socialist *Bürgerblock*, of Radicals, Catholic Conservatives and peasants, which dominated Swiss politics from 1919 onwards, was a completely multi-class party, including some of the poorest elements in the nation: Italian-speaking Catholics, who felt discriminated against by progressive, French- and German-speaking Protestant liberals. Conservatism became a powerful negative force, able to block plebiscitory change.[94] Secondly, by preventing the radicalization of the workers, Conservative populism drove the Socialists towards the centre. In 1935 the Swiss Social Democrat Party became the first to renounce the principle of class struggle and two years later negotiated a 'Peace Agreement' in the engineering industry. This opened the way for a Socialist to join the Federal government in 1943, and in turn to the creation of an integrated bourgeois–Social-democrat state, based on conservative negativism.

The negative approach paradoxically promoted the dynamism of the Swiss economy, especially in its biggest growth industry, banking. During the 1960s and 1970s, it was the refusal of conservative elements to accept the Social Democrat demand to 'democratize' and 'open' Swiss banking which allowed the economy to continue to grow and the banks to survive the 'Chiasso Affair' of 1977 (which involved a branch of Credit Suisse and Italian currency smugglers). Swiss banks were forbidden to divulge information about accounts by a law passed in 1934 to prevent the Nazi government from tracking down the savings of German Jews. Information is made available through Interpol in cases of kidnapping and robbery and (since 1980) to the US government to deal with certain cases of organized crime. But Switzerland resolutely refused to divulge financial data for political purposes, although it came under a great deal of pressure when the Shah of Iran was ejected in 1979. There are many thousands of numbered 'political' accounts in Switzerland, including many from behind the Iron Curtain. But they represent only a tiny fraction of the Swiss banking trade, which at the end of 1978 held foreign deposits of $115.06 billion, plus a further $123.7 billion in securities.[95] By the early 1980s total Swiss bank holdings were in the trillion-dollar range and to 'democratize' the system would, Conservatives argued, destroy the efficiency of a system whose secrecy is linked with informality, speed and hatred of bureaucracy. Since banking was the source of Swiss industrial growth (in 1980 the three largest Swiss banks held 2,200 seats on 1,700 Swiss corporations), a flight of capital would send the entire economy into recession. To defend banking secrecy is perhaps the most unpopular cause anyone could now support in the late-twentieth century. Yet thanks to Swiss plebiscitory democracy, which has made it easy to construct negative coalitions, the line was held throughout the 1970s, the Swiss economy remained buoyant, the Swiss franc one of the world's strongest currencies and Swiss *per capita* income pulled ahead of Scandinavian and North American levels.

The high performance and the democratic stability of the Swiss and Scandinavian countries, generally classified as 'Protestant', fitted in with the theories, first advanced in France in the 1830s and culminating in Max Weber's 'Protestant ethic' thesis, that religious belief tended to determine economic patterns. This was demolished on a historical basis in the 1940s and 1950s, but even more interesting was its practical refutation, during the post-war period, by the development of the south European, 'non-Protestant' economies. Italian Switzerland caught up with the French and German cantons. Italy had its industrial 'miracle' in the 1950s, France in the 1960s. Even more impressive, in view of past performance, was the political and social progress of the Iberian peninsula and Greece.

António Salazar in Portugal and Franco in Spain proved not only the most durable but by far the most successful of the pre-war dictators, and history is likely to take a far more favourable view of both than was fashionable even in the early 1980s. Salazar took over finance in 1928, the prime ministership in 1932 and survived until 1970, the only tyrant ever to be overthrown by that dangerous instrument, a collapsing deckchair. He was also the only one to run a dictatorship of intellectuals (though Lenin came near to it). Between 1932 and 1961, university professors never made up less than 21 per cent of Salazar's cabinet. They held half the cabinet posts 1936–44; about one in four of the dictator's colleagues came from a single department, the law faculty at Coimbra University. This *catedratiocracia*, or rule by dons, was highly successful in promoting slow but steady economic growth, maintaining a strong currency, holding back inflation and, above all, in giving Portugal what it had never possessed in modern times: political stability. The last was achieved partly by a small but highly efficient secret police force, the PIDE (International Police for the Defence of the State), which dated from 1926. Salazar defended the interests of the possessing classes but often went against their wishes, especially in hanging on, at great expense, to Portugal's African possessions, long after business wanted to compromise. He saw the head of the PIDE every day and supervised its smallest movement. He gaoled his enemies for long periods: in the mid-1970s, the twenty-two members of the Communist Central Committee claimed they had served a total of 308 years in prison, an average of fourteen.[96] But he would not impose the death penalty, even though he allowed the PIDE an occasional unofficial murder, such as the killing of General Delgado, the leader of the opposition, in February 1965.[97] Because the PIDE was discreet in its brutality it was remarkably hard to expose and even enjoyed some esteem. Its commander, Agostinho Lourenco, was head of Interpol in Paris in the late 1940s, and when Pope Paul VI visited Fatima in 1967 he decorated several senior PIDE officers.

When Salazar, as a result of his deckchair mishap, lost his senses in 1969, the professors were sent back to their universities and the PIDE 'abolished' or rather renamed. Like most bureaucratic reforms, this produced a big increase in numbers and a catastrophic reduction in efficiency (though not in cruelty and lawlessness). The secret police were taken by surprise by the uprising which overthrew the regime on 25 April 1974.[98] Portugal was democratized, the empire vanished, the economy stumbled, inflation increased. But after three years of confusion Portugal retreated from the headlines and reverted to basic Salazarian economic patterns. The astonishing and encouraging aspect was that Portugal was able to make the transition from a durable police state to a working democracy not only without a bloodbath but while conserving most of the achievements of the old regime.

Spain underwent a similar, and in the circumstances still more remarkable, experience in the 1970s. When Franco handed over his authority in summer 1974 to Juan Carlos (crowned King in November 1975 immediately after Franco's death), he had held effective power for thirty-eight years, an achievement even Philip II might have respected. He was probably right in thinking that a Republican victory would have produced another civil war and that his regime was the one 'which divides us least', for there were two bitterly divided monarchical factions, a fascist and a traditional conservative faction as well as the mortal enmity between the CP and other Republicans. In October 1944, after the liberation of France, 2,000 republicans 'invaded' across the Pyranees, expecting a general insurrection: nothing happened. A Republican government was formed 26 August 1945: a non-event. The Allies would not act against Franco because they did not want civil war in Spain. To please them he gave up the fascist salute (which he had never liked) but would not ban the Falange, much as he deplored its posturings, because it was a safety-valve for the extremist Right, and controllable.

In essence Franco was a non-political figure, who ruled through men acceptable to the Church, the landed classes and business. That was what the army wanted and the army had a veto on policy which long antedated Franco. Franco, like the army, was a negative force. He kept the state immobile and unadventurous; he prevented professional politicians from doing things. He described himself dourly to senior army officers as 'the sentry who is never relieved, the man who receives the unwelcome telegrams and dictates the answers, the man who watches while others sleep.'[99] If he had been a younger man he might have devised a plebiscitory framework. As it was, on 6 July 1947 he submitted a 'Law of Succession', embodying the monarchical principle, to a vote. Out of an electorate of nearly 17,200,000, 15,200,000 cast their votes and 14,145,163 voted 'Yes', under conditions which observers testified to be fair.[100]

With that out of the way Franco educated and coached Juan Carlos as his successor. In the meantime, within the framework of negative government, not unlike Salazar's or, for that matter, the Swiss Confederation's, the economy modernized itself with the help of market forces. In the twenty years 1950–70, Spain was transformed. Those living in towns over 20,000 rose from 30 per cent to nearly 50 per cent of the population. Illiteracy dropped from 19 to 9 per cent in thirty years, and in a mere fifteen years the student population doubled. Spain was in some ways more successful in modernizing its backward south than Italy. Physically and visually the landscape of Andalucia was transformed in the quarter-century 1950–75, and the rapidly falling rural population probably benefited more, in terms of real wages, than the industrial workers of the swelling towns. But the important change was in expectation: surveys showed that workers could expect much better jobs, in pay and prestige, than their fathers; that a man had higher expectations at forty than at twenty. The old hopelessness of Spain, the source of its sullen misery and occasionally of its frantic violence, had gone.[101] During the 1950s and 1960s, in effect, Spain became part of the general modern European economy, sharing its successes and failures and its overall prosperity: the Pyrenees ceased to be a cultural-economic wall.

The relative prosperity made possible by Franconian stability and political negativism helps to explain the success of the transition. It was characteristic of Franco's attitude that his last Prime Minister, and King Juan Carlos's first, Carlos Arias, was not a politician or a technocrat or a member of the Falange, but a protégé of an important army general.[102] It was equally characteristic of Spain's grudging acknowledgement of Franco's virtues that the first true Prime Minister of the democratic regime, Adolfo Suarez, though born only in 1932, had created his Right-Centre party, the Union of the Spanish People (UDPE), on the principle of *continuismo*. Suarez was assisted by the experience of Gaullism: both by its intrinsic success and by its ability to survive the death of its creator. He got his political reform through Franco's last Cortes without having to dissolve it, had it approved by a 94.2 per cent 'Yes' vote (15 December 1976), and in the eleven months before the elections he abolished Franco's monopoly party structure, introduced a multi-party system (including the CP), legalized trade unions, restored freedom of speech and the press, besides setting up the poll itself, the first free voting since February 1936. The system was biased in favour of rural areas: the fifteen smallest provinces, with 3.4 million population, had fifty-three seats in the Cortes, while Barcelona, with 4.5 million, had only thirty-three. But this allowed the emergence in the June 1977 vote of a quadripartite structure (as in France), with Suarez's re-named Union of the Democratic Centre as the strongest, with 34 per cent, followed by the Socialists (29 per cent), and Communists and Conservatives equal on the wings.[103]

The concentration of power in the centre was important, for the new Cortes had authority to write the constitution. The document which was eventually produced and approved by referendum in December 1978 defined Spain as a 'social and democratic state ruled by law', whose form of government was 'parliamentary monarchy'; but it also guaranteed the 'nationalities' autonomy, a major departure from the centralism not merely of Franco but of Spain itself ever since it accepted Castilian dominance in the late fifteenth century. The King was made head of the armed forces as well as the state, a point which was to prove vital during the attempted *putsch* of 1981: Spain remains a country where the army is accorded a special role, though it is not, curiously enough, a large force (220,000, plus 46,600 in the navy and 35,700 in the air force). The constitution abolished the death penalty, gave recognition, though not official status, to the Catholic Church, opened the way to divorce, and gave legal status to unions and parties. It raised a host of problems by laying down very complicated procedures for regional devolution, the issue likely to dominate Spanish politics in the 1980s. Indeed, being a parliamentary text and not a *diktat*, it was long (169 articles), as well as complex, absurdly detailed and gruesomely ill-written. Its great merit, however, was that it represented a consensus: Spain's first constitution which did not express a single ideology or a party monopoly of power.[104] By the early 1980s, the new Spanish establishment, led by a cool and cunning monarch (who showed his self-confidence by making Suarez a duke in 1981, Europe's first new non-royal one since the war), isolated both radical terrorism on the one hand, and army conspiracy on the other, and successfully pushed both out of the public mainstream, so that in 1982 the first Socialist government since 1936 was able to take office peacefully. Hence in a political sense, too, Spain now joined the European culture.

What was still more striking, and would have gladdened the shade of Lloyd George, was that poor, battered Greece at last merged itself with that culture too. Eleftherios Venizelos's democratic Greece, an intended major beneficiary of Versailles, had in fact gained little, though for her the Great War had lasted an entire decade, 1912–22. Its wartime Chief of Staff, General John Metaxas, attempted a *putsch* as early as 1923 and finally succeeded in setting up a dictatorship in 1936. He promised to 'discipline' the Greek people, replace Greek individualism with *ernst*, 'the serious German spirit'; he was 'the First Peasant', 'the First Worker', the 'National Father'. All the same it was Metaxas who defeated the Italians in 1940 (he died early in 1941), and it was the army, rather than any other institution, which emerged with the most honour from Greece's long war and post-war agony. Churchill's famous telegram to General Scobie may have saved Greece for the West, but Communist resistance survived in the north. Not until the summer of 1949 did Metaxas's old chief of staff, Field-Marshal Papagos, establish the government's authority over the whole country. For Greece, the

Second World War, too, lasted an entire decade. The civil war killed 80,000 Greeks, sent 20,000 to prison (including 5,000 executions or life-sentences), turned 700,000 into refugees and forced 10 per cent of the population to change home.[105]

There had been sixteen transitory governments between 1946 and 1952, but in the 1952 elections Papagos, who had created a 'national' party on the lines of de Gaulle's RPF, won an overwhelming victory and began eleven years of right-wing rule. When he died in 1955, Constantine Karamanlis took over his party, winning the 1958 and 1961 elections. This was the only kind of democratic 'normalcy' the army would accept. When George Papandreou, who had reconstructed the old Venizelos Centre-Left coalition, ousted Karamanlis in 1963 and drove him into exile, a period of confusion followed, terminating in an army *putsch*, under a group of middle-ranking officers led by Colonel George Papadopoulos.

As in Spain, the army considered itself more of a national institution than any of the parties. They were run by hereditary castes of the middle and upper classes, who operated a spoils system. The army, by contrast, claimed it was run on merit, most of its officers being recruited from the peasantry. It was closer to the Church, too; its hatred of professional politicians was widely shared. The Papadopoulos regime echoed Metaxas, with its accent on 'discipline' and 'Helleno–Christian civilization'. It produced a new, authoritarian constitution in 1968 and in 1973 ended Greece's always unsatisfactory monarchy. It aroused little opposition among workers and peasants; not much enthusiasm either. It imprisoned and occasionally tortured its middle-class enemies. It might have survived indefinitely, but Papadopoulos lost the confidence of his colleagues, was deposed, and the junta then dabbled clumsily in Cyprus politics, provoking the Turkish invasion of 1974. Defeated, it dissolved in chaos. Karamanlis was summoned from his Paris exile. He won an overwhelming electoral victory (219 seats out of 300) and so was able to push through in 1975 a constitution with a strong executive on Gaullist lines – yet another example of the extraordinary impact de Gaulle had on the Europe of the 1960s and 1970s. This resilient framework produced some confidence that the next electoral victory of the Papandreou clan, which duly occurred in 1981 on a socialist platform, would not introduce another cycle of constitutional instability.

What mattered to most Greeks was not the political ballet, or indeed the very exercise of professional politics, but the fact that in 1952 Papagos had introduced a long era of social and economic progress. This continued, at roughly the same pace, under Karamanlis, under the military, and then under Karamanlis again. It illustrated one of the lessons which emerge from a study of modern times. Political activities rarely promoted economic well-being, though they might, if intense and protracted enough, undermine it. The most useful function of government was to hold the ring, within which individuals could advance their own interests, benefiting the communal one in the process. The improvement in the fortunes of ordinary Greeks in the three decades 1950–80 was by far the most substantial in the country's history.[106] This was reflected in the one reliable index of popular approval: movement. Men and women are most sincere when they vote not with their ballot-papers but with their feet. Greeks had emigrated since the eighth century BC. During the 1970s, of 13 million Greeks, 4 million lived abroad, 3 million of them permanently. Emigration reached a peak of 117,167 in 1965, but that appears to have been the turning-point. During the later years of the military regime, the emigration rate fell fast, except to the United States, and more and more overseas Greeks began returning home. By 1974, for the first time since statistics were compiled in 1850, the number of Greeks joining the home economy was greater than those leaving it for work abroad. By 1979, when emigration had dropped below 20,000, remittances from abroad ($1.2 billion) had fallen behind tourism ($1.7 billion) and shipping ($1.5 billion) as Greece's prime source of income. Indeed during the 1970s, the Greek economy's growth-rates, averaging 5–6 per cent, with only 2 per cent unemployment, were much superior to those of Western Europe.[107] By the early 1980s, Greece was quickly approaching West European living-standards, and that was an added reason to suppose her new political and social stability might be lasting.

The process whereby, over thirty-five years, some 300 million people in Europe west and south of the Iron Curtain achieved relative affluence within a democratic framework and under the rule of law was one of the most striking in the whole of history. It might be termed unexpected, too, since it followed hard upon two attempts at continental suicide which had come close to success. Yet there was a paradox in this new stability and prosperity. In the early 1980s, three-and-a-half decades after the end of the war, democratic Europe, despite its accruing wealth, was still dependent for its security not merely on the guarantees of transatlantic America but on the continuing physical presence of American forces. This was anomalous. The history of America in the 1960s and 1970s suggested it was also dangerous.

EIGHTEEN

America's Suicide Attempt

The Eisenhower years were the culmination of the American paramountcy. A wall of collective security was completed around the
perimeter of the Communist bloc. Behind its ramparts, first America,
then Western Europe, enjoyed unprecedented prosperity. So both the
diplomatic and economic lessons of the inter-war period had been
learnt. Or so it was thought. It was Twenties prosperity over again,
but less frenetic and more secure, with a far wider social spread and
on both sides of the Atlantic. The Fifties was the decade of affluence,
a word popularized by the fashionable economist J.K.Galbraith in
his 1958 best-seller, *The Affluent Society*. The book attacked the old
'conventional wisdom'. In doing so it created a new one. Galbraith
and his school argued that the days of shortage were over. The world
was abundant in resources. The advanced economies had mastered
the difficulty of producing goods. The economic problem was solved.
What remained was a political one: distributing them equitably. The
state should play a creative role by employing 'private affluence' to
end 'public squalor' and cure dangerous imbalances in wealth not
only within nations but between them. Eisenhower did not share this
optimism. He thought the American economy could easily be
wrecked by excessive spending on arms or welfare, let alone both
together. Indeed it was notable that, unlike the Twenties, it was not
the Right but the Left who now believed that prosperity would go on
for ever and who turned the Sixties into the decade of illusion.

By 1960 Eisenhower was the oldest man ever to occupy the White
House. He appeared comatose. The cry was for activism, to 'get
America moving again'. America was presented as falling behind not
only in welfare provision but in military strength. There was talk of a
'missile gap'.[1] The Republican candidate in the 1960 election,
Vice-President Richard Nixon, was young (forty-seven) but asso-
ciated with the Administration's immobility and, as a hard-line
Californian, detested by the dominant East Coast media-liberals. The

Democrat, John Kennedy, was younger still (forty-three), rich and handsome. His strength lay in public relations and in an efficient and ruthless political machine, run by his brother Robert. These won him the election; that is, if he did win it legally. Of nearly 69 million votes cast, Kennedy had a margin of only 120,000, and this was clouded by rival interpretations of the vote in Alabama. Kennedy had a majority of 84 in the electoral college, which was what mattered. But here again irregularities in Texas and, still more, in Illinois by the notorious Daley machine, cast doubt on the validity of the Kennedy victory. Nixon did not challenge the result because he thought it would damage the presidency, and so America.[2] Such restraint earned him no credit. Kennedy's contempt for Nixon emerged in his post-election comment in 1960: 'He went out the way he came in – no class.'[3]

Kennedy had 'class'. He was the first president since Roosevelt who had never had to earn his living. Like FDR, he turned Washington into a city of hope; that is to say, a place where middle-class intellectuals flocked for employment. His wife Jackie was a society beauty with a taste for high culture. With such a glamorous couple in the White House, some spoke of Kennedy's Washington as 'the new Camelot'. Others were less impressed. The Kennedy invasion, one visiting statesman observed, was 'like watching the Borgia brothers take over a respectable north Italian town'. The first beneficiary of the new regime was the 'military-industrial complex', as the distrustful Eisenhower had branded it. Spending both on conventional and nuclear forces increased sharply. In some ways Kennedy and his Secretary of State, Dean Rusk, proved the most enthusiastic of the Cold Warriors, though not the most skilful. Kennedy gave a universalist twist to America's overseas obligations which was entirely new. The classical American attitude had been defined by Secretary of State John Quincy Adams in 1821. 'Wherever the standard of freedom and independence has been or shall be unfurled,' he promised, 'there will be America's heart, her benedictions and her prayers.' But, he added, 'she goes not abroad in search of monsters to destroy. She is the well-wisher to the freedom and independence of all. She is the champion and vindicator only of her own.'[4] Under Truman and Eisenhower, the doctrine had been modified, for 'her own' could be extended to include allies whose survival was vital to American self-interest.

Kennedy went further. He was conscious that the old-style Cold War, which Stalin waged by pushing forward his frontiers from a central base, was no longer the only one. Stalin's successors had introduced a war of movement, in which America's defensive barriers could be overlept. Nikita Khrushchev actually defined the new policy, in reality a policy as old as Lenin which Russia now had the resources to push vigorously, in a speech of 6 January 1961, shortly before Kennedy took over. The Communist victory, Khrushchev said, would not take place through nuclear war, which would destroy humanity, nor through conventional war, which might soon become nuclear, but through 'national liberation wars' in Africa, Asia and Latin America, the 'centres of revolutionary struggle against imperialism'. Since 'Communists are revolutionaries', they would 'take advantage' of these 'new opportunities'. Kennedy interpreted this as a kind of declaration of war, and he used his Inaugural Address to take up the challenge. He declared the time to be an 'hour of maximum danger' for freedom. His generation had been given the role of defending it. 'I do not shrink from this responsibility,' he said, 'I welcome it.' America would 'pay any price, bear any burden, meet any hardship, support any friend, oppose any foe, to ensure the survival and the success of liberty.'[5] That was an extraordinary guarantee; a blank cheque tossed at the world's feet.

Kennedy made this expansive gesture because he and his advisers believed that America could successfully compete with Soviet Russia for the allegience of the poorer peoples by promoting the emergence of liberal, democratic regimes to serve them. A variety of devices advanced this new 'action diplomacy': the Peace Corps of young US volunteers to serve abroad, the Green Berets for more forceful activities, termed 'counter-insurgency', campaigns for winning 'hearts and minds', the 'Alliance for progress' for Latin America; increased economic and military aid almost everywhere.[6] But this was to ignore the central lesson of the British Empire, that the best any possessing power can hope to settle for is stability, however imperfect. To promote dynamism is to invite chaos. In the end, a possessing power always had to defend its system by force, or watch it disintegrate, as Britain had done. America had now created a new, post-colonial system, as Kennedy's Inaugural acknowledged. But it was still a possessing one, dependent on stability for its well-being. America's resources were far greater than Britain's had been. But they were still limited. The art, therefore, lay in selecting those positions which must be defended and could only be defended by force, and devising workable alternatives for the others. Therein lay the weakness of Kennedy's universalism.

The problem immediately arose in an acute form in Latin America. Under the Monroe Doctrine of 1823 the United States had policed the hemisphere, in theory to preserve the independence of its nations from European covetousness, in reality to protect America's own interests. This often involved military intervention, especially in Central America and the Caribbean. The Monroe Doctrine was based on the reasoning that the Caribbean was America's 'inland sea' and part of the US economic structure. In Cuba, which America had liberated from Spain, the US right of intervention was actually written into the Cuban constitution, through the so-called 'Platt Amendment'. In the inter-war period, under the impact of Wilsonian doctrines of self-determination, the system foundered. In the 1928 Clark Memorandum, the State Department itself argued that Monroe did not justify US intervention since 'it states a case of United States vs. Europe, not the United States vs. Latin America'.[7] Roosevelt accepted this logic, scrapped the Platt Amendment in 1934 and introduced instead a 'Good Neighbour' policy, which in theory treated the Latin American states as equals. This might in time have worked very well, with the larger nations forming the same kind of relationship with their giant patron as Canada.

The most likely candidate for this role was Argentina, whose economy in the inter-war period was developing on the lines of Canada's and Australia's. Like Canada it had boomed from 1900 to 1914, experienced slower growth in the 1920s, a sharp setback from 1929 to 1933, but thereafter a long period of growth at an average of 2–3 per cent a year, with steady progress in the manufacturing, mining, oil, public utilities and electrical sectors: achieving, in fact, economic take-off – the first Latin American country to do so.[8] It had a market economy, minimum government, a growing middle class, a free press and the rule of law. During the Second World War it enjoyed a prosperity unknown in the southern hemisphere outside Australia, with wages rising to West European levels. It accumulated what was then the princely reserves of $1,500 million in dollar and sterling balances – more than Britain, Argentina's chief economic partner, had been able to invest there in over seventy years.[9] If the money had been used to create steel, petroleum and other import-substitution industries, the likelihood is that Argentina would have achieved dynamic, self-sustaining economic growth during the 1950s, and the whole history of Latin America would have been different.

Instead, Argentina fell victim to both the twin evils which poison Latin America: militarism and politics. In the nineteenth century the military *coup* had become a standard means to change government. This disastrous practice continued after the arrival of universal suffrage. In the years 1920–66, for instance, there were eighty successful military *coups* in eighteen Latin-American countries, Ecuador and Bolivia leading with nine each, Paraguay and Argentina following with seven each.[10] The key one in Argentina came in 1943. The junta appointed to the Labour Ministry a certain Colonel Juan Perón, the son of a poor farmer who had done well in the army; a handsome ski and fencing champion, flashy in mind and body, student of sociology, a pseudo-intellectual of the type that was to become very common in the post-war era. The military had hitherto stamped on unions. Perón discovered that, by patronizing labour, he could build himself a mass-following. As Labour Minister, he took over the unions. Hitherto, union leaders had been bribed personally. Perón bribed the entire labour movement.[11]

Perón's career illustrated the essential identity of the Marxist and the fascist will to power, for at times he borrowed from Lenin, Mussolini, Hitler, Franco and Stalin. He had great personal charm; a superb speaking voice; a gift for ideological verbiage. He spoke of his labour followers as 'the shirtless ones' (they were in fact well paid). He called his philosophy *Justicialismo*, the first of the bogus 'isms' of what was to become the Third World. Perón could claim to be the prototype not merely of a new kind of Latin-American dictator but of all the post-colonial charismatics of Africa and Asia. He was the link between the old-style mountebank dictator and the new Bandung model. He showed how to manipulate head-counting democracy. He had no substance. When he quarrelled with his military colleagues in 1945, all he could think of was to fall on his knees and beg for mercy. It was his mistress Eva Duarte, a militant feminist, who roused the workers and got him released. By marrying her he squared the church. Then he swept on to a handsome victory (24 February 1945) in one of the few free elections in Argentina's history.[12]

As President, Perón gave a classic demonstration, in the name of socialism and nationalism, of how to wreck an economy. He nationalized the Central Bank, railways, telecommunications, gas, electricity, fishing, air-transport, steel and insurance. He set up a state marketing agency for exports. He created Big Government and a welfare state in one bound: spending on public services, as percentage of GNP, rose from 19.5 to 29.5 per cent in five years.[13] He had no system of priorities. He told the people they would get everything at once. In theory they did. The workers were given thirteen months' pay for a year's work; holidays with pay; social benefits at a Scandinavian level. He would track down a highly successful firm which spent lavishly on its workers and force all firms to copy its practices, regardless of their resources. At the same time he carried out a frontal assault on the agricultural sector, Argentina's main source of internal capital. By 1951 he had exhausted the reserves and decapitalized the country, wrecked the balance of payments and built wage-inflation into the system. Next year drought struck the land and brought the crisis into the open. Seeing his support vanish, Perón turned from economic demagoguery to political tyranny. He destroyed the Supreme Court. He took over the radio station and *La Prensa*, the greatest newspaper in Latin America. He debauched the universities and fiddled with the constitution. Above all, he created public 'enemies': Britain, America, all foreigners, the Jockey Club, which his gangs burnt down in 1953, destroying its library and art collection. Next year he turned on Catholicism, and in 1955 his labour mobs destroyed Argentina's two finest churches, San Francisco and Santo Domingo, and many others.

That was the last straw. The army turned him out. He fled on a Paraguayan gunboat. But his successors could never get back to the minimum government which had allowed Argentina to become wealthy. Too many vested interests had been created: a huge, parasitical state, over-powerful unions, a vast army of public employees. It is one of the dismal lessons of the twentieth century that, once a state is allowed to expand, it is almost impossible to contract it. Perón's legacy proved more durable than his verbiage. But he himself proved durable enough. In 1968 the head of the military, General Alejandro Lanusse, swore: 'If that man . . . should set foot in this land again, one of us, he or I, will leave it feet first, because I shall not let my sons suffer what I have.' Five years later, as President, he organized the elections which swept Perón back into power, aged seventy-nine: a case, as Dr Johnson said of second marriage, of 'the triumph of hope over experience'.[14] By this point the whole course of Argentina's history had been changed. It had forfeited its chance of becoming an advanced economy and had been permanently downgraded to the status of a second-rate Latin-American republic, condemned to industrial backwardness, political instability and military tyranny. In the late 1970s and early 1980s, the public life of Argentina became increasingly savage, and in 1982 it even embarked on a reckless military adventure against Britain's Falkland Isles, which ended in humiliating defeat.

The Perónist revolution was a wider disaster for Latin America as a whole, and for the USA also. The Canadian analogy receded. In frustration and despair, demagoguery flourished; and demagogues, as Perón himself had done, took the easy way out and blamed America. Moreover, Perón himself remained a potent exemplar. He had 'stood up to the *Yanquis*'; he had made his country truly independent for the first time. His economic failure was forgotten; his political success was remembered and imitated.

Perón's shadow fell over Cuba. It, like Argentina before Perón, was one of the richest Latin-American countries. But its economic structure was very different. It was really part of the US economy. When it became independent in 1898 it should, in logic, have become a US state, like Texas or New Mexico, or a colony, like Puerto Rico, to be later upgraded. In 1924 US investment in Cuba was already $1.2 billion. Cuba got 66 per cent of its imports from the US and sent it 83 per cent of its exports, chiefly sugar. In 1934 the Reciprocal Trade Agreement forbade Cuba to impose tariffs or quotas on a wide range of US imports; the quid pro quo, the Jones–Costigan Act, guaranteed the USA would take the Cuban sugar crop at generous prices. The arrangement was termed by Earl Babst, head of the American Sugar Refining Company, 'a step in the direction of a sound colonial policy'.[15] After 1945 the dominance of the USA in the Cuban economy slowly declined. But even in the 1950s the US Ambassador in Havana, as one of them testified, was 'the second most important man in Cuba; sometimes even more important than the president'.[16] Cuba, in fact, was a kind of US satellite. But the ending of the Platt Amendment had made it a full independent country – in theory. Therein lay the source of much anger.

Like the vast majority of Latin-American dictators, Cuba's had always begun as liberals and ended as tyrants, usually becoming reconciled to the US paramountcy in the process. The last old-style dictator, a former liberal, of course, had been Gerardo Machado, thrown out in 1933 by an NCOs' *coup* led by Fulgencio Batista. This sergeant-stenographer was a genuine man of the people, half-Indian, whose father had been a sugar-worker. He had worked on the plantations himself. He was an extreme radical. The US ambassador, Sumner Welles, thought his regime 'frankly communistic' and wanted battleships sent.[17] The Communist leader, Blas Roca, called Batista the father of the Popular Front, 'this magnificent reserve of Cuban democracy', 'the people's idol, the great man of our national politics'.[18] Batista ruled as president himself, 1940–4, but usually through others. He was in league with the radical students, and his favourite substitute as president was their leader, Ramón Grau San Martin, who created the Authentic Revolutionary Movement (*Auténticos*, as opposed to *Ortodoxos*, the opposition revolutionaries). But Grau turned out a crook, a weak man run by a grasping mistress. 'Have a word with Paulina' was his system of government. By the time that Batista took power himself again, in 1952, the damage was done, and he himself was sucked into the morass of graft. So was virtually everyone else in public life.

In the 1940s and 1950s, Cuba became a radical gangster society. In the old days America would have intervened and imposed somebody honest. Now that was ruled out. But America was necessarily involved in all major Cuban transactions. In the age of *Peronismo*, it was blamed for everything. Cuba illustrated the gap between words and reality which was to become the most striking characteristic of the Third World. Everyone in politics talked revolution and practised graft. Of course corruption was linked to violence. The presidency of the students' union at Havana University, an institution almost as important as the army, was settled by guns. The police were not allowed on campus. The campus police were murdered or terrorized. Many students carried Forty-fives, and lectures were punctuated by shots. The Communists were as corrupt as anyone. Grau used to say, when they greeted him with clenched-fist salutes, 'Don't worry: tomorrow they will open their fists!'[19] The only opponents of corruption were a few rich men, such as the eccentric Eduardo Chibás, leader of the *Ortodoxos*, and even he joined in the violence by fighting duels. The various police forces fought gang-battles with each other; most gangsters held police as well as political rank. The political *pistoleros*, organized in 'action groups', and spouting Marxist, fascist or Perónist slogans, were reminiscent of Germany in the early 1920s. Students supplied the worst killers and the most pathetic victims.

One of the student gunmen was Fidel Castro. His father came from Galicia, from a family of right-wing Carlists, and like most Spanish immigrants hated the Americans. He worked for United Fruit, got a farm himself, prospered and ended with 10,000 acres and a labour force of five hundred. His son Fidel became a professional student politician – he never seems to have wanted any other occupation than politics – and, being rich, supported Chibas's *Ortodoxos*. On his own admission, he carried a gun as a student.[20] In 1947, aged twenty, he took part in an invasion of the Dominican Republic by an 'action group', armed with a sub-machine gun. The next year he was involved in appalling violence in Bogota, during the Pan-American Conference; he was said to have helped to organize the riots, in which 3,000 were killed.[21] The same year he was in a gun-battle with Cuban police, and ten days later was accused of murdering the Minister for Sport. Batista, hearing he was an exceptionally gifted political gangster, tried to enlist him. Castro declined for what he termed 'generational reasons'. According to a fellow law-student, he was 'a power-hungry person, completely unprincipled, who would throw in his lot with any group he felt could help his political career'.[22] He later claimed his 'vocation' was 'being a revolutionary'. He had the urges, in short, of a Lenin as well as a Hitler: the two streams came together in his violent personality. But, like Perón, he modelled his political prose-style on the Spanish proto-fascist Primo de Rivera until he adopted Marxist clichés.[23]

Castro's chance came in 1951–2, when Chibás went mad and shot himself, leaving the 'idealist' role vacant, and Batista, in an attempt to end gangsterism, abolished the parties and made himself dictator. His 'freedom *coup*' was popular with the workers and he would probably have restored constitutional rule eventually, as he had done before. But Castro did not give him time. He seems to have welcomed the *coup* as a chance to get down to serious fighting: *Le hora es de lucha*, as he put it in his first political statement. He took to the Sierra with 150 other gunmen. His guerrilla campaign was never very serious, though urban terrorism cost many lives. The Cuban economy continued to flourish until 1957. In all essentials, the battle for Cuba was a public relations campaign, fought in New York and Washington. Castro's principal advocate was Herbert Matthews of the *New York Times*, who presented him as the T.E.Lawrence of the Caribbean.[24] Just as the Hearst press helped to make the Cuban revolution in 1898, so the *Times* sponsored Castro. This swung round the State Department. William Wieland, in charge of the Caribbean desk, had hitherto taken the view, 'I know Batista is considered by many as a sonofabitch ... but American interests come first ... at least he is our sonofabitch.'[25] Now Wieland changed sides. Earl Smith, appointed Ambassador to Havana in 1957, was told: 'You are assigned to Cuba to preside over the downfall of Batista. The decision has been taken that Batista has to go.' Wieland sent him to be briefed by Matthews, who told him: 'it would be in the best interests of Cuba and ... the world ... if Batista were removed.' Roy Rubottom, Assistant Secretary of State, was also pro-Castro, as were the CIA in Havana.[26]

Once in Cuba, however, Smith grasped that a Castro victory would be a disaster for America, and sought to prevent it. He insisted on flying to Washington, at his own expense (Rubottom refused to authorize it from state funds), to hold a warning press conference, at which he said that 'the US government' would never be able 'to do business with Fidel Castro' because he 'would not honour international obligations'.[27] Thereafter the State Department worked behind his back. The pattern of muddle, duplicity and cross-purpose recalled Roosevelt diplomacy at its worst, and attempts by some State Department officials to undermine the Shah of Iran in 1979. On 13 March 1958 Smith saw Batista in his study lined with busts of Lincoln, and agreement was reached to hold free elections and for Batista to stand down on 24 February 1959. The next day, unknown to Smith, Washington took the decision to suspend all official arms sales to Cuba. A shipment of Garrand rifles was stopped at the New York dockside. As Castro's American well-wishers continued to subscribe for arms to him, America was now, from early 1958, arming one side: the rebels. The US arms embargo was the turning-point in Castro's road to power. Before it, he had never had more than three-hundred men. After it, the Cubans concluded the Americans had changed their policy and switched sides accordingly.

Castro's support rocketed up; the economy plummeted. Even so, Castro never had more than 3,000 followers. His 'battles' were public relations exercises. In the so-called 'Battle of Santa Clara' his losses were six, and only forty in the defeat of Batista's 1958 summer offensive, the largest engagement in the 'war'. Batista's total losses were only 300. The real fighters were the anti-Batista elements in the towns, of whom between 1,500 and 2,000 were killed. The 'guerrilla war' was largely propaganda.[28] As Che Guevara admitted, after it was over: 'The presence of a foreign journalist, American for preference, was more important for us than a military victory.'[29] Apart from America's switch, the morale of the Batista regime was destroyed by the urban bands, which were non-Castroist. At the last minute, in November 1958, the American government sought to organize the succession of a non-Castro government, characteristically without telling their Ambassador.[30] But by then it was too late. Batista got out in January 1959, and Cuba was at Castro's mercy.

At what point Castro became a Leninist is unclear. He had obviously studied carefully the methods both Lenin and Hitler had used to make themselves absolute masters. When he took over in January 1959 he had himself made Commander-in-Chief and, using as his excuse the necessity to prevent the re-emergence of gangsterism, secured for himself a monopoly of force. All police forces were placed under himself, not the Interior Ministry, and key posts in both police and army were rapidly taken over by his guerrilla colleagues. The critical moment was when he got the rival anti-Batista forces, especially the democratic *Directorio Revolucionario*, to lay down their arms.[31] Thereafter he could do what he liked; and did so. The provisional president, Judge Manuel Urrutia, was made to agree with Castro's demand to postpone elections for eighteen months, with rule by decree in the meantime. This was the Lenin technique. One of the first decrees abolished all political parties, his paper, *Revolución*, explaining: 'Worthy men who belong to definite political parties already have posts in the provisional government . . . . The others . . . would do better to be silent' (7 January 1959). That was the Hitler touch. So was the decree of 7 February, described as 'a fundamental law of the republic', investing legislative power in the cabinet – the equivalent of Hitler's Enabling Law. Immediately after it, Castro took over as Prime Minister, banning the President from cabinet meetings.[32] Thus, within weeks of the take-over, the liberals and democrats had been effectively excluded from power. The cabinet was the Politburo; and, within it, thanks to his relations and cronies, Castro was dictator, exactly like Batista. But Batista had the saving grace of caring for money as well as power. Castro wanted power alone.

Castro had already been running purge courts-martial to kill his enemies. The first unambiguous act of tyranny came on 3 March 1959, after forty-four Batista air force men, accused of 'war crimes', were acquitted in a Santiago court for lack of evidence. Castro immediately announced on TV that the trial was a mistake. There would be another. The president of the court was found dead. A creature of the Castros was appointed in his place. The men were retried and sentenced to twenty to thirty years' imprisonment. Castro announced: 'Revolutionary Justice is based not upon legal precepts but on moral conviction.' It was the end of the rule of law in Cuba.[33] When Grau asked when elections would be held, Castro replied when the agrarian reform was complete, when all children went free to school and could read and write, when all had free access to medicine and doctors. Never, in short. He got rid of Urrutia over the Agrarian Reform law in summer 1959. The President fled to the Venezuelan Embassy and then out of the country.

The movement to Soviet Russia began at the same time. The truth is, Cuba had, and has, a dependent economy. If America was unacceptable as a patron, another great power had to fill the role. And America was unacceptable, in the sense that Castro, like other Third World dictators, needed an enemy. After Batista went, it had to be America. And with America as enemy, he needed an ally; it had to be Soviet Russia. With Russia as ally and, from mid-1959, paymaster, Castro's ideology had to be Marxism, which fitted in well with his Left–fascist brand of domestic autocracy. Castro was never an orthodox Marxist-Leninist ruler in that he governed not merely by secret committee but by public oratory, in the tradition of Mussolini, Hitler and Perón. But in the second half of 1959 he signed his treaty with Mephistopheles by getting Soviet arms, advisers and KGB assistance in organizing his security services. He was hooked. From now on, for a Cuban just to hold anti-Communist views was enough for arrest. At the same time, the first gangland killing of Castro's opponents started, with the mysterious death of the army Commander-in-Chief Camilo Cienfuegos. Purge-trials of old Castro associates, such as Hubert Matos, who would not accept his totalitarian system, began in December 1959. By the end of the year Cuba was a Communist dictatorship.[34]

For an island only forty miles from America to transform itself abruptly from a dependent ally into a Soviet satellite was in itself a momentous shift in the world balance of power, especially since Castro himself, in a four-thousand-word manifesto published in 1957, had openly proclaimed that, once in power, he would pursue an active foreign policy against, as he put it, 'other Caribbean dictators'.[35] America would have been within her rights to reverse the development by any means, including force. Perhaps the best analogy was with neutral Finland, whose foreign and defence policy, because of the proximity to Russia, were conducted subject to a Soviet veto. But by the end of 1959, Dulles was dead and Eisenhower was a lame-duck president not running for re-election. Nothing definite was done, though many plans were considered. When Kennedy took over, early in 1961, he found a proposal, supported by the CIA and the chairman of the Joint Chiefs of Staff, for 12,000 armed Cuban exiles, known as the Cuban Liberation Corps, to land in Cuba's Bay of Pigs and detonate a popular rising against Castro. It is hard to believe the wily and experienced Eisenhower would have given final approval to the scheme. It had all the disadvantages of involving America morally and politically (the first two men to step ashore were CIA operatives[36]) with none of the real advantages of US air and naval participation. Naïvely and weakly, Kennedy allowed it to go ahead on 17 April. It proved a fiasco. The invasion should have got full American backing, or been dropped. This was Kennedy's instinct. As he said to his brother Robert, he would 'rather be called an aggressor than a bum'.[37] But in the event he lacked the resolution: in its political and military miscalculations, the Bay of Pigs raised uneasy echoes of Eden's Suez misadventure.[38] For Cuba it was a disaster, for it gave Castro the opportunity to wage a terror-campaign against the opposition. Most of those already in custody were shot. Perhaps as many as 100,000 were arrested. They included the real underground, most of the CIA's 2,500 agents, and 20,000 counter-revolutionary sympathizers.[39] On 1 May Castro announced that Cuba was now a socialist state. There would be no more elections: there was, he said, an election every day in Cuba since the revolutionary regime expressed the will of the people.[40]

American opinion was outraged by the Bay of Pigs failure and would have supported direct intervention. One senior policy-maker, Chester Bowles, thought a decision by Kennedy 'to send in troops or drop bombs or whatever . . . would have had the affirmative votes of at least 90 per cent of the people'. Richard Nixon, consulted, told the President: 'I would find a proper legal cover and I would go in.'[41] But the Administration dithered. Defence Secretary Robert McNamara admitted: 'We were hysterical about Castro at the time of the Bay of Pigs and thereafter.'[42] At various times, there were plans to employ gangsters to attack Cuban officials, to spread the rumour that Castro was Antichrist and a Second Coming imminent, with a submarine letting off star-shells, to attack sugar-workers with non-lethal chemicals, to use thallium salts to make Castro's beard fall out, to lace his cigars with disorienting chemicals or impregnate them with deadly botulinus, to give his mistress, Marie Lorenz, poison capsules, to use Cuban–American gangsters to assassinate him under contract, to give him a scuba-diving suit impregnated with a tuberculus bacillus and a skin-fungus, and to plant a rare seashell, filled with an explosive device, in the area where he dived. Richard Helms, whom Kennedy had made head of the CIA, later testified:

It was the policy at the time to get rid of Castro, and if killing him was one of the things that was to be done . . . we felt we were acting well within the guidelines . . . . Nobody wants to embarrass a President . . . by discussing the assassination of foreign leaders in his presence.[43]

None of these wild schemes came to anything. In the event it was Khrushchev who provided Kennedy with another opportunity to settle the Cuban problem. Khrushchev, too, had his 'missile gap', real or imaginary. By stationing medium-range missiles in Cuba he would alter the strategic nuclear equation drastically in Russia's favour at virtually no extra expense. Once they were installed and properly defended, they could not be attacked without nuclear war, thus ensuring the inviolability of the Castro regime – Khrushchev was, it appears, scared of 'losing' Cuba to America and being blamed by his colleagues.[44] According to Castro's account, given to two French journalists, the 'initial idea originated with the Russians and with them alone . . . . It was not in order to ensure our own defence but primarily to strengthen socialism on the international plane.' Castro said he finally agreed because it was 'impossible for us not to share the risks which the Soviet Union was taking to save us . . . . It was in the final analysis a question of honour.'[45]

In fact honour had nothing to do with it. The cost to Russia of maintaining the Cuban economy and financing Castro's ambitious scheme was mounting rapidly, and Castro had no alternative but to provide his island as a missile-base in return. He also thought his regime, though not the Cuban people, would be safer with the missiles than without them. The scheme was as crackbrained as the Bay of Pigs venture and infinitely more dangerous. Castro claimed that Khrushchev boasted his move was something Stalin would never have dared. His colleague Anastas Mikoyan told a secret briefing of Soviet diplomats in Washington that it was designed to achieve 'a definite shift in the power relationship between the socialist and the capitalist worlds'.[46] What made the venture still more reckless was that Khrushchev deliberately lied to Kennedy. He admitted that Russia was arming Castro but gave secret assurances that only short-range surface-to-air missiles would be installed. In no circumstances would long-range strategic missiles be sent. In fact he sent forty-two medium-range 1,100-miles nuclear missiles and twenty-four 2,200-miles missiles (the latter never arrived), together with twenty-four SAM anti-aircraft missile groups and 22,000 Soviet troops and technicians.

There was never any possibility of concealing this activity, and its
true nature, from US air observation. The sites were photographed
by a U-2 aircraft on 15 October. It was clear that by December at least
fifty strategic missiles would be deployed, armed with nuclear
weapons and strongly protected, only a few miles from American
territory. From 16 October the Administration debated what to do.
It divided into 'Hawks' and 'Doves', as they were now termed. The
Hawks, led by Dean Acheson, who was brought into the secret
debate, advocated, as he put it, 'cleaning the missile bases out
decisively with an air attack', without further warning. The Doves,
led by Robert Kennedy and Robert McNamara, deplored the idea of
a 'Pearl Harbor in reverse', which would be sure to kill 'several
thousand' Russians as well as Cuban civilians – the Chiefs of Staff
calculated that 800 sorties would be required. Moscow, argued
McNamara, would feel obliged to make 'a very major response. In
such an event the United States would lose control of the situation
which could escalate to general war.' Instead they urged a blockade
or (to use the more cunning term Roosevelt had applied to Japan) a
'quarantine', which would give Russia a chance to retreat from the
brink without too much loss of face.[47]

President Kennedy wavered from one side to the other. He ordered
preparations for an air-strike to continue but finally opted for
quarantine and announced it publicly on 22 October, with a deadline
two days later. The deadline was put in because by 23 October four
out of six medium-range missile sites were operational and it was
essential to prevent the Russians from working on the sites under
cover of diplomatic delays. On 24 October, Soviet missile-carrying
cargo ships approached the quarantine line and stopped. But it
remained to get the existing missiles out. So the following day
President Kennedy cabled Khrushchev asking for 'a restoration of the
earlier situation' (i.e., removal of the missiles). Khrushchev sent two
replies. The first, on 26 October, indicated compliance in return for
an American pledge not to invade Cuba. The second, the next day,
demanded a further US concession: removal of its own medium-
range Jupiter missiles from Turkey. Kennedy ignored the second
letter and accepted the non-invasion deal proposed in the first. It was
on this basis that Khrushchev agreed to remove the missiles on 28
October.[48]

President Kennedy's handling of the missile crisis was much
praised at the time and for some years thereafter. Khrushchev was
blamed by his own colleagues. When the Soviet Presidium dismissed
him in October 1964, it referred to his 'hairbrained scheming, hasty
conclusions, rash decisions and actions based on wishful thinking'.[49]
There was no doubt the world came close to large-scale nuclear war.

On 22 October all American missile crews were placed on 'maximum alert'. Some 800 B47s, 550 B52s, and seventy B58s were prepared with bomb-bays closed for immediate take-off from their dispersal positions. Over the Atlantic were ninety B52s carrying multi-megaton bombs. Nuclear war-heads were activated on 100 Atlas, fifty Titans and twelve Minuteman missiles, and on American carriers, submarines and overseas bases. All commands were in a state of Defcon-2, the highest state of readiness next to war itself.[50] Robert Kennedy spoke of '60 million Americans killed and as many Russians or more'. Khrushchev himself claimed that in arguing with his own military he warned of 'the death of 500 million human beings'.[51] He took a gigantic risk, but pulled back from the brink when his bluff was called. Castro, who was not consulted about the climb-down, was furious when he got the news. According to Che Guevara, who was present, he swore, kicked the wall and smashed a looking-glass.[52] More than a decade later, however, he told George McGovern: 'I would have taken a harder line than Khrushchev. I was furious when he compromised. But Khrushchev was older and wiser. I realize in retrospect that he reached the proper settlement with Kennedy. If my position had prevailed there might have been a terrible war.'[53]

In fact both Castro and Russia did very well out of Khrushchev's brinkmanship. Before Russia started arming Cuba on a big scale in September 1962, Castro was an easy target for American intervention. No American president was under any contractual restraints in handling the danger. Properly considered, Khrushchev's installation of strategic missiles was tantamount to a major act of aggression. When Kennedy called Khrushchev's bluff, he had Russia at a disadvantage. As de Gaulle rightly perceived, Russia really had no alternative but to back down completely. Khrushchev admitted this himself: 'Cuba was 11,000 kilometres from the Soviet Union. Our sea and air communications were so precarious that an attack against the United States was unthinkable.'[54] The missile crisis took place at a time when the strategic nuclear equation was still strongly in America's favour, and in a theatre where America enjoyed overwhelming advantage in conventional power. Kennedy was thus in a position to demand an absolute restoration of the *status quo ante*. He could have gone further: he could have insisted on punishment – on Soviet acceptance of a neutral, disarmed Cuba: the Finnish analogy. As Dean Acheson rightly observed: 'So long as we had the thumbscrew on Khrushchev, we should have given it another turn every day.'[55]

Instead, Kennedy, while winning a public relations victory, rewarded the aggressive Soviet act with two substantial concessions.

The minor one was the withdrawal of the Jupiter missiles, supposedly on the grounds of their obsolescence.[56] Far more important, however, was Kennedy's acquiescence in the continuation of a Communist regime in Cuba, in open military alliance with Soviet Russia.[57] On the practical issue of Cuba and Caribbean security, Kennedy lost the missile crisis. It was an American defeat: the worst it had so far suffered in the Cold War.

Thus in an area which, by any definition, was vital to America's interests, Castro survived to become, for a quarter of a century, her most persistent and successful enemy; to export revolution to South America in the 1960s and, far more successfully, to Central America in the late 1970s and early 1980s; to vilify American 'imperialism' systematically at Third World gatherings, while posing as a 'non-aligned' power; and, in the 1970s, to send no less than three expeditionary forces to Africa as executants of Soviet policy. With remarkable audacity, Castro posed as a defender of the oppressed in the United States itself, and was rewarded by the adulation of a segment of American progressive opinion. To Saul Landau, Castro was 'steeped in democracy', to Leo Huberman and Paul Sweezy he was 'a passionate humanitarian', and other visitors testified to his 'encyclopaedic knowledge'. He made them think of 'the connection between socialism and Christianity'. He was 'soft-spoken, shy, sensitive' and, at the same time, vigorous, handsome, informal, undogmatic, open, humane, superbly accessible and warm. Norman Mailer thought him 'the first and greatest hero to appear in the world since the Second World War'. When Castro stood erect, wrote Abbie Hoffman, 'he is like a mighty penis coming to life, and when he is tall and straight the crowd immediately is transformed'.[58] Many of the Western liberal fantasies once woven around Stalin were transferred to Castro. Mao's eventual fall from grace left Castro the last charismatic of the totalitarian world.

The ordinary Cubans, by contrast, voted with their feet and their outboard motors: in the 1960s alone over a million fled from Castro. By 1980, in which year alone 150,000 political refugees were added to the total, about a fifth of the population were living in exile, most of them in the USA. In 1981 it was calculated that, since Castro took charge, Cuba had had an annual growth-rate *per capita* of minus 1.2 per cent; that from being one of the richest Latin-American countries it had become one of the poorest, and with a national income of only $810 per head, worse off than neighbouring Jamaica, the Dominican Republic, Colombia and Mexico; and, finally, that with armed forces of 200,000 (a quarter abroad on active service), it was the largest military power in Latin America, except for Brazil – indeed, *per capita*, probably had more men under arms than any other country in the world.[59] That was Castro's work; and Kennedy's legacy.

President Kennedy's handling of Cuba suggested an imperfect understanding of America's vital interests and a failure to distinguish between image and reality. These weaknesses, which were characteristic of Kennedy's public-relations approach to politics, were exhibited in other fields, notably the space programme and Vietnam. With the assistance of captured German scientists, Soviet Russia had given highest priority (next to the nuclear-weapons programme itself) to heavy, long-range rockets. The rewards began to come in the late 1950s. On 4 October 1957 Americans were stunned when Russia put Sputnik 1, a 184-pound satellite, into orbit. The next month a much larger one weighing 1,120 pounds followed, with a dog Laika inside it. The first American satellite, Explorer 1, did not go into orbit until 31 January 1958, and it weighed only thirty pounds. An American general was quoted as saying, 'We captured the wrong generals.' In fact America was building big rockets too, including the army's enormous Saturn rocket, developed by Werner Von Braun in Huntsville, Alabama. Equally important was American progress in miniaturization, which explains America's greater willingness to accept low payloads.[60] It was all a question of aims, priorities and finance. Eisenhower, rightly obsessed as he was with the strength of the US economy, would not invest heavily in space beyond the pragmatic needs of the defence programme. He was flatly opposed to luxurious space ventures run for the purpose of 'prestige', a word he detested. He took no notice of the post-Sputnik panic.

With Kennedy in office the priorities changed totally. His Vice-President, the Texan Lyndon Johnson, who was placed in charge of Space, was a big-spending Texan with many connections in the aerospace business world. He picked James Webb, a publicity-conscious business operator, as director of the National Aeronautics and Space Administration. On 12 April 1961, less than three months after Kennedy had taken over, Russia launched the first man, Yuri Gagarin, into orbit, beating the Americans by nearly four weeks. We have a vivid record of a frenzied meeting Kennedy held two days later in the White House, storming:

Is there any place where we can catch them? What can we do? Can we go around the Moon before them? Can we put a man on the Moon before them? . . . Can we leapfrog? . . . If somebody can just tell me how to catch up! Let's find somebody, anybody. I don't care if it's the janitor over there, if he knows how.[61]

Three days later came the Bay of Pigs disaster, and on 19 April a grim Kennedy summoned Johnson for a forty-five-minute session, followed by an excited directive (20 April 1961), ordering him to find out: 'Do we have a chance of beating the Soviets by putting a laboratory in space, or by a trip round the Moon, or by a rocket to land on the Moon, or by a rocket to go to the Moon and back with a man? Is there any other space programme which promises dramatic results in which we could win?'[62] The wording was characteristic: 'beating', 'dramatic results', 'win'.

There was a sense in which Kennedy was a professional sportsman, a propagandist and a political huckster rather than a man of state. In May he publicly committed America to the Apollo programme, with its aim to land a manned spacecraft on the Moon 'before this decade is out'. It was a project typical of Sixties illusion, with its contempt for finance, its assumption that resources were limitless. The programme got going in 1963, and for the next ten years, America spent up to $5 billion a year on space. Of course the aim was achieved. On 20 July 1969, Apollo 11 landed Neil Armstrong and Edwin Aldrin on the moon. There were four more Moon landings by 1972, when the programme petered out. By then America and Russia had launched over 1,200 satellites and space-probes, at a combined cost of something like $100 billion. In the more austere conditions of the mid-1970s, the space-effort shifted from propaganda to pragmatism, to space laboratories and shuttles. In 1981 NASA created the first genuine space-ship, the shuttle, while the Russians developed a 300-foot freighter, capable of lifting 220,000 pounds into low earth-orbit. The showbiz era of space-travel was over.

While President Kennedy was launching America on the Moon-race to reassert her prestige and leadership in technology, he was looking for an area in which his foreign policy, too, could produce a resounding success, especially after the Bay of Pigs humiliation. A National Security Council member advised him: 'It is very important that the government have a major anti-Communist victory to its credit . . . here [Vietnam] the odds are still in our favour.' On 1 May 1961, two weeks after the Bay of Pigs, the Defense Department produced a report outlining how Vietnam could be 'saved'; eleven days later, Kennedy approved the plan in NSC Memorandum 52, which authorized various actions to achieve a clearly stated objective, 'to prevent Communist domination of South Vietnam'. The next month, after the Vienna Summit with Khrushchev, Kennedy told a journalist: 'Now we have a problem in making our power credible and Vietnam looks like the place.'[63]

Yet the blame heaped on Kennedy for involving America in Vietnam is only partly merited. He inherited a crisis. Immediately after his Inauguration, he was handed a report written by Edward

Lansdale (the CIA agent portrayed by Graham Greene in his 1956 novel, *The Quiet American*) advising him that the situation in Saigon was deteriorating fast. He commented, 'This is the worst one we've got, isn't it?'[64] The Indo-China War, which began soon after the collapse of the Japanese occupation and continued into the 1980s, has been surrounded by more mythology than any other post-war event. It was complicated enough to baffle any western statesman, as it eventually baffled the Chinese. Every American president contributed his quota of error. Roosevelt, knowing nothing about it, offered the country to China. Immediately after his death, the fervent anti-colonialists of his Office of Strategic Services (the precursor of the CIA) worked hard to set up a left-wing nationalist regime. Three weeks after the Japanese surrender, the Communist leader Ho Chi Minh, sponsored by the OSS, staged a *putsch*, known as the 'August Revolution', which ousted the abdicating Emperor of Vietnam. The man who, in effect, crowned Ho as the new ruler was an OSS agent, Archimedes Patti.[65]

It is important to grasp that America never had any territorial ambitions in Indo-China, either as a base or in any other capacity. But its policy was usually muddled and invariably indecisive. In the first phase it was entirely Europe-oriented. Truman, on taking office, was advised that Indo-China was secondary to the absolute necessity to bolster France as a stabilizing power in Europe and assist her 'morally as well as physically, to regain her strength and influence'.[66] To feel confident again, France needed to get back her Indo-China empire (or so it was argued); and in December 1946 the French drove Ho into the jungle and brought the Emperor Bao Dai back from Hong-Kong. Reluctantly the Americans acquiesced in the French creation of three puppet nations, Laos, Cambodia and Vietnam, and gave them recognition as independent states within the French Union on 7 February 1950. At the same time Russia and China recognized Ho's regime. It was at this point that the struggle became an international one. Russia and China poured in arms. In May America did the same, and with the outbreak of the Korean War the next month the US aid programme accelerated fast. In 1951 it was $21.8 million in economic and $425.7 in military assistance. By next year the military aid had risen to over half a billion dollars: 40 per cent of France's costs. Dean Acheson was warned by State Department officials that America was 'moving into a position in Indo-China' in which 'our responsibilities tend to supplant rather than complement those of the French'. But he decided that 'having put our hand to the plough, we would not look back'. He argued that the situation in Europe was too dangerous for America to think of deserting the French in the east.[67] By 1953–4, America was paying for 80 per cent of the French war effort.

Then, on 8 May 1954, the French fortress at Dien Bien Phu surrendered. The defeat was made possible by the unexpected scale of the arms assistance now being provided by Russia and China to Ho's forces. The French asked for direct participation by American air-power, and when this was refused they formed a new government under Pierre Mendès-France to negotiate a French withdrawal and a political settlement. The cease-fire agreement, signed at Geneva in July, provided for a division of the country along the 17th parallel, the Communists keeping the North, the West the rest, unity to be brought about by elections in two years' time under an International Control Commission.

It was at this point that Eisenhower's customary good sense failed him: indeed, it can be argued that he was more responsible for the eventual mess in Vietnam than any other American. He should have signed the accords and compelled the premier of the South, Ngo Dinh Diem, to abide by them. It is possible Ho would have won free elections and become ruler of a united Communist country. Would that have been a disaster for America? Even Acheson, in his famous 'perimeter' speech of January 1950, had not considered a non-Communist government in Indo-China essential to American security.[68] George Kennan, in a memo dated 21 August 1950, argued that it was 'preferable to permit the turbulent political currents of that country to find their own level . . . even at the probable cost of an eventual deal between Vietnam and Vietminh, and the spreading over the whole country of Vietminh authority.'[69] This was Eisenhower's own feeling. He said he could not 'conceive of a greater tragedy for America than to get heavily involved'. 'There is going to be no involvement,' he repeated. If America did go in, it would only be in agreement with her principal Allies and with explicit constitutional approval from Congress. He worked on the Chiefs of Staff and got from them the assurance (May 1954) that 'Indo-China is devoid of decisive military objectives and the allocation of more than token US armed forces to that area would be a serious diversion of limited US capabilities.'[70]

But Eisenhower was in two minds. He popularized the theory that, if Vietnam was 'lost', the whole of Indo-China would vanish into Communist hands; and that if Indo-China was swallowed, other countries in South-East Asia must follow. He spoke of 'a cork in a bottle', a 'chain-reaction' and 'falling dominoes'.[71] Not only did he refuse to sign the Geneva Accords himself, but he acquiesced in Diem's refusal to submit to the test of free elections. That was a fundamental departure from American global policy in the Cold War, which had always rested on the contention that conflict between East and West should be decided not by force of arms but by the test of an honest poll. Diem was permitted to evade this basic principle and, indeed, was rewarded by American military and economic assistance, for the first time direct and not through a French intermediary. Thus it was Eisenhower who committed America's original sin in Vietnam. In default of unitary elections, the Vietcong emerged in 1957 and a new war started up in the South. Eisenhower made America a party to that war, claiming, in his last major statement on the subject (4 April 1959): 'The loss of South Vietnam would set in motion a crumbling process that could, as it progressed, have grave consequences for us and for freedom.'[72]

When Kennedy reached the White House, Vietnam was already one of America's largest and costliest commitments anywhere in the world. It is hard to understand why he made no attempt to get back to the Geneva Accords and hold unified free elections. In Paris on 31 May 1961, de Gaulle urged him urgently to disengage: 'I predict you will sink step by step into a bottomless military and political quagmire.'[73] Nevertheless, in November that year Kennedy authorized the despatch to Vietnam of the first 7,000 American troops, for 'base security'. General Maxwell Taylor, who recommended the step, warned him that, if things got worse, 'it will be difficult to resist the pressure to reinforce' and that 'there is no limit to our possible commitment'.[74] Kennedy himself shared the unease. He told his colleague Arthur Schlesinger: 'The troops will march in; the bands will play; the crowds will cheer; and in four days everyone will have forgotten. Then we will be told to send in more troops. It's like taking a drink. The effect wears off, and you have to take another.'[75] That was an accurate prediction. Kennedy's instinct was either to stay out or bring things to a head by a direct American attack on Hanoi. An American invasion of the North, which would have been successful at this stage, would at least have had the merit of putting the clock back to 1954 and the Geneva Accords. There could be no fundamental moral objection to such a course, since by 1961 the North had effectively invaded the South. It must always be borne in mind, when analysing the long tragedy of Indo-China, that it was the determination of Ho, his colleagues and successors, to dominate the entire country, including Laos and Cambodia, which was, from 1945 onwards, the principal dynamic of the struggle and the ultimate cause of all the bloodshed. America's errors were merely a contributory factor. Nevertheless they were serious. Unwilling to leave the country to its fate, or to carry the land-war to the North, Kennedy settled for a hopeless compromise, in which military aid, in ever-growing but never decisive quantities, was given to a client-government he could not control. Diem was by far the ablest of the

Vietnam leaders and he had the great merit of being a civilian. Lyndon Johnson, then Vice-President, termed him with some exaggeration 'the Churchill of South-East Asia', and told a journalist, 'Shit, man, he's the only boy we got out there.'[76] But Kennedy, exasperated by his failure to pull a resounding success out of Vietnam, blamed the agent rather than the policy. In the autumn of 1963 he secretly authorized American support for an anti-Diem *coup*. It duly took place on 1 November, Diem being murdered and the CIA providing $42,000 in bribes for the soldiers who set up a military junta. This was America's second great sin: 'the worst mistake we ever made', as Lyndon Johnson put it.[77] Three weeks later Kennedy himself was murdered and Johnson was president.

Johnson was no more decisive than Kennedy, whose compromise policy he continued in irresolute fashion until August 1964, when North Vietnam attacked American destroyers in the Gulf of Tonkin. There is no evidence, as was later alleged, that the incident was contrived, to get America deeper into the war.[78] In fact Johnson was very reluctant to escalate: he was entering a presidential campaign on a peace platform against the Republican Barry Goldwater, who wanted to use nuclear weapons, if necessary, to win the war. But Congress, by an overwhelming majority (out of 535 members of both houses, only Senators Wayne Morse and Ernest Gruening voted against), passed what became known as the 'Tonkin Gulf Resolution' authorizing the President to take vigorous measures to protect US forces. Senator William Fulbright, then a supporter of the war, who steered the motion through the Senate, said it effectively gave Johnson the right to go to war without further authorization. Johnson made no use of it for nearly six months. Then, having won an overwhelming electoral victory on an anti-escalation platform, he behaved like Wilson and Roosevelt before him, and proceeded to do the opposite. In February 1965, following heavy US casualties in a Vietcong attack on a barracks, he ordered the bombing of the North.[79]

This was the third critical American mistake. Having involved itself, America should have followed the logic of its position and responded to aggression by occupying the North. To bomb was a weak compromise, absolutely characteristic of the irresolution which dogged American policy throughout the tragedy. Once aircraft from Da Nang began to bomb the North, security had to be provided for the base: so on 8 March 3,500 marines were landed at Da Nang. The troop level rose to 82,000 in April. In June a demand came for forty-four more battalions. On 28 July Johnson announced: 'I have today ordered to Vietnam the Airmobile Division and certain other forces which will raise our fighting strength ... to 125,000 men almost immediately. Additional forces will be needed later and they will be sent as requested.'[80] There was no attempt by the military to deceive the politicians (as Kennedy had suspected). The Joint Chiefs reported on 14 July: 'There seems to be no reason we cannot win if such is our will – and *if that will is manifested in strategy and tactical operations.*' The underlining was in the original.[81] When Johnson asked General Wheeler of the JCS, 'Bus, what do you think it will take to do the job?', the answer was 700,000 to a million men and seven years.[82] Johnson went into the war with his eyes open. He whistled to keep his courage up: 'After the Alamo,' he said, 'no one thought Sam Houston would wind it up so quick.'[83]

But Johnson was no Sam Houston. Even as a bomber he was indecisive. The Air Force told him they could promise results if the offensive was heavy, swift, repeated endlessly and without restraint. That was the whole lesson of the Second World War. They promised nothing if it was slowed and restricted.[84] Yet that was precisely what Johnson did. From start to finish, the bombing was limited by restrictions which were entirely political. Every Tuesday Johnson held a lunch at which he determined targets and bomb-weights: it was Eden and Suez all over again. Johnson was not the ruthless man he liked to impersonate: he was paralysed by moral restraints. As his biographer, Doris Kearns, shrewdly observed, to him 'limited bombing was seduction, not rape, and seduction was controllable, even reversible'.[85] Thus the bombing intensified very slowly and the Vietminh had time to build shelters and adjust. When Soviet Russia moved in defensive missiles, American bombers were not allowed to attack while the sites were under construction. There were, in addition, sixteen 'bombing pauses', none of which evoked the slightest response, and seventy-two American 'peace initiatives', which fell on deaf ears.[86] Unlike the Americans, the North Vietnamese leaders never once wavered in their determination to secure their political aim – total domination of the entire country – at any cost. They do not seem to have been influenced in the smallest degree by the casualties their subjects suffered or inflicted. There was thus a bitter irony in the accusations of genocide hurled at the Americans. An examination of classified material in the Pentagon archives revealed that all the charges made against US forces at the 1967 Stockholm 'International War Crimes tribunal' were baseless. Evacuation of civilians from war zones to create 'free fire' fields not only saved civilian lives but was actually required by the 1949 Geneva Convention. The heavy incidence of combat in civilian areas was the direct result of Vietcong tactics in converting villages into fortified strongholds, itself a violation of the Geneva agreement. It was the restrictions on American bombing to protect civilian lives and property which made it so ineffective. The proportion of civilians killed, about 45 per cent of all war-deaths, was about average for twentieth-century wars. In fact the population increased steadily during the war, not least because of US medical programmes. In the South, the standard of living rose quite fast.[87]

But the experience of the twentieth century indicates that self-imposed restraints by a civilized power are worse than useless. They are interpreted by friend and foe alike as evidence, not of humanity, but of guilt and lack of righteous conviction. Despite them, indeed because of them, Johnson lost the propaganda battle, not only in the West as a whole but especially in the USA, where it mattered most. Initially the Vietnam war had the support of the moderate liberal consensus. 'The US has a major interest in the defence of Vietnam,' the *Washington Post* wrote, 7 April 1961. 'American prestige is very much involved in the effort to protect the Vietnamese people from Communist absorption.' The *New York Times* admitted, 12 March 1963, that 'The cost [of saving Vietnam] is large, but the cost of South-East Asia coming under the domination of Russia and Communist China would be still larger.' On 21 May 1964 the *Times* urged: 'If we demonstrate that we will make whatever military and political effort [denying victory to Communism] requires, the Communists sooner or later will also recognize reality.' The *Post* insisted, 1 June 1964, that America continue to show in Vietnam that 'persistence in aggression is fruitless and possibly deadly'. But the *Times* deserted Johnson early in 1966, the *Post* in summer 1967.[88] About the same time the TV networks became neutral, then increasingly hostile.

What the Administration came to fear was not editorial censure so much as the tendentious presentation of the news. The US media became strongly biased in some cases. More often it was misled, skilfully and deliberately; or misled itself. A much publicized photograph of a 'prisoner' being thrown from a US helicopter was in fact staged. Accounts of American 'tiger cages' at Con Son island were inaccurate and sensationalized. Another widely used photo of a young girl burned by napalm created the impression, which was in fact quite untrue, that many thousands of children had been incinerated by Americans.[89]

Even more serious was the notion increasingly conveyed by the media that Vietcong victory was inevitable. This came to a decisive head in the handling of the Vietcong 'Tet Offensive' on 30 January 1968. It was the first major offensive in the open the Communists had tried. It was designed to achieve complete tactical success and detonate a mass-uprising. In fact it failed on both counts. For the first time the Vietcong suffered heavy casualties in conventional combat, and their army emerged from the engagement very much weaker militarily.[90] But the media, especially TV, presented it as a decisive Vietcong victory, an American Dien Bien Phu. An elaborate study of the coverage, published in 1977, showed exactly how this reversal of the truth, which was not on the whole deliberate, came about.[91] The image not the reality of Tet was probably decisive, especially among influential East Coast liberals. In general, American public opinion strongly backed the war, which was throughout more popular than the Korean War. According to the pollsters the only hostile category was what they described as 'the Jewish sub-group'.[92] Johnson's popularity rating rose whenever he piled on the pressure: it leapt 14 per cent when he started the bombing.[93] Throughout the fighting, far more Americans were critical of Johnson for doing too little than for doing too much. The notion of a great swing away from the war in public opinion, and above all the axiom that the young opposed it, was an invention. In fact support for withdrawal was never over 20 per cent until after the November 1968 election, by which time the decision to get out had already been taken. Support for intensifying the war was always greater among the under thirty-fives than among older people; young white males were the most consistent group backing escalation.[94]

It was not the American people which lost its stomach for the kind of sacrifices Kennedy had demanded in his Inaugural. It was the American leadership. In the last months of 1967, and especially after Tet, the American establishment crumpled. The Defence Secretary, Clark Clifford, turned against the war; so did old Dean Acheson. Senate hard-liners began to oppose further reinforcements.[95] Finally Johnson himself, diffidently campaigning for re-election, lost heart on 12 March 1968 when his vote sagged in the New Hampshire primary. He threw in the electoral towel and announced he would spend the rest of his term making peace. It was not the end of the war. But it was the end of America's will and effort to win it. The trouble with the American ruling class was that it believed what it read in the newspapers, and they saw New Hampshire as a victory for peace. In fact, among the anti-Johnson voters the Hawks outnumbered the Doves by three to two.[96] Johnson lost the primary, and with it the war, because he was not tough enough.

There was, however, an additional and more sinister factor which knocked the stuffing out of the President, whose slogan was 'All the Way with LBJ'. In March 1968, when the Vietnam command asked for an additional 206,000 men, the Treasury Secretary, Henry Fowler, protested. To grant the request, he warned, would mean cutting not only other defence programmes but major domestic programmes as well; and, even so, the dollar would suffer.[97] The move recalled Macmillan's chilling intervention in the cabinet debates during Britain's Suez crisis. It was a significant turning-point in American history: the first time the Great Republic, the richest nation on earth, came up against the limits of its financial resources.

For Johnson himself the warning was a particularly bitter blow. More than Kennedy even, more perhaps than anyone, he had revelled in the illusions of the 1960s. No one had believed more passionately in the strength of the West and in particular in the boundless capacity of the American economy to deliver. He was not merely the last, he was the greatest, of the big spenders. He referred to his domestic spending programme as 'the beautiful woman'. He told his biographer: 'I was determined to be a leader of war *and* a leader of peace. I wanted both, I believed in both and I believed America had the resources to provide for both.'[98] Under Truman and Eisenhower, defence was the biggest item in Federal spending. Spending on housing, education, welfare and other 'human resources' (as they were termed) was only about a quarter of the budget and less than 5 per cent of GNP. Some attempt was made to balance the budget, except in a bad recession year. Until Eisenhower retired, American public finance was run in all essentials on conventional lines.

The big change in principle came under Kennedy. In the autumn of 1962 the Administration committed itself to a new and radical principle of creating budgetary deficits even when there was no economic emergency, the budget being already in deficit and the economy moving upward. Having thus given himself financial leeway, Kennedy introduced a new concept of 'big government': the 'problem-eliminator'. Every area of human misery could be classified as a 'problem'; then the Federal government could be armed to 'eliminate' it. 'The poverty problem' had been made a fashionable subject in the early 1960s by Michael Harrington's best-seller, *The Other America* (1962), which Kennedy found shocking and stimulating. In 1963 he introduced his 'poverty programme', along with a mass of other high-spending legislation. Kennedy found it difficult to re-educate Congress to his new expansionist ideas, and his legislation piled up. But resistance was beginning to collapse even before Kennedy was murdered;[99] and Lyndon Johnson was able to use the emotional response to the assassination, plus his own wonderful skills as a Congressional manager, to push through the greatest and most expensive legislative programme in American history.

In his first State of the Union address, 8 January 1964, Johnson announced: 'This Administration today, here and now, declares unconditional war on poverty.' When he signed his first anti-poverty bill, the Equal Opportunities Act, on 20 August 1964, he boasted: 'Today, for the first time in the history of the human race, a great nation is able to make and is willing to make a commitment to eradicate poverty among its people.'[100] That summer, preparing for his election campaign, he turned his 'beautiful woman' into flesh: the 'Great Society'. America, he said, had to acquire 'the 'wisdom to use wealth to enrich and elevate our national life', to move not only to 'the rich society and the powerful society but upward to the Great Society', which rested on 'abundance and liberty to all', where 'every child' would 'find knowledge to enrich his mind and enlarge his talents' and everyone would be able to satisfy 'the desire for beauty and the hunger for community'.[101]

The Great Society was supposedly endorsed in the November 1964 elections, which Johnson won overwhelmingly against an exceptionally weak opponent. The bills came rolling out: the Elementary and Secondary Education Act, the Medicare Act, the Rent Supplement Act, various poverty acts. Johnson called 20–27 July 1965 'the most productive and most historic legislative week in Washington during this century'. 'They say Jack Kennedy had style,' he snorted, 'but I'm the one who got the bills passed.' One liberal journalist, Tom Wicker, exulted in the *New York Times*: 'They are rolling the bills out of Congress these days the way Detroit turns super-sleek, souped-up autos off the assembly-line.' The first session of the 89th Congress was the most productive in fundamental legislation since the early days of Woodrow Wilson. Johnson had a 68 per cent success-rate, the highest in history, for his bills, 207 of which were made law, 'the building-blocks of a better America', as he called them.[102] He drew a conscious parallel with the war in Vietnam, also – as he saw it – an exercise in idealism, by the blatant use of military metaphor. He created ten anti-poverty 'task forces'. He told housing bureaucrats: 'I'm going to convert you from armchair generals to front-line commanders.' There was a Youth corps for 'neighbourhoods', a Job corps for 'dropouts', Head Start for pre-school children, Outward Bound for college students, and countless other schemes. The cost soared: $30 billion a year in the first poverty programme; then another $30 billion added towards the end of the term.[103] These sums soon became built into the structure of the Federal outlay and proved impossible to reduce. Indeed they were increased. Thanks to Johnson's efforts, by 1971, for the first time, government spent more on welfare than defence. Between 1949 and 1979, defence costs rose ten times (from $11.5 billion to $114.5 billion) but remained roughly 4–5 per cent of GNP. But welfare spending rose twenty-five times, from $10.6 billion to $259 billion, its share of the budget went up to more than half, and the proportion of the GNP it absorbed tripled to nearly 12 per cent.[104]

This momentous change in the fundamental purpose and cost of American central government began to impose growing strains even before Johnson ceased to be president. By that stage, the government's slice of the GNP had risen from 28.7 per cent under Eisenhower to 33.4 per cent. Treasury control disintegrated. Under Eisenhower, the very efficient Bureau of the Budget (as it was called up to 1970) operated as Harding had conceived it: as an objective agency, rather like a court of law, to supervise all spending. Under Kennedy, characteristically, the Office was politicized and under Johnson it became activist: the Budget Director had to share big-spending values.[105] Moreover, though Congress would vote for the programmes, it was much less willing to provide the taxes to pay for them. Johnson quarrelled bitterly with the House finance-boss, Wilbur Mills, and the Republican leader Gerald Ford. Unable to get the taxes, he printed money. His fear of inflation and his inability to cope with it was a hidden factor in his decision to leave public life in 1968. 'I told [Mills] that whether he realized it or not, the country's economy was about to go down the drain.'[106]

By that time some of Johnson's own illusions about the virtues of big spending had been undermined. It was no longer clear to him that the results justified the damaging impact on the economy. The most important one, and certainly the most permanent, was unintentional: the government's share of all workers doubled and by 1976 one in six (over 13 million) was directly on Washington's payroll. But the beneficiaries of this shift were overwhelmingly middle class. Johnson claimed that, during his time in office, of the 35 million 'trapped in poverty' in 1964, he 'lifted out' 12.4 million or almost 36 per cent.[107] But this was only one way of looking at the statistics. As living standards rose, the definition of poverty changed, and the poor 'felt' just as poor as before, though their real incomes had risen. The danger of the kind of welfare state Johnson was creating was that it pushed people out of the productive economy permanently and made them dependents of the state. Poverty increased when families split up, either by old people living apart or by divorce, with consequent divisions of income.[108] Legislation often promoted these processes. It emerged that perhaps the biggest single cause of poverty in the USA was the instability of black marriages. Daniel P. Moynihan, Johnson's Assistant-Secretary of Labour, argued in the *Moynihan Report* (March 1965) that half the black population suffered from a 'social pathology' whose source was the black family, where husbands deserted wives and children in distressingly large numbers. The object of policy should be 'the establishment of a stable family structure'.[109] But the poverty war did not do this. It did the opposite, for often the structure of welfare provision made it pay for a poor family to split up. By the time Johnson was ready to quit, Moynihan was arguing that the whole poverty programme was misconceived and ill-directed.[110]

Even more tragic and painful was the loss of illusions over education. This was, indeed, the central mirage of the decade of illusion. It was an old liberal belief, popularized by Macaulay, that universal education alone could make democracy tolerable. That accomplished manufacturer of progressive clichés, H. G. Wells, had defined modern history as 'a race between education and catastrophe'. This belief survived the melancholy fact that the nation which took Hitler to its heart and waged his fearful war with passionate industry was easily the best-educated on earth. In the 1950s the myth that education was the miracle cure for society emerged stronger than ever. No one believed in it more devotedly than Johnson. As President he said: 'The answer for all our national problems comes in a single world. That word is education.'[111]

Johnson reflected the conventional wisdom of his day. In the late 1950s, C. P. Snow had argued that there was a direct causal link between the amount of money invested in higher education and a country's GNP.[112] E. F. Denison showed that, over the three decades 1930–60, half America's growth was accounted for by the expansion of education, especially of the universities. The same year, 1962, Fritz Machlup calculated that the 'knowledge industry' accounted for 29 per cent of America's GNP and was growing at twice the rate of the economy as a whole.[113] In the 1963 Godkin Lectures at Harvard, the President of Berkeley, Clark Kerr, America's leading academic statesman, argued that knowledge was now the 'leading sector' in the growth of the economy. 'What the railways did for the second half of the last century and the automobile for the first half of this century', he argued, 'may be done for the second half of this century by the knowledge industry: that is, to serve as the focal point for national growth.'[114]

Against this background, the 1960s became the most explosive decade in the entire history of educational expansion. The process in America had begun with the 1944 'GI bill', allocating public funds for the college education of returned veterans, and continued with the 1952 Korean War GI bill. The 1958 National Defense Education Act doubled the Federal education budget and, for the first time, made central government the financial dynamic of education. The number of state teachers grew from 1 million in 1950 to 2.3 million in 1970, as spending per person rose by over 100 per cent. The growth of higher education was the most marked because it was now contended it should be universally available. 'The important question', an official report argued, 'need be not "Who deserves to be admitted?" but "Whom can the society, in conscience and self-interest, exclude?"', since nobody could be 'justly' denied a university education unless 'his deficiencies are so severe' that even the 'most flexible and dedicated institution' could not help him.[115] The phenomenon was international in the West. In Britain the 1963 Robbins Report led to the doubling of university places within a decade, with a projected student body of 2 million by 1981. Similar expansion plans were adopted in France, Canada, Australia, West Germany and elsewhere. The American experience was most striking because of the statistics involved. Between 1960 and 1975, the number of American colleges and universities rose from 2,040 to 3,055. During the 'golden years' of expansion, new ones were opening at the rate of one a week. Students rose from 3.6 million in 1960 to 9.4 million in 1975, the bulk of the increase (4 million) coming in the public sector. Including non-degree students, they passed the 11-million mark in 1975, at an annual cost of $45 billion.[116]

It was confidently expected that this vast investment in human resources would not only stimulate growth still further but achieve moral and social purposes by furthering the *embourgeoisement* of the working class. It would make 'middle-class democracy . . . with all its freedoms', as Clark Kerr put it, 'the wave of the future', thus ensuring general contentment and political stability, and in particular underpinning the enlightened capitalist system which made it all possible. In fact the reverse happened. At the pre-college level, while spending doubled, then trebled, educational performance fell. Some decline had been expected as the system absorbed large minority groups, but not of this precipitous magnitude. The best index, Scholastic Aptitude Test scores, showed over the years 1963–77 a forty-nine-point decline in verbal and thirty-two-point decline in mathematical skills (on a scale of 800).[117] In the mid-1970s a rash of gloomy reports suggested that more, and more expensive, education did not solve any social problems.[118] Crime-rates among children in full-time education rose inexorably. In the second half of the 1970s, opinion turned against the education process, as cities and states cut their teacher forces. The end of the post-war 'baby boom bulge' was only one factor. The chief reason was loss of confidence in the economic advantages of more education. Over the years 1970–8, some 2,800 public-sector schools and colleges were shut, the first time this had ever happened in American history. By the mid-1980s, public-sector enrollments were expected to decline by 4 million.[119] By 1978, American workers had an average of 12½ years schooling, and 17 per cent had a college degree. But graduates (especially women) were finding it increasingly difficult to get professional or managerial employment. The ratio between length of education and salary declined sharply. Equalizing educational opportunity, it was found, did not promote greater equality among adults.[120] So the attractions of university declined. The proportion of young men starting college, which rose rapidly to 44 per cent in the 1960s, fell to 34 per cent by 1974. It levelled off among women, too.

Nor did more education promote stability. Quite the contrary. As it happened, this had been foreseen by Joseph Schumpeter, who had been born in the same year as Keynes, and who had some claim to rival him as the greatest economist of modern times. It was Schumpeter's view, first expressed in an article he wrote in 1920, expanded into *Capitalism, Socialism and Democracy* (1942), that capitalism tended to promote its own self-destruction in a number of ways. Among them was its propensity to create, and then give full rein to, by virtue of its commitment to freedom, an ever-expanding class of intellectuals, who inevitably played a socially destructive role.[121] This point was overlooked in the university-expansion plans of the 1950s and 1960s, though it had in fact already been vindicated, to some extent, in the 1930s. At all events, Schumpeter was certainly proved right in the Lyndon Johnson era. The first signs of radical student interest in social and political issues appeared in 1958. In spring 1960 came the first 'sit-in' protests, demonstrations in San Francisco against the House Un-American Activities Committee, and West Coast 'vigils' against the execution of the fashionable murderer, Caryl Chessman. Protests against university training corps, loyalty affidavits, fraternity and sorority discrimination and other matters of university discipline – or simple civil rights issues – broadened into directly political campaigns.

At first, student activism was welcomed, as a sign of 'maturity' and 'awareness'. The earliest sign of large-scale violence came during 'freedom summer' in 1964, at Clark Kerr's own university, Berkeley. What was supposed to be the 'leading sector' in GNP growth became a leading sector in something quite different: the 'student revolt'. By December the Governor of California had called in the riot police and Berkeley had become the world's chief 'political' campus.[122] Johnson's Great Society programme merely poured fuel into this gathering conflagration. The next year 25,000 students invaded Washington to protest against the Vietnam war. In 1966–7, more and more campuses were 'radicalized'. The 'campus riot' became part of the college culture, as university presidents compromised, surrendered or abdicated. On 23 April 1968 there was a devastating smash-up at Columbia, one of America's leading universities. Professor Archibald Cox of the Harvard Law School was called in to report, and did so in the smug optimism of the time: 'The present generation of young people in our universities are the best informed, the most intelligent and the most idealistic this country has ever known.' As Lionel Trilling sourly commented, Cox 'celebrated as knowledge and intelligence' what was in fact 'merely a congerie of "advanced" public attitudes'. Cox, he insisted, was deriving his values not from knowledge and experience but from the young: their 'certification' was enough to prove them sound.[123]

Whether or not the students were the most intelligent in history, they were certainly the most destructive. Cox-type complacency did not survive summer 1968, especially after the wild Paris student riots in May, which began a new and much more savage cycle of student violence all over the world but especially in America. The National Student Association claimed there were 221 major demonstrations at universities in America during 1968.[124] It was student radicals who ran the campaign of Eugene McCarthy, which knocked Johnson out of the presidential race in New Hampshire. But student power was essentially negative. At the Chicago Democratic Convention in August 1968 students fought a pitched battle with 11,900 of Mayor Daley's police, 7,500 of the Illinois National Guard, and 1,000 FBI and Secret Service agents. They won the media contest in that they succeeded in branding Daley's law-enforcement a 'police riot', but they could not get McCarthy the nomination, nor could they prevent the man they hated most, Richard Nixon, from becoming president. When in 1972 they finally secured the Democratic nomination for their own choice, George McGovern, the only result was to secure Nixon a landslide.

What student violence did above all was to damage American higher education and demoralize its teachers. Reflecting on it in 1971, Professor Louis Kampf, in his presidential address to the Modern Languages Association, said that since 1968 'the young go into the profession with dread, the old can scarcely wait for retirement, and those of the middle years yearn for sabbaticals'.[125] The great German scholar Fritz Stern, noting the 'excremental language' of student activists, saw it as the only novelty: the rest reproduced the pattern of extremist behaviour among the students who led Germany in putting Hitler into power.[126]

The promotion of student violence by the well-intended expansion of higher education was an excellent example of the 'law of unintended effect'. The attempt by successive presidents to obtain justice for American blacks was another. Here again, good intentions produced death and destruction. The problem was seen as threefold. First, to end segregation, especially in education. Second, to enable blacks to exercise voting rights. Third, to bring black incomes into line with white ones. It was believed that if the first two were solved, the third would ultimately solve itself. In 1954 the Supreme Court had ruled that public-sector education must be integrated. The problem was to get the law enforced in practice. In 1957, when Governor Orval Faubus of Arkansas defied the Supreme Court, Eisenhower dispatched troops to Little Rock to enforce compliance. Again, in 1962, Kennedy used troops to enable a black student, James Meredith, to attend the hitherto all-white state university of Mississippi. It was Kennedy's policy to proceed by executive action: that is, to use Federal power to make the existing law stick. The difficulty with this procedure was that it moved from one public confrontation to another, and in the process a huge and increasingly militant civil rights movement was created, from which white liberals were progressively eliminated. Physical action was seen by blacks as the answer, and as with the agitation Gandhi created in India, protest tended to degenerate into violence. The real solution was to get blacks voting quickly, because once politicians needed their votes, concessions would follow, even in the deep South. Eisenhower had put through Congress two weak Civil Rights acts, in 1957 and 1960. Kennedy eventually tabled a much stronger one, but it was blocked in Congress. Johnson was much more successful. He pushed through a monumental Civil Rights Act in 1964 and immediately after his November election victory he got to work on a bill which became the decisive Voting Rights Act of 1965. In the state of Mississippi, which had a higher proportion of blacks (36 per cent) than any other, only 6 per cent were registered to vote, because of complicated tests and other barriers. The new Act had the right to vote enforced by Federal examiners, and within thirty days of its enactment, black registration in Mississippi rose 120 per cent. By the end of 1970, the percentage of registered black voters in the state was comparable to white registrations (71 to 82 per cent) and in 1971 fifty blacks were elected to public office in the state.[127] By the early 1970s, the black vote had become a significant factor in many states of the old South, thus bringing about a progressive transformation of Southern politics.[128]

But voting could not equalize black and white incomes. Nor could the huge and increasing sums of Federal money which Johnson poured into the black 'problem'. The more progress made, the more cash available, the more black anger increased. In the 1950s and early 1960s, Federal power had been used to protect blacks from white violence. In the course of the series of enforcement battles staged under Kennedy, the initiative in violence shifted to the blacks. The turning-point was the night of 10 May 1962, in Birmingham, Alabama. There was a black riot, with police forced onto the defensive and white shops demolished: 'Let the whole fucking city burn,' shouted a mob-leader, 'This'll show the white motherfuckers!' This was a new cry, and a new attitude, in American race-politics, and it could not be confined to the South.[129]

To Johnson's consternation, the scale and intensity of black violence, especially in the big cities outside the South, advanced step by step with his vigorous and effective efforts to secure black rights. The first really big and ugly black riots broke out in Harlem and Brooklyn on 18 July 1964, only two weeks after the epoch-making Civil Rights Act was passed. The violence spread to Rochester in New York State, to Jersey City, Patterson and Elizabeth in New Jersey, to Dixmoor in Chicago, and Philadelphia. In August 1965 the Watts riots in Los Angeles lasted six days, involved 15,000 National Guardsmen, killed thirty-four, injured 856 and destroyed $200 million of property. Thereafter, large-scale riots by blacks in the inner cities became a recurrent feature of the Sixties, in sinister counterpoint and sometimes in deliberate harmony with student violence on the campuses. The riots in Detroit on 24–28 July 1967 were among the most serious in American history, killing forty-three people and forcing a distraught President Johnson to move in the 18th Airborne Corps of paratroopers, whose commander said he entered a city 'saturated with fear'.[130] By 1968, with the Vietnam War moving to its sickly climax, students rioting on over 200 campuses, and blacks putting some of the biggest cities to fire, Johnson seemed a failure. His decision not to seek re-election was an admission of defeat. He was the first major casualty of the Sixties illusions. But not the last. America's troubles were only beginning.

Nor was Johnson a victim of lost illusions alone. He was also, in a real sense, a victim of the media, and especially of the East Coast liberals who controlled the most influential newspapers and the big three TV networks. The two points were connected, for one of the deepest illusions of the Sixties was that many forms of traditional authority could be diluted: the authority of America in the world, and of the president within America. Lyndon Johnson, as a powerful and in many ways effective president, stood for the authority principle. That was, for many, a sufficient reason for emasculating him. Another was that he did not share East Coast liberal assumptions, in the way that Roosevelt and Kennedy had done. He had been doubtful about running for president even in 1964 for this reason: 'I did not believe . . . that the nation would unite definitely behind any Southerner. One reason . . . was that the Metropolitan press would never permit it.'[131] The prediction proved accurate, though its fulfilment was delayed. By August 1967, the Washington Correspondent of the St Louis Post-Dispatch, James Deakin, reported, 'the relationship between the President and the Washington press corps has settled into a pattern of chronic disbelief'.[132] Media misrepresentation of the Tet Offensive was immediately responsible for Johnson's departure. But more fundamental still was its habitual presentation of any decisive and forceful act by the White House as in some inescapable sense malevolent.

This was quite a new development. Opposition to a strong presidency had hitherto come, as was natural, from the legislature, especially from the senate. As Roosevelt had put it, 'the only way to do anything in the American government was to bypass the senate'.[133] His Republican opponent, Wendell Wilkie, had spoken of devoting his life to 'saving America from the Senate'.[134] Under Roosevelt and Truman the press and academic constitutionalists had strongly supported firm presidential leadership, especially in foreign policy, and contrasted it with Congressional obscurantism.[135] During the McCarthy investigations, Eisenhower had been severely criticized by the press for failing to defend executive rights against Congressional probing. The *New Republic* commented (1953): 'The current gravitation of power into the hands of Congress at the expense of the Executive is a phenomenon so fatuous as to be incredible if the facts were not so patent.'[136] When Eisenhower invoked 'executive privilege' to deny information about government acts to the Un-American Activities Committee, he was warmly applauded by the liberal media. The Committee, said the *New York Times*, had no right 'to know the details of what went on in these inner Administration councils'. Eisenhower, wrote the *Washington Post*, was 'abundantly right' to protect 'the confidential nature of executive conversations'.[137] Until the mid-1960s, the media continued to support resolute presidential leadership on civil rights, on social and economic issues and, above all, on foreign policy, endorsing Kennedy's dictum (1960): 'It is the President alone who must make the major decisions on our foreign policy.'[138]

The change came after the Tonkin Gulf resolution. By the time Johnson handed over the White House to Richard Nixon in 1969, the East Coast media, along with many other vociferous elements in the nation, had moved into permanent opposition. As one commentator put it, 'The men and the movement that broke Lyndon Johnson's authority in 1968 are out to break Richard Nixon in 1969 . . . breaking a president is, like most feats, easier to accomplish the second time around.'[139] Nixon was peculiarly vulnerable. He was a Californian whom the Eastern press had hated since the late 1940s. He felt the media had helped to deprive him of the presidency in 1960 and had made a concerted effort to destroy his political career for good in 1963; he returned their antipathy with interest. 'Remember,' he told his staff, 'the press is the enemy. When news is concerned, nobody in the press is a friend. They are all enemies.'[140] In 1968 Nixon won despite the media, but only just. He got 43.4 per cent of the vote to Hubert Humphrey's 42.7. This was the smallest

proportion of the popular vote of any president since 1912, and as
the poll was low (61 per cent), it meant only 27 per cent of all voters
favoured him. He did not carry a single big city.[141] In parts of the
media there was an inclination to deny his legitimacy as president
and to seek to reverse the verdict by non-constitutional means.

Despite these handicaps, Nixon had considerable success in clearing up the anarchic heritage of the Johnson–Kennedy years, and
especially in his skilful disengaging from Vietnam. He proclaimed the
same objective as all his predecessors: 'We seek the opportunity for
the South Vietnamese people to determine their own political future
without outside interference.'[142] So long as he was fully in charge of
American policy this aim was upheld, but at far smaller cost. In four
years he reduced American forces in Vietnam from 550,000 to
24,000. Spending declined from $25 billion a year under Johnson to
less than $3 billion.[143] This was made possible by a more intelligent
and flexible use of American force, in Cambodia in 1970, in Laos in
1971, in bombing North Vietnam in 1972, which kept the determined men in Hanoi perplexed and apprehensive about America's
intentions. At the same time Nixon actively pursued peace-
negotiations with the North Vietnamese. More important, he did
something neither Kennedy nor Johnson had dared: he exploited the
logic of the Sino–Soviet dispute and reached an understanding with
China.

It was Nixon's Californian orientation which inclined him towards Peking; he saw the Pacific as the world-arena of the future. He
began his new China policy on 31 January 1969, only eleven days
after he started work in the White House. The policy was embodied
in National Security Study Memorandum 14 (4 February 1969), and
it was reinforced by a conversation Nixon had with André Malraux,
who told him it was a 'tragedy' that 'the richest and most productive
people in the world' should be at odds with 'the poorest and most
populous people in the world'.[144] Because of Chinese fears, the moves
towards a *rapprochement* with China were conducted in private, and
Nixon went to considerable lengths to get pledges of secrecy from the
Congressional leaders he consulted. He told his staff: 'A fourth of the
world's people live in Communist China. Today they're not a
significant power, but twenty-five years from now they could be
decisive. For the US not to do what it can at this time, when it can,
would lead to a situation of great danger. We could have total
détente with the Soviet Union, but that would mean nothing if the
Chinese are outside the international community.'[145]

The new China policy, and the change in US military strategy,
made possible peace with Hanoi. On 27 January 1973 in Paris,
Nixon's Secretary of State, William Rogers, and Nguyen Duy Trinh of

North Vietnam signed an 'Agreement on Ending the War and Restoring Peace in Vietnam'. The merit of this understanding, which made it possible for America to leave Vietnam, was that it reserved Nixon's right to maintain carriers in Indo-Chinese waters and to use aircraft stationed in Taiwan and Thailand if the accords were broken by Hanoi.[146] So long as Nixon held power, that sanction was a real one. Granted the situation he had inherited and the mistakes of his predecessors, Nixon had performed a notable feat of extrication.

But America, and more tragically the peoples of Indo-China, were denied the fruits of this success because, by 1973, Nixon and the nation were already engulfed in the maelstrom of hysteria known as 'Watergate'. America seems peculiarly prone to these spasms of self-righteous political emotion in which all sense of perspective and the national interest is lost. The outbreak of xenophobia in 1918–20 was the work of right-wing Democrats. The anti-Communist scare of the late 1940s and early 1950s was largely directed by conservative Republicans. The Watergate witch-hunt, by contrast, was run by liberals in the media. In their eyes Nixon's real offence was popularity. Though he won narrowly in 1968, he successfully appealed, as president, over the heads of opinion-formers and a Democratic Congress, to unfashionable, inarticulate 'middle Americans', family-loving, church-going, patriotic, industrious and anti-liberal. On 3 November 1969 he made a highly successful speech appealing for support in his foreign policy to those he termed 'you, the great, silent majority of my fellow Americans'. This ended, for the time being, the 'breaking of Nixon' campaign by the media.[147] In the 1972 campaign, Nixon was delighted when the Democrats nominated the ultra-liberal George McGovern. 'Here is a situation', he told his staff, 'where the Eastern Establishment media finally has a candidate who almost totally shares their views.' The 'real ideological bent of the *New York Times*, the *Washington Post*, *Time*, *Newsweek* and the three TV networks' was 'on the side of amnesty, pot, abortion, confiscation of wealth (unless it is theirs), massive increases in welfare, unilateral disarmament, reduction of our defences and surrender in Vietnam.' At last, he concluded, 'the country will find out whether what the media has been standing for during these last five years really represents the majority thinking.'[148] Whether or not that was the issue, Nixon won by a landslide, carrying the electoral college by 521 to 17 and securing 60.7 of the popular vote, only just short of Johnson's record in 1964.[149]

Among the media there were many who were not merely humiliated by Nixon's triumph but genuinely frightened. As one powerful editor put it: 'There's got to be a bloodletting. We've got to make sure nobody even thinks of doing anything like this again.'[150] The aim was to use publicity to reverse the electoral verdict of 1972, which was felt to be, in some metaphysical sense, illegitimate – rather as conservative Germans had regarded Weimar as illegitimate. The Nixon White House played into the hands of this desire by the use of extra-legal means to protect the President and his policies. The tradition of presidential skulduggery had begun with Franklin Roosevelt. He had created his own 'intelligence unit', responsible only to himself, with a staff of eleven and financed by State Department 'Special Emergency' money.[151] He used Hoover's FBI and the Justice Department to harass his enemies, especially in the press, and to tap their phones – the mineworkers' leader John L. Lewis being one victim.[152] He made a desperate effort to 'get' the *Chicago Tribune*, which he hated, in the courts. He even used the intelligence service to bug his wife's hotel room.[153] Though Truman and Eisenhower kept clear of clandestine activities by their staffs and the CIA, they were aware of them, considering that, in dealing with Soviet Russia and other totalitarian-terror regimes, they were unavoidable. Kennedy and his brother Robert positively revelled in the game, and Kennedy's chief regret was that he had not made Robert head of the CIA, to bring it under close family control. At the Justice Department, Robert Kennedy in 1962 had FBI agents carry out dawn raids on the homes of executives of US Steel who had defied his brother's policies.[154] In their civil rights campaign, the Kennedy brothers exploited the Federal contracts system and used executive orders in housing finance (rather than legislation) to get their way.[155] They plotted against right-wing radio and TV stations.[156] Under Kennedy and Johnson, phone-tapping increased markedly.[157] So did executive 'bugging': the large-scale womanizing of the civil rights leader, Martin Luther King, was tapped and then played to newspaper editors.[158] Johnson used secret government files, the Internal Revenue Service and other executive devices to protect himself against exposure in the Bobby Baker scandal of 1963, potentially the biggest since Teapot Dome.

Until the Nixon presidency the media was extremely selective in its publicizing of any presidential misdemeanours. Working journalists protected Roosevelt from the exposure of his love-affairs.[159] They did the same for Kennedy, concealing the fact that, while President, he kept a Washington apartment for his mistresses, one of whom he shared with a gangster.[160] In Johnson's struggle to extricate himself from the Bobby Baker scandal, the *Washington Post* actually helped him to blacken his chief accuser, Senator John Williams.[161] Johnson, as Vice-President, accepted bribes, as did Nixon's Vice-President, Spiro Agnew: Agnew was exposed and convicted; Johnson went on to the White House.[162]

Nixon enjoyed no such forbearance from the media. Quite the contrary. But then it is likely that, in certain respects, he went further than any of his predecessors. This was partly a matter of size: the White House was expanding out of control. Lincoln had to pay a secretary out of his own pocket. Hoover had to struggle hard to get three. Roosevelt appointed the first six 'administrative assistants' in 1939. Kennedy had twenty-three. The total White House staff had risen to 1,664 in Kennedy's last year. Under Johnson it was forty times the size of Hoover's. Under Nixon it rose to 5,395 in 1971, the cost jumping from $31 million to $71 million.[163] Much of the expansion was the work of Henry Kissinger, Nixon's Security Assistant and later Secretary of State, who controlled the Vietnam negotiations. It was Kissinger who fundamentally expanded the phone-tapping operations, in theory to assist his peace offensive.[164] Vietnam, where world peace and American lives were at stake, was the ostensible, and for Nixon the real, justification for many questionable activities. He saw secrecy as paramount to success. In 1971 a huge series of secret Administration papers (the 'Pentagon Papers') were stolen and given to the *New York Times*, which published them. In Britain and most other Western democracies, those concerned would have been gaoled under government secrecy laws. That was not possible in the USA, where the press enjoys constitutional privileges under the First Amendment. To Nixon, as one of his colleagues put it, this publication was 'a challenge by the élite, unelected press to the primacy of power of the democratically elected government. A moral issue was at stake.'[165] A 'Special Investigations unit' of the Executive was authorized to use illegal means (including a break-in) to nail the leaker. This 'plumbing' unit became the prototype for other task-forces, one of which broke into Democratic Party headquarters, in the Watergate building, in late-May 1972 and again on 17 June. On the second occasion, about which the Democrats may have known in advance, the 'plumbers' were arrested.[166]

Political espionage, even theft, had never hitherto been taken seriously in America. Johnson had 'bugged' Goldwater in 1964. The NBC TV network had bugged Democratic Party headquarters in 1968. Both the *Washington Post* and the *New York Times* published purloined material, of an extremely valuable nature (the Haldeman and Kissinger memoirs), during this period. But the *Washington Post*, in a series of articles beginning on 10 October 1972, decided to make the Watergate break-in a major moral issue, a lead followed by the rest of the East Coast media. This in itself might not have been serious. It failed to prevent the Nixon landslide. But it caught the attention of a publicity-hungry federal judge, John Sirica, known as 'Maximum John' for the severity of his sentences – and not, in any other circumstances, a justice likely to enjoy the approval of the liberal press. When the burglars came before him, he gave them provisional life sentences to force them to provide evidence against members of the Administration. That he was serious was indicated by the fact that he sentenced the only man who refused to comply, Gordon Liddy, to twenty years in prison, plus a fine of $40,000, for a first offence of breaking and entering, in which nothing was stolen and no resistance offered to police.[167] This act of judicial terrorism, which would have been impossible in any other country under the rule of law, was to be sadly typical of the juridical witch-hunt by means of which members of the Nixon Administration were hounded, convicted (in some cases pleading guilty to save the financial ruin of an expensive defence) and sentenced.[168] But it had the desired effect and 'broke' the Watergate scandal, that is, it allowed the machinery of Congressional investigation, where of course the Democrats enjoyed majority control, to make a frontal assault on the 'imperial presidency'. In the process the notion of executive privilege, once so hotly defended by the liberal media, was scrapped. Indeed, in the overwhelming desire to destroy Nixon, all considerations of national security were cast aside.

Matters were made easy for the witch-hunters by the admission, on Friday 13 July 1973, by one of the White House staff, that all Nixon's working conversations were automatically taped. Again, there was nothing new in this. Roosevelt had stationed stenographers in a specially constructed cubicle beneath his office to eavesdrop on callers. In 1982 it was revealed that in 1940 he had also used secret tapes, with the help of the Radio Corporation of America, which owned one of the big networks. At the same time it emerged that Truman had made tapes, that Eisenhower used a combination of tapes and dicta-belts, that Kennedy secretly taped visitors (and his wife) for the last sixteen months of his presidency, and that Johnson was an inveterate taper.[169] In fact one of Nixon's first acts, in February 1969, was to have Johnson's taping system ripped out: he thought it wrong. Then, in February 1971, worried that liberal historians of the future would misrepresent his Vietnam policy, he ordered a new system to be installed. His Chief of Staff, Bob Haldeman, picked one which was indiscriminate and voice-activated, 'the greatest single disservice a presidential aide ever performed for his chief'.[170] These transcribed tapes, which the courts and Congressional investigators insisted that Nixon surrender – under the ironic gaze, presumably, of a ghostly Senator Joe McCarthy – were used to mount a putative impeachment of the President. Whether Nixon was actually guilty of an attempt to interfere with the course of justice, as alleged, and whether such an attempt, if made, was covered by a legitimate interpretation of *raison d'état*, was never established. Nixon never put his side of the case since, rather than risk the prolonged national convulsion of an impeachment, which might have lasted years, he resigned in August 1974. Thus the electoral verdict of 1972 was overturned by what might be described as a media *putsch*. The 'imperial presidency' was replaced by the 'imperial press'.[171]

The fall of Nixon was made the occasion for a radical shift in the balance of power back towards the legislature. Some movement in this direction was perhaps overdue. In the event it proceeded much too far in the opposite direction. In 1973 the War Powers Resolution, passed over Nixon's veto, imposed unprecedented restraints on the power of the President to commit US forces abroad, compelling him in any event to seek Congressional authority within sixty days. Further limitations on presidential foreign policy were imposed by the Jackson–Vanik and Stevenson Amendments of 1973–4. In July–August 1974 Congress paralysed the President's handling of the Cyprus crisis; in the autumn it imposed restrictions on the use of the CIA. In 1975 it effectively hamstrung the President's policy in Angola. Later that year it passed the Arms Export Control Act, removing the President's discretion in the supply of arms. It used financial controls to limit severely the system of 'presidential agreements' with foreign powers, over 6,300 of which had been concluded from 1946–74 (as opposed to only 411 treaties, which required Congressional sanction). It reinforced its aggressive restrictions on presidential power by enabling no less than seventeen Senatorial and sixteen House committees to supervise aspects of foreign policy, and by expanding its expert staff to over 3,000 (the House International Relations Committee staff tripled, 1971–7), to monitor White House activities.[172] By the late 1970s, it was calculated that there were no less than seventy limiting Amendments on the presidential conduct of foreign policy. It was even argued that a test of the War Powers Act would reveal that the President was no longer Commander-in-Chief and that the decision whether or not American troops could be kept abroad or withdrawn might have to be left to the Supreme Court.[173]

The immediate, and in terms of human life the most serious, impact of the Watergate hysteria was the destruction of free institutions in the whole of Indo-China. Nixon's policy of withdrawal made sense only if the North Vietnamese were kept guessing about America's willingness to provide forceful backing to its allies in the South. The War Powers Act, the 1974 Congressional ban on American military involvement, and Congress's further reductions of all assistance to the South, the direct results of the Watergate *dégringolade*, ended the necessary ambiguities about American policy. Nixon and his successor, Gerald Ford, were powerless to prevent the North Vietnamese from breaking the accords and taking everything. Some French experts had argued all along that the true cause of the Indo-Chinese struggle, and the dynamic throughout, was the aggressive expansionism of the North Vietnamese and their centuries-old desire, which Communist organization and ruthlessness provided the means to gratify, to dominate all the peoples of Indo-China. That thesis was now strengthened by events. As US aid tailed off, the military balance shifted decisively to the North in 1973. By the end of the year the North had achieved a two-to-one superiority and launched a general invasion. In January 1975 the whole of central Vietnam had to be evacuated, and a million refugees fled towards Saigon. In a last desperate appeal to Congress, President Ford pleaded: 'American unwillingness to provide adequate assistance to allies fighting for their lives could seriously affect our credibility throughout the world as an ally.'[174] But Congress did nothing. At his news conference on 26 March Ford appealed again, warning of 'a massive shift in the foreign policies of many countries and a fundamental threat . . . to the security of the United States'.[175] The face of Congress remained averted. Less than four weeks later, on 21 April, the Vietnamese government abdicated. Marine helicopters lifted American officials, and a few Vietnamese friends, from the rooftop of the US embassy in Saigon. Nine days later Communist tanks entered the city. It was the gravest and most humiliating defeat in American history. For the peoples of the region it was a catastrophe.

The Communist élites which seized power by force all over Indo-China in April 1975 immediately embarked on nationwide programmes of social engineering which recalled Stalin's collectivization of the peasants, though in some respects they were even more inhuman. The best-documented is the 'ruralization' conducted in Cambodia by the Communist Khmer Rouge, which entered the capital Phnom Penh in mid-April, the American embassy having been evacuated on the 12th. The atrocities began on 17 April. They were carried out mainly by illiterate peasant soldiers, but they had been planned two years before by a group of middle-class ideologues who called themselves *Angka Loeu* ('the Higher Organization'). Details of their plan had been obtained by a State Department expert, Kenneth Quinn, who circulated it in a report dated 20 February 1974.[176] The scheme was an attempt to telescope, in one terrifying *coup*, the social changes brought about over twenty-five years in Mao's China. There was to be 'total social revolution'. Everything about the past was 'anathema and must be destroyed'. It was necessary to 'psychologically reconstruct individual members of society'. It entailed 'stripping away, through terror and other means, the traditional bases, structures and forces which have shaped and guided an individual's life' and then 'rebuilding him according to party doctrines by substituting a series of new values'.[177] *Angka Loeu* consisted of about twenty professional political intellectuals, mainly teachers and bureaucrats. Of the eight leaders, all in their forties (one a woman), five were teachers, one a university professor, one an economist, one a bureaucrat. All had studied in France in the 1950s, where they had absorbed the doctrines of 'necessary violence' preached on the radical Left. They were Sartre's children. It is notable that, while this group of ideologues preached the virtues of rural life, none had in fact ever engaged in manual labour or had any experience at all of creating wealth. Like Lenin, they were pure intellectuals. They epitomized the great destructive force of the twentieth century: the religious fanatic reincarnated as professional politician. What they did illustrated the ultimate heartlessness of ideas. In any other age or place, the plans of these savage pedants would have remained in their fevered imaginations. In Cambodia in 1975 it was possible to put them into practice.

On 17 April over 3 million people were living in Phnom Penh. They were literally pushed into the surrounding countryside. The violence started at 7 am with attacks on Chinese shops; then general looting. The first killings came at 8.45 am. Fifteen minutes later troops began to clear the Military Hospital, driving doctors, nurses, sick and dying into the streets. An hour later they opened fire on anyone seen in the streets, to start a panic out of the city. At noon the Preah Ket Melea hospital was cleared: hundreds of men, women and children, driven at gunpoint, limped out into midday temperatures of over 100 Fahrenheit. Of 20,000 wounded in the city, all were in the jungle by nightfall. One man humped his son, who had just had both legs amputated; others pushed the beds of the very ill, carrying bottles of plasma and serum. Every hospital in the city was emptied. All papers and records in the city were destroyed. All books were thrown into the Mekong River or burned on the banks. The paper money in the Banque Khmer de Commerce was incinerated. Cars, motorbikes and bicycles were impounded. Rockets and bazookas were fired at houses where any movement was detected. There were many summary executions. The rest were told, 'Leave immediately or we will shoot all of you.' By evening the water-supply was cut off. What gave the episode its peculiar Kafkaesque horror was the absence of any visible authority. The peasant-soldiers simply killed and terrified, obeying orders, invoking the commands of *Angka Loeu*. Nothing was explained. The intellectuals who had planned it all never appeared.[178]

On 23 April troops began emptying the other cities, with populations ranging from 15,000 to 200,000. There were many atrocities. In Siem Reap over one-hundred patients in the Monte Peth hospital were murdered in their beds with clubs and knives; forty more were killed in the military hospital. Following the pattern of Stalin in Poland, there were massacres of officers: at Mongkol Borei, for instance, a group of two-hundred were driven into a minefield laid specially for the purpose. At the Svay Pagoda near Sisophon, eighty-eight pilots were clubbed to death. Other groups murdered *en masse* were street beggars, prostitutes, the seriously wounded and incurably sick found in hospitals, civil servants, teachers and students. As in the big Indonesia massacre, the families of the 'guilty' were slaughtered to prevent 'revenge': Khmer Rouge girl-soldiers took off the women and small children to the death-pits. But little attempt was made to hide the killings: bodies were left to decompose or floated in scores down the rivers.[179]

By June 3,500,000 people from the cities and 500,000 from 'bad' villages had been scattered over the countryside, and set to work to build new villages, often with their bare hands. Slackers were told they would be 'ground down by the wheel of History', a striking image of Leninism in practice. Sexual intercourse was forbidden; adultery or fornication punished by death, the sentence being carried our ruthlessly. Married couples were forbidden to have prolonged conversations together: this was known as 'arguing' and punished by death on the second offence. As famine and epidemic developed, the old and sick and the very young (especially if orphans) were abandoned. Executions were in public, relatives being forced to watch while their brother, mother or child was garotted or decapitated, stabbed, bludgeoned or axed to death. Sometimes entire families were executed together. Former officials were often tortured to death, or mutilated before execution. At Do Nauy, Colonel Saray Savath had his nose and ears cut off and was then crucified to a tree, dying the third day. In the same place a teacher called Tan Samay, who disobeyed orders not to teach his pupils anything except soil-tilling, was hanged, his own pupils, aged eight to ten, being forced to carry out the execution, and to shout 'Unfit teacher!' as they did so.[180] The sickening list of cruelties is endless.

In April 1976, the leader of the *Angka Loeu*, Khieu Samphan, became head of state, being succeeded as head of government by another middle-class fanatic intellectual, Pol Pot. As head of state, Khieu attended a conference of so-called non-aligned nations in Colombo in August 1976, and in a confused interview with an Italian magazine appeared to admit that a million 'war criminals', as he termed them, had died since the Khmer Rouge took over. At that time large-scale murders were continuing. According to one set of calculations, based on interviews with over 300 witnesses and the work of the French scholar François Ponchaud, who questioned many more, about 100,000 Cambodians were executed, 20,000 died trying to flee, 400,000 died in the forced exodus from the towns, a further 430,000 died in the camps and 'villages' before the end of 1975, and 250,000 more in 1976. Hence between April 1975 and the beginning of 1977, the Marxist-Leninist ideologues ended the lives of 1,200,000 people, a fifth of the population.[181]

Although the Cambodia atrocities attracted the most attention in the West, social engineering of a similar kind took place in Laos and South Vietnam. In Laos the middle class had been destroyed or driven out to Thailand by the end of 1975, when a People's Democratic Republic was declared, in reality a cover for colonization by North Vietnamese. Minorities were destroyed or expelled and in the north mass-settlement by North Vietnamese peasants took place in the years 1977–8. In July 1976, South Vietnam was 'unified' with the North under Northern control. As in Cambodia, large but unknown numbers of city-dwellers were moved by force into the countryside. The Secretary-General of the Vietnamese Communist Party, Le Duan, announced that living standards would now fall. 'People in the South', he said, had 'attained living-standards too high for the country's economy'. Such a 'consumer society' was the 'complete opposite of a truly happy and civilized life'. So that was that. The party journal wrote of 'our entire people's submission to the will of the advanced class representing society'. By January 1977 there were 200,000 political prisoners, in addition to many thousands of executions. In December 1978 the North Vietnam élite finally broke with the Pol Pot regime in Cambodia, invaded the country and occupied Phnom Penh on 7 January 1979. The whole of Indo-China was now in practical terms 'united' under a North Vietnamese military dictatorship, with 200,000 Viet troops in Kampuchea (as Cambodia was now called) and 20,000 in Laos. By 1980, Vietnam had well over 1 million in its armed forces, next to Cuba the largest, *per capita*, in the world.[182] It was a gruesome climax to the 'liberation struggle', which now entered a new phase, with guerrilla movements, supported by China, taking the field against Hanoi, and with Soviet Russia supplying the North Vietnamese imperialists with the helicopter gunships to maintain their paramountcy. But the twentieth century has been crowded with such ironies.

These events were viewed apathetically in America, and indeed in the West as a whole. They were merely one marginal aspect of the process of disillusionment so characteristic of the Seventies decade, and which centred increasingly on the flagging performance of the world economy. The Vietnam War and its bitter sequel, the Great Society and its collapse, the Imperial Presidency and its demolition: these constituted, in combination, a suicide attempt by the super-power of the West. They were powerful factors in ending the great post-war economic expansion and in returning international society to the fear and disarray of the 1930s. Equally important, they undermined the capacity of American leadership to respond to the new instability.

NINETEEN

The Collectivist Seventies

Economic disorder precedes the military disorder of war. The economic collapse of the early 1930s undoubtedly made possible the Second World War. In its aftermath, Western statesmen earnestly sought guidance to prevent this pattern recurring. The result was the Keynesian age. He had defined the essence of his philosophy in his famous letter to the *New York Times* in 1933: 'I lay overwhelming emphasis on the increase of national purchasing power resulting from governmental expenditure, which is financed by loans.'[1] During the 1950s and 1960s this Keynesian emphasis became the leading principle of economic policy in all the major Western economies. Moreover, Keynesianism was adopted at the international level. In July 1944 at Bretton Woods in New Hampshire, he and the American Treasury official Harry Dexter White created the World Bank and the International Monetary Fund. The haughty King's man found White intolerably rude: he had 'not the faintest conception' of 'civilized behaviour'. White called Keynes 'Your Royal Highness'. But in practice these two men, both of whom had guilty secrets, worked well together. Keynes contended that London's pre-1914 role of running the international money system had been left vacant, because of British weakness, between the wars: hence the disaster. The new system was to fill the gap. It extended 'the principles of local banking to the international field . . . when one chap wants to leave his resources idle, those resources are not therefore withdrawn from circulation but are made available to another chap who is prepared to use them – and to make this possible without the former losing his liquidity.'[2]

The new system came into existence in May 1946. It worked very well, mainly because the US economy boomed, and American policy-makers were prepared to run the world on Keynesian lines. There was a world-wide, insatiable demand for dollars, and Washington was prepared to provide them either through Marshall Aid, other foreign aid programmes, or cheap loans. The result was the most rapid and prolonged economic expansion in world history. World trade, which had actually contracted by 3 per cent in the early 1930s, and only recovered the lost ground in the late 1930s, grew over the quarter-century 1948–71 at the remarkable average annual rate of 7.27 per cent.[3] Nothing like this had ever been experienced before. Even in the brief 1926–9 frenzy, the rate had been only 6.74 per cent. Industrial expansion was comparably exotic. In the 260-odd years for which reasonable figures are available, 1705–1971, the quantity of industrial production in the world rose 1,730 times. Considerably over half this increase came in the post-1948 quarter-century. The growth in industrial production over the whole world averaged 5.6 per cent, sustained year after year.[4]

The framework of stability which made possible this phenomenal material improvement in the human condition was provided by the dollar as a generously administered international currency. But the reliability of the dollar depended on the strength of the American economy. And in the 1960s successive American presidents placed that economy under growing strain. Moreover, America's was essentially a businessman's economy. Its success lay in great part in the existence of a favourable climate, in which businessmen felt safe and esteemed. That climate had existed in the 1920s. It had disappeared in the 1930s. It had reappeared in the war, when business was needed to destroy Hitler, and it had been sustained until the end of the Eisenhower administration. In the 1960s came a great change. The national climate turned hostile to business. The first sign of trouble was a return to the vigorous enforcement of anti-trust legislation. The Justice Department made a frontal assault on the electric industry. Early in 1961, top officials of General Electric and Westinghouse, and the companies themselves, were convicted of price-fixing. Sentencing alone took two days. Seven leading business-men went to gaol; the fines totalled nearly $2 million.[5]

That was only a foretaste. The Kennedy brothers had been brought up by their speculator-father to hate businessmen.[6] The result was the 1962 attack on the steel industry, led by the Attorney-General, Robert Kennedy, who had learnt the techniques of harassment and judicial manipulation as one of Joe McCarthy's staff. The *Christian Science Monitor* asked: 'After this display of naked power . . . how free will the American economy be?' The *Wall Street Journal* complained that the government was coercing the steel industry 'by the pressure of fear – by naked power, by threats, by agents of the state security police'.[7] The result was the first big post-war fall in the New York stock market. It recovered, but stocks in some industries never again kept ahead of inflation. In 1966, with inflation passing the 3 per cent barrier for the first time, and with interest-rates pushing up to the then-daunting level of $5\frac{1}{2}$ per cent, the sparkle went out of the Great Bull Market. In 1968, the culminating year of Lyndon Johnson's troubles, the growth of stocks ended completely, with the Dow-Jones industrial index short of the magic 1,000-mark. Twelve years later, adjusted for inflation, it had fallen to about 300.[8] In the decade of the 1970s alone the value of common stocks on the New York Stock Exchange fell by about 42 per cent.[9] Cumulatively, the loss of confidence in stocks – that is, in the American business economy – was as great as in the Hoover collapse, though spread over a much longer period.

The flagging stock exchange was only the beginning of the troubles of American business. In 1961 Rachel Carson published *The Sea Around Us* and the next year *The Silent Spring*, in which she drew attention to the alarming pollution of natural resources and the destruction of organic life caused by the processes of booming modern economies, especially the dumping of toxic chemicals and the use of insecticides to raise agricultural production. In 1965 Ralph Nader published *Unsafe at Any Speed*, presenting the characteristic product of the American auto industry, the very heart of the industrial economy, as a death-trap. These books were necessary correctives to the harmful side-effects of rapid growth. But they introduced an era in which the protection of the environment and the consumer became a quasi-religious crusade, fought with increasingly fanatical zeal. It had a peculiar appeal to the hundreds of thousands of graduates now pouring off the campuses as a result of the expansion of higher education, keen to find ways to express the radicalism they absorbed there. Nothing was more calculated to produce a climate hostile to business than the growth of the health and safety lobby. It became a salient feature of American life from the mid-1960s onwards and was soon reflected in a mass of regulatory legislation. With his extraordinary capacity to get laws through Congress, Lyndon Johnson began the process: in 1964 the Multiple Use Act and the Land and Water Act; in 1965 the Water Pollution Act and the Clean Air Act; in 1966 the Clean Water Restoration Act. When Johnson faltered, the 'Conservation Congress' of 1968 took the initiative and held it into the 1970s, when a series of gigantic Acts imposed what was termed 'Ecotopia' on American business: the Environmental Protection Act, the Toxic Substances Control Act, the Occupational Health and Safety Act, the Clean Air Amendments Act and a whole series of Food and Drug Acts. By 1976 it was calculated that compliance with the new regulations was costing business $63 billion a year, plus a further $3 billion to the taxpayer to maintain the government regulatory agencies. Total costs rose to over $100 billion by 1979.[10]

Equally serious was the effect on productivity. One example was the coal industry, where production stood at 19.9 tons per worker per day in 1969. By 1976, when the full effects of the 1969 Coal-Mine Health and Safety Act (in some ways a highly desirable statute) had been felt, production had slipped to 13.6 tons, a fall of 32 per cent.[11] In 1975, over the whole of American industry, productivity was 1.4 per cent lower than otherwise as a result of meeting government pollution and job-safety regulations.[12] During the late 1960s and throughout the 1970s, therefore, excessive government regulation was applying the same kind of destructive friction to the American economy as trade union legal privilege in Britain. As a result, in the decade 1967–77, productivity in American manufacturing industry grew by only 27 per cent, about the same as in Britain (the corresponding figure for West Germany was 70 per cent, for France 72 per cent and for Japan 107 per cent). From the mid-1970s onwards, American productivity actually declined. The most detailed analysis of this stagnation and decline in American economic dynamism suggested the causes were mainly political: failure to control the money supply, excessive tax burdens and above all government intervention and regulation.[13]

But the anti-business climate was not the creation of politics alone. It was also the work of the courts, which in the 1960s entered a period of aggressive expansion – part of the movement towards a litigious society – led by the Supreme Court. Chief Justice Waite had laid down the correct principle in 1877: 'For protection against abuses by legislatures, the people must resort to the polls, not the courts.' But in the 1950s and early 1960s, liberal America had appealed to the courts to remedy the refusal of Congress to pass effective civil rights legislation. The courts responded and, having acquired the taste for power, indulged it long after the essential civil rights battle was won. They eroded the legitimate sphere not only of Congress but of the presidency, not only in the area of rights but in the conduct of the economy. Thus the early 1970s saw the birth not only of the 'imperial press' but of the 'imperial judiciary'.

The animus of the courts was directed particularly against businessmen, notably when the judiciary, by an extension of the civil rights concept, embraced the principle of 'affirmative action' (that is, discrimination in favour of 'underprivileged groups') and began the process of imposing 'race quotas'. This was only one aspect of 'rights': the rights of women, homosexuals, the handicapped and many other collective entities were interpreted by the courts as enforceable against powerful institutions, such as business or government. The Supreme Court in effect reinterpreted the constitution to sustain the particular political and legislative preferences of the judiciary, which were liberal. Hence constitutional principles, and the legal practice derived from them, changed with frightening speed.[14] A growing proportion of business resources and executive time was devoted to responding to litigation: in the 1970s, America had four times as many lawyers *per capita* as West Germany, twenty times as many as Japan.[15]

The courts also moved to make it difficult for government, at local, state or federal level, to reduce the size and cost of the public sector. When Nixon provided no funds for the 1974 Office of Economic Opportunity, which meant closing down its nine hundred Community Action agencies (a bureaucratic extravaganza of no great practical value), a federal judge ruled the action illegal.[16] The courts also ruled that a governing authority failing to provide social or welfare services in such a way as to infringe the civil rights of citizens was liable for damages; that an authority which reduced prison staff as an economy measure damaged the civil rights of prisoners; that for Congress to refuse funds in a specific civil rights area (e.g., the right to abortion) was unconstitutional; and that all government departments, and all private companies receiving government funds or contracts, must employ races by quota.[17] The cumulative effect of these and many similar decisions was to make it exceedingly difficult to reverse the growth of government expenditure and create room for a revival of business confidence and efficiency.

The peak post-war year for the American economy, relative to the rest of the world, was 1968, when American industrial production was more than one-third (34 per cent) of the world total. It was also the climax of the American global paramountcy, the year of Lyndon Johnson's agony, the point at which the combined burden of foreign and domestic spending became too great to bear. Thereafter all was decadence. And with America's relative economic decline came a progressive softening of the dollar as a reserve currency. This inevitably undermined the Bretton Woods arrangements. From the late 1960s Washington ceased to control the world monetary system. To some extent it ceased to control its own currency since the quantity of unrepatriated dollars – what de Gaulle stigmatized as 'America's export of her own inflation' – now reached catastrophic proportions. The age of the dollar was over. The age of the Eurodollar dawned.

As long ago as 1949 the Communist Chinese, fearing America might block any dollars they earned, decided to keep their dollars outside the US in a Soviet Paris bank. Its cable address was 'Eurobank' – hence the term Eurodollar. America first went into deficit in 1958, and thereafter the flow of dollars into Europe increased steadily. A British financier, Sir George Bolton, of the Bank of London and South America, now grasped the idea that here, for the first time, was a currency growing up outside national supervision, an expatriate currency capable of providing colossal amounts of credit. He made London the centre of the new Eurodollar system.[18] The Eurodollar market tripled in 1959 alone; doubled again in 1960. Attempts by Kennedy to break it up by controls merely boosted its attractiveness. Similar measures by European governments were equally counter-productive. It was a good example of the way in which the market defies the suppressive puritanism of governments and world agencies. As Walter Wriston of New York's Citibank put it, the Eurocurrency market was 'fathered by controls'. It was, in fact, a kind of black market world financial system. Freed of government interference, it was able to make the maximum use of the new electronic communications devices which became available in the 1960s and 1970s. To quote Wriston again: 'Mankind now has a completely integrated international financial and information marketplace, capable of moving money and ideas to any place on this planet within minutes.'[19]

But of course the Eurodollar market, the product of American inflation, was itself highly inflationary. It reproduced some of the worst features of the 1920s New York money market, especially in its international loans. It increased the volatile nature of money, stacked up credit in multiple tiers of borrowings, thus creating 'dollars' which did not exist.[20] Eurobonds and Eurocredits were invented. All the world's major banks came into the market, and formed syndicates to handle loans to governments on a scale never before imagined. The first Eurodollar syndicated loan was to the Shah's Iran in 1969. It was for $80 million. Italy got a $200 million loan later that year. Soon up to two hundred banks joined syndicates, and the size and number of loans, and the speed at which they were packaged, grew dramatically. The billion-dollar loan became routine. Commercial banks replaced wealthy Western governments and development aid as the chief source of finance for the Third World. In 1967, commercial banks accounted for only 12 per cent of external public debt in the world. By the end of 1975 they passed the 50 per cent mark at a trot.[21]

As the banks took over the international monetary system, the supervisory role of Washington collapsed. In 1971 the Nixon administration lost or abandoned control of what was happening.[22] Two years later, in March 1973, Nixon cut the link between gold and dollars, and thereafter most major currencies floated, either singly or in groups. The float revealed the weakness of the dollar, which lost 40 per cent of its value against the Deutschmark between February and March 1973. It also increased the speed and hysteria of monetary movements which, thanks to electronic gadgetry, surged backwards and forwards across frontiers in gigantic masses (in the late 1970s, money transactions in New York alone averaged $23 billion a day[23]). In short, by autumn 1973, the financial underpinning of the world economy was coming apart. To produce disaster, all that was required was a sudden shock. What happened was by no means a mere shock: it was an earthquake.

It was no accident that the earthquake emanated from the Middle East. The great post-war boom had been propelled by cheap energy. Between 1951 and 1972, the price of fuel declined consistently compared to the price of manufactured goods. It fell sharply in relative terms 1953–69, and in the years 1963–9 it actually fell in absolute terms.[24] This fall in price was made possible by the rapid increase of exports of cheap Middle East oil. It is significant that the three leading sectors in the Western economic boom, motors, chemicals and electricity, were all energy-intensive, indeed oil-intensive.[25] By assuming energy would remain cheap, all the industrial nations were short-sighted. But American energy policy was a particularly sad tale of improvidence, since government intervention kept domestic prices well below world averages. From being a world exporter of energy America became a net importer – 7 per cent of the total by 1960 – with her energy consumption increasing fast every year (5 per cent annually in the second half of the 1960s). Her imports of petroleum products were particularly disturbing: in 1960 she imported 10 per cent; by 1968 28 per cent; by 1973 36 per cent.[26] America's own oil production peaked in 1970 and thereafter declined.

The rulers of the Middle East oil states noted this growing dependence of the West and Japan on their oil exports, and the failure to devise supplementary or alternative sources of energy. Some of them, and especially the Shah of Iran, were impressed by the arguments of the ecologists that the advanced industrial nations, especially America, were using up natural resources too fast because they were underpriced. In 1972–3 there were already signs that raw materials and other commodities, such as farm products, were rising in price, and oil began to follow. The Shah sought to persuade his fellow-rulers that the oil-exporting countries of the Middle East would do better to expand production more slowly and push up prices: thus their oil in the ground would increase in value. But to heed his advice they required not only a reason but an emotion – hatred of Israel, and of Israel's ally America.

Strictly speaking, there had been no paramount power in the Middle East since the Suez fiasco of 1956–7. But though Britain kept a much lower profile she was quite active and surprisingly effective in the area for the next few years. British military interventions in Jordan in 1958, in Oman in 1959, in Kuwait in 1961, were successful in keeping the area reasonably stable. It was the progressive British military withdrawal from Aden and from the Gulf in the late 1960s which made the real difference.[27] Thereafter the area lacked an international policeman. The late Dag Hammarskjöld's UN force was, in fact, a force working for instability, since under the UN doctrine of sovereignty President Nasser could ask for its withdrawal as soon as he felt strong enough to overwhelm Israel. That is precisely what he did on 16 May 1967. The UN complied three days later and the same evening Cairo Radio announced: 'This is our chance, Arabs, to deal Israel a mortal blow of annihilation.' Nasser, 27 May: 'Our basic objective will be the destruction of Israel.' President Aref of Iraq, 31 May: 'Our goal is clear: to wipe Israel off the map.' Ahmed Shukairy, Chairman of the Palestine Liberation Organization, 1 June: 'The Jews of Palestine will have to leave . . . . Any of the old Jewish Palestine population who survive may stay, but it is my impression that none of them will survive.'

In view of the withdrawal of the UN, these threats, and the concentration on her borders of armies outnumbering her own by three to one, heavily armed with modern Soviet material, Israel launched a preventive war on 4 June, beginning with strikes against Egyptian air-power. It lasted six days and was wholly successful. The Egyptian, Jordanian and Syrian forces were routed, and in Egypt's case humiliated. Sinai and the West Bank were occupied. The Syrian Golan Heights, which made possible the bombardment of the Israeli settlements in Upper Galilee, were stormed. Above all, Old Jerusalem, including the Wailing Wall and the Holy Places, the great prize which had eluded Israel in 1948, was now brought into the new state. Thus the war corrected a painful anomaly. In its 4,000-year history, Jerusalem had been besieged, occupied, destroyed and rebuilt repeatedly, under Canaanites, Jebusites, Jews, Babylonians, Assyrians, Persians, Romans, Byzantines, Arabs, Crusaders, Mamelukes, Ottomans and British. But it had never been divided, except during the years 1948–67. The reunification of the city under the Israelis made possible an agreed administration of the Holy Places by Muslims, Jews and Christians, within the framework of a national capital.[28]

In other respects the Israeli victory brought no permanent gains. Nasser survived, thanks to some adroit crowd-manipulation.[29] His forces were rearmed by Soviet Russia, at more than twice the strength of the 1967 level. The thrust of his propaganda became increasingly anti-American, summed up in his endlessly repeated slogan 'Israel is America and America is Israel.' It was one of

Nasser's arguments that to strike at America was to hurt Israel and that America's growing dependence on Middle East oil was a means to do so. But Egypt was not an oil power. Nasser died on 28 September 1970 of a heart-attack, a propagandist of genius, a total failure as a military and political leader. There was no one to replace him as the cynosure of Arab hopes, delusory though they might be. But Nasser's destructive role as an advocate and practitioner of violence was soon filled by Colonel Mohammed Gadafy of Libya. A year before, he and other young officers had overthrown the country's pro-Western monarchy rather as Nasser had despatched Farouk. In many ways Gadafy modelled himself on Nasser and repeated his Pan-Arabist and anti-Israeli rhetoric word-for-word. Libya was one of the smallest Arab states with only 2 million inhabitants. But it was by far the largest Arab oil producer west of Suez, and the importance of its geographical location was stressed in the aftermath of the 1967 war, when the canal was closed and Middle East oil supplies to the West disrupted. From the earliest days of his dictatorship Gadafy stressed the importance of the oil weapon in hitting back at 'western imperialism' for its support of Israel.

Gadafy proved extremely adroit in bargaining with the oil companies and the consumer nations, showing that both could successfully be divided and blackmailed separately. When he took power Libyan oil was virtually the cheapest in the world. In a series of negotiations, in 1970, 1971 and again in 1973, he obtained the biggest oil price increases ever granted to an Arab power, with additional upward adjustments to account for the fall in the dollar. The importance of his success was that it was quickly imitated by the Arab-dominated Organization of Petroleum Exporting Countries. OPEC had been formed as a defensive body to protect the oil price when it fell. Hitherto it had engaged in no collective action except to agree a royalty formula in 1965. In 1971, following Gadafy's move, the OPEC states of the Gulf bargained together as a group against the oil companies for the first time.[30] At Teheran on 14 February 1971, they secured a 40-cents-on-the-barrel price increase. This was the beginning of the energy price revolution. The new agreement was to hold for five years, 'a solemn promise', as Henry Kissinger put it, 'that must hold a world record in the scale and speed of its violation'.[31]

The likelihood that the oil weapon would now be used more skilfully was much increased in July 1972 when Nasser's successor, General Anwar Sadat, threw off the Soviet alliance, expelled his Soviet advisers and technicians, and aligned Egypt with Saudi Arabia and the other oil states of the Gulf. Sadat was not a verbalizer like Nasser. In spirit he was not of the Bandung generation. He was a realist. He recognized that the Egypt–Israel antagonism was opposed to Egypt's historic tradition and detrimental to her current interests, especially economic. He wanted to end it. But to have the power to make peace he first needed the prestige of military victory. On Saturday 6 October 1973, on the festival of Yom Kippur or Day of Atonement, the holiest day in the Jewish calendar, he launched a co-ordinated Egyptian–Syrian attack on Israel. The initial success was considerable. The Israeli 'Bar-Lev line' in Sinai was pierced. A large part of the Israeli air force was destroyed by Soviet ground-to-air missiles. Golda Meir, the Israeli Prime Minister, appealed in some panic to Washington. Some $2.2 billion of the latest American arms was airlifted to Israel. From 8 October the Israelis began counter-attacking. Before a cease-fire was signed on 24 October, Israel had recovered the lost territory, advanced to within range of Damascus, established a bridgehead on the western side of the Suez Canal, and surrounded a large part of the Egyptian army.[32] Egypt had demonstrated an unexpected military capacity, and that was enough for Sadat; Israel had shown she could survive initial disaster.

The war brought out the ultimate military dependence of Israel on American will. It also drew attention to the damage inflicted on America's leadership of the West by the pursuit of the Watergate affair by the American media and the Congressional Democratic majority. When Israel counter-attacked successfully, Sadat appealed for Soviet support and Brezhnev sent a message to Nixon on 24 October warning that Soviet troops might be sent to fight the Israelis without further warning. Though Nixon had earlier ordered full logistical backing for the Israelis and now agreed to an alert of US forces throughout the world, the first on such a scale since the Cuban missile crisis of 1962, he was so cocooned in the Watergate tangle that he felt obliged to hand over control of the crisis to Kissinger, now the Secretary of State. It was Kissinger, not the President, who presided over the White House meeting which responded to the Brezhnev message; and he issued the orders for the alert. To the charge by some of the Watergate witch-hunters that the crisis had been engineered to divert attention from Nixon's difficulties, Kissinger scornfully replied (press conference, 25 October):

We are attempting to conduct the foreign policy of the United States with regard for what we owe not just to the electorate but to future generations. And it is a symptom of what is happening to our country that it could even be suggested that the United States would alert its forces for domestic reasons.[33]

With the American President paralysed by his domestic enemies, there was no one to lead the West on behalf of the world's oil consumers when the Arab OPEC states responded to Israel's survival by employing the oil weapon with brutal violence. Already, on 16 October, they politicized oil exports, cut oil production and (with non-Arab producers) raised the price 70 per cent. On 23 December they again raised the price, this time by 128 per cent. As a result, crude oil prices quadrupled in less than a year. The decision, as Kissinger put it, 'was one of the pivotal events in the history of this century'.[34] It transformed a general but gradual rise in prices into a price-revolution of a kind the world had never before experienced over so short a period. The worst hit were the poorest countries, most of which had acute debt-burdens and imported all their energy. In countries with *per capita* incomes around or below the $100 a year mark, where a billion people lived, and whose incomes had been rising slowly (about 2 per cent a year) in the 1960s decade, a downturn in growth was already occurring before the oil-price revolution hit them. For them it was a catastrophe.[35] They found themselves worse off at the end of the 1970s than they were when the decade opened, the first such reversal in modern times. At such low levels, such a direct fall in incomes meant malnutrition and related epidemics. The number of Africans and Asians who died in consequence of Arab oil policy in the decade after 1973 must be calculated in tens of millions.

The world as a whole experienced a decline in wealth since the loss of output was worth twice the extra funds transferred to the oil-producing countries. For the industrialized countries, the result was a form of economic malady which Keynesianism had not envisaged: stagflation. From a 5.2 per cent rate of growth with 4.1 per cent average price increases, the world moved in 1974–5 to nil or minus growth with 10–12 per cent average price increases a year. This was high inflation, and in many countries it accelerated into hyper-inflation. The price revolution, with the oil jump at its heart, spanned the years 1972–6. It was by far the most destructive economic event since 1945. It acted as a fierce brake on the energy-intensive leading sectors responsible for the prolonged expansion in the American, West European and Japanese economies, producing abrupt declines in output and unemployment on a scale unknown since the 1930s.[36] By the early 1980s, the number of unemployed in America and West Europe alone was 25 million.

The disaster might have been still more serious but for the resiliency of the banking system. In November 1973, in the immediate aftermath of the Middle East crisis, a big London fringe bank, the London and County, tottered. The Bank of England hastily launched a 'lifeboat', getting the major banks to provide $3 billions support for twenty-six other fringe banks. A bad moment occurred in the following June, when the German Herstatt Bank collapsed, owing huge sums to British and American banks, and with disturbing echoes of the fall of Credit Anstalt in 1931. But again the support system worked. At the end of 1974, the Comptroller of Currency in Washington was keeping under special observation some 150 US banks, including two of the biggest, which were known to be under strain. In London the property boom foundered, dragging down some glittering companies. The *Financial Times* index, 543 in March 1972, fell to 146 at the beginning of 1975, with shares worth less, in real terms, than at the depths of the war in 1940. In America, New York city finances, long suspect, finally succumbed when the banks refused further loans. The richest city in the world appealed to the White House, but Gerald Ford refused to intervene, an event celebrated in a famous *New York Daily News* headline: 'Ford to City: Drop Dead'.[37] But by then the worst of the money crisis was over and all the banks and institutions that really mattered were still erect.

Indeed the commercial banks, whose Eurodollar frenzy had contributed to the instability, now used similar methods to produce some kind of order out of the chaos. The problem was as follows. The oil price revolution meant that the OPEC countries took an extra $80 billion a year out of the world economy. That was 10 per cent of all world exports. Saudi Arabia and Kuwait alone, with tiny populations, received an extra $37 billion a year, enough over twenty-five years to buy all the major companies on all the world's stock exchanges. There was real terror that the Arabs would use the new 'money weapon' as they used the oil weapon. In any case it was essential to get the cash back into the world's productive economy quickly. Washington, still paralysed by Watergate, could provide no leadership. Happily, the extra-governmental Eurodollar system, used to responding to pure market needs without bureaucratic help or hindrance, was waiting to be used. Eurodollars were renamed petrodollars. A new term, 'recycling,' came into use. The petrodollars were quickly packaged into huge loans for the hard-hit advanced industrial countries and for the still more disturbed developing countries, like Indonesia, Zaïre, Brazil, Turkey and even new competitors for the Arab oil producers, like Mexico.

The Arabs had no wish to help the Third World, except through government loans with strings attached. But once they put their money into the world banking system, they lost sight of it. And they had nowhere else to put it. Like Croesus, they were baffled. They did not like what was happening. But not as yet having a banking system of their own, for Koranic reasons, there was nothing they could do. As a Congressional witness put it: 'All they have is an IOU in a bank account which can be frozen at any time in the United States or in

Germany or wherever it is.'[38] If a nation has more money than it can spend, it has to share the use, willingly or unwillingly. America did so willingly, in the years after 1945, in the form of Marshall Aid, Point Four Aid, and in the military containment of Soviet expansion. The Arabs had no such altruism, but they could not stop the banks lending their money. Walter Wriston of Citibank put the situation neatly:

If Exxon pays Saudi Arabia $50 million, all that happens is that we debit Exxon and credit Saudi Arabia. The balance-sheet of Citibank remains the same. And if they say they don't like American banks, they'll put it in Credit Suisse, all we do is charge Saudi Arabia and credit Credit Suisse: our balance sheet remains the same. So when people run around waiting for the sky to fall there isn't any way that money can leave the system. It's a closed circuit.[39]

It would, of course, have been a different matter if the Arabs had possessed a sophisticated banking network, as they belatedly realized. By the time they had begun to build up their own international banks, in the early 1980s, the industrial nations had tapped alternative sources of energy, including non-Arab oil, world oil supplies were in surplus, and the problem of petrodollars was unlikely to recur, at any rate in such an intense form. The point of maximum Arab power had passed. That point came in the years 1974–7, when the Arabs had half the world's liquidity. Thanks to the commercial banking system, the world's financial black market, the money vanished into the bottomless pit of the needs of the developing nations. By 1977, they owed the commercial banks $75 billion, more than half of it to American banks. Nearly all of this was Arab money. In global terms it was less efficient than the pre-1973 pattern, which kept the industrial West expanding steadily. Indonesia borrowed over $6 billion, most of which was wasted, before defaulting. One official put $80 million into his own accounts.[40] Zaïre, which had borrowed $3 billion by 1979, was an equally bad case of folly and corruption.[41] The biggest borrowers, Brazil and Mexico, made on the whole productive use of what they received. And much of the money ended up where it started, in the industrial economies. But the huge total of indebtedness led to recurrent fears of a world banking crisis. Hence the Seventies were a period of deepening dismay for the West. The comforting facts of recycling took some time to make themselves felt. In the meantime the recession had a political as well as an economic impact. As we have noted, the Great Depression of the Thirties demoralized the democracies, producing a lack of will to deal with aggression, or of energy to devise collective security against the growth of illegitimate power and the practice of violence. This time, fortunately, NATO and other regional pacts already existed. They continued to function after a fashion. But leadership was lacking to devise responses to new threats or variations on old ones. The relative decline in American power and will was greatly accelerated by the price revolution and the recession. The dollar lost half its value in the later 1970s. The 'American Century' seemed to have ended only twenty-five years after it began. From virtual self-sufficiency, America had moved into world-wide dependence. It imported half its oil, from Canada, Venezuela, Mexico, Nigeria and Indonesia as well as the Arab states, and most of its chrome, bauxite, manganese, nickel, tin and zinc, from all over the Western Hemisphere and from Malaysia, Zambia, Australia, Zaïre and South Africa.[42] While reliance on the sea-lanes had grown, the ability to keep them open had declined. Secretary of Defense Donald Rumsfeld, in his budget report for 1977, noted that the 'current [US] fleet can control the North Atlantic sea-lanes to Europe' but only after 'serious losses' to shipping. The 'ability to operate in the eastern Mediterranean would be, at best, uncertain'. The Pacific fleet could 'hold open the sea-lanes to Hawaii and Alaska' but 'would have difficulty in protecting our lines of communication into the Western Pacific'. In a global war America, he warned, would be hard put to protect allies like Japan or Israel, or reinforce NATO.[43] This was a radical change from the 1950s or even the early 1960s. And waning physical power was further undermined by the collapse of leadership. The 1970s was the nadir of the American presidency. After the spring of 1973, the Nixon presidency was rendered totally ineffectual by the Watergate witch-hunt. His successor, Gerald Ford, had only two years in office, lacking the mandate of election. He spent the first desperately disentangling the Administration from Watergate, the second in a bid to put together a coalition to get himself elected. Behind the orderly façade of the Ford White House there were inconclusive battles for power among rival subordinates, which Ford lacked the authority and the savagery to end. As a colleague put it, 'Good old Gerry was too damned good for his own good.'[44] Ford's views, on the rare occasions when they emerged, usually turned out to be sensible. But he lacked *gravitas*. In public, he developed an unfortunate tendency to fall over.[45]

His successor was far worse. Despite Watergate and all his disabilities, Ford nearly got himself elected in 1976 and would certainly have done so if he had been allowed to pick his Vice-President, Nelson Rockefeller, as running-mate. By this date, as a result of media harassment, the presidency was regarded as an almost impossible assignment. The competition was meagre and the Democratic nomination went to a lacklustre Georgian, Jimmy Carter, who was sold as a TV package by a clever Atlanta advertising executive, Gerald Rafshoon.[46] He won the presidency by a tiny margin against the weakest incumbent in history and became a still weaker one. Carter carried on the Nixon–Kissinger policy of *détente* with Soviet Russia long after events had rendered obsolete whatever validity it once possessed and its authors had themselves lost faith in it.[47] By the mid-Seventies, the first Strategic Arms Limitation agreement (known as SALT I), signed in May 1972, was having an unforeseen impact on American defence policy. It created an arms-control lobby within the Washington bureaucracy, especially in the State Department, which secured the right to examine new weapons programmes at their research and development stage, and seek to veto them if they posed special problems of control which would upset the SALT I arrangements.[48] Carter's policies promoted this disturbing development.

Even more damaging was Carter's ill-considered 'human rights' policy, based upon an agreement signed in Helsinki, under which the signatories undertook to seek to end violations of human rights throughout the world. The idea was to force Soviet Russia to liberalize its internal policy. The effect was quite different. Behind the Iron Curtain, the Helsinki Accords were ignored and voluntary groups set up to monitor observance were arrested. In the West, America found itself campaigning against some of its oldest allies. Again, a human rights lobby grew up within the Administration, including an entire bureau of the State Department, which worked actively against American interests. In September 1977 Brazil reacted to State Department criticisms by cancelling all its four remaining defence agreements with the US, two of which went back to 1942. Argentina was similarly estranged. The State Department played a significant role in the overthrow of the Somoza regime in Nicaragua. An Assistant Secretary, Viron Vaky, announced on behalf of the US government: 'No negotiation, mediation or compromise can be achieved any longer with a Somoza government. The solution can only begin with a sharp break from the past.'[49] The 'sharp break' took the form, in 1979, of the replacement of Somoza, a faithful if distasteful ally of the West, by a Marxist regime whose attitude to human rights was equally contemptuous and which immediately campaigned against American allies in Guatemala, El Salvador and elsewhere in Central America. Again, in 1978, the State Department's Bureau of Human Rights actively undermined the Shah's regime in Iran, playing a significant part in its destruction in 1979 and replacement by a violently anti-Western terrorist regime.[50] American human rights policy, however worthwhile in theory, was naïve in practice.

Policy under Carter was so confused, however, as to lack salient characteristics, other than a propensity to damage friends and allies. The internal battles under Ford were as nothing to the triangular tug of war under Carter between his Secretary of State, Cyrus Vance, his Security Adviser, Zbigniew Brzezinski, and his Georgian assistant, Hamilton Jordan, much of which was conducted in public – leaving aside the freelance activities of Carter's boozy brother, Billy, who acted as a paid lobbyist for the anti-American Libyan government. The only point on which Carter's men seemed agreed was America's inability to control events. Cyrus Vance thought that to 'oppose Soviet or Cuban involvement in Africa would be futile'. 'The fact is', he added, 'that we can no more stop change than Canute could still the waters.' Brzezinski insisted 'the world is changing under the influences of forces no government can control'. Carter himself said America's power to influence events was 'very limited'. Feeling itself impotent, the Administration took refuge in cloudy metaphor, for which Brzezinski had a talent. Vietnam had been 'the Waterloo of the WASP élite': no such intervention could ever again be undertaken by America. 'There are many different axes of conflict in the world,' he noted; 'the more they intersect, the more dangerous they become.' West Asia was 'the arc of crisis'. But: 'the need is not for acrobatics but for architecture.'[51] No foreign policy architecture in fact appeared, however. When the Iranian terrorist government seized the American Embassy staff as hostages, acrobatics were eventually resorted to, ending in a charred heap of burnt-out American helicopters in the desert in May 1980, perhaps the lowest point of America's fortunes in this century.

America's decline in the Seventies seemed even more precipitous in contrast with the apparent solidity and self-confidence of the Soviet regime. In 1971 Soviet Russia passed America in numbers of strategic land-based and submarine-launched nuclear missiles. The same year Andrei Gromyko boasted that, all over the world, 'No question of any significance . . . can now be decided without the Soviet Union or in opposition to it.'[52] He himself was a symbol both of internal stability and the external consistency of Soviet policy, since he had been Deputy Foreign Minister as long ago as 1946 and, since 1957, Foreign Minister, a post he was to hold well into the Eighties.

Not that the internal history of post-Stalin Russia was uneventful. Beria, Stalin's last secret police boss, did not long survive his master: he knew too much about everybody at the top. His colleagues drew up an indictment which, according to Stalin's daughter Svetlana, took three hours to read, and half of which was devoted to his sexual antics – epitomized by the poet Yevtushenko in his memoirs: 'I saw the vulture face of Beria, half hidden by a muffler, glued to the window of his limousine as he drove slowly by the kerb hunting down a woman for the night.'[53] Beria was arrested on 26 June 1953 and officially shot in December, after trial. But Khrushchev, the Party Secretary, told an Italian Communist in 1956 that he was in fact murdered at the time of his arrest: while reaching for a gun, he was seized by Malenkov, Mikoyan, Marshal Konev and Marshal Moshkalenko and strangled (another Khrushchev version had him shot).[54] In 1955 Khrushchev ousted Malenkov as leader of the post-Stalin oligarchy. Two years later he confirmed his power by driving from office the 'Anti-Party Group' of such old Stalinists as Molotov and Kaganovich, who had made common cause with Malenkov and his successor as premier, Bulganin. According to Khrushchev's own account, they had a majority against him on the Presidium, but with the help of Marshal Zhukov he airlifted to Moscow his allies on the Central Committee and had the decision reversed. Four months later he turned on Zhukov, whom he accused of harbouring 'Bonapartist aspirations' and 'violating Leninist norms'. Finally in 1958 he dismissed Bulganin and took over his job. Thereafter he was paramount for six years.

There was, however, no 'de-Stalinization'. The term was never used inside Soviet Russia. All that the post-Stalin changes and Khrushchev's 'Secret Session' speech at the twentieth Party Congress in 1956 involved was the end of mass-terrorism against party members, that is those inside the ruling system.[55] The totalitarian structure of the Leninist state, giving an absolute monopoly of power to the party – meaning in practice the tiny élite which controlled it – remained in its entirety, sustained as before by the secret police and the army, itself controlled by an internal structure of party officers. The autocratic plinth endured; and at any moment a ruthless man could build a superstructure of mass terror on it. Khrushchev behaved in many ways like an autocrat, and had to be removed like one. His colleagues disliked his adventurism. They came to see him as a disturbing influence. He tried to introduce more democracy within the party, a non-Leninist notion. His idea of 'the state of the whole people', implying the end of party power-monopoly, was throughly anti-Leninist. In some ways Khrushchev, unlike Lenin, was a Marxist: that is, he believed Communism to be attainable. At the twenty-second Party Congress in 1961 he laid down as his programme the outstripping of American living-standards in the 1960s, the beginning of Communism (rent-free housing, free public transport, etc) in the 1970s, and its completion in the 1980s. He might be described as yet another optimist who succumbed to the illusions of the Sixties. His Presidium critics thought that such promises, which could not conceivably be fulfilled, would merely produce disappointment and anger, as had his Cuban missile venture in 1962 and his 'virgin lands' scheme of 1954 to cultivate 100 million untilled acres in Soviet Central Asia and Siberia, which in June 1960 produced the biggest dust-storms in history. While he was on holiday in the Crimea in October 1964, the Presidium voted him out of office and had their decision confirmed by the Central Committee the next day. The plot was designed by the ultra-Leninist chief theoretician of the party, Michael Suslov, and executed by the head of the KGB, Alexander Shelepin, who was waiting at the airport for Khrushchev when he was flown back to Moscow under heavy police guard.[56] The object and manner of the *coup* confirmed the organic connection between 'Leninist norms' and secret policemanship.

Suslov, who preferred to remain behind the scenes, assisted the new First Secretary, Leonid Brezhnev, in his ascent to paramountcy. Brezhnev was designated Secretary-General in 1966, Head of State and Chairman of the Presidium in 1977, and Chairman of the Council of Defence, as well as being made Marshal of the Soviet Union in 1976 and receiving the Lenin Prize for Peace (1972) and Literature (1979). This glittering concentration of offices and honours was the reward conferred by Brezhnev's elderly peers in the leadership of the party for bringing to the direction of Soviet affairs a new stability, reliability and predictability, based upon an absolute determination to concentrate power in the Communist élite.[57] Brezhnev summed up this philosophy of government in the code-phrase 'trust in cadres' – that is, a consolidation and perpetuation of a privileged ruling class, a division of the country into rulers and ruled. There must be no argument about where the line was drawn, no question of surrendering the smallest iota of power to a wider franchise than the party leadership. Positions of power, once acquired, were never to be relinquished, and the principle applied externally as well as internally. As he himself put it to the liberal Czech Communist Dubček in 1968, 'Don't talk to me about "Socialism". What we have, we hold.'[58]

Brezhnev's Russia was a fulfilled rather than an expectant society. It offered more of the same rather than qualitative change. He admitted at the twenty-sixth Party Congress in February 1981 that the 1961 targets were obsolete: there would be no more specific 'Communist' goals. He restored Stalinist priority to armaments, which remained the most favoured and by far the most flourishing sector of the economy; in the 1960s and 1970s military spending grew in real terms about 3 per cent a year, meaning that, between the fall of Khrushchev and the mid-1970s, Russia spent on arms, in relation to resources, about twice the rate of America.[59] The Soviet economy as a whole grew more slowly. By 1978, according to one calculation, GNP was $1,253.6

billion, against $2,107.6 billion for the USA, giving a *per capita* income of $4,800 for Russia, $9,650 for the USA.[60] The difficulty about such figures is that income per head means little in a society overwhelmingly dominated by the public sector; and in any case they are based on statistics compiled by the Soviet government for which no independent check is available. As Khrushchev characteristically observed of the officials who run the Soviet Bureau of Statistics, 'They're the sort who can melt shit into bullets.'[61] During the 1960s and 1970s Brezhnev made available for ordinary consumers considerable quantities of low-quality goods. One estimate was that, by the end of the 1970s, the living standard of the Soviet worker was approximately that of the American worker at the beginning of the 1920s.[62] But this comparison was subject to three important qualifications. In Soviet Russia urban housing did not keep pace with the movement to the cities, which had only 19 per cent of the population in 1926 and about 62 per cent fifty years later. As a result, the Russians had the poorest living accommodation of any industrialized nation, with *per capita* floor-space only about 72 square feet (1,200 in America). Secondly, only one Russian in forty-six owned a car (though road deaths were higher than in the USA). Thirdly, the food situation deteriorated under Brezhnev, particularly in the late 1970s and early 1980s.[63]

Yet Russia was prosperous enough for Brezhnev's purposes. He wanted no 'revolution of rising expectations'. The regime had no other purpose than to perpetuate itself. As Alexander Herzen said of the Tsarist regime: 'It wields power in order to wield power.' But the comparison does not do justice to the Tsars, who were often motivated by a genuine desire to raise up their people. In exile in America, Alexander Solzhenitsyn repeatedly and angrily repudiated the notion that the Soviet regime was in any sense whatever a continuation of the Tsarist autocracy.[64] Politically and morally the Soviet regime was a totalitarian society of an altogether different kind: more a self-perpetuating conspiracy than a legitimate form of government. Though the Chicago-style gangsterism of Stalin had been replaced by the low-key Mafia of Brezhnev and his associates, the essential criminality remained. The regime rested on a basis not of law but of force. In economic terms it was, perhaps, best defined by the pseudonymous Fedor Zniakov in his *samizdat* '*Memorandum*' circulated in May 1966, as 'super-monopoly capitalism', with all significant ownership concentrated in a single centre.[65] Brezhnev's political problem was to ensure that the profits of this super-monopoly were distributed among the ruling class. This could be considered as three-tiered. Of Russia's 260 millions, about 15 million belonged to the party in 1976. These constituted not the ruling class itself but potential members of it. By the exercise of industry and subservience a fraction of them graduated to actual membership of the class. Others were eliminated at the rate of 300,000 a year by the refusal of authority to renew their party cards. The true ruling class consisted of 500,000 full-time party and senior government officials (plus their families). They were rewarded by administrative power, made possible by the enormous size of the state machine and the existence of a vast Soviet empire with high-sounding jobs throughout the world – 'enough pasture for all the sheep', as Sir Robert Walpole used to put it – and by economic privileges based upon access to a closed distributive system, including food and other consumer goods shops, housing, foreign travel, health-care, resorts and higher education. The Soviet establishment thus became a true ruling class, in the old-fashioned feudal (and Marxist) sense, in that it was distinguished from the rest of society not by comparative wealth alone but by superior, clearly distinguished legal and administrative rights. Under Lenin and Stalin, and still more under Brezhnev, Soviet society became stratified throughout. At the science settlement at Norosibrisk in the 1970s, for instance, housing was allocated as follows. A full Academy member had a villa; a Corresponding member half a villa; a Senior Research Officer an apartment with a three-metre ceiling height; a Junior Research Officer an apartment with 2.25 metre ceiling height and only a communal bathroom.[66] The real division, however, came between the top half-million and the rest: they were the true élite, the 'them' as opposed to the 'us' of the Russian masses. Of this ruling class, 426 exercised actual political power as members of the Central Committee. About 200 held ministerial rank. What they demanded of Brezhnev, and what he gave them, were extensive privileges, safety of life and property, and security of employment. In 1976, for instance, 83.4 per cent of the CC were re-elected, a typical proportion. By the end of the 1970s, most of the top 200 were over sixty-five, many in their mid-seventies. Because of its isolation from the rest of society, its special access to the highest quality of higher education, and its tendency to intermarriage, the new ruling class was already becoming hereditary, Brezhnev's own family being a case in point.

Under Stalin, as in Germany under Hitler, opposition was conspiratorial or non-existent. A totalitarian regime does not normally become internally vulnerable until it attempts to liberalize itself. There were some tentative moves in this direction under Khrushchev. Part of the Gulag structure was dismantled, though its core remained. On 25 December 1958 new 'Fundamental Principles of Criminal Law and Procedure' were enacted, giving theoretical rights to the accused and provoking the first legal debate ever held in the Soviet press. But this reform from above was bound to produce instability, and so reversal, since Soviet Russia was not a society under the rule of law. Marxism had never produced a philosophy of law. The only true Soviet legal philosopher, Evgeny Pashukanis, argued that in the socialist society Law would be replaced by Plan.[67] This was logical, since the notion of an independent legal process was incompatible with the notion of an inevitable historical process interpreted by a ruling Marxist élite. Pashukanis's own case proved it: law was replaced by plan – Stalin's – and he was murdered in the 1930s. The 1958 enactment could not be applied in practice because it would have given the courts the beginnings of an independent status and so allowed them to erode the monopoly of power enjoyed by the party. Even under Khrushchev no Soviet court ever returned a verdict of 'not guilty' in a political case; nor did a Soviet appeal court ever overturn a guilty verdict in a political case – thus preserving an unbroken record of entire subservience to the ruling party from Lenin's first year of power until the present.[68]

More important was Khrushchev's relaxation of censorship. The Presidium refused his request to change the system, so he authorized some publications on his own responsibility.[69] Heterodox material appeared in the press and in book form. In 1962 Alexander Solzhenitsyn was able to publish *One Day in the Life of Ivan Denisovich*, perhaps the most influential book to circulate freely in Russia since the Revolution. But the same year there were mass protests at Novocherkassk against food price increases. On 2 June troops fired on the mob, killing many. Riots were and are a recurrent feature of Soviet society, serving as in feudal times the role of strikes and politics, to draw attention to grievances. The June riot was on an unusually large scale and may have played a part in Khrushchev's downfall two years later. Even before he disappeared, however, he refused to allow publication of any more books about the camps. According to Roy Medvedev, our most valuable informant, the dissent movement dated from 1965, the year after Khrushchev's fall, and there was something approaching mass protest in 1966–7, when the *samizdat*-type of underground publication was at its peak.[70] The repression began at the same time, with the trial of two leading dissenters, Sinyavsky and Daniel, in February 1966. This ended any pretence of judicial reform or liberalization generally. Shortly after it two high-ranking secret police officers were appointed judges of the Soviet Supreme Court. The worst phase of the repression was 1968–70, beginning with the 'trial of the four' (Galanskov, Ginzburg, Dobrovolsky and Lashkova) in January 1968. This, one of the best-documented of Soviet trials, was a predetermined political farce, which showed that the Soviet system remained, in essentials, a totalitarian tyranny, no more capable of self-reform than of the squaring of the circle.[71]

After 1970, there was some relaxation of the new terror. Those in the West who, as part of the *détente* policy, urged acceptance of the Soviet demand for the Helsinki Conference on 'European Security and Co-operation' (July 1973 – July 1975), argued that the Soviet leaders could be forced to respect human rights as part of the agreement. This became the official policy of the Ford and Carter administrations. Under Principle Seven of the Helsinki Accords, the Soviet government undertook to 'respect human rights and fundamental freedoms'. But this was merely another treaty to be broken. In fact the Helsinki process led directly to a resumption of widespread repression, not only in Soviet Russia but elsewhere behind the Iron Curtain. For it encouraged dissenters to come out into the open. They formed monitoring groups 'To Promote Observance of the Helsinki Accords' in Moscow, the Ukraine, Georgia, Armenia and Lithuania. Similar movements sprang up in Czechoslovakia, East Germany, Poland and other satellites. Information about violations of the Accords was passed to Western journalists.

A wave of violent persecution followed, beginning in 1975 and reaching a climax in the years after 1977. Leaders of the monitoring groups were the chief victims. In some cases the KGB followed a new policy of issuing dissenters with exit visas and driving them out of their own country. But many others got long prison sentences with forced labour. Thus the Helsinki Accords radically increased the volume and ferocity of human rights violations in Soviet Russia. The farce culminated in the follow-up meeting in Belgrade, 1977–8, when the Soviet delegation produced elaborate documentation about persecution of Catholics in Ulster and blacks in America but flatly refused to discuss Soviet practice. Immediately after the meeting broke up, two members of the Ukrainian monitoring group got seven years' hard labour each, the founder of the Moscow group, already held fifteen months in custody without trial, was sentenced to seven years in a 'strict' camp, and the most famous of Soviet dissidents, Andrei Sakharov, was accused of 'hooliganism', followed by house arrest and internal exile.[72] The trials of the Georgian monitoring group evoked sinister echoes of the Stalin period, with fabricated charges of spying for Western intelligence agencies, and suggestions of torture and forced confessions.[73]

In one respect Soviet policy towards opposition elements was consistent, from the first phase of Lenin's rule to the early 1980s: dissent has always been treated as a mental disease, and dissenters have always been liable to suffer 'treatment' in special Soviet psychiatric hospitals. The first known case was in 1919, when Lenin had Maria Spiridonova, a leader of the Socialist Revolutionary Party, sentenced by the Moscow Revolutionary Tribunal to internment in a sanatorium.[74] The large-scale, systematic use of psychiatric punishment began in the late 1930s, when the NKVD built a special 400-bed penal establishment in the grounds of the regular mental hospital in Kazan. By the late 1940s, the Serbsky Institute, the main Soviet centre for teaching and research in criminal psychiatry, had a special department for 'political' work.[75] By the early 1950s, at least three establishments 'treated' cases of political prisoners, since we know of one man, Ilya Yarkov, who suffered in all of them. Psychiatric punishment was given chiefly to offenders under the catch-all Article 58 of the criminal code, dealing with 'anti-Soviet acts': Yarkov's fellow-inmates included Christians, surviving Trotskyists, opponents of Lysenko, heterodox writers, painters and musicians, Latvians, Poles and other nationalists.[76] The system, far from being abandoned, greatly expanded under Khrushchev, who was anxious to persuade the world that Soviet Russia no longer imprisoned political offenders, merely the unbalanced, and was quoted by *Pravda* (1959) as saying: 'A crime is a deviation from the generally recognized standards of behaviour, frequently caused by mental disorder . . . . To those who might start calling for opposition to Communism . . . clearly the mental state of such people is not normal.'[77]

The West first became aware of Soviet penal psychiatry in 1965 with the publication of Valery Tarsis's *Ward 7*, and thereafter efforts were made within the psychiatric profession to obtain documentation of specific cases and to raise the issue at meetings of the World Psychiatric Association.[78] These efforts were partly frustrated by the anxiety of some (chiefly American) psychiatrists to preserve Iron Curtain participation in the body at any cost, partly by the skill with which the Soviet psychiatric establishment covered its tracks and, in 1973, arranged a Potemkin-type visit to the Serbsky.[79] Nevertheless during the period 1965–75 details of 210 fully authenticated cases were obtained.[80] In addition to the first psychiatric punishment prison in Kazan, at least thirteen other Special Psychiatric Hospitals were opened in the 1960s and 1970s. No Westerner, whether psychiatrist or not, was allowed to visit an SPH. But it was established they were under the control of the Ministry of the Interior (MVD) not the Ministry of Health, were headed by military officers and run administratively like prisons. Reports from former prisoners showed the SPHs bore a marked resemblance to the experimental prison-clinics run by SS doctors as part of Himmler's race-programme, in both the cruelties practised and the type of doctor in charge. The most common torture, the wet canvas 'roll-up' method, appears to have been invented by a Dr Elizaveta Lavrit-skaya, one of the most hardened of the creatures described by Yarkov.[81] Details of tortures, beatings and the punitive use of drugs were provided at US Senate hearings in 1972.[82] The worst offenders were identified as Professor Andrei Snezhnevsky, Director of the Institute of Psychiatry at the Academy of Medical Sciences, who led the campaign to diagnose dissent as a form of schizophrenia; Professor Ruben Nadzharov, his deputy; Dr Georgy Morozov, head of the Serbsky; and Professor Daniel Lunts, regarded by the dissenters as the worst of the practitioners of psycho-terror. As with the SS, some of the doctors held military rank: Lunts was variously identified as a KGB colonel or a major-general in the MVD. These men were allowed to travel abroad to represent Soviet psychiatry, had salaries three times as large as other psychiatrists, and enjoyed access to the luxuries and privileges of the higher echelons of the Soviet ruling class.[83]

Psychiatric punishment expanded greatly under Brezhnev, though following the campaign of exposure in the West it was confined largely to the humble worker-protester unlikely to attract outside attention. For the prominent, there were many increasingly severe grades of oppression, none of which need even involve a trial. Commenting on the exile of Sakharov to Gorky, Medvedev noted: 'From Gorky Sakharov could be sent to Irkutsk in Siberia, to Tomsk, or to Chita. Worse every time . . . . The important thing is that the victim must always have something to lose, therefore something to be afraid of.'[84] At the end of March 1977, Brezhnev made it brutally clear that a return to liberalization was out of the question:

In our country it is not forbidden 'to think differently' from the majority . . . . It is quite another matter if a few individuals who have . . . actively come out against the socialist system, embark on the road of anti-Soviet activity, violate laws and, finding no support inside their own country, turn for support abroad, to imperialist subversive centres . . . . Our people demand that such . . . activists be treated as opponents of socialism, as persons acting against their own motherland, as accomplices if not actual agents of imperialism . . . . We have taken and will continue to take against them measures envisaged by our law.[85]

The identification of political criticism with treason, indeed with active treachery, was of course the basis of the Lenin–Stalin terror. Brezhnev made it clear it could be resumed at any moment. Provision for it was made in the new version of the constitution, ratified by the Supreme Soviet on 7 October 1977. Article 6 affirmed the total monopoly of political power and state activity of the Communist

Party. Article 62 read: 'Citizens of the USSR are obliged to safeguard the interests of the Soviet states, and to enhance its power and prestige.' The first of these contradicted Article 2, which said all power belonged to the people. The second contradicted Article 49, which gave the citizen the right to criticize state bodies. Articles 6 and 62 were thus the totalitarian heart of the constitution, giving the ruling class all the authority it needed to subject internal opponents to whatever degree of terror was thought necessary. Dissent continued even under the Brezhnev repression. In 1977–80, for instance, twenty-four *samizdat* publications appeared regularly. The number of individual *samizdat* items circulating passed the 100,000-mark in 1980.[86] But any kind of organized political activity, or wide diffusion of heterodox views, became totally impossible. During the 1970s, in short, while the legitimate authority of American government was being recklessly eroded, the autocratic power of Soviet government was being systematically reinforced. The process reached a logical conclusion after the death of Brezhnev in 1982, when Yuri Andropov, who had been head of the KGB for fifteen years, during which he had institutionalized psychiatric punishment of dissidents, became the Soviet ruler.

Operating from a base of political stability, Soviet global power expanded steadily during the Seventies. The most striking and visible sign of this expansion was the spectacular growth of the Soviet navy. In many ways it was comparable to the German naval programme of the 1890s and 1900s: it was not justified by any need to protect traditional lines of supply and communications but was deliberately aimed to change the existing balance of maritime power.[87] Like the British navy in the nineteenth century, American sea–air power was the great stabilizing fact in the post-war world. In 1945 America had 5,718 ships in active service, including ninety-eight aircraft carriers, twenty-three battleships, seventy-two cruisers and over 700 destroyers and escorts. As late as June 1968, the USA had 976 ships in commission.[88] But in the 1970s the American fleet shrank rapidly, to thirteen carriers and their escorts. Meanwhile the Soviet navy expanded. At the end of 1951 it was still possible for Admiral Carney, commander of NATO forces in Southern Europe, to dismiss Soviet naval power in the Mediterranean: 'He said it was possible there were a few "maverick" Soviet submarines in the Mediterranean and they might be able to push in some others in preparation for a war. But they couldn't support them long.'[89] The big change came after 1962, when the Cuban missile crisis persuaded the Soviet leadership that, if they wished to expand Communism outside the Eurasian land-mass, they would have to build a big surface navy. The new strategy was the work of Admiral Gorshkov, whose

writings constituted a body of doctrine comparable to Admiral
Mahan's, and whose advocacy of a huge submarine fleet plus a
global surface force became established policy in the early 1960s.[90]
In the fourteen-year period following the missile crisis, Soviet Russia
built a total of 1,323 ships of all classes (compared to 302 American), including 120 major surface combat ships, eighty-three amphibious and fifty-three auxiliaries. By the same date (1976), Gorshkov had accumulated a fleet of 188 nuclear submarines, forty-six of
them carrying strategic missiles.[91] In the late 1970s, the first genuine
Soviet carriers appeared. The impact of the new Soviet navy on
geopolitics became undeniable in the 1967 Arab–Israeli war, when a
large Soviet naval presence in the Eastern Mediterranean was
established on a permanent basis. By 1973, during the Yom Kippur
war, the position of the American fleet in this theatre was described
by one of its commanders as 'very uncomfortable' for the first time
since the destruction of Japanese naval power.[92] By this point the
Soviet navy, already predominant in the North-East Atlantic and
North-West Pacific, was ready to move into the South Atlantic and
the Indian Ocean.

Naval power was one element in the Soviet descent on black Africa
which was a major feature of the later 1970s. The other was the use
of Cuba as a satellite-mercenary. In the 1960s Soviet Russia bought
Cuban allegiance comparatively cheaply: less than half a billion
dollars a year. In return it got verbal support: Castro loudly defended
the Soviet invasion of Czechoslovakia in 1968. By the early 1970s
the Cuban economy was degenerating fast and in 1972 there was an
agonizing reappraisal of Soviet–Cuban relations. The Cuban debt to
Russia now stood at nearly $4 billion, and Brezhnev saw no
alternative but to defer all interest and principal payments to 1986
and in the meantime bail Cuba out.[93] The cost to Russia rose first to
$8 million, then $10 million and (by the early 1980s) $12 million a
day: nearly $4.5 billion a year. In return, however, Brezhnev
acquired a valuable instrument for the penetration of sub-Saharan
Africa. Soviet Russia had of course been active in Arab Africa since
the Nasser deal in 1955. But Soviet military and economic missions
had often made themselves unpopular; and, being white, were easily
accused of 'imperialism'. As one of the Arab premiers, Mahgoub of
the Sudan, put it, Arab states got 'obsolete machinery' from Soviet
Russia in return for primary products, 'a form of barter'; and the
Soviet bloc 'often resold the raw materials obtained from us to the
capitalist West' at below-market prices, with 'disastrous effects on
our countries producing the raw materials'.[94] One of the many
advantages of using Cuban surrogates was that, by an inexplicable
paradox, Cuba was a member of the 'non-aligned bloc', though in

fact the most vociferously faithful of the Soviet client-states. Cuban soldiers, being non-white (in many cases black), were not easily presented as imperialists. Castro had already earned his keep by defending Soviet Russia from the charge of imperialism at the 1973 Algiers Conference of the non-aligned. Where, he asked, were Russia's 'monopoly corporations'? Where its 'participation in the multinational companies'? 'What factories, what mines, what oilfields does it own in the underdeveloped world? What worker is exploited in any country of Asia, Africa or Latin America by Soviet capital?'[95] Now he was asked to go further and provide non-imperialist invasion forces. In December 1975, under Soviet naval escort, the first Cuban troops landed in Angola. In 1976 they moved into Abyssinia, now in the Soviet camp, and into Central and East Africa. As far back as 1963, the old colony of French Congo proclaimed itself the People's Republic of the Congo, the first Marxist-Leninist state in Africa. It did not always behave like one. European political categories did not always translate into African realities.[96] But by the end of the 1970s there were ten such African states, providing Soviet Russia, in varying degrees, with diplomatic and propaganda support, economic advantages and military bases. And in 1979, in Nicaragua, Cuba acquired the first satellite of its own, in Central America.

The extension of the Cold War, during the Seventies, to virtually every part of the globe, gave the decade the air of chronic insecurity so characteristic of the Thirties – the same syndrome of unemployment, economic decay, armaments and aggression. Soviet policy was by no means the only factor. America was in part responsible for the drift to violence. To offset the drop in arms purchases with the end of the Vietnam war, American industry moved into international arms sales on an unprecedented scale. In 1970 America sold $952 millions worth of arms abroad. The figure had jumped to over $10 billion by 1977–8. But others were in the race. In the 1960s and 1970s, French arms sales multiplied over thirty times. Soviet arms-exports increased even faster than America's. In 1979–81 America ceased to be the leading arms-exporter, falling into third place behind Soviet Russia and France (with Britain a poor fourth). By the early 1980s, international arms sales were approaching an annual value of about $70 billion, nearly all of them negotiated at a state-to-state level. One Soviet tank factory alone covered twenty square miles and exported to thirty countries, most of them poor. The old free enterprise Merchants of Death looked innocent by comparison with modern states, competing to sell destruction by the megaton.

It is true that none of the great powers sold nuclear weapons. But they failed to prevent their proliferation. In the 1950s, well-meaning scientists spread the notion that plutonium for 'peace' reactors was not normally suitable for bombs. On this quite fallacious assumption, America launched 'operation candour' in December 1953 with the 'Atoms for Peace' programme. It released over 11,000 classified papers, including details of the Purex method of producing the pure plutonium vital for big explosions.[97] Some of the details of the assistance programmes were sloppily drafted, so that when a clear breach took place – for instance when India exploded a bomb in 1974 – American officials could pretend that it had not. The Non-Proliferation Treaty negotiated by America, Russia and Britain in July 1968, quickly ratified by forty other powers, really made little difference since even countries which signed it could, under its rules, get very close to a nuclear capability and attain it rapidly after the three-month notice of withdrawal under Article Eleven.

In fact nuclear powers did not multiply as fast as pessimists predicted. In 1960 it was calculated twelve new countries would go nuclear by 1966.[98] But nuclear umbrella alliances, such as NATO, SEATO and CENTO, tended to discourage states from independent ventures. Proliferation occurred as a result of antagonistic 'pairing'. China's bomb in 1964 was a function of her quarrel with Russia; India's 1974 bomb was the direct result of China's: Pakistan's putative bomb was the offspring of India's. Both Israel and South Africa became covert nuclear powers in the 1970s, largely because they were not members of reliable military pacts which included nuclear coverage. Israel's bomb provoked an Iraqi nuclear-weapons programme, frustrated in 1981 when Israeli aircraft destroyed Iraq's French-built 'peaceful' reactor.

There was also a tendency for advanced powers to drift into nuclear weapons programmes. This was what happened in France under the Fourth Republic, long before de Gaulle took the decision to make bombs. As one official put it, 'the manufacture of an atomic bomb . . . welded itself into our public life as a sort of by-product of an officially peaceful effort'.[99] That was the most likely route West Germany and Japan, hitherto encouraged to remain non-nuclear by American guarantees, would pursue towards the bomb. By the end of the 1970s, Japan had developed a large and innovatory space industry and was in a position not merely to produce nuclear warheads very fast but to develop an advanced delivery system on the lines of the American Trident. But to become a first-class nuclear power involved by this stage developing protection, counter-detection and second-strike capabilities, all dauntingly expensive.[100] Barring a retreat by America into isolation, Germany and Japan looked unlikely to join the club. The danger lay, rather, in a ragged development of marginal nuclear capacity by unstable Arab powers or states which, for one reason or another, felt themselves insecure and inadequately protected by alliances, such as Brazil, Argentina, South Korea, Taiwan and Indonesia. By the early 1980s, twenty-two powers (in addition to Israel and South Africa) were in a position to develop nuclear weapons at comparatively low cost and over a one- to four-year time span.[101]

In practice, however, the world was less disturbed during the 1970s by the possibility of nuclear war than by the growing reality of other forms of violence. More than thirty conventional wars were fought in the decade, most of them in Africa. Less costly in human life, but politically and psychologically far more disturbing for the world, was the growth of international terrorism. Many historical strands went into this new phenomenon. There was the Muslim tradition of politico-religious terrorism, going back to the Persian–Sunni sect of the Assassins in the Middle Ages. It was born again in the Arab–Israeli struggle in inter-war Palestine, taking final shape in the Palestine Liberation Organization, which in the Sixties and Seventies was the largest, richest, best-armed and most active of all terrorist groups, with its own training camps of which many other, quite unrelated terrorist movements took advantage.

Secondly there was the Russian tradition, transmuted by Lenin (who repudiated individual terrorism as a form of 'infantile Leftism') into state-terrorism, both for internal use and for export. Through-out this period Soviet Russia maintained a terrorist training scheme, directed from the military academy at Simteropol in the Crimea, from which foreign 'guerrillas' and 'saboteurs' graduated for service in the Middle East, Latin America and Africa. Most PLO experts and instructors benefited from this course.[102]

Thirdly there was the European, chiefly German, tradition of intellectualizing violence as a moral necessity. The first large-scale modern phase of political terrorism took place, as we have seen, in Germany 1919–22, when right-wing killers murdered 354 people. It was the failure of society to bring these people to book which prepared the way for the state terror of Hitler. This took many forms, including kidnapping, practised by the Brown Sisters of the SS, who scoured concentration camps for blond, blue-eyed children under six. The German terrorist tradition found philosophical ex-pression in Existentialism, popularized in the post-war period by Sartre, who remained fascinated by violence throughout his life and whose pupil, Franz Fanon, published in 1961 the most influential of all terrorist handbooks, *Les damnés de la terre*.

Fourthly, there was the non-political tradition of Mediterranean piracy, going back to the second millennium before Christ. Pompey had ended piracy in the first century BC, and it was a sinister sign of Rome's fading power when the pirates returned in force in the middle of the third century AD. In the eighteenth century the British navy eliminated piracy on the oceans, but the Barbary menace remained until 1830, when the French occupied Algiers. For the next 130 years, the age of colonialism, large-scale piracy and kidnapping virtually ceased to exist. It rapidly returned as the imperialist tide receded, especially in its traditional centres, Algiers and Tripoli, with the end of the Algerian war and Gadafy's 1969 *coup*. But it now had a distinct political coloration, with the Algerian leaders in the 1960s, and Gadafy in the 1970s, providing money, arms, training facilities, refuges and orchestration. These four strands, coming together in the 1970s, made the problem of terrorism immensely complex and difficult to define. It could not be seen as a simple Soviet conspiracy to destabilize legitimate states. In fact the democratic state most seriously damaged by terrorism in the 1970s, Italy, was the victim more of commercial violence, especially kidnappings which netted $100 million in the years 1975–80, than of purely political terror.[103]

Yet there was no doubt that individual terrorist movements, such as the Baader-Meinhof gang in West Germany, the IRA in Ulster, the Red Brigades in Italy, Basque separatists in Spain, the PLO and perhaps a score of other Arab, Latin-American and black African terror groups, benefited from an international radical network, whose moving spirits, such as the Venezuelan assassin known as 'Carlos', were all Communists.[104] Two incidents, selected from scores, illustrate the international and Marxist character of the movement. The massacre of twenty-six pilgrims, mostly Puerto Ricans, at Israel's Lod airport in 1972, was carried out by Japanese Marxists, trained by the PLO in Lebanon, armed with Japanese weapons delivered to them in Rome by Carlos himself. Again, the Basque killers who murdered a Spanish admiral in 1974 had been trained in Cuba and the South Yemen by East Germans, Palestinians and Cubans, and used explosives acquired from IRA gangsters who first met the Basques in Algiers, under the auspices of the KGB.[105]

It is significant that, during the Seventies, as relative American power declined, and Soviet power rose, international terrorist incidents (explosions, bombings, assassinations, hostage-taking, kidnapping, etc) increased steadily, from 279 in 1971 to 1,709 in 1980. The number of assassinations, in which the KGB and its antecedents had always specialized, increased spectacularly, from seventeen in 1971 to 1,169 in 1980.[106] Totalitarian societies, with all-pervasive secret police permitted to arrest and imprison without trial, to torture and to practise judicial murder and assassination themselves, had little to fear from terrorism. Liberal-democratic societies had a great deal. The lesson of the Seventies was that terrorism actively, systematically and necessarily assisted the spread of the totalitarian state; that it distinguished between lawful and totalitarian states in favour of the latter; that it exploited the apparatus of freedom in liberal societies and thereby endangered it; and that it sapped the will of a civilized society to defend itself.[107]

In a more fundamental sense, the political terrorism of the Seventies was a product of moral relativism. In particular, the unspeakable cruelties it practised were made possible only by the Marxist habit of thinking in terms of classes instead of individuals. Young radical ideologues who kept their victims, usually diplomats or businessmen chosen solely by occupation, chained in tiny, underground concrete dungeons, blindfolded, their ears sealed with wax, for weeks or months, then dispatched them without pity or hesitation, did not see those they tortured and murdered as human beings but as pieces of political furniture. In the process they dehumanized themselves as well as those they destroyed and became lost souls, like the debased creatures Dostoevsky described in his great anti-terrorist novel, *The Devils*.

As a threat to the stability of all societies under the rule of law, international terrorism should have been the primary concern of the United Nations. But by the 1970s, the UN was a corrupt and demoralized body, and its ill-considered interventions were more inclined to promote violence than to prevent it. Truman's fatal mistake in allowing executive power to slip towards the General Assembly in 1950, compounded by Eisenhower's error in 1956, when he allowed Hammarskjöld to hound Britain and France as aggressors, now yielded a bitter and abundant harvest. The UN was founded by fifty-one states, the great majority of them democracies. By 1975 there were 144 members, with plans for 165, all but twenty-five of them totalitarian or one-party states, mainly of the Left. The Soviet, Arab–Muslim and African states together constituted a working majority. There was thus no question of taking action against terrorism. On the contrary. As we have already noted, Idi Amin, a terrorist himself and a patron and beneficiary of terrorism, was given a standing ovation in 1975 when he advocated genocide. Yasser Arafat, head of the PLO, the world's largest terrorist organization, was actually given a seat in the Assembly. The UN Secretariat had long since ceased to apply the principles of the Charter. The Secretary-General functioned as a mere post-office. Communist members of the Secretariat lived in their national compounds and handed in their hard-currency salary cheques to their embassy finance officers. Their senior member, the Under-Secretary-General for the Security Council, Arkady Shevchenko, had a KGB 'minder' all to himself.[108]

Broadly speaking, during the 1970s the UN majority concentrated on three issues: organizing the destruction of South Africa and Israel, and condemning 'imperialism' as personified by America. In 1974, the credentials of South Africa, a founder-member, were rejected, as a substitute for expulsion. At the UN meeting of non-aligned states held at Havana, a Soviet satellite capital, in March 1975, a plan was outlined to expel Israel, but dropped when the US threatened to leave the Assembly and discontinue its financial contribution. Instead, the UN Third Committee passed an anti-Semitic resolution, condemning Israel as 'racist', by 70 votes to 29 with 27 abstentions. The resolution was produced by Cuba, Libya and Somalia, all then Soviet satellites. As the American delegate Leonard Garment pointed out, the resolution was 'ominous' because it used 'racism' not as the word 'for a very real and concrete set of injustices but merely as an epithet to be flung at whoever happens to be one's adversary'. It turned 'an idea with a vivid and obnoxious meaning' into 'nothing more than an ideological tool'.[109] Some of the speeches in favour of the motion were openly anti-Semitic and would have evoked roars of applause at Nuremberg. Of the seventy states which voted for it, only eight had the most remote claims to be considered democracies and more than two-thirds of them practised varieties of official racism. In Moscow Andrei Sakharov, who had not yet been arrested, remarked that the resolution 'can only contribute to anti-Semitic tendencies in many countries by giving them the appearance of international legality'. Even more serious was the fear that the vote might subsequently be used as justification, in morality and international law, for a concerted attempt by Arab states to exterminate the Israeli people, who had founded the state precisely as a refuge from racism and race-murder. The American Ambassador to the UN angrily announced, when the General Assembly ratified the vote 67–55: 'The United States rises to declare before the General Assembly of the United Nations and before the world, that it does not acknowledge, it will not abide by and it will never acquiesce in this infamous act.'[110] It was true that the vote was merely on paper. But the real danger of the UN was that paper majorities tended to grow into real policies: the corrupt arithmetic of the Assembly, where in the Seventies votes could be bought by arms or even by personal bribes to delegates, tended to become imperceptibly the conventional wisdom of international society.

This was particularly true of the attacks on America, now increasingly isolated and, as the economic crisis of the 1970s deepened, blamed as the source of the world's ills. It was a striking consequence of UN arithmetic that the Arab oil states, whose price-increases added $70 billion a year to their incomes in the year 1974–5, all of it at the expense of the industrial nations and underdeveloped countries, were never once criticized in any resolution by the Assembly or a UN committee. Nor was any attempt made by the UN majority to get them to disgorge these excess profits in the form of mandatory aid. The synthetic anger of the UN was concentrated wholly on America, one of the chief victims, and by extension to the West as a whole. It is illuminating to trace the genesis of this assault. The original Marxist thesis was that capitalism would collapse. That had not happened. The first fall-back position (Khrushchev's) was that the 'socialist bloc' would overtake the West in living standards. That had not happened either. The second fall-back position, used from the early 1970s onwards, which was sold to the Third World and became the UN orthodoxy, was that high Western living standards, far from being the consequence of a more efficient economic system, were the immoral wages of the deliberate and systematic impoverishment of the rest of the world. Thus in 1974 the UN adopted a 'Charter of Economic Rights and Duties of States' which condemned the workings of Western economies. The 1974 UN World Population Conference was a prolonged attack on US selfishness. The 1974 UN World Food Conference denounced America and other states, the only ones actually to produce food surpluses. The Indian Food Minister thought it 'obvious' they were 'responsible for the present plight' of the poor nations, and had a 'duty' to help them. Such help was not 'charity' but 'deferred compensation for what has been done to them in the past by the developed nations'. Next February the 'non-aligned' countries castigated 'the obstinacy of the imperialist powers in preserving the structures of colonial and neo-colonial exploitation which nurture their luxurious and superfluous consumer societies while they keep a large part of humanity in misery and hunger.'

The attack was particularly unreasonable since during the previous fourteen years alone (1960–73), official development aid from the advanced nations direct to the poorer countries, or through agencies, amounted to $91.8 billion, the largest voluntary transfer of resources in history.[111] Whether the money was effectively used, of course, was another matter. Much of it served merely to keep in power inefficient and tyrannical regimes practising various forms of 'socialism', such as Julius Nyerere's in Tanzania, and so to perpetuate backwardness. The argument that the West was somehow to blame for world poverty was itself a Western invention. Like decolonization, it was a product of guilt, that prime dissolvent of order and justice. It reflected the same tendency to categorize people morally not as individuals but as members of classes which was the fundamental fallacy of Marxism. The nation-structure was analogous to the class-structure. We have already noted the effect of the

'Third World' concept on the Bandung generation. Like many clever but misleading ideas, it came from France. In 1952 the demographer Alfred Sauvy had written a famous article, 'Three Worlds, One Planet', in which he quoted Sièyes's famous remarks in 1789: 'What is the Third Estate? Everything. What has it been hitherto in the political order? Nothing. What does it ask? To become something.' The Cold War, he argued, was essentially a struggle between the capitalist world and the Communist world for the Third World. That 'Third World', ignored, exploited, despised, like the Third Estate, it too wants to be something.[112] Gradually the term 'Third World' became one of the great cant phrases of the post-war period.[113] It was never defined, for the good and simple reason that, the moment anyone attempted to do so, the concept was seen to be meaningless and collapsed. But it was immensely influential. It satisfied the human longing for simple moral distinctions. There were 'good' nations (the poor ones) and 'bad' nations (the rich ones). Nations were rich precisely because they were bad, and poor because they were innocent. It became the dynamic of the UN General Assembly. It led to the creation of the UN Conference on Trade and Development (UNCTAD) in 1962, which popularized the fallacy. It inspired the guilt-ridden Pearson Report of 1969, which surveyed the whole aid programme 1950–67 and blamed its failures on the people who had supplied the money.

In due course the term 'Third World' began to seem a little threadbare from overuse. The Paris intellectual fashion-factory promptly supplied a new one: 'North–South'. It was coined in 1974, when the French President, Giscard d'Estaing, called a conference of 'oil-importing, oil-exporting and non-oil developing nations'. The idea was to link guilt to 'the North' and innocence to 'the South'. This involved a good deal of violence to simple geography, as well as to economic facts. The so-called 'South' was represented by Algeria, Argentina, Brazil, Cameroon, Egypt, India, Indonesia, Iraq, Iran, Jamaica, Mexico, Nigeria, Pakistan, Peru, Saudi Arabia, Venezuela, Yugoslavia, Zaïre and Zambia. The 'North' consisted of Canada, the EEC powers, Japan, Spain, Australia, Sweden, Switzerland and the USA. Eleven of the 'South' states were actually north of the equator, and one of them, Saudi Arabia, had the world's highest *per capita* income. Australia, the only continent entirely south of the equator, had to be classified as 'North', presumably because it was predominantly white and capitalist. The Soviet bloc was omitted altogether, though entirely in the North. In short the concept was meaningless, except for purposes of political abuse. But for this it served very well. It led to an elaborate gathering in Paris in May–June 1977.[114] In due course it inspired a document called the Brandt Report (1980), which like the Pearson Report blamed the West, now termed 'the North', and proposed an international system of taxation, under which the North should subsidize the South, on the analogy of national welfare states.[115]

Inevitably America was presented as the primary villain in the North–South melodrama. It was also the target of another term of Seventies abuse: the 'multinational'. This too came from France. In 1967 the French publicist Jean-Jacques Servan-Schreiber produced a sensational book, Le Défi Americain, drawing attention to expansion of American firms abroad. By the 1980s, he predicted, the 'third industrial power in the world' would not be Europe but 'American investments in Europe'. The 'multinational' was 'the American challenge' to the world. The notion was eagerly taken up by European intellectuals of the Left, and translated into 'Third World' terms, with the multinational, overriding the sovereignty of states, as the spearhead of 'American imperialism'. At the UN General Assembly of April–May 1974, the multinational was held up to global obloquy, almost on a level with South Africa and Israel. Like most intellectual fashions, it was misconceived and already out of date. Multinationals were simply businesses operating in many countries. They dated from the 1900s, when Gillette, Kodak and other firms set up in Europe, and they included banks and oil companies and others whose business was essentially international. They were by far the most cost-efficient means for the export of capital, technology and skills from richer to poorer countries. Equally important, in the post-war period they learnt much faster than governments how to merge into the local landscape and adjust to national prejudices. Studies of American multinationals in Chile and Peru, for instance, showed that their political influence, considerable up to 1939, had long been declining rapidly by the time the term became fashionable.[116] Within America, the power of international companies was more than balanced by labour and ethnic lobbies. The 'multinational explosion' was really a phenomenon of the 1950s and early 1960s, and was near its climax when Servan-Schreiber wrote. In 1959 America had 111 or 71 per cent of the world's largest firms. By 1976, the number had dropped to sixty-eight and the percentage to forty-four. The peak year for US multinationals was 1968, as it was the apogee of the American paramountcy as a whole, when 540 US overseas subsidiaries were established or acquired. By 1974–5, however, the 187 largest American multinationals were breeding only 200 a year.[117] It is true that, over the decade 1967–77, US investment in Europe rose from $16 billion to $55 billion.[118] But Servan-Schreiber's apocalyptic vision seemed absurd by the mid-1970s, when West German and Japanese firms were expanding overseas much faster than their American competitors. In 1970 the ten biggest banks were all American. By 1980 only two were, the rest being French (four), German (two), Japanese and British (one each). The Japanese held six places out of the top twenty, and another was held by Brazil.[119] All the evidence shows that during the 1970s international economic power was becoming far more widely diffused. Yet the multinational scare was immensely damaging to America, just at the time when its relative influence was declining fast. Far from wielding excessive power, American companies were increasingly discriminated against. 'I can tell you', complained an official of Chase Manhattan, 'that as a US bank in Mexico we get treated like dirt by the Mexican authorities.'[120] This was despite the fact that Mexico, together with Brazil, owed $69 billion of floating interest-rate debt, much of it to Chase.[121] The artificially created hostility to US multinationals even penetrated back into America itself, where an attempt was made to pass the Foreign Trade and Investment Act (1971), calling for control over export of US capital and technology and heavier taxation of multinational profits. The ensuing struggle was highly damaging to American economic interests.[122]

The attacks on America during the 1970s were so venomous and for the most part so irrational as to merit the description of an international witch-hunt. One might say that the most ubiquitous form of racism during this decade was anti-Americanism. The adage, 'to know all is to forgive all', does not work in international affairs. One reason why America was attacked so much was because so much was known about her, chiefly thanks to the American media and academia, which poured forth a ceaseless torrent of self-critical material.[123] But a more fundamental reason was that America as a great power and still more Americanism as a concept stood for the principle of individualism as opposed to collectivism, for free will as opposed to determinism. The spirit of the late Sixties, and still more of the early and mid-Seventies, was strongly collectivist and deterministic.

Much of this was again due to intellectual trends in Paris, which France's new-found economic dynamism helped to project forcefully onto the world stage. In the Forties and Fifties, Sartre had at least believed in free will. It was indeed the essence of his philosophy, which made it fundamentally incompatible with Marxism, however much he might league himself with Marxists at a purely political level. Sartre lived on until 1980, but he was already an intellectual antique by the time of the student revolt of 1968. The mandarins who took his place were all, in varying degrees, influenced by Marxist determinism, which denies any importance to the individual or to free will or to moral conscience in shaping the world. Unlike the orthodox Marxists, they did not see economic forces, operating through classes, as the sole dynamic of human history. Each advanced alternative or complementary explanations. But all accepted Marx's starting-point that events were determined not by human will, as had been traditionally supposed, but by the hidden structures of society. As Marx put it: 'the *final pattern* of economic relatives as seen on the surface . . . is very much different from, and indeed quite the reverse of, their *inner but concealed essential pattern* and the *conception corresponding* to it.'[124] Man was imprisoned in structures: twentieth-century man in bourgeois structures. In *Structural Anthropology*, first widely read and translated in 1963, Claude Lévi-Strauss insisted that, though social structures were not visible to the eye or even detectable by empirical observations, they were present, just as molecular structures existed though undiscoverable by all but the electron microscope. These structures determined the cast of mind, so what appeared to be acts of human will were merely concordance with the structure. For Lévi-Strauss, as for Marx, history was not a succession of events but a discernible pattern working according to discoverable laws. A variation of this argument was provided by the French historians of the *Annales* school, especially by Fernand Braudel, whose *Mediterranean and the Mediterranean World in the Age of Philip II* (1949) proved by far the most influential historical work published since the Second World War. They dismissed narrative as superficial and individuals as unimportant and preached a doctrine of geographical and economic determinism in history, whose long-term course was decided wholly by such structures. In psychology, Jacques Lacan reinterpreted Freud (hitherto largely ignored in France) to provide a new determinism of human behaviour, based on signs, signals, codes and conventions which, when analysed, left little room for human choice. In literature Roland Barthes argued that a novelist did not create by an act of imaginative will so much as in response to the social structures from which he derived his impulses, expressed in the symbols he used, which could be codified by the new science of semiology. In linguistics, the American scholar Noam Chomsky dismissed the physical characteristics of speech and language as superficial, determined by the so-called deep structures of linguistic rules.

What all the structuralists had in common was the Marxist assumption that human attributes and activities were governed by laws in a way analogous to the way scientific laws governed inanimate nature. Hence it was the function of the social sciences to discover such laws, and then for society to act upon their discoveries. The emergence of this new form of intellectual Utopianism, with its strong suggestion of compulsory social engineering at the end of the road, coincided exactly with the rapid expansion of higher education, especially of the social science disciplines, in the late Fifties and throughout the Sixties. Between the mid-1950s and the late 1960s, the average annual increase in expenditure on higher education was nearly 10 per cent in Britain, over 11 per cent in America, Spain and Japan, 13.3 per cent in France, over 15 per cent in Italy, Belgium, the Netherlands and Denmark, and over 16 per cent in Canada and West Germany. University enrolments rose by an annual average of over 12 per cent in this period.[125] By a historical accident, which had nothing to do with structures, deep or otherwise, the Structuralists thus had an influence quite disproportionate to the intrinsic plausibility of their theories, and they attained their maximum impact on society during the Seventies, when millions of new graduates poured out of the universities.

The heyday of Structuralism coincided with the demoralization of America and with the steady expansion of Soviet power and influence. It reinforced both tendencies, for Structuralism, like the Marxism from which it sprang, was anti-empirical, denying the real world in favour of the theoretical world, discounting facts in favour of 'explanations'. Communists had always been infuriated by the tendency of facts to get in the way of Marxist theses. One might say that the whole of Stalin's dictatorship had been a campaign against facts, or rather a superhuman attempt to transform the awkward facts of humanity into new 'deep structures', under six feet of earth. To Structuralists, facts were by definition on the surface, and therefore misleading. To attempt to marshal them in the form of argument was, obviously, nothing more than a shameless defence of the status quo.[126] Structuralism fitted well into the Potemkin world of the United Nations, where facts were unimportant, where North was South, and vice-versa, where wealth created poverty, where Zionism was racism and sin was the White Man's monopoly. The multinational, that sinister infrastructure of international injustice, was a quintessentially structuralist concept. Structuralism, like Marxism, was a form of gnosticism, that is an arcane system of knowledge, revealed to the élite. Both expanded rapidly in the Sixties and, in conjunction, were intellectually predominant in the Seventies. But reality cannot for long be banished from history. Facts have a way of making their presence felt. The pattern of the Seventies, so dismaying to the few democratic societies which remained under the rule of law, was beginning to break up before the decade ended.

TWENTY

The Recovery of Freedom

From the initial tragedy of the First World War, 1914–18, the twentieth century had appeared to many a relentless succession of moral and physical disasters. These had occurred despite the rapid increase in wealth, notably in the advanced countries, and the steady forward march of scientific discovery. As early as 1945 H. G. Wells, once the prophet of ever-accelerating human progress, had given up in despair, publishing his gloomy testament, *Mind at the End of Its Tether*.[1] Thereafter a further declension appeared to have taken place, the 1970s being a decade of exceptional anxiety and disillusionment when concern about the environment and the exhaustion of raw materials were added to the spread of Cold War competition throughout the world and the ravages of collectivism in Eastern Europe, most of Africa and large parts of Asia and Latin America. Everywhere, democracy and the rule of law that gave it meaning appeared on the defensive, even in its heartlands. In 1979 President Carter referred publicly to the 'crisis that strikes at the very heart and soul and spirit of our national will . . . The erosion of our confidence in the future is threatening to destroy the social and political fabric of America.'[2]

Yet, with the 1980s, there came a great wind of change in the affairs of mankind which, gathering momentum throughout the decade and beyond into the 1990s, swept all before it and left the global landscape transformed beyond recognition. The 1980s formed one of the watersheds of modern history. The spirit of democracy recovered its self-confidence and spread. The rule of law was re-established in large parts of the globe and international predation checked and punished. The United Nations, and especially its Security Council, began for the first time to function as its founders intended. Capitalist economies flourished mightily and, almost everywhere, there was growing recognition that the market system was not merely the surest but the only way to increase wealth and raise living standards. As an intellectual creed, collectivism collapsed and the process of abandoning it got under way even in its strongholds. Stalin's empire, the last of the colonial conglomerates, disintegrated. The Soviet system itself came under increasing strain, and Russia's multiplying problems undermined both its status as a superpower and its rulers' will to continue the Cold War. By the early 1990s, the nightmare vision of thermonuclear conflict faded and the world seemed safer, more stable and, above all, more hopeful. How did this dramatic counter-revolution come about?

It was essentially the work of outstanding popular leaders, who mirrored the thoughts, desires and faith of ordinary men and women. It was certainly not the work of the intelligentsia, of philosophers, economists and political theorists, or of academics generally. The universities had little or nothing to do with it, just as they had played virtually no part in the first Industrial Revolution of the late eighteenth century.[3] Indeed while Marxism was being progressively abandoned by the governments which had once ardently propagated it, it continued to be upheld and taught only in that traditional home of lost causes, the university campus.

It is important to look in a little detail at the failure of intellectual leadership in the twentieth century, or rather at its apparent inability to offer clear and firm guidance to a perplexed humanity, because this failure or inability lay at the root of the tragedies of the age. In the seven decades which followed the First World War, knowledge itself expanded more rapidly than ever. Yet in many ways an educated man in the 1990s was less equipped with certitudes than an ancient Egyptian in 2500 BC. At least the Egyptian of the Old Kingdom had a clear cosmology. In 1915 Einstein had undermined the Newtonian universe, and the cosmology substituted for it was merely speculative, since the General Theory of Relativity was a classical explanation and could not be used to describe a singularity such as the conditions at the moment of creation. The mathematical model of the Big Bang, in which matter expanded from zero some 6,000–10,000 million years ago, with everything essential occurring in the first twenty minutes, was no more demonstrable than the Judeo-Christian hypothesis first crudely described in Chapter One of the Book of Genesis, which it strikingly resembled. During the next three-quarters of the century, empirical knowledge of the universe accumulated at impressive speed, above all in the 1970s and 1980s, when data from space probes began to reach the earth in prodigious quantities. The measurement of microwave background radiation which fills the universe indicated the near-certainty of a Big Bang.[4] But one cosmologist laconically observed: 'Our universe is simply one of thousands which happen from time to time.'[5] A clear picture of primal events was as elusive as ever.

Indeed the historian of the modern world is sometimes tempted to reach the depressing conclusion that progress is destructive of certitude. In the eighteenth and nineteenth centuries the Western élites were confident that men and progress were governed by reason. A prime discovery of modern times is that reason plays little part in our affairs. Even scientists are not moved by it. As Max Planck sorrowfully observed: 'A new scientific truth is not usually presented in a way to convince its opponents. Rather, they die off, and a rising generation is familiarized with the truth from the start.'[6] Three years after Einstein's General Theory of Relativity was verified by Eddington, ending belief in fixed space and time, Ludwig Wittgenstein, one of the key figures of our period, published his *Tractatus Logico-Philosophicus*, which cumulatively over the decades tended to destroy confidence in philosophy as a guide to human reason. For half a century Wittgenstein's influence on academic philosophy was immense. By the early 1990s doubts were raised about his sanity: was he a genius, or simply a madman?[7] But by then much damage had been done. A leading Logical Positivist like Sir A.J.Ayer, who at the time of his death in 1989 was widely regarded as the world's leading philosopher, remarked with some complacency that philosophy demonstrated that man was ignorant rather than knowledgeable: '[It] tends to show that we can't really know lots of things which we think we know.' Empirical popular knowledge, usually termed 'common sense', had been dismissed contemptuously by Bertrand Russell as 'the metaphysics of savages'.[8] But if academic philosophers thought the world was peopled by fools, most made little or no attempt to enlighten them on the great issues of the day, and even Russell, who wrote on such matters, drew an absolute distinction between his popular journalism and his 'serious' work.[9] The negative and destructive nature of twentieth-century philosophy, its obsession with the inadequacies and failures of language, above all its failure to address itself to the immense problems confronting humanity, was a source of shame to the few who tried to grapple with them, notably Karl Popper: 'I cannot say that I am proud of being called a philosopher,' he wrote.[10]

Moreover, growing uncertainty surrounded even the one tool which the academic philosophers felt they could trust: logic. Two centuries before, Kant had asserted in his *Logik* (1800): 'There are but few sciences that can come into a permanent state, which admits of no further alteration. To these belong Logic . . . We do not require any further discoveries in Logic, since it contains merely the form of thought.' As late as 1939, a British philosopher asserted: 'Dictators may be powerful today, but they cannot alter the laws of logic, nor indeed can even God do so.'[11] Thirteen years later the American philosopher Willard Quine calmly accepted that the definition of logic was undergoing fundamental change: 'What difference is there in principle between such a shift and the shift whereby Kepler succeeded Ptolemy, or Einstein Newton, or Darwin Aristotle?'[12] In the decades that followed, many rival systems to classical logic emerged: Bochvar's many-valued logic, new systems by Birkhoff and Destouches-Février and Reichenbach, minimal logic, deontic logics, tense logics. It became possible to speak of empirical proof or disproof of logic.[13] What would be the consequences for the theory of truth, asked one worried logician, '. . . of the adoption of a non-standard system'?[14] Another, observing systems of modal logic, observed: 'One gets an uneasy feeling as one discerns and studies more of the systems belonging to this family that it is literally a family, and has the power of reproducing and multiplying, proliferating new systems [of logic] without limit.'[15]

In a world in which even the rules of logic shifted and disintegrated, it is not surprising that modern times did not develop in ways the generation of 1920 would have considered 'logical'. What is important in history is not only the events that occur but the events that obstinately do not occur. The outstanding event of modern times was the failure of religious belief to disappear. For many millions, especially in the advanced nations, religion ceased to play much or any part in their lives, and the ways in which the vacuum thus lost was filled, by fascism, Nazism and Communism, by attempts at humanist utopianism, by eugenics or health politics, by the ideologies of sexual liberation, race politics and environmental politics, form much of the substance of the history of our century. But for many more millions – for the overwhelming majority of the human race, in fact – religion continued to be a huge dimension in their lives. Nietzsche, who had so accurately predicted the transmutation of faith into political zealotry and the totalitarian will to power, failed to see that the religious spirit could, quite illogically, coexist with secularization, and so resuscitate his dying God. What looked antiquated, even risible, in the 1990s was not religious belief but the confident prediction of its demise once provided by Feuerbach and Marx, Durkheim and Frazer, Lenin, Wells, Shaw, Gide, Sartre and many others. By the end of our period, even the term 'secularization' was in dispute. 'The whole concept appears a tool of counter-religious ideologies,' wrote one professor of sociology angrily, 'which identify the "real" element in religion for polemical purposes, and then arbitrarily relate it to the notion of a unitary and irreversible process . . . [It] should be erased from the sociological vocabulary.'[16] The secularist movement, that is militant atheism, appears to have peaked in the West in the 1880s at exactly the same time as its great rival, Protestant Nonconformity, so that Lenin was a survivor rather than a precursor, and his secularization programme was put through by force, not established by argument.[17] By the 1990s, the Museums of Anti-God and Chairs of Scientific Atheism he had established were merely historical curiosities, or had been dismantled and scrapped. The once-influential alternatives to religion, such as Positivism, had vanished almost without trace, confirming John Henry Newman's observation: 'True religion is slow in growth and, when once planted, is difficult of dislodgement; but its intellectual counterfeit has no root in itself; it springs up suddenly, it suddenly withers.'[18] Perhaps the most spectacular testimony to this truth was to be found in Russia, where the collapse of belief in the Communist ideology Lenin had implanted revealed, in the growing climate of freedom of 1989–91, that both Orthodox and Catholic Christianity had survived all the assaults made upon them by the regime, and were strong and spreading.[19] Throughout the world, while spiritual bewilderment, neatly classified as 'agnosticism', was widespread, it is likely that there were fewer real atheists in 1990 than in 1890.

Yet organized religion was full of paradoxes. Many of these were personified in Karol Wojtyla, who on 16 October 1978 became the 263rd Roman pontiff, with the title of Pope John Paul II. He was the first non-Italian to be elected pope since 1522, the youngest since 1846, the first from the Slavic East. Wojtyla had been Cardinal-Archbishop of Cracow. The choice was now highly appropriate for Poland had become the heartland of Catholicism. First Hitler, then Stalin and his successors had done everything in their power to destroy the Polish Church. Hitler had closed its schools, universities and seminaries, and murdered a third of its clergy. When the Red Army imposed the Lublin government in 1945, they were confident that the Church would disappear within a generation. Yet pre-war Poland, where the Church enjoyed special status, proved a less favourable environment for Catholicism than the post-war People's Republic, where it was actively persecuted. The new frontiers turned Poland into one of the most homogeneous states on earth: more than 95 per cent of the population were now ethnic Poles, virtually all of them baptized Catholics. Catholicism became the focus of resistance to the alien Communist regime. By the 1960s, the Catholic priesthood was back to its pre-war strength of 18,000. The number of religious – i.e. priests, nuns and monks – 22,000 in 1939, had grown to 36,500. There were 50 per cent more monastic foundations, priories and convents than before the war. Some 92–95 per cent of children received Holy Communion after instruction at 18,000 catechetical centres. Over 90 per cent of Poles were buried according to Catholic rites. The movement of peasants into the towns re-evangelized the urban population. Up to three-quarters of town-dwellers were married in church. Sunday Mass attendance was over 50 per cent even in the cities. These figures could not be matched anywhere in the world.[20] Moreover, Catholicism was the driving force behind the new Polish independent trade union, baptized Solidarity, which began to function in the Gdansk shipyard in June 1980, achieved reluctant legal recognition from the regime two months later, and, under its fervent Catholic leader, Lech Walesa, gradually undermined the regime during the decade. A further eight-year legal ban, imposed in 1981, was finally ended in April 1989, when Communist authority began to collapse. Four months later, on 24 August, Poland became the first country in the Soviet bloc to appoint a non-Communist government, with Walesa's colleague, Tadeusz Mazowiecki, editor of a Catholic newspaper, as Prime Minister. The destruction of Communism was completed in 1990–91, when Walesa himself became President, and all remaining religious restraints were removed. This largely peaceful change of regime showed how powerful the alliance between the human longing for personal freedom and the force of religious belief could be.

The new Pope personified the paradoxical vigour of this ebullient Polish religious spirit springing from within the framework of an atheist state. He was a paradox in himself: an intellectual, a poet, a playwright, a professional philosopher trained in the Phenomenologist tradition which sought to Christianize Existentialism; yet also a passionate devotee of the culture of populist Catholicism: shrines, miracles, pilgrimages, saints, the rosary and the Virgin. He had been one of the most active members of the Second Vatican Council, summoned by the reforming Pope John XXIII in 1962 to bring about what he called the *aggiornamento* (updating) of the Church, and which for four years modernized every aspect of its activities, introducing a new, vernacular liturgy and forms of consultative democracy. The Council reflected the optimism and illusions of the 1960s. The mood did not survive 1968, a climactic year for Catholicism as well as for secular society, when a new Pope, Paul VI, refused to lift the Church's ban on artificial contraception, condemning it once again in his encyclical *Humanae Vitae*. For much of the Church, as for the world outside it, the 1970s were a period of disillusionment, of falling attendances, of declining authority, bitter internal divisions and fading faith, with thousands of priests renouncing their vocations. The Jesuits, the largest and most influential of the Church's orders, were one example. When the Council opened, there were 36,000 of them, twice as many as there had been in the 1920s. This expansion was reversed in the second half of the 1960s, and in the 1970s the Jesuits declined by a third; the number of students and novices dropped from 16,000 to a mere 3,000.[21]

Pope John Paul II, reflecting the new spirit of realism, conservatism and the return to authority which characterized the transition from the 1970s to the 1980s, carried through a restoration of traditional Catholicism. Just as the railway age of the nineteenth century, taking pilgrims to Rome, Lourdes and other devotional centres, had reinvigorated Catholicism under papal leadership, so now John Paul used the jet and the helicopter to make global travel a routine part of his pontificate, and drove in a specially constructed glass-topped vehicle, known as the Popemobile, to show himself to the largest possible number. Throughout the 1980s and even, despite his age, into the 1990s, he visited virtually all parts of the world, often several times, and attracted some of the largest crowds in history. By the end of 1990 over 200 million had attended his services. In May 1981 he survived an assassination attempt and resumed his foreign tours as soon as he had recovered. In Africa and Latin America, congregations of a million or more assembled for his open-air services. In Ireland half the entire population turned out to hear him. In Poland at Czestochowa, a notable shrine of the Virgin, there was a congregation of 3.5 million, the largest crowd ever recorded.[22]

These gatherings showed both the reach of Christianity and how much it was changing demographically. When John Paul II took office in 1978, there were 739,126,000 Roman Catholics – about 18 per cent of a total world population of 4,094,110,000. This body was a powerful educational and cultural force, since it ran 79,207 primary and over 28,000 secondary schools and provided nearly a million university places. In the early 1960s, Catholics from the traditional European heartlands (plus North America) still made up 51.5 per cent of the whole. But by John Paul II's accession, Catholicism had become essentially a Third World religion. Of the sixteen countries with Catholic populations of over 10 million, eight were Third World, the order being Brazil (with over 100 million Catholics and by far the largest contingent of bishops, 330, in the Church), Mexico, Italy, Argentina, Colombia, Peru, Venezuela, France, Spain, Poland, West Germany, Czechoslovakia, the United

States, Zaire and the Philippines.[23] By the year 1990 well over 60 per cent of Catholics lived in developing countries, chiefly in Latin America and Africa, and it was calculated that, by the end of the 1990s, the figure would rise to 70 per cent. Catholicism was not only ceasing to be predominantly European: it was becoming urban, indeed megapolitan. By 2000 AD a high proportion of Catholics would live in giant cities of over 5 million, many in the two largest cities of all, Mexico City, with a projected population of 31 million, and São Paulo with 26 million.[24] While the highest numbers of Catholics were in Latin America, as a result of high birth-rates which had more than doubled the population since 1945, Catholicism was actually growing through conversion fastest in black Africa. A mid-1970s survey showed that Catholicism, which had doubled the number of its missionaries since 1950, had spread most in the general expansion of Christianity in Africa, from about 25 million in 1950 to some 100 million in 1975.[25] By the early 1990s the number of Catholics in Southern, Central and East Africa was believed to be about 125 million.

Yet in the advanced countries, even Catholicism – despite all the efforts of Pope John Paul II – was not immune to erosion. In the United States, the figures suggest that regular church and chapel attendance on Sunday, *per capita*, peaked in the 1950s (as against the late 1880s in Europe). Attendance among Catholics, as opposed to most other mainstream Christian churches, continued to rise until the mid-1970s, when it reached a plateau; during the late 1980s there was evidence of an aggregate decline, prompted by serious disagreements within the Church in North America over contraception, annulment of marriages (which became markedly more difficult to obtain under John Paul II), the treatment of homosexuals, the role of women in the clergy and other contentious issues, on all of which the Pope took conservative positions. Similar patterns were reported in France, Italy and Spain, though not in Poland and Germany. In Britain, where total Christian regular church attendance on Sunday fell below the 10-per-cent mark in the 1980s, an authoritative survey, the English Church Census, published in March 1991, concluded that during the ten years 1981–90, the English churches as a whole had lost 500,000 regular Sunday worshippers. Apart from Baptists, attendance at all the mainstream churches had fallen. The Church of England, the third largest group, had forfeited 9 per cent of its faithful; but the Roman Catholic Church, though still the largest, had lost an alarming 14 per cent. The chief gainers had been the charismatic and fundamentalist sects on the fringes of Nonconformity.[26]

What the world witnessed, during the late 1970s, throughout the

1980s and into the 1990s, was a widespread retreat from the churches and established religious bodies which had sought to rationalize their beliefs and come to terms with societies which in general were non-religious; and simultaneously, the growth of fundamentalism, which bypassed rationalism, stressed the overwhelming importance of faith and miraculous revelation and rejected the idea of compromise with institutions based on non-belief. The outstanding symbol of 'rationalizing' religion was the World Council of Churches, which throughout the 1980s had stressed ecumenicalism, minimalist beliefs and the need to reach agreement with Marxism and other anti-religious creeds. It lost support throughout the decade, and came close to discrediting itself finally in February 1991 during its meeting in Canberra. Some delegates were shocked to find in the foyer a stall advocating more women clergy, which 'displayed pornographic cartoons including a couple performing an unnatural act'; one well-known religious leader attending the meeting 'asked a female delegate to perform a sexual act on him' and then 'beat her over the head until she surrendered to his demand'.[27] Another form of rationalizing Christianity was the so-called 'liberation theology', ultimately derived from Germany, which sought to transform Catholic activism into a radical political force, operating from 'basic communities' organized on the Communist cell principle, and even advocating violence for the overthrow of oppressive governments of the Right. During the 1970s and 1980s it attracted much attention in the media and was said to be flourishing in Brazil and Central America. In Castro's Communist satellite, Nicaragua, four Catholic priests professing this radicalized form of Christianity held ministerial office in 1979, and two years later refused to obey orders from their bishops to return to their pastoral duties. A section of the Latin American clergy, which hitherto had usually underwritten established authority, had become strongly antinomian during the years 1965–80.[28] Yet this politicization of Catholicism, though a source of fascination to the media, was confined to a small portion of the élites. Most priests and bishops remained strongly traditionalist; the laity still more so. When liberation theology was put to any kind of popular test, it failed to make much impact. Nicaragua's Sandinista government, led by the Marxist Daniel Ortega and including the supporters of liberation theology who backed and worked with him, was decisively defeated the first time it was subjected to free elections in 1990.

Indeed, the two outstanding religious phenomena in Latin America during the 1970s, and still more in the 1980s, both attracting wide popular support almost everywhere, were fundamentalist. The first was evangelical Protestantism, hitherto banned from proselytizing in Latin America as a result of concordats between states and the Catholic Church, or laws granting Catholicism privileged status. The lifting of these prohibitions led to a large-scale missionary effort by Protestant groups, mainly directed and financed from the United States, where evangelicalism, making full use of television, radio and cable, made huge advances in the 1960s, 1970s and 1980s, constituting what was popularly known as 'the Moral Majority'. Its efforts in Latin America, especially in Mexico, Central America, Colombia, Brazil and Venezuela, met with remarkable success, and by the late 1980s a new generation of trained Latin American evangelists were at work. The Catholic response was the growth, which seems to have been quite spontaneous in origin, of a form of religious observance not essentially different from Protestant evangelicalism, and known as *religiosidad popular*, anti-political, anti-intellectual, spontaneous, devotional, fervent and with a strong mass appeal among the poor. But whereas Protestant fundamentalism stressed the Bible, Catholic fundamentalism was characterized by the cult of saints (often unofficial local ones), relics and shrines.

John Paul II gave the movement the stamp of his approval in January 1979, when he insisted on visiting the shrine of the Virgin of Guadalupe and placed the people of Mexico under the protection of that Indian-style Madonna. But of course these popular cults were often heterodox, mixtures of paganism and Christianity, nurtured in villages and then brought by migrating peasants into the sprawling cities to protect themselves from urban alienation. These syncretistic forms of Christianity have always tended to appear in periods of rapid population growth, racial and cultural mingling, movement and change. They were particularly marked in Brazil, where the large black population whose forebears had been slaves retained modes of belief and worship ultimately drawn from Africa.[29] They were a still more important feature in Africa itself, a boiling maelstrom of expansion, revivalism, strange sects, gnosticism, evangelism, Christian Zionism, fervent orthodoxy and fanatic zeal, rather as primitive Christianity had been in Asia Minor and the Balkans in the third century AD.[30] While theologians at the Universities of Tübingen and Utrecht were diminishing the total of Christian belief, strange charismatics in the slums of Mexico City and São Paulo, of Recife and Rio, of Cape Town, Johannesburg, Lagos and Nairobi, were adding to it. The first group spoke for thousands; the second for scores of millions.

The fundamentalist spirit of Islam, gathering force in the third quarter of the twentieth century, became a powerful, popular and, to many, frightening phenomenon in the 1980s. It affected all the great religions, often in response to fundamentalist outbreaks in their traditional rivals. Thus the revival of Islamic extremism, which began in the 1950s and by the early 1990s had spread to most of the Muslim world, provoked violent reactions. In India, for instance, the Hindu-based Janata Dal Party had, by the end of the 1980s, been goaded into forms of religious extremism by Islamic pressure, and early in 1991 there was widespread violence in northern India as Hindus fought to reclaim the shrines of their gods where mosques had been built. Islamic fundamentalism also helped along the revival of Jewish ultra-Orthodoxy, started in New York under the Rabbi Meir Kahane, then transferring itself to Israel to promote both the expanding 'historical' frontiers of the Kingdom of David, and the transformation of Israel into a Jewish theocracy. This led to running legal battles and street fights with the Israeli authorities, and more serious violence between fundamentalist Jewish settlers and Arabs in the West Bank.[31]

Islamic militancy was the most important of the new fundamentalist forces because of the vast numbers involved and the huge geographical spread, curving in a long crescent from West Africa, through the southern Mediterranean, the Balkans, Asia Minor and the Middle East, across the interior of Southwest Asia, the Indian subcontinent and down into Malaysia and the Philippines. Its political, military and indeed cultural impact was felt over three continents. It was advancing in black Africa, often with the aid of Arab money, arms and indeed force. In the 1960s the ruling northern élite in the Sudan sought to impose Islam on the Christian south. In the 1970s and 1980s Gadafy tried to convert all of Chad by fire and sword, or rather by napalm and helicopter, just as Amin tried to Islamize Uganda by mass-murder. But Islam enjoyed natural growth as well and a new dynamism fuelled by its own internal revival. One reason for this was the increase of Muslim self-confidence, indeed stridency, as a result of the new wealth from oil. By filtering down to the masses it also made possible an unprecedented expansion in the number of Mecca pilgrims, flown by chartered jet to kiss the *Kaaba* and returning full of zeal for Islam, which is a far more political and this-worldly faith than Christianity. The prime beneficiaries of the new Islamic zealotry were not the orthodox Sunni Muslims, who constituted the majority, especially among Arabs, and represented the right-thinking, conservative, static establishment of Islam, including the two chief ruling families, the Hashemites and the Saudis. The effect of the revival was to reanimate the dramatic bifurcation of Islam in the seventh and eighth centuries, when Islamic nonconformity, in the shape of the Shi'ites and the many heterodox sects they spawned, such as the Druzes, the

Ismailis and the Alawites, made their appearance. Shi'ia Islam, with its messianic belief in the 'hidden Imam' and its consequent millennarianism, its cult of martyrs and suffering, its puritanism and not least its addiction to violence (the Assassins were Shi'ia Ismailis), has always been a source of disorder in the Muslim world, especially in Syria, the Lebanon and Iraq, where they are numerous, and Iran, where they form the majority. They claimed that the Sunnis always, when possible, treated them like second-class citizens. The Islamic revival led them to demand a new deal for themselves as well as producing a new assertiveness by Islam towards the infidel world. They created a belt of crisis which cut across the familiar Cold War patterns.

The first consequence was the destruction of the Lebanon, a small but highly civilized country, the sole Arab democracy, whose survival was made possible only by a series of gentleman's agreements among the élites of the main religious groups: Maronites (Eastern Christians in communion with Rome), Orthodox Christians, Sunni and Shi'ia Muslims and Druzes. Such agreements were made workable only by self-denying ordinances among all the religions and sects to forswear fanaticism. The Arab–Israeli dispute made such restraint increasingly difficult. In 1949 Lebanon had been obliged to accommodate 300,000 Palestine refugees, 100,000 of them in fifteen major camps, five of them ringing the capital, Beirut, and controlling all routes in and out of it. Each successive Arab–Israeli crisis dealt massive blows to Lebanon's fragile unity. In 1958, following the Suez invasion, there was the first hint of civil war, which produced an American intervention at the request of the dominant Maronites. The 1967 war doubled the number of refugees in Jordan, and when King Hussein threw the militant Palestinians out of his kingdom by force in 1970–1, they moved into Lebanon, defying the legitimate authorities and forming militant enclaves ruled by the terrorists of the PLO. In 1975, following the Yom Kippur War, President Sadat of Egypt, with the encouragement of the United States, took the historic step of opening peace negotiations with Israel. The 'Camp David process', named after the presidential mountain retreat in Maryland where President Carter first brought Sadat and Prime Minister Begin of Israel together, ended in a peace treaty of immense benefit to both parties: the one potentially mortal threat to Israel was removed, and Egypt was released from the burden of a vendetta which had nothing to do with her and which was wrecking all her economic aspirations. The Israel–Egypt Peace Treaty was one of the few creative acts of a dismal decade, and made peace between Israel and all her neighbours not only possible but, in the long run, inevitable.

The word 'inevitable' is justified because whereas, up to the 1980s, Arab confidence in the eventual failure of Israel (indeed the extermination of Zionism, frequently stated as an object of Arab policy in Arabic broadcasts) had been buoyed up by demographic trends, both within Israel and the 'occupied territories', and in the Middle East as a whole, at the end of the 1980s the trend was reversed. On 3 January 1985 it was revealed that a secret airlift, operated with the consent of Sudan, had enabled 25,000 Falashas, black Jews of a tribe which for centuries had lived in Ethiopia, to be brought to Israel as settlers (a further 10,000 were flown to Israel in 1991). This was only a foretaste of a mass emigration by Russian Jews, allowed to leave the Soviet Union as a result of political changes there, which reached 100,000 in 1989, rose to over 200,000 in 1990, and continued to accelerate. Israeli authorities had always assumed that no more than 1.5 million Jews lived in Russia. By the end of 1990 it was clear that the total was very much larger, and might be as high as 4 million, almost all of whom wished to leave. By a decision of the Soviet government such emigrants were obliged to proceed straight to Israel. This mass immigration into Israel, actual and potential, had the effect of altering the demographic prospect completely, and strengthened the likelihood that other states, notably Syria, would eventually want to follow Egypt's example and make peace.

But in the meantime the Israel–Egypt Peace Treaty, signed finally on 26 March 1979, led directly to Lebanese civil war, started by the PLO and broadened by the intervention of Syria, whose ruling Awali sect wished to capture from Egypt the leadership of the Arab world. The precarious balance of communal power in Lebanon was thus destroyed. It had been preserved hitherto by the conciliatory attitude of the local Higher Muslim Council, which spoke for all Muslim sects including the Druzes, and was dominated by an old-fashioned Sunni establishment. This was overthrown when the Shi'ites, led by a Persian fundamentalist of Lebanese origin called the Imam Moussa Sadr, called for a separate Shi'ia Muslim Higher Council. The Shi'ites formed a destructive alliance with the secular Left of the PLO. All the sects, Christian and Muslim, produced private armies. In the ensuing fighting, which raged fiercely in 1975–6, 1982, 1988–90 and sporadically in the intervals, Israel as well as Syria was forced to intervene, back-street gangsters flourished as respectable guerrilla and political leaders, 40,000 people were killed, Beirut was destroyed as a commercial centre, Lebanon ceased to exist as an independent country, the ancient Christian community lost its paramountcy, though it held on to its main settlement areas, and a light of reason in the Arab world was extinguished.[32]

In 1982 Israel felt obliged to conduct a full-scale invasion. This led to the expulsion and dispersal of the PLO, first to Tunisia, then also to Iraq. But Israel quickly found herself blamed for a massacre of Palestinian refugees, carried out by Christian militiamen at the Sabra and Chatila camps in West Beirut, and as early as spring 1983 she was beginning to withdraw her forces, keeping only a security zone in the south of the country. Gradually, Syrian forces filled the vacuum of power in Lebanon, though they found it no easier to establish a secure presence there than did the Israelis. By the early 1990s, Lebanon, once the richest and most civilized Arab state, found itself fragmented and almost destitute, with no focus of unity, though violence was now sporadic rather than continuous.

The Islamic fundamentalists, mainly but not exclusively Shi'ites, struck again and again at the forces of stability in the Middle East. They tried hard to overthrow the regime in Egypt and finally succeeded in murdering Sadat in 1981. In 1979 they seized the shrine of Mecca by force, in an attempt to destroy the Saudi royal family, and were ejected from its underground labyrinth of tunnels only after a week of bitter fighting. There was another gruesome incident on 30 July 1987 when 155,000 Iranian Shi'ite pilgrims rioted, tried to seize Mecca, and were slaughtered in their hundreds by Saudi police. But their most resounding success came in 1978–9 when they toppled the Shah of Iran from his Peacock Throne. This cataclysmic event, much misunderstood, casts a searchlight on the forces at work in modern times. The regime should have been immensely strong. It had been armed to the teeth by the Americans and British, as the residual 'stabilizing force' in the Gulf after the Western military withdrawal. The monarchy, immensely ancient and respected as an institution, was the one unifying force in a country which was essentially a collection of racial, religious, cultural, linguistic and geographical minorities, most of whom hated each other and many of whom looked to the throne for protection. By contrast, the Shi'ite fundamentalists of Qum and Meshed spoke only for a section of the Muslims, and their leader, the Ayatollah Khomeini, was much hated as well as loved and feared. The Shah was not overthrown because he was pro-West, or a capitalist, or corrupt, or cruel – most Middle Eastern rulers were cruel and by their standards he was a liberal – and least of all because he was king. The truth is he destroyed himself by succumbing to the fatal temptation of modern times: the lure of social engineering. He fell because he tried to be a Persian Stalin.

It was in the blood. His father was a Persian Cossack officer who seized power in 1925 and modelled himself on Ataturk, the great secularizer; later he came to admire and envy the ruthlessness with which Stalin collectivized the peasants. He said grimly: 'I have made the Iranians realize that when they get up in the morning they must go to work, and work hard all day long.'[33] He personally defenestrated an idle minister. His son came to the throne as a child in 1944, ruled from the age of twenty-one but entered on his grandiose visions only in the 1960s with the rapid increase in oil revenues. He began by giving away the royal lands to the peasants, then changed his mind and decided, like Stalin, to modernize the country in his own lifetime. There was no more popular demand for this than in Soviet Russia: it was revolution from above, what the Shah called the 'White Revolution'. His schemes changed from simple investment planning to megalomaniac social engineering in a series of leaps. Planning was first introduced in the late 1940s: the first Seven Year Plan involved a modest investment of $58 million mainly in agriculture, primary products, roads and cement. The second Seven Year Plan, 1955–62, jumped to a billion dollars, on roads, railways and dams for power and irrigation. A third, Five Year Plan spent $2.7 billion, 1963–8, on pipelines, steel and petrochemical industries and, moving into the social field, began to shove people around for the first time. The Fourth Plan, 1968–72, spent $10 billion on roads, ports, airports, dams, natural gas, water, housing, heavy metallurgy and agro-business. The Stalinist phase began with the Fifth Plan, 1973–8, which started with a spending target of $36 billion, quickly jacked up to $70 billion when oil prices quadrupled.[34] For the financial year 1978–9, the Shah's last, some $17.2 billion went on development alone, three hundred times the cost of the entire first plan, plus a further $8.5 billion on health, education and welfare, as well as $10 billion on military spending.[35]

The planners, educated abroad and known as *massachuseti* (after the famous Institute of Technology, MIT), had the arrogance of party *apparatchiks* and a Stalinist faith in centralized planning, the virtues of growth and bigness. Above all, they lusted for change. There was an inferno of extractive expansion: gold, salt, lime, phosphorus, gypsum, marble, alabaster, precious stones, coal, lead, zinc, chromite, iron, and the sixth-largest copper industry in the world, newly built in Central Iran with 25,000 miners living in brick barracks. Four nuclear reactors were started, plus a nationwide rash of factories producing cars, diesel engines, elevators, bicycles, water-meters, asbestos, foundry-sand, glucose, aluminium, clothes, tractors, machine-tools and arms. The Shah boasted that his White Revolution combined 'the principles of capitalism . . . with socialism, even communism . . . . There's never been so much change in 3,000 years. The whole structure is [being turned] upside down.'[36] By trying to spend too much too fast he bought himself inflation. To put the brake on inflation, he organized student-gangs to arrest 'profiteering' merchants and small businessmen. This merely gave youth a taste for violence and cost the throne the bazaar.

That might not have mattered for the Shahs had hitherto always been able to invoke the conservative countryside to tame urban radicalism. But the Shah's gravest error was to alienate the countryside, whose peasant sons formed his army. Having given the royal lands and the confiscated estates of the clergy to the peasants, he found, predictably, that output declined. In 1975, having thus turned Iran from a food-exporting to a food-importing nation, he changed the policy and embarked on collectivization. The model was the 1972–5 Dez irrigation project in northern Khuzestan, which had taken back 100,000 hectares of prime farmland, given to the peasants only five years before, and turned everything and everybody over to what was called 'consolidated agricultural management'. Thus yeoman farmers were turned into a rural proletariat, earning a dollar a day and living in cinder-block two-room houses, back-to-back in new 'model towns' called *shahraks*.[37] The law of June 1975 in effect extended this model to the whole country, forcing the independent peasants into several hundred 'agro-business units' or vast 'farm corporations' or into 2,800 co-operatives. It is true that the peasants, while relinquishing their freeholds, got shares in the new companies. But in essentials it was not very different from forced collectivization.[38] The scheme involved knocking 67,000 small villages into 30,000 larger ones, each big enough to justify clinics, schools, piped water and roads. Large families were broken up. Menacing convoys of bulldozers and earth-moving equipment, often of stupendous size, would descend, without warning or explanation, upon 2,000-year-old village communities, and literally uproot them. The place-names of tiny hamlets, even orchards, were changed. The agricultural planners and the 'justice corpsmen', as they were called, behaved with all the arrogance of the party activists Stalin used to push through his programme, though there was no resistance and no actual brutality.[39] The programme as a whole was a deliberate assault on tribal diversity, local patriarchs, family cohesion, provincial accents and tongues, regional dress, customs and interest groups, anything in fact which offered alternative centres of influence to the all-powerful central state. It was fundamental to the White Revolution that the ultimate freehold of all land and property resided in the crown, that is the state. Thus the Shah, despite his liberalism and his public posture as a pillar of the West, was pursuing a policy of radical totalitarianism. He argued: 'It shows that if you think that it is only through bloodshed that you can make a revolution, you are wrong.'[40] But it was the Shah who was wrong. The elders were pushed into the *shahraks* but their grown sons went into the cities and formed the Ayatollah's mob; and their brothers in the army were reluctant to shoot them when the time came. The Shah was reluctant too. Collectivization is impossible without terror; and he had not the heart for it. When it came to the point, at the close of 1978, he felt he had been betrayed by his ally, President Carter.[41] But he also betrayed himself. In the end he lacked the will to power.

Both Shah and President betrayed the Iranians. They handed over a nation, including many defenceless minorities, to a priesthood which had no tradition or training for the exercise of political power.[42] The result was a barbarous terror exercised by a small group of fundamentalist despots, acting in the name of an 'Islamic Republic' established in February 1979. In the first two years of its existence it executed over 8,000 people, convicted in Islamic courts of being 'enemies of Allah'.[43] The Khomeini terror moved first against the former regime, slaughtering twenty-three generals, 400 other army and police officers and 800 civilian officials; then against supporters of rival Ayatollahs, 700 of whom were executed; then against its former liberal-secular allies (500) and the Left (100). From the start it organized the execution or murder of leaders of ethnic and religious minorities, killing over 1,000 Kurds, 200 Turkomans, and many Jews, Christians, Shaikhis, Sabeans and members of dissident Shi'ia sects as well as orthodox Sunnis.[44] Its persecution of the Bahais was particularly ferocious.[45] Churches and synagogues were wrecked, cemeteries desecrated, shrines vandalized or demolished. The judicially murdered ranged from the Kurdish poet Allameh Vahidi, aged 102, to a nine-year-old girl, convicted of 'attacking revolutionary guards'.

Khomeini's harassment of Iran's Sunni minority (many of them Iraqis), and reciprocal measures against Persian Shi'ites in Iraq, resurrected Iran–Iraq border disputes, which have poisoned their relations ever since the creation of Iraq by Britain in 1920–2. In September 1980, reports that most of Iran's senior officers had been murdered or fled, and that its armed forces, especially its once formidable air force, were in disarray, tempted Iraq's Baathist dictator, Saddam Hussein, to launch a full-scale invasion of Iran, beginning with air attacks on the world's largest oil refinery at Abadan. He hoped to secure control of the Shatt-al-Arab, the main sea-outlet of the Tigris–Euphrates, and possibly Iran's oilfields. In fact the war, instead of being a quick Iraqi triumph, lasted eight years, and cost (on both sides) over a million dead. Saddam ended up with very little: a few miles of unimportant territory, which he quickly relinquished in 1990 when he found himself in trouble with the West.

During the war itself, however, the West, though neutral, tended to assist Iraq. It was well aware of the cruelty and gangsterism of Saddam's regime. But it was still more hostile to Khomeini's Iran, which had invaded the American embassy and held hostage its staff (releasing them only in return for a ransom), as well as financing and arming various anti-Western terrorist groups.

So Western warships patrolled the Gulf, clearing Iranian mines from the sea-lanes used by tankers exporting Arab oil, while doing nothing to impede Iraqi air attacks on Iranian tankers. Indeed, when Iraqi jets, on 27 May 1987, mistakenly fired Exocet missiles at the American frigate *Stark*, killing thirty-seven of its crew, Washington's protest was muted; and American readiness to attack Iranian targets deemed hostile was demonstrated on 3 July 1988, when the US Navy Warship *Vincennes* mistakenly shot down an Iranian civil airliner, killing 290 people, in the belief that it was a warplane. Most serious of all, however, was the complacency with which the West, while denying arms to Iran, sold them to Saddam, who was also receiving huge supplies, particularly of modern tanks, artillery, armoured troop carriers and aircraft, from the Soviet Union.

The Iran–Iraq war came to an inconclusive end on 8 August 1988. But Saddam, far from disarming, actually increased the size of his armed forces, which by 1990 were the fourth-largest in the world. With Western agreement, he had been subsidized militarily during the war by the Sunni-dominated Gulf oil states, in addition to Iraq's own enormous oil revenues (by the end of the 1980s it was the second largest oil producer, after Saudi Arabia, in the Middle East); virtually all these huge sums, amounting during the 1980s to something approaching $100 billion, went on creating a war machine. The Israelis did not share the West's indifference to Iraq's growing military power, especially when their intelligence sources revealed that a French-built nuclear reactor, near Baghdad, was being used to produce material for nuclear bombs. On 7 June 1981 Israeli aircraft destroyed the reactor. But Saddam continued to scour the world for weapons of mass destruction and the means to make them; by the end of the 1980s he had acquired both a chemical and a biological warfare capability, and indeed in 1989 he killed over 5,000 Kurds, alleged to be rebels, by dropping chemical bombs on their villages.

Saddam was well-known to Western governments as a man of exceptional depravity, from a clan of professional brigands.[46] He had acquired his first gun at the age of ten (and committed his first murder, it was claimed, two years later). As head of the secret police from 1968, and as president from 1979, his career had been punctuated both by the slaughter of his colleagues and rivals, often by his own hand, and by atrocities on the largest possible scale, not least mass public hangings of Jews. A tract he published testified to his ambition to extend Iraq's borders on the model of the ancient Babylonian empire. Nonetheless, while American and British military assistance tapered off in the 1980s, France continued to supply modern weapons, West Germany provided hi-tech military expertise (some of it illegally), and the Russians not only poured in arms but kept over a thousand military experts in Iraq to train Saddam's armed forces in their use, and in tactics and strategy.

Soviet policy, which became increasingly confused as the 1980s progressed, was dictated by its assumption that the Baathist regimes were its most reliable allies in the Middle East; so it armed Baathist Syria, as well as Baathist Iraq, though the two were irreconcilable enemies. The West felt it must lean, if anything, towards Iraq since Iran was identified with international terrorism, and especially with the kidnapping by Shi'ite militias of Western citizens in Beirut. It is true that terrorism in the 1980s took a variety of forms. An Indian terrorist group was probably responsible for the mid-Atlantic destruction of an Air India Boeing, all aboard perishing; and Sikh terrorists assassinated the Indian Prime Minister, Mrs Indira Gandhi, on 31 October 1984. A Tamil terrorist was believed responsible for the murder of Rajiv Gandhi in May 1991. During the early 1980s the Russian KGB was still training terrorists from various nations in special camps in the Crimea and elsewhere, and the Soviet government itself was guilty of a terrorist act on 1 September 1983 when, quite deliberately and without warning, it shot down a civil airliner, a Boeing 747 of (South) Korean Airways, which had strayed off course into Soviet territory.

Some murderous acts remained mysteries: the Swedish police were unable to discover who killed the country's Prime Minister, Olaf Palme, on 28 February 1986, the only suspect they produced being acquitted. On the other hand, there was no doubt that the Irish Republican Army was responsible for an attempt to murder the entire British Cabinet on 12 October 1984 in a Brighton hotel during the annual Conservative Party conference, and for a further shot at the Cabinet in January 1991, when home-made mortar bombs were unsuccessfully fired at 10 Downing Street. The IRA got its Semtex explosives from Czechoslovakia, the makers; when Vaclav Havel became the Czech President in 1990 he reported that Semtex records showed the IRA had been supplied by the Communist regime with enough explosives to last one hundred years. But the IRA also received vast quantities of weapons (some of them intercepted and identified) from Gadafy's Libya, from other

Middle Eastern states and from the PLO. Iranian-supported groups were responsible for perhaps the most successful terrorist assault of all, two coordinated suicide-bomb attacks in Beirut on 23 October 1983, which killed 241 American marines and 58 French paratroopers, guarding their embassies. Middle Eastern groups, financed by Iran, Libya or possibly both, also blew up a West Berlin discotheque patronized by American soldiers, on 5 April 1986, and a Pan Am 747 over Lockerbie in Scotland on 21 December 1988, killing its 258 passengers and crew and eleven on the ground, a crime for which two Libyan intelligence agents were indicted by the US and British governments.

All these outrages, and many more minor ones, without exception, failed in their political objectives. During the 1980s and still more into the 1990s, the West was less inclined than in the 1970s to have any kind of dealings with terrorist groups; indeed, international policing became highly coordinated, and it became progressively easier to secure the extradition of wanted terrorists. The effect of international and especially state-backed terrorism was, rather, to distort the West's judgement in dealing with certain Middle Eastern states. In particular, America's obsession with hostile Iran, which in turn always referred to the United States as 'the Great Satan', led it to underestimate the growing threat from Iraq. Rarely in diplomacy was the old adage 'My enemy's enemy is my friend' more apt.

So Iran found itself isolated. As a rule, a non-white nationalist leader who treated Washington as his prime enemy could expect a sympathetic response from the Western intelligentsia. But Khomeini had a unique talent for alienating potential allies. In 1988 the Anglo-Indian author Salman Rushdie, who had been a minor literary celebrity since he won the Booker Prize for his novel *Midnight's Children* in 1981, published another controversial work of fiction, *The Satanic Verses*. The title referred to certain verses cut from the Koran by the Prophet Mohammed because he believed they were inspired by Satan. Many found the book obscure; nonetheless it was on the bestseller list in London, disposing of 40,000 hardback copies in three months. But it angered British Muslims, who pronounced it blasphemous. On 14 January 1989, Muslims in Bradford publicly burned copies of the book. It was then drawn to the attention of the Ayatollah himself, and on 14 February he publicly announced: 'I inform the proud Muslim people of the world that the author of *The Satanic Verses* book, which is against Islam, the Prophet and the Koran, and all those involved in its publication who were aware of its content, are sentenced to death.'[47] Muslims were enjoined to carry out this *fatwah* or religious ruling.

There was some argument among Muslim religious authorities as to whether the book was indeed blasphemous, and whether the Ayatollah was authorized to pass a death-sentence (it was confirmed by his successors when he finally went to eternity, aged eighty-six, on 4 June 1989). But no one was taking any chances. The novel had long since been banned in Pakistan, India and Saudi Arabia. Now, it was taken off display by Britain's biggest book-chain, W. H. Smith, German, French and Italian publishers scrapped plans to bring out translations, Penguin Books postponed, then dropped, plans to bring out a paperback, and Rushdie himself cancelled an American promotional tour and went into hiding. The world-wide publicity sold the book in prodigious quantities, making Rushdie a multi-millionaire, though also a voluntary prisoner, perhaps for life. The literary and arts intelligentsia on both sides of the Atlantic – the 'beautiful people' in New York and the 'chattering classes' in London – joined hands to denounce the Ayatollah, his successors and their regime. The Left in general became almost as hostile to Iran as the White House, a strange conjunction. However, some British Labour MPs with large Pakistani minorities in their constituencies appeared curiously reluctant to stand up for freedom of publication; and the intellectuals lost a lot of enthusiasm for Rushdie's cause when, abruptly in December 1990, in what may have been a genuine conversion but looked to many like a desperate (and unsuccessful, as it turned out) attempt to get the *fatwah* lifted, he announced his re-conversion to Islam and apologized for any offence caused – a step from which he later retreated.

The Khomeini regime could thus inspire fear but it could not make friends in any quarter. The only merit of its isolation was that it ended the Shah's social engineering. The confiscation of its foreign assets, the eight-year war with Iraq, the virtual cessation for a time of oil production, and the flight of the middle class abroad or into hiding, brought the modern sector of the Iranian economy to a juddering halt, from which it was scarcely beginning to recover even in the early 1990s. The inevitable consequences followed: unemployment, breakdown of health and other basic services, mass epidemics, malnutrition and even starvation. Iran's horrifying experiences illustrated yet again the law of unintended effect. The Shah's state road to Utopia led only to Golgotha.

The Islamic revival, the Shah's fall and the fundamentalist terror contributed directly to the beginning of civil war in Afghanistan in December 1979. Here was another case of social engineering leading to barbarism, though in this case, as so often, the Utopian impulse came from the Communist camp. The episode was important because of its eventual colossal impact on the entire Soviet empire. The British had fought three Afghan Wars (1838–42,

1878–80 and 1919), all well-meaning in a sense; none served to establish stability in this unruly country or 'solve' the Afghan 'problem'. Undeterred by this experience, the Soviet Union, from a mixture of fear, greed and good intentions, plunged into the Afghan maze and lost itself there. Up to 1979, the Soviet government had aimed for the long term. It supported the non-Marxist Prince Mohammed Daud when he set up a constitutional monarchy in 1953; and again twenty years later when he threw out the King and made himself President. In the 1950s it gave a little money; in the 1960s it built roads from the north (ultimately to be used by its troops); in the 1970s it concentrated on building up a united Marxist party. This last object was achieved, so it thought, in 1977 when it brought together in the People's Democratic Party three revolutionary factions led by Babrak Karmal, Mur Muhammad Taraki and Hafizullah Amin. By 1978 it was considered time for the social engineering to begin, and in April a Soviet-sanctioned *putsch* overthrew Daud.[48]

But the experience of the twentieth century shows emphatically that Utopianism is never far from gangsterism. The Soviet leaders could start revolution in Afghanistan; they could not control it. The trio now in power were not unlike the saturnine ideologues who launched the terror in Cambodia. Amin, the most forceful of them, was a maths teacher, who turned eagerly from the abstractions of numbers to quantitative bloodletting. His first act was to have thirty members of Daud's family shot before his eyes; then members of the government; then Daud himself.[49] According to Amnesty International, 12,000 prisoners were held without trial; many were tortured. Pushing through the Marxist-Leninist 'plan', as in Cambodia, involved the destruction of entire villages. According to one report of eye-witness accounts:

While the soldiers started pulling down and burning the houses, thirteen children were rounded up and stood in line in front of their parents. Some of the soldiers then poked out the children's eyes with steel rods. The mutilated children were then slowly strangled to death. Next it was the parents' turn . . . The surrounding fields were bulldozed, all trees and shrubs uprooted, and the entire site reduced to an ash-strewn scar.[50]

Though Karmal later accused Amin of being a 'bloodthirsty hangman' and 'liquidating collectively', the evidence shows he was equally guilty of such atrocities until March 1979, when Amin made himself sole dictator and packed Karmal off to Prague as 'ambassador'. He intensified the terror, primarily because the new Khomeini regime was now giving aid to Muslim insurgents within Afghanistan. Indeed he seems to have nursed the idea of stamping out Islam entirely. Violence increased throughout 1979. The American Ambassador, an insurgency expert, was murdered, probably by the Russians. On 12 August, thirty Russian advisers were skinned alive near the Muslim shrine of Kandahar. General Alexei Yepishev, the senior party official within the Red Army, who had handled the political side of the 1968 Czech invasion, went to Kabul, and on his return Taraki, regarded as the most 'reliable' of the trio, was ordered to remove Amin. But in the course of a lively discussion at the Soviet Embassy, it was Taraki who was shot, and Moscow was obliged to send Amin a telegram (17 September 1979) congratulating him on surviving a 'counter-revolutionary plot'. The next week, at Amin's request, three Soviet battalions moved into the country and, on 17 December, paratroops. Unknown to Amin they had Karmal in their baggage and on Christmas Day Soviet Russia began a full-scale invasion, using two of its seven airborne divisions. These were the 4th and 105th, all 'Greater Russians' (i.e., white Europeans). The main body of the 80,000-strong expeditionary force came down the new roads, built for this very purpose. Amin was murdered two days later, together with his wife, seven children, a nephew and twenty to thirty of his staff.[51] The Soviet general in charge of the *putsch*, Viktor Papertin, committed suicide. Karmal set up a new government, but the new year revealed him as nothing more than a Soviet puppet facing a general uprising.[52]

The initial Soviet army of 80,000 men gradually rose to 120,000, and occasionally was much higher. The war lasted a decade, and at no point were the Russians and their allies able to control much more than the main towns and strategic roads. At the time and since, the Soviet venture into Afghanistan was compared to American involvement in Vietnam, a miscalculation which turned into a disaster and shocked national self-confidence. But the parallels should not be drawn too closely. For one thing, Soviet generals fought the war with a ruthlessness which the Americans rarely showed in any part of Indo-China. They used tanks, gunships, bombing, napalm, chemical warfare and the systematic destruction of what they termed 'bandit villages'. The war inflicted horrific damage on Afghanistan and created social and even political upheaval in all the neighbouring countries. Hundreds of thousands of Afghans were slaughtered (one estimate puts the death toll at one million). During the fighting the Red Army lost 16,000 killed and 30,000 wounded. Vast numbers of Afghans fled the country. Out of a population estimated by the UN in 1985 at 18,136,000, it was calculated that, by the time the fighting slackened after a decade of savagery, about 6 million, or nearly a third, were refugees, chiefly in

Pakistan but also in Iran. It is a dismal fact that, during the 1970s and 1980s, the policies followed by Russia and its Cuban, Ethiopian and Indo-Chinese satellites added around 12–15 million to the world total of displaced persons: not unworthy of comparison with the horrific statistical achievements of Stalin or Hitler.

As the Soviet leaders gradually discovered, moreover, the entire military operation they had launched was futile. The *mujaheddin*, as the nationalist rebels were called, could not be finally defeated, or even contained, by non-Afghan forces. Indeed, the man the Soviets finally installed as dictator-President in 1987, Dr Najibullah, did better without Soviet direct assistance than with it. The cost of the war to the already strained and declining Soviet economy was unbearable, and it undoubtedly played a major role in bringing about the fundamental changes in Moscow's thinking which began in the mid-1980s. On 8 February 1988, the new Soviet leader, Mikhail Gorbachev, announced to an initially sceptical world that Soviet troops would pull out of Afghanistan completely. The actual withdrawal started on 15 May and was completed by 15 February 1989.

One reason why the Soviet leaders were, in the end, anxious to get out of Afghanistan was their fear that the guerrilla warfare might spread into the nearby Muslim areas of Soviet Asia. Soviet state theory had no clearer answer to the problem of Islamic fundamentalism than Marxism had had. The Bolsheviks had attached little weight to Islam as a whole. 'The putrescent tissue of Islam', Trotsky thought, 'will vanish at the first puff.' It was Islam which had to fear change, from 'the Eastern Woman, who is to be the great centre of future revolutions'.[53] Stalin and still more Khrushchev and Brezhnev sought to run Islam as they ran the Orthodox Church, through pliable state clerics. At the 1970 Tashkent Muslim Conference, the Mufti Ahmed Habibullak Bozgoviev praised Soviet leaders who, though infidels, shaped their social policies according to 'laws that were dictated by God and expounded by his Prophet'. Another delegate said: 'We admire the genius of the Prophet who preached the social principles of socialism.'[54] In the 1970s and 1980s, growth of pilgrimages, cults of sheiks (saints), living and dead, Sufism and excited crowd movements testified to the Muslim revival within Soviet territory, with the Muslim leaders trying, sometimes desperately, to make Muslim practice, including public prayers, Ramadan and other fasts, fit in with Soviet rules, to 'legitimize Islam' in terms of Communist society. They sought to encourage Muslims, especially young people, to join Soviet social organizations 'as Muslims'.[55] But Muslim clerics working for the Shah had done exactly the same.

The Islamic revival was part of the wider problem of the Soviet empire, the great unresolved anomaly of the late twentieth century. In the preface to the 1921 edition of his *Imperialism*, Lenin admitted that it was written 'with an eye to the Tsarist censorship', which allowed it to be published in spring 1916 provided that, while attacking all the other empires, it left Tsarist imperialism alone. Hence, said Lenin, 'I was forced to take as an example . . . Japan! The careful reader will easily substitute Russia for Japan.'[56] Lenin's theory of imperialism, therefore, contained no attack on its Russian variety, a fact which he and still more his successors found mightily convenient when they came to power and decided to keep as many of the Tsarist possessions as they could. Greater Russian imperialism therefore continued, with the Tsarist provinces and territories transformed into internal satellites christened 'socialist republics'. In the 1950s Khrushchev introduced a cosmetic process of 'decolonization' by issuing decrees (29 August 1957, 22 June 1959) enlarging the powers of cabinets in the federated republics and judicial and administrative independence. But some of his colleagues did not like even these timid measures, and they were reversed after his fall. The 1977 constitution kept a formal federal system in Article 70 and even the dreamlike 'right of secession' in Article 72. But in every other respect it was a monolithic document making the aim centralization, unity and the emergence of the 'Soviet people' as a new historic community, embracing and eventually superseding the fifty-three principal national communities of the USSR.[57]

Hence in essential respects Soviet imperial policy resembled France's: a union in which the 'colonies' would gradually acquire the cultural and economic advantages of equality with the Greater Russians in return for relinquishing their national aspirations. The policy, like France's, was based on fake elections and administrative *diktat*. Much more so indeed, since imperial policy was enacted by the party which had a monopoly of all political power, speech and writing, something the French imperialists had never possessed, or even sought. Under the 1977 constitution the principal instruments of integration were the armed forces and the party, with Slavs (chiefly Greater Russians) forming 95 per cent of all general officers and the Supreme Soviet. Slavs dominated all the key state bodies and, through the party, controlled the selection of political, administrative and technical cadres at all levels in the non-Russian republics.[58] As late as the 1980s, language was used as the dissolvent of national cohesion, the number of schools teaching in Russian rising fast and knowledge of Russian being essential for social advancement. Even when a complete national system of education existed, Russian was made obligatory from start to finish.[59] Where national education systems were incomplete, a change to Russian at some stage became mandatory. As a result, national groups whose languages were in decline from the 1950s included the Baltic peoples, the Belorussians, the Moldavians, the 1.8 million Germans and the Jews. Even in the Ukraine, there were accusations that Russian was taking over from Ukrainian in higher education. Teaching in national languages as a proportion of the total was in decline throughout Soviet Russia.[60]

As we have seen, however, French assimilationist imperialism failed, not least for demographic reasons. One of the lessons of the twentieth century is that high birth-rates in the subject peoples are a mortal enemy of colonialism. Until the coming of Bolshevism, Russia had one of the world's most dynamic populations. The total 'demographic deficit' caused by the First World War, the Civil War and Lenin's famine, Stalin's famine and the Great Purges, and the Second World War amounted to 60 million over the whole period, partly offset by the 20 million gained by the acquisition of the Baltic States, Bessarabia, Karelia, Soviet Poland, Bukovina and other territories.[61] There was some demographic dynamism 1945–58 and the annual growth-rate 1959–70 was 1.34 per cent, high by European standards, though falling. In the 1970s it seems to have averaged less than 1 per cent. Soviet demographers expected the 1970 census to produce a figure of over 250 million, with a projection of 350 million by the end of the century. In fact the 1970 total fell 10 million short and the 1979 figure produced only 262,436,000, meaning a population of not much over 300 million in 2000 AD. What the 1970 census revealed for the first time was a dual birth-rate: low in Slavic and Baltic Russia, high in the eastern USSR, Central Asia and the Caucasus. In the 1960s alone the Muslim population leapt from 24 to 35 million, adding another 14 million in the 1970s, giving a total of about 50 million by the beginning of the 1980s. By this point it was clear that at the turn of the century Central Asia and Caucasia would contribute about 100 million, that is a third, of the total.[62] Even by 1979, the 137 million Great Russians, a markedly ageing population compared to the non-Slavs, felt demographically on the defensive, their growth rate well under 1 per cent, against 2.5 to 3.5 per cent for Soviet Muslims. It was significant, too, that among Muslims knowledge of Russian was declining.[63]

Soviet Russia was not the only country worried by demographic trends. Total world population had been 1,262 million in 1900; by 1930 it had passed the 2-billion-mark; it was 2,515 million by 1950, passed the 3-billion-mark by 1960 and the 4-billion-mark by 1975. By 1987 it was over 5 billion, and was increasing at the rate of 80 million a year or 150 a minute. One calculation put the estimated world population in the year 2000 at 6,130 million, a five-fold increase during the century.[64] How were these additional billions to be fed? Modern developing societies go through a cycle known as the 'demographic transition'. In the first phase, scientific medicine and public health reduce infant mortality and infectious diseases, thus cutting the death-rate, while the birth-rate remains high at its old replacement rate. So population rises fast. In the second phase, rising living standards cause the birth-rate to fall. The rate of population increase slows down and eventually comes into balance. Between the first and second phases, however, population jumps alarmingly and may produce violent political consequences. In Europe the 'transition' began with the Industrial Revolution, 1760–1870, and was virtually complete by the 1970s, by which time the birth-rate had fallen below the critical 20-per-thousand mark even in Russia (1964), Yugoslavia (1967) and Portugal and Spain (1969). The European demographic transition spans and helps to explain the whole cycle of colonization and decolonization. Japan followed a similar pattern somewhat later than the European average. In the 1920s its birth-rate was still 34-per-thousand and the death-rate was falling precipitously, from 30-per-thousand at the beginning of the decade to 18 at the end. Hence Japan's growing desperation. But even in the inter-war period the second phase was beginning, since in the later 1930s the birth-rate dipped below the 30-mark for the first time. Despite an immediately post-war upturn (a universal phenomenon) it continued to fall thereafter, moving below the 20-mark in the second half of the 1950s.[65] Japan's population problem, once so threatening, was therefore 'solved' by the 1960s.

The conclusions to be drawn from the theory of the demographic transition were twofold. First, there was no need to panic even when the first phase produced its maximum effects in Asia, Latin America and Africa. But second, there was a real need to try to improve industrial growth-rates in the developing countries in order to reach the second phase there as rapidly as possible. Birth-control programmes and techniques were helpful but not decisive since effective use of contraception was a symptom, rather than a cause, of the decelerating birth-rate, which was the consequence of economic betterment. The great thing was to push up living standards: this was the real answer to those who opposed growth policies on environmental grounds.

It is true that a rising GNP does not necessarily bring down the birth-rate immediately or, when it does so, at a uniform rate. But there were encouraging signs in the 1970s that China was entering the second phase of the transition, though death-rates had still a good deal to fall before they stabilized. In 1979, the US Census Bureau estimated the population of China at 1,010 million and calculated that it had undergone a sharp drop in the rate of increase; this largely accounted for the deceleration in the world growth-rate, which fell from an average of 2.1 per cent a year in the late 1960s and 1.9 per cent in the early 1970s to 1.7 per cent in the late 1970s. By the early 1980s the Asian growth-rate as a whole was under 1.9 per cent, not much more than the world average. The Latin-American growth-rate had slowed to 2.4 per cent. The only area where the growth rate had actually increased, from 2.5 to 2.9 per cent (1979 figures), was Africa, which was exactly what demographers had expected.[66] The most important news during the 1980s, perhaps, was that the population of China appeared virtually to have stabilized. A nationwide census in July 1982 gave a total population of 1,008,175,288; and a UN estimate three years later reported 1,059,521,000, though a figure of 1,072,200,000 was also published in the late 1980s. The news from India caused rather more concern: the 1981 census reported a population of 685,184,692; a 1985 UN estimate showed a rise to approximately 750,900,000, though another estimate put the total at not much over 748 million. These figures too indicated deceleration, though at a slower rate than in China.[67] Throughout the 1980s and into the 1990s, the areas of highest population increase remained Central America and, above all, Africa, though in most of the latter accurate figures were increasingly difficult to obtain. Calculations made in the early 1960s indicated that the point at which higher living standards began to affect the birth-rate was when *per capita* incomes passed the barrier of $400 (at 1964 value). By the early 1990s, and allowing for inflation which raised the figure to about $2,000, few Central American and virtually no black African states had broken through this barrier. The experience of the 1970s and 1980s appeared, in general, to confirm the theory of population growth and deceleration. In short, the 'population explosion' was not an explosion at all but a curve linked to economic development: it could be contained by sensible growth policies.

How could such policies be promoted? The problem was not technical. Scientific farming was practised on a prodigious scale in the advanced countries in the years after 1945; knowledge, and its dissemination, increased steadily. The capitalist, market-orientated agricultural systems of the United States, Canada, Australia, Argentina and Western Europe produced huge and increasing surpluses in the 1970s and still more in the 1980s. These areas alone could feed the entire world, if necessary, and at a price. The problem, rather, was political, and especially the adoption of collectivist systems of agriculture, with their lack of financial incentives to farmers, their gross inefficiency, and not least their neglect of market factors and the need for an efficient distribution system. Lenin, like Marx, had been a victim of the 'physical fallacy': the belief that only those who made goods or grew food were 'honest' workers; all middlemen were parasites. Lenin had denounced them as 'bagmen', 'thieves', 'plunderers', 'economic bandits' and the like. Such attitudes persisted in the Soviet system and were exported to Eastern Europe, and to wherever in Asia, Africa and Latin America the collectivist, Soviet-style system was implemented.

The result was calamitous as a rule. In India, though Soviet influence was strong, serious efforts were made to give peasant-farmers incentives to modernize, and both funds and technical instruction were made available on a large scale. As a result, India was able to feed itself in the 1980s and even to achieve an overall, if modest, surplus for export. In China investment and the promotion of some market practices, combined with a refusal to echo Lenin's contempt for the middleman – the Chinese are particularly gifted at running distribution systems, both at home and as expatriates – enabled China, too, to feed itself in the 1980s. In most other collectivist areas, however, the picture was dismal.

An egregious example was Soviet Russia itself. Until 1914, agricultural modernization and the creation of large and relatively efficient peasant farms (and voluntary cooperatives) meant that Russia was one of the world's largest exporters of agricultural goods, sending up to 40 per cent of its produce abroad. Under Lenin it became a net importer of food, and the deficit widened as the years passed. Stalin's collectivization policy led to the murder or death by starvation of most of Russia's best peasant farmers. It branded a mark of Cain on the brow of the regime, which burned more deeply over the decades. The 1963 harvest was the first of the big post-war Soviet agricultural disasters. Khrushchev complained it would have been even worse but for his virgin-land wheat. But his policy, like Stalin's, was confused and subject to abrupt reversals. His much-boosted virgin lands scheme was a total failure and silently abandoned. He oscillated between state farms and collectives, between centralization and decentralization. In retirement, he complained bitterly of food shortages. Even in a Moscow hospital reserved for high party officials, he whined, the food was disgusting. And Moscow, as always, was the food-showplace of Soviet Russia. It was far worse in the provinces. He met people from traditional food-producing areas who 'tell me loudly and bitterly how eggs and meat are simply unavailable, and how they had to take a couple of days and travel to Moscow by train', for the privilege of queuing for groceries. Why, he asked, should eggs and meat be unobtainable 'after fifty years of Soviet power'? 'I look forward to the day', he wrote, 'when a camel would be able to walk from Moscow to Vladivostok without being eaten by hungry peasants on the way.'[68] But, while he had the power, he never dared to suggest handing back the land to the private sector. Brezhnev and his immediate successors evolved more stable policies – this period was later officially branded 'the years of stagnation' – and kept agriculture wholly collectivized. So the food problem grew slowly but steadily worse. Though the Soviet Union had twice as much land under cultivation as any other country, including some of the best soil on earth in the Ukraine, together with a relatively low population density, its import demands, sometimes 15 million tons of grain a year, sometimes 30 million, tended to increase. During the 1970s and 1980s, meat and eggs became scarce in the non-privileged shops even in Moscow.

In the late 1980s, the regime's agricultural policy changed marginally; a private sector was allowed to develop within strict limits and sell its produce at market (i.e., high) prices. This merely served to reveal the inefficiency and confusion of the state and collectivized sector. Attempts in 1988–91 to introduce 'realistic' accounting and sales, while retaining all the basic principles of collectivism, merely made matters worse, especially since the distribution system remained primitive, corrupt and grotesquely inefficient. It was calculated that 40 per cent of the food produced never reached consumers; it rotted in warehouses and railway sidings, or was eaten by rats. By the winter of 1990–91 there was a real threat of starvation in parts of Russia, and the proud Soviet regime was forced to beg for Western food aid. Food-rationing was reintroduced, followed in March 1991 by huge increases in state-determined food prices. It was characteristic of Soviet realities that during the referendum held on 16 March 1991 to determine whether the USSR should remain a unity, the regime, to encourage a high turnout, sold meat and vegetables from its secret reserves at polling stations; but even these had run out by lunchtime.[69] At the root of all Soviet difficulties was a theory based on dishonest use of statistical evidence, compounded by sheer ignorance. No Marxist ever seems to have held sensible views on agriculture, perhaps because neither Marx nor Lenin was really interested in it. Marxism is an essentially urban religion.

The Soviets were not alone in their doctrinaire improvidence. Poland, a big food exporter in the 1930s, also became a major net importer, despite her uncollectivized peasantry, because the regime insisted on a socialized distribution system; the position began to improve slowly in the years 1989–91, with the replacement of Communism by a freely-elected government. Romania, another huge exporter in the 1930s, kept up some exports, to earn hard currency for the ferocious Nicolae Ceausescu regime, only by starving its own people. Hungary, from 1985 onwards, when it began to adopt the market system, slowly raised productivity, so by 1991 it was again a net exporter. Bulgaria followed, belatedly, but Yugoslavia was another net importer of food in the 1980s. Hence the COMECON group as a whole, once an area with immense surpluses, became a burden on the world, and was often kept going by low-cost sales from the European Community's food mountains, themselves the objectionable consequence of an ill-conceived system of subsidies. Thus one unsatisfactory agricultural system served to make bearable – just – another which was an unrelieved disaster.

The Marxist-collectivist influence on agriculture had calamitous results in virtually all the Third World countries which came under its spell. Iraq and Syria, both under radical military dictatorships, and embracing the Utopian mirage of Big Government and state management as a solution to all problems, turned surpluses into deficit. Iran was another example. Indonesia, under Sukarno's brand of socialism, ceased to export rice, and his successors did only marginally better. Socialist Burma also became a net rice importer. Some of the worst cases occurred in post-colonial Africa, whose leaders eagerly embarked on socialist agricultural experiments, especially in Ghana, which rapidly turned itself from the richest black African territory into one of the poorest, and in Tanzania, which also became a net food-importer, despite receiving more foreign aid *per capita* than any other country in the world. Africa's food-producing problems, essentially political in origin, were compounded by border troubles and especially civil wars, provoked by oppressive regimes which persecuted minorities for tribal, racial or religious reasons, and so created uprisings. This led to widespread starvation, during the 1980s, in Mozambique and Chad, to give only two examples. During the 1980s and into the 1990s, the most distressing and widespread famines occurred in the Sudan and Ethiopia, partly as a result of rain-failure but chiefly caused by the civil war raging between north and south Sudan, endemic internal unrest in Ethiopia provoked by its Marxist government, which shifted huge masses of peasants from their traditional farming and grazing areas and bombed their villages, and the regime's wars with its neighbours, Eritrea and Somalia.

By the end of the 1980s, even the few black African states which, in the 1970s, had appeared to be making a success of independence, such as the Ivory Coast, Kenya and Malawi, were experiencing increasing economic difficulties and social unrest. The plight of Liberia, oldest of the black states (it was founded in 1822), was pitiful: in 1990 it was torn between three murderous personal armies, run by rival contenders to the presidency, a conflict compounded by a supposed 'peacekeeping force' provided by neighbouring states which joined in the general pillage, while the unarmed starved. Many of the poorer African states, indeed, had virtually dropped out of the international economy by the 1990s. There were signs, however, of a process of self-education among the ruling élites. Mozambique, for instance, began to dismantle its collectivist economy in 1988 and return to a market system, inviting back Western firms it had once expelled. The same year South Africa reached a cease-fire agreement with Angola, which likewise was repudiating its collectivist structure; and this in turn made possible independence and free elections in the former mandatory territory of South West Africa (Namibia), which also chose a non-radical path.

But the most important change of all came in South Africa itself, which from early 1989 moved decisively away from its peculiar system of ethnic socialism, apartheid. Events in South Africa were of special significance, not only because of the immense interest the outside world took in its racial problems but because, in many ways, South Africa was a microcosm of the global problems which confronted humanity in the early 1990s. There is no other country on earth whose characteristics, and the difficulties they create, are closer to those of the world as a whole. The point is worth enlarging in a little detail. In the early 1990s, the world was composed of a white minority, with low birth-rates, and a non-white majority, with (on the whole) high birth-rates. So was South Africa: in 1989–90 there were about 5 million whites and 30 million non-whites living there, the ratio being of the same order of magnitude as the world's. South African differentials in annual population growth, ranging from 0.77 per cent for whites, through 1.64 for Asians and 1.89 for 'coloureds' (mixed race), to 2.39 for blacks (1988 figures) were similar to those for the world.[70] Like the world too, South Africa, with eleven major languages, had no one tongue written or spoken by a majority of its inhabitants. Like the world, it was a combination of a First World economy and a Third World one. Power, including military power, was distributed between whites and non-whites in a similar fashion to that in the world as a whole. Income ratios between whites and non-whites were also comparable to the world's. Rapid urbanization, which enlarged the proportion of the population, of all races, living in towns and cities from 25 per cent in 1900 to over 60 per cent in 1989, also followed the overall world pattern and led to similar consequences: the growth of huge, megapolitan slums and horrifying urban crime-rates. Again, like over a hundred other countries throughout the world, South Africa had attempted to solve the resulting problems by enlarging its state sector and adopting a 'command economy' attitude, and had thereby merely compounded them.

The flagging of the once vigorous South African economy as a result of apartheid-style Big Government, was, in fact, the compelling reason why F.W. de Klerk, who became leader of the ruling South African Nationalist Party on 2 February 1989, and President of the country on the following 6 September, introduced fundamental changes in the social, economic and political system. He began a dialogue with the black nationalists on 8 July 1989 when he visited the unofficial leader of the African National Congress, Nelson Mandela, in jail, where he had been held for twenty-six years after being convicted of sabotage. The release of Mandela, and of many other 'political' prisoners, the lifting of the state of emergency, the unbanning of the ANC and similar measures followed later in 1989–91. One result, however, was an increase in violence between blacks (mainly Xhosa) supporting the ANC and blacks (mainly Zulu) belonging to the Inkatha movement. De Klerk also acted on the social front. Some aspects of the apartheid legal structure, such as the ban on sexual relations between the races, had been abolished in the 1980s; others had become inoperative under the pressure of population movements and economic change. In February 1991 de Klerk announced fundamental legal changes which ended restrictions on the movement of non-whites, residence and the ownership of houses and land – the economic core of apartheid – leaving only the voting system as the last operative relic of racial discrimination. In the hope of negotiating some form of multi-racial power-sharing which fell short of a straight one-man-one-vote system, de Klerk called, and won overwhelmingly, a referendum in March 1992, by which the many sanctions, the sporting ones, had been lifted. Here again, the dilemma was mirrored in the world as a whole. A world government elected by universal adult suffrage would place the whites in a small, permanent majority, made progressively smaller by demographic trends; that was the prospect universal suffrage held for South African whites too.[71]

One reason why, during the 1980s, Third World countries which had unsuccessfully tried to operate collectivist economies began to turn towards reform and the market was the manifest and growing success of the enterprise states of East Asia. These states, of which Japan, Hong Kong (a British crown colony), Singapore (a former British crown colony, self-governing from 1959, independent from

1965), Taiwan and South Korea, were the most important, had all begun the post-war period with high birth-rates and low *per capita* incomes ($100 a year or below in every case except Japan). All rejected the collectivist solution, in industry and agriculture. All adopted the market system. Each illustrated the way in which rising *per capita* incomes tended to produce falls in the birth-rate, thus stimulating further wealth-creation. In 1960, Hong Kong, Singapore, Taiwan and South Korea had birth-rates ranging from 36 (Hong Kong) to 42.9 (South Korea) per 1,000. In all four territories, living standards rose faster in the 1960s than anywhere else in the world. By 1971, Hong Kong's birth-rate was below the 20-per-1,000 mark, Singapore's almost there, and both Taiwan and South Korea were below the 30-per-1,000 mark.[72] These trends accelerated in the 1980s. By the late 1980s, Hong Kong's *per capita* income, despite a huge influx of penniless immigrants from China, was believed to be not far below $10,000, Singapore's (1987) was $7,464, Taiwan's (1987) $5,075 and South Korea's (1988) $3,450. In short, these countries were rapidly ceasing to be Third World states and were becoming part of the First World. In fact during the 1970s and 1980s, the growth of the Pacific enterprise state was perhaps the most encouraging material aspect of human society.

The process started in Japan in the late 1940s. As in West Germany in 1948–9 and France in 1958, the foundation was an excellent constitution. As we have seen, Japan's pre-war constitution was a shambles and its whole system of law primitive and unstable. The Occupation, under which America had sole power, in effect vested in an autocrat, General MacArthur, proved a decisive blessing. He was able to play the role of enlightened despot, and impose on Japan a revolution from above, like the Meiji Restoration of the 1860s which launched the Japanese as a modern nation. The 1947 constitution, drawn up in MacArthur's headquarters, was not an inter-party compromise, representing the lowest common denominator of agreement, but a homogeneous concept, incorporating the best aspects of the British and US constitutions and (like de Gaulle's) steering a skilful median between executive and legislature and between central and devolved power.[73] Taken in conjunction with other Occupation laws creating free trade unions, a free press and devolved control of the police (the armed forces as such were abolished), the constitution, and the 'American era' which it epitomized, succeeded in destroying the mesmeric hold the state had hitherto exercised over the Japanese people. The American occupation of Japan was probably the greatest constructive achievement of American overseas policy in the whole post-war period, and it was carried through virtually single-handed.[74] And, as with Britain's creation of a model trade union movement for West Germany, it raised up a mighty competitor.

What the constitutional reforms essentially did was to persuade the Japanese that the state existed for its citizens, and not vice-versa. It laid the foundations of a new and healthy individualism by encouraging the emergence, as an alternative centre of loyalty to the state, of the family and of the many Japanese institutions which embody the family metaphor. As in post-war Germany and Italy, the family, both in its biological and its extended forms, provided the natural antidote to the totalitarian infection. This was assisted by a highly effective land reform, which gave freehold tenure to 4.7 million tenant farmers and raised the proportion of owner-farmed land to over 90 per cent. Local government reform completed the process of creating strong, democratic, property-owning local communities, as in Christian Democrat West Europe.[75] The independence of the judiciary and an American-style Supreme Court underwrote individual property rights and civil liberties at the expense of the state and the collective.[76] On these foundations was raised an exceptionally stable parliamentary structure, run by a liberal-conservative alliance (eventually called the Liberal Democratic Party), whose internal factions, modelled on extended families, provided flexibility and change, but whose external unity gave the country's economy a consistent free enterprise framework. The Liberal Democrats thus provided the same cohesion as the Christian Democrats in Germany and Italy, and the Gaullist-Independents in Fifth Republic France. The parallel went further. MacArthur's post-war purges made possible the emergence of an elderly political genius who, like Adenauer, de Gasperi and de Gaulle, had been in opposition under the pre-war regime. Yoshida Shigeru was a former diplomat and thus from the background closest to Anglo-Saxon traditions of democracy and the rule of law. He was sixty-seven when he became Prime Minister in 1946 and held the job with brilliant tenacity for nearly nine years, as one observer put it 'like a veteran *bonsai* [plum tree], of some antiquity, on whose gnarled branches white blossoms flower year by year'. [77] He carried the new system through from adolescence to maturity, and by the time he retired in 1954 the pattern of stability was set not only for the 1950s but for the next quarter-century and beyond.

As a result, Japan had completed its post-war reconstruction by 1953, only four years after Germany, and then embarked on a twenty-year period of growth which averaged 9.7 per cent annually. This was nearly twice the rate of any other major industrial nation in the post-war period. The only true comparison is with the spectacular growth of the American economy in the forty years up to 1929.[78] The 'miracle' was based on the car, with the growth of passenger car production in the intense period 1966–72 at the astonishing rate of nearly 29 per cent a year, with Japanese car ownership rising by a third annually.[79] Between the end of the 1950s and the end of the 1970s, Japanese car production increased one hundred times, reaching over 10 million in 1979, roughly the American total, and overtaking it decisively in the early 1980s. Of this production about half was exported. From cars the Japanese spread over virtually the whole range of consumer goods. In 1979 they became the world's leading watch producer, with 60 million (50 million for Switzerland). They ousted America as the leading producer of radios in the 1960s, and of television sets in the 1970s, the same decade they took the lead from Germany in camera production. During the 1970s, Japan's *per capita* industrial production equalled America's and in certain important respects she became the world's leading industrial power. In 1978 she had an industrial trade surplus of $76 billion (against a US industrial trade deficit of $5 billion). By the end of the decade she had a steel capacity as big as America's and almost as big as the entire EEC. In the 1980s, in many fields, Japan overtook the United States and European producers in quality too, particularly in high-technology areas such as jets, machine-tools, robots, semi-conductors, calculators and copiers, computers and telecommunications, advanced energy-systems, including nuclear power, and rocketry. By 1980 her investment was twice America's *per capita*, and in some years during the 1980s exceeded it in absolute terms.[80]

Japan's rate of economic growth slowed a little in the 1980s but it continued to make spectacular advances in the financial sector. It weathered the stock market crash of October 1987 with remarkable aplomb and within a year had pushed the United States into second place as the world's largest banking nation. Right through the decade it maintained the largest trading surplus. It bought heavily into the United States economy, by taking up huge quantities of American Treasury bonds and making it possible for the United States to run a large and growing budget deficit throughout the period, and by investing in, or taking over, American businesses, thus enabling the US to run a large and continuing deficit on visible trade. It also invested heavily in such territories as Australia, source of many of its raw materials, to the point where this former British political colony was in danger of becoming a Japanese economic colony. It also invested heavily in Britain, as a means of sliding under the European Community's tariff barriers. This took a variety of forms. On 12 November 1981, for instance, one of Japan's leading car-makers, Honda, signed an agreement with British Leyland, last of the major independent British car firms, to develop a joint product for the 1990s, involving the mass production of matching components in both countries. On 8 September 1986, to give a second example, another major Japanese manufacturer, Nissan, opened a new £430 million car plant near Sunderland, in northern England, with a production capacity of 100,000 a year. By the early 1990s, the Japanese possessed not only by far the world's biggest investment portfolio but one, in relative size and influence, which compared with Britain's in the period up to 1914. Japan's success, and the inability of Western producers to penetrate far into Japan's own market, aroused accusations of unfair trading practices, particularly in the United States Congress and from the European Community. In some cases Japan accepted voluntary quotas on its manufacturing exports, and it showed its nervousness over the issue in March 1991 when, in a self-denying ordinance, it forbade Japanese contractors to bid for work in restoring Kuwait, where the United States and Britain, having done the lion's share in liberating the country, were expecting the lion's share of the post-war reconstruction business. By this stage Japan had easily overtaken the Soviet Union as the world's second largest economy, and it continued to invest heavily in high technology, new equipment and, not least, in education and training. By the late 1980s, 93 per cent of Japanese children were attending secondary school up to the age of eighteen, and well over a third were going on to higher education, up to the age of twenty-one or twenty-two, at one or other of Japan's 1,000-plus universities and colleges, the vast majority of which were privately maintained.

There was nothing miraculous about this miracle. It was a straightforward case of Adam Smith economics, with no more than a touch of Keynesianism. A high percentage of fixed capital formation, very little of it in non-productive investment. Moderate taxation. Low defence and government spending. A very high rate of personal saving, efficiently channelled into industry through the banking system. Shrewd import of foreign technology under licence. Very fast replacement rate of existing plant, made possible by remarkable wage restraint, with productivity running well ahead of wages. Labour was plentiful because of contraction in the agricultural sector, and exceptionally well-educated and skilled because Japan (and the Asian market states generally) geared the educational expansion noted already closely to industrial needs and not to social science ideologies. Indeed, the East Asian market states were the only ones to gain economically from the revolution in higher education of the 1960s, which in Europe and North America proved such a handicap. It is true that Japan benefited substantially from the windfalls of first the Korean then the Vietnam wars. But all the other factors were of her own making. The Japanese government provided a degree of external protection and export support. But its chief contribution was to erect a framework of intense internal competition, on an Adam Smith model, and a climate of benevolence towards business.[81]

What was unique to Japan, and perhaps her most creative contribution to the modern world, was the way in which business used the principle of anthropomorphism and the new anti-collective stress on the family, already mentioned, to humanize the industrial process and so reduce the destructive impact of class warfare. Trade unions were by no means inactive in Japan: there were, in fact, 34,000 of them by 1949.[82] Nor were they unsuccessful. Plant bargaining and productivity improvements, with the pressure coming from fellow-workers rather than management, meant that Japanese wage-rates rose faster in real terms than those of any other major industrial country during the 1970s and 1980s, with the highest degree of job security and the lowest unemployment, an average of 2.6 per cent in the late 1980s. Equally important, by the 1970s Japan had achieved greater equality of income distribution than any other industrial economy and, with the possible exception of the Scandinavian economies, had moved further than other market economies to eliminate absolute poverty.[83] But most Japanese firms supplemented the efforts of unions by enveloping the worker in a familial embrace which included housing, meals, medical care, ethical guidance, sport and holidays. The anthropomorphism extended to the product and even the customers. At the Kubota Iron and Machinery Works, for instance, the workers were taught to see their machines as mothers and fathers, engendering sons and daughters – the company's finished products – which were then 'married' to customers, using salesmen as marriage-brokers. Kubota dealers then provided 'postnatal aftercare', to the satisfaction of both 'bride' and 'bridegroom'. In the company's chief product, a mechanical tiller, the casing of the machine was treated as the body, the engine as the heart. Visitors to the factory were 'family relations', 'friends of the family'. The workers ran highly critical 'self-improvement committees' to promote productivity and sales, composed and calligraphed hortatory banners and were supplied with masses of production and investment figures on which to brood. They contributed enthusiastic poetry to the works magazine.[84] The kind of collectivized production propaganda which failed so signally in Soviet Russia, and even in China where it was applied far more skilfully, worked in the non-totalitarian context of Japan, where it was given a human scale, a voluntary impulse and a familial imagery and, not least, was seen to produce immediate and substantial gains in personal consumption.

The huge and sustained expansion of the Japanese economy was decisive in creating a dynamic market environment for the entire Pacific area. It acted both by direct stimulus and by example. The most striking example was South Korea. A World Bank team reported in 1977: 'The sustained high rate of expansion in incomes over fifteen years has transformed Korea from one of the poorest developing countries, with heavy dependence on agriculture and weak balance of payments, to a semi-industrialized middle-income nation with an increasingly strong external payments position.[85] Taiwan's progress followed the same course. In 1949, when the now totally discredited KMT regime took over, the economy was substantially pre-industrial. The transformation, like Japan's, began with a highly successful land reform, followed by a rapid rise in farmers' incomes, creating a local market for new factories. Over 90 per cent of agricultural land passed into the hands of the farmers who tilled it. No-strike laws were agreed and enforced. Duty-free processing zones were created. At times in the 1970s and 1980s, exports rose to 90 per cent of GNP, the highest proportion in the world, and growth-rates occasionally hit the 12-per-cent mark. Thus, on top of a sound agricultural base, a complex industrial economy was created, revolving around shipbuilding, textiles, petrochemicals and electronic equipment.[86] Hong Kong's progress was, in some ways, even more impressive, since it had to absorb about 5 million refugees from mainland China, about five times the number of Palestinians the entire Arab world had failed to resettle. Here again, as in Taiwan and Japan, stability of government (provided by the Colonial Governor, advised by a local Legislative Council), and consistency of economic policy over forty years, provided the ideal hospitable environment for business, though in Hong Kong's case the future, during the early 1990s, became overshadowed by the approaching merger with the Chinese Communist Republic, set for 1997.

Singapore, after some instability in the decade after 1945, at last found a solid government framework in 1959 under Lee Kuan Yew's People's Action Party which began as a socialist movement but soon became a passionate and masterful instrument of the market. As Lee put it, after two decades of successful wealth-creation: 'The question was how to make a living . . . a matter of life and death for two million people . . . How this was to be achieved, by socialism or free enterprise, was a secondary matter. The answer turned out to be free enterprise, tempered with the socialist philosophy of equal opportunities for education, jobs, health and housing.'[87] In the 1980s, Lee was frequently accused in the Western media of authoritarianism, putting pressure on the courts and local newspapers, and bullying the (tiny) opposition. On the other hand, during his rule of over thirty years (he went into semi-retirement in 1991), he had some claim to be considered the most successful of all the post-war statesmen, in terms of the material benefits he conferred on his country and its people.

Singapore was notable for possessing no natural resources at all, other than its geographical position. Japan, Korea and Taiwan (but not Hong Kong) had some reasonably good agricultural land; otherwise none of these enterprise states began their ascent with any physical advantages, other than a potentially strong work-force. As one report put it: 'The success is almost entirely due to good policies and the ability of the people, scarcely at all to favourable circumstances or a good start.'[88] The way in which these rugged market economies flourished from the 1960s onwards encouraged better-endowed Pacific neighbours to switch to the free market for both agriculture and business. Thailand's growth accelerated rapidly after it acquired a stable pro-market government in 1958, and achieved economic 'takeoff' in the 1960s with growth rates at one time of 9 per cent annually. It was one of the few Third World countries that managed to sustain its agricultural export position, by raising productivity by 15 per cent a year and expanding acreages.[89] During the 1980s its *per capita* income had risen to $810 (1986), more than four times that of its once-richer but now long-socialist neighbour Burma, at $200 (1986). During the 1970s and 1980s Malaysia also did well, thanks partly to handsome natural resources but mainly to political stability and economic realism, pushing itself into the middle-income bracket with $1,850 *per capita* (1986). Indonesia, one of the world's best-endowed nations in natural resources, began to recover from a disastrous start under the Sukarno regime, and even the Philippines, bedevilled by Muslim-Catholic clashes, the pilfering of the monstrous Marcos regime and insurgency then and thereafter, made some progress, achieving a *per capita* income of $614 by 1986.

Hence during the quarter-century 1965–90, the Pacific, defying the tyranny of its vast distances, became the prime trade development area of the world, thanks to market economics. Former Pacific colonies like Fiji and New Caledonia leapt into the over–$1,000-a-year *per capita* income bracket. The tiny island of Nauru, rich in phosphates, was not only the world's smallest republic, with a population of about 8,000, but became 'acre for acre and body for body' one of the world's wealthiest nations, with average incomes of $9,091 (1985).[90] There was a rebirth of the free-market spirit on the eastern fringe of the Pacific. The most interesting case was Chile. In the mid-1960s, Christian Democrat Chile, under President Eduardo Frei, was regarded by the United States as the best hope, along with Romulo Betancourt's Venezuela, for Kennedy's Alliance for Progress. But Chile had chronic inflation: about 20 per cent a year in the late 1950s, 26.6 per cent in 1968, 32.5 per cent in 1970. Virtually the sole cause was government overspending and money-printing. In the 1970 elections, the reforming socialist Salvador Allende, at his fourth attempt, at last won the presidency because of a split in the anti-socialist vote, which nevertheless got 62 per cent combined against Allende's 36.2. The new president had a mandate for nothing, and, on Thomas Jefferson's principle that great innovations should not rest on narrow majorities, he should have concentrated on good housekeeping.

But Allende was a weak man with a divided, part-revolutionary following, which quickly slipped from his control. While he embarked on a programme of wholesale nationalization, which isolated Chile from the world trading community, the militants of his Left wing were not prepared to accept any of the restraints of constitutionalism. They launched 'People's Power', consisting of Peasant Councils which seized farms in the countryside and Workers' Assemblies which occupied factories.[91] The strategy was Leninist – 'The task of the moment,' said the Socialist Party, 'is to destroy parliament' – but the real parallel was with Spain in 1936, where the divisions on the Left and the drift to violence produced Civil War. Allende was caught in a nutcracker with his revolutionaries forming one arm and the other constituted by an increasingly outraged middle class, with the army, originally reluctant to intervene, gradually politicized by the collapse of order.

At the time Allende took over, in January 1971, inflation had actually fallen to about 23 per cent. Within months it was hyper-inflation. In 1972 it was 163 per cent. In the summer of 1973 it reached 190 per cent, by far the highest in the world.[92] This was before the quadrupling of oil prices: the Allende inflation was entirely his own doing. In November 1971 Chile declared a unilateral moratorium on its foreign debts (i.e., went bankrupt). The banks cut off credit; capital fled; with the farms in chaos, producing little, the factories occupied, producing less, exports vanished, imports soared, then vanished too as the money ran out. The shops emptied. The middle class started to strike. The workers, finding their wages cut in real terms, struck too. The official price structure became irrational and then irrelevant as the black market took over. The Left began to smuggle in arms in July 1971 and began serious political violence in May the next year. They had in fact more weapons (30,000) than the army, which numbered only 26,000 men plus 25,000 armed police.[93] Allende oscillated between ordering the police to fight the Far Left and accusing the army of plotting a coup. But he also countenanced a plan to arm Leftist guerrillas and on 4 September 1973 permitted a demonstration by 750,000 on the anniversary of the elections. A week later his own appointment, General Augusto Pinochet, led a united *coup* by all three armed forces. Chile had hitherto had an exceptionally good record, by Latin American standards, for constitutionalism and stability. The coup was by no means bloodless. Allende was killed or committed suicide, and the official body-count at the Santiago morgue was 2,796.[94] Most of the resistance came from non-Chilean political refugees, of whom there were 13,000 in Santiago at the time. The failure of the workers occupying factories, or the peasants on the seized farms, or even of the armed 'revolutionary bands' to fight seriously, suggests that the Far Left commanded little enthusiasm.

The opposition to Pinochet, though noisy, came chiefly from abroad, at least at the beginning of his rule. It was cleverly orchestrated from Moscow, though in fact Soviet Russia had flatly refused to bail Allende out with credits: he was more use to them dead than alive.[95] Though foreign criticism concentrated on the repressive aspect of Pinochet's military regime, the more important one was the decision to reverse the growth of the public sector, which Allende had merely accelerated, and open the economy to market forces, on the lines of the other Pacific economies. It was notable that virtually all the Pacific enterprise states, except Japan, had been accused at one time or another of running repressive regimes. But the degree to which the state was representative and elected was only one issue; equally important was the extent of national life it controlled. That was why, living as he did in a *laissez-faire*, minimalist state, Dr Samuel Johnson was able to declare with conviction: 'I would not give half a guinea to live under one form of government rather than another. It is of no moment in the happiness of an individual.'[96] Market economics by definition involved a withdrawal by the state from a huge area of decision-making, which was left to the individual. Economic and political liberty were inseparably linked. Freedom of the market inevitably led to erosion of political restraints: that was the lesson of Thailand, Taiwan and South Korea.

The lesson applied equally to Chile. The disaster of 1973 produced complete political and economic breakdown. The reconstruction of the economy had to begin against a background of world recession. The merit of the regime was that it was able to reverse a course of government-led inflation that had persisted for many decades and become part of the structure of the Chilean economy.[97] This was painful and unpopular and led initially to a falling GNP and high unemployment. But it allowed the economy to be refloated on a market basis with the help of IMF loans. During the later 1970s, with inflation at last under control, growth was resumed and by the beginning of 1980 the World Bank was able to report: 'Under extra-ordinarily unfavourable circumstances, the Chilean authorities have engineered an economic turnaround without precedent in the history of Chile.'[98] The economic improvement explained why, on 11 September 1980, a referendum showed 69.14 per cent of those Chileans who voted favouring an eight-year extension of Pinochet's term. But as the 1980s progressed, economic freedom led to ever-increasing demands for political freedom. Pinochet was unwilling to grant it. In June 1983, there was nationwide rioting against the regime; two months later the government admitted that seventeen people had been killed in demonstrations. The victims of Pinochet's political police, the Dina, were far more numerous. An official report, commissioned after democracy was restored, calculated that during the sixteen years of Pinochet's rule, 1973–89, 1,068 people had been killed by the Dina or people working for them; a further 957 had 'disappeared'.[99] But fear of the Dina did not deter Chileans from following the logic of a free economy and pressing for a return to full voting rights. Pinochet agreed to hold another referendum on his presidency, and on 14 December 1989 the opposition candidate, Patricio Aylwin, won the presidential election with 52.4 per cent of the votes, bringing the dictatorship to an end, though Pinochet himself remained commander of the army. Aylwin not only commissioned the report into the regime's excesses, he also set up a permanent foundation in March 1991 to investigate the fate of its victims case by case. But he was careful to continue, on the whole, the regime's well-tried economic policies.

The success of the free enterprise economies of the Pacific undoubtedly helped to rekindle belief in the market system both in North America and in Europe. The 1970s, as we have seen, were a discouraging decade for capitalism. It became fashionable among the intelligentsia, including many economists, to speak of 'zero growth', of 'late capitalism' or even of 'post-capitalism', as though the system that had created, for the first time in history, what even its opponents dubbed the Affluent Society was now moribund. The most widely approved form of government in the West was the so-called 'mixed society', with the state sector absorbing between 40 and 60 per cent of the GNP, administering welfare services on a growing scale, and reserving the actual wealth-creating role to the private sector operating about half the economy. But the weaknesses of this Euro-American formula were reflected in the low growth-rates, the phenomenon known as 'stagflation' which marked most of their economies as the decade progressed, and the evidence of widespread popular dissatisfaction reflected in a growing number of strikes. Towards the end of the decade, as high-quality, low-priced Japanese (and South Korean and Taiwanese) goods began increasingly to penetrate Western markets, there was a growing demand for changes which would bring about Japanese-style efficiency.

The watershed year was 1979, and the battlefield was Britain. After an unprecedented series of strikes, especially in the public sector, dubbed by the media 'the winter of discontent', Margaret Thatcher, the first woman to become leader of a British political party (in 1975), became Britain's first woman Prime Minister on 4 May 1979, having led the Conservatives to a 43-seat electoral victory. Mrs Thatcher, soon dubbed by the Brezhnev regime 'the Iron Lady' (a title she relished), called herself a 'conviction' politician, as opposed to a consensus one. She implicitly repudiated much of Conservative post-war policy, and especially its tacit agreement with the Labour Party that whole areas of British public life, including the welfare state and the nationalized sector, were sacrosanct. Her first task was to curb the legal power of the trade unions which, as we have seen, had been growing steadily since 1945. A previous attempt at reform by the Conservative government in 1971, the comprehensive and ultra-complex Industrial Relations Act, had proved unworkable and had been promptly scrapped by the incoming Labour Cabinet in 1974. Mrs Thatcher's government, having learned the lesson, set about the problem on a step-by-step basis, enacting in all five separate acts, over the space of three parliaments, which progressively ended a whole series of special union legal privileges, made many strikes and forms of picketing unlawful, and subjected unions that broke the law to severe financial penalties. Mrs Thatcher also made it clear that the police, in dealing with 'mass', 'flying' and 'secondary' pickets, which had made it virtually impossible in the 1970s for employers to resist strike demands and so inflicted grievous damage on both the private and public sector, would be fully backed by her government.

The new policy was soon put to the test. The trade unions had effectively destroyed the governments of Harold Wilson in 1968–70, Edward Heath in 1974 and James Callaghan in 1979. The National Union of Mineworkers, following aggressive tactics created by Arthur Scargill, leader of the Yorkshire miners, who became president of the NUM in 1981, had played a major role in these victories, which threatened to make syndicalism, rather than parliamentary democracy, the ruling force in Britain, at least in a negative sense. The British coal industry had been taken into public ownership in 1946 precisely to create industrial peace in the mines. But the NUM had always treated the National Coal Board as if it were as grasping and antisocial as the worst private pit-owner, thus defeating the central object of nationalization. On 6 March 1984, the NCB, which was already losing over £100 million a year, announced the closure of twenty uneconomic pits. Scargill had twice failed to bring about a general miners' strike, which under NUM rules required a 55 per cent majority in a national pit-head ballot. On this occasion, Scargill evaded the rule-book procedures. As his Vice-President Mick McGahey put it: 'We shall not be constitutionalized out of a strike. Area by area will decide, and there will be a domino effect.'[100] Hence the decision to strike was taken not by the union's members but by the more militant delegates; and the strike having begun on 10 March, a special delegate conference on 20 April rejected demands for a national ballot by 69–54. The fact that the strike was called undemocratically and unconstitutionally was a strong point in the government's favour in resisting it. Harold Macmillan had frequently observed: 'There are three institutions in Britain so powerful that no government is wise to take them on: the Brigade of Guards, the Roman Catholic Church, and the National Union of Mineworkers.' Margaret Thatcher was encouraged in defying this dictum by the attitude of the Nottinghamshire miners, who resented Scargill's tactics, voted in a ballot four-to-one against a strike, kept their pits open, despite much intimidation, and eventually formed a separate union, thus splitting the NUM irretrievably; on 7 August 1985 they won a High Court action which, four months later, enabled the new Union of Democratic Miners to achieve legal status as a trade union.

The Scargill strike of 1984–5 merits examination in some detail because it was, in effect, an attempt to destroy a democratically-elected government, and its failure was an epochal event in British industrial history. It was beaten by a combination of the courts, enacting the new reforms governing union activities, and by effective coordination between the various locally-commanded police forces of Britain. By mid-April 1984 Scargill's men had shut down 131 out of 174 pits and they planned to 'picket out' the rest, using the fear-inspiring methods they had employed so successfully in the 1970s. This time, however, the police were prepared to stop them, with the backing of the law. On 22 October the police won a High Court ruling that they had the right to stop buses carrying militant miners to areas of disturbance with the object of committing a breach of the peace. By road control, and by mass policing at functioning pit-heads, the police managed to make it possible for miners wishing to work to do so, though some were victimized at home. Thus Scargill's primary objective of shutting all pits failed. The strike was extremely costly: it added £2,750 million to government expenditure, £1,850 million to the NCB's losses, cost British Steel £300 million, British Rail £250 million and the electricity supply industry £2,200 million.[101] It was also extremely violent, and cost five lives; on 16 May 1985 two South Wales miners were found guilty of murdering a taxi-driver taking non-striking miners to work, though the conviction was reduced to manslaughter on appeal. Between March and end-November 1984, for example, 7,100 striking miners were charged with various offences, and a total of 3,483 cases were eventually heard, with 2,740 convictions; the cost of policing alone rose to £300 million.

But with the government determined on no surrender, the futility of the strike became gradually apparent. Ignoring the lessons of the 1920s, Scargill had struck at the wrong time of year, the spring. The NCB and its consumers had long seen the crisis coming, and had built up huge stocks. As a result, there was no need for power-cuts throughout the winter of 1984–5, and on 8 January 1985 the highest peak demand for electricity ever recorded in Britain was met without difficulty. Scargill's strike funds were augmented by huge subsidies provided by Gadafy's Libyan government, a fact denied by the NUM at the time but subsequently established, beyond doubt, by the *Daily Mirror* in 1990. Despite this, miners began to drift back, and by the end of February 1985, over half the 170,000 employees on the NCB's books were back at work. On 5 March a national miners' delegate conference assented to what was, in effect, unconditional surrender. Court fines had already cost the NUM £1.4 million, and its funds were sequestrated. Some 700 strikers were sacked for 'gross industrial misconduct', and 30,000 were made redundant, 10,000 more than the pre-strike planned figure. Indeed, with the creation of the breakaway UDM, the NUM itself, once the largest union in Europe, soon shrank to a mere 80,000 members, and, from being one of the richest in Britain, became among the poorest.

It was perhaps the most unsuccessful major strike in British history, though by one of the fundamental axioms of British trade unionism – security of tenure for officials – Scargill remained in charge, even if echoes of the dispute rumbled on. In 1990 he was accused of using Libyan-supplied funds to facilitate the purchase of a new home, grand by miners' standards, and it was said, 'Scargill started out with a big union and a small house, and ended with a big house and a small union.' Mrs Thatcher rightly regarded the defeat of the NUM as the most important reversal for militant trade unionism since the General Strike of 1926, rejoicing (6 April 1985), that she had 'seen off' what she called 'the enemy within'. Two days later she added: 'Despite cruel intimidation, the working miners insisted on their right to continue to work, and they found they had an employer and a government prepared to stand up for them. I hope and believe the lesson will not be lost on others.'[102]

Nor was it. Perhaps the most strongly entrenched group of workers in British industry were the printers, consisting chiefly of the National Graphical Association (compositors) and the Society of Graphic and Allied Trades '82, or SOGAT '82, comprising other manual workers in the industry. In the London area in particular they operated a rigid closed (or union) shop system, underwritten by tight conditions of entry and financed by some of the highest wages in the country. Overmanning and restrictive practices, known in the trade as 'old Spanish customs', were uniquely costly, even by the standards of British industry. Moreover, throughout the 1970s and into the 1980s, work stoppages, involving the non-appearance of national newspapers, were becoming more frequent, and there was a still more disturbing tendency for compositors to censor copy, news stories as well as comment, with which they did not agree. In 1983 the *Financial Times* was shut down by a strike from 1 June to 8 August, and all national newspapers from 25–27 November (two of them did not appear till 30 November).

Next month, however, the print unions suffered their first big defeat under the new union legislation when the NGA was fined (9 December 1983) the massive sum of £525,000 for contempt in refusing to obey a court order (plus £150,000 for earlier contempts). They had been trying to stop the appearance of a new daily, *Today*, founded by the Asian-born Eddy Shah, and manned and operated outside the traditional conventions of the industry. *Today* thus continued to appear and the point was not lost on Rupert Murdoch, biggest and most enterprising of the British newspaper proprietors and publisher of the *Times*, the *Sunday Times*, the *News of the World* and the *Sun*, with a combined circulation of about 11 million copies. Having secretly constructed (1984–6) a high-technology printing plant at Wapping in East London, which embodied all the latest developments in electronic setting and make-up, he responded to a shutdown by the NGA and SOGAT in the traditional Fleet Street area, where his papers were printed, by sacking the entire workforce on 24 January 1986 and transferring his papers to Wapping. There, he had already made arrangements with the independent-minded Electrical, Electronic, Telecommunication and Plumbing Union for its members to operate the new machinery. Once again, the unions tried to use force, and Wapping was repeatedly the scene of pitched battles. But Murdoch had had the plant constructed with a siege in mind and not for nothing did it become known as Fortress Wapping. Again, a combination of court injunctions, using the new legislation, and efficient policing ensured that force was defeated. The Wapping victory and the ensuing collapse of the power of the print unions ended unofficial censorship of the press in Britain, revitalized an ailing industry, made national newspapers profitable again, and so enabled new ones, such as the *Independent* (1986), to be successfully created. But, together with the defeat of the miners' strike, it also effectively ended the union threat to the British constitutional and political system. It was the prelude to a new era of peace in British industry, so that in the years 1987–90 the number of working days lost through strikes fell to their lowest level for more than half a century, and the 'English disease' appeared cured.

The decline of union restrictive practices and of overmanning in many sectors produced a rise in productivity in Britain which, in several years during the decade, was the highest in Europe; and for much of the 1980s the British economy expanded rapidly: in mid-1988, for instance, it was still growing at 4 per cent after seven years of continuous expansion, a record unique in the post-war period.[103] But what particularly struck foreigners about the performance of the Thatcher government was its success in reducing the state sector, by the process known as 'privatization'. This had two aspects. The first was the transfer of nationalized industries, such as Cable & Wireless, British Steel, British Airways, British Telecommunications, British Gas, and the water and the electricity supply and distribution industry, into private ownership and management. Many of these nationalized bodies were incurring huge losses and were a heavy burden on the taxpayer. Privatization rapidly transformed the loss-makers into profitable companies. British Steel, for instance, had incurred the largest loss in corporate history, some £500 million, the year before it was privatized; by the end of the 1980s it had the highest productivity rates in the European steel industry and was the most profitable steel company in the world. The turnaround at British Airways was scarcely less spectacular. The second aspect was the way in which the privatization was managed by 'floating' the companies through the Stock Exchange in ways which encouraged small savers to buy into them. The British Telecom flotation, for example, was the largest public share offer in history. The net effect was that, during the 1980s, the number of individual shareholders in Britain rose from 2.5 million to nearly 10 million, giving some substance to the notion, which came into fashion as the 1980s advanced, of 'democratic capitalism'. The rapid reduction of losses in the public sector, plus the proceeds of these sales, enabled the government not merely to reduce direct taxation, the standard rate falling from 37½ to 25 per cent and top rates from 94 and 87 per cent to 40 per cent, but to run big budget surpluses and repay over one-fifth of the entire national debt. Privatization was one of the great success stories of the 1980s and found many imitators abroad, especially in Europe but also in Latin America, Australasia, Africa and Asia. Even Japan, which was teaching the West so much, followed Britain's example and privatized its rail network on 1 April 1987.

By such means, Mrs Thatcher made herself one of the most consistently successful politicians of her age. On 19 June 1983 she got her party re-elected with a huge overall majority of 144 seats over all other parties, and she repeated her landslide success on 12 June 1987, when the Conservatives won 375 against 229 for the Labour opposition. No British prime minister had ever won three general elections in a row since the Great Reform Bill of 1832. When Mrs Thatcher was finally forced out of office by her own party on 20 November 1990 she had been head of the government for a longer continuous period, eleven and a half years, than any of her predecessors since the Earl of Liverpool (Prime Minister 1812–27). Mrs Thatcher's last year in office, however, coincided with the end of a trade cycle, and in 1991–2 Britain was in deep recession. Moreover, it was notable that Mrs Thatcher aroused much hostility as well as enthusiastic support, and in the three elections she won her party never secured as much as 50 per cent of the votes cast. In many ways, she resembled de Gaulle: like him, she was good at saying no, and meaning it; like him, she restored her nation's self-confidence and pride; she ruled with great authority for almost exactly the same span; and, like de Gaulle, she fell attempting a fundamental reform of local government, in her case seeking to replace the outmoded and inequitable way in which it was financed.

Mrs Thatcher, and 'Thatcherism', had a global influence during the 1980s which went well beyond the new fashion for privatization and reducing the state sector. The 1980s was a radical conservative decade, and even in states where socialist or Labour governments were elected, the drift away from Marxism, collectivism and all the traditional 'isms' of the Left was marked. The process was particularly notable in France. The election of the socialist François Mitterrand as President in 1981, after twenty-three years of Gaullism and its successors, introduced a brief period of socialist egalitarianism and anti-business policies, which led in rapid succession to three devaluations of the franc; thereafter, the French Socialist Party moved sharply to the Right and to free-market policies; and in the later 1980s and early 1990s, alternations in power between socialist and Conservative prime ministers appeared to make little difference, in economic policy, defence or foreign affairs. The German Social Democrats had renounced Marxism, or anything approaching it, a generation before. In Portugal, Dr Mário Soares, elected premier for the first time in 1976 and President in 1987, under the new and liberal 1982 constitution, gradually steered Portuguese socialism into the free-market camp during the 1980s. There was a similar movement in Spain, where the Socialist Party, under its moderate leader Felipe Gonzalez, far from exploiting its landslide victory of 1982, reinforced the enterprise culture which had transformed the Spanish economy during the years 1950–75. In Australia Bob Hawke's Labour Party, which returned to power in March 1983 and was later re-elected three times, moved consistently towards the Right; indeed in March 1991, Hawke himself made a ringing declaration, warning the country that it could no longer afford to impose irksome restraints on business, for socialist, environmental or any other reasons. In New Zealand, the Labour leader David Lange, who became Prime Minister in 1984, took his party and government in the same direction, though evidently not fast enough for some of his colleagues, who in effect forced his resignation in August 1989, as a result of a right-wing caucus *putsch*. In Britain, following the Labour Party's third successive electoral defeat in 1987, its leader, Neil Kinnock, began the painful process of dropping traditional Labour policies, and by 1990–1 had made Labour, at least in theory, electable again.

In Labour or democratic socialist parties across the world, the term 'social market' came into fashion, implying acceptance of market forces subject to certain essential restraints to protect the poor and the underprivileged. But the phase was used on the Right too. 'I like the expression,' declared Norman Lamont in March 1991, immediately after delivering his first budget as Chancellor of the Exchequer in the government John Major formed to replace Mrs Thatcher's.[104] Another political *cliché* that came into fashion in the early 1990s, reflecting the Left's acceptance of the market, was 'the enabling state', as opposed to Big Government: the state was there, the argument went, not to do things itself, so much as to make it possible for people to do things on their own behalf. Conservatives were equally content to use this formulation of government's role. To some extent, then, there was a convergence of views in the world's democracies during the 1980s and early 1990s, but it was a convergence on the terms of the Right. Indeed, the 'ratchet effect', a phrase coined by the British Conservative ideologue Sir Keith (later Lord) Joseph in the 1970s, whereby policies initiated by left-wing governments were endorsed by their right-wing successors, thus replacing the swing of the pendulum by a collectivist ratchet, was now reversed: it was the radicals of the Right who were now moving societies permanently in the direction of economic liberalism.

The same process was at work in the North American continent, though here it was affected by geographical factors too. Mexico, like Chile, was affected by the new Pacific enterprise culture, though like Chile it had earlier suffered from a grandiose experiment in state-directed collectivism. The economy grew very fast 1940–70, and in the 1970s President Luís Echeverria sought to make Mexico the leader of the Third World as a model Big Government state. He increased the state's share of the economy by 50 per cent and the number of state-owned corporations from eighty-six to 740. The predictable result was hyper-inflation and a balance-of-payments crisis. José Lopez Portillo came to power in 1976 and wrenched Mexico back towards the market.[105] He told the IMF that he feared the 'South Americanization' of Mexico life: coups and dictatorships of Left or Right.[106] He was helped by the major oil discoveries of 1977, which suggested Mexico might eventually be a producer in the same class as Kuwait or even Saudi Arabia. On the other hand the structure of Mexico, essentially a one-party state run by an élite through the Institutional Revolutionary Party (PRI), made cutting state employment (and patronage) difficult.[107] By the early 1980s, Mexico's foreign debts exceeded even Brazil's. In the summer of 1982 it was unable to meet its interest payments and nationalized the banks. But the economy moved back in a liberal direction during the years 1985–90, making possible a historic trade agreement with the United States.

The Mexican economy, indeed, was merging into the North-East Pacific economy formed by the Western United States, West Canada and Alaska. Some 70 per cent of Mexican exports went to America in the 1970s and 1980s; 60 per cent of its imports were American. There were perhaps as many as 10 million illegal Mexican immigrants in the US; one in seven families in California, and one in three in New Mexico, were Hispanic. It was true that Mexico's was also a Caribbean economy. So was America's, especially since the Hispanization of the economy of Florida, which grew rapidly in the quarter-century, 1965–90, tilted it in a Latin-American direction. But from the 1970s both the Mexican and the American economies felt the pull of the Pacific, increasingly a free-market pull.

The shift of America's centre of gravity, both demographic and economic, from the North-East to the South-West was one of the most important changes of modern times. In the 1940s, the geographer E.L.Ullman located the 'core area' of the US economy in the North-East. Though only 8 per cent of the total land area, it had 43 per cent of the population and 68 per cent of manufacturing employment.[108] The pattern remained stable for most of the 1950s. The geographer H.S.Perloff, writing in 1960, saw what he called 'the manufacturing belt' as 'still the very heart of the national economy.'[109] But even while he was writing the pattern was changing. In 1940–60 the North still gained population (2 million) but this was entirely accounted for by low-income, largely unskilled blacks from the South. It was already suffering a net loss of whites; this soon became an absolute loss. The change came in the 1960s and became pronounced in the 1970s. In the years 1970–7, the North-East lost 2.4 million by migration; the South-West gained 3.4 million, most of them skilled whites. As the shift was essentially from the frost-belt to the sun-belt, it was reinforced by the rise in energy prices, as the 1980 census showed. Regional variations in income, once heavily in favour of the old 'core area', converged, then moved in favour of the South-West. Investment followed population. The 'core area's' share of manufacturing employment fell from 66 per cent in 1950 to 50 per cent in 1977. The South-West's rose from 20 to 30 per cent.[110]

The demographic shift brought changes in political power and philosophy. At the election of Kennedy in 1960, the frost-belt had 286 electoral college votes to the sun-belt's 245. By 1980 the sun-belt led by four and Census Bureau projections showed that for the 1984 election the sun-belt would have a lead of twenty-six.[111] The shift marked the end of the old Roosevelt interventionist coalition, dominant for two generations, and the emergence of a South-West coalition wedded to the free market.

Richard Nixon's landslide victory of November 1972 was a foretaste of the political consequences of this shift, but that was overshadowed by Watergate and its aftermath. On 4 November 1980, however, the trend became unmistakable when Ronald Reagan, a successful two-term Governor of California – and from one of California's most powerful interest-groups, the movie industry – trounced Jimmy Carter, the first elected sitting president to be defeated since Herbert Hoover in 1932. Reagan won by a huge popular margin, taking 43.9 million votes to Carter's 35.4 million. On 6 November 1984 he repeated his success by an even bigger margin, taking 59 per cent of the popular vote, with majorities in every major bloc of voters except blacks, Jews and trade unionists. He beat his Democratic opponent, Walter Mondale, in all but one of the fifty states. It was no coincidence that the 1980s, when California, already the richest, became the most populous state in the USA with the most electoral college votes, was in many ways the Californian Decade.

But Reagan's dominance during the 1980s was by no means mainly due to changing demographics. Better than any other politician except Margaret Thatcher herself, he caught the spirit of the age. He was undoubtedly inspired by her victory and example – she was his John the Baptist or, to put it another way, he was her aptest pupil – and for eight years, with one exception, they formed a mutual admiration society of two. But most of his few, simple and popular ideas had entered his head long before. 'By 1960,' he wrote, 'I realized the real enemy wasn't big business, it was big government.'[112] Twenty years later, he was a man whose time had come. Oddly enough, he did not succeed substantially in reducing the size of government. In this respect he was the victim of a growing dichotomy in American politics: a tendency to elect Republican presidents and Democratic congresses. His party controlled the Senate for a time but never the House of Representatives. There, indeed, the Democratic grip tightened during the 1980s. As the cost of electioneering rose, the chances of displacing a sitting congressman declined, until by the end of the decade the turnover was less than 10 per cent; and Congressional tenure depended to a growing extent on satisfying groups of interests through federal spending. Hence it was beyond the power of Reagan, or indeed his Republican successor George Bush, to cut federal domestic spending. What Reagan could and did do however was cut taxes. The result was the steady growth of the budget deficit. In the first six years after the initial tax cuts came into effect in late 1981, the resulting stimulation of the economy actually increased tax revenues by $375 billion. But during the same period Congress increased domestic spending by $450 billion.[113] The budget deficit was accompanied by a growing trade imbalance which during the four years of Reagan's second term reached the cumulative total of $541,243 million. The budget deficit began to fall in 1988 but remained large and that year total government debt passed the $2,000,000-million mark. [114] The sale of government bonds and private business to finance these two deficits meant that foreign holders and investors, with Japan in the lead but Britain not far behind in the investment field, were securing a significant grip on the American economy, or so many Americans feared.

On the other hand, Reagan's policies, or Reaganomics as they were called by friends and enemies alike, produced a dynamism America had not known since the Eisenhower years. Over six years, 1982–87, GNP (adjusted for inflation) rose by 27 per cent, manufacturing by 33 per cent, median incomes by 12 per cent (against a decline of 10.5 per cent during the 1970s).[115] An estimated 20 million new jobs were created. Moreover, Reagan succeeded in getting across at the popular level the notion that America was a dynamic, successful nation again, after the doubts of the 1970s. He won for himself, from an initially hostile media, the grudging accolade of 'The Great Communicator'. The result was that America, as a nation, began to recover its self-confidence, lost during the 1970s' suicide attempt. Research conducted by the high-level Commission on Long-Term Strategy, which Reagan appointed, reported in January 1988 that between 1990 and 2010 the United States economy would grow from $4.6 trillion to nearly $8 trillion, and at the later date would still be nearly twice as large as the world's next biggest economy.[116] In the meantime, however, the early 1990s found the US in sharp recession.

Nonetheless, the recovered self-respect during the 1980s went far to end the masochism caused by Vietnam, and enabled Reagan, who had no inhibitions about the legitimate use of America's enormous power, to perform on the world stage with growing aplomb. He was not a rash man, and certainly not a bellicose man, but he was a staunch believer in absolute values of conduct with a clear view of the difference between right and wrong in international affairs. When he felt the need to act, he acted; not without careful deliberation, but without any feelings of guilt or *arrières-pensées*. But here again Mrs Thatcher served as a mentor. On Friday 2 April 1982, without warning or any declaration of war, large Argentinian amphibious forces invaded and occupied the British crown colony of the Falkland Islands. (They also occupied South Georgia, to the east.) These islands, known to Argentinians as the Malvinas, had been in dispute for two centuries (Dr Johnson had published a pamphlet on the subject, rejecting British claims of ownership). However, all the inhabitants were of British descent, from settlers who arrived in the 1820s, and were thus natives by right of six generations of ownership. The head of the then Argentine military junta, General Leopoldo Galtieri, was (as it happened) himself a second-generation immigrant from Europe, a distinction he shared, interestingly enough, with Ian Smith, leader of the Rhodesian whites, and Fidel Castro, the Cuban dictator. Argentine claims that they were engaged in an act of anti-colonial liberation carried little conviction, and the United Nations Security Council voted 10–1 in favour of an immediate Argentine withdrawal (Resolution 502). The British, however, were caught completely unprepared, with no forces of any significance in the area. Their Foreign Secretary, Lord Carrington, felt it right to resign to atone for the failure of his department to foresee the aggression. Margaret Thatcher, followed by her cabinet, determined to recover the islands, by diplomacy if possible, by force if necessary.

The first British warships left for the south Atlantic two days after the invasion. A week later Britain declared a 200-mile exclusion zone around the islands, a variation on the 'quarantine' President Kennedy had imposed on the Cuban area during the 1962 missile crisis. It was a hazardous decision to send an expeditionary force 8,000 miles, with naval escort but without full air cover (the two British carriers were equipped only with subsonic Harrier jump-jets, whereas Argentine supersonic aircraft could operate from airfields on her mainland, as well as the Port Stanley airport on the Falklands itself). It aroused the admiration of, among other people, Ronald Reagan himself, who throughout the operation not only gave the British government full diplomatic support at the United Nations and elsewhere but provided covert intelligence assistance. The daring operation succeeded. On 25 April South Georgia was recovered. Exactly a week later, the Argentine heavy cruiser *Belgrano* was sunk by the British submarine *Conqueror*, with the loss of 385 lives; thereafter, the Argentine navy retired to harbour and took no further part in the conflict. The Argentine air force fought rather better, using missiles to sink a total of four British warships and transports, though loss of life was tiny. Otherwise the amphibious operation proceeded according to plan. On 21 May the British army established a bridgehead at San Carlos; a week later paratroopers took Port Darwin and Goose Green, and on 14 June the entire Argentine garrison surrendered. Some 255 British and 652 Argentine lives were lost in the land fighting. Three days afterwards, Galtieri was ousted. Indeed, the British victory led directly to the end of military rule in Argentina and the restoration of democracy. On 10 December 1983, Raúl Alfonsín was elected Argentina's first civilian and democratic president for eight years, an immediate investigation was begun into the thousands of dissidents who had 'disappeared' during the junta's rule, and Galtieri and many of his colleagues were sentenced to long terms of imprisonment.

The effect on Reagan was also striking. The Falklands action served to reinvigorate the Western sense of the proprieties of international behaviour and to remind the United States of her responsibilities as the leading democracy and defender of the rule of law. The first geopolitical consequences occurred late in 1983. On 19 October Maurice Bishop, premier of the small West Indian island of Grenada, which was a member of the British Commonwealth, was murdered during a left-wing *putsch*, aided and possibly planned by Cubans. Two days later, the leaders of Grenada's neighbours, Jamaica, Barbados, St Vincent, St Lucia, Dominica and Antigua, reported a large Cuban military build-up on the island and, fearing for the safety of their own democratic governments, secretly petitioned for US military intervention. Reagan, on a golfing weekend in Georgia, was woken at four o'clock on a Saturday morning with this news. Informed by the Joint Chiefs of Staff that a 'rescue operation' could be mounted within forty-eight hours, his response was, 'Do it.' As Cuban reinforcements were feared, and eight hundred United States medical students were in Grenada, all potential hostages, the highest secrecy was imposed.[117] This had one unhappy consequence; Mrs Thatcher was not informed of what Reagan planned to do, and as Grenada was a Commonwealth country, she (and the Queen) took umbrage, and she made her view public, an unfortunate error.[118] This was the only serious disagreement she and Reagan had in eight years, and she later privately admitted she had been mistaken. Otherwise the operation was well received and attained all its objectives. US troops landed on 25 October, restored constitutional authority, and began withdrawing promptly on 2 November.

Nor was this the only forceful action the Reagan administration undertook as an unofficial world policeman and in defence of America's legitimate interests. On 8 July 1985 Reagan had branded five nations, Iran, North Korea, Cuba, Nicaragua and Libya, as 'members of a confederation of terrorist states', carrying out 'outright acts of war' against the United States. They were 'outlaw states run by the strangest collection of misfits, loony-tunes and squalid criminals since the advent of the Third Reich'. This statement, to the American Bar Association, was characteristic of the President's robust style and much relished by ordinary Americans; it was part of his populism. He privately regarded Colonel Gadafy of Libya as the most dangerous of the 'collection', on the grounds that, 'He's not only a barbarian, he's flaky.'[119] As already noted, on 5 April 1986, a bomb exploded in a Berlin disco frequented by US sevicemen, killing one, and a Turkish woman, and injuring two hundred. US intercepts established beyond doubt that Libya had a hand in the outrage, and on 13 April Reagan authorized US F-111 bombers to carry out an attack on Gadafy's military headquarters and barracks in Tripoli. It took place on the night of 14–15 April. Mrs Thatcher gave her permission for US aircraft to operate from their bases in Britain, but France and Italy refused permission to fly over their airspace, making necessary a 1,000-mile detour over the Atlantic and Mediterranean. The attack succeeded in its primary object: thereafter, Gadafy took a notably less prominent and active part in assisting international terrorism.

This growing willingness of the United States to assert its legitimate rights and use its power continued under Reagan's successor, George Bush. On 21 December 1989, the White House, exasperated both by the treatment General Manuel Noriega, the dictator of Panama, meted out to his democratic opponents, and by his participation in a narcotics ring which smuggled billions of dollars' worth of drugs into the United States (Noriega was wanted on serious criminal charges in Florida), authorized an American military intervention. The immediate pretext was the murder of an American soldier in the US canal zone. Some two hundred civilians, nineteen US soldiers and fifty-nine members of the Panamanian forces were believed killed in the fighting. But Noriega himself was quickly overthrown, took refuge in the Vatican nunciature, surrendered and was flown to trial in Florida. In Panama, as in Grenada, democracy was restored and the American forces withdrew quickly. These police actions were much criticized by some members of the Western intelligentsia, but appeared popular among the public, and served to deter some, though unfortunately not all, Third World dictators from aggressive and antisocial behaviour. They also prepared both the American leadership, and public opinion, to meet a more serious challenge to world order, as we shall see.

In the early 1980s, however, President Reagan was more concerned with recovering some of the ground lost, in both a physical and a psychological sense, to the Soviet Union, her satellites and surrogates, during the collectivist 1970s. When Reagan became president, he discovered that the Soviet Union was spending 50 per cent more each year on weapons than the United States, and gaining ground in both the conventional and nuclear fields. Particularly disturbing was the large-scale deployment in Eastern Europe of intermediate-range, multiple-warhead SS-20 rockets. On 17 June 1980 Mrs Thatcher had negotiated with President Carter an agreement whereby, to counter the SS-20s, American Cruise missiles were deployed in Britain. On the basis of this first move, Reagan and Mrs Thatcher were able to persuade other NATO members to provide sites for the Cruise network. In Europe the extreme Left organized coordinated demonstrations against the deployment: on 22 October 1983 some 250,000 were claimed (by the organizers) to have marched in London; a 'human chain' was formed across Paris; in Germany, the Left said a million had protested; at Greenham Common in England, where some Cruise missiles were based, a Women's Peace camp was set up. But such protests were ineffective, and there is no evidence they enjoyed working-class support anywhere. The Greenham women, in particular, soon made themselves unpopular with the local inhabitants.

Deploying Cruise served to notify the Moscow leadership that the era of indecision in White House policy was over.[120] At the same time, from the very first days of his presidency, Reagan launched an across-the-board rearmament programme. As he put it, 'I asked [the Joint Chiefs of Staff] to tell me what new weapons they needed to achieve military superiority over our potential enemies.' If it came to a choice between national security and the deficit, 'I'd have to come down on the side of national defence.'[121] Additional defence spending was soon running at the rate of about $140 billion a year. It included the expansion and training of rapid-deployment forces, de-mothballing World War Two battleships and equipping them with Cruise missiles, and the development of the radar-resistant Stealth bomber and a range of high-technology laser-guided missiles, including anti-ballistic weapons, known collectively as the Star Wars programme. Strategic planning and tactical training of all the US armed forces were redesigned around the use, for both nuclear and conventional purposes, of these advanced weapons systems, a change which was to prove of critical importance in 1991.[122]

However, the principal impact of the rearmament programme was, as intended, political, and in two senses. Reagan was anxious, first, to show to the peoples of Western Europe (and indeed the satellite populations behind the Iron Curtain, who were beginning to look increasingly to the West), that America's commitment to collective security was as strong as ever. This brought a positive response from most European governments.[123] Equally important, however, was the calculated impact on Soviet policy-making. As Reagan quickly discovered from intelligence assessments, Russia was running into increasing economic turbulence in the early 1980s. The Afghanistan war was unpopular and expensive; and by supplying the rebels with small, highly-mobile anti-aircraft and anti-tank weapons, America was able to raise the human and financial cost of the war to Russia at little expense to herself. The Russian gerontocracy, the phalanx of elderly party managers and generals who had controlled the country since the Khrushchev era, was also running into severe leadership problems. Until the early 1980s, the so-called Brezhnev Doctrine was the basis of Soviet foreign and defence policy; this held that once a 'Socialist State', such as Cuba or Vietnam, had been established, any threat to its government was to be regarded as a threat to the Soviet Union's vital interests. Whether the doctrine would have been enforced in every case is arguable; but it was never put to the test, and the principle itself seems to have died with the old man on 10 November 1982. He was succeeded two days later as Party General Secretary, and on 16 June 1983 as President, by Yuri Andropov, who had been head of the KGB for fifteen years.

On 8 March 1983, Reagan took the opportunity of warning the new Soviet leadership of how he regarded their expanded system, and what he intended to do to resist any further encroachments. In Orlando, Florida, he made what became known as the 'evil empire' speech. As he put it, he delivered the speech, 'and others like it, with malice aforethought' (and against the advice of his formidable wife Nancy) because 'I wanted to remind the Soviets we knew what they were up to.'[124] The much stiffer attitude of the White House, fully backed as it was by the Thatcher government in London, had repercussions in Moscow, where there was increasing uncertainty in the Soviet leadership. Seven months after he became President, Andropov died (9 February 1984), and his successor, Konstantin Chernenko, hastily installed as General Secretary and President (13 February, 11 April), lasted little over a year, dying on 10 March 1985. The Soviet élite then took the momentous step of skipping a generation and electing the 52-year-old Mikhail Gorbachev, a party *apparatchik*, born in the Caucasus but of Ukrainian descent (on his mother's side), who had advanced under the aegis of Andropov.[125]

Gorbachev began to consolidate his position by making many thousands of personnel changes at all levels of the Soviet government, central and regional; but he never seems to have exercised the unquestioned authority which even Brezhnev had taken for granted. Increasingly, in the years 1987–91, his apparent orders were ignored or imperfectly executed, and actions took place without his sanction, or indeed knowledge. By the standards of the Soviet Communist Party, he was a liberal; but he dismissed the very idea of a multi-party system in Russia as 'complete nonsense'. He toured the country extensively, making many exhortatory speeches: his theme was, 'We have to change everything,' but he added, 'I am a Communist.' He seems to have assumed that Communism could reform itself from within, without abandoning its basic doctrines, especially its Leninist principles of how the state and economy should be organized. But, as we have seen, it was Lenin's system, not its Stalinist superstructure, which was at the root of Russia's problems. Again on 7 November 1989 Gorbachev told Soviet TV viewers: 'We have to advance faster and faster,' without indicating clearly what the country was advancing to. He said he believed in introducing the market system, thus showing he had caught, or at least was aware of, the spirit of the 1980s. But what this meant in practice was a small extension of the area of land open to individual cultivation, and greater accountability for industrial enterprises. But the first move, under which 5 per cent of the land under cultivation (by smallholders) was soon producing 50 per cent of the food available in the markets, merely drew attention to the failure of the state farms and collectives, which remained intact; and the second, by reducing central subsidies to industry, led to an accelerating fall in output. Thus in the second half of the 1980s, and still more in the early 1990s, goods available in Soviet shops diminished sharply, and a growing proportion of the entire economy operated by barter, not just individually but between factories and through the black market. Gorbachev introduced the policy of *glasnost*, or 'openness', whereby the press and, to some extent, state broadcasting were allowed to criticize and call the government to account. He restrained the activities of the KGB.[126] Some archives were opened. Independent-minded Soviet historians became more daring. Mass graves, dating from Stalin's time, were opened and publicized, and the number of Stalin's victims was constantly revised upwards. Bukharin and nine others, judicially murdered in 1938, were rehabilitated. Fewer people were sent to prison or psychiatric hospitals for political offences.

The net result was to remove, to some extent, the climate of fear in which the Soviet Union had lived for seventy years. But that, in turn, relaxed the discipline, based on fear, which alone kept the Soviet Communist system working at all. Absenteeism increased. Strikes became common. There was a huge increase in crime, in illicit vodka distillation and hence in drunkenness. Gorbachev first imposed a limited form of prohibition; then, faced with a collapse of state revenues from vodka duties, he abandoned it. There was a series of demoralizing disasters, both natural and caused by human failure and carelessness. On 26 April 1986, one of the nuclear reactors at Chernobyl, near Kiev in the Ukraine, blew up, constituting the worst calamity in the history of nuclear power, with casualties, fallout and long-term effects over a huge area. Four months later, on 31 August, the Soviet passenger liner *Admiral Nakhimov* sank in the Black Sea, with the loss of over 400 lives. Five weeks later, on 6 October, a Soviet nuclear submarine, with sixteen multiple nuclear warheads, disappeared without trace in mid-Atlantic. In December 1988, an earthquake in the Armenian districts of Soviet Transcaucasia killed over 20,000 people and devastated an entire region; the relief services functioned badly. On 4 June 1989, an explosion of gas from a leaking Siberian pipeline, which should have registered on the monitoring system, blew up two passing passenger trains, killing over 800, including many children on holiday.

These and many other incidents provided evidence of a system which was showing signs of general breakdown, and which Gorbachev's economic reform programme, which he called *perestroika* or 'remodelling', in some respects aggravated. The CIA and other agencies had been reporting to the White House, with growing conviction, evidence of economic and technological failure in the Soviet Union since the early 1980s. It was affecting all areas of life, including public health. Even in the field of energy, once a major source of Soviet strength because of its abundant natural resources – the USSR remained the world's largest oil exporter even in the early 1990s – difficulties were growing, on account of inefficient extraction and other technological failures.[127] To some extent, the Soviet military-industrial complex was isolated from the worst of Russia's economic difficulties by receiving absolute priority in supplies of materials and skilled manpower. But part of the object of Reagan's rearmament programme was, by raising the pace of high-technology development in the arms race, to turn the screw on the Soviet economy generally, and force the leadership to ask itself hard questions. Was it prepared to match the US high-tech military effort at the expense of the civil economy, at the very time the Soviet people were being promised change and improvements? Could it, indeed, match the US effort, even if it wished? The answer to both these questions was no. A third question then arose: was the Soviet leadership prepared to respond to the American arms build-up by agreeing to come to the negotiating table and engage in realistic disarmament negotiations? The answer to this was yes. On 19 November 1985 Reagan and Gorbachev met in Geneva for the first of what was to prove a series of summit meetings. Reagan proposed monitored arms reductions, using the Russian phrase, *Doverey no provorey*, 'trust but verify', and warned Gorbachev that the alternative was continuing the arms race, 'and I have to tell you if it's an arms race, you must know it's an arms race you can't win.'[128]

Historians will argue for many years whether the Reagan–Thatcher strategy of rearming and deploying advanced weapons in Europe, while offering the USSR a way out through verified disarmament, was effective in bringing about a fundamental change in Soviet foreign and defence policy, which ended the Cold War.[129] The evidence of timing seems to suggest that the strategy helped to push Gorbachev in a direction he was already inclined to take, and in particular to win over doubting colleagues. In 1986–7 there were still real doubts about Gorbachev's sincerity and the reality of the changes he was introducing. In the words of Henry Kissinger, 'Afghanistan will be the test.'[130] Gorbachev had told Reagan at Geneva that the first he had heard of the Soviet invasion was on the radio, indicating he had no responsibility for it, 'and little enthusiasm,' added Reagan.[131] Hence the announcement of the withdrawal, and its completion on schedule, came as a welcome reassurance to Western leaders, and thereafter they – and particularly Reagan, his successor Bush and Mrs Thatcher – regarded

Gorbachev as the man they wished to remain in charge of the USSR. This was of some importance to him, since from 1987 his own popularity at home, once considerable, began to fall steadily. What Western leaders did not then know, however, was that a decision even more important than the withdrawal from Afghanistan had been taken in Moscow: a determination not to use the Red Army (as in 1953, 1956 and 1968) to prop up failing Communist regimes in Eastern Europe.

Once this decision was taken, events moved swiftly, though the process that destroyed Stalin's satellite empire is not entirely clear. Most of the East European regimes were slipping into the same kind of economic crisis that had engulfed Russia in the 1980s, and for the same reason: the cumulative failure of the collectivist system and the so-called 'command economy'. The detonator was, in all probability, a malfunction in the capitalist world itself. The years of growth in the West which were distinguished by 'Thatcherism' and 'Reaganomics', and by the rapid development of world financial centres, led to breakneck rises in stocks and the inevitable *dégringolade*. This came first on 19 October 1987, when the Dow Jones index in New York fell 508 points, or 23 per cent, in one day. It was not, as some feared, a repeat of the 'Black Thursday' of 1929, but the prolegomenon to the end of a long period of economic expansion, and in due course it produced a recession in 1990–1. At the time it was a warning to many banks that their credit lines were over-extended. Banks which were heavy lenders to East European governments and their agencies were already concerned by their credit-worthiness, and after October 1987 no further cash was available east of the Oder–Neiser line; indeed pressure to repay capital and interest intensified. This in turn led to domestic measures by East European governments which reduced goods in the shops and raised their prices. Public anger grew, especially as the feeling spread that the 'evil empire' – the phrase was much relished by its subjects – was losing the will to govern by force.

Thus the year 1989, which the Left throughout the world had planned as a celebration of the bicentennial of the French Revolution – the beginning of modern radical politics, as it was argued – turned into something quite different: a Year of Revolutions indeed, but of revolutions against the established order of Marxism-Leninism. Not all of them succeeded. In March 1989 riots in Tibet against the Chinese occupation and its policy of genocide were put down with savage force. The next month, Chinese students in Peking used the occasion of the death and funeral (22 April) of the Communist leader Hu Yaobang, who had been popular with the masses but deposed by hardliners in 1987, to stage a

major demonstration. By 27 April this had developed into an occupation by students of the vast Tiananmen Square in central Peking.
Other mass demonstrations occurred in various Chinese cities,
including Shanghai. On 15 May, student demonstrators, to the
shame and fury of the Chinese leadership, disrupted a visit by
Gorbachev to Peking, designed to be the first Sino-Soviet summit
for thirty years. On 30 May, a 30-foot fibre-and-glass replica of the
Statue of Liberty was erected in the square. This seems to have
goaded the authorities, who had been holding inconclusive discussions with student leaders about 'reforms', into action. Large forces
of China's Red Army, overwhelmingly drawn from peasant soldiers
from remote regions, to whom city-dwellers were natural enemies
and students 'parasites', were concentrated around Peking. On the
night of 4 June, the regime attacked, using tanks and infantry in
overwhelming numbers, clearing Tiananmen Square, and in the process killing 2,600 people and injuring over 10,000. Despite rumours
of divisions in the leadership and army commanders, the unrest was
put down everywhere with great severity, and thousands were
jailed.

In Europe, however, it was a different story. The lead was
taken by Hungary, which had earlier been in the van in introducing market factors into its crumbling 'command economy'.
Its much-hated leader, János Kádar, had been removed in May 1988
as Party General Secretary; now, on 8 May, he was dismissed as
Party Chairman, and in due course the Hungarian Communist Party
voted itself out of existence (10 October 1989), being replaced by a
multi-party system. More important, however, was Hungary's decision to dismantle the Iron Curtain itself, as this had a knock-on
effect on other satellites. On 2 May Hungary began to roll up its
border fence with Austria, opening the frontier to East–West traffic
at will. Even more sensational was Czechoslovakia's decision to
open its border to East Germany on 10 September.

The gathering force of anti-Marxist revolutionary fervour made
this a move of critical significance. The Polish Communist Party
had suffered a crushing defeat at the polls on 5 June, the day after
the Tiananmen Square massacre, and on 12 September the first
non-Communist government took over in Warsaw. The people of
East Germany, who had been so brutally repressed by Soviet tanks
in 1953, were unwilling to see their Slav and Hungarian neighbours
liberate themselves while they remained chained to the gruesomely
unpopular regime of Erich Honecker. Once the Czech frontier was
opened, many of them poured across it, en route to West Germany.
The Iron Curtain thus had a huge hole in it, and the effect was to
destabilize the East German government, long regarded as one of

the most Stalinist and secure. While some East Germans fled, others began to demonstrate. The same day the Hungarian CP dissolved itself, mass marches began throughout East Germany, but especially in Berlin and Leipzig. Gorbachev, paying a long-arranged visit (7 October), was asked by an anxious Honecker to send in troops and tanks. He refused. He told the old Stalinist he must either enact reforms, quickly, or get out while he could. Publicly, Gorbachev said all the East European regimes were in danger unless they responded to what he called 'the impulse' of the times. Thus abandoned by his ally, Honecker resigned on 18 October, his colleagues having refused to authorize troops to open fire on the demonstrators. He was succeeded by 'a brief and embarrassed phantom' (to use Disraeli's phrase) called Egon Krentz, who lasted exactly seven weeks. On 4 November a million marched in East Berlin. Five days later, at a historic press conference held by the East Berlin party boss, Gunter Schabowski, it was announced that frontier police would no longer try to prevent East Germans from leaving the country. A *Daily Telegraph* reporter asked the key question: 'What about the Berlin Wall?' and was told it was no longer an exit-barrier.[132]

That night the Berlin Wall, the ugly and despised testament to Communist oppression, where so many hundreds of German democrats had died trying to escape, was the scene of a wild orgy of rejoicing and destruction, as young Germans hacked at it with pickaxes. Television carried these historic scenes around the world and in other East European capitals, and, to use, ironically, a phrase of Marx's, 'the enflamed masses began to scream *ça ira, ça ira!*'[133] In Czechoslovakia, another satellite with a hardline Stalinist government, demonstrations began eight days later, on 17 November, and the following day in Bulgaria. There, the fall of the Stalinist government of Todor Zhivkov was followed, on 16 December, by the Bulgarian Communist Party renouncing its monopoly on political power and opening the way to a multi-party system. Meanwhile on 24 November, after almost continuous demonstrations in Prague, the entire Communist leadership resigned and a non-Communist government was formed under the writer Vaclav Havel, later elected President. In most cases, these momentous changes were brought about without much violence, or even peacefully. There was, happily, no lynch law, though the nature and number of the crimes committed by outgoing Communist leaders, which now came to light, were horrific. In East Germany, for instance, the secret police had been involved not only in international terrorism but in large-scale drug smuggling to the West, producing hard currency profits which had gone into Swiss bank accounts kept for the benefit of party leaders. Honecker saved his own skin by entering an army hospital in a military zone controlled by the Soviet forces, from whence he was spirited to Moscow early in 1991. Many other satellite leaders, like Zhivkov, were arrested and in some cases brought to trial.

The one exception to the non-violent revolutionary pattern was Romania. The 24-year dictatorship of the party boss there, Nicolae Ceausescu, like that of his predecessor Gheorghiu-Dej, was exceptionally brutal and corrupt even by the standards of most Marxist regimes, his rule reinforced by a secret police organization known as the Securitate. Its members were recruited largely from state orphanages. Ceausescu, dreaming of a nation of 100 million Romanians, refused to allow the sale of contraceptives, banned abortions and penalized the unmarried and childless. In consequence there were large numbers of illegitimate or unwanted children. Suitable male orphans were taken into cadet battalions in their early teens and were trained, under Ceausescu's supervision, to regard the regime as their parents and to serve it with fanatical loyalty. As adult members of the Securitate, they were given special privileges, and indeed were among the few Romanians who regularly got enough to eat. The Securitate was in some ways organized like Hitler's SS, with its own tanks and aircraft, and had built a complex network of tunnels and strongpoints under Bucharest. Protected by this formidable force, Ceausescu engaged in large-scale exercises in social engineering, rather like the Shah's in Iran, which involved the progressive destruction of over 8,000 traditional villages, and the herding of their inhabitants into big agricultural 'towns'.

Curiously enough, Ceausescu was not unpopular in the West; indeed he was praised for his unwillingness to follow all the twists and turns of Soviet foreign and defence policy, and for his ability to service and repay his debts and pay for Western goods on the nail – a policy made possible by starving the mass of the people of all but the barest necessities, leaving the rest for export.[134] But Western support evaporated when the nature and scale of his rural destruction became known, as it did from 1988 onwards. Moreover, this policy brought the regime into direct conflict with its large Hungarian minority, and its troubles started in earnest when discontent burst into active revolt at the mainly Hungarian-speaking town of Timisoara. The Securitate hit back viciously, and it was later claimed that a mass grave had been discovered there filled by 4,630 bodies of their victims.[135]

Ceausescu believed himself secure from the tides of revolution toppling his Marxist colleagues elsewhere. At his last great party gathering, early in December, there were no less than sixty-seven standing ovations during his five-hour speech, and he felt safe enough to carry out a scheduled state visit to Iran. But news that the Hungarian unrest was spreading, even into the capital, brought him scurrying back. On 21 December he addressed the crowd in front of his presidential palace. As a rule, Ceausescu's oratory was listened to by the citizens of Bucharest in silence, with cheers and applause supplied by recordings piped from loudspeakers – all part of the political surrealism which characterized his gruesome regime. On this occasion, however, the crowd shouted and hurled abuse, and Ceausescu, accompanied by his furious wife Elena, equally hated, stumped back into the palace: an electrifying little scene, recorded on video. The following day he was forced to flee the palace by helicopter. What happened next is mysterious. His plans to hole up in a Securitate redoubt clearly misfired, and it may be that he was abandoned by close colleagues, who regarded his personal unpopularity as a threat to their own lives: his eventual successor, Ion Iliescu, was one of them. At all events, the Conducator, as he called himself, was captured, along with Elena; both were tried by a military court on Christmas Day, charged with 'crimes against the people', genocide and the murder of 60,000 men, women and children, convicted and immediately executed by firing squad. These events too were recorded on video. The fall of the Ceausescus had been made possible by a change of allegiance of the army, and its political masters, even though both had played a role in earlier Ceausescu-authorized killings. The Securitate, however, remained loyal to its master, even after he was dead, and fighting continued for a fortnight in tunnels and bunkers, as the army gradually established its control. Casualties were reported to be enormous but proved, on closer examination, to number a thousand or less.[136] Listeners all over the world were moved to hear, on Christmas Day, the church bells of Bucharest ringing out, for the first time in forty-five years, to celebrate the death of 'the Anti-Christ', as he was called.

The aftermath, however, was less satisfactory for democracy. The changes in Romania, as in Bulgaria also, turned out to be more of persons than of regimes; in both countries the old Communist *nomenklatura* clung on to their police and military power, changed their titles and party names, got back control of broadcasting stations and newspapers, and staged 'elections', in the course of 1990, which kept them in power. In both countries there was unfinished business. Much the same could be said of Albania, most Stalinist of all the East European regimes, where trouble started in earnest early in 1991, and in Yugoslavia, where the unpopularity of the federal Communist regime was complicated by regional divisions. As we have already noted, the smouldering inter-racial tensions in this union of South Slavs had been deplored by its architect, Professor Seton-Watson, as far back as the 1920s. The death of Marshal Tito in 1984 removed the one figure who commanded respect, or at any rate fear, and in the later 1980s and early 1990 the country sank slowly into bankruptcy and chaos. The heartland of Yugoslav Communism remained Serbia, which controlled 70 per cent of the federal army. But in 1990 both Slovenia and Croatia, the two most advanced states, voted non-Communist state governments into power, and by summer 1991 the stage was set either for civil war or for a break-up of the state.

In East Germany, Poland, Czechoslovakia and Hungary, however, the changes were fundamental and permanent, and by the middle of 1991 democracy appeared to be firmly established in all four. Indeed, one of them, East Germany, had ceased to exist, since the last remnants of the Allied occupation, in Berlin, had been dissolved, and, with the consent of Russia, the United States, France and Britain, the Germans had agreed to unify themselves. *Länder* elections had taken place in October 1990 and federal elections in December, confirming the Christian Democrat leader Helmut Kohl as first Chancellor of a united Federal Republic of all Germany. The merger was not without grave economic problems, for it had been accompanied, much against the advice of the head of the West German Bundesbank, Karl Otto Pohl, by a financial arrangement which put the West and East German marks at parity. Since East German industry was grotesquely inefficient and under-capitalized by comparison with West Germany's, the foreseeable result was the collapse of many East German firms, unemployment soaring to 25 per cent of the population, and more mass demonstrations, especially in Leipzig – this time against the workings of the capitalist system.[137] On the other hand, East Germany, now part of the Federal Republic, was also part of the European Community, and few doubted that, in the medium term, the former East Germans could be absorbed into the Community system and made affluent like the rest.

But if the Prussians and the Saxons could be part of the EC, as of right, how could entry be denied to other historic European races: the Poles, the Hungarians, the Czechs and Slovaks, and indeed the Slovenes and Croats, if they could prise themselves loose from the grip of Serbian Belgrade? That was the question confronting the Community in the early 1990s. No one doubted that, now these East European peoples had chosen to repudiate Communism and embrace the market, much responsibility rested on the wealthy members of the EC to help finance what would inevitably be an expensive transfer. The infrastructures, transport systems, industries and educational provisions of these states were all inadequate and run-down, and, the more closely they were examined, the higher the bill mounted to make them competitive with Western Europe. The cost would run into hundreds, perhaps thousands of millions of dollars, and would clearly have to be spread over many years. There were also debts. Many Western banks had already made provisions to regard East European debts as unrecoverable, and, as a gesture, the United States government, in March 1991, wrote off all loans to Poland. But what of future finance, urgently required?

The question was linked to the entire long-term strategy of the Community. As a free-trade area it had done exceptionally well, and by the end of the 1980s all members had passed legislation to complete the process of abolishing customs duties during 1992, making what was termed a 'single market' (with special transitional provisions for some countries). But two questions remained open, both of them serious. The first concerned external barriers. Was the EC to remain an outward-looking group, with low external tariffs, abetting the process begun in the late 1940s by the General Agreement on Tariffs and Trade, whose ultimate aim was a single world market? Or was it, rather, to be inward-looking, with a high tariff wall against the world outside? This question was itself linked to the future of farming subsidies, part of the Common Agricultural Policy, which by the end of the 1980s was being slowly dismantled. The world's leading agricultural exporters, especially the United States, Canada and Australia, accused the EC of excessive protectionism and conduct likely to destroy the whole GATT structure. A conference in 1990, called to resolve the argument, not only failed to do so but ended in acrimony.

The second question concerned the way in which the EC itself was to develop. Now that the single market was established, some members, notably the French, led by the Socialist President of the European Commission, Jacques Delors, wished to proceed rapidly to financial, economic and political union, involving, in the first place, a common currency and a Community Central Bank. The British, especially while Margaret Thatcher was still in charge of their affairs, argued that a common currency was either going to displace national currencies, or prove a failure, and that not enough homework had been done on how it would work, or on what powers the new Central Bank would exercise. If the currency displaced national ones, and the Central Bank ran it, then national parliaments would sacrifice a huge part of their sovereignty, and political union would have to follow, whether or not public opinion was ready for it. In Britain's case it was not, and there was a strong suspicion that the same was true of France and Germany, whatever their leaders might say in public. Not everyone in British politics agreed with Mrs Thatcher, and her hostile attitude to further European unity was one reason why she was overthrown in November 1990. On the other hand, Germany's enthusiasm for a common currency, strong in 1989–90, waned noticeably as the experience of blending the Eastern and Western mark revealed how difficult it was to bring currencies into a satisfactory alignment; in 1991 Pohl moved closer to the British position, before resigning. There was also a school of thought which argued that, instead of concentrating on vertical progress – that is, uniting the economies and political systems of existing members and deepening the Community – it should rather expand horizontally, and devote its resources and energies to taking in the newly-liberated states of Eastern Europe. In 1991–2, the EC adopted both approaches: the Maastricht Agreement of December 1991 deepened the intercommunion of the Twelve. But its free trade area was widened to include the EFTA states, and in principle invitations to join were extended to various countries in Eastern Europe. This growing movement towards a pan-European entity, however, was threatened by the dramatic increase in refugees fleeing the collapsed economies and the civil commotions of the former Communist states, which in turn led to the rapid growth of extremist, anti-immigrant parties in most EC states.

There remained, moreover, the unresolved problem of Russia. Was it part of Europe, and therefore a future candidate-member of the EC, or not? Gorbachev indicated repeatedly that Russia was European. De Gaulle himself had spoken of 'a Europe from the Atlantic to the Urals'. He had also made the point, in the early 1960s, before Britain became a member, that the community was not so much an economic or political as a cultural concept; he referred to 'the Europe of Dante, of Goethe and of Chateaubriand'. After Britain's entry, it was fair to add 'and of Shakespeare'. But if Europe was a cultural federation, not only was it wrong to exclude the countries which had produced Liszt, Chopin, Dvořák and Kafka, it was also unacceptable to deny – in the long term – the homeland of Tolstoy and Turgenev, Chekhov, Tchaikovsky and Stravinsky. This was certainly a question the Community would have to resolve, if not in the 1990s then in the early decades of the twenty-first century.

In the meantime, however, Russia's internal problems mounted. The Union of Soviet Socialist Republics was a paper edifice, in which all real power was exercised by Greater Russians from Moscow. In short it was, as Reagan had said, an empire, though in the later 1980s it became marginally less evil. As it became less evil, however, and its subjects less frightened of their masters, the constitution of the USSR tended to become less of a construct and more of a reality. While Gorbachev's failure to implement market economics raised ever more serious economic problems, the decline of the fear factor produced ever-growing regional ones. The two were of course connected; the more the centre failed to fill the shops, the more the regions wanted to take charge of their own affairs. The most easily managed were the central Asian republics, run in effect by the KGB. But from 1989 all three of the Baltic republics, Estonia, Latvia and Lithuania, began to campaign not merely for greater autonomy but for outright independence, such as they had enjoyed between 1918 and 1940, when they fell victim to Stalin under the terms of the 1939 Soviet–Nazi pact and its secret protocols. In March 1991, all three held referenda, in which the demand for independence was endorsed by overwhelming majorities, including majorities among their Russian-speaking minorities. Georgia too, demanded independence, and in the Ukraine, largest and wealthiest of the Republics if we exclude Russia itself, there was a similar drift towards autonomy, if not yet outright independence. South of the Caucasus, the Christian Armenians and the Muslim Azerbaijanis actually fought each other, and large numbers of Soviet troops had to be despatched to separate the combatants.

Gorbachev's regional problems were compounded by the behaviour of Russia itself (as opposed to the USSR, 'the centre') with its 150 million inhabitants, its vast territories, including almost all of Siberia, and its natural resources. It was a standing grievance of all the USSR's satellites, and all its republics, that they were the victims of Russian exploitation; it was equally the passionate conviction of the Russians themselves that they were being milked by satellites and republics alike: 'We poor Russians pay for all,' as they put it. The fact, of course, was that Russians, republics and satellites alike had been the victims of an incorrigibly inefficient system. In so far as anyone did the exploiting, it was the *nomenklatura*, the privileged caste of high Communist Party officials and army officers, which existed in all of them. Perhaps Gorbachev's most fundamental mistake was not to abolish the caste and its privileges right from the beginning: then all those in positions of authority, brought up against the reality of shortages, would have accepted the inevitability of abolishing Leninism itself. But he left the privileges intact, and the USSR remained two nations: the ruling class and the *hoi polloi*, just like a society in antiquity. The Gorbachev family enjoyed the perks as much as anyone; in New York, during the Gorbachev–Reagan summit in Washington in December 1987, Mrs

Raisa Gorbachev went shopping with an American Express Gold card, illegal in Russia and punishable with a long prison term. But she was above the law: a *nomenklatura* wife.

It is not, therefore, surprising that, as Gorbachev's popularity plunged, the man who replaced him in the affections of ordinary Russians was Boris Yeltsin, a high functionary who had voluntarily relinquished, for himself and his family, the privileges of party rank. The former Moscow party leader, he had been sacked by Gorbachev in 1987 for complaining publicly that the reforms were not proceeding fast or far enough. He then stood for the first fairly contested elections for the Congress of People's Deputies, held on 28 March 1989, and, in the Moscow constituency of 7 million people, was returned with 90 per cent of the votes. Subsequently, and despite much hostile manoeuvring by Gorbachev and his henchmen, Yeltsin was elected President (that is, head of the government) of the Russian Republic, the largest constituent of the USSR.

The stage was thus set for a constitutional crisis which, as in Yugoslavia, had undertones of a *putsch* or possibly civil war. Yeltsin had his critics, as did Gorbachev. But Yeltsin was popular, which Gorbachev was not (except abroad). Moreover, Yeltsin had been elected by the people, whereas Gorbachev was President of the USSR only by courtesy of a Party caucus. Yeltsin stood for regionalism, Gorbachev for 'the centre'. When Gorbachev held a countrywide referendum in March 1991, asking Soviet citizens if they wished to remain part of the USSR, some of the republics, including all the Baltic states, refused to take part; others, including Russia and the Ukraine, asked additional questions not framed by 'the centre'. Yeltsin's Russia was asked: do you want the Presidents of the Republics elected by universal suffrage? Both Gorbachev and Yeltsin got the answers they wanted, or said they had. So little was resolved by this democratic exercise, such as it was. In June 1991, however, Yeltsin strengthened his position by becoming the first Russian president to be directly elected, winning nearly 60 per cent of the vote.

In the meantime, two processes seemingly outside the control of either Gorbachev or Yeltsin appeared to proceed inexorably. The first was the recovery of the Communist hardliners, especially in the army, the KGB and the bureaucracy, who in 1990–1 began to regain some of their lost confidence and pulled 'the centre' more in their direction. They evaded orders they did not like and took actions which the Kremlin, or at any rate Gorbachev himself, claimed he had not sanctioned, such as seizing broadcasting stations, newspaper buildings and other emblems of regionalism in the Baltic republics, in one case with considerable loss of life. In the autumn of 1990, Gorbachev's liberal Foreign Minister, Eduard Shevard-nadze, resigned in protest at the behaviour of what he called 'these occult forces'. By the spring of 1991, Soviet Russia was suffering from an absence of clear lines of authority. In many countries, this would have constituted the curtain-raiser to a military coup. However, it was worth noting that Russia had no tradition of generals seizing power; the only occasion when such had been attempted, the famous Decembrist movement of 1825, had ended in complete fiasco. Moreover the army at home, swollen by troops who had left their comfortable quarters in Eastern Europe reluctantly to return to overcrowded barracks and empty shops, was demoralized.

It was against this background that Gorbachev negotiated a new Union treaty with Yeltsin and other leaders of the republics in the summer of 1991. Four of the republics, Lithuania, Latvia, Estonia and Georgia, refused to take part in the negotiations, claiming full independence. Others, such as Yeltsin's Russia, expressed reservations about the text, which provided a considerable devolution of authority away from the centre but kept the USSR itself in being. Nevertheless, Gorbachev, who had been taking a brief holiday at his villa in the Crimea, was planning to return to Moscow to sign the treaty formally on Tuesday 20 August. For the hardliners, the treaty was the sticking point. They regarded it as the prelude to the disintegration of the USSR and decided to abort its birth at all costs. Over the weekend of 17–18 August, KGB troops surrounded Gorbachev's villa, cut off its communications, and placed him and his family under house arrest. On Monday 19 August, the *putsch* was publicly announced on state broadcasting services and at a press conference in Moscow. The cover-story was that Gorbachev was sick and unable to perform his duties, which devolved on his deputy-president. A Committee of Eight had been formed to rescue the country from the multiplicity of crises which faced it, and to restore order.

The conspirators were a mixture of men who disposed of real power, such as the Defence Minister, the head of the KGB and the Minister of the Interior, and others who were little more than figureheads, though holding senior posts in the state machine and its trade union structure. Virtually all had been appointed by Gorbachev himself, and some were old and trusted colleagues of his. Their move was supported by the state media, where censorship was hastily reimposed, and by many prominent Communist Party officials. It was announced with evident relief by Peking radio and television and hailed with enthusiasm by such international outcasts as Saddam Hussein in Iraq, Colonel Gadafy in Libya and Fidel Castro in Cuba. The rest of the world responded with shocked silence or, as in the case of the United States and Great Britain, with open hostility and predictions that the new regime had no long-term future.

Those who remembered the Decembrist fiasco, however, felt it would unravel much more quickly, and proved to be right. As their press conference demonstrated, right at the start, the Committee of Eight had no agreed ideological base for what they were doing. Notably absent from their self-justification was any element of Marxist-Leninist theory. The collapse of belief in Communism had evidently spread even to those diehards still clinging desperately to its state structure, and the privileged life it provided for the party élite. The rationale of their seizure of power was the simple, crude fact that they controlled the armed forces and the police. But did they? Doubts soon arose. The *putsch* appeared to have no leadership. There was no Lenin, to supply will; no Trotsky to take decisive military action. The members of the Committee disagreed on their aims and methods – as the Decembrists had done – and were soon quarrelling among themselves. Every tactical and strategic mistake was made. Though Gorbachev was held against his will, his life was spared, he was allowed to retain his personal bodyguards, and over his radio he heard BBC World Service announcements giving the world's hostile reaction to the conspiracy: this undoubtedly strengthened his resolve to do no deal with the Committee. More important, they failed to seize their arch-enemy, Yeltsin. Five hours after he heard the announcement of the *putsch*, Yeltsin was able to make his way to his stronghold, the Russian Parliament or 'White House' on Manezh Square, which was not even sealed off by police or troops. Yeltsin was not able to communicate his defiance to the Russian people by radio or TV, but his phone-links were left intact. He was thus able to speak to President Bush and to John Major, and receive their support and encouragement. Moreover, he was able to convey this news, and his own calls for resistance, to many cities and organizations in Russia by fax-lines, which were also uncut. Tanks and armoured personnel carriers were out on the streets of Moscow, but without clear orders. Some made their way to the White House and their crews announced they were siding with the Russian parliamentarians. Late on Monday, Yeltsin came out of the White House, climbed on a tank turret, and proclaimed to the crowds that the *putschists* would be arrested and put on trial.

The climax came on the night of Tuesday 20 August, when after a day of indecision, a group of armoured vehicles opened fire on insurgent civilians on Moscow's outer ring-road, and three young men were killed. At that point, the military commanders in the Moscow area refused to give any further fire-orders, and in some cases the tanks began to return to barracks. In Leningrad, where the democrats were in full control, army units were ordered not to enter the city, and complied. The air force command had already refused to carry out any orders from the Committee, and naval units declined to take action against the Baltic republics, where only the special Interior Ministry troops, or Black Berets, were prepared to obey Committee instructions. Between midnight on Tuesday, and noon the following day, the *putsch* faltered, then collapsed in ignominy and dissention. The Interior Minister committed suicide. Two of his co-conspirators flew to the Crimea, in a forlorn attempt to explain themselves to Gorbachev. But with the tide turning, they found themselves prisoners. In Moscow, Yeltsin took charge of the government, and soon all the tanks were off the streets. By Thursday, Gorbachev was on his way back to the Kremlin, a free man, and all seven of the Committee still alive were under arrest. Marx had noted the tendency of history to repeat itself, the first time as tragedy, the second as farce. By a superlative stroke of irony, the rise and fall of the horrific totalitarian state which embodied his teachings illustrated his maxim. Lenin's *putsch* of October 1917, which set it up, was a tragedy, for Russia and for the world; the *putsch* of August 1991, which brought it crashing down, was farce.

By Friday 23 August, it became clear that the failure of the conspiracy had brought about the nemesis it had been designed to prevent: the destruction of the Communist state and of its imperial framework, the Union of Soviet Socialist Republics. Gorbachev returned to Moscow intending to resume his gradualist programme, and replaced the arrested functionaries with other Party stalwarts, in most cases their deputies. He was quickly made to realize that, in his absence, a decisive shift of power had taken place, from the centre to the republics, and from himself to Yeltsin. The three crucial days had, in effect, reversed the Leninist revolution which had occurred seventy-four years before. The change was marked by symbolic gestures, recalling scenes in the former satellites in 1989: notably, the destruction of the giant statue of Felix Dzerzhinsky, founder of Lenin's secret police, which stood outside the Lubyianka, headquarters of the KGB, in Moscow. In response to the demands of the crowd, who threatened to tear it down with their bare hands, it was removed by power-cranes of the Moscow City Public Works Department, and dumped across the road from Gorky Park, where it was joined by huge images of Jacob Sverdlov, Mikhail Kalinin and heads of Stalin which had somehow survived earlier bouts of iconoclasm. Statues of Lenin were removed in many republics, a decision was made to close his tomb in Red Square and remove his embalmed body for reburial alongside his mother's remains, and

Leningrad itself reverted to its historic name of St Petersburg, following a referendum of its citizens.

The key scene, however, took place in the Russian Parliament, on the afternoon of Friday 23 August. Gorbachev had been invited there by Yeltsin to give his own account of the conspiracy, and the occasion was televised live, not only to Russian viewers but to the entire world. Yet Gorbachev was not allowed to conduct the business in his own way. During his address, Yeltsin, sitting alongside him as Russian President, handed him a document proving that his entire Cabinet, senior ministers whom he himself had selected, had supported the *coup*. Gorbachev (protesting): 'But I have not yet read this.' Yeltsin (jabbing with his finger): 'Then read it now, out loud.' Gorbachev, caught at a disadvantage, complied, and no episode, etched as it was on the memories of those who watched, more tellingly summed up the transfer of authority from one leader to another. Yeltsin pushed home his advantage shortly afterwards when, to Gorbachev's evident dismay, he announced he was signing a decree suspending the Communist Party throughout the Russian republic, and ordering its property to be seized, and its papers to be sealed and examined by the authorities. He then put his pen to the document, as the Russian Parliament cheered.

During the next fortnight, the implications of this dramatic scene were worked out in detail. The suspension of the Communist Party was extended to all the territory of the USSR. Over five thousand of its buildings, usually in prime city sites, were taken over by the public, its bank accounts and foreign holdings were sequestered, and its files were impounded. The KGB likewise had its files taken over, its numbers and functions drastically reduced and a new head was appointed to liberalize its methods. All the main institutions in the old USSR, such as the Defence Ministry, the KGB, the Interior Ministry and the Foreign Office, lost their collegiums, the instruments through which party control was primarily exercised. Gorbachev was obliged to appoint yet another set of men, all liberals this time, to the top offices in the state. But, as August became September, he found it increasingly difficult to persuade influential men to accept his invitation to join him, as the power of the centre manifestly withered, and his own authority shrank from day to day.

Gorbachev's own power-base had been the Communist Party itself, now in effect dissolved, and the USSR Parliament. In the first week in September it met in the Kremlin, still overwhelmingly hardline in composition. But deprived of its Speaker, now under arrest, and with many of its leaders behind bars or absent in hiding, it meekly agreed to measures dismantling the power of the

Communist Party and the super-state it controlled. Estonia, Latvia and Lithuania were accorded their independence without further argument, and their freedom was underlined by the withdrawal, in some disarray, of the remaining Interior Ministry special forces still holding out there. Denmark was the first Western state to recognize, or rather reaffirm, the sovereignty of the three republics (their occupation, under the Nazi-Soviet Pact, had never been accepted as valid), followed quickly by the other EC powers and the United States. One by one, all the component parts of the Soviet Union, led by the Ukraine, next in size and importance to Russia itself, declared their *de facto* independence, as a basis for negotiating new pragmatic links with each other. Early in September, Gorbachev and the republican leaders proposed, and the USSR parliament endorsed, a decision to transform the old USSR into a lose confederation of sovereign states. The process began of working out how trade between these states would be conducted, who would control defence (including the ownership, siting and firing of nuclear weapons) and foreign policy, and who would manage a common currency, if any were to exist. Thus the old tsarist empire, as remodelled by Stalin, the grim entity which was rightly called 'the prison of peoples', was at last thrown open and its inmates left free to go their separate ways or seek such mutual cooperation as they found useful.

These momentous changes, ending three-quarters of a century of Soviet Communist totalitarianism, and redrawing not only the ideological map of Eastern Europe, but its political map too, took place against an accelerating decline of the Soviet economy as a whole. Food shortages have been noted earlier. In fact, the industrial sector was performing more sluggishly than agriculture, which at least was still producing food, even if the state could not distribute it. On 9 March 1991, someone in Moscow leaked a secret report from Gosplan, the USSR's central planning agency, giving a forecast for 1991–2.[138] This predicted that, during the year, agricultural production would fall by 5 per cent, industrial production by an alarming 15 per cent and GNP as a whole by 11.5 per cent. It envisaged what it called 'an imminent collapse' in capital investment, and concluded that the country was facing 'an economic catastrophe'. These figures had to be revised downwards during the summer as political disorder spread, central control slackened, and the republics drifted apart; and by early autumn it was clear that the harvest would be much smaller than in 1990, necessitating larger imports of food payable in hard currency, which neither the USSR as a whole, nor its individual republics, possessed. Gorbachev had pressed the Western leaders for the right to attend the G-7 summit of the advanced industrial powers, held in London in July 1991. Participation was refused, but he was allowed to address the assembled heads of state or government, on the Soviet Union's increasing need for help. After his retirement, Boris Yeltsin, who as President of Russia was now the most important leader in the former Soviet Union, attended part of the 1992 G-7 summit. This was an important stage in the rehabilitation of Russia as a 'normal' great power.

Until the failure of the August 1991 *putsch*, and the subsequent downfall of the Communist Party, the West had hesitated to provide material relief to its once-mighty antagonist. There was, rightly, concern in Washington and London at the mood of the Soviet armed forces, or their commanders; and evidence that some of the disarmament agreements, drawn up by Reagan and Bush, and by Gorvachev, were being evaded by the Soviets. There was also a useful nineteenth-century diplomatic adage, probably coined by Talleyrand, which runs: 'Russia is never as strong as it looks; Russian is never as weak as it looks.' But it was clear that, during the later 1980s and early 1990s, some things in the great power relationships had changed permanently. Following a shipboard summit held off Malta on 3 December 1989, the Soviet spokesman, Gennady Gerasimov, had been emboldened to say: 'The Cold War ended at 12.45 today.' That remained a fact. Increasingly in the 1990s the United States, Russia and other leading powers were able to discuss issues in the traditional, realistic terms of old-style power politics, without ideological overtones. This was not a formula for Utopia, but it was progress of a sort. The Warsaw Pact was disbanded, and there was even talk of expanding Nato into a world security agency, sharing some responsibilities with the Soviet republics. The notion of a thermonuclear exchange between the two superpowers receded into the realm of practical impossibility. Indeed, it was no longer plausible, by the autumn of 1991, to see the shrunken and divided entity of Soviet Russia as a true superpower; the United States was, in practice, the only one.[139]

The ending of the Cold War not only sharply diminished the thermonuclear threat. It also, for the first time, made it possible for the United Nations Security Council to function in the way its creators intended, as an instrument to deal quickly and effectively with aggression. The occasion arose on 2 August 1990 when, without warning, Iraqi forces invaded and occupied Kuwait in the course of a single day. As we have already noted, Iraq had built up immense armed forces, with some help from the United States and Britain, but chiefly through Soviet Russia, China, France and (in specialist technical fields) West Germany. The assault was not without a prolegomenon. Iraq not only had a border dispute with Kuwait, involving part of one of its oilfields, but a much larger claim that the entire country was, in terms of the old Ottoman administrative divisions, Iraq's 'lost province'. This had no historical basis, since Kuwait had been internationally recognized as a separate entity long before Iraq had been put together by the British as a League of Nations mandate in 1920–2. But it was part of Saddam Hussein's vision of a resurrected Greater Babylonia; that was why he had acquired such immense armed forces. A further grievance against Kuwait was that it had lent him immense sums, to finance his eight-year war against Iran, and was now demanding repayment of the capital, or at least some interest. Saddam also accused all the Gulf states (17 July 1990) of 'conspiring with the United States' to cut the price of crude oil and 'stabbing Iraq in the back with a political dagger'. Five days later he began to move troops and armour toward the border. On 27 July, under Iraqi pressure, the Organization of Petroleum Exporting Countries (OPEC) did in fact raise the so-called target price for oil to $21 a barrel. The same day, however, the US Senate ended farm credits for Iraq and prohibited any further transfers of military technology. By 31 July some 100,000 Iraqi troops were on the Kuwait border, and talks between Iraqi and Kuwaiti plenipotentiaries, held in Jeddah the same day, broke down after two hours. At the time it was widely reported that the American ambassador in Baghdad, in conversation with Saddam Hussein, had failed to warn him that an occupation of Kuwait would be regarded by Washington as a threat to America's vital interests; but this was denied in evidence before the Senate Foreign Affairs Committee in March 1991.[140] One thing is clear, however: there was a failure of US (and British) intelligence, and the actual invasion came as a surprise and a shock.

By a stroke of good fortune, however, this act of aggression coincided with an international meeting in Aspen, Colorado, attended by, among others, Margaret Thatcher. She was thus able to meet President Bush immediately. Together they determined on a joint Anglo-American approach which remained solid throughout the many anxious months of diplomacy and military build-up which followed, and the actual hostilities. In fact at no time since the Second World War had the 'special relationship' between the Anglo-Saxon powers (as de Gaulle used to call them caustically) functioned so successfully.

The first Allied priority was to prevent Saddam invading Saudi Arabia, and indeed rolling south to absorb all the rich oil states of the Gulf. With such resources, it was believed, Iraq could, within a few years, acquire not only nuclear weapons but the means to deliver them over immense distances, thus threatening Europe (and possibly even the United States) as well as Israel and other Middle East countries. It was at this point that the new self-confidence created among the civilized Western powers by the events of the 1980s, including the successful conduct of the Falklands campaign, the liberation of Grenada, the Libyan raid and the intervention in Panama, paid handsome dividends. George Bush and Margaret Thatcher determined from the start not merely to protect Saudi Arabia by force, but to liberate Kuwait too, whatever it cost. Moreover, they agreed to proceed at every stage with the full backing of the UN Security Council and, following its resolutions, to build up the most broadly based international force possible, including Arab states.

The involvement of the UN, which would have been impossible so long as the Cold War continued, was the best possible proof that it had in fact ended. Soviet Russia also cooperated with the Anglo-American diplomatic effort throughout, in private even more wholeheartedly than in public. It was, of course, influenced by self-interest. On the one hand, its military investment in Iraq was enormous (including over 1,000 technicians and advisers), and it wished to avoid an armed conflict if possible; hence it stressed throughout the desirability of a non-violent solution. On the other hand, its need for American financial and economic assistance was becoming daily more pressing, and this inclined Moscow to follow the American lead in the last resort and to get the Gulf problem disposed of as quickly as possible.

Hence, not without some argument and difficulty, the Security Council complied with the overall Anglo-American strategy. On 2 August Security Council Resolution 660 condemned the invasion and demanded an unconditional withdrawal of Iraqi forces. The phrase was reinforced by a statement from Bush: the United States, he insisted, required 'the immediate, complete and unconditional withdrawal of all Iraqi forces from Kuwait'. On 6 August, SC Resolution 661 imposed a trade embargo on Iraq. On 9 August, SCR 662 ruled that Iraq's annexation of Kuwait, announced in Baghdad, was unlawful, null and void. On 18 August, SCR 664 rescinded Iraq's order closing down diplomatic missions in Kuwait and demanded the right of all foreign nationals to leave. On 25 August the Security Council went an important step further and authorized the use of force to make sanctions work. Finally, on 29 November, SCR 678 authorized 'all necessary means' to drive Iraqi forces out of Kuwait if they had not left by a deadline fixed at midnight on 15 January 1991. The text of 678 also permitted steps to be taken to ensure peace and stability in the area. All these resolutions, of which the last was by far the most important, were passed with the agreement of the five permanent members of the Security Council (two Marxist non-permanent members, Cuba and Yemen, voted against certain resolutions, but had no power of veto). The resolutions were negotiated beforehand with Russia, and indeed on 19 November George Bush and Gorbachev met privately in Paris to discuss the whole strategy in detail. Russia did not contribute to the Allied forces building up in the Gulf, but it was a consenting party to their use, and it actively assisted the process of UN authorization; it also privately provided various forms of military intelligence about the capability, siting and command-structures of Iraqi weapons systems which Russia had itself supplied to Saddam's forces. The operation was thus the first positive result of the new relationship between the former Cold War powers.[141]

The Gulf War was able to demonstrate how effective the Security Council could be in resisting an aggressor and forcing him to disgorge, providing that – and this was a critical qualification – the United States, as the democratic superpower, and its leading allies, such as Britain, were willing to discharge their responsibilities to the UN Charter. The crisis was also the first one to be conducted, and indeed fought, entirely in front of the TV cameras, with many networks, such as the US-based Cable News Network, and the British-based Sky, providing twenty-four-hour coverage. Public opinion, therefore, played a prominent part throughout, and the American government, in the light of the bitter Vietnam experience, had to be careful to carry opinion with it in everything that was done. In fact the polls showed American voters moving steadily towards full backing of a forceful ejection of the Iraqi aggressor, and though Bush secured only a narrow majority in the Senate authorizing him to use force, his actions were later overwhelmingly endorsed by both Houses of Congress and by poll ratings sometimes as high as 90 per cent. British opinion was always behind the original Thatcher determination (wholly endorsed by her successor John Major) by large majorities (75–80 per cent). The 'special relationship' was thus able to supply the core of the enormous expeditional force which was assembled in the Gulf between August 1990 and January 1991 with the approval of the American and British electorates. French opinion also favoured forceful intervention; the French government was less enthusiastic, and indeed almost until the last moment President Mitterrand tried to play a lone game of negotiations with the Iraqi dictator, though to no purpose; and in the end the French made a major contribution both to the Allied force and to its success. Opinion in other Western countries varied, though most made some contribution. West Germany and Japan claimed they were precluded from sending their armed forces by constitutional limitations, but they provided funds to finance the Allied war effort. By skilful diplomacy, the Anglo-Saxon powers also secured a large Arab military participation, not only by Saudi Arabia, Kuwait itself and other Gulf states, but by Egypt and Syria. Saddam Hussein's efforts to reach over the heads of hostile Arab governments and arouse their peoples to his defence met little success. Nor did his hasty signature of a final peace agreement with Iran, on 15 August, by which he surrendered all the meagre territorial gains he had acquired at such cost in eight years of fighting, bring him any support from that direction. Hence the twenty-eight-strong Allied coalition which eventually participated in reversing the Iraqi aggression represented a large cross-section of the world community, and this too was a significant precedent and a major strengthening of the UN's authority.[142]

The entire diplomatic-military exercise might still have foundered in doubt and acrimony if the operation itself, code-named Desert Storm, had proved a long and costly affair. Public support, especially in the United States, might have been eroded, and the Arab part of the coalition might have unravelled if Saddam had been able to register any major successes. As it was, he attempted to undermine the support of Arab governments for the US-led coalition by launching numerous missile attacks on Israeli cities, inflicting some casualties on civilians. He hoped to provoke an Israeli military response, and so be able to portray the Egyptian, Saudi and Syrian governments as Israel's *de facto* allies. But Israel wisely held its hand, assisted by the prompt supply of US anti-missile Patriot rockets, which proved remarkably effective; so the Iraqi tactic failed. Desert Storm itself was planned with great care and executed with brilliant success. The Commander-in-Chief, General Norman Schwarzkopf, proved himself not merely an outstanding military supremo in directing one of the most complex international campaigns in history, involving sea, land and air forces, but showed himself well aware of the TV and public-opinion dimension of the operation. Indeed he proved himself an accomplished performer in front of the cameras at his regular briefings. His summary of Allied strategy, after the campaign was completed, immediately became a TV classic: it was as if one had watched the Duke of Wellington describing the Battle of Waterloo the day after it took place.

The Allied air assault began almost immediately after the 15 January deadline was reached and continued remorselessly up to and beyond the date set for the ground offensive on 24 February. The aim was to use precision weapons, involving the latest military technology (the Stealth bomber, Cruises, so-called 'Smart' bombs and laser guidance systems, and infra-red night-bombing equip-

ment) to pinpoint identified military targets, avoid civilian areas
and minimize non-military casualties. This aim largely succeeded;
civilian casualties were minimal, and this helped the Allies to win
the media war at home, as well as the actual one. Targeting proceeded systematically from command-and-control systems, radar
and missile sites, airfields and chemical, biological and nuclear
weapons establishments, to all systems of communications. Thence
it spread to the pinpointing and carpet-bombing of Iraqi ground
forces deployed in Kuwait and southern Iraq. The Iraqi air force
was either destroyed or opted out of the combat at an early stage,
and this greatly assisted the Allied air offensive, which eventually
consisted of nearly 140,000 sorties.

The object was to win the war, in so far as it was possible, by the
use of air power, thus minimizing Allied ground casualties. The
strategy proved, in the event, more successful than even
Schwarzkopf and his advisers, chief of whom was the Commander
of British Forces Middle East, General Sir Peter de la Billière, had
dared to hope. The land offensive, launched on 24 February,
involved an elaborate deception plan, which worked. Iraqi resistance, thanks to the sustained air offensive, was lighter than expected, and by 28 February, forty out of forty-two Iraqi divisions in the
war zone had been destroyed or rendered ineffective. Preliminary
figures indicated that the Iraqis had lost 50,000 killed and 175,000
missing or captured. Allied casualties were 166 dead, 207 wounded
and 106 missing or captured.[143] Anxious not to exceed the terms of
the UN mandate, and unwilling to go on to Baghdad and get
dragged into Iraqi internal politics, Bush ordered a temporary cease
fire on 28 February, provided Iraq accepted all Allied conditions,
which Saddam agreed to do three days later. He himself was shortly
involved in a struggle to retain power against his numerous internal
enemies, and allied troops were obliged to move into northern Iraq
to protect the Kurds from his vengeance. Thus an unprovoked
aggression was decisively reversed by firm leadership from the
civilized powers, within the strict framework of the United Nations,
and in full accordance with international law. This augured well for
the future of collective security, not merely throughout the 1990s
but in the coming twenty-first century, and suggested that some, at
least, of the lessons of the twentieth century were at last being
learned.

The cost, however, was heavy in some ways; Iraq's infrastructure
had been damaged or destroyed, and Saddam himself had looted
and wrecked much of Kuwait's. The bills ran into many hundreds
of billions of dollars though, by one of those ironies of modernity,
the task of rebuilding the two countries was to act as a stimulant to

Western economies and help to pull them out of recession. Saddam, however, in his rage and frustration, had committed two huge crimes, not just against Kuwait but against all humanity. He had released millions of tons of crude oil into the Gulf, which slowly drifted southwards and polluted a huge area of sea, seabed and coast; and he had set fire to about five hundred oil wells in the vast Kuwaiti fields. At the end of March 1991, it was calculated it would take at least two years to extinguish them, though in the event the resources of modern technology enabled the job to be done much faster.

These barbarous deeds reinforced fears that mankind, in its anxiety to acquire higher living standards by exploiting the earth's natural resources, was damaging the planet irreparably. The ecological fears of the 1980s and early 1990s were in some ways similar to the panics of the 1970s, in which the world was warned it was running out of key raw materials; that is, they were both marked by emotionalism masquerading as science, gross exaggeration and reckless (even dishonest) use of statistics. Nonetheless some of the much-publicized worries had substance. There was, for instance, justified concern at the rapid destruction of the tropical rainforests, especially in Brazil, for commercial purposes. The rainforest area was calculated at about 1.6 billion hectares before deforestation by humans began in earnest in the nineteenth century. By 1987 it had been reduced to 1.1 billion, and about 80,000 square kilometres, an area the size of Austria, was being lost every year. The result was erosion of soil, floods, drought and appreciable effects on the world's atmosphere. An additional point, beloved of ecologists but perhaps of less concern to most people, was the loss of insect species caused by deforestation. Some 30 million species of insects lived in the rainforests during the 1980s; they were being destroyed at the rate of six an hour, and 10–30 per cent of the earth's species, it was reckoned, would be extinct by the end of the century.[144]

Tropical deforestation was linked to a problem which, in the later 1980s, came increasingly to be seen as serious not only by ecological pressure groups but by science and government: the 'greenhouse effect'. The earth's ozone layer, which keeps out harmful ultra-violet radiation from the sun, was being progressively weakened, it was argued, by a number of factors, chiefly the burning of fossil fuels, producing carbon dioxide which acted like the glass of a greenhouse, trapping the sun's heat; and by the growing use of chlorofluorocarbons, used for instance as propellants in aerosols and in refrigeration and air-conditioning. Sweden had passed a law banning aerosol sprays as long ago as January 1978; but then Sweden passed many laws banning supposed harmful human activities. The

first serious and documented warning about the ozone layer came
in March 1984 from a team at the University of East Anglia. The
'greenhouse effect' was calculated to produce warmer summers,
milder winters, but also violent storms, floods and drought. British
people in particular began to believe there was some truth in it during the 1980s, which produced some of the warmest summers on
record and, on 16 October 1987, the most violent hurricane since
the early eighteenth century, which destroyed millions of trees,
including many prize specimens at Kew Gardens. The month
before, seventy nations, meeting in Montreal, had agreed (16
September) on a programme of measures to freeze chlorofluoro-
carbon emissions at existing levels and reduce them by 50 per cent
before 1999. In 1992 an even bigger 'Earth Summit' in Rio indicated the world was slowly waking up to its responsibilities as a
preserver of the planet, as well as its exploiter.[145]

Yet if the industrial use of technology, such as the immense
machines which were tearing down the Brazilian rainforests, could
damage the earth, technological advances, including sophisticated
monitoring systems, could help to preserve it, by telling us exactly
what was happening and what we were doing wrong. In any case,
there was no halting the march of science and its application, which
proceeded at an ever-accelerating pace throughout the twentieth
century, both assisting man in his barbarism and reducing its worst
consequences. The winning of the Gulf War by high-technology
weapons, thus reducing casualties (at least on the Allied side) to a
minimum, was both an exemplar and a pointer to the future. In
purely physical terms, the exact sciences fulfilled all their promises
in the twentieth century. Modern times, in earlier phases, were
dominated by physics, especially nuclear physics and astro-physics.
The physicist carried man to the brink of the pit but then halted
him and bade him look down. It may be that, after the seeming
inevitability of two world wars, the creation of nuclear weapons
was an admonitory gift, which spared us a third clash of great
nations and introduced what had become, by the early 1990s,
the longest period of general peace ever recorded. The end of the
Cold War, too, and the partial reconciliation of the two leading
thermonuclear powers, suggested that they would be prepared to
take joint steps to prevent the spread of such weapons to states
foolish enough to use them. In this sense physics seems to have
served an important political purpose in the second half of the
century.

But physics seemed to have come to the end of its paramountcy
during the 1960s. In any case, it could not tell people what they
increasingly demanded to know: what had gone wrong with

humanity. Why had the promise of the nineteenth century been dashed? Why had much of the twentieth century turned into an age of horror or, as some would say, evil? The social sciences, which claimed such questions as their province, could not provide the answer. Nor was this surprising: they were part, and a very important part, of the problem. Economics, sociology, psychology and other inexact sciences – scarcely sciences at all in the light of modern experience – had constructed the juggernaut of social engineering, which had crushed beneath it so many lives and so much wealth. The tragedy was that the social sciences only began to fall into disfavour in the 1970s, after they had benefited from the great afflatus of higher education. The effect of the social science fallacy would therefore still be felt until the turn of the century.

Indeed, in the early 1990s, social scientists at Western universities, including some with high, if falling, reputations, were still trying to practise social engineering. At Oxford, and to a lesser extent at Cambridge, for instance, some colleges pursued a policy of discriminating, in their admissions procedures, against high-performing boys and girls from fee-paying schools, in favour of lower-performing applicants from state schools.[146] The object was the purely social and non-academic one of correcting supposed 'social and financial imbalances' in the general population. The consequence, however, was simply a lowering of standards. But standards themselves came under attack. One senior academic at the University of Pennsylvania, who opposed the whole idea of a hierarchy of merit in literature and the arts, and who wrote that distinguishing between the work of Virginia Woolf and Pearl Buck was 'no different from choosing between a hoagy and a pizza', declared publicly that he was 'one whose career is dedicated to the day when we have a disappearance of those standards'. The fact that he was elected to be the 1992 president of the Modern Languages Association of America demonstrated the power of deconstructionists, as they were called, in academia.[147] But if, as deconstructionists maintained, 'hierarchical' systems of judgement, which favoured the study of Shakespeare's plays over, say, comic books, were a source of social evil, what was the point of universities, whose traditional purpose was the pursuit of excellence?

Some universities now argued that the function of the campus was to correct social abuses. At Harvard, Yale, Stanford and elsewhere, social engineering operated in a variety of ways. While it was difficult to expel students for organizing violent demonstrations on behalf of approved causes, or indeed for doing no academic work at all, it was comparatively easy to extrude them summarily for offending against the code of liberal censorship by using words condemned by organized pressure groups. At Smith, once one of the best women's colleges in the world, forbidden activities included not merely racism, sexism, 'ageism', heterosexism and other narrowly-defined antisocial evils, but 'lookism', said to 'oppress' ugly people by 'supposing a standard for beauty and attractiveness'. A visiting professor at Harvard Law School, once the best law school in the world, committed the particularly heinous crime of 'sexism' by quoting Byron's famous line, 'And whispering I will ne'er consent – consented'. In 1991 Stanford was reported to be working on a 'speech code', in which such words as 'girls' and 'ladies' were forbidden as 'sexist'; instead of 'girl', the term 'pre-woman' had to be employed, though on this point there was some disagreement, since some female pressure groups insisted the word 'woman' should be spelt 'womyn', and others 'wimman'.[148] Significantly, just as in Marxist states social engineering went hand in hand with financial corruption of the most blatant kind, the same conjunction appeared in 'progressive' American universities. Early in 1991, the House of Representatives' Energy and Commerce Committee, under the chairmanship of John Dingell, began a vigorous investigation into the use of $9.2 billion a year funded to American universities by the federal government in the form of research contracts. They discovered that at Stanford, which had received $1.8 billion during the previous ten years, about $200 million had been syphoned off into unjustifiable expenditure, designed chiefly to give the academic staff, from the university's president downwards, a higher standard of living.[149] Such scandals contributed to the process which, by the early 1990s, had begun to undermine the standing of the universities in general, and the social sciences in particular, among the public.

But if physics seemed to have entered, by comparison with its triumphs in the first half of the century, a period of relative quiescence, and if the social sciences were discredited, a new era of biology began from the 1950s onwards. Hitherto, the exact sciences had been able to tell us far too little about life, as opposed to matter. By the 1950s, the way in which the non-organic world operated was generally known; what began to mature in the next thirty years was knowledge of the laws of life. Such law-systems proved to be unitary and holistic. Just as Einstein's recasting of the laws of physics applied both in the ordering of gigantic stellar congregations and in the minute structures of subatomic particles, so the evolving biological rules applied over the whole spectrum of living matter, from the smallest to the greatest.

In the mid-nineteenth century, Charles Darwin's theory of evolution for the first time provided a scientific organizing principle to explain why plants and animals developed the characteristics they exhibit. It was not a deductive system, permitting the prediction of future developments or even the reconstruction of the past: in this sense it was unlike Newton's laws or Einstein's modifications of them. Darwin himself always stressed the limits of his discoveries. He discouraged those who sought to build ambitious projections on them. That was why he gave no licence to the theories of the 'social Darwinists', which terminated in Hitler's Holocaust, and why he likewise brushed off Marx's attempts to appropriate Darwinism for his own theories of social determinism, which eventually produced the mass murders of Stalin, Mao Tse-tung and Pol Pot. In the second half of the twentieth century, however, there were at last signs of a unified theory emerging from the laboratory and reaching to both ends of the spectrum.

At the microcosmic end, molecular biology, neurophysiology, endocrinology and other new disciplines began to explain such processes as the mechanism of genetic inheritance and programming. The most important of the micro-level discoveries came at Cambridge University in 1953 when James Watson and Francis Crick succeeded in deciphering the double-helix configuration of the molecule of deoxyribonucleic acid (DNA).[150] They found that molecules of DNA, which determine the structure and function of every living animal or plant, were in the shape of a double coil, like a spiral ladder, built up of sugars and phosphates and formed into rungs containing various acids. The structure, like a magnificently complex, living computer, constitutes the particular code telling the cell what protein to make, the heart of the creative operation.[151] More striking still was the speed with which this discovery was given a multitude of practical applications. The gap between the theoretical basis of nuclear physics and actual nuclear power was half a century. In the new biology the gap was less than twenty years. In 1972 scientists in California discovered 'restriction enzymes', which allowed the DNA to be split in highly specific ways and then recombined or spliced for a particular purpose. The recombinant DNA was put back into its cell or bacterium and, operating according to normal biological principles, divided and reduplicated itself to form new protein material. The man-made micro-organism was then fed with nutrients and fermented by procedures in use by the pharmaceutical industry for half a century in the production of antibiotics.[152]

Once DNA had been explored, the formidable resources of modern commercial chemistry had no difficulty in devising a range of products for immediate use. The process of mass production and marketing began in June 1980, when the US Supreme Court, in a historic decision, granted the protection of the patent law to man-made organisms. Earlier fears of 'Frankenstein monster viruses' being secretly developed and then 'escaping' from laboratories quickly evaporated. In America, where gene-splicing was concentrated, the restrictive regulatory structure on DNA research was replaced, in September 1981, by a voluntary code.[153] In the late 1970s less than a score of laboratories and firms specialized in splicing. By the early 1990s there were many thousands. With its immediate and multiplying applications over animal and vegetable food production, energy and, above all, medical science and pharmaceutical products, the new industrial biology promised to be a primary dynamic of the last years of the century.

The speed with which the DNA discovery was developed and applied to practical problems raised questions about the macroscopic end of the biological spectrum: the process of explaining the evolution of social behaviour in terms of the growth and age-structure of whole animal populations, humanity included, and in terms of their genetic constitution. Granted the unitary nature of biological laws, if a scientific revolution could occur at one end of the range, was it not to be expected (or feared) at the other? It was in this area that the social sciences had most conspicuously failed, not least because they had been penetrated by Marxist superstition. The academic imperialism of some social scientists prevented much serious work being done on the lines Darwin's discoveries had suggested: that minds and mental attitudes evolved like bodies, and that behaviour could be studied like other organic properties, by means of comparative genealogies and evolutionary analysis. Such approaches were, quite irrationally, discredited by the weird racist eugenics which the inter-war fascists (and, in the 1920s, the Communists also) believed and practised.

In the 1930s, however, the Chicago scientist Warder Alee published *Animal Aggregations* (1931) and *The Social Life of Animals* (1938), which gave illuminating examples of the effect of evolution on social behaviour. The real breakthrough came at roughly the same time as the Watson–Crick discovery, when the British ecologist V.C. Wynne-Edwards published *Animal Dispersion in Relation to Social Behaviour* (1962). He showed that virtually all social behaviour, such as hierarchies and pecking-orders, securing territory, bird-flocking, herding and dances, were means to regulate numbers and prevent species exceeding available food supplies. Socially subordinate members were prevented from breeding; each animal sought to maximize its own reproduction; the fittest succeeded. In 1964 another British geneticist, W.D. Hamilton, showed in *The Genetic Evolution of Social Behaviour* how important devotion to one's own genes was in ordering social behaviour: parental 'protection' was a case of concern for others in proportion as they shared parents' genes. Unselfishness or altruism found in natural selection, therefore, was not moral in origin, nor implied a conscience or personal motivation: there were altruistic chickens, even viruses. Genetic kin theory stated that occurrence of altruistic behaviour increased in proportion to the number of genes shared by common ancestry. It had a cost-benefit element, being more likely to occur when the cost to the donor was small, the recipient's benefit large. Kin theory was refined by the Harvard biologist Robert Trivers, who developed the notions of 'reciprocal altruism' (a form of enlightened self-interest) and 'parental investment', which enhanced the offspring's chances of survival at the cost of parents' ability to invest in subsequent offspring. Females invested more than males, since eggs 'cost' more than sperm. Female choice was largely responsible for the evolution of mating systems, being attuned to the maximizing of evolutionary fitness. As this new methodology developed, it became possible to show that social patterns in almost any species had their origins in evolutionary natural selection.

In 1975 the Harvard scientist Edward Wilson brought together two decades of specialist research in his book, *Sociobiology: the New Synthesis*.[154] His own work lay with insects but he drew on a vast array of detailed empirical studies to mount his case that the time was ripe for a general theory analogous to the laws of Newton or Einstein. This book, and other studies, drew attention to the biological process of self-improvement which is going on all the time and is a vital element in human progress. They suggested the process should be studied by empirical science, not metaphysics, and by the methodology so brilliantly categorized by Karl Popper, in which theory is made narrow, specific and falsifiable by empirical data, as opposed to the all-purpose, untestable and self-modifying explanations offered by Marx, Freud, Lévi-Strauss, Lacan, Barthes and other prophets.

What was clear, by the last decade of the century, was that Alexander Pope had been right in suggesting, 'The proper study of mankind is man.'[155] For man, as a social being, was plainly in need of radical improvement. He was, indeed, capable of producing scientific and technical 'miracles' on an ever-increasing scale. The ability to create new substances further accelerated the communications and electronics revolution that had started in the 1970s and gathered pace throughout the 1980s and into the 1990s. As the number of circuits which could be imprinted on a given area multiplied, calculators and computers grew in capacity and fell in price. The first true pocket calculator, on which mankind had been working since the time of Pascal in the mid-seventeenth century, was produced by Clive Sinclair in 1972 and cost £100; by 1982 a far more powerful model cost £7. The emergence of the silicon chip led directly to the development of micro-processors. Whereas complex electronic controls had previously to be specifically constructed for each job, the micro-processor was a general-purpose device which could be cheaply made in vast numbers. Its emergence was followed, in December 1986, by high-temperature super-conductors, materials which lose all resistance to electric currents at very low temperatures. These, and other new materials and processes, not only advanced the frontiers of high technology, thus making possible the kind of long-distance space probes common in the 1980s and early 1990s, advanced laser surgery and the devastating military technology employed in the Gulf War, but introduced mass-manufactured, low-cost devices which affected the life and work of hundreds of millions of ordinary people. Video machines and micro-discs transformed popular entertainment. Portable phones and car phones gave a new, and often unattractive, dimension to work. Conventional telephone cables were replaced by fibre-optic ones, whose signals coded as light-pulses enabled thousands of phone conversations and scores of TV channels to be carried simultaneously along a single circuit. While the capacity of specialist computers enabled governments and businesses to perform prodigies of computations in micro-seconds, word-processors transformed office work throughout the advanced nations and were employed by ever-widening ranges of people, even including humble world-historians. Machines, often of astonishing complexity, now entered and often dominated the lives of the masses.

Yet, in the early 1990s, as many people died of starvation as ever before in world history. Moreover, many innovations designed to increase human happiness ended by diminishing it. In the West, the spread of contraception, in a variety of forms, and the growing availability of abortion on demand, made fortunes for pharmaceutical firms and clinics, but, in a hedonistic and heedless society, did not appreciably diminish the number of unwanted children. One striking and unwelcome phenomenon of the 1970s and still more of the 1980s was the growth of what were euphemistically termed 'one-parent families', in most cases mothers, usually dependent on welfare payments, looking after children on their own. These deprived children were the products of promiscuity and divorce-by-consent. The numbers of illegitimate children, in societies which called themselves advanced, grew at an astonishing rate in the 1980s. By 1992, more than one in four live births in Britain was illegitimate; in parts of Washington DC, capital of the richest nation on earth, the proportion was as high as 90 per cent. There was no point in trying to pretend that one-parent families and illegitimacy were anything other than grave social evils, devastating for the individuals concerned and harmful for society, leading, as they inevitably did in many cases, to extreme poverty and crime. Crime-rates rose everywhere, fuelled by growing abuse of alcohol and drugs. The spread of unlawful drug habits was just as likely to be prompted by affluence as by poverty. By the end of the 1980s it was calculated that the illegal use of drugs in the United States now netted its controllers over $110 billion a year. On 6 September 1989, President Bush announced plans to reduce drug abuse in the United States by half by the year 2000, and to spend $7.86 billion in federal funds on the effort. Few expressed much confidence in the project.

Another self-inflicted wound in the advanced nations was the spread of AIDS (Acquired Immune Deficiency Syndrome). The origins of this fatal and seemingly incurable disease, which destroys the body's self-defence system against infection, remained obscure even in the early 1990s, despite much research. It appeared to be spreading most rapidly in black Africa, where heterosexuals acted as transmitters. In the West, however, it was largely confined to male homosexuals and (to a much lesser extent) to drug-users. It was the product of drug abuse and, far more seriously, of the homosexual promiscuity which, often in extreme form, had followed the decriminalization of homosexuality in the 1960s and 1970s. Some male homosexuals were shown to have had 300 or more sexual partners in a single year, and against this background the disease spread rapidly. First reports of its seriousness came on 31 December 1981, when 152 cases had emerged, chiefly in San Francisco, Los Angeles and New York; one was an intravenous drug-abuser; the rest were male homosexuals. By 13 October 1985 the World Health Organization declared that the disease had reached epidemic proportions. By February 1989 it was widely reported that those tested for AIDS with positive results were being denied life insurance; others were losing their jobs. Drugs like azidothymidine (AZT) were used to delay (not cure) the progress of the disease, but often with horrific side effects. On 9 February 1989 it was announced that a new antibody called CD4 had been developed in San Francisco; this promised to delay the fatal consequences of AIDS for possibly years, and with minimal side-effects. But no actual cure appeared in sight despite vast expenditure and effort. Uncertainties about the disease produced bitter political arguments. Governments were particularly anxious to prevent its spread among the community as a whole, and spent many millions on advertising campaigns designed to reduce heterosexual promiscuity, and encourage the use of condoms.

Again, the pharmaceutical industry benefited, but whether government expenditure had any other effect, no one knew. By the early
1990s it was generally believed that the likelihood of an epidemic
among heterosexuals, once confidently forecast by the homosexual
lobby, was negligible.

Hugely expensive and probably ineffectual government campaigns against drug-abuse and AIDS saw the modern state in a characteristic twentieth-century posture – trying to do collectively what
the sensible and morally educated person did individually. The disillusion with socialism and other forms of collectivism, which became
the dominant spirit of the 1980s, was only one aspect of a much
wider loss of faith in the state as an agency of benevolence. The
state was, up to the 1980s, the great gainer of the twentieth century;
and the central failure. Before 1914 it was rare for the public sector
to embrace more than 10 per cent of the economy; by the end of the
1970s, and even beyond, the state took up to 45 per cent or more of
the GNP in liberal countries, let alone totalitarian ones. But whereas,
at the time of the Versailles Treaty in 1919, most intelligent people
believed that an enlarged state could increase the sum total of
human happiness, by the 1990s this view was held by no one outside a small, diminishing and dispirited band of zealots, most of
them academics. The experiment had been tried in innumerable
ways; and it had failed in nearly all of them. The state had proved
itself an insatiable spender, an unrivalled waster. It had also proved
itself the greatest killer of all time. By the 1990s, state action had
been responsible for the violent or unnatural deaths of some 125
million people during the century, more perhaps than it had succeeded in destroying during the whole of human history up to 1900.
Its inhuman malevolence had more than kept pace with its growing
size and expanding means.

The fall from grace of the state likewise, by the early 1990s, had
begun to discredit its agents, the activist politicians, whose phenomenal rise in numbers and authority was one of the most important
and baleful human developments of modern times. It was Jean-
Jacques Rousseau who had first announced that human beings
could be transformed for the better by the political process, and
that the agency of change, the creator of what he termed the 'new
man', would be the state, and the self-appointed benefactors who
controlled it for the good of all. In the twentieth century his theory
was finally put to the test, on a colossal scale, and tested to destruction. As we have noted, by the year 1900 politics was already
replacing religion as the chief form of zealotry. To archetypes of the
new class, such as Lenin, Hitler and Mao Tse-tung, politics – by
which they meant the engineering of society for lofty purposes –

was the one legitimate form of moral activity, the only sure means of improving humanity. This view, which would have struck an earlier age as fantastic, even insane, became to some extent the orthodoxy everywhere: diluted in the West, in virulent form in the Communist countries and much of the Third World. At the democratic end of the spectrum, the political zealot offered New Deals, Great Societies and welfare states; at the totalitarian end, cultural revolutions; always and everywhere, Plans. These zealots marched across the decades and hemispheres: mountebanks, charismatics, *exaltés*, secular saints, mass murderers, all united by their belief that politics was the cure for human ills: Sun Yat-sen and Ataturk, Stalin and Mussolini, Khrushchev, Ho Chi Minh, Pol Pot, Castro, Nehru, U Nu and Sukarno, Perón and Allende, Nkrumah and Nyerere, Nasser, Shah Pahlevi, Gadafy and Saddam Hussein, Honecker and Ceausescu. By the 1990s, this new ruling class had lost its confidence and was rapidly losing ground, and power, in many parts of the world. Most of them, whether alive or dead, were now execrated in their own homelands, their grotesque statues toppled or defaced, like the sneering head of Shelley's Ozymandias. Was it possible to predict that 'the age of politics', like the 'age of religion' before it, was now drawing to a close?

Certainly, by the last decade of the century, some lessons had plainly been learned. But it was not yet clear whether the underlying evils which had made possible its catastrophic failures and tragedies – the rise of moral relativism, the decline of personal responsibility, the repudiation of Judeo-Christian values, not least the arrogant belief that men and women could solve all the mysteries of the universe by their own unaided intellects – were in the process of being eradicated. On that would depend the chances of the twenty-first century becoming, by contrast, an age of hope for mankind.

Source Notes

1 A Relativistic World

1 A. Einstein, in *Annalen der Physik*, 17 (Leipzig 1905), 891ff.

2 Banesh Hoffman, *Einstein* (London 1975 ed.), 78; John White, *The Birth and Rebirth of Pictorial Space* (London 1967 ed.), 236–73.

3 Hoffman, op cit., 81–2.

4 A. Vibert Douglas, *The Life of Arthur Stanley Eddington* (London 1956), 39–40.

5 *Daily Telegraph*, 25 June 1980; D. W. Sciama, *The Physical Foundations of General Relativity* (New York 1969).

6 Karl Popper, *Conjectures and Refutation* (London 1963), 34ff.; and Popper, *Unended Quest: an Intellectual Autobiography* (London 1976 ed.), 38.

7 A. N. Whitehead, *Science and the Modern World* (London 1925).

8 A. Einstein, *Out of My Later Years* (London 1950), 41.

9 *The Born–Einstein Letters 1916–1955* (London 1971).

10 Ibid., 149.

11 Ernest Jones, *The Life and Work of Sigmund Freud*, ed. Lionel Trilling and Steven Marcus (New York 1961), 493ff.

12 Ibid., 493.

13 B. A. Farrell, *The Standing of Psychoanalysis* (Oxford 1981); Anthony Clare, *The Times Literary Supplement*, 26 June 1981, 735.

14 P. B. Medawar, *The Hope of Progress* (London 1972).

15 Jones, op. cit., 493.

16 Letter of 18 December 1912. William McGuire (ed.), *The Freud–Jung Letters*, (tr. London 1971), 534–5.

17 See Freud's essay, 'Psychoanalysis Exploring the Hidden Recesses of the Mind', in the Encyclopaedia Brittania survey, *These Eventful Years: the Twentieth Century in the Making*, 2 vols (New York 1924), II 511ff.

18 Sigmund Freud, *The Future of an Illusion* (London 1927), 28.

19 Quoted by Richard Buckle, *Diaghilev* (New York 1979), 87.

20 Walter Laqueur, *Weimar: a Cultural History, 1918–1933* (London 1974).

21 There is no evidence they met. The conjunction forms the setting for Tom Stoppard's play *Travesties* (1977).

22 George Painter, *Marcel Proust*, 2 vols (New York 1978), II 293ff.

23 Theodore Zeldin, *France 1848–1945*, 2 vols (Oxford, 1977), vol. II *Intellect, Taste, Anxiety*, 370ff.

24 Quoted in Lionel Trilling, *The Last Decade: Essays and Reviews 1965–1977* (New York 1979), 28.

25 Painter, op. cit., II 339.

26 Camille Vettard, 'Proust et Einstein', *Nouvelle Revue Française*, August 1922.

27 Trilling, op. cit., 28–9.

28 Karl Marx, *A Contribution to the Critique of Political Economy*, 20.

29 Sigmund Freud, *Beyond the Pleasure Principle* (1920) 70–81.

30 Quoted in Fritz Stern, *The Failure of Illiberalism* (London 1972), 'Bethmann Hollweg and the War', 77–118.

31 Frederick R. Karl, *Joseph Conrad: the Three Lives* (New York 1979), 737–8.

32 J.B. Bury, *The Idea of Progress* (London 1920), 352; see I.F. Clarke, *The Pattern of Expectation, 1744–2001* (London 1979).

33 Quoted by Martin Gilbert in R.S. Churchill and Martin Gilbert, *Winston S. Churchill*, 5 vols (to date) with companion volumes (London, 1966–) IV 913–14.

34 Randolph Bourne, *Untimely Papers* (New York 1919), 140.

35 Foster Rhea Dulles, *The United States Since 1865* (Ann Arbor 1959), 263.

36 Figure given by Karl Deutsch, 'The Crisis of the State', *Government and Opposition* (London School of Economics), Summer 1981.

37 W.W. Rostow, *The World Economy: History and Prospect* (University of Texas 1978), 59.

38 Margaret Miller, *The Economic Development of Russia, 1905–1914* (London 1926), 299.

39 Olga Crisp, *Studies in the Russian Economy Before 1914* (London 1976).

40 G. Garvy, 'Banking under the Tsars and the Soviets', *Journal of Economic History*, XXXII (1972), 869–93.

41 Stephen White, *Political Culture and Soviet Politics* (London 1979), 50.

42 Stern, op. cit., 91.

43 E.H. Carr, *The Bolshevik Revolution, 1917–1923*, 2 vols (London 1952) II 81.

44 Riezler's diary, 4 August 1917; Stern, op. cit., 118.

45 Hajo Holborn, *A History of Modern Germany 1840–1945* (London 1969), 466, 454.

46 Arthur M. Schlesinger, *The Crisis of the Old Order 1919–1933* (Boston 1957), 20ff.

47 Dulles, op. cit., 260–1.

48 John Dewey, 'The Social Possibilities of War', *Characters and Events*, 2 vols (New York 1929) II 552–7.

49 Dulles, op. cit., 262.

50 See Henry Kissinger, *A World Restored: Castlereagh, Metternich and the Restoration of Peace* (London 1957).

51 Harold Nicolson, *Peacemaking 1919* (London 1945 ed.), 25.

52 Quoted by Robert Wohl, *The Generation of 1914* (London 1980), 44.

53 Ibid., 25ff.

54 Professor Carl Pribham and Professor Karl Brockhausen, 'Austria' in *These Eventful Years*.

55 Carr, op. cit., I 254.

56 F. Lorimer, *The Population of the Soviet Union* (Geneva 1946), gives full list, Table 23, 55–61.

57 Nicolson, op. cit., 200–1.

58 *Papers Respecting Negotiations for an Anglo–French Pact*, Cmnd 2169 (London 1924), 5–8.

59 For the secret treaties see Nicolson, op. cit., 108ff.; Howard Elcock, *Portrait of a Decision: the Council of Four and the Treaty of Versailles,* (London 1972), chapter 1.

60 P.S. Wandycz, *France and Her Eastern Allies* (Minneapolis 1962), 11–14.

61 H. and C. Seton-Watson, *The Making of a New Europe: R.W. Seton-Watson and the last years of Austria–Hungary* (London 1981).

62 Peter A. Poole, *America in World Politics: Foreign Policy and Policymakers since 1898* (New York 1975), 39.

63 Ibid., 46.

64 L.E. Gelfand, *The Inquiry: American Preparations for Peace, 1917–1919* (Yale 1963).

65 Nicolson, op. cit., 21–2.

66 Ibid., 31–3.

67 Holborn, op. cit., 502.

68 For the armistice negotiations see Harold Temperley, *A History of the Peace Conference of Paris,* 4 vols (London 1920–4), I 448ff.

69 For the 'Commentary', see C. Seymour (ed.), *The Intimate Papers of Colonel House*, 4 vols (London 1928), IV 159ff.

70 Keith Middlemas (ed.), *Thomas Jones: Whitehall Diary,* I 1916–1925 (Oxford 1969), 70.

71 Nicolson, op. cit., 83–4.
72 For this episode, see Robert Lansing's own account, *The Peace Negotiations: a Personal Narrative* (Boston 1921).
73 Nicolson, op. cit., 79–82.
74 Elcock, op. cit., 241.
75 Ibid., 242.
76 Nicolson, op. cit., 270.
77 Elcock, op. cit., 270–89.
78 *Foreign Relations of the United States: Paris Peace Conference 1919*, 13 vols (Washington DC 1942–7), XI 600.
79 François Kersaudy, *Churchill and de Gaulle* (London 1981).
80 Elcock, op. cit., 320–1.
81 André Tardieu, *The Truth About the Treaty* (London 1921), 287.
82 Elcock, op. cit., 310.
83 *Paris Peace Conference*, XI 547–9.
84 Lansing, op. cit., 3.
85 *Paris Peace Conference*, XI 570–4.
86 Walter Lippmann, letter to R.B.Fosdick, 15 August 1919, in *Letters on the League of Nations* (Princeton 1966).
87 Howard Elcock, 'J.M.Keynes at the Paris Peace Conference' in Milo Keynes (ed.), *Essays on John Maynard Keynes* (Cambridge 1975), 162ff.
88 *Collected Writings of J.M.Keynes*, XVI *Activities 1914–1919* (London 1971), 313–34.
89 Ibid., 375 (the paper is 334–83).
90 Ibid., 418–19.
91 H.Roy Harrod, *Life of John Maynard Keynes* (London 1951), 246.
92 Drafts in Lloyd George Papers, Beaverbrook Library (F/7/2/27 and F/3/34) quoted in Elcock, 'Keynes at the Paris Peace Conference'.
93 See for example Arthur Walworth, *America's Moment 1918: American Diplomacy at the end of World War One* (New York 1977).
94 Keynes, *Collected Writings*, XVI, 438.
95 Harrod, op. cit., 250.
96 Elcock, *Keynes*, 174; Harrod, op. cit., 253.
97 Paul Levy, 'The Bloomsbury Group' in Milo Keynes, op. cit., 68.
98 Quotations from ibid., 67, 69.

99 For Cecil see Kenneth Rose, *The Later Cecils* (London 1975), 127–84.
100 Hankey minute, 1916, Foreign Policy Committee 27/626/, FP (36) 2; Crowe memo, 12 October 1916: Admiralty minute 23 December 1918 CAB 27/626/, FP(36)2. Quoted in Corelli Barnett, *The Collapse of British Power* (London 1972), 245.
101 G.Clemenceau, *Grandeur and Misery of a Victory* (London 1930); A.Tardieu, op. cit.
102 Henry Cabot Lodge, *The Senate and the League of Nations* (New York 1925).
103 R.S.Baker and W.E.Dodds (eds), *The Public Papers of Woodrow Wilson*, 6 vols, (New York 1925–7), VI 215.
104 For the details of Wilson's last eighteen months in office, see Gene Smith, *When the Cheering Stopped: the last years of Woodrow Wilson* (New York 1964).
105 Ibid., 153.
106 Ibid., 107, 111–13, 126–8.
107 Dulles, op. cit., 273.
108 G. Smith, op. cit., 149; Robert Murray, *The Harding Era: Warren G.Harding and his Administration* (University of Minnesota 1969), 91.
109 For the importance of Article 19 *see* Nicolson, op. cit., 73–5.
110 See Table of Wholesale Prices, *US Federal Reserve Bulletin* (1924).
111 See R.L.Schuettinger and E.F.Butler, *Forty Centuries of Wage and Price Controls* (Washington DC 1979).
112 *These Eventful Years*, vol I; this gives complete table of international indebtedness, 410.
113 A.J.P.Taylor, *English History 1914–45* (London 1970 ed.), 74, 169.
114 See Dulles's essay, 'Reparations' in *These Eventful Years*, vol I.
115 Karl Popper, *Conjectures and Refutations* (London 1972 ed.), 367–9.
116 Stern, op. cit., 119.
117 Martin Kaplan and Robert Webster, 'The Epidemiology of Influenza', *Scientific American*, December 1977.

118 Lee Williams, *Anatomy of Four Race Riots 1919–1921* (University of Mississippi 1972).

119 S.W.Horrall, 'The Royal NW Mounted Police and Labour Unrest in Western Canada 1919', *Canadian Historical Review*, June 1980.

120 Jones, *Whitehall Diary*, I 132–6.

121 For this and the following paragraphs, see Roy Mellor, *Eastern Europe: a Geography of the Comecon Countries* (London 1975), 65ff.

122 Quoted by Norman Stone, *The Times Literary Supplement*, 2 October 1981, 1131.

123 Mellor, op. cit., 73.

124 H. and S.Seton-Watson (eds), *R.W.Seton-Watson and the Yugoslavs: Correspondence 1906–1941*, 2 vols (London 1979), II 97.

125 Mellor, op. cit., 75–7.

126 4 January 1918. Stephen Roskill, *Hankey: Man of Secrets*, 3 vols (London 1970–4), I 479.

127 *Statistics of the Military Effort of the British Empire during the Great War* (London 1922), 756.

128 See S.F.Waley, *Edwin Montagu* (London 1964).

129 Barnett, op. cit., 144ff.

130 Nicholas Mansergh, *The Commonwealth Experience* (London 1969), 256.

131 *Report on Indian Constitutional Reforms*, Cmnd 9109 (1918), 3; quoted in Barnett, op. cit., 147.

132 Ibid, 120; quoted in Barnett, 148.

133 See 'History and Imagination', Hugh Trevor-Roper's valedictory lecture, Oxford University, 20 May 1980, published in Hugh Lloyd-Jones *et al.* (eds), *History and Imagination* (London 1981).

134 S.W.Roskill, *Naval Policy Between the Wars*, 2 vols (London 1968), I 70.

135 John Gallagher, 'Nationalism and the Crisis of Empire 1919–22', in Christopher Baker *et al.* (eds), *Power, Profit and Politics: essays on imperialism, nationalism and change in twentieth-century India* (Cambridge 1981).

136 C.E.Callwell, *FM Sir Henry Wilson*, 2 vols (London 1927) II 240–1.

137 Jones, *Whitehall Diary*, I 101.

138 Philip Woodruff, *The Men Who Ruled India*, 2 vols (London 1954), I 370.

139 *Guardian* (London), 21 September 1981.

140 Percival Griffiths, *To Guard My People: the History of the Indian Police* (London 1971), 243ff; Dyer's entry in the *Dictionary of National Biography*; Alfred Draper, *Amritsar: the Massacre that Ended the Raj* (London 1981), and the review of it in *Booknews*, September 1981, by Brigadier Sir John Smyth, who was also commanding security forces in the Punjab in April 1919.

141 Gilbert: op. cit., IV, chapter 23, 401–11.

142 Jawaharlal Nehru, *Autobiography* (Indian edition 1962), 43–4; Nehru, *India and the World* (London 1936), 147.

143 Woodruff, op. cit., II 243.

144 Griffith, op. cit., 247ff.

145 Quoted by J.P.Stern, *Nietzsche* (London 1978), 93. The passage is from the fifth part of *The Joyous Science*, translated as *The Gay Science* (New York 1974).

2 The First Despotic Utopias

1 For a discussion of *Revolutionierungspolitik*, see G.Katkof, *The February Revolution* (London 1967).

2 There are various eye-witness accounts of Lenin's return to Russia. See Edmund Wilson, *To the Finland Station* (London 1966 ed.), 468ff.

3 Carr, op. cit., I 77 (and footnote 2), 78; Wilson, op. cit., 477–8.

4 David Shub, *Lenin: A Biography* (London 1966), 13–16.

5 Ibid., 39.

6 J.M.Bochenski, 'Marxism-Leninism and Religion' in B.R.Bociurkiw *et al.* (eds), *Religion and Atheism in the USSR and Eastern Europe* (London 1975).

7 V.I.Lenin, 'Socialism and Religion', *Collected Works*, XII 142; all the relevant texts are in *V.I.Lenin ob ateisme i tserkvi* (V.I.Lenin on Atheism and the Church) (Moscow 1969).

8 Krupskaya, *Memories of Lenin* (tr. London 1930), 35.

9 Maxim Gorky, *Days with Lenin* (tr. London 1932), 52.

10 Lenin, *Collected Works*, IV 390–1.

11 G.V.Plekhanov, *Collected Works*, XIII 7, 90–1.

12 *Iskra* No. 70, 25 July 1904.

13 Isaac Deutscher, *The Prophet Armed: Trotsky 1879–1921* (London 1954), 91–6.

14 Shub, op. cit., 137.

15 Ibid., 153–4.

16 Ibid., 180.

17 Ibid., 88.

18 Lenin, 'Materialism and Empiro-Criticism', *Collected Works*, XIV 326.

19 Nikolai Valentinov, *My Talks with Lenin* (New York 1948), 325.

20 Lenin, *Collected Works*, XX 102, XXVI 71.

21 Trotsky, *O Lenine* (Moscow 1924), 148.

22 Jean Variot, *Propos de Georges Sorel* (Paris 1935), 55.

23 F.Engels, *The Class War in Germany*, 135.

24 Lenin, *Collected Works*, V 370ff.

25 Lenin, *Collected Works*, IV 447, 466–9.

26 Vera Zasulich in *Iskra*, 25 July 1904.

27 Rosa Luxemburg, *Neue Zeit*, XXII (Vienna 1903–4).

28 Rosa Luxemburg, *The Russian Revolution and Leninism and Marxism* (tr. Ann Arbor 1961), 82–95.

29 A.James Gregor, *Italian Fascism and Development Dictatorship* (Princeton 1979). Olivetti's article was published in *Pagine libere* 1 July 1909.

30 Benito Mussolini, *Opera Omnia*, 36 vols (Florence 1951–63), II 32, 126.

31 Ibid., I 92, 103, 185–9.

32 Ibid., V 69.

33 Ernst Nolte, *Three Faces of Fascism* (tr. London 1965), 155; see also Nolte's essay 'Marx und Nietzsche im Sozialismus des jungen Mussolini', *Historische Zeitschrift*, CXCI 2.

34 Nolte, *Three Faces of Fascism*, 154.

35 Mussolini, *Opera Omnia*, V 346.

36 A.James Gregor, *Young Mussolini and the Intellectual Origins of Fascism* (Berkeley 1979); Denis Mack Smith, *Mussolini* (London 1982), 10–12, 17, 23.

37 Lenin, *Collected Works*, XVIII 44–6.

38 Ibid., XIX 357.

39 Stalin, *Collected Works*, VI 333–4.

40 The 'April Theses' were published in *Pravda*, 7 April 1917.

41 Carr, op. cit., I 40–1.

42 Ibid., 82.

43 John L.H.Keep, *The Russian Revolution: a study in mass-mobilization* (London 1976), 9.

44 D.J.Male, *Russian Peasant Organization before Collectivization* (Cambridge 1971); T. Shanin, *The Awkward Class: Political Sociology of the Peasantry in a Developing Society: Russia 1910–1925* (Oxford 1972); Moshe Lewin, *Russian Peasants and Soviet Power* (tr. London 1968).

45 Keep, op. cit., 172–85.

46 Ibid., 207ff., 216.

47 M.Ferro, *La Révolution* (Paris 1967), 174, 183.

48 Carr, op. cit., I 80.

49 Ibid., 83–6.

50 Ibid., 89.

51 I asked Kerensky in a BBC TV interview why he did not have Lenin shot. He replied: 'I did not consider him important.'

52 Lenin, *Collected Works*, XXI 142–8.

53 Carr, op. cit., I 94–9.

54 Stalin, *Collected Works*, VI 347.

55 John Reed, *Ten Days that Shook the World* (Penguin ed. 1966), 38–40, 61, 117.

56 See decree in Mervyn Matthews (ed.), *Soviet Government: A selection of official Documents on Internal Policies* (London 1974).

57 Boris Pasternak, *Doctor Zhivago* (London 1961), 194.
58 Quoted in Victor Woroszynski, *The Life of Mayakovsky* (London 1972), 194.
59 Nicholas Sukhanov, *The Russian Revolution* (Oxford 1955), 518.
60 G. Vellay (ed.), *Discourses et Rapports de Robespierre* (Paris 1908), 332.
61 *Karl Marx–Friedrich Engels: Historisch-Kritische Gesamtausgabe*, Ier Teil, VII 423; see Carr, op. cit., I 155.
62 *Bericht über den Gründungsparteitag der Kommunistischen Partei Deutschlands (Spartakusbund)* (Berlin 1919), 52.
63 Figure quoted by Alexander Solzhenitsyn, speech in Washington, 30 June 1975, *Alexander Solzhenitsyn Speaks to the West* (London 1978).
64 Carr, op. cit., I 153, footnote 2.
65 Lenin, *Collected Works*, IV 108.
66 V. Adoratsky, *Vospominaniya o Lenine* (1939), 66–7; V. Bonch-Bruevich, *Na Boevykh Postakh Fevral'skoi i Oktyabr'skoi Revolyutsii* (1930), 195; both quoted in Carr, op. cit., I 156–7 footnote 4.
67 Trotsky, *Collected Works*, II 202.
68 See Lenin, *Collected Works*, XXII 78.
69 Carr. op. cit., I 158, footnote 3; *The History of the Civil War in the USSR*, II (tr. London 1947), 599–601; J. Bunyan and H.H. Fisher, *The Bolshevik Revolution 1917–1918* (Stanford 1934), 297–8.
70 Carr, op. cit., I 157.
71 George Leggett, *The Cheka: Lenin's Political Police* (Oxford 1981).
72 Solzhenitsyn, op. cit.
73 Carr, op. cit., I 158–9.
74 Ibid., 159.
75 Leggett, op. cit.
76 Lenin, *Collected Works*, XXII 166–7, 243, 449, 493.
77 *Pravda*, 23 February 1918; Bunyan and Fisher, op. cit., 576.
78 Quoted in Leggett, op. cit.
79 Ibid.

80 Douglas Brown, *Doomsday 1917: the Destruction of Russia's Ruling Class* (London 1975), 173–4.
81 A. Solzhenitsyn, *The Gulag Archipelago* (London 1974), 3 vols, I 28.
82 Quoted in Harrison Salisbury, *Black Night, White Snow: Russia's Revolutions, 1905–1917* (London 1978), 565
83 Lenin, *Collected Works*, XXII 109–10.
84 Ibid., XXII 131–4.
85 *Izvestiya*, 22 December 1917.
86 Carr, op. cit., I 117–18.
87 Ibid., 119 footnote 2, 120.
88 Holborn, op. cit., 490.
89 Gilbert, op. cit., IV 220.
90 J.M. Thompson, *Russia, Bolshevism and the Versailles Peace* (Princeton 1966).
91 Gilbert, op. cit., IV 225.
92 Ibid., 227, 278, 235, 275, 362–4.
93 Ibid., 257–9.
94 Ibid., 244, 228, 305–6, 261.
95 Ibid., 342, footnote 2.
96 Ibid., 316.
97 E.g., General Sir H.C. Holman's telegram to Churchill of 8 January 1920, printed Gilbert, op. cit., IV 366–7.
98 Carr, op. cit., I 263ff., 291–305, and note B 410ff.
99 Stalin, *Collected Works*, IV 31–2.
100 Leon Trotsky, *Stalin* (New York 1946), 279.
101 Carr, op. cit., I 364.
102 Ibid., 380–409.
103 Ibid., 141.
104 Ibid., 143.
105 Bertrand Russell, *The Practice and Theory of Bolshevism* (London 1920), 26.
106 For the Kronstadt affair see Leonard Schapiro, *The Origin of the Communist Autocracy* (London 2nd ed., 1977), 301–14.
107 Lenin, *Collected Works*, XXVI 352.
108 Ibid., XXVI 208.
109 Carr, op. cit., 221–2.
110 Ibid., 205–8.
111 S. Liberman, *Building Lenin's Russia* (Chicago 1945), 13.
112 Lydia Bach, *Le Droit et les Institutions de la Russie Soviétique* (Paris 1923), 48.

113 See George L.Yaney, *The Systematization of Russian Government . . . 1711–1905* (Urbana, Illinois, 1973).

114 T.H.Rigby, *Lenin's Government: Sovnarkom, 1917–1922* (Cambridge 1979), 230–5.

115 Shapiro, op. cit., 343.

116 Carr, op. cit., I 190 footnote 3.

117 Lenin, *Collected Works*, XXVI 227.

118 Quoted in Schapiro, op. cit., 320.

119 Rigby, op. cit., 236–7.

120 Schapiro, op. cit., 322; Carr, op. cit., I 204–5.

121 Carr, op. cit., I 213.

122 Lenin, *The State and the Revolution* (1917).

123 Lenin, *Collected Works*, XXVII 239–40.

124 Ibid., XXVII 296.

125 Rigby, op. cit., 191–2.

126 Ronald Hingley, *Joseph Stalin: Man and Legend* (London 1974), 141.

127 Schapiro, op. cit., 320.

128 Hingley, op. cit., 144–5.

129 Lincoln Steffens, *Autobiography* (New York 1931), 791–2; William Bullitt, *The Bullitt Mission to Russia* (New York 1919).

130 Carr, op. cit., II 24.

131 Keep, op. cit., 261.

132 A.Moriset, *Chez Lénine et Trotski à Moscou* (Paris 1922), 240–2.

133 K.Marx, *Capital*, II chapter XVI; *Communist Manifesto; Critique of the Gotha Programme*.

134 Lenin, *Collected Works*, XXII 378.

135 Ibid., XXII 516–17. Lenin later dropped this reference to Peter the Great, the only time he ever openly compared himself to the Tsars.

136 Carr, op. cit., II 68.

137 Lenin, *Collected Works*, XXII 493.

138 Carr, op. cit., II 102–8.

139 Lenin, *Collected Works*, XX 417.

140 Carr, op. cit., II 109–10.

141 Ibid., 202 footnote 2.

142 Ibid., 209–10.

143 Legal enactments are: *Sobranie Uzakonenii, 1919*, No. 12 article 124; No. 20 article 235; No. 12 article 130 etc.

144 Carr, op. cit., II 212–13; *Izvestia*, 2 April 1920; *Sobranie Uzakonenii 1920*, No. 35 article 169.

145 Carr, op. cit., II 215–16.

146 *Sobranie Uzakonenii, 1918*, Article 11 (e).

147 Lenin, *Collected Works*, XXII 356–7.

148 Ibid., XXVI 204.

149 For NEP see Carr, op. cit., II 273–82.

150 Lenin, *Collected Works*, XXVII 35.

151 Lenin, *Collected Works*, XXV 389, 491; *Pravda*, 22 February 1921.

152 Holborn, op. cit., 512–13, 526–32; Sebastian Haffner, *Failure of a Revolution: Germany 1918–1919* (London 1973).

153 For Gömbös, see Carlile A.MacCartney, *October 15: A History of Modern Hungary 1929–1945*, 2 vols (Edinburgh 1956).

154 David O.Roberts, *The Syndicalist Tradition and Italian Fascism* (Manchester 1979).

155 Mussolini, *Opera Omnia*, XIII 170.

156 Nolte, op. cit., 10.

157 Mussolini, *Opera Omnia*, III 206; V 67.

158 Luigi Barzini, *From Caesar to the Mafia: sketches of Italian life* (London 1971), 139.

159 Figure given in Giordano Bruno Guerri, *Galeazzo Ciano: una vita 1903–1944* (Milan 1980).

160 G. d'Annunzio, 'Il Trionfo della Norte', *Prose di Romani* (Milan 1954), I 958.

161 Mussolini, *Opera Omnia*, VI 82; VI 248.

162 Ibid., XIV 60.

163 See Walter L. Adamson, *Hegemony and Revolution: Antonio Gramsci's Political and Cultural Theory* (University of California 1980).

164 Quoted in Angelo Tasca, *Nascita e avvento del fascismo* (Florence 1950), 78.

165 For socialist violence, see Giorgio Alberto Chiurco, *Storia della rivoluzione fascista*, 5 vols (Florence 1929–), II 78, 168.

166 Mussolini, *Opera Omnia*, XV 267.

167 Giorgio Rochat, *Italo Balbo: aviatore e ministro dell'aeronautica, 1926–1933* (Bologna 1979).

168 Mussolini, *Opera Omnia*, XVI 31, XI 344, XVI 44, 276, 288, 241.

169 Tasca, op. cit., 276; Nolte, op. cit., 210–11.
170 Mussolini, *Opera Omnia*, XVIII 581.
171 The incident is described in Ivone Kirkpatrick, *Mussolini: Study of a Demagogue* (London 1964), 144.
172 Mussolini, *Opera Omnia*, XIX 196.
173 Gaetano Salvemini, *La Terreur Fasciste* (Paris 1930).
174 Mussolini, *Opera Omnia*, XX 379.
175 Ibid., XXII 109.
176 Ibid., XXIX 2.
177 Quoted in Roberts, op. cit., 301.
178 13th Plenary Session of the Executive Committee of the Communist International, December 1933; quoted in Nolte, op. cit.
179 Arthur Koestler, 'Whereof one cannot speak', *Kaleidoscope* (London 1981), 323ff.
180 For the malaria problem, see Norman Douglas, *Old Calabria* (London 1915), chapter 34.
181 Sergio Romano, *Giuseppe Volpi: Industria e finanza tra Giolitti e Mussolini* (Milan 1979).

3 Waiting for Hitler
1 Adolf Hitler, *Mein Kampf*, 202–4; Joachim Fest, *Hitler* (tr. London 1977), 117.
2 Holborn, op. cit., 487.
3 Ibid., 561.
4 Ibid., 602.
5 Translated as F. Fischer, *Germany's Aims in the First World War* (London 1967).
6 For the Fischer controversy, see Fritz Stern, *The Failure of Illiberalism* (London 1972); *International Affairs* (1968).
7 J. Tampke, 'Bismarck's Social Legislation: a Genuine Breakthrough?' in W. J. Mommsen (ed.), *The Emergence of the Welfare State in Britain and Germany, 1850–1950* (London 1981), 71ff.
8 Fritz Fischer, *The War of Illusions: German Policies from 1911 to 1914* (tr. London 1975).
9 Riezler's diary, 18 April 1915. Quoted in Stern, op. cit.
10 Ibid., 4 October 1915.
11 Ibid., 1 October 1918.

12 Holborn, op. cit., 562–3.
13 Stern, op. cit., 118.
14 Gerhard Ritter, *Staatskunst und Kriegshandwerk* (2nd ed., Munich 1965), 2 vols, II 129.
15 Holborn, op. cit., 514.
16 Ibid., 519–21.
17 George L. Mosse, *The Crisis of German Ideology* (London 1966); Fritz Stern, *The Politics of Cultural Despair* (Berkeley 1961).
18 Laqueur, op. cit., 27–30.
19 Martin Esslin, *Brecht: the Man and his Work* (London 1959); John Willett, *The Theatre of Bertolt Brecht* (London 1959).
20 H. F. Garten, *Modern German Drama* (London 1958).
21 Laqueur, op. cit., 36.
22 Frederich V. Grunfeld, *Prophets Without Honour: a Background to Freud, Kafka, Einstein and their World* (New York 1979).
23 Laqueur, op. cit., 155.
24 Roger Manvell and Heinrich Fraenkel, *The German Cinema* (London 1971); Lotte Eisner, *The Haunted Screen* (London 1969).
25 Walter Gropius, *The New Architecture and the Bauhaus* (London 1965); Barbara Miller Lane, *Architecture and Politics in Germany, 1918–1945* (New York 1970).
26 Arts Council, *Neue Sachlichkeit and German Realism of the Twenties* (London 1979).
27 Kurt Tucholsky, *Deutchland, Deutchland uber alles* (Berlin 1931). See Harold Poor, *Kurt Tucholsky and the Ordeal of Germany 1914–1935* (New York 1969).
28 Quoted in Laqueur, op. cit., 81.
29 See Ruth Fischer, *Stalin and German Communism* (London 1948).
30 See Fritz Stern, *Gold and Iron* (London 1977).
31 Grunfeld, op. cit., 26–7: Laqueur, op. cit., 73.
32 F. Nietzsche, *Zur Genealogie der Moral* (1887).
33 *Die Tat*, April 1925.
34 Gerhard Loose, 'The Peasant in Wilhelm Heinrich Riehl's Sociological and Novelistic Writings', *Germanic Review*, XV (1940).

35 Mosse, op. cit., 23.
36 Ibid., 171ff., 112, 82.
37 Laqueur, op. cit., 87.
38 For Lagarde and Lengbehn, see Fritz Stern, *The Politics of Cultural Despair*.
39 Mosse, op. cit., 96–7.
40 Ibid., 143.
41 Quoted in Laqueur, op. cit., 75.
42 Ibid., 76.
43 Fest, op. cit., 138.
44 H-P Ullmann, 'German Industry and Bismarck's Social Security System', in Mommsen, op. cit., 133ff.
45 Max Weber, 'Politics as Vocation', printed as *Gesammelte Politische Schriften* (Munich 1921).
46 K.Hornung, *Der Jungdeutsche Orden* (Dusseldorf 1958).
47 Georg Franz-Willing, *Die Hitlerbewegung* 2 vols (Hamburg 1926), I 82.
48 Holborn, op. cit., 585.
49 Ibid., 586.
50 Figures from E.J.Gumpel, *Vier Jahre politischer Mord* (Berlin 1922); quoted in Grunfeld, op. cit., 211, footnote.
51 Fritz K.Ringer, *The Decline of the German Mandarins: the German Academic Community, 1890–1933* (Harvard 1969), 446; Laqueur, op. cit., 189.
52 Holborn, op. cit., 658.
53 Joseph Bendersky, 'The Expendable *Kronjurist*: Carl Schmitt and National Socialism 1933–6', *Journal of Contemporary History*, 14 (1979), 309–28.
54 For van den Bruck see Fritz Stern, *The Politics of Cultural Despair*.
55 Michael Steinberg, *Sabres and Brownshirts: the German Students' Path to National Socialism 1918–1935* (Chicago 1977), 7.
56 Laqueur, op. cit., 186.
57 Istavan Meszaros, *Marx's Theory of Alienation* (London 1970), 29–30.
58 Robert S. Wistrich, *Revolutionary Jews from Marx to Trotsky* (London 1976).
59 Quoted in Robert S. Wistrich, 'Marxism and Jewish Nationalism: the Theoretical Roots of Contradiction' in *The Left Against Zion* (London 1981), 3.
60 Laqueur, op. cit., 103. Hubert Lanzinger's portrait of Hitler as a knight is reproduced as plate 31 in Joseph Wulf, *Die Gildenden Künste im Dritten Reich* (Gutersloh 1963).
61 Fest, op. cit., 76.
62 Ibid., 32.
63 August Kubizek, *Young Hitler: the story of our friendship* (tr. London 1954), 140f.
64 Wilfried Daim, *Der Mann, der Hitler, die Ideengab* (Munich 1958).
65 Hans Jürgen Syberberg, 'Hitler, Artiste d'Etat et l'Avant-Garde Méphistophélique du XXe siècle' in *Les Réalismes 1919–1939* (Paris 1980), 378–403.
66 Adolf Hitler, *Monologe im Führerhauptquartier 1941–1944* (Hamburg 1980), 54, 90, 331.
67 Hitler, *Mein Kampf*, 474ff.
68 Fest, op. cit., 482.
69 William Carr, *Hitler: a Study in Personality and Politics* (London 1978), 2–3.
70 Fest, op. cit., 489.
71 H.P.Knickerbocker, *The German Crisis* (New York 1932), 227.
72 Weigand von Miltenberg, *Adolf Hitler Wilhelm III* (Berlin 1931), II.
73 Max H.Kele, *The Nazis and the Workers* (Chapel Hill 1972) argues that Hitler had a powerful working-class following; J. Noakes, *The Nazi Party in Lower Saxony 1921–1933* (Oxford 1971), and R.Heberle, *From Democracy to Nazism* (Baton Rouge 1970) put the opposite case.
74 W.Carr, op. cit., 6.
75 Holborn, op. cit., 596–8.
76 Fest, op. cit., 271–88.
77 Ernst Hanstaengl, *Zwischen weissem und brannten Haus* (Munich 1970), 114.
78 Werner Maser, *Hitler's Mein Kampf: an Analysis* (London 1970); see also his *Hitler: Legend, Myth and Reality* (New York 1973).
79 Hitler, *Mein Kampf*, 654.
80 Lawrence's 'Letter' was first published in the *New Statesman*, 13 October 1924; reprinted in *Phoenix* (London 1936), 107–10.

81 Hans Frank, *Im Angesicht des Galgens* (2nd ed., Neuhaus 1955), 47.
82 Otto Dietrich, *Zwölf Jahre mit Hitler* (Munich 1955), 180.

4 Legitimacy in Decadence

1 Pierre Miquel, *Poincaré* (Paris 1961).
2 Harold Nicolson, *Curzon: the Last Phase 1919–1925* (London 1934), 273–4.
3 Charles Petrie, *Life of Sir Austen Chamberlain*, 2 vols (London 1939), II 263.
4 Lord Murray of Elibank, *Reflections on Some Aspects of British Foreign Policy Between the World Wars* (Edinburgh 1946), 10.
5 See D'Abernon's *An Ambassador of Peace*, 3 vols (London 1929–30), I 14.
6 Barnett, op. cit., 323; Lord Vansittart, *The Mist Procession* (London 1958), 341.
7 L.B.Namier, *Facing East* (London 1947), 84.
8 Zeldin, op. cit., II 949–50.
9 J.M.Read, *Atrocity Propaganda 1914–19* (Yale 1941); Alfred Sauvy, *Histoire Économique de la France entre les deux guerres*, 4 vols (Paris 1967–75).
10 André Bisson: *L'Inflation française 1914–1952* (Paris 1953).
11 Zeldin, op. cit., 961, 971.
12 Ibid., 78–81.
13 Ibid., 623–5, 637–42.
14 Sauvy, op. cit.
15 Richard Kuisel, *Ernest Mercier, French Technocrat* (University of California 1967); J.N.Jeanneney, *François de Wendel en République: l'Argent et le pouvoir 1914–1940* (Paris 1976).
16 Zeldin, op. cit., 324–9.
17 François Chatelet, *La Philosophie des professeurs* (Paris 1970).
18 G. Pascal, *Alain educateur* (Paris 1969); B. de Huszar (ed.), *The Intellectuals* (Glencoe, Illinois, 1960).
19 Zeldin, op. cit., 1032.
20 Jean Pélissier, *Grandeur et servitudes de l'enseignment libre* (Paris 1951).

21 Joseph de Maistre, *Les Soirées de Saint-Petersbourg*, 7e entretien; *Du Pape* (1819), Book 3, chapter 2; *Les Soirées*, 2e entretien. Quoted in Nolte, op. cit., 34–5.
22 See Erich Maria Rémarque, *Arch de Triomphe* (New York 1946).
23 Zeldin, op. cit., 15–16.
24 Jacques Barzun, *Race: a Study in Modern Superstition* (London 1938), 227–41.
25 These were Maurras's own claims in his posthumous book, *Le Bienhereux Pie X, sauveur de la France* (Paris 1953), 52, 71.
26 Eugen Weber, *Action Française* (Stanford University, 1962), 189.
27 Anatole France, *L'Orme du Mail* (Paris n.d.), 219; quoted in Nolte, op. cit., 267.
28 Quotations from *Le nouveau Kiel et Tanger; Enquète sur la monarchie; Le Mauvais traité.*
29 Jacques Bainville, *Journal*, 2 vols (Paris 1948), II 172, 174.
30 Nolte, op. cit., 79.
31 Keith Middlemass and John Barnes, *Baldwin: a Biography* (London 1969), 356.
32 Barnett, op. cit., 332.
33 Committee of Imperial Defence meeting of 13 December 1928; Barnett, op. cit., 324.
34 'A Forecast of the World's Affairs', *These Eventful Years* (New York 1924), II 14.
35 Christopher Andrew and A.S.Kanya-Forstner, *France Overseas: the Great War and the Climax of French Imperial Expansion* (London 1981), 208–9, 226–7.
36 J.L.Miller, 'The Syrian Revolt of 1925', *International Journal of Middle East Studies*, VIII (1977).
37 Andrew and Forstner, op. cit., 248, 238.
38 Quoted in W.P.Kirkman, *Unscrambling an Empire: a Critique of British Colonial Policy 1955–1966* (London 1966), 197.
39 A.P.Thornton, *Imperialism in the Twentieth Century* (London 1978), 136.
40 Andrew and Forstner, op. cit., 245.

41 Robin Bidwell, *Morocco under Colonial Rule: French Administration of Tribal Areas 1912–1956* (London 1973); Alan Scham, *Lyautey in Morocco: Protectorate Administration 1912–1925* (University of California 1970).

42 J.L.Hymans, *Léopold Sedar Senghor: an Intellectual Biography* (Edinburgh 1971).

43 Andrew and Forstner, op. cit., 244–5.

44 Quoted in H. Grimal, *Decolonization* (London 1978).

45 A.Savvant, *Grandeur et Servitudes Coloniales* (Paris 1931), 19.

46 Alistair Horne, *A Savage War of Peace: Algeria 1954–1962* (London 1977), 37.

47 Ronald Robinson and John Gallagher, 'The Imperialism of Free Trade', *Economic History Review*, 2nd series, 6 (1953), 1–15.

48 Donald Winch, *Classical Political Economy and Colonies* (Harvard 1965).

49 Quoted in Raymond Betts, *The False Dawn: European Imperialism in the Nineteenth Century* (Minneapolis 1976).

50 J.S.Mill, *Principles of Political Economy* (London 1848).

51 Bernard Porter, *Critics of Empire: British Radical Attitudes to Colonialism in Africa, 1895–1914* (London 1968), 168–79.

52 J.A.Hobson, *Imperialism* (London 1954 ed.), 94.

53 Richard Koebner, 'The Concept of Economic Imperialism', *Economic History Review*, 2 (1949), 1–29.

54 J.Schumpeter, *Imperialism and Social Classes* (New York 1951); quoted in Fieldhouse, *Colonialism 1870–1945: An Introduction* (London 1981), 20.

55 A.S.Kanya-Forstner, *The Conquest of the Western Sudan* (Cambridge 1968).

56 Quoted in Andrew and Forstner, op. cit., 11.

57 Ibid., 13.

58 Fieldhouse, op. cit.

59 D.K.Fieldhouse, *Unilever Overseas* (London 1978), chapter 9.

60 H.S.Ferns, *Britain and Argentina in the Nineteenth Century* (Oxford 1960).

61 David S. Landes, 'Some Thoughts on the Nature of Economic Imperialism', *Journal of Economic History*, 21 (1961), 496–512.

62 A.F.Cairncross, *Home and Foreign Investment 1870–1913* (Cambridge 1953), 88; S.G.Checkland, 'The Mind of the City 1870–1914', *Oxford Economic Papers* (Oxford 1957).

63 Lord Lugard, *The Dual Mandate* (London 1926 ed.), 509.

64 C.Segre, *Fourth Shore: The Italian Colonization of Libya* (Chicago 1974).

65 Fieldhouse, *Colonialism*, 93–5. For India see D.H.Buchanan, *The Development of Capitalist Enterprise in India, 1900–1939* (London 1966 ed.); A.K.Bagchi, *Private Investment in India 1900–1939* (Cambridge 1972).

66 I.Little et al., *Industry and Trade in Some Developing Countries* (London 1970).

67 For this debate see C.Furtado, *Development and Underdevelopment* (University of California 1964); Andre G. Frank, *Development Accumulation and Underdevelopment* (London 1978); H.Myint, *Economic Theory and the Underdeveloped Countries* (Oxford 1971).

68 J.J.Poquin, *Les Relations économique extérieures des pays d'Afrique noire de l'Union française 1925–1955* (Paris 1957), 102–4; printed as table in Fieldhouse, *Colonialism*, 87.

69 V.Purcell, *The Chinese in South-East Asia* (London 1962 ed.); H. Tinker, *A New System of Slavery* (London 1974).

70 J.S.Furnivall, *Netherlands India: a study of plural economy* (New York 1944), chapter 5.

71 Lord Hailey, *An African Survey* (Oxford 1975 ed.), 1362–75.

72 E.J.Berg in the *Quarterly Journal of Economics*, 75 (1961).

73 Betts, op. cit., 193 footnote 7.

74 B.R.Tomlinson, *The Political Economy of the Raj, 1914–1947* (London 1979).

75 Malcom Muggeridge, *Chronicles of Wasted Time* (London 1972), I 101.

76 Evelyn Waugh, *Remote People* (London 1931).

77 L.S.Amery, *My Political Life*, II 1914–1929 (London 1953), 336.

78 H.Montgomery Hyde, *Lord Reading* (London 1967), 317–27.

79 Jones, *Whitehall Diary*, I 274.

80 George Orwell, 'Shooting an Elephant', *New Writing* 2 (1936).

81 For an examination of British casualties see John Terraine, *The Smoke and the Fire: Myths and Anti-Myths of War 1861–1945* (London 1980), 35–47.

82 Paul Fussell, *The Great War and Modern Memory* (Oxford 1975).

83 See Brian Gardener (ed.), *Up the Line to Death: War Poets 1914–1918* (London 1976 ed.)

84 H.J.Massingham, *The English Countryman* (London 1942), 101.

85 C.F.G.Masterman, *England After the War* (London 1923), 31–2.

86 H.Williamson, *The Story of a Norfolk Farm* (London 1941), 76–7.

87 J.M.Keynes, *General Theory of Employment, Interest and Money* (London 1954 ed.); 333, 348–9; Gilbert, op. cit., v 99–100.

88 Evelyn Waugh, *Brideshead Revisited* (London 1945), Book Two, chapter Three.

89 Rostow, *World Economy*, Table III–42, 220.

90 Alan Wilkinson, *The Church of England and the First World War* (London 1979).

91 Sidney Dark (ed.), *Conrad Noel: an Autobiography* (London 1945), 110–20.

92 F.A.Iremonger, *William Temple* (Oxford 1948), 332–5.

93 Ibid., 340.

94 Ibid., 438–9.

95 Quoted in Barnett, op. cit., 241.

96 Peter Allen, *The Cambridge Apostles: the early years* (Cambridge 1978), 135.

97 Michael Holroyd, *Lytton Strachey* (London, Penguin ed. 1971), 37–8, 57ff.

98 G.E.Moore, *Principia Ethica* (Cambridge 1903), 'The Ideal'.

99 Strachey to Keynes, 8 April 1906, quoted in Holroyd, op. cit., 211–12.

100 From E.M.Forster, 'What I Believe' (1939), printed in *Two Cheers for Democracy* (London 1951).

101 Leon Edel, *Bloomsbury: a House of Lions* (London 1979).

102 P.Allen, op. cit., 71.

103 Jo Vallacott, *Bertrand Russell and the Pacifists in the First World War* (Brighton 1980).

104 Holroyd, op. cit., 629.

105 Letter to C.R.L.Fletcher, quoted in Charles Carrington, *Rudyard Kipling* (London 1970 ed.), 553.

106 Holroyd, op. cit., 200.

107 Noël Annan, 'Georgian Squares and Charmed Circles', *The Times Literary Supplement*, 23 November 1979, 19–20.

108 E.M.Forster, *Goldsworthy Lowes Dickinson* (London 1934).

109 Frank Swinnerton, *The Georgian Literary Scene* (London 1935), 291.

110 Holroyd, op. cit., 738, 571.

111 Kingsley Martin, *Father Figures* (London 1966), 120.

112 Ibid., 121.

113 Holroyd, op. cit., 200.

114 Quoted in Paul Levy, *G.E.Moore and the Cambridge Apostles* (London 1979), 176.

115 Alan Wood, *Bertrand Russell: the Passionate Sceptic* (London 1957), 87–8.

116 Holroyd, op. cit., 164–5.

117 John Pearson, *Façades: Edith, Osbert and Sacheverell Sitwell* (London 1978), 124, 126.

118 Quoted in Ronald Clark, *The Life of Bertrand Russell* (London 1975), 380.

119 Ibid., 395.

120 Lionel Trilling, *E.M.Forster: a Study* (London 1944), 27.

121 Clarke, op. cit., 386–7.

122 Barnett, op. cit., 174

123 John Darwin, 'Imperialism in Decline? Tendencies in British Imperial Policy between the Wars', *Cambridge Historical Journal*, XXIII (1980), 657–79.

124 Barnett, op. cit., 252.

125 R.W.Curry, *Woodrow Wilson and Far Eastern Policy 1913–1921* (New York 1957).

126 H.C.Allen, *The Anglo–American Relationship since 1783* (London 1959).

127 Microfilm, AR/195/76 US Navy Operational Archives, Historical Section, Washington Navy Yard, Washington DC.

128 Barnett, op. cit., 252–65.

129 Vincent Massey, *What's Past is Prologue* (London 1963), 242.

130 H.C.Allen, op. cit., 737.

131 Gilbert, *Churchill*, v 69–70.

132 Barnett, op. cit., 217–18.

133. Gilbert, *Churchill*, v, (Companion Volume) Part I, 303–7.

5 An Infernal Theocracy, a Celestial Chaos

1 L.Mosley, *Hirohito: Emperor of Japan* (London 1966), 2, 21, 23 footnote.

2 David James, *The Rise and Fall of the Japanese Empire* (London 1951), 175.

3 See Kurt Singer, *Mirror, Sword and Jewel: a study of Japanese characteristics* (London 1973), 98–100.

4 Fosco Maraini, *Japan: Patterns of Continuity* (Palo Alto 1971), 191.

5 Chie Nakane, *Japanese Society* (London 1970), 149.

6 George Macklin Wilson, 'Time and History in Japan', in Special Issue, 'Across Cultures: Meiji Japan and the Western World', *American Historical Review*, June 1980, 557–72.

7 Singer, op. cit., 147; Tetsuro Watsuji, *A Climate: a Philosophical Study* (Tokyo 1961).

8 W.G.Beasley, *The Modern History of Japan* (London 1963 ed.), 212–17.

9 Robert E. Ward and Dankwart A. Rustow (eds), *Political Modernization in Japan and Turkey* (Princeton 1964).

10 Singer, op. cit., 57–8, 71ff.

11 I. Nitobe, *Bushido* (London 1907); see also Sir George Sansom, *Japan: a short cultural history* (New York 1943), 495.

12 B.Hall Chamberlain, *Things Japanese* (London 1927), 564.

13 In William Stead (ed.), *Japan by the Japanese* (London 1904), 266, 279.

14 Ito Hirobumi, 'Some Reminiscences' in S.Okuma (ed.), *Fifty Years of New Japan*, 2 vols (London 1910), I 127.

15 Chie Nakane, *Kinship and Economic Organization in Rural Japan* (London 1967); and his *Japanese Society* (London 1970).

16 Ozaki Yukio, *The Voice of Japanese Democracy* (Yokohama 1918), 90f.

17 Beasley, op. cit., 226–7.

18 A.M.Young, *Japan under Taisho Tenno* (London 1928), 280.

19 Beasley, op. cit., 237–9.

20 James, op. cit., 162.

21 Hugh Byas, *Government by Assassination* (London 1943), 173–92.

22 Ibid., 173–92.

23 Quoted in Harold S. Quigley and John E. Turner: *The New Japan: Government and Politics* (Minneapolis 1956), 35.

24 James, op. cit., Appendix VIII, 376.

25 Ibid., 163–4.

26 Richard Storry, *The Double Patriots* (London 1957), 52.

27 A.M.Young, *Imperial Japan 1926–1928* (London 1938), 179–80.

28 Byas, op. cit., 17–31, 41–2.

29 For examples see Young, *Japan under Taisho Tenno*.

30 Joyce Lebra, *Japan's Greater East-Asia Co-Prosperity Sphere in World War Two* (London 1975).

31 M.D.Kennedy, *The Estrangement of Great Britain and Japan 1917–1935* (Manchester 1969).

32 James, op. cit., 16; Beasley, op. cit., 218.

33 Quoted in W.T.deBary (ed.), *Sources of the Japanese Tradition* (New York 1958), 796–7.

34 James, op. cit., 166.

35 Ibid., 134.

36 Ibid., 138.

37 Singer, op. cit., 39–40.

38 Charles Drage, *Two-Gun Cohen* (London 1954), 131.

39 Stuart Schram, *Mao Tse-tung* (London 1966), 25, 36.

40 Joseph Levenson, *Confucian China and its Modern Fate* (London 1958).

41 Drage, op. cit., 130–1.

42 Hallett Abend, *Tortured China* (London 1931), 14–15.
43 Schram, op. cit., 74.
44 Drage, op. cit., 154–5.
45 Schram, op. cit., 79.
46 Ibid., 83 footnote.
47 Ibid., 93.
48 Abend, op. cit., 39.
49 Conrad Brandt, *Stalin's Failure in China 1924–1927* (Harvard 1958), 178.
50 Drage, op. cit., 167ff; John Tolland, *The Rising Sun: the decline and fall of the Japanese Empire, 1936–1945* (London 1971), 38, footnote.
51 Abend, op. cit., 49–50, 61, 251.
52 Hsiao Hsu-tung, *Mao Tse-tung and I were Beggars* (Syracuse 1959).
53 Benjamin Schwartz, *In Search of Wealth and Power: Yen Fu and the West* (Harvard 1964).
54 Chow Tse-tung, *The May Fourth Movement: Intellectual Revolution in Modern China* (Harvard 1960).
55 *Far Eastern Review*, December 1923.
56 Reminiscences of Professor Pai Yu, quoted in Schram, op. cit., 73.
57 Sun Yat-sen, lecture 3 February 1924, quoted by John Gittings, *The World and China 1922–1975* (London 1974), 43; Stalin, *Collected Works*, ıx 225.
58 Gittings, op. cit., 39–40.
59 Cf. Mao's poem 'Snow', written February 1936; Schram, op. cit., 107–8.
60 Stuart Schram, *The Political Thought of Mao Tse-tung* (London 1964), 94–5.
61 Chalmers A. Johnson, *Peasant Nationalism and Communist Power: the Emergence of Revolutionary China 1937–1945* (Stanford 1962).
62 Schram, *Mao Tse-tung*, 127.
63 Ibid., 153.
64 Abend, op. cit., 147–8.
65 Ibid., 80, 67.
66 Ibid., 75, 82.
67 James, op. cit., 139.
68 John Tolland, op. cit., 7 footnote.
69 Quoted in Dulles, op. cit., 281.

6 The Last Arcadia
1 The figure 106 (which includes many sub-groups) is used in Stephan Thernstrom and Ann Orlov, *Harvard Encyclopaedia of Ethnic Groups* (New York 1980).
2 Madison Grant, *The Passing of the Great Race* (New York 1916), 3–36.
3 'The Klan's Fight for Americans', *North American Review*, March 1926.
4 William C. Widenor, *Henry Cabot Lodge and the Search for an American Foreign Policy* (University of California 1980); Robert Murray, *The Harding Era* (University of Minnesota 1969), 64.
5 John Morton Blum, *The Progressive Presidents: Roosevelt, Wilson, Roosevelt, Johnson* (New York 1980), 97.
6 Dulles, op. cit., 295.
7 A. Mitchell Palmer, 'The Case Against the Reds', *Forum*, February 1920.
8 Quoted in Arthur Ekirch, *Ideologies and Utopias and the Impact of the New Deal on American Thought* (Chicago 1969), 13–14.
9 *Baltimore Evening Sun*, 27 September 1920.
10 Horace Kellen, *Culture and Democracy in the United States* (New York 1924).
11 V. W. Brooks, 'Towards a National Culture' and 'The Culture of Industrialism', *Seven Arts*, April 1917.
12 V. W. Brooks, 'Trans-National America', *Atlantic Monthly*, 1916.
13 Van Wyck Brooks, *An Autobiography* (New York 1965), 253–6.
14 James Hoopes, *Van Wyck Brooks in Search of American Culture* (Amherst 1977), 130.
15 William Jennings Bryan (and Mary Baird Bryan), *Memoirs* (Philadelphia 1925), 448.
16 Ibid., 479–84.
17 *New Republic*, 10 May 1922.
18 Robert Sklar (ed.), *The Plastic Age 1917–1930* (New York 1970), 14.

19 Albert E. Sawyer, 'The Enforcement of National Prohibition', *Annals*, September 1932.

20 Alan Block, *East Side, West Side: Organized Crime in New York 1930–1950* (Cardiff 1980).

21 *The Illinois Crime Survey* (Chicago 1929), 909–19.

22 Lloyd Wendt and Herman Cogan, *Big Bill of Chicago* (Indianapolis 1953), 271ff.

23 Charles Fecher, *Mencken: a Study of his Thought* (New York 1978), 159.

24 *Sidney Bulletin*, 20 July 1922; for non-enforcement, see Charles Merz, *The Dry Decade* (New York 1931), 88, 107, 123–4, 144, 154.

25 T.K.Derry, *A History of Modern Norway 1814–1972* (Oxford 1973), 301–4.

26 *The Prohibition Amendment: Hearings before the Committee of the Judiciary, 75th Congress, Second Session* (Washington DC 1930), Part I, 12–31.

27 Mark H. Haller, 'The Changing Structure of American Gambling in the Twentieth Century', *Journal of Social Issues*, XXXV, (1979), 87–114.

28 For instance, Annelise Graebner Anderson, *The Business of Organized Crime: a Cosa Nostra Family* (Stanford 1979).

29 Quoted in Seymour Martin Lipset, 'Marx, Engels and America's Political Parties', *Wilson Review*, Winter 1979.

30 David Shannon, *The Socialist Party of America: a History* (New York 1955).

31 Theodore Draper, *The Roots of American Communism* (New York 1957).

32 John Hicks, *The Republican Ascendancy 1921–1933* (New York 1960).

33 Robert Murray, *The Harding Era* (University of Minnesota 1969), 67.

34 Dulles, op. cit., 302.

35 Murray, op. cit., 70.

36 Ibid., 420.

37 Andrew Turnbull (ed.), *Letters of F. Scott Fitzgerald* (New York 1963), 326.

38 Murray, op. cit., 112.

39 Quoted in Murray N. Rothbard, *America's Great Depression* (Los Angeles 1972), 167.

40 Murray, op. cit., 178–9.

41 *New York Times*, 14 October 1922; see Fritz Marx, 'The Bureau of the Budget: its Evolution and Present Role', *American Political Science Review*, August 1945.

42 Murray, op. cit., 168–9.

43 Ibid., 117–19.

44 Ibid., 108.

45 *Investigation of Veterans Bureau: Hearings before Select Committee, US Senate* (Washington DC 1923).

46 Burl Noggle, 'The Origins of the Teapot Dome Investigation', *Mississippi Valley Historical Review*, September 1957; M.R.Werner and John Starr, *Teapot Dome* (New York 1959), 194–277; Murray, op. cit., 473.

47 Murray, op. cit., 486–7.

48 Alice Roosevelt Longworth, *Crowded Hours* (New York 1933), 324–5.

49 Arthur M. Schlesinger, 'Our Presidents: a Rating by Seventy-five Historians', *New York Times Magazine*, 29 July 1962; for a full analysis of the historiography of Harding, see Murray, op. cit., 487–528.

50 William Allen White, *A Puritan in Babylon* (New York 1938), 247.

51 Donald McCoy, *Calvin Coolidge: the Quiet President* (New York 1967), 33, 158ff., 139–41.

52 Ishbel Ross, *Grace Coolidge and her Era* (New York 1962), 65.

53 Mark de Wolf Howe (ed.), *The Holmes–Laski Letters 1916–1935*, 2 vols (Harvard 1953), I 673.

54 Quoted in Sklar, op. cit., 297.

55 McCoy, op. cit., 256–63.

56 Gamaliel Bradford, *The Quick and the Dead* (Boston 1931), 241.

57 McCoy, op. cit., 99, 58, 208ff., 255.

58 Calvin Coolidge, *Autobiography* (New York 1929).

59 Howard Quint and Robert Ferrell (eds), *The Talkative President: Off-the-Record Press Conferences of Calvin Coolidge* (Amhurst 1964), preface.

60 McCoy, op. cit., 384, 395.

61 Ibid., 53–5.
62 Calvin Coolidge: 'Government and Business' in *Foundations of the Republic: Speeches and Addresses* (New York 1926), 317–32.
63 F. Scott Fitzgerald, *The Crack-up*, ed. by Edmund Wilson (New York 1945).
64 Letter to Maxwell Geismar, 10 June 1942, in Elena Wilson (ed.), *Edmund Wilson: Letters on Literature and Politics 1912–1972* (New York 1977), 385.
65 James Truslow Adams, *The Epic of America* (Boston 1931), 400.
66 Michael Rostovtzeff, *A Social and Economic History of the Roman Empire* (Yale 1926), 487.
67 Stuart Chase, *Prosperity: Fact or Myth?* (New York 1930).
68 George Soule, *Prosperity Decade from War to Depression 1917–1929* (New York 1947).
69 Cited in Sklar, op. cit.
70 Rostow, *World Economy* 209 and Table III–38; Harold Underwood Faulkner, *American Economic History* (New York 7th ed. 1954), 622.
71 Faulkner, op. cit., 624.
72 Ibid., 607–8.
73 Sinclair Lewis, 'Main Street's Been Paved!' *Nation*, 10 September 1924.
74 Herbert Blumer, *Movies and Conduct* (New York 1933), 243–7, 220–3.
75 Sophia Breckenridge, 'The Activities of Women Outside the Home' in *Recent Social Trends in the US* (New York 1930), 709–50.
76 Samuel Schmalhausen and V.F.Calverton (eds), *Woman's Coming of Age: a Symposium* (New York 1931), 536–49.
77 R.S. and H.R.Lynd, *Middletown: a Study in Modern American Culture* (New York 1929), 251–63.
78 Lewis L. Lorwin, *The American Federation of Labour: History, Policies and Prospects* (New York 1933), 279.
79 R.W.Dunn, *The Americanization of Labour* (New York 1927), 153, 193–4.
80 Kenneth M. Goode and Harford Powel, *What About Advertising?* (New York 1927).

81 Warren Suzman (ed.), *Culture and Commitment 1929–1945* (New York 1973).
82 See Leon Edel, *The Life of Henry James* (London 1977 ed.), I Chapter 84: 'A Storm in the Provinces'.
83 Nathaniel Hawthorne, Preface to *A Marble Faun* (Boston 1860).
84 Lionel Trilling, 'Manners, Morals and the Novel', printed in *The Liberal Imagination* (1950).
85 E.g., 'Best Sort of Mother', written for J.M.Barrie's burlesque *Rosy Rapture*; see Gerald Boardman, *Jerome Kern: his Life and Music* (Oxford 1980).
86 See the Introduction by Edward Jablonski to *Lady, Be Good!* in the Smithsonian Archival Reproduction Series, the Smithsonian Collection R008 (Washington DC 1977).
87 Quoted in McCoy, op. cit., 392.
88 Charles and Mary Beard, *The Rise of American Civilization*, 2 vols (New York 1927), II 800.
89 Walter Lippmann, *Men of Destiny* (New York 1927), 23ff.
90 Lincoln Steffens, *Individualism Old and New* (New York 1930), 35ff.

7 Dégringolade
1 Norman Mursell, *Come Dawn, Come Dusk* (London 1981).
2 Gilbert, op. cit., V, (Companion Volume) Part 2, 86–7.
3 J.K.Galbraith, *The Great Crash 1929* (Boston 3rd ed. 1972), 83.
4 Ibid., 104–16.
5 William Williams, 'The Legend of Isolationism in the 1920s', *Science and Society* (Winter 1954).
6 William Williams, *The Tragedy of American Diplomacy* (New York 1962); Carl Parrini, *The Heir to Empire: US Economic Diplomacy 1916–1923* (Pittsburg 1969).
7 See Jude Wanninski's letter in the *Wall Street Journal*, 16 June 1980.
8 Rothbard, op. cit., 86.
9 Federal Reserve Bank, *Annual Report 1923* (Washington DC 1924), 10.
10 Seymour E. Harriss, *Twenty Years of Federal Reserve Policy* (Harvard 1933), 91.

11 Rothbard, op. cit., 128–30.
12 Harris Gaylord Warren, *Herbert Hoover and the Great Depression* (Oxford 1959) 27.
13 *Congressional investigation of Stock Exchange Practises: Hearings 1933*, 2091ff; *Report 1934*, 220–1. Galbraith, op. cit., 186–7.
14 Rothbard, op. cit., 158ff.
15 For Strong, see Lester V. Chandler, *Benjamin Strong, Central Banker* (Washington DC 1958).
16 Rothbard, op. cit., 133.
17 Melchior Palyi, 'The Meaning of the Gold Standard', *Journal of Business*, July 1941.
18 Rothbard, op. cit., 139.
19 Quoted in Lionel Robbins, *The Great Depression* (New York 1934), 53. Lord Robbins repudiated this book in his *Autobiography of an Economist* (London 1971), 154–5, written just before the great Seventies recession brought Keynesianism down in ruins.
20 Quoted in Chandler, op. cit., 379–80.
21 Rostow, *World Economy*, Table II–7, 68.
22 Rothbard, op. cit., 157–8; R.G.Hawtrey, *The Art of Central Banking* (London 1932), 300.
23 Galbraith, op. cit., 180.
24 Dulles, op. cit., 290.
25 Schmalhausen and Calverton, op. cit., 536–49.
26 Selma Goldsmith *et al.*: 'Size Distribution of Income Since the Mid-Thirties', *Review of Economics and Statistics*, February 1954; Galbraith, op. cit., 181.
27 Walter Bagehot, *Lombard Street* (London 1922 ed.), 151.
28 For the collected sayings of 'experts', see Edward Angly, *Oh Yeah?* (New York 1931).
29 Galbraith, op. cit., 57ff.
30 *Securities and Exchange Commission in the Matter of Richard Whitney, Edwin D. Morgan etc* (Washington DC 1938).
31 Bagehot, op. cit., 150.
32 Galbraith, op. cit., 140.
33 Ibid., 147.

34 The principal works are: E.K.Lindley, *The Roosevelt Revolution. First phase* (New York 1933); Raymond Moley, *After Seven Years* (New York 1939); Dixon Wecter, *The Age of the Great Depression* (New York 1948); Richard Hofstadter, *The American Political Tradition* (New York 1948); Robert Sherwood, *Roosevelt and Hopkins* (New York 1950); Rexford Tugwell, *The Democratic Roosevelt* (New York 1957); and, not least, the many writings of J.K.Galbraith and Arthur M.Schlesinger, especially the latter's *The Crisis of the Old Order 1919–1933* (Boston 1957).
35 See John P.Diggins, *The Bard of Savagery: Thorstein Veblen and Modern Social Theory* (London 1979).
36 For Hoover's early life see David Burner, *Herbert Hoover: a Public Life* (New York 1979).
37 Quoted in William Manchester, *The Glory and the Dream, a Narrative History of America 1932–1972* (New York 1974), 24.
38 Murray Rothbard: 'Food Diplomacy' in Lawrence Gelfand (ed.), *Herbert Hoover: the Great War and its Aftermath, 1914–1923* (University of Iowa 1980).
39 J.M.Keynes, *Economic Consequences of the Peace* (London 1919), 257, footnote.
40 The letter was to Hugh Gibson and Hoover preserved it in his files; now in the Hoover Papers.
41 Herbert Hoover, *Memoirs*, 3 vols (Stanford 1951–2), II 42–4.
42 Ibid., II 41–2.
43 Martin Fasault and George Mazuzan (eds), *The Hoover Presidency: a Reappraisal* (New York 1974), 8; Murray Benedict, *Farm Policies of the United States* (New York 1953).
44 Murray, *The Harding Era*, 195.
45 Ellis Hawley: 'Herbert Hoover and American Corporatism 1929–33' in Fasault and Mazuzan, op. cit.
46 Eugene Lyons, *Herbert Hoover, a Biography* (New York 1964), 294.

47 Joan Hoff Wilson, *American Business and Foreign Policy 1920–1933* (Lexington 1971), 220; Donald R.McCoy's 'To the White House' in Fasault and Mazuzan, op. cit., 55; for Wilson's anti-Semitism, David Cronon (ed.), *The Cabinet Diaries of Josephus Daniels 1913–1921* (Lincoln, Nebraska 1963), 131, 267, 497; for FDR's, Walter Trohan, *Political Animals* (New York 1975), 99.

48 Quoted in Galbraith, op. cit., 143.

49 Hoover to J.C.Penney, quoted by Donald McCoy in Fasault and Mazuzan, op. cit., 52–3.

50 Hoover to General Peyton Marsh at the War Food Administration; quoted in Arthur Schlesinger, *The Crisis of the Old Order*, 80.

51 Rothbard, *The Great Depression*, 187.

52 Hoover, op. cit., II 108.

53 Ibid., III 295.

54 *American Federation*, January, March 1930.

55 Harrod, op. cit., 437–48.

56 Galbraith, op. cit., 142.

57 Rothbard, op. cit., 233–4.

58 Hoover, Republican Convention acceptance speech, 11 August 1932; speech at Des Moines, 4 October 1932.

59 Rothbard, op. cit., 268.

60 Ibid., 291.

61 Rostow, *World Economy*, Table III–42, 220.

62 *Fortune*, September 1932.

63 Manchester, op. cit., 40–1.

64 C.J.Enzler, *Some Social Aspects of the Depression* (Washington DC 1939), chapter 5.

65 Ekirch, op. cit., 28–9.

66 Don Congdon (ed.), *The Thirties: a Time to Remember* (New York 1962), 24.

67 James Thurber, *Fortune*, January 1932; Rothbard, op. cit., 290.

68 Thomas Wolfe, *You Can't Go Home Again* (New York 1934), 414.

69 Edmund Wilson: 'The Literary Consequences of the Crash', *The Shores of Light* (New York 1952), 498.

70 *Harper's*, December 1931.

71 Charles Abba, *Business Week*, 24 June 1931.

72 Fausold and Mazuzan, op. cit., 10.

72 Quoted by Albert Romasco, 'The End of the Old Order or the Beginning of the New', in Fausold and Mazuzan, op. cit., 80.

74 Ibid., 91, 92.

75 H.G.Wells, *An Experiment in Autobiography* (London 1934).

76 Roger Daniels, *The Bonus March: an Episode in the Great Depression* (Westport 1971), esp. chapter 10, 'The Bonus March as Myth'.

77 Theodore Joslin, *Hoover Off the Record* (New York 1934); Donald J.Lision, *The President and Protest: Hoover, Conspiracy and the Bonus Riot* (University of Missouri 1974), 254ff.

78 James MacGregor Burns, *Roosevelt: the Lion and the Fox* (New York 1956), 20.

79 Quoted in Ekirch, op. cit.

80 Ekirch, op. cit., 87–90.

81 Letter to Christian Gaus, 24 April 1934, in Elena Wilson (ed.), op. cit., 245.

82 Hoover, speech at Madison Square Garden 31 October 1932.

83 Roosevelt, acceptance speech at Democratic Party Convention.

84 Frank Freidel, 'The Interregnum Struggle Between Hoover and Roosevelt', in Fausold and Mazuzan, op. cit., 137.

85 Ibid., 137–8. In the Hoover papers there is a document entitled 'My personal relations with Mr' Roosevelt'.

86 Burns, op. cit., 162.

87 Trohan, op. cit., 83–4.

88 For composition of this speech, see Samuel I. Rosenman, *Working with Roosevelt* (New York 1952), 81–99. The idea came from Thoreau.

89 Moley, op. cit., 151.

90 Burns, op. cit., 148–9.

91 Press conferences of 24 March and 19 and 26 April 1933.

92 Burns, op. cit., 167, 172; Elliot Roosevelt (ed.), *FDR: His Personal Letters*, 4 vols (New York 1947–50), I 339–40, letter to Josephus Daniels 27 March 1933; Trohan, op. cit., 64.

93 J.M.Keynes in *New York Times*, 31 December 1933.

94 Joan Robinson, 'What Has Become of the Keynesian Revolution?' in Milo Keynes (ed.) op. cit., 135; Raymond Moley, *The First New Deal* (New York 1966), 4.

95 Faulkner, op. cit., 658–62.

96 Arthur M. Schlesinger, *The Coming of the New Deal* (Boston 1958), 123; Manchester, op. cit., 89.

97 Leverett S. Lyon et al., *The National Recovery Administration* (Washington DC 1935).

98 Quoted in Eric Goldman, *Rendezvous with Destiny* (New York 1952).

99 Broadus Mitchel, *et al.*, *Depression Decade* (New York 1947).

100 Walter Lippmann, 'The Permanent New Deal', *Yale Review*, 24 (1935), 649–67.

101 For example, William Myers and Walter Newton, *The Hoover Administration: a Documented Narrative* (New York 1936).

102 Francis Sill Wickware in *Fortune*, January 1940; *Economic Indicators: Historical and Descriptive Supplement, Joint Committee on the Economic Report* (Washington DC 1953); Galbraith, op. cit., 173; Rostow, *World Economy*, Table III–42.

103 Keynes in *New Republic*, 29 July 1940.

104 Trohan, op. cit., 59ff., 67–8, 115.

105 Joseph P. Lash, *Eleanor and Franklyn* (New York 1971), 220ff.; Doris Feber, *The Life of Lorena Hickok, ER's Friend* (New York 1980), *passim*; Richard W. Steele, 'Franklin D. Roosevelt and his Foreign Policy Critics', *Political Science Quarterly*, Spring 1979.

106 'The Hullabaloo over the Brains Trust', *Literary Review*, CXV 1933.

107 Bernard Sternsher, *Rexford Tugwell and the New Deal* (Rutgers 1964), 114–15; Otis Graham: 'Historians and the New Deals', *Social Studies*, April 1963.

108 Manchester, op. cit., 84.

109 Lippmann, *Saturday Review of Literature*, 11 December 1926.

110 Fecher, op. cit.

111 George Wolfskill and John Hudson, *All But the People: Franklyn D. Roosevelt and his Critics* (New York 1969), 5–16.

112 Elizabeth Nowell (ed.), *The Letters of Thomas Wolfe* (New York 1956), 551ff.

113 Quoted in Ekirch, op. cit., 27–8.

114 Stuart Chase, *The New Deal* (New York 1932), 252.

115 Frank Warren, *Liberals and Communism* (Bloomington 1966), chapter 4.

8 The Devils

1 Dmitri Shostakovitch, *Memoirs*.

2 Boris I. Nicolaevsky, *Power and the Soviet Elite: 'The Letter of an Old Bolshevik' and Other Essays* (New York 1965), 3–65.

3 Quoted in K. E. Voroshilov, *Stalin and the Armed Forces of the USSR* (Moscow 1951), 19.

4 Albert Seaton, *Stalin as Warlord* (London 1976), 29ff.

5 Stephen F. Cohen, *Bukharin and the Bolshevik Revolution* (London 1974).

6 E. H. Carr, *From Napoleon to Stalin and Other Essays* (London 1980), 156.

7 Isaac Deutscher's three-volume life of Trotsky is *The Prophet Armed* (Oxford 1954), *The Prophet Unarmed* (1959), *The Prophet Outcast* (1963), but it is his *Stalin: a Political Biography* (1949, 1966, 1967) which gives his best-known presentation of the Stalin–Trotsky dichotomy. For an exposure of his work, see Leopold Labedz, 'Isaac Deutscher's "Stalin": an Unpublished Critique', *Encounter*, January 1979, 65–82.

8 W. H. Chamberlin, *The Russian Revolution 1917–1921*, 2 vols (New York 1935), II 119.

9 Hingley, op. cit., 162–3; Paul Avrich, *Kronstadt 1921* (Princeton 1970), 176–8, 211.

10 Leon Trotsky, *Their Morals and Ours* (New York 1942), 35.

11 Kolakowski, op. cit., III 186, 199.

12 Leonard Schapiro, *The Communist Party of the Soviet Union* (2nd ed. London 1970), 353.

13 Boris Bajanov, *Avec Staline dans le Kremlin* (Paris 1930), 74–7, 91, 145, 156ff.

14 Trotsky, *My Life* (London 1930), 433, claimed he was deliberately misinformed of the time of the funeral.

15 Ian Grey, *Stalin: Mán of History* (London 1979), 199–200.

16 Stalin, *Collected Works*, vi 328.

17 The circumstances of Frunze's death are described in Boris Pilnyak's novel, *Tale of the Unextinguished Moon*; and in Trotsky's *Stalin: an Appraisal of the Man and his Influence*, 2 vols (tr. London 1969), ii 250–1.

18 Hingley, op. cit., 168.

19 Quoted in Deutscher, *Stalin*, 311.

20 E.H.Carr and R.W.Davies, *Foundations of a Planned Economy* (London 1974 ed.), i 84–5.

21 Carr, *Foundations*, ii 65–6; Hingley, op. cit., 191; Deutscher, *Stalin*, 314; B.Souvarine, *Stalin* (London, n.d.), 485.

22 Stalin, *Collected Works*, x 191.

23 Eugene Lyons, *Assignment in Utopia* (London 1937), 117, 123, 127.

24 Abdurakhman Avtorkhanov, *Stalin and the Soviet Communist Party* (London 1959), 28–9.

25 Hingley, op. cit., 197.

26 Lyons, op. cit., 372.

27 Stalin, *Collected Works*, xii 14.

28 Cohen, op. cit., 372.

29 Hingley, op. cit., 201; Souvarine, op. cit., 577.

30 Hingley, op. cit., 200.

31 Schapiro, *Communist Party*, 368.

32 Kolakowski, op. cit., iii 25ff.

33 Stalin, *Collected Works*, viii 142; Carr, *Foundations*, i 28–9.

34 For figures see Carr, *Foundations*, i 120–1.

35 M.Fainsod, *Smolensk under Soviet Rule* (London 1958), 46; Stalin, *Collected Works*, xi, 44–5, 48.

36 Tatiana Chernavin, *Escape from the Soviets* (tr. London 1933), 37.

37 Robert C. Williams, 'The Quiet Trade: Russian Art and American Money', *Wilson Quarterly*, Winter 1979.

38 Stalin, *Collected Works*, xi 90.

39 Carr, *Foundations*, i 201.

40 M.Hindus, *Red Bread* (London 1931), 335; Carr, op. cit., 223.

41 T.H.Rigby (ed.), *The Stalin Dictatorship: Khrushchev's 'Secret Session' Speech and Other Documents* (Sydney 1968).

42 Carr, *Foundations*, i 283.

43 Deutscher, *Stalin*, 320; Stalin, *Collected Works*, xii 170.

44 Deutscher, *Stalin*, 325 footnote 1.

45 Lewin, op. cit., 514.

46 Kolakowski, op. cit., iii 38.

47 Winston Churchill, *The Second World War*, 12 vols (London 1964), viii 78.

48 S. Swianiewicz, *Forced Labour and Economic Development: an Inquiry into the Experience of Soviet Industrialization* (London 1965), 123; Lewin, op. cit., 508.

49 Kolakowski, op. cit., iii 39.

50 Robert Conquest, *The Great Terror: Stalin's Purge of the Thirties* (London 1969), 22.

51 Deutscher, *Stalin*, 325; Roy Medvedev, *Let History Judge: the Origins and Consequences of Stalinism* (tr. New York 1971), 90–1; figures from *Istoriia sssr* (1964), No. 5, p. 6.

52 See the summary-article, 'Revising Stalin's Legacy', *Wall Street Journal*, 23 July 1980; M.Msksudov, 'Pertes subies par la population de l'URSS 1918–1958', *Cahier du monde russe et sovietique*, March 1977.

53 Kolakowski, op. cit., iii 43.

54 Cohen, op. cit., 364.

55 Alexander Orlov, *The Secret History of Stalin's Crimes* (London 1954), 317–18; Alexander Barmine, *One Who Survived* (New York 1945), 256, 264; Svetlana Alliluyeva, *Twenty Letters to a Friend* (tr., London 1967), 351.

56 Svetlana Allíluyeva, *Only One Year* (New York 1969), 143.

57 Wolfgang Leonhard, *Kreml ohne Stalin* (Cologne 1959), 95; Nicolaevsky, op. cit., 93–4.

58 Stalin, *Collected Works*, xiii 161–215.

59 Borys Lewytzkyj, *Die rote Inquisition: die Geschichte der sowjetischen Sicherheitsdienste* (Frankfurt 1967), 76.

60 Hingley, op. cit., 214.

61 Albert Speer, *The Slave State* (London 1981), 303.

62 Muggeridge, op. cit., I 234–5.
63 Victor Serge, *Memoirs of a Revolutionary* (tr., New York 1963), 250.
64 Paul Hollander, *Political Pilgrims: Travels of Western Intellectuals to the Soviet Union, China and Cuba 1928–1978* (Oxford 1981), chapter 4.
65 Amabel Williams-Ellis, *The White Sea Canal* (London 1935), introduction; Sidney and Beatrice Webb, *Soviet Communism: a New Civilization?* (London 1935); Harold Laski, *Law and Justice in Soviet Russia* (London 1935); Anna Louise Strong, *This Soviet World* (New York 1936); G.B.Shaw, *The Rationalization of Russia* (London 1931); Solzhenitsyn's account of the Canal is in *The Gulag Archipelago* (New York 1975), II 80–102.
66 Julian Huxley, *A Scientist Among the Soviets* (London 1932), 67; Lyons, op. cit., 430; Shaw, op. cit., 28.
67 Hesketh Pearson, *GBS: a Full-Length Portrait* (New York 1942), 329–31.
68 Wells, *Autobiography*, 799–807; for other refs. see Hollander, op. cit., 167–73.
69 Williams, op. cit.
70 Muggeridge, op. cit., 254.
71 Edward N.Peterson, *The Limits of Hitler's Power* (Princeton 1969), 154.
72 Mosse, op. cit., 294ff.
73 Bendersky, op. cit.
74 Mosse, op. cit., 280.
75 Holborn, op. cit., 658.
76 Fritz Stern, 'Adenauer in Weimar: the Man and the System' in *The Failure of Illiberalism*, 178–87; Paul Weymar, *Konrad Adenauer* (Munich 1955), 129–43; the quotation is from Adenauer's letter to M.Tirard, chairman of the Allied Rhineland Committee in 1923, in the Stresemann Papers; see Henry Turner, *Stresemann and the Politics of the Weimar Republic* (Princeton 1963).
77 For instance his secret report to the cabinet, 31 March 1931, cited in Barnett, op. cit., 340.
78 Michael Balfour, *West Germany* (London 1968), 85–6.
79 Rostow, *World Economy*, Table III–42; Holborn, op. cit., 639–40.
80 Holborn, op. cit., 732.
81 Laqueur, op. cit., 257.
82 Holborn, op. cit., 687.
83 Karl Dietrich Bracher, *The German Dictatorship: the Origins, Structure and Effects of National Socialism* (tr., London 1970), 6.
84 Chrisopher Isherwood, *The Berlin Stories* (New York 1945 ed.), 86.
85 Fest, op. cit., 517.
86 Francis Carsten, *Reichswehr und Politik 1918–1933* (Cologne 1964), 377.
87 Fest, op. cit., 545.
88 Ibid., 507.
89 Ibid., 546.
90 Thomas Mann, *Betrachtungen eines Unpolitischen* (Berlin 1918).
91 Quoted in E.K.Bramstedt, *Dictatorship and Political Police* (Oxford 1945), 98.
92 See Arnold Brecht, *Prelude to Silence: the End of the German Republic* (New York 1944).
93 Quoted by Fest, op. cit., 618.
94 Roger Manvell and Heinrich Fraenkel, *Goering* (New York 1962) 296.
95 Manvel and Fraenkel, *Heinrich Himmler* (London 1965), 10–15, 31–2.
96 Ibid., 34.
97 *Neueste Nachrichten* (Munich), 21 March 1933.
98 Quoted in Manvell and Fraenkel, *Himmler*, 35–6.
99 Ibid., 41.
100 Ibid., 38–9.
101 Grunfeld, op. cit., 126–9.
102 Peterson, op. cit., 14; Hans Buchheim, *ss und Polizei im NS Staat* (Duisberg 1964).
103 Hans Frank, *Im Angesicht des Galgens* (Munich 1953).
104 *Hitler's Secret Conversations* (New York 1953), 420.
105 Peterson, op. cit., 70–1.
106 *Hitler's Secret Conversations*, 306; Peterson, op. cit., 72.
107 Peterson, op. cit., 133–42.
108 Frank, op. cit., 167; Lutz Graf Schwerin von Krosigk, *Es geschah in Deutschland* (Tübingen 1951).
109 Paul Seabury, *The Wilhelmstrasse: a Study of German Diplomacy under the Nazi Regime* (Berkeley 1954).

110 Herbert Jacob, *German Administration Since Bismarck* (New Haven 1963), 113; Peterson, op. cit., 37.

111 Helmut Heiber, *Adolf Hitler* (Berlin 1960), 92ff.; Alan Bullock, *Hitler: a Study in Tyranny* (London 1964), 386; Joseph Nyomarkay, *Charisma and Factionalism in the Nazi Party* (Minneapolis 1967).

112. Fest, op. cit., 807.

113 Otto Dietrich, *Zwölf Jahre mit Hitler* (Munich 1955), 153.

114 Thomas Hobbes, *Leviathan*, Part 1, chapter XI.

115 Peterson, op. cit., 75–6.

116 David Schoenbaum, *Hitler's Social Revolution* (New York 1966), 159–86, 200–1, 285.

117 Heinrich Uhlig, *Die Warenhäuser im Dritten Reich* (Cologne 1956).

118 Friedrich Facius, *Wirtschaft und Staat (Schriften des Bundesarchiv)* (Koblenz 1959) 147.

119 Raul Hilberg, *The Destruction of the European Jews* (Chicago 1961), 98.

120 This is the view of E.K.Bramsted, *Goebbels and National Socialist Propaganda* (Lansing 1965); Helmut Heiber, *Josef Goebbels* (Berlin 1962) argues that Goebbels was not anti-Semitic.

121 Bullock, op. cit., 121.

122 Arthur Schweitzer, *Big Business in the Third Reich* (London 1964), 643, note 25.

123 Hermann Rauschning, *Hitler's Revolution of Destruction* (London 1939).

124 Quoted Holborn, op. cit., 753.

125 Joseph Borking, *The Crime and Punishment of I.G.Farben* (London 1979), 56–60.

126 For Todt's ability see Alan Milward, *The German Economy at War* (London 1965).

127 Speer, op. cit., 4ff.

128 David Schoenbaum, *Die braune Revolution* (Cologne 1968), 150.

129 Fest, op. cit., 559.

130 David Carlton, *Anthony Eden* (London 1981), 46.

131 Hans Gisevius, *Adolf Hitler* (Munich 1963), 173.

132 Holborn, op. cit., 745–7; Manvell and Fraenkel, *Himmler*, 42–6.

133 Fest, op. cit., 705.

134 Nicholaevsky, op. cit., 28–30.

135 For the influence of the Roehm purge on Stalin, see George Kennan, *Russia and the West Under Lenin and Stalin* (New York 1960), 285.

136 Conquest, op. cit., 44.

137 Medvedev, op. cit., 157ff.; Hingley, op. cit., 236ff.; Conquest, op. cit., 47ff.

138 Orlov, op. cit., 17–18, 129.

139 Orlov, op. cit., 350.

140 Rigby, *The Stalin Dictatorship*, 39–40.

141 W.G.Krivitsky, *I Was Stalin's Agent* (London 1940), 166.

142 Ibid., 228.

143 Paul Blackstock, *The Secret Road to World War Two: Soviet versus Western Intelligence 1921–1939* (Chicago 1969); Hingley, op. cit., 292ff.

144 John Erickson, *The Soviet High Command, a Military and Political History, 1918–1941* (London 1962), 374; Conquest, op. cit., 224; Hingley, op. cit., 258–9.

145 Schapiro, *Communist Party*, 440.

146 Medvedev, op. cit., 294–6.

147 Ibid., 219–23.

148 Fitzroy Maclean, *Eastern Approaches* (London 1966 ed.) 119–20.

149 For details of the use of torture, see Medvedev, op. cit., 259–70, 286.

150 Simon Wolin and Robert M.Slusser, *The Soviet Secret Police* (New York 1957), 194; Antoni Ekart, *Vanished Without Trace* (London 1954), 244.

151 Medvedev, op. cit., 239; Conquest, op. cit., 525–35; see also Iosif Dyadkin's calculations, *Wall Street Journal*, 23 July 1980, which are similar.

152 Laqueur, op. cit., 266–7.

153 For right-wing intellectuals, see Richard Griffiths, *Fellow-Travellers of the Right: British Enthusiasts for Nazi Germany 1933–1938* (London 1980), and Alastair Hamilton, *The Appeal of Fascism: a Study of Intellectuals and Fascism 1919–1945* (London 1971); see also Malcolm Muggeridge, *The Thirties* (London 1940), 281–2.

154 For Stalin's anti-Semitism, see Medvedev, op. cit., 493ff.; he gives a list of books banned by Stalin on p. 524; for Gorky, see Hingley, op. cit., 241–2.

155 *The Letters of Lincoln Steffens*, ed. E. Winter and G. Hicks, 2 vols (New York 1938), II 1001.

156 Shaw, *The Rationalization of Russia* (Bloomington, Ind., 1964 ed.), 112.

157 Quoted by Jean Lacourure, *André Malraux* (New York 1975), 230.

158 Quoted by Sidney Hook in *Encounter*, March 1978.

159 Cohen, op. cit., 376.

160 Muggeridge, *Chronicles of Wasted Time*, 254–5.

161 Walter Duranty, *The Kremlin and the People* (New York 1941), 65.

162 Quoted in Hollander, op. cit., 164.

163 Trilling, in *The Last Decade*, 'Art, Will and Necessity'.

164 Ibid., 'A Novel of the Thirties'.

9 **The High Noon of Aggression**

1 Manchester, op. cit., 7.

2 James Margach, *The Abuse of Power* (London 1978).

3 Barnett, op. cit., 291; Mary Agnes Hamilton, *Arthur Henderson* (London 1938).

4 Beasley, op. cit., 245.

5 *Documents on British Foreign Policy*, 2, IX No. 43; see Ian Nish, *Japanese Foreign Policy, 1869–1942* (London 1977), 260ff.

6 Barnett, op. cit., 300.

7 Middlemass and Barnes, op. cit., 729.

8 James Neidpath, *The Singapore Naval Base and the Defence of Britain's Eastern Empire 1919–1941* (Oxford 1981).

9 James, op. cit., 167.

10 Harold S. Quigley and John E. Turner, *The New Japan: Government and Politics* (Minneapolis 1956), 38–9.

11 Quoted by Hugh Byas, op. cit., 265–6.

12 Ibid., 97.

13 Mosley, op. cit., 154–5.

14 Tolland, op. cit., 13.

15 Byas, op. cit., 119ff.; Tolland, op. cit., 13–33; Beasley, op. cit., 250; James, op. cit., 170ff.

16 Tolland, op. cit., 21.

17 Ibid, 33 footnote; for Sorge, see William Deakin and G. R. Storry, *The Case of Richard Sorge* (London 1964).

18 Anthony Garavente, 'The Long March', *China Quarterly*, 22 (1965), 84–124.

19 Edgar Snow, *Red Star over China* (London 1938); Chen Chang-Feng, *On the Long March with Chairman Mao* (Peking 1959); *The Long March: Eyewitness Accounts* (Peking 1963).

20 Edgar Snow, *Random Notes on Red China* (Harvard 1957), 1–11; J. M. Betram, *Crisis in China: the Only Story of the Sian Mutiny* (London 1937).

21 Agnes Smedley, *Battle Hymn of China* (London 1944), 96–143.

22 Tolland, op. cit., 44–7; see also James B. Crowley in the *Journal of Asian Studies*, May 1963, and C. P. Fitzgerald, *The Birth of Communist China* (Baltimore 1964).

23 Nish, op. cit., 232; Katsu Young, 'The Nomohan Incident: Imperial Japan and the Soviet Union', *Monumenta Nipponica*, 22 (1967), 82–102.

24 Tolland, op. cit., 44 footnote.

25 Ibid., 47.

26 Mosley, op. cit., 177–81; Tolland, op. cit., 50.

27 Quoted by Nish, op. cit., 260.

28 Hugh Byas in *New York Times*, 31 July 1938.

29 Hans Frank, *Im Angesicht des Galgens* (Munich 1953), 92; Joseph Goebbels, *Der Faschismus und seine praktischen Ergebnisse* (1935).

30 Nolte, op. cit., 230.

31 Mussolini, *Opera Omnia*, XXVI 233.

32 Barnett, op. cit., 344–8.

33 Ibid., 379–80; Carlton, op. cit., 68.

34 Carlton, op. cit., 84–6.

35 Barnett, op. cit., 381.

36 *Ciano's Diplomatic Papers* (London 1948), 56.

37 For Italian fascist racialism, see Antonio Spinosa, 'Le persecuzioni razziali in Italia', *Il Ponte* VIII (1952), 964–78, 1078–96, 1604–22, IX (1953), 950ff.

38 Salvador de Madariaga, *Spain: a Modern History* (London 1961), 455.

39 Quoted in Paul Preston, *The Coming of the Spanish Civil War* (London 1978), 15.

40 Largo Caballero, *Mis Recuerdos* (Mexico City 1954), 37.

41 Mariano Perez Galan, *La Ensenanza en la II Republica espanola* (Madrid 1975), 332–3.

42 See articles by Luis Araquistain, *El Sol* (Madrid), 18, 21, 24 July 1931.

43 Preston, op. cit., 107.

44 Stanley Payne, *The Spanish Revolution* (New York 1970), 108.

45 Eye-witness 1933, quoted Ramón Sender, *Viaje a la aldea del crimen* (Madrid 1934), 33–42.

46 J. Arrarás Irribaren (ed.), *Historia de la Cruzada Española*, 8 vols (Madrid 1940–4), II 263; J. A. Ansaldo, *Para Qui? De Alfonso XIII a Juan III* (Buenos Aires 1951), 51.

47 George Dimitrov, *The Working Classes Against Fascism* (London 1935), 47.

48 Hugh Thomas, *The Spanish Civil War* (London 1961 ed.), 95; George Hills, *Franco: the Man and his Nation* (London 1967), 210.

49 J. W. D. Trythall, *Franco: a Biography* (London 1970), 80.

50 R. A. H. Robinson, *The Origins of Franco's Spain* (Newton Abbot 1970), 12.

51 Thomas, op. cit., 5.

52 Preston, op. cit., 162–3, 172.

53 Trythall, op. cit., 81; Preston, op. cit., 176.

54 Burnett Bolloten, *The Grand Camouflage* (London 2nd ed. 1968), 115–16; Juan-Simeon Vidarte, *Todos fuimos culpables* (Mexico 1973), 56–7.

55 Robinson, op. cit., 259–60; Preston, op. cit, 185.

56 Vidarte, op. cit., 100, 115–27; Idalecio Prieto, *Convulciones de Espana*, 3 vols (Mexico 1967–9), III 143–4.

57 Constancia de la Mora, *In Place of Splendour* (London 1940), 214–15; Claud Bowers, *My Mission to Spain* (London 1954), 200–8; Henry Buckley, *Life and Death of the Spanish Republic* (London 1940), 129; Stanley Payne, *Falange: a History of Spanish Fascism* (Stanford 1961), 98–105; Ian Gibson, *La Represion nacionalista de Granada en 1936* (Paris 1971) 40–3.

58 Thomas, op. cit., 5; Robles's figures were broadly correct.

59 Vidarte, op. cit., 213–17.

60 J. Gutiérrez-Ravé, *Gil Robles: caudillo frustrado* (Madrid 1967), 198–9.

61 Thomas, op. cit. 52–4.

62 Ibid., 269, footnote 1.

63 Antonio Montero, *La Persecucion religiosa en Espagna 1936–1939* (Madrid 1961), 762.

64 Thomas, op. cit., 270–2.

65 Arthur Koestler, *The Invisible Writing* (London 1954), 347; Ignacio Escobar, *Asi empezo* (Madrid 1974).

66 Thomas, op. cit., 270 footnote 2.

67 Juan de Iturralde, *El Catolicismo y la cruzada de Franco*, 2 vols (Bayonne 1955), II 88–9.

68 Ignacio de Azpiazu, *Siete meses y siete dias en la Espana de Franco* (Caracas 1964), 115.

69 Georges Bernanos, *Les Grands Cimitières sous la lune* (Paris 1938), 72–3; Koestler, *Invisible Writing*, 333–5.

70 Thomas, op. cit., 265, citing authorities in footnotes; Ian Gibson, *The Death of Lorca* (London 1973), 167–9.

71 Trythall, op. cit., 94.

72 S. G. Payne, *Politics and the Military in Modern Spain* (Stanford 1967), 371–2.

73 Thomas, op. cit., 1977 edition, gives details of foreign intervention in Appendix 7, 974–85; see also Jesus Salas, *Intervencion extrajeras en la guerra de Espana* (Madrid 1974).

74 D. C. Watt, 'Soviet Aid to the Republic', *Slavonic and East European Review*, June 1960; Thomas, op. cit., 981–2.

75 Thomas, op. cit., 982 footnote 2; Neal Wood, *Communism and British Intellectuals* (London 1959), 56.

76 Quoted by Trythall, op. cit., 65; Luis de Galinsoga, *Centinela del Occidente: Semblanza biográfica de Francisco Franco* (Barcelona 1956), 134–9.

77 Rudolf Timmermans, *General Franco* (Olten 1937), 135; Francisco Franco, *Diario de una Bandera* (Madrid 1922), 46, 179; Trythall, op. cit., 58.

78 Alekandro Vicuna, *Franco* (Santiago de Chile 1956) 222–3; Ignacio Gonzalez, *La Guerra nacional espagnola ante la moral y el derecho* (Salamanca 1937); Jay Allen, *Chicago Tribune*, 29 July 1936; *Cruzada Espanola*, II 84.

79 Thomas, op. cit., Appendix 5, 971.

80 Ibid., 974–7; Salas, op. cit., 510.

81 Carlos Baker, *Ernest Hemingway* (Penguin 1972), 472.

82 Thomas, op. cit., 533.

83 Jesús Hernández Tomas, *La Grande Trahison* (Paris 1953), 66; Thomas, op. cit., 650–1.

84 Thomas, op. cit., 664 footnote 1; Manuel Azana, *Obras Completas*, 4 vols (Mexico City 1966–8), IV 867; Caballero, op. cit., 204; Incalecio Prieto, *Convulciones de Espagna*, 3 vols (Mexico City 1967–9) III 220.

85 George Orwell, *Homage to Catalonia* (London 1938), 169ff.; Thomas, op. cit., 651ff.

86 Hernández, op. cit., 124–6.

87 Thomas, op. cit., 705–6; Bernard Crick, *George Orwell: a Life* (London 1980), 224–6.

88 Krivitsky managed to publish his book, *I Was Stalin's Agent*, (London 1940) first; Hingley, op. cit., 268ff.

89 Thomas, op. cit., 702–3 and footnote.

90 Orlov, op. cit.

91 Thomas, op. cit., 624–7, Appendix 8, 986–91; Vincente Talon, *Arde Guernica* (Madrid 1970); Herbert Southworth, *La Destruction de Guernica* (Paris 1975); Adolf Galland, *The First and the Last* (London 1957).

92 Allen Guttmann, *The Wound in the Heart: America and the Spanish Civil War* (New York 1962).

93 Koestler, *Invisible Writing*.

94 *New English Weekly*, 29 July, 2 September 1937; for this celebrated episode, see Kingley Martin, *Editor, 1931–1945* (London 1968), 218; George Orwell, *Collected Essays*, etc., 4 vols (Penguin 1970), I 333ff.; Crick, op. cit., 227ff.

95 Sean Day-Lewis, *C. Day-Lewis: an English Literary Life* (London 1980), 94, 102.

96 Cyril Connolly, 'Some Memories' in Stephen Spender (ed.), *W. H. Auden: a tribute* (London 1975), 70.

97 Hugh Thomas, 'The Lyrical Illusion of Spain 1936' in Mestine de Courcel (ed.), *Malraux: Life and Work* (London 1976), 42–3.

98 Carlos Baker, op. cit., 465.

99 Martin, op. cit., 219–20.

100 Stephen Spender, *World within World* (London 1951), 242–3.

101 Ibid., 223.

102 Orwell, 'Notes on the Spanish Militias', *Collected Essays*, I 350–64.

103 Jose Diaz de Villegas, *La Guerra de liberacion* (Barcelona 1957), 384.

104 Thomas, op. cit., 926–7.

105 Text of Law in *Boletín Oficial del Estado*, 13 February 1939; Trythall, op. cit., 141.

106 *Ciano's Diplomatic Papers*, 293–4.

107 Quoted by Max Gallo, *Spain under Franco: a History* (tr. London 1973), 88. The figure of 193,000 is given in Charles Foltz, *The Masquerade in Spain* (Boston 1948), 97; see Thomas, op. cit., 924–5.

108 Trythall, op. cit., 142ff.

10 The End of Old Europe

1 H. A. Jacobsen, *Der Zweite Weltkrieg: Grundzüge der Politik und Strategie in Dokumenten* (Frankfurt 1965), 180–1; quoted in Andreas Hillgruber, *Germany and the Two World Wars* (tr., Harvard 1981), 56–7.

2 Notes taken by Lt-General Liebmann, quoted in Hillgruber, op. cit., 57.

3 Rudolph Binion, *Hitler among the Germans* (New York 1976), 61–3, 78–82.

4 *Hitlers Zweites Buch: Ein Dokument aus dem Jahre 1928* (Stuttgart 1961); tr. as *Hitler's Secret Book* (New York 1962).
5 Quoted in Fest, op. cit., 793.
6 *Hitlers Zweites Buch*, 130.
7 Hillgruber, op. cit., 50.
8 Fest, op. cit., 796–7.
9 Herbert Agar, 'Culture v. Colonialism in America', *Southern Review*, 1 (July 1935), 1–19.
10 George Kennan, *Memoirs, 1925–1950* (Boston 1967), 53.
11 C.A.MacDonald, *The United States, Britain and Appeasement 1936–1939* (London 1981).
12 Kennan, *Memoirs 1925–1950*, 84.
13 Ibid., 86; Daniel Yergin, *Shattered Peace: the Origins of the Cold War and the National Security State* (Boston 1977), 34–5.
14 Fest, op. cit., 869.
15 Gilbert, *Churchill*, v 459–62.
16 Quoted in Montgomery Hyde, *Carson* (London 1953), 387.
17 Roland Hunt and John Harrison, *The District Officer in India 1930–1947* (London 1980).
18 B.R.Tomlinson, 'Foreign private investment in India 1920–50', *Modern Asian Studies*, XII 4 (1978).
19 Gilbert, op. cit., 399ff.; 480–1.
20 Andrew Boyle, *The Climate of Treason* (London 1979), with corrections in Noel Annan's review, *The Times Literary Supplement*, 7 December 1979, 83–4.
21 Stuart Macintyre, *A Proletarian Science: Marxism in Britain 1917–1933* (Cambridge 1980).
22 Middlemas and Barnes, op. cit., 745.
23 Quoted in John Gross, *The Rise and Fall of the Man of Letters* (London 1969), 283.
24 Gisela Lebzelter, *Political Anti-Semitism in England 1918–1939* (New York 1978).
25 J.R.M.Butler, *Lord Lothian* (London 1960), 206.
26 Viscount Templewood, *Nine Troubled Years* (London 1954), 133.
27 *Daily Telegraph*, 28 January 1935.
28 Martin Gilbert, *The Roots of Appeasement* (London 1966), 354–5; Barnett, op. cit., 389ff.
29 Nicolson, *Diaries*, 23 March 1936.
30 Gilbert, *Churchill*, v 456.
31 V. K.Krishna Menon (ed.), *Young Oxford and War* (London 1934).
32 Barnett, op. cit., 423–4.
33 Christopher Thorne, 'Viscount Cecil, the Government and the Far Eastern Crisis of 1931', *Cambridge Historical Journal*, XIV (1971), 805–26.
34 See Donald S. Birn, *The League of Nations Union 1918–1945* (Oxford 1981).
35 Letter to the *Manchester Guardian*, 26 February 1932.
36 Michael Pugh, 'Pacifism and Politics in Britain 1931–1935', *Cambridge Historical Journal*, XXIII (1980), 641–56.
37 For an explanation (not justification) of the concession, see Paul Haggie, *Britannia at Bay* (Oxford 1981).
38 Anthony Eden, speech, 30 January 1941.
39 Paul Schmidt, *Hitler's Interpreter* (tr. London 1951), 320.
40 Barnett, op. cit., 409–10.
41 The conference is described in Friedrich Hossbach, *Zwischen Wehrmacht und Hitler 1934–1938* (Hanover 1949); Fest, op. cit., 800.
42 Fest, op. cit., 809–10.
43 See Stefan Zweig, *The World of Yesterday* (New York 1943).
44 Jones, *Life and Work of Freud*, 636ff.
45 Barnett, op. cit., 474–5.
46 Robert J. O'Neill, *The German-Army and the Nazi Party 1933–1939* (London 1966), 152–9.
47 Peter Hoffman, *Widerstand, Staatsstreich, Attentat: Der Kampf der Opposition gegen Hitler* (Munich 1969), 83; Fest, op. cit., 829ff., and 1174–5 notes 20–3 for sources.
48 O'Neill, op. cit., 163–5.
49 Fest, op. cit., 832–3.
50 'Letter to Runciman', 15 September 1938; *Opera Omnia*, XIX 143.
51 Holborn, op. cit., 780ff.
52 Gilbert, *Churchill*, v 999ff.
53 André Beauffre, *1940: the Fall of France* (tr. London 1967), 84; Barnett, op. cit., 526–7.
54 Holborn, op. cit., 777.

55 William Shirer, *The Rise and Fall of the Third Reich* (London 1960), 399.

56 Fest, op. cit., 892; Kennan, *Memoirs 1925–1950*, 108.

57 See Franklin Reid Gannon, *The British Press and Germany 1936–1939* (Oxford 1971); Martin, *Editor*, 254–7.

58 Barnett, op. cit., 560.

59 *The Times*, leading article, 1 April 1939; Gilbert, *Churchill*, v 1052–3.

60 Hillgruber, op. cit., 61–2.

61 Ibid., 66.

62 Barnett, op. cit., 569.

63 Fest, op. cit., 917; Hillgruber, op. cit., 63.

64 Fest, op. cit., 869.

65 Hubertus Lupke, 'Japans Russlandpolitik von 1939 bis 1941', *Schriften des Instituts für Asienkunde in Hamburg*, x (Frankfurt 1962), 7–24.

66 Fest, op. cit., 884–5; for sources see 1177–8, note 27.

67 Hans Gunther Seraphim (ed.), *Das politische Tagebuch Alfred Rosenbergs* (Gottingen 1956), 82; Gustav Hilder and Alfred G. Meyer, *The Incompatible Allies: a Memoir-History of the German–Soviet Relationship, 1918–1941* (New York 1953), 315.

68 Fest, op. cit., 879–80.

69 Albert Tarulis, *Soviet Policy towards the Baltic States 1919–1940* (Notre Dame 1959), 154–5.

70 Michael Freund, *Weltgeschichte der Gegenwart in Dokumenten* (Freiburg 1954–6), III 166ff.

71 F. La Ruche, *La Neutralité de la Suède* (Paris 1953).

72 Henri Michel, *The Second World War* (tr. London 1975), for details.

73 A. Rossi, *Deux Ans d'alliance germano–sovietique* (Paris 1949), 88–90; *Hitler's Table-Talk* (tr. London 1953), 8.

74 Carl Burckhardt, *Meine Danzinger Mission 1937–1979* (Munich 1960), 348; quoted in Hillgruber, op. cit., 69.

75 Fest, op. cit., 908; sources, 1179, note 7.

76 Ibid., 906, 921–2.

77 J.-B. Duraselle, *La Décadence 1932–1939* (Paris 1979).

78 Dominique Leca, *La Rupture de 1940* (Paris 1979).

79 François Bedarida (ed.), *La Strategie sécrète de la Drole de Guerre* (Paris 1979); see also *Français et Britanniques dans la Drole de Guerre: Actes du Colloque Franco–Britannique de decembre 1975* (Paris 1978).

80 Fest, op. cit., 940, 1181 note 10; Helmut Heiber (ed.), *Hitlers Lagebesprechungen* (Stuttgart 1962), 30.

81 Marc Bloch, *Strange Defeat* (tr. Oxford 1949), 36–7.

82 See Dr Pierre Renchnick in *Médeciné et Hygène* (Geneva, September 1981).

83 Bloch, op. cit., 28.

84 Henri Michel, *Le Procès de Riom* (Paris 1979).

85 Richard Griffith, *Marshal Pétain* (London 1970); Judith Hughes, *To the Maginot Line: the Politics of French Military Preparation in the 1920s* (Harvard 1971).

86 Quoted in Raymond Tournoux, *Pétain et la France* (Paris 1980).

87 Quoted in Robert Aron, *The Vichy Regime 1940–1944* (tr. London 1958), 122.

88 Alan Milward, *The New Order and the French Economy* (Oxford 1970), 272–88.

89 Trythall, op. cit., 161–3; *Documenti Diplomatici Italiani* 9th series (Rome 1954), IV No. 260.

90 Schmidt, op. cit., 191–4; *Ciano's Diplomatic Papers*, 412.

91 Franz Halder, *Kriegstagebuch: Tägliche Aufzeichnungen des Chefs des Generalstabes des Heeres 1939–1942* (Stuttgart 1962) I 308.

92 Karl Klee, *Das Unternehmen 'Seelöwe'* (Gottingen 1958), 189–90.

93 Halder, op. cit., I 375.

94 Quoted in Hillgruber, op. cit., 354n.

95 Daniel Benjamin and Levis Kochin, 'Voluntary Unemployment in Interwar Britain', *The Banker*, February 1979.

96 A.J.Younger, *Britain's Economic Growth 1920–1966* (London 1967), 112.
97 R.S.Sayers in *Economic Journal*, June 1950.
98 Younger, op. cit., 107ff.; H. W. Richardson, *Economic Recovery in Britain 1932–1939* (London 1967).
99 Barnett, op. cit., 482–3.
100 See M.M.Postan, D. Hay and J.D.Scott, *The Design and Development of Weapons* (London 1964).
101 For Churchill's popularity in summer 1940, see Brian Gardner, *Churchill in his Time: a Study in a Reputation 1939–1945* (London 1968), 65–96.
102 Carlton, op. cit., 163.
103 Robert Rhodes James (ed.), *Chips: the Diaries of Sir Henry Channon* (Penguin 1967), 19 July 1940, 320.
104 Cecil's *aide-mémoire* is printed in Hugh Cudlipp, *Publish and Be Damned* (London 1953), 144.
105 Winston Churchill, *The Second World War: Their Finest Hour* (London 1949), 567.
106 See, for instance, Taylor, op. cit., 629ff. and note C 648–9.
107 Quoted in Gardner, op. cit., 69.
108 H.Duncan Hall, *North American Supply* (London 1955), 247ff.
109 Taylor, op. cit., 623–4, 647.

11 The Watershed Year
1 Erickson, op. cit., 587.
2 G.Zhukov, *The Memoirs of Marshal Zhukov* (tr., London 1971), 268; Kennan, *Memoirs 1925–1950*, 324; Rigby, *Stalin*, 57; Stalin, *Collected Works*, xv 3; Ivan Maiski in *Novy Mir*, Moscow 1964, 12, 162–3.
3 Seaton, op. cit., 95; Hingley, op. cit., 309; Rigby, op. cit., 55.
4 J.K.Zawodny, *Death in the Forest: the story of the Katyn Forest Massacre* (London 1971), 127; Hilder and Meyer, op. cit., 330; Hingley, op. cit., 301ff.
5 Margarete Buber-Neuman, *Als Gefangene bei Stalin und Hitler: eine Welt im Dünkel* (Stuttgart 1958), 179.
6 Conquest, op. cit., 449.

7 Seaton, op. cit., 91.
8 *Akten zur deutscher auswartigen Politik, 1918–1945* (Bonn 1966–   ), Series D, XI, No. 329, 472.
9 Fest, op. cit., 957–8; Bullock, op. cit., 639.
10 Fest, op. cit., 952–5; *Le Testament politique de Hitler*, 93ff.
11 Halder, op. cit., II 6.
12 Fest, op. cit., 1104.
13 Heinz Hohne, *Canaris* (tr. London 1980).
14 Hillgruber, op. cit., 80–1; Fest, op. cit., 955.
15 For the 'Marcks Plan' see Alfred Philippi, *Das Pripjetproblem: Eine Studie über die operative Bedeuting des Pripjets-Gebietes für den Feldzug des Jahres 1941* (Frankfurt 1956), 69ff.
16 Fest, op. cit., 962, 1091.
17 Matthew Cooper, *The German Air Force 1933–1945: an Anatomy of Failure* (London 1981).
18 Postan, op. cit.
19 Erickson, op. cit., 584.
20 Alexander Werth, *Russia at War 1941–1945* (London 1964), 401; Seaton, op. cit., 271.
21 Hillgruber, op. cit., 90.
22 Fest, op. cit., 972.
23 Ibid., 978.
24 Ibid., 996.
25 Ibid., 962.
26 Halder, op. cit., II 335–8.
27 Hans-Adolf Jacobsen, 'The *Kommissarbefehl* and Mass Executions of Soviet Russian Prisoners of War' in Hans Buchheim *et al.*, *Anatomy of the SS State* (tr. New York 1968).
28 Hillgruber, op. cit., 86–7.
29 *Hitler's Table-Talk*, 426; Fest, op. cit., 1017, 1021ff.
30 Adolf Hitler, *Monologe im Führerhauptquartier 1941–1944* (Hamburg 1980), 54, 90, 331.
31 Fest, op. cit., 1025.
32 Nuremberg Document NOKW 1692; printed along with other relevant documents in Jacobsen, op. cit.; Fest, op. cit., 968–9.
33 Boris Pasternak, *Doctor Zhivago* (tr. London 1958), 453.
34 Seaton, op. cit., 91.
35 J.Stalin, *War Speeches and Orders of the Day* (London 1945), 26.

36 Deutscher, *Stalin*, 468–9.
37 Gustav Herling, *A World Apart* (London 1951), 59.
38 Conquest, op. cit., 486–90.
39 Albert Seaton, *The Russo–German War 1941–1945* (London 1971), 90.
40 Hingley, op. cit., 318.
41 Robert Conquest, *The Nation-Killers: the Soviet Deportation of Nationalities* (London 1970), 65, 102; Hingley, op. cit., 348.
42 Deaton, *Stalin as Warlord*, 131–3.
43 Ibid., 126.
44 Ibid., 265–6.
45 Kennan, *Memoirs 1925–1950*, 133–4.
46 R.J.M.Butler, *Grand Strategy* (London 1957), II 543–4.
47 Carlton, op. cit., 184–5. Harvey's uncensored *Diaries* are London, British Library, Add. MS 56398.
48 A.J.P.Taylor, *Beaverbrook* (London 1972), 487.
49 Churchill, *War Memoirs*, x 210.
50 See F.H.Hinsley *et al.*, *British Intelligence in the Second World War* (London 1981), II.
51 Haggie, op. cit.; Neidpath, op. cit.
52 Nish, op. cit., 232.
53 Ibid., 242.
54 Ibid., 246; B. Martin, *Deutschland und Japan in 2. Weltkrieg* (Gottingen 1969), chapter 1.
55 Kennan, *Memoirs 1925–1950*, 135.
56 Tolland, op. cit., 244.
57 Ibid., 95.
58 Nobutaka Ike, *Japan's Decision for War: records of the 1941 policy conferences* (Stanford 1967), 133ff.; Mosley, op. cit., 215.
59 Mosley, op. cit., 207 and footnote.
60 Tolland, op. cit., 94, 148; Mosley, op. cit., 200 footnote.
61 Barbara Teters, 'Matsuoka Yusuke: the diplomacy of bluff and gesture' in R.B.Burns and E.M.Bennett (eds), *Diplomats in Crisis: United States, Chinese, Japanese Relations 1919–1941* (Oxford 1974).
62 Tolland, op. cit., 75 footnote, 77.
63 Robert Craigie, *Behind the Japanese Mask* (London 1945).
64 Nish, op. cit., 235.
65 Tolland, op. cit., 179 and footnote.

66 R.J.C.Butow, *Tojo and the Coming of War* (Princeton 1961), 172.
67 Ike, op. cit., 151 footnote 36; Mosley, op. cit., 216–20.
68 Mosley, op. cit., 200.
69 Tolland, op. cit., 112.
70 Ike, op. cit., 188.
71 Tolland, op. cit., 133.
72 Ibid., 47, 68 footnote.
73 Ibid., 82.
74 Ike, op. cit., 201.
75 Ibid., 189–92.
76 Mosley, op. cit., 205 footnote.
77 Tolland, op. cit., 150 footnote.
78 Ibid., 225, 235ff.
79 Ike, op. cit., 233.
80 Tolland, op. cit., 273–5.
81 Martin, *Deutschland und Japan*, chapter 1.
82 See Masatake Okumiya, *Midway: the Battle that Doomed Japan* (Annapolis 1955).
83 Tolland, op. cit., 339.
84 Hans-Adolf Jacobsen, *1939–1945: Der Zweite Weltkrieg in Chronik und Dokumenten* (Darmstadt 1961) 290.
85 Hillgruber, op. cit., 96.

12 Superpower and Genocide

1 George Bruce, *Second Front Now: the Road to D-Day* (London 1979); Ian Colvin, *Flight 777* (London 1957) for Leslie Howard.
2 Tolland, op. cit., 75–6 and footnote.
3 Ibid., 441–4; Burke Davis, *Get Yamamoto* (New York 1969).
4 Barbara Tuchman, *The Zimmerman Telegram* (New York 1958).
5 David Kahn, 'Codebreaking in World Wars I and II: the Major Successes and Failures, their Causes and their Effects', *Cambridge Historical Journal*, September 1980.
6 Richard Woytak, *On the Border of War and Peace: Polish Intelligence and Diplomacy in 1939 and the Origins of the Ultra Secret* (Boulder 1979).
7 It was first revealed by F.W.Winterbotham, *The Ultra Secret* (London 1974), written from memory.

8 Ralph Bennett, 'Ultra and Some Command Decisions', *Journal of Contemporary History*, 16 (1981), 131–51.

9 Vice-Admiral B.B.Schofield, 'The Defeat of the U-boats During World War Two', ibid., 119–29; P.Beesley, *Very Special Intelligence* (London 1977), 152–85; see also Jürgen Rohwer and Eberhard Jackel (eds), *Die Funkaufklarung und ihre Rolle in 2 Weltkrieg* (1979), report on international conference held 15–18 November 1978 on reasons for U-boat defeat.

10 John Masterman, *The Double-Cross System in the War of 1939–1945* (Yale 1972).

11 Edward Van Der Rhoer, *Deadly Magic: a personal account of communications intelligence in World War Two in the Pacific* (New York 1978); W.J.Holmes, *Double-Edged Secrets: US Naval Intelligence Operations in the Pacific during World War Two* (Annapolis 1979).

12 Harold Deutsch, 'The Historical Impact of Revealing the Ultra Secret', US Army War College: *Parameters*, VII 3 (1978).

13 Tolland, op. cit, 444–6.

14 Milward, *German Economy at War*.

15 Andreas Hillgruber, *Hitlers Strategie: Politik und Kriegführung 1940 bis 1941* (Frankfurt 1965), 38 footnote; Fest, op. cit., 1179–80, note 11.

16 Quoted in Seaton, *Stalin as Warlord*, 263.

17 Fest, op. cit., 980.

18 Ibid., 974.

19 Tolland, op. cit., 327.

20 Susman (ed.), op. cit.

21 Charles Murphy, 'The Earth Movers Organize for War', *Fortune*, August–October 1943.

22 Gilbert Burck, 'GE Does IT', *Fortune*, March 1942.

23 Tolland, op. cit., 426.

24 Ike, op. cit., XXVI; Bruce, op. cit., for Churchill episode.

25 See Geoffrey Best, *Humanity in Warfare* (London 1981); and the article by Hans Blix in *British Yearbook of International Law* (London 1978).

26 Charles Webster and Noble Frankland, *The Strategic Air Offensive Against Germany*, 4 vols (London 1961), I 323.

27 Ibid., III 287; Taylor, *English History 1914–45*, 693.

28 Taylor, *English History, 1914–45*, 692, footnote 4.

29 David Irving, *The Destruction of Dresden* (London 1963), 44–5; Martin Middlebrook, *The Battle of Hamburg* (London 1980).

30 Irving, op. cit., 51–2, 99–100.

31 Ibid., 154–8, 175, 142–3.

32 Hugo Young, Brian Silcock and Peter Dunn, *Journey to Tranquillity: the History of Man's Assault on the Moon* (London 1969), 29–32.

33 David Irving, *The Mare's Nest* (London 1964), 299, 306–14.

34 Nils Bohr and J.A.Wheeler, *Physics Review*, 56 (1939), 426.

35 Margaret Gowing, *Britain and Atomic Energy, 1939–1945* (London 1964), 54.

36 See Freeman Dyson, *Disturbing the Universe* (New York 1979).

37 Gowing, op. cit., 45–51.

38 Ibid., 76–8.

39 Richard Hewlett and Oscar Anderson, *The New World 1939–1946* (Washington DC 1972).

40 Stephane Groueff, *Manhattan Project* (Boston 1967), 62; Leslie Groves, *Now It Can Be Told: the Story of the Manhattan Project* (New York 1962), 107.

41 Peter Pringle and James Spigelman, *The Nuclear Barons* (London 1982), 26ff.

42 David Holloway, 'Entering the Nuclear Arms Race: the Soviet Decision to Build the Atomic Bomb 1939–45', *Working Paper N. 9*, Woodrow Wilson Center (Washington DC 1979).

43 Strobe Talbot (ed.), *Khrushchev Remembers: the Last Testament* (London 1974), 60.

44 Deborah Shapley, 'Nuclear Weapons History: Japan's Wartime Bomb-projects Revealed', *Science*, 13 January 1978.

45 Rauschning, op. cit.

46 Nolte, op. cit., 234.

47 Mussolini, *Opera Omnia*, XXXI
223.
48 Ibid., XXXII 1–5, 190.
49 Fest, op. cit., 1031.
50 Michael Balfour, 'The Origins of
the Formula "Unconditional
Surrender" in World War Two',
Armed Forces and Society
(Chicago University, Winter 1979).
51 Hans Speidel, *Invasion 1944*
(Tübingen 1961), 155.
52 Quoted in Schmidt, op. cit.
53 *Hitler's Table-Talk*, 657, 661, 666,
684; Fest, op. cit., 1057, 1063.
54 Fest, op. cit., 1057–9.
55 See Hugh Trevor-Roper, 'Thomas
Carlyle's Historical Philosophy',
The Times Literary Supplement,
26 June 1981, 731–4.
56 Quoted in Hugh Trevor-Roper,
The Last Days of Hitler (London
1947), 51.
57 Albert Zollar, *Hitler privat*
(Dusseldorf 1949), 150.
58 Fest, op. cit., 1069ff., 1077,
1104–12.
59 A.Mitscherlich and F.Mielke, *The
Death Doctors* (London 1962),
236ff.; Manvell and Fraenkel,
Himmler, 87ff.; Holborn, op. cit.,
811.
60 Manvell and Fraenkel, *Himmler*,
117.
61 Fest, op. cit., 1011.
62 Manvell and Fraenkel, *Himmler*,
118–19.
63 Ibid., 120–2.
64 Borkin, op. cit., 122–3.
65 For a selection see Raul Hilberg
(ed.), *Documents of Destruction:
Germany and Jewry 1933–1945*
(New York 1971), and his
Destruction of the European Jews
(New York 1961).
66 Martin Gilbert, *Final Journey: the
Fate of the Jews in Nazi Europe*
(London 1979), 69–70.
67 Quoted from Gerald Reitlinger,
The Final Solution (London 1953).
68 Gilbert, *Final Journey*, 77–8.
69 Speer, op. cit., 302–4.
70 Ibid., 368 note 23.
71 See Benjamin B. Ferencz, *Less than
Slaves: Jewish Forced Labor and
the Quest for Compensation*
(Harvard 1981).

72 *Trial of the Major War Criminals
before the International Military
Tribunal,* ed. L.D.Egbert, 42 vols
(Nuremberg 1947–9), I 245.
73 Borkin, op. cit., 111–27.
74 Gilbert, *Final Journey*, 78.
75 Manvell and Fraenkel, *Himmler*,
91.
76 Ibid., 104–11. See also
Mitscherlich and Mielke, op. cit.
77 Manvell and Fraenkel, *Himmler*,
Appendix B, 252–3.
78 Ibid., 136–7, 196–7.
79 Gilbert, *Final Journey*, 70; Luba
Krugman Gurdus, *The Death
Train* (New York 1979).
80 See, for a discussion of this aspect,
Rainer C. Baum, *The Holocaust
and the German Elite: Genocide
and National Suicide in Germany
1871–1945* (London 1982).
81 Gerald Reitlinger, *The SS: Alibi of
a Nation, 1922–1945* (London
1956), 377.
82 Maurice Raisfus, *Les Juifs dans la
Collaboration: L'UGIF
1941–1944* (Paris 1981).
83 Michael R. Marrus and Robert O.
Paxton, *Vichy France and the Jews*
(New York 1981).
84 Martin Gilbert, *Auschwitz and the
Allies* (London 1981), 267–70.
85 Quoted in ibid.
86 John Wheeler-Bennett and
Anthony Nicholls, *The Semblance
of Peace: the Political Settlement
after the Second World War* (New
York 1972), 146–8, 166;
Alexander Werth, *Russia at War
1941–1945* (New York 1965),
267–8.
87 Aaron Goldman, 'Germans and
Nazis: the controversy over
"Vansittartism" in Britain during
the Second World War', *Journal of
Contemporary History*, 14 (1979),
155–91.
88 Manvell and Fraenkel, *Himmler*,
157, 169–70, 266 footnote 20.
89 Borkin, op. cit., 135–56.
90 Figures from Ferencz, *Less than
Slaves.*
91 Tolland, op. cit., 499 footnote.
92 James, op. cit., 322.
93 Tolland, op. cit., 477–8.
94 James, op. cit., 246–7, 321, 396.

95　Ibid., 299; Tolland, op. cit., 468.
96　Tolland, op. cit., 469–71.
97　James, op. cit., 246–7.
98　Ibid, 293.
99　Lansing Lamont, *Day of Trinity* (New York 1965), 235.
100　For the bomb decision, see Martin Sherwin, *A World Destroyed: the Atomic Bomb and the Grand Alliance* (New York 1975), chapter 8.
101　Tolland, op. cit., 756.
102　Calculation of Professor Shogo Nagaoka, First curator of the Peace Memorial in Hiroshima, Tolland, op. cit., 790 footnote.
103　James, op. cit., 328; Shapley, op. cit.
104　Tolland, op. cit., 813 footnote.
105　Text in R.J.C.Butow, *Japan's Decision to Surrender* (Stanford 1954) 248.
106　Beaseley, op. cit., 277–8.
107　See the International Military Tribunal for the Far East, *Proceedings*, 3 May 1946 to 16 April 1946, *Judgement*, November 1948, Tokyo.
108　James, op. cit., 259–60.
109　Philip R. Piccigallo, *The Japanese on Trial: Allied War Crimes Operations in the East 1945–1951* (Austin 1979), 27.
110　Ibid., 23, for dissenting opinions.
111　Quoted in Mosley, op. cit.
112　Samuel Eliot Morrison, *History of the US Naval Operations in World War Two:* VII *Aleutians, Gilberts and Marshalls* (Washington DC 1951).
113　Tolland, op. cit., 677 footnote.
114　Sherwin, op. cit., 302.
115　Poole, op. cit., 130.
116　James, op. cit., 335–40.
117　Nicholas Bethell, *The Last Secret: Forcible Repatriation to Russia 1944–1947* (London 1974), 5.
118　Ibid., 8–13; Carlton, op. cit., 239–42.
119　Ibid.; Bethell, op. cit., 57–60.
120　Joseph Hecomovic, *Tito's Death-Marches and Extermination Camps* (New York 1962) 23.
121　Bethell, op. cit., 82, 101, 131–3, 142–3.

13　Peace by Terror

1　Rhodes James (ed.), op. cit., 505.
2　Quoted in Charles Bohlen, *Witness to History 1929–1969* (New York 1973), 26–9.
3　Robert Sherwood, *Roosevelt and Hopkins*, 2 vols (New York 1950), I 387–423; Adam B. Ulam, *Stalin: the Man and his Era* (New York 1973), 539–42, 560–1.
4　Yergin, op. cit., 54.
5　Winston Churchill, *Wartime Correspondence* (London 1960), 196.
6　Cairo Conference 1943. Quoted in Terry Anderson, *The United States, Great Britain and the Cold War 1944–1947* (Colombia 1981), 4.
7　Quoted in Robert Garson, 'The Atlantic Alliance, East Europe and the Origin of the Cold War' in H.C.Allen and Rogert Thompson (eds), *Contrast and Connection* (Athens, Ohio 1976), 298–9.
8　Lord Moran, *Churchill: the Struggle for Survival, 1940–1944* (London 1968), 154.
9　John Wheeler-Bennett and Anthony Nicholls, *The Semblance of Peace: the Political Settlement after the Second World War* (New York 1972), 290.
10　Anderson, op. cit., 15.
11　John R.Deane, *The Strange Alliance: the Story of American Efforts at Wartime Co-operation with Russia* (London 1947), 298.
12　Lisle A.Rose, *Dubious Victory: the United States and the End of World War Two* (Kent, Ohio 1973), I 6–7.
13　Foreign Office Memo 21 March 1944, 'Essentials of an American Policy'.
14　The minute is in the Inverchapel Papers in the PRO; see Carlton, op. cit., 244; Churchill, *Second World War*, VI 196–7.
15　Diary of Sir Pierson Dixon, 4 December 1944, quoted in Carlton, op. cit., 248–9; Churchill, *Second World War*, VI 252.
16　Quoted Carlton, op. cit., 248.
17　Averell Harriman and Elie Abel, *Special Envoy to Churchill and Stalin 1941–1946* (New York 1975), 390.

18 Churchill, *Second World War*, VI 337.
19 William D.Leahy, *I Was There* (New York 1950), 315–16.
20 Anderson, op. cit., 47.
21 Ibid., 50.
22 Viscount Montgomery, *Memoirs* (New York 1958), 296–7.
23 Harry S.Truman, *Memoirs*, 2 vols (New York 1955–6), I 81–2.
24 Omar Bradley, *A Soldier's Story* (New York 1951), 535–6; Forrest Pogue, *George C. Marshall: Organizer of Victory* (New York 1973), 573–4.
25 Thomas Campbell and George Herring, *The Diaries of Edward R.Stettinius Jr, 1943–1946* (New York 1975), 177–8.
26 Anderson, op. cit., 69.
27 Moran, op. cit., 305.
28 Victor Rothwell, *Britain and the Cold War 1941–1947* (London 1982).
29 *Forrestal Diaries* (New York 1951), 38–40, 57.
30 Z.Stypulkowski, *Invitation to Moscow* (London 1951).
31 Anderson, op. cit., 75–6.
32 Patricia Dawson Ward, *The Threat of Peace: James F. Byrnes and the Council of Foreign Ministers 1945–6* (Kent, Ohio 1979).
33 Yergin, op. cit., 160–1; George Curry, 'James F. Byrnes' in Robert H. Ferrell and Samuel Flagg Bemiss (eds), *The American Secretaries of State and their Diplomacy* (New York 1965).
34 Kennan, *Memoirs 1925–1950*, 294.
35 Text of speech in Robert Rhodes James, *Churchill Complete Speeches* (London 1974), VII 7283–96; Jerome K. Ward, 'Winston Churchill and the Iron Curtain Speech', *The History Teacher*, January 1968.
36 Leahy Diaries, 24 January, 7 February 1946.
37 John Morton Blun, *The Price of Vision: the Diary of Henry A. Wallace* (Boston 1973), 589–601; Yergin, op. cit., 253–4.
38 Dean Acheson, *Present at the Creation* (New York 1969), 219; Yergin, op. cit., 281–2.
39 Acheson, op. cit., 234.
40 See 'Overseas Deficit', dated 2 May 1947, Dalton Papers; Harry Bayard Price, *The Marshall Plan and its Meaning* (Cornell 1955).
41 Yergin, op. cit., 348–50.
42 Jean Edward Smith (ed.), *The Papers of General Lucius D. Clay: Germany, 1945–1949* (Bloomington 1974), 734–7.
43 Yergin, op. cit., 380.
44 Talbot (ed.) op. cit., 205.
45 David Alan Rosenberg, 'American Atomic Strategy and the Hydrogen Bomb Decision', *Journal of American History*, June 1979; David Lilienthal, *Atomic Energy: a New Start* (New York 1980).
46 W.PhillipsDavison, *The Berlin Blockade* (Princeton 1958).
47 Kennan, *Memoirs 1925–1950*, 354ff.
48 Warner Schilling *et al.*, *Strategy, Politics and Defence Budgets* (Colombia 1962), 298–330.
49 Richard Hewlett and Francis Duncan, *Atomic Shield 1947–1952* (Pennsylvania 1969), 362–9.
50 Anderson, op. cit., 184.
51 Churchill, *Second World War*, VI: *Triumph and Tragedy* (London 1954), 701.
52 Samuel I. Rosenman (ed.), *Public Papers and Addresses of Franklin D. Roosevelt: Victory and the Threshold of Peace 1944–1945* (New York 1950), 562.
53 Schram, op. cit., 220ff.; Tang Tsou, *America's Failure in China 1941–1950* (Chicago 1963), 176ff.
54 Schram, op. cit., 228–9; Tang Tsou, op. cit., 100–24.
55 Milovan Djilas, *Conversations with Stalin* (London 1962), 182; Vladimir Dedijer, *Tito Speaks* (London 1953), 331.
56 Schram, op. cit., 232–3.
57 Wolfram Eberhard, *History of China* (4th ed., London 1977), 344.
58 Derk Bodde, *Peking Diary: a Year of Revolution* (tr. London 1951), 32.
59 Quoted in Noel Barber, *The Fall of Shanghai: the Communist Takeover in 1949* (London 1979), 42.
60 Bodde, op. cit., 47.

61 Barber, op. cit., 49–50.
62 Ibid., 51.
63 Tang Tsou, op. cit., 482–4, 497–8; Schram, op. cit., 245.
64 Mao Tse-Tung, *Selected Works*, IV 201–2, order of 13 February 1948.
65 Kennan, *Memoirs 1925–1950*, 376.
66 Samuel Wells, 'The Lessons of the Korean War', in Francis Heller (ed.), *The Korean War: a 25-Year Perspective* (Kansas 1977).
67 Duncan Wilson, *Tito's Yugoslavia* (Cambridge 1979), 50 footnote.
68 Djilas, op. cit., 129, 141.
69 Hingley, op. cit., 385; D. Wilson, op. cit., 55.
70 D.Wilson, op. cit., 61.
71 Ibid., 87.
72 Robert Conquest, *The Soviet Police System* (London 1968), 41.
73 Hingley, op. cit., 388.
74 S.Wells, op. cit.
75 Kennan, *Memoirs, 1925–1950*, 490.
76 *New York Times*, 3 August 1980; S.Wells, op. cit.
77 Talbot (ed.), op. cit., 269; *China Quarterly*, April–June 1964.
78 Yergin, op. cit., 407; S.Wells, op. cit.
79 Robert C. Tucher, 'Swollen State, Spent Society: Stalin's Legacy to Brezhnev's Russia', *Foreign Affairs*, 60 (Winter 1981–2), 414–45.
80 Kolakowski, op. cit., III 132–5; Hingley, op. cit., 380–2.
81 Zhores A. Medvedev, *The Rise and Fall of T.D.Lysenko* (tr. New York 1969), 116–17.
82 Robert Payne, *The Rise and Fall of Stalin* (London 1968), 664.
83 *Pravda*, 17 February 1950, quoted Hingley, op. cit., 508.
84 Rigby, *Stalin*, 71; Marc Slonim, *Soviet Russian Literature* (New York 1964), 289.
85 Svetlana Alliluyeva, *Twenty Letters*, 171, 193, 197, 206; Talbot (ed.), op. cit., 263.
86 Robert Conquest, *Power and Policy in the USSR* (London 1961), 100.
87 Grey, op. cit., 453–4.
88 Kennan, *Memoirs 1950–1963*, 154–6.
89 Hingley, op. cit., 404.

90 Rigby, *Stalin*, 81.
91 Conquest, *Power and Policy*, 165–6; Rigby, *Stalin*, 66–7; Hingley, op. cit., 414.
92 Svetlana Alliluyeva, *After One Year*, 365; Hingley, op. cit., 393–5, 416.
93 K.P.S.Menon, *The Flying Troika: extracts from a diary* (London 1963), 27–9.
94 Svetlana Alliluyeva, *Twenty Letters*, 13–18.
95 Hingley, op. cit., 424, 427.
96 Sidney Olson, 'The Boom', *Fortune*, June 1946.
97 Kennan, *Memoirs 1950–1963* 191–2.
98 Alan Harper, *The Politics of Loyalty* (New York 1969).
99 Roy Cohn, *McCarthy* (New York 1968), 56ff.
100 Richard Rovere, *Senator Joe McCarthy* (London 1960), 51.
101 Quoted in Arthur Schlesinger, *Robert Kennedy and his Times* (Boston 1978).
102 Edwin R.Bayley, *Joe McCarthy and the Press* (University of Wisconsin 1981), 66–87, 214–22.
103 Kennan, *Memoirs 1950–1963*, 220.
104 Barton J. Bernstein, 'New Light on the Korean War', *International History Review*, 3 (1981), 256–77.
105 Robert Griffith, *The Politics of Fear: Joseph McCarthy and the Senate* (Lexington 1970); Richard M. Fried, *Men Against McCarthy* (New York 1976).
106 Fred I. Greenstein, 'Eisenhower as an Activist President: a look at new evidence', *Political Science Quarterly*, Winter 1979–80; Robert Wright, 'Ike and Joe: Eisenhower's White House and the Demise of Joe McCarthy', unpublished thesis (Princeton 1979).
107 Trohan, op. cit., 292.
108 Emmet John Hughes, *Ordeal of Power: a Political Memoir of the Eisenhower Years* (New York 1963), 329–30.
109 Richard Nixon, *Six Crises* (New York 1962), 161.
110 Greenstein, op. cit.; see also Douglas Kinnaird, *President Eisenhower and Strategic Management* (Lexington 1977).

111 Sherman Adams, *First Hand Report* (New York 1961), 73.
112 Trohan, op. cit., 111.
113 Robert H.Ferrell, *The Eisenhower Diaries* (New York 1981), 230–2.
114 Kennan, *Memoirs 1950–1963*, 196.
115 Verno A. Walters, *Silent Missions* (New York 1978), 226.
116 See Robert A. Divine, *Eisenhower and the Cold War* (Oxford 1981).
117 *Public Papers of Dwight D. Eisenhower 1954* (Washington 1960), 253, 206.
118 See Richard H. Immerman, 'The US and Guatemala 1954', unpublished PhD thesis (Boston College 1978), quoted in Greenstein, op. cit.; Richard Cotton, *Nationalism in Iran* (Pittsburg 1964).
119 Joseph B. Smith, *Portrait of a Cold Warrior* (New York 1976), 229–40; Schlesinger, *Robert Kennedy*, 455, 457.
120 C.L.Sulzburger, *A Long Row of Candles* (New York 1969), 767–9.
121 Kennan, *Memoirs 1950–1963*, 183.
122 Sherman Adams, op. cit., chapter 17, 360ff.
123 See Joan Robinson, 'What has become of the Keynesian Revolution?' in Milo Keynes (ed.), op. cit., 140.
124 Arthur Larsen, *Eisenhower: the President that Nobody Knew* (New York 1968), 34.

14 The Bandung Generation
1 E.L.Woodward, *British Foreign Policy in the Second World War* (London 1970), I XLIV.
2 16 June 1943; quoted in David Dilks (ed.), *Retreat from Power* (London 1981), II *After 1939*.
3 William Roger Louis, *Imperialism at Bay: the United States and the Decolonization of the British Empire 1941–1945* (Oxford 1978).
4 Entry in Admiral Leahy's diary, 9 February 1945, quoted in Anderson, op. cit.
5 W.K.Hancock and Margaret Gowing, *The British War Economy* (London 1949), 546–9.
6 Dalton Diary, 10 September 1946.
7 *Harold Nicolson: Diaries and Letters 1945–1962* (London 1968), 115–16.
8 A.Goldberg, 'The Military Origins of the British Nuclear Deterrent', *International Affairs*, XL (1964).
9 Edward Spiers, 'The British Nuclear Deterrent: problems, possibilities', in Dilks, op. cit., II 183–4.
10 M.H.Gowing, *Independence and Deterrence, Britain and Atomic Energy 1945–52*, 2 vols (London 1974), I 131.
11 Ibid., 182–3.
12 Ibid., 406.
13 Dilks, op. cit., II 161.
14 For end of war statistics see James, op. cit.
15 Ibid., 251–3.
16 Robert Rhodes James, *Memoirs of a Conservative: J.C.C.Davidon's Letters and Papers 1910–1937* (London 1969), 390.
17 John Wheeler-Bennett, *King George VI: his Life and Times* (London 1958), 703.
18 Ved Mehta, *Mahatma Gandhi and his Apostles* (New York 1976), 33ff.
19 Ibid., 13–16.
20 Ibid., 44.
21 Ibid., 56.
22 Orwell, *Collected Essays*, etc., IV 529.
23 Quoted in Sarvepalli Gopal, *Jawaharlal Nehru: a biography* (London 1965), I 38–9.
24 Ibid., 79, 98, 236; Leonard Woolf, *Downhill All the Way* (London 1967), 230.
25 Speech by Nehru at Ootacamund, 1 June 1948; Gopal, op. cit., II 308.
26 Richard Hughes, *Foreign Devil* (London 1972), 289–92.
27 Richard Hough, *Mountbatten* (London 1980), 216.
28 R. Jeffrey, 'The Punjab Boundary Force and the problem of order, August 1947', *Modern Asian Studies* (1974), 491–520.
29 M.Masson, *Edwina Mountbatten* (London 1958), 206–7.
30 Gopal, op. cit., II 13.

31 Penderal Mood, *Divide and Quit* (London 1961), gives 200,000; G.D.Khosla, *Stern Reckoning* (Delhi n.d.), 4–500,000; Ian Stephens, *Pakistan* (London 1963), 500,000; M.Edwardes, *Last Years of British India* (London 1963), 600,000.

32 Gopal, op. cit., II 21, 42.

33 Letter from Nehru to Krishna Menon, 24 August 1949.

34 Walter Lippmann in *Herald Tribune*, 10 January 1949; Acheson, op. cit., 336; *Christian Science Monitor*, 26 October 1949; *Manchester Guardian*, 26 May 1954; W.Johnson (ed.), *The Papers of Adlai E. Stevenson* (Boston 1973), III 181.

35 Nehru, letter dated 9 June 1951.

36 Gopal, op. cit., 311.

37 Letter from Nehru to Rajagopalachari, 3 July 1950; cable to President Nasser, 31 October 1956; cable to J.F.Dulles, same date.

38 Quoted Gopal, op. cit., II 246.

39 S.Dutt, *With Nehru at the Foreign Office* (Calcutta 1977), 177.

40 Letter from Nehru to Ernest Bevin, 20 November 1950.

41 Gopal, op. cit., II 194–5, 227.

42 J.K.Galbraith, *A Life in Our Times* (London 1981), chapter 27, 420ff.

43 Keith Irvine, *The Rise of the Coloured Races* (London 1972), 540ff.; G. McT. Kahin, *The Asian–African Conference, Bandung* (Ithaca 1956).

44 J.D.Legge, *Sukarno: A Political Biography* (London 1972), 264–5.

45 Richard Wright, *The Colour Curtain* (London 1965), 15.

46 Harry J. Benda, 'Christian Snouck Hurgronje and the Foundation of Dutch Islamic Policy in Indonesia', *Journal of Modern History*, xxx (1958), 338–47.

47 E.H.Kossman, *The Low Countries, 1780–1940* (Oxford 1978), 672ff.

48 See Sukarno's book, *The Birth of Pantja Sila* (Djakarta 1950).

49 D.S.Lev, *The Transition to Guided Democracy: Indonesia Politics 1957–1959* (Ithaca 1966).

50 For slogans, see Legge, op. cit., 288–90, 324, 332–3, 359 and *passim*.

51 Talbot (ed.), op. cit., 322.

52 Legge, op. cit., 387; John Hughes, *The End of Sukarno* (London 1968), 44.

53 J.R.Bass, 'The PKI and the attempted coup', *Journal of SE Asian Studies*, March 1970; for critical bibliography of the *coup* see Legge, op. cit., 390 footnote 45.

54 Hughes, op. cit., chapter 16.

55 Howard M. Sachar, *Britain Leaves the Middle East* (London 1974), 391.

56 *Petroleum Times*, June 1948; *Oil Weekly*, 6 March 1944.

57 *Forrestal Diaries*, 356–7.

58 Sachar, op. cit., 395.

59 Churchill, *Second World War*, IV 952.

60 Sachar, op. cit., 442.

61 Chaim Weizmann, *Trial and Error* (Philadelphia 1949), II 437.

62 Yehudah Bauer, *From Diplomacy to Resistance: a History of Jewish Palestine 1939–1945* (Philadelphia 1970), 230.

63 Sachar, op. cit., 447.

64 *New York Post*, 21 May 1946.

65 Nicholas Bethell, *The Palestine Triangle: the struggle between the British, the Jews and the Arabs, 1935–1948* (London 1979), 254–5.

66 Bethell, *The Palestine Triangle*, 261ff., based on records released in 1978.

67 *Jerusalem Post*, 1 August 1947.

68 Bethell, *The Palestine Triangle*, 243–4.

69 Jon and David Kimche, *Both Sides of the Hill: Britain and the Palestine War* (London 1960), 21–2.

70 Bauer, op. cit., 230.

71 *The Jewish Case for the Anglo–American Committee of Inquiry on Palestine* (Jerusalem 1947), 6–7, 74–5.

72 Joseph Schechtman, *The US and the Jewish State Movement* (New York 1966), 110.

73 Quoted in Alfred Steinberg, *The Man from Missouri: the life and times of Harry S. Truman* (New York 1952), 301.

74 Truman, *Memoirs*, II 135.

75 *Petroleum Times*, June 1948.

76 *Forrestal Diaries*, 324, 344, 348.

77 Howard Sachar, 'The Arab–Israeli issue in the light of the Cold War', *Sino–Soviet Institute Studies* (Washington DC), 1966, 2.

78 Sachar, *Europe Leaves the Middle East*, 546–7.

79 Ibid., 518ff.

80 Kimche, op. cit., 60.

81 Netanel Lorch, *The Edge of the Sword: Israel's War of Independence 1947–1948* (New York 1961), 90.

82 David Horowitz, *State in the Making* (New York 1953), 232–5.

83 Rony E. Gabbay, *A Political Study of the Arab–Jewish Conflict* (Geneva 1959), 92–3.

84 Sachar, *Europe Leaves the Middle East*, 550–1; Walid Khalidi, 'Why Did the Palestinians Leave?', *Middle East Forum*, July 1955; Erkine B. Childers, 'The Other Exodus', *Spectator*, 12 May 1961. Arab League instructions were printed in *Al-Kayat* (Lebanon, 30 April, 5–7 May 1948).

85 Colonial Office transcript (CO 733 477) quoted in Bethell, *The Palestine Triangle*, 355.

86 Walter Pinner, *How Many Arab Refugees?* (New York 1959), 3–4.

87 Sachar, op. cit., 191; for distribution of Jewish exodus, see Martin Gilbert, *The Arab–Israeli Conflict: its History in Maps* (London 1974), 50.

88 Jon Kimche, *Seven Fallen Pillars* (London 1954), 46.

89 Francis Williams: *A Prime Minister Remembers* (London 1961), 175–6.

90 Bethell, *The Palestine Triangle*, 358.

91 Sachar, *Europe Leaves the Middle East*, 51.

92 For an incisive portrait by a fellow-Muslim ruler see Mohammed Ahmed Mahgoub, *Democracy on Trial: Reflections on Arab and African Politics* (London 1974).

93 Constantine Zurayak, *The Meaning of the Disaster* (Beirut 1956), 2.

94 For the dam project see P.K.O'Brien, *The Revolution in Egypt's Economic System* (London 1966) and Tom Little, *High Dam at Aswan* (London 1965).

95 Carlton, op. cit., 416.

96 Ibid., 389.

97 André Beaufre, *The Suez Expedition 1956* (tr. London 1969), 28–34; Hugh Stockwell, 'Suez: Success or Disaster?', *Listener*, 4 November 1976.

98 See Eden's own account in *Memoirs: Full Circle* (London 1960); Selwyn Lloyd, *Suez 1956: a Personal Account* (London 1978).

99 Moshe Dayan, *Story of My Life* (London 1976), 181.

100 Dwight D. Eisenhower, *The White House Years: Waging Peace 1956–1961* (New York 1965), 666–7.

101 Carlton, op. cit., 451–3.

102 Brian Urquhart, *Hammarskjöld* (London 1973), 26.

103 Ibid., 170, 174, 185–9.

104 Horne, op. cit. (London 1977), 60.

105 See Robert Aron *et al.*, *Les Origines de la guerre d'Algérie* (Paris 1962).

106 Albert-Paul Lentin, *L'Algérie des colonels* (Paris 1958).

107 Horne, op. cit., 72.

108 Ibid., 91–2, 101; Pierre Leulliette, *St Michael and the Dragon* (tr. London 1964).

109 Horne, op. cit., 132–5.

110 C.Marighela, *For the Liberation of Brazil* (Penguin 1971).

111 Horne, op. cit., 98–9.

112 Germaine Tillion, *L'Algérie en 1957* (Paris 1957); Vincent Monteil, *Soldat de fortune* (Paris 1966).

113 Jacques Soustelle, *Aimée et Souffrante Algérie* (Paris 1956).

114 Horne, op. cit., 117–18.

115 Albert Camus, *Chroniques Algériennes 1939–1958* (Paris 1958).

116 Horne, op. cit., 187.

117 Jacques Massu, *La Vrai Bataille d'Alger* (Paris 1971).

118 Henri Alleg, *La Question* (Paris 1958).

119 Horne, op. cit., 201.

120 For examples, see J.-R.Tournoux, *Secret d'Etat* (Paris 1960); J.J.Servan-Schreiber, *Lieutenant en Algérie* (Paris 1957).

121 Charles de Gaulle: *Memoirs of Hope* (tr. London 1970–1), I 12.

122 Ibid., 15.

123 Simone de Beauvoir, *La Force des choses* (Paris 1963).

124 Horne, op. cit., 291.

125 De Gaulle, op. cit., 47.

126 Horne, op. cit., 376–8.

127 Ibid., 515–16.

128 Ibid., 495.

129 Ibid., 506.

130 Mouloud Feraoun, *Journal 1955–1962* (Paris 1962).

131 Horne, op. cit., 524.

132 Ibid., 540–3.

133 Ibid., 537–8.

134 De Gaulle, op. cit., I 126.

135 Ben Bella, interview with Radio Monte Carlo: *Daily Telegraph*, 19 March 1982.

15 **Caliban's Kingdoms**

1 Mark Amory (ed.), *Letters of Evelyn Waugh* (London 1980), 517.

2 James, op. cit., 193.

3 Quoted in Dorothy Pickles, *French Politics: the First Years of the Fourth Republic* (London 1953), 151.

4 Stewart Easton, *The Twilight of European Colonialism* (London 1961).

5 *Le Monde*, 21 June 1951.

6 De Gaulle, op. cit., I 66.

7 Ibid., 68.

8 Quoted in Easton, op. cit.

9 Michael Blundell, *So Rough a Wind* (London 1964).

10 *Weekend Telegraph*, 12 March 1965.

11 Miles Hudson, *Triumph or Tragedy: Rhodesia to Zimbabwe* (London 1981), 38–9.

12 Jean Labrique, *Congo Politique* (Leopoldville 1957), 199–219.

13 Comnd 9109 (1918), 3, quoted in Barnett, op. cit., 147.

14 Kirkman, op. cit., 15ff.

15 For the elaboration of this theory, see P.A.Baran, *The Political Economy of Growth* (New York 1957); C. Leys, *Underdevelopment in Kenya: the Political Economy of Neo-Colonialism 1964–71* (London 1975).

16 Quoted in Mahgoub, op. cit., 250ff.

17 Tawia Adamafio, *A Portrait of the Osagyefo, Dr Kwame Nkrumah* (Accra 1960), 95.

18 Mahgoub, op. cit., 284.

19 John Rogge, 'The Balkanization of Nigeria's Federal System', *Journal of Geography*, April–May 1977.

20 J.L.Lacroix, *Industrialization au Congo* (Paris 1966), 21ff.

21 Easton, op. cit., 445; see also R.Anstey, *King Leopold's Legacy: the Congo Under Belgian Rule 1908–1960* (Oxford 1966).

22 See G.Heinz and H.Donnay, *Lumumba: the Last Fifty Days* (New York 1969).

23 Urquhart, op. cit., 392–3, 397.

24 Paul-Henri Spaak, *Combats Inachevés* (Paris 1969), 244–5.

25 Urquhart, op. cit., 385.

26 Ibid., 507.

27 Urquhart, op. cit., 587; Conor Cruise O'Brien, *To Katanga and Back* (London 1962), 286.

28 *Sunday Times*, 11 October 1964.

29 Ali Mazrui, 'Moise Tschombe and the Arabs, 1960–8' in *Violence and Thought: Essays on Social Tension in Africa* (London 1969).

30 *Wall Street Journal*, 25–26 June 1980; Patrick Marnham, *Fantastic Invasion* (London 1980), 203 note 10.

31 K.W.Grundy, *Conflicting Images of the Military in Africa* (Nairobi 1968).

32 Samuel Decalo, *Coups and Army Rule in Africa* (Yale 1976), 5–6 and Tables 1.1 and 1.2.

33 A point made in Shiva Naipaul, *North of South: an African Journey* (London 1978).

34 *African Standard*, Nairobi, 12 April 1965; quoted in Mazrui, op. cit., 210–11.

35 Marvin Harris, *Portugal's African 'Wards'* (New York 1958); James Duffy, *Portuguese Africa* (Harvard 1959).

36 Marcello Caetano, *Colonizing Traditions: Principles and Methods of the Portuguese* (Lisbon 1951).

37 Easton, op. cit., 506.
38 T.R.H.Davenport, *South Africa: a Modern History* (London 1977), 346.
39 W.K.Hancock, *Smuts* (London 1968), II.
40 For these sects see Bengt G.M.Sundkler, *Bantu Prophets in South Africa* (2nd ed. Oxford 1961) and *Zulu Zion and some Swazi Zionists* (Oxford 1976).
41 Davenport, op. cit., 176ff.
42 Ibid., 207; for Native bills see M. Ballinger, *From Union to Apartheid* (London 1969).
43 B.Patchai, *The International Aspects of the South African Indian Question 1860–1971* (London 1971).
44 N.M.Stultz, *Afrikaaner Politics in South Africa 1934–48* (London 1974).
45 G.D.Scholtz, *Dr H.F.Verwoerd* (London 1974).
46 Ambrose Reeves, *Shooting at Sharpeville* (London 1961).
47 Davenport, op. cit., 270–1.
48 Ibid., 296–7, with diagram of population growth.
49 Ibid., 304–5.
50 Ibid., 376 for mineral map.
51 *Wall Street Journal*, 10 July 1980.
52 Ibid., 4 August 1980.
53 Naipaul, op. cit., 231.
54 Richard West, *The White Tribes Revisited* (London 1978), 16ff.
55 Naipaul, op. cit., 232–3.
56 Quoted in Marnham, op. cit., 196.
57 West, op. cit., 147.
58 Marnham, op. cit., 112.
59 Ibid., 125ff.
60 *Inside East Africa*, August–September 1960.
61 *Sunday News* (Dar es Salaam), 26 January 1964.
62 'One Party Government', *Transition*, December 1961.
63 *Report of the Presidential Commission on the Establishment of a Democratic One Party State*, (Dar es Salaam 1965), 2.
64 Lionel Cliffe (ed.), *One-Party Democracy in Tanzania* (Nairobi 1967).
65 Mazrui, op. cit., 255ff.
66 *The Arusha Declaration and Tanu's Policy on Socialism and Self-Reliance* (Dar es Salaam 1967); Marzui, op. cit., 48.
67 Naipaul, op. cit., 144ff.
68 Quoted ibid., 200–1.
69 *Daily Nation*, Nairobi, 6 February 1968.
70 Ali Mazrui, 'Mini-skirts and Political Puritanism', *Africa Report*, October 1968.
71 *Reporter*, Nairobi, 23 February 1968.
72 Naipaul, op. cit., 237–8.
73 *The Times*, 7 October 1965.
74 Marnham, op. cit., 199.
75 West, op. cit., 146.
76 *Annual Register* (London), 1980.
77 Pierre Kalck, *Central African Republic: a Failure of Decolonization* (New York 1971).
78 Winston Churchill, *My African Journey* (London 1908).
79 George Ivan Smith, *Ghosts of Kampala* (London 1980), 34.
80 Ibid., 51ff.
81 West, op. cit., 24–5.
82 Quoted Smith, op. cit., 96.
83 Ibid., 101 for text of memorandum.
84 Henry Kyemba, *State of Blood* (London 1977).
85 Smith, op. cit., 111–12.
86 Ibid, 124–31.
87 Ibid., 166–7.
88 Daniel Patrick Moynihan, *A Dangerous Place* (London 1978), 154–5.
89 Quoted Smith, op. cit., 181.
90 J.J.Jordensen, *Uganda: a Modern History* (London 1981); Wadada Nabundere, *Imperialism and Revolution in Uganda* (Tanzania 1981).
91 Victoria Brittain, 'After Amin', *London Review of Books*, 17 September 1981.
92 For instance, *Daily Telegraph*, 5 September 1981.
93 Mazrui, *Violence and Thought*, 37–9.
94 Colin Legum *et al.*, *Africa in the 1980s* (New York 1979).
95 West, op. cit., 6–7.
96 For detailed figures see *New York Times*, 11 May 1980.
97 Marnham, op. cit., 165, 205.
98 Ibid., 168.
99 David Lomax, 'The civil war in Chad', *Listener*, 4 February 1982.

100 Genganne Chapin and Robert
    Wasserstrom, 'Agricultural
    production and malarial
    resurgence in Central America and
    India', *Nature*, 17 September
    1981.
101 *New York Times*, 11 May 1980.
102 Marnham, op. cit., 240.
103 Compiled from *Annual Register*
    (London 1980, 1981) and *New
    York Times*.

16 Experimenting with Half Humanity
  1 Jack Chen, *Inside the Cultural
    Revolution* (London 1976),
    219–20.
  2 Hollander, op. cit., chapter 7, 'The
    Pilgrimage to China', 278ff.
  3 Ibid., 326–30.
  4 Talbot (ed.), op. cit., 249.
  5 John Gittings, *The World and
    China, 1922–1975* (London
    1974), 236.
  6 Bill Brugger, *China: Liberation
    and Transformation 1942–1962*
    (New Jersey 1981), 212.
  7 Ross Terrill, *Mao: a Biography*
    (New York 1980), 383.
  8 Quoted in Han Suyin, *Wind in the
    Tower: Mao Tse-Tung and the
    Chinese Revolution 1949–1975*
    (London 1976), 291.
  9 Talbot (ed.), op. cit., 249.
 10 Schram, op. cit., 253–4.
 11 Ibid., 295.
 12 Ibid., 291.
 13 Talbot (ed.), op. cit., 255.
 14 Terrill, op. cit., 53.
 15 Roger Garside, *Coming Alive:
    China After Mao* (London 1981),
    45.
 16 Ibid., 46–7.
 17 Robert Jay Lifton, *Revolutionary
    Immortality* (London 1969), 72–3.
 18 Garside, op. cit., 50.
 19 Brugger, op. cit., 44–55.
 20 Schram, op. cit., 267, footnote; see
    Jacques Guillermaz, *La Chine
    Populaire* (3rd ed., Paris 1964).
 21 Robert Jay Lifton, *Thought
    Reform and the Psychology of
    Totalism: a Study of Brainwashing
    in China* (New York 1961),
    chapter 19.
 22 Schram, op. cit., 271 footnote.
 23 Ibid., 277.
 24 Talbot (ed.), op. cit., 272.

 25 Jerome A. Cohen, 'The criminal
    process in the People's Republic of
    China: an introduction', *Harvard
    Law Review*, January 1966.
 26 Editorials, *Peking Review*, 6, 13,
    20 September 1963.
 27 Quoted Schram, op. cit., 253.
 28 Brugger, op. cit., 174ff.
 29 Talbot (ed.), op. cit., 272–8.
 30 Brugger, op. cit., 212.
 31 K. Walker, *Planning in Chinese
    Agriculture: Socialization and the
    Private Sector 1956–62* (London
    1965), 444–5.
 32 Bill Brugger, *China: Radicalism
    and Revisionism 1962–1972* (New
    Jersey 1981), 36.
 33 Ibid., 47.
 34 Roxane Witke, *Comrade Chiang
    Ching* (London 1977), 162.
 35 Ibid., 154; Chiang Ching confided
    at great length in Witke.
 36 Colin Mackerras, *The Chinese
    Theatre in Modern Times*
    (Amherst, Mass., 1975).
 37 Witke, op. cit., 383.
 38 Ibid., 158–9.
 39 Ibid., 309–10.
 40 Ibid., 312–14.
 41 Terrill, op. cit., 305 footnote.
 42 Ibid., 304–9.
 43 Witke, op. cit., 318.
 44 For the long-term origins of the
    Cultural Revolution, see Roderick
    MacFarquhar, *The Origins of the
    Cultural Revolution, 1
    Contradictions Among the People
    1956–7* (London 1974).
 45 *China Quarterly*, 45.
 46 Terrill, *Mao*, 315.
 47 Witke, op. cit., 320, 356ff.
 48 Naranarayan Das, *China's Hundred
    Weeds: a Study of the Anti-Rightist
    Campaign in China 1957–1958*
    (Calcutta 1979); Garside, op. cit.,
    69.
 49 Chen, op. cit., 388.
 50 Ibid., 226.
 51 Ibid., 211.
 52 Garside, op. cit., 70, 91; Witke,
    op. cit., 379; Terrill, op. cit., 315;
    Chen, op. cit., 226ff.
 53 Chen, op. cit., 221–4.
 54 Anita Chan, *et al.*, 'Students and
    class warfare: the social roots of
    the Red Guard conflict in
    Guangzhon (Canton)', *China
    Quarterly*, 83, September 1980.

55 Chen, op. cit., 228–31.
56 See Simon Leys in *The Times Literary Supplement*, 6 March 1981, 259–60.
57 Witke, op. cit., 324–5.
58 Witke, op. cit., 328.
59 William Hinton, *Hundred Days War: the Cultural Revolution at Tsinghua University* (New York 1972), 101–4.
60 Terrill, op. cit., 319.
61 Witke, op. cit., 388–90.
62 Ibid., 435.
63 Ibid., 391–2, 402.
64 Parris Chang, 'Shanghai and Chinese politics before and after the Cultural Revolution' in Christopher Howe (ed.), *Shanghai* (Cambridge 1981).
65 Philip Bridgham, 'Mao's Cultural Revolution in 1967' in Richard Baum and Louis Bennett (eds), *China in Ferment* (Yale 1971), 134–5; Thomas Robinson, 'Chou En-lai and the Cultural Revolution in China' in Baum and Bennett (eds), *The Cultural Revolution in China* (Berkeley 1971), 239–50.
66 Witke, op. cit., 349; Edward Rice, *Mao's Way* (Berkeley 1972), 376–8.
67 *Far Eastern Economic Review*, 2 October 1969; Terrill, op. cit., 321–8.
68 Terrill, op. cit., 328–30.
69 Chen, op. cit., 344ff.; Terrill, op. cit., 345ff.
70 Terrill, op. cit., 369; Witke, op. cit., 365.
71 Terrill, op. cit., 387–90; Witke, op. cit., 475–6.
72 Terrill, op. cit., 402 footnote.
73 Ibid., 381, 420.
74 Quoted in Ross Terrill, *The Future of China After Mao* (London 1978), 121.
75 Ibid., 115–17.
76 Witke, op. cit., 472ff.; Terrill, *China After Mao*, 121–3.
77 *Daily Telegraph*, 9 January 1981, quoting *Zheng Ming* magazine.
78 Garside, op. cit., 67ff.
79 Ibid., 73ff.
80 Leys, op. cit.
81 Michael Oksenberg, 'China Policy for the 1980s', *Foreign Affairs*, 59 (Winter 1980–1), 304–22.
82 *Guardian*, 5 February 1982.

83 M.D.Morris *et al.*, (eds), *Indian Economy in the Nineteenth Century* (Delhi 1969); W.J.Macpherson, 'Economic Development in India under the British Crown 1858–1947' in A.J.Youngson (ed.), *Economic Development in the Long Run* (London 1972), 126–91; Peter Robb, 'British rule and Indian "Improvement"', *Economic History Review*, XXXIV (1981), 507–23.
84 J.Nehru, *The Discovery of India* (London 1946).
85 Dom Moraes, *Mrs Gandhi* (London 1980), 127.
86 Dom Moraes, *The Tempest Within* (Delhi 1971).
87 Moraes, *Mrs Gandhi*, 224.
88 Shahid Javed Burki, *Pakistan under Bhutto 1971–1977* (London 1979).
89 Moraes, *Mrs Gandhi*, 250.
90 Victoria Schofield, *Bhutto: Trial and Execution* (London 1980).
91 Moraes, *Mrs Gandhi*, 319.
92 Parliamentary statement by Minister of State for Home Affairs, 15 March 1981.
93 *The Times*, 3 February 1981.
94 *Daily Telegraph*, 2 February 1981.
95 See, for instance, James Freeman, *Untouchable: an Indian Life History* (London 1980).
96 *New York Times*, 20 July 1980.
97 R.Kipling, *From Sea to Sea* (London 1899).
98 Ved Mehta, *Portrait of India* (London 1970), Part VII, 362.
99 See, for instance, *Daily Telegraph*, 8 February 1982.

17 **The European Lazarus**
1 Jacques Dumaine, *Quai d'Orsay 1945–1951* (tr. London 1958), 13.
2 Simone de Beauvoir, *Force of Circumstance* (tr. London 1965), 38ff.
3 David Pryce-Jones, *Paris in the Third Reich: A history of the German Occupation 1940–1944* (London 1981).
4 Bernard-Henri Levy, *L'Idéologie française* (Paris 1981).
5 Quoted in Herbert R. Lottman, *Camus* (London 1981 ed.), 705.

6 Ibid., 322.
7 Guillaume Hanoteau, *L'Age d'or de St-Germain-des-Près* (Paris 1965); Herbert Lottman, 'Splendours and miseries of the literary café', *Saturday Review*, 13 March 1963, and *New York Times Book Review*, 4 June 1967.
8 Popper, *Conjectures and Refutations*, 363.
9 Terence Prittie, *Konrad Adenauer 1876–1967* (London 1972), 35–6.
10 Maria Romana Catti, *De Gasperi uomo solo* (Milan 1964), 81–2.
11 Elisa Carrillo, *Alcide de Gasperi: the Long Apprenticeship* (Notre Dame 1965), 9.
12 Ibid., 23.
13 Catti, op. cit., 104–11; Carrillo, op. cit., 83–4.
14 Prittie, op. cit., 224, 312.
15 Ibid., 97.
16 Ibid., 106–10.
17 Lewis J. Edinger, *Kurt Schumacher* (Stanford 1965), 135–6.
18 Arnold J. Heidenheimer, *Adenauer and the CDU* (The Hague 1960).
19 For the speech see Leo Schwering, *Frühgeschichte der Christlich-Demokratische Union* (Recklinghausen 1963), 190–3.
20 Quoted in Prittie, op. cit., 171.
21 Frank Pakenham, *Born to Believe* (London 1953), 198–9.
22 *Die Welt*, 30 November 1946.
23 Konrad Adenauer, *Memoirs*, 4 vols (tr. London 1966), i 180–2.
24 Aidan Crawley, *The Rise of West Germany 1945–1972* (London 1973), chapter 12.
25 Walter Henkels, *Gar nicht so Pingelig* (Dusseldorf 1965), 161.
26 Hans-Joachim Netzer (ed.), *Adenauer und die Folgen* (Munich 1965), 159.
27 Prittie, op. cit., 173 footnote 7.
28 Henkels, op. cit.
29 Prittie, op. cit., 236.
30 Adenauer, *Memoirs*, ii 509ff.
31 Rudolf Augstein, *Konrad Adenauer* (tr. London 1964), 94.
32 Radio broadcast, 2 July 1954; Prittie, op. cit., 173.
33 Quoted in J. Galtier-Boissière, *Mon Journal pendant l'occupation* (Paris 1945).
34 Philippe Bauchard, *Les Technocrates et le pouvoir* (Paris 1966); Zeldin, op. cit., 1068–9.
35 G. Wright, *Rural Revolution in France* (Stanford 1964), chapter 5.
36 Zeldin, op. cit., 687.
37 W. D. Halls, *The Youth of Vichy France* (Oxford 1981); Zeldin, op. cit., 1141.
38 Robert Aron, *Histoire de l'Épuration* 3 vols (Paris 1967); Peter Novick, *The Resistance v. Vichy* (New York 1968).
39 Herbert Lüthy, *The State of France* (tr. London 1955), 107.
40 André Rossi, *Physiologie du parti communiste français* (Paris 1948), 83, 431–2.
41 Annie Kriegel, *The French Communists: Profile of a People* (Chicago 1972).
42 See Herbert Lüthy, 'Why Five Million Frenchmen Vote Communist', *Socialist Commentary*, December 1951, p. 289.
43 Quoted Lüthy, *State of France*, 117.
44 Philip Williams, *Politics in Post-War France* (London 1954 ed.), 17–19.
45 Lüthy, *State of France*, 123.
46 Zeldin, op. cit., 1045ff.
47 Jean Monnet, *Memoirs* (tr. London 1978).
48 *Bulletin mensuel de statistique* (Paris), October 1952, p. 44.
49 Lüthy, *State of France*, 432.
50 Joseph Hours in *Année politique et économique*, spring 1953.
51 Quoted Lüthy, op. cit., 385.
52 Jean-Raymond Tournoux, *Pétain and de Gaulle* (tr. London 1966), 7.
53 Zeldin, op. cit., 1121.
54 Gaston Palewski, 'A Surprising Friendship: Malraux and de Gaulle' in Martine de Curcel (ed.), *Malraux: Life and Work* (London 1976), 70.
55 Ibid., 69.
56 *Goethe's Faust* (Penguin Classics), Part i, 71.
57 De Gaulle, speech, 17 April 1948.
58 De Gaulle, speeches of 13 April 1963; 22 November 1944; 1 March 1941; 25 November 1943; see Philip Cerny, *The Politics of Grandeur: Ideological Aspects of de Gaulle's Foreign Policy* (Cambridge 1980).

59 De Gaulle, op. cit., 235.
60 Ibid., 18.
61 Quoted in Jacques Fauvet, *La Quatrième République* (Paris 1959), 64, note.
62 David Schoenbrun, *Three Lives of Charles de Gaulle* (London 1965), 94–5.
63 J.R.Frears, *Political Parties and Elections in the French Fifth Republic* (London 1977), 18ff.
64 De Gaulle, op. cit., 144–6.
65 John Ardagh, *The New France: a Society in Transition 1945–1977* (London, 3rd ed., 1977), 31–2.
66 Zeldin, op. cit., 625, 635–6.
67 Ibid., 300–30.
68 Quoted in Lüthy, *State of France*, 382.
69 Albert Sorel, *Europe and the French Revolution* (tr. London 1968), I 277ff.
70 De Gaulle, op. cit., 173–4.
71 Adenauer, op. cit., III 434.
72 Text in Uwe Kitzinger, *The European Common Market and Community* (London 1967), 33–7.
73 Quoted in Anthony Sampson, *Macmillan* (London 1967), 146.
74 Prittie, op. cit., 268–9.
75 Adenauer, op. cit., III 434.
76 Prittie, op. cit., 268.
77 Transcript of press conference in Harold Wilson, *The Labour Government 1964–1970* (London 1971), 392–4.
78 For de Gaulle's vetoes, see Uwe Kitzinger, *Diplomacy and Persuasion: how Britain joined the Common Market* (London 1973), 37–8.
79 Rostow, *World Economy*, 234–5 and Table III–47.
80 Kitzinger, *Diplomacy and Persuasion*, Table p. 29.
81 Quoted in B. Simpson, *Labour: the Unions and the Party* (London 1973), 39.
82 A.Flanders, *Trades Unions* (London 1968); John Burton, *The Trojan Horse: Union Power in British Politics* (Leesburg 1979), 48, 50.
83 Sydney and Beatrice Webb, *The History of Trade Unionism* (London 1920); *Dicey's Law and Public Opinion in England* (London 1963 ed.).

84 *BBC v. Hearn and Others* (1977); see J.H.Bescoby and C.G.Hanson, 'Continuity and Change in Recent Labour Law', *National Westminster Bank Quarterly Review*, February 1976; *Trade Union Immunities* (London, HMSO, 1981), 34–101.
85 F.W.Paish, 'Inflation, Personal Incomes and Taxation', *Lloyds Bank Review*, April 1975.
86 Geoffrey Fry, *The Growth of Government* (London 1979), 2–3; A.T.Peacock and J.Wiseman, *The Growth of Public Expenditure in the UK* (London, 2nd ed., 1967); M.Abramovitz and V.F.Eliasberg, *The Growth of Public Employment in Great Britain* (London 1957).
87 J.M.Buchanan, John Burton and R.E.Wagner, *The Consequences of Mr Keynes* (London, Institute of Economic Affairs, 1978), 67 and Table II, p. 34.
88 Rostow, *World Economy*, Table III–42, p. 220; *League of Nations Statistical Yearbook 1933–4* (Geneva 1934), Table 10.
89 Derry, *Norway*, 325; P.M.Hayes, *Quisling* (Newton Abbot 1971).
90 T.K.Derry, *A History of Scandinavia* (London 1979), 322–4; Rostow, *World Economy*, 220.
91 E.D.Simon, *The Smaller Democracies* (London 1939); Marquis Childs, *Sweden: the Middle Way* (New York 1936).
92 Derry, *Scandinavia*, 336–7.
93 Christopher Hughes, *Switzerland* (London 1975), 167–72.
94 Urs Altermatt, 'Conservatism in Switzerland: a study in anti-Modernism', *Journal of Contemporary History*, 14 (1979), 581–610.
95 *Wall Street Journal*, 23 June 1980.
96 Kenneth Maxwell, 'Portugal under Pressure', *New York Review of Books*, 29 May 1975, 20–30.
97 Tom Gallagher, 'Controlled Repression in Salazar's Portugal', *Journal of Contemporary History*, 14 (1979) 385–402; for the PIDE see 'Para a Historia do Fascismo Portugues: a Pide', *Portugal Informaca*, June–July 1977.

98 Neil Bruce, *Portugal: the Last Empire* (Newton Abbot 1975), 108.
99 Franco, speech at Madrid Army Museum, 9 March 1946, quoted in Trythall, op. cit.
100 Ibid., 206.
101 *Estudios sociológicos sobre la situación social de España 1975* (Madrid 1976).
102 Raymond Carr and Juan Pablo Fusi, *Spain: Dictatorship to Democracy* (London 1979), 195ff.
103 Stanley Meisler, 'Spain's New Democracy', *Foreign Affairs*, October 1977.
104 Carr and Fusi, op. cit., 246.
105 Richard Clogg, *A Short History of Modern Greece* (Cambridge 1979), 164–5.
106 William McNeil, *Metamorphosis of Greece since World War II* (Chicago 1978).
107 *New York Times*, 6 July 1980.

18 America's Attempted Suicide

1 Edgar M. Bottome, *The Missile Gap* (Rutherford, N.J. 1971).
2 Schlesinger, *Robert Kennedy*, 220 footnote; William Safire, *Before the Fall: an inside view of the pre-Watergate White House* (New York 1975), 152–3.
3 Pierre Salinger, *With Kennedy* (New York 1966), 51.
4 Quoted by William F. Buckley Jr, 'Human Rights and Foreign Policy', *Foreign Affairs*, Spring 1980.
5 J.F.Kennedy, *Public Papers etc.*, 3 vols (Washington DC 1963–4), 1 1ff.
6 R.J.Walton, *Cold War and Counter-revolution: the Foreign Policy of John F. Kennedy* (New York 1972).
7 Poole, op. cit., 28.
8 Rostow, *World Economy*, 222ff.; Carlos Diáz Alejandro, *Essays on the Economic History of the Argentine Republic* (Yale 1970).
9 H.S.Ferns, *Argentina* (London 1969), 184ff.
10 Claudio Veliz (ed.), *The Politics of Conformity in Latin America* (Oxford 1967), Appendix, 'Successful Military Coups 1920–1966', 278.

11 Ferns, *Argentina*, 173.
12 Walter Little, 'The Popular Origins of Peronism' in David Rock (ed.), *Argentina in the Twentieth Century* (London 1975).
13 Ferns, *Argentina*, 190.
14 David Rock, 'The Survival and Restoration of Peronism', in *Argentina in the Twentieth Century*.
15 Martin Shermin and Peter Winn, 'The US and Cuba', *Wilson Review*, Winter 1979.
16 Earl Smith in congressional testimony, Senate Judiciary Committee, 30 August 1960.
17 Hugh Thomas, *Cuba, or the Pursuit of Freedom* (London 1971), 639.
18 Blas Roca, *En Defensa del Pueblo* (1945), 41–3; quoted in Thomas, *Cuba*, 736.
19 E. Suarez Rivas, *Un Pueblo Crucificado* (Miami 1964), 18; quoted in Thomas, *Cuba*.
20 *America Libre*, Bogota, 22 May 1961; Thomas, *Cuba*, 811.
21 Thomas, *Cuba*, 814–16.
22 Quoted ibid., 819.
23 For Castro, see Luis Conte Aguero, *Fidel Castro, Psiquiatria y Politica* (Mexico City 1968 ed.), which is critical; and Herbert Matthews, *Castro: a Political Biography* (London 1969), which is more favourable.
24 Thomas, *Cuba*, 946.
25 Quoted ibid., 977.
26 For US policy to Batista and Castro, see Earl Smith, *The Fourth Floor* (New York 1962) and *Communist Threat to the USA through the Caribbean: Hearings of the Internal Security Sub-committee, US Senate* (Washington DC 1959–62).
27 Smith, *Fourth Floor*, 60.
28 Thomas, *Cuba*, 1038–44.
29 E. Guevara, *Ouevres Révolutionaires 1959–1967* (Paris 1968), 25.
30 Smith, *Fourth Floor*, 170.
31 Thomas, *Cuba*, 1071ff.
32 Ibid., 1197.
33 Ibid., 1202–3.
34 Ibid., 1233–57.
35 Ibid., 969–70.
36 Schlesinger, *Robert Kennedy*, 452.
37 Ibid., 445.

38 For J.F.Kennedy's handling of the Bay of Pigs, see Haynes Johnson, *The Bay of Pigs* (New York 1964) and Arthur Schlesinger, *A Thousand Days* (Boston 1965), chapters 10–11.

39 Thomas, *Cuba*, 1365.

40 Ibid., 1371.

41 Schlesinger, *Robert Kennedy*, 472; *Readers' Digest*, November 1964.

42 *Alleged Assassination Plots involving Foreign Leaders* (Washington DC 1975), 14.

43 Ibid., interim and final reports; Schlesinger, *Robert Kennedy*, chapter 21.

44 H.S.Dinerstein, *The Making of a Missile Crisis* (Baltimore 1976), 156; see also Talbot (ed.), op. cit.

45 Jean Daniel in *L'Express*, 14 December 1963 and *New Republic*, 21 December 1963; Claude Julien, *Le Monde*, 22 March 1963.

46 Schlesinger, *Robert Kennedy*, 504–5.

47 Ibid., 507–11.

48 For an inside account of the missile crisis, see Robert Kennedy, *Thirteen Days: a memoir of the Cuban Missile Crisis* (New York 1971 ed.).

49 Quoted in Michel Tatu, *Power in the Kremlin: from Khrushchev to Kosygin* (New York 1969), 422.

50 *Newsweek*, 28 October 1963.

51 Edwin Guthman, *We Band of Brothers* (New York 1971), 26; *Saturday Review*, 15 October 1977.

52 Thomas, *Cuba*, 1414.

53 Quoted Schlesinger, *Robert Kennedy*, 531.

54 Talbot (ed.), op. cit., 511.

55 Quoted Schlesinger, *Robert Kennedy*, 530–1.

56 Ibid., 523 and footnote.

57 Thomas, *Cuba*, 1418.

58 Quoted in Hollander, op. cit., chapter 6: 'Revolutionary Cuba and the discovery of the New World', esp. 234ff.

59 Hugh Thomas in *The Times Literary Supplement*, 10 April 1981, 403.

60 See Werner Von Braun and F.I.Ordway, *History of Rocketry and Space-Travel* (New York, revised ed. 1969).

61 Quoted by Hugh Sidey, who was present, in his *John F. Kennedy: Portrait of a President* (London 1964).

62 H.Young *et al.*, *Journey to Tranquillity: the History of Man's Assault on the Moon* (London 1969), 109–10.

63 Quoted in Leslie H. Gelb and Richard K. Betts, *The Irony of Vietnam: the System Worked* (Washington DC 1979), 70–1.

64 W.W.Rostow, *The Diffusion of Power: an essay in recent history* (New York 1972), 265.

65 See Archimedes L.A.Patti, *Why Viet Nam? Prelude to America's Albatros* (University of California 1981); but see Dennis Duncanson, *The Times Literary Supplement*, 21 August 1981, 965.

66 Truman, op. cit., I 14–15.

67 Acheson, op. cit., 675–6.

68 Acheson, National Press Club speech, *Department of State Bulletin*, 23 January 1950, 115f.

69 Kennan, *Memoirs 1950–1963*, 59.

70 D. Eisenhower, *Public Papers* (1954), 253, 306; Gelb and Betts, op. cit., 60.

71 Eisenhower, press conference, 7, 26 April 1954; Gelb and Betts, op. cit., 59.

72 Eisenhower, *Public Papers* (1959), 71.

73 De Gaulle, op. cit., 256.

74 J.F.Kennedy, *Public Papers*, II 90.

75 Schlesinger, *A Thousand Days*, 547.

76 David Halberstam, *The Best and the Brightest* (New York 1972), 135.

77 Quoted in Henry Graff, *The Tuesday Cabinet: Deliberation and Decision in Peace and War under Lyndon B. Johnson* (New York 1970), 53.

78 Gelb and Betts, op. cit., 104 footnote 31; but see also Joseph C. Goulden, *Truth is the First Casualty: the Gulf of Tonkin Affair* (New York 1969), 160.

79 Gelb and Betts, op. cit., 117–18.

80 Ibid., 120–3.

81 Lyndon Johnson, *Public Papers*, IV 291.

82 Quoted in Halberstam, op. cit., 596.

83 Graff, op. cit., 81.

84 Gelb and Betts, op. cit., 135ff.
85 Doris Kearns, *Lyndon Johnson and the American Dream* (New York 1976), 264.
86 Gelb and Betts, op. cit., 139–43.
87 Guenther Lewy, 'Vietnam: New Light on the Question of American Guilt', *Commentary*, February 1978.
88 Gelb and Betts, op. cit., 214–15.
89 Lewy, op. cit.
90 Gelb and Betts, op. cit., 171.
91 Peter Braestrup, *Big Story: How the American Press and TV Reported and Interpreted the Crisis of Tet 1968 in Vietnam and Washington*, 2 vols (Boulder 1977).
92 John Mueller, *War, Presidents and Public Opinion* (New York 1973).
93 Gelb and Betts, op. cit., 130.
94 William Lunch and Peter Sperlich, 'American Public Opinion and the War in Vietnam', *Western Political Quarterly*, Utah, March 1979.
95 Don Oberdorfer, *Tet!* (New York 1971), 289–90.
96 Sidney Verba *et al.*, *Vietnam and the Silent Majority* (New York 1970); Stephen Hess, 'Foreign Policy and Presidential Campaigns', *Foreign Policy*, Autumn 1972.
97 Herbert Y. Shandler, *The Unmaking of a President: Lyndon Johnson and Vietnam* (Princeton 1977), 226–9.
98 Kearns, op. cit., 286, 282–3.
99 Schlesinger, *Robert Kennedy*, 1002.
100 Lyndon Baines Johnson, *The Vantage Point: perspectives of the Presidency 1963–1969* (New York 1971), 81.
101 Johnson, address to University of Michigan, May 1964, quoted in Lawrence J. Wittner, *Cold War America: from Hiroshima to Watergate* (New York 1974), 239–40.
102 Johnson, *Vantage Point*, 322–4; *New York Times*, 10 August 1965; Wittner, op. cit., 247–8.
103 Johnson, *Vantage Point*, 330, 172–3.
104 *Office of Management and Budget: Federal Government Finances* (Washington DC 1979); for a slightly different calculation, see Rostow, *World Economy*, 272, Table III–65.
105 Larry Berman, *The Office of Management and Budget and the Presidency 1921–1979* (Princeton 1979).
106 Johnson, *Vantage Point*, 435, 442ff., 450–1.
107 Ibid., 87.
108 Stanley Lebergott, *Wealth and Want* (Princeton 1975), 11–12.
109 Daniel P. Moynihan, *The Negro Family* (New York 1965).
110 Daniel P. Moynihan, *Maximum Feasible Misunderstanding* (New York 1968).
111 Quoted by Diane Divoky, 'A Loss of Nerve', *Wilson Review*, Autumn 1979.
112 C.P. Snow, *The Two Cultures and the Scientific Revolution* (Cambridge 1959).
113 Edward F. Denison, *Sources of Economic Growth* (New York 1962); Fritz Machlup, *The Production and Distribution of Knowledge in the United States* (Princeton 1962).
114 Clark Kerr, *The Uses of the University* (New York 1966).
115 Quoted by Lewis B. Mayhew, *Higher Education in the Revolutionary Decades* (Berkeley 1967), 101ff.
116 Charles E. Finn, *Scholars, Dollars and Bureaucrats* (Washington DC 1978), 22.
117 *On Further Examination: Report of the Advisory Panel on the Scholastic Aptitude Test score decline* (College Entrance Examination Board, New York 1977).
118 For instance, *National Institute of Education Compensatory Education Study* (New York 1978).
119 Divoky, op. cit.
120 Christopher Jenks, *Who Gets Ahead? The Determinants of Economic Success in America* (New York 1979).
121 See Arnold Heertje (ed.), *Schumpeter's Vision: Capitalism, Socialism and Democracy after Forty Years* (Eastbourne 1981).
122 Wittner, op. cit., 246–7.
123 Trilling, *Last Decade*, 174.

124 Wittner, op. cit., 292.
125 Quoted by Trilling, *Last Decade*, 111.
126 Fritz Stern, 'Reflections on the International Student Movement', *The American Scholar*, 40 (Winter 1970–1), 123–37.
127 Paul Joubert and Ben Crouch, 'Mississippi blacks and the Voting Rights Act of 1965', *Journal of Negro Education*, Spring 1977.
128 Jack Bass and Walter de Vries, *The Transformation of Southern Politics* (New York 1976).
129 Quoted Schlesinger, *Robert Kennedy*, 330; see D.W. Matthews and J.R. Prothero, *Negroes and the New Southern Politics* (New York 1966), 240ff.
130 *Report of the National Advisory Commission on Civil Disorders* (Washington DC 1968), 56.
131 Johnson, *Vantage Point*, 95.
132 Quoted in Wittner, op. cit., 283.
133 Bohlen, op. cit., 210.
134 Quoted in Arthur Schlesinger, *The Imperial Presidency* (Boston 1973), 123.
135 Thomas Cronic, 'The Textbook Presidency and Political Science', *Congressional Record*, 5 October 1970.
136 Wilfred Binkley, *New Republic*, 18 May 1953.
137 *New York Times*, 18 May 1954; *Washington Post*, 20 May 1954.
138 Schlesinger, *Imperial Presidency*, 169.
139 David Broder quoted in Safire, op. cit., 171.
140 Ibid., 70, 75.
141 Wittner, op. cit., 300–1.
142 Richard Nixon, *Public Papers, 1969* (Washington DC 1971), 371.
143 Gelb and Betts, op. cit., 350.
144 Safire, op. cit., 369.
145 Ibid., 375–9.
146 Test of Agreement in *State Department Bulletin*, 12 February 1973; Gelb and Betts, op. cit., 350.
147 Safire, op. cit., 117–18.
148 Ibid., 360.
149 Wittner, op. cit., 370–1.
150 Quoted in Safire, op. cit., 264.
151 Richard W. Steele, 'Franklin D. Roosevelt and his Foreign Policy Critics', *Political Science Quarterly*, Spring 1979, 22 footnote 27.
152 Ibid., 18; Saul Alindky, *John L. Lewis* (New York 1970), 238; Safire, op. cit., 166.
153 Trohan, op. cit., 179; *Daily Telegraph*, 4 March 1982.
154 Schlesinger, *Robert Kennedy*, 403ff.; Roger Blough, *The Washington Embrace of Business* (New York 1975).
155 Schlesinger, *Robert Kennedy*, 311–12.
156 Fred Friendly, *The Good Guys, the Bad Guys and the First Amendment* (New York 1976), chapter 3.
157 Safire, op. cit., 166.
158 Schlesinger, *Robert Kennedy*, 362ff.; Senate Select Committee (on) Intelligence Activities (Church Committee), *Final Report* (Washington 1976), II 154, III 158–60.
159 Trohan, op. cit., 136–7.
160 Ibid., 326; Judith Exner, *My Story* (New York 1977).
161 Alfred Steinberg, *Sam Johnson's Boy* (New York 1968), 671.
162 For Johnson's misdemeanours, see Robert A. Caro, *The Years of Lyndon Johnson* (New York 1982 and forthcoming).
163 Charles Roberts, *LBJ's Inner Circle* (New York 1965), 34; Schlesinger, *Imperial Presidency*, 221; see 'The Development of the White House Staff', *Congressional Record*, 20 June 1972.
164 Safire, op. cit., 166ff.
165 Ibid., 357.
166 Fred Thompson, *At That Point in Time* (New York 1980).
167 *Will: the Autobiography of G. Gordon Liddy* (London 1981), 300.
168 See, for instance, Maurice Stans, *The Terrors of Justice: the untold side of Watergate* (New York 1979), and James Nuechterlein, 'Watergate: towards a Revisionist View', *Commentary*, August 1979. Sirica provided his own account: John J. Sirica, *To Set the Record Straight* (New York 1979).
169 *Daily Telegraph*, 15 January and 5–6 February 1982.
170 Anthony Lukas, *Nightmare: the Underside of the Nixon Years* (New York 1976), 375ff.; Safire, op. cit., 292.

171 Tom Bethell and Charles Peters,
     'The Imperial Press', *Washington
     Monthly*, November 1976.
172 Lee H. Hamilton and Michael H.
     Van Dusen, 'Making the
     Separation of Powers Work',
     Foreign Affairs, Autumn 1978.
173 Georgetown University Conference
     on Leadership, Williamsburg,
     Virginia, reported in *Wall Street
     Journal*, 15 May 1980.
174 Gerald Ford, *Public Papers 1975*
     (Washington DC 1977), 119.
175 *State Department Bulletin*,
     14 April 1975.
176 *Political Change in Wartime: the
     Khmer Krahom Revolution in
     Southern Cambodia 1970–4*,
     paper given at American Political
     Science Association Convention,
     San Francisco, 4 September 1975.
177 Ibid.
178 Evidence collected from over 300
     refugees in camps in Thailand,
     Malaysia, France and the USA,
     October 1975–October 1976,
     printed in John Barron and
     Anthony Paul, *Peace with Horror*
     (London 1977), 10–31.
179 Ibid., 66–85; *New York Times*,
     9 May 1974, 31 October 1977,
     13 May 1978; *Washington Post*,
     21 July 1977, 2, 3, 4 May and 1
     June 1978.
180 Barron and Paul, op. cit., 136–49.
181 Ibid., 202ff.
182 *Annual Register* 1981 (London
     1982).

19 The Collectivist Seventies
 1 *New York Times*, 31 December
    1933.
 2 Letter to Montagu Norman,
    Collected Writings of J. M. Keynes
    XXV 98–9.
 3 Rostow, *World Economy*, 68
    Table II–7.
 4 Ibid., 49.
 5 Richard Austin Smith, 'The
    Incredible Electrical Conspiracy',
    Fortune, April–May 1961.
 6 Schlesinger, *Robert Kennedy*, 405.
 7 *Christian Science Monitor*,
    16 April 1962; *Wall Street Journal*,
    19 April 1962.
 8 Robert Sobell, *The Last Bull
    Market: Wall Street in the 1960s*
    (New York 1980).

 9 James Lorie, 'The Second Great
    Crash', *Wall Street Journal*, 2 June
    1980.
10 Robert DeFina, *Public and Private
    Expenditures for Federal
    Regulation of Business*
    (Washington University, St Louis
    1977); Murray L. Weidenbaum,
    *Government Power and Business
    Performance* (Stanford 1980).
11 Weidenbaum, op. cit.
12 Edward F. Denison in *Survey of
    Current Business* (US Department
    of Commerce, Washington DC),
    January 1978.
13 Denison, *Survey of Current
    Business*, August 1979 (Part II);
    and his *Accounting for Slower
    Economic Growth: the United
    States in the 1970s* (Washington
    DC 1980).
14 R. A. Maidment, 'The US Supreme
    Court and Affirmative Action: the
    Cases of Bakka, Weber and
    Fullilove', *Journal of American
    Studies*, December 1981.
15 Laurence H. Silberman, 'Will
    Lawyers Strangle Democratic
    Capitalism?', *Regulation*
    (Washington DC), March/April
    1978.
16 John Osborne, *White House
    Watch: the Ford Years*
    (Washington DC 1977), 68.
17 *Washington Star*, 16 April 1980;
    Washington Post, 18 April 1980;
    Wall Street Journal, 24 April 1980;
    Carl Cohen, 'Justice Debased: the
    Weber Decision', *Commentary*,
    September 1979.
18 Richard Fry (ed.), *A Banker's
    World* (London 1970), 7.
19 Speech, International Monetary
    Conference, London, 11 June
    1979; quoted in Anthony
    Sampson, *The Money Lenders:
    Bankers in a Dangerous World*
    (London 1981), chapter 7, 106ff.,
    describes the origin of the
    Euro-dollar system.
20 Geoffrey Bell, *The Euro-dollar
    Market and the International
    Financial System* (New York
    1973).
21 Irving Friedman, *The Emerging
    Role of Private Banks in the
    Developing World* (New York
    1977).

22 Charles Coombs, *The Arena of International Finance* (New York 1976), 219.
23 Geoffrey Bell, 'Developments in the International Monetary System Since Floating', *Schroders International*, November 1980.
24 Rostow, *World Economy*, 248–9.
25 Ibid., 260–1 and Table III–59.
26 Ibid., 254–5.
27 J.B.Kelly, *Arabia, the Gulf and the West* (London 1980).
28 Teddy Kollek, 'Jerusalem', *Foreign Affairs*, July 1977.
29 P.J.Vatikiotis, *Nasser and his Generation* (London 1978).
30 Ruth First, *Libya: the Elusive Revolution* (Harmondsworth 1974), 201–4.
31 Henry Kissinger, *Years of Upheaval* (London 1982).
32 Martin Gilbert, *The Arab–Israel Conflict* (London 1974), 97.
33 Quoted in Poole, op. cit., 247; Scott Sagan, 'The Yom Kippur Alert', *Foreign Policy*, Autumn 1979.
34 Kissinger, op. cit.
35 Rostow, *World Economy*, 295.
36 Ibid., 290–5.
37 Charles R. Morris, *The Cost of Good Intentions: New York City and the Liberal Experiment* (New York 1980), 234.
38 *House Banking Committee: International Banking Operations, hearings* (Washington DC 1977), 719.
39 Quoted in Sampson, *The Money Lenders*, 126–7.
40 Seth Lipsky, *The Billion Dollar Bubble* (Hong Kong 1978).
41 *Wall Street Journal*, 25–26 June 1980.
42 Bruce Palmer (ed.), *Grand Strategy for the 1980s* (Washington DC 1979), 5.
43 *Annual Defence Department Report, Financial Year 1977* (Washington DC 1977), section V.
44 Osborne, op. cit., XXXIII.
45 Ibid., 32.
46 Paula Smith: 'The Man Who Sold Jimmy Carter', *Dun's Review* (New York), August 1976.
47 Robert W. Tucker, 'America in Decline: the Foreign Policy of "Maturity"', *Foreign Affairs*, 58 (Autumn 1979), 450–84.
48 Papers by Judith Reppy and Robert Lyle Butterworth in Symposium on American Security Policy and Policy-Making, *Policy Studies Journal*, Autumn 1979.
49 Quoted by Jeane Kirkpatrick, 'Dictatorships and Double Standards: a Critique of US Policy', *Commentary*, November 1979.
50 Michael A. Ledeen and William H. Lewis, 'Carter and the Fall of Shah: the Inside Story', *Washington Quarterly*, Summer 1980, 15ff.
51 Quoted in Thomas L. Hughes: 'Carter and the Management of Contradictions', *Foreign Policy*, 31 (Summer 1978), 34–55; Simon Serfaty, 'Brzezinski: Play it Again, Zbig', *Foreign Policy*, 32 (Autumn 1978), 3–21; Elizabeth Drew, 'Brzezinski', *New Yorker*, 1 May 1978; and Kirkpatrick, op. cit.
52 See Robert Legvold, 'The Nature of Soviet Power', *Foreign Affairs*, 56 (Autumn 1977), 49–71.
53 Quoted in Ronald Hingley, *The Russian Secret Police* (London 1970), 222.
54 Robert Payne, *The Rise and Fall of Stalin* (London 1968), 718–19.
55 Kolakowski, op. cit., III 'Destalinization'.
56 For the *coup*, see Michel Tatu, *Power in the Kremlin* (tr. London 1969); Hingley, *Russian Secret Police*, 43–5.
57 Hélène Carrère d'Encausse, *Le Pouvoir Confisqué: Gouvernants et Gouvernés en URSS* (Paris 1981).
58 Quoted in Robert C. Tucker, 'Swollen State, Spent Society: Stalin's Legacy to Brezhnev's Russia', *Foreign Affairs*, 60 (Winter 1981–2), 414–25.
59 See CIA, *A Dollar Comparison of Soviet and US Defence Activities 1967–1977* (Washington DC January 1978); Les Aspin, 'Putting Soviet Power in Perspective', *AEI Defense Review* (Washington DC), June 1978.
60 National Foreign Assessment Center, *Handbook of Economic Statistics 1979* (Washington DC).
61 Talbot (ed.), op. cit., 131.

62 Arcadius Kahan and Blair Rible (eds), *Industrial Labour in the USSR* (Washington DC 1979).

63 See Joint Economic Committee, Congress of the USA, *Soviet Economy in a Time of Change* (Washington DC 1979).

64 See Solzhenitsyn's 'Misconceptions about Russia are a Threat to America', *Foreign Affairs*, 58 (Spring 1980), 797–834.

65 *Arkhiv samizdata*, Document Number 374, quoted in Tucker, op. cit.

66 Mark Popovsky, *Manipulated Science: the Crisis of Science and Scientists in the Soviet Union Today* (tr. New York 1979), 179.

67 See Evgeny Pashukanis, *Selected Writings on Marxism and Law* (tr. London 1980); Eugene Kamenka, 'Demythologizing the Law', *The Times Literary Supplement*, 1 May 1981, 475–6.

68 Tufton Beamish and Guy Hadley, *The Kremlin Dilemma: the struggle for Human Rights in Eastern Europe* (London 1979), 24.

69 Roy Medvedev, *On Soviet Dissent: interviews with Piero Ostellino* (tr. London 1980), 61.

70 Ibid., 53–4.

71 Bavel Litvinov (ed.), *The Trial of the Four* (London 1972).

72 Beamish and Hadley, op. cit., 216ff.

73 Ibid., 221ff.

74 I.Z.Steinberg, *Spiridonova: Revolutionary Terrorist* (London 1935), 241–2; in fact she was kept in the Kremlin guardroom until her escape in April 1919.

75 Sidney Bloch and Peter Reddaway, *Russia's Political Hospitals: the Abuse of Psychiatry in the Soviet Union* (London 1977), 51–3.

76 Yarkov's *samizdat* autobiography was smuggled to the West in 1970.

77 *Pravda*, 24 May 1959.

78 See the evidence of forty-four British psychiatrists in C. Mee (ed.), *The Internment of Soviet Dissenters in Mental Hospitals* (London 1971).

79 Bloch and Reddaway, op. cit., 311ff.; see also I.F.Stone, *New York Review of Books*, 10 February 1972, 7–14.

80 All are summarized in Bloch and Reddaway, op. cit., Appendix I, 347–98.

81 Ibid., 57.

82 *Abuse of Psychiatry for Political Repression in the Soviet Union*, US Senate Judiciary Committee (Washington DC 1972).

83 Bloch and Reddaway, op. cit., 220–30.

84 Medvedev, *On Soviet Dissent*, 142–3.

85 *Reprints from the Soviet Press*, 30 April 1977, 22–3.

86 *Index on Censorship* (London), No. 4 1980; Vladimir Bukovsky, 'Critical Masses: the Soviet Union's Dissident Many,' *American Spectator*, August 1980; see also Joshua Rubenstein, *Soviet Dissidents: their Struggle for Human Rights* (Boston 1981).

87 Alva M. Bowen, 'The Anglo–German and Soviet–American Naval Rivalries: Some Comparisons', in Paul Murphy (ed.), *Naval Power and Soviet Policy* (New York 1976).

88 James L. George (ed.), *Problems of Sea-Power as we approach the 21st Century* (Washington DC 1978), 18.

89 Sulzberger, op. cit., 698.

90 Gorshkov's collected articles are published in translation by the US Naval Institute (Annapolis) as *Red Star Rising at Sea* and *Sea-Power and the State*.

91 George, op. cit., 17.

92 Admiral Elmo Zumwalt, *On Watch* (New York 1976), 444–5.

93 Richard Fagen, 'Cuba and the Soviet Union', *Wilson Review*, Winter 1979.

94 Mahgoub, op. cit., 277.

95 Quoted in Fagen, op. cit.

96 Jonathan Kwitny, '"Communist" Congo, "Capitalist" Zaire', *Wall Street Journal*, 2 July 1980.

97 Albert Wohlstetter (ed.), *Swords from Ploughshares: the Military Potential of Civilian Nuclear Energy* (Chicago, 1979), XIII.

98 Ibid., 17.

99 Lawrence Scheinman, *Atomic Policy in France under the Fourth Republic* (Princeton 1965), 94–5.

100 For Japan, see Wohlstetter, op. cit., chapter 5, 111–25; Geoffrey Kemp, *Nuclear Forces for Medium Powers* (London 1974).
101 Wohlstetter, op. cit., 44–5.
102 See Claire Sterling, *The Terror Network* (New York 1981).
103 Caroline Moorehead, *Fortune's Hostages: Kidnapping in the World Today* (London 1980).
104 Christopher Dobson and Ronald Payne, *The Carlos Complex: a pattern of violence* (London 1977), 30–44.
105 For these two cases see Sterling, op. cit.
106 'The Most Sinister Growth Industry', *The Times*, 27 October 1981.
107 This argument is elaborated in Paul Johnson, 'The Seven Deadly Sins of Terrorism', Jerusalem Conference on International Terrorism, published by the Jonathan Institute, Jerusalem 1979.
108 Moynihan, *A Dangerous Place*, 86.
109 Quoted ibid., 157–8.
110 Ibid., 197.
111 Rostow, *World Economy*, Table II–71, 285.
112 Alfred Sauvy, *L'Observateur*, 14 August 1952.
113 Carl E. Pletsch, 'The Three Worlds, or the Division of Social Scientific Labour, 1950–75', *Comparative Studies in Society and History*, October 1981.
114 Jahangir Amuzegar, 'A Requiem for the North–South Conference', *Foreign Affairs*, 56 (October 1977), 136–59.
115 *North–South: a Programme for Survival* (Massachusetts Institute of Technology, March 1980).
116 Theodore Moran, *Multinational Corporations and the Politics of Dependence: Copper in Chile* (Princeton 1974); Charles Goodsell, *American Corporations and Peruvian Politics* (Harvard 1974).
117 Lawrence Franco, 'Multinationals: the end of US dominance', *Harvard Business Review*, Nov.–Dec. 1978.
118 'Finis for the American Challenge?', *Economist*, 10 September 1977.

119 *The Banker* (London), June 1980; Sampson, *The Moneylenders*, 200–2.
120 *Euromoney*, July 1980; quoted by Sampson in *The Moneylenders*, 257.
121 World Bank estimates, December 1981.
122 Richard Baricuck, 'The Washington Struggle over Multinationals', *Business and Society Review*, Summer 1976.
123 Paul Hollander, 'Reflections on Anti-Americanism in our time', *Worldview*, June 1978.
124 Marx, *A Contribution to the Critique of Political Economy*, quoted in Maurice Gordelier, 'Structuralism and Marxism', in Tom Bottomore (ed.), *Modern Interpretations of Marx* (Oxford 1981).
125 Rostow, *World Economy*, Table III–68, 279.
126 Ernest Gellner, 'What is Structuralism?', *The Times Literary Supplement*, 31 July 1981, 881–3.

20 The Recovery of Freedom

1 Published in London 1945, in New York 1946; see also *Sunday Express*, 21, 28 October, 4 November 1945; David C. Smith: *H.G. Wells: Desperately Mortal* (Yale 1986), 476ff.
2 President Jimmy Carter, Address to the Nation, 16 July 1979.
3 An exception was Adam Smith, who had been Professor of Moral Philosophy at Glasgow University, 1752–64, though he had left academic life by the time he wrote his *The Wealth of Nations*, published in 1776.
4 John Gribbin, *Our Changing Universe: the New Astronomy* (London 1976).
5 Dr Edward Tryon in *Nature*, 246 (1973), 393.
6 *Wissenschaftliche Selbstbiographie* (Leipzig 1948), quoted by Thomas Kuhn in A.C. Crombie (ed.), *Scientific Change* (London 1963), 348.

7 See Dr John Smythies in *Nature*, March 1991; Robert Matthews in the *Sunday Telegraph*, 17 March 1991; and correspondence in the *Independent*, 21 and 23 March 1991.

8 Quotations from Ayer and Russell are in Bryan Magee, *Modern British Philosophers* (London 1971).

9 See my essay on Russell in *Intellectuals* (London 1988), 197–224.

10 Karl Popper, *Unended Quest: an Intellectual Autobiography* (London 1976).

11 A.C Ewing, 'The linguistic theory of a priori propositions', *Proceedings of the Aristotelian Society*, XI 1939–40, 217.

12 W.V.O. Quine, *From a Logical Point of View* (New York 1953).

13 H. Putnam, 'Is Logic Empirical?', in R.S. Cohen (ed.), *Boston Studies in the Philosophy of Science*, V 1969.

14 Susan Haack, *Deviant Logic: some philosophical issues* (London 1974), *xi*.

15 J. Jay Zeman, *Modal Logic: the Lewis-modal Systems* (Oxford 1973).

16 David Martin, *The Religious and the Secular* (London 1969).

17 Edward Royle, *Victorian Infidels* (Manchester 1974).

18 John Henry Newman, *The Idea of a University* (London 1953).

19 Michael Bourdeaux, *Gorbachev, Glasnost and the Gospel* (London 1990), 87–108.

20 Vincent C. Chrypinski, 'Polish Catholicism and Social Change', in Bociurkiw *et al.* (eds), op. cit., 241–59; Peter Raina, *Political Opposition in Poland 1954–77* (London 1978), 406ff.

21 J.C.H. Aveling, *The Jesuits* (London 1981), 355–65.

22 *Annuario Ufficiale* (Vatican City), 1978.

23 Peter Nichols, *The Pope's Divisions; The Roman Catholic Church Today* (London 1981), 22–38.

24 Ibid., 35ff.

25 Edward Fashole-Like *et al., Christianity in Independent Africa* (London 1979).

26 For a comprehensive summary of the report see the *Daily Telegraph*, Tuesday 12 March 1991.

27 See reports in the press for the week 24 February–2 March 1991, and Christopher Booker in the *Sunday Telegraph*, 24 February 1991.

28 For two views on this process see Ivan Vallier, *Catholicism, Social Control and Modernization in Latin America* (Santa Cruz 1970), and Edward Norman, *Christianity in the Southern Hemisphere* (Oxford 1981).

29 Roger Bastide, *The African Religions of Brazil* (Baltimore 1978); J.H. Rodrigues, *Brazil and Africa* (Berkeley 1965).

30 Bengt G.M. Sundkler, *Zulu Zion and Some Swasi Zionists* (Oxford 1976).

31 For a discussion of the battle between Orthodox fundamentalism and secularism in Israel see Emile Marmorstein, *Heaven at Bay: the Jewish Kulturkampf in the Holy Land* (Oxford 1969); see also Paul Johnson, *A History of the Jews* (London 1987), 546–56.

32 For an account of the background see John Bulloch, *Death of a Country: Civil War in Lebanon* (London 1977).

33 William Forbis, *Fall of the Peacock Throne* (New York 1980), 45.

34 Kayhan Research Associates, *Iran's Fifth Plan* (Teheran 1974); Jahangir Amuzegar, *Iran: an Economic Profile* (Washington DC 1977).

35 Forbis, op. cit., 237ff.

36 Ibid., 73–4.

37 Grace Goodell, 'How the Shah De-Stabilized Himself', *Policy Review* (Washington, DC), Spring 1981.

38 Forbis, op. cit., 259–61.

39 Goodell, op. cit.

40 Forbis, op. cit., 74.

41 Michael A. Ledeen and William H. Lewis, 'Carter and the Fall of the Shah', *Washington Quarterly*, Summer 1980.

42 Shahrough Akhavi, *Religion and Politics in Contemporary Iran: Clergy–State Relations in the Pahlavi Period* (New York 1980).

43 Figures given by the former Iran Bar Associations in a letter to the UN Secretary-General, August 1981.

44 See report by Amir Taheri, *Sunday Times*, 23 August 1981.

45 *Sunday Times*, 6 September 1981.

46 For Saddam Hussein's family background and childhood see John Bulloch, 'The Violent Boy from Al-Ouja', in the *Independent on Sunday*, 6 January 1991.

47 *The Times* and *Daily Telegraph*, 15 February 1989.

48 For different versions of Soviet involvement see M.E. Yapp in *The Times Literary Supplement*, 3 July 1981, 753, and 25 September 1981, 1101, and Anthony Arnold, *The Soviet Invasion of Afghanistan in Perspective* (Stanford 1981), 68–71.

49 John Griffiths, *Afghanistan: Key to a Continent* (London 1981).

50 *The Times*, 21 January 1980.

51 *Daily Telegraph*, 21 February 1980.

52 Nancy Peabody Newell and Richard S. Newell, *The Struggle for Afghanistan* (Cornell 1981).

53 Quoted in Cecil Kaye, *Communism in India*, edited by Subodh Roy (Calcutta 1971), 272.

54 Hélène Carrère d'Encausse, *Decline of an Empire: the Soviet Socialist Republics in Revolt* (tr. New York 1979), 239.

55 Ibid., 237, 240.

56 Lenin, *Imperialism*, preface to 1921 edition.

57 Carrère d'Encausse, op. cit., 122–3, and 42–3 for nationalities map.

58 Ibid., 155.

59 This was particularly true of the 1960s and 1970s; see Brian Silver; 'The status of national minority languages in Soviet education: an assessment of recent changes', *Soviet Studies*, 25 No. 1 (1974).

60 Y. Bilinsky, 'Politics, Purge and Dissent in the Ukraine', in L. Kamenetsky (ed.), *Nationalism and Human Rights: Processes of Modernization in the USSR* (Colorado 1977); P. Botychnyi (ed.), *The Ukraine in the Seventies* (Oakville, Ontario 1975), 246; Carrère d'Encausse, op. cit., 170–1, 180 (Table 37).

61 Msksudov, op. cit.; Carrère d'Encausse, op. cit., 50–1.

62 Carrère d'Encausse, op cit., 67ff.

63 Ibid., 173–4.

64 This was the view of John D. Durand, 'The Modern Expansion of World Population', *Proceedings of the American Philosophical Society*, III (June 1967), 136–59; but demographic projections are notoriously liable to error.

65 Rostow, *World Economy*, Table I–13, 25.

66 UN *Demographic Yearbook 1971*; *Washington Post* and *Wall Street Journal*, 10 July 1980.

67 See *Whitaker's Almanac* for 1988, 1989, 1990; *Chronicle of the Year 1989* (London 1990).

68 Talbot (ed.), op cit., 120ff., 139–43.

69 *Daily Telegraph, The Times*, 17, 18 March 1991.

70 See 'Demographic Trends', *South Africa 1989–90, Official Yearbook* (Pretoria, Cape Town 1990), 79–90.

71 For a discussion of this and other aspects of South Africa's difficulties and their global significance, see Martin Schneider (ed.), *South Africa: the Watershed Years* (Cape Town 1991), especially 29ff., 42ff., 60ff., 70ff., 136ff.

72 Rostow, *World Economy*, Table I–15, 30.

73 Text of constitution in H. Borton, *Japan's Modern Century* (New York 1955), 490–507.

74 For a general treatment of the occupation, see Kazuo Kawai, *Japan's American Interlude* (Chicago 1960).

75 R.P. Dore, *Land Reform in Japan* (Oxford 1959); Kurt Steiner, *Local Government in Japan* (Stanford 1965).

76 John M. Maki, *Court and Constitution in Japan* (Seattle 1964).

77 Richard Storry, *The Times Literary Supplement*, 5 September 1980, 970; see J.W. Dower, *Empire and Aftermath: Yoshida Shigeru and the Japanese Experience, 1878–1954* (Harvard 1980).

78 Andra Boltho, *Japan: an Economic Survey* (Oxford 1975), 8 footnote; S. Kuznets, *Economic Growth of Nations* (Harvard 1971), 30–1, 38–40.

79 Rostow, *World Economy*, 275.

80 Ezra F. Vogel, 'The Challenge from Japan', Harvard Conference on US Competitiveness, 25 April 1980.

81 J.A.A. Stockwin, *Japan: Divided Politics in a Growth Economy* (London 1975), 1–3.

82 Beasley, op. cit., 286.

83 Boltho, op. cit., 167–8.

84 James Kirkup, *Heaven, Hell and Hara-Kiri* (London 1974), 248–52.

85 Quoted by Frank Gibney, 'The Ripple Effect in Korea', *Foreign Affairs*, October 1977.

86 See Special Issue of *Wilson Review*, Autumn 1979, for Taiwan's spectacular progress in the 1960s and 1970s.

87 Quoted by Sampson, *The Moneylenders*, 183–4.

88 I.M.D. Little: 'The experience and causes of rapid labour-intensive development in Korea, Taiwan, Hong Kong and Singapore, and the possibilities of emulation', *ILO Working Paper* (Bangkok 1979).

89 Rostow, *World Economy*, 548–51.

90 See David Nevin, *The American Touch in Micronesia* (New York 1977); *Chronicle of the Year 1989* (London 1990), 117.

91 Stefan de Vylder, *Allende's Chile: the political economy of the rise and fall of the Unidad Popular* (Cambridge, Mass., 1976); Brian Loveman, *Struggle in the Countryside: politics and rural labour in Chile, 1919–1973* (Indiana 1976).

92 Ian Roxborough *et al.*, *Chile: the State and Revolution* (London 1977), 146–7. Allende had told me as far back as 1960 that he had no chance of winning an election except through a split on the Right, and that the result was likely to be high inflation and a middle-class revolt.

93 Ibid., 226.

94 *Newsweek*, 8 October 1973.

95 Joseph L. Nogee and John W. Sloan, 'Allende's Chile and the Soviet Union', *Journal of International Studies and World Affairs*, August 1979.

96 James Boswell, *Life of Johnson* II (London 1934), 170.

97 W. Baer and I. Kerstenetsky (eds), *Inflation and Growth in Latin America* (Homewood, Illinois 1964).

98 Quoted in Sampson, *The Moneylenders*, 303.

99 *Daily Telegraph*, 6 March 1991.

100 *Annual Review 1984* (London 1985), 8.

101 *Annual Review 1985* (London 1986), 8–9.

102 Statement, House of Commons, 8 April 1985.

103 Hugo Young, *The Iron Lady: a Biography of Margaret Thatcher* (London 1989), 532–3.

104 Norman Lamont, MP, on the *Today Programme*, BBC Radio 4, 20 March 1991.

105 *Wilson Quarterly*, Special Issue on Mexico, Summer 1979; Michael Meyer and William Sherman, *The Course of Mexican History* (Oxford 1979).

106 Richard R. Fagen: 'The Realities of Mexico–American Relations', *Foreign Affairs*, July 1977.

107 Richard R. Fagen, *Labyrinths of Power: Political Recruitment in 20th Century Mexico* (Princeton 1979).

108 E.L. Ullman: 'Regional Development and the Geography of Concentration', *Papers and Proceedings of the Regional Science Association*, 4 (1958), 197–8.

109 H.S. Perloff *et al.*, *Regions, Resources and Economic Growth* (University of Nebraska 1960), 50.

110 Robert Estall, 'The Changing Balance of the Northern and Southern Regions of the United States', *Journal of American Studies* (Cambridge), December 1980.

111 Ben J. Wattenburg: 'A New Country: America 1984', *Public Opinion* (Washington DC), Oct–Nov 1979.

112 Ronald Reagan, *An American Life: an Autobiography* (New York 1990), 135.

113 Ibid., 335–6.

114 *The Statesman's Yearbook 1990–1*, 1399ff, 1413.

115 *An American Life*, 334 –5.

116 *Discriminate Deterrence: Report of the Commission on Integrated Long-Term Strategy* (Washington DC 1988), 5–7.

117 *An American Life*, 449–51.

118 See my article in the *Observer*, 30 October 1983.

119 *An American Life*, 517–8.

120 For the events which led up to the S-20s and Cruise deployment, see Jonathan Haslam: *The Soviet Union and the Politics of Nuclear Weapons in Europe, 1969–77* (Cornell UP 1990).

121 *An American Life*, 234–5.

122 For a general discussion of the US rearmament programme as it evolved in the 1980s see the account by Reagan's Defence Secretary, Caspar Weinberger, *Fighting For Peace* (New York 1990).

123 See Paul Johnson, 'Europe and the Reagan Years', and Robert W. Tucker, 'Reagan's Foreign Policy', in 'America and the World, 1988–9', a special issue of *Foreign Affairs*, 68 (1989).

124 *An American Life*, 568–70, which gives the key passages from the Orlando speech.

125 No personal biography of the Soviet leader has been published and details of Gorbachev's life proved difficult to obtain; some were published in the *Sunday Correspondent* colour supplement, 25 February 1990.

126 For details of the changes in Russia during the 1980s, see Geoffrey Hosking, *The Awakening of the Soviet Union* (Harvard 1990), who shows that some of the changes began before Gorbachev.

127 For an overall view of this subject see Thane Gustafson, *Crisis and Plenty: the Politics of Soviet Energy under Brezhnev and Gorbachev* (Princeton 1989).

128 Reagan's detailed personal account of the Geneva meeting is in *An American Life*, 633–41.

129 For contrasting views see 'The American 1980s: Disaster or Triumph: a Symposium', special issue of *Commentary*, September 1990; see also Larry Berman (ed.), *Looking Back on the Reagan Presidency* (Baltimore 1990), and W.G. Hyland, *The Cold War is Over* (New York 1990).

130 To the author; this was also Margaret Thatcher's view.

131 *An American Life*, 639.

132 The *Telegraph* reporter was the author's eldest son, Daniel Johnson.

133 From *Marx-Engels Werke* (East Berlin 1956–68), iii 569–71.

134 For the Ceausescu regime, see Edward Behr, *Kiss the Hand You Cannot Bite* (London 1991); John Sweeney, *The Life and Evil Times of Nicolae Ceaucescu* (London 1991).

135 This figure, like most others connected with recent Romanian events, is unreliable; Sweeney, op. cit., believes no more than fifty were shot.

136 Ibid.

137 See, for instance, 'The End of the Honeymoon', *Daily Telegraph*, 25 March 1991.

138 Reported on the BBC *Money Programme*, 10 March 1991.

139 See M.E. Porter, *The Competitive Advantage of Nations* (New York 1990).

140 For the events leading up to the war, see John Bulloch and Harvey Morris, *Saddam's War: the origins of the Kuwait conflict and the international response* (London 1991).

141 For details and dates of the events leading up to the Iraqi invasion, and the Allied response, see the following special newspaper supplements: London *Times*, 16 January 1991; *Daily Mail*, 1 March 1991; *Daily Telegraph*, 2 March 1991; *Sunday Telegraph*, 3 March 1991.

142 The major ground components of the Allied force were: United States 320,000; United Kingdom 25,000; Saudi Arabia 40,000; Syria 12,000; France 10,000; Egypt 35,000.

143 Figures vary and must be regarded as estimates until official war histories are published; I have taken these from the *Daily Telegraph* supplement of 2 March 1991.

144 For these and other figures see *Chronicle of the Twentieth Century*, 1294–5.

145 For various examples see David Israelson, *Silent Earth: the Politics of Survival* (Ontario 1990), esp. 227–50.

146 Sarah Johnson in the *Sunday Telegraph*, 4 February 1991.

147 Conor Cruise O'Brien: 'Devaluing the University', London *Times*, 5 March 1991; David Lehman, *Signs of the Times: Deconstruction and the Fall of Paul de Man* (New York 1991).

148 See Dinesh D'Sousa, *Illiberal Education: The Politics of Race and Sex on Campus* (New York 1991).

149 Martin Fletcher in the *Times*, 16 March 1991.

150 James Watson, *The Double Helix: being a personal account of the discovery of the structure of* DNA (New York 1977).

151 Franklin Portugal and Jack Cohen, *A Century of* DNA: *a history of the discovery of the structure and function of the genetic substance* (Massachusetts Institute of Technology 1977).

152 Nicholas Wade, *The Ultimate Experiment: man-made evolution* (New York 1977).

153 *Nature*, 17 September 1981, 176.

154 Quotations from Edward Wilson, *Sociobiology* (Harvard 1975) and *On Human Nature* (Harvard 1979).

155 Alexander Pope, *An Essay on Man* (London 1733–4), Ep., I, line 2.

Index

Kempei Tai (special police), 184
Kennan, George, 344, 345, 356, 385, 437, 442, 460, 462, 464, 632
Kennedy, John F., 586, 640, 647, 650, 664; universalist policy, 614–15; and Cuban problem, 624–9; space programme, 629–30; and Vietnam, 630, 633–4, 635; poverty programme, 638; and civil rights, 645
Kennedy, Joseph, 345, 370
Kennedy, Robert, 459, 614, 624, 626, 627, 650, 660
Kenseikai party, 183
Kenya, 517, 518, 728; race discrimination, 159, 520, 527
Kenyatta, Jomo, 518, 531
Kerekou, Mathieu, 542
Kerensky, Alexander, 21, 61, 63, 66, 92, 198
Kern, Jerome, 227
Kerr, Clark, 641, 642
Ketsumedian society, 184
Keynes, John Maynard, 29–30, 152, 356; and Versailles Treaty, 28–9, 30, 34, 106, 108, 139, 348; and German financial policy, 134, 136; on economics as ethics, 166; on return to gold, 164; and Bloomsbury Group, 167, 169, 170; and credit-inflation, 233, 235, 240; and stabilization, 235; on Hoover, 242, 244; and reflation by deficit finance, 255; on war stimulus to US economic recovery, 257; 1945 bankruptcy report, 466, 467
Keynesianism, 241, 248, 659, 669
KGB (Committee of State Security), 535, 688, 689, 771
Khachaturian, Aram, 453
Khama, Seretse, 526
Khan, Marshal Ayub, 568
Khan, General Tikka, 569
Khieu Samphan, 656
Khmer Rouge, 654, 656
Khomeini, Ayatollah, 710, 713, 716–17
Khrushchev, Nikita, 302, 449, 451, 479, 551, 677; criticism of Stalin, 270, 300, 372, 441, 454, 455, 549–50; on Mao, 545, 546; on Communist victory through 'national liberation wars', 615; brinkmanship in Cuban missile crisis, 625–7; his leadership, 675–6; attempts at liberalization, 675, 678, 679; ousted, 676; use of penal psychiatry, 681; 'decolonization', 721; agricultural policy, 725–6
kibbutz movement, 488 729
Kielce pogrom (1946), 482
Kim II-sung, 450
King, Cecil, 368
King, Mackenzie, 174
King, Martin Luther, 650
Kingoro, Hashimoto, 189
Kinnock, Neil, 746

Kipling, Rudyard, 169
Kirov, Sergei, 299–300
Kissinger, Henry, 651, 667, 668, 669
Klausener, Ernst 298
Klee, Paul, 114
Kleist-Schwenzin, Ewald von, 353
Klerk, F.W. de, 729
Knickerbocker, H.R., 132
Kodo ('Imperial Way'), 315
Koestler, Arthur, 303, 328
Kohl, Helmut, 763
Kokoschka, Oskar, 114
Kokuryukai sect, 183
Kolakowski, Leszek, 271, 728
Kolchak, Admiral, 75
Koltzov, Michael, 335
Kolyma death camps, 304
Konovalek Evhen, 335
Konoye, Prince Fumimaro, 428
Korea, 187; Korean War, 450–1, 452, 460–1, 463, 493, 548, 631; South Korea, 730, 735, 736
Kornilov, General 63
Korsah, Sir Arku, 511
Kortner, Fritz, 116
Kosygin, Alexei, 302, 555
Koussevitsky, Serge, 227
Kovarev, S.V., 304
Krauch, Karl, 422
Krim, Belkachem, 497
Kristallnacht (Nov. 1938), 293
Krivitzky, Walter, 335
Kronstadt mutiny (1921), 79–80, 82, 93, 263
Krupps, 139, 282, 293, 422
Krupskaya, Nadezhda, 50, 51, 87
Krzhizhanovskaya, Madame, 52
Ku-Klux Klan, 203, 204, 206
Kubota Iron and Machinery Works, 722
Kuibyshev, V.V., 84
kulaks, 60, 269, 270–2
Kulturbolschewismus, 114
Kun, Béla, 95, 122, 242, 302
Kuominchun,195
Kuomintang (KMT), 192, 194–5, 196, 199, 315–16, 317, 444, 446, 458
Kurchatov, Igor, 409
Kurds, 714, 773
Kuwait, 666, 670, 733, 773–9
Kuznetsov, A. A., 455
Kuznetsov, Admiral N.G., 372
Kwajalein, 423
Kwantung army, 202
Kyemba, Henry, 534
Kyemba, Teresa, 535

La Chambre, Guy, 365
Labour Party, British, 122, 348, 368, 436, 601–3, 746
Lacalle, García, 337
Lacan, Jacques, 695
Lacoste, Robert, 500, 501